Financial Statement Analysis

CFA® PROGRAM CURRICULUM • VOLUME 3

Cover photograph courtesy of Getty Images.

Printed in the United States of America

10 9 8 7 6 5 4 3 2 1

ISBN 0-536-34180-X

2006160825

AG/JS

Please visit our web site at *www.pearsoncustom.com*

PEARSON CUSTOM PUBLISHING
501 Boylston Street, Suite 900, Boston, MA 02116
A Pearson Education Company

CONTENTS

HOW TO USE THE CFA PROGRAM CURRICULUM

Congratulations on your decision to enter the Chartered Financial Analyst (CFA®) Program. This exciting and rewarding program of study reflects your desire to become a serious investment professional. You are embarking on a program noted for its high ethical standards and the breadth of knowledge, skills, and abilities it develops. Your commitment to the CFA Program should be educationally and professionally rewarding.

The credential you seek is respected around the world as a mark of accomplishment and dedication. Each level of the program represents a distinct achievement in professional development. Successful completion of the program is rewarded with membership in a prestigious global community of investment professionals. CFA charterholders are dedicated to life-long learning and maintaining currency with the ever-changing dynamics of a challenging profession.

The CFA examination measures your degree of mastery of the assigned CFA Program curriculum. Effective study and preparation based on that curriculum are keys to your success on the examination.

Curriculum Development

The CFA Program curriculum is grounded in the practice of the investment profession. CFA Institute regularly conducts a practice analysis survey of investment professionals around the world to determine the knowledge, skills, and abilities that are relevant to the profession. The survey results define the Candidate Body of Knowledge (CBOK™), an inventory of knowledge and responsibilities expected of the investment management professional at the level of a new CFA charterholder. The survey also determines how much emphasis each of the major topic areas receives on the CFA examinations.

A committee made up of practicing charterholders, in conjunction with CFA Institute staff, designs the CFA Program curriculum to deliver the CBOK to candidates. The examinations, also written by practicing charterholders, are designed to allow you to demonstrate your mastery of the CBOK as set forth in the CFA Program curriculum. As you structure your personal study program, you should emphasize mastery of the CBOK and the practical application of that knowledge. For more information on the practice analysis, CBOK, and development of the CFA Program curriculum, please visit www.cfainstitute.org/toolkit.

Organization

The Level I CFA Program curriculum is organized into 10 topic areas. Each topic area begins with a brief statement of the material and the depth of knowledge expected.

Each topic area is then divided into one or more study sessions. These study sessions—18 sessions in the Level I curriculum—should form the basic structure of your reading and preparation.

Each study session includes a statement of its structure and objective, and is further divided into specific reading assignments. The outline on the inside front cover of each volume illustrates the organization of these 18 study sessions.

The reading assignments are the basis for all examination questions, and are selected or developed specifically to teach the CBOK. These readings are drawn from textbook chapters, professional journal articles, research analyst reports, CFA Program-commissioned content, and cases. Many readings include problems and solutions as well as appendices to help you learn.

Reading-specific Learning Outcome Statements (LOS) are listed in the pages introducing each study session as well as at the beginning of each reading. These LOS indicate what you should be able to accomplish after studying the reading. We encourage you to review how to properly use LOS, and the descriptions of commonly used LOS "command words," at www.cfainstitute.org/toolkit. The command words signal the depth of learning you are expected to achieve from the reading. You should use the LOS to guide and focus your study, as each examination question is based on an assigned reading and one or more LOS. However, the readings provide context for the LOS and enable you to apply a principle or concept in a variety of scenarios. It is important to study the whole of a required reading.

Features of the Curriculum

- **Required vs. Optional Segments** - You should read all of the pages for an assigned reading. In some cases, however, we have reprinted an entire chapter or article and marked those parts of the reading that are not required as "optional." The CFA examination is based only on the required segments, and the optional segments are included only when they might help you to better understand the required segments (by seeing the required material in its full context). When an optional segment begins, you will see an icon and a solid vertical bar in the outside margin that will continue until the optional segment ends, accompanied by another icon. *Unless the material is specifically marked as optional, you should assume it is required.* Keep in mind that the optional material is provided strictly for your convenience and will not be tested. You should rely on the required segments and the reading-specific LOS in preparing for the examination.

- **Problems/Solutions** - *All questions and problems in the readings as well as their solutions (which are provided in an appendix at the end of each volume) are required material.* When appropriate, we have included problems after the readings to demonstrate practical application and reinforce your understanding of the concepts presented. The questions and problems are designed to help you learn these concepts. Many of the questions are in the same style and format as the actual CFA examination and will give you test-taking experience in that format. Examination questions that come from a past CFA examination are marked with the CFA logo in the margin.

CFA 2006 exam

- **Margins** - The wide margins in each volume provide space for your note-taking.
- **Two-color Format** - To enrich the visual appeal and clarity of the exhibits, tables, and text, the curriculum is printed in a two-color format.
- **Six-volume Structure** - For portability of the curriculum, the material is spread over six volumes.
- **Glossary and Index** - For your convenience, we have printed a comprehensive glossary and index in each volume. Throughout the curriculum, a **bolded blue** word in a reading denotes a term defined in the glossary.

Designing Your Personal Study Program

Create a Schedule - An orderly, systematic approach to examination preparation is critical. You should dedicate a consistent block of time every week to reading and studying. Complete all reading assignments and the associated problems and solutions in each study session. Review the LOS both before and after you study each reading to ensure that you have mastered the applicable content and can demonstrate the knowledge, skill, or ability described by the LOS and the assigned reading.

CFA Institute estimates that you will need to devote a minimum of 10–15 hours per week for 18 weeks to study the assigned readings. Allow a minimum of one week for each study session, and plan to complete them all at least 30–45 days prior to the examination. This schedule will allow you to spend the final four to six weeks before the examination reviewing the assigned material and taking multiple online sample examinations.

At CFA Institute, we believe that candidates need to commit to a *minimum* of 250 hours reading and reviewing the curriculum, and taking online sample examinations, to master the material. This recommendation, however, may substantially underestimate the hours needed for appropriate examination preparation depending on your individual circumstances, relevant experience, and academic background.

You will undoubtedly adjust your study time to conform to your own strengths and weaknesses, and your educational and professional background. You will probably spend more time on some study sessions than on others. You should allow ample time for both in-depth study of all topic areas and additional concentration on those topic areas for which you feel least prepared.

Preliminary Readings - The reading assignments in Economics assume candidates already have a basic mastery of the concepts typically presented in introductory university-level economics courses. Information on suggested readings to improve your knowledge of these topics precedes the relevant study sessions.

Candidate Preparation Toolkit - We have created the online toolkit to provide a single comprehensive location for resources and guidance for candidate preparation. In addition to in-depth information on study program planning, the CFA Program curriculum, and the online sample examinations, the toolkit also contains curriculum errata, printable study session outlines, sample examination questions, and more. Errata identified in the curriculum are corrected and listed periodically in the errata listing in the toolkit. We encourage you to use the toolkit as your central preparation resource during your tenure as a candidate. Visit the toolkit at www.cfainstitute.org/toolkit.

Online Sample Examinations - After completing your study of the assigned curriculum, use the CFA Institute online sample examinations to measure your knowledge of the topics and to improve your examination-taking skills. After each question, you will receive immediate feedback noting the correct response and indicating the assigned reading for further study. The sample examinations are designed by the same people who create the actual CFA examinations, and reflect the question formats, topics, and level of difficulty of the actual CFA examinations, in a timed environment. Aggregate data indicate that the CFA examination pass rate was higher among candidates who took one or more online sample examinations than among candidates who did not take the online sample examinations. For more information on the online sample examinations, please visit www.cfainstitute.org/toolkit.

Preparatory Providers - After you enroll in the CFA Program, you may receive numerous solicitations for preparatory courses and review materials. Although preparatory courses and notes may be helpful to some candidates, you should view these resources as *supplements* to the assigned CFA Program curriculum. The CFA examinations reference only the CFA Institute assigned curriculum—no preparatory course or review course materials are consulted or referenced.

Before you decide on a supplementary prep course, do some research. Determine the experience and expertise of the instructors, the accuracy and currency of their content, the delivery method for their materials, and the provider's claims of success. Most importantly, make sure the provider is in compliance with the CFA Institute Prep Provider Guidelines Program. Three years of prep course products can be a significant investment, so make sure you're getting a sufficient return. Just remember, there are no shortcuts to success on the CFA examinations. Prep products can enhance your learning experience, but the CFA curriculum is the key to success. For more information on the Prep Provider Guidelines Program, visit www.cfainstitute.org/cfaprog/resources/prepcourse.html.

SUMMARY

Every question on the CFA examination is based on specific pages in the required readings and on one or more LOS. Frequently, an examination question is also tied to a specific example highlighted within a reading or to a specific end-of-reading question/problem and its solution. To make effective use of the curriculum, please remember these key points:

1. All pages printed in the Custom Curriculum are required reading for the examination except for occasional sections marked as optional. You may read optional pages as background, but you will not be tested on them.
2. All questions/problems printed at the end of readings and their solutions in the appendix to each volume are required study material for the examination.
3. Make appropriate use of the CFA Candidate Toolkit, the online sample examinations, and preparatory courses and review materials.
4. Commit sufficient study time to cover the 18 study sessions, review the materials, and take sample examinations.

Feedback

At CFA Institute, we are committed to delivering a comprehensive and rigorous curriculum for the development of competent, ethically grounded investment professionals. We rely on candidate and member feedback as we work to incorporate content, design, and packaging improvements. You can be assured that we will continue to listen to your suggestions. Please send any comments or feedback to curriculum@cfainstitute.org. Ongoing improvements in the curriculum will help you prepare for success on the upcoming examinations, and for a lifetime of learning as a serious investment professional.

FINANCIAL STATEMENT ANALYSIS

STUDY SESSIONS

TOPIC LEVEL LEARNING OUTCOME

The candidate should be able to demonstrate a thorough knowledge of financial accounting procedures and the rules that govern disclosure. Emphasis is on basic financial statements and how alternative accounting methods affect those statements and the analysis of financial statement relationships.

STUDY SESSION 7
FINANCIAL STATEMENT ANALYSIS:
An Introduction

The readings in this study session discuss the general principles of the financial reporting system, underscoring the critical role of the analysis of financial reports in investment decision making.

The first reading introduces the range of information that an analyst may use in analyzing the financial performance of a company, including the principal financial statements (the income statement, balance sheet, cash flow statement, and statement of changes in owners' equity), notes to those statements, and management discussion and analysis of results. A general framework for addressing most financial statement analysis tasks is also presented.

A company's financial statements are the end-products of a process for recording the business transactions of the company. The second reading illustrates this process, introducing such basic concepts as the accounting equation and accounting accruals.

The presentation of financial information to the public by a company must conform to the governing set of financial reporting standards applying in the jurisdiction in which the information is released. The final reading in this study explores the role of financial reporting standard-setting bodies worldwide and the International Financial Reporting Standards framework promulgated by one key body, the International Accounting Standards Board. The movement towards worldwide convergence of financial reporting standards is also introduced.

Note:
New rulings and/or pronouncements issued after the publication of the readings in Study Sessions 7 through 10 in financial statement analysis may cause some of the information in these readings to become dated. Candidates are expected to be familiar with the overall analytical framework contained in the study session readings, as well as the implications of alternative accounting methods for financial analysis and valuation, as provided in the assigned readings. For the purpose of Level I questions on financial statement analysis, when a ratio is defined and calculated differently in various texts, candidates should use the definitions given in the CFA Institute copyrighted readings by Robinson, et al. Variations in ratio definitions are part of the nature of practical financial analysis.

READING ASSIGNMENTS

Reading 29 Financial Statement Analysis: An Introduction
Reading 30 Financial Reporting Mechanics
Reading 31 Financial Reporting Standards

LEARNING OUTCOMES

Reading 29: Financial Statement Analysis: An Introduction

The candidate should be able to:

a. discuss the roles of financial reporting and financial statement analysis;

b. discuss the role of key financial statements (income statement, balance sheet, cash flow statement and statement of changes in owners' equity) in evaluating a company's performance and financial position;

c. discuss the importance of financial statement notes and supplementary information (including disclosures of accounting methods, estimates and assumptions), and management's discussion and analysis;

d. discuss the objective of audits of financial statements, the types of audit reports, and the importance of effective internal controls;

e. identify and explain information sources other than annual financial statements and supplementary information that analysts use in financial statement analysis;

f. describe the steps in the financial statement analysis framework.

Reading 30: Financial Reporting Mechanics

The candidate should be able to:

a. identify the groups (operating, investing, and financing activities) into which business activities are categorized for financial reporting purposes and classify any business activity into the appropriate group;

b. explain the relationship of financial statement elements and accounts, and classify accounts into the financial statement elements;

c. explain the accounting equation in its basic and expanded forms;

d. explain the process of recording business transactions using an accounting system based on the accounting equations;

e. explain the need for accruals and other adjustments in preparing financial statements;

f. prepare financial statements, given account balances or other elements in the relevant accounting equation, and explain the relationships among the income statement, balance sheet, statement of cash flows, and statement of owners' equity;

g. describe the flow of information in an accounting system;

h. explain the use of the results of the accounting process in security analysis.

Reading 31: Financial Reporting Standards

The candidate should be able to:

a. explain the objective of financial statements and the importance of reporting standards in security analysis and valuation;

b. explain the role of standard-setting bodies, such as the International Accounting Standards Board and the U.S. Financial Accounting Standards Board, and regulatory authorities such as the International Organization of Securities Commissions, the U.K. Financial Services Authority, and the U.S. Securities and Exchange Commission in establishing and enforcing financial reporting standards;

- **c.** discuss the ongoing barriers to developing one universally accepted set of financial reporting standards;
- **d.** describe the International Financial Reporting Standards (IFRS) framework, including the objective of financial statements, their qualitative characteristics, required reporting elements, and the constraints and assumptions in preparing financial statements;
- **e.** explain the general requirements for financial statements;
- **f.** compare and contrast key concepts of financial reporting standards under IFRS and alternative reporting systems, and discuss the implications for financial analysis of differing financial reporting systems;
- **g.** identify the characteristics of a coherent financial reporting framework and barriers to creating a coherent financial reporting network;
- **h.** discuss the importance of monitoring developments in financial reporting standards and evaluate company disclosures of significant accounting policies.

FINANCIAL STATEMENT ANALYSIS: AN INTRODUCTION

by Thomas R. Robinson, Hennie van Greuning, Elaine Henry, and Michael A. Broihahn

READING

29

LEARNING OUTCOMES

The candidate should be able to:

a. discuss the roles of financial reporting and financial statement analysis;

b. discuss the role of key financial statements (income statement, balance sheet, cash flow statement and statement of changes in owners' equity) in evaluating a company's performance and financial position;

c. discuss the importance of financial statement notes and supplementary information (including disclosures of accounting methods, estimates and assumptions), and management's discussion and analysis;

d. discuss the objective of audits of financial statements, the types of audit reports, and the importance of effective internal controls;

e. identify and explain information sources other than annual financial statements and supplementary information that analysts use in financial statement analysis;

f. describe the steps in the financial statement analysis framework.

THEME

The information presented in financial reports, including the financial statements, financial notes, and management's discussion and analysis, allows the financial analyst to assess a company's performance and financial position. An analyst may be called upon to perform a financial analysis for a variety of reasons, including the valuation of equity securities, the assessment of credit risk, the performance of due diligence in an acquisition, and the evaluation of a subsidiary's performance relative to other business units. Major considerations in both equity analysis and credit analysis are evaluating a company's financial position, ability to generate profits and cash flow, and ability to generate future growth in profits and cash flow.

1 INTRODUCTION

Analysts are employed in a number of functional areas. Commonly, analysts evaluate an investment in some type of security that has characteristics of equity (representing an ownership position) or debt (representing a lending position). In arriving at investment decisions or recommendations, analysts need to evaluate the performance, financial position, and value of the company issuing the securities. Company financial reports, which include financial statements and other data, provide the information necessary to evaluate the company and its securities. Consequently, the analyst must have a firm understanding of the information provided in each company's financial reports, including the financial notes and other forms of supplementary information.

This reading is organized as follows: Section 2 discusses the scope of financial statement analysis. Section 3 describes the sources of information used in financial statement analysis, including the primary financial statements (income statement, balance sheet, and **cash flow statement**). Section 4 provides a framework for guiding the financial statement analysis process. A summary of the key points and practice problems in the CFA Institute multiple-choice format conclude the reading.

2 SCOPE OF FINANCIAL STATEMENT ANALYSIS

The role of financial reporting by companies is to provide information about their performance, financial position, and changes in financial position that is useful to a wide range of users in making economic decisions.[1] The role of financial statement analysis is to take financial reports prepared by companies, combined with other information, to evaluate the past, current, and prospective performance and financial position of a company for the purpose of making investment, credit, and other economic decisions.

In evaluating financial reports, analysts typically have an economic decision in mind. Examples include the following:

- Evaluating an equity investment for inclusion in a portfolio.
- Evaluating a merger or acquisition candidate.
- Evaluating a subsidiary or operating division of a parent company.
- Deciding whether to make a venture capital or other private equity investment.
- Determining the **creditworthiness** of a company that has made a loan request.
- Extending credit to a customer.

[1] See paragraph 12 of the "Framework for the Preparation and Presentation of Financial Statements," originally published by the International Accounting Standards Committee in 1989 and then adopted by the International Accounting Standards Board in 2001.

- Examining compliance with debt covenants or other contractual arrangements.
- Assigning a debt rating to a company or bond issue.
- Valuing a security for making an investment recommendation to others.
- Forecasting future net income and cash flow.

There are certain themes in financial analysis. In general, analysts seek to examine the performance and financial position of companies as well as forecast future performance and financial position. Analysts are also concerned about factors that affect risks to the company's future performance and financial position. An examination of performance can include an assessment of a company's profitability (the ability to earn a profit from delivering goods and services) and its cash flow generating ability (the ability to produce cash receipts in excess of cash disbursements). Profit and cash flow are not equivalent. Profit represents the excess of the prices at which goods or services are sold over all the costs of providing those goods and services (regardless of when cash is received or paid). Example 1 illustrates the distinction between profit and cash flow.

EXAMPLE 1

Profit versus Cash Flow

Sennett Designs (SD) sells imported furniture on a retail basis. SD began operations during December 2006 and sold furniture for cash of €250,000. The furniture that was sold by SD was delivered by the supplier during December, but the supplier has granted SD credit terms according to which payment is not due until January 2007. SD is obligated to pay €220,000 in January for the furniture it sold during December.

1. How much is SD's profit for December 2006 if no other transactions occurred?
2. How much is SD's cash flow for December 2006?

Solution to 1: SD's profit for December 2006 is the excess of the sales price (€250,000) over the cost of the goods that were sold (€220,000), or €30,000.

Solution to 2: The December 2006 cash flow is €250,000.

Although profitability is important, so is the ability to generate positive cash flow. Cash flow is important because, ultimately, cash is needed to pay employees, suppliers, and others to continue as a going concern. A company that generates positive **cash flow from operations** has more flexibility in funding needed investments and taking advantage of attractive business opportunities than an otherwise **comparable company** without positive cash flow. Additionally, cash flow is the source of returns to providers of capital. Therefore, the expected magnitude of future cash flows is important in valuing corporate securities and in determining the company's ability to meet its obligations. The ability to meet short-term obligations is generally referred to as **liquidity**, and the ability to meet long-term obligations is generally referred to as **solvency**. However, as shown in Example 1, cash flow in a given period is not a complete measure of performance in that period; for example, a company may be obligated to make future cash payments as a result of a transaction generating positive cash flow in the current period.

As noted earlier, profits reflect the ability of a company to deliver goods and services at prices in excess of the costs of delivering the goods and services. Profits also provide useful information about future (and past) cash flows. If the transaction of Example 1 were repeated year after year, the long-term average annual cash flow of SD would be €30,000, its annual profit. Many analysts not only evaluate past profitability but also forecast future profitability.

Exhibit 1 shows how news media coverage of corporate earnings announcements places corporate results in the context of analysts' expectations. Furthermore, analysts frequently use earnings in valuation, for example, when they

EXHIBIT 1 **An Earnings Release and Analyst Reaction**

Panel A. Excerpt from Apple Earnings Release

Apple Reports Third Quarter Results
Posts Second Highest Quarterly Revenue and Earnings in Company's History

CUPERTINO, California—July 19, 2006—Apple® today announced financial results for its fiscal 2006 third quarter ended July 1, 2006. The Company posted revenue of $4.37 billion and a net quarterly profit of $472 million, or $.54 per diluted share. These results compare to revenue of $3.52 billion and a net profit of $320 million, or $.37 per diluted share, in the year-ago quarter. Gross margin was 30.3 percent, up from 29.7 percent in the year-ago quarter. International sales accounted for 39 percent of the quarter's revenue.

Apple shipped 1,327,000 Macintosh® computers and 8,111,000 iPods during the quarter, representing 12 percent growth in Macs and 32 percent growth in iPods over the year-ago quarter. . . .

Panel B. Excerpt from CNET News.com Report

"Mac Sales Up 12 Percent as Apple Profits Soar" by Tom Krazit

Apple Computer's third-quarter revenue fell a little short of expectations, but profitability was far higher than expected and Mac sales increased at a healthy clip.

. . . Net income was $472 million, or 54 cents per share, an improvement of 48 percent compared with last year's results of $320 million in net income and 37 cents per share. Analysts surveyed by Thomson First Call had been expecting Apple to report $4.4 billion in revenue and earn 44 cents per share.

. . . The outlook for the next period will probably disappoint some investors. The company predicted fourth-quarter revenue would be about $4.5 billion to $4.6 billion, less than the $4.9 billion analysts had been expecting. Apple executives will hold a conference call later Wednesday to discuss results.

Sources: www.apple.com/pr/library/2006/jul/19results.html and http://news.com.com/Mac+sales+up+12+percent+as+Apple+profits+soar/2100-1047_3-6096116.html.

value shares of a company on the basis of the price-to-earnings ratio (P/E) in relation to peer companies' P/Es or when they use a present value model of valuation that is based on forecasted future earnings.

Analysts are also interested in the current financial position of a company. The financial position can be measured by comparing the resources controlled by the company in relation to the claims against those resources. An example of a resource is cash. In Example 1, if no other transactions occur, the company should have cash at 31 December 2006 of €250,000. This cash can be used by the company to pay the obligation to the supplier (a claim against the company) and may also be used to make distributions to the owner (who also has a claim against the company for any profits that have been earned). Financial position is particularly important in **credit analysis**, as depicted in Exhibit 2.

EXHIBIT 2 Grupo Imsa Press Release Dated 18 January 2005

Standard & Poor's and Fitch Upgrade Grupo Imsa's Credit Rating

MONTERREY, Mexico: Grupo Imsa (NYSE:IMY) (BMV:IMSA) announces that Standard & Poor's has recently upgraded the Company's local currency corporate credit rating from BBB– to BBB and its national scale rating from mxAA to mxAA+. Fitch Mexico also increased Grupo Imsa's domestic rating from AA(mex) to AA+(mex). These rating upgrades reflect the positive results of Grupo Imsa's main businesses and the strengthening of its financial position, combined with the Company's geographic diversification, market leadership, state-of-the-art technology and high operational efficiency.

Mr. Marcelo Canales, Grupo Imsa's CFO, explained: "Grupo Imsa follows a policy of maintaining a solid financial position that ensures the Company's continuity for the benefit of our employees, shareholders and creditors. We take our financial commitments very seriously, as can be seen from the fact that during our 70 years of existence we have always complied with our financial obligations. The change in rating also reflects the strength of our business model and its capacity to generate cash." Mr. Canales added: "These upgrades in credit rating should translate into a better valuation of our debt to reflect Grupo Imsa's new financial reality."

Grupo Imsa, a holding company, dates back to 1936 and is today one of Mexico's leading diversified industrial companies, operating in three core businesses: steel processed products; steel and plastic construction products; and aluminum and other related products. With manufacturing and distribution facilities in Mexico, the United States, Europe and throughout Central and South America, Grupo Imsa currently exports to all five continents. Grupo Imsa's shares trade on the Mexican Stock Exchange (IMSA) and, in the United States, on the NYSE (IMY).

This document contains forward-looking statements relating to Grupo Imsa's future performance or its current expectations or beliefs, including statements regarding the intent, belief or current expectations of the Company and its management. Investors are cautioned that any such forward-looking statements are not guarantees of future performance and involve a number of risks and uncertainties pertaining to the industries in which the Company participates. Grupo Imsa does not intend, and does not assume any obligation, to update these forward-looking statements.

Source: Business Wire, 18 January 2005.

In conducting a financial analysis of a company, the analyst will regularly refer to the company's financial statements, financial notes and supplementary schedules, and a variety of other information sources. The next section introduces the major financial statements and most commonly used information sources.

3 MAJOR FINANCIAL STATEMENTS AND OTHER INFORMATION SOURCES

In order to perform an equity or credit analysis of a company, an analyst must collect a great deal of information. The nature of the information will vary based on the individual task but will typically include information about the economy, industry, and company as well as information about comparable peer companies. Much of this information will come from outside the company, such as economic statistics, industry reports, trade publications, and databases containing information on competitors. The company itself provides some of the core information for analysis in its financial reports, press releases, and conference calls and webcasts.

Companies prepare financial reports to report to investors and creditors on financial performance and financial strength at regular intervals (annually, semi-annually, and/or quarterly). Financial reports include financial statements and supplemental information necessary to assess the performance and financial position of the company. Financial statements are the end results of an accounting recordkeeping process that records the economic activities of a company. They summarize this information for use by investors, creditors, analysts, and others interested in a company's performance and financial position. In order to provide some assurances as to the information provided in the financial statements and related notes, the financial statements are audited by independent accountants who express an opinion on whether the financial statements fairly portray the company's performance and financial position.

3.1 Financial Statements and Supplementary Information

The key financial statements that are the focus of analysis are the income statement, balance sheet, statement of cash flows, and statement of changes in owners' equity. The income statement and **statement of cash flows** portray different aspects of a company's performance over a period of time. The balance sheet portrays the company's financial position at a given point in time. The statement of changes in **owners' equity** provides additional information regarding the changes in a company's financial position. In addition to the financial statements, a company provides other information in its financial reports that is useful to the financial analyst. As part of his or her analysis, the financial analyst should read and assess this additional information, which includes:

- notes to the financial statements (also known as footnotes) and supplementary schedules;
- management's discussion and analysis (MD&A); and
- the external auditor's report(s).

The following sections illustrate the major financial statements.

3.1.1 Income Statement

The income statement presents information on the financial results of a company's business activities over a period of time. The income statement communicates how much revenue the company generated during a period and what costs it incurred in connection with generating that revenue. Net income (revenue minus all costs) on the income statement is often referred to as the "bottom line" because of its proximity to the bottom of the income statement.[2] Income statements are reported on a consolidated basis, meaning that they include the revenues and expenses of affiliated companies under the control of the parent (reporting) company. The income statement is sometimes referred to as a statement of operations or profit and loss (P&L) statement. The basic equation underlying the income statement is Revenue − Expenses = Net income.

In Exhibit 3, the income statement is presented with the most recent year in the first column and the earliest year in the last column. Although this is a common presentation, analysts should be careful when reading an income statement because in other cases, the years may be listed from most distant to most recent.

Exhibit 3 shows that Wal-Mart's total revenue for the fiscal year ended 31 January 2005 was (in millions) $287,989. Wal-Mart then subtracted its operating costs and expenses to arrive at an operating income (profit) of $17,091. Operating income reflects a company's profits from its usual business activities, before deducting interest expense or taxes. Operating income is thus often referred to as EBIT, or earnings before interest and taxes. Operating income reflects the company's underlying performance independent of the use of financial leverage. Wal-Mart's total interest cost (net of the interest income that was earned from investments) for 2005 was $986; its earnings before taxes were, therefore, $16,105. Total income tax expense for 2005 was $5,589, and the minority interest expense (income earned by the minority shareholders from Wal-Mart subsidiary companies) was $249. After deducting these final expenses, Wal-Mart's net income for fiscal 2005 was $10,267.

Companies present their basic and diluted earnings per share on the face of the income statement. Earnings per share represents the net income divided by the number of shares of stock outstanding during the period. **Basic earnings per share** uses the weighted-average number of common shares that were actually outstanding during the period, whereas diluted earnings per share uses **diluted shares**—the number of shares that would be outstanding if potentially dilutive claims on common shares (e.g., stock options) were exercised by their holders. Wal-Mart's basic earning per share for 2005 was $2.41 ($10,267 net income ÷ 4,259 basic shares outstanding). Likewise, Wal-Mart's diluted earnings per share for 2005 was also $2.41 ($10,267 net income ÷ 4,266 diluted shares).

An analyst examining the income statement might note that Wal-Mart was profitable in each year and that revenue, operating income, net income, and earnings per share—all measures of profitability—increased over the three-year period. The analyst might formulate questions related to profitability, such as the following:

- Is the growth in revenue related to an increase in units sold, an increase in prices, or some combination?
- After adjusting for growth in the number of stores, is the company still more profitable over time?
- How does the company compare with other companies in the industry?

[2] "Net income" is also referred to as "net earnings" or "net profit." In the event that costs exceed revenues, it is referred to as "net loss."

EXHIBIT 3 Wal-Mart Consolidated Statements of Income (in millions except per share data)

Fiscal Years Ended 31 January	2005	2004	2003
Revenues:			
Net sales	$285,222	$256,329	$229,616
Other income, net	2,767	2,352	1,961
	287,989	258,681	231,577
Costs and expenses:			
Cost of sales	219,793	198,747	178,299
Operating, selling, general, and administrative expenses	51,105	44,909	39,983
Operating income	17,091	15,025	13,295
Interest:			
Debt	934	729	799
Capital lease	253	267	260
Interest income	(201)	(164)	(132)
Interest, net	986	832	927
Income from continuing operations before income taxes and minority interest	16,105	14,193	12,368
Provision for income taxes:			
Current	5,326	4,941	3,883
Deferred	263	177	474
Total	5,589	5,118	4,357
Income from continuing operations before minority interest	10,516	9,075	8,011
Minority interest	(249)	(214)	(193)
Income from continuing operations	10,267	8,861	7,818
Income from discontinued operations, net of tax	–	193	137
Net income	$ 10,267	$ 9,054	$ 7,955
Basic net income per common share:			
Income from continuing operations	$ 2.41	$ 2.03	$ 1.77
Income from discontinued operations	–	0.05	0.03
Basic net income per common share	$ 2.41	$ 2.08	$ 1.80
Diluted net income per common share:			
Income from continuing operations	$ 2.41	$ 2.03	$ 1.76
Income from discontinued operations	–	0.04	0.03
Diluted net income per common share	$ 2.41	$ 2.07	$ 1.79
Weighted-average number of common shares:			
Basic	4,259	4,363	4,430
Diluted	4,266	4,373	4,446
Dividends per common share	$ 0.52	$ 0.36	$ 0.30

Answering such questions requires the analyst to gather, analyze, and interpret facts from a number of sources, including the income statement. The reading on understanding the income statement will explain the income statement in greater detail. The next section illustrates the balance sheet, the second major financial statement.

3.1.2 Balance Sheet

The **balance sheet** (also known as the statement of financial position or statement of financial condition) presents a company's current financial position by disclosing resources the company controls (assets) and what it owes (liabilities) at a specific point in time. Owners' equity represents the excess of assets over liabilities. This amount is attributable to the owners or shareholders of the business; it is the residual interest in the assets of an entity after deducting its liabilities. The three parts of the balance sheet are formulated in an accounting relationship known as the accounting equation: Assets = Liabilities + Owners' equity (that is, the total amount for assets must *balance* to the combined total amounts for liabilities and owners' equity). Alternatively, the three parts of the balance sheet of the accounting relationship may be formulated as Assets − Liabilities = Owners' equity. Depending on the form of the organization, owners' equity also goes by several alternative titles, such as "partners' capital" or "shareholders' equity."

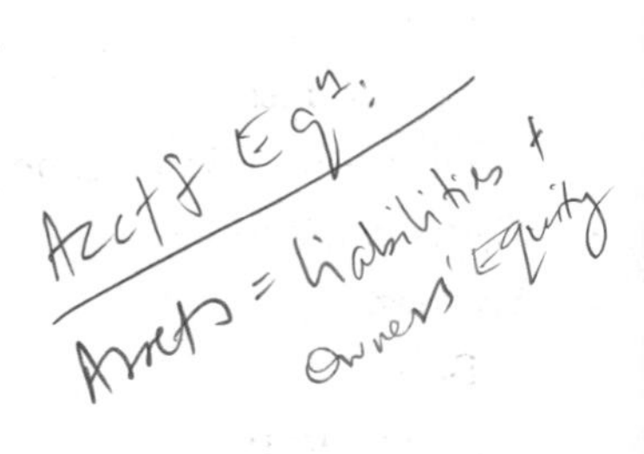

Exhibit 4 presents Wal-Mart's consolidated balance sheets for the fiscal years ended 31 January 2004 and 2005.

EXHIBIT 4 Wal-Mart Consolidated Balance Sheets (in millions except per share data)

Fiscal Years Ended 31 January	2005	2004
Assets		
Current assets:		
Cash and cash equivalents	$ 5,488	$ 5,199
Receivables	1,715	1,254
Inventories	29,447	26,612
Prepaid expenses and other	1,841	1,356
Total current assets	38,491	34,421
Property and equipment, at cost:		
Land	14,472	12,699
Buildings and improvements	46,582	40,192
Fixtures and equipment	21,461	17,934
Transportation equipment	1,530	1,269
Property and equipment, at cost	84,045	72,094
Less accumulated depreciation	18,637	15,684
Property and equipment, net	65,408	56,410

(Exhibit continued on next page . . .)

EXHIBIT 4 (continued)

Property under capital lease:		
Property under capital lease	4,997	4,286
Less accumulated amortization	1,838	1,673
Property under capital lease, net	3,159	2,613
Goodwill	10,803	9,882
Other assets and deferred charges	2,362	2,079
Total assets	$120,223	$105,405
Liabilities and shareholders' equity		
Current liabilities:		
Commercial paper	$ 3,812	$ 3,267
Accounts payable	21,671	19,425
Accrued liabilities	12,155	10,671
Accrued income taxes	1,281	1,377
Long-term debt due within one year	3,759	2,904
Obligations under capital leases due within one year	210	196
Total current liabilities	42,888	37,840
Long-term debt	20,087	17,102
Long-term obligations under capital leases	3,582	2,997
Deferred income taxes and other	2,947	2,359
Minority interest	1,323	1,484
Shareholders' equity:		
Preferred stock ($0.10 par value; 100 shares authorized, none issued)	–	–
Common stock ($0.10 par value; 11,000 shares authorized, 4,234 and 4,311 issued and outstanding in 2005 and 2004, respectively)	423	431
Capital in excess of par value	2,425	2,135
Other accumulated comprehensive income	2,694	851
Retained earnings	43,854	40,206
Total shareholders' equity	49,396	43,623
Total liabilities and shareholders' equity	$120,223	$105,405

At 31 January 2005, Wal-Mart's total resources or assets were $120,223 (in millions). **Shareholders' equity** (in millions) was $49,396. Although Wal-Mart does not give a total amount for all the balance sheet liabilities, it may be determined from the accounting relationship as Total assets − Total shareholders' equity or $120,223 − $49,396 = $70,827.[3] Using the balance sheet and applying financial statement analysis, the analyst will be able to answer such questions as:

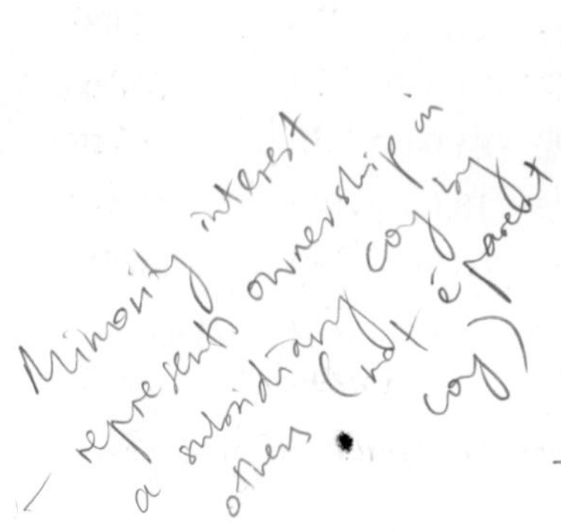

[3] Note that this computation includes an amount labeled "minority interest in liabilities." Minority interest represents ownership in a subsidiary company by others (not the parent company). Accounting rulemakers are currently considering reclassifying this amount as part of owners' equity.

- Has the company's liquidity (ability to meet short-term obligations) improved?
- Is the company solvent (does it have sufficient resources to cover its obligations)?
- What is the company's financial position relative to the industry?

The reading on understanding the balance sheet will cover the analysis of the balance sheet in more depth. The next section illustrates the cash flow statement.

3.1.3 Cash Flow Statement

Although the income statement and balance sheet provide a measure of a company's success in terms of performance and financial position, cash flow is also vital to a company's long-term success. Disclosing the sources and uses of cash helps creditors, investors, and other statement users evaluate the company's liquidity, solvency, and financial flexibility. **Financial flexibility** is the ability to react and adapt to financial adversities and opportunities. The cash flow statement classifies all company cash flows into operating, investing, and financing activity cash flows. **Operating activities** involve transactions that enter into the determination of net income and are primarily activities that comprise the day-to-day business functions of a company. **Investing activities** are those activities associated with the acquisition and disposal of **long-term assets**, such as equipment. **Financing activities** are those activities related to obtaining or repaying capital to be used in the business.

Exhibit 5 presents Wal-Mart's consolidated statement of cash flows for the fiscal years ended 31 January 2003, 2004, and 2005.

EXHIBIT 5 Wal-Mart Consolidated Statements of Cash Flows (in millions)

Fiscal Years Ended 31 January	2005	2004	2003
Cash flows from operating activities:			
Income from continuing operations	$ 10,267	$ 8,861	$ 7,818
Adjustments to reconcile net income to net cash provided by operating activities:			
Depreciation and amortization	4,405	3,852	3,364
Deferred income taxes	263	177	474
Other operating activities	378	173	685
Changes in certain assets and liabilities, net of effects of acquisitions:			
Decrease (increase) in accounts receivable	(304)	373	(159)
Increase in inventories	(2,635)	(1,973)	(2,219)
Increase in accounts payable	1,694	2,587	1,748
Increase in accrued liabilities	976	1,896	1,212
Net cash provided by operating activities of continuing operations	15,044	15,946	12,923
Net cash provided by operating activities of discontinued operations	–	50	82
Net cash provided by operating activities	15,044	15,996	13,005

(Exhibit continued on next page . . .)

EXHIBIT 5 (continued)

Cash flows from investing activities:			
Payments for property and equipment	(12,893)	(10,308)	(9,245)
Investment in international operations	(315)	(38)	(749)
Proceeds from the disposal of fixed assets	953	481	311
Proceeds from the sale of McLane	–	1,500	–
Other investing activities	(96)	78	(73)
Net cash used in investing activities of continuing operations	(12,351)	(8,287)	(9,756)
Net cash used in investing activities of discontinued operations	–	(25)	(83)
Net cash used in investing activities	(12,351)	(8,312)	(9,839)
Cash flows from financing activities:			
Increase in commercial paper	544	688	1,836
Proceeds from issuance of long-term debt	5,832	4,099	2,044
Purchase of company stock	(4,549)	(5,046)	(3,383)
Dividends paid	(2,214)	(1,569)	(1,328)
Payment of long-term debt	(2,131)	(3,541)	(1,261)
Payment of capital lease obligations	(204)	(305)	(216)
Other financing activities	113	111	(62)
Net cash used in financing activities	(2,609)	(5,563)	(2,370)
Effect of exchange rate changes on cash	205	320	(199)
Net increase in cash and cash equivalents	289	2,441	597
Cash and cash equivalents at beginning of year	5,199	2,758	2,161
Cash and cash equivalents at end of year	$ 5,488	$ 5,199	$ 2,758
Supplemental disclosure of cash flow information:			
Income tax paid	$ 5,593	$ 4,358	$ 4,539
Interest paid	1,163	1,024	1,085
Capital lease obligations incurred	377	252	381

In the cash flows from operating activities section of Wal-Mart's cash flow statement, the company reconciles its net income to net cash provided by operating activities. This emphasizes the different perspectives of the income statement and cash flow statement. Income is reported when earned, not necessarily when cash is received. The cash flow statement presents another aspect of performance: the ability of a company to generate cash flow from running its business. Ideally, the analyst would like to see that the primary source of cash flow is from operating activities (as opposed to investing or financing activities). Note that Wal-Mart had a large amount of operating cash flow, which increased from 2003 to 2004 but decreased slightly in 2005. Although operating cash flow was high, an analyst might question why net income increased but operating cash flow decreased in 2005.

The summation of the net cash flows from operating, investing, and financing activities and the effect of exchange rates on cash equals the net change in cash during the fiscal year. For Wal-Mart, the summation of these four cash flow activities in 2005 was $289, which thus increased the company's cash from $5,199 at 31 January 2004 (beginning cash balance) to $5,488 at 31 January 2005 (ending cash balance). Note that these beginning and ending cash balances agree with the cash reported on Wal-Mart's balance sheets in Exhibit 4.

The cash flow statement will be treated in more depth in the reading on understanding the cash flow statement.

3.1.4 Statement of Changes in Owners' Equity

The income statement, balance sheet, and cash flow statements represent the primary financial statements used to assess a company's performance and financial position. A fourth financial statement is also available, variously called a "statement of changes in owners' equity," "statement of shareholders' equity," or "**statement of retained earnings**." This statement primarily serves to report changes in the owners' investment in the business over time and assists the analyst in understanding the changes in financial position reflected on the balance sheet.

3.1.5 Financial Notes and Supplementary Schedules

Financial notes and supplementary schedules are an integral part of the financial statements. By way of example, the financial notes and supplemental schedules provide explanatory information about the following:

- business acquisitions and disposals;
- commitments and contingencies;
- legal proceedings;
- stock option and other employee benefit plans;
- related-party transactions;
- significant customers;
- subsequent events;
- business and geographic segments; and
- quarterly financial data.

Additionally, the footnotes contain information about the methods and assumptions used to prepare the financial statements. Comparability of financial statements is a critical requirement for objective financial analysis. Financial statement comparability occurs when information is measured and reported in a similar manner over time and for different companies. Comparability allows the analyst to identify and analyze the real economic substance differences and similarities between companies. The International Accounting Standards Board based in London sets forth standards under which international financial statements should be prepared. These are referred to as international financial reporting standards (IFRS). Similarly, the Financial Accounting Standards Board (FASB) in the United States sets forth standards (called statements of financial accounting standards) that constitute the key part of the body of principles known as generally accepted accounting principles (U.S. GAAP). These two organizations are working to make their standards similar, but there are key differences. When comparing a U.S. company with a European company, an analyst must understand differences in these standards, which can relate, for example, to the period in which to report revenue.

Even within each of these sets of standards there can be choices for management to make that can reduce comparability between companies. Both IFRS and U.S. GAAP allow the use of alternative accounting methods to measure company financial performance and financial condition where there are differences in economic environments between companies. Additionally, some principles require the use of estimates and assumptions in measuring performance and financial condition. This flexibility is necessary because, ideally, a company will select those methods, estimates, and assumptions within the principles that fairly reflect the unique economic environment of the company's business and industry. Although this flexibility in accounting principles ostensibly meets the divergent needs of many businesses, it creates a problem for the analyst because comparability is lost when flexibility occurs. For example, if a company acquires a piece of equipment to use in its operations, accounting standards require that the cost of the asset be reported as an expense in a systematic manner over the life of the equipment (estimating the process of the equipment wearing out). This allocation of the cost is known as **depreciation**. The standards permit a great deal of flexibility, however, in determining the manner in which each year's expense is determined. Two companies may acquire similar equipment but use different methods and assumptions to record the expense over time. Comparing the companies' performance directly is then impaired by this difference.

A company's accounting policies (methods, estimates, and assumptions) are generally presented in the notes to the financial statements. A note containing a summary of significant accounting policies reveals, for example, how the company recognizes its revenues and depreciates its capital assets. Analysts must be aware of the methods, estimates, and assumptions used by a company to determine if they are similar to those of other companies that are being used as benchmarks. If they are not similar, the analyst who understands accounting techniques can make adjustments to make the financial statements more comparable.

3.1.6 Management's Discussion and Analysis

Publicly held companies are often required to include in their financial reports a section called management's discussion and analysis (MD&A). In it, management must highlight any favorable or unfavorable trends and identify significant events and uncertainties that affect the company's liquidity, capital resources, and results of operations. The MD&A must also provide information about the effects of inflation, changing prices, or other material events and uncertainties that may cause the future operating results and financial condition to materially depart from the current reported financial information. Companies should also provide disclosure in the MD&A that discusses the critical accounting policies that require management to make subjective judgments and that have a significant impact on reported financial results. The MD&A section of a company's report provides a good starting place for understanding what is going on in the financial statements. Nevertheless, it is only one input for the analyst in seeking an objective and independent perspective on a company's performance and prospects.

3.1.7 Auditor's Reports

Financial statements presented in company annual financial reports are often required to be audited (examined) by an independent accounting firm that then expresses an opinion on the financial statements. Audits may be required by contractual arrangement, law, or regulation. Just as there are standards for preparing financial statements, there are standards for auditing and for expressing the resulting auditor's opinion. International standards for auditing have been developed by the International Auditing and Assurance Standards Board of the International Federation of Accountants. These standards have been adopted by many countries. Other countries, such as the United States, have developed their own standards. With the enactment of the **Sarbanes–Oxley Act** in the United States, auditing standards are being promulgated by the Public Company Accounting Oversight Board (PCAOB). Under International Standard on Auditing 200:

> The objective of an audit of financial statements is to enable the auditor to express an opinion whether the financial statements are prepared, in all material respects, in accordance with an applicable financial reporting framework.[4]

Publicly traded companies may also have requirements set by regulators or stock exchanges, such as appointing an independent audit committee of the board of directors to oversee the audit process. The audit process provides a basis for the independent auditor to express an audit opinion on the fairness of the financial statements that were audited. Because audits are designed and conducted by using audit sampling techniques, independent auditors cannot express an opinion that provides absolute assurance about the accuracy or precision of the financial statements. Instead, the independent audit report provides *reasonable assurance* that the financial statements are *fairly presented,* meaning that there is a high degree of probability that the audited financial statements are free from *material* error, fraud, or illegal acts that have a direct effect on the financial statements.

The standard independent audit report for a publicly traded company normally has several paragraphs under both the international and U.S. auditing standards. The first or "introductory" paragraph describes the financial statements that were audited and the responsibilities of both management and the independent auditor. The second or "scope" paragraph describes the nature of the audit process and provides the basis for the auditor's expression about reasonable assurance on the fairness of the financial statements. The third or "opinion" paragraph expresses the auditor's opinion on the fairness of the audited financial statements. An *unqualified* audit opinion states that the financial statements give a "true and fair view" (international) or are "fairly presented" (international and U.S.) in accordance with applicable accounting standards. This is often referred to as a "clean" opinion and is the one that analysts would like to see in a financial report. There are several other types of opinions. A *qualified* audit opinion is one in which there is some limitation or exception to accounting standards. Exceptions are described in the audit report with additional explanatory paragraphs so that the analyst can determine the importance of the exception. An *adverse* audit opinion occurs when the financial statements materially depart from accounting standards and are not fairly presented. An adverse opinion makes analysis of the financial statements easy: Don't bother, because the company's financial statements cannot be relied upon. Finally, a *disclaimer of opinion* occurs when, for some reason, the auditors are unable to issue an opinion. Exhibit 6 presents the independent auditor's report for Wal-Mart. Note that Wal-Mart received a "clean" or unqualified audit opinion from Ernst & Young LLP for the company's fiscal year ended 31 January 2005.

---

[4] International Federation of Accountants, *Handbook of International Auditing, Assurance, and Ethics Pronouncements,* 2006 edition, p. 230, available at www.ifac.org.

EXHIBIT 6 Wal-Mart's Independent Audit Report

Report of Independent Registered Accounting Firm
WAL-MART

The Board of Directors and Shareholders,
Wal-Mart Stores, Inc.

We have audited the accompanying consolidated balance sheets of Wal-Mart Stores, Inc. as of January 31, 2005 and 2004, and the related consolidated statements of income, shareholders' equity and cash flows for each of the three years in the period ended January 31, 2005. These financial statements are the responsibility of the company's management. Our responsibility is to express an opinion on these financial statements based on our audits.

We conducted our audits in accordance with the standards of the Public Company Accounting Oversight Board (United States). Those standards require that we plan and perform the audit to obtain reasonable assurance about whether the financial statements are free of material misstatement. An audit includes examining on a test basis, evidence supporting the amounts and disclosures in the financial statements. An audit also includes assessing the accounting principles used and significant estimates made by management, as well as evaluating the overall financial statement presentation. We believe that our audits provide a reasonable basis for our opinion.

In our opinion, the financial statements referred to above present fairly, in all material respects, the consolidated financial position of Wal-Mart Stores, Inc. at January 31, 2005 and 2004, and the consolidated results of its operations and its cash flows for each of the three years in the period ended January 31, 2005, in conformity with U.S. generally accepted accounting principles.

We also have audited, in accordance with the standards of the Public Accounting Oversight Board (United States), the effectiveness of Wal-Mart Stores, Inc.'s internal control over financial reporting as of January 31, 2005, based on criteria established in *Internal Control—Integrated Framework* issued by the Committee of Sponsoring Organizations of the Treadway Committee and our report dated March 25, 2005 expressed an unqualified opinion thereon.

Ernst & Young LLP
Rogers, Arkansas
March 25, 2005

Source: 2005 Wal-Mart Stores, Inc., Annual Report.

In the United States, under the Sarbanes–Oxley Act, the auditors must also express an opinion on the company's internal control systems. This information may be provided in a separate opinion or incorporated as a fourth paragraph in the opinion related to the financial statements. The internal control system is the company's internal system that is designed, among other things, to ensure that the company's process for generating financial reports is sound.

Although management has always been responsible for maintaining effective internal control, the Sarbanes–Oxley Act greatly increases management's responsibility for demonstrating that the company's internal controls are effective. Publicly traded companies in the United States are now required by securities regulators to:

- accept responsibility for the effectiveness of internal control;
- evaluate the effectiveness of internal control using suitable control criteria;
- support the evaluation with sufficient competent evidence; and
- provide a report on internal control.

The Sarbanes–Oxley Act specifically requires management's report on internal control to:

- state that it is management's responsibility to establish and maintain adequate internal control;
- identify management's framework for evaluating internal control;
- include management's assessment of the effectiveness of the company's internal control over financial reporting as of the end of the most recent year, including a statement as to whether internal control over financial reporting is effective;
- include a statement that the company's auditors have issued an attestation report on management's assessment; and
- certify that the company's financial statements are fairly presented.

Exhibit 7 presents Wal-Mart management's report on internal control to its company's shareholders. Note that Wal-Mart has fully complied with each of the reporting criterion that were discussed in the preceding paragraph.

EXHIBIT 7 Wal-Mart's Report to Shareholders on Corporate Governance and Internal Control

Management's Report to Our Shareholders
WAL-MART

Management of Wal-Mart Stores, Inc. ("Wal-Mart") is responsible for the preparation, integrity and objectivity of Wal-Mart's consolidated financial statements and other financial information contained in this Annual Report to Shareholders. Those consolidated financial statements were prepared in conformity with accounting principles generally accepted in the United States. In preparing those consolidated financial statements, Management was required to make certain estimates and judgments, which are based upon currently available information and Management's view of current conditions and circumstances.

The Audit Committee of the Board of Directors, which consists solely of independent directors, oversees our process of reporting financial information and the audit of our consolidated financial statements. The Audit Committee stays informed of the financial condition of Wal-Mart and regularly reviews Management's financial policies and procedures, the independence of our independent auditors, our internal control and the objectivity of our financial reporting. Both the independent financial auditors and the internal auditors have free access to the Audit Committee and meet with the Audit Committee periodically, both with and without Management present.

(Exhibit continued on next page . . .)

EXHIBIT 7 (continued)

We have retained Ernst & Young LLP, an independent registered public accounting firm, to audit our consolidated financial statements found in this annual report. We have made available to Ernst & Young LLP all of our financial records and related data in connection with their audit of our consolidated financial statements.

We have filed with the Securities and Exchange Commission the required certifications related to our consolidated financial statements as of and for the year ended January 31, 2005. These certifications are attached as exhibits to our Annual Report on Form 10-K for the year ended January 31, 2005. Additionally, we have also provided to the New York Stock Exchange the required annual certification of our Chief Executive Officer regarding our compliance with the New York Stock Exchange's corporate governance listing standards.

Report on Internal Control over Financial Reporting

Management has responsibility for establishing and maintaining adequate internal control over financial reporting. Internal control over financial reporting is a process designed to provide reasonable assurance regarding the reliability of financial reporting and the preparation of financial statements for external reporting purposes in accordance with accounting principles generally accepted in the United States. Because of its inherent limitations, internal control over financial reporting may not prevent or detect misstatements. Management has assessed the effectiveness of the company's internal control over financial reporting as of January 31, 2005. In making its assessment, Management has utilized the criteria set forth by the Committee of Sponsoring Organizations ("COSO") of the Treadway Commission in *Internal Control – Integrated Framework.* Management concluded that based on its assessment, Wal-Mart's internal control over financial reporting was effective as of January 31, 2005. Management's assessment of the effectiveness of the company's internal control over financial reporting as of January 31, 2005 has been audited by Ernst & Young LLP, an independent registered public accounting firm, as stated in their report which appears in this Annual Report to Shareholders.

Evaluation of Disclosure Controls and Procedures

We maintain disclosure controls and procedures designed to provide reasonable assurance that information, which is required to be timely disclosed, is accumulated and communicated to Management in a timely fashion. Management has assessed the effectiveness of these disclosure controls and procedures as of January 31, 2005 and determined that they were effective as of that date to provide reasonable assurance that information required to be disclosed by us in the reports we file or submit under the **Securities Exchange Act of 1934**, as amended, is accumulated and communicated to Management, as appropriate, to allow timely decisions regarding required disclosure and are effective to provide reasonable assurance that such information is recorded, processed, summarized and reported within the time periods specified by the SEC's rules and forms.

Report on Ethical Standards

Our company was founded on the belief that open communications and the highest standard of ethics are necessary to be successful. Our long-standing "Open Door" communication policy helps Management be aware of and address issues in a timely and effective manner. Through the open door policy all associates are encouraged to inform Management at the appropriate level when they are concerned about any matter pertaining to Wal-Mart.

Wal-Mart has adopted a Statement of Ethics to guide our associates in the continued observance of high ethical standards such as honesty, integrity and compliance with the law in the conduct of Wal-Mart's business. Familiarity and compliance with the Statement of Ethics is required of all associates who are part of Management. The company also maintains a separate Code of Ethics for our senior financial officers. Wal-Mart also has in

(Exhibit continued on next page . . .)

EXHIBIT 7 (continued)

place a Related-Party Transaction Policy. This policy applies to all of Wal-Mart's Officers and Directors and requires material related-party transactions to be reviewed by the Audit Committee. The Officers and Directors are required to report material related-party transactions to Wal-Mart. We maintain an ethics office which oversees and administers an ethics hotline. The ethics hotline provides a channel for associates to make confidential and anonymous complaints regarding potential violations of our statement of ethics, including violations related to financial or accounting matters.

H. Lee Scott
President and Chief Executive Officer

Thomas M. Schoewe
Executive Vice President and Chief Financial Officer

Source: 2005 Wal-Mart Stores, Inc., Annual Report.

Although these reports provide some assurances to analysts, they are not infallible. The analyst must always use a degree of healthy skepticism when analyzing financial statements.

3.2 Other Sources of Information

The information described in the previous section is generally provided to shareholders on an annual basis. Interim reports are also provided by the company either semiannually or quarterly. Interim reports generally present the four key financial statements and footnotes but are not audited. These interim reports provide updated information on a company's performance and financial position since the last annual period. Companies also prepare proxy statements for distribution to shareholders on matters that are to be put to a vote at the company's annual (or special) meeting of shareholders. The proxy statement typically provides useful information regarding management and director compensation and company stock performance and discloses any potential conflicts of interest that may exist between management, the board, and shareholders. Companies also provide relevant current information on their websites and in press releases and as part of conference calls. When performing financial statement analysis, analysts should review all these company sources of information as well as information from external sources regarding the economy, the industry, the company, and peer (comparable) companies. Information on the economy, industry, and peer companies is useful in putting the company's financial performance and position in perspective and in assessing the company's future. The next section presents a framework for using all this information in financial statement analysis.

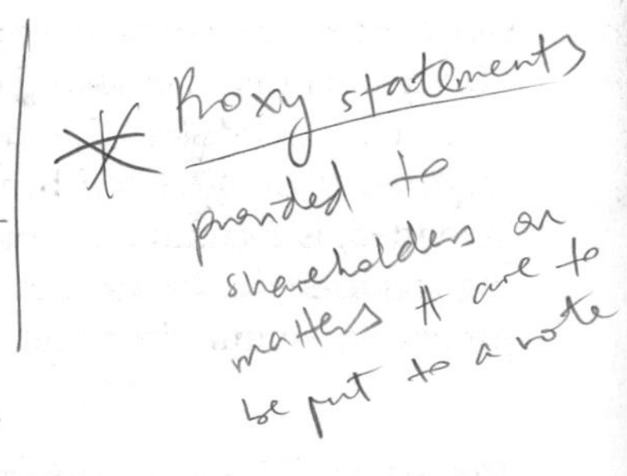

4 FINANCIAL STATEMENT ANALYSIS FRAMEWORK

Analysts work in a variety of positions. Some are equity analysts whose main objective is to evaluate potential equity (share) investments to determine whether a prospective investment is attractive and what an appropriate purchase price might be. Others are credit analysts who evaluate the creditworthiness of a company to decide whether (and with what terms) a loan should be made or what credit rating should be assigned. Analysts may also be involved in a variety of other tasks, such as evaluating the performance of a subsidiary company, evaluating a private equity investment, or finding stocks that are overvalued for purposes of taking a short position. This section presents a generic framework for financial statement analysis that can be used in these various tasks. The framework is summarized in Exhibit 8.[5]

The following sections discuss the individual phases of financial statement analysis.

4.1 Articulate the Purpose and Context of Analysis

Prior to undertaking any analysis, it is essential to understand the purpose of the analysis. An understanding of the purpose is particularly important in financial statement analysis because of the numerous available techniques and the substantial amount of data.

Some analytical tasks are well defined, in which case articulating the purpose of the analysis requires little decision making by the analyst. For example, a periodic credit review of an investment-grade debt portfolio or an equity analyst's report on a particular company may be guided by institutional norms such that the purpose of the analysis is given. Furthermore, the format, procedures, and/or sources of information may also be given.

For other analytical tasks, articulating the purpose of the analysis requires the analyst to make decisions. The purpose of an analysis guides further decisions about the approach, the tools, the data sources, the format in which to report results of the analysis, and the relative importance of different aspects of the analysis.

When facing a substantial amount of data, a less experienced analyst may be tempted to just start crunching numbers and creating output. It is generally advisable to resist the temptation and thus avoid the black hole of pointless number crunching. Consider the questions: If you could wave a magic wand and have all the numbers crunched, what conclusion would you be able to draw? What question would you be able to answer? What decision would your answer support?

The analyst should also define the context at this stage. Who is the intended audience? What is the end product—for example, a final report explaining conclusions and recommendations? What is the time frame (i.e., when is the report due)? What resources and resource constraints are relevant to completion of the analysis? Again, the context may be predefined (i.e., standard and guided by institutional norms).

Having clarified the purpose and context of the financial statement analysis, the analyst should next compile the specific questions to be answered by the analysis. For example, if the purpose of the financial statement analysis (or, more

[5] Components of this framework have been adapted from van Greuning and Bratanovic (2003, p. 300) and from Benninga and Sarig (1997, pp. 134–156).

EXHIBIT 8 Financial Statement Analysis Framework

Phase	Sources of Information	Output
1. Articulate the purpose and context of the analysis.	▶ The nature of the analyst's function, such as evaluating an equity or debt investment or issuing a credit rating. ▶ Communication with client or supervisor on needs and concerns. ▶ Institutional guidelines related to developing specific work product.	▶ Statement of the purpose or objective of analysis. ▶ A list (written or unwritten) of specific questions to be answered by the analysis. ▶ Nature and content of report to be provided. ▶ Timetable and budgeted resources for completion.
2. Collect data.	▶ Financial statements, other financial data, questionnaires, and industry/economic data. ▶ Discussions with management, suppliers, customers, and competitors. ▶ Company site visits (e.g., to production facilities or retail stores).	▶ Organized financial statements. ▶ Financial data tables. ▶ Completed questionnaires, if applicable.
3. Process data.	▶ Data from the previous phase.	▶ Adjusted financial statements. ▶ Common-size statements. ▶ Ratios and graphs. ▶ Forecasts.
4. Analyze/interpret the processed data.	▶ Input data as well as processed data.	▶ Analytical results.
5. Develop and communicate conclusions and recommendations (e.g., with an analysis report).	▶ Analytical results and previous reports. ▶ Institutional guidelines for published reports.	▶ Analytical report answering questions posed in Phase 1. ▶ Recommendation regarding the purpose of the analysis, such as whether to make an investment or grant credit.
6. Follow up.	▶ Information gathered by periodically repeating above steps as necessary to determine whether changes to holdings or recommendations are necessary.	▶ Updated reports and recommendations.

likely, the particular stage of a larger analysis) is to compare the historical performance of three companies operating in a particular industry, specific questions would include: What has been the relative growth rate of the companies and what has been the relative profitability of the companies?

4.2 Collect Data

Next, the analyst obtains the data required to answer the specific questions. A key part of this step is obtaining an understanding of the company's business, financial performance, and financial position (including trends over time and in comparison with peer companies). For historical analyses, financial statement data alone are adequate in some cases. For example, to screen a large number of alternative companies for those with a minimum level of profitability, financial statement data alone would be adequate. But to address more in-depth questions, such as why and how one company performed better or worse than its competitors, additional information would be required. As another example, to compare the historical performance of two companies in a particular industry, the historical financial statements would be sufficient to determine which had faster growing sales or earnings and which was more profitable; however, a broader comparison with overall industry growth and profitability would obviously require industry data.

Furthermore, information on the economy and industry is necessary to understand the environment in which the company operates. Analysts often take a top-down approach whereby they (1) gain an understanding of the macroeconomic environment, such as prospects for growth in the economy and inflation, (2) analyze the prospects of the industry in which the subject company operates based on the expected macroeconomic environment, and (3) determine the prospects for the company in the expected industry and macroeconomic environments. For example, an analyst may need to forecast future growth in earnings for a company. To project future growth, past company data provide one basis for statistical forecasting; however, an understanding of economic and industry conditions can improve the analyst's ability to forecast a company's earnings based on forecasts of overall economic and industry activity.

4.3 Process Data

After obtaining the requisite financial statement and other information, the analyst processes this data using appropriate analytical tools. For example, processing the data may involve computing ratios or growth rates; preparing common-size financial statements; creating charts; performing statistical analyses, such as regressions or Monte Carlo simulations; performing equity valuation; performing sensitivity analyses; or using any other analytical tools or combination of tools that are available and appropriate to the task. A comprehensive financial analysis at this stage would include the following:

- Reading and evaluating financial statements for each company subject to analysis. This includes reading the footnotes and understanding what accounting standards have been used (for example, IFRS or U.S. GAAP), what accounting choices have been made (for example, when to report revenue on the income statement), and what operating decisions have been made that affect reported financial statements (for example, leasing versus purchasing equipment).
- Making any needed adjustments to the financial statements to facilitate comparison, when the unadjusted statements of the subject companies reflect differences in accounting standards, accounting choices, or operating decisions. Note that commonly used databases do not make such analyst adjustments.

- Preparing or collecting common-size financial statement data [which scale data to directly reflect percentages (e.g., of sales) or changes (e.g., from the prior year)] and financial ratios (which are measures of various aspects of corporate performance based on financial statement elements). On the basis of common size financial statements and financial ratios, analysts can evaluate a company's relative profitability, liquidity, leverage, efficiency, and valuation in relation to past results and/or peers' results.

4.4 Analyze/Interpret the Processed Data

Once the data have been processed, the next step—critical to any analysis—is to interpret the output. The answer to a specific financial analysis question is seldom the numerical answer alone; the answer to the analytical question relies on the interpretation of the output and the use of this interpreted output to support a conclusion or recommendation. The answers to the specific analytical questions may themselves achieve the underlying purpose of the analysis, but usually, a conclusion or recommendation is required. For example, an equity analysis may require a buy, hold, or sell decision or a conclusion about the value of a share of stock. In support of the decision, the analysis would cite such information as target value, relative performance, expected future performance given a company's strategic position, quality of management, and whatever other information was important in reaching the decision.

4.5 Develop and Communicate Conclusions/Recommendations

Communicating the conclusion or recommendation in an appropriate format is the next step in an analysis. The appropriate format will vary by analytical task, by institution, and/or by audience. For example, an equity analyst report would typically include the following components:[6]

- summary and investment conclusion;
- business summary;
- risks;
- valuation; and
- historical and pro forma tables.

The contents of reports may also be specified by regulatory agencies or professional standards. For example, the CFA Institute *Standards of Practice Handbook* (SOPH) dictates standards that must be followed in communicating recommendations. The SOPH provides, in part:

> Standard V(B) states the responsibility of members and candidates to include in their communications those key factors that are instrumental to the investment recommendation presented. A critical part of this requirement is to distinguish clearly between opinions and facts. In preparing a research report, the member or candidate must present the basic characteristics of the security being analyzed, which will allow the reader to evaluate the report and incorporate information the reader deems relevant to his or her investment decision making process.[7]

---

[6] Stowe, Robinson, Pinto, and McLeavey (2002, p. 27).

[7] *Standards of Practice Handbook* (2006, p. 105).

The SOPH requires that limitations to the analysis and any risks inherent to the investment be disclosed. Furthermore, the SOPH requires that any report include elements important to the analysis and conclusions so that readers can evaluate the conclusions themselves.

4.6 Follow Up

The process does not end with the report. If an equity investment is made or a credit rating assigned, periodic review is required to determine if the original conclusions and recommendations are still valid. In the case of a rejected investment, follow up may not be necessary but may be appropriate to determine if the analysis process should be refined (for example, if a rejected investment turns out to be successful in the market). Follow up may involve repeating all the above steps in the process on a periodic basis.

SUMMARY

This reading has presented an overview of financial statement analysis. Among the major points covered are the following:

- The primary purpose of financial reports is to provide information and data about a company's financial position and performance, including profitability and cash flows. The information presented in financial reports—including the financial statements, financial notes, and management's discussion and analysis—allows the financial analyst to assess a company's financial position and performance and trends in that performance.
- Key financial statements that are a primary focus of analysis include the income statement, balance sheet, cash flow statement, and statement of owners' equity.
- The income statement presents information on the financial results of a company's business activities over a period of time. The income statement communicates how much revenue the company generated during a period and what costs it incurred in connection with generating that revenue. The basic equation underlying the income statement is Revenue − Expense = Net income.
- The balance sheet discloses what a company owns (assets) and what it owes (liabilities) at a specific point in time. Owners' equity represents the portion belonging to the owners or shareholders of the business; it is the residual interest in the assets of an entity after deducting its liabilities. The three parts of the balance sheet are formulated in the accounting relationship of Assets = Liabilities + Owners' equity.
- Although the income statement and balance sheet provide a measure of a company's success, cash and cash flow are also vital to a company's long-term success. Disclosing the sources and uses of cash in the cash flow statement helps creditors, investors, and other statement users evaluate the company's liquidity, solvency, and financial flexibility.
- The statement of changes in owners' equity reflects information about the increases or decreases to a company's owners' equity.
- In addition to the financial statements, a company provides other sources of financial information that are useful to the financial analyst. As part of his or her analysis, the financial analyst should read and assess the information presented in the company's financial note disclosures and supplementary schedules as well as the information contained in the management's discussion and analysis (MD&A). Analysts must also evaluate footnote disclosures regarding the use of alternative accounting methods, estimates, and assumptions.
- A publicly traded company must have an independent audit performed on its year-end financial statements. The auditor's opinion provides some assurance about whether the financial statements fairly reflect a company's performance and financial position. In addition, for U.S. publicly traded companies, management must demonstrate that the company's internal controls are effective.

- The financial statement analysis framework provides steps that can be followed in any financial statement analysis project, including the following:
  - articulate the purpose and context of the analysis;
  - collect input data;
  - process data;
  - analyze/interpret the processed data;
  - develop and communicate conclusions and recommendations; and
  - follow up.

PRACTICE PROBLEMS FOR READING 29

1. Providing information about the performance and financial position of companies so that users can make economic decisions best describes the role of
   A. auditing.
   B. financial reporting.
   C. financial statements.
   D. financial statement analysis.
2. A company's current financial position would *best* be evaluated using the
   A. balance sheet.
   B. income statement.
   C. cash flow statement.
   D. statement of owners' equity.
3. A company's profitability for a period would *best* be evaluated using the
   A. balance sheet.
   B. income statement.
   C. cash flow statement.
   D. statement of owners' equity.
4. Accounting methods, estimates, and assumptions used in preparing financial statements are found
   A. in footnotes.
   B. in the auditor's report.
   C. in the proxy statement.
   D. nowhere in financial statements.
5. Information about management and director compensation would *best* be found
   A. in footnotes.
   B. in the auditor's report.
   C. in the proxy statement.
   D. nowhere in financial statements.
6. Information about material events and uncertainties would *best* be found in
   A. footnotes.
   B. the auditor's report.
   C. the proxy statement.
   D. management's discussion and analysis.
7. What type of audit opinion is preferred when analyzing financial statements?
   A. Qualified.
   B. Adverse.
   C. Disclaimer.
   D. Unqualified.

8. Ratios are an input into which step in the financial analysis framework?

A. Process data.

B. Collect input data.

C. Analyze/interpret the processed data.

D. Develop and communicate conclusions and recommendations.

Note: They are an output of the "Process data" step.

FINANCIAL REPORTING MECHANICS

by Thomas R. Robinson, Hennie van Greuning,
Karen O'Connor Rubsam, Elaine Henry, and Michael A. Broihahn

READING

30

LEARNING OUTCOMES

The candidate should be able to:

a. identify the groups (operating, investing, and financing activities) into which business activities are categorized for financial reporting purposes and classify any business activity into the appropriate group;

b. explain the relationship of financial statement elements and accounts, and classify accounts into the financial statement elements;

c. explain the accounting equation in its basic and expanded forms;

d. explain the process of recording business transactions using an accounting system based on the accounting equations;

e. explain the need for accruals and other adjustments in preparing financial statements;

f. prepare financial statements, given account balances or other elements in the relevant accounting equation, and explain the relationships among the income statement, balance sheet, statement of cash flows, and statement of owners' equity;

g. describe the flow of information in an accounting system;

h. explain the use of the results of the accounting process in security analysis.

THEME

The mechanics of the accounting process is the foundation for financial reporting. Understanding those mechanics enables an analyst to understand the interrelationships of financial accounts and statements and, therefore, to better assess a company's financial performance.

1 INTRODUCTION

The financial statements of a company are end-products of a process for recording transactions of the company related to operations, financing, and investment. The structures of financial statements themselves reflect the system of recording and organizing transactions. To be an informed user of financial statements, the analyst must be knowledgeable about the principles of this system. This reading will supply that essential knowledge, taking the perspective of the user rather than the preparer. Learning the process from this perspective will enable an analyst to grasp the critical concepts without being overwhelmed by the detailed technical skills required by the accountants who prepare financial statements that are a major component of financial reports.

This reading is organized as follows: Section 2 describes the three groups into which business activities are classified for financial reporting purposes. Any transaction affects one or more of these groups. Section 3 describes how the elements of financial statements relate to accounts, the basic content unit of classifying transactions. The section is also an introduction to the linkages among the financial statements. Section 4 provides a step-by-step illustration of the accounting process. Section 5 explains the consequences of timing differences between the elements of a transaction. Section 6 provides an overview of how information flows through a business's accounting system. Section 7 introduces the use of financial reporting in security analysis. A summary of the key points and practice problems in the CFA Institute multiple-choice format conclude the reading.

2 THE CLASSIFICATION OF BUSINESS ACTIVITIES

Accountants give similar accounting treatment to similar types of business transactions. Therefore, a first step in understanding financial reporting mechanics is to understand how business activities are classified for financial reporting purposes.

Business activities may be classified into three groups for financial reporting purposes: operating, investing, and financing activities.

- **Operating activities** are those activities that are part of the day-to-day business functioning of an entity. Examples include the sale of meals by a restaurant, the sale of services by a consulting firm, the manufacture and sale of ovens by an oven-manufacturing company, and taking deposits and making loans by a bank.
- **Investing activities** are those activities associated with acquisition and disposal of long-term assets. Examples include the purchase of equipment or sale of surplus equipment (such as an oven) by a restaurant (contrast this to the sale of an oven by an oven manufacturer, which would be an operating activity), and the purchase or sale of an office building, a retail store, or a factory.
- **Financing activities** are those activities related to obtaining or repaying capital. The two primary sources for such funds are owners (shareholders) or creditors. Examples include issuing common shares, taking out a bank loan, and issuing bonds.

Understanding the nature of activities helps the analyst understand where the company is doing well and where it is not doing so well. Ideally, an analyst would prefer that most of a company's profits (and cash flow) come from its operating activities. Exhibit 1 provides examples of typical business activities and how these activities relate to the elements of financial statements described in the following section.

EXHIBIT 1 Typical Business Activities and Financial Statement Elements Affected

Operating activities	▶ Sales of goods and services to customers: (R) ▶ Costs of providing the goods and services: (X) ▶ Income tax expense: (X) ▶ Holding short-term assets or incurring short-term liabilities directly related to operating activities: (A), (L)
Investing activities	▶ Purchase or sale of assets, such as property, plant, and equipment: (A) ▶ Purchase or sale of other entities' equity and debt securities: (A)
Financing activities	▶ Issuance or repurchase of the company's own preferred or common stock: (E) ▶ Issuance or repayment of debt: (L) ▶ Payment of distributions (i.e., dividends to preferred or common stockholders): (E)

Assets (A), Liabilities (L), Owners' Equity (E), Revenue (R), and Expenses (X).

Not all transactions fit neatly in this framework for purposes of financial statement presentation. For example, interest received by a bank on one of its loans would be considered part of operating activities because a bank is in the business of lending money. In contrast, interest received on a bond investment by a restaurant may be more appropriately classified as an investing activity because the restaurant is not in the business of lending money.

The next section discusses how transactions resulting from these business activities are reflected in a company's financial records.

ACCOUNTS AND FINANCIAL STATEMENTS 3

Business activities resulting in transactions are reflected in the broad groupings of financial statement elements: Assets, Liabilities, Owners' Equity, Revenue, and Expenses.[1] In general terms, these elements can be defined as follows: **assets** are

[1] International Financial Reporting Standards use the term "income" to include revenue and gains. Gains are similar to revenue; however, they arise from secondary or peripheral activities rather than from a company's primary business activities. For example, for a restaurant, the sale of surplus restaurant equipment for more than its cost is referred to as a gain rather than revenue. Similarly, a loss is like an expense but arises from secondary activities. Gains and losses may be considered part of operations on the income statement (for example, a loss due to a decline in value of inventory) or may be part of nonoperating activities (for example, the sale of nontrading investments). Under U.S. GAAP, financial statement elements are defined to include assets, liabilities, owners' equity, revenue, expenses, gains, and losses. To illustrate business transactions in this reading, we will use the simple classification of revenues and expenses. All gains and revenue will be aggregated in revenue, and all losses and expenses will be aggregated in expenses.

the economic resources of a company; **liabilities** are the creditors' claims on the resources of a company; **owners' equity** is the residual claim on those resources; **revenues** are inflows of economic resources to the company; and **expenses** are outflows of economic resources or increases in liabilities.[2]

Accounts provide individual records of increases and decreases in a *specific* asset, liability, component of owners' equity, revenue, or expense. The financial statements are constructed using these elements.

3.1 Financial Statement Elements and Accounts

Within the financial statement elements, accounts are subclassifications. **Accounts** are individual records of increases and decreases in a specific asset, liability, component of owners' equity, revenue, or expense. For financial statements, amounts recorded in every individual account are summarized and grouped appropriately within a financial statement element. Exhibit 2 provides a listing of common accounts. These accounts will be described throughout this reading or in following readings. Unlike the financial statement elements, there is no standard set of accounts applicable to all companies. Although almost every company has certain accounts, such as cash, each company specifies the accounts in its accounting system based on its particular needs and circumstances. For example, a company in the restaurant business may not be involved in trading securities and, therefore, may not need an account to record such an activity. Furthermore, each company names its accounts based on its business. A company in the restaurant business might have an asset account for each of its ovens, with the accounts named "Oven-1" and "Oven-2." In its financial statements, these accounts would likely be grouped within long-term assets as a single line item called "Property, plant, and equipment."

A company's challenge is to establish accounts and account groupings that provide meaningful summarization of voluminous data but retain enough detail to facilitate decision making and preparation of the financial statements. The actual accounts used in a company's accounting system will be set forth in a **chart of accounts.** Generally, the chart of accounts is far more detailed than the information presented in financial statements.

Certain accounts are used to offset other accounts. For example, a common asset account is accounts receivable, also known as "trade accounts receivable" or "trade receivables." A company uses this account to record the amounts it is owed by its customers. In other words, sales made on credit are reflected in accounts receivable. In connection with its receivables, a company often expects some amount of uncollectible accounts and, therefore, records an estimate of the amount that may not be collected. The estimated uncollectible amount is recorded in an account called **allowance for bad debts**. Because the effect of the allowance for bad debts account is to reduce the balance of the company's accounts receivable, it is known as a "contra asset account." Any account that is offset or deducted from another account is called a "**contra account**." Common contra asset accounts include allowance for bad debts (an offset to accounts receivable for the amount of accounts receivable that are estimated to be uncollectible), **accumulated depreciation** (an offset to property, plant, and equipment reflecting the amount of the cost of property, plant, and equipment that has

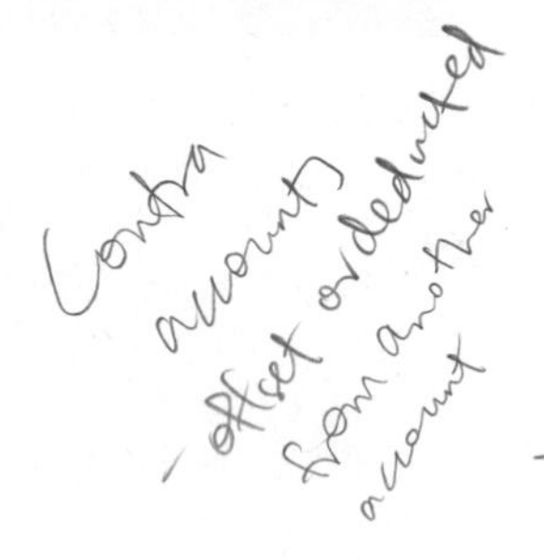

[2] The authoritative accounting standards provide significantly more detailed definitions of the accounting elements. Also note that "owners' equity" is a generic term and more specific titles are often used such as "shareholders' equity," "stockholders' equity," or "partners' capital." The broader terms "equity" and "capital" are also used on occasion.

been allocated to current and previous accounting periods), and **sales returns and allowances** (an offset to revenue reflecting any cash refunds, credits on account, and discounts from sales prices given to customers who purchased defective or unsatisfactory items).

EXHIBIT 2 Common Accounts

Assets	▶ Cash and cash equivalents
	▶ Accounts receivable, trade receivables
	▶ Prepaid expenses
	▶ Inventory
	▶ Property, plant, and equipment
	▶ Investment property
	▶ **Intangible assets** (patents, trademarks, licenses, copyright, goodwill)
	▶ Financial assets, **trading securities**, investment securities
	▶ Investments accounted for by the equity method
	▶ Current and deferred tax assets
	▶ [for banks, Loans (receivable)]
Liabilities	▶ Accounts payable, trade payables
	▶ Provisions or accrued liabilities
	▶ Financial liabilities
	▶ Current and deferred tax liabilities
	▶ Reserves
	▶ Minority interest
	▶ Unearned revenue
	▶ Debt payable
	▶ Bonds (payable)
	▶ [for banks, Deposits]
Owners' equity	▶ Capital, such as common stock par value
	▶ Additional paid-in capital
	▶ Retained earnings
	▶ Other comprehensive income
Revenue	▶ Revenue, sales
	▶ Gains
	▶ Investment income (e.g., interest and dividends)
Expense	▶ **Cost of goods sold**
	▶ Selling, general, and administrative expenses "SG&A" (e.g., rent, utilities, salaries, advertising)
	▶ Depreciation and amortization
	▶ Interest expense
	▶ Tax expense
	▶ Losses

For presentation purposes, assets are sometimes categorized as "current" or "noncurrent." For example, Tesco (a large European retailer) presents the following major asset accounts in its 2006 financial reports:

Noncurrent assets

- Intangible assets including goodwill
- Property, plant, and equipment
- Investment property
- Investments in joint ventures and associates

Current assets

- Inventories
- Trade and other receivables
- Cash and cash equivalents

Noncurrent assets are assets that are expected to benefit the company over an extended period of time (usually more than one year). For Tesco, these include the following: intangible assets, such as goodwill;[3] property, plant, and equipment used in operations (e.g., land and buildings); other property held for investment, and investments in the securities of other companies.

Current assets are those that are expected to be consumed or converted into cash in the near future, typically one year or less. Inventories are the unsold units of product on hand (sometimes referred to as inventory stock). **Trade receivables** (also referred to as commercial receivables, or simply accounts receivable) are amounts customers owe the company for products that have been sold as well as amounts that may be due from suppliers (such as for returns of merchandise). **Other receivables** represent amounts owed to the company from parties other than customers. Cash refers to cash on hand (e.g., petty cash and cash not yet deposited to the bank) and in the bank. Cash equivalents are very liquid short-term investments, usually maturing in 90 days or less. The presentation of assets as current or noncurrent will vary from industry to industry and from country to country. Some industries present current assets first, whereas others list noncurrent assets first. This is discussed further in later readings.

3.2 Accounting Equations

The five financial statement elements noted previously serve as the inputs for equations that underlie the financial statements. This section describes the equations for three of the financial statements: balance sheet, income statement, and statement of retained earnings. A statement of retained earnings can be viewed as a component of the statement of stockholders' equity, which shows *all* changes to owners' equity, both changes resulting from retained earnings and changes resulting from share issuance or repurchase. The fourth basic financial statement, the statement of cash flows, will be discussed in a later section.

The **balance sheet** presents a company's financial position at a *particular point in time.* It provides a listing of a company's assets and the claims on those assets (liabilities and equity claims). The equation that underlies the balance

[3] **Goodwill** is an intangible asset that represents the excess of the purchase price of an acquired company over the value of the net assets acquired.

sheet is also known as the "basic accounting equation." A company's financial position is reflected using the following equation:

$$\text{Assets} = \text{Liabilities} + \text{Owners' equity} \quad \textbf{(30-1a)}$$

Presented in this form, it is clear that claims on assets are from two sources: liabilities or owners' equity. Owners' equity is the **residual claim** of the owners (i.e., the owners' remaining claim on the company's assets after the liabilities are deducted). The concept of the owners' residual claim is well illustrated by the slightly rearranged balance sheet equation, roughly equivalent to the structure commonly seen in the balance sheets of U.K. companies:

$$\text{Assets} - \text{Liabilities} = \text{Owners' equity} \quad \textbf{(30-1b)}$$

Other terms are used to denote owners' equity, including shareholders' equity, stockholders' equity, net assets, equity, net worth, **net book value**, and partners' capital. The exact titles depend upon the type of entity, but the equation remains the same. Owners' equity at a given date can be further classified by its origin: capital contributed by owners, and earnings retained in the business up to that date:[4]

$$\text{Owners' equity} = \text{Contributed capital} + \text{Retained earnings} \quad \textbf{(30-2)}$$

The income statement presents the performance of a business for a *specific period of time.* The equation reflected in the income statement is the following:

$$\text{Revenue} - \text{Expenses} = \text{Net income (loss)} \quad \textbf{(30-3)}$$

Note that net income (loss) is the difference between two of the elements: revenue and expenses. When a company's revenue exceeds its expenses, it reports net income; when a company's revenues are less than its expenses, it reports a net loss. Other terms are used synonymously with revenue, including sales and turnover (in the United Kingdom). Other terms used synonymously with net income include net profit and net earnings.

Also, as noted earlier, revenue and expenses generally relate to providing goods or services in a company's primary business activities. In contrast, gains (losses) relate to increases (decreases) in resources that are not part of a company's primary business activities. Distinguishing a company's primary business activities from other business activities is important in financial analysis; however, for purposes of the accounting equation, gains are included in revenue and losses are included in expenses.

The balance sheet and income statement are two of the primary financial statements. Although these are the common terms for these statements, some variations in the names occur. A balance sheet can be referred to as a "statement of financial position" or some similar term that indicates it contains balances at a point in time. Income statements can be titled "statement of operations,"

[4] This formula reflects the fundamental origins of owners' equity and reflects the basic principles of accounting. The presentation is somewhat simplified. In practice, the owners' equity section of a company's balance sheet may include other items, such as treasury stock (which arises when a company repurchases and holds its own stock) or other comprehensive income. **Comprehensive income** includes all income of the company. Some items of comprehensive income are not reported on the income statement. These items as a group are called **other comprehensive income**; such items arise, for example, when there are changes in the value of assets or liabilities that are not reflected in the income statement.

"statement of income," "statement of profit and loss," or some other similar term showing that it reflects the company's operating activity for a period of time. A simplified balance sheet and income statement are shown in Exhibit 3.

EXHIBIT 3 Simplified Balance Sheet and Income Statement

ABC Company, Inc. Balance Sheet As of 31 December 20X1		ABC Company, Inc. Income Statement For the Year Ended 31 December 20X1	
Assets	2,000	Revenue	250
Liabilities	500	Expense	50
Owners' equity	1,500	Net income	200
	2,000		

The balance sheet represents a company's financial position at a point in time, and the income statement represents a company's activity over a period of time. The two statements are linked together through the retained earnings component of owners' equity. Beginning retained earnings is the balance in this account at the beginning of the accounting period, and ending retained earnings is the balance at the end of the period. A company's ending retained earnings is composed of the beginning balance (if any), plus net income, less any distributions to owners (dividends). Accordingly, the equation underlying retained earnings is:

$$\text{Ending retained earnings} = \text{Beginning retained earnings} + \text{Net income} - \text{Dividends} \quad \textbf{(30-4a)}$$

Or, substituting Equation 30-3 for Net income, equivalently:

$$\text{Ending retained earnings} = \text{Beginning retained earnings} + \text{Revenues} - \text{Expenses} - \text{Dividends} \quad \textbf{(30-4b)}$$

As its name suggests, retained earnings represent the earnings (i.e., net income) that are retained by the company—in other words, the amount not distributed as dividends to owners. Retained earnings is a component of owners' equity and links the "as of" balance sheet equation with the "activity" equation of the income statement. To provide a combined representation of the balance sheet and income statement, we can substitute Equation 30-2 into Equation 30-1a. This becomes the expanded accounting equation:

$$\text{Assets} = \text{Liabilities} + \text{Contributed capital} + \text{Ending retained earnings} \quad \textbf{(30-5a)}$$

Or equivalently, substituting Equation 30-4b into Equation 30-5a, we can write:

$$\text{Assets} = \text{Liabilities} + \text{Contributed capital} + \text{Beginning retained earnings} + \text{Revenue} - \text{Expenses} - \text{Dividends} \quad \textbf{(30-5b)}$$

The last five items, beginning with contributed capital, are components of owners' equity.

The statement of retained earnings shows the linkage between the balance sheet and income statement. Exhibit 4 shows a simplified example of financial statements for a company that began the year with retained earnings of $250 and recognized $200 of net income during the period. The example assumes the company paid no dividends and, therefore, had ending retained earnings of $450.

The basic accounting equation reflected in the balance sheet (Assets = Liabilities + Owners' equity) implies that every recorded transaction affects at least two accounts in order to keep the equation in balance, hence the term **double-entry accounting** that is sometimes used to describe the accounting process. For example, the use of cash to purchase equipment affects two accounts (both asset accounts): cash decreases and equipment increases. As another example, the use of cash to pay off a liability also affects two accounts (one asset account and one liability account): cash decreases and the liability decreases. With each transaction, the accounting equation remains in balance, which is a fundamental accounting concept. Example 1 presents a partial balance sheet for an actual company and an application of the accounting equation. Examples 2 and 3 provide further practice for applying the accounting equations.

EXHIBIT 4 Simplified Balance Sheet, Income Statement, and Statement of Retained Earnings

Point in Time: Beginning of Period Balance Sheet		Change over Time: Income Statement *and* Changes in Retained Earnings		Point in Time: End of Period Balance Sheet	
ABC Company, Inc. (Beginning) Balance Sheet As of 31 December 20X0		**ABC Company, Inc. Income Statement Year Ended 31 December 20X1**		**ABC Company, Inc. (Ending) Balance Sheet As of 31 December 20X1**	
Assets	2,000	Revenue	250	Assets	2,200
		Expense	50		
Liabilities	500	Net income	200	Liabilities	500
Contributed equity	1,250			Combined equity	1,250
Retained earnings	**250**			**Retained earnings**	**450**
Owners' equity	1,500			Owners' equity	1,700
	2,000				2,200

ABC Company, Inc.
Statement of Retained Earnings
Year Ended 31 December 20X1

Beginning retained earnings	**250**
Plus net income	200
Minus dividends	0
Ending retained earnings	**450**

EXAMPLE 1

Using Accounting Equations (1)

Canon is a manufacturer of copy machines and other electronic equipment. Abbreviated balance sheets as of 31 December 2004 and 2005 are presented below.

Canon and Subsidiaries
Consolidated Balance Sheets
(millions of yen)

	31 Dec 2005	31 Dec 2004
Assets		
Total assets	¥4,043,553	¥3,587,021
Liabilities and stockholders' equity		
Total liabilities	1,238,535	1,190,331
Total stockholders' equity	?	2,396,690
Total liabilities and stockholders' equity	¥4,043,553	¥3,587,021

Using Equation 30-1a, address the following:

1. Determine the amount of stockholders' equity as of 31 December 2005.
2. A. Calculate and contrast the absolute change in total assets in 2005 with the absolute change in total stockholders' equity in 2005.
   B. Based on your answer to 2A, state and justify the relative importance of growth in stockholders' equity and growth in liabilities in financing the growth of assets over the two years.

Solution to 1: Total stockholders' equity is equal to assets minus liabilities; in other words, it is the residual claim to the company's assets after deducting liabilities. For 2005, the amount of Canon's total stockholders' equity was thus ¥4,043,553 million − ¥1,238,535 million = ¥2,805,018 million in 2005.

Solution to 2:

A. Total assets increased by ¥4,043,553 million − ¥3,587,021 million = ¥456,532 million. Total stockholders' equity increased by ¥2,805,018 million − ¥2,396,690 million = ¥408,328 million. Thus, in 2005, total assets grew by more than total stockholders' equity (¥456,532 million is larger than ¥408,328 million).

B. Using the relationship Assets = Liabilities + Owners' equity, the solution to 2A implies that total liabilities increased by the difference between the increase in total assets and the increase in total stockholders' equity, that is, by ¥456,532 million − ¥408,328 million = ¥48,204 million. (If liabilities had not increased by ¥48,204 million, the accounting equation would not be in balance.) Contrasting the growth in total stockholders' equity (¥408,328 million) with the growth in total liabilities (¥48,204 million), we see that the growth in stockholders' equity was relatively much more important than the growth in liabilities in financing total asset growth in 2005.

EXAMPLE 2

Using Accounting Equations (2)

An analyst has collected the following information regarding a company in advance of its year-end earnings announcement (amounts in millions):

Estimated net income	$ 150
Beginning retained earnings	$2,000
Estimated distributions to owners	$ 50

The analyst's estimate of ending retained earnings (in millions) should be closest to

A. $2,000.
B. $2,100.
C. $2,150.
D. $2,200.

Solution: B is correct. Beginning retained earnings is increased by net income and reduced by distributions to owners: $2,000 + $150 − $50 = $2,100.

EXAMPLE 3

Using Accounting Equations (3)

An analyst has compiled the following information regarding RDZ, Inc.

Liabilities at year-end	€1,000
Contributed capital at year-end	€1,000
Beginning retained earnings	€500
Revenue during the year	€4,000
Expenses during the year	€3,800

There have been no distributions to owners. The analyst's estimate of total assets at year-end should be closest to

A. €2,000.
B. €2,300.
C. €2,500.
D. €2,700.

Solution: D is correct. Ending retained earnings is first determined by adding revenue minus expenses to beginning retained earnings to obtain €700. Total assets would be equal to the sum of liabilities, contributed capital, and ending retained earnings: €1,000 + €1,000 + €700 = €2,700.

Having described the components and linkages of financial statements in abstract terms, we now examine more concretely how business activities are recorded. The next section illustrates the accounting process with a simple step-by-step example.

4 THE ACCOUNTING PROCESS

The accounting process involves recording business transactions such that periodic financial statements can be prepared. This section illustrates how business transactions are recorded in a simplified accounting system.

4.1 An Illustration

Key concepts of the accounting process can be more easily explained using a simple illustration. We look at an illustration in which three friends decide to start a business, Investment Advisers, Ltd. (IAL). They plan to issue a monthly newsletter of securities trading advice and to sell investment books. Although they do not plan to manage any clients' funds, they will manage a trading portfolio of the owners' funds to demonstrate the success of the recommended strategies from the newsletter. Because this illustration is meant to present accounting concepts, any regulatory implications will not be addressed. Additionally, for this illustration, we will assume that the entity will not be subject to income taxes; any income or loss will be passed through to the owners and be subject to tax on their personal income tax returns.

As the business commences, various business activities occur. Exhibit 5 provides a listing of the business activities that have taken place in the early stages of operations. Note that these activities encompass the types of operating, investing, and financing business activities discussed above.

4.2 The Accounting Records

If the owners want to evaluate the business at the end of January 2006, Exhibit 5 does not provide a sufficiently meaningful report of what transpired or where the company currently stands. It is clear that a system is needed to track this information and to address three objectives:

- Identify those activities requiring further action (e.g., collection of outstanding receivable balances).
- Assess the profitability of the operations over the month.
- Evaluate the current financial position of the company (such as cash on hand).

EXHIBIT 5 Business Activities for Investment Advisers, Ltd.

#	Date	Business Activity
1	31 December 2005	► File documents with regulatory authorities to establish a separate legal entity. Initially capitalize the company through deposit of $150,000 from the three owners.
2	2 January 2006	► Set up a $100,000 investment account and purchase a portfolio of equities and fixed-income securities.
3	2 January 2006	► Pay $3,000 to landlord for office/warehouse. $2,000 represents a refundable deposit, and $1,000 represents the first month's rent.
4	3 January 2006	► Purchase office equipment for $6,000. The equipment has an estimated life of two years with no salvage value.[5]
5	3 January 2006	► Receive $1,200 cash for a one-year subscription to the monthly newsletter.
6	10 January 2006	► Purchase and receive 500 books at a cost of $20 per book for a total of $10,000. Invoice terms are that payment from IAL is due in 30 days. No cash changes hands. These books are intended for resale.
7	10 January 2006	► Spend $600 on newspaper and trade magazine advertising for the month.
8	15 January 2006	► Borrow $12,000 from a bank for working capital. Interest is payable annually at 10 percent. The principal is due in two years.
9	15 January 2006	► Ship first order to a customer consisting of five books at $25 per book. Invoice terms are that payment is due in 30 days. No cash changes hands.
10	15 January 2006	► Sell for cash 10 books at $25 per book at an investment conference.
11	30 January 2006	► Hire a part-time clerk. The clerk is hired through an agency that also handles all payroll taxes. The company is to pay $15 per hour to the agency. The clerk works six hours prior to 31 January, but no cash will be paid until February.
12	31 January 2006	► Mail out the first month's newsletter to customer. This subscription had been sold on 3 January. See item 5.
13	31 January 2006	► Review of the investment portfolio shows that $100 of interest income was earned and the market value of the portfolio has increased by $2,000. The balance in the investment account is now $102,100. The securities are classified as "trading" securities.

An accounting system will translate the company's business activities into usable financial records. The basic system for recording transactions in this illustration is a spreadsheet with each of the different types of accounts represented by a column. The accounting equation provides a basis for setting up this system. Recall the accounting Equation 30-5b:

Assets = Liabilities + Contributed capital + Beginning retained earnings + Revenue − Expenses − Dividends

[5] **Salvage value** is the amount the company estimates that it can sell the asset for at the end of its useful life.

The specific accounts to be used for IAL's system include the following:

- Asset Accounts:
  Cash
  Investments
  Prepaid rent (cash paid for rent in advance of recognizing the expense)
  Rent deposit (cash deposited with the landlord, but returnable to the company)
  Office equipment
  Inventory
  Accounts receivable
- Liability Accounts:
  Unearned fees (fees that have not been earned yet, even though cash has been received)
  Accounts payable (amounts owed to suppliers)
  Bank debt
- Equity Accounts:
  Contributed capital
  Retained earnings
    Income
      Revenue
      Expenses
    Dividends

Exhibit 6 presents the spreadsheet representing IAL's accounting system for the first 10 transactions. Each event is entered on a new row of the spreadsheet as it occurs. To record events in the spreadsheet, the financial impact of each needs to be assessed and the activity expressed as an accounting transaction. In assessing the financial impact of each event and converting these events into accounting transactions, the following steps are taken:

1. Identify which accounts are affected, by what amount, and whether the accounts are increased or decreased.
2. Determine the element type for each account identified in Step 1 (e.g., cash is an asset) and where it fits in the basic accounting equation. Rely on the economic characteristics of the account and the basic definitions of the elements to make this determination.
3. Using the information from Steps 1 and 2, enter the amounts in the appropriate column of the spreadsheet.
4. Verify that the accounting equation is still in balance.

At any point in time, basic financial statements can be prepared based on the subtotals in each column.

EXHIBIT 6 Accounting System for Investment Advisers, Ltd.

	Assets =			Liabilities		+	Owners' Equity			
#	**Cash**	**Other Assets**	**Account**	**Amount**	**Account**	**Contributed Capital**	**Beginning Retained Earnings**	**Revenue**	**Expense**	**Dividends**
Beg. Balance	0	0		0		0	0	0	0	0
1 Capitalize	150,000					150,000				
2 Investments	(100,000)	100,000	Investments							
3 Pay landlord	(3,000)	1,000	Prepaid rent							
		2,000	Rent deposit							
4 Buy equipment	(6,000)	6,000	Office equipment							
5 Sell subscription	1,200			1,200	Unearned fees					
6 Buy books		10,000	Inventory	10,000	Accounts payable					
7 Advertise	(600)								(600)	
8 Borrow	12,000			12,000	Bank debt					
9 Sell books on account		125	Accounts receivable					125	(100)	
		(100)	Inventory							
10 Cash sale	250	(200)	Inventory					250	(200)	
Subtotal	**53,850**	**118,825**		**23,200**			**150,000**	**375**	**(900)**	

The following discussion identifies the accounts affected and the related element (Steps 1 and 2) for the first 10 events listed in Exhibit 5. The accounting treatment shows the account affected in bold and the related element in brackets. The recording of these entries into a basic accounting system (Steps 3 and 4) is depicted on the spreadsheet in Exhibit 6.

Because this is a new business, the accounting equation begins at zero on both sides. There is a zero beginning balance in all accounts.

31 December 2005

#	Business Activity	Accounting Treatment
1	▶ File documents with regulatory authorities to establish a separate legal entity. Initially capitalize the company through deposit of $150,000 from the three owners.	▶ **Cash [A]** is increased by $150,000, and **contributed capital [E]**[6] is increased by $150,000.

Accounting elements: Assets (A), Liabilities (L), Equity (E), Revenue (R), and Expenses (X).

This transaction affects two elements: assets and equity. Exhibit 6 demonstrates this effect on the accounting equation. The company's balance sheet at this point in time would be presented by subtotaling the columns in Exhibit 6:

Investment Advisers, Ltd.
Balance Sheet
As of 31 December 2005

Assets	
Cash	$150,000
Total assets	$150,000
Liabilities and owners' equity	
Contributed capital	$150,000
Total liabilities and owners' equity	$150,000

The company has assets (resources) of $150,000, and the owners' claim on the resources equals $150,000 (their contributed capital) as there are no liabilities at this point.

[6] The account title will vary depending upon the type of entity (incorporated or not) and jurisdiction. Alternative account titles are "common shares," "common stock," "members' capital," "partners' capital," etc.

For this illustration, we present an unclassified balance sheet. An **unclassified balance sheet** is one that does not show subtotals for current assets and current liabilities. Assets are simply listed in order of liquidity (how quickly they are expected to be converted into cash). Similarly, liabilities are listed in the order in which they are expected to be satisfied (or paid off).

2 January 2006

#	Business Activity	Accounting Treatment
2	▶ Set up a $100,000 investment account and purchase a portfolio of equities and fixed-income securities.	▶ **Investments [A]** were increased by $100,000, and **cash [A]** was decreased by $100,000.

Accounting elements: Assets (A), Liabilities (L), Equity (E), Revenue (R), and Expenses (X).

This transaction affects two accounts, but only one element (assets) and one side of the accounting equation, as depicted in Exhibit 6. Cash is reduced when the securities are purchased. Another type of asset, investments, increases. We examine the other transaction from 2 January before taking another look at the company's balance sheet.

2 January 2006

#	Business Activity	Accounting Treatment
3	▶ Pay $3,000 to landlord for office/warehouse. $2,000 represents a refundable deposit, and $1,000 represents the first month's rent.	▶ **Cash [A]** was decreased by $3,000, **deposits [A]** were increased by $2,000, and **prepaid rent [A]** was increased by $1,000.

Accounting elements: Assets (A), Liabilities (L), Equity (E), Revenue (R), and Expenses (X).

Once again, this transaction affects only asset accounts. Note that the first month's rent is initially recorded as an asset, prepaid rent. As time passes, the company will incur rent expense, so a portion of this prepaid asset will be transferred to expenses and thus will appear on the income statement as an expense.[7] This will require a later adjustment in our accounting system. Note that the

[7] An argument can be made for treating this $1,000 as an immediate expense. We adopt the approach of recording a prepaid asset in order to illustrate accrual accounting. A situation in which a company prepays rent (or insurance or any similar expense) for a time span covering multiple accounting periods more clearly requires the use of accrual accounting.

transactions so far have had no impact on the income statement. At this point in time, the company's balance sheet would be:

Investment Advisers, Ltd.
Balance Sheet
As of 2 January 2006

Assets	
Cash	$ 47,000
Investments	100,000
Prepaid rent	1,000
Deposits	2,000
Total assets	$150,000
Liabilities and owners' equity	
Contributed capital	$150,000
Total liabilities and owners' equity	$150,000

Note that the items in the balance sheet have changed, but it remains in balance; the amount of total assets equals total liabilities plus owners' equity. The company still has $150,000 in resources, but the assets now comprise cash, investments, prepaid rent, and deposits. Each asset is listed separately because they are different in terms of their ability to be used by the company. Note also that the owners' equity claim on these assets remains $150,000 because the company still has no liabilities.

3 January 2006

#	Business Activity	Accounting Treatment
4	▶ Purchase office equipment for $6,000 in cash. The equipment has an estimated life of two years with no salvage value.	▶ **Cash** [A] was decreased by $6,000, and **office equipment** [A] was increased by $6,000.

Accounting elements: Assets (A), Liabilities (L), Equity (E), Revenue (R), and Expenses (X).

The company has once again exchanged one asset for another. Cash has decreased while office equipment has increased. Office equipment is a resource that will provide benefits over multiple future periods and, therefore, its cost must also be spread over multiple future periods. This will require adjustments to our accounting records as time passes. **Depreciation** is the term for the process of spreading this cost over multiple periods.

3 January 2006

#	Business Activity	Accounting Treatment
5	▶ Receive $1,200 cash for a one-year subscription to the monthly newsletter.	▶ **Cash [A]** was increased by $1,200, and **unearned fees [L]** was increased by $1,200.

Accounting elements: Assets (A), Liabilities (L), Equity (E), Revenue (R), and Expenses (X).

In this transaction, the company has received cash related to the sale of subscriptions. However, the company has not yet actually earned the subscription fees because it has an obligation to deliver newsletters in the future. So, this amount is recorded as a liability called **unearned fees** (or **unearned revenue**). In the future, as the company delivers the newsletters and thus fulfills its obligation, this amount will be transferred to revenue. If the company fails to deliver the newsletters, the fees will need to be returned to the customer. As of 3 January 2006, the company's balance sheet would appear as

Investment Advisers, Ltd.
Balance Sheet
As of 3 January 2006

Assets	
Cash	$ 42,200
Investments	100,000
Prepaid rent	1,000
Deposits	2,000
Office equipment	6,000
Total assets	$151,200
Liabilities and owners' equity	
Liabilities	
Unearned fees	$ 1,200
Equity	
Contributed capital	$150,000
Total liabilities and owners' equity	$151,200

The company now has $151,200 of resources, against which there is a claim by the subscription customer of $1,200 and a residual claim by the owners of $150,000. Again, the balance sheet remains in balance, with total assets equal to total liabilities plus equity.

10 January 2006

#	Business Activity	Accounting Treatment
6	▶ Purchase and receive 500 books at a cost of $20 per book for a total of $10,000. Invoice terms are that payment from IAL is due in 30 days. No cash changes hands. These books are intended for resale.	▶ **Inventory [A]** is increased by $10,000, and **accounts payable [L]** is increased by $10,000.

Accounting elements: Assets (A), Liabilities (L), Equity (E), Revenue (R), and Expenses (X).

The company has obtained an asset, inventory, which can be sold to customers at a later date. Rather than paying cash to the supplier currently, the company has incurred an obligation to do so in 30 days. This represents a liability to the supplier that is termed accounts payable.

10 January 2006

#	Business Activity	Accounting Treatment
7	▶ Spend $600 on newspaper and trade magazine advertising for the month.	▶ **Cash [A]** was decreased by $600, and **advertising expense [X]** was increased by $600.

Accounting elements: Assets (A), Liabilities (L), Equity (E), Revenue (R), and Expenses (X).

Unlike the previous expenditures, advertising is an expense, not an asset. Its benefits relate to the current period. Expenditures such as advertising are recorded as an expense when they are incurred. Contrast this expenditure with that for equipment, which is expected to be useful over multiple periods and thus is initially recorded as an asset, and then reflected as an expense over time. Also, contrast this treatment with that for rent expense, which was paid in advance and can be clearly allocated over time, and thus is initially recorded as a prepaid asset and then reflected as an expense over time. The advertising expenditure in this example relates to the current period. If the company had paid in advance for several years worth of advertising, then a portion would be capitalized (i.e., recorded as an asset), similar to the treatment of equipment or prepaid rent and expensed in future periods. We can now prepare a partial income statement for the company reflecting this expense:

Investment Advisers, Ltd.
Income Statement
For the Period 1 January through 10 January 2006

Total revenue		$ 0
Expenses		
Advertising	600	
Total expense		600
Net income (loss)		$ (600)

Because the company has incurred a $600 expense but has not recorded any revenue (the subscription revenue has not been earned yet), an income statement for Transactions 1 through 7 would show net income of minus $600 (i.e., a net loss). To prepare a balance sheet for the company, we need to update the retained earnings account. Beginning retained earnings was $0 (zero). Adding the net loss of $600 (made up of $0 revenue minus $600 expense) and deducting any dividend ($0 in this illustration) gives ending retained earnings of minus $600. The ending retained earnings covering Transactions 1–7 is included in the interim balance sheet:

Investment Advisers, Ltd.
Balance Sheet
As of 10 January 2006

Assets	
Cash	$ 41,600
Investments	100,000
Inventory	10,000
Prepaid rent	1,000
Deposits	2,000
Office equipment	6,000
Total assets	$160,600
Liabilities and owners' equity	
Liabilities	
Accounts payable	$ 10,000
Unearned fees	1,200
Total liabilities	11,200
Equity	
Contributed capital	150,000
Retained earnings	(600)
Total equity	149,400
Total liabilities and owners' equity	$160,600

As with all balance sheets, the amount of total assets equals total liabilities plus owners' equity—both are $160,600. The owners' claim on the business has been reduced to $149,400. This is due to the negative retained earnings (sometimes referred to as a retained "deficit"). As noted, the company has a net loss after the first seven transactions, a result of incurring $600 of advertising expenses but not yet producing any revenue.

15 January 2006

#	Business Activity	Accounting Treatment
8	▶ Borrow $12,000 from a bank for working capital. Interest is payable annually at 10 percent. The principal is due in two years.	▶ **Cash [A]** is increased by $12,000, and **bank debt [L]** is increased by $12,000.

Accounting elements: Assets (A), Liabilities (L), Equity (E), Revenue (R), and Expenses (X).

Cash is increased, and a corresponding liability is recorded to reflect the amount owed to the bank. Initially, no entry is made for interest that is expected to be paid on the loan. In the future, interest will be recorded as time passes and interest accrues (accumulates) on the loan.

15 January 2006

#	Business Activity	Accounting Treatment
9	▶ Ship first order to a customer consisting of five books at $25 per book. Invoice terms are that payment is due in 30 days. No cash changes hands.	▶ **Accounts receivable [A]** increased by $125, and **revenue [R]** increased by $125. Additionally, **inventory [A]** decreased by $100, and **cost of goods sold [X]** increased by $100.

Accounting elements: Assets (A), Liabilities (L), Equity (E), Revenue (R), and Expenses (X).

The company has now made a sale. Sale transaction records have two parts. One part represents the $125 revenue to be received from the customer, and the other part represents the $100 cost of the goods that have been sold. Although payment has not yet been received from the customer in payment for the goods, the company has delivered the goods (five books) and so revenue is recorded. A corresponding asset, accounts receivable, is recorded to reflect amounts due from the customer. Simultaneously, the company reduces its inventory balance by the cost of the five books sold and also records this amount as an expense termed **cost of goods sold**.

15 January 2006

#	Business Activity	Accounting Treatment
10	► Sell for cash 10 books at $25 per book at an investment conference.	► **Cash [A]** is increased by $250, and **revenue [R]** is increased by $250. Additionally, **inventory [A]** is decreased by $200, and **cost of goods sold [X]** is increased by $200.

Accounting elements: Assets (A), Liabilities (L), Equity (E), Revenue (R), and Expenses (X).

Similar to the previous sale transaction, both the $250 sales proceeds and the $200 cost of the goods sold must be recorded. In contrast with the previous sale, however, the sales proceeds are received in cash. Subtotals from Exhibit 6 can once again be used to prepare a preliminary income statement and balance sheet to evaluate the business to date:

Investment Advisers, Ltd.
Income Statement
For the Period 1 January through 15 January 2006

Total revenue		$ 375
Expenses		
Cost of goods sold	300	
Advertising	600	
Total expenses		900
Net income (loss)		$ (525)

Investment Advisers, Ltd.
Balance Sheet
As of 15 January 2006

Assets	
Cash	$ 53,850
Accounts receivable	125
Investments	100,000
Inventory	9,700
Prepaid rent	1,000
Deposits	2,000
Office equipment	6,000
Total assets	$172,675

(Continued on next page . . .)

(continued)

Liabilities and owners' equity	
Liabilities	
Accounts payable	$ 10,000
Unearned fees	1,200
Bank debt	12,000
Total liabilities	23,200
Equity	
Contributed capital	150,000
Retained earnings	(525)
Total equity	149,475
Total liabilities and owners' equity	$172,675

An income statement covering Transactions 1–10 would reflect revenue to date of $375 for the sale of books minus the $300 cost of those books and minus the $600 advertising expense. The net loss is $525, which is shown in the income statement as $(525) using the accounting convention that indicates a negative number using parentheses. This net loss is also reflected on the balance sheet in retained earnings. The amount in retained earnings at this point equals the net loss of $525 because retained earnings had $0 beginning balance and no dividends have been distributed. The balance sheet reflects total assets of $172,675 and claims on the assets of $23,200 in liabilities and $149,475 owners' equity. Within assets, the inventory balance represents the cost of the 485 remaining books (a total of 15 have been sold) at $20 each.

Transactions 1–10 occurred throughout the month and involved cash, accounts receivable, or accounts payable; accordingly, these transactions clearly required an entry into the accounting system. The other transactions, items 11–13, have also occurred and need to be reflected in the financial statements, but these transactions may not be so obvious. In order to prepare complete financial statements at the end of a reporting period, an entity needs to review its operations to determine whether any accruals or other adjustments are required. A more complete discussion of accruals and adjustments is set forth in the next section, but generally speaking, such entries serve to allocate revenue and expense items into the correct accounting period. In practice, companies may also make adjustments to correct erroneous entries or to update inventory balances to reflect a physical count.

In this illustration, adjustments are needed for a number of transactions in order to allocate amounts across accounting periods. The accounting treatment for these transactions is shown in Exhibit 7. Transactions are numbered sequentially, and an "a" is added to a transaction number to denote an adjustment relating to a previous transaction. Exhibit 8 presents the completed spreadsheet reflecting these additional entries in the accounting system.

EXHIBIT 7 **Investment Advisers, Ltd., Accruals and Other Adjusting Entries on 31 January 2006**

#	Business Activity	Accounting Treatment
11	▶ Hire a part-time clerk. The clerk is hired through an agency that also handles all payroll taxes. The company is to pay $15 per hour to the agency. The clerk works six hours prior to 31 January, but no cash will be paid until February.	▶ The company owes $90 for wages at month end. Under accrual accounting, expenses are recorded when incurred, not when paid. ▶ **Accrued wages [L]** is increased by $90, and **payroll expense [X]** is increased by $90. The accrued wage liability will be eliminated when the wages are paid.
12	▶ Mail out the first month's newsletter to customer. This subscription had been sold on 3 January.	▶ One month (or 1/12) of the $1,200 subscription has been satisfied, so $100 can be recognized as revenue. ▶ **Unearned fees [L]** is decreased by $100, and **fee revenue [R]** is increased by $100.
13	▶ Review of the investment portfolio shows that $100 of interest income was earned and the market value of the portfolio has increased by $2,000. The balance in the investment account is now $102,100. The securities are classified as "trading" securities.	▶ **Interest income [R]** is increased by $100, and the **investments** account **[A]** is increased by $100. ▶ The $2,000 increase in the value of the portfolio represents unrealized gains that are part of income for traded securities. The **investments** account **[A]** is increased by $2,000, and **unrealized gains [R]** is increased by $2,000.
3a	▶ In item 3, $3,000 was paid to the landlord for office/warehouse, including a $2,000 refundable deposit and $1,000 for the first month's rent ▶ Now, the first month has ended, so this rent has become a cost of doing business.	▶ To reflect the full amount of the first month's rent as a cost of doing business, **prepaid rent [A]** is decreased by $1,000, and **rent expense [X]** is increased by $1,000.
4a	▶ In item 4, office equipment was purchased for $6,000 in cash. The equipment has an estimated life of two years with no salvage value. ▶ Now, one month (or 1/24) of the useful life of the equipment has ended, so a portion of the equipment cost has become a cost of doing business.	▶ A portion (1/24) of the total $6,000 cost of the office equipment is allocated to the current period's cost of doing business. ▶ **Depreciation expense [X]** is increased by $250, and **accumulated depreciation [A]** (a contra asset account) is increased by $250. ▶ Accumulated depreciation is a contra asset account to office equipment.
8a	▶ The company borrowed $12,000 from a bank on 15 January, with interest payable annually at 10 percent and the principal due in two years. ▶ Now, one-half of one month has passed since the borrowing.	▶ One-half of one month of interest expense has become a cost of doing business. $12,000 × 10% = $1,200 of annual interest, equivalent to $100 per month or $50 for one-half month. ▶ **Interest expense [X]** is increased by $50, and **interest payable [L]** is increased by $50.

Accounting elements: Assets (A), Liabilities (L), Equity (E), Revenue (R), and Expenses (X).
Notes: Items 11–13 are repeated from Exhibit 5. Items 3a, 4a, and 8a reflect adjustments relating to items 3, 4, and 8 from Exhibit 5.

EXHIBIT 8 Accounting System for Investment Advisers, Ltd.

	Assets =			Liabilities		+	Owners' Equity			
#	**Cash**	**Other Assets**	**Account**	**Amount**	**Account**	**Contributed Capital**	**Beginning Retained Earnings**	**Revenue**	**Expense (enter as negative)**	**Dividends (enter as negative)**
Beg. Bal	0	0		0		0	0	0	0	0
1 Capitalize	150,000					150,000				
2 Investments	(100,000)	100,000	Investments							
3 Pay landlord	(3,000)	1,000	Prepaid rent							
		2,000	Rent deposit							
4 Buy equipment	(6,000)	6,000	Office equipment							
5 Sell subscript.	1,200			1,200	Unearned fees					
6 Buy books		10,000	Inventory	10,000	Accounts payable					
7 Advertise	(600)								(600)	
8 Borrow	12,000			12,000	Bank debt					
9 Sell books on account		(100)	Inventory					125	(100)	
		125	Accounts receivable							
10 Cash sale	250	(200)	Inventory					250	(200)	
11 Accrue wages				90	Accrued wages				(90)	
12 Earn subscription fees				(100)	Unearned fees			100		
13 Investment income		100	Investments					100		
		2,000	Investments					2,000		
3a Rent expense		(1,000)	Prepaid rent						(1,000)	
4a Depreciate equipment		(250)	Accumulated depreciation (equipment)						(250)	
8a Accrue interest				50	Interest payable				(50)	
Subtotal	**53,850**	**119,675**		**23,240**		**150,000**		**2,575**	**(2,290)**	

A final income statement and balance sheet can now be prepared reflecting all transactions and adjustments.

Investment Advisers, Ltd.
Income Statement
For the Period 1 January through 31 January 2006

Revenues	
Fee revenue	$ 100
Book sales	375
Investment income	2,100
Total revenues	$ 2,575
Expenses	
Cost of goods sold	$ 300
Advertising	600
Wage	90
Rent	1,000
Depreciation	250 → for mth
Interest	50
Total expenses	2,290
Net income (loss)	$ 285

Investment Advisers, Ltd.
Balance Sheet
As of 31 January 2006

Assets	
Cash	$ 53,850
Accounts receivable	125
Investments	102,100
Inventory	9,700
Prepaid rent	0
Office equipment, net	5,750
Deposits	2,000
Total assets	$173,525
Liabilities and owners' equity	
Liabilities	
Accounts payable	$ 10,000
Accrued wages	90
Interest payable	50
Unearned fees	1,100
Bank debt	12,000

(Continued on next page . . .)

(continued)

Total liabilities	23,240
Equity	
Contributed capital	150,000
Retained earnings	285
Total equity	150,285
Total liabilities and owners' equity	$173,525

From the income statement, we can determine that the business was profitable for the month. The business earned $285 after expenses. The balance sheet presents the financial position. The company has assets of $173,525, and claims against those assets included liabilities of $23,240 and an owners' claim of $150,285. The owners' claim reflects their initial investment plus reinvested earnings. These statements are explored further in the next section.

4.3 Financial Statements

The spreadsheet in Exhibit 8 is an organized presentation of the company's transactions and can help in preparing the income statement and balance sheet presented above. Exhibit 9 presents all financial statements and demonstrates their relationships. Note that the data for the income statement come from the revenue and expense columns of the spreadsheet (which include gains and losses). The net income of $285 (revenue of $2,575 minus expenses of $2,290) was retained in the business rather than distributed to the owners as dividends. The net income, therefore, becomes part of ending retained earnings on the balance sheet. The detail of retained earnings is shown in the statement of owners' equity.

The balance sheet presents the financial position of the company using the assets, liabilities, and equity accounts from the accounting system spreadsheet. The statement of cash flows summarizes the data from the cash column of the accounting system spreadsheet to enable the owners and others to assess the sources and uses of cash. These sources and uses of cash are categorized according to group of business activity: operating, investing, or financing. The format of the statement of cash flows presented here is known as the **direct format**, which refers to the operating cash section appearing simply as operating cash receipts less operating cash disbursements. An alternative format for the operating cash section, which begins with net income and shows adjustments to derive operating cash flow, is known as the **indirect format**. The alternative formats and detailed rules are discussed in Reading 34.

EXHIBIT 9 Investment Advisers, Ltd., Financial Statements

Investment Advisers, Ltd.
Balance Sheet
As of

	12/31/2005	1/31/2006
Assets		
Cash	150,000	53,850
Accounts receivable	0	125
Investments	0	102,100
Inventory		9,700
Office equipment, net		5,750
Deposits		2,000
Total assets	150,000	173,525
Liabilities		
Accounts payable	0	10,000
Accrued expenses		140
Unearned fees		1,100
Bank debt		12,000
Total liabilities		23,240
Owners' equity		
Contributed capital	150,000	150,000
Retained earnings	0	285
Total equity	150,000	150,285
Total liabilities and equity	150,000	173,525

Investment Advisers, Ltd.
Income Statement
For the Month Ended 1/31/2006

Fee revenue	100
Book sales revenue	375
Investment income	2,100
Total revenue	2,575
Cost of goods sold	300
Other expense	1,990
Total expense	2,290
Net income (loss)	285

Investment Advisers, Ltd.
Statement of Cash Flows
For the Month Ended 1/31/2006

Cash received from customers	1,450
Cash paid to landlord	(3,000)
Cash paid for advertising	(600)
Investments in trading securities	(100,000)
Operating cash flows	(102,150)
Capital expenditures	(6,000)
Investing cash flows	(6,000)
Borrowing	12,000
Financing cash flows	12,000
Net decrease in cash	(96,150)
Cash at 12/31/05	150,000
Cash at 1/31/06	53,850

Investment Advisers, Ltd.
Statement of Owners' Equity
31 January 2006

	Contributed Capital	Retained Earnings	Total
Balance at 12/31/05	150,000	0	150,000
Issuance of stock			
Net income (loss)		285	285
Distributions			
Balance at 1/31/06	150,000	285	150,285

Financial statements use the financial data reported in the accounting system and present this data in a more meaningful manner. Each statement reports on critical areas. Specifically, a review of the financial statements for the IAL illustration provides the following information:

- **Balance Sheet**. This statement provides information about a company's financial position at a point in time. It shows an entity's assets, liabilities, and owners' equity at a particular date. Two years are usually presented so that comparisons can be made. Less significant accounts can be grouped into a single line item. One observation from the IAL illustration is that although total assets have increased significantly (about 16 percent), equity has increased less than 0.2 percent—most of the increase in total assets is due to the increase in liabilities.
- **Income Statement**. This statement provides information about a company's profitability over a period of time. It shows the amount of revenue, expense, and resulting net income or loss for a company during a period of time. Again, less significant accounts can be grouped into a single line item—in this illustration, expenses other than cost of goods sold are grouped into a single line item. The statement shows that IAL has three sources of revenue and made a small profit in its first month of operations. Significantly, most of the revenue came from investments rather than subscriptions or book sales.
- **Statement of Cash Flows**. This statement provides information about a company's cash flows over a period of time. It shows a company's cash inflows (receipts) and outflows (payments) during the period. These flows are categorized according to the three groups of business activities: operating, financing, and investing. In the illustration, IAL reported a large negative cash flow from operations ($102,150), primarily because its trading activities involved the purchase of a portfolio of securities but no sales were made from the portfolio. (Note that the purchase of investments for IAL appears in its operating section because the company is in the business of trading securities. In contrast, for a nontrading company, investment activity would be shown as investing cash flows rather than operating cash flows.) IAL's negative operating and investing cash flows were funded by $12,000 bank borrowing and a $96,150 reduction in the cash balance.
- **Statement of Owners' Equity**. This statement provides information about the composition and changes in owners' equity during a period of time. In this illustration, the only change in equity resulted from the net income of $285. A Statement of Retained Earnings (not shown) would report the changes in a company's retained earnings during a period of time.

These statements again illustrate the interrelationships among financial statements. On the balance sheet, we see beginning and ending amounts for assets, liabilities, and owners' equity. Owners' equity increased from $150,000 to $150,285. The statement of owners' equity presents a breakdown of this $285 change. The arrow from the statement of owners' equity to the owners' equity section of the balance sheet explains that section of the balance sheet. In the

IAL illustration, the entire $285 change resulted from an increase in retained earnings. In turn, the increase in retained earnings resulted from $285 net income. The income statement presents a breakdown of the revenues and expenses resulting in this $285. The arrow from the income statement to the net income figure in the owners' equity section explains how reported net income came about.

Also on the balance sheet, we see that cash decreased from $150,000 at the beginning of the month to $53,850 at the end of the month. The statement of cash flows provides information on the increases and decreases in cash by group of business activity. The arrow from the cash flow statement to the ending cash figure shows that the cash flow statement explains in detail the ending cash amount.

In summary, the balance sheet provides information at a point in time (financial position), whereas the other statements provide useful information regarding the activity during a period of time (profitability, cash flow, and changes in owners' equity).

ACCRUALS AND VALUATION ADJUSTMENTS

5

In a simple business model such as the investment company discussed in the illustration above, many transactions are handled in cash and settled in a relatively short time frame. Furthermore, assets and liabilities have a fixed and determinable value. Translating business transactions into the accounting system is fairly easy. Difficulty usually arises when a cash receipt or disbursement occurs in a different period than the related revenue or expense, or when the reportable values of assets vary. This section will address the accounting treatment for these situations—namely, accruals and valuation adjustments.

5.1 Accruals

Accrual accounting requires that revenue be recorded when earned and that expenses be recorded when incurred, irrespective of when the related cash movements occur. The purpose of accrual entries is to report revenue and expense in the proper accounting period. Because accrual entries occur due to timing differences between cash movements and accounting recognition of revenue or expense, it follows that there are only a few possibilities. First, cash movement and accounting recognition can occur at the same time, in which case there is no need for accruals. Second, cash movement may occur before or after accounting recognition, in which case accruals are required. The possible situations requiring accrual entries are summarized into four types of accrual entries shown in Exhibit 10 and discussed below. Each type of accrual involves an originating entry and at least one adjusting entry at a later date or dates.

EXHIBIT 10 Accruals

	Cash Movement prior to Accounting Recognition	Cash Movement in the Same Period as Accounting Recognition	Cash Movement after Accounting Recognition
Revenue	**UNEARNED (DEFERRED) REVENUE** ▶ **Originating entry**–record cash receipt and establish a liability (such as unearned revenue) ▶ **Adjusting entry**–reduce the liability while recording revenue	Settled transaction –no accrual entry needed	**UNBILLED (ACCRUED) REVENUE** ▶ **Originating entry**–record revenue and establish an asset (such as unbilled revenue) ▶ **Adjusting entry**–When billing occurs, reduce unbilled revenue and increase accounts receivable. When cash is collected, eliminate the receivable.
Expense	**PREPAID EXPENSE** ▶ **Originating entry**–record cash payment and establish an asset (such as prepaid expense) ▶ **Adjusting entry**–reduce the asset while recording expense		**ACCRUED EXPENSES** ▶ **Originating entry**–establish a liability (such as accrued expenses) and record an expense ▶ **Adjusting entry**–reduce the liability as cash is paid

Unearned (or deferred) revenue arises when a company receives cash prior to earning the revenue. In the IAL illustration, in Transaction 5, the company received $1,200 for a 12-month subscription to a monthly newsletter. At the time the cash was received, the company had an obligation to deliver 12 newsletters and thus had not yet earned the revenue. Each month, as a newsletter is delivered, this obligation will decrease by 1/12th (i.e., $100). And at the same time, $100 of revenue will be earned. The accounting treatment involves an originating entry (the initial recording of the cash received and the corresponding liability to deliver newsletters) and, subsequently, 12 future adjusting entries, the first one of which was illustrated as Transaction 12. Each adjusting entry reduces the liability and records revenue.

In practice, a large amount of unearned revenue may cause some concern about a company's ability to deliver on this future commitment. Conversely, a positive aspect is that increases in unearned revenue are an indicator of future revenues. For example, a large liability on the balance sheet of an airline relates to cash received for future airline travel. Revenue will be recognized as the travel occurs, so an increase in this liability is an indicator of future increases in revenue.

Unbilled (or **accrued**) **revenue** arises when a company earns revenue prior to receiving cash but has not yet recognized the revenue at the end of an accounting period. In such cases, the accounting treatment involves an originating entry to record the revenue earned through the end of the accounting period and a related receivable reflecting amounts due from customers. When the company receives payment (or if goods are returned), an adjusting entry eliminates the receivable.

Accrued revenue specifically relates to end-of-period accruals; however, the concept is similar to any sale involving deferred receipt of cash. In the IAL illustration, in Transaction 9, the company sold books on account, so the revenue was recognized prior to cash receipt. The accounting treatment involved an entry to record the revenue and the associated receivable. In the future, when the company receives payment, an adjusting entry (not shown) would eliminate the receivable. In practice, it is important to understand the quality of a company's receivables (i.e., the likelihood of collection).

Prepaid expense arises when a company makes a cash payment prior to recognizing an expense. In the illustration, in Transaction 3, the company prepaid one month's rent. The accounting treatment involves an originating entry to record the payment of cash and the prepaid asset reflecting future benefits, and a subsequent adjusting entry to record the expense and eliminate the prepaid asset. (See the boxes showing the accounting treatment of Transaction 3, which refers to the originating entry, and Transaction 3a, which refers to the adjusting entry.) In other words, prepaid expenses are assets that will be subsequently **expensed**. In practice, particularly in a valuation, one consideration is that prepaid assets typically have future value only as future operations transpire, unless they are refundable.

Accrued expenses arise when a company incurs expenses that have not yet been paid as of the end of an accounting period. Accrued expenses result in liabilities that usually require future cash payments. In the IAL illustration, the company had incurred wage expenses at month end, but the payment would not be made until after the end of the month (Transaction 11). To reflect the company's position at the end of the month, the accounting treatment involved an originating entry to record wage expense and the corresponding liability for wages payable, and a future adjusting entry to eliminate the liability when cash is paid (not shown because wages will be paid only in February). Similarly, the IAL illustration included interest accrual on the company's bank borrowing. (See the boxes showing the accounting treatment of Transaction 8, where Transaction 8 refers to the originating entry, and Transaction 8a, which refers to the adjusting entry.)

As with accrued revenues, accrued expenses specifically relate to end-of-period accruals. Accounts payable are similar to accrued expenses in that they involve a transaction that occurs now but the cash payment is made later. Accounts payable is also a liability but often relates to the receipt of inventory (or perhaps services) as opposed to recording an immediate expense. Accounts payable should be listed separately from other accrued expenses on the balance sheet because of their different nature.

Overall, in practice, complex businesses require additional accruals that are theoretically similar to the four categories of accruals discussed above but which require considerably more judgment. For example, there may be significant lags between a transaction and **cash settlement**. In such cases, accruals can span many accounting periods (even 10–20 years!), and it is not always clear when revenue has been earned or an expense has been incurred. Considerable judgment is required to determine how to allocate/distribute amounts across periods. An example of such a complex accrual would be the estimated annual revenue for a contractor on a long-term construction project, such as building a nuclear power plant. In general, however, accruals fall under the four general types and follow essentially the same pattern of originating and adjusting entries as the basic accruals described.

5.2 Valuation Adjustments

In contrast to accrual entries that allocate revenue and expenses into the appropriate accounting periods, valuation adjustments are made to a company's assets or liabilities—only where required by accounting standards—so that the accounting records reflect the current market value rather than the historical cost. In this discussion, we focus on valuation adjustments to assets. For example, in the IAL illustration, Transaction 13 adjusted the value of the company's investment portfolio to its current market value. The income statement reflects the $2,100 increase (including interest), and the ending balance sheets report the investment portfolio at its current market value of $102,100. In contrast, the equipment in the IAL illustration was not reported at its current market value and no valuation adjustment was required.

As this illustration demonstrates, accounting regulations do not require all types of assets to be reported at their current market value. Some assets (e.g., trading securities) are shown on the balance sheet at their current market value, and changes in that market value are reported in the income statement. Some assets are shown at their historical cost (e.g., specific classes of investment securities being held to maturity). Other assets (e.g., a particular class of investment securities) are shown on the balance sheet at their current market value, but changes in market value bypass the income statement and are recorded directly into shareholders' equity under a component referred to as "other comprehensive income." This topic will be discussed in more detail in later readings.

In summary, where valuation adjustment entries are required for assets, the basic pattern is the following for increases in assets: An asset is increased with the other side of the equation being a gain on the income statement or an increase to other comprehensive income. Conversely for decreases: An asset is decreased with the other side of the equation being a loss on the income statement or a decrease to other comprehensive income.

6 ACCOUNTING SYSTEMS

The accounting system set forth for the IAL illustration involved a very simple business, a single month of activity, and a small number of transactions. In practice, most businesses are more complicated and have many more transactions. Accordingly, actual accounting systems, although using essentially the same logic as discussed in the illustration, are both more efficient than a spreadsheet and more complex.

6.1 Flow of Information in an Accounting System

Accounting texts typically discuss accounting systems in detail because accountants need to understand each step in the process. While analysts do not need to know the same details, they should be familiar with the flow of information through a financial reporting system. This flow and the key related documents are described in Exhibit 11.

EXHIBIT 11 Accounting System Flow and Related Documents

Journal entries and adjusting entries

A journal is a document or computer file in which business transactions are recorded in the order in which they occur (chronological order). The general journal is the collection of all business transactions in an accounting system sorted by date. All accounting systems have a general journal to record all transactions. Some accounting systems also include special journals. For example, there may be one journal for recording sales transactions and another for recording inventory purchases.

Journal entries—recorded in journals—are dated, show the accounts affected, and the amounts. If necessary, the entry will include an explanation of the transaction and documented authorization to record the entry. As the initial step in converting business transactions into financial information, the journal entry is useful for obtaining detailed information regarding a particular transaction.

Adjusting journal entries, a subset of journal entries, are typically made at the end of an accounting period to record items such as accruals that are not yet reflected in the accounting system.

⇩

General ledger and T- accounts

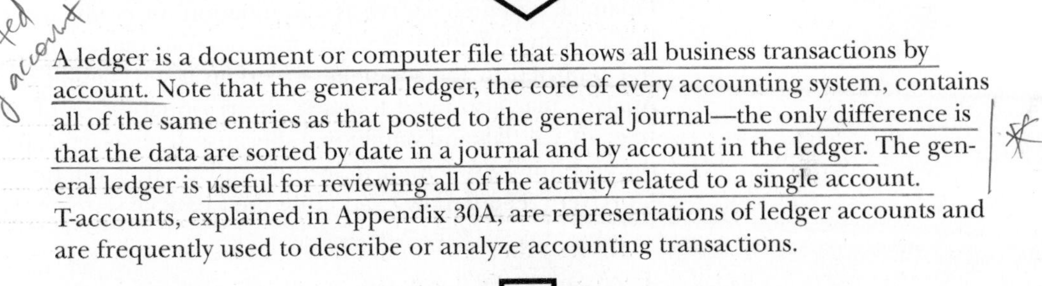

A ledger is a document or computer file that shows all business transactions by account. Note that the general ledger, the core of every accounting system, contains all of the same entries as that posted to the general journal—the only difference is that the data are sorted by date in a journal and by account in the ledger. The general ledger is useful for reviewing all of the activity related to a single account. T-accounts, explained in Appendix 30A, are representations of ledger accounts and are frequently used to describe or analyze accounting transactions.

⇩

Trial balance and adjusted trial balance

A trial balance is a document that lists account balances at a particular point in time. Trial balances are typically prepared at the end of an accounting period as a first step in producing financial statements. A key difference between a trial balance and a ledger is that the trial balance shows only total ending balances. An initial trial balance assists in the identification of any adjusting entries that may be required. Once these adjusting entries are made, an adjusted trial balance can be prepared.

⇩

Financial statements

The financial statements, a final product of the accounting system, are prepared based on the account totals from an adjusted trial balance.

6.2 Debits and Credits

Reviewing the example of IAL, it is clear that the accounting treatment of every transaction involved at least two accounts and the transaction either increased or decreased the value of any affected account. Traditionally, accounting systems have used the terms debit and credit to describe changes in an account resulting from the accounting processing of a transaction. The correct usage of "debit" and "credit" in an accounting context differs from how these terms are used in everyday language.[8] The accounting definitions of debit and credit ensure that, in processing a transaction, the sum of the debits equals the sum of the credits, which is consistent with the accounting equation (i.e., Equation 30-7) always remaining in balance.

Although mastering the usage of the terms "debit" and "credit" is essential for an accountant, an analyst can still understand financial reporting mechanics without speaking in terms of debits and credits. In general, this text avoids the use of debit/credit presentation; however, for reference, Appendix 30A presents the IAL illustration in a debit and credit system.

The following section broadly describes some considerations for using financial statements in security analysis.

7 USING FINANCIAL STATEMENTS IN SECURITY ANALYSIS

Financial statements serve as a foundation for credit and equity analysis, including security valuation. Analysts may need to make adjustments to reflect items not reported in the statements (certain assets/liabilities and future earnings). Analysts may also need to assess the reasonableness of management judgment (e.g., in accruals and valuations). Because analysts typically will not have access to the accounting system or individual entries, they will need to infer what transactions were recorded by examining the financial statements.

7.1 The Use of Judgment in Accounts and Entries

Quite apart from deliberate misrepresentations, even efforts to faithfully represent the economic performance and position of a company require judgments and estimates. Financial reporting systems need to accommodate complex business models by recording accruals and changes in valuations of balance sheet accounts. Accruals and valuation entries require considerable judgment and thus create many of the limitations of the accounting model. Judgments could prove wrong or, worse, be used for deliberate earnings manipulation. An important first step in analyzing financial statements is identifying the types of accruals and valuation entries in an entity's financial statements. Most of these items will be noted in the critical accounting policies/estimates section of management's discussion and analysis (MD&A) and in the significant accounting policies footnote, both found in the annual report. Analysts should use this disclosure to identify the key accruals and valuations for a company. The analyst needs to be aware, as Example 4 shows, that the manipulation of earnings and assets can take place within the context of satisfying the mechanical rules governing the recording of transactions.

[8] In accounting, debits record increases of asset and expense accounts or decreases in liability and owners' equity accounts. Credits record increases in liability, owners' equity, and revenue accounts or decreases in asset accounts. Appendix 30A provides more details.

EXAMPLE 4

The Manipulation of Accounting Earnings

As discussed in this reading, the accounting equation can be expressed as Assets = Liabilities + Contributed capital + Ending retained earnings (Equation 30-5a). Although the equation must remain in balance with each transaction, management can improperly record a transaction to achieve a desired result. For example, when a company spends cash and records an expense, assets are reduced on the left side of the equation and expenses are recorded, which lowers retained earnings on the right side. The balance is maintained. If, however, a company spent cash but did not want to record an expense in order to achieve higher net income, the company could manipulate the system by reducing cash and increasing another asset. The equation would remain in balance and the right-hand side of the equation would not be affected at all. This was one of the techniques used by managers at WorldCom to manipulate financial reports, as summarized in a U.S. Securities and Exchange Commission complaint against the company (emphasis added):

> In general, WorldCom manipulated its financial results in two ways. First, WorldCom reduced its operating expenses by improperly releasing certain reserves held against operating expenses. Second, **WorldCom improperly reduced its operating expenses by recharacterizing certain expenses as capital assets.** Neither practice was in conformity with generally accepted accounting principles ("GAAP"). Neither practice was disclosed to WorldCom's investors, despite the fact that both practices constituted changes from WorldCom's previous accounting practices. Both practices falsely reduced WorldCom's expenses and, accordingly, had the effect of artificially inflating the income WorldCom reported to the public in its financial statements from 1999 through the first quarter of 2002.[9]

In 2005, the former CEO of WorldCom was sentenced to 25 years in prison for his role in the fraud.[10] The analyst should be aware of the possibility of manipulation of earnings and be on the lookout for large increases in existing assets, new unusual assets, and unexplained changes in financial ratios.

7.2 Misrepresentations

It is rare in this age of computers that the mechanics of an accounting system do not work. Most computer accounting systems will not allow a company to make one-sided entries. It is important to note, however, that just because the mechanics work does not necessarily mean that the judgments underlying the financial statements are correct. An unscrupulous accountant could structure entries to achieve a desired result. For example, if a manager wanted to record fictitious

[9] SEC vs. WorldCom, 5 November 2002: www.sec.gov/litigation/complaints/comp17829.htm.

[10] "Ebbers Is Sentenced to 25 Years For $11 Billion WorldCom Fraud," *Wall Street Journal*, 14 July 2005, A1.

revenue, a fictitious asset (a receivable) could be created to keep the accounting equation in balance. If the manager paid for something but did not want to record an expense, the transaction could be recorded in a prepaid asset account. If cash is received but the manager does not want to record revenue, a liability could be created. Understanding that there has to be another side to every entry is key in detecting inappropriate accounting because—usually in the course of "fixing" one account—there will be another account with a balance that does not make sense. In the case of recording fictitious revenue, there is likely to be a growing receivable whose collectibility is in doubt. Ratio analysis, which is discussed further in later readings, can assist in detecting suspect amounts in these accounts. Furthermore, the accounting equation can be used to detect likely accounts where aggressive or even fraudulent accounting may have occurred.

SUMMARY

The accounting process is a key component of financial reporting. The mechanics of this process convert business transactions into records necessary to create periodic reports on a company. An understanding of these mechanics is useful in evaluating financial statements for credit and equity analysis purposes and in forecasting future financial statements. Key concepts are as follows:

- Business activities can be classified into three groups: operating activities, investing activities, and financing activities.
- Companies classify transactions into common accounts that are components of the five financial statement elements: assets, liabilities, equity, revenue, and expense.
- The core of the accounting process is the basic accounting equation: Assets = Liabilities + Owners' equity.
- The expanded accounting equation is Assets = Liabilities + Contributed capital + Beginning retained earnings + Revenue − Expenses − Dividends.
- Business transactions are recorded in an accounting system that is based on the basic and expanded accounting equations.
- The accounting system tracks and summarizes data used to create financial statements: the balance sheet, income statement, statement of cash flows, and statement of owners' equity. The statement of retained earnings is a component of the statement of owners' equity.
- Accruals are a necessary part of the accounting process and are designed to allocate activity to the proper period for financial reporting purposes.
- The results of the accounting process are financial reports that are used by managers, investors, creditors, analysts, and others in making business decisions.
- An analyst uses the financial statements to make judgments on the financial health of a company.
- Company management can manipulate financial statements, and a perceptive analyst can use his or her understanding of financial statements to detect misrepresentations.

A DEBIT/CREDIT ACCOUNTING SYSTEM

OPTIONAL SEGMENT BEGINS

The main section of this reading presented a basic accounting system represented as a spreadsheet. An alternative system that underlies most manual and electronic accounting systems uses debits and credits. Both a spreadsheet and a debit/credit system are based on the basic accounting equation:

Assets = Liabilities + Owners' equity

Early generations of accountants desired a system for recording transactions that maintained the balance of the accounting equation and avoided the use of negative numbers (which could lead to errors in recording). The system can be illustrated with T-accounts for every account involved in recording transactions. The T-account is so named for its shape:

T-Account

Debit	Credit

The left-hand side of the T-account is called a "debit," and the right-hand side is termed a "credit." The names should not be construed as denoting value. A debit is not better than a credit and vice versa. Debit simply means the left side of the T-account, and credit simply means the right side. Traditionally, debit is abbreviated as "DR," whereas credit is abbreviated "CR." The T-account is also related to the balance sheet and accounting equation as follows:

Balance Sheet

Assets	Liabilities Owners' Equity

Assets are referred to as the left side of the balance sheet (and accounting equation) and hence are on the left side of the T-account. Assets are, therefore, recorded with a debit balance. In other words, to record an increase in an asset, an entry is made to the left-hand side of a T-account. A decrease to an asset is recorded on the right side of a T-account. Liabilities and owners' equity are referred to as the right side of the balance sheet (and accounting equation). Increases to liabilities and owners' equity are recorded on the right side of a T-account; decreases to liabilities and owners' equity are recorded on the left side.

At any point in time, the balance in an account is determined by summing all the amounts on the left side of the account, summing all the amounts on the right side of the account, and calculating the difference. If the sum of amounts on the left side of the account is greater than the sum of amounts on the right side of the account, the account has a debit balance equal to the difference. If the sum of amounts on the right side of the account is greater than the sum of amounts on the left side of the account, the account has a credit balance.

EXHIBIT A-1 Balance Sheet T-Accounts for Investment Advisers, Ltd.

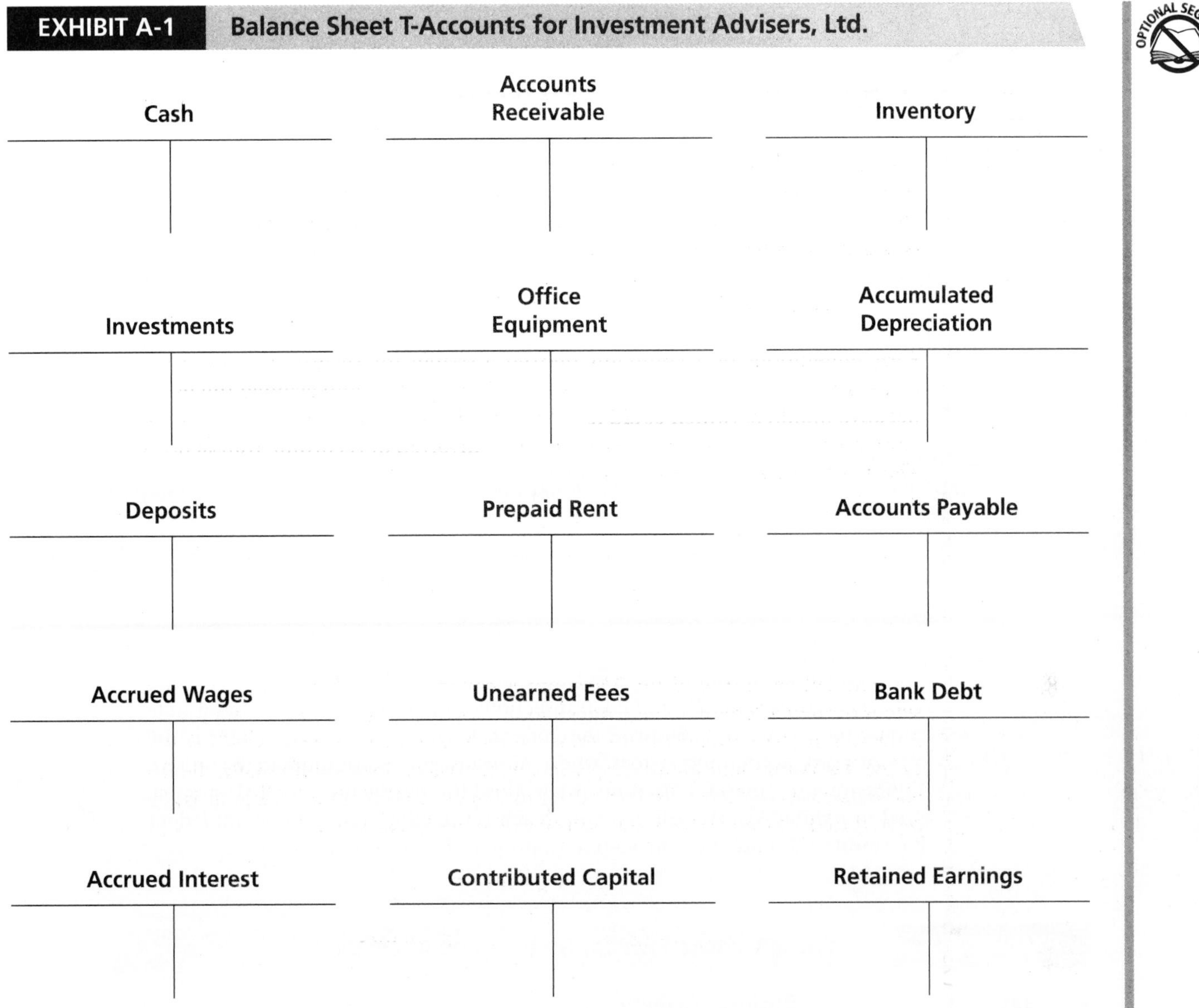

OPTIONAL SEGMENT

A T-account is created for each asset account, liability account, and owners' equity account. The collection of these T-accounts at the beginning of the year for a fictitious company, Investment Advisers, Ltd. (IAL), is presented in Exhibit A-1. Each balance sheet T-account is termed a "permanent" or "real" account because the balance in the account carries over from year-to-year.

T-accounts are also set up for each income statement account. These T-accounts are referred to as "temporary" or "nominal" accounts because they are transferred at the end of each fiscal year by transferring any net income or loss to the balance sheet account, Retained Earnings. Income statement T-accounts for IAL are presented in Exhibit A-2.

EXHIBIT A-2 Income Statement T-Accounts for Investment Advisers, Ltd.

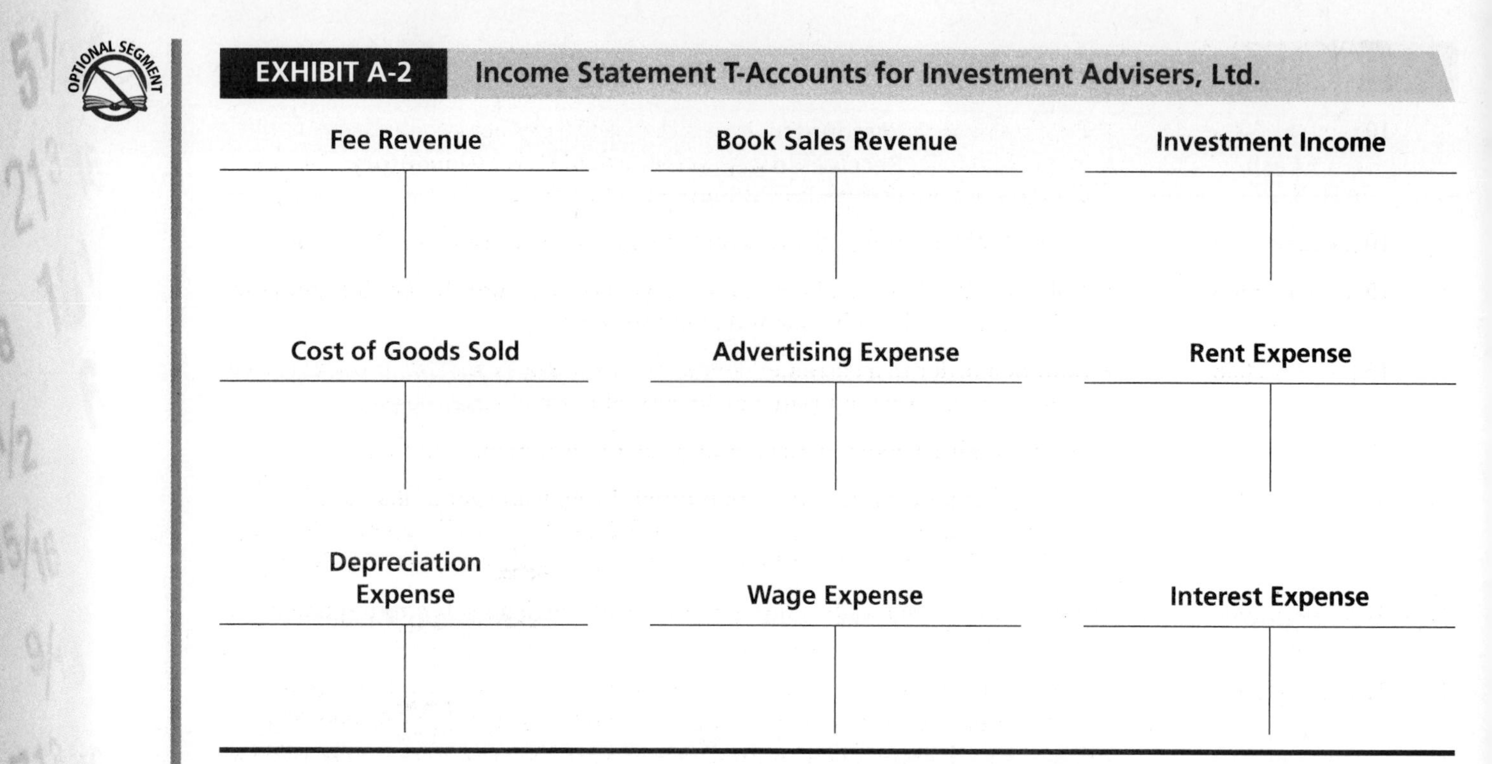

The collection of all business transactions sorted by account, real and temporary, for a company comprise the general ledger. The general ledger is the core of every accounting system, where all transactions are ultimately entered. To illustrate the use of T-accounts, we will use the transactions for IAL summarized in Exhibit A-3. We will first enter each transaction into the general ledger T-accounts, then use the information to prepare financial statements.

EXHIBIT A-3 Business Transactions for Investment Advisers, Ltd.

#	Date	Business Activity
1	31 December 2005	▶ File documents with regulatory authorities to establish a separate legal entity. Initially capitalize the company through deposit of $150,000 from the three owners.
2	2 January 2006	▶ Set up a $100,000 investment account and purchase a portfolio of equities and fixed-income securities.
3	2 January 2006	▶ Pay $3,000 to landlord for office/warehouse. $2,000 represents a refundable deposit, and $1,000 represents the first month's rent.
4	3 January 2006	▶ Purchase office equipment for $6,000. The equipment has an estimated life of two years with no salvage value.
5	3 January 2006	▶ Receive $1,200 cash for a one-year subscription to the monthly newsletter.

(Exhibit continued on next page . . .)

OPTIONAL SEGMENT

EXHIBIT A-3 (continued)

6	10 January 2006	▶ Purchase and receive 500 books at a cost of $20 per book for a total of $10,000. Invoice terms are that payment from IAL is due in 30 days. No cash changes hands. These books are intended for resale.
7	10 January 2006	▶ Spend $600 on newspaper and trade magazine advertising for the month.
8	15 January 2006	▶ Borrow $12,000 from a bank for working capital. Interest is payable annually at 10 percent. The principal is due in two years.
9	15 January 2006	▶ Ship first order to a customer consisting of five books at $25 per book. Invoice terms are that payment is due in 30 days. No cash changes hands.
10	15 January 2006	▶ Sell for cash 10 books at $25 per book at an investment conference.
11	30 January 2006	▶ Hire a part-time clerk. The clerk is hired through an agency that also handles all payroll taxes. The company is to pay $15 per hour to the agency. The clerk works six hours prior to 31 January, but no cash will be paid until February.
12	31 January 2006	▶ Mail out the first month's newsletter to customer. This subscription had been sold on 3 January. See item 5.
13	31 January 2006	▶ Review of the investment portfolio shows that $100 of interest income was earned and the market value of the portfolio has increased by $2,000. The balance in the investment account is now $102,100. Securities are classified as "trading" securities.

Because this is a new business, the company's general ledger T-accounts initially have a zero balance.

31 December 2005 (excerpt from Exhibit A-3)

#	Business Activity	Accounting Treatment
1	▶ File documents with regulatory authorities to establish a separate legal entity. Initially capitalize the company through deposit of $150,000 from the three owners.	▶ **Cash [A]** is increased by $150,000, and **contributed capital [E]**[11] is increased by $150,000.

Accounting elements: Assets (A), Liabilities (L), Equity (E), Revenue (R), and Expenses (X).

[11] The account title will vary depending upon the type of entity (incorporated or not) and jurisdiction. Alternative account titles are "common shares," "common stock," "members' capital," "partners' capital," etc.

This transaction affects two accounts: cash and contributed capital. (Cash is an asset, and contributed capital is part of equity.) The transaction is entered into the T-accounts as shown below. The number in parenthesis references the transaction number.

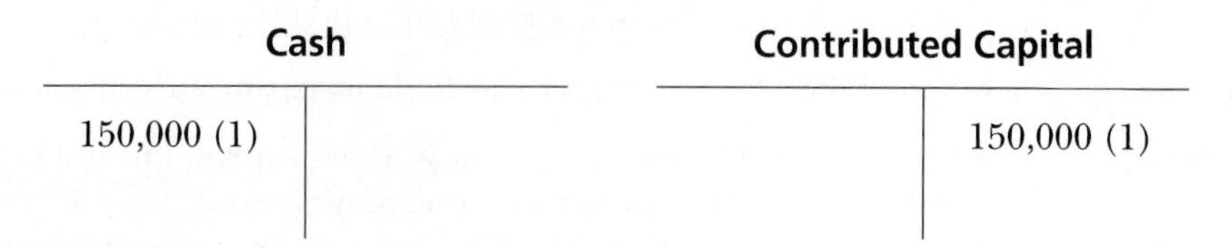

Cash is an asset account, and assets are on the left-hand side of the balance sheet (and basic accounting equation); therefore, cash is increased by recording the $150,000 on the debit (left) side of the T-account. Contributed capital is an equity account, and equity accounts are on the right-hand side of the balance sheet; therefore, contributed capital is increased by recording $150,000 on the credit (right) side of the T-account. Note that the sum of the debits for this transaction equals the sum of the credits:

$$DR = \$150,000$$
$$CR = \$150,000$$
$$DR = CR$$

Each transaction must always maintain this equality. This ensures that the accounting system (and accounting equation) is kept in balance. At this point in time, the company has assets (resources) of $150,000, and the owners' claim on the resources equals $150,000 (their contributed capital) because there are no liabilities at this point.

Transactions are recorded in a journal, which is then "posted to" (recorded in) the general ledger. When a transaction is recorded in a journal, it takes the form:

Date	Account		DR	CR
13 Dec 2005	Cash		150,000	
		Contributed Capital		150,000

This kind of entry is referred to as a "journal entry," and it is a summary of the information that will be posted in the general ledger T-accounts.

2 January 2006 (excerpt from Exhibit A-3)

#	Business Activity	Accounting Treatment
2	▶ Set up a $100,000 investment account and purchase a portfolio of equities and fixed-income securities.	▶ **Investments [A]** were increased by $100,000, and **cash [A]** was decreased by $100,000.

Accounting elements: Assets (A), Liabilities (L), Equity (E), Revenue (R), and Expenses (X).

This transaction affects two accounts but only one side of the accounting equation. Cash is reduced when the investments are purchased. Another type of asset, investments, increases. The T-account entries are shown below:

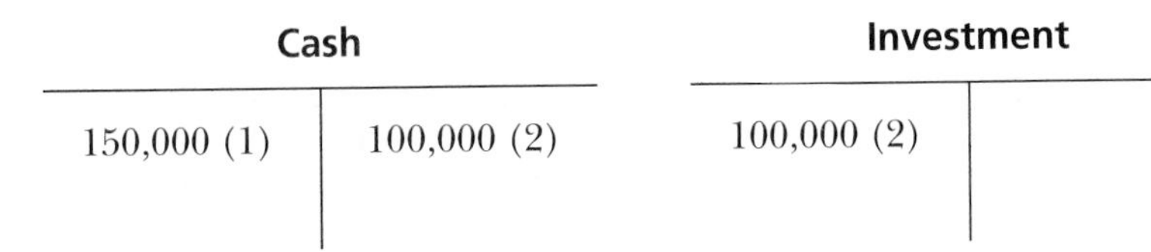

Cash		Investment	
150,000 (1)	100,000 (2)	100,000 (2)	

The cash account started with a $150,000 debit balance from the previous transaction. Assets are reduced by credit entries, so the reduction in cash is recorded by entering the $100,000 on the credit (right) side of the cash T-account. The investment account is also an asset, and the increase in investments is recorded by entering $100,000 on the debit side of the investments T-account. Transaction 2 balances because Transaction 2 debits equal Transaction 2 credits.

Going forward, we will use the traditional accounting terms of debit (debiting, debited) to indicate the action of entering a number in the debit side of an account, and credit (crediting, credited) to indicate the action of entering an amount on the credit side of an account.

2 January 2006 (excerpt from Exhibit A-3)

#	Business Activity	Accounting Treatment
3	▶ Pay $3,000 to landlord for office/warehouse. $2,000 represents a refundable deposit, and $1,000 represents the first month's rent.	▶ **Cash [A]** was decreased by $3,000, **deposits [A]** were increased by $2,000, and **prepaid rent [A]** was increased by $1,000.

Accounting elements: Assets (A), Liabilities (L), Equity (E), Revenue (R), and Expenses (X).

Cash is reduced once again by crediting the account by $3,000. On the other side of the transaction, two asset accounts increase. Deposits are increased by debiting the account for $2,000, while prepaid rent is increased by debiting that account for $1,000:

Cash		Deposits		Prepaid Rent	
150,000 (1)	100,000 (2)	2,000 (3)		1,000 (3)	
	3,000 (3)				

The sum of the debits for Transaction 3 equals the sum of the credits (i.e., $3,000).

3 January 2006 (excerpt from Exhibit A-3)

#	Business Activity	Accounting Treatment
4	▶ Purchase office equipment for $6,000 in cash. The equipment has an estimated life of two years with no salvage value.	▶ **Cash [A]** was decreased by $6,000, and **office equipment [A]** was increased by $6,000.

Accounting elements: Assets (A), Liabilities (L), Equity (E), Revenue (R), and Expenses (X).

Cash is credited for $6,000, while office equipment is debited for $6,000. Both are asset accounts, so these entries reflect a reduction in cash and an increase in office equipment.

Cash		Office Equipment	
150,000 (1)	100,000 (2)	6,000 (4)	
	3,000 (3)		
	6,000 (4)		

3 January 2006 (excerpt from Exhibit A-3)

#	Business Activity	Accounting Treatment
5	▶ Receive $1,200 cash for a one-year subscription to the monthly newsletter.	▶ **Cash [A]** was increased by $1,200, and **unearned fees [L]** was increased by $1,200.

Accounting elements: Assets (A), Liabilities (L), Equity (E), Revenue (R), and Expenses (X).

In this transaction, the company has received cash related to the sale of subscriptions. However, the company has not yet actually earned the subscription fees because it has an obligation to deliver newsletters in the future. So, this amount is recorded as a liability called "unearned fees" (or "unearned revenue"). In the future, as the company delivers the newsletters and thus fulfills its obligation, this amount will be transferred to revenue. If they fail to deliver the newsletters, the fees will need to be returned to the customer. To record the transaction, cash is debited (increased), while a liability account, unearned fees, is credited. Liabilities are on the right-hand side of the balance sheet and are, therefore, increased by crediting the T-account.

OPTIONAL SEGMENT

Cash	
150,000 (1)	100,000 (2)
1,200 (5)	3,000 (3)
	6,000 (4)

Unearned Fees	
	1,200 (5)

The sum of Transaction 5 debits and credits each equal $1,200.

10 January 2006 (excerpt from Exhibit A-3)

#	Business Activity	Accounting Treatment
6	▶ Purchase and receive 500 books at a cost of $20 per book for a total of $10,000. Invoice terms are that payment from IAL is due in 30 days. No cash changes hands. These books are intended for resale.	▶ **Inventory [A]** is increased by $10,000, and **accounts payable [L]** is increased by $10,000.

Accounting elements: Assets (A), Liabilities (L), Equity (E), Revenue (R), and Expenses (X).

The company has obtained an asset, inventory, which can be sold to customers at a later date. Rather than paying cash to the supplier currently, the company has an obligation to do so in 30 days. This represents a liability ("accounts payable") to the supplier. Inventory is debited for $10,000, while the liability, accounts payable, is credited for $10,000. Note that there is no impact on the cash account.

Inventory	
10,000 (6)	

Accounts Payable	
	10,600 (6)

10 January 2006 (excerpt from Exhibit A-3)

#	Business Activity	Accounting Treatment
7	▶ Spend $600 on newspaper and trade magazine advertising for the month.	▶ **Cash [A]** was decreased by $600, and **advertising expense [X]** was increased by $600.

Accounting elements: Assets (A), Liabilities (L), Equity (E), Revenue (R), and Expenses (X).

OPTIONAL SEGMENT

Unlike the previous expenditures, advertising is not an asset. Its future economic benefits are unclear, unlike equipment, which is expected to be useful over multiple periods. Expenditures such as advertising are recorded as an expense when they are incurred. To record the advertising expense, cash is credited for $600, and advertising expense is debited for $600. Expenses reduce net income, and thus reduce retained earnings. Decreases in retained earnings, as with any equity account, are recorded as debits. The entries with respect to retained earnings will be presented later in this section after the income statement.

Cash	
150,000 (1)	100,000 (2)
1,200 (5)	3,000 (3)
	6,000 (4)
	600 (7)

Advertising Expense	
600 (7)	

15 January 2006 (excerpt from Exhibit A-3)

#	Business Activity	Accounting Treatment
8	▶ Borrow $12,000 from a bank for working capital. Interest is payable annually at 10 percent. The principal is due in two years.	▶ **Cash [A]** is increased by $12,000, and **Bank debt [L]** is increased by $12,000.

Accounting elements: Assets (A), Liabilities (L), Equity (E), Revenue (R), and Expenses (X).

Cash is debited, and a corresponding liability is credited. Initially, no entry is made for interest that is expected to be paid on the loan. Interest will be recorded in the future as time passes and interest accrues (accumulates) on the loan.

Cash	
150,000 (1)	100,000 (2)
1,200 (5)	3,000 (3)
12,000 (8)	6,000 (4)
	600 (7)

Bank Debt	
	12,000 (8)

The debits and credits of Transaction 8 each total $12,000.

15 January 2006 (excerpt from Exhibit A-3)

#	Business Activity	Accounting Treatment
9	▶ Ship first order to a customer consisting of five books at $25 per book. Invoice terms are that payment is due in 30 days. No cash changes hands.	▶ **Accounts receivable [A]** increased by $125, and **book sales revenue [R]** increased by $125. Additionally, **inventory [A]** decreased by $100, and **cost of goods sold [X]** increased by $100.

Accounting elements: Assets (A), Liabilities (L), Equity (E), Revenue (R), and Expenses (X).

The company has now made a sale. Sale transaction records have two parts. One part records the $125 revenue to be received from the customer, and the other part records the $100 cost of the goods that have been sold. For the first part, accounts receivable is debited (increased) for $125, and a revenue account is credited for $125.

Accounts Receivable

Debit	Credit
125 (9)	

Book Sales Revenue

Debit	Credit
	125 (9)

For the second part, inventory is credited (reduced) for $100, and an expense, cost of goods sold, is debited (increased) to reflect the cost of inventory sold.

Inventory

Debit	Credit
10,000 (6)	100 (9)

Cost of Goods Sold

Debit	Credit
100 (9)	

Note that the sum of debits and the sum of credits for Transaction 9 both equal $225. The $225 is not meaningful by itself. What is important is that the debits and credits balance.

15 January 2006 (excerpt from Exhibit A-3)

#	Business Activity	Accounting Treatment
10	▶ Sell for cash 10 books at $25 per book at an investment conference.	▶ **Cash [A]** is increased by $250, and **book sales revenue [R]** is increased by $250. Additionally, **inventory [A]** is decreased by $200, and **cost of goods sold [X]** is increased by $200.

Accounting elements: Assets (A), Liabilities (L), Equity (E), Revenue (R), and Expenses (X).

Similar to the previous transaction, both the sales proceeds and cost of the goods sold must be recorded. In this case, however, the sales proceeds are received in cash. To record the sale proceeds, the entries include a debit to cash for $250 and a corresponding credit to book sales revenue for $250. To record cost of goods sold, the entries include a debit to cost of goods sold and a credit to inventory.

Cash

Debit	Credit
150,000 (1)	100,000 (2)
1,200 (5)	3,000 (3)
12,000 (8)	6,000 (4)
250 (10)	600 (7)

Book Sales Revenue

Debit	Credit
	125 (9)
	250 (10)

Inventory

Debit	Credit
10,000 (6)	100 (9)
	200 (10)

Cost of Goods Sold

Debit	Credit
100 (9)	
200 (10)	

Transaction 10's debits and credits are equal, maintaining the accounting system's balance.

30 January 2006 (excerpt from Exhibit A-3)

#	Business Activity	Accounting Treatment
11	▶ Hire a part-time clerk. The clerk is hired through an agency that also handles all payroll taxes. The company is to pay $15 per hour to the agency. The clerk works six hours prior to 31 January, but no cash will be paid until February.	▶ The company owes $90 for wages at month-end. Under accrual accounting, expenses are recorded when incurred, not when paid. ▶ **Accrued wages [L]** is increased by $90, and **wage expense [X]** is increased by $90. The accrued wage liability will be eliminated when the wages are paid.

Accounting elements: Assets (A), Liabilities (L), Equity (E), Revenue (R), and Expenses (X).

Accrued wages is a liability that is increased by crediting that account, whereas payroll is an expense account that is increased with a debit.

Accrued Wages

Debit	Credit
	90 (11)

Wage Expense

Debit	Credit
90 (11)	

OPTIONAL SEGMENT

31 January 2006 (excerpt from Exhibit A-3)

#	Business Activity	Accounting Treatment
12	▶ Mail out the first month's newsletter to customer. This subscription had been sold on 3 January.	▶ One month (or 1/12) of the $1,200 subscription has been satisfied, and thus $100 can be recognized as revenue. ▶ **Unearned fees [L]** is decreased by $100, and **fee revenue [R]** is increased by $100.

Accounting elements: Assets (A), Liabilities (L), Equity (E), Revenue (R), and Expenses (X).

To record the recognition of one month of the subscription fee, the account fee revenue is credited (increased) by $100, and the related liability is debited (decreased) by $100.

Fee Revenue

Debit	Credit
	100 (12)

Unearned Fees

Debit	Credit
100 (12)	1,200 (5)

31 January 2006 (excerpt from Exhibit A-3)

#	Business Activity	Accounting Treatment
13	▶ Review of the investment portfolio shows that $100 of interest income was earned and the market value of the portfolio has increased by $2,000. The balance in the investment account is now $102,100. The securities are classified as "trading" securities.	▶ **Investment income [R]** is increased by $100, and the **investments** account **[A]** is increased by $100. ▶ The $2,000 increase in the value of the portfolio represents unrealized gains that are part of income for traded securities. The **investments** account **[A]** is increased by $2,000, and **investment income [R]** is increased by $2,000.

Accounting elements: Assets (A), Liabilities (L), Equity (E), Revenue (R), and Expenses (X).

The investments account is an asset account that is debited (increased) for $2,100, and investment income is a revenue account that is credited (increased) by $2,100.

Investments

Debit	Credit
100,000 (2)	
2,100 (13)	

Investment Income

Debit	Credit
	2,100 (13)

OPTIONAL SEGMENT

These entries complete the recording of the first 13 transactions. In this illustration, there are three adjustments. An adjustment must be made related to Transaction 3 to account for the fact that a month has passed and rent expense has been incurred. We refer to this as Transaction 3a. Adjustments must also be made for an estimate of the depreciation of the office equipment (Transaction 4a) and for interest that has accrued on the loan (Transaction 8a).

31 January 2006

#	Business Activity	Accounting Treatment
3a	▶ In item 3, $3,000 was paid to the landlord for office/warehouse, including a $2,000 refundable deposit and $1,000 for the first month's rent ▶ Now, the first month has ended, so this rent has become a cost of doing business.	▶ To reflect the full amount of the first month's rent as a cost of doing business, **prepaid rent [A]** is decreased by $1,000, and **rent expense [X]** is increased by $1,000.

Accounting elements: Assets (A), Liabilities (L), Equity (E), Revenue (R), and Expenses (X).

Prepaid rent (an asset) is credited for $1,000 to reduce the balance, and rent expense is debited for the same amount to record the fact that the expense has now been incurred. After this entry, the balance of the prepaid rent asset account is $0.

Prepaid Rent

1,000 (3)	1,000 (3a)

Rent Expense

1,000 (3a)	

31 January 2006

#	Business Activity	Accounting Treatment
4a	▶ In item 6, office equipment was purchased for $6,000 in cash. The equipment has an estimated life of two years with no salvage value. ▶ Now, one month (or 1/24) of the useful life of the equipment has ended so a portion of the equipment cost has become a cost of doing business.	▶ A portion (1/24) of the total $6,000 cost of the office equipment is allocated to the current period's cost of doing business. ▶ **Depreciation expense [X]** is increased by $250, and **accumulated depreciation** is increased by $250. ▶ Accumulated depreciation is a contra asset account to office equipment

Accounting elements: Assets (A), Liabilities (L), Equity (E), Revenue (R), and Expenses (X).

Because some time has passed, accounting principles require that the estimated depreciation of the equipment be recorded. In this case, one could directly credit office equipment for $250; however, a preferred method is to credit an account called "accumulated depreciation," which is associated with the office equipment account. This accumulated depreciation account "holds" the cumulative amount of the depreciation related to the office equipment. When financial reports are prepared, a user is able to see both the original cost of the equipment as well as the accumulated depreciation. The user, therefore, has insight into the age of the asset, and perhaps how much time remains before it is likely to be replaced. Accumulated depreciation is termed a "contra" asset account and is credited for $250, while depreciation expense is debited (increased) for $250.

Accumulated Depreciation	
	250 (4a)

Depreciation Expense	
250 (4a)	

31 January 2006

#	Business Activity	Accounting Treatment
8a	▶ The company borrowed $12,000 from a bank on 15 January, with interest payable annually at 10 percent and the principal due in two years. ▶ Now, one-half of one month has passed since the borrowing.	▶ One-half of one month of interest expense has become a cost of doing business. $12,000 times 10% equals $1,200 of annual interest, equivalent to $100 per month and $50 for one-half month. ▶ **Interest expense [X]** is increased by $50, and **accrued interest [L]** is increased by $50.

Accounting elements: Assets (A), Liabilities (L), Equity (E), Revenue (R), and Expenses (X).

Accrued interest is a liability that is credited (increased) for $50, and interest expense is debited (increased) for $50. Accrued interest is also sometimes referred to as "interest payable."

Accrued Interest	
	50 (8a)

Interest Expense	
50 (8a)	

Exhibit A-4 summarizes the general ledger T-accounts for IAL at this point in time. For accounts with multiple entries, a line is drawn and the debit and credit columns are summed and netted to determine the current balance in the account. The balance is entered below the line. These individual account totals are then summarized in a trial balance as depicted in Exhibit A-5. A trial balance is a summary of the account balances at a point in time. An accountant can prepare a trial balance at any time to ensure that the system is in balance and to review current amounts in the accounts. Note that the debit and credit columns each total $176,065, confirming that the system is in balance. Any difference in the column totals would indicate an error had been made. The trial balance totals have no particular significance and are not used in preparing financial statements. These totals are simply the sum of debits and credits in the accounting system at that point in time.

OPTIONAL SEGMENT

EXHIBIT A-4 General Ledger T-Accounts for Investment Advisors, Ltd.

Cash

150,000 (1)	100,000 (2)
1,200 (5)	3,000 (3)
12,000 (8)	6,000 (4)
250 (10)	600 (7)
53,850	

Accounts Receivable

125 (9)	

Inventory

10,000 (6)	100 (9)
	200 (10)
9,700	

Investments

100,000 (2)	
2,100 (13)	
102,100	

Office Equipment

6,000 (4)	

Accumulated Depreciation

	250 (4a)

Deposits

2,000 (3)	

Prepaid Rent

1,000 (3)	1,000 (3a)
0	

Accounts Payable

	10,000 (6)

Accrued Wages

	90 (11)

Unearned Fees

100 (12)	1,200 (5)
	1,100

Bank Debt

	12,000 (8)

Accrued Interest

	50 (8a)

Contributed Capital

	150,000 (1)

Retained Earnings

Fee Revenue

	100 (12)

Book Sales Revenue

	125 (9)
	250 (10)
	375

Investment Income

	2,100 (13)

Cost of Goods Sold

100 (9)	
200 (10)	
300	

Advertising Expense

600 (7)	

Rent Expense

1,000 (3a)	

Depreciation Expense

250 (4a)	

Wage Expense

90 (11)	

Interest Expense

50 (8a)	

OPTIONAL SEGMENT

EXHIBIT A-5 Investment Advisers, Ltd., Trial Balance

	DR	CR
Cash	53,850	
Accounts receivable	125	
Inventory	9,700	
Investments	102,100	
Office equipment	6,000	
Accumulated depreciation		250
Deposits	2,000	
Prepaid rent	0	
Accounts payable		10,000
Accrued wages		90
Unearned fees		1,100
Bank debt		12,000
Accrued interest		50
Contributed capital		150,000
Retained earnings		
Fee revenue		100
Book sales revenue		375
Investment income		2,100
Cost of goods sold	300	
Advertising expense	600	
Rent expense	1,000	
Depreciation expense	250	
Wage expense	90	
Interest expense	50	
Total	**176,065**	**176,065**

After ensuring that the balances in the trial balance are correct (if there are errors, they are corrected and an adjusted trial balance is prepared), we prepare the financial statements. The trial balance provides the information necessary to prepare the balance sheet and the income statement. The detail in the general ledger must be reviewed to prepare the statement of cash flows and statement of owners' equity. After the income statement is prepared, the temporary accounts are closed out (i.e., taken to a zero balance) by transferring each of their balances to retained earnings. This typically occurs at year-end and is termed the "closing process." Exhibits A-6 and A-7 show the post-closing general ledger and trial balance, respectively.

OPTIONAL SEGMENT

EXHIBIT A-6 Post-Closing General Ledger T-Accounts for Investment Advisors, Ltd.

Cash	
150,000 (1)	100,000 (2)
1,200 (5)	3,000 (3)
12,000 (8)	6,000 (4)
250 (10)	600 (7)
53,850	

Accounts Receivable	
125 (9)	

Inventory	
10,000 (6)	100 (9)
	200 (10)
9,700	

Investments	
100,000 (2)	
2,100 (13)	
102,100	

Office Equipment	
6,000 (4)	

Accumulated Depreciation	
	250 (4a)

Deposits	
2,000 (3)	

Prepaid Rent	
1,000 (3)	1,000 (3a)
0	

Accounts Payable	
	10,000 (6)

Accrued Wages	
	90 (11)

Unearned Fees	
100 (12)	1,200 (5)
	1,100

Bank Debt	
	12,000 (8)

Accrued Interest	
	50 (8a)

Contributed Capital	
	150,000 (1)

Retained Earnings	
	285

Fee Revenue	
	0

Book Sales Revenue	
	0

Investment Income	
	0

Cost of Goods Sold	
0	

Advertising Expense	
0	

Rent Expense	
0	

Depreciation Expense	
0	

Wage Expense	
0	

Interest Expense	
0	

EXHIBIT A-7 **Investment Advisers, Ltd., Post-Closing Trial Balance**

	DR	CR
Cash	53,850	
Accounts receivable	125	
Inventory	9,700	
Investments	102,100	
Office equipment	6,000	
Accumulated depreciation		250
Deposits	2,000	
Prepaid rent	0	
Accounts payable		10,000
Accrued wages		90
Unearned fees		1,100
Bank debt		12,000
Accrued interest		50
Contributed capital		150,000
Retained earnings		285
Fee revenue		0
Book sales revenue		0
Investment income		0
Cost of goods sold	0	
Advertising expense	0	
Rent expense	0	
Depreciation expense	0	
Wage expense	0	
Interest expense	0	
Total	**173,775**	**173,775**

Financial statements are identical whether using a spreadsheet approach or a debit/credit approach. Accordingly, the financial statements for IAL that would be prepared using the trial balances are identical to those presented in the main body of the reading as Exhibit 9.

PRACTICE PROBLEMS FOR READING 30

1. Which of the following items would most likely be classified as an operating activity?
   A. Issuance of debt.
   B. Acquisition of a competitor.
   C. Sale of automobiles by an automobile dealer.
   D. Sale of surplus office equipment by an accounting firm.
2. Which of the following items would most likely be classified as a financing activity?
   A. Issuance of debt.
   B. Payment of income taxes.
   C. Investments in the stock of a supplier.
   D. Receipt of dividends from a stock investment.
3. Which of the following elements represents an economic resource?
   A. Asset.
   B. Revenue.
   C. Liability.
   D. Owners' equity.
4. Which of the following elements represents a residual claim?
   A. Asset.
   B. Expense.
   C. Liability.
   D. Owners' equity.
5. An analyst has projected that a company will have assets of €2,000 at year-end and liabilities of €1,200. The analyst's projection of total owners' equity should be closest to
   A. €800.
   B. €1,200.
   C. €2,000.
   D. €3,200.
6. An analyst has collected the following information regarding a company in advance of its year-end earnings announcement (in millions):

Estimated net income	$ 200
Beginning retained earnings	$1,400
Estimated distributions to owners	$ 100

   The analyst's estimate of ending retained earnings (in millions) should be closest to
   A. $1,100.
   B. $1,300.
   C. $1,500.
   D. $1,700.

7. An analyst has compiled the following information regarding Rubsam, Inc.

Liabilities at year-end	€1,000
Contributed capital at year-end	€500
Beginning retained earnings	€600
Revenue during the year	€5,000
Expenses during the year	€4,300

There have been no distributions to owners. The analyst's most likely estimate of total assets at year-end should be closest to

A. €1,400.

B. €2,100.

C. €2,300.

D. €2,800.

8. A group of individuals formed a new company with an investment of $500,000. The most likely effect of this transaction on the company's accounting equation at the time of the formation is an increase in cash and

A. an increase in revenue.

B. a decrease in liabilities.

C. an increase in liabilities.

D. an increase in contributed capital.

9. HVG, LLC paid $12,000 of cash to a real estate company upon signing a lease on 31 December 2005. The payment represents a $4,000 security deposit and $4,000 of rent for each of January 2006 and February 2006. Assuming that the correct accounting is to reflect both January and February rent as prepaid, the most likely effect on HVG's accounting equation in December 2005 is

A. no net change in assets.

B. a decrease in assets of $4,000.

C. a decrease in assets of $8,000.

D. a decrease in assets of $12,000.

10. TRR Enterprises sold products to customers on 30 June 2006 for a total price of €10,000. The terms of the sale are that payment is due in 30 days. The cost of the products was €8,000. The most likely net change in TRR's total assets on 30 June 2006 related to this transaction is

A. €(8,000).

B. €0.

C. €2,000.

D. €10,000.

11. On 30 April 2006, Pinto Products received a cash payment of $30,000 as a deposit on production of a custom machine to be delivered in August 2006. This transaction would most likely result in which of the following on 30 April 2006?

A. No effect on liabilities.

B. A decrease in assets of $30,000.

C. An increase in revenue of $30,000.

D. An increase in liabilities of $30,000.

12. Squires & Johnson, Ltd., recorded €250,000 of depreciation expense in December 2005. The most likely effect on the company's accounting equation is
    - **A.** no affect on assets.
    - **B.** a decrease in assets of €250,000.
    - **C.** an increase in assets of €250,000.
    - **D.** an increase in liabilities of €250,000.
13. An analyst who is interested in assessing a company's financial position is most likely to focus on which financial statement?
    - **A.** Balance sheet.
    - **B.** Income statement.
    - **C.** Statement of cash flows.
    - **D.** Statement of owners' equity.
14. The statement of cash flows presents the flows into which three groups of business activities?
    - **A.** Operating, nonoperating, and financing.
    - **B.** Operating, investing, and financing.
    - **C.** Operating, nonoperating, and investing.
    - **D.** Operating, investing, and owners' equity.
15. Which of the following statements about cash received prior to the recognition of revenue in the financial statements is *most* accurate? The cash is recorded as
    - **A.** accrued revenue, an asset.
    - **B.** deferred revenue, an asset.
    - **C.** accrued revenue, a liability.
    - **D.** deferred revenue, a liability.
16. When, at the end of an accounting period, a revenue has been recognized in the financial statements but no billing has occurred and no cash has been received, the accrual is to
    - **A.** unbilled (accrued) revenue, an asset.
    - **B.** deferred revenue, an asset.
    - **C.** unbilled (accrued) revenue, a liability.
    - **D.** deferred revenue, a liability.
17. When, at the end of an accounting period, cash has been paid with respect to an expense incurred but not yet recognized in the financial statements, the business should then record
    - **A.** an accrued expense, an asset.
    - **B.** a prepaid expense, an asset.
    - **C.** an accrued expense, a liability.
    - **D.** a prepaid expense, a liability.

18. When, at the end of an accounting period, cash has not been paid with respect to an expense that has been incurred but not recognized yet in the financial statements, the business should then record

A. an accrued expense, an asset.

B. a prepaid expense, an asset.

C. an accrued expense, a liability.

D. a prepaid expense, a liability.

19. The collection of all business transactions sorted by account in an accounting system is referred to as

A. a trial balance.

B. a general ledger.

C. a general journal.

D. an adjusted trial balance.

20. If a company reported fictitious revenue, it would most likely try to cover up its fraud by

A. decreasing assets.

B. increasing liabilities.

C. creating a fictitious asset.

D. creating a fictitious liability.

FINANCIAL REPORTING STANDARDS

by Thomas R. Robinson, Hennie van Greuning,
Karen O'Connor Rubsam, Elaine Henry, and Michael A. Broihahn

READING

31

LEARNING OUTCOMES

The candidate should be able to:

a. explain the objective of financial statements and the importance of reporting standards in security analysis and valuation;

b. explain the role of standard-setting bodies, such as the International Accounting Standards Board and the U.S. Financial Accounting Standards Board, and regulatory authorities such as the International Organization of Securities Commissions, the U.K. Financial Services Authority, and the U.S. Securities and Exchange Commission in establishing and enforcing financial reporting standards;

c. discuss the ongoing barriers to developing one universally accepted set of financial reporting standards;

d. describe the International Financial Reporting Standards (IFRS) framework, including the objective of financial statements, their qualitative characteristics, required reporting elements, and the constraints and assumptions in preparing financial statements;

e. explain the general requirements for financial statements;

f. compare and contrast key concepts of financial reporting standards under IFRS and alternative reporting systems, and discuss the implications for financial analysis of differing financial reporting systems;

g. identify the characteristics of a coherent financial reporting framework and barriers to creating a coherent financial reporting network;

h. discuss the importance of monitoring developments in financial reporting standards and evaluate company disclosures of significant accounting policies.

THEME

Financial statements are created based on a conceptual framework established by standard-setting bodies and regulatory authorities. Understanding the principles underlying this financial reporting framework will allow an analyst to assess the securities valuation implications of any financial statement element or transaction.

1 INTRODUCTION

Financial reporting standards determine the types and amounts of information that must be provided to investors and creditors so that they may make informed decisions. This reading focuses on the broad framework within which these standards are created. An understanding of the underlying framework of financial reporting standards, which is broader than knowledge of specific accounting rules, will allow an analyst to assess the valuation implications of *any* financial statement element or transaction—including newly developed transactions that are not specifically addressed by the standards.

Section 2 of this reading discusses the objective of financial statements and the importance of financial standards in security analysis and valuation. Section 3 describes the financial reporting standard-setting bodies and regulatory authorities that establish financial reporting standards. Section 4 examines the trend toward convergence of global financial reporting standards. The International Financial Reporting Standards (IFRS) framework is presented in Section 5, and Section 6 compares IFRS with alternative reporting systems.[1] Section 7 discusses the characteristics of an effective financial reporting framework. Section 8 discusses the importance of monitoring developments in financial reporting standards. A summary of the key points and practice problems in the CFA Institute multiple-choice format conclude the reading.

2 THE OBJECTIVE OF FINANCIAL REPORTING

Financial reporting begins with a simple enough premise. The International Accounting Standards Board (IASB), which is the international accounting standard-setting body, expresses it as follows in its *Framework for the Preparation and Presentation of Financial Statements:*

> The objective of financial statements is to provide information about the financial position, performance, and changes in financial position of an entity; this information should be useful to a wide range of users for the purpose of making economic decisions.[2]

[1] The body of standards issued by the IASB is referred to as "International Financial Reporting Standards," which include previously issued International Accounting Standards (IAS). "Financial reporting" is a broad term including reporting on accounting, financial statements, and other information found in company financial reports.

[2] *Framework for the Preparation and Presentation of Financial Statements,* International Accounting Standards Committee, 1989, adopted by IASB 2001, paragraph 12.

Until recently, financial reporting standards were developed mostly independently by each country's standard-setting body. This has created a wide range of standards, some of which are quite comprehensive and complex, and others more general. Recent accounting scandals have raised awareness of the need for more uniform global financial reporting standards and provided the impetus for stronger coordination among the major standard-setting bodies. Such coordination is also a natural outgrowth of the increased globalization of capital markets.

Developing financial reporting standards is complicated because the underlying economic reality is complicated. The financial transactions and organizations that financial statements purport to represent are complicated. There is often uncertainty about transactions, resulting in the need for accruals and estimates. These accruals and estimates necessitate judgment. Judgment varies from one preparer to the next. Accordingly, standards are needed to achieve some type of consistency in these judgments. Even with such standards there will be no one right answer. Nevertheless, financial reporting standards try to limit the range of acceptable answers to ensure some measure of consistency in financial statements.

EXAMPLE 1

Estimates in Financial Reporting

In order to make comparisons across companies (**cross-sectional analysis**) and over time for a single company (time-series analysis), it is important that accounting methods are comparable and consistently applied. However, accounting standards must be flexible enough to recognize that there are differences in the underlying economics between businesses.

Suppose two companies buy the same model of machinery to be used in their respective businesses. The machine is expected to last for several years. Financial reporting standards should require that both companies account for this equipment by initially recording the cost of the machinery as an asset. Without such a standard, the companies could report the purchase of the equipment differently. For example, one company might record the purchase as an asset and the other might record the purchase as an expense. An accounting standard ensures that both companies would be required to record the transaction in a similar manner.

Accounting standards typically would require the cost of the machine to be apportioned over the **estimated useful life** of an asset as an expense called depreciation. Because the two companies may be operating the machinery differently, financial reporting standards must retain some flexibility. One company might operate the machinery only a few days per week, whereas the other company operates the equipment continuously throughout the week. Given the difference in usage, it would not be appropriate for the two companies to report an identical amount of depreciation expense each period. Financial reporting standards must allow for some discretion such that management can match their financial reporting choices to the underlying economics of their business while ensuring that similar transactions are recorded in a similar manner between companies.

The IASB and the U.S. Financial Accounting Standards Board (FASB) have developed similar financial reporting frameworks, both of which specify the overall objective and qualities of information to be provided. Financial reports are intended to provide information to many users, including investors, creditors, employees, customers, and others. As a result of this multipurpose nature, financial reports are *not* designed with only asset valuation in mind. However, financial reports provide important inputs into the process of valuing a company or the securities a company issues. Understanding the financial reporting framework—including how and when judgments and estimates can affect the numbers reported—enables an analyst to evaluate the information reported and to use the information appropriately when assessing a company's financial performance. Clearly, such an understanding is also important in assessing the financial impact of business decisions and in making comparisons across entities.

3 FINANCIAL REPORTING STANDARD-SETTING BODIES AND REGULATORY AUTHORITIES

A distinction needs to be made between standard-setting bodies and regulatory authorities. Standard-setting bodies, such as the IASB and FASB, are typically private sector organizations consisting of experienced accountants, auditors, users of financial statements, and academics. Regulatory authorities, such as the SEC in the United States and the FSA in the United Kingdom, are governmental entities that have the legal authority to enforce financial reporting requirements and exert other controls over entities that participate in the capital markets within their jurisdiction.

In other words, *generally*, standard-setting bodies make the rules and regulatory authorities enforce the rules. Note, however, that regulators often retain the legal authority to establish financial reporting standards in their jurisdiction and can overrule the private sector standard-setting bodies.

EXAMPLE 2

Industry-Specific Regulation

In certain cases, there exist multiple regulatory bodies that affect a company's financial reporting requirements. For example, in almost all jurisdictions around the world, banking-specific regulatory bodies establish requirements related to risk-based capital measurement, minimum capital adequacy, provisions for doubtful loans, and minimum monetary reserves. An awareness of such regulations provides an analyst with the context to understand a bank's business, including the objectives and scope of allowed activities.

In the United States, the Office of the Comptroller of the Currency charters and regulates all national banks. In the United Kingdom, the FSA regulates the financial services industry. In some countries, a single entity serves both as the central bank and as the regulatory body for the country's financial institutions.

This section provides a brief overview of the most important international standard-setting body, the IASB, followed by a description of the International Organization of Securities Commissions (IOSCO), capital markets regulation in the **European Union (EU)**, and an overview of the U.S. Securities and Exchange Commission (SEC).

3.1 International Accounting Standards Board

The IASB is the standard-setting body responsible for developing international financial reporting and accounting standards. The four goals of the IASB are:

> (a) to develop, in the public interest, a single set of high quality, understandable and enforceable global accounting standards that require high quality, transparent and comparable information in financial statements and other financial reporting to help participants in the world's capital markets and other users make economic decisions;
>
> (b) to promote the use and rigorous application of those standards;
>
> (c) in fulfilling the objectives associated with (a) and (b), to take account of, as appropriate, the special needs of small and medium-sized entities and emerging economies; and
>
> (d) to bring about convergence of national accounting standards and International Accounting Standards and International Financial Reporting Standards to high quality solutions.[3]

The predecessor of the IASB, the International Accounting Standards Committee (IASC), was founded in June 1973 as a result of an agreement by accountancy bodies in Australia, Canada, France, Germany, Japan, Mexico, the Netherlands, the United Kingdom and Ireland, and the United States. By 1998, the IASC had expanded membership to 140 accountancy bodies in 101 countries. In 2001, the IASC was reconstituted into the IASB. The IASB has 14 full-time board members who deliberate new financial reporting standards.[4]

The IASB is overseen by the International Accounting Standards Committee Foundation, which has 19 trustees who appoint the members of the IASB, establish the budget, and monitor the IASB's progress. The IASB is advised by the Standards Advisory Council, which is composed of about 50 members representing organizations and individuals with an interest in international financial reporting.

3.2 International Organization of Securities Commissions

The IOSCO, formed in 1983 as the successor organization of an inter-American regional association (created in 1974), has 181 members that regulate more than 90 percent of the world's financial capital markets.

[3] *International Accounting Standards Committee Foundation Constitution*, IASCF, July 2005, part A, paragraph 2.

[4] Although the name of the IASB incorporates "Accounting Standards" and early standards were titled International Accounting Standards (IAS), the term "International Financial Reporting Standards" is being used for new standards. The use of the words "financial reporting" recognizes the importance of disclosures outside of the core financial statements, such as management discussion of the business, risks, and future plans.

In 1998, IOSCO adopted a comprehensive set of *Objectives and Principles of Securities Regulation*, which is recognized as international benchmarks for all markets. IOSCO sets out three core objectives of securities regulation:

- protecting investors;
- ensuring that markets are fair, efficient, and transparent; and
- reducing **systematic risk**.

Standards related to financial reporting, including accounting and auditing standards, are key components in achieving these objectives. The IOSCO's *Objectives and Principles of Securities Regulation* states:

> Full disclosure of information material to investors' decisions is the most important means for ensuring investor protection. Investors are, thereby, better able to assess the potential risks and rewards of their investments and, thus, to protect their own interests. As key components of disclosure requirements, accounting and auditing standards should be in place and they should be of a high and internationally acceptable quality.[5]

Historically, regulation and related financial reporting standards were developed within individual countries and were often based on the cultural, economic, and political norms of each country. As financial markets have become more global, it has become desirable to establish comparable financial reporting standards internationally. Ultimately, laws and regulations are established by individual jurisdictions, so this also requires cooperation among regulators. In order to ensure adherence to international financial standards, it is important to have uniform regulation across national boundaries. The IOSCO aims to assist in attaining this goal of uniform regulation.

3.3 Capital Markets Regulation in Europe

Each individual member state of the EU regulates capital markets in its jurisdiction. There are, however, certain regulations that have been adopted at the EU level. These include standards and directives related to enforcement of IFRS, a proposed directive to adopt International Standards on Auditing, and proposed directives concerning the board of directors' responsibility for a company's financial statements. The EU, under its Accounting Regulation, will likely serve a role similar to the SEC in the United States as it must endorse each international standard for use in Europe.

In 2001, the European Commission established two committees related to securities regulation: the European Securities Committee (ESC) and the Committee of European Securities Regulators (CESR). The ESC consists of high-level representatives of member states and advises the European Commission on securities policy issues. The CESR is an independent advisory body composed of representatives of regulatory authorities of the member states.

As noted earlier, regulation still rests with the individual member states and, therefore, requirements for registering shares and filing periodic financial reports vary from country to country. Over time, this process is expected to become more uniform in the EU.

[5] *Objectives and Principles of Securities Regulation*, IOSCO, May 2003, section 4.2.1.

3.4 Capital Markets Regulation in the United States

Any company issuing securities within the United States, or otherwise involved in U.S. capital markets, is subject to the rules and regulations of the U.S. SEC. The SEC, one of the oldest and most developed regulatory authorities, originated as a result of reform efforts made after the great stock market crash of 1929, sometimes referred to as simply the "Great Crash."

3.4.1 Significant Securities-Related Legislation

There are numerous SEC rules and regulations affecting reporting companies, broker/dealers, and other market participants. From a financial reporting and analysis perspective, the most significant of these acts are the Securities Acts of 1933 and 1934 and the Sarbanes–Oxley Act of 2002.

- **Securities Act of 1933 (The 1933 Act)**—This act specifies the financial and other significant information that investors must receive when securities are sold, prohibits misrepresentations, and requires initial registration of all public issuances of securities.
- **Securities Exchange Act of 1934 (The 1934 Act)**—This act created the SEC, gave the SEC authority over all aspects of the securities industry, and empowered the SEC to require periodic reporting by companies with publicly traded securities.
- **Sarbanes–Oxley Act of 2002**—The Sarbanes–Oxley Act of 2002 created the Public Company Accounting Oversight Board (PCAOB) to oversee auditors. The SEC is responsible for carrying out the requirements of the act and overseeing the PCAOB. The act addresses auditor independence; for example, it prohibits auditors from providing certain nonaudit services to the companies they audit. The act strengthens corporate responsibility for financial reports; for example, it requires the chief executive officer and the chief financial officer to certify that the company's financial reports fairly present the company's condition. Furthermore, Section 404 of the Sarbanes–Oxley Act requires management to report on the effectiveness of the company's internal control over financial reporting and to obtain a report from its external auditor attesting to management's assertion about the effectiveness of the company's internal control.

3.4.2 SEC Filings: Key Sources of Information for Analysts

Companies satisfy compliance with these acts principally through the completion and submission (i.e., filing) of standardized forms issued by the SEC. There are more than 50 different types of SEC forms that are used to satisfy reporting requirements; the discussion herein will be limited to those forms most relevant for financial analysts.

In 1993, the SEC began to mandate electronic filings of the required forms through its Electronic Data Gathering, Analysis, and Retrieval (EDGAR) system. As of 2005, most SEC filings are required to be made electronically. EDGAR has made corporate and financial information more readily available to investors and the financial community. Most of the SEC filings that an analyst would be interested in can be retrieved from the Internet from one of many websites, including the SEC's own website. Some filings are required upon the initial offering of securities, whereas others are required on a periodic basis thereafter. The following are some of the more common information sources used by analysts.

- **Securities Offerings Registration Statement**—The 1933 Act requires companies offering securities to file a registration statement. New issuers as well as previously registered companies that are issuing new securities are required to file these statements. Required information and the precise form vary depending upon the size and nature of the offering. Typically, required information includes: (1) disclosures about the securities being offered for sale, (2) the relationship of these new securities to the issuer's other capital securities, (3) the information typically provided in the annual filings, (4) recent audited financial statements, and (5) risk factors involved in the business.

EXAMPLE 3

Initial Registration Statement

In 2004, Google filed a Form S-1 registration statement with the U.S. SEC to register its initial public offering of securities (Class A Common Stock). In addition to copious amounts of financial and business information, the registration statement provided a 20-page discussion of risks related to Google's business and industry. This type of qualitative information is helpful, if not essential, in making an assessment of a company's credit or investment risk.

- **Forms 10-K, 20-F, and 40-F**—These are forms that companies are required to file *annually*. Form 10-K is for U.S. registrants, Form 40-F is for certain Canadian registrants, and Form 20-F is for all other non-U.S. registrants. These forms require a comprehensive overview, including information concerning a company's business, financial disclosures, legal proceedings, and information related to management. The financial disclosures include a historical summary of financial data (usually 10 years), management's discussion and analysis (MD&A) of the company's financial condition and results of operations, and audited financial statements.

- **Annual Report**—In addition to the SEC's annual filings (e.g., form 10-K), most companies prepare an annual report to shareholders. This is not a requirement of the SEC. The annual report is usually viewed as one of the most significant opportunities for a company to present itself to shareholders and other external parties; accordingly, it is often a highly polished marketing document with photographs, an opening letter from the chief executive officer, financial data, market segment information, research and development activities, and future corporate goals. In contrast, the Form 10-K is a more legal type of document with minimal marketing emphasis. Although the perspectives vary, there is considerable overlap between a company's annual report and its Form 10-K. Some companies elect to prepare just the Form 10-K or a document that integrates both the 10-K and annual report.

- **Proxy Statement/Form DEF-14A**—The SEC requires that shareholders of a company receive a proxy statement prior to a shareholder meeting. A proxy is an authorization from the shareholder giving another party the right to cast its vote. Shareholder meetings are held at least once a year, but any special meetings also require a proxy statement. Proxies, especially annual meeting proxies, contain information that is often useful to financial analysts. Such information typically includes proposals that require a shareholder vote, details of security ownership by management and principal owners, biographical information on directors, and disclosure of executive compensation. Proxy statement information is filed with the SEC as Form DEF-14A.

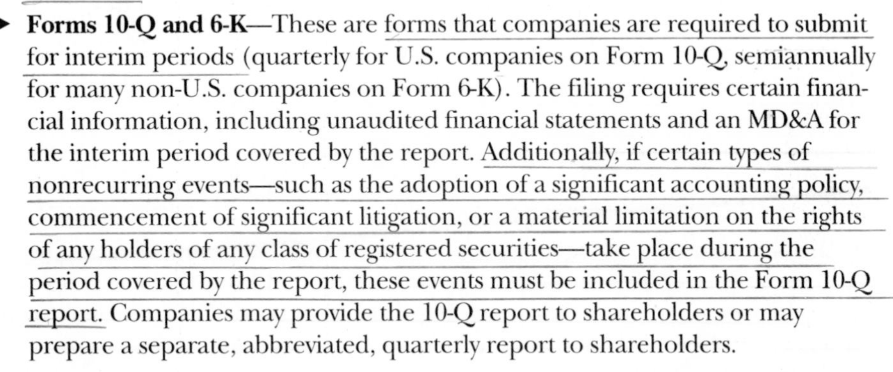

- **Forms 10-Q and 6-K**—These are forms that companies are required to submit for interim periods (quarterly for U.S. companies on Form 10-Q, semiannually for many non-U.S. companies on Form 6-K). The filing requires certain financial information, including unaudited financial statements and an MD&A for the interim period covered by the report. Additionally, if certain types of nonrecurring events—such as the adoption of a significant accounting policy, commencement of significant litigation, or a material limitation on the rights of any holders of any class of registered securities—take place during the period covered by the report, these events must be included in the Form 10-Q report. Companies may provide the 10-Q report to shareholders or may prepare a separate, abbreviated, quarterly report to shareholders.

3.4.3 Other Filings

There are other SEC filings that a company or its officers make—either periodically, or, if significant events or transactions have occurred, in between the periodic reports noted above. By their nature, these forms sometimes contain the most interesting and timely information and may have significant valuation implications.

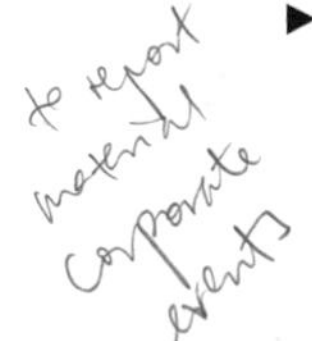

- **Form 8-K**—In addition to filing annual and interim reports, SEC registrants must report material corporate events on a more current basis. Form 8-K (6-K for non-U.S. registrants) is the "current report" companies must file with the SEC to announce such major events as acquisitions or disposals of corporate assets, changes in securities and trading markets, matters related to accountants and financial statements, corporate governance and management changes, and Regulation FD disclosures.[6]
- **Form 144**—This form must be filed with the SEC as notice of the proposed sale of restricted securities or securities held by an affiliate of the issuer in reliance on Rule 144. Rule 144 permits limited sales of restricted securities without registration.
- **Forms 3, 4, and 5**—These forms are required to report beneficial ownership of securities. These filings are required for any director or officer of a registered company as well as beneficial owners of greater than 10 percent of a class of registered equity securities. Form 3 is the initial statement, Form 4 reports changes, and Form 5 is the annual report. These forms, along with Form 144, can be used to examine purchases and sales of securities by officers, directors, and other affiliates of the company.

[6] Regulation FD provides that when an issuer discloses material nonpublic information to certain individuals or entities—generally, securities market professionals such as stock analysts or holders of the issuer's securities who may trade on the basis of the information—the issuer must make public disclosure of that information. In this way, the rule aims to promote full and fair disclosure.

- **Form 11-K**—This is the annual report of employee stock purchase, savings, and similar plans. It might be of interest to analysts for companies with significant employee benefit plans because it contains more information than that disclosed in the company's financial statements.

4 CONVERGENCE OF GLOBAL FINANCIAL REPORTING STANDARDS

Recent activities have moved the goal of one set of universally accepted financial reporting standards out of the theoretical sphere into the realm of reality.

In 2002, the IASB and FASB each acknowledged their commitment to the development of high-quality, compatible accounting standards that could be used for both domestic and cross-border financial reporting (in an agreement referred to as "The Norwalk Agreement"). Both the IASB and FASB pledged to use their best efforts to (1) make their existing financial reporting standards fully compatible as soon as practicable, and (2) to coordinate their future work programs to ensure that, once achieved, compatibility is maintained. The Norwalk Agreement was certainly an important milestone, and both bodies are working toward convergence through an ongoing short-term convergence project, a convergence research project, and joint projects such as revenue recognition and business combinations.

In 2004, the IASB and FASB agreed that, in principle, any significant accounting standard would be developed cooperatively. It is likely to take considerable time to work out differences on existing IFRS and U.S. generally accepted accounting principles (GAAP) because of other pressing priorities and honest differences in principles. Development of one universally accepted financial reporting framework is a major undertaking and is expected to take a number of years. Exhibit 1 provides a summary of the worldwide adoption status of IFRS.

In some ways, the move toward one global set of financial reporting standards has made the barriers to full convergence more apparent. Standard-setting bodies and regulators can have differing views. In addition, they may be influenced by strong industry lobbying groups and others that will be subject to these reporting standards. For example, the FASB faced strong opposition when it first attempted to adopt standards requiring companies to expense employee stock compensation plans.[7] The IASB has experienced similar political pressures. The issue of political pressure is compounded when international standards are involved, simply because there are many more interested parties and many more divergent views and objectives. The integrity of the financial reporting framework depends on the standard setter's ability to balance various points of view.

5 THE INTERNATIONAL FINANCIAL REPORTING STANDARDS FRAMEWORK

The IFRS *Framework for the Preparation and Presentation of Financial Statements* (referred to here as the "Framework") sets forth the concepts that underlie the preparation and presentation of financial statements for external uses. The Framework is designed to assist the IASB in developing standards and to instruct preparers of financial statements on the principles of financial statement con-

[7] The second attempt was successful and FASB Statement 123R now requires the expensing of stock options.

EXHIBIT 1 International Adoption Status of IFRS as of December 2006

Region	Status
Europe	▶ The EU requires companies listed in EU countries to adopt IFRS for the 2005 financial statements. ▶ The IASB decides in late 2006 that it will not require the application of new IFRS or major amendments to existing standards before 1 January 2009. ▶ Switzerland requires that multinational main board companies must choose either U.S. GAAP or IFRS.
United States	▶ The SEC accepts IFRS for non-U.S. registrants but currently requires a reconciliation to U.S. GAAP. It has indicated that it will revisit this requirement after the filing of 2005 financial statements. ▶ The FASB is engaged in numerous projects with the IASB to achieve convergence of U.S. GAAP to IFRS. Full convergence, however, is not expected to be completed in the foreseeable future.
Canada	▶ In 2006, Canada's Accounting Standards Board decided to converge Canadian GAAP with IFRS.
Central and South America	▶ Guatemala, Costa Rica, Ecuador, Nicaragua, Panama, Peru, and Honduras require IFRS for all domestic listed companies. ▶ Venezuela required adoption of IFRS beginning in 2006 for listed companies and 2007 for others. ▶ El Salvador permits IFRS for domestic listed companies.
Caribbean	▶ Bahamas, Barbados, Jamaica, Trinidad and Tobago, Dominican Republic, and Haiti require IFRS for all domestic listed companies.
Asia Pacific countries	▶ Bangladesh requires the use of IFRS, and Australia and New Zealand have adopted IFRS "equivalent" standards for the 2005 and 2007, respectively, financial statements. ▶ Japan has launched a joint project with the IASB to reduce differences between Japanese accounting standards and IFRS. ▶ China requires IFRS for some domestic listed companies. ▶ Hong Kong and Philippines have adopted national standards that are equivalent to IFRS except for some effective dates and transition. ▶ Singapore has adopted many IFRS. ▶ Myanmar and Sri Lanka permit the use of IFRS for domestic listed companies.
Africa and the Middle East	▶ South Africa, Tanzania, Kenya, Egypt, and Malawi require IFRS for all domestic listed companies.
Russian Federation and former Soviet Union	▶ The Russian Federation requires IFRS for banks and has proposed phasing in requiring all domestic listed companies to use IFRS beginning in 2006.

Sources: Based on data from www.iasb.org and www.iasplus.com.

struction. Importantly, the Framework is also designed to assist users of financial statements—including financial analysts—in interpreting the information contained therein.

The Framework is diagrammed in Exhibit 2. The top part shows how the objective of financial statements determines the characteristics that the reporting elements (relating to performance and financial position) should embody. In practice, decisions in financial statement preparation must satisfy a number of constraints, such as cost–benefit trade-offs. Finally, underlying financial statement preparation, and, therefore, placed at the bottom of the exhibit, are certain important assumptions.

EXHIBIT 2 IFRS Framework for the Preparation and Presentation of Financial Statements

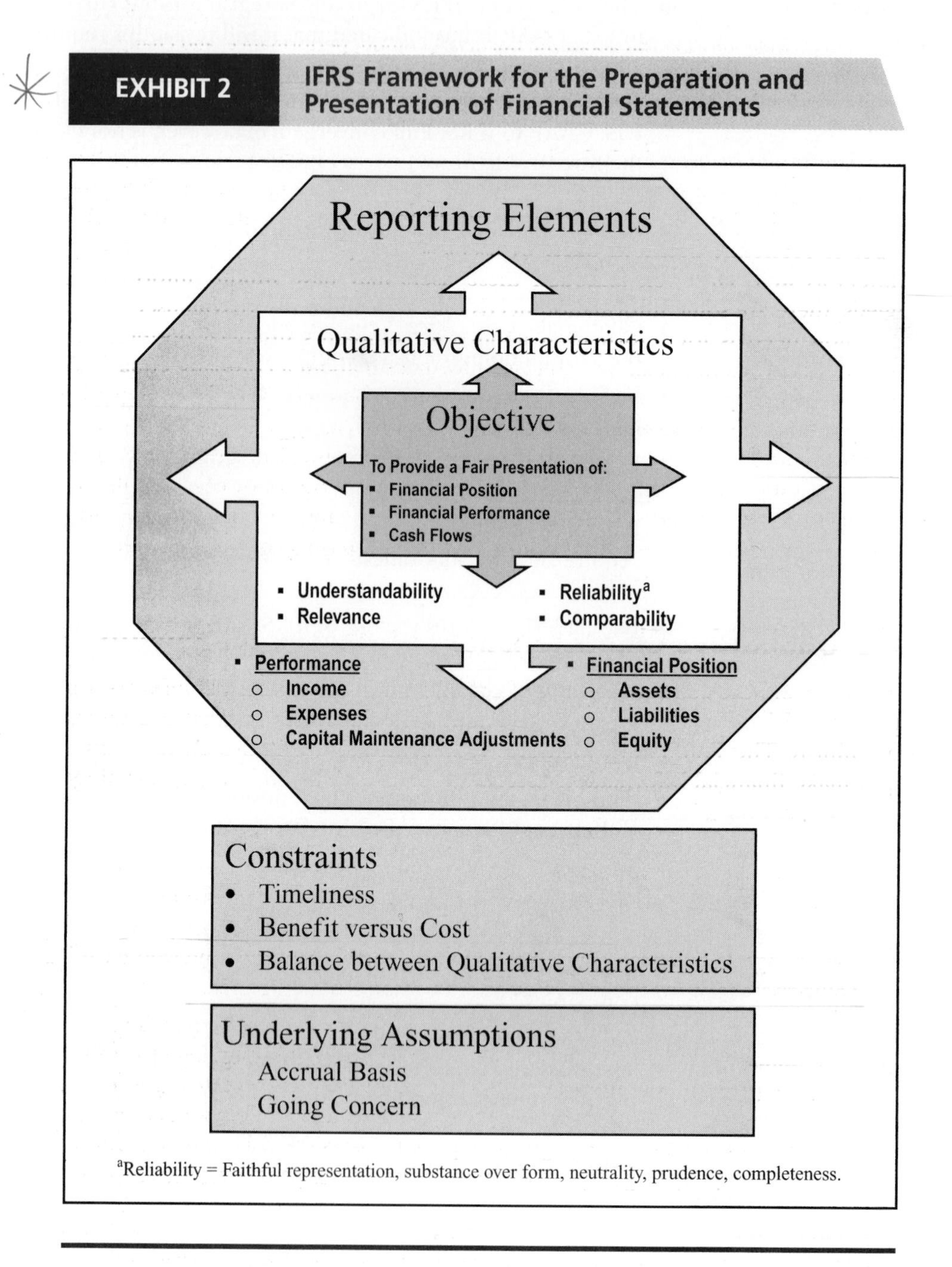

[a]Reliability = Faithful representation, substance over form, neutrality, prudence, completeness.

In the following, we discuss the Framework starting at the center: the objective of financial statements.

5.1 Objective of Financial Statements

At the center of the Framework is the objective: fair presentation of the company's financial position, its financial performance, and its cash flows. All other aspects of the Framework flow from that central objective.

Fair presentation to whom? And for what purpose? The introduction to the Framework states that the objective of financial statements is:

> . . . to provide information about the financial position, performance, and changes in financial position of an entity; this information should be useful to a wide range of users for the purpose of making economic decisions.[8]

The range of users includes investors, employees, lenders, suppliers, other creditors, customers, government agencies, the public, and analysts. The purpose of all this information is to be useful in making economic decisions. The types of economic decisions differ by users, so the specific information needed differs as well. However, although these users may have unique information needs, there are some information needs that are common across all users. One common need is for information about the company's financial position: its resources and its financial obligations. Information about a company's financial performance explains how and why the company's financial position changed in the past and can be useful in evaluating potential changes in the future. The third common information need reflected in the Framework diagram is the need for information about a company's cash. How did the company obtain cash? By selling its products and services, borrowing, other? How did the company use cash? Paying expenses, investing in new equipment, paying dividends, other?

5.2 Qualitative Characteristics of Financial Statements

Flowing from the central objective of providing a *fair presentation* of information that is *useful* to decision makers, the Framework elaborates on what constitutes usefulness. The Framework identifies four principal qualitative characteristics that make financial information useful: understandability, relevance, reliability, and comparability.[9]

1. *Understandability.* Understandability of information is defined in terms of who should be able to understand it. The Framework specifies that the information should be readily understandable by users who have a basic knowledge of business, economic activities, and accounting, and who have a willingness to study the information with reasonable diligence.
2. *Relevance.* Relevance of information is defined in terms of whether the information influences economic decisions of users, helping them to evaluate past, present, and future events, or to confirm or correct their past evaluations. Relevant information is typically timely, rather than dated. Relevant information is detailed enough to help users assess the risks and opportunities of a company (e.g., information on business segments or geographical

[8] *Framework for the Preparation and Presentation of Financial Statements*, IASC, 1989, adopted by IASB 2001, paragraph 12.

[9] Ibid., paragraphs 24–42.

segments). In choosing the level of detail to present, a criterion of materiality is applied. **Materiality** means that omission or misstatement of the information could make a difference to users' decisions.

3. *Reliability.* Reliable information is free from material error and bias. It is information that a user can depend upon to represent a company's financial situation faithfully and completely (within the bounds of materiality and cost). Reliable information also reflects economic reality, not just the legal form of a transaction or event. The following factors contribute to reliability:

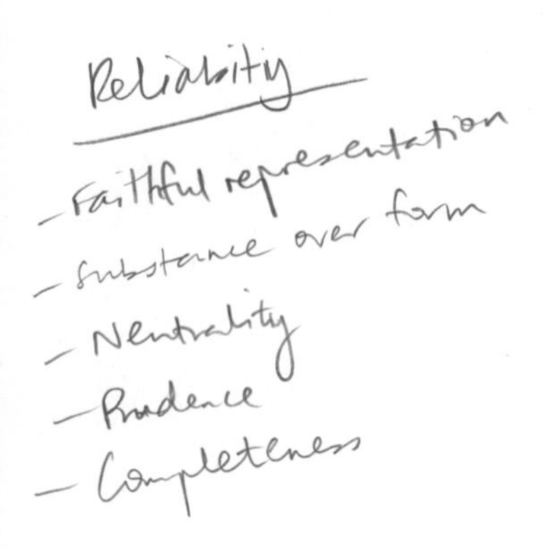

   - *Faithful representation.* Information must represent faithfully the transactions and other events it either purports to represent or could reasonably be expected to represent.
   - *Substance over form.* It is necessary that transactions and other events be accounted for and represented in accordance with their substance and economic reality and not merely their legal form.
   - *Neutrality.* Information contained in the financial statements must be neutral—that is, free from bias.
   - *Prudence.* Prudence is the inclusion of a degree of caution in making the estimates required under conditions of uncertainty. It does not, however, allow the deliberate misstatement of elements in the financial statements in an attempt to be conservative by providing for hidden reserves or excessive provisions.
   - *Completeness.* Financial statements must be complete within the bounds of materiality and cost.

4. *Comparability.* Information should be presented in a consistent manner over time and in a consistent manner between entities to enable users to make significant comparisons.

Financial information exhibiting these principal qualitative characteristics normally results in fair presentation (sometimes termed a "true and fair view").

5.3 Constraints on Financial Statements

Although it would be ideal for financial statements to exhibit all of these qualitative characteristics and thus to achieve maximal usefulness, there are several constraints in achieving this goal.[10]

One constraint is the necessity for trade-offs across the desirable characteristics. For example, to be relevant, information must be timely; however, it may take considerable time to ensure the information is error-free (i.e., reliable). The aim is a balance between relevance and reliability.

Another constraint on useful financial information is the cost of providing this information. Optimally, benefits derived from information should exceed the cost of providing it. Again, the aim is a balance between costs and benefits.

A further constraint involves what financial statements omit. Financial statements, by necessity, omit information that is nonquantifiable. For example, the creativity, innovation, and competence of a company's work force are not directly captured in the financial statements. Similarly, customer loyalty, a positive corporate culture, environmental respectfulness, and many other nonquantifiable aspects about a company are not directly reflected in the financial

[10] Ibid., paragraphs 43–45.

statements. Of course, to the extent that these nonquantifiable items result in superior financial performance, a company's financial reports will reflect the results.

EXAMPLE 4

Balancing Qualitative Characteristics of Useful Information

A trade-off between qualitative characteristics often occurs. For example, when a company records sales revenue, it is required to simultaneously estimate and record an expense for potential bad debts (uncollectible accounts). This is considered to provide relevant information about the net profits for the accounting period. However, because bad debts may not be known with certainty until a later period, there is a sacrifice of reliability. The bad debt expense is simply an estimate. It is apparent that it is not always possible to simultaneously fulfill all qualitative characteristics.

5.4 The Elements of Financial Statements

Financial statements portray the financial effects of transactions and other events by grouping them into broad classes (elements) according to their economic characteristics.

Three elements of financial statements are directly related to the measurement of the financial position: assets, liabilities, and equity.[11]

- **Assets**—Resources controlled by the enterprise as a result of past events and from which future economic benefits are expected to flow to the enterprise. Assets are what a company owns (e.g., inventory and equipment).
- **Liabilities**—Present obligations of an enterprise arising from past events, the settlement of which is expected to result in an outflow of resources embodying economic benefits. Liabilities are what a company owes (e.g., bank borrowings).
- **Equity** (commonly known as "shareholders' equity")—Assets less liabilities. Equity is the residual interest in the assets after subtracting the liabilities.

The elements of financial statements directly related to the measurement of performance are income and expenses.[12]

- **Income**—Increases in economic benefits in the form of inflows or enhancements of assets, or decreases of liabilities that result in an increase in equity (other than increases resulting from contributions by owners). Income includes both revenues and gains. Revenues represent income from the ordinary activities of the enterprise (e.g., the sale of products). Gains may result from ordinary activities or other activities (the sale of surplus equipment).

[11] Ibid., paragraph 49.

[12] Ibid., paragraph 70.

- **Expenses**—Decreases in economic benefits in the form of outflows or depletions of assets, or increases in liabilities that result in decreases in equity (other than decreases because of distributions to owners). Expenses include losses, as well as those items normally thought of as expenses, such as the cost of goods sold or wages.

5.4.1 *Underlying Assumptions in Financial Statements*

At the base of the Framework, two important assumptions underlying financial statements are shown: accrual basis and going concern. These assumptions determine how financial statement elements are recognized and measured.[13]

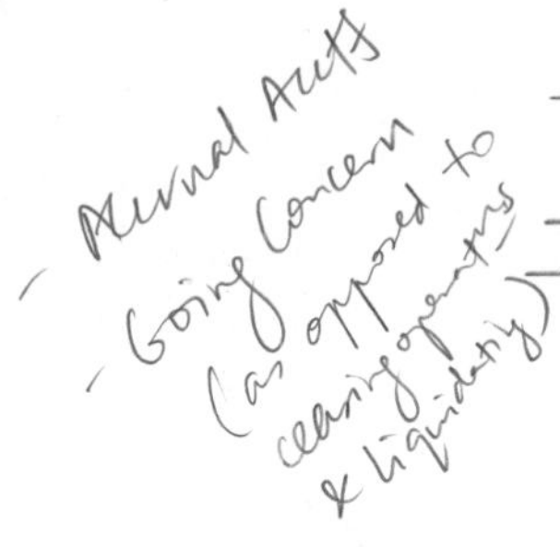

"Accrual basis" refers to the underlying assumption that financial statements aim to reflect transactions when they actually occur, not necessarily when cash movements occur. For example, accrual accounting specifies that a company reports revenues *when they are earned*, regardless of whether the company received cash before delivering the product, after delivering the product, or at the time of delivery.

"Going concern" refers to the assumption that the company will continue in business for the foreseeable future. To illustrate, consider the value of a company's inventory if it is assumed that the inventory can be sold over a normal period of time versus the value of that same inventory if it is assumed that the inventory must all be sold in a day (or a week). Companies with the intent to liquidate or materially curtail operations would require different information for a fair presentation.

EXAMPLE 5

Going Concern

In reporting the financial position of a company that is assumed to be a going concern, it may be appropriate to list assets at some measure of a current value based upon normal market conditions. However, if a company is expected to cease operations and be liquidated, it may be more appropriate to list such assets at an appropriate liquidation value, namely, a value that would be obtained in a forced sale.

5.4.2 *Recognition of Financial Statement Elements*

Recognition is the process of incorporating in the balance sheet or income statement an item that meets the definition of an element and satisfies the criteria for recognition. A financial statement element (assets, liabilities, equity, income, and expenses) should be recognized in the financial statements if:[14]

- it is *probable* that any future economic benefit associated with the item will flow to or from the enterprise; and
- the item has a cost or value that can be *measured with reliability*.

[13] Ibid., paragraphs 22 and 23.

[14] Ibid., paragraph 83.

5.4.3 Measurement of Financial Statement Elements

Measurement is the process of determining the monetary amounts at which the elements of the financial statements are to be recognized and carried in the balance sheet and income statement. The following alternative bases of measurement are used to different degrees and in varying combinations to measure assets and liabilities:

- **Historical cost.** Historical cost is simply the amount of cash or cash equivalents paid to purchase an asset, including any costs of acquisition and/or preparation. If the asset was not bought for cash, historical cost is the fair value of whatever was given in order to buy the asset. When referring to liabilities, the historical cost basis of measurement means the amount of proceeds received in exchange for the obligation.
- **Current cost.** In reference to assets, current cost is the amount of cash or cash equivalents that would have to be paid to buy the same or an equivalent asset today. In reference to liabilities, the current cost basis of measurement means the undiscounted amount of cash or cash equivalents that would be required to settle the obligation today.
- **Realizable (settlement) value.** In reference to assets, realizable value is the amount of cash or cash equivalents that could currently be obtained by selling the asset in an orderly disposal. For liabilities, the equivalent to realizable value is called "settlement value"—that is, settlement value is the undiscounted amount of cash or cash equivalents expected to be paid to satisfy the liabilities in the normal course of business.
- **Present value.** For assets, present value is the present discounted value of the future net cash inflows that the asset is expected to generate in the normal course of business. For liabilities, present value is the present discounted value of the future net cash outflows that are expected to be required to settle the liabilities in the normal course of business.
- **Fair value.** Fair value is the amount at which an asset could be exchanged, or a liability settled, between knowledgeable, willing parties in an arm's-length transaction, which may involve either market measures or present value measures.

5.5 General Requirements for Financial Statements

The Framework provides a basis for establishing standards and the elements of financial statements, but it does not address the contents of the financial statements. Having discussed the Framework, we now need to address the general requirements for financial statements.

The required financial statements, the fundamental principles underlying their presentation, and the principles of presentation are provided by International Accounting Standard (IAS) No. 1, *Presentation of Financial Statements.* These general requirements are illustrated in Exhibit 3 and described in the subsections below.

EXHIBIT 3 IASB General Requirements for Financial Statements

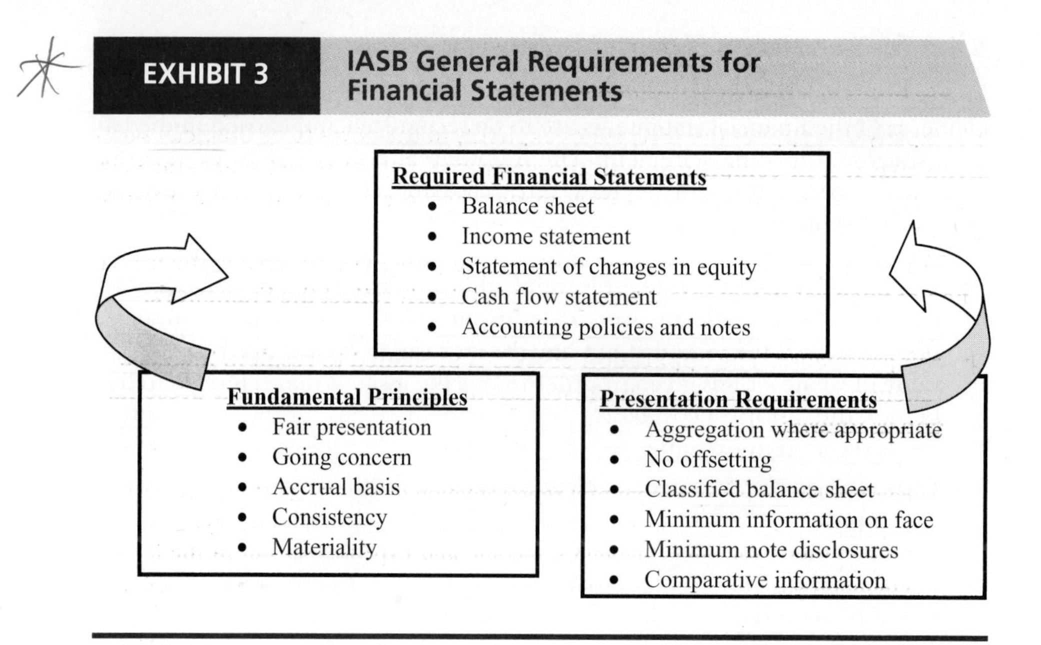

In the following, we discuss required financial statements, the fundamental principles underlying the preparation of financial statements, and the principles of presentation in greater detail.

5.5.1 Required Financial Statements

Under IAS No. 1, a complete set of financial statements includes:[15]

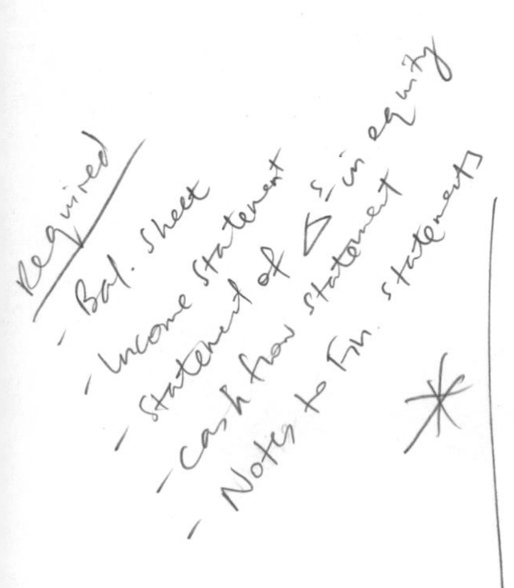

- a balance sheet;
- an income statement;
- a statement of changes in equity showing either:
  - all changes in equity, or
  - changes in equity other than those arising from transactions with equityholders acting in their capacity as equityholders;[16]
- a cash flow statement; and
- notes comprising a summary of significant accounting policies and other explanatory notes.

Entities are encouraged to furnish other related financial and nonfinancial information in addition to the financial statements. Financial statements need to present fairly the financial position, financial performance, and cash flows of an entity.

[15] IAS No. 1, *Presentation of Financial Statements*, paragraph 8.

[16] Examples of transactions with equityholders acting in their capacity as equityholders include sale of equity securities to investors, distributions of earnings to investors, and repurchases of equity securities from investors.

5.5.2 Fundamental Principles Underlying the Preparation of Financial Statements

A company that applies the IFRS states explicitly in the notes to its financial statements that it is in compliance with the standards. Except in extremely rare circumstances, such a statement is only made when a company is in compliance with *all* requirements of IFRS.

IAS No. 1 specifies a number of fundamental principles underlying the preparation of financial statements. These principles clearly reflect the Framework.

- *Fair presentation.* The application of IFRS is presumed to result in financial statements that achieve a fair presentation. The IAS describes fair presentation as follows:

> Fair presentation requires faithful representation of the effects of transactions, events and conditions in accordance with the definitions and recognition criteria for assets, liabilities, income and expenses set out in the Framework.[17]

- *Going concern.* Financial statements are prepared on a going concern basis unless management either intends to liquidate the entity or to cease trading, or has no realistic alternative but to do so. If not presented on a going concern basis, the fact and rationale should be disclosed.
- *Accrual basis.* Financial statements (except for cash flow information) are to be prepared using the accrual basis of accounting.
- *Consistency.* The presentation and classification of items in the financial statements are usually retained from one period to the next. Comparative information of prior periods is disclosed for all amounts reported in the financial statements, unless an IFRS requires or permits otherwise.
- *Materiality.* Omissions or misstatements of items are material if they could, individually or collectively, influence the economic decisions of users taken on the basis of the financial statements. Any material item shall be presented separately.

5.5.3 Presentation Requirements

IAS No. 1 also specifies a number of principles that guide the presentation of financial statements. These principles include the following:

- *Aggregation.* Each material class of similar items is presented separately. Dissimilar items are presented separately unless they are immaterial.
- *No offsetting.* Assets and liabilities, and income and expenses, are not offset unless required or permitted by an IFRS.
- *Classified balance sheet.* The balance sheet should distinguish between current and noncurrent assets, and between current and noncurrent liabilities unless a presentation based on liquidity provides more relevant and reliable information (e.g., in the case of a bank or similar financial institution).

[17] IAS No. 1, *Presentation of Financial Statements,* paragraph 13.

- *Minimum information on the face of the financial statements.* IAS No. 1 specifies the minimum line item disclosures on the face of, or in the notes to, the balance sheet, the income statement, and the statement of changes in equity. For example, companies are specifically required to disclose the amount of their plant, property, and equipment as a line item on the face of the balance sheet. The specific requirements are listed in Exhibit 4.
- *Minimum information in the notes* (or on face of financial statements). IAS No. 1 specifies disclosures about information to be presented in the financial statements. This information must be provided in a systematic manner and cross-referenced from the face of the financial statements to the notes. The required information is summarized in Exhibit 5.
- *Comparative information.* For all amounts reported in a financial statement, comparative information should be provided for the previous period unless another standard requires or permits otherwise. Such comparative information allows users to better understand reported amounts.

EXHIBIT 4 IAS No. 1: Minimum Required Line Items in Financial Statements

On the face of the balance sheet	▶ Plant, property, and equipment ▶ Investment property ▶ Intangible assets ▶ Financial assets (not listed in other line items) ▶ Investments accounted for using the equity method ▶ Biological assets ▶ Inventories ▶ Trade and other receivables ▶ Cash and cash equivalents ▶ Trade and other payables ▶ Provisions ▶ Financial liabilities (not listed in other line items) ▶ Liabilities and assets for current tax ▶ Deferred tax liabilities and deferred tax assets ▶ Minority interest, presented within equity ▶ Issued capital and reserves attributable to equityholders of the parent
On the face of the income statement	▶ Revenue ▶ Finance costs ▶ Share of the profit or loss of associates and joint ventures accounted for using the equity method ▶ Pretax gain or loss recognized on the disposal of assets or settlement of liabilities attributable to discontinuing operations ▶ Tax expense ▶ Profit or loss ▶ Profit or loss attributable to minority interest ▶ Profit or loss attributable to equityholders of the parent

(Exhibit continued on next page . . .)

EXHIBIT 4 (continued)

On the face of the statement of changes in equity	▶ Profit or loss for the period ▶ Each item of income and expense for the period that, as required by other Standards or by Interpretations, is recognized directly in equity, and the total of these items ▶ Total income and expense for the period, showing separately the total amounts attributable to equityholders of the parent and to minority interest ▶ For each component of equity, the effects of changes in accounting policies and corrections of errors recognized in accordance with IAS No. 8

EXHIBIT 5 Summary of IFRS Required Disclosures in the Notes to the Financial Statements

Disclosure of accounting policies	▶ Measurement bases used in preparing financial statements ▶ Each accounting policy used even if not covered by the IFRS ▶ Judgments made in applying accounting policies that have the most significant effect on the amounts recognized in the financial statements
Estimation uncertainty	▶ Key assumptions about the future and other key sources of estimation uncertainty that have a significant risk of causing material adjustment to the carrying amount of assets and liabilities within the next year
Other disclosures	▶ Description of the entity, including its domicile, legal form, country of incorporation, and registered office or business address ▶ Nature of operations or principal activities, or both ▶ Name of parent and ultimate parent

COMPARISON OF IFRS WITH ALTERNATIVE REPORTING SYSTEMS

The recent adoption of IFRS as the required financial reporting standard by the EU and other countries has advanced the goal of global convergence. Nevertheless, there are still significant differences in financial reporting in the global capital markets. Arguably, the most critical are the differences that exist between IFRS and U.S. GAAP. After the EU adoption of IFRS in 2005, these two reporting standards account for a significant number of the world's listed companies.

This section will discuss the differences between IFRS and U.S. GAAP that affect the framework and general financial reporting requirements. The readings on individual financial statements will review in more detail the differences in these financial reporting standards as they apply to specific financial statements. The reading on the convergence of international standards also makes relevant points.

6.1 U.S. GAAP

The FASB or its predecessor organizations have been issuing financial reporting standards in the United States since the 1930s. Currently, the FASB is the primary body setting these standards. There are, however, several other organizations that have issued guidance in the past. These include the American Institute of Certified Public Accountants' (AICPA) Accounting Standards Executive Committee (AcSEC), the Emerging Issues Task Force (EITF), and the FASB staff. Since the introduction of the Sarbanes–Oxley Act, changes have been made that essentially limit these other bodies from providing any new guidance unless it is directly under the direction of the FASB. The EITF has come under the more formal oversight of the FASB, and the AICPA AcSEC will no longer issue new standards applicable to public companies.

6.1.1 U.S. GAAP Authoritative Guidance

Together, the standards and interpretations issued by these bodies comprise U.S. GAAP. A "GAAP hierarchy" was established to provide guidance as to the order of authority of the various sources of accounting pronouncements. In other words, the GAAP hierarchy defines the sources of accounting principles and a framework for selecting the right principle. This hierarchy is especially important for new transactions and those policies where there is no explicit authoritative guidance. The GAAP hierarchy was originally established in the auditing area rather than the accounting area, but it is currently being re-examined by the FASB. The FASB is also working on a project to bring all authoritative guidance from these various sources into one set of authoritative literature called the "Codification."

The top level of the hierarchy includes standards issued by the FASB. If an answer is not found at that level, preparers and auditors consider other sources of GAAP. The literature referred to in the GAAP hierarchy that comprises U.S. GAAP is extensive. The FASB has stated that there are more than 2,000 pronouncements comprising U.S. GAAP. The FASB alone has issued 7 Concept Statements, 153 Standards, 47 Interpretations, and numerous Technical Bulletins. Recently, the FASB began issuing FASB Staff Positions, which provide still another source of U.S. GAAP.

As these standards have been developed over many years and by various bodies, they are more a patchwork than a cohesive framework. Although U.S. GAAP does have an explicit conceptual framework that was developed in the late 1970s/early 1980s, not all of the standards adhere completely to the framework. Some standards were developed prior to the framework and certain of the more recent standards are rule based as preparers and auditors request detailed rules and clear-cut do's and don'ts in an effort to reduce the need for judgment.

6.1.2 Role of the SEC in U.S. GAAP

U.S. GAAP, as established by the standard-setting bodies noted above, is officially recognized as authoritative by the SEC (Financial Reporting Release No. 1, Section 101, and reaffirmed in the April 2003 Policy Statement). However, the SEC retains the authority to establish standards. Although it has rarely overruled the FASB, the SEC does issue Staff Accounting Bulletins (SABs). SABs reflect the SEC's views regarding accounting-related disclosure practices and can be found on the SEC website.

6.1.3 Convergence of the U.S. GAAP and IASB Framework

A joint IASB–FASB project was begun in October 2004 to develop a common conceptual framework. The project, which currently has a five-year timetable, is divided into seven phases. The initial focus is on achieving the convergence of the frameworks and improving particular aspects of the framework dealing with objectives, qualitative characteristics, elements recognition, and measurement. A December 2004 discussion paper presented the broad differences between the two frameworks. These differences are summarized in Exhibit 6. Additionally, under U.S. GAAP, there is not a single standard like IAS No. 1 that specifies the presentation of financial statements; instead, standards for presentation of financial statements are dispersed in many different FASB pronouncements and SEC regulations.

EXHIBIT 6 Summary of Differences between IFRS and U.S. GAAP Frameworks

	U.S. GAAP (FASB) Framework
Purpose of the framework	The FASB framework is similar to the IASB framework in its purpose to assist in developing and revising standards, but it resides at a lower level in the hierarchy—a very important difference. Under IFRS, management is expressly required to consider the framework if there is no standard or interpretation for that issue. The FASB framework does not have a similar provision.
Objectives of financial statements	There is general agreement on the objectives of financial statements: Both frameworks have a broad focus to provide relevant information to a wide range of users. The principal difference is that the U.S. GAAP framework provides separate objectives for business entities versus nonbusiness entities rather than one objective as in the IASB framework.
Underlying assumptions	Although the U.S. GAAP framework recognizes the importance of the accrual and going concern assumptions, these are not given as much prominence as in the IASB framework. In particular, the going concern assumption is not well developed in the FASB framework.
Qualitative characteristics	The U.S. GAAP framework identifies the same qualitative characteristics but also establishes a hierarchy of those characteristics. Relevance and reliability are considered primary qualities, whereas comparability is deemed to be a secondary quality under the FASB framework. The fourth qualitative characteristic, understandability, is treated as a user-specific quality in the U.S. GAAP framework and is seen as a link between the characteristics of individual users and decision-specific qualities of information. The FASB framework indicates that it cannot base its decisions on the specific circumstances of individual users.
Constraints	There is similar discussion of the constraints in both frameworks.

(Exhibit continued on next page . . .)

EXHIBIT 6 (continued)

Financial statement elements (definition, recognition, and measurement)	► *Performance elements.* The FASB framework includes three elements relating to financial performance in addition to revenue and expenses: gains, losses, and comprehensive income. Comprehensive income is a more encompassing concept than net income, as it includes all changes in equity during a period except those resulting from investments by and distributions to owners. ► *Financial position elements.* The FASB framework defines an asset as "a future economic benefit" rather than the "resource" from which future economic benefits are expected to flow to the entity as in the IASB framework. It also includes the term "probable" to define the assets and liabilities elements. As discussed below, the term "probable" is part of the IASB framework recognition criteria. Additionally, the frameworks have different meanings of probable. ► *Recognition of elements.* The FASB framework does not discuss the term "probable" in its recognition criteria, whereas the IASB framework requires that it is probable that any future economic benefit flow to/from the entity. The FASB framework also has a separate recognition criterion of relevance. ► *Measurement of elements.* Measurement attributes (historical cost, current cost, settlement value, current market value, and present value) are broadly consistent, and both frameworks lack fully developed measurement concepts. Furthermore, the FASB framework prohibits revaluations except for certain categories of financial instruments, which have to be carried at fair value.

6.2 Implications of Other Reporting Systems

As more countries adopt IFRS, the need to examine other financial reporting systems will be minimized. Additionally, the IASB and FASB are considering frameworks from other jurisdictions in developing their joint framework. Nevertheless, analysts are likely to encounter financial statements that are prepared on a basis other than IFRS. Although the number and relevance of different local GAAP reporting systems are likely to decline, industry-specific financial reports—such as those required for banking or insurance companies—will continue to exist.

6.3 Reconciliation of Financials Prepared According to Different Standards

When analyzing financial statements created under different frameworks, reconciliation schedules and disclosures regarding the significant differences between the reporting bases are usually available. For example, the SEC currently requires reconciliation for foreign private issuers that do not prepare financial statements in accordance with U.S. GAAP. The EU is currently considering requiring reconciliations for companies trading on European markets that do not prepare financial statements using IFRS. Such reconciliations can reveal additional information related to the more judgmental components of the financial statements and can have important implications for security valuation.

A first look at the disclosure related to any such differences can sometimes be daunting, particularly if the reconciliation is lengthy. For example, Syngenta's 2005 U.S. SEC Form 20-F filing discusses these differences in Note 33, "Significant Differences between IFRS and United States Generally Accepted Accounting Principles." This note is longer than 15 pages!

Given the length of reconciliation disclosure, a systematic method to quickly digest the information can be helpful. A good starting point is the chart that provides the numerical reconciliation of net income and shareholders' equity (see Exhibit 7). These reconciliations can be reviewed to identify the significant items; large amounts should be examined in more detail. The Syngenta disclosure indicates that the company's 2005 net income based on U.S. GAAP was $556 million, compared with the $622 million of net income reported under IFRS. The reconciliation indicates that most significant differences relate to accounting for acquisitions (purchase accounting adjustments include a $7 million decrease and an $80 million decrease), accounting for pension provisions ($15 million), and accounting for various tax-related items. In some instances, further analysis would be undertaken to determine the implications of each significant difference based on disclosures in the indicated notes.

EXHIBIT 7 Reconciliation of GAAP Income—Syngenta (US$ in millions)

	2005	2004	2003 (adjusted)
Net income (loss) reported under IFRS attributable to Syngenta AG shareholders	622	460	248
U.S. GAAP adjustments:			
Purchase accounting: Zaneca agrochemicals business	(7)	62	43
Purchase accounting: other acquisitions	(80)	(62)	(67)
Restructuring charges	(9)	47	32
Pension provisions (including post-retirement benefits)	(15)	43	2
Deferred taxes on stock-based compensation	3	(3)	2
Deferred taxes on unrealized profit in inventory	(33)	(61)	36
Impairment losses	(7)	(1)	
Other items	28	(17)	(4)
Valuation allowance against deferred tax assets	26	(34)	–
Tax on undistributed earnings of subsidiaries	1	(27)	–
Deferred tax affect of U.S. GAAP adjustments	27	(55)	(42)
Net income/(loss) reported under U.S. GAAP	556	352	250

Source: 2005 U.S. SEC Form 20-F.

7 EFFECTIVE FINANCIAL REPORTING

A discussion of the characteristics of an effective framework and the barriers to the creation of such a framework offer additional perspective on the financial reporting frameworks reviewed above.

7.1 Characteristics of an Effective Financial Reporting Framework

Any effective financial reporting system needs to be a coherent one (i.e., a framework in which all the pieces fit together according to an underlying logic). Such frameworks have several characteristics:

- *Transparency.* A framework should enhance the transparency of a company's financial statements. Transparency means that users should be able to see the underlying economics of the business reflected clearly in the company's financial statements. Full disclosure and fair presentation create transparency.
- *Comprehensiveness.* To be comprehensive, a framework should encompass the full spectrum of transactions that have financial consequences. This spectrum includes not only transactions currently occurring but also new types of transactions as they are developed. So, an effective financial reporting framework is based on principles that are universal enough to provide guidance for recording both existing and newly developed transactions.
- *Consistency.* An effective framework should ensure reasonable consistency across companies and time periods. In other words, similar transactions should be measured and presented in a similar manner regardless of industry, company size, geography, or other characteristics. Balanced against this need for consistency, however, is the need for sufficient flexibility to allow companies sufficient discretion to report results in accordance with underlying economic activity.

7.2 Barriers to a Single Coherent Framework

Although effective frameworks all share the characteristics of transparency, comprehensiveness, and consistency, there are some conflicts that create inherent limitations in any financial reporting standards framework. Specifically, it is difficult to completely satisfy all these characteristics concurrently, so any framework represents an attempt to balance the relative importance of these characteristics. Three areas of conflict include valuation, standard-setting approach, and measurement.

- *Valuation.* As discussed, various bases for measuring the value of assets and liabilities exist, such as historical cost, current cost, realizable value, and present value. Historical cost valuation, under which an asset's value is its initial cost, requires minimal judgment. In contrast, other valuation approaches require considerable judgment. Over time, both the IASB and FASB have recognized that it may be more appropriate to measure certain elements of financial statements using some fair value method in spite of the judgment required.[18] Fair value is the amount at which an asset could

[18] The FASB is currently developing a Fair Value Measurement standard that will also be reviewed by the IASB. This standard is expected to be effective for fiscal years beginning after 15 November 2007 in the United States.

be exchanged, or a liability settled, between knowledgeable willing parties in an arm's-length transaction; clearly, in many cases, determining fair value requires considerable judgment. Fair value may be more relevant, whereas historical cost may be more reliable.

- *Standard-setting approach.* Financial reporting standards can be established based on (1) principles, (2) rules, or (3) a combination of principles and rules (sometimes referred to as "objectives oriented"). A principles-based approach provides a broad financial reporting framework with little specific guidance on how to report a particular element or transaction. Such principles-based approaches require the preparers of financial reports and auditors to exercise considerable judgment in financial reporting. In contrast, a rules-based approach establishes specific rules for each element or transaction. Rules-based approaches are characterized by a list of yes-or-no rules, specific numerical tests for classifying certain transactions (known as "bright-line tests"), exceptions, and alternative treatments. The third alternative, an objectives-oriented approach, combines the other two approaches by including both a framework of principles and appropriate levels of implementation guidance.

  IFRS has been referred to as a "principles-based approach." The FASB, which has been criticized for having a rules-based approach in the past, has explicitly stated that it is moving to adopt a more objectives-oriented approach to standard setting. There is a joint project underway to develop a common conceptual framework, and this is likely to be more objectives oriented.

- *Measurement.* The balance sheet presents elements at a point in time, whereas the income statement reflects changes during a period of time. Because these statements are related, standards regarding one of the statements have an effect on the other statement. Financial reporting standards can be established taking an "asset/liability" approach, which gives preference to proper valuation of the balance sheet, or a "revenue/expense" approach that focuses more on the income statement. This conflict can result in one statement being reported in a theoretically sound manner, but the other statement reflecting less relevant information. In recent years, standard setters have predominantly used an asset/liability approach.

EXAMPLE 6

Conflicts between Measurement Approaches

Prime Retailers (PR), a U.S.-based distributor of men's shirts, has a policy of marking its merchandise up by $5 per unit. At the beginning of 2005, PR had 10,000 units of inventory on hand, which cost $15 per unit. During 2006, PR purchased 100,000 units of inventory at a cost of $22 per unit. Also during 2006, PR sold 100,000 units of inventory at $27 per unit. How shall PR reflect the cost of the inventory sold: $15 or $22?

In order to match current costs with current revenues, PR (which does not operate in an IFRS jurisdiction) may decide that it is appropriate to use a method of inventory costing that assumes that the most recently purchased inventory is sold first. So, the assumption is that the

100,000 units of sales had a cost of $22. A partial income statement for PR would be:

Sales	$2,700,000
Cost of sales	$2,200,000
Gross profit	$500,000

The **gross profit** reflected in this manner reflects the current cost of goods matched with the current level of revenues.

But PR still has 10,000 units of inventory on hand. The assumption must be that the 10,000 remaining units had a cost of $15 per unit. Therefore, the value of the inventory reflected on the balance sheet would be $150,000.

Although the income statement reflects current costs, the remaining inventory on the balance sheet does not reflect current information. The inventory is reflected at the older cost of $15 per unit. An analyst would likely find this older cost less relevant than the current cost of that inventory.

8 MONITORING DEVELOPMENTS IN FINANCIAL REPORTING STANDARDS

In studying financial reporting and financial statement analysis in general, the analyst needs to be aware that reporting standards are evolving rapidly. Analysts need to monitor ongoing developments in financial reporting and assess their implications for security analysis and valuation. The need to monitor developments in financial reporting standards does not mean that analysts should be accountants. An accountant monitors these developments from a preparer's perspective; an analyst needs to monitor from a user's perspective. More specifically, analysts need to know how these developments will affect financial reports.

Analysts can remain aware of developments in financial reporting standards by monitoring three areas: new products or transactions, actions of standard setters and other groups representing users of financial statements (such as CFA Institute), and company disclosures regarding critical accounting policies and estimates.

8.1 New Products or Types of Transactions

New products and new types of transactions can have unusual or unique elements to them such that no explicit guidance in the financial reporting standards exists. New products or transactions typically arise from economic events, such as new businesses (e.g., the Internet), or from a newly developed financial instrument or financial structure. Financial instruments, exchange traded or not, are typically designed to enhance a company's business or to mitigate inherent risks. However, at times, financial instruments or structured transactions have been developed primarily for purposes of financial report "window dressing."

Although companies might discuss new products and transactions in their financial reports, the analyst can also monitor business journals and the capital markets to identify such items. Additionally, when one company in an industry develops a new product or transaction, other companies in the industry often do the same. Once new products, financial instruments, or structured transactions are identified, it is helpful to gain an understanding of the business purpose. If necessary, an analyst can obtain further information from a company's management, which should be able to describe the economic purpose, the financial statement reporting, significant estimates, judgments applied in determining the reporting, and future cash flow implications for these items. The financial reporting framework presented here is useful in evaluating the potential effect on financial statements even though a standard may not have been issued as to how to report a particular transaction.

8.2 Evolving Standards and the Role of CFA Institute

Although the actions of standard setters and regulators are unlikely to be helpful in identifying new products and transactions given the lag between new product development and regulatory action, monitoring the actions of these authorities is, nonetheless, important for another reason: Changes in regulations can affect companies' financial reports and, thus, valuations. This is particularly true if the financial reporting standards change to require more explicit identification of matters affecting asset/liability valuation or financial performance. For example, a recent regulatory change requires companies to report the value of employee stock options as an expense in the income statement. Prior to the required expensing, an analyst could assess the impact of stock options on a company's performance and the dilutive effect to shareholders by reviewing information disclosed in the notes to the financial statements. To the extent that some market participants do not examine financial statement details and thus ignore this expense when valuing a company's securities, more explicit identification could affect the value of the company's securities.

The IASB and FASB have numerous major projects underway that will most likely result in new standards. It is important to keep up to date on these evolving standards. The IASB (www.iasb.org) and FASB (www.fasb.org) provide a great deal of information on their websites regarding new standards and proposals for future changes in standards. In addition, the IASB and FASB seek input from the financial analyst community—those who regularly use financial statements in making investment and credit decisions. When a new standard is proposed, an exposure draft is made available and users of financial statements can draft comment letters and position papers for submission to the IASB and FASB in order to evaluate the proposal.

CFA Institute is active through its CFA Centre for Financial Market Integrity in advocating improvements to financial reporting. Volunteer members of CFA Institute serve on several liaison committees that meet regularly to make recommendations to the IASB and FASB on proposed standards and to draft comment letters and position papers. You can view the CFA Centre's positions on financial reporting issues at www.cfainstitute.org/cfacentre/.

In October 2005, the CFA Centre issued a position paper titled *A Comprehensive Business Reporting Model: Financial Reporting for Investors*, which provides a suggested model for significantly improving financial reporting. The position paper states:

> Corporate financial statements and their related disclosures are critical to sound investment decision making. The well being of the world's financial markets, and of the millions of investors who entrust their financial present and future to those markets, depends directly on the quality of the information financial statements and disclosures provide. Consequently, the quality of the information drives global financial markets. The quality, in turn, depends directly on the quality of the

principles and standards by which managers recognize and measure the economic activities and events affecting their companies' operations. To succeed, a partnership is needed among standard setters, common shareowners, and other investors to bring full transparency and the highest integrity to the standards and the processes by which those standards are developed. CFA Institute and the CFA Centre for Financial Market Integrity are committed to join in a partnership to improve financial market integrity in the 21st century.[19]

Among other principles, the proposed model stresses the importance of information regarding the current fair value of assets and liabilities, of neutrality in financial reporting, and of providing detailed information on cash flows to investors through the choice of the so-called direct format for the cash flow statement.[20]

In summary, analysts can improve their investment decision making by keeping current on financial reporting standards, and various web-based sources provide the means to do so. In addition, analysts can contribute to improving financial reporting by sharing their users' perspective with standard-setting bodies, which typically invite comments concerning proposed changes.

8.3 Company Disclosures

A good source for obtaining information regarding the effect of financial reporting standards on a company's financial statements is typically the company itself. This information is provided in the footnotes to the financial statements and accompanying discussion.

8.3.1 Disclosures Relating to Critical and Significant Accounting Policies

As noted earlier, financial reporting standards need to restrict alternatives but retain flexibility in allowing enterprises to match their accounting methods with underlying economics. As a result, companies choose among alternative accounting policies (e.g., depreciation methods) and use estimates (e.g., depreciable lives of assets). Under both IFRS and U.S. GAAP, companies are required to disclose their accounting policies and estimates in the footnotes to the financial statements. Public companies must discuss their accounting policies and estimates in management's discussion and analysis (MD&A). This disclosure indicates the policies that management deems most important. Although many of the policies are discussed in both the MD&A and the footnotes to the financial statements, there is typically a distinction between the two discussions. The MD&A disclosure relates to those policies that require significant judgments and estimates, whereas the footnote discusses all accounting policies, irrespective of whether judgment was required. Each disclosure has value.

In analyzing financial reporting disclosures, the following questions should be addressed:

- What policies have been discussed?
- Do these policies appear to cover all of the significant balances on the financial statements?

[19] *A Comprehensive Business Reporting Model: Financial Reporting for Investors*, CFA Institute Centre for Financial Market Integrity, 24 October 2005, p. 3.

[20] See the reading on the cash flow statement for further information on the direct format.

- Which policies are identified as requiring significant estimates?
- Have there been any changes in these disclosures from one year to the next?

Example 7 summarizes the accounting policies discussed in Disney's 2004 annual report MD&A and Note 2, "Summary of Significant Accounting Policy."

Two items usually requiring significant judgment include revenue recognition and timing of reporting the related expenses. As a result, the types of judgments and estimates in revenue recognition and expense reporting are usually discussed in both the MD&A and in the footnotes.

8.3.2 Disclosures Regarding the Impact of Recently Issued Accounting Standards

Internationally, public companies face disclosure requirements related to recently issued accounting standards. In the United States, the SEC (in its SABs) also requires public companies to provide information regarding the likely future impact of recently issued accounting standards. Under IFRS, IAS No. 8

EXAMPLE 7

List of Significant Accounting Policy Disclosures: Disney MD&A Notes

- Film and television revenue and costs
- Revenue recognition
- Pension and post-retirement benefit plan actuarial assumptions
- Goodwill, intangible assets, **long-lived assets**, and investments
- Contingencies and litigation
- Income tax audit
- Principles of consolidation
- Accounting changes
- Use of estimates
- Advertising expenses
- Cash and cash equivalents
- Investments
- Translation policy
- Inventories
- Film and television costs
- Capitalized software costs
- Parks, resorts, and other property
- Goodwill and other intangible assets
- Risk management contracts
- Earnings per share
- Stock options
- Reclassifications

similarly requires discussion about pending implementations of new standards and the known or estimable information relevant to assessing the impact of the new standards. These disclosures can alert an analyst to significant changes in reported financial statement amounts that could affect security valuation. Although each discussion will be different, the conclusions that a company can reach about a new standard include:

1. the standard does not apply;
2. the standard will have no material impact;
3. management is still evaluating the impact; or
4. the impact of adoption is discussed.

Exhibit 8 provides some of the disclosures provided by Syngenta in its 2004 Form 20-F relating to recently issued accounting standards. In the exhibit, "IFRIC" refers to the International Financial Reporting Interpretations Committee—formerly known as the "Standing Interpretations Committee" or "SIC"—which is responsible for interpreting IAS and IFRS.

Clearly, disclosures indicating the expected impact provide the most meaningful information. In addition, disclosures indicating that the standard does not apply or will not have a material effect are also helpful. However, disclosures indicating that management is still evaluating the impact of a new standard create some uncertainty about whether the change might materially affect the company.

EXHIBIT 8 Impact of Recently Issued Accounting Standards: Syngenta

Standard does not apply	IFRIC amendment to SIC-12, "Special Purpose Entities," was published in October 2004 and requires employee share trusts and similar entities established under share participation plans to be consolidated with effect from 1 January 2005. *Syngenta operates its employee share participation plans without using entities of this type, and the amendment will have no effect on the consolidated financial statements.*
No material impact	Amendment to IAS No. 39, "Transition and Initial Recognition of Financial Assets and Financial Liabilities," was issued in December 2004. It will be effective from Syngenta as from 1 January 2005. The amendment changes the transitional requirements on adoption of IAS No. 39 (revised December 2003). *Syngenta does not expect the amendment to have a material effect on its consolidated financial statements.*
Evaluating the impact	IFRIC 4, "Determining Whether an Arrangement Contains a Lease," was issued in December 2004 and requires contracts for the supply of goods or services that depend upon the use of a specific asset to be treated in certain circumstances as containing a lease of that asset in addition to a supply contract. IFRIC 4 will be mandatory for Syngenta with effect from 1 January 2006. *During 2005, Syngenta will assess the impact on its consolidated financial statements from adopting IFRIC 4.*
Impact described	As stated in Note 2 above, Syngenta will apply IFRS 3, "Business Combinations," and the related revisions to IAS No. 36 and IAS No. 38, to all previous business combinations with effect from 1 January 2005. *Goodwill amortization expense will no longer be recorded. Goodwill amortization expense on these acquisitions in 2004 was US$56 million. The related tax credit was US$2 million because in most cases the amortization is not tax deductible. Syngenta will test goodwill for impairment annually.*

Note: Emphasis added.

SUMMARY

An awareness of the reporting framework underlying financial reports can assist in security valuation and other financial analysis. The framework describes the objectives of financial reporting, desirable characteristics for financial reports, the elements of financial reports, and the underlying assumptions and constraints of financial reporting. An understanding of the framework, broader than knowledge of a particular set of rules, offers an analyst a basis from which to infer the proper financial reporting, and thus security valuation implications, of *any* financial statement element or transaction.

We have discussed how financial reporting systems are developed, the conceptual objectives of financial reporting standards, the parties involved in standard-setting processes, and how financial reporting standards are converging into one global set of standards. A summary of the key points for each section is noted below:

- *The objective of financial reporting:*
  - The objective of financial statements is to provide information about the financial position, performance, and changes in financial position of an entity; this information should be useful to a wide range of users for the purpose of making economic decisions.[21]
  - Financial reporting requires policy choices and estimates. These choices and estimates require judgment, which can vary from one preparer to the next. Accordingly, standards are needed to attempt to ensure some type of consistency in these judgments.
- *Financial reporting standard-setting bodies and regulatory authorities.* Private sector standard-setting bodies and regulatory authorities play significant but different roles in the standard-setting process. In general, standard-setting bodies make the rules, and regulatory authorities enforce the rules. However, regulators typically retain legal authority to establish financial reporting standards in their jurisdiction.
- *Convergence of global financial reporting standards.* The IASB and FASB, along with other standard setters, are working to achieve convergence of financial reporting standards. Listed companies in many countries are adopting IFRS. Barriers to full convergence still exist.
- *The IFRS Framework.* The IFRS Framework sets forth the concepts that underlie the preparation and presentation of financial statements for external users, provides further guidance on the elements from which financial statements are constructed, and discusses concepts of capital and capital maintenance.
  - The objective of fair presentation of useful information is the center of the Framework. The qualitative characteristics of useful information include understandability, relevance, reliability, and comparability.
  - The IFRS Framework identifies the following elements of financial statements: assets, liabilities, equity, income, expense, and capital maintenance adjustments.

[21] *Framework for the Preparation and Presentation of Financial Statements,* IASC, 1989, adopted by IASB 2001, paragraph 12.

- The Framework is constructed based on the underlying assumptions of accrual basis and going concern but acknowledges three inherent constraints: timeliness, benefit versus cost, and balance between qualitative characteristics.

- *IFRS financial statements.* IAS No. 1 prescribes that a complete set of financial statements includes a balance sheet, an income statement, a statement of changes in equity, a cash flow statement, and notes. The notes include a summary of significant accounting policies and other explanatory information.
  - Financial statements need to adhere to the fundamental principles of fair presentation, going concern, accrual basis, consistency, and materiality.
  - Financial statements must also satisfy the presentation requirements of appropriate aggregation, no offsetting, and a classified balance sheet. Statements must provide the required minimum information on the face of the financial statements and note disclosures.
- *Comparison of IFRS with alternative reporting systems.* A significant number of the world's listed companies report under either IFRS or U.S. GAAP. Although these standards are moving toward convergence, there are still significant differences in the framework and individual standards. Frequently, companies provide reconciliations and disclosures regarding the significant differences between reporting bases. These reconciliations can be reviewed to identify significant items that could affect security valuation.
- *Characteristics of a coherent financial reporting framework.* Effective frameworks share three characteristics: transparency, comprehensiveness, and consistency. Effective standards can, however, have conflicting approaches on valuation, the bases for standard setting (principle or rules based), and resolution of conflicts between balance sheet and income statement focus.
- *Monitoring developments.* Analysts can remain aware of ongoing developments in financial reporting by monitoring three areas: new products or transactions, standard setters' and regulators' actions, and company disclosures regarding critical accounting policies and estimates.

PRACTICE PROBLEMS FOR READING 31

1. Which of the following is not an objective of financial statements as expressed by the International Accounting Standards Board?
   - **A.** To provide information about the performance of an entity.
   - **B.** To provide information about the financial position of an entity.
   - **C.** To provide information about the users of an entity's financial statements.
   - **D.** To provide information about changes in the financial position of an entity.
2. International accounting standards are currently developed by which entity?
   - **A.** The European Union.
   - **B.** The Financial Services Authority.
   - **C.** The International Accounting Standards Board.
   - **D.** The International Accounting Standards Committee.
3. U.S. Financial Accounting Standards are currently developed by which entity?
   - **A.** The United States Congress.
   - **B.** The Financial Services Authority.
   - **C.** The Financial Accounting Standards Board.
   - **D.** The Public Company Accounting Oversight Board.
4. The SEC requires which of the following be issued to shareholders before a shareholder meeting?
   - **A.** Form 10-K.
   - **B.** Statement of cash flow.
   - **C.** Form S-1.
   - **D.** Proxy statement.
5. According to the *Framework for the Preparation and Presentation of Financial Statements*, which of the following is a qualitative characteristic of information in financial statements?
   - **A.** Accuracy.
   - **B.** Precision.
   - **C.** Timeliness. — Constraint
   - **D.** Comparability.
6. Which of the following is *not* a constraint on the financial statements according to the IFRS Framework?
   - **A.** Timeliness.
   - **B.** Understandability.
   - **C.** Benefit versus cost.
   - **D.** Balancing of qualitative characteristics.

7. The assumption that an entity will continue to operate for the foreseeable future is called
   A. accrual basis.
   B. comparability.
   C. going concern.
   D. faithful representation.
8. The assumption that the effects of transactions and other events are recognized when they occur, not when the cash flows, is called
   A. accrual basis.
   B. going concern.
   C. relevance.
   D. completeness.
9. Neutrality of information in the financial statements most closely contributes to which qualitative characteristic?
   A. Relevance.
   B. Reliability.
   C. Comparability.
   D. Understandability.
10. Does fair presentation entail full disclosure and transparency?

	Full Disclosure	Transparency
A.	No	No
B.	No	Yes
C.	Yes	No
D.	Yes	Yes

11. Valuing assets at the amount of cash or equivalents paid or the fair value of the consideration given to acquire them at the time of acquisition most closely describes which measurement of financial statement elements?
    A. Current cost.
    B. Present value.
    C. Realizable cost.
    D. Historical cost.
12. The valuation technique under which assets are recorded at the amount that would be received in an orderly disposal is
    A. Current cost.
    B. Present value.
    C. Historical cost.
    D. Realizable value.
13. Which of the following is not a required financial statement according to IAS No. 1?
    A. Balance sheet.
    B. Income statement.
    C. Statement of changes in equity.
    D. Statement of changes in income.

14. Which of the following elements of financial statements is most closely related to measurement of performance?

A. Assets.

B. Equity.

C. Expenses.

D. Liabilities.

15. Which of the following elements of financial statements is most closely related to measurement of financial position?

A. Equity.

B. Income.

C. Expenses.

D. Capital maintenance adjustments.

16. Which of the following is not a characteristic of a coherent financial reporting framework?

A. Timeliness.

B. Consistency.

C. Transparency.

D. Comprehensiveness.

17. In the past, the Financial Accounting Standards Board has been criticized as having

A. a rules-based approach to standards.

B. an asset/liability approach to standards.

C. a principles-based approach to standards.

D. an objectives-oriented approach to standards.

18. Which of the following types of discussions regarding new accounting standards in management's discussion would provide the most meaningful information to an analyst?

A. The standard does not apply.

B. The impact of adoption is discussed.

C. The standard will have no material impact.

D. Management is still evaluating the impact.

STUDY SESSION 8
FINANCIAL STATEMENT ANALYSIS:
The Income Statement, Balance Sheet, and Cash Flow Statement

Each reading in this study session focuses on one of the three major financial statements: the balance sheet, the income statement, and the statement of cash flows. For each financial statement, the chapter details its purpose, construction, pertinent ratios, and common-size analysis. Understanding these concepts allows a financial analyst to evaluate trends in performance over several measurement periods and to compare the performance of different companies over the same period(s). Additional analyst tools such as the earnings per share calculation are also described.

READING ASSIGNMENTS

LEARNING OUTCOMES

Reading 32: Understanding the Income Statement

The candidate should be able to:

a. describe the components of the income statement and construct an income statement using the alternative presentation formats of that statement;

b. explain the general principles of revenue recognition and accrual accounting, demonstrate specific revenue recognition applications (including accounting for long-term contracts, installment sales, barter transactions, and gross and net reporting of revenue), and discuss the implications of revenue recognition principles for financial analysis;

c. discuss the general principles of expense recognition, such as the matching principle, specific expense recognition applications (including depreciation of long-term assets and inventory methods), and the implications of expense recognition principles for financial analysis;

d. determine which method of depreciation, accounting for inventory, or amortizing intangibles is appropriate, based on facts that might influence the decision;

e. demonstrate the depreciation of long-term assets using each approved method, accounting for inventory using each approved method, and amortization of intangibles;

f. distinguish between the operating and nonoperating components of the income statement;

g. discuss the financial reporting treatment and analysis of nonrecurring items (including discontinued operations, extraordinary items, and unusual or infrequent items), and changes in accounting standards;

h. describe the components of earnings per share and calculate a company's earnings per share (both basic and diluted earnings per share) for both a simple and complex capital structure;

i. distinguish between dilutive and antidilutive securities, and discuss the implications of each for the earnings per share calculation;

j. evaluate a company's financial performance using common-size income statements and financial ratios based on the income statement;

k. state the accounting classification for items that are excluded from the income statement but affect owners' equity, and list the major types of items receiving that treatment;

l. describe and calculate comprehensive income.

Reading 33: Understanding the Balance Sheet

The candidate should be able to:

a. illustrate and interpret the components of the assets, liabilities, and equity sections of the balance sheet, and discuss the uses of the balance sheet in financial analysis;

b. describe the various formats of balance sheet presentation;

c. explain how assets and liabilities arise from the accrual process;

d. compare and contrast current and noncurrent assets and liabilities;

e. explain the measurement bases (e.g., historical cost and fair value) of assets and liabilities, including current assets, current liabilities, tangible assets, and intangible assets;

f. discuss off-balance-sheet disclosures;

g. demonstrate the appropriate classifications and related accounting treatments for marketable and non-marketable financial instruments held as assets or owed by the company as liabilities;

h. list and explain the components of owners' equity;

i. interpret balance sheets, common-size balance sheets, the statement of changes in equity, and commonly used balance sheet ratios.

Reading 34: Understanding the Cash Flow Statement

The candidate should be able to:

a. compare and contrast cash flows from operating, investing, and financing activities, and classify cash flow items as relating to one of these three categories, given a description of the items;

b. describe how noncash investing and financing activities are reported;

c. compare and contrast the key differences in cash flow statements prepared under international financial reporting standards and U.S. generally accepted accounting principles;

d. demonstrate the difference between the direct and indirect methods of presenting cash from operating activities and explain the arguments in favor of each;

e. demonstrate how the cash flow statement is linked to the income statement and balance sheet;

f. demonstrate the steps in the preparation of direct and indirect cash flow statements, including how cash flows can be computed using income statement and balance sheet data;

g. describe the process of converting a statement of cash flows from the direct to the indirect method of presentation;

h. analyze and interpret a cash flow statement using both total currency amounts and common-size cash flow statements;

i. explain and calculate free cash flow to the firm, free cash flow to equity, and other cash flow ratios.

UNDERSTANDING THE INCOME STATEMENT

by Thomas R. Robinson, Hennie van Greuning, Elaine Henry, and Michael A. Broihahn

READING

32

LEARNING OUTCOMES

The candidate should be able to:

a. describe the components of the income statement and construct an income statement using the alternative presentation formats of that statement;

b. explain the general principles of revenue recognition and accrual accounting, demonstrate specific revenue recognition applications (including accounting for long-term contracts, installment sales, barter transactions, and gross and net reporting of revenue), and discuss the implications of revenue recognition principles for financial analysis;

c. discuss the general principles of expense recognition, such as the matching principle, specific expense recognition applications (including depreciation of long-term assets and inventory methods), and the implications of expense recognition principles for financial analysis;

d. determine which method of depreciation, accounting for inventory, or amortizing intangibles is appropriate, based on facts that might influence the decision;

e. demonstrate the depreciation of long-term assets using each approved method, accounting for inventory using each approved method, and amortization of intangibles;

f. distinguish between the operating and nonoperating components of the income statement;

g. discuss the financial reporting treatment and analysis of nonrecurring items (including discontinued operations, extraordinary items, and unusual or infrequent items), and changes in accounting standards;

h. describe the components of earnings per share and calculate a company's earnings per share (both basic and diluted earnings per share) for both a simple and complex capital structure;

i. distinguish between dilutive and antidilutive securities, and discuss the implications of each for the earnings per share calculation;

j. evaluate a company's financial performance using common-size income statements and financial ratios based on the income statement;

k. state the accounting classification for items that are excluded from the income statement but affect owners' equity, and list the major types of items receiving that treatment;

l. describe and calculate comprehensive income.

THEME

The income statement presents results of a company's performance during a period of time. Recognizing income in the period earned is a basic objective of accrual accounting. Accrual accounting, therefore, requires companies to choose appropriate revenue and expense recognition policies and to estimate certain related parameters. Understanding a company's accounting choices and estimates enables an analyst to assess a company's performance, to evaluate trends in performance, and to compare different companies' performance.

1 INTRODUCTION

The income statement presents information on the financial results of a company's business activities over a period of time. The income statement communicates how much revenue the company generated during a period and what costs it incurred in connection with generating that revenue. The basic equation underlying the income statement is Revenue minus Expense equals Net income. The income statement is also called the "statement of operations" or "statement of earnings," or, sometimes, in business jargon, it is called the "P&L" for profit and loss.

Investment analysts intensely scrutinize companies' income statements. Equity analysts are interested in them because equity markets often reward relatively high- or low-earnings growth companies with above-average or below-average valuations, respectively. Fixed-income analysts examine the components of income statements, past and projected, for information on companies' abilities to make promised payments on their debt over the course of the business cycle. Corporate financial announcements frequently emphasize income statements more than the other financial statements.

This reading is organized as follows. Section 2 describes the components of the income statement and its format. Section 3 describes basic principles and selected applications related to the recognition of revenue, and Section 4 describes basic principles and selected applications related to the recognition of expenses. Section 5 covers nonrecurring items and nonoperating items. Section 6 explains the calculation of earnings per share. Section 7 introduces income statement analysis. Section 8 explains comprehensive income and its reporting. A summary of the key points and practice problems in the CFA Institute multiple-choice format complete the reading.

2 COMPONENTS AND FORMAT OF THE INCOME STATEMENT

On the top line of the income statement, companies typically report revenue. **Revenue** refers to amounts charged for the delivery of goods or services in the ordinary activities of a business. The term **net revenue** means that the revenue number is shown after adjustments (e.g., for estimated returns or for amounts unlikely to be collected). "Revenue" is often used synonymously with "sales."[1] Exhibits 1 and 2 show the income statements for Groupe Danone, a French food

or Turnover

EXHIBIT 1 Groupe Danone Consolidated Statements of Income (in millions of euro)

	Year Ended 31 December		
	2002	**2003**	**2004**
Net sales	13,555	13,131	13,700
Cost of goods sold	(6,442)	(5,983)	(6,369)
Selling expenses	(4,170)	(4,176)	(4,294)
General and administrative expenses	(964)	(977)	(997)
Research and development expenses	(133)	(130)	(131)
Other (expense) income	(256)	(261)	(204)
Operating income	1,590	1,604	1,705
Nonrecurring items	458	(60)	(105)
Interest expense, net	(110)	(70)	(73)
Income before provision for income taxes and minority interests	1,938	1,474	1,527
Provision for income taxes	(490)	(488)	(457)
Income before minority interests	1,448	986	1,070
Minority interests	(182)	(184)	(189)
Share in net income of affiliates	17	37	(564)
Net income	1,283	839	317

[1] **Sales** is sometimes understood to refer to the sale of goods, whereas "revenue" can include the sale of goods or services; however, the terms are often used interchangeably. In some countries, **turnover** is used in place of "revenue."

manufacturer, and Kraft Foods, a U.S. food manufacturer. For the year ended 31 December 2004, Danone reports €13.7 billion of net sales, whereas Kraft reports $32.2 billion of net revenues.[2]

EXHIBIT 2 **Kraft Foods and Subsidiaries Consolidated Statements of Earnings (in millions of dollars, except per-share data)**

	Year Ended 31 December		
	2004	**2003**	**2002**
Net revenues	$32,168	$30,498	$29,248
Cost of sales	20,281	18,531	17,463
Gross profit	11,887	11,967	11,785
Marketing, administration, and research costs	6,658	6,136	5,644
Integration costs and a loss on sale of a food factory		(13)	111
Asset impairment and exit costs	603	6	142
Losses (gains) on sales of businesses	3	(31)	(80)
Amortization of intangibles	11	9	7
Operating income	4,612	5,860	5,961
Interest and other debt expense, net	666	665	847
Earnings from continuing operations before income taxes and minority interest	3,946	5,195	5,114
Provision for income taxes	1,274	1,812	1,813
Earnings from continuing operations before minority interest	2,672	3,383	3,301
Minority interest in earnings from continuing operations, net	3	4	4
Earnings from continuing operations	2,669	3,379	3,297
(Loss) earnings from discontinued operations, net of income taxes	(4)	97	97
Net earnings	$2,665	$3,476	$3,394

Note that Groupe Danone lists the years in increasing order from left to right with the most recent year in the last column, whereas Kraft lists the years in decreasing order with the most recent year listed in the first column. These alternative formats are common. There are also differences in presentations of items, such as expenses. Groupe Danone shows expenses such as cost of goods sold in parenthesis to explicitly show that these are subtracted from revenue. Kraft, on

[2] Following net income, the income statement will also present **earnings per share**, the amount of earnings per common share of the company. Earnings per share will be discussed in detail later in this reading, and the per-share display has been omitted from these exhibits to focus on the core income statement.

the other hand, does not place cost of sales in parenthesis. Rather, it is implicitly understood that this is an expense and is subtracted in arriving at subtotals and totals. The analyst should always verify the order of years and presentation of negative items before analysis is begun because there is flexibility in how companies may present the income statement.

At the bottom of the income statement, companies report net income (or, essentially synonymously, net earnings or profit). For 2004, Danone reports €317 million of net income and Kraft reports $2,665 million of net earnings. Net income is often referred to as "the bottom line." The basis for this expression is that net income is the final—or bottom—line in an income statement. Because net income is often viewed as the single most relevant number to describe a company's performance over a period of time, the term "bottom line" sometimes is used in general business jargon to mean any final or most relevant result.

Net income also includes **gains** and **losses,** which are asset inflows and outflows, respectively, not directly related to the ordinary activities of the business. For example, if a company sells products, these are reported as revenue and the costs are listed separately. However, if a company sells surplus land that is not needed, the cost of the land is subtracted from the sales price and the net result is reported as a gain or a loss.

In addition to presenting the net income, income statements also present subtotals that are significant to users of financial statements. Some of the subtotals are specified by international financial reporting standards (IFRS), particularly nonrecurring items, but other subtotals are not specified.[3] International Accounting Standard (IAS) No. 1, *Presentation of Financial Statements,* requires that certain items, such as revenue, finance costs, and tax expense, be separately stated on the face of the income statement. IAS No. 1 also requires that headings and subtotals should also "be presented on the face of the income statement when such presentation is relevant to an understanding of the entity's financial performance."[4] IAS No. 1 states that expenses may be grouped together either by their nature or function. For example, grouping together expenses such as depreciation on manufacturing equipment and depreciation on administrative facilities into a single line item called "depreciation" represents a **grouping by nature** of the expense. An example of **grouping by function** would be grouping together expenses into a category such as cost of goods sold, which would include some salaries (e.g., salespeople's), material costs, depreciation, and other direct sales-related expenses.

One subtotal often shown in an income statement is **gross profit** (or, synonymously, **gross margin**). When an income statement shows a gross profit subtotal, it is said to use a **multi-step format** rather than a **single-step format.** The Kraft Foods income statement is an example of the multi-step format, whereas the Danone income statement is a single step. For manufacturing and merchandising companies, for whom gross profit is most relevant, gross profit is calculated as revenue minus the cost of the goods that were sold.[5] For service companies, gross profit is calculated as revenue minus the cost of services that were

[3] The body of standards issued by the International Accounting Standards Board is now referred to as International Financial Reporting Standards, which include previously issued International Accounting Standards. "Financial reporting" is a broad term including reporting on accounting, financial statements, and other information found in company financial reports.

[4] IAS No. 1, *Presentation of Financial Statements,* paragraph 83.

[5] Later readings will provide additional information about alternative methods to calculate cost of goods sold.

provided. In summary, gross profit is the amount of revenue available after subtracting the costs of delivering goods or services such as material and labor. Other expenses related to running the business are subtracted after gross profit.

Another important subtotal shown on the income statement is **operating profit** (or, synonymously, operating income). Operating profit further deducts operating expenses such as selling, general, administrative, and research and development expenses. Operating profit reflects a company's profits on its usual business activities before deducting taxes. For financial firms, interest expense would be included in operating expenses and subtracted in arriving at operating profit. For nonfinancial companies, interest expense would not be included in operating expenses and would be subtracted after operating profit because it relates to nonoperating activities for such companies. For some companies composed of a number of separate business segments, operating profit can be useful in evaluating the performance of the individual businesses, reflecting the reality that interest and tax expenses are more relevant at the level of the overall company rather than an individual segment level. For example, in its Investor Relations information, DaimlerChrysler notes, "Especially on the pre-tax level, Operating Profit is the principal earnings indicator for the Segments, Divisions and Business Units."[6] The specific calculations of gross margin and operating profit may vary by company, and a reader of financial statements can consult the notes to the statements to identify significant variations across companies.

Note that both Groupe Danone and Kraft Foods include a line item on their income statements referring to minority interest. Danone and Kraft both consolidate subsidiaries over which they have control. Consolidation means that they include all of the revenues and expenses of those subsidiaries even if they own less than 100 percent. Minority interest represents the portion of income that belongs to minority shareholders of these consolidated subsidiaries, as opposed to the parent company.

Exhibit 3 shows the income statement for CRA International (then known as Charles River Associates), a company providing management consulting services. These examples illustrate basic points about the income statement, including variations across the statements—some of which depend on the industry, whereas others reflect differences in accounting policies and practices of a particular company. In addition, some differences within an industry are primarily differences in terminology, whereas others are more fundamental accounting differences. Footnotes to the financial statements are helpful in identifying such differences.

Having introduced the components and format of an income statement, the next objective is to understand the actual reported numbers in it. To accurately interpret reported numbers, the analyst needs to be familiar with the principles of revenue and expense recognition—that is, how revenue and expenses are measured and attributed to a given accounting reporting period. Revenue and expense recognition are our next topics.

[6] DaimlerChrysler/Investor Relations/Basic Information/Controlling systems at www.daimlerchrysler.com.

EXHIBIT 3 Charles River Associates Incorporated Consolidated Statements of Income (in thousands, except per-share data)

	Year Ended		
	27 Nov. 2004 (52 weeks)	29 Nov. 2003 (52 weeks)	30 Nov. 2002 (53 weeks)
Revenues	$216,735	$163,458	$130,690
Cost of services	127,716	100,168	80,659
Gross profit	89,019	63,290	50,031
Selling, general, and administrative expenses	57,286	43,055	36,600
Income from operations	31,733	20,235	13,431
Interest income	904	429	486
Interest expense	(1,751)	(38)	(120)
Other expense	(260)	(306)	(29)
Income before provision for income taxes and minority interest	30,626	20,320	13,768
Provision for income taxes	(13,947)	(8,737)	(5,879)
Income before minority interest	16,679	11,583	7,889
Minority interest	(335)	(154)	547
Net income	$16,344	$11,429	$8,436

REVENUE RECOGNITION 3

Revenue is the top line in an income statement, so we begin the discussion with revenue recognition. A first task is to explain some relevant accounting terminology.

The terms "revenue," "sales," "gains," "losses," and "net income" ("profit," "net earnings") have been previously briefly defined. The IFRS *Framework for the Preparation and Presentation of Financial Statements* (referred to here as "the Framework" for short) provides further relevant details. The Framework provides that profit is a frequently used measure of performance that is composed of income and expenses.[7] It defines **income** as follows:

> Income is increases in economic benefits during the accounting period in the form of inflows or enhancements of assets or decreases of liabilities that result in increases in equity, other than those relating to contributions from equity participants.[8]

International Financial Reporting Standards use the term "income" to include revenue and gains. Gains are similar to revenue; however, they arise from secondary or peripheral activities rather than from a company's primary business activities. For example, for a restaurant, the sale of surplus restaurant equipment for more than its cost is referred to as a gain rather than as revenue. Similarly, a

[7] IASB, *International Framework for the Preparation and Presentation of Financial Statements*, paragraph 69.

[8] Ibid., paragraph 70.

loss is like an expense but arises from secondary activities. Gains and losses may be considered part of operating activities (e.g., a loss due to a decline in the value of inventory) or may be considered part of nonoperating activities (e.g., the sale of nontrading investments).

In a simple hypothetical scenario, revenue recognition would not be an issue. For instance, a company sells goods to a buyer for cash with no returns allowed: When should the company recognize revenue? In this instance, it is clear that revenue should be recognized when the exchange of goods for cash takes place. In practice, however, determining when revenue should be recognized can be somewhat more complex for a number of reasons discussed in the following sections.

3.1 General Principles

An important concept concerning revenue recognition is that it can occur independently of cash movements. For example, assume a company sells goods to a buyer on credit and so does not actually receive cash until some later time. A fundamental principle of accrual accounting is that revenue is recognized when it is earned, so the company's financial records reflect the sale when it is made and a related accounts receivable is created. Later, when cash changes hands, the company's financial records simply reflect that cash has been received to settle an account receivable. Similarly, there are situations when a company receives cash upfront and actually delivers the product or service later, perhaps over a period of time. In this case, the company would record **unearned revenue**, which is then recognized as being earned over time. (One example would be a subscription payment received up front for a publication that is to be delivered periodically over time, the accounting for which was illustrated earlier.)

The basic revenue recognition principles promulgated by accounting regulators deal with the definition of "earned." The International Accounting Standards Board (IASB) provides that revenue for the sale of goods is to be recognized (reported on the income statement) when the following conditions are satisfied:[9]

- the entity has transferred to the buyer the significant risks and rewards of ownership of the goods;
- the entity retains neither continuing managerial involvement to the degree usually associated with ownership nor effective control over the goods sold;
- the amount of revenue can be measured reliably;
- it is probable that the economic benefits associated with the transaction will flow to the entity; and
- the costs incurred or to be incurred in respect of the transaction can be measured reliably.

The IASB notes that the transfer of the risks and rewards of ownership normally occurs when goods are delivered to the buyer or when legal title to goods transfers. However, as noted by the above remaining conditions, transfer of goods will not always result in the recognition of revenue. For example, if goods are delivered to a retail store to be sold on consignment and title is not transferred, the revenue would not yet be recognized.[10]

[9] IASB, IAS No. 18, *Revenue*, paragraph 14.

[10] IAS No. 18 describes a "consignment sale" as one in which the recipient undertakes to sell the goods for the shipper. Revenue is recognized when the recipient sells the goods to a third party. IAS No. 18, Appendix, paragraph 2.

The Financial Accounting Standards Board (FASB)[11] specifies that revenue should be recognized when it is "realized or realizable and earned." The U.S. Securities and Exchange Commission (SEC),[12] motivated in part because of the frequency with which overstating revenue occurs in connection with fraud and/or misstatements, provides guidance on how to apply the accounting principles. This guidance names four criteria to determine when revenue is realized or realizable and earned:

1. There is evidence of an arrangement between buyer and seller. For instance, this would disallow the practice of recognizing revenue in a period by delivering the product just before the end of an accounting period and then completing a sales contract *after* the period end.
2. The product has been delivered, or the service has been rendered. For instance, this would preclude revenue recognition when the product has been shipped but the *risks and rewards of ownership have not actually passed* to the buyer.
3. The price is determined, or determinable. For instance, this would preclude a company from recognizing revenue that is based on some *contingency*.
4. The seller is reasonably sure of collecting money. For instance, this would preclude a company from recognizing revenue when the customer is *unlikely to pay*.

The IASB standards separately deal with the recognition of revenue for services:[13]

- When the outcome of a transaction involving the rendering of services can be estimated reliably, revenue associated with the transaction shall be recognized by reference to the stage of completion of the transaction at the balance sheet date.
- The outcome of a transaction can be estimated reliably when all the following conditions are satisfied:
  - the amount of revenue can be measured reliably;
  - it is probable that the economic benefits associated with the transaction will flow to the entity;
  - the stage of completion of the transaction at the balance sheet date can be measured reliably; and
  - the costs incurred for the transaction and the costs to complete the transaction can be measured reliably.

Companies must disclose their revenue recognition policies in the footnotes to their financial statements. Analysts should review these policies carefully to understand how and when a company recognizes revenue, which may differ depending upon the types of product sold and services rendered. Exhibit 4 presents a portion of the revenue recognition footnote for DaimlerChrysler from its 2005 annual report prepared under IFRS.

[11] See Statement of Financial Accounting Concepts No. 5, paragraph 83(b).

[12] See SEC Staff Accounting Bulletin 101.

[13] IASB, IAS No. 18, paragraph 20.

EXHIBIT 4 Partial Revenue Recognition Footnote for DaimlerChrysler

Revenue for sales of vehicles, service parts and other related products is recognized when persuasive evidence of an arrangement exists, delivery has occurred or services have been rendered, the price of the transaction is fixed and determinable, and collectibility is reasonably assured.

Revenues are recognized net of discounts, cash sales incentives, customer bonuses and rebates granted. Non-cash sales incentives that do not reduce the transaction price to the customer are classified within cost of sales. Shipping and handling costs are recorded as cost of sales in the period incurred.

DaimlerChrysler uses price discounts to adjust market pricing in response to a number of market and product factors, including: pricing actions and incentives offered by competitors, economic conditions, the amount of excess industry production capacity, the intensity of market competition, and consumer demand for the product. The Group may offer a variety of sales incentive programs at any point in time, including: cash offers to dealers and consumers, lease subsidies which reduce the consumer's monthly lease payment, or reduced financing rate programs offered to consumers.

The Group records as a reduction to revenue at the time of sale to the dealer the estimated impact of sales incentives programs offered to dealers and consumers. This estimated impact represents the incentive programs offered to dealers and consumers as well as the expected modifications to these programs in order for the dealers to sell their inventory.

The topic of revenue recognition remains important, and new challenges have evolved, particularly in areas of e-commerce and services such as software development. Standard setters continue to evaluate current revenue recognition standards and issue new guidance periodically to deal with new types of transactions. Additionally, there are occasional special cases for revenue recognition, as discussed in the next section.

3.2 Revenue Recognition in Special Cases

The general principles discussed above are helpful for dealing with most revenue recognition issues. There are some areas where revenue recognition is more difficult to determine. For example, in limited circumstances, revenue may be recognized before or after goods are delivered or services are rendered, as summarized in Exhibit 5.

The following sections discuss revenue recognition in the case of long-term contracts, installment sales, and barter.

3.2.1 Long-Term Contracts

A **long-term contract** is one that spans a number of accounting periods. Such contracts raise issues in determining when the earnings process has been completed. How should a company apportion the revenue earned under a long-term

EXHIBIT 5 Revenue Recognition in Special Cases

Before **Goods Are Delivered or Services Rendered**	***At the Time*** **Goods Are Delivered or Services Rendered**	***After*** **Goods Are Delivered or Services Rendered**
For example, with long-term contracts where the outcome can be reliably measured, the percentage-of-completion method is used.	Recognize revenues using normal revenue recognition criteria (IAS, FAS, SEC).	For example, with real estate sales where there is doubt about the buyer's ability to complete payments, the installment method and cost recovery method are appropriate.

contract to each accounting period? If, for example, the contract is a service contract or a licensing arrangement, the company may recognize the revenue ratably over the period of time of the contract rather than at the end of the contract term. As stated in IAS No. 18 regarding the rendering of services:

> The recognition of revenue by reference to the stage of completion of a transaction is often referred to as the percentage-of-completion method. Under this method, revenue is recognized in the accounting periods in which the services are rendered. The recognition of revenue on this basis provides useful information on the extent of service activity and performance during a period. IAS 11 *Construction Contracts* also requires the recognition of revenue on this basis. The requirements of that Standard are generally applicable to the recognition of revenue and the associated expenses for a transaction involving the rendering of services.[14]

As noted in IAS No. 18, construction contracts are another example of contracts that may span a number of accounting periods. IAS No. 11 provides that when the outcome of a construction contract can be measured reliably, revenue and expenses should be recognized in reference to the stage of completion. U.S. generally accepted accounting principles (U.S. GAAP) have a similar requirement. In both cases, the percentage-of-completion method of accounting is used. Under the **percentage-of-completion** method, in each accounting period, the company estimates what percentage of the contract is complete and then reports that percentage of the total contract revenue in its income statement. Contract costs for the period are expensed against the revenue. Therefore, net income or profit is reported each year as work is performed.

Under IAS No. 11, if the outcome of the contract cannot be measured reliably, then revenue is only reported to the extent of contract costs incurred (if it is probable the costs will be recovered). Costs are expensed in the period incurred. Under this method, no profit would be reported until completion of the contract. Under U.S. GAAP, a different method is used when the outcome cannot be measured reliably, termed the "completed contract method." Under the **completed contract** method, the company does not report any revenue until the contract is finished. Under U.S. GAAP, the completed contract method is also appropriate when the contract is not a long-term contract. Note, however, that when a contract is started and completed in the same period, there is no difference between the percentage-of-completion and completed contract methods.

[14] IAS No. 18, paragraph 21.

Examples 1, 2, and 3 provide illustrations of these revenue recognition methods. As shown, the percentage-of-completion method results in revenue recognition sooner than the completed contract method and thus may be considered a less conservative approach. In addition, the percentage-of-completion method relies on management estimates and is thus not as objective as the completed contract method. However, an advantage of the percentage-of-completion method is that it results in better matching of revenue recognition with the accounting period in which it was earned. Because of better matching with the periods in which work is performed, the percentage-of-completion method is the preferred method of revenue recognition for long-term contracts and is required when the outcome can be measured reliably under both IFRS and U.S. GAAP. Under both IFRS and U.S. GAAP, if a loss is expected on the contract, the loss is reported immediately, not upon completion of the contract, regardless of the method used (e.g., percentage-of-completion or completed contract).

EXAMPLE 1

Revenue Recognition for Long-Term Contracts: Recognizing Revenue Ratably

New Era Network Associates has a five-year license to provide networking support services to a customer. The total amount of the license fee to be received by New Era is $1 million. New Era recognizes license revenue ratably regardless of the time at which cash is received. How much revenue will New Era recognize for this license?

Solution: For this license, New Era Network Associates will recognize $200,000 each year for five years (calculated as $1 million divided by 5).

EXAMPLE 2

Revenue Recognition for Long-Term Contracts: Percentage-of-Completion Method

Stelle Technology has a contract to build a network for a customer for a total sales price of $10 million. The network will take an estimated three years to build, and total building costs are estimated to be $6 million. Stelle recognizes long-term contract revenue using the percentage-of-completion method and estimates percentage complete based on expenditure incurred as a percentage of total estimated expenditures.

1. At the end of Year 1, the company has spent $3 million. Total costs to complete are estimated to be another $3 million. How much revenue will Stelle recognize in Year 1?
2. At the end of Year 2, the company has spent $5.4 million. Total costs to complete are estimated to be another $0.6 million. How much revenue will Stelle recognize in Year 2?
3. At the end of Year 3, the contract is complete. The company spent a total of $6 million. How much revenue will Stelle recognize in Year 3?

Solution to 1: Stelle has spent 50 percent of the total project costs ($3 million divided by $6 million), so in Year 1, the company will recognize 50 percent of the total contract revenue (i.e., $5 million).

Solution to 2: Because Stelle has spent 90 percent of the total project costs ($5.4 million divided by $6 million), by the end of Year 2, it will need to have recognized 90 percent of the total contract revenue (i.e., $9 million). Stelle has already recognized $5 million of revenue in Year 1, so in Year 2, the company will recognize $4 million revenue ($9 million minus $5 million).

Solution to 3: Because Stelle has spent 100 percent of the total project costs, by the end of Year 3, it will need to have recognized 100 percent of the total contract revenue (i.e., $10 million). Stelle had already recognized $9 million of revenue by the end of Year 2, so in Year 3, the company will recognize $1 million revenue ($10 million minus $9 million).

	Year 1	Year 2	Year 3	Total
Revenue	$5 million	$4 million	$1 million	$10 million

EXAMPLE 3

Revenue Recognition for Long-Term Contracts: Completed Contract Method

Kolenda Technology Group has a contract to build a network for a customer for a total sales price of $10 million. This network will take an estimated three years to build, but considerable uncertainty surrounds total building costs because new technologies are involved. Kolenda recognizes contract revenue using the completed contract method.

1. At the end of Year 1, Kolenda has spent $3 million. How much revenue will the company recognize in Year 1?
2. At the end of Year 2, Kolenda has spent $5.4 million. How much revenue will the company recognize in Year 2?
3. At the end of Year 3, the contract is complete. Kolenda spent a total of $6 million. How much revenue will the company recognize in Year 3?

Solution to 1: No revenue will be recognized until the contract is complete. In Year 1, Kolenda will recognize $0.

Solution to 2: No revenue will be recognized until the contract is complete. In Year 2, Kolenda will recognize $0.

Solution to 3: Because the contract is complete, Kolenda will recognize the total contract revenue (i.e., $10 million).

	Year 1	Year 2	Year 3	Total
Revenue	$0 million	$0 million	$10 million	$10 million

3.2.2 Installment Sales

As noted above, revenue is normally reported when goods are delivered or services are rendered, independent of the period in which cash payments for those goods or services are received. This principle applies even to **installment** sales—sales in which proceeds are to be paid in installments over an extended period. Under limited circumstances, recognition of revenue or profit may be required to be deferred for some installment sales.

An example of such deferral arises for certain sales of real estate on an installment basis. Revenue recognition for sales of real estate[15] varies depending on specific aspects of the sale transaction. Under normal conditions, sales of real estate are reported at the time of sale using the normal revenue recognition conditions. International standards note that in the case of real estate sales, the time at which legal title transfers may differ from the time at which the buyer acquires a vested interest. Continuing involvement in the real estate by the seller may also indicate that risks and rewards of ownership of the property have not been transferred. There may also be significant doubt of the ability of the buyer to complete payment for a real estate sales contract. IAS No. 18 provides that in the case of real estate where the down payment and payments received do not provide sufficient evidence of the commitment of the buyer, revenue should only be reported to the extent cash is received. This is a conservative treatment because the reporting of revenue is deferred. Similar provisions exist under U.S. GAAP except that under U.S. GAAP the full revenue is shown in the year of sale but some of the profit is deferred.

Two methods may be appropriate in these limited circumstances and relate to the amount of profit to be recognized each year from the transaction: the **installment method** and the **cost recovery method**. Under the installment method, the portion of the total profit of the sale that is recognized in each period is determined by the percentage of the total sales price for which the seller has received cash. Exhibit 6 presents an example of a disclosure of an installment sale of real estate under U.S. GAAP where a portion of the profit was recognized and the remainder was deferred.

[15] IAS No. 18, Appendix, paragraph 9, and FASB Statement No. 66, *Accounting for Sales of Real Estate.*

EXHIBIT 6 Installment Sale Disclosure for First Bancshares

On June 22, 2004, an agreement was entered into to sell the property and equipment of South Central Missouri Title Company, Inc., for $252,000. In addition, South Central entered into a covenant not to compete agreement with the purchaser. Expense related to the sale totaled $61,512. As of the date of the sale, the assets sold had a net book value of $100,166. The majority of the sales price was in the form of a promissory note to South Central with a five year maturity. The transaction closed on July 16, 2004. As a result of this sale, the subsidiary will no longer offer sales of title insurance or real estate closing services. The company accounted for this sale on the installment method because the initial investment by the buyer was not substantial enough to warrant full recognition of the gain. However, the recovery of the cost of the property is reasonably assured if the buyer defaults. The following schedule summarizes certain information for the transaction:

Revenue	$252,000
Cost of sale	161,678
Deferred gain	90,322
Deferred gain recognized during FY 2005	8,026
Deferred gain at June 30, 2005	$82,296

Source: First Bancshares Form 10K, filed 11/1/2005.

The cost recovery method of revenue recognition is an appropriate alternative for many of the same situations as the installment method. Under the cost recovery method, the seller does not report any profit until the cash amounts paid by the buyer—including principal and interest on any financing from the seller—are greater than all the seller's costs of the property. Example 4 below provides an example of the differences between the installment method and the cost recovery method.

Installment sales and cost recovery treatment of revenue recognition are rare for financial reporting purposes, especially for assets other than real estate. IAS No. 18 provides that installment sales other than real estate generally require revenue to be recognized at the time of sale; however, it further provides that the guidance found in IAS No. 18 must be considered in light of local laws regarding the sale of goods in a particular country.

EXAMPLE 4

The Installment and Cost Recovery Methods of Revenue Recognition

Assume the total sales price and cost of a property are $2,000,000 and $1,100,000, respectively, so that the total profit to be recognized is $900,000. The amount of cash received by the seller as a down payment is $300,000, with the remainder of the sales price to be received over a 10-year period. It has been determined that there is significant doubt about

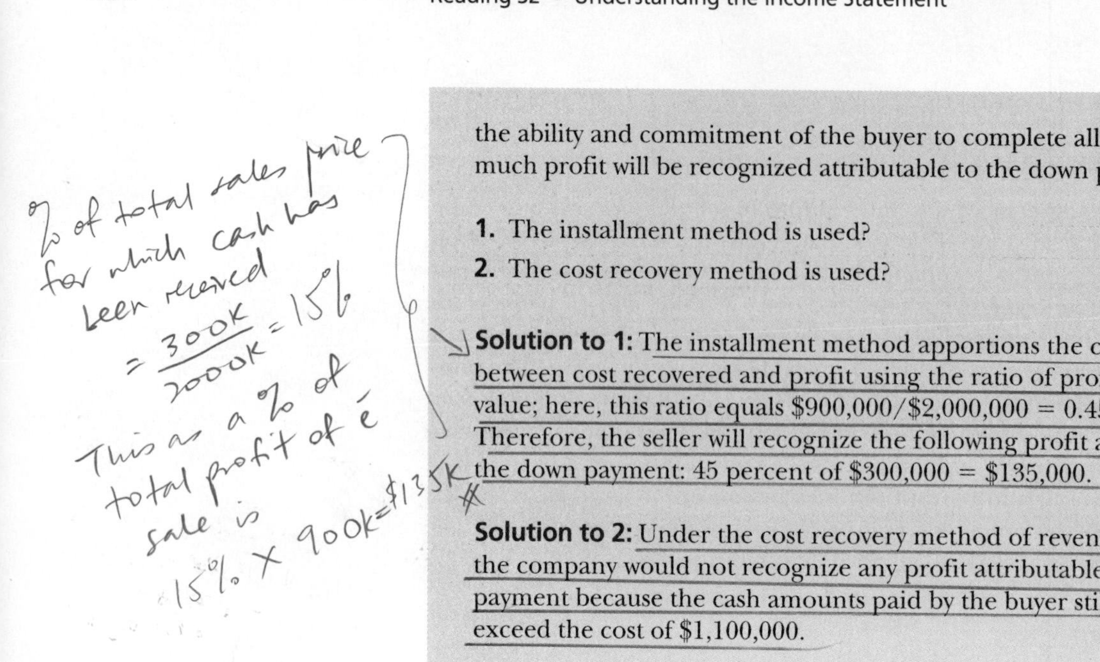

the ability and commitment of the buyer to complete all payments. How much profit will be recognized attributable to the down payment if:

1. The installment method is used?
2. The cost recovery method is used?

Solution to 1: The installment method apportions the cash receipt between cost recovered and profit using the ratio of profit to sales value; here, this ratio equals \$900,000/\$2,000,000 = 0.45 or 45 percent. Therefore, the seller will recognize the following profit attributable to the down payment: 45 percent of \$300,000 = \$135,000.

Solution to 2: Under the cost recovery method of revenue recognition, the company would not recognize any profit attributable to the down payment because the cash amounts paid by the buyer still do not exceed the cost of \$1,100,000.

3.2.3 Barter

Revenue recognition issues related to barter transactions became particularly important as e-commerce developed. As an example, if Company A exchanges advertising space for computer equipment from Company B but no cash changes hands, can Company A and B both report revenue? Such an exchange is referred to as a "barter transaction."

An even more challenging revenue recognition issue evolved from barter transactions—round-trip transactions. As an example, if Company A sells advertising services (or energy contracts, or commodities) to Company B and almost simultaneously buys an almost identical product from Company B, can Company A report revenue at the fair value of the product sold? Because the company's revenue would be approximately equal to its expense, the net effect of the transaction would have no impact on net income or cash flow. However, the amount of revenue reported would be higher, and the amount of revenue can be important to a company's valuation. In the earlier stages of e-commerce, for example, some equity valuations were based on sales (because many early internet companies reported no net income).

Under IFRS, revenue from barter transactions must be measured based on the fair value of revenue from similar nonbarter transactions with unrelated parties (parties other than the barter partner).[16] Similarly, the FASB states that revenue can be recognized at fair value only if a company has historically received cash payments for such services and can thus use this historical experience as a basis for determining fair value.[17]

3.2.4 Gross versus Net Reporting

Another revenue recognition issue that became particularly important with the emergence of e-commerce is the issue of gross versus net reporting. Merchandising companies typically sell products that they purchased from a supplier. In

[16] IASB, SIC Interpretation 31, Revenue—Barter Transactions Involving Advertising Services, paragraph 5.

[17] See Emerging Issues Task Force EITF 99-17, "Accounting for Advertising Barter Transactions."

accounting for their sales, the company records the amount of the sale proceeds as sales revenue and their cost of the products as the cost of goods sold. As Internet-based merchandising companies developed, many sold products that they had never held in inventory; they simply arranged for the supplier to ship the products directly to the end customer. In effect, many such companies were agents of the supplier company, and the net difference between their sales proceeds and their costs was equivalent to a sales commission. What amount should these companies record as their revenues—the gross amount of sales proceeds received from their customers, or the net difference between sales proceeds and their cost?

U.S. GAAP indicates that the approach should be based on the specific situation and provides guidance for determining when revenue should be reported gross versus net.[18] To report gross revenues, the following criteria are relevant: The company is the primary obligor under the contract, bears inventory risk and credit risk, can choose its supplier, and has reasonable latitude to establish price. If these criteria are not met, the company should report revenues net. Example 5 provides an illustration.

EXAMPLE 5

Gross versus Net Reporting of Revenues

Flyalot has agreements with several major airlines to obtain airline tickets at reduced rates. The company pays only for tickets it sells to customers. In the most recent period, Flyalot sold airline tickets to customers over the internet for a total of $1.1 million. The cost of these tickets to Flyalot was $1 million. The company's direct selling costs were $2,000. Once the customers receive their ticket, the airline is responsible for providing all services associated with the customers' flight.

1. Demonstrate the reporting of revenues under:
   - **A.** gross reporting.
   - **B.** net reporting.
2. Determine and justify the appropriate method for reporting revenues.

Solution to 1: The table below shows how reporting would appear on a gross and a net basis.

	A. Gross Reporting	B. Net Reporting
Revenues	$1,100,000	$100,000
Cost of sales	1,002,000	2,000
Gross margin	$98,000	$98,000

[18] See Emerging Issues Task Force EITF 99-19, "Reporting Revenue Gross as a Principal versus Net as an Agent."

Solution to 2: Flyalot should report revenue on a net basis. Flyalot pays only for tickets it sells to customers and thus did not bear inventory risk. In addition, the airline—not Flyalot—is the primary obligor under the contract. Revenues should be reported as $100,000.

3.3 Implications for Financial Analysis

As we have seen, companies use a variety of revenue recognition methods. Furthermore, a single company may use different revenue recognition policies for different businesses. Companies disclose their revenue recognition policies in the footnotes to their financial statement, often in the first note.

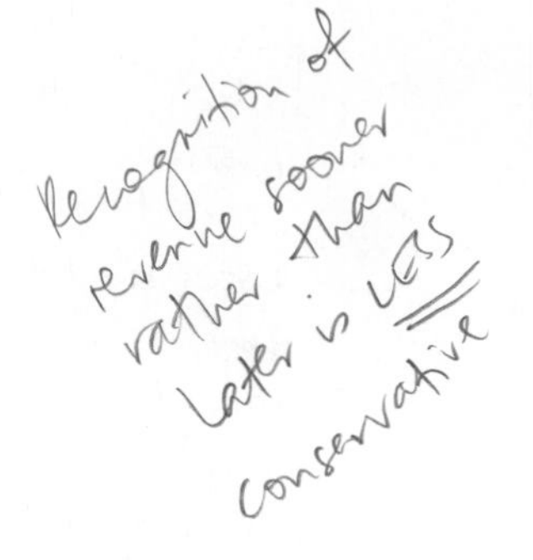

The following aspects of a company's revenue recognition policy are particularly relevant to financial analysis: whether a policy results in recognition of revenue sooner rather than later (sooner is less conservative), and to what extent a policy requires the company to make estimates. In order to analyze a company's financial statements, and particularly to compare one company's financial statements with those of another company, it is helpful to understand any differences in their revenue recognition policies. Although it may not be possible to calculate the monetary effect of differences between particular companies' revenue recognition policies and estimates, it is generally possible to characterize the relative conservatism of a company's policies and to qualitatively assess how differences in policies might affect financial ratios.

With familiarity of the basic principles of revenue recognition in hand, the next section begins a discussion of expense recognition.

EXAMPLE 6

Revenue Recognition Policy for Motorola

As disclosed in the footnotes to the financial statements shown below (emphasis added), Motorola (NYSE:MOT) uses different revenue recognition policies depending on the type of revenue-producing activity, including product sales, long-term contracts, contracts involving unproven technology, revenue for services, and revenue for licensing agreements.

> **Revenue Recognition:** The Company recognizes revenue for ***product sales*** when title transfers, the risks and rewards of ownership have been transferred to the customer, the fee is fixed and determinable, and collection of the related receivable is probable, which is generally at the time of shipment. Accruals are established, with the related reduction to revenue, for allowances for discounts and price protection, product returns and incentive programs for distributors and end customers related to these sales based on actual historical exposure at the time the related revenues are recognized. For ***long-term contracts***, the Company uses the percentage-of-completion method to recognize revenues and costs based on the percentage of costs incurred to date compared to the total estimated contract costs. For ***contracts involving new unproven technologies***, revenues and profits are deferred until technological feasibility is established, customer acceptance is obtained and other contract-specific terms have been completed. Provisions for losses are

recognized during the period in which the loss first becomes apparent. ***Revenue for services*** is recognized ratably over the contract term or as services are being performed. ***Revenue related to licensing agreements*** is recognized over the licensing period or at the time the Company has fulfilled its obligations and the fee to be received is fixed and determinable.

Source: Motorola 10-K financial statement footnotes for the year ended 31 December 2004, as filed with the SEC. Emphasis added.

EXAMPLE 7

Revenue Recognition of i2 Technologies

On 9 June 2004, the SEC announced it had settled a securities fraud case against i2 Technologies (NASDAQ: ITWO) involving the misstatement of approximately $1 billion in revenues. The SEC announcement explains that the company recognized revenue up front on its software licenses, which was inappropriate because some of the software lacked complete functionality either for general use or for use by a particular customer.

Source: SEC Accounting and Auditing Enforcement Release No. 2034.

EXPENSE RECOGNITION

4

Expenses are deducted against revenue to arrive at a company's net profit or loss. Under the IASB Framework, **expenses** are "decreases in economic benefits during the accounting period in the form of outflows or depletions of assets or incurrences of liabilities that result in decreases in equity, other than those relating to distributions to equity participants."[19]

The IASB Framework also states:

> The definition of expenses encompasses losses as well as those expenses that arise in the course of the ordinary activities of the enterprise. Expenses that arise in the course of the ordinary activities of the enterprise include, for example, cost of sales, wages and depreciation. They usually take the form of an outflow or depletion of assets such as cash and cash equivalents, inventory, property, plant and equipment.
>
> Losses represent other items that meet the definition of expenses and may, or may not, arise in the course of the ordinary activities of the enterprise. Losses represent decreases in economic benefits and as such they are no different in nature from other expenses. Hence, they are not regarded as a separate element in this Framework.
>
> Losses include, for example, those resulting from disasters such as fire and flood.[20]

[19] IASB *Framework for the Preparation and Presentation of Financial Statements*, paragraph 70.

[20] Ibid., paragraphs 78-80.

Similar to the issues with revenue recognition, in a simple hypothetical scenario, expense recognition would not be an issue. For instance, assume a company purchased inventory for cash and sold the entire inventory in the same period. When the company paid for the inventory, absent indications to the contrary, it is clear that the inventory cost has been incurred and should be recognized as an expense (cost of goods sold) in the financial records. Assume also that the company paid all operating and administrative expenses in cash within each accounting period. In such a simple hypothetical scenario, no issues of expense recognition would arise. In practice, however, as with revenue recognition, determining when expenses should be recognized can be somewhat more complex.

4.1 General Principles

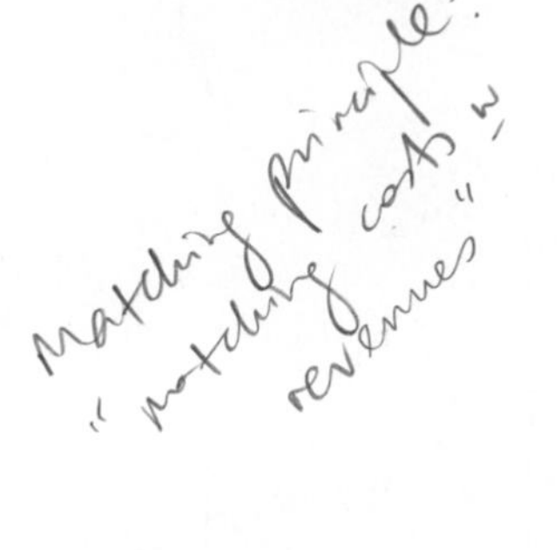

In general, a company recognizes expenses in the period that it consumes (i.e., uses up) the economic benefits associated with the expenditure, or loses some previously recognized economic benefit.[21]

A general principle of expense recognition is the **matching principle,** also known as the "matching of costs with revenues."[22] Under the matching principle, a company directly matches some expenses (e.g., cost of goods sold) with associated revenues. Unlike the simple scenario in which a company purchases inventory and sells all of the inventory within the same accounting period, in practice, it is more likely that some of the current period's sales are made from inventory purchased in a previous period. It is also more likely that some of the inventory purchased in the current period will remain unsold at the end of the current period and so will be sold in the following period. The matching principle requires that the company match the cost of goods sold with the revenues of the period.

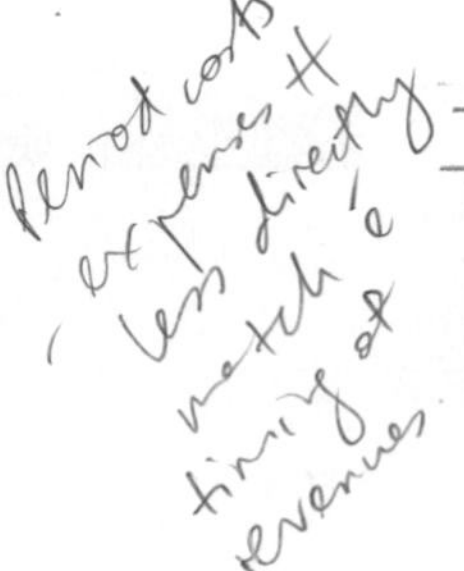

Period costs, expenditures that less directly match the timing of revenues, are reflected in the period when a company makes the expenditure or incurs the liability to pay. Administrative expenses are an example of period costs. Other expenditures that also less directly match the timing of revenues relate more directly to future expected benefits; in this case, the expenditures are allocated systematically with the passage of time. An example is depreciation expense (discussed below).

Examples 8 and 9 demonstrate the matching principle applied to inventory and cost of goods sold.

[21] Ibid., paragraph 94.

[22] Ibid., paragraph 95.

EXAMPLE 8

The Matching of Inventory Costs with Revenues

Kahn Distribution Limited (KDL) purchases inventory items for resale. During 2006, Kahn had the following transactions:

Quarter	Inventory Purchases
First quarter	2,000 units at $40 per unit
Second quarter	1,500 units at $41 per unit
Third quarter	2,200 units at $43 per unit
Fourth quarter	1,900 units at $45 per unit
Total	7,600 units at a total cost of $321,600

Inventory sales during the year were 5,600 units at $50 per unit. KDL determines that there were 2,000 remaining units of inventory and specifically identifies that 1,900 were those purchased in the fourth quarter and 100 were purchased in the third quarter. What are the revenue and expense associated with these transactions during 2006?

Solution: The revenue for 2006 would be $280,000 (5,600 units × $50 per unit). Initially, the total cost of the goods purchased would be recorded as inventory (an asset) in the amount of $321,600. During 2006, the cost of the 5,600 units sold would be expensed (matched against the revenue) while the cost of the 2,000 remaining unsold units would remain in inventory as follows:

Cost of Goods Sold		
From the first quarter	2,000 units at $40 per unit =	$ 80,000
From the second quarter	1,500 units at $41 per unit =	$ 61,500
From the third quarter	2,100 units at $43 per unit =	$ 90,300
Total cost of goods sold		$231,800
Cost of Goods Remaining in Inventory		
From the third quarter	100 units at $43 per unit =	$ 4,300
From the fourth quarter	1,900 units at $45 per unit =	$85,500
Total remaining (or ending) inventory cost		$89,800

To confirm that total costs are accounted for:
$231,800 + $89,800 = $321,600
The cost of the goods sold would be expensed against the revenue of $280,000 as follows:

Revenue	$280,000
Cost of goods sold	231,800
Gross profit	$ 48,200

The remaining inventory amount of $89,800 will be matched against revenue in a future year when the inventory items are sold.

EXAMPLE 9

Alternative Inventory Costing Methods

In Example 8, KDL was able to specifically identify which inventory items were sold and which remained in inventory to be carried over to later periods. That method is called the **specific identification method.** It is not always possible to specifically identify which items were sold, so the accounting standards permit the assignment of inventory costs to costs of goods sold and to ending inventory using cost flow assumptions. Under both IFRS and U.S. GAAP, companies may use either of two methods to assign costs: the First In, First Out (FIFO) method, or the weighted average cost method. Under the **FIFO method**, it is simply assumed that the earliest items purchased were sold first. Ending inventory would, therefore, include only the latest purchases. It turns out that those items specifically identified as sold in Example 8 were also the first items purchased, so in this example, under FIFO, the cost of goods sold would also be $231,800, calculated as above. The **weighted average cost method** simply averages the total available costs over the total available units.

For KDL, the weighted average cost would be

$321,600/7,600 units = $42.3158 per unit

Cost of goods sold using the weighted average cost method would be

5,600 units at $42.3158 = $236,968

Ending inventory using the weighted average cost method would be

2,000 units at $42.3158 = $ 84,632

Another method is available under U.S. GAAP but is not permitted under IFRS. This method is the Last In, First Out (LIFO) method. Under the **LIFO method**, it is assumed that the most recent items purchased were sold first. Although this may seem contrary to common sense, it is logical in certain circumstances. For example, lumber in a lumberyard may be stacked up with the oldest lumber on the bottom. As lumber is sold, it is sold from the top of the stack, so the last lumber in is the first lumber out. Theoretically, a company should choose this method under U.S. GAAP if the physical inventory flows in this manner.[23] Under the LIFO method, in the KDL example, it would be assumed that the 2,000 units remaining in ending inventory would have come from the first quarter's purchases:[24]

Ending inventory 2,000 units at $40 per unit = $80,000

The remaining costs would be allocated to cost of goods sold under LIFO:

Total costs of $321,600 less $80,000 remaining in ending inventory = $241,600

[23] Practically, the reason some companies choose to use LIFO in the United States is to reduce taxes. When prices and inventory quantities are rising, LIFO will normally result in lower income and hence lower taxes. U.S. tax regulations require that if LIFO is used on a company's tax return, it must also be used on the company's GAAP financial statements.

[24] If data on the precise timing of quarterly sales were available, the answer would differ because the cost of goods sold would be determined during the quarter rather than at the end of the quarter.

Alternatively, the cost of the last 5,600 units purchased is allocated to cost of goods sold under LIFO:

1,900 units at $45 per unit + 2,200 units at $43 per unit + 1,500 units at $41 per unit = $241,600

Exhibit 7 summarizes and compares inventory costing methods.

EXHIBIT 7 Summary Table on Inventory Costing Methods

Method	Description	Cost of Goods Sold When Prices Are Rising, Relative to Other Two Methods	Ending Inventory When Prices Are Rising, Relative to Other Two Methods
FIFO (first in, first out)	Assumes that earliest items purchased were sold first	Lowest	Highest
LIFO (last in, first out)	Assumes most recent items purchased were sold first	Highest[a]	Lowest[a]
Weighted average cost	Averages total costs over total units available	Middle	Middle

[a]Assumes no LIFO layer liquidation. **LIFO layer liquidation** occurs when the volume of sales rises above the volume of recent purchases so that some sales are made from existing, relatively low-priced inventory rather than from more recent purchases.

4.2 Issues in Expense Recognition

The following sections cover applications of the principles of expense recognition to certain common situations.

4.2.1 Doubtful Accounts

When a company sells its products or services on credit, it is likely that some customers will ultimately default on their obligations (i.e., fail to pay). At the time of the sale, it is not known which customer will default. (If it were known that a particular customer would ultimately default, presumably a company would not sell on credit to that customer.) One possible approach to recognizing credit losses on customer receivables would be for the company to wait until such time as a customer defaulted and only then recognize the loss (**direct write-off method**). Such an approach would usually not be consistent with generally accepted accounting principles.

Under the matching principle, at the time revenue is recognized on a sale, a company is required to record an estimate of how much of the revenue will ultimately be uncollectible. Companies make such estimates based on previous experience with uncollectible accounts. Such estimates may be expressed as a proportion of the overall amount of sales, the overall amount of receivables, or the amount of receivables overdue by a specific amount of time. The company records its estimate of uncollectible amounts as an expense on the income statement, not as a direct reduction of revenues.

4.2.2 Warranties

At times, companies offer warranties on the products they sell. If the product proves deficient in some respect that is covered under the terms of the warranty, the company will incur an expense to repair or replace the product. At the time of sale, the company does not know the amount of future expenses it will incur in connection with its warranties. One possible approach would be for a company to wait until actual expenses are incurred under the warranty and to reflect the expense at that time. However, this would not result in a matching of the expense with the associated revenue.

Under the matching principle, a company is required to estimate the amount of future expenses resulting from its warranties, to recognize an estimated warranty expense in the period of the sale, and to update the expense as indicated by experience over the life of the warranty.

4.2.3 Depreciation and Amortization

Companies commonly incur costs to obtain long-lived assets. **Long-lived assets** are assets expected to provide economic benefits over a future period of time greater than one year. Examples are land (property), plant, equipment, and **intangible assets** (assets lacking physical substance) such as trademarks. The costs of most long-lived assets are allocated over the period of time during which they provide economic benefits. The two main types of long-lived assets whose costs are *not* allocated over time are land and those intangible assets with indefinite useful lives.

Depreciation is the process of systematically allocating costs of long-lived assets over the period during which the assets are expected to provide economic benefits. "Depreciation" is the term commonly applied to this process for physical long-lived assets such as plant and equipment (land is not depreciated), and **amortization** is the term commonly applied to this process for intangible long-lived assets with a finite useful life.[25] Examples of intangible long-lived assets with a finite useful life include an acquired mailing list, an acquired patent with a set expiration date, and an acquired copyright with a set legal life. The term "amortization" is also commonly applied to the systematic allocation of a premium or discount relative to the face value of a fixed-income security over the life of the security.

IAS No. 16, *Property, Plant, and Equipment,* requires that the depreciable amount (cost less residual value) be allocated on a systematic basis over the remaining useful life of the asset. The method used to compute depreciation must reflect the pattern over which the economic benefits of the asset are expected to be consumed. IAS No. 16 does not prescribe a particular method for computing depreciation but notes that several methods are commonly used, such as the straight-line method, diminishing balance method (accelerated depreciation), and the units of **production method** (depreciation varies depending upon production or usage).

The **straight-line method** allocates evenly the cost of long-lived assets less estimated residual value over the estimated useful life of an asset. (The term

[25] Under SFAS No. 142, intangible assets with indefinite life are not amortized. Instead, they are tested at least annually for impairment (i.e., if the current value of an intangible asset is materially lower than its value in the company's books, the value of the asset is considered to be impaired and its value must be decreased).

"straight line" derives from the fact that the annual depreciation expense, if represented as a line graph over time, would be a straight line. In addition, a plot of the cost of the asset minus the cumulative amount of annual depreciation expense, if represented as a line graph over time, would be a straight line with a negative downward slope.) Calculating depreciation and amortization requires two significant estimates: the estimated useful life of an asset and the estimated residual value (also known as "salvage value") of an asset. Under IAS No. 16, the residual value is the amount that the company expects to receive upon sale of the asset at the end of its useful life. Example 10 assumes that an item of equipment is depreciated using the straight-line method and illustrates how the annual depreciation expense varies under different estimates of the useful life and estimated residual value of an asset. As shown, annual depreciation expense is sensitive to both the estimated useful life and to the estimated residual value.

EXAMPLE 10

Sensitivity of Annual Depreciation Expense to Varying Estimates of Useful Life and Residual Value

Using the straight-line method of depreciation, annual depreciation expense is calculated as

$$\frac{\text{Cost} - \text{Residual value}}{\text{Estimated useful life}}$$

Assume the cost of an asset is $10,000. If, for example, the residual value of the asset is estimated to be $0 and its useful life is estimated to be 5 years, the annual depreciation expense under the straight-line method would be ($10,000 − $0)/5 years = $2,000. In contrast, holding the estimated useful life of the asset constant at 5 years but increasing the estimated residual value of the asset to $4,000 would result in annual depreciation expense of only $1,200 [calculated as ($10,000 − $4,000)/5 years]. Alternatively, holding the estimated residual value at $0 but increasing the estimated useful life of the asset to 10 years would result in annual depreciation expense of only $1,000 [calculated as ($10,000 − $0)/10 years]. Exhibit 8 shows annual depreciation expense for various combinations of estimated useful life and residual value.

EXHIBIT 8 Annual Depreciation Expense (in dollars)

Estimated Useful Life (years)	Estimated Residual Value					
	0	1,000	2,000	3,000	4,000	5,000
2	5,000	4,500	4,000	3,500	3,000	2,500
4	2,500	2,250	2,000	1,750	1,500	1,250
5	2,000	1,800	1,600	1,400	1,200	1,000
8	1,250	1,125	1,000	875	750	625
10	1,000	900	800	700	600	500

Generally, alternatives to the straight-line method of depreciation are called **accelerated methods of depreciation** because they accelerate (i.e., speed up) the timing of depreciation. Accelerated depreciation methods allocate a greater proportion of the cost to the early years of an asset's useful life. These methods are appropriate if the plant or equipment is expected to be used up faster in the early years (e.g., an automobile). A commonly used accelerated method is the **diminishing balance method,** as mentioned in IAS No. 16 (also known as the **declining balance method**). The diminishing balance method is demonstrated in Example 11.

EXAMPLE 11

An Illustration of Diminishing Balance Depreciation

Assume the cost of computer equipment was $11,000, the estimated residual value is $1,000, and the estimated useful life is five years. Under the diminishing or declining balance method, the first step is to determine the straight-line rate, the rate at which the asset would be depreciated under the straight-line method. This rate is measured as 100 percent divided by the useful life or 20 percent for a five-year useful life. Under the straight-line method, 1/5 or 20 percent of the **depreciable cost** of the asset (here, $11,000 − $1,000 = $10,000) would be expensed each year for five years: The depreciation expense would be $2,000 per year.

The next step is to determine an acceleration factor that approximates the pattern of the asset's wear. Common acceleration factors are 150 percent and 200 percent. The latter is known as **double declining balance depreciation** because it depreciates the asset at double the straight-line rate. Using the 200 percent acceleration factor, the diminishing balance rate would be 40 percent (20 percent × 2.0). This rate is then applied to the remaining undepreciated balance of the asset each period (known as the **net book value**).

At the beginning of the first year, the net book value is $11,000. Depreciation expense for the first full year of use of the asset would be 40 percent of $11,000, or $4,400. Under this method, the residual value, if any, is generally not used in the computation of the depreciation each period (the 40 percent is applied to $11,000 rather than to $11,000 minus residual value). However, the company will stop taking depreciation when the salvage value is reached.

At the beginning of Year 2, the net book value is measured as

Asset cost	$11,000
Less: Accumulated depreciation	(4,400)
Net book value	$ 6,600

For the second full year, depreciation expense would be $6,600 × 40 percent, or $2,640. At the end of the second year (i.e., beginning of the third year), a total of $7,040 ($4,400 + $2,640) of depreciation would have been recorded. So, the remaining net book value at the beginning of the third year would be

Asset cost	$11,000
Less: Accumulated depreciation	(7,040)
Net book value	$ 3,960

For the third full year, depreciation would be \$3,960 × 40 percent, or \$1,584. At the end of the third year, a total of \$8,624 (\$4,400 + \$2,640 + \$1,584) of depreciation would have been recorded. So, the remaining net book value at the beginning of the fourth year would be

Asset cost	\$11,000
Less: Accumulated depreciation	(8,624)
Net book value	\$ 2,376

For the fourth full year, depreciation would be \$2,376 × 40 percent, or \$950. At the end of the fourth year, a total of \$9,574 (\$4,400 + \$2,640 + \$1,584 + \$950) of depreciation would have been recorded. So, the remaining net book value at the beginning of the fifth year would be

Asset cost	\$11,000
Less: Accumulated depreciation	(9,574)
Net book value	\$ 1,426

For the fifth year, if deprecation were determined as in previous years, it would amount to \$570 (\$1,426 × 40 percent). However, this would result in a remaining net book value of the asset below its estimated residual value of \$1,000. So, instead, only \$426 would be depreciated, leaving a \$1,000 net book value at the end of the fifth year.

Asset cost	\$11,000
Less: Accumulated depreciation	(10,000)
Net book value	\$ 1,000

Companies often use a zero or small residual value, which creates problems for diminishing balance depreciation because the asset never fully depreciates. In order to fully depreciate the asset over the initially estimated useful life when a zero or small residual value is assumed, companies often adopt a depreciation policy that combines the diminishing balance and straight-line methods. An example would be a deprecation policy of using double-declining balance depreciation and switching to the straight-line method halfway through the useful life.

Under accelerated depreciation methods, there is a higher depreciation expense in early years relative to the straight-line method. This results in higher expenses and lower net income in the early depreciation years. In later years, there is a reversal with accelerated depreciation expense lower than straight-line depreciation. Accelerated deprecation is sometimes referred to as a "conservative" accounting choice because it results in lower net income in the early years of asset use.

For those intangible assets that must be amortized (those with an identifiable useful life), the process is the same as for depreciation; only the name of the expense is different. IAS No. 38, *Intangible Assets*, states that if a pattern cannot be determined over the useful life, then the straight-line method should be used. In most cases under international accounting standards and U.S. GAAP, amortizable intangible assets are amortized using the straight-line method with no residual value. **Goodwill**[26] and intangible assets with indefinite life are not amortized. Instead, they are tested at least annually for impairment (i.e., if the current value of an intangible asset or goodwill is materially lower than its value in the company's books, the value of the asset is considered to be impaired and its value in the company's books must be decreased).

In summary, to calculate depreciation and amortization, a company must choose a method, estimate the asset's useful life, and estimate residual value. Clearly, different choices have a differing effect on depreciation or amortization expense and, therefore, on reported net income.

4.3 Implications for Financial Analysis

A company's estimates for doubtful accounts and/or for warranty expenses can affect its reported net income. Similarly, a company's choice of depreciation or amortization method, estimates of assets' useful lives, and estimates of assets' residual values can affect reported net income. These are only a few of the choices and estimates that affect a company's reported net income.

As with revenue recognition policies, a company's choice of expense recognition can be characterized by its relative conservatism. A policy that results in recognition of expenses later rather than sooner is considered less conservative. In addition, many items of expense require the company to make estimates that can significantly affect net income. Analysis of a company's financial statements, and particularly comparison of one company's financial statements with those of another, requires an understanding of differences in these estimates and their potential impact.

If, for example, a company shows a significant year-to-year change in its estimates of uncollectible accounts as a percentage of sales, warranty expenses as percentage of sales, or estimated useful lives of assets, the analyst should seek to understand the underlying reasons. Do the changes reflect a change in business operations (e.g., lower estimated warranty expenses reflecting recent experience of fewer warranty claims because of improved product quality)? Or are the changes seemingly unrelated to changes in business operations and thus possibly a signal that a company is manipulating estimates in order to achieve a particular effect on its reported net income?

As another example, if two companies in the same industry have dramatically different estimates for uncollectible accounts as a percentage of their sales, warranty expenses as a percentage of sales, or estimated useful lives as a percentage of assets, it is important to understand the underlying reasons. Are the differences consistent with differences in the two companies' business operations (e.g., lower uncollectible accounts for one company reflecting a different, more creditworthy customer base or possibly stricter credit policies)? Another difference consistent with differences in business operations would be a difference in estimated useful lives of assets if one of the companies employs newer equipment. Or, alternatively, are the differences seemingly inconsistent with differences in the two companies' business operations, possibly signaling that a company is manipulating estimates?

Information about a company's accounting policies and significant estimates are described in the footnotes to the financial statements and in the management discussion and analysis section of a company's annual report.

[26] Goodwill is recorded in acquisitions and is the amount by which the price to purchase an entity exceeds the amount of net identifiable assets acquired (the total amount of identifiable assets acquired less liabilities assumed).

When possible, the monetary effect of differences in expense recognition policies and estimates can facilitate more meaningful comparisons with a single company's historical performance or across a number of companies. An analyst can use the monetary effect to adjust the reported expenses so that they are on a comparable basis.

Even when the monetary effects of differences in policies and estimates cannot be calculated, it is generally possible to characterize the relative conservatism of the policies and estimates and, therefore, to qualitatively assess how such differences might affect reported expenses and thus financial ratios.

NONRECURRING ITEMS AND NONOPERATING ITEMS

5

From a company's income statements, we can see its earnings from last year and in the previous year. Looking forward, the question is: What will the company earn next year and in the years after?

To assess a company's future earnings, it is helpful to separate those prior years' items of income and expense that are likely to continue in the future from those items that are less likely to continue.[27] Some items from prior years are clearly not expected to continue in the future periods and are separately disclosed on a company's income statement. Two such items are (1) discontinued operations, and (2) extraordinary items (the latter category is no longer permitted under IFRS). These two items, if applicable, must be reported separately from continuing operations.[28]

For other items on a company's income statement, such as unusual items, accounting changes, and nonoperating income, the likelihood of their continuing in the future is somewhat less clear and requires the analyst to make some judgments.

5.1 Discontinued Operations

When a company disposes of or establishes a plan to dispose of one of its component operations and will have no further involvement in the operation, the income statement reports separately the effect of this disposal as a "discontinued" operation under both IFRS and U.S. GAAP. Financial standards provide various criteria for reporting the effect separately, which are generally that the discontinued component must be separable both physically and operationally.[29]

Because the discontinued operation will no longer provide earnings (or cash flow) to the company, an analyst can eliminate discontinued operations in formulating expectations about a company's future financial performance.

In Exhibit 2, Kraft reported a loss from discontinued operations of $4 million in 2004 and earnings of $97 million in both 2003 and 2002. In Footnote 5 of its financial statements, Kraft explains that it sold substantially all of its sugar confectionary business (including brands such as Life Savers and Altoids). The $4 million loss and $97 million earnings refer to the amount of loss (earnings) of the sugar confectionary business in each of those years.

[27] In business writing, items expected to continue in the future are often described as "persistent" or "permanent," whereas those not expected to continue are described as "transitory."

[28] These requirements apply to material amounts.

[29] IFRS No. 5, *Non-Current Assets Held for Sale and Discontinued Operations*, paragraphs 31–33.

5.2 Extraordinary Items

IAS No. 1 prohibits classification of any income or expense items as being "extraordinary."[30] Under U.S. GAAP, an extraordinary item is one that is both unusual in nature and infrequent in occurrence. Extraordinary items are presented separately on the income statement and allow a reader of the statements to see that these items are not part of a company's operating activities and are not expected to occur on an ongoing basis. Extraordinary items are shown net of tax and appear on the income statement below discontinued operations. An example of an extraordinary item is provided in Example 12.

EXAMPLE 12

Extraordinary Gain: Purchase of a Business for Less than the Fair Value of the Identifiable Net Assets

Vicon Industries in its annual report made the following disclosure:

> On October 1, 2004, the Company entered into an agreement to purchase all of the operating assets of Videotronic Infosystems GmbH ("Videotronic"), a Germany based video system supplier which was operating under insolvency protection, for 700,000 Eurodollars [sic] (approximately $868,000)... During the year ended September 30, 2005, the Company recognized a $211,000 extraordinary gain on the recovery of Videotronic net assets in excess of their allocated purchase price. Such gain includes adjustments to assigned values of accounts receivable, inventories, trade payables and severance liabilities.

Source: Vicon Industries 10-K Report for fiscal year ended 30 September 2005, filed 29 December 2005: Note 15.

Companies apply judgment to determine whether an item is extraordinary based on guidance from accounting standards (Accounting Practices Board Opinion No. 30). Judgment on whether an item is unusual in nature requires consideration of the company's environment, including its industry and geography. Determining whether an item is infrequent in occurrence is based on expectations of whether it will occur again in the near future. Standard setters offer specific guidance in some cases. For example, following Hurricanes Katrina and Rita in 2005, the American Institute of Certified Public Accountants issued Technical Practice Aid 5400.05, which states (the material in square brackets has been added): "A natural disaster [such as a hurricane, tornado, fire, or earthquake] of a type that is reasonably expected to re-occur would not meet both conditions [for classification as an extraordinary item]."

Given the requirements for classification of an item as extraordinary—unusual and infrequent—an analyst can generally eliminate extraordinary items from expectations about a company's future financial performance unless there is some indication that such an extraordinary item may reoccur.

[30] IAS No. 1, *Presentation of Financial Statements*, paragraph 85, effective 2005. In prior years, classification of items as extraordinary was permitted.

5.3 Unusual or Infrequent Items

Items that do not meet the definition of extraordinary are shown as part of a company's continuing operations. Items that are unusual or infrequent—but not both—cannot be shown as extraordinary. For example, restructuring charges, such as costs to close plants and employee termination costs, are considered part of a company's ordinary activities. As another example, gains and losses arising when a company sells an asset or part of a business for more or less than its carrying value are also disclosed separately on the income statement but are not considered extraordinary because such sales are considered ordinary business activities.[31]

Highlighting the unusual or infrequent nature of these items assists an analyst in judging the likelihood that such items will reoccur.

In Exhibit 2, Kraft's income statement showed several such infrequent but not unusual items, all of which are included as part of operating income. The company reported a $111 million loss in 2002 from "integration costs and a loss on sale of a food factory," followed by a $13 million reduction of these costs in 2003. In Note 14 of its financial statements, the company explains that these costs arose from consolidating production lines in North America. Also, the company reported $142 million, $6 million, and $603 million in 2002, 2003, and 2004, respectively, for "**asset impairment** and exit costs" and explains in the footnotes that the large costs in 2004 are related to its restructuring program and reflect asset disposals, severance, and other implementation aspects.

Finally, Kraft reported an $80 million gain on the sale of businesses in 2002 and a $31 million gain in 2003, followed by a $3 million loss on the sale of businesses in 2004. In Note 14 of its financial statements, Kraft explains that the $80 million gain in 2002 arose from the sale of its Latin American bakery ingredient business and several small food businesses; the $31 million gain in 2003 arose from the sale of a European rice business and an Italian fresh cheese business; and the $3 million loss in 2004 arose from the sale of a Brazilian snack nuts business and Norwegian candy business trademarks. An analyst would seek to understand how these disposals fit with the company's strategy and what effect, if material, these disposals would have on the company's future operations.

Generally, in forecasting future operations, an analyst would assess whether the items reported are likely to reoccur and also possible implications for future earnings. It is generally not advisable simply to ignore all unusual items.

5.4 Changes in Accounting Standards

At times, standard setters issue new pronouncements that require companies to change accounting principles. In other cases, changes in accounting principles (e.g., from one acceptable inventory costing method to another) are made for other reasons, such as providing a better reflection of the company's performance. Changes in accounting principles are reported through retrospective application,[32] unless it is impractical to do so. *Retrospective application* means that the financial statements for all fiscal years shown in a company's financial report are presented as if the newly adopted accounting principle had been used

[31] In its financial statement footnotes, Groupe Danone provides a reconciliation between operating income under French GAAP, which excludes certain exceptional items (such as gains and losses on disposals), and U.S. GAAP.

[32] IAS No. 8, *Accounting Policies, Changes in Accounting Estimates and Errors*, and FASB Financial Accounting Statement No. 154, *Accounting Changes and Error Corrections*.

throughout the entire period. Footnotes to the financial statements describe the change and explain the justification for the change.

Because changes in accounting principles are retrospectively applied, the financial statements that appear within a financial report are comparable. So, if a company's annual report for 2006 includes its financial statements for fiscal years 2004, 2005, and 2006, all of these statements will be comparable.

In years prior to 2005, under both IFRS and U.S. GAAP, the cumulative effect of changes in accounting policies was typically shown at the bottom of the income statement in the year of change instead of using retrospective application. It is possible that future accounting standards may occasionally require a company to report the change differently than retrospective application. Footnote disclosures are required to explain how the transition from the old standard to the new one was handled. During the period when companies make the transition from the old standard to the new, an analyst would examine disclosures to ensure comparability across companies.

In contrast to changes in accounting policies (such as whether to expense the cost of employee stock options), companies sometimes make *changes in accounting estimates* (such as the useful life of a depreciable asset). Changes in accounting estimates are handled prospectively, with the change affecting the financial statements for the period of change and future periods.[33] No adjustments are made to prior statements, and the adjustment is not shown on the face of the income statement. Significant changes should be disclosed in the footnotes.

Another possible adjustment is a *correction of an error for a prior period* (e.g., in financial statements issued for an earlier year). This cannot be handled by simply adjusting the current period income statement. Correction of an error for a prior period is handled by restating the financial statements (including the balance sheet, statement of owners' equity, and cash flow statement) for the prior periods presented in the current financial statements.[34] Footnote disclosures are required regarding the error. These disclosures should be examined carefully because they may reveal weaknesses in the company's accounting systems and financial controls.

5.5 Nonoperating Items: Investing and Financing Activities

Nonoperating items are reported separately from operating income. For example, if a nonfinancial service company invests in equity or debt securities issued by another company, any interest, dividends, or profits from sales of these securities will be shown as nonoperating income. In general, for nonfinancial services companies,[35] nonoperating income that is disclosed separately on the income statement (or in the notes) includes amounts earned through investing activities.

Among nonoperating items on the income statement (or accompanying notes), nonfinancial service companies also disclose the interest expense on their debt securities, including amortization of any discount or premium. The amount of interest expense is related to the amount of a company's borrowings and is generally described in the financial footnotes. For financial service companies, interest income and expense are likely components of operating activities.

[33] Ibid.

[34] Ibid.

[35] Examples of financial services firms are insurance companies, banks, brokers, dealers, and investment companies.

In practice, investing and financing activities may be disclosed on a net basis, with the components disclosed separately in the footnotes. In its income statement for 2004, Kraft, for example, disclosed net interest and other debt expense of $666 million. The financial statement footnotes (not shown) further disclose that Kraft's total interest expense was $679 million and interest income was $13 million, thus the net $666 million. Groupe Danone's footnotes provide similar disclosures.

For purposes of assessing a company's future performance, the amount of financing expense will depend on the company's financing policy (target capital structure) and borrowing costs. The amount of investing income will depend on the purpose and success of investing activities. For a nonfinancial company, a significant amount of financial income would typically warrant further exploration. What are the reasons underlying the company's investments in the securities of other companies? Is the company simply investing excess cash in short-term securities to generate income higher than cash deposits, or is the company purchasing securities issued by other companies for strategic reasons, such as access to raw material supply or research?

EARNINGS PER SHARE 6

One metric of particular importance to an equity investor is earnings per share (EPS). EPS is an input into ratios such as the price/earnings ratio. Additionally, each shareholder in a company owns a different number of shares. A presentation of EPS, therefore, enables each shareholder to compute his or her share of the company's earnings. Under IFRS, IAS No. 33, *Earnings Per Share*, requires the presentation of EPS on the face of the income statement for net profit or loss (net income) and profit or loss (income) from continuing operations. Similar presentation is required under U.S. GAAP by Financial Accounting Statement No. 128, *Earnings Per Share*. This section outlines the calculations for EPS and explains how the calculation differs for a simple versus complex capital structure.

6.1 Simple versus Complex Capital Structure

A company's capital is composed of its equity and debt. Some types of equity have preference over others, and some debt (and other instruments) may be converted into equity. Under IFRS, the type of equity for which EPS is presented are ordinary shares. **Ordinary shares** are those equity shares that are subordinate to all other types of equity. This is the basic ownership of the company—the equityholders who are paid last in a liquidation of the company and who benefit the most when the company does well. Under U.S. GAAP, this equity is referred to as **common stock** or **common shares**, reflecting U.S. language usage. The terms "ordinary shares," "common stock," and "common shares" are used equivalently in the remaining discussion.

When a company has any securities that are potentially convertible into common stock, it is said to have a complex capital structure. Specific examples of securities that are potentially convertible into common stock include **convertible bonds**, convertible preferred stock, employee stock options, and warrants.[36] If a

[36] A warrant is a call option typically attached to securities issued by a company, such as bonds. A warrant gives the holder the right to acquire the company's stock from the company at a specified price within a specified time period. IFRS and U.S. GAAP standards regarding earnings per share apply equally to call options, warrants, and equivalent instruments.

company's capital structure does not include securities that are potentially convertible into common stock, it is said to have a simple capital structure.

The distinction between simple versus complex capital structure is relevant to the calculation of EPS because any securities that are potentially convertible into common stock could, as a result of conversion, potentially dilute (i.e., decrease) EPS. Information about such a potential dilution is valuable to a company's current and potential shareholders; therefore, accounting standards require companies to disclose what their EPS would be if all dilutive securities were converted into common stock. The EPS that would result if all dilutive securities were converted is called **diluted EPS**. In contrast, **basic EPS** is calculated using the actual earnings available to common stock and the weighted average number of shares outstanding.

Companies are required to report both their basic EPS and their diluted EPS. In Exhibit 2, Kraft reported basic EPS of $1.56 and diluted EPS of $1.55 for 2004, lower than EPS (from continuing operations) of $1.95 for 2003. In Exhibit 1, Danone reported basic EPS of 1.26 and diluted EPS of 1.25 for 2004, much lower than 2003. An analyst would try to determine the causes underlying the changes in EPS, a topic we will address following an explanation of the calculations of both basic and diluted EPS.

6.2 Basic EPS

Basic EPS is the amount of income available to common shareholders divided by the weighted average number of common shares outstanding over a period. The amount of income available to common shareholders is the amount of net income remaining after preferred dividends (if any) have been paid. Thus, the formula to calculate basic EPS is:

$$\text{Basic EPS} = \frac{\text{Net income} - \text{Preferred dividends}}{\text{Weighted average number of shares outstanding}} \qquad \textbf{(32-1)}$$

The weighted average number of shares outstanding is a time weighting of common shares outstanding, and the methodology applies to calculating diluted EPS. As an example, assume a company began the year with 2,000,000 shares outstanding and repurchased 100,000 shares on 1 July. The weighted average number of shares outstanding would be the sum of 2,000,000 shares × 1/2 year + 1,900,000 shares ×1/2 year, or 1,950,000 shares. So, the company would use 1,950,000 shares in calculating its basic EPS.

If the number of shares of common stock increases as a result of a **stock dividend**, stock bonus, or a **stock split** (all three represent the receipt of additional shares by existing shareholders), the EPS calculation reflects the change retroactively to the beginning of the period.

Examples of a basic EPS computation are presented in Examples 13, 14, and 15.

EXAMPLE 13

A Basic EPS Calculation (1)

For the year ended 31 December 2006, Shopalot Company had net income of $1,950,000. The company had an average of 1,500,000 shares of common stock outstanding, no preferred stock, and no convertible securities. What was Shopalot's basic EPS?

Solution: Shopalot's basic EPS was $1.30, calculated as $1,950,000 divided by 1,500,000 shares.

EXAMPLE 14

A Basic EPS Calculation (2)

For the year ended 31 December 2006, Angler Products had net income of $2,500,000. The company declared and paid $200,000 of dividends on preferred stock. The company also had the following common stock share information:

Shares outstanding on 1 January 2006	1,000,000
Shares issued on 1 April 2006	200,000
Shares repurchased (treasury shares) on 1 October 2006	(100,000)
Shares outstanding on 31 December 2006	1,100,000

1. What is the company's weighted average number of shares outstanding?
2. What is the company's basic EPS?

Solution to 1: The weighted average number of shares outstanding is determined by the length of time each quantity of shares was outstanding:

1,000,000 × (3 months/12 months) =	250,000
1,200,000 × (6 months/12 months) =	600,000
1,100,000 × (3 months/12 months) =	275,000
Weighted average number of shares outstanding	1,125,000

Solution to 2: Basic EPS is (Net income − Preferred dividends)/Weighted average number of shares = ($2,500,000 − $200,000)/1,125,000 = $2.04

EXAMPLE 15

A Basic EPS Calculation (3)

Assume the same facts as in Example 14 except that on 1 December 2006, the company institutes a 2 for 1 stock split. Each shareholder receives two shares in exchange for each current share that he or she owns. What is the company's basic EPS?

Solution: For EPS calculation purposes, a stock split is treated as if it occurred at the beginning of the period. The weighted average number of shares would, therefore, be 2,250,000, and the basic EPS would be $1.02

6.3 Diluted EPS

If a company has a simple capital structure (i.e., one with no potentially dilutive securities), then its basic EPS is equal to its diluted EPS. If, however, a company has dilutive securities, its diluted EPS is lower than its basic EPS. The sections below describe the effects of three types of potentially dilutive securities: convertible preferred, convertible debt, and employee stock options.

6.3.1 Diluted EPS When a Company Has Convertible Preferred Stock Outstanding

When a company has convertible preferred stock outstanding, diluted EPS is calculated using the **if-converted method** (i.e., what EPS would have been *if* the convertible preferred securities had been converted at the beginning of the period). What would have been the effect if the securities had been converted? If the convertible preferred securities had converted, these securities would no longer be outstanding; instead, additional common stock would be outstanding. Therefore, if such a conversion had taken place, the company would not have paid preferred dividends and would have had more shares of common stock.

The diluted EPS using the if-converted method for convertible preferred stock is equal to the amount of net income divided by the weighted average number of shares outstanding plus the new shares of common stock that would be issued upon conversion of the preferred. Thus, the formula to calculate diluted EPS using the if-converted method for preferred stock is:

$$\text{Diluted EPS} = \frac{(\text{Net income})}{(\text{Weighted average number of shares outstanding} + \text{New common shares that would have been issued at conversion})} \quad \textbf{(32-2)}$$

A diluted EPS calculation using the if-converted method for preferred stock is provided in Example 16.

EXAMPLE 16

A Diluted EPS Calculation Using the If-Converted Method for Preferred Stock

For the year ended 31 December 2006, Bright-Warm Utility Company had net income of $1,750,000. The company had an average of 500,000 shares of common stock outstanding, 20,000 shares of convertible preferred, and no other potentially dilutive securities. Each share of preferred pays a dividend of $10 per share, and each is convertible into five shares of the company's common stock. Calculate the company's basic and diluted EPS.

Solution: If the 20,000 shares of convertible preferred had each converted into 5 shares of the company's common stock, the company would have had an additional 100,000 shares of common stock (5 shares of common for each of the 20,000 shares of preferred). If the conversion had taken place, the company would not have paid preferred dividends of $200,000 ($10 per share for each of the 20,000 shares of preferred). As shown in Exhibit 9, the company's basic EPS was $3.10 and its diluted EPS was $2.92.

EXHIBIT 9 Calculation of Diluted EPS for Bright-Warm Utility Company Using the If-Converted Method: Case of Preferred Stock

	Basic EPS	Diluted EPS Using If-Converted Method
Net income	$1,750,000	$1,750,000
Preferred dividend	−200,000	0
Numerator	$1,550,000	$1,750,000
Weighted average number of shares outstanding	500,000	500,000
If converted	0	100,000
Denominator	500,000	600,000
EPS	**$3.10**	**$2.92**

6.3.2 *Diluted EPS When a Company Has Convertible Debt Outstanding*

When a company has convertible debt outstanding, the diluted EPS calculation is similar to the calculation for convertible preferred: Diluted EPS is calculated using the if-converted method (i.e., what EPS would have been *if* the convertible debt had been converted at the beginning of the period). If the convertible debt had been converted, the debt securities would no longer be outstanding; instead, additional common stock would be outstanding. Therefore, if such a conversion had taken place, the company would not have paid interest on the convertible debt and would have had more shares of common stock.

To calculate diluted EPS using the if-converted method for convertible debt, the amount of net income available to common shareholders must be increased by the amount of after-tax interest related to the convertible debt. In addition, the weighted average number of shares in the denominator increases by the number of new shares of common stock that would be issued upon conversion of the convertible debt. Thus, the formula to calculate diluted EPS using the if-converted method for convertible debt is:

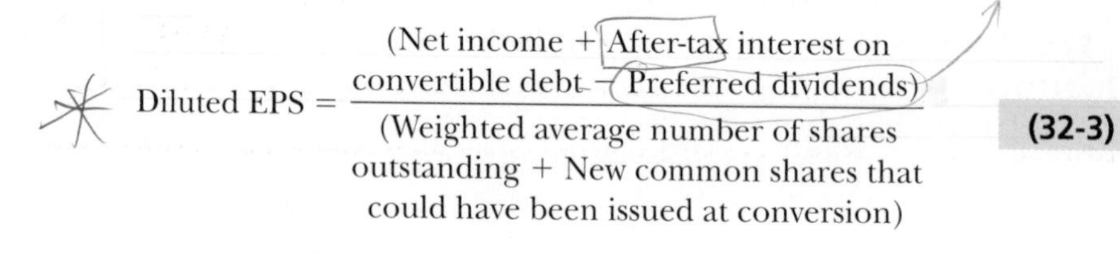

$$\text{Diluted EPS} = \frac{(\text{Net income} + \text{After-tax interest on convertible debt} - \text{Preferred dividends})}{(\text{Weighted average number of shares outstanding} + \text{New common shares that could have been issued at conversion})} \quad \textbf{(32-3)}$$

A diluted EPS calculation using the if-converted method for convertible debt is provided in Example 17.

EXAMPLE 17

A Diluted EPS Calculation Using the If-Converted Method for Convertible Debt

Oppnox Company reported net income of $750,000 for the year ended 31 December 2005. The company had an average of 690,000 shares of common stock outstanding. In addition, the company has only one potentially dilutive security: $50,000 of 6 percent convertible bonds, convertible into a total of 10,000 shares. Assuming a tax rate of 30 percent, calculate Oppnox's basic and diluted EPS.

Solution: If the convertible debt had been converted, the debt securities would no longer be outstanding; instead, an additional 10,000 shares of common stock would be outstanding. Also, if such a conversion had taken place, the company would not have paid interest on the convertible debt of $3,000, equivalent to $3,000(1 − 0.30) = $2,100 on an after-tax basis. To calculate diluted EPS using the if-converted method for convertible debt, the amount of net income available to common shareholders is increased by $2,100. Also, the weighted average number of shares in the denominator increases by 10,000 shares.

EXHIBIT 10 **Calculation of Diluted EPS for Oppnox Company Using the If-Converted Method: Case of a Convertible Bond**

	Basic EPS	Diluted EPS Using If-Converted Method
Net income	$750,000	$750,000
After-tax cost of interest		2,100
Numerator	$750,000	$752,100
Weighted average number of shares outstanding	690,000	690,000
If converted	0	10,000
Denominator	690,000	700,000
EPS	**$1.09**	**$1.07**

6.3.3 Diluted EPS When a Company Has Stock Options, Warrants, or Their Equivalents Outstanding

Under U.S. GAAP, when a company has stock options, warrants, or their equivalents[37] outstanding, the diluted EPS is calculated using the **treasury stock method** (i.e., what EPS would have been *if* the options had been exercised and the company had used the proceeds to repurchase common stock). If the options had been exercised, the company would have received cash for the amount of the option exercise price. The options would no longer be outstanding; instead, additional common stock would be outstanding. Under the treasury stock method, a further calculation is made to adjust the number of shares outstanding by the number of shares that could have been purchased with the cash received upon exercise of the options.

To calculate diluted EPS using the treasury stock method for options, the weighted average number of shares in the denominator increases by the number of new shares of common stock that would be issued upon exercise of the options minus the number of shares that could have been purchased with the cash received upon exercise of the options. No change is made to the numerator. Thus, the formula to calculate diluted EPS using the treasury stock method for options is

$$\text{Diluted EPS} = \frac{(\text{Net income} - \text{Preferred dividends})}{\begin{array}{c}(\text{Weighted average number of shares} \\ \text{outstanding} + \text{New shares that could} \\ \text{have been issued at option exercise} - \\ \text{Shares that could have been purchased} \\ \text{with cash received upon exercise})\end{array}} \qquad \textbf{(32-4)}$$

[37] Hereafter, options, warrants, and their equivalents will be referred to simply as "options" because the accounting treatment is interchangeable for these instruments under IFRS and U.S. GAAP.

A diluted EPS calculation using the treasury stock method for options is provided in Example 18.

EXAMPLE 18

A Diluted EPS Calculation Using the Treasury Stock Method for Options

Hihotech Company reported net income of $2.3 million for the year ended 30 June 2005 and had an average of 800,000 common shares outstanding. The company has outstanding 30,000 options with an exercise price of $35 and no other potentially dilutive securities. Over the year, the company's market price has averaged $55 per share. Calculate the company's basic and diluted EPS.

Solution: Using the treasury stock method, we first calculate that the company would have received $1,050,000 ($35 for each of the 30,000 options exercised) if all the options had been exercised. The options would no longer be outstanding; instead, 30,000 new shares of common stock would be outstanding. Under the treasury stock method, we reduce the number of new shares by the number of shares that could have been purchased with the cash received upon exercise of the options. At an average market price of $55 per share, the $1,050,000 proceeds from option exercise could have purchased 19,091 shares of treasury stock. Therefore, the net new shares issued would have been 10,909 (calculated as 30,000 minus 19,091). No change is made to the numerator. As shown in Exhibit 11, the company's basic EPS was $2.88 and the diluted EPS was $2.84.

EXHIBIT 11 Calculation of Diluted EPS for Hihotech Company Using the Treasury Stock Method: Case of Stock Options

	Basic EPS	Diluted EPS Using Treasury Stock Method
Net income	$2,300,000	$2,300,000
Numerator	$2,300,000	$2,300,000
Weighted average number of shares outstanding	800,000	800,000
If converted	0	10,909
Denominator	800,000	810,909
EPS	**$2.88**	**$2.84**

Under IFRS, IAS No. 33 requires a similar computation but does not refer to it as the "treasury stock method." The company is required to consider that any assumed proceeds are received from the issuance of new shares at the average market price for the period. These new "inferred" shares would be disregarded in the computation of diluted EPS, but the excess of the new shares issued under options contracts over the new "inferred" shares would be added into the weighted average number of shares outstanding. The results are similar to the treasury stock method, as shown in Example 19.

EXAMPLE 19

Diluted EPS for Options under IFRS

Assuming the same facts as in Example 18, calculate the weighted average number of shares outstanding for diluted EPS under IFRS.

Solution: If the options had been converted, the company would have received $1,050,000. If this amount had been received from the issuance of new shares at the average market price of $55 per share, the company would have sold 19,091 shares. The excess of the shares issued under options (30,000) over the shares the company could have sold at market prices (19,091) is 10,909. This amount is added to the weighted average number of shares outstanding of 800,000 to get diluted shares of 810,909. Note that this is the same result as that obtained under U.S. GAAP; it is just derived in a different manner.

6.3.4 Other Issues with Diluted EPS

It is possible that some potentially convertible securities could be **antidilutive** (i.e., their inclusion in the computation would result in an EPS higher than the company's basic EPS). Under accounting standards, antidilutive securities are not included in the calculation of diluted EPS. In general, diluted EPS reflects maximum potential dilution. Example 20 provides an illustration of an antidilutive security.

EXAMPLE 20

An Antidilutive Security

For the year ended 31 December 2006, Dim-Cool Utility Company had net income of $1,750,000. The company had an average of 500,000 shares of common stock outstanding, 20,000 shares of convertible preferred, and no other potentially dilutive securities. Each share of preferred pays a dividend of $10 per share, and each is convertible into three shares of the company's common stock. What was the company's basic and diluted EPS?

Solution: If the 20,000 shares of convertible preferred had each converted into 3 shares of the company's common stock, the company would have had an additional 60,000 shares of common stock (3 shares of common for each of the 20,000 shares of preferred). If the conversion had taken place, the company would not have paid preferred dividends of $200,000 ($10 per share for each of the 20,000 shares of preferred). The effect of using the if-converted method would be EPS of $3.13, as shown in Exhibit 12. Because this is greater than the company's basic EPS of $3.10, the securities are said to be antidilutive and the effect of their conversion would not be included in diluted EPS. Diluted EPS would be the same as basic EPS (i.e., $3.10).

EXHIBIT 12 Calculation for an Antidilutive Security

	Basic EPS	Diluted EPS Using If-Converted Method
Net income	$1,750,000	$1,750,000
Preferred dividend	−200,000	0
Numerator	$1,550,000	$1,750,000
Weighted average number of shares outstanding	500,000	500,000
If converted	0	60,000
Denominator	500,000	560,000
EPS	**$3.10**	**$3.13**[a]

[a]Exceeds basic EPS; security is antidilutive and, therefore, not included.

7 ANALYSIS OF THE INCOME STATEMENT

In this section, we apply two analytical tools to analyze the income statement: **common-size analysis** and income statement ratios. In analyzing the income statement, the objective is to assess a company's performance over a period of time—compared with its own historical performance or to the performance of another company.

7.1 Common-Size Analysis of the Income Statement

Common-size analysis of the income statement can be performed by stating each line item on the income statement as a percentage of revenue.[38] Common-size statements facilitate comparison across time periods (time-series analysis) and across companies of different sizes (cross-sectional analysis).

To illustrate, Panel A of Exhibit 13 presents an income statement for three hypothetical companies. Company A and Company B, each with $10 million in sales, are larger (as measured by sales) than Company C, which has only $2 million in sales. In addition, Companies A and B both have higher operating profit: $2 million and $1.5 million, respectively, compared with Company C's operating profit of only $400,000.

EXHIBIT 13

Panel A: Income Statements for Companies A, B, and C ($)

	A	B	C
Sales	$10,000,000	$10,000,000	$2,000,000
Cost of sales	3,000,000	7,500,000	600,000
Gross profit	7,000,000	2,500,000	1,400,000
Selling, general, and administrative expenses	1,000,000	1,000,000	200,000
Research and development	2,000,000	–	400,000
Advertising	2,000,000	–	400,000
Operating profit	2,000,000	1,500,000	400,000

Panel B: Common-Size Income Statements for Companies A, B, and C (%)

	A	B	C
Sales	100%	100%	100%
Cost of sales	30	75	30
Gross profit	70	25	70
Selling, general, and administrative expenses	10	10	10
Research and development	20	0	20
Advertising	20	0	20
Operating profit	20	15	20

Note: Each line item is expressed as a percentage of the company's sales.

[38] This format can be distinguished as "vertical common-size analysis." As the reading on financial statement analysis discusses, there is another type of common-size analysis, known as "**horizontal common-size analysis**," that states items in relation to a selected base year value. Unless otherwise indicated, text references to "common-size analysis" refer to **vertical analysis**.

How can an analyst meaningfully compare the performance of these companies? By preparing a common-size income statement, as illustrated in Panel B, an analyst can readily see that the percentages of Company C's expenses and profit relative to its sales are exactly the same as for Company A. Furthermore, although Company C's operating profit is lower than Company B's in absolute dollars, it is higher in percentage terms (20 percent for Company C compared with only 15 percent for Company B). For each $100 of sales, Company C generates $5 more operating profit than Company B. In other words, Company C is more profitable than Company B based on this measure.

The common-size income statement also highlights differences in companies' strategies. Comparing the two larger companies, Company A reports significantly higher gross profit as a percentage of sales than does Company B (70 percent compared with 25 percent). Given that both companies operate in the same industry, why can Company A generate so much higher gross profit? One possible explanation is found by comparing the operating expenses of the two companies. Company A spends significantly more on research and development and on advertising than Company B. Expenditures on research and development likely result in products with superior technology. Expenditures on advertising likely result in greater brand awareness. So, based on these differences, it is likely that Company A is selling technologically superior products with a better brand image. Company B may be selling its products more cheaply (with a lower gross profit as a percentage of sales) but saving money by not investing in research and development or advertising. In practice, differences across companies are more subtle, but the concept is similar. An analyst, noting significant differences, would seek to understand the underlying reasons for the differences and their implications for the future performance of the companies.

For most expenses, comparison to the amount of sales is appropriate. However, in the case of taxes, it is more meaningful to compare the amount of taxes with the amount of pretax income. Using financial footnote disclosure, an analyst can then examine the causes for differences in effective tax rates. To project the companies' future net income, an analyst would project the companies' pretax income and apply an estimated effective tax rate determined in part by the historical tax rates.

Vertical common-size analysis of the income statement is particularly useful in cross-sectional analysis—comparing companies with each other for a particular time period or comparing a company with industry or sector data. The analyst could select individual peer companies for comparison, use industry data from published sources, or compile data from databases based on a selection of peer companies or broader industry data. For example, Exhibit 14 presents common-size income statement data compiled for the components of the Standard & Poor's 500 classified into the 10 S&P/MSCI Global Industrial Classification System (GICS) sectors using 2005 data. Note that when compiling aggregate data such as this, some level of aggregation is necessary and less detail may be available than from peer company financial statements. The performance of an individual company can be compared with industry or peer company data to evaluate its relative performance.

EXHIBIT 14 Common-Size Income Statement Statistics for the S&P 500 Classified by S&P/MSCI GICS Sector Data for 2005

Panel A: Median Data

	Energy	Materials	Industrials	Consumer Discretionary	Consumer Staples	Health Care	Financials	Information Technology	Telecom. Services	Utilities
No. observations	29	30	49	85	36	52	87	73	9	31
Operating margin	17.24	11.85	11.94	11.15	12.53	16.73	34.62	12.59	22.85	13.52
Pretax margin	19.17	10.95	10.55	10.17	10.76	14.03	23.28	13.60	18.18	9.27
Taxes	5.63	2.87	2.94	3.59	3.26	4.69	6.51	4.06	4.27	3.12
Profit margin	13.97	7.68	7.28	6.87	6.74	9.35	16.09	11.60	10.91	6.93
Cost of goods sold	66.52	68.35	69.02	63.29	56.24	45.29	42.29	47.17	41.76	76.79
Selling, general, and administrative expenses	3.82	10.20	15.88	22.46	25.07	31.77	28.98	31.81	22.40	4.91

Panel B: Mean Data

	Energy	Materials	Industrials	Consumer Discretionary	Consumer Staples	Health Care	Financials	Information Technology	Telecom. Services	Utilities
No. observations	29	30	49	85	36	52	87	73	9	31
Operating margin	23.13	14.12	13.16	12.69	14.51	17.84	35.45	15.13	20.66	14.60
Pretax margin	23.96	12.58	11.09	10.38	12.03	15.83	23.42	15.25	15.19	8.00
Taxes	7.72	3.38	3.33	3.94	3.81	4.94	6.65	4.98	5.14	2.48
Profit margin	16.02	8.58	7.69	6.32	8.15	10.80	16.37	10.26	9.52	5.68
Cost of goods sold	62.36	67.87	68.92	62.41	56.62	49.20	51.47	46.65	40.61	76.51
Selling, general, and administrative expenses	5.44	13.05	17.45	22.82	25.88	30.48	27.68	33.06	22.81	4.91
Average tax rate computed on mean	32.22	26.89	30.04	37.98	31.65	31.21	28.40	32.66	33.82	30.99

Source: Based on data from Compustat.

7.2 Income Statement Ratios

One aspect of financial performance is profitability. One indicator of profitability is **net profit margin**, also known as **profit margin** and **return on sales**, which is calculated as net income divided by revenue (or sales).[39]

$$\text{Net profit margin} = \frac{\text{Net income}}{\text{Revenue}}$$

Net profit margin measures the amount of income that a company was able to generate for each dollar of revenue. A higher level of net profit margin indicates higher profitability and is thus more desirable. Net profit margin can also be found directly on the common-size income statements.

For Kraft Foods, net profit margin for 2004 was 8.3 percent (calculated as earnings from continuing operations of $2,669 million, divided by net revenues of $32,168 million). To judge this ratio, some comparison is needed. Kraft's profitability can be compared with that of another company or with its own previous performance. Compared with previous years, Kraft's profitability has declined. In 2003, net profit margin was 11.1 percent, and in 2002, it was 11.3 percent.

Another measure of profitability is the gross profit margin. Gross profit is calculated as revenue minus cost of goods sold, and the **gross profit margin** is calculated as the gross profit divided by revenue.

$$\text{Gross profit margin} = \frac{\text{Gross profit}}{\text{Revenue}}$$

The gross profit margin measures the amount of gross profit that a company generated for each dollar of revenue. A higher level of gross profit margin indicates higher profitability and thus is generally more desirable, although differences in gross profit margins across companies reflect differences in companies' strategies. For example, consider a company pursuing a strategy of selling a differentiated product (e.g., a product differentiated based on brand name, quality, superior technology, or patent protection). The company would likely be able to sell the differentiated product at a higher price than a similar, but undifferentiated, product and, therefore, would likely show a higher gross profit margin than a company selling an undifferentiated product. Although a company selling a differentiated product would likely show a higher gross profit margin, this may take time. In the initial stage of the strategy, the company would likely incur costs to create a differentiated product, such as advertising or research and development, which would not be reflected in the gross margin calculation.

Kraft's gross profit (shown in Exhibit 2) was $11,785 in 2002 and $11,887 in 2004. In other words, in absolute terms, Kraft's gross profit increased. However, expressing gross profit as a percentage of net revenues,[40] it is apparent that Kraft's gross profit margin declined, as Exhibit 15 illustrates. From over 40 percent in 2002, Kraft's profit margin declined to 36.95 percent in 2004.

[39] In the definition of margin ratios of this type, "sales" is often used interchangeably with "revenue." "Return on sales" has also been used to refer to a class of **profitability ratios** having revenue in the denominator.

[40] Some items disclosed separately in Kraft's actual income statement have been summarized as "other operating costs (income)" for this display.

EXHIBIT 15 Kraft's Gross Profit Margin

	2004		2003		2002	
	$ millions	**%**	**$ millions**	**%**	**$ millions**	**%**
Net revenues	32,168	100.00	30,498	100.00	29,248	100.00
Cost of sales	20,281	63.05	18,531	60.76	17,463	59.71
Gross profit	11,887	**36.95**	11,967	**39.24**	11,785	**40.29**

The net profit margin and gross profit margin are just two of the many subtotals that can be generated from common-size income statements. Other "margins" used by analysts include the **operating margin** (operating income divided by revenue) and **pretax margin** (earnings before taxes divided by revenue).

COMPREHENSIVE INCOME 8

The general expression for net income is revenue minus expenses. There are, however, certain items of revenue and expense that, by accounting convention, are excluded from the net income calculation. To understand how reported shareholders' equity of one period links with reported shareholders' equity of the next period, we must understand these excluded items, known as **other comprehensive income.**

Comprehensive income is defined as "the change in equity [net assets] of a business enterprise during a period from transactions and other events and circumstances from nonowner sources. It includes all changes in equity during a period except those resulting from investments by owners and distributions to owners."[41] So, comprehensive income includes *both* net income and other revenue and expense items that are excluded from the net income calculation (other comprehensive income). Assume, for example, a company's beginning shareholders' equity is €110 million, its net income for the year is €10 million, its cash dividends for the year are €2 million, and there was no issuance or repurchase of common stock. If the company's actual ending shareholders' equity is €123 million, then €5 million [€123 − (€110 + €10 − €2)] has bypassed the net income calculation by being classified as other comprehensive income. (If the company had no other comprehensive income, its ending shareholders' equity would have been €118 million [€110 + €10 − €2].)

In U.S. financial statements, according to U.S. GAAP, four types of items are treated as other comprehensive income.

- Foreign currency translation adjustments. In consolidating the financial statements of foreign subsidiaries, the effects of translating the subsidiaries' balance sheet assets and liabilities at current exchange rates are included as other comprehensive income.

[41] See SFAS No. 130, Concepts Statement 6, paragraph 70.

- Minimum pension liability adjustments. Accounting for pensions involves numerous mechanisms designed to smooth the effects of market volatility on the value of plan assets as well as numerous assumptions; consequently, over time, the company's pension obligation that would be calculated on a market valuation basis will probably diverge from the amount recorded on its balance sheet. When this divergence becomes too large (as defined by various criteria), the company adjusts the liability on its balance sheet and commensurately reflects the adjustment (decrease or increase) as part of other comprehensive income.
- Unrealized gains or losses on derivatives contracts accounted for as hedges. Changes in the fair value of derivatives are recorded each period, but these changes in value for certain derivatives (those considered hedges) are treated as other comprehensive income and thus bypass the income statement.
- Unrealized holding gains and losses on a certain category of investment securities, namely, available-for-sale securities.

The last type of item is perhaps the simplest to illustrate. Holding gains on securities arise when a company owns securities over an accounting period, during which time the securities' value increases. Similarly, holding losses on securities arise when a company owns securities over a period during which time the securities' value decreases. If the company has not sold the securities (i.e., realized the gain or loss), its holding gain or loss is said to be unrealized. The question is: Should the company reflect these unrealized holding gains and losses in its income statement?

According to accounting standards, the answer depends on how the company has categorized the securities. Categorization depends on what the company intends to do with the securities. If the company intends to actively trade the securities, the answer is yes; the company should categorize the securities as **trading securities** and reflect unrealized holding gains and losses in its income statement. However, if the company does not intend to actively trade the securities, the securities may be categorized as **available-for-sale securities**. For available-for-sale securities, the company does not reflect unrealized holding gains and losses in its income statement. Instead, unrealized holding gains and losses on available-for-sale securities bypass the income statement and go directly to shareholders' equity.

Even though unrealized holding gains and losses on available-for-sale securities are excluded from a company's net income, they are *included* in a company's comprehensive income.

SFAS No. 130 allows companies to report comprehensive income at the bottom of the income statement, on a separate statement of comprehensive income, or as a column in the statement of shareholders' equity; however, presentation alternatives are currently being reviewed by both U.S. and non-U.S. standard setters.

Particularly in comparing financial statements of two companies, it is relevant to examine significant differences in comprehensive income.

EXAMPLE 21

Other Comprehensive Income

Assume a company's beginning shareholders' equity is €200 million, its net income for the year is €20 million, its cash dividends for the year are €3 million, and there was no issuance or repurchase of common stock. The company's actual ending shareholders' equity is €227 million.

1. What amount has bypassed the net income calculation by being classified as other comprehensive income?
   - **A.** €0.
   - **B.** €7 million.
   - **C.** €10 million.
   - **D.** €30 million.
2. Which of the following statements best describes other comprehensive income?
   - **A.** Income earned from diverse geographic and segment activities.
   - **B.** Income earned from activities that are not part of the company's ordinary business activities.
   - **C.** Income related to the sale of goods and delivery of services.
   - **D.** Income that increases stockholders' equity but is not reflected as part of net income.

Solution to 1: C is correct. If the company's actual ending shareholders' equity is €227 million, then €10 million [€227− (€200 + €20 − €3)] has bypassed the net income calculation by being classified as other comprehensive income.

Solution to 2: D is correct. Answers A and B are not correct because they do not specify whether such income is reported as part of net income and shown in the income statement. Answer C is not correct because such activities would typically be reported as part of net income on the income statement.

EXAMPLE 22

Other Comprehensive Income in Analysis

An analyst is looking at two comparable companies. Company A has a lower **price/earnings (P/E) ratio** than Company B, and the conclusion that has been suggested is that Company A is undervalued. As part of examining this conclusion, the analyst decides to explore the question: What would the company's P/E look like if total comprehensive income per share—rather than net income per share—were used as the relevant metric?

	Company A	Company B
Price	$35	$30
EPS	$1.60	$0.90
P/E ratio	21.9×	33.3×
Other comprehensive income (loss) $ million	$(16.272)	$(1.757)
Shares (millions)	22.6	25.1

Solution: As shown by the following table, part of the explanation for Company A's lower P/E ratio may be that its significant losses—accounted for as other comprehensive income (OCI)—are not included in the P/E ratio.

	Company A	Company B
Price	$35	$30
EPS	$1.60	$0.90
OCI (loss) $ million	($16.272)	$(1.757)
Shares (millions)	22.6	25.1
OCI (loss) per share	$(0.72)	$(0.07)
Comprehensive EPS = EPS + OCI per share	$0.88	$0.83
Price/Comprehensive EPS ratio	39.8×	36.1×

SUMMARY

This reading has presented the elements of income statement analysis. The income statement presents information on the financial results of a company's business activities over a period of time; it communicates how much revenue the company generated during a period and what costs it incurred in connection with generating that revenue. A company's net income and its components (e.g., gross margin, operating earnings, and pretax earnings) are critical inputs into both the equity and credit analysis processes. Equity analysts are interested in earnings because equity markets often reward relatively high- or low-earnings growth companies with above-average or below-average valuations, respectively. Fixed-income analysts examine the components of income statements, past and projected, for information on companies' abilities to make promised payments on their debt over the course of the business cycle. Corporate financial announcements frequently emphasize income statements more than the other financial statements. Key points to this reading include the following:

- The income statement presents revenue, expenses, and net income.
- The components of the income statement include: revenue; cost of sales; sales, general, and administrative expenses; other operating expenses; non-operating income and expenses; gains and losses; nonrecurring items; net income; and EPS.
- An income statement that presents a subtotal for gross profit (revenue minus cost of goods sold) is said to be presented in a multi-step format. One that does not present this subtotal is said to be presented in a single-step format.
- Revenue is recognized in the period it is earned, which may or may not be in the same period as the related cash collection. Recognition of revenue when earned is a fundamental principle of accrual accounting.
- In limited circumstances, specific revenue recognition methods may be applicable, including percentage of completion, completed contract, installment sales, and cost recovery.
- An analyst should identify differences in companies' revenue recognition methods and adjust reported revenue where possible to facilitate comparability. Where the available information does not permit adjustment, an analyst can characterize the revenue recognition as more or less conservative and thus qualitatively assess how differences in policies might affect financial ratios and judgments about profitability.
- The general principles of expense recognition include the matching principle. Expenses are matched either to revenue or to the time period in which the expenditure occurs (period costs) or to the time period of expected benefits of the expenditures (e.g., depreciation).
- In expense recognition, choice of method (i.e., depreciation method and inventory cost method), as well as estimates (i.e., uncollectible accounts, warranty expenses, assets' useful life, and salvage value) affect a company's reported income. An analyst should identify differences in companies' expense recognition methods and adjust reported financial statements where possible to facilitate comparability. Where the available information does not permit adjustment, an analyst can characterize the policies and estimates as more or less conservative and thus qualitatively assess how differences in policies might affect financial ratios and judgments about companies' performance.

- To assess a company's future earnings, it is helpful to separate those prior years' items of income and expense that are likely to continue in the future from those items that are less likely to continue.
- Some items from prior years clearly are not expected to continue in future periods and are separately disclosed on a company's income statement. Two such items are (1) discontinued operations and (2) extraordinary items. Both of these items are required to be reported separately from continuing operations.
- For other items on a company's income statement, such as unusual items and accounting changes, the likelihood of their continuing in the future is somewhat less clear and requires the analyst to make some judgments.
- Nonoperating items are reported separately from operating items. For example, if a nonfinancial service company invests in equity or debt securities issued by another company, any interest, dividends, or profits from sales of these securities will be shown as nonoperating income.
- Basic EPS is the amount of income available to common shareholders divided by the weighted average number of common shares outstanding over a period. The amount of income available to common shareholders is the amount of net income remaining after preferred dividends (if any) have been paid.
- If a company has a simple capital structure (i.e., one with no potentially dilutive securities), then its basic EPS is equal to its diluted EPS. If, however, a company has dilutive securities, its diluted EPS is lower than its basic EPS.
- Diluted EPS is calculated using the if-converted method for convertible securities and the treasury stock method for options.
- Common-size analysis of the income statement involves stating each line item on the income statement as a percentage of sales. Common-size statements facilitate comparison across time periods and across companies of different sizes.
- Two income-statement-based indicators of profitability are net profit margin and gross profit margin.
- Comprehensive income includes *both* net income and other revenue and expense items that are excluded from the net income calculation.

PRACTICE PROBLEMS FOR READING 32

1. Expenses on the income statement may be grouped by

A. nature, but not by function.

B. function, but not by nature.

C. either function or nature.

D. neither function nor nature.

2. An example of an expense classification by function is

A. tax expense.

B. interest expense.

C. depreciation.

D. cost of goods sold.

3. Denali Limited, a manufacturing company, had the following income statement information:

Revenue	$4,000,000
Cost of goods sold	$3,000,000
Other operating expenses	$ 500,000
Interest expense	$ 100,000
Tax expense	$ 120,000

Denali's gross profit is equal to

A. $280,000.

B. $400,000.

C. $500,000.

D. $1,000,000.

4. Under IFRS, income includes increases in economic benefits from

A. increases in owners' equity related to owners' contributions.

B. decreases in assets not related to owners' contributions.

C. increases in liabilities not related to owners' contributions.

D. enhancements of assets not related to owners' contributions.

5. Fairplay had the following information related to the sale of its products during 2006, which was its first year of business:

Revenue	$1,000,000
Returns of goods sold	$ 100,000
Cash collected	$ 800,000
Cost of goods sold	$ 700,000

Under the accrual basis of accounting, how much net revenue would be reported on Fairplay's 2006 income statement?

A. $200,000.

B. $800,000.

C. $900,000.

D. $1,000,000.

6. If the outcome of a long-term contract can be measured reliably, the preferred accounting method under both IFRS and U.S. GAAP is
   A. the installment method.
   B. the cost recovery method.
   C. the completed contract method.
   D. the percentage-of-completion method.
7. At the beginning of 2006, Florida Road Construction entered into a contract to build a road for the government. Construction will take four years. The following information as of 31 December 2006 is available for the contract:

Total revenue according to contract	$10,000,000
Total expected cost	$ 8,000,000
Cost incurred during 2006	$ 1,200,000

   Under the completed contract method, how much revenue will be reported in 2006?
   A. None.
   B. $300,000.
   C. $1,500,000.
   D. $10,000,000.
8. During 2006, Argo Company sold 10 acres of prime commercial zoned land to a builder for $5,000,000. The builder gave Argo a $1,000,000 down payment and will pay the remaining balance of $4,000,000 to Argo in 2007. Argo purchased the land in 1999 for $2,000,000. Using the installment method, how much profit will Argo report for 2006?
   A. None.
   B. $600,000.
   C. $1,000,000.
   D. $3,000,000.
9. Using the same information as in Question 8, how much profit will Argo report for 2006 by using the cost recovery method?
   A. None.
   B. $600,000.
   C. $1,000,000.
   D. $3,000,000.
10. Under IFRS, revenue from barter transactions should be measured based on the fair value of revenue from
   A. similar barter transactions with related parties.
   B. similar barter transactions with unrelated parties.
   C. similar nonbarter transactions with related parties.
   D. similar nonbarter transactions with unrelated parties.

11. Apex Consignment sells items over the internet for individuals on a consignment basis. Apex receives the items from the owner, lists them for sale on the internet, and receives a 25 percent commission for any items sold. Apex collects the full amount from the buyer and pays the net amount after commission to the owner. Unsold items are returned to the owner after 90 days. During 2006, Apex had the following information:

- Total sales price of items sold during 2006 on consignment was €2,000,000.
- Total commissions retained by Apex during 2006 for these items was €500,000.

How much revenue should Apex report on its 2006 income statement?

A. None.
B. €500,000.
C. €2,000,000.
D. €1,500,000.

12. During 2007, Accent Toys Plc., which began business in October of that year, purchased 10,000 units of its most popular toy at a cost of £10 per unit in October. In anticipation of heavy December sales, Accent purchased 5,000 additional units in November at a cost of £11 per unit. During 2007, Accent sold 12,000 units at a price of £15 per unit. Under the First In, First Out (FIFO) method, what is Accent's cost of goods sold for 2007?

A. £105,000.
B. £120,000.
C. £122,000.
D. £124,000.

13. Using the same information as in Question 12, what would Accent's cost of goods sold be under the weighted average cost method?

A. £105,000.
B. £120,000.
C. £122,000.
D. £124,000.

14. Which inventory method is least likely to be used under IFRS?

A. First In, First Out (FIFO).
B. Last In, First Out (LIFO).
C. Weighted average.
D. Specific identification.

15. At the beginning of 2007, Glass Manufacturing purchased a new machine for its assembly line at a cost of $600,000. The machine has an estimated useful life of 10 years and estimated residual value of $50,000. Under the straight-line method, how much depreciation would Glass take in 2008 for financial reporting purposes?

A. None.
B. $55,000.
C. $60,000.
D. $65,000.

16. Using the same information as in Question 15, how much depreciation would Glass take in 2007 for financial reporting purposes under the double-declining balance method?

A. $60,000.

B. $110,000.

C. $120,000.

D. $550,000.

17. Which combination of depreciation methods and useful lives is most conservative in the year a depreciable asset is acquired?

A. Straight-line depreciation with a long useful life.

B. Straight-line depreciation with a short useful life.

C. Declining balance depreciation with a long useful life.

D. Declining balance depreciation with a short useful life.

18. Under IFRS, a loss from the destruction of property in a fire would most likely be classified as

A. continuing operations.

B. an extraordinary item.

C. discontinued operations.

D. a prior period adjustment.

19. For 2007, Flamingo Products had net income of $1,000,000. At 1 January 2007, there were 1,000,000 shares outstanding. On 1 July 2007, the company issued 100,000 new shares for $20 per share. The company paid $200,000 in dividends to common shareholders. What is Flamingo's basic earnings per share for 2007?

A. $0.73.

B. $0.80.

C. $0.91.

D. $0.95.

20. Cell Services (CSI) had 1,000,000 average shares outstanding during all of 2007. During 2007, CSI also had 10,000 options outstanding with exercise prices of $10 each. The average stock price of CSI during 2007 was $15. For purposes of computing diluted earnings per share, how many shares would be used in the denominator?

A. 1,000,000.

B. 1,003,333.

C. 1,006,667.

D. 1,010,000.

UNDERSTANDING THE BALANCE SHEET

by Thomas R. Robinson, Hennie van Greuning, Elaine Henry, and Michael A. Broihahn

READING 33

LEARNING OUTCOMES

The candidate should be able to:

a. illustrate and interpret the components of the assets, liabilities, and equity sections of the balance sheet, and discuss the uses of the balance sheet in financial analysis;

b. describe the various formats of balance sheet presentation;

c. explain how assets and liabilities arise from the accrual process;

d. compare and contrast current and noncurrent assets and liabilities;

e. explain the measurement bases (e.g., historical cost and fair value) of assets and liabilities, including current assets, current liabilities, tangible assets, and intangible assets;

f. discuss off-balance sheet disclosures;

g. demonstrate the appropriate classifications and related accounting treatments for marketable and non-marketable financial instruments held as assets or owed by the company as liabilities;

h. list and explain the components of owners' equity;

i. interpret balance sheets, common-size balance sheets, the statement of changes in equity, and commonly used balance sheet ratios.

THEME

The balance sheet presents the financial position of a company at a point in time. The information in a balance sheet allows the financial analyst to better assess a company's ability to meet debt obligations, generate future cash flows, and make distributions to owners. However, the balance sheet has limitations, especially as it relates to the measurement of assets and liabilities. The analyst must understand the measurement of assets and liabilities and the structure of the balance sheet in order to accurately assess the financial position of a company.

1 INTRODUCTION

The starting place for analyzing a company's financial position is typically the balance sheet. Creditors, investors, and analysts recognize the value of the balance sheet and also its limitations. The balance sheet provides such users with information on a company's resources (assets) and its sources of capital (its equity and liabilities/debt). It normally also provides information about the future earnings capacity of a company's assets as well as an indication of cash flows that may come from receivables and inventories.

However, the balance sheet does have limitations, especially relating to how assets and liabilities are measured. Liabilities and, sometimes, assets may not be recognized in a timely manner. Furthermore, the use of historical costs rather than fair values to measure some items on the balance sheet means that the financial analyst may need to make adjustments to determine the real (economic) net worth of the company. By understanding how a balance sheet is constructed and how it may be analyzed, the reader should be able to make appropriate use of it.

This reading is organized as follows. In Section 2, we describe and illustrate the format, structure, and components of the balance sheet. Section 3 discusses the measurement bases for assets and liabilities. Section 4 describes the components of equity and illustrates the statement of changes in shareholders' equity. Section 5 introduces balance sheet analysis. A summary of the key points and practice problems in the CFA Institute mulitple-choice format conclude the reading.

2 COMPONENTS AND FORMAT OF THE BALANCE SHEET

The **balance sheet** discloses what an entity owns and what it owes at a specific point in time; thus, it is also referred to as the **statement of financial position.**[1]

The financial position of an entity is described in terms of its assets, liabilities, and equity:

- **Assets (A)** are resources controlled by the company as a result of past events and from which future economic benefits are expected to flow to the entity.
- **Liabilities (L)** represent obligations of a company arising from past events, the settlement of which is expected to result in an outflow of economic benefits from the entity.
- **Equity (E)** Commonly known as **shareholders' equity** or **owners' equity**, equity is determined by subtracting the liabilities from the assets of a company, giving rise to the accounting equation: **A = L + E** or **A − L = E.** Equity can be viewed as a residual or balancing amount, taking assets and liabilities into account.

[1] The balance sheet is also known as the **statement of financial condition**.

Assets and liabilities arise as a result of business transactions (e.g., the purchase of a building or issuing a bond.) The accounting equation is useful in assessing the impact of transactions on the balance sheet. For example, if a company borrows money in exchange for a note payable, assets and liabilities increase by the same amount. Assets and liabilities also arise from the accrual process. As noted in earlier readings, the income statement reflects revenue and expenses reported on an accrual basis regardless of the period in which cash is received and paid. Differences between accrued revenue and expenses and cash flows will result in assets and liabilities. Specifically:

- Revenue reported on the income statement before cash is received; this results in accrued revenue or accounts receivable, which is an asset. This is ultimately reflected on the balance sheet as an increase in accounts receivable and an increase in retained earnings.
- Cash received before revenue is to be reported on the income statement; this results in a deferred revenue or unearned revenue, which is a liability. For example, if a company pays in advance for delivery of custom equipment, the balance sheet reflects an increase in cash and an increase in liabilities.
- Expense reported on the income statement before cash is paid; this results in an accrued expense, which is a liability. This is reflected on the balance sheet as an increase in liabilities and a decrease in retained earnings.
- Cash paid before an expense is to be reported on the income statement; this results in a deferred expense, also known as a "prepaid expense," which is an asset. On the balance sheet, cash is reduced and prepaid assets are increased.

Exhibit 1 illustrates what an unformatted balance sheet might look like, providing examples of a selection of assets and liabilities. The account "trade creditors" (also known as "accounts payable") arises when goods are purchased on credit and received into inventory before their purchase price is paid in cash. Because an expense is recognized before cash is paid, it is an example of the type of accrual described in the third bullet point.

EXHIBIT 1 Listing of Assets, Liabilities, and Owners' Equity Funds

Element	20X7	20X6	Financial Statement Element	Equation
Inventory	€20,000	€16,000	Asset	+ A
Property, plant, and equipment	53,000	27,000	Asset	
Subtotal	**73,000**	**43,000**		
Trade creditors	(14,000)	(7,000)	Liability	– L
Bond repayable in 5 years' time	(37,000)	(16,000)	Liability	
Owners' equity	**€22,000**	**€20,000**	**Equity** (balancing amount)	= E

2.1 Structure and Components of the Balance Sheet

As noted above, the balance sheet presents the financial position of a company. The financial position shows the relative amounts of assets, liabilities, and equity held by the enterprise at a particular point in time.

2.1.1 Assets

Assets are generated either through purchase (investing activities), or generated through business activities (operating activities), or financing activities, such as issuance of debt.

Through the analysis of the liabilities and equity of an entity, the analyst is able to determine *how* assets are acquired or funded. Funding for the purchase may come from shareholders (financing activities) or from creditors (either through direct financing activities, or indirectly through the surplus generated through operating activities that may be funded by current liabilities/trade finance).

Reading 31, on financial reporting standards, defined **assets** as "resources controlled by the enterprise as a result of past events and from which future economic benefits are expected to flow to the enterprise." This formal definition of an asset tells us that its essence lies in its capability to generate future benefits, which, therefore, alerts the reader of the financial statements about the future earnings capability of the entity's assets. A simpler definition of an asset is that it is a store of wealth (such as cash, marketable securities, and property).

Turning back to the official definition of assets, we note that financial statement elements (such as assets) should only be recognized in the financial statements if:

- it is probable that any future economic benefit associated with the item will flow to the entity; and
- the item has a cost or value that can be *measured* with reliability (this aspect will be discussed more fully in Section 3 of this reading).

Values that are typically included in assets will include amounts that have been spent but which have not been recorded as an expense on the income statement (as in the case of inventories) because of the matching principle, or amounts that have been reported as earned on an income statement but which have not been received (as in the case of accounts receivable).

Exhibit 1 included inventories as well as property, plant, and equipment as examples of assets. Exhibit 2 provides a more complete list of assets that may be found on the face of the balance sheet.

EXHIBIT 2 Typical Assets Disclosed on the Balance Sheet

Cash and cash equivalents
Inventories
Trade and other receivables
Prepaid expenses
Financial assets
Deferred tax assets
Property, plant, and equipment
Investment property
Intangible assets — eg: Goodwill
Investments accounted for using the equity method
Natural resource assets
Assets held for sale

2.1.2 Liabilities

Liabilities (and equity capital) represent the ways in which the funds were raised to acquire the assets. **Liabilities** are technically defined as probable future sacrifices of economic benefits arising from present obligations of an entity to transfer assets or provide services to other entities in the future as a result of past transactions or events. Alternatively, a liability can be described as:

- Amounts received but which have not been reported as revenues or income on an income statement and/or will have to be repaid (e.g., notes payable).
- Amounts that have been reported as expenses on an income statement but which have not been paid (e.g., accounts payable, accruals, and taxes payable).

Exhibit 1 included trade creditors as well as a long-term bond payable as examples of liabilities. Exhibit 3 provides a more complete list of liabilities that may be found on the face of the balance sheet.

EXHIBIT 3 Typical Liabilities Disclosed on the Balance Sheet

Bank borrowings/notes payable
Trade and other payables
Provisions
Unearned revenues
Financial liabilities
Accrued liabilities
Deferred tax liabilities

2.1.3 Equity

Equity represents the portion belonging to the owners or shareholders of a business. **Equity** is the residual interest in the assets of an entity after deducting its liabilities, also referred to as **net asset value**:

Equity = Assets − Liabilities

Equity is increased by contributions by the owners or by profits (including gains) made during the year and is decreased by losses or withdrawals in the form of dividends.

Almost every aspect of a company is either directly or indirectly influenced by the availability and/or the cost of equity capital. The adequacy of equity capital is one of the key factors to be considered when the safety and soundness of a particular company is assessed. An adequate equity base serves as a safety net for a variety of risks to which any entity is exposed in the course of its business. Equity capital provides a cushion to absorb possible losses and thus provides a basis for maintaining creditor confidence in a company. Equity capital also is the ultimate determinant of a company's borrowing capacity. In practice, a company's balance sheet cannot be expanded beyond a level determined by its equity capital without increasing the risk of financial distress to an unacceptable level; the availability of equity capital consequently determines the maximum level of assets.

The cost and amount of capital affect a company's competitive position. Because shareholders expect a return on their equity, the obligation to earn such a return impacts the pricing of company products. There is also another important aspect to the level of capital, namely, the perspective of the market. The issuance of debt requires public confidence in a company, which, in turn, can best be established and maintained by an equity capital buffer. If a company faces a shortage of equity capital or if the cost of capital is high, a company stands to lose business to its competitors.

The key purposes of equity capital are to provide stability and to absorb losses, thereby providing a measure of protection to creditors in the event of liquidation. As such, the capital of a company should have three important characteristics:

- It should be permanent.
- It should not impose mandatory fixed charges against earnings (in the case of banks).
- It should allow for legal subordination to the rights of creditors.

Exhibit 4 provides a list of equity information that is disclosed on the balance sheet.

EXHIBIT 4 Typical Equity Information Disclosed on the Balance Sheet

Minority interest, presented within equity
Issued capital and paid-in capital attributable to equityholders of the parent
Earnings retained in the company
Parent shareholders' equity

Information that is usually disclosed for each class of equity on the face of the balance sheet or in notes to the financial statements includes:

- Number of shares authorized
- Number of shares issued and fully paid
- Number of shares issued and not fully paid
- Par (or stated) value per share, or a statement that it has no par (stated) value
- Reconciliation of shares at beginning and end of reporting period
- Rights, preferences, and restrictions attached to that class
- Shares in the entity held by entity, subsidiaries, or associates
- Shares reserved for issue under options and sales contracts

The total amount of equity capital is of fundamental importance. Also important is the nature of the company ownership—the identity of those owners who can directly influence the company's strategic direction and risk management policies. This is particularly critical for financial institutions, such as banks. For example, a bank's ownership structure must ensure the integrity of its capital, and owners must be able to supply more capital if and when needed.

2.2 Format of the Balance Sheet

As the balance sheet provides information about the financial position of the company, it should distinguish between major categories and classifications of assets and liabilities.

Detail and formats of balance sheets vary from company to company. The basic information contained in balance sheets is the same though, regardless of the format. When using the **report format**, assets, liabilities, and equity are listed in a single column. The **account format** follows the pattern of the traditional general ledger accounts, with assets at the left and liabilities and equity at the right of a central dividing line. The report format is most commonly preferred and used by financial statement preparers.

If a company were to have many assets and liabilities, the balance sheet might become quite difficult to read. Grouping together the various classes of assets and liabilities, therefore, results in a balance sheet format described as a **classified balance sheet**.

"Classification," in this case, is the term used to describe the grouping of accounts into subcategories—it helps readers to gain a quick perspective of the company's financial position. Classification assists in drawing attention to specific amounts and also to groups of accounts.

Classifications most often distinguish between current and noncurrent assets/liabilities, or by financial and nonfinancial categories—all in order to provide information related to the liquidity of such assets or liabilities (albeit indirectly in many cases).

2.2.1 Current and Noncurrent Distinction

The balance sheet should distinguish between current and noncurrent assets and between current and noncurrent liabilities unless a presentation based on liquidity provides more relevant and reliable information (e.g., in the case of a bank or similar financial institution).

From Exhibit 5, it should be clear that in essence, the current/noncurrent distinction is also an attempt at incorporating liquidity expectations into the structure of the balance sheet. Assets expected to be liquidated or used up within one year or one operating cycle of the business, whichever is greater, are classified as current assets. A company's operating cycle is the amount of time that elapses between spending cash for inventory and supplies and collecting the cash from its sales to customers. Assets not expected to be liquidated or used up within one year or **one operating cycle** of the business, whichever is greater, are classified as noncurrent (long-term) assets.

The excess of current assets over current liabilities is called **working capital**. The level of working capital tells analysts about the ability of an entity to meet liabilities as they fall due. Yet, working capital should not be too large because funds could be tied up that could be used more productively elsewhere.

EXHIBIT 5 Balance Sheet: Current versus Noncurrent Distinction

Apex Corporation	20X7	20X6
Assets		
Current assets	€20,000	€16,000
Noncurrent assets	53,000	27,000
Total assets	**€73,000**	**€43,000**
Liabilities and equity		
Current liabilities	14,000	7,000
Noncurrent liabilities	37,000	16,000
Total liabilities	**51,000**	**23,000**
Equity	**22,000**	**20,000**
Total liabilities and equity	**€73,000**	**€43,000**

Some **current assets** are allocated to expenses immediately (e.g., inventory) when sales or cash transactions take place, whereas noncurrent assets are allocated over the useful lives of such assets. Current assets are maintained for operating purposes and represent cash or items expected to be converted into cash or used up (e.g., prepaid expenses) in the current period. Current assets, therefore, tell us more about the operating activities and the operating capability of the entity.

Noncurrent assets represent the infrastructure from which the entity operates and are not consumed or disposed in the current period. Such assets represent potentially less-liquid investments made from a strategic or longer-term perspective (e.g., to secure trading advantages, supply lines, or other synergies, such as equity securities held, investments in associates, or investments in subsidiaries).

A **current liability** is a liability that satisfies any of the following criteria:

- It is expected to be settled in the entity's normal operating cycle.
- It is held primarily for the purpose of being traded.
- It is due to be settled within one year after the balance sheet date.
- The entity does not have an unconditional right to defer settlement of the liability for at least one year after the balance sheet date.

Financial liabilities are classified as current if they are due to be settled within one year after the balance sheet date, even if the original term was for a period longer than one year. All other liabilities are classified as **noncurrent**.

International Accounting Standard (IAS) No. 1 specifies that some current liabilities, such as trade payables and some accruals for employee and other operating costs, are part of the working capital used in the entity's normal operating cycle. Such operating items are classified as current liabilities even if they will be settled more than one year after the balance sheet date. When the entity's normal operating cycle is not clearly identifiable, its duration is assumed to be one year.

Noncurrent liabilities include financial liabilities that provide financing on a long-term basis, and they are, therefore, not part of the working capital used in the entity's normal operating cycle; neither are they due for settlement within one year after the balance sheet date.

2.2.2 *Liquidity-Based Presentation*

Paragraph 51 of IAS No. 1 requires the use of the current/noncurrent format of presentation for the balance sheet, except when a presentation based on liquidity provides information that is reliable and is more relevant. When that exception applies, all assets and liabilities shall be presented broadly in order of liquidity.

Entities such as banks are clearly candidates for such a liquidity-based presentation in their balance sheets. Exhibit 6 shows how the asset side of a bank's balance sheet could be ordered using a liquidity-based presentation.

EXHIBIT 6 Bank Balance Sheet: Asset Side Order Using a Liquidity-Based Presentation

Assets

1. Cash and balances with the central bank
2. Trading securities
3. Securities held for stable liquidity portfolio purposes
4. Placements with and loans to banks and credit institutions (net of specific provisions)
5. Loans and advances to other customers
6. Investments—long-term interests in other entities
7. Property, plant, and equipment
8. Other assets (prepayments, etc.)
Total Assets

2.2.3 *IFRS and U.S. GAAP Balance Sheet Illustrations*

This section illustrates actual corporate balance sheets prepared under international financial reporting standards (IFRS) and generally accepted accounting principles (GAAP) via examples from Roche Group and Sony Corporation, respectively.

Roche is a leading international healthcare company based in Switzerland and prepares its financial statements in accordance with IFRS. Exhibit 7 presents the comparative balance sheets from the company's annual report for the fiscal years ended 31 December 2005 and 2004.

Roche prepares its balance sheets using the report format. The balance sheet also gives noncurrent assets before current assets and long-term liabilities before current liabilities, following common practice under IFRS. Note also that Roche shows the minority interest for its consolidated subsidiary companies in the shareholders' equity section as required under IFRS. **Minority interest** represents the portion of consolidated subsidiaries owned by others. For example, if a company owns 85 percent of a subsidiary, 100 percent of the subsidiary's assets and liabilities are included in the consolidated balance sheet. Minority interest represents the 15 percent of the net assets of the subsidiary not owned by the parent company.

EXHIBIT 7 Roche Group Consolidated Balance Sheets (CHF millions)

	31 December	
	2005	**2004**
Noncurrent assets		
Property, plant, and equipment	15,097	12,408
Goodwill	6,132	5,532
Intangible assets	6,256	6,340
Investments in associated companies	58	55
Financial long-term assets	2,190	1,227
Other long-term assets	660	484
Deferred income tax assets	1,724	1,144
Post-employment benefit assets	1,622	1,577
Total noncurrent assets	**33,739**	**28,767**
Current assets		
Inventories	5,041	4,614
Accounts receivables	7,698	7,014
Current income tax assets	299	159
Other current assets	1,703	2,007
Receivable from Bayer Group collected on 1 January 2005	—	2,886
Marketable securities	16,657	10,394
Cash and cash equivalents	4,228	2,605
Total current assets	**35,626**	**29,679**
Total assets	**69,365**	**58,446**
Noncurrent liabilities		
Long-term debt	(9,322)	(7,077)
Deferred income tax liabilities	(3,518)	(3,564)
Post-employment benefit liabilities	(2,937)	(2,744)
Provisions	(1,547)	(683)
Other noncurrent liabilities	(806)	(961)
Total noncurrent liabilities	**(18,130)**	**(15,029)**
Current liabilities		
Short-term debt	(348)	(2,013)
Current income tax liabilities	(811)	(947)
Provisions	(833)	(1,223)
Accounts payable	(2,373)	(1,844)

(Exhibit continued on next page . . .)

EXHIBIT 7 **(continued)**

	31 December	
	2005	**2004**
Accrued and other current liabilities	(5,127)	(4,107)
Total current liabilities	**(9,492)**	**(10,134)**
Total liabilities	**(27,622)**	**(25,163)**
Total net assets	**41,743**	**33,283**
Equity		
Capital and reserves attributable to Roche shareholders	34,922	27,998
Equity attributable to minority interests	6,821	5,285
Total equity	**41,743**	**33,283**

Sony Corporation and its consolidated subsidiaries are engaged in the development, design, manufacture, and sale of various kinds of electronic equipment, instruments, and devices for consumer and industrial markets. Sony is also engaged in the development, production, and distribution of recorded music and image-based software. Sony Corporation has prepared a set of consolidated financial statements in accordance with U.S. GAAP. Exhibit 8 presents the comparative balance sheets from the company's U.S. GAAP annual report for the fiscal years ended 31 March 2005 and 2004.

Sony prepares its balance sheets using the report format. Under U.S. GAAP, current assets are presented before long-term assets, and current liabilities are presented before long-term liabilities. The current/long-term presentation rule is applicable for all manufacturing, merchandising, and service companies, although there are some regulated industry exceptions (e.g., utility companies) where the presentation is reversed (similar to the common IFRS practice of presenting long-term assets before current assets and long-term liabilities before current liabilities). Note also that Sony shows the minority interest for its consolidated subsidiary companies in an "in-between" or "mezzanine" section between the liabilities and shareholders' equity sections. This mezzanine presentation for minority interest is common under U.S. GAAP; however, minority interest may also be shown under either liabilities or shareholders' equity. By contrast, under IFRS, a minority interest is presented in the shareholders' equity section. The Financial Accounting Standards Board (FASB) is considering a change to U.S. GAAP to conform their standards to IFRS.

EXHIBIT 8 **Sony Corporation Consolidated Balance Sheets (¥ millions)**

	31 March	
	2005	**2004**
Assets		
Current assets:		
Cash and cash equivalents	779,103	849,211
Time deposits	1,492	4,662

(Exhibit continued on next page . . .)

EXHIBIT 8 (continued)

	31 March	
	2005	2004
Marketable securities	460,202	274,748
Notes and accounts receivable, trade	1,113,071	1,123,863
Allowance for doubtful accounts and sales returns	(87,709)	(112,674)
Inventories	631,349	666,507
Deferred income taxes	141,154	125,532
Prepaid expenses and other current assets	517,509	431,506
Total current assets	3,556,171	3,363,355
Film costs	278,961	256,740
Investments and advances:		
Affiliated companies	252,905	86,253
Securities investments and other	2,492,784	2,426,697
	2,745,689	2,512,950
Property, plant, and equipment:		
Land	182,900	189,785
Buildings	925,796	930,983
Machinery and equipment	2,192,038	2,053,085
Construction in progress	92,611	98,480
Less—Accumulated depreciation	(2,020,946)	(1,907,289)
	1,372,399	1,365,044
Other assets:		
Intangibles, net	187,024	248,010
Goodwill	283,923	277,870
Deferred insurance acquisition costs	374,805	349,194
Deferred income taxes	240,396	203,203
Other	459,732	514,296
	1,545,880	1,592,573
Total assets	9,499,100	9,090,662
Liabilities and Stockholders' Equity		
Current liabilities:		
Short-term borrowings	63,396	91,260
Current portion of long-term debt	166,870	383,757
Notes and accounts payable, trade	806,044	778,773
Accounts payable, other and accrued expenses	746,466	812,175
Accrued income and other taxes	55,651	57,913
Deposits from customers in the banking business	546,718	378,851
Other	424,223	479,486
Total current liabilities	2,809,368	2,982,215

(Exhibit continued on next page . . .)

EXHIBIT 8 (continued)

	31 March	
	2005	**2004**
Long-term liabilities:		
Long-term debt	678,992	777,649
Accrued pension and severance costs	352,402	368,382
Deferred income taxes	72,227	96,193
Future insurance policy benefits and other	2,464,295	2,178,626
Other	227,631	286,737
	3,795,547	3,707,587
Minority interest in consolidated subsidiaries	23,847	22,858
Stockholders' equity:		
Subsidiary tracking stock, no par value—		
Authorized 100,000,000 shares, outstanding 3,072,000 shares	3,917	3,917
Common stock, no par value—		
2004-Authorized 3,500,000,000 shares, outstanding 926,418,280 shares		476,350
2005-Authorized 3,500,000,000 shares, outstanding 997,211,213 shares	617,792	
Additional paid-in capital	1,134,222	992,817
Retained earnings	1,506,082	1,367,060
Accumulated other comprehensive income—		
Unrealized gains on securities	62,669	69,950
Unrealized losses on derivative investments	(2,490)	(600)
Minimum pension liability adjustments	(90,030)	(89,261)
Foreign currency translation adjustments	(355,824)	(430,048)
	(385,675)	(449,959)
Treasury stock, at cost		
Subsidiary tracking stock (2004—0 shares, 2005—32 shares)	(0)	(0)
Common stock (2004—2,468,258 shares, 2005—1,118,984 shares)	(6,000)	(12,183)
	2,870,338	2,378,002
Total liabilities and stockholders' equity	9,499,100	9,090,662

3 MEASUREMENT BASES OF ASSETS AND LIABILITIES

In portraying an asset or liability on the balance sheet, the question arises as to how it should be measured. For example, an asset may have been acquired many years ago at a cost of $1,000,000 but may have a current value of $5,000,000. Should this asset be listed at its historic cost or its current value? On the one hand, historical cost provides a reliable and objectively determined measurement base—there would be no dispute regarding what the asset cost. On the other hand, users of financial statements (e.g., creditors) may prefer to know what the asset could be sold for currently if the company needed to raise cash. Some assets and liabilities can be more objectively valued in the marketplace than others (e.g., when an established market exists in which the asset or liability trades regularly, such as an investment in another publicly traded company). As a result, the balance sheet under current standards is a mixed model: Some assets and liabilities are reported based on historical cost, sometimes with adjustments, whereas other assets and liabilities are measured based upon a current value intended to represent the asset's fair value. Fair value and historical value can be defined as follows.

- **Fair value.** Fair value is the amount at which an asset could be exchanged, or a liability settled, between knowledgeable willing parties in an arm's length transaction. When the asset or liability trades regularly, its fair value is usually readily determinable from its market price (sometimes referred to as **fair market value**).
- **Historical cost.** The historical cost of an asset or liability is its cost or fair value at acquisition, including any costs of acquisition and/or preparation.

In limited circumstances other measurement bases are sometimes used, such as **current cost** (the cost to replace an asset) or **present value** (the present discounted value of future cash flows). The key question for analysts is how the reported measures of assets and liabilities on the balance sheet relate to economic reality and to each other. To answer this question, the analyst needs to understand the accounting policies applied in preparing the balance sheet and the measurement bases used. Analysts may need to make adjustments to balance sheet measures of assets and liabilities in assessing the investment potential or creditworthiness of a company. For example, land is generally reported at historical cost on the balance sheet because this measure is objective and any measure of current value (other than an actual sale) would be very subjective. Through diligent research, an analyst may find companies that own valuable land that is not adequately reflected on the balance sheet.[2]

For all of these reasons, the balance sheet value of total assets should not be accepted as an accurate measure of the total value of a company. The value of a company is a function of many factors, including future cash flows expected to be generated by the company and current market conditions. The balance sheet provides important information about the value of some assets and information about future cash flows but does not represent the value of the company as a whole.

Once individual assets and liabilities are measured, additional decisions may be necessary as to how these measures are reflected on the balance sheet. Accounting standards generally prohibit the offsetting of assets and liabilities other than in limited circumstances. For example, if a building is purchased for $10,000,000 subject to a mortgage of $8,000,000, the building is reported as an asset for $10,000,000 while the mortgage is shown separately as a liability ($8,000,000). It is important that these assets and liabilities be reported separately. Offsetting in the balance sheet, except when offsetting reflects the substance of the transaction or other event, detracts from the ability of users to understand the transactions, events, and conditions that have occurred and to assess the entity's future cash flows. However, disclosing or measuring assets net of valuation allowances (e.g., obsolescence allowances on inventories and doubtful accounts allowances on receivables) is not considered to be offsetting. Offsetting is also permitted in limited circumstances where there are restrictions on the availability of assets (such as with pension plans).

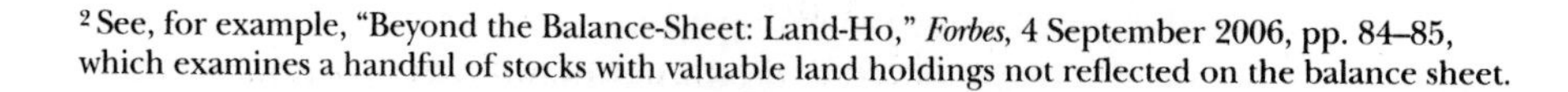

[2] See, for example, "Beyond the Balance-Sheet: Land-Ho," *Forbes*, 4 September 2006, pp. 84–85, which examines a handful of stocks with valuable land holdings not reflected on the balance sheet.

According to IFRS, fair presentation requires the faithful representation on the balance sheet of the effects of transactions, other events, and conditions in accordance with the definitions and recognition criteria for assets, liabilities, income, and expenses set out in the IFRS Framework, as presented in Reading 31 on financial reporting standards. The application of IFRS is presumed to result in fair presentation.

The financial statements should disclose the following information related to the measures used for assets and liabilities shown on the balance sheet:

- accounting policies, including the cost formulas used;
- total carrying amount of inventories and amount per category;
- amount of inventories carried at fair value less costs to sell;
- amount of any write-downs and reversals of any write-down;
- circumstances or events that led to the reversal of a write-down;
- inventories pledged as security for liabilities; and
- amount of inventories recognized as an expense.

The notes to financial statements and management's discussion and analysis are integral parts of the U.S. GAAP and IFRS financial reporting processes. They provide important required detailed disclosures, as well as other information provided voluntarily by management. This information can be invaluable when determining whether the measurement of assets is comparable to other entities being analyzed. The notes include information on such topics as the following:

- specific accounting policies that were used in compiling the financial statements;
- terms of debt agreements;
- lease information;
- off-balance-sheet financing;
- breakdowns of operations by important segments;
- contingent assets and liabilities; and
- detailed pension plan disclosure.

The notes would also provide information in respect of:

Disclosure of accounting policies	▶ Measurement bases used in preparing financial statements. ▶ Each accounting policy used. ▶ Judgments made in applying accounting policies that have the most significant effect on the amounts recognized in the financial statements.
Estimation uncertainty	▶ Key assumptions about the future and other key sources of estimation uncertainty that have a significant risk of causing material adjustment to the carrying amount of assets and liabilities within the next year.
Other disclosures	▶ Description of the entity, including its domicile, legal form, country of incorporation, and registered office or business address. ▶ Nature of operations or principal activities, or both. ▶ Name of parent and ultimate parent.

EXAMPLE 1

Analysis of Off-Balance-Sheet Disclosures

Hewitt Associates (NYSE: HEW) posted the following table on page 43 of its SEC Form 10K for the fiscal year ending 30 September 2005. The table was included in the Management Discussion and Analysis.

Contractual Obligations
(in millions)

		Payments Due in Fiscal Year			
	Total	**2006**	**2007–08**	**2009–10**	**Thereafter**
Operating leases (1)	737	89	149	123	376
Capital leases:					
Principal	80	4	9	11	56
Interest	41	6	11	9	15
Total leases:	121	10	20	20	71
Debt:					
Principal	259	36	50	30	143
Interest	50	12	18	13	7
Total debt:	309	48	68	43	150
Purchase commitments	73	34	37	2	—
Other long-term liabilities	72	8	16	9	39
Total contractual obligations	$1,312	$189	$290	$197	$636

On pages 56–57 of the 10K, Hewitt posted the following balance sheet (abbreviated below). Of the obligations listed above, only the capital leases and other long-term liabilities are included explicitly on the balance sheet.

Hewitt Associates, Inc.
Consolidated Balance Sheets

(dollars in thousands except share and per-share amounts)

	30 September	
	2005	**2004**
Assets		
Current assets:		
Cash and cash equivalents	$ 163,928	$ 129,481
Short-term investments	53,693	183,205
Client receivables and unbilled work in process	595,691	522,882
Refundable income taxes	23,100	—
Prepaid expenses and other current assets	60,662	50,546
Funds held for clients	97,907	14,693
Deferred income taxes, net	5,902	246
Total current assets	1,000,883	901,053
Noncurrent assets:		
Deferred contract costs	253,505	162,602
Property and equipment, net	302,875	236,099
Capitalized software, net	110,997	85,350
Other intangible assets, net	261,999	107,322
Goodwill	694,370	285,743
Other assets, net	32,711	29,805
Total noncurrent assets	1,656,457	906,921
Total assets	2,657,340	1,807,974
Liabilities		
Current liabilities:		
Accounts payable	57,412	20,909
Accrued expenses	156,575	83,226
Funds held for clients	97,907	14,693
Advanced billings to clients	156,257	106,934
Accrued compensation and benefits	141,350	181,812
Short-term debt and current portion of long-term debt	35,915	13,445
Current portion of capital lease obligations	3,989	5,373
Employee deferred compensation and accrued profit sharing	30,136	49,450
Total current liabilities	679,541	475,842
Long-term liabilities:		
Deferred contract revenues	140,474	118,025
Debt, less current portion	222,692	121,253
Capital lease obligations, less current portion	76,477	79,982

(continued on next page . . .)

	30 September	
	2005	**2004**
Other long-term liabilities	127,376	83,063
Deferred income taxes, net	99,423	70,456
Total long-term liabilities	666,442	472,779
Total liabilities	1,345,983	948,621
Commitments and contingencies (Notes 12 and 17)		
Stockholders' Equity		
Total stockholders' equity	1,311,357	859,353
Total liabilities and stockholders' equity	$2,657,340	$1,807,974

Operating leases represent assets used by the company but for which accounting standards do not currently require the assets or related obligations to be reported on the company's balance sheet. Analysts, however, frequently prefer to adjust the balance sheet to determine how it would look if the assets had been purchased and financed. Credit analysts, such as Standard & Poor's, also make this adjustment to better reflect the creditworthiness of the company. Ideally, the analyst would like to know the implied interest rate in the lease agreements and use this to determine the present value of the asset and related liability, because each lease payment effectively has an interest and a principal component. For this initial example, we will use a shortcut method. Assuming operating leases can be segregated into principal and interest components at approximately the same rate as the capital leases, they represent a liability worth nearly $500 million that is not recorded on the balance sheet. The analyst would adjust the balance sheet by adding that amount to fixed assets and liabilities to examine the current economic position. This information would not have been uncovered based solely upon a review of the balance sheet. Important disclosures about assets and liabilities can be found in the footnotes to the financial statements and in management's discussion of the financial statements.

3.1 Current Assets

Current assets are assets expected to be realized or intended for sale or consumption in the entity's normal operating cycle. Typical current assets that appear on the face of the balance sheet include:

- Assets held primarily for trading.
- Assets expected to be realized within 12 months after the balance sheet date.
- Cash or cash equivalents, unless restricted in use for at least 12 months.
- Marketable securities—Debt or equity securities that are owned by a business, traded in a public market, and whose value can be determined from price information in a public market. Examples of marketable securities

include treasury bills, notes, bonds, and equity securities, such as common stocks and mutual fund shares.

- Trade receivables—Amounts owed to a business by its customers for products and services already delivered are included as trade receivables. Allowance has to be made for bad debt expenses, reducing the gross receivables amount.
- Inventories—Physical products on hand such as goods that will eventually be sold to an entity's customers, either in their current form (finished goods) or as inputs into a process to manufacture a final product (raw materials and work-in-process).
- Other current assets—Short-term items not easily classifiable into the above categories (e.g., prepaid expenses).

Exhibit 9 illustrates how the current asset amounts of €20,000 (20X7) and €16,000 (20X6) have been expanded from the one amount shown in Exhibit 5. In the sections below, some of the issues surrounding the measurement principles for inventories and prepaid expenses are discussed.

EXHIBIT 9 Apex Current Assets

	20X7	20X6
Current assets	**€20,000**	**€16,000**
Cash and cash equivalents	3,000	2,000
Marketable securities	3,000	4,000
Trade receivables	5,000	3,000
Inventories	7,000	6,000
Other current assets—prepaid expenses	2,000	1,000

3.1.1 Inventories

Inventories should be measured at the lower of cost or net realizable value. The cost of inventories comprises all costs of purchase, costs of conversion, and other costs incurred in bringing the inventories to their present location and condition. The following amounts should be excluded in the determination of inventory costs:

- abnormal amounts of wasted materials, labor, and overheads;
- storage costs, unless they are necessary prior to a further production process;
- administrative overheads; and
- selling costs.

The net realizable value (NRV) is the estimated selling price less the estimated costs of completion and costs necessary to make the sale.

Accounting standards allow different valuation methods. For example, IAS No. 2 allows only the first-in, first-out (FIFO), weighted average cost (WAC), and specific identification methods. Some accounting standard setters (such as U.S. GAAP) also allow LIFO (last-in, first-out) as an additional inventory valuation method, whereas LIFO is not allowed under IFRS.

The following techniques can be used to measure the cost of inventories if the resulting valuation amount approximates cost:

- **Standard cost**, which should take into account the normal levels of materials, labor, and actual capacity. The standard cost should be reviewed regularly in order to ensure that it approximates actual costs.
- The **retail method** in which the sales value is reduced by the gross margin to calculate cost. An average gross margin percentage should be used for each homogeneous group of items. In addition, the impact of marked-down prices should be taken into consideration.

EXAMPLE 2

Analysis of Inventory

Cisco Systems is the world's leading provider of networking equipment. In its third quarter 2001 Form 10-Q filed with the U.S. Securities and Exchange Commission (U.S. SEC) on 1 June 2001, the company made the following disclosure:

> We recorded a provision for inventory, including purchase commitments, totaling $2.36 billion in the third quarter of fiscal 2001, of which $2.25 billion related to an additional excess inventory charge. Inventory purchases and commitments are based upon future sales forecasts. To mitigate the component supply constraints that have existed in the past, we built inventory levels for certain components with long lead times and entered into certain longer-term commitments for certain components. Due to the sudden and significant decrease in demand for our products, inventory levels exceeded our requirements based on current 12-month sales forecasts. This additional excess inventory charge was calculated based on the inventory levels in excess of 12-month demand for each specific product. We do not currently anticipate that the excess inventory subject to this provision will be used at a later date based on our current 12-month demand forecast.

Even after the inventory charge, Cisco held approximately $2 billion of inventory on the balance sheet, suggesting that the write-off amounted to half its inventory. In addition to the obvious concerns raised as to management's poor performance anticipating how much they would need, many analysts were concerned about how the write-off would affect Cisco's future reported earnings. When this inventory is sold in a future period, a "gain" could be reported based on a lower cost basis for the inventory. In this case, management indicated that the intent was to scrap the inventory. When the company subsequently released its annual earnings, the press release stated:[3]

> Net sales for fiscal 2001 were $22.29 billion, compared with $18.93 billion for fiscal 2000, an increase of 18%. Pro forma net income, which excludes the effects of acquisition charges, payroll tax on stock option exercises, restructuring costs and other special charges, excess inventory charge (benefit), and net gains realized on minority investments, was $3.09 billion or $0.41 per share for fiscal 2001, compared with pro forma net income of $3.91 billion or $0.53 per share for fiscal 2000, decreases of 21% and 23%, respectively.

[3] Cisco Press Release dated 7 August 2001 from www.cisco.com.

Actual net loss for fiscal 2001 was $1.01 billion or $0.14 per share, compared with actual net income of $2.67 billion or $0.36 per share for fiscal 2000.

Note that the company focused on "pro forma earnings" initially, which excluded the impact of many items, including the inventory write-off. The company only gave a brief mention of actual (U.S. GAAP) results.

3.1.2 Prepaid Expenses

Prepaid expenses are normal operating expenses that have been paid in advance. The advance payment creates an asset out of a transaction that would normally have resulted in an expense. Examples might include prepaid rent or prepaid insurance. Prepaid expenses will be expensed in future periods as they are used up. Generally, expenses are reported in the period in which they are incurred as opposed to when they are paid. If a company pays its insurance premium for the next calendar year on 31 December, the expense is not incurred at that date; the expense is incurred as time passes (in this example, 1/12 in each following month).

3.2 Current Liabilities

Current liabilities are those liabilities that are expected to be settled in the entity's normal operating cycle, held primarily for trading and due to be settled within 12 months after the balance sheet date.

Exhibit 10 illustrates how the current liabilities amounts of €14,000 (20X7) and €7,000 (20X6) have been expanded from the one amount shown in Exhibit 5. In the sections below, some of the issues surrounding the measurement principles for payables, accrued liabilities, and unearned revenue are discussed.

Noncurrent interest-bearing liabilities to be settled within 12 months after the balance sheet date can be classified as noncurrent liabilities if:

- the original term of the liability is greater than 12 months;
- it is the intention to refinance or reschedule the obligation; or
- the agreement to refinance or reschedule the obligation is completed on or before the balance sheet date.

EXHIBIT 10 Apex Current Liabilities

	20X7	20X6
Current liabilities	**€14,000**	**€7,000**
Trade and other payables	5,000	2,000
Notes payable	3,000	1,000
Current portion of noncurrent borrowings	2,000	1,000
Current tax payable	2,000	2,000
Accrued liabilities	1,000	500
Unearned revenue	1,000	500

3.2.1 Trade and Other Payables (Accounts Payable)

Accounts payable are amounts that a business owes its vendors for goods and services that were purchased from them but which have not yet been paid.

3.2.2 Notes Payable

Notes payable are amounts owed by a business to creditors as a result of borrowings that are evidenced by a (short-term) loan agreement. Examples of notes payable include bank loans and other current borrowings other than those arising from trade credit. Notes payable may also appear in the long-term liability section of the balance sheet if they are due after one year or the operating cycle, whichever is longer.

3.2.3 Current Portion of Noncurrent Borrowings

By convention, liabilities expected to be repaid or liquidated within one year or one operating cycle of the business, whichever is greater, are classified as current liabilities. Other liabilities are classified as noncurrent. For example, Exhibit 10 shows that €2,000 of Apex's noncurrent borrowings will come due within a year; therefore, the €2,000 constitutes a current liability.

3.2.4 Current Tax Payable

Current taxes payable are tax expenses that have been determined and recorded on a company's income statement but which have not yet been paid.

3.2.5 Accrued Liabilities

Accrued liabilities (also known as **accrued expenses**) are expenses that have been reported on a company's income statement but which have not yet been paid because there is no legal obligation to pay them as of the balance sheet date. Common examples of accrued liabilities are accrued interest payable and accrued wages payable.

3.2.6 Unearned Revenue

Unearned revenue (also known as deferred revenue) is the collection of money in advance of delivery of the goods and services associated with the revenue. Examples include rental income received in advance, advance fees for servicing office equipment, and advance payments for magazine subscriptions received from customers.

3.3 Tangible Assets

Tangible assets are long-term assets with physical substance that are used in company operations. These noncurrent assets are carried at their historical cost less any accumulated depreciation or accumulated depletion. Historical cost generally consists of vendor invoice cost, freight cost, and any other additional costs incurred to

EXAMPLE 3

Analysis of Unearned Revenue

Germany's SAP AG is one of the world's leading providers of business software solutions and one of the world's three largest independent software companies based on market capitalization. At year-end 2005, SAP reported the following assets and liabilities on its balance sheet (in € thousands):[4]

	2005	2004
Assets		
Goodwill	€626,546	€456,707
Other intangible assets	139,697	68,186
Property, plant, and equipment	1,094,965	999,083
Financial assets	534,155	100,382
Fixed assets	2,395,363	1,624,358
Inventories	19,376	11,692
Accounts receivable, net	2,251,027	1,929,100
Other assets	635,554	537,645
Accounts receivable and other assets	2,886,581	2,466,745
Marketable securities	209,565	10,164
Liquid assets	3,213,572	3,196,542
Nonfixed assets	6,329,094	5,685,143
Deferred taxes	250,698	205,601
Prepaid expenses and deferred charges	87,587	70,370
Total assets	€9,062,742	€7,585,472
thereof total current assets	6,241,125	4,849,537
Shareholders' equity and liabilities		
Subscribed capital	316,458	316,004
Treasury stock	(775,318)	(569,166)
Additional paid-in capital	372,767	322,660
Retained earnings	5,986,186	4,830,156
Accumulated other comprehensive loss	(117,855)	(305,401)
Shareholders' equity	5,782,238	4,594,253
Minority interests	7,615	21,971
Pension liabilities and similar obligations	183,619	139,690
Other reserves and accrued liabilities	1,839,140	1,768,723
Reserves and accrued liabilities	2,022,759	1,908,413
Bonds	6,927	7,277
Other liabilities	838,778	728,838

[4] In its annual report, SAP AG chose to provide the subtotal of current assets and current liabilities at the bottom of the respective portions of the balance sheet rather than within the balance sheet to distinguish how much of its nonfixed assets are current. According to Footnote 1 of SAP AG's 2005 annual report: "Non-fixed assets are comprised of Inventories, Accounts receivable, Other assets, Marketable securities, and Liquid assets including amounts to be realized in excess of one year."

	2005	2004
Other liabilities	845,705	736,115
Deferred income	404,425	324,720
Total shareholders' equity and liabilities	€9,062,742	€7,585,472
thereof current liabilities	2,781,685	2,591,872

The final line shows that deferred income rose nearly 25 percent to end 2005 with a value of $404.4 million. SAP describes the line as follows:

> Deferred income consists mainly of prepayments for maintenance and deferred software license revenues. Such amounts will be recognized as software, maintenance, or service revenue, depending upon the reasons for the deferral when the basic criteria in SOP 97-2 have been met (see Note 3).

Although investors prefer to see many liabilities minimized, deferred revenue represents money the company has already been paid for services that will be delivered in the future. Because it will then be recognized as revenue, many investors monitor the deferred income line (when significant) as an indicator of future revenue growth.

make the asset operable. Examples of tangible assets include land, buildings, equipment, machinery, furniture, and natural resources owned by the company, such as copper mines, oil and gas properties, and timberlands. If any of these assets are not used in company operations, they must be classified as investment assets.

3.4 Intangible Assets

Intangible assets are amounts paid by a company to acquire certain rights that are not represented by the possession of physical assets. A distinction can be made between identifiable intangibles and unidentifiable intangibles. An **identifiable intangible** can be acquired singly and is typically linked to specific rights or privileges having finite benefit periods. Examples include patents and trademarks. An **unidentifiable tangible** cannot be acquired singly and typically possesses an indefinite benefit period. An example is accounting goodwill, discussed further in Section 3.4.2.

A company should assess whether the useful life of an intangible asset is finite or infinite and, if finite, the length of its life, or number of production or similar units constituting its useful life. Amortization and impairment principles apply as follows:

- An intangible asset with a finite useful life is amortized on a systematic basis over the best estimate of its useful life.
- An intangible asset with an infinite useful life should be tested for impairment annually but not amortized.

The balance sheet and notes should disclose the gross carrying amount (book value) less accumulated amortization for each class of asset at the beginning and the end of the period.

Companies may also have intangible assets that are not recorded on their balance sheets. These intangible assets might include management skill, valuable trademarks and name recognition, a good reputation, proprietary products, and so forth. Such assets are valuable and would fetch their worth if a company were to be sold.

Financial analysts have traditionally viewed the values assigned to intangible assets, particularly unidentifiable tangibles, with caution. Consequently, in assessing financial statements, they often exclude the book value assigned to intangibles, particularly unidentifiable intangibles, reducing net equity by an equal amount and increasing pretax income by any amortization expense or impairment associated with the intangibles. An arbitrary assignment of zero value to intangibles is not advisable. The analyst should examine each listed intangible and assess whether an adjustment should be made.

3.4.1 Specifically Identifiable Intangibles

Under IFRS, specifically identifiable intangible assets are nonfinancial assets without physical substance but which can be identified. Such assets are recognized on the balance sheet if it is probable that future economic benefits will flow to the company and the cost of the asset can be measured reliably. Examples of identifiable intangible assets include patents, trademarks, copyrights, franchises, and other rights. Identifiable intangible assets may have been created or purchased by a company. Determining the cost of internally created intangible assets can be difficult and subjective. For these reasons, internally created identifiable intangibles are less likely to be reported on the balance sheet under IFRS or U.S. GAAP. IAS No. 38 applies to all intangible assets that are not specifically dealt with in other international accounting standards. This standard determines that the intangible assets reported on a balance sheet are only those intangibles that have been *purchased* or *created* (in strictly limited instances).

IAS No. 38 provides that for internally created intangible assets, the company must identify the research phase and the development phase. The research phase includes activities that seek new knowledge or products. The development phase occurs after the research phase and includes design or testing of prototypes and models. IAS No. 38 prohibits the capitalization of costs as intangible assets during the research phase. Instead, these costs must be expensed on the income statement. Costs incurred in the development stage can be capitalized as intangible assets if certain criteria are met, including technological feasibility, the ability to use or sell the resulting asset, and the ability to complete the project.

All other expenses related to the following categories are **expensed**. They include:

- internally *generated* brands, mastheads, publishing titles, **customer lists**, etc.
- start-up costs
- training costs
- administrative and other general overhead costs
- advertising and promotion
- relocation and reorganization expenses
- redundancy and other termination costs

GAAP
- R+D expensed

U.S. GAAP prohibits the capitalization as an asset of almost all research and development costs. All such costs usually must be expensed. Generally, under U.S. GAAP, acquired intangible assets are reported as separately identifiable intangibles (as opposed to goodwill) if they arise from contractual rights (such as a licensing agreement), other legal rights (such as patents), or have the ability to be separated and sold (such as a customer list).

EXAMPLE 4

Measuring Intangible Assets

Alpha, Inc., a motor vehicle manufacturer, has a research division that worked on the following projects during the year:

Project 1: Research aimed at finding a steering mechanism that does not operate like a conventional steering wheel but reacts to the impulses from a driver's fingers.

Project 2: The design of a prototype welding apparatus that is controlled electronically rather than mechanically, which has been determined to be technologically feasible.

The following is a summary of the expenses of the particular department (in thousands of euro):

	General	Project 1	Project 2
Material and services	€128	€935	€620
Labor			
Direct labor	—	620	320
Administrative personnel	720	—	—
Overhead			
Direct	—	340	410
Indirect	270	110	60

Five percent of administrative personnel costs can be attributed to each of Projects 1 and 2. Explain the capitalization of Alpha's development costs for Projects 1 and 2 under IFRS.

Solution: Under IFRS, the capitalization of development costs for Projects 1 and 2 would be as follows:

Project 1: Classified as research so all costs are recognized as expenses.	NIL
Project 2: (620 + 320 + 410 + 60)	€1,410

Note that Project 2 is in the development stage and costs related to the project should be capitalized under IFRS. However, under IAS No. 38, administrative personnel costs should be expensed.

3.4.2 Goodwill

In a purchase acquisition, the excess of the cost of acquisition over the acquirer's interest in the fair value of the identifiable assets and liabilities acquired is described as goodwill and is recognized as an asset.

The subject of recognizing goodwill in financial statements has found both proponents and opponents among professionals. The proponents of goodwill recognition assert that goodwill is the "present value of excess returns that a company is able to earn." This group claims that determining the present value of these excess returns is analogous to determining the present value of future cash flows associated with other assets and projects. Opponents of goodwill recognition claim that the prices paid for acquisitions often turn out to be based on unrealistic expectations, thereby leading to future write-offs of goodwill.

Analysts should distinguish between accounting goodwill and economic goodwill. Economic goodwill is based on the economic performance of the entity, whereas accounting goodwill is based on accounting standards and only reported for past acquisitions. Economic goodwill is what should concern analysts and investors, and it is often not reflected on the balance sheet. This economic goodwill should be reflected in the stock price. Many analysts believe that goodwill should not be listed on the balance sheet, as it cannot be sold separately from the entity. These analysts believe that only assets that can be separately identified and sold be reflected on the balance sheet. Other financial statement users may desire to analyze goodwill and any subsequent impairment charges to assess management's performance on prior acquisitions.

Under IFRS and U.S. GAAP, goodwill should be capitalized and tested for impairment annually. Goodwill is not amortized. Impairment of goodwill is a noncash expense. If goodwill is deemed to be impaired, it is charged against income in the current period. This charge reduces current earnings. Assets are also reduced, so some performance measures, such as return on assets (net income divided by average total assets), may actually increase in future periods.

Under IFRS No. 3, the purchase method of accounting can be summarized by the following steps:

- The cost of acquisition is determined.
- The fair value of the acquiree's assets is determined.
- The fair value of the acquiree's liabilities and contingent liabilities is determined.
- Calculate the goodwill arising from the purchase as follows:
  - The book value of the acquirer's assets and liabilities should be combined with the fair value adjustments of the acquiree's assets, liabilities, and contingent liabilities.
  - Any goodwill should be recognized as an asset in the combined entity's balance sheet.

Despite the clear guidance incorporated in IFRS No. 3, many analysts believe that the determination of fair values involves considerable management discretion. Values for intangible assets, such as computer software, might not be easily validated when analyzing purchase acquisitions.

Management judgment can be particularly apparent in the allocation of the excess purchase price (after all other allocations to assets and liabilities). If, for example, the remaining excess purchase price is allocated to goodwill, there will be no impact on the company's net income because goodwill is not amortized (but is tested for impairment). If the excess were to be allocated to fixed assets, depreciation would rise, thus reducing net income and producing incorrect financial statements. (**Depreciation** is the allocation of the costs of a long-term [tangible] asset over its useful life.)

Goodwill can significantly affect the comparability of financial statements between companies using different accounting methods. As such, an analyst should remove any distortion that the recognition, amortization, and impairment of goodwill might create by adjusting the company's financial statements. Adjustments should be made by:

- computing financial ratios using balance sheet data that exclude goodwill;
- reviewing operating trends using data that exclude the amortization of goodwill or impairment to goodwill charges; and
- evaluating future business acquisitions by taking into account the purchase price paid relative to the net assets and earnings prospects of the acquired company.

IFRS No. 3 requires disclosure of the factors that contributed to goodwill and a description of each intangible asset that was not recognized separately from goodwill.

EXAMPLE 5

Goodwill Impairment

Vodafone Group, PLC, is a leading international provider of mobile communications services. It entered many of its international markets by acquiring local carriers. On 27 February 2006, Vodafone issued a press release that included the following information:

> Reflecting the increasingly competitive environment in the industry, Vodafone has incorporated into its latest ten year plan a lower view of growth prospects for a number of key operating companies, particularly in the medium to long term, than those it has used previously.
>
> The result of these factors is that Vodafone expects to report:
>
> - An impairment of the Group's goodwill in the range of GBP 23 billion to GBP 28 billion in respect of reductions in the aggregate goodwill for Vodafone Germany, Vodafone Italy and, potentially, Vodafone Japan. It is expected that most of the total will be attributable to Vodafone Germany.
> - No impairment for any other subsidiary, joint venture or investment in associated undertakings.
> - No impairment in respect of finite lived assets.

A summary of the Group's goodwill in respect of subsidiary undertakings and joint ventures as of 30 September 2005 follows.

GBP billion	
Germany	35.5
Italy	19.7
Japan	9.0
Spain	10.3
U.K.	0.7
Other subsidiaries and joint ventures	6.3
	81.5

How significant is this goodwill impairment and, with reference to acquisition prices, what might it indicate?

Solution: Given that the goodwill impairment was approximately equal to one-third the total value of goodwill recorded, it would appear to be significant. According to the press release, the impairment has arisen due to a competitive environment and lower expected growth rates. The operations involved appear now to be worth less than the price that was paid for their acquisition.

3.5 Financial Instruments: Financial Assets and Financial Liabilities

International accounting standards define a financial instrument as a contract that gives rise to a financial asset of one entity, and a financial liability or equity instrument of another entity. Financial instruments, both assets and liabilities, come in a variety of forms. Financial assets include investments in stocks and bonds and similar instruments. Financial liabilities include bonds, notes payable, and similar instruments. Some financial instruments may be classified as either an asset or a liability depending upon the contractual terms and current market conditions. One example of such a complex financial instrument is a derivative. A **derivative** is a financial instrument for which the value is derived based on some underlying factor (interest rate, exchange rate, commodity price, security price, or credit rating) and for which little or no initial investment is required. Derivatives may be used to hedge business transactions or for speculation.

Mark-to-market (fair value adjustments to financial assets and liabilities) is the process whereby the value of most trading assets (e.g., those held for trading and that are available for sale) and trading liabilities are adjusted to reflect current fair value. Such adjustments are often made on a daily basis, and cumulative balances are reversed on the subsequent day, prior to recalculating a fresh cumulative mark-to-market adjustment.

All financial assets and financial liabilities (including derivatives) should be recognized when the entity becomes a party to the contractual provisions of an instrument. For the purchase or sale of financial assets where market convention determines a fixed period between trade and settlement dates, the trade or settlement date can be used for recognition. Interest is not normally accrued between trade and settlement dates, but mark-to-market adjustments are made regardless of whether the entity uses trade date or settlement date accounting. Although IAS No. 39 allows the use of either date, trade date accounting is preferred by most treasury accountants.

Exhibit 11 provides a summary of how various financial assets and liabilities are classified and measured.

From Exhibit 11, marketable securities such as stocks and bonds may be classified as trading, available for sale, and held to maturity. To illustrate the different accounting treatments of the gains and losses on marketable securities, consider an entity that invests €100,000,000 in a 5 percent coupon fixed-income security portfolio. After six months, the company receives the first coupon payment of €2,500,000. Additionally, interest rates have declined and the value of the fixed-income securities has increased by €2,000,000. Exhibit 12 illustrates how this situation will be portrayed in the balance sheet assets and equity, as well as the income statement of the entity concerned, under each of the following three accounting policies for marketable securities: assets held for trading purposes, assets available for sale, and held-to-maturity assets.

EXHIBIT 11 Measurement of Financial Assets and Liabilities

Measured at Fair Value	Measured at Cost or Amortized Cost
Financial Assets	**Financial Assets**
Financial assets held for trading (e.g., stocks and bonds)	Unlisted instruments (investments where the fair value is not reliably measurable)
Available-for-sale financial assets (e.g., stocks and bonds)	Held-to-maturity investments (bonds intended to be held to maturity)
Derivatives whether stand-alone or embedded in nonderivative instruments	Loans and receivables
Nonderivative instruments (including financial assets) with fair value exposures *hedged* by derivatives	
Financial Liabilities	**Financial Liabilities**
Derivatives	All other liabilities (such as bonds payable or notes payable)
Financial liabilities held for trading	
Nonderivative instruments (including financial liabilities) with fair value exposures *hedged* by derivatives	

EXHIBIT 12 Accounting for Gains and Losses on Marketable Securities

Balance Sheet **As of 30 June 200X**	**Trading Portfolio**	**Available-for-Sale Portfolio**	**Held to Maturity**
Assets			
Deposits	2,500,000	2,500,000	2,500,000
Cost of securities	100,000,000	100,000,000	100,000,000
Unrealized gains (losses) on securities	2,000,000	2,000,000	—
	104,500,000	104,500,000	102,500,000
Liabilities			
Equity			
Paid-in capital	100,000,000	100,000,000	100,000,000
Retained earnings	4,500,000	2,500,000	2,500,000
Other comprehensive income (losses)	—	2,000,000	—
	104,500,000	104,500,000	102,500,000

Income Statement **For Period 1 January–30 June 200X**			
Interest income	2,500,000	2,500,000	2,500,000
Unrealized gains (losses)	2,000,000	—	—
	4,500,000	2,500,000	2,500,000

In the case of marketable securities classified as either trading or available for sale, the investments are listed under assets at fair market value. For exposition purposes, Exhibit 12 shows the unrealized gain on a separate line. Practically, the investments would be listed at their fair value of €102,000,000 on one line within assets. In the case of trading securities, the unrealized gain is included on the income statement and thus reflected in retained earnings. In the case of available-for-sale securities, the unrealized gain is not included on the income statement; rather, it is deferred as part of other comprehensive income within owners' equity. As noted in Reading 32, on the income statement, other comprehensive income includes gains and losses that have not yet been reported on the income statement due to particular accounting standards. In the case of **held-to-maturity securities**, the unrealized gain is not reflected on either the balance sheet or income statement.

In the case of liabilities such as bonds issued by a company, these are normally reported at amortized cost on the balance sheet, as noted in Exhibit 11. For example, if a company issues bonds with a total par value of $10,000,000 at a price of $9,750,000 (issued at a discount), the bonds are reported as a liability of $9,750,000 (cost). As time passes, the discount of $250,000 is amortized such that the bond will be listed as a liability of $10,000,000 at maturity. Similarly, any bond premium would be amortized for bonds issued at a premium.

4 EQUITY

Equity is the residual claim on a company's assets after subtracting liabilities. It represents the claim of the owner against the company. Equity includes funds directly invested in the company by the owners, as well as earnings that have been reinvested over time. Equity can also include items of gain or loss that are not yet recognized on the company's income statement.

4.1 Components of Equity

IFRS and U.S. GAAP both define equity (or net assets) as the residual interest in the assets of an entity that remain after deducting its liabilities. There are five potential components that comprise the owners' equity section of the balance sheet:

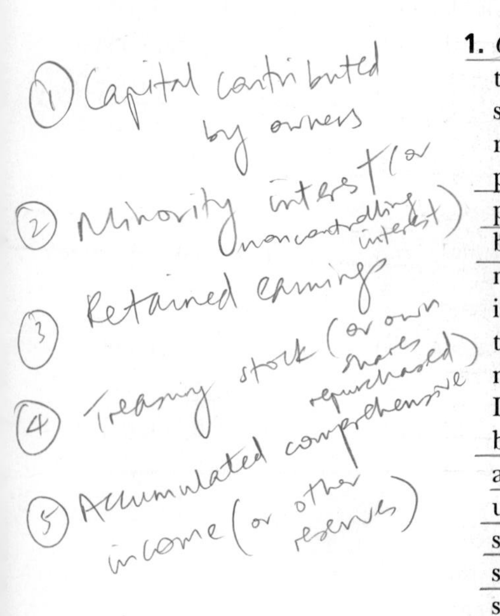

1. *Capital contributed by owners.* Capital ownership in a corporation is evidenced through the issuance of common stock, although preferred stock (a hybrid security with some characteristics of debt) may be issued by some companies in addition to common stock. Preferred shares have rights that take precedence over the rights of common shareholders—rights that generally pertain to receipt of dividends (not always cumulative if omitted by the board of directors) and receipt of assets if the company is liquidated. Common and preferred shares may have a par value (or stated value) or may be issued as no par shares (depending on governmental requirements at the time of incorporation). Where par or stated value requirements exist, it must be disclosed in the stockholders' equity section of the balance sheet. In addition, the number of shares authorized, issued, and outstanding must be disclosed for each class of stock issued by the company. The number of authorized shares is the number of shares that may be sold by the company under its articles of incorporation. The number of issued shares is those shares that have been sold to investors while the number of outstanding shares consists of the issued shares less those shares repurchased (treasury stock) by the company.
2. *Minority interest (or noncontrolling interest).* The equity interests of minority shareholders in the subsidiary companies that have been consolidated by the parent (controlling) company but that are not wholly owned by the parent company.
3. *Retained earnings (or retained deficit).* Amounts that have been recognized as cumulatively earned in the company's income statements but which have not been paid to the owners of the company through dividends.
4. *Treasury stock (or own shares repurchased).* The repurchase of company shares may occur when management considers the shares undervalued or when it wants to limit the effects of dilution from various employee stock compensation plans. Treasury stock is a reduction of shareholders' equity and a reduction of total shares outstanding. Treasury shares are nonvoting and do not receive dividends if declared by the company.
5. *Accumulated comprehensive income (or other reserves).* Amounts that may either increase or decrease total shareholders' equity but are not derived from the income statement or through any company transactions in its own equity shares.

In June 1997, the FASB released Statement of Financial Accounting Standard (SFAS) No. 130, *Reporting of Comprehensive Income*. This statement established certain standards for reporting and presenting comprehensive income in the general-purpose financial statements. SFAS No. 130 was issued in response to users' concerns that certain changes in assets and liabilities were bypassing the income statement and appearing in the statement of changes in stockholders' equity. The purpose of SFAS No. 130 was to report all items that met the definition of "comprehensive income" in a prominent financial statement for the same period in which they were recognized. In accordance with the definition provided by Statement of Financial Accounting Concepts No. 6, **comprehensive income** was to include all changes in owners' equity that resulted from transactions of the business entity with non-owners. Comprehensive income can be defined as:

Comprehensive income = Net income + Other comprehensive income

According to SFAS No. 130, **other comprehensive income** (OCI) is part of total comprehensive income but generally excluded from net income. Prior to SFAS No. 130, these three items—foreign currency translation adjustments, minimum pension liability adjustments, and unrealized gains or losses on available-for-sale investments—were disclosed as separate components of stockholders' equity on the balance sheet. Under SFAS No. 130, they are to be reported as OCI. Furthermore, they must be reported separately, as the FASB decided that information about each component is more important than information about the aggregate. Later, under SFAS No. 133, net unrealized losses on derivatives were also included in the definition of OCI. The intent of SFAS No. 130 was that "if used with related disclosures and other information in financial statements, the information provided by reporting comprehensive income would assist investors, creditors, and other financial statement users in assessing an enterprise's economic activities and its timing and magnitude of future cash flows."

Although the FASB required that "an enterprise shall display total comprehensive income and its components in a financial statement that is displayed with the same prominence as other financial statements that constitute a full set of financial statements," it did not specify which format was required, except that net income should be shown as a component of comprehensive income in that financial statement. According to SFAS No. 130, three alternative formats are allowed for presenting OCI and total comprehensive income:

- below the line for net income in a traditional income statement (as a combined statement of net income and comprehensive income);
- in a separate statement of comprehensive income that begins with the amount of net income for the year; or
- in a statement of changes in stockholders' equity.

Under IFRS, the component changes are also reported in the statement of equity; however, it is not presently required that a comprehensive income amount be reported.

Exhibit 13 illustrates how the equity amounts of €22,000 (20X7) and €20,000 (20X6) have been expanded from the one amount shown in Exhibit 5.

EXHIBIT 13 Apex Stockholders' Equity

	20X7	20X6
Equity	**€22,000**	**€20,000**
Share capital	10,000	10,000
Preferred shares	2,000	2,000
Share premium (paid-in capital)	—	—
Other reserves (unrealized gains and losses)	1,000	—
Retained earnings	9,000	8,000
Own shares repurchased (treasury shares)	—	—

4.2 Statement of Changes in Shareholders' Equity

The **statement of changes in shareholders' equity** reflects information about the increases or decreases to a company's net assets or wealth. With respect to comprehensive income, the following items, if present, must be disclosed:

- unrealized gains or losses on available-for-sale investments;
- gains or losses from derivatives that qualify as net investment hedges or cash flow hedges;
- minimum pension liability adjustments from underfunded defined-benefit plans; and
- foreign currency translation adjustments on foreign subsidiary companies.

Other information in the changes in equity statement or in notes includes the following:

- capital transactions with owners and distributions to owners;
- reconciliation of the balance of accumulated profit or loss (retained earnings) at the beginning and end of the year; and
- reconciliation of the carrying amount of each class of equity capital, share premium (paid-in capital), and accumulated comprehensive income (reserve) at the beginning and end of the period.

Exhibit 14 presents Sony Corporation's Consolidated Statement of Changes in Stockholders' Equity for the fiscal years ended 31 March 2004 and 2005. In this statement, Sony complies with the reconciliation and disclosure requirements that were discussed above.

EXHIBIT 14 Sony Corporation and Consolidated Subsidiaries Consolidated Statement of Changes in Stockholders' Equity (¥ millions)

	Subsidiary Tracking Stock	Common Stock	Additional Paid-In Capital	Retained Earnings	Accumulated Other Comprehensive Income	Treasury Stock, at Cost	Total
Balance at 31 March 2003	3,917	472,361	984,196	1,301,740	(471,978)	(9,341)	2,280,895
Conversion of convertible bonds		3,989	3,988				7,977
Stock issued under exchange offering			5,409				5,409
Comprehensive income:							
Net income				88,511			88,511
Other comprehensive income, net of tax							
Unrealized gains on securities:							
Unrealized holding gains or losses arising during period					57,971		57,971
Less: Reclassification adjustment for gains or losses included in net income					(5,679)		(5,679)
Unrealized losses on derivative instruments:							
Unrealized holding gains or losses arising during period					7,537		7,537
Less: Reclassification adjustment for gains or losses included in net income					(3,344)		(3,344)
Minimum pension liability adjustment					93,415		93,415
Foreign currency translation adjustments:							
Translation adjustments arising during period					(129,113)		(129,113)
Less: Reclassification adjustment for losses included in net income					1,232		1,232
Total comprehensive income							110,530
Stock issue costs, net of tax				(53)			(53)
Dividends declared				(23,138)			(23,138)
Purchase of treasury stock						(8,523)	(8,523)
Reissuance of treasury stock			(776)			5,681	4,905
Balance at 31 March 2004	**3,917**	**476,350**	**992,817**	**1,367,060**	**(449,959)**	**(12,183)**	**2,378,022**

(Exhibit continued on next page . . .)

EXHIBIT 14 (continued)

	Subsidiary Tracking Stock	Common Stock	Additional Paid-In Capital	Retained Earnings	Accumulated Other Comprehensive Income	Treasury Stock, at Cost	Total
Balance at 31 March 2004	3,917	476,350	992,817	1,367,060	(449,959)	(12,183)	2,378,022
Exercise of stock acquisition rights		52	53				105
Conversion of convertible bonds		141,390	141,354				282,744
Stock-based compensation			340				340
Comprehensive income:							
Net income				163,838			163,838
Other comprehensive income, net of tax							
Unrealized gains on securities:							
Unrealized holding gains or losses arising during period					5,643		5,643
Less: Reclassification adjustment for gains or losses included in net income					(12,924)		(12,924)
Unrealized losses on derivative instruments:							
Unrealized holding gains or losses arising during period					(209)		(209)
Less: Reclassification adjustment for gains or losses included in net income					(1,681)		(1,681)
Minimum pension liability adjustment					(769)		(769)
Foreign currency translation adjustments:							
Translation adjustments arising during period					74,224		74,224
Total comprehensive income							228,122
Stock issue costs, net of tax				(541)			(541)
Dividends declared				(24,030)			(24,030)
Purchase of treasury stock						(416)	(416)
Reissuance of treasury stock			(342)	(245)		6,599	6,012
Balance at 31 March 2005	**3,917**	**617,792**	**1,134,222**	**1,506,082**	**(385,675)**	**(6,000)**	**2,870,338**

USES AND ANALYSIS OF THE BALANCE SHEET

5

The classified sections of Apex Corporation's balance sheets have been discussed and illustrated throughout this reading. Exhibit 15 now presents the complete detailed balance sheets for Apex, which we will use as the basis for a discussion of how to analyze a balance sheet.

EXHIBIT 15 Apex Detailed Balance Sheets

Balance Sheet (000)	20X7	20X6
Assets		
Current assets	**€20,000**	**€16,000**
Cash and cash equivalents	3,000	2,000
Marketable securities: 3 types	3,000	4,000
Trade receivables	5,000	3,000
Inventories	7,000	6,000
Other current assets	2,000	1,000
Noncurrent assets	**53,000**	**27,000**
Property, plant, and equipment	35,000	20,000
Goodwill	5,000	1,000
Other intangible assets	3,000	1,000
Noncurrent investments (subsidiaries, associates, joint ventures)	10,000	5,000
Total assets	**€73,000**	**€43,000**
Liabilities and Equity		
Current liabilities	**14,000**	**7,000**
Trade and other payables	5,000	2,000
Current borrowings	3,000	1,000
Current portion of noncurrent borrowings	2,000	1,000
Current tax payable	2,000	2,000
Accrued liabilities	1,000	500
Unearned revenue	1,000	500
Noncurrent liabilities	**37,000**	**16,000**
Noncurrent borrowings	30,000	10,000
Deferred tax	6,000	5,000
Noncurrent provisions	1,000	1,000
Total liabilities	**51,000**	**23,000**
Equity	**22,000**	**20,000**
Share capital	10,000	10,000
Preference shares	2,000	2,000
Share premium (paid-in capital)	—	—
Other reserves (unrealized gains and losses)	1,000	—
Retained earnings	9,000	8,000
Own shares repurchased (treasury shares)	—	—
Total liabilities and shareholders' equity	**€73,000**	**€43,000**

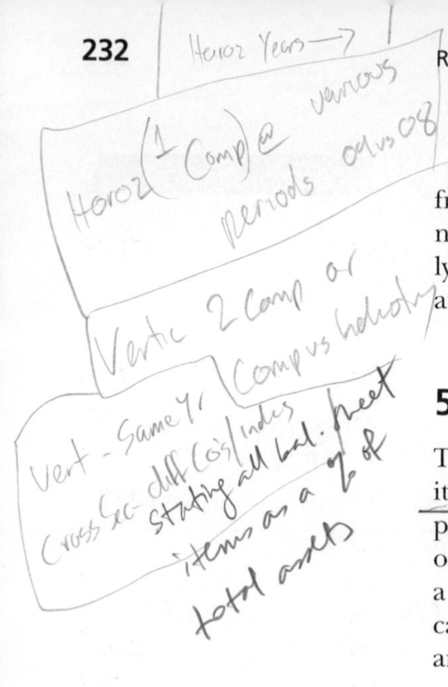

If a company is growing or shrinking, comparing balance sheet amounts from year to year may not clearly show trends. Additionally, comparing companies is difficult unless adjustments are made for size. Two techniques used to analyze balance sheets adjusted for differences or changes are common-size analysis and ratio analysis.

5.1 Common-Size Analysis of the Balance Sheet

The first technique, common-size analysis, involves stating all balance sheet items as a percentage of total assets.[5] Common-size statements are useful in comparing a company's current balance sheet with prior-year balance sheets or to other companies in the same industry. Horizontal common-size analysis provides a format to accomplish the former but not the latter. Exhibit 16 illustrates vertical common-size balance sheets for Apex Corporation. Horizontal common-size analysis is demonstrated in a later reading.

EXHIBIT 16 Apex Common-Size Balance Sheets

Balance Sheet (Percent of Total Assets)	20X7	20X6
Assets		
Current assets	**27.4**	**37.2**
Cash and cash equivalents	4.1	4.7
Marketable securities: 3 types	4.1	9.3
Trade receivables	6.8	7.0
Inventories	9.6	14.0
Other current assets	2.7	2.3
Noncurrent assets	**72.6**	**62.8**
Property, plant, and equipment	47.9	46.5
Goodwill	6.8	2.3
Other intangible assets	4.1	2.3
Noncurrent investments (subsidiaries, associates, joint ventures)	13.7	11.6
Total assets	**100.0**	**100.0**

(Exhibit continued on next page . . .)

[5] This format can be distinguished as "vertical common-size analysis." As the reading on financial statement analysis will discuss, another type of common-size analysis, known as "horizontal common-size analysis," states quantities in terms of a selected base-year value. Unless otherwise indicated, text references to "common-size analysis" refer to vertical analysis.

EXHIBIT 16 (continued)

Balance Sheet (Percent of Total Assets)	20X7	20X6
Liabilities and Equity		
Current liabilities	**19.2**	**16.3**
Trade and other payables	6.8	4.7
Current borrowings	4.1	2.3
Current portion of noncurrent borrowings	2.7	2.3
Current tax payable	2.7	4.7
Accrued liabilities	1.4	1.2
Unearned revenue	1.4	1.2
Noncurrent liabilities	**50.7**	**37.2**
Noncurrent borrowings	41.1	23.3
Deferred tax	8.2	11.6
Noncurrent provisions	1.4	2.3
Total liabilities	**69.9**	**53.5**
Shareholders' equity	**30.1**	**46.5**
Share capital	13.7	23.3
Preference shares	2.7	4.7
Share premium (paid-in capital)	—	—
Other reserves (unrealized gains and losses)	1.4	—
Retained earnings	12.3	18.6
Own shares repurchased (treasury shares)	—	—
Total liabilities and shareholders' equity	**100.0**	**100.0**

The common-size analysis for Apex clearly shows that for 20X7, the company is less liquid and is more leveraged than it was in 20X6. Regarding liquidity, current assets have decreased and current liabilities have increased when compared with the prior year. With respect to leverage, both noncurrent and total liabilities have increased when compared with the prior year.

EXAMPLE 6

Common-Size Analysis

Applying common-size analysis to the Roche Group balance sheets presented in Exhibit 7, which one of the following line items increased in 2005 relative to 2004?

A. Goodwill.
B. Inventories.
C. Long-term debt.
D. Accounts receivables.

Solution: C is correct. Long-term debt increased as a percentage of total assets from 12.1 percent of total assets in 2004 (CHF7,077 ÷ CHF58,446) to 13.4 percent in 2005 (CHF9,322 ÷ CHF69,365).

Although goodwill, inventories, and accounts receivables all increased in absolute Swiss franc amounts during 2005, they declined as a percentage of total assets when compared with the previous year.

Vertical common-size analysis of the balance sheet is particularly useful in cross-sectional analysis—comparing companies to each other for a particular time period or comparing a company with industry or sector data. The analyst could select individual peer companies for comparison, use industry data from published sources, or compile data from databases. Some common sources of published data are:

- *Annual Statement Studies*, published by the Risk Management Association (RMA). This volume provides abbreviated common-size (and ratio) data by industry. The source of data includes both public and nonpublic company data collected by financial institutions and may reflect non-GAAP, unaudited data.
- *Almanac of Business and Industrial Financial Ratios*, by Leo Troy. This is an annually revised publication, currently published by CCH.

When analyzing a company, many analysts prefer to select the peer companies for comparison or to compile their own industry statistics. For example, Exhibit 17 presents common-size balance sheet data compiled for the 10 sectors of Standard & Poor's 500 using 2005 data. The sector classification follows the S&P/MSCI Global Industrial Classification System (GICS). The exhibit presents mean and median common-size balance sheet data for those companies in the S&P 500 for which 2005 data was available in the Compustat database.[6]

[6] An entry of zero for an item (e.g., current assets) was excluded from the data, except in the case of preferred stock. Note that most financial institutions did not provide current asset or current liability data, so these are reported as not available in the database.

EXHIBIT 17 Common-Size Balance Sheet Statistics for the S&P 500 Grouped by S&P/MSCI GICS Sector (in Percent Except No. of Observations; Data for 2005)

Panel A. Median Data

	Energy	Materials	Industrials	Consumer Discretionary	Consumer Staples	Health Care	Financials	Information Technology	Telecom Services	Utilities
No. observations	29	30	49	85	36	52	87	73	9	31
Cash	7.55	6.07	4.89	7.60	4.50	18.50	5.32	28.35	2.05	1.61
Receivables	11.16	13.56	16.50	9.60	9.92	11.91	28.95	10.64	4.71	5.49
Inventories	3.98	10.21	10.38	15.43	14.67	7.49	1.37	5.52	0.95	2.13
Other current	1.64	2.51	3.59	3.33	2.75	3.85	0.98	4.00	1.49	4.59
Current assets	27.29	35.65	36.58	43.92	33.18	41.61	NA	56.05	10.06	16.89
PPE	54.70	37.21	15.79	20.99	27.53	13.70	1.06	9.80	42.57	55.04
Accts payable	7.50	7.01	6.91	6.99	8.54	4.54	34.73	4.14	2.49	3.89
Current liabilities	17.94	20.18	24.48	27.13	29.55	23.87	NA	22.90	13.70	17.13
LT debt	14.77	19.86	17.43	17.81	21.39	11.43	11.98	8.01	23.13	29.35
Total liabilities	50.72	63.82	62.29	56.73	65.36	47.87	89.81	37.10	58.39	75.28
Preferred stock	0.00	0.00	0.00	0.00	0.00	0.00	0.00	0.00	0.00	0.28
Common equity	49.28	36.18	37.71	43.27	34.64	52.13	10.19	62.90	41.61	22.89
Total equity	49.28	36.18	37.71	43.27	34.64	52.13	10.19	62.90	41.61	24.72

LT = long term, PPE = property, plant, and equipment.

(Exhibit continued on next page . . .)

EXHIBIT 17 (continued)

Panel B. Mean Data

	Energy	Materials	Industrials	Consumer Discretionary	Consumer Staples	Health Care	Financials	Information Technology	Telecom Services	Utilities
No. observations	29	30	49	85	36	52	87	73	9	31
Cash	7.56	9.16	7.91	10.19	7.45	19.55	10.49	33.43	3.32	2.85
Receivables	11.83	14.30	17.92	12.46	9.92	12.96	34.02	12.78	5.16	6.78
Inventories	5.32	10.82	10.21	19.36	15.54	9.23	6.88	6.51	0.94	2.62
Other current	2.98	2.73	4.07	3.74	3.09	4.08	1.09	4.60	2.49	6.44
Current assets	27.14	36.82	36.41	40.18	36.35	44.62	NA	56.71	11.59	18.60
PPE	54.84	35.70	24.83	25.38	30.77	16.76	1.92	13.05	48.53	57.48
Accts payable	9.07	8.80	7.12	10.46	9.82	8.75	35.09	7.03	2.76	4.53
Current liabilities	19.00	21.02	25.48	27.71	28.66	25.50	NA	23.99	13.56	18.92
LT debt	17.84	20.18	18.78	19.05	23.51	14.83	18.16	10.60	31.00	31.94
Total liabilities	53.16	61.72	61.10	57.64	64.67	48.88	80.50	40.05	65.74	76.83
Preferred stock	0.50	0.76	0.14	0.11	0.01	0.18	0.93	0.06	0.04	0.60
Common equity	46.33	37.52	38.76	42.25	35.32	50.94	18.60	59.89	34.22	22.57
Total equity	46.84	38.28	38.90	42.36	35.33	51.12	19.50	59.95	34.26	23.17

LT = long term, PPE = property, plant, and equipment.

Source: Based on data from Compustat.

Some interesting general observations can be made from these data:

- Energy and utility companies have the largest amounts of property, plant, and equipment. Utilities also have the highest level of long-term debt and use some preferred stock.
- Financial companies have the greatest percentage of liabilities.
- Telecommunications services and utility companies have the lowest level of receivables.
- Inventory levels are highest for consumer discretionary and consumer staples companies.
- Information technology companies use the least amount of leverage as evidenced by the entries for long-term debt and total liabilities.

Example 7 shows an analyst using cross-sectional common-size balance sheet data.

EXAMPLE 7

Cross-Sectional Common-Size Analysis

Jason Lu is examining four companies in the computer industry to evaluate their relative financial position as reflected on their balance sheet. He has compiled the following vertical common-size data for Dell, Hewlett-Packard Co., Gateway, and Apple Computer.

Cross-Sectional Analysis

Consolidated Balance Sheets (in percent of total assets)

Company Fiscal year	DELL 3 Feb 2006	HPQ 31 Oct 2005	GTW 31 Dec 2005	AAPL 30 Sep 2005
Assets				
Current assets:				
Cash and cash equivalents	30.47	17.99	21.99	30.22
Short-term investments	8.72	0.02	8.50	41.30
Accounts receivable, net	17.69	16.11	17.97	7.75
Financing receivables, net	5.90	n/a	n/a	n/a
Inventories	2.49	8.89	11.42	1.43
Other current assets	11.34	13.03	22.06	8.48
Total current assets	76.62	56.05	81.94	89.17
Property, plant, and equipment, net	8.68	8.34	4.33	7.07
Investments	11.64	9.70	0.00	0.00
Long-term financing receivables, net	1.41	n/a	n/a	n/a
Other assets	1.65	25.91	13.73	3.76
Total Assets	100.00	100.00	100.00	100.00

Company Fiscal year	DELL 3 Feb 2006	HPQ 31 Oct 2005	GTW 31 Dec 2005	AAPL 30 Sep 2005
Liabilities and Stockholders' Equity				
Current liabilities:				
Accounts payable	42.58	13.22	39.66	15.40
Short-term debt	0.00	2.37	2.60	0.00
Accrued and other	26.34	25.10	23.60	14.76
Total current liabilities	68.92	40.69	65.86	30.16
Long-term debt	2.18	4.39	15.62	0.00
Other liabilities	11.03	6.84	2.98	5.20
Commitments and contingent liabilities	0.00	0.00	0.00	0.00
Total liabilities	82.13	51.92	84.46	35.36
Stockholders' equity				
Total stockholders' equity	17.87	48.08	15.54	64.64

HPQ = Hewlett-Packard Co., GTW = Gateway, AAPL = Apple Computer, n/a = not available.
Source: Based on data from Bloomberg.

From this data, Lu learns the following:

- All four companies have a high level of cash, consistent with the information technology sector. Dell and Apple have a much higher than normal balance in cash and investments combined. This may reflect their business models, which have generated large operating cash flows in recent years.
- Apple has the lowest level of accounts receivable. Further research is necessary to learn if this is related to Apple's cash sales through retail stores or if the company has been selling/factoring receivables to a greater degree than the other companies.
- Dell and Apple both have an extraordinarily low level of inventory. Both utilize a just-in-time inventory system and rely on suppliers to hold inventory until needed. Additional scrutiny of the footnotes accompanying their annual reports reveals that Dell includes some "in-transit" inventory in other current assets and that Apple regularly makes purchase commitments that are not currently recorded as inventory and uses contract manufacturers to assemble and test some finished products. Dell has a smaller relative amount of purchase commitments. Hewlett-Packard has similar purchase commitments to Apple, and all of the companies make some use of contract manufacturers, but no mention is made of them about the extent that inventory may be "understated" through such use. Overall, it appears that the inventory levels may be understated somewhat for Dell and Apple but that, all things considered, they have been more efficient at managing inventory than Hewlett-Packard or Gateway.
- All four companies have a level of property, plant, and equipment below that of the sector, with Gateway having the lowest level.

Financial ratio analysis is limited by:

- The use of alternative accounting methods. Accounting methods play an important role in the interpretation of financial ratios. It should be remembered that ratios are usually based on data taken from financial statements. Such data are generated via accounting procedures that might not be comparable among companies because companies have latitude in the choice of accounting methods. This lack of consistency across companies makes comparability difficult to analyze and limits the usefulness of ratio analysis. Some accounting alternatives currently found include the following:
  - first-in-first-out (FIFO) or last-in-first-out (LIFO) inventory valuation methods;
  - cost or equity methods of accounting for unconsolidated associates;
  - straight-line or accelerated consumption pattern methods of depreciation; and
  - capitalized or operating lease treatment.
- The homogeneity of a company's operating activities. Many companies are diversified with divisions operating in different industries. This makes it difficult to find comparable industry ratios to use for comparison purposes. It is better to examine industry-specific ratios by lines of business.
- The need to determine whether the results of the ratio analysis are mutually consistent. One set of ratios might show a problem and another set might indicate that this problem is short term in nature.
- The need to use judgment. The analyst must use judgment when performing ratio analysis. A key issue is whether a ratio for a company is within a reasonable range for an industry, with this range being determined by the analyst. Although financial ratios are used to help assess the growth potential and risk of a business, they cannot be used alone to directly value a company or determine its creditworthiness. The entire operation of the business must be examined, and the external economic and industry setting in which it is operating must be considered when interpreting financial ratios.

SUMMARY

The starting place for analyzing a company is typically the balance sheet. It provides users such as creditors or investors with information regarding the sources of finance available for projects and infrastructure. At the same time, it normally provides information about the future earnings capacity of a company's assets as well as an indication of cash flows implicit in the receivables and inventories.

The balance sheet has many limitations, especially relating to the measurement of assets and liabilities. The lack of timely recognition of liabilities and, sometimes, assets, coupled with historical costs as opposed to fair value accounting for all items on the balance sheet, implies that the financial analyst must make numerous adjustments to determine the economic net worth of the company.

The balance sheet discloses what an entity owns (assets) and what it owes (liabilities) at a specific point in time, which is why it is also referred to as the statement of financial position. Equity represents the portion belonging to the owners or shareholders of a business. Equity is the residual interest in the assets of an entity after deducting its liabilities. The value of equity is increased by any generation of new assets by the business itself or by profits made during the year and is decreased by losses or withdrawals in the form of dividends.

The analyst must understand the structure and format of the balance sheet in order to evaluate the liquidity, solvency, and overall financial position of a company. Key points are:

- The "report format" of the balance sheet lists assets, liabilities, and equity in a single column. The "account format" follows the pattern of the traditional general ledger accounts, with assets at the left and liabilities and equity at the right of a central dividing line.
- The balance sheet should distinguish between current and noncurrent assets and between current and noncurrent liabilities unless a presentation based on liquidity provides more relevant and reliable information.
- Assets expected to be liquidated or used up within one year or one operating cycle of the business, whichever is greater, are classified as current assets. Assets not expected to be liquidated or used up within one year or one operating cycle of the business, whichever is greater, are classified as noncurrent assets.
- Liabilities expected to be settled or paid within one year or one operating cycle of the business, whichever is greater, are classified as current liabilities. Liabilities not expected to be settled or paid within one year or one operating cycle of the business, whichever is greater, are classified as noncurrent liabilities.
- Asset and liability values reported on a balance sheet may be measured on the basis of fair value or historical cost. Historical cost values may be quite different from economic values. Balance sheets must be evaluated critically in light of accounting policies applied in order to answer the question of how the values relate to economic reality and to each other.
- The notes to financial statements are an integral part of the U.S. GAAP and IFRS financial reporting processes. They provide important required detailed disclosures, as well as other information provided voluntarily by management. This information can be invaluable when determining whether the measurement of assets is comparable to other entities being analyzed.

- Tangible assets are long-term assets with physical substance that are used in company operations.
- Intangible assets are amounts paid by a company to acquire certain rights that are not represented by the possession of physical assets. A company should assess whether the useful life of an intangible asset is finite or infinite and, if finite, the length of its life.
- Under IFRS and U.S. GAAP, goodwill should be capitalized and tested for impairment annually. Goodwill is not amortized.
- Financial instruments are contracts that give rise to both a financial asset of one entity and a financial liability of another entity. Financial instruments come in a variety of instruments, including derivatives, hedges, and marketable securities.
- There are five potential components that comprise the owners' equity section of the balance sheet: contributed capital, minority interest, retained earnings, treasury stock, and accumulated comprehensive income.
- The statement of changes in equity reflects information about the increases or decreases to a company's net assets or wealth.
- Ratio analysis is used by analysts and managers to assess company performance and status. Another valuable analytical technique is common-size (relative) analysis, which is achieved through the conversion of all balance sheet items to a percentage of total assets.

PRACTICE PROBLEMS FOR READING 33

1. Resources controlled by a company as a result of past events are
A. equity.
B. assets.
C. liabilities.
D. other comprehensive income.

2. Equity equals
A. Assets − Liabilities.
B. Liabilities − Assets.
C. Assets + Liabilities.
D. Assets × Liabilities.

3. Distinguishing between current and noncurrent items on the balance sheet and presenting a subtotal for current assets and liabilities is referred to as
A. the report format.
B. the account format.
C. a classified balance sheet.
D. an unclassified balance sheet.

4. All of the following are current assets *except*
A. cash.
B. goodwill.
C. inventories.
D. accounts receivable.

5. Debt due within one year is considered
A. current.
B. preferred.
C. long term.
D. convertible.

6. Money received from customers for products to be delivered in the future is recorded as
A. revenue and an asset.
B. an asset and a liability. — ↑ in cash (A), ↑ in deferred revenue or unearned revenue (L)
C. revenue and a liability.
D. an asset and shareholders' equity.

7. The carrying value of inventories reflects
A. their original cost.
B. their current value.
C. the lower of original cost or net realizable value.
D. the higher of original cost or net realizable value.

8. When a company pays its rent in advance, its balance sheet will reflect a reduction in
   A. assets and liabilities.
   B. assets and shareholders' equity.
   C. liabilities and shareholders' equity.
   D. one category of assets and an increase in another.

9. Accrued liabilities are
   A. balanced against an asset.
   B. expenses that have been paid.
   C. created when another liability is reduced.
   D. expenses that have been reported on the income statement.

10. The initial measurement of goodwill is
   A. not subject to management discretion.
   B. based on an acquisition's purchase price.
   C. based on the acquired company's book value.
   D. based on the fair value of the acquirer's assets and liabilities.

11. Defining total asset turnover as revenue divided by average total assets, all else equal, impairment write downs of long-lived assets owned by a company will most likely result in an increase for that company in
   A. the debt-to-equity ratio but not the total asset turnover.
   B. the total asset turnover but not the debt-to-equity ratio.
   C. both the debt-to-equity ratio and the total asset turnover.
   D. neither the debt-to-equity ratio nor the total asset turnover.

12. For financial assets classified as trading securities, how are unrealized gains and losses reflected in shareholders' equity?
   A. They are not recognized.
   B. As an adjustment to paid-in capital.
   C. They flow through income into retained earnings.
   D. As a separate line item (other comprehensive income).

13. For financial assets classified as available for sale, how are unrealized gains and losses reflected in shareholders' equity?
   A. They are not recognized.
   B. As an adjustment to paid-in capital.
   C. They flow through retained earnings.
   D. As a separate line item (other comprehensive income).

14. For financial assets classified as held to maturity, how are unrealized gains and losses reflected in shareholders' equity?
   A. They are not recognized.
   B. As an adjustment to paid-in capital.
   C. They flow through retained earnings.
   D. As a separate line item (valuation gains/losses).

15. Under IFRS, the minority interest in consolidated subsidiaries is presented on the balance sheet as

A. a long-term liability.

B. separately, but as a part of shareholders' equity.

C. a mezzanine item between liabilities and shareholders' equity.

D. either a long-term liability, shareholders' equity, or as a mezzanine item between liabilities and shareholders' equity.

16. Retained earnings are a component of

A. assets.

B. liabilities.

C. minority interest.

D. owners' equity.

17. When a company buys shares of its own stock to be held in treasury, it records a reduction in

A. both assets and liabilities.

B. both assets and shareholders' equity.

C. assets and an increase in shareholders' equity.

D. liabilities and an increase in shareholders' equity.

18. A common-size analysis of the balance sheet is most likely to signal investors that the company

A. has increased sales.

B. is using assets efficiently.

C. is becoming more leveraged.

D. can meet its short-term obligations.

19. An investor concerned whether a company can meet its near-term obligations is most likely to calculate the

A. current ratio.

B. debt-to-equity ratio.

C. return on total capital.

D. financial leverage ratio.

20. The most stringent test of a company's liquidity is its

A. cash ratio.

B. quick ratio.

C. current ratio.

D. inventory turnover.

21. An investor worried that a company may go bankrupt would most likely examine its

A. current ratio.

B. return on equity.

C. debt-to-equity ratio.

D. total asset turnover.

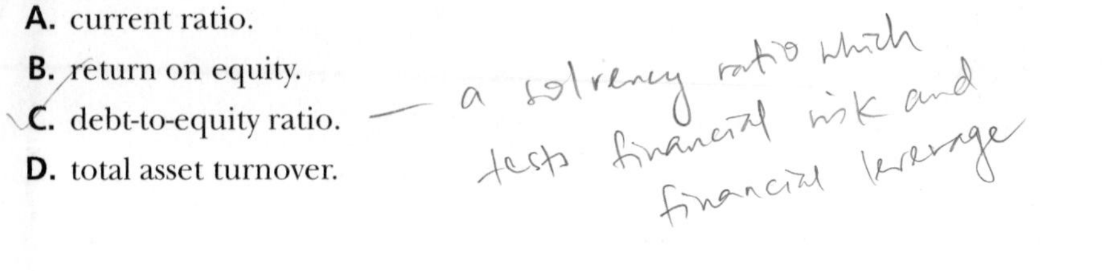

22. Using the information presented in Exhibit 8, the quick ratio for Sony Corp. at 31 March 2005 is *closest* to

A. 0.44.

B. 0.81.

C. 0.84.

D. 1.04.

cash + mktable securities + receivables / Current liabilities

= 779103 + 460202 + 1113071 + 1492 − 87709 / 2809368

time deposits

Allowance for doubtful a/cs & sales returns

23. Applying common-size analysis to the Sony Corp. balance sheets presented in Exhibit 8, which one of the following line items increased in 2005 relative to 2004?

A. Goodwill.

B. Securities investments and other.

C. Notes and accounts payable, trade.

D. Deferred insurance acquisition costs.

24. Using the information presented in Exhibit 8, the financial leverage ratio for Sony Corp. at 31 March 2005 is *closest* to

A. 2.30.

B. 2.81.

C. 3.31.

D. 3.82.

Total Assets / Total Equity = 9499100 / 2870338 = 3.31

Liquidity ratios (Ability to meet current liabilities)

1. Current ratio → CA / CL
2. Quick ratio → cash + mktable securities + Receivables / CL
3. Cash ratio → cash + mktable securities / CL

Level of stringency

Solvency ratios (Financial risk and financial leverage)

1. Long-term debt to equity → Total long-term debt / Total equity
2. Debt to equity → Total debt / Total equity
3. Total debt → Total debt / Total assets
4. Financial leverage → Total assets / Total equity

UNDERSTANDING THE CASH FLOW STATEMENT

by Thomas R. Robinson, Hennie van Greuning, Elaine Henry, and Michael A. Broihahn

READING

34

LEARNING OUTCOMES

The candidate should be able to:

a. compare and contrast cash flows from operating, investing, and financing activities, and classify cash flow items as relating to one of these three categories, given a description of the items;

b. describe how noncash investing and financing activities are reported;

c. compare and contrast the key differences in cash flow statements prepared under international financial reporting standards and U.S. generally accepted accounting principles;

d. demonstrate the difference between the direct and indirect methods of presenting cash from operating activities and explain the arguments in favor of each;

e. demonstrate how the cash flow statement is linked to the income statement and balance sheet;

f. demonstrate the steps in the preparation of direct and indirect cash flow statements, including how cash flows can be computed using income statement and balance sheet data;

g. describe the process of converting a statement of cash flows from the direct to the indirect method of presentation;

h. analyze and interpret a cash flow statement using both total currency amounts and common-size cash flow statements;

i. explain and calculate free cash flow to the firm, free cash flow to equity, and other cash flow ratios.

THEME

The information in a cash flow statement helps financial analysts assess a company's historical ability to generate cash that can be invested in additional assets or distributed to its capital providers. The cash flow statement classifies all cash flows as being provided by (or used for) operating, investing, or financing activities and has two major presentation formats: indirect and direct. The analysis of a company's cash flow statements can provide useful information for understanding the company's business and reported earnings, and helps in uncovering relationships that can be useful in the prediction of future cash flows.

1 INTRODUCTION

The cash flow statement provides information about a company's *cash receipts* and *cash payments* during an accounting period, showing how these cash flows link the ending cash balance to the beginning balance shown on the company's balance sheet. The cash-based information provided by the cash flow statement contrasts with the accrual-based information from the income statement. For example, the income statement reflects revenues when earned rather than when cash is collected; in contrast, the cash flow statement reflects cash receipts when collected as opposed to when the revenue was earned. A reconciliation between reported income and cash flows from operating activities provides useful information about when, whether, and how a company is able to generate cash from its operating activities. Although income is an important measure of the results of a company's activities, cash flow is also essential. As an extreme illustration, a hypothetical company that makes all sales on account, without regard to whether it will ever collect its accounts receivable, would report healthy sales on its income statement and might well report significant income; however, with zero cash inflow, the company would not survive. The cash flow statement also provides a reconciliation of the beginning and ending cash on the balance sheet.

In addition to information about cash generated (or, alternatively, cash used) in operating activities, the cash flow statement provides information about cash provided (or used) in a company's investing and financing activities. This information allows the analyst to answer such questions as:

- Does the company generate enough cash from its operations to pay for its new investments, or is the company relying on new debt issuance to finance them?
- Does the company pay its dividends to common stockholders using cash generated from operations, from selling assets, or from issuing debt?

Answers to these questions are important because, in theory, generating cash from operations can continue indefinitely, but generating cash from selling assets, for example, is possible only as long as there are assets to sell. Similarly, generating cash from debt financing is possible only as long as lenders are willing to lend, and the lending decision depends on expectations that the company will ultimately have adequate cash to repay its obligations. In summary, information about the sources and uses of cash helps creditors, investors, and other statement users evaluate the company's liquidity, solvency, and financial flexibility.

This reading explains how cash flow activities are reflected in a company's cash flow statement. The reading is organized as follows. Section 2 describes the components and format of the cash flow statement, including the classification of cash flows under international financial reporting standards (IFRS) and U.S. generally accepted accounting principles (GAAP) and the direct and indirect formats for presenting the cash flow statement. Section 3 discusses the linkages of the cash flow statement with the income statement and balance sheet and the steps in the preparation of the cash flow statement. Section 4 demonstrates the analysis of cash flow statements, including the conversion of an indirect cash flow statement to the direct method and how to use common-size cash flow analysis, free cash flow measures, and cash flow ratios used in security analysis. A summary of the key points and practice problems in CFA Institute multiple-choice format conclude the reading.

2 COMPONENTS AND FORMAT OF THE CASH FLOW STATEMENT

The analyst needs to be able to extract and interpret information on cash flows from financial statements prepared according to any allowable format. The basic components and allowable formats of the cash flow statement are well established.

- The cash flow statement has subsections relating specific items to the operating, investing, and financing activities of the company.
- Two presentation formats are available: the direct and the indirect.

The following discussion presents these topics in greater detail.

2.1 Classification of Cash Flows and Noncash Activities

All companies engage in operating, investing, and financing activities. These activities are the classifications used in the cash flow statement under both IFRS and U.S. GAAP. Under IFRS, International Accounting Standard No. 7, (IAS No. 7), *Cash Flow Statements*, provides that cash flows are categorized as follows:[1]

- **Operating activities** include the company's day-to-day activities that create revenues, such as selling inventory and providing services. Cash inflows result from cash sales and from collection of accounts receivable. Examples

[1] IAS No. 7 became effective on 1 January 1994.

include cash receipts from the provision of services and royalties, commissions, and other revenue. To generate revenue, companies undertake activities such as manufacturing inventory, purchasing inventory from suppliers, and paying employees. Cash outflows result from cash payments for inventory, salaries, taxes, and other operating-related expenses and from paying accounts payable. Additionally, operating activities include cash receipts and payments related to securities held for dealing or trading purposes (as opposed to being held for investment, as discussed below).

- **Investing activities** include purchasing and selling investments. Investments include property, plant, and equipment; intangible assets; other long-term assets; and both long-term and short-term investments in the equity and debt (bonds and loans) issued by other companies. For this purpose, investments in equity and debt securities exclude: (a) any securities considered cash equivalents (very short-term, highly liquid securities) and (b) **dealing** or **trading securities**, the purchase and sale of which are considered operating activities even for companies where this is not a primary business activity. Cash inflows in the investing category include cash receipts from the sale of nontrading securities; property, plant, and equipment; intangibles; or other **long-term assets**. Cash outflows include cash payments for the purchase of these assets.
- **Financing activities** include obtaining or repaying capital, such as equity and long-term debt. The two primary sources of capital are shareholders and creditors. Cash inflows in this category include cash receipts from issuing stock (common or preferred) or bonds and cash receipts from borrowing. Cash outflows include cash payments to repurchase stock (e.g., treasury stock), to pay dividends, and to repay bonds and other borrowings. Note that indirect borrowing using accounts payable is not considered a financing activity—such borrowing would be classified as an operating activity.

EXAMPLE 1

Net Cash Flow from Investing Activities

A company recorded the following in Year 1:

Proceeds from issuance of long-term debt	$300,000
Purchase of equipment	$200,000
Loss on sale of equipment	$ 70,000
Proceeds from sale of equipment	$120,000
Equity in earnings of affiliate	$ 10,000

On the Year 1 statement of cash flows, the company would report net cash flow from investing activities *closest* to

A. −$150,000.
B. −$80,000.
C. $200,000.
D. $300,000.

Solution: The only two items that would affect the investing section are the purchase of equipment and the proceeds from sale of equipment. The loss on sale of equipment and the equity in earnings of affiliate affect net income but are not investing cash flows. The issuance of debt is a financing cash flow. B is correct: (\$200,000) + \$120,000 = (\$80,000).

Under IFRS, there is some flexibility in reporting some items of cash flow, particularly interest and dividends. IAS No. 7 notes that while for a financial institution interest paid and received would normally be classified as operating activities, for other entities, alternative classifications may be appropriate. For this reason, under IFRS, interest received may be classified either as an operating activity or as an investing activity. Under IFRS, interest paid may be classified as either an operating activity or as a financing activity. Furthermore, under IFRS, dividends received may be classified as either an operating activity or an investing activity. On the other hand, dividends paid may be classified as either an operating activity or a financing activity. Companies must use a consistent classification from year to year and disclose where the amounts are reported.

Under U.S. GAAP, this discretion is not permitted: Interest received and paid is reported as operating activities for all companies.[2] Under U.S. GAAP, dividends received are always reported as operating activities and dividends paid are always reported as financing activities.

EXAMPLE 2

Operating versus Financing Cash Flows

On 31 December 2006, a company issued a \$30,000, 90-day note at 8 percent to pay for inventory purchased that day and issued \$110,000 long-term debt at 11 percent annually to pay for new equipment purchased that day. Which of the following *most* accurately reflects the combined effect of both transactions on the company's cash flows for the year ended 31 December 2006 under U.S. GAAP? Cash flow from

A. operations increases \$30,000.
B. financing increases \$110,000.
C. operations decreases \$30,000.
D. financing decreases \$110,000.

Solution: C is correct because the increase in inventories would decrease cash flow from operations. The issuance of both short-term and long-term debt is part of financing activities. Equipment purchased is an investing activity. Note that because no interest was paid or received in this example, the answer would be the same under IFRS.

[2] See Financial Accounting Standard No. 95, *Statement of Cash Flows.* This was originally issued in 1987 and modified somewhat in recent years.

Companies may also engage in **noncash investing and financing transactions**. A noncash transaction is any transaction that does not involve an inflow or outflow of cash. For example, if a company exchanges one nonmonetary asset for another nonmonetary asset, no cash is involved. Similarly, no cash is involved when a company issues common stock either for dividends or in connection with conversion of a convertible bond or convertible preferred stock. Because no cash is involved in noncash transactions (by definition), these transactions are not incorporated in the cash flow statement. However, any significant noncash transaction is required to be disclosed, either in a separate note or a supplementary schedule to the cash flow statement.

2.2 A Summary of Differences between IFRS and U.S. GAAP

As highlighted in the previous section, there are some differences in cash flow statements prepared under IFRS and U.S. GAAP that the analyst should be aware of when comparing the cash flow statements of companies using U.S. GAAP or IFRS. The key differences are summarized in Exhibit 1. In short, the IASB allows more flexibility in the reporting of items such as interest paid or received and dividends paid or received, and in how income tax expense is classified.

U.S. GAAP classifies interest and dividends received from investments as operating activities, whereas IFRS allows companies to classify those items as either operating or investing cash flows. Likewise, U.S. GAAP classifies interest

EXHIBIT 1 Cash Flow Statements: Differences between IFRS and U.S. GAAP

Topic	IFRS	U.S. GAAP
Classification of cash flows:		
Interest received	Operating or investing	Operating
Interest paid	Operating or financing	Operating
Dividends received	Operating or investing	Operating
Dividends paid	Operating or financing	Financing
Bank overdrafts	Considered part of cash equivalents	Not considered part of cash and cash equivalents and classified as financing
Taxes paid	Generally operating, but a portion can be allocated to investing or financing if it can be specifically identified with these categories	Operating
Format of statement	Direct or indirect; direct is encouraged	Direct or indirect; direct is encouraged. If direct is used, a reconciliation of net income and operating cash flow must also be provided

(Exhibit continued on next page . . .)

EXHIBIT 1 (continued)

Disclosures	Tax cash flows must be separately disclosed in the cash flow statement	Interest and taxes paid must be disclosed in footnotes if not presented on the statement of cash flows

Sources: IAS No. 7, FAS No. 95, and "Similarities and Differences: A Comparison of IFRS and U.S. GAAP," PricewaterhouseCoopers, October 2004, available at www.pwc.com.

expense as an operating activity, even though the principal amount of the debt issued is classified as a financing activity. IFRS allows companies to classify interest expense as either an operating activity or a financing activity. U.S. GAAP classifies dividends paid to stockholders as a financing activity, whereas IFRS allows companies to classify dividends paid as either an operating activity or a financing activity.

U.S. GAAP classifies all income tax expenses as an operating activity. IFRS also classifies income tax expense as an operating activity, unless the tax expense can be specifically identified with an investing or financing activity (e.g., the tax effect of the sale of a discontinued operation could be classified under investing activities). Under either of the two sets of standards, companies currently have a choice of formats for presenting cash flow statements, as discussed in the next section.

2.3 Direct and Indirect Cash Flow Formats for Reporting Operating Cash Flow

There are two acceptable formats for reporting **cash flow from operations** (also known as **cash flow from operating activities** or **operating cash flow**), defined as the net amount of cash provided from operating activities: the direct and the indirect methods. The *amount* of operating cash flow is identical under both methods; only the *presentation format* of the operating cash flow section differs. The presentation format of the cash flows from investing and financing is exactly the same, regardless of which method is used to present operating cash flows.

The **direct method** shows the specific cash inflows and outflows that result in reported cash flow from operating activities. It shows each cash inflow and outflow related to a company's cash receipts and disbursements, adjusting income statement items to remove the effect of accruals. In other words, the direct method eliminates any impact of accruals and shows only cash receipts and cash payments. The primary argument in favor of the direct method is that it provides information on the specific sources of operating cash receipts and payments in contrast to the indirect method, which shows only the net result of these receipts and payments. Just as information on the specific sources of revenues and expenses is more useful than knowing only the net result—net income—the analyst gets additional information from a direct-format cash flow statement. The additional information is useful in understanding historical performance and in predicting future operating cash flows.

The **indirect method** shows how cash flow from operations can be obtained from reported net income as the result of a series of adjustments. The indirect format begins with net income. To reconcile net income with operating cash flow, adjustments are made for noncash items, for nonoperating items, and for the net changes in operating accruals. The main argument for the indirect approach is that it shows the reasons for differences between net income and operating cash flows. (It may be noted, however, that the differences between net income and operating cash flows are equally visible on an indirect-format cash flow statement and in the supplementary reconciliation required if the company uses the direct method.) Another argument for the indirect method is that it mirrors a forecasting approach that begins by forecasting future income and then derives cash flows by adjusting for changes in balance sheet accounts that occur due to the timing differences between accrual and cash accounting.

Under IFRS, IAS No. 7 encourages the use of the direct method but permits either. Similarly, under U.S. GAAP, the Financial Accounting Standards Board (FASB) in Financial Accounting Standard No. 95 encourages the use of the direct method but allows companies to use the indirect method. Under FAS No. 95, if the direct method is presented, footnote disclosure must also be provided of the indirect method. If the indirect method is chosen, no direct-format disclosures are required. As a result, few U.S. companies present the direct format for operating cash flows.

Many users of financial statements prefer the direct format, particularly analysts and commercial lenders, because of the importance of information about operating receipts and payments to assessing a company's financing needs and capacity to repay existing obligations. In 1987, at the time the FASB was adopting FAS No. 95, some companies argued that it is less costly to adjust net income to operating cash flow, as in the indirect format, than it is to report gross operating cash receipts and payments, as in the direct format. With subsequent progress in accounting systems and technology, it is not clear that this argument remains valid. CFA Institute has advocated that standard setters require the use of the direct format for the main presentation of the cash flow statement, with indirect cash flows as supplementary disclosure.[3]

2.3.1 An Indirect-Format Cash Flow Statement Prepared under IFRS

Exhibit 2 presents cash flow statements prepared under IFRS from Roche Group's annual report for the fiscal years ended 31 December 2005 and 2004, which show the use of the indirect method. Roche is a leading international healthcare company based in Switzerland.[4]

In the cash flows from operating activities section of Roche's cash flow statement, the company reconciles its net income to net cash provided by operating activities. Under IFRS, payments for interest and taxes are disclosed in the body of the cash flow statement. Note that Roche discloses the income taxes paid (CHF 1,997 million in 2005) as a separate item in the cash flows from operating activities section. Separate disclosure of this is not useful if an analyst is trying to assess the impact on cash flow of changes in tax rates (income tax expense provided on the income statement does not reflect the flow of cash due to prepaid and deferred items). Roche reports its interest paid in the cash flows from

[3] *A Comprehensive Business Reporting Model: Financial Reporting for Investors,* CFA Institute Centre for Financial Market Integrity, October 2005, p. 27.

[4] The cash flow statement presented here includes a reconciliation of net income to cash generated from operations, which Roche Group reported in the footnotes to the financial statement rather than on the statement itself.

EXHIBIT 2 Roche Group Consolidated Cash Flow Statements (millions of CHF)

Fiscal Years Ended 31 December	2005	2004
Cash flows from operating activities:		
Net income	6,730	7,063
Add back nonoperating (income) expense:		
Income from associated companies	(1)	43
Financial income	(678)	(369)
Financing costs	382	602
Exceptional income from bond conversion and redemption	–	(872)
Income taxes	2,224	1,865
Discontinued businesses	12	(2,337)
Operating profit	8,669	5,995
Depreciation of property, plant, and equipment	1,302	1,242
Amortization of goodwill	–	572
Amortization of intangible assets	1,011	1,000
Impairment of long-term assets	66	39
Changes in group organization	–	199
Major legal cases	356	–
Expenses for defined-benefit postemployment plans	313	532
Expenses for equity-settled equity compensation plans	364	169
Other adjustments	455	(335)
Cash generated from continuing operations	12,526	9,413
Operating cash flows generated from discontinued businesses	(5)	335
Cash generated from operations	12,521	9,748
(Increase) decrease in working capital	488	227
Vitamin case payments	(82)	(66)
Major legal cases	(98)	(65)
Payments made for defined-benefit postemployment plans	(303)	(653)
Utilization of restructuring provisions	(119)	(163)
Utilization of other provisions	(310)	(128)
Other operating cash flows	(125)	(75)
Income taxes paid	(1,997)	(1,490)
Total cash flows from operating activities	9,975	7,335
Cash flows from investing activities:		
Purchase of property, plant, and equipment	(3,319)	(2,344)
Purchase of intangible assets	(349)	(191)
Disposal of property, plant, and equipment	353	196
Disposal of intangible assets	2	12
Disposal of products	56	431

(Exhibit continued on next page . . .)

EXHIBIT 2 (continued)

Fiscal Years Ended 31 December	2005	2004
Acquisitions of subsidiaries and associated companies	(233)	(1,822)
Divestments of discontinued businesses and associated companies	2,913	696
Interest and dividends received	383	255
Sales of marketable securities	9,859	4,965
Purchases of marketable securities	(15,190)	(4,281)
Other investing cash flows	(161)	64
Total cash flows from investing activities	(5,686)	(2,019)
Cash flows from financing activities:		
Proceeds from issue of long-term debt instruments	2,565	–
Repayment of long-term debt instruments	(1,178)	(3,039)
Increase (decrease) in other long-term debt	(1,083)	(1,156)
Transactions in own equity instruments	779	237
Increase (decrease) in short-term borrowings	(422)	(939)
Interest and dividends paid	(1,983)	(1,971)
Exercises of equity-settled equity compensation plans	1,090	643
Genentech and Chugai share repurchases	(2,511)	(1,699)
Other financing cash flows	(38)	61
Total cash flows from financing activities	(2,781)	(7,863)
Net effect of currency translation on cash and cash equivalents	115	(124)
Increase (decrease) in cash and cash equivalents	1,623	(2,671)
Cash and cash equivalents at 1 January	2,605	5,276
Cash and cash equivalents at 31 December	4,228	2,605

financing activities section, showing a total of CHF 1,983 million in interest and dividends paid in 2005. As noted earlier under U.S. GAAP, interest paid—or the reconciliation adjustment for the net change in interest payable—must be reported in the operating section of the cash flow statement. Furthermore, U.S. GAAP does not require that interest and taxes paid be disclosed as separate line items on the cash flow statement; however, it does require that these amounts be provided in a supplemental note.

Roche reports its dividends and interest received (CHF 383 million in 2005) in the cash flows from investing activities section. Under U.S. GAAP, investment income received (or the reconciliation adjustment for the net change in investment income receivable) must be reported in the operating section of the cash flow statement.

2.3.2 *A Direct-Format Cash Flow Statement Prepared under IFRS*

Exhibit 3 presents a direct-method format cash flow statement prepared under IFRS for Telefónica Group, a diversified telecommunications company based in Madrid.[5] Note that in this format of the cash flow statement, the cash received from customers, as well as other operating items, is clearly shown. The analyst can then contrast the change in revenues from the income statement with the change in cash received from customers. An increase in revenues coupled with a decrease in cash received from customers could signal collection problems. However, in the case of Telefónica Group, cash received from customers has increased.

EXHIBIT 3 **Telefónica Group Consolidated Cash Flow Statements (millions of euros)**

Fiscal Years Ended 31 December	2005	2004
Cash flows from operating activities		
Cash received from customers	44,353.14	36,367.10
Cash paid to suppliers and employees	(30,531.54)	(24,674.10)
Dividends received	70.58	71.24
Net interest and other financial expenses paid	(1,520.00)	(1,307.11)
Taxes paid	(1,233.04)	(326.00)
Net cash from operating activities	11,139.14	10,131.13
Cash flows from investing activities		
Proceeds on disposals of property, plant, and equipment and intangible assets	113.20	241.27
Payments on investments in property, plant, and equipment and intangible assets	(4,423.22)	(3,488.15)
Proceeds on disposals of companies, net of cash, and cash equivalents disposed	501.59	531.98
Payments on investments in companies, net of cash, and cash equivalents acquired	(6,571.40)	(4,201.57)
Proceeds on financial investments not included under cash equivalents	147.61	31.64
Payments made on financial investments not included under cash equivalents	(17.65)	(76.35)
Interest received on short-term investments not included under cash equivalents	625.18	1,139.51
Capital grants received	32.67	13.51
Net cash used in investing activities	(9,592.02)	(5,808.16)

(Exhibit continued on next page . . .)

[5] Excludes supplemental cash flow reconciliation provided at the bottom of the original cash flow statement by the company.

EXHIBIT 3 (continued)

Fiscal Years Ended 31 December	2005	2004
Cash flows from financing activities		
Dividends paid	(2,768.60)	(2,865.81)
Proceeds from issue of stock	(2,054.12)	(1,938.56)
Proceeds on issue of debentures and bonds	875.15	572.99
Proceeds on loans, credits, and promissory notes	16,533.96	10,135.11
Cancellation of debentures and bonds	(3,696.52)	(1,790.57)
Repayments of loans, credits, and promissory notes	(9,324.54)	(8,049.77)
Net cash from financing activities	(434.67)	(3,936.61)
Effect of foreign exchange rate changes on collections and payments	165.73	74.18
Effect of changes in consolidation methods and other nonmonetary effects	9.62	(36.76)
Net increase (decrease) in cash and cash equivalents during the year	1,287.80	423.78
Cash and cash equivalents at beginning of year	914.35	490.57
Cash and cash equivalents at end of year	2,202.15	914.35

2.3.3 Illustrations of Cash Flow Statements Prepared under U.S. GAAP

Previously, we presented a cash flow statement prepared under IFRS. In this section, we illustrate cash flow statements prepared under U.S. GAAP. This section presents the cash flow statements of two companies, Tech Data Corporation and Wal-Mart. Tech Data reports its operating activities using the direct method, whereas Wal-Mart reports its operating activities using the more common indirect method.

Tech Data Corporation is a leading distributor of information technology products. Exhibit 4 presents comparative cash flow statements from the company's annual report for the fiscal years ended 31 January 2005 and 2004.[6]

Tech Data Corporation prepares its cash flow statements under the direct method. In the cash flows from operating activities section of Tech Data's cash flow statements, the company identifies the amount of cash it received from customers, $19.7 billion for 2005, and the amount of cash that it paid to suppliers and employees, $19.6 billion for 2005. Net cash provided by operating activities of $106.9 million was adequate to cover the company's investing activities, primarily purchases of property and equipment ($25.9 million) and software development ($17.9 million). In 2005, the company issued $32.7 million of common stock, providing net cash from financing activities of $12.2 million after its debt repayments. Overall, the company's cash increased by $86.3 million, from $108.8 million at the beginning of the year to $195.1 million at the end of the year.

[6] Under U.S. GAAP, companies present three years of the cash flow statement. For purposes of presentation and comparison with the IFRS statements presented above, only two years are presented here.

EXHIBIT 4 Tech Data Corporation and Subsidiaries Consolidated Cash Flow Statements (in thousands)

Fiscal Years Ended 31 January	2005	2004
Cash flows from operating activities:		
Cash received from customers	$19,745,283	$17,390,674
Cash paid to suppliers and employees	(19,571,824)	(17,027,162)
Interest paid	(18,837)	(17,045)
Income taxes paid	(47,677)	(43,233)
Net cash provided by operating activities	106,945	303,234
Cash flows from investing activities:		
Acquisition of businesses, net of cash acquired	–	(203,010)
Proceeds from sale of property and equipment	5,130	4,484
Expenditures for property and equipment	(25,876)	(31,278)
Software development costs	(17,899)	(21,714)
Net cash used in investing activities	(38,645)	(251,518)
Cash flows from financing activities:		
Proceeds from the issuance of common stock	32,733	28,823
Net repayments on revolving credit loans	(11,319)	(138,039)
Principal payments on long-term debt	(9,214)	(1,492)
Net cash provided by (used in) financing activities	12,200	(110,708)
Effect of exchange rate changes on cash	5,755	10,602
Net increase (decrease) in cash and cash equivalents	86,255	(48,390)
Cash and cash equivalents at beginning of year	108,801	157,191
Cash and cash equivalents at end of year	$ 195,056	$ 108,801
Reconciliation of net income to net cash provided by operating activities:		
Net income	$ 162,460	$ 104,147
Adjustments to reconcile net income to net cash provided by operating activities:		
Depreciation and amortization	55,472	55,084
Provision for losses on accounts receivable	13,268	29,214
Deferred income taxes	(3,616)	7,369
Changes in operating assets and liabilities, net of acquisitions:		
Accounts receivable	(44,305)	(15,699)
Inventories	(119,999)	(140,203)
Prepaid and other assets	(32,193)	14,713
Accounts payable	55,849	300,350
Accrued expenses and other liabilities	20,000	(51,741)
Total adjustments	(55,515)	199,087
Net cash provided by operating activities	$ 106,945	$ 303,234

Whenever the direct method is used, FAS No. 95 mandates a disclosure note and schedule that reconciles net income with the net cash flow from operating activities. Tech Data shows this reconciliation at the bottom of its consolidated statements of cash flows. The disclosure note and reconciliation schedule are exactly the information that would have been presented in the body of the cash flow statement if the company had elected instead to use the indirect method.

Wal-Mart is a global retailer that conducts business under the names of Wal-Mart and Sam's Club. Exhibit 5 presents the comparative cash flow statements from the company's annual report for the fiscal years ended 31 January 2005 and 2004.[7]

EXHIBIT 5 Wal-Mart Cash Flow Statements (in millions)

Fiscal Years Ended 31 January	2005	2004
Cash flows from operating activities:		
Income from continuing operations	$10,267	$ 8,861
Adjustments to reconcile net income to net cash provided by operating activities:		
Depreciation and amortization	4,405	3,852
Deferred income taxes	263	177
Other operating activities	378	173
Changes in certain assets and liabilities, net of effects of acquisitions:		
Decrease (increase) in accounts receivable	(304)	373
Increase in inventories	(2,635)	(1,973)
Increase in accounts payable	1,694	2,587
Increase in accrued liabilities	976	1,896
Net cash provided by operating activities of continuing operations	15,044	15,946
Net cash provided by operating activities of discontinued operations	–	50
Net cash provided by operating activities	15,044	15,996
Cash flows from investing activities:		
Payments for property and equipment	(12,893)	(10,308)
Investment in international operations	(315)	(38)
Proceeds from the disposal of fixed assets	953	481
Proceeds from the sale of McLane	–	1,500
Other investing activities	(96)	78
Net cash used in investing activities of continuing operations	(12,351)	(8,287)
Net cash used in investing activities discontinued operations	–	(25)
Net cash used in investing activities	(12,351)	(8,312)

(Exhibit continued on next page . . .)

[7] Under U.S. GAAP, companies present three years of the cash flow statement. For purposes of presentation and comparison with the IFRS statements presented above, only two years are presented here.

EXHIBIT 5 (continued)

Cash flows from financing activities:		
Increase in commercial paper	544	688
Proceeds from issuance of long-term debt	5,832	4,099
Purchase of company stock	(4,549)	(5,046)
Dividends paid	(2,214)	(1,569)
Payment of long-term debt	(2,131)	(3,541)
Payment of capital lease obligations	(204)	(305)
Other financing activities	113	111
Net cash used in financing activities	(2,609)	(5,563)
Effect of exchange rate changes on cash	205	320
Net increase in cash and cash equivalents	289	2,441
Cash and cash equivalents at beginning of year	5,119	2,758
Cash and cash equivalents at end of year	$ 5,488	$ 5,199
Income tax paid	$ 5,593	$ 4,358
Interest paid	1,163	1,024
Capital lease obligations incurred	377	252

Wal-Mart prepares its cash flow statements under the indirect method. In the cash flows from operating activities section of Wal-Mart's cash flow statement, the company reconciles its net income of $10.3 billion to net cash provided by operating activities of $15 billion. Whenever the indirect method is used, U.S. GAAP mandates a supplemental note that discloses how much cash was paid for interest and income taxes. Wal-Mart discloses the amount of cash paid for income tax ($5.6 billion), interest ($1.2 billion), and capital lease obligations (i.e., the interest expense component of the capital lease payments) at the bottom of its cash flow statements.

3 THE CASH FLOW STATEMENT: LINKAGES AND PREPARATION

The indirect format of the cash flow statement demonstrates that changes in balance sheet accounts are an important factor in determining cash flows. The next section addresses the linkages between the cash flow statement and other financial statements.

3.1 Linkages of the Cash Flow Statement with the Income Statement and Balance Sheet

Recall the accounting equation that summarizes the balance sheet:

$$\text{Assets} = \text{Liabilities} + \text{Owners' equity}$$

Cash is an asset. The statement of cash flows ultimately shows the change in cash during an accounting period. The beginning and ending balances of cash are shown on the company's balance sheets for the previous and current years, and the bottom of the cash flow statement reconciles beginning cash with ending cash. For example, the Roche Group's cash flow statement for 2005, presented in Exhibit 2, shows that operating, investing, and financing activities during the year imply a CHF 1,623 increase in cash and cash equivalents, which is the amount by which end-of-year cash and cash equivalents (CHF 4,228) exceeds beginning-of-year cash and cash equivalents (CHF 2,605). The relationship, stated in general terms, is as shown below.

Beginning Balance Sheet at 31 December 20X6	Statement of Cash Flows for Year Ended 31 December 20X7		Ending Balance Sheet at 31 December 20X7
Beginning cash	Plus: Cash receipts (from operating, investing, and financing activities)	Less: Cash payments (for operating, investing, and financing activities)	Ending cash

In the case of cash held in foreign currencies, there would also be an impact from changes in exchange rates. The body of the cash flow statement shows why the change in cash occurred; in other words, it shows the company's operating, investing, and financing activities (as well as the impact of foreign currency translation). The beginning and ending balance sheet values of cash and cash equivalents are linked through the cash flow statement. The linkage is similar to the one that relates net income and dividends as shown in the income statement to the beginning and ending values of retained earnings in the owners' equity section of the balance sheet, as shown below.

Beginning Balance Sheet at 31 December 20X6	Statement of Owners' Equity for Year Ended 31 December 20X7		Ending Balance Sheet at 31 December 20X7
Beginning retained earnings	Plus: Net income or minus net loss from the income statement for year ended 31 December 20X7	Minus: Dividends	Ending retained earnings

A company's operating activities are reported on an accrual basis in the income statement, and any differences between the accrual basis and the cash basis of accounting for an operating transaction result in an increase or decrease in some (usually) short-term asset or liability on the balance sheet. For example, if revenue reported using accrual accounting is higher than the cash actually collected, the result will be an increase in accounts receivable. If expenses reported using accrual accounting are lower than cash actually paid, the result will be a decrease in accounts payable.

A company's investing activities typically relate to the long-term asset section of the balance sheet, and its financing activities typically relate to the equity and long-term debt sections of the balance sheet. Each item on the balance sheet is also related to the income statement and/or cash flow statement through the change in the beginning and ending balance. Consider, for example, accounts receivable:

Beginning Balance Sheet at 31 December 20X6	Income Statement for Year Ended 31 December 20X7	Statement of Cash Flows for Year Ended 31 December 20X7	Ending Balance Sheet at 31 December 20X7
Beginning accounts receivable	Plus: Revenues	Minus: Cash collected from customers	Ending accounts receivable

Knowing any three of these four items makes it easy to compute the fourth. For example, if you know beginning accounts receivable, revenues, and cash collected from customers, you can easily compute ending accounts receivable. Understanding these interrelationships between the balance sheet, income statement, and cash flow statement is useful in not only understanding the company's financial health but also in detecting accounting irregularities. The next section demonstrates the preparation of cash flow information based upon income statement and balance sheet information.

3.2 Steps in Preparing the Cash Flow Statement

The preparation of the cash flow statement uses data from both the income statement and the comparative balance sheets.

As noted earlier, companies often only disclose indirect operating cash flow information, whereas analysts prefer direct-format information. Understanding how cash flow information is put together will enable you to take an indirect statement apart and reconfigure it in a more useful manner. The following demonstration of how a cash flow statement is prepared uses the income statement and the comparative balance sheets for Acme Corporation (a fictitious retail company) shown in Exhibits 6 and 7.

EXHIBIT 6 **Acme Corporation Income Statement Year Ended 31 December 2006 (in thousands)**

Revenue		$23,598
Cost of goods sold		11,456
Gross profit		12,142
Salary and wage expense	4,123	
Depreciation expense	1,052	
Other operating expenses	3,577	
Total operating expenses		8,752
Operating profit		3,390

(Exhibit continued on next page . . .)

EXHIBIT 6 (continued)

Other revenues (expenses):		
Gain on sale of equipment	205	
Interest expense	(246)	(41)
Income before tax		3,349
Income tax expense		1,139
Net income		$ 2,210

EXHIBIT 7 Acme Corporation Comparative Balance Sheets 31 December 2006 and 2005 (in thousands)

	2006	2005	Net Change
Cash	$ 1,011	$ 1,163	$ (152)
Accounts receivable	1,012	957	55
Inventory	3,984	3,277	707
Prepaid expenses	155	178	(23)
Total current assets	6,162	5,575	587
Land	510	510	–
Buildings	3,680	3,680	–
Equipment[a]	8,798	8,555	243
Less: accumulated depreciation	(3,443)	(2,891)	(552)
Total long-term assets	9,545	9,854	(309)
Total assets	$15,707	$15,429	278
Accounts payable	$ 3,588	$ 3,325	$ 263
Salary and wage payable	85	75	10
Interest payable	62	74	(12)
Income tax payable	55	50	5
Other accrued liabilities	1,126	1,104	22
Total current liabilities	4,916	4,628	288
Long-term debt	3,075	3,575	(500)
Common stock	3,750	4,350	(600)
Retained earnings	3,966	2,876	1,090
Total liabilities and equity	$15,707	$15,429	278

[a] During 2006, Acme purchased new equipment for a total cost of $1,300. No items impacted retained earnings other than net income and dividends.

The first step in preparing the cash flow statement is to determine the total cash flows from operating activities. The direct method of presenting cash from operating activities will be illustrated first, followed by the indirect method. Cash flows from investing activities and from financing activities are identical under either method.

3.2.1 Operating Activities: Direct Method

We first determine how much cash Acme received from its customers, followed by how much cash was paid to suppliers and to employees as well as how much cash was paid for other operating expenses, interest, and income taxes.

3.2.1.1 Cash Received from Customers The income statement for Acme reported revenue of $23,598 (in thousands) for the year ended 31 December 2006. To determine the cash receipts from its customers, it is necessary to adjust this revenue amount by the net change in accounts receivable for the year. If accounts receivable increase during the year, revenue on an accrual basis is higher than cash receipts from customers, and vice versa. For Acme Corporation, accounts receivable increased by $55, so cash received from customers was $23,543, as follows:

Revenue	$23,598
Less: Increase in accounts receivable	(55)
Cash received from customers	**$23,543**

Cash received from customers affects the accounts receivable account as follows:

Beginning accounts receivable	$ 957
Plus revenue	23,598
Minus cash collected from customers	**(23,543)**
Ending accounts receivable	$ 1,012

The accounts receivable account information can also be presented as follows:

Beginning accounts receivable	$ 957
Plus revenue	23,598
Minus ending accounts receivable	(1,012)
Cash collected from customers	**$23,543**

EXAMPLE 3

Computing Cash Received from Customers

Blue Bayou, an advertising company, reported revenues of $50 million, total expenses of $35 million, and net income of $15 million in the most recent year. If accounts receivable decreased by $12 million, how much cash did the company receive from customers?

A. $62 million.
B. $50 million.
C. $38 million.
D. $15 million.

Solution: A is correct. Revenues of $50 million plus the decrease in accounts receivable of $12 million equals $62 million cash received from customers. The decrease in accounts receivable means that the company received more in cash than the amount of revenue it reported.

"Cash received from customers" is sometimes referred to as "cash collections from customers" or "cash collections."

3.2.1.2 Cash Paid to Suppliers For Acme, the cash paid to suppliers was $11,900, determined as follows:

Cost of goods sold	$11,456
Plus: Increase in inventory	707
Equals purchases from suppliers	$12,163
Less: Increase in accounts payable	(263)
Cash paid to suppliers	**$11,900**

There are two pieces to this calculation: the amount of inventory purchased and the amount paid for it. To determine purchases from suppliers, cost of goods sold is adjusted for the change in inventory. If inventory increased during the year, then purchases during the year exceeded cost of goods sold, and vice versa. Acme reported cost of goods sold of $11,456 for the year ended 31 December 2006. For Acme Corporation, inventory increased by $707, so purchases from suppliers was $12,163. Purchases from suppliers affects the inventory account, as shown below:

Beginning inventory	3,277
Plus purchases	12,163
Minus cost of goods sold	(11,456)
Ending inventory	3,984

Acme purchased $12,163 of inventory from suppliers this year, but is this the amount of cash that Acme paid to its suppliers during the year? Not necessarily. Acme may not have yet paid for all of these purchases and may yet owe for some of the purchases made this year. In other words, Acme may have paid less cash to its suppliers than the amount of this year's purchases, in which case Acme's liability (accounts payable) will have increased by the difference. Alternatively, Acme may have paid even more to its suppliers than the amount of this year's purchases, in which case Acme's accounts payable will have decreased.

Therefore, once purchases have been determined, cash paid to suppliers can be calculated by adjusting purchases for the change in accounts payable. If the company made all purchases for cash, then accounts payable would not change and cash outflows would equal purchases. If accounts payable increased during the year, then purchases on an accrual basis are higher than they are on a cash basis, and vice versa. In this example, Acme made more purchases than it paid in cash, so the balance in accounts payable has increased. For Acme, the cash paid to suppliers was $11,900, determined as follows:

Purchases from suppliers	$12,163
Less: Increase in accounts payable	(263)
Cash paid to suppliers	**$11,900**

The amount of cash paid to suppliers is reflected in the accounts payable account, as shown below:

Beginning accounts payable	$ 3,325
Plus purchases	12,163
Minus cash paid to suppliers	**(11,900)**
Ending accounts payable	$ 3,588

EXAMPLE 4

Computing Cash Paid to Suppliers

Orange Beverages Plc., a manufacturer of tropical drinks, reported cost of goods sold for the year of $100 million. Total assets increased by $55 million, but inventory declined by $6 million. Total liabilities increased by $45 million, but accounts payable decreased by $2 million. How much cash did the company pay to its suppliers during the year?

A. $110 million.
B. $108 million.
C. $104 million.
D. $96 million.

Solution: D is correct. Cost of goods sold of $100 million less the decrease in inventory of $6 million equals purchases from suppliers of $94 million. The decrease in accounts payable of $2 million means that the company paid $96 million in cash ($94 million plus $2 million).

3.2.1.3 Cash Paid to Employees To determine the cash paid to employees, it is necessary to adjust salary and wage expense by the net change in salary and wage payable for the year. If salary and wage payable increased during the year, then salary and wage expense on an accrual basis is higher than the amount of cash paid for this expense, and vice versa. For Acme, salary and wage payable increased by $10, so cash paid for salary and wages was $4,113, as follows:

Salary and wage expense	$4,123
Less: Increase in salary and wage payable	(10)
Cash paid to employees	**$4,113**

The amount of cash paid to employees is reflected in the salary and wage payable account, as shown below:

Beginning salary and wages payable	$ 75
Plus salary and wage expense	4,123
Minus cash paid to employees	**(4,113)**
Ending salary and wages payable	$ 85

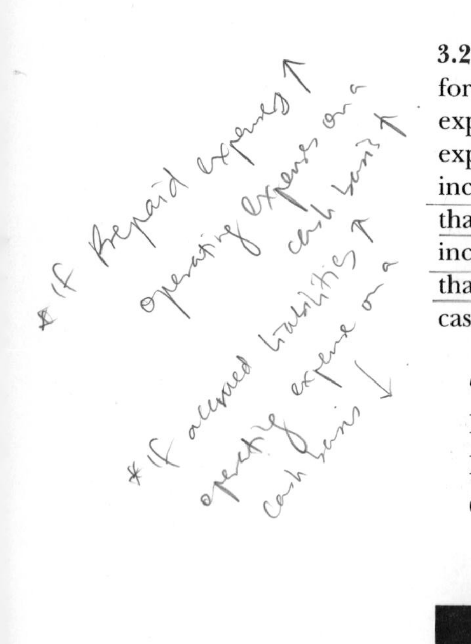

3.2.1.4 Cash Paid for Other Operating Expenses To determine the cash paid for other operating expenses, it is necessary to adjust the other operating expenses amount on the income statement by the net changes in prepaid expenses and accrued expense liabilities for the year. If prepaid expenses increased during the year, other operating expenses on a cash basis were higher than on an accrual basis, and vice versa. Likewise, if accrued expense liabilities increased during the year, other operating expenses on a cash basis were lower than on an accrual basis, and vice versa. For Acme Corporation, the amount of cash paid for operating expenses in 2006 was $3,532, as follows:

Other operating expenses	$3,577
Less: Decrease in prepaid expenses	23
Less: Increase in other accrued liabilities	(22)
Cash paid for other operating expenses	**$3,532**

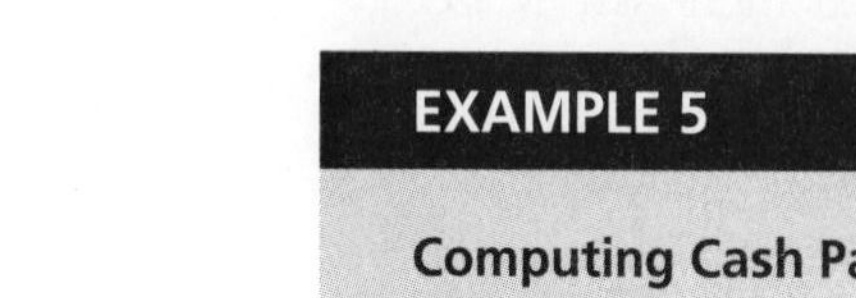

Computing Cash Paid for Other Operating Expenses

Black Ice, a sportswear manufacturer, reported other operating expenses of $30 million. Prepaid insurance expense increased by $4 million, and accrued utilities payable decreased by $7 million. Insurance and utilities are the only two components of other operating expenses. How much cash did the company pay in other operating expenses?

A. $41 million.
B. $33 million.
C. $27 million.
D. $19 million.

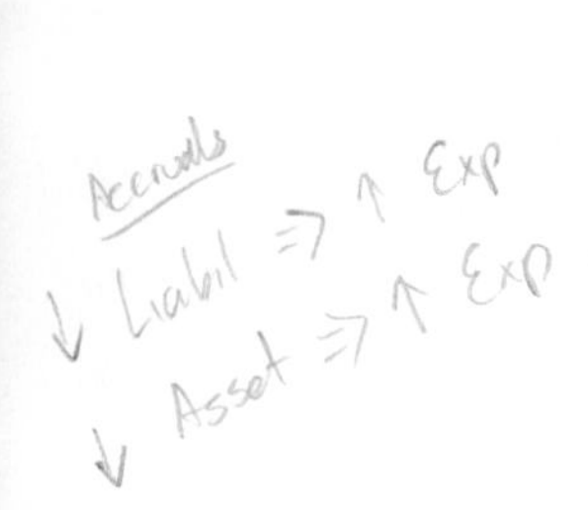

Solution: A is correct. Other operating expenses of $30 million plus the increase in prepaid insurance expense of $4 million plus the decrease in accrued utilities payable of $7 million equals $41 million.

3.2.1.5 Cash Paid for Interest The company is either subject to U.S. GAAP, which requires that interest expense be included in operating cash flows, or it is subject to IFRS, which gives companies the option to treat interest expense in this manner. To determine the cash paid for interest, it is necessary to adjust interest expense by the net change in interest payable for the year. If interest payable increases during the year, then interest expense on an accrual basis is higher than the amount of cash paid for interest, and vice versa. For Acme Corporation, interest payable decreased by $12 and cash paid for interest was $258, as follows:

Interest expense	$246
Plus: Decrease in interest payable	12
Cash paid for interest	**$258**

Alternatively, cash paid for interest may also be determined by an analysis of the interest payable account, as shown below:

Beginning interest payable	$ 74
Plus interest expense	246
Minus cash paid for interest	**(258)**
Ending interest payable	$ 62

3.2.1.6 Cash Paid for Income Taxes To determine the cash paid for income taxes, it is necessary to adjust the income tax expense amount on the income statement by the net changes in taxes receivable, taxes payable, and deferred income taxes for the year. If taxes receivable or deferred tax assets increase during the year, income taxes on a cash basis will be higher than on an accrual basis, and vice versa. Likewise, if taxes payable or deferred tax liabilities increase during the year, income tax expense on a cash basis will be lower than on an accrual basis, and vice versa. For Acme Corporation, the amount of cash paid for income taxes in 2006 was $1,134, as follows:

Income tax expense	$1,139
Less: Increase in income tax payable	(5)
Cash paid for income taxes	**$1,134**

3.2.2 Investing Activities: Direct Method

The second and third steps in preparing the cash flow statement are to determine the total cash flows from investing activities and from financing activities. The presentation of this information is identical, regardless of whether the direct or indirect method is used for operating cash flows. Investing cash flows are always presented using the direct method.

Purchases and sales of equipment were the only investing activities undertaken by Acme in 2006, as evidenced by the fact that the amounts reported for land and buildings were unchanged during the year. An informational note in Exhibit 7 tells us that Acme *purchased* new equipment in 2006 for a total cost of $1,300. However, the amount of equipment shown on Acme's balance sheet increased by only $243 (ending balance of $8,798 minus beginning balance of $8,555); therefore, Acme must have also *sold* some equipment during the year. To determine the cash inflow from the sale of equipment, we analyze the equipment and accumulated depreciation accounts as well as the gain on the sale of equipment from Exhibits 6 and 7.

The historical cost of the equipment sold was $1,057. This amount is determined as follows:

Beginning balance equipment (from balance sheet)	$8,555
Plus equipment purchased (from informational note)	1,300
Minus ending balance equipment (from balance sheet)	(8,798)
Equals historical cost of equipment sold	$1,057

The accumulated depreciation on the equipment sold was $500, determined as follows:

Beginning balance accumulated depreciation (from balance sheet)	$2,891
Plus depreciation expense (from income statement)	1,052
Minus ending balance accumulated depreciation (from balance sheet)	(3,443)
Equals accumulated depreciation on equipment sold	$500

The historical cost information, accumulated depreciation information, and information from the income statement about the gain on the sale of equipment can be used to determine the cash received from the sale.

Historical cost of equipment sold (calculated above)	$1,057
Less accumulated depreciation on equipment sold (calculated above)	(500)
Equals: Book value of equipment sold	557
Plus: Gain on sale of equipment (from the income statement)	205
Equals: Cash received from sale of equipment	**$762**

EXAMPLE 6

Computing Cash Received from the Sale of Equipment

Copper, Inc., a brewery and restaurant chain, reported a gain on the sale of equipment of $12 million. In addition, the company's income statement shows depreciation expense of $8 million, and the cash flow statement shows capital expenditure of $15 million, all of which was for the purchase of new equipment.

Balance sheet item	12/31/2005	12/31/2006	Change
Equipment	$100 million	$109 million	$9 million
Accumulated depreciation—equipment	$30 million	$36 million	$6 million

–ve Asset do not combine

Using the above information from the comparative balance sheets, how much cash did the company receive from the equipment sale?

A. $16 million.
B. $9 million.
C. $6 million.
D. $3 million.

Solution: A is correct. Selling price (cash inflow) minus book value equals gain or loss on sale; therefore, gain or loss on sale plus book value equals selling price (cash inflow). The amount of gain is given, $12 million. To calculate the book value of the equipment sold, find the historical cost of the equipment and the accumulated depreciation on the equipment.

- Beginning balance of equipment of $100 million plus equipment purchased of $15 million minus ending balance of equipment of $109 million equals historical cost of equipment sold, or $6 million.
- Beginning accumulated depreciation on equipment of $30 million plus depreciation expense for the year of $8 million minus ending balance of accumulated depreciation of $36 million equals accumulated depreciation on the equipment sold, or $2 million.
- Therefore, the book value of the equipment sold was $6 million minus $2 million, or $4 million.
- Because the gain on the sale of equipment was $12 million, the amount of cash received must have been $16 million.

3.2.3 Financing Activities: Direct Method

As with investing activities, financing activities are always presented using the direct method.

3.2.3.1 Long-Term Debt and Common Stock The change in long-term debt, based on the beginning and ending balance sheets in Exhibit 7, was a decrease of $500. Absent other information, this indicates that Acme retired $500 of long-term debt. Retiring long-term debt is a cash outflow relating to financing activities.

Similarly, the change in common stock during 2006 was a decrease of $600. Absent other information, this indicates that Acme repurchased $600 of its common stock. Repurchase of common stock is also a cash outflow related to financing activity.

3.2.3.2 Dividends Recall the following relationship:

Beginning retained earnings + Net income − Dividends
= Ending retained earnings

Based on this relationship, the amount of cash dividends paid in 2006 can be determined from an analysis of retained earnings, as follows:

Beginning balance of retained earnings (from the balance sheet)	$2,876
Plus net income (from the income statement)	2,210
Minus ending balance of retained earnings (from the balance sheet)	(3,966)
Equals dividends paid	**$1,120**

3.2.4 Overall Statement of Cash Flows: Direct Method

Exhibit 8 summarizes the information about Acme's operating, investing, and financing cash flows in the statement of cash flows. At the bottom of the statement, the total net change in cash is shown to be a decrease of $152 (from $1,163 to $1,011). This can also be seen on the comparative balance sheet in Exhibit 7. The cash provided by operating activities of $2,606 was adequate to cover the net cash used in investing activities of $538; however, the company's debt repayments, cash payments for dividends, and repurchase of common stock (i.e., its financing activities) of $2,220 resulted in an overall decrease of $152.

EXHIBIT 8 Acme Corporation Cash Flow Statement (Direct Method) for Year Ended 31 December 2006 (in thousands)

Cash flow from operating activities:	
Cash received from customers	$23,543
Cash paid to suppliers	(11,900)
Cash paid to employees	(4,113)
Cash paid for other operating expenses	(3,532)
Cash paid for interest	(258)
Cash paid for income tax	(1,134)
Net cash provided by operating activities	2,606
Cash flow from investing activities:	
Cash received from sale of equipment	762
Cash paid for purchase of equipment	(1,300)
Net cash used for investing activities	(538)
Cash flow from financing activities:	
Cash paid to retire long-term debt	(500)
Cash paid to retire common stock	(600)
Cash paid for dividends	(1,120)
Net cash used for financing activities	(2,220)
Net decrease in cash	(152)
Cash balance, 31 December 2005	1,163
Cash balance, 31 December 2006	$ 1,011

direct cash movements

3.2.5 *Overall Statement of Cash Flows: Indirect Method*

Using the alternative approach to reporting cash from operating activities, the indirect method, we will present the same amount of cash provided by operating activities. Under this approach, we reconcile Acme's net income of $2,210 to its operating cash flow of $2,606.

To perform this reconciliation, net income is adjusted for the following: (a) any nonoperating activities; (b) any noncash expenses; and (c) changes in operating working capital items.

The only nonoperating activity in Acme's income statement, the sale of equipment, resulted in a gain of $205. This amount is removed from the operating cash flow section; the cash effects of the sale are shown in the investing section.

Acme's only noncash expense was depreciation expense of $1,052. Under the indirect method, depreciation expense must be added back to net income because it was a noncash deduction in the calculation of net income.

Changes in working capital accounts include increases and decreases in the current operating asset and liability accounts. The changes in these accounts arise from applying accrual accounting; that is, recognizing revenues when they are earned and expenses when they are incurred instead of when the cash is received or paid. To make the working capital adjustments under the indirect method, any increase in a current operating asset account is subtracted from net income while a net decrease is added to net income. As described above, the increase in accounts receivable, for example, resulted from Acme recording income statement revenue higher than the amount of cash received from customers; therefore, to reconcile back to operating cash flow, that increase in accounts receivable must be deducted from net income. For current operating liabilities, a net increase is added to net income while a net decrease is subtracted from net income. As described above, the increase in wages payable, for example, resulted from Acme recording income statement expenses higher than the amount of cash paid to employees.

Exhibit 9 presents a tabulation of the most common types of adjustments that are made to net income when using the indirect method to determine net cash flow from operating activities.

EXHIBIT 9 Adjustments to Net Income Using the Indirect Method

Additions
- Noncash items
  - Depreciation expense of tangible assets
  - Amortization expense of intangible assets
  - Depletion expense of natural resources
  - Amortization of bond discount
- Nonoperating losses
  - Loss on sale or write down of assets
  - Loss on retirement of debt
  - Loss on investments accounted for under the equity method
- Increase in deferred income tax liability
- Changes in working capital resulting from accruing higher expenses than cash payments, or lower revenues than cash receipts

(Exhibit continued on next page . . .)

EXHIBIT 9 (continued)

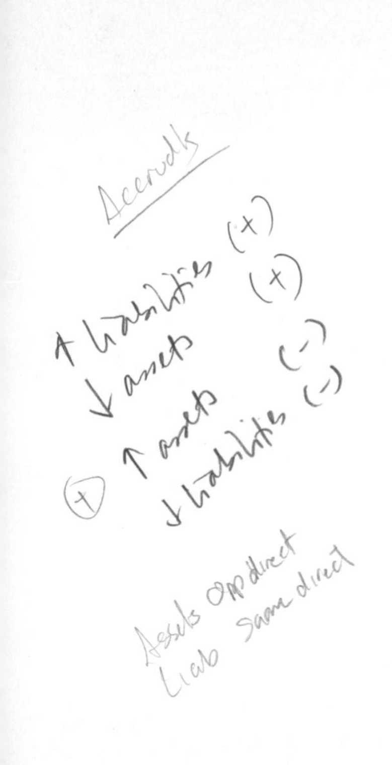

	Increase in current operating liabilities (e.g., accounts payable and accrued expense liabilities)
	Decrease in current operating assets (e.g., accounts receivable, inventory, and prepaid expenses)
Subtractions	Noncash items (e.g., amortization of bond premium)
	Nonoperating items
	Gain on sale of assets
	Gain on retirement of debt
	Income on investments accounted for under the equity method
	Decrease in deferred income tax liability
	Changes in working capital resulting from accruing lower expenses than cash payments, or higher revenues than cash receipts
	Decrease in current operating liabilities (e.g., accounts payable and accrued expense liabilities)
	Increase in current operating assets (e.g., accounts receivable, inventory, and prepaid expenses)

Accordingly, for Acme Corporation, the $55 increase in accounts receivable and the $707 increase in inventory are subtracted from net income while the $23 decrease in prepaid expenses is added to net income. For Acme's current liabilities, the increases in accounts payable, salary and wage payable, income tax payable, and other accrued liabilities ($263, $10, $5, and $22, respectively) are added to net income while the $12 decrease in interest payable is subtracted from net income. Exhibit 10 presents the cash flow statement for Acme Corporation under the indirect method by using the information that we have determined from our analysis of the income statement and the comparative balance sheets. Note that the investing and financing sections are identical to the statement of cash flows prepared using the direct method.

EXHIBIT 10 Acme Corporation Cash Flow Statement (Indirect Method) Year Ended 31 December 2006 (in thousands)

Cash flow from operating activities:	
Net income	$2,210
Depreciation expense	1,052
Gain on sale of equipment	(205)
Increase in accounts receivable	(55)
Increase in inventory	(707)

(Exhibit continued on next page . . .)

EXHIBIT 10 (continued)

Decrease in prepaid expenses	23
Increase in accounts payable	263
Increase in salary and wage payable	10
Decrease in interest payable	(12)
Increase in income tax payable	5
Increase in other accrued liabilities	22
Net cash provided by operating activities	2,606
Cash flow from investing activities:	
Cash received from sale of equipment	762
Cash paid for purchase of equipment	(1,300)
Net cash used for investing activities	(538)
Cash flow from financing activities:	
Cash paid to retire long-term debt	(500)
Cash paid to retire common stock	(600)
Cash paid for dividends	(1,120)
Net cash used for financing activities	(2,220)
Net decrease in cash	(152)
Cash balance, 31 December 2005	(1,163)
Cash balance, 31 December 2006	$ 1,011

EXAMPLE 7

Adjusting Net Income to Compute Operating Cash Flow

Based on the following information for Pinkerly Inc., what are the total adjustments that the company would make to net income in order to derive operating cash flow?

	Year Ended
Income statement item	12/31/2006
Net income	$30 million
Depreciation	$7 million

Balance sheet item	12/31/2005	12/31/2006	Change
Accounts receivable	$15 million	$30 million	$15 million
Inventory	$16 million	$13 million	($3 million)
Accounts payable	$10 million	$20 million	$10 million

A. Add \$5 million.
B. Add \$29 million.
C. Subtract \$5 million.
D. Subtract \$29 million.

Solution: A is correct. To derive operating cash flow, the company would make the following adjustments to net income: add depreciation (a noncash expense) of \$7 million; add the decrease in inventory of \$3 million; add the increase in accounts payable of \$10 million; and subtract the increase in accounts receivable of \$15 million. Total additions would be \$20 million, and total subtractions would be \$15 million for net additions of \$5 million.

3.3 Conversion of Cash Flows from the Indirect to the Direct Method

An analyst may desire to review direct-format operating cash flow to review trends in cash receipts and payments (such as cash received from customers or cash paid to suppliers). If a direct-format statement is not available, cash flows from operating activities reported under the indirect method can be converted to the direct method. Accuracy of conversion depends on adjustments using data available in published financial reports. The method described here is sufficiently accurate for most analytical purposes.

The three-step conversion process is demonstrated for Acme Corporation in Exhibit 11. Referring again to Exhibits 6 and 7 for Acme Corporation's income statement and balance sheet information, begin by disaggregating net income of \$2,210 into total revenues and total expenses (Step 1). Next, remove any nonoperating and noncash items (Step 2). For Acme, we therefore remove the nonoperating gain on the sale of equipment of \$205 and the noncash depreciation expense of \$1,052. Then, convert accrual amounts of revenues and expenses to cash flow amounts of receipts and payments by adjusting for changes in working capital accounts (Step 3). The results of these adjustments are the items of information for the direct format of operating cash flows. These line items are shown as the results of Step 3.

EXHIBIT 11 Conversion from the Indirect to the Direct Method

Step 1	Total revenues	\$23,803
Aggregate all revenue and all expenses	Total expenses	21,593
	Net income	\$ 2,210
Step 2	Total revenue less noncash item revenues:	
Remove all noncash items from aggregated revenues and expenses and break out remaining items into relevant cash flow items	(\$23,803 − \$205) =	\$23,598
	Revenue	\$23,598
	Total expenses less noncash item expenses:	
	(\$21,593 − \$1,052) =	\$20,541

(Exhibit continued on next page . . .)

EXHIBIT 11 (continued)

	Cost of goods sold	$11,456
	Salary and wage expenses	4,123
	Other operating expenses	3,577
	Interest expense	246
	Income tax expense	1,139
	Total	$20,541
Step 3 Convert accrual amounts to cash flow amounts by adjusting for working capital changes	Cash received from customers[a]	$23,543
	Cash paid to suppliers[b]	11,900
	Cash paid to employees[c]	4,133
	Cash paid for other operating expenses[d]	3,532
	Cash paid for interest[e]	258
	Cash paid for income tax[f]	1,134

Calculations for Step 3

[a] Revenue of $23,598 less increase in accounts receivable of $55.

[b] Cost of goods sold of $11,456 plus increase in inventory of $707 less increase in accounts payable of $263.

[c] Salary and wage expense of $4,123 less increase in salary and wage payable of $10.

[d] Other operating expenses of $3,577 less decrease in prepaid expenses of $23 less increase in other accrued liabilities of $22.

[e] Interest expense of $246 plus decrease in interest payable of $12.

[f] Income tax expense of $1,139 less increase in income tax payable of $5.

CASH FLOW STATEMENT ANALYSIS

The analysis of a company's cash flows can provide useful information for understanding a company's business and earnings and for predicting its future cash flows. This section describes tools and techniques for analyzing the statement of cash flows, including the analysis of major sources and uses of cash, cash flow, common-size analysis, conversion of the cash flow statement from the indirect method to the direct method, and computation of free cash flow and cash flow ratios.

4.1 Evaluation of the Sources and Uses of Cash

Evaluation of the cash flow statement should involve an overall assessment of the sources and uses of cash between the three main categories as well as an assessment of the main drivers of cash flow within each category, as follows:

1. Evaluate where the major sources and uses of cash flow are between operating, investing, and financing activities.
2. Evaluate the primary determinants of operating cash flow.
3. Evaluate the primary determinants of investing cash flow.
4. Evaluate the primary determinants of financing cash flow.

Step 1 The major sources of cash for a company can vary with its stage of growth. For a mature company, it is desirable to have the primary source of cash be operating activities. Over the long term, a company must generate cash from its operating activities. If operating cash flow were consistently negative, a company would need to borrow money or issue stock (financing activities) to fund the shortfall. Eventually, these providers of capital need to be repaid from operations or they will no longer be willing to provide capital. Cash generated from operating activities can either be used in investing or financing activities. If the company has good opportunities to grow the business or other investment opportunities, it is desirable to use the cash in investing activities. If the company does not have profitable investment opportunities, the cash should be returned to capital providers, a financing activity. For a new or growth stage company, operating cash flow may be negative for some period of time as it invests in inventory and receivables (extending credit to new customers) in order to grow the business. This cannot sustain itself over the long term, so eventually the cash must start to come primarily from operating activities so that capital can be returned to the providers of capital. Lastly, it is desirable that operating cash flows are sufficient to cover capital expenditures (in other words, the company has free cash flow as discussed further below). In summary, major points to consider at this step are:

- What are the major sources and uses of cash flow?
- Is operating cash flow positive and sufficient to cover capital expenditures?

Step 2 Turning to the operating section, the analysts should examine the most significant determinates of operating cash flow. Some companies need to raise cash for use in operations (to hold receivables, inventory, etc.), while occasionally a company's business model generates cash flow (e.g., when cash is received from customers before it needs to be paid out to suppliers). Under the indirect method, the increases and decreases in receivables, inventory, payables, and so on can be examined to determine whether the company is using or generating cash in operations and why. It is also useful to compare operating cash flow with net income. For a mature company, because net income includes noncash expenses (depreciation and amortization), it is desirable that operating cash flow exceeds net income. The relationship between net income and operating cash flow is also an indicator of earnings quality. If a company has large net income but poor operating cash flow, it may be a sign of poor earnings quality. The company may be making aggressive accounting choices to increase net income but not be generating cash for its business. You should also examine the variability of both earnings and cash flow and consider the impact of this variability on the company's risk as well as the ability to forecast future cash flows for valuation purposes. In summary:

- What are the major determinants of operating cash flow?
- Is operating cash flow higher or lower than net income? Why?
- How consistent are operating cash flows?

Step 3 Within the investing section, you should evaluate each line item. Each line item represents either a source or use of cash. This enables you to understand where the cash is being spent (or received). This section will tell you how much cash is being invested for the future in property, plant, and equipment; how much is used to acquire entire companies; and how much is put aside in liquid investments, such as stocks and bonds. It will also tell you how much cash is being raised by selling these types of assets. If the company is making major capital investments, you should consider where the cash is coming from to cover these investments (e.g., is the cash coming from excess operating cash flow or from the financing activities described in Step 4?).

Step 4 Within the financing section, you should examine each line item to understand whether the company is raising capital or repaying capital and what the nature of its capital sources are. If the company is borrowing each year, you should consider when repayment may be required. This section will also present dividend payments and repurchases of stock that are alternative means of returning capital to owners.

Example 8 provides an example of a cash flow statement evaluation.

EXAMPLE 8

Analysis of the Cash Flow Statement

Derek Yee, CFA, is preparing to forecast cash flow for Groupe Danone as an input into his valuation model. He has asked you to evaluate the historical cash flow statement of Groupe Danone, which is presented in Exhibit 12. Groupe Danone prepares its financial statements in conformity with International Financial Reporting Standards as adopted by the European Union.

EXHIBIT 12 **Groupe Danone Consolidated Financial Statements Consolidated Statements of Cash Flows (millions of euro)**

Fiscal Years Ended 31 December	2004	2005
Net income	449	1,464
Minority interests in net income of consolidated subsidiaries	189	207
Net income from discontinued operations	(47)	(504)
Net income (loss) of affiliates	550	(44)
Depreciation and amortization	481	478
Dividends received from affiliates	45	45
Other flows	(93)	70
Cash flows provided by operations	1,574	1,716
(Increase) decrease in inventories	(70)	(17)
(Increase) decrease in trade accounts receivable	(27)	(87)
Increase (decrease) in trade accounts payable	143	123
Changes in other working capital items	74	112
Net change in current working capital	120	131
Cash flows provided by operating activities	1,694	1,847
Capital expenditures	(520)	(607)
Purchase of businesses and other investments net of cash and cash equivalent acquired	(98)	(636)

(Exhibit continued on next page . . .)

EXHIBIT 12 (continued)

Proceeds from the sale of businesses and other investments net of cash and cash equivalent disposed of	650	1,659
(Increase) decrease in long-term loans and other long-term assets	130	(134)
Changes in cash and cash equivalents of discontinued operations	52	30
Cash flows provided by investing activities	214	312
Increase in capital and additional paid-in capital	38	61
Purchases of treasury stock (net of disposals)	(213)	(558)
Dividends	(456)	(489)
Increase (decrease) in noncurrent financial liabilities	(290)	(715)
Increase (decrease) in current financial liabilities	(536)	(191)
(Increase) decrease in marketable securities	(415)	(210)
Cash flows used in financing activities	(1,872)	(2,102)
Effect of exchange rate changes on cash and cash equivalents	(21)	53
Increase (decrease) in cash and cash equivalents	15	110
Cash and cash equivalents at beginning of period	451	466
Cash and cash equivalents at end of period	466	576
Supplemental disclosures:		
Cash paid during the year:		
Interest	152	172
Income tax	439	424

Yee would like answers to the following questions:

- What are the major sources of cash for Groupe Danone?
- What are the major uses of cash for Groupe Danone?
- What is the relationship between net income and cash flow from operating activities?
- Is cash flow from operating activities sufficient to cover capital expenditures?
- Other than capital expenditures, is cash being used or generated in investing activities?
- What types of financing cash flows does Groupe Danone have?

Solution: The major categories of cash flows can be summarized as follows (in millions of euro):

	2004	2005
Cash flows from operating activities	1,694	1,847
Cash flows from investing activities	214	312
Cash flows from financing activities	(1,872)	(2,102)
Exchange rate effects on cash	(21)	53
Increase in cash	15	110

The primary source of cash for Groupe Danone is operating activities. The secondary source of cash is investing activities. Most of this cash flow is being spent in financing activities. The fact that the primary source of cash is from operations is a good sign. Additionally, operating cash flow exceeds net income in both years—a good sign. Operating cash flows are much higher than capital expenditures, indicating that the company can easily fund capital expenditures from operations. The company has generated investing cash flows by selling business and investments in the two years presented. In the financing category, Groupe Danone is spending cash by repurchasing its own stock, paying dividends, and paying down debt. This could be an indicator that the company lacks investment opportunities and is, therefore, returning cash to the providers of capital.

4.2 Common-Size Analysis of the Statement of Cash Flows

In common-size analysis of a company's income statement, each income and expense line item is expressed as a percentage of net revenues (net sales). For the common-size balance sheet, each asset, liability, and equity line item is expressed as a percentage of total assets. For the common-size cash flow statement, there are two alternative approaches. The first approach is to express each line item of cash inflow (outflow) as a percentage of total inflows (outflows) of cash, and the second approach is to express each line item as a percentage of net revenue.

Exhibit 13 demonstrates the total cash inflows/total outflows method for Acme Corporation. Under this approach, each of the cash inflows is expressed as a percentage of the total cash inflows, whereas each of the cash outflows is expressed as a percentage of the total cash outflows. In Panel A, Acme's common-size statement is based on a cash flow statement using the direct method of presenting operating cash flows. Operating cash inflows and outflows are separately presented on the cash flow statement and, therefore, the common-size cash flow statement shows each of these operating inflows (outflows) as a percentage of total inflows (outflows). In Panel B, Acme's common-size statement is based on a cash flow statement using the indirect method of presenting operating cash flows. When a cash flow statement has been presented using the indirect method, operating cash inflows and outflows are not separately presented; therefore, the common-size cash flow statement shows only the net operating cash flows as a percentage of total inflows or outflows, depending on whether the net amount was an in- or out-cash flow. Because Acme's net operating cash flow is positive, it is shown as a percentage of total inflows.

EXHIBIT 13 Acme Corporation Common-Size Cash Flow Statement: Year Ended 31 December 2006

Panel A. Direct Format for Operating Cash Flow

Inflows		Percentage of Total Inflows
Receipts from customers	$23,543	96.86%
Sale of equipment	762	3.14
Total	$24,305	100.00%

Outflows		Percentage of Total Outflows
Payments to suppliers	$11,900	48.66%
Payments to employees	4,113	16.82
Payments for other operating expenses	3,532	14.44
Payments for interest	258	1.05
Payments for income tax	1,134	4.64
Purchase of equipment	1,300	5.32
Retirement of long-term debt	500	2.04
Retirement of common stock	600	2.45
Dividend payments	1,120	4.58
Total	$24,457	100.00%

Panel B. Indirect Format for Operating Cash Flow

Inflows		Percentage of Total Inflows
Operations	$ 2,606	77.38%
Sale of equipment	762	22.62
Total	$ 3,368	100.00%

Outflows		Percentage of Total Outflows
Purchase of equipment	1,300	36.93%
Retirement of long-term debt	500	14.20
Retirement of common stock	600	17.05
Dividend payments	1,120	31.82
Total	$ 3,520	100.00%

Exhibit 14 demonstrates the net revenue common-size cash flow statement for Acme Corporation. Under the net revenue approach, each line item in the cash flow statement is shown as a percentage of net revenue. The common-size statement in this exhibit has been developed based on Acme's cash flow statement using the indirect method for operating cash flows. Each line item of the reconciliation between net income and net operating cash flows is expressed as a percentage of net revenue. The common-size format makes it easier to see trends in cash flow rather than just looking at the total amount. This method is also useful to the analyst in forecasting future cash flows because individual items in the common-size statement (e.g., depreciation, fixed capital expenditures, debt borrowing, and repayment) are expressed as a percentage of net revenue. Thus, once the analyst has forecast revenue, the common-size statement provides a basis for forecasting cash flows.

EXHIBIT 14 Acme Corporation Common-Size Cash Flow Statement: Indirect Format Year Ended 31 December 2006

		Percentage of Net Revenue
Cash flow from operating activities:		
Net income	$2,210	9.37
Depreciation expense	1,052	4.46
Gain on sale of equipment	(205)	(0.87)
Increase in accounts receivable	(55)	(0.23)
Increase in inventory	(707)	(3.00)
Decrease in prepaid expenses	23	0.10
Increase in accounts payable	263	1.11
Increase in salary and wage payable	10	0.04
Decrease in interest payable	(12)	(0.05)
Increase in income tax payable	5	0.02
Increase in other accrued liabilities	22	0.09
Net cash provided by operating activities	2,606	11.04
Cash flow from investing activities:		
Cash received from sale of equipment	762	3.23
Cash paid for purchase of equipment	(1,300)	(5.51)
Net cash used for investing activities	(538)	(2.28)
Cash flow from financing activities:		
Cash paid to retire long-term debt	(500)	(2.12)
Cash paid to retire common stock	(600)	(2.54)
Cash paid for dividends	(1,120)	(4.75)
Net cash used for financing activities	(2,220)	(9.41)
Net decrease in cash	$ (152)	(0.64)

EXAMPLE 9

Analysis of a Common-Size Cash Flow Statement

Andrew Potter is examining an abbreviated common-size cash flow statement based on net revenues for Dell, which is reproduced below:

	Period Ending				
	3 Feb 2006	**28 Jan 2005**	**30 Jan 2004**	**31 Jan 2003**	**1 Feb 2002**
Net income	**6.39%**	**6.18%**	**6.38%**	**5.99%**	**4.00%**
Cash flows—operating activities					
Depreciation	0.70	0.68	0.63	0.60	0.77
Net income adjustments	0.93	−0.56	−0.92	−0.61	4.57
Changes in operating activities					
Accounts receivable	−1.84	0.00	−1.96	0.54	0.71
Inventory	−0.21	0.00	−0.13	−0.06	0.36
Other operating activities	−0.54	4.49	−0.34	−0.50	−0.20
Liabilities	3.22	0.00	5.19	4.04	1.98
Net cash flow—operating	**8.66%**	**10.79%**	**8.86%**	**9.99%**	**12.18%**
Cash flows—investing activities					
Capital expenditures	−1.30	−1.07	−0.79	−0.86	−0.97
Investments	8.24	−3.64	−4.88	−3.04	−6.28
Other investing activities	0.00	0.00	−1.12	0.00	0.00
Net cash flows—investing	**6.94%**	**−4.71%**	**−6.79%**	**−3.90%**	**−7.25%**
Cash flows—financing activities					
Sale and purchase of stock	−11.14	−6.36	−3.34	−5.72	−8.68
Other financing activities	0.00	0.00	0.00	0.00	0.01
Net cash flows—financing	**−11.14%**	**−6.36%**	**−3.34%**	**−5.72%**	**−8.67%**
Effect of exchange rate	−0.35	1.15	1.48	1.30	−0.33
Net cash flow	**4.10%**	**0.87%**	**0.21%**	**1.67%**	**−4.07%**

Based on the information in the above exhibit, address the following:

1. Characterize the importance of
   - **A.** depreciation.
   - **B.** capital expenditures.
2. Contrast Dell's operating cash flow as a percentage of revenue with Dell's net profit margin (on a cash basis).
3. Identify Dell's major use of its positive operating cash flow.

Solution to 1:

A. Dell has very little depreciation expense (less than 1 percent), which is added back to determine operating cash flow.

B. Dell's level of capital expenditures is relatively small, less than 1 percent of revenues in most years, but this increased in the most recent year. This is consistent with Dell's low amount of depreciation.

Solution to 2: Dell's operating cash flow as a percentage of revenue is consistently much higher than net profit margin. Dell's business model appears to generate cash flow instead of requiring working capital, as many companies do. Dell collects cash flow from customers, on average, sooner than cash is paid out to suppliers.

Solution to 3: Most of Dell's operating cash flow has been used to repurchase large amounts of its own stock (financing activities).

4.3 Free Cash Flow to the Firm and Free Cash Flow to Equity

In the initial evaluation of the cash flow statement above, it was mentioned that it is desirable that operating cash flows are sufficient to cover capital expenditures. The excess of operating cash flow over capital expenditures is known generically as **free cash flow**. For purposes of valuing a company or its equity securities, an analyst may want to determine a more precise free cash flow measure, such as **free cash flow to the firm** (FCFF) or **free cash flow to equity** (FCFE).

FCFF is the cash flow available to the company's suppliers of debt and equity capital after all operating expenses (including income taxes) have been paid and necessary investments in working capital and fixed capital have been made. FCFF can be computed starting with net income as[8]

$$\text{FCFF} = \text{NI} + \text{NCC} + \text{Int}(1-\text{Tax rate}) - \text{FCInv} - \text{WCInv}$$

where

NI = Net income

NCC = Noncash charges (such as depreciation and amortization)

Int = Interest expense

FCInv = Capital expenditures (fixed capital, such as equipment)

WCInv = Working capital expenditures

The reason for adding back interest is that FCFF is the cash flow available to the suppliers of debt capital as well as equity capital. Conveniently, FCFF can also be computed from cash flow from operating activities as

$$\text{FCFF} = \text{CFO} + \text{Int}(1-\text{Tax rate}) - \text{FCInv}$$

[8] See Stowe, Robinson, Pinto, and McLeavy (2002) for a detailed discussion of free cash flow computations.

CFO represents cash flow from operating activities under U.S. GAAP or under IFRS where the company has chosen to place interest expense in operating activities. Under IFRS, if the company has placed interest and dividends received in investing activities, these should be added back to CFO to determine FCFF. Additionally, if dividends paid were subtracted in the operating section, these should be added back in to compute FCFF.

The computation of FCFF for Acme Corporation (based on the data from Exhibits 6, 7, and 8) is as follows:

CFO	$2,606
Plus: Interest paid times (1 − income tax rate) {$258 [1 − ($1,139 ÷ $3,349)]}	170
Less: Net investments in fixed capital ($1,300 − $762)	(538)
FCFF	$2,238

FCFE is the cash flow available to the company's common stockholders after all operating expenses and borrowing costs (principal and interest) have been paid and necessary investments in working capital and fixed capital have been made. FCFE can be computed as

$$\text{FCFE} = \text{CFO} - \text{FCInv} + \text{Net borrowing} - \text{Net debt repayment}$$

The computation of FCFE for Acme Corporation (based on the data from Exhibits 6, 7, and 8) is as follows:

CFO	$2,606
Less: Net investments in fixed capital [$1,300 − $762]	538
Less: Debt repayment	(500)
FCFE	$1,568

Positive FCFE means that the company has an excess of operating cash flow over amounts needed for investments for the future and repayment of debt. This cash would be available for distribution to owners.

4.4 Cash Flow Ratios

The statement of cash flows provides information that can be analyzed over time to obtain a better understanding of the past performance of a company and its future prospects. This information can also be effectively used to compare the performance and prospects of different companies in an industry and of different industries. There are several ratios based on cash flow from operating activities that are useful in this analysis. These ratios generally fall into cash flow performance (profitability) ratios and cash flow coverage (solvency) ratios. Exhibit 15 summarizes the calculation and interpretation of some of these ratios.

EXHIBIT 15 Cash Flow Ratios

Performance Ratios	Calculation	What It Measures
Cash flow to revenue	CFO ÷ Net revenue	Cash generated per dollar of revenue
Cash return on assets	CFO ÷ Average total assets	Cash generated from all resources
Cash return on equity	CFO ÷ Average shareholders' equity	Cash generated from owner resources
Cash to income	CFO ÷ Operating income	Cash-generating ability of operations
Cash flow per share	(CFO − Preferred dividends) ÷ number of common shares outstanding	Operating cash flow on a per-share basis

Coverage Ratios	Calculation	What It Measures
Debt coverage	CFO ÷ Total debt	Financial risk and financial leverage
Interest coverage	(CFO + Interest paid + Taxes paid) ÷ Interest paid	Ability to meet interest obligations
Reinvestment	CFO ÷ Cash paid for long-term assets	Ability to acquire assets with operating cash flows
Debt payment	CFO ÷ Cash paid for long-term debt repayment	Ability to pay debts with operating cash flows
Dividend payment	CFO ÷ Dividends paid	Ability to pay dividends with operating cash flows
Investing and financing	CFO ÷ Cash outflows for investing and financing activities	Ability to acquire assets, pay debts, and make distributions to owners

EXAMPLE 10

A Cash Flow Analysis of Comparables

Andrew Potter is comparing the cash-flow-generating ability of Dell with that of several other computer manufacturers: Hewlett Packard, Gateway, and Apple. He collects the following information:

	Operating Cash Flow		
Revenue	2005	2004	2003
DELL	8.66%	10.79%	8.86%
HPQ	9.26%	6.37%	8.29%
GTW	−0.65%	−11.89%	2.15%
AAPL	18.20%	11.28%	4.66%

Average Total Assets	2005	2004	2003
DELL	20.89%	24.97%	21.10%
HPQ	10.46%	6.75%	8.33%
GTW	−1.35%	−22.84%	3.22%
AAPL	25.87%	12.57%	4.41%

AAPL = Apple, GTW = Gateway, HPQ = Hewlett Packard.

What is Potter likely to conclude about the relative cash-flow-generating ability of these companies?

Solution: Dell has consistently generated operating cash flow relative to both revenue and assets. Hewlett Packard also has a good level of operating cash flow relative to revenue, but its operating cash flow is not as strong as Dell relative to assets. This is likely due to Dell's lean business model and lack of a need for large amounts of property, plant, and equipment. Gateway has poor operating cash flow on both measures. Apple has dramatically improved its operating cash flow over the three years and in 2005 had the strongest operating cash flow of the group.

SUMMARY

The cash flow statement provides important information about a company's cash receipts and cash payments during an accounting period as well as information about a company's operating, investing, and financing activities. Although the income statement provides a measure of a company's success, cash and cash flow are also vital to a company's long-term success. Information on the sources and uses of cash helps creditors, investors, and other statement users evaluate the company's liquidity, solvency, and financial flexibility. Key concepts are as follows:

- Cash flow activities are classified into three categories: operating activities, investing activities, and financing activities. Significant noncash transaction activities (if present) are reported by using a supplemental disclosure note to the cash flow statement.
- The cash flow statement under IFRS is similar to U.S. GAAP; however, IFRS permits greater discretion in classifying some cash flow items as operating, investing, or financing activities.
- Companies can use either the direct or the indirect method for reporting their operating cash flow:
  - The direct method discloses operating cash inflows by source (e.g., cash received from customers, cash received from investment income) and operating cash outflows by use (e.g., cash paid to suppliers, cash paid for interest) in the operating activities section of the cash flow statement.
  - The indirect method reconciles net income to net cash flow from operating activities by adjusting net income for all noncash items and the net changes in the operating working capital accounts.
- The cash flow statement is linked to a company's income statement and comparative balance sheets and is constructed from the data on those statements.
- Although the indirect method is most commonly used by companies, the analyst can generally convert it to the direct format by following a simple three-step process.
- The analyst can use common-size statement analysis for the cash flow statement. Two prescribed approaches are the total cash inflows/total cash outflows method and the percentage of net revenues method.
- The cash flow statement can be used to determine FCFF and FCFE.
- The cash flow statement may also be used in financial ratios measuring a company's profitability, performance, and financial strength.

PRACTICE PROBLEMS FOR READING 34

1. The three major classifications of activities in a cash flow statement are
   A. revenues, expenses, and net income.
   B. inflows, outflows, and balances.
   C. beginning balance, ending balance, and change.
   D. operating, investing, and financing.
2. The sale of a building for cash would be classified as what type of activity on the cash flow statement?
   A. Operating.
   B. Investing.
   C. Financing.
   D. This activity would not appear on the cash flow statement.
3. Which of the following is an example of a financing activity on the cash flow statement under U.S. GAAP?
   A. Payment of dividends.
   B. Receipt of dividends.
   C. Payment of interest.
   D. Receipt of interest.
4. A conversion of a face value $1,000,000 convertible bond for $1,000,000 of common stock would most likely be
   A. reported as a $1,000,000 financing cash outflow and inflow.
   B. reported as supplementary information to the cash flow statement.
   C. reported as a $1,000,000 financing cash outflow and a $1,000,000 investing cash inflow.
   D. reported as a $1,000,000 investing cash outflow and a $1,000,000 financing cash inflow.
5. Interest expense may be classified as an operating cash flow
   A. under U.S. GAAP, but may be classified as either operating or investing cash flows under IFRS.
   B. under IFRS, but may be classified as either operating or investing cash flows under U.S. GAAP.
   C. under U.S. GAAP, but may be classified as either operating or financing cash flows under IFRS.
   D. under IFRS, but may be classified as either operating or financing cash flows under U.S. GAAP.
6. Tax cash flows
   A. must be separately disclosed in the cash flow statement under IFRS only.
   B. must be separately disclosed in the cash flow statement under U.S. GAAP only.
   C. are not separately disclosed in the cash flow statement under IFRS or U.S. GAAP.
   D. must be separately disclosed in the cash flow statement under both IFRS and U.S GAAP.

7. Which of the following components of the cash flow statement may be prepared under the indirect method under both IFRS and U.S. GAAP?
   A. Operating.
   B. Investing.
   C. Financing.
   D. The impact of exchange rates on cash balances.

8. Which of the following is most likely to appear in the operating section of a cash flow statement under the indirect method under U.S. GAAP?
   A. Net income.
   B. Cash paid for interest.
   C. Cash paid to suppliers.
   D. Cash received from customers.

9. Red Road Company, a consulting company, reported total revenues of $100 million, total expenses of $80 million, and net income of $20 million in the most recent year. If accounts receivable increased by $10 million, how much cash did the company receive from customers?
   A. $210 million.
   B. $110 million.
   C. $90 million.
   D. $30 million.

10. Green Glory Corp., a garden supply wholesaler, reported cost of goods sold for the year of $80 million. Total assets increased by $55 million, including an increase of $5 million in inventory. Total liabilities increased by $45 million, including an increase of $2 million in accounts payable. How much cash did the company pay to its suppliers during the year?
    A. $90 million.
    B. $83 million.
    C. $77 million.
    D. $70 million.

11. Purple Fleur S.A., a retailer of floral products, reported cost of goods sold for the year of $75 million. Total assets increased by $55 million, but inventory declined by $6 million. Total liabilities increased by $45 million, and accounts payable increased by $2 million. How much cash did the company pay to its suppliers during the year?
    A. $85 million.
    B. $79 million.
    C. $69 million.
    D. $67 million.

12. White Flag, a women's clothing manufacturer, reported wage expense of $20 million. The beginning balance of wages payable was $3 million, and the ending balance of wages payable was $1 million. How much cash did the company pay in wages?

A. $24 million.
B. $23 million.
C. $22 million.
D. $18 million.

2005 exam

13. An analyst gathered the following information from a company's 2004 financial statements ($ millions):

Year Ended 31 December	2003	2004
Net sales	245.8	254.6
Cost of goods sold	168.3	175.9
Accounts receivable	73.2	68.3
Inventory	39.0	47.8
Accounts payable	20.3	22.9

Based only on the information above, the company's 2004 statement of cash flows prepared using the direct method would include amounts ($ millions) for cash received from customers and cash paid to suppliers, respectively, that are *closest* to:

	Cash received from customers	Cash paid to suppliers
A.	249.7	169.7
B.	249.7	182.1
C.	259.5	169.7
D.	259.5	182.1

14. Golden Cumulus Corp., a commodities trading company, reported interest expense of $19 million and taxes of $6 million. Interest payable increased by $3 million, and taxes payable decreased by $4 million. How much cash did the company pay for interest and taxes?

A. $22 million for interest and $2 million for taxes.
B. $22 million for interest and $10 million for taxes.
C. $16 million for interest and $2 million for taxes.
D. $16 million for interest and $10 million for taxes.

15. An analyst gathered the following information from a company's 2005 financial statements ($ millions):

CFA 2005 exam

Balances as of Year Ended 31 December	2004	2005
Retained earnings	120	145
Accounts receivable	38	43
Inventory	45	48
Accounts payable	36	29

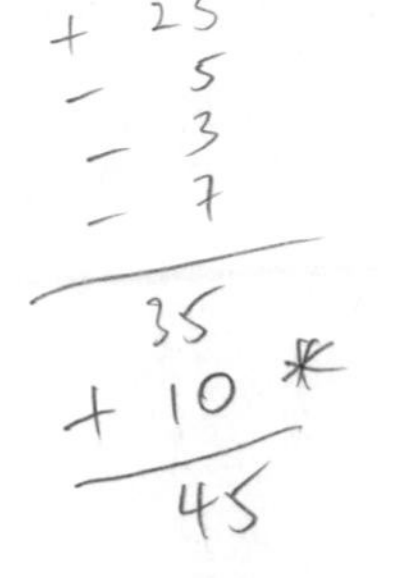

The company declared and paid cash dividends of $10 million in 2005 and recorded depreciation expense in the amount of $25 million for 2005. The company's 2005 cash flow from operations ($ millions) was *closest* to

A. 25.
B. 35.
C. 45.
D. 75.

16. Silverago Incorporated, an international metals company, reported a loss on the sale of equipment of $2 million. In addition, the company's income statement shows depreciation expense of $8 million, and the cash flow statement shows capital expenditure of $10 million, all of which was for the purchase of new equipment. Using the following information from the comparative balance sheets, how much cash did the company receive from the equipment sale?

Balance Sheet Item	12/31/2005	12/31/2006	Change
Equipment	$100 million	$105 million	$5 million
Accumulated depreciation—equipment	$40 million	$46 million	$6 million

A. $6 million.
B. $5 million.
C. $1 million.
D. $0.

17. Jaderong Plinkett Stores reported net income of $25 million, which equals the company's comprehensive income. The company has no outstanding debt. Using the following information from the comparative balance sheets (in millions), what should the company report in the financing section of the statement of cash flows?

Balance Sheet Item	12/31/2005	12/31/2006	Change
Common stock	$100	$102	$2
Additional paid-in capital common stock	$100	$140	$40
Retained earnings	$100	$115	$15
Total stockholders' equity	$300	$357	$57

A. Issuance of common stock $42 million; dividends paid of $10 million.
B. Issuance of common stock $38 million; dividends paid of $10 million.
C. Issuance of common stock $42 million; dividends paid of $40 million.
D. Issuance of common stock $38 million; dividends paid of $40 million.

18. Based on the following information for Pinkerly Inc., what are the total net adjustments that the company would make to net income in order to derive operating cash flow?

Income Statement Item		Year Ended 12/31/2006	
Net income		$20 million	
Depreciation		$2 million	
Balance Sheet Item	**12/31/2005**	**12/31/2006**	**Change**
Accounts receivable	$25 million	$22 million	($3 million)
Inventory	$10 million	$14 million	$4 million
Accounts payable	$8 million	$13 million	$5 million

A. Add $6 million.
B. Add $8 million.
C. Subtract $6 million.
D. Subtract $8 million.

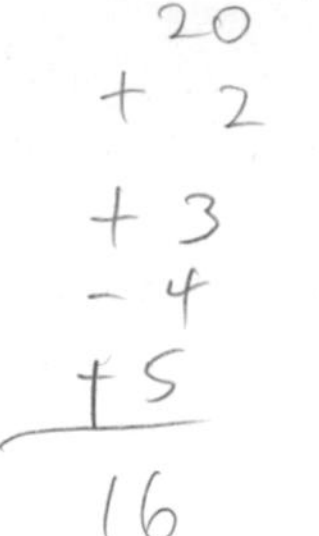

19. The first step in evaluating the cash flow statement should be to examine

A. individual operating cash flow items.

B. individual investing cash flow items.

C. individual financing cash flow items.

D. the major sources and uses of cash.

20. Which of the following would be valid conclusions from an analysis of the cash flow statement for Telefónica Group presented in Exhibit 3?

A. The company does not pay dividends.

B. The primary use of cash is financing activities.

C. The primary source of cash is operating activities.

D. Telefónica classifies interest received as an operating activity.

21. Which is an appropriate method of preparing a common-size cash flow statement?

A. Begin with net income and show the items that reconcile net income and operating cash flows.

B. Show each line item on the cash flow statement as a percentage of net revenue.

C. Show each item of revenue and expense as a percentage of net revenue.

D. Show each line item on the cash flow statement as a percentage of total cash outflows.

22. Which of the following is an appropriate method of computing free cash flow to the firm?

A. Add operating cash flows plus capital expenditures and deduct after-tax interest payments.

B. Add operating cash flows plus after-tax interest payments and deduct capital expenditures.

C. Add capital expenditures and after-tax interest payments and deduct operating cash flows.

D. Deduct both after-tax interest payments and capital expenditures from operating cash flows.

23. An analyst has calculated a ratio using as the numerator the sum of operating cash flow, interest, and taxes, and as the denominator the amount of interest. What is this ratio, what does it measure, and what does it indicate?

A. This ratio is an interest coverage ratio, measuring a company's ability to meet its interest obligations and indicating a company's solvency.

B. This ratio is an effective tax ratio, measuring the amount of a company's operating cash flow used for taxes and indicating a company's efficiency in tax management.

C. This ratio is an operating profitability ratio, measuring the operating cash flow generated accounting for taxes and interest and indicating a company's liquidity.

D. This ratio is a reinvestment ratio, measuring the amount of operating cash used for interest and indicating a company's profitability.

STUDY SESSION 9
FINANCIAL STATEMENT ANALYSIS:
Inventories, Long-Term Assets, Deferred Taxes, and On- and Off-Balance-Sheet Debt

The readings in this study session examine specific categories of assets and liabilities that are particularly susceptible to the impact of alternative accounting policies and estimates. Analysts must understand the effects of alternative policies on financial statements and ratios, and be able to execute appropriate adjustments to enhance comparability between companies. In addition, analysts must be alert to differences between a company's reported financial statements and economic reality.

The description and measurement of inventories require careful attention because the investment in inventories is frequently the largest current asset for merchandizing and manufacturing companies. For these companies, the measurement of inventory cost (i.e., cost of goods sold) is a critical factor in determining gross profit and other measures of company profitability. Long-term operating assets are often the largest category of assets on a company's balance sheet. The analyst needs to scrutinize management's choices with respect to recognizing expenses associated with the operating assets because of the potentially large impact such choices can have on reported earnings.

A company's accounting policies (such as depreciation choices) can cause differences in taxes reported in financial statements and taxes reported on tax returns. The reading "Analysis of Income Taxes" discusses several issues that arise relating to deferred taxes.

Both on- and off-balance-sheet debt affect a company's liquidity and solvency, and have consequences for its long-term growth and viability. The notes of the financial statements must be carefully reviewed to ensure that all potential liabilities (e.g., leasing arrangements and other contractual commitments) are appropriately evaluated for their conformity to economic reality. Adjustments to the financial statements may be required to achieve comparability when evaluating several companies, and may also be required to improve credit and investment decision-making.

READING ASSIGNMENTS

Reading 35 Analysis of Inventories
Reading 36 Analysis of Long-Lived Assets:
Part I—The Capitalization Decision
Reading 37 Analysis of Long-Lived Assets:
Part II—Analysis of Depreciation and Impairment
Reading 38 Analysis of Income Taxes
Reading 39 Analysis of Financing Liabilities
Reading 40 Leases and Off-Balance-Sheet Debt

LEARNING OUTCOMES

Reading 35: Analysis of Inventories

The candidate should be able to:

a. compute ending inventory balances and cost of goods sold using the LIFO, FIFO, and average cost methods to account for product inventory;

b. explain the relationship among and the usefulness of inventory and cost of goods sold data provided by the LIFO, FIFO, and average cost methods when prices are (1) stable or (2) changing;

c. compare and contrast the effect of the different methods on cost of goods sold and inventory balances and discuss how a company's choice of inventory accounting method affects other financial items such as income, cash flow, and working capital;

d. compare and contrast the effects of the choice of inventory method on profitability, liquidity, activity, and solvency ratios;

e. indicate the reasons that a LIFO reserve might decline during a given period and evaluate the implications of such a decline for financial analysis;

f. illustrate how inventories are reported in the financial statements and how the lower-of-cost-or-market principle is used and applied.

Reading 36: Analysis of Long-Lived Assets: Part I—The Capitalization Decision

The candidate should be able to:

a. demonstrate the effects of capitalizing versus expensing on net income, shareholders' equity, cash flow from operations, and financial ratios;

b. determine which intangible assets, including software development costs and research and development costs, should be capitalized, according to U.S. GAAP and international accounting standards.

Reading 37: Analysis of Long-Lived Assets: Part II—Analysis of Depreciation and Impairment

The candidate should be able to:

a. demonstrate the different depreciation methods and explain how the choice of depreciation method affects a company's financial statements, ratios, and taxes;

b. demonstrate how modifying the depreciation method, the estimated useful life, and/or the salvage value used in accounting for long-lived assets affect financial statements and ratios;

c. determine the average age and average depreciable life of a company's assets using the company's fixed asset disclosures;

d. explain and illustrate the use of impairment charges on long-lived assets, and analyze the effects of taking such impairment charges on a company's financial statements and ratios;

e. discuss accounting requirements related to remedying environmental damage caused by operating assets and explain the financial statement and ratio effects that result from the application of those requirements.

Reading 38: Analysis of Income Taxes

The candidate should be able to:

a. explain the key terms related to income tax accounting and the origin of deferred tax liabilities and assets;

b. demonstrate the liability method of accounting for deferred taxes;

c. discuss the use of valuation allowances for deferred tax assets, and their implications for financial statement analysis;

d. explain the factors that determine whether a company's deferred tax liabilities should be treated as a liability or as equity for purposes of financial analysis;

e. distinguish between temporary and permanent items in pretax financial income and taxable income;

f. calculate and interpret income tax expense, income taxes payable, deferred tax assets, and deferred tax liabilities;

g. calculate and interpret the adjustment(s) to the deferred tax accounts related to a change in the tax rate;

h. interpret a deferred tax footnote disclosure that reconciles the effective and statutory tax rates;

i. analyze disclosures relating to, and the effect of, deferred taxes on a company's financial statements and financial ratios;

j. compare and contrast a company's deferred tax items and effective tax rate reconciliation (1) between reporting periods and (2) with the comparable items reported by other companies.

Reading 39: Analysis of Financing Liabilities

The candidate should be able to:

a. distinguish between operating and trade debt related to operating activities and debt generated by financing activities, and discuss the analytical implications of a shift between the two types of liabilities;

b. determine the effects of debt issuance and amortization of bond discounts and premiums on financial statements and financial ratios;

c. analyze the effect on financial statements and financial ratios of issuing zero-coupon debt;

d. classify a debt security with equity features as a debt or equity security and demonstrate the effect of issuing debt with equity features on the financial statements and ratios;

e. describe the disclosures relating to financing liabilities, and discuss the advantages/disadvantages to the company of selecting a given financing instrument and the effect of the selection on a company's financial statements and ratios;

f. determine the effects of changing interest rates on the market value of debt and on financial statements and ratios;

g. calculate and describe the accounting treatment of, and economic gains and losses resulting from, the various methods of retiring debt prior to its maturity;

h. analyze the implications of debt covenants for creditors and the issuing company.

Reading 40: Leases and Off-Balance-Sheet Debt

The candidate should be able to:

a. discuss the incentives for leasing assets instead of purchasing them, and the incentives for reporting the leases as operating leases rather than capital leases;

b. contrast the effects of capital and operating leases on the financial statements and ratios of lessees and lessors;

c. describe the types of off-balance-sheet financing and analyze their effects on selected financial ratios;

d. distinguish between sales-type leases and direct financing leases and explain the effects of these types of leases on the financial statements of lessors.

ANALYSIS OF INVENTORIES

by Gerald I. White, Ashwinpaul C. Sondhi, and Dov Fried

READING 35

LEARNING OUTCOMES

The candidate should be able to:

a. compute ending inventory balances and cost of goods sold using the LIFO, FIFO, and average cost methods to account for product inventory;

b. explain the relationship among and the usefulness of inventory and cost of goods sold data provided by the LIFO, FIFO, and average cost methods when prices are (1) stable or (2) changing;

c. compare and contrast the effect of the different methods on cost of goods sold and inventory balances and discuss how a company's choice of inventory accounting method affects other financial items such as income, cash flow, and working capital;

d. compare and contrast the effects of the choice of inventory method on profitability, liquidity, activity, and solvency ratios;

e. indicate the reasons that a LIFO reserve might decline during a given period and evaluate the implications of such a decline for financial analysis;

f. illustrate how inventories are reported in the financial statements and how the lower-of-cost-or-market principle is used and applied.

INTRODUCTION 1

During 1999, the **spot price** of crude oil[1] rose from less than $10 per barrel to more than $25 per barrel, an increase of more than 150%. Crude oil continued to rise in early 2000, nearing $32 per barrel in March. Simultaneously, the price of gasoline sold at the pump increased dramatically in most countries. Consumers and politicians criticized oil companies for immediately raising the price of gasoline sold at the retail level. They argued that the gasoline being sold had been refined

[1] Measured by the Brent Crude "near contract generic future" as reported on Bloomberg.

from oil purchased at a price of $10 per barrel and, hence, raising the price of this "old" gasoline resulted in windfall profits.

The oil companies countered that since the market price of oil had risen, replacing the old oil now cost more and thus raising the price of gasoline was justified by current market conditions.

The accounting choice of last-in, first-out (LIFO) versus first-in, first-out (FIFO) for inventory and cost of goods sold (COGS) mirrors this debate as to the more appropriate measure of income. The choice affects the firm's income statement, balance sheet, and related ratios. Perhaps more important, in contrast to most financial reporting choices, the choice of inventory method has real cash flow effects as it affects income taxes paid by the firm.

2 INVENTORY AND COST OF GOODS SOLD: BASIC RELATIONSHIPS

The inventory account is affected by two events: the purchase (or manufacture) of goods (P) and their subsequent sale (COGS). The relationship between these events and the balance of beginning inventory (BI) and ending inventory (EI) can be expressed as

$$EI = BI + P - \text{COGS or} \quad \textbf{(35-1a)}$$

$$BI + P = \text{COGS} + EI \quad \textbf{(35-1b)}$$

For any period, prior to the preparation of financial statements for the period, the left side of the second equation is known: the beginning inventory plus purchases (cost of goods acquired for sale during the period). Preparation of the income statement and balance sheet for the period requires the allocation of these costs ($BI + P$) between COGS and ending inventory. This process is illustrated under two scenarios:

Beginning inventory: 200 units @ $10/unit = $2,000 =BI

		Scenario 1: Stable Prices		Scenario 2: Rising Prices	
Quarter	**Purchases Units**	**Unit Cost**	**Purchases Dollars**	**Unit Cost**	**Purchases Dollars**
1	100	$10	$1,000	$11	$1,100
2	150	10	1,500	12	1,800
3	150	10	1,500	13	1,950
4	100	10	1,000	14	1,400
Total	500		$5,000		$6,250
			$BI + P =$ $7,000		$BI + P =$ $8,250

Units sold: 100 units per quarter for a total of 400 units.
Ending inventory: 300 units.

Scenario 1: Stable Prices

Beginning inventory plus purchases equals $7,000. Since unit costs are constant at $10 per unit and 400 units were sold, the COGS equals $4,000 (400 × $10) and the cost of the 300 units in ending inventory equals $3,000 (300 × $10).

$$BI + P = \text{COGS} + EI$$
$$\$2{,}000 + \$5{,}000 = \$4{,}000 + \$3{,}000$$

However, perfectly stable prices are the exception rather than the norm. In addition to general inflationary pressures, costs and prices for specific goods are constantly changing. Accounting for inventory and COGS in such an environment, as a result, becomes more complex.

Scenario 2: Rising Prices

Beginning inventory plus purchases equals $8,250. Unlike the case of stable prices, the allocation between COGS and the cost of ending inventory requires an assumption as to the flow of costs. Essentially, three alternative assumptions are possible: *FIFO, LIFO,* and *weighted-average cost.*

FIFO accounting assumes that the costs of items *first purchased* are deemed to be the costs of items *first sold* and these costs enter COGS; ending inventory is made up of the cost of the most recent items purchased.

At the opposite extreme is LIFO accounting where items *last purchased* are assumed to be the ones *first sold* and the ending inventory is made up of the earliest costs incurred.

Finally, as its name implies, weighted-average cost accounting uses the (same) average cost for both the items sold and those remaining in closing inventory.

In our example, *the assumptions of rising prices and an increase in the inventory balance generate three alternative allocations of the cost of goods available for sale* ($BI + P$), on the income statement and balance sheet (the calculations are shown in Exhibit 1):

Method	*BI*	+	*P*	=	COGS	+	*EI*
FIFO	$2,000	+	$6,250	=	$4,300	+	$3,950
Weighted-average	2,000	+	6,250	=	4,714	+	3,536
LIFO	2,000	+	6,250	=	5,150	+	3,100

3 COMPARISON OF INFORMATION PROVIDED BY ALTERNATIVE METHODS

This section compares the information provided by the three alternative accounting methods.

Balance Sheet Information: Inventory Account

The ending inventory consists of 300 units. At current replacement cost (i.e., the fourth-quarter unit cost of $14), the inventory would have a carrying value of $4,200. The FIFO inventory of $3,950 comes closest to this amount because FIFO

EXHIBIT 1 Allocation of Costs Under Different Inventory Methods, Scenario 2

A. FIFO

The 400 units sold (COGS) are assumed to carry the earliest costs incurred and the 300 units left in inventory carry the latest costs:

COGS		Ending Inventory	
200 @ $10 = $2,000		100 @ $14 = $1,400	
100 @ $11 = $1,100		150 @ $13 = $1,950	
100 @ $12 = $1,200		50 @ $12 = $ 600	
400	$4,300	300	$3,950

B. LIFO

The 400 units sold (COGS) are assumed to carry the latest costs incurred and the 300 units left in inventory carry the earliest costs:

COGS		Ending Inventory	
100 @ $14 = $1,400		200 @ $10 = $2,000	
150 @ $13 = $1,950		100 @ $11 = $1,100	
150 @ $12 = $1,800			
400	$5,150	300	$3,100

C. Weighted-Average

The total costs for the 700 units = $8,250. On a per-unit basis, this results in a weighted-average unit cost of:

$$\frac{\$8,250}{700} = \$11.786$$

$$\text{COGS} = 400 \times \$11.786 = \$4,714$$

$$\text{Ending inventory} = 300 \times \$11.786 = \$3,536$$

allocates the earliest costs to COGS, leaving the most recent costs in ending inventory.

Conversely, the LIFO balance of $3,100 is furthest from the current cost as LIFO accounting allocates the earliest (outdated) costs to ending inventory. In fact, the cost of ending inventory for many companies using LIFO may be decades old[2] and virtually useless as an indicator of the current or replacement cost of inventories on hand.

[2] For example, Caterpillar has stated that the LIFO method "was first adopted for the major portion of inventories in 1950."

From a balance sheet perspective, therefore, inventories based on FIFO are preferable to those presented under LIFO, as carrying values most closely reflect current cost. In other words, FIFO provides a measure of inventory that is closer to its current (economic) value.

The carrying amount of inventory can also be affected by changes in market value as discussed below.

Inventory Valuation: Lower of Cost or Market

GAAP requires the use of the lower-of-cost-or-market valuation basis (LCM) for inventories, with market value defined as replacement cost.[3] The LCM valuation basis follows the principle of conservatism (on both the balance sheet and income statement) since it recognizes losses or declines in market value as they occur, whereas increases are reported only when inventory is sold. LCM can be used with LIFO for financial statement purposes. However, for tax purposes LIFO cannot be combined with LCM. Firms using LIFO cannot recognize (and obtain tax benefits from) writedowns and declines in market value for tax purposes.[4]

Income Statement Information: Cost of Goods Sold

Consider a situation where an item purchased for $6 is sold for $10 at a time when it costs $7 to replace it. Prior to replacement of the item, reported income is $4 ($10 − $6). However, if income is defined as the amount available for distribution to shareholders without impairing the firm's operations, then it can be argued that income is only $3, as $7 (not the original cost of $6) are needed to replace the item in inventory and continue operations. The $1 difference between the original cost of the item and the cost of replacement is referred to as a holding gain or inventory profit,[5] and it is debatable whether this amount should be considered income.[6]

In our hypothetical case, *only if the item were not replaced* would there be $10 to distribute to shareholders, indicating income of $4. Under a going-concern assumption, however, firms that sell their inventory need to replenish it constantly for sales in the future. Thus, income should be measured after providing for the replacement of inventory. In addition, the increase in inventory costs suggests that income of $3 is a better indicator of expected future income than $4.

In our example, the replacement cost of the items sold (using the unit cost for each quarter) is $5,000[7] [(100 × $11) + (100 × $12) + (100 × $13) + (100 × $14)]. As U.S. GAAP uses a historical cost framework, however, replacement cost accounting is not permitted. LIFO allocates the most recent purchase prices

[3] However, replacement cost cannot exceed the net realizable value or be below the net realizable value less the normal profit margin.

[4] Otherwise, the firm could have the best of both worlds and obtain tax savings whether costs were rising or declining.

[5] If we use terminology, economic income equals $4. As the holding gain is $1, sustainable (future) income is $3. Jennings, Simko, and Thompson (1996) confirm that LIFO-based cost of goods sold is a more useful indicator of the firm's future resource outflows than ("as-if") non-LIFO cost of goods sold as LIFO-based income statements explained more of the variation in equity valuations than non-LIFO income statements. However, in contrast to our earlier argument, they did not find ("as-if") non-LIFO balance sheets to be more informative than LIFO-based balance sheets.

[6] The situation is analogous to having purchased a home before a rapid increase in real estate prices and not being able to benefit from your good fortune because any replacement home would cost as much as the home you live in now.

[7] If the computation were done on an annual basis, the replacement cost would be $5,600 (400 × $14) using the most recent purchase price to measure replacement cost.

to COGS. The reported LIFO COGS of $5,150 is, therefore, closest to the replacement cost, with the FIFO COGS of $4,300 furthest from this cost. *During periods of changing prices and stable or growing inventories, LIFO is the most informative accounting method for income statement purposes, in that it provides a better measure of current income and future profitability.* This leaves us in something of a quandary, since FIFO provides the best measure for the balance sheet.[8]

The preceding discussion implied the use of a single method for all inventories of the firm. In practice, firms often use more than one inventory method. They may use different methods for their foreign operations since LIFO is rarely used outside the United States, or they may use different methods for particular business segments. This factor serves to disguise further the impact of reported inventory on the income statement and balance sheet.

Additionally, the LIFO measurements are based on assumptions and estimates that are complex in a multiproduct environment and are affected by management choice.

Finally, the use of FIFO, LIFO, or weighted-average for the allocation of cost of goods available for sale is preceded by the measurement of costs included in inventory. In a manufacturing environment, as Box 1 illustrates, such measurement is also affected by management choice.

From an analyst's perspective the use of different methods is not so grim. Information is often available to permit restatement of financial statements from one method to the other. Such restatement is illustrated later in this reading. Our discussion now, however, turns to the financial statement effects of the choice between LIFO and FIFO.

4 LIFO VERSUS FIFO: INCOME, CASH FLOW, AND WORKING CAPITAL EFFECTS

- LIFO better for Current Cost Accting

The above example illustrates that, in periods of rising prices and stable or increasing inventory quantities, the use of LIFO results in higher COGS expense and lower reported income. In the absence of income taxes, there would be no difference in cash flow. Cash flow would equal payments made for inventory purchases and be independent of the accounting method used.

When LIFO is a permitted method for income taxes, however, lower income translates into lower taxes and thus higher operating cash flows. In the United States, unlike other accounting policy choices that allow differing methods of accounting for financial statements and tax purposes, *IRS regulations require that the same method of inventory accounting used for tax purposes also be used for financial reporting.* From an economic perspective, given rising prices, LIFO is the better choice, as taxes will be lower and cash flows will be higher despite the lower reported income.[9]

It was noted that working capital is used as a broad liquidity measure because it includes cash and near-cash assets. Inventory accounting can distort the working

[8] The weighted-average method falls someplace in between the FIFO and LIFO methods both in terms of the balance sheet and income statement. It is seen by some as a compromise method. Alternatively, we can argue that it is the worst of the three choices: Unlike LIFO and FIFO, which provide good information on one financial statement, the weighted-average method does not do so for either statement. Practically speaking, however, the weighted-average method tends to be closer to FIFO than LIFO, especially with respect to inventory costs on the balance sheet.

[9] The question of why, given the foregoing, all firms do not use LIFO will be considered later in the reading.

BOX 1 INVENTORY COSTING IN A MANUFACTURING ENVIRONMENT

Accounting for inventories in a manufacturing environment adds another dimension to the problem of inventory costing. Unlike merchandising operations, which carry only finished goods inventory, manufacturing operations carry three types of inventory: (1) raw material, (2) work in process, and (3) finished goods.

Inventories include raw material costs as well as labor and overhead costs required to transform the raw materials into finished goods. Determining the amount of overhead (indirect) costs poses the most problems. Included in (factory) overhead are items such as: supervisors' salaries, depreciation/rent of factory plant and equipment, utilities, repairs and maintenance, and quality control costs.

Such costs are *joint costs* and, in a multiproduct environment, are difficult to allocate among products. As the inventory carrying amount of any one product line depends on the allocation procedure, that amount can be somewhat arbitrary and capable of manipulation. For example, a manufacturer can increase reported income by choosing an allocation method that charges more of the joint costs to slower moving items. These costs then remain in inventory longer, and products with higher turnover rates appear more profitable.

A second aspect of this problem is the fixed nature (in the short run) of items such as depreciation, rent, or supervisors' salaries. Allocating such costs to products involves an averaging process that is affected by changing levels of production. A simple example in a single-product environment will illustrate this effect.

Assume a company has factory rent of $12,000 and it sells 10,000 units. If it produces 10,000 units, the full $12,000 of factory rent will be expensed through COGS (at a rate of $1.20/unit). If production increases to 12,000 units, then factory rent is allocated to inventory at $1.00/unit. But if only 10,000 units are sold, then only $10,000 is expensed as part of COGS and $2,000 of unallocated (but incurred) rent remains in inventory. Income increases by changing production levels rather than increasing sales.

The income effect of changing production rates can be the result of either intentional management decision (manipulation) or the unintended result of sales levels that differ from expectation. In either case it is imperative for the analyst to recognize:

- the accounting policies used by different firms in the same industry
- the effects of fluctuations in production on COGS and reported income

Finally, which costs are charged to inventory (and expensed when sold) and which costs are expensed as incurred vary among firms. Schiff (1987) notes that, although it is commonly suggested in accounting textbooks that fixed overhead costs must be allocated to inventory, in practice, many companies[a] have (historically) charged certain overhead costs (e.g., depreciation, pension costs, and property taxes) directly to expense. For such companies, variations in production and inventory levels will not affect the amount expensed. However, for firms that allocate such costs to inventory, when inventory levels increase, the amount expensed will be less than the amount actually incurred, with the difference remaining in inventory. On the balance sheet, those firms that capitalize more indirect costs in inventory will have higher carrying values of inventory, working capital, and equity balances. Unfortunately, not all companies disclose their practices in this respect. This can make comparisons between companies difficult.[b]

[a] The steel industry is one example noted by Schiff.

[b] The matter is further complicated by the increased emphasis in recent years in improvements in manufacturing processes. As a result, many firms have adjusted their method of inventory costing. [Bartley and Chen (1992) also report tax-related motivations for firms to switch from expensing to capitalization of certain items.]

capital measure and lead to erroneous and contradictory conclusions. LIFO accounting results in higher cash flows, but it reports lower working capital because the inventory balances retain earlier (lower) costs and the cash saved is only a percentage (the marginal tax rate) of the difference in inventory values.

In periods of rising prices and stable or increasing inventory quantities, the impact of LIFO and FIFO on the financial statements can be summarized as:

	LIFO	FIFO
COGS	Higher	Lower
Income before taxes	Lower	Higher
Income taxes	Lower	Higher
Net Income	Lower	Higher
Cash flow	**Higher**	**Lower**
Inventory balance	Lower	Higher
Working capital	Lower	Higher

Cash flow has been highlighted because it is the only amount with direct economic impact. The others are accounting constructs and their economic significance is indirect and informational.

Continuing with the previous numeric example and assuming that 400 units are sold for $10,000 (average price of $25) with a tax rate of 40%, we can illustrate the above differences as follows. The resulting income statements are:

			LIFO
	FIFO	**LIFO**	**Higher/(Lower) By**
Sales	$10,000	$10,000	$ 0
COGS	(4,300)	(5,150)	850
Income before tax	$ 5,700	$ 4,850	$(850)
Income tax @ 40%	(2,280)	(1,940)	(340)
Net income	$ 3,420	$ 2,910	$(510)

If we assume that sales are for cash and payments for purchases and taxes are made immediately, then cash flows are:

			LIFO
	FIFO	**LIFO**	**Higher/(Lower) By**
Sales inflows	$10,000	$10,000	$ 0
Purchases	(6,250)	(6,250)	0
Inflows before tax	$ 3,750	$ 3,750	$ 0
Income tax paid	(2,280)	(1,940)	(340)
Operating cash flow	$ 1,470	$ 1,810	$340

Therefore, changes in balance sheet accounts are:

Assets			
			LIFO
	FIFO	LIFO	Higher/(Lower) By
Operating cash[a]	$1,470	$1,810	$340
Inventory[b]	1,950	1,100	(850)
Working capital	$3,420	$2,910	$(510)
Liabilities and Stockholders' Equity			
Retained earnings[c]	$3,420	$2,910	$(510)

[a] Net cash flow for period.
[b] Purchases less COGS.
[c] Net income for period.

The difference in net income of $510 and the difference in cash flows of $340 are related to the difference in COGS (equivalently the difference in inventory balances) of $850 as follows:

Income Difference	=	(1 − Tax Rate)	×	COGS Difference
$510	=	0.6	×	$850
Cash Flow Difference	=	Tax Rate	×	COGS Difference
$340	=	0.4	×	$850

However, these differences are in *opposite directions,* with higher income for the FIFO firm and higher operating cash flows for the LIFO firm. The difference in working capital is the net of the difference in inventory balance and cash flow:

$510 = $850 − $340

This results in misleading liquidity measures for the LIFO firm as its working capital is understated.[10] The increase in cash is more than offset by the understatement of inventory.

Our illustration shows that the choice of inventory method can greatly affect reported operating results. Moreover, depending on whether the focus is the balance sheet or income statement, differing methods may be preferred. Thus, the analyst needs to be able to adjust between LIFO and FIFO in order to:

- Eliminate differences between firms due to accounting methods so that any remaining differences reflect economic and operating variations.
- Obtain the measure(s) most relevant for their analytical purpose.

The next sections describe how such adjustments can be made.

[10] Johnson and Dhaliwal (1988) studied firms that abandoned LIFO in favor of FIFO. Their evidence suggests one possible motivation for the abandonment decision was to increase their reported working capital. Compared to firms that retained LIFO, the abandonment firms had tighter working capital constraints under their debt covenants.

5 ADJUSTMENT FROM LIFO TO FIFO

Adjustment of Inventory Balances

LIFO inventory balances generally contain older costs with little or no relationship to current costs. Because of this deficiency, firms are required to disclose the *LIFO reserve.* The LIFO reserve (usually shown in the financial statement footnotes, but sometimes on the face of the balance sheet) is the difference between the inventory balance shown on the balance sheet and the (approximately current or replacement cost) amount that would have been reported had the firm used FIFO.

To adjust inventory balances of firms using LIFO to current or FIFO cost, we must add the LIFO reserve to the LIFO inventory amount. We can express this as

$$\text{LIFO Reserve} = \text{Inventory}_F - \text{Inventory}_L$$

or

$$\text{Inventory}_F = \text{Inventory}_L + \text{LIFO Reserve}$$

where the subscripts F and L represent the accounting methods FIFO and LIFO, respectively.

Adjustment of Cost of Goods Sold

COGS can be derived using the opening and closing inventory balances and purchases for the period:

$$\text{COGS} = BI + P - EI$$

Thus, to arrive at FIFO cost of goods sold (COGS_F), these amounts must be restated from LIFO to FIFO. The adjustment of inventory balances was illustrated earlier. Purchases (which are not a function of the accounting method

EXAMPLE 1

Sunoco

Exhibit 2 contains details of inventory and portions of financial statement footnotes from the 1996–1999 annual reports of Sunoco, a large U.S. oil refiner. Sunoco uses the LIFO method to account for virtually all crude oil and refined product inventories.

Exhibit 3A shows the adjustment of inventory from LIFO to FIFO, adding the LIFO reserve to the LIFO inventory. Sunoco's LIFO reserve is large, indicating that the balance sheet carrying amount significantly understates inventories. This understatement is typical of firms whose products have risen in price and that have used LIFO for many years. In the case of Sunoco, the LIFO cost of inventories is only 30% of the FIFO cost in 1999. As the price of oil is volatile, the difference between Inventory_F and Inventory_L is highly variable over the period shown in Exhibit 3.

EXHIBIT 2 Sunoco

Inventory Disclosures

Inventories of crude oil and refined products are valued at the lower of cost or market. The cost of such inventories is determined principally using LIFO.

	Inventories[a] at December 31 (in $millions)			
	1996	**1997**	**1998**	**1999**
Crude oil	$157	$150	$184	$158
Refined products	252	214	219	163
Inventories valued at LIFO	**$409**	**$364**	**$403**	**$321**

The current replacement cost of all inventories valued at LIFO exceeded their carrying cost by $780, $492, $205, and $763 million at December 31, 1996 through 1999, respectively.

	1996	**1997**	**1998**	**1999**
Cost of goods sold (in $millions)	$8,718	$7,610	$5,646	$7,365

[a] The above data only include inventories intended for resale. Sunoco also carries materials and supplies on its balance sheet as inventories.

Source: Sunoco, 1996–1999 annual reports.

EXHIBIT 3 Sunoco

Adjustment from LIFO to FIFO, 1996–1999

A. Adjusting LIFO Inventory to FIFO (Current Cost)

	1996	**1997**	**1998**	**1999**
Inventories carried at LIFO	$ 409	$364	$403	$ 321
LIFO reserve	780	492	205	763
Inventories adjusted to FIFO	$1,189	$856	$608	$1,084

B. Adjusting LIFO COGS to FIFO COGS

	1996	**1997**	**1998**	**1999**
Cost of goods sold at LIFO ($COGS_L$)		$7,610	$5,646	$7,365
Less: LIFO effect[a]		(288)	(287)	558
Equals: cost of goods sold at FIFO ($COGS_F$)		$7,898	$5,933	$6,807

[a] Change in LIFO reserve from previous year-end.

Source: Data from Sunoco, 1996–1999 annual reports.

used) need not be adjusted and can be derived directly from the (opening and closing) inventory balances and COGS reported in the financial statements:

$$P = \text{COGS}_L + EI_L - BI_L$$

EXAMPLE 2

Sunoco

Sunoco's purchases for 1999 can be calculated (in $millions) as

$$\begin{aligned} P &= \$7{,}365 \text{ million} + \$321 \text{ million} - \$403 \text{ million} \\ &= \$7{,}283 \text{ million} \end{aligned}$$

Using 1999 purchases, just calculated, and the FIFO inventory amounts derived in Exhibit 3A yields the 1999 COGS on a FIFO basis for Sunoco:

$$\begin{aligned} \text{COGS}_F &= BI_F + P - EI_F \\ &= \$608 \text{ million} + \$7{,}283 \text{ million} - \$1{,}084 \text{ million} \\ &= \$6{,}807 \text{ million} \end{aligned}$$

Thus COGS on a FIFO basis is lower than on a LIFO basis by $558 million ($7,365 million − $6,807 million). The astute reader will note that this amount equals the increase in the LIFO reserve during the year (from $205 to $763 million). This is no coincidence and the adjustment from LIFO to FIFO COGS can be made directly from the LIFO reserve accounts without going through the intermediate steps of calculating purchases and adjusting inventories. The direct adjustment (shown in Exhibit 3B) is[11]

$$\text{COGS}_F = \text{COGS}_L - \text{Change in LIFO Reserve}$$

or

$$\begin{aligned} \text{COGS}_F &= \text{COGS}_L - (\text{LIFO Reserve}_E - \text{LIFO Reserve}_B) \\ \$6{,}807 \text{ million} &= \$7{,}365 \text{ million} - (\$763 \text{ million} - \$205 \text{ million}) \end{aligned}$$

where the subscripts E and B refer to ending (inventory) and beginning (inventory), respectively. The change in LIFO reserve during the year, sometimes called the *LIFO effect* for the year, is thus the difference between the COGS computed under the two methods.

[11] For those with a more mathematical bent, this result can be proven as follows:

Purchases ($P = \text{COGS} + EI - BI$) are identical for both accounting methods.
Thus $\text{COGS}_F + EI_F - BI_F = \text{COGS}_L + EI_L - BI_L$.
Rearranging terms yields $\text{COGS}_F = \text{COGS}_L - [(EI_F - EI_L) - (BI_F - BI_L)]$
or $\text{COGS}_F = \text{COGS}_L - [(\text{LIFO Reserve}_E - \text{LIFO Reserve}_B)]$.

Before leaving this discussion, consider two questions. First, why does conversion to FIFO in 1996 to 1998 increase COGS (see Exhibit 3B) when we normally expect $COGS_F$ to be lower than $COGS_L$? Second, why did the LIFO reserve decrease in those years?

The answer to both questions is the same: Oil prices decreased. This decline reduced the difference between inventory cost on a LIFO basis and cost on a FIFO basis. The LIFO reserve, which represents this difference, is thus reduced. In both years, use of the LIFO method reduced COGS by almost $290 million, increasing pretax earnings by an equal amount. The lesson here should be clear: *When prices are declining, LIFO produces lower COGS and, therefore, higher earnings.*

In 1999, when prices (and the LIFO reserve) increased, the expected effect was obtained. $COGS_L$ was higher and pretax income was reduced by the amount of increase in the LIFO reserve. In industries such as oil and gas, based on volatile commodity prices, fluctuations in the LIFO reserve due to price changes are common.

ADJUSTMENT OF INCOME TO CURRENT COST INCOME

6

This section discusses the adjustment of FIFO (and weighted-average) COGS to reflect current costs.[12] There are two reasons for making this adjustment. One is to estimate the impact of price changes on a firm's COGS and earnings; we wish to separate **price effects** from operating effects. The second reason is to compare the firm with other firms in the same industry using LIFO accounting.

Note that *only the adjustment of COGS to LIFO COGS is relevant.* Adjustments of inventory balances to LIFO serve no purpose, as LIFO inventory costs are outdated and almost meaningless.

Unlike the adjustment from LIFO to FIFO discussed in the previous section, information needed to adjust COGS to LIFO is not generally provided in the financial statements of firms using FIFO (or average cost). An approximate adjustment, however, is often possible.[13]

This adjustment requires multiplying the opening inventory by the (specific) inflation rate and adding the result to $COGS_F$ to arrive at $COGS_L$.

$$COGS_L = COGS_F + (BI_F \times r)$$

[12] Although we use the terms LIFO and current cost COGS interchangeably, our objective is to estimate current cost COGS. Generally, as long as the firm does not deplete any of its opening inventory, these two are equivalent. When opening inventory quantities are reduced (known as a LIFO liquidation), LIFO COGS and income are both distorted, as old costs flow into the income statement and COGS no longer reflects the current cost of inventory sold. When a LIFO liquidation occurs, LIFO COGS does not equal current cost COGS; in a subsequent section of the reading we illustrate how to adjust for this distortion.

[13] A more complex adjustment taking into consideration the firm's inventory turnover is possible. Falkenstein and Weil (1977) discuss the use of turnover, but note (p. 51 of their article) that estimates from the more basic procedure (used here) have always approximated the estimates from the more complex methods.

More formally, where r is the *specific inflation rate appropriate for the products in which the firm deals.*[14]

To the extent that a firm's inventory purchases are steady throughout the period, the above adjustment will approximate the actual FIFO-to-LIFO (current cost) adjustment.

Weighted-average COGS (with subscript w) can be similarly adjusted to current cost (LIFO); the adjustment to opening inventory can be appoximated[15] by one-half the (specific) inflation rate:

$$COGS_L = COGS_W + (BI_W \times r/2)$$

Obtaining r. The inflation rate needed for the adjustment is not a general producer or consumer price index, but rather should be the specific price index appropriate to the firm in question. (For a multi-industry firm, the calculation should be done on a segmented basis.) Many industry indices are readily available, published by government or private sources. For companies whose inputs are commodities (oil, coffee, steel scrap), the spot price for the commodity may be used.

Alternatively, the specific price level change, r, for a given FIFO (or weighted average) firm can be estimated from data of a competing (LIFO) firm (in the same industry) by making use of the following relationship:[16]

$$r = \frac{\Delta \text{LIFO reserve}}{BI_F}$$

This procedure provides a reasonable approximation of r as long as the LIFO firm has not had a *significant* reduction of its inventory from year to year. The example that follows illustrates the adjustment procedure to LIFO.

---

[14] The appropriateness of the approximation can be illustrated by the following proof. Assume that a firm carries a *quantity Q* of inventory and this quantity is equal to three months of inventory. The inventory level Q is replenished every three months. Assume further that the inflation rate over the year is equal to r. Finally, let P be the unit cost at which the opening inventory Q_o was purchased at the end of the previous year. Thus, the unit cost of the inventory at the end of the current year will equal $P(1 + r)$. The following illustrates the actual flow of goods purchased throughout the year:

Beginning inventory =	Q_0	= Sales during 1st Quarter
End of 1st Quarter Purchase =	Q_1	= Sales during 2nd Quarter
End of 2nd Quarter Purchase =	Q_2	= Sales during 3rd Quarter
End of 3rd Quarter Purchase =	Q_3	= Sales during 4th Quarter
End of 4th Quarter Purchase =	Q_4	= Ending Inventory

Under FIFO, the cost of Q_0, Q_1, Q_2, and Q_3 will appear in COGS. Under LIFO, the cost of Q_1, Q_2, Q_3, and Q_4 will appear in COGS. Thus, the difference between the two methods lies in the difference between the cost of the beginning (Q_0) and ending (Q_4) inventory. Hence, the difference between LIFO and FIFO equals

$$Q_4P(1 + r) - Q_0P = Q_0Pr$$

since the inventory quantity purchased each period is the same.

[15] When weighted-average cost is used, the inventory turnover rate affects the adjustment.

[16] This can be proven since

$$COGS_F = COGS_L - \Delta \text{LIFO reserve}$$

and

$$COGS_L = COGS_F + (r \times BI_F)$$

Therefore

$$(r \times BI_F) = \Delta \text{ LIFO reserve}$$

and

$$r = \frac{\Delta \text{ LIFO reserve}}{BI_F}$$

EXAMPLE 3

Caltex Australia

Exhibit 4 part A contains relevant income statement and balance sheet information for Caltex Australia, a major oil producer and refiner in Australia. LIFO is not permitted under Australian GAAP, and Caltex Australia uses the weighted-average cost method to account for inventory. Our objective is to demonstrate the adjustment of COGS and earnings to a current cost basis using the methodology described previously.

One advantage of using Caltex Australia as our example is that the company discloses (Exhibit 4, part B) the estimated effects of inventory holding gains on its earnings. Thus, we can double-check our estimates with those provided by management. The company states that it provides this information because:

> As a general rule using the historic cost basis of accounting, rising crude prices will result in increased operating profit for Caltex, falling crude oil prices will result in decreased operating profit. This movement in operating profit, often referred to as an inventory gain or loss, can create large variations in Caltex's results as calculated by the historic cost method. *Consequently, in order to provide a better insight into the operating performance of the company, Caltex's Financial reporting now includes earnings on a replacement cost of sales basis.* Replacement cost of sales earnings exclude inventory gains and losses and are calculated by restating cost of sale using the replacement cost of goods sold rather than the historic cost. (Caltex Australia's *1999 Annual Review*, emphasis added.)

The price of crude oil increased dramatically in 1999. In Australia, the price increased from \$10.60/barrel at the beginning of the year to \$23.85/barrel at year-end.[17] This implies a specific price index (r) of 125% for oil products.[18] The adjustment to Caltex Australia's weighted average COGS (the LIFO effect) is

$$(BI_W \times r / 2) = (\$AUS\ 235 \text{ million} \times 1.25/2) = \$AUS\ 147 \text{ million}$$

where the \$AUS 235 million is the inventory balance at the beginning of 1999.

This \$AUS 147 million is the holding gain included in income reported under the weighted-average method. Removing the holding gain from income (adding it to COGS) results in a better measure of reported income (\$AUS in millions):

Operating income (reported)	\$AUS 217
Adjustment for holding gain	(147)
Operating income (approximate current cost)	\$AUS 70

[17] *Source:* U.S. Energy Information Administration, Department of Energy.

[18] This estimate of r reflects the price increase in U.S. dollars. To more accurately measure the effect on Caltex Australia, the analysis should be done with oil prices expressed in Australian dollars, thereby taking into account exchange rate effects as well. However, as the method demonstrated is only an approximation and the exchange rate effect is relatively small, for ease of exposition we have ignored this technicality. (Exhibit 4 indicates that the exchange rate effect was only \$3.2 million of the total \$142 million effect.)

EXHIBIT 4 Caltex Australia

Selected Income, Balance Sheet and Replacement Cost Disclosures (in $AUS millions)

A. Income Statement and Balance Sheet Data

	1998	1999
Net revenue	$2,891	$3,153
Operating costs and expenses	(2,693)	(2,936)
Operating profit (before interest, income tax, and abnormal items)	$ 198	$ 217
Ending inventory	234.8	429.0

Caltex Australia uses the weighted-average method to account for its inventory.

B. Replacement Cost of Sales Basis of Accounting

- To assist in understanding the company's operating performance, the directors have provided additional disclosure of the company's results for the year on a replacement-cost-of-sales basis, which excludes net inventory gains and losses adjusted for foreign exchange.
- Operating profit before interest, income tax, and abnormal items on a replacement-cost-of-sales basis was $75.0 million, a reduction of $221.8 million over 1998.

	1995	1996	1997	1998	1999	Total
Historical cost operating profit before interest, income tax, and abnormal items	$263.7	$272.6	$200.6	$216.7	$198.2	$1,151.8
Add/(deduct) inventory losses/(gains)[a]	(15.5)	(27.9)	53.4	98.6	(141.7)	(33.1)
Replacement cost operating profit before interest, income tax, and abnormal items	$248.2	$244.7	$254.0	$296.8	$ 75.0	$1,118.7

[a] Historical cost results includes gross inventory gains or losses from the movement in crude prices, net of the related exchange impact. In 1999, historical cost result includes $141.7 million net inventory gain (1998: $98.6 million net inventory loss) from the increase in crude oil prices, made up of **$144.9** million in inventory gains (1998: $124.7 million in inventory losses) net of an unfavorable exchange impact of $3.2 million (1998: $26.1 million gain).

Source: Caltex Australia, *Annual Review 1999.*

Note that this approximation almost equals the estimated ($AUS 144.9 million) inventory holding gain provided by the firm itself in the footnote to part B of Exhibit 4.

An alternative approach to arrive at the specific price index appropriate for the oil refining industry would be to examine the financial statements of a competing firm in that industry using LIFO. The LIFO reserve information presented earlier in Exhibit 3 for Sunoco Company can be used to approximate the effect of inflation on Caltex Australia.

The 1999 increase in Sunoco's LIFO reserve of $558 million ($205 to $763 million) represents the increase in current costs during 1999. The specific inflation rate *r* was, therefore,

$$\$558 \text{ million}/\$608 \text{ million} = 92\%$$

where $608 million is Sunoco's Inventory_F on December 31, 1998.

This estimated *r* of 92% is considerably smaller than the estimated *r* of 125% derived from the spot price of oil. However, from Exhibit 3, we see that Sunoco's *physical* inventory must have been reduced by approximately 20%. Inventory_L decreased from $403 million to $321 million. As noted, the estimate of *r* is biased when inventory is reduced dramatically, and the greater the change in the relevant price index, the greater the distortion.

We can eliminate the distortion by estimating *r* based on only 80% of the opening inventory:

Estimating *r* from Sunoco Data after Adjusting for Reduction in Inventory

	1999 Opening Inventory	80% of 1999 Opening Inventory	1999 Closing Inventory
Inventory_L	$403	**$321**	**$321**
LIFO reserve	205	**164**	**763**
Inventory_F	$608	**$485**	**$1,084**

Using the second and third columns, the change in the LIFO Reserve equals $599 ($763 − $164) and BI_F = $485. By using the price change (LIFO effect) only for those inventories that Sunoco retained the whole year, our estimate of *r* becomes 123.5% ($599/$485). This estimate is virtually identical to the 125% estimate using the alternative methodology and, as we showed earlier, is consistent with Caltex Australia's estimate of 1999 inventory holding gains.

Before proceeding to the next section it is worthwhile to explore further Caltex Australia's estimates of its inventory holding gains/losses for the years 1997–1999.

First, compare the pattern of Caltex Australia's adjustments to replacement cost with the pattern of Sunoco's COGS on a FIFO and LIFO basis (Exhibit 3). For both companies, the effect of declining prices in 1997 and 1998 was that replacement cost income exceeded operating income ($COGS_L < COGS_F$); in 1999, when prices rose, the situation reversed.

The data in Exhibit 4 speak for themselves. Historical cost profit experienced a sharp decline in 1997–1998 relative to 1995–1996 and then recovered slightly in 1999. When holding gains and losses are excluded, however, a different picture emerges: replacement cost profit rose steadily from 1995–1998 (20% increase) and experienced a dramatic 75% decrease in 1999 as prices rose. *Reported operating earnings over this time period were significantly affected by inventory holding gains or losses virtually every year.*

If we recall our discussion of the meaning of income, it seems clear that replacement cost profit is a better measure of earnings. Holding gains and losses are not predictable. Moreover, holding gains must be reinvested in inventory for the firm to remain in business; they are not available for distribution.

Although Caltex Australia, given wide swings in the price of oil, may be an extreme case, it illustrates the necessity of analyzing the inventory accounting of a firm to understand the impact of changing prices on its earnings and net worth.

FINANCIAL RATIOS: LIFO VERSUS FIFO

Exhibit 5, based on Dopuch and Pincus (1988), compares selected financial characteristics of FIFO and LIFO firms.[19] The comparison is made first on the basis of amounts reported in financial statements (part A) and again after adjusting to the alternative accounting method (part B).

Using reported financial data, part A shows that, based on median values, LIFO firms have higher turnover ratios, less inventory as a percentage of sales or total assets, and lower variation in inventory levels and pretax income.[20] However, for the most part, these differences are not real operating differences but rather are differences due to the accounting choice. In part B the FIFO firms are adjusted to LIFO and the LIFO firms are adjusted to FIFO. The appropriate comparison can now be made with all firms using the same accounting method; that is, the numbers in part B should be compared with those directly above them in part A.

Once the data are adjusted for accounting methods, the differences tend to disappear. For example, the inventory turnover ratio as reported is 4.97 for LIFO firms and 3.88 for FIFO firms—a difference of 28%. After we adjust to the same method, the turnover ratios are:

- With all firms on FIFO, 4.03 for LIFO-reporting firms and 3.88 for FIFO-reporting firms—a difference of only 4%.

[19] Although the data used in their sample (1963–1981) may be outdated, (the direction and degree of) distortion resulting from inventory accounting differences remains relevant.

[20] The variation in inventory and pretax income is measured by the coefficient of variation—(standard deviation divided by the mean).

- With all firms on a LIFO basis, 4.97 versus 4.72, respectively—a difference of only 5%.

Similar patterns exist for the other variables.

With Exhibit 5 as a prologue, we now focus on how the FIFO/LIFO choice distorts measures of financial performance.

The FIFO/LIFO choice impacts reported profitability, liquidity, activity, and leverage ratios. For some ratios, LIFO provides a better measure, whereas for others, FIFO does. The LIFO-to-FIFO and FIFO-to-LIFO adjustment procedures discussed earlier, however, allow the analyst to make the appropriate adjustments to arrive at the "correct" ratio regardless of the firm's choice of accounting method. *The general guideline is to use LIFO numbers for ratio components that are income related and FIFO-based data for components that are balance sheet related.*

Profitability: Gross Profit Margin

The argument that LIFO better measures current income can be made with reference to gross profit margins. When input prices increase, firms pass along the added costs to customers. Moreover, they try to mark up not only those items purchased at the higher price but also all goods previously purchased. (This

EXHIBIT 5 Analysis of FIFO/LIFO Firms Based on Median Data, 1963–1981

A. Data as Reported

	LIFO	FIFO
COGS/average Inventory	4.97	3.88
Inventory/sales	0.16	0.20
Inventory/assets	0.21	0.29
C.V. inventory[a]	0.42	0.63
C.V. pretax income	0.74	0.79

B. FIFO Firms Adjusted to LIFO and LIFO Firms to FIFO

	FIFO to LIFO	LIFO to FIFO
COGS/average inventory	4.72	4.03
Inventory/sales	0.17	0.22
Inventory/assets	0.25	0.24
C.V. inventory	0.52	0.67
C.V. pretax income	0.81	0.77

[a] C.V. is the coefficient of variation (standard deviation divided by the mean).

Source: Nicholas Dopuch and Morton Pincus, "Evidence of the Choice of Inventory Accounting Methods: LIFO Versus FIFO," *Journal of Accounting Research* (Spring 1988), pp. 28–59, Tables 4 and 5, p. 44 (adapted).

policy is economically defensible using the argument made earlier that the real cost of an item sold is its replacement cost.)

Thus, if the pricing policy of the firm in our opening example is to mark up cost by 100% (implying gross profit margin of 50% of sales), the $10,000 of sales in our example would have been arrived at as follows:

Sales: 100 Units per Quarter for a Total of 400 Units

Sales Price: Assume 100% Markup over Current Costs

	Unit		Sales	
Quarter	**Cost**	**Price**	**Units**	**Dollars**
1	$11	$22	100	$ 2,200
2	12	24	100	2,400
3	13	26	100	2,600
4	14	28	100	2,800
Total			400	$10,000

Gross profit margin under FIFO and LIFO would be

Method	Sales	–	COGS	=	Gross Profit	Percent Margin
FIFO	$10,000	–	$4,300	=	$5,700	$5,700/$10,000 = 57.0%
LIFO	$10,000	–	$5,150	=	$4,850	$4,850/$10,000 = 48.5%

The 48.5% gross profit margin reported when LIFO is used is clearly closer to the profit margin intended by the firm's pricing policy. FIFO accounting, in times of rising (falling) prices, will tend to overstate (understate) reported profit margins.

The gross profit margin, by measuring the profitability of current sales, also provides an indication of the future profitability of a firm. Clearly, FIFO net income (which includes holding gains resulting from rising prices) inflates expectations regarding future profitability as future holding gains may be smaller (or negative) if future price increases are lower (or prices fall). *LIFO gives a more accurate forecast of the firm's prospects by removing the impact of price changes.*

Liquidity: Working Capital

LIFO misstates working-capital-based ratios because, as discussed, the inventory component of working capital reports outdated costs. As the purpose of the current ratio is to compare a firm's cash or near-cash assets and liabilities, use of the current value of inventory (FIFO) results in the better measure.

For Sunoco, working capital and current ratios for 1996 to 1999 based on reported data are:

Sunoco
Current Position Based on Reported LIFO Inventory

	Years Ended December 31 (in $millions)			
	1996	**1997**	**1998**	**1999**
Current assets	$1,535	$1,248	$1,180	$1,456
Current liabilities	(1,817)	(1,464)	(1,384)	(1,766)
Working capital	**$ (282)**	**$ (216)**	**$ (204)**	**$ (310)**
Current ratio	**0.84**	**0.85**	**0.85**	**0.82**

Adjusting LIFO inventory (and hence current assets) to current cost (FIFO) by adding the LIFO reserves (see Exhibits 2 and 3) changes Sunoco's current position to:

Sunoco
Adjusted Current Position Based on Current Cost (FIFO) Inventory

	Years Ended December 31 (in $millions)			
	1996	**1997**	**1998**	**1999**
Current assets	$1,535	$1,248	$1,180	$1,456
LIFO reserve	780	492	205	763
Adjusted current assets	$2,315	$1,740	$1,385	$2,219
Current liabilities	(1,817)	(1,464)	(1,384)	(1,766)
Adjusted working capital	**$ 498**	**$ 276**	**$ 1**	**$ 453**
Adjusted current ratio	**1.27**	**1.19**	**1.00**	**1.26**

The adjustments convert negative working capital to a positive measure for each year. Similarly, adjusted current ratios are (approximately 20–50%) higher than the unadjusted measures. The adjusted current ratio is also more volatile than the original ratio, reflecting the volatility of the current cost of oil-based inventories.

Activity: Inventory Turnover

Inventory turnover, defined as COGS/average inventory, is often meaningless for LIFO firms due to the mismatching of costs. The numerator represents current costs, whereas the denominator reports outdated historical costs. Thus, the turnover ratio under LIFO will, when prices increase, trend higher irrespective of the trend of physical turnover.

This point is illustrated in Exhibit 6. We assume an actual physical turnover of four times per year; that is, the average inventory is sufficient for one quarter. Further, it is assumed that unit costs increase 10% per quarter.

The FIFO inventory ratio is unaffected by the change in price, and at 3.77 is a rough approximation of the actual physical turnover of 4. The

EXHIBIT 6 Illustration of Turnover Ratio under LIFO and FIFO

Year	Quarter	Purchases = Sales	Cost per Unit	Total	For Entire Year		
Opening inventory		100	$10.00	$1,000			
1	1	100	$11.00	$1,100	FIFO	COGS	$4,641
1	2	100	$12.10	$1,210		Avg. inv.	$1,232
1	3	100	$13.31	$1,331	LIFO	COGS	$5,105
1	4	100	$14.64	$1,464		Avg. inv.	$1,000
2	1	100	$16.11	$1,611	FIFO	COGS	$6,795
2	2	100	$17.72	$1,772		Avg. inv.	$1,804
2	3	100	$19.49	$1,949	LIFO	COGS	$7,474
2	4	100	$21.44	$2,144		Avg. inv.	$1,000

	Turnover Ratios	
	Year 1	**Year 2**
FIFO	3.77	3.77
LIFO	5.11	7.47
Current cost	4.14	4.14

LIFO-based ratios of 5.11 and 7.47 are, however, far from the actual measure of 4, and the discrepancy grows over time. *Thus, to arrive at a reasonable approximation of the inventory turnover ratio for a LIFO firm, we must first convert stated inventory to FIFO.*

The preferred measure of inventory turnover (labeled "current cost" in Exhibit 6), however, is based solely on current cost. It combines the two methods, using LIFO COGS in the numerator and the FIFO inventory balance in the denominator. This approach provides the best matching of costs, as current costs are used in both the numerator and denominator. The current cost ratio (4.14) comes closest to the actual measure (based on physical units) of 4.

Using data for Sunoco (Exhibit 3), the computed inventory turnover ratios for 1998 and 1999 are (in $millions).

	1998		1999	
Method	**Turnover**	**#Days**	**Turnover**	**#Days**
LIFO (reported)	$\frac{\$5,646}{(\$364 + \$403)/2} = 14.72$	25	$\frac{\$7,365}{(\$403 + \$321)/2} = 20.34$	18
FIFO (adjusted)	$\frac{\$5,933}{(\$856 + \$608)/2} = 8.10$	45	$\frac{\$6,807}{(\$608 + \$1,084)/2} = 8.04$	45
Current cost	$\frac{\$5,646}{(\$856 + \$608)/2} = 7.71$	47	$\frac{\$7,365}{(\$608 + \$1,084)/2} = 8.70$	42

Comparing the 1998 and 1999 inventory turnover ratios for Sunoco, we see the importance of making current cost adjustments. Based on reported data, it appears that Sunoco turns its inventory very rapidly and increased its efficiency (turnover ratio) by almost 50% in 1999. After adjustment to current cost, however, a different picture emerges as the adjusted ratios imply a six-week rather than a three-week supply of inventory on hand and a much smaller year-to-year improvement in turnover.

Note also the small differences between the FIFO turnover ratios and the more refined current cost ratios. The ratio levels are similar although the current cost ratio shows higher turnover in 1999 whereas the FIFO ratio does not. The similarity is empirically true in most situations and for all practical purposes these two ratio calculations are equivalent as long as prices are not rising too rapidly (as was the case for 1999 oil prices).

Our example illustrates the usefulness of the LIFO-to-current cost adjustment for the analysis of a given company's turnover ratio. The same methodology can be used to compare two companies in the same industry when one uses FIFO and the other LIFO. The first step would be to adjust the LIFO turnover ratio to current cost. *Having made the ratios comparable (by eliminating the effect of different accounting methods), the analyst can then look for other explanations for any difference in the current cost turnover ratio.*

Inventory Theory and Turnover Ratios

Computing the inventory turnover ratio implies that there is some standard against which to measure or that there is an optimal ratio. As for all turnover ratios, one's first instinct is to believe that higher is better, that more rapid inventory turnover indicates a more efficient use of capital. In practice, however, that assumption may be overly simplistic.

The management science literature has devoted much study to the design of optimal inventory ordering policies. The traditional literature in the United States has focused on the economic order quantity (EOQ). More recently, in line with developments in Japanese management practices, focus has turned to just-in-time inventory policies. It is worthwhile to note the implications of these theories for the interpretation of the turnover ratio.

Economic Order Quantity

The construction and use of ratios for cross-sectional and time-series comparisons implicitly assume that the relationship between the numerator and denominator is linear. Applying this assumption to the inventory turnover ratio implies that, as demand increases, the quantity of inventory held should increase proportionately. The EOQ model, however, argues that the optimal level of inventory is proportionate to the *square root* of demand.

Thus, for example, if demand (COGS) increases by four times, one would expect average inventory to double (2 = the square root of 4). As a result, the turnover ratio would also double. Generally, under the EOQ model, turnover ratios should rise as sales increase and smaller firms should have lower turnover ratios. A high turnover ratio for a small firm might not be a sign of efficiency but, on the contrary, an indication that the firm was not managing its inventories in the most economic fashion.

Just in Time

Japanese management practices strive for the ideal that firms should not hold any inventory but rather should receive and ship orders "just in time" (JIT) as needed. Carried to its ultimate conclusion, this would argue for a turnover ratio approaching infinity with zero inventory held. Hence, we would expect the turnover ratios of Japanese firms to be considerably higher than those of American firms. To the extent that U.S. firms adopt these practices, they can be expected to have higher turnover ratios in the future.

One interesting byproduct of the trend toward JIT inventory is that it renders the LIFO/FIFO choice less meaningful. If a firm has no inventories (or relatively small quantities), then there is no significant difference between FIFO and LIFO.[21]

The FIFO/LIFO Choice and Inventory Holding Policy

Another important consideration is that the LIFO/FIFO choice may be related to a firm's actual inventory holding policy. Biddle (1980) found that LIFO firms tend to maintain higher inventory balances (in units) than comparably sized FIFO firms.[22] This finding is consistent with the following three factors:

1. Firms with higher inventory balances have larger potential tax savings from the use of LIFO. Thus, the higher inventory levels that result from the firm's production and operating environment may explain why the firm chose LIFO in the first place.
2. These higher balances may result from the LIFO choice, as LIFO firms attempt to get the most advantage from it by increasing their inventory levels.
3. To avoid LIFO liquidations and consequent higher income taxes, LIFO firms must buy (produce) at least as many items as they sell each year. For LIFO firms it is costly to reduce inventory levels, even when lower expected levels of demand might dictate lower levels.

Solvency: Debt-to-Equity Ratio

We have argued that, to compute liquidity ratios, understated LIFO inventory balances should be restated to current cost by adding the LIFO reserve. For the same reason, the firm's stockholders' equity should be increased by the same amount.[23] The rationale for this adjustment is that the reported equity of the

[21] However, suppliers may hold inventory and if a firm owns or controls its suppliers, it may indirectly bear the residual risk usually borne by the suppliers. To properly include the effect of captive suppliers, turnover ratios and other inventory measures should be based on consolidated financial statements, where consolidation reflects economic rather than legal or regulatory control. Admittedly, such consolidation is not always feasible given the paucity of disclosure regarding such relationships.

[22] Barlev et al. (1984) examined Canadian and Israeli firms that were not permitted to use LIFO but used an alternative method of tax adjustment for inflation. They found that inventory balances were higher for firms with large tax benefits from the inflation adjustment.

[23] Lasman and Weil (1978) suggest that the LIFO reserve should not be adjusted for taxes unless a liquidation of LIFO layers is assumed. Further, as liquidations are reported in reverse LIFO order (latest layers are liquidated first), the largest gains reside in the earliest layers. Thus, there is a low probability that the tax effect of "minor" liquidations will be significant and (if we assume that the firm remains in business) extensive liquidations are unlikely, also arguing against tax adjustment. Note that firms have strong incentives to avoid liquidations that would result in significant tax payments. See, however, the discussion regarding the Dhaliwal, Trezevant and Wilkins (2000) paper.

firm is understated because the firm owns inventory whose current value exceeds its carrying value.[24]

For analytical purposes, the inventory choice should be treated like other accounting choices. The fact that the Internal Revenue Service does not permit any difference between financial reporting and tax accounting methods should not tie the hands of the analyst. The valuation of a LIFO firm should not be penalized because it takes advantage of the tax savings inherent in LIFO.

DECLINES IN LIFO RESERVE 8

LIFO reserves can decline for either of the following reasons:

- liquidation of inventories
- price declines

In either case, COGS will be smaller (and income larger) relative to what it would have been had the reserve not declined. *The response of the analyst should not be the same in both cases, however.* For LIFO liquidations, the analyst should exclude the effects of the LIFO liquidation to arrive at a better measure of the firm's operating performance. In the second case, no adjustment is required, as price decreases are a normal part of the firm's operating results (just as much as price increases).

LIFO Liquidations

The discussion of LIFO in this reading thus far has assumed that inventory quantities are stable or increasing. When more goods are sold than are purchased (or manufactured), goods held in opening inventory are included in COGS. For LIFO companies, this results in the liquidation of LIFO layers established in prior years, and such *LIFO liquidations* can materially distort reported operating results.

The carrying cost of the old (in an accounting sense) inventories (which becomes the cost of goods sold associated with the inventory reduction) may be abnormally low and the gross profit margin abnormally high. Thus, LIFO cost no longer approximates current cost. For companies whose base inventory is very old, the distortion from these "paper profits" can be quite large;[25] for analysis, that distortion needs to be removed.

The higher income resulting from LIFO liquidations translates into increased income taxes and lower operating cash flows as taxes that were postponed through the use of LIFO must now be paid. To postpone taxes indefinitely, purchases (production) must always be greater than or equal to sales.[26]

---

[24] Using FIFO values for equity does not contradict our statement that the optimal choice for income presentation is LIFO. Recalling the example in footnote 6, the fact that your house doubled in value from $100,000 to $200,000 at a time when all houses doubled in value means that you do not benefit from selling the house as you will need the larger amount to buy a replacement house. The value of (your equity in) your house is, nevertheless, $200,000.

[25] Schiff (1983) showed that in the recession of 1980–1981, LIFO layers that were liquidated dated back as far as World War II.

[26] See Biddle (1980) for a discussion of the impact of LIFO/FIFO on inventory purchases and holding policy.

LIFO liquidations may result from inventory reductions because of strikes, recession, or declining demand for a particular product line.[27] The paradoxical result is that companies may report surprisingly high profits during economic downturns, as production cuts result in the liquidation of low-cost LIFO inventories. Given the trend toward lower inventory levels in recent years as companies move toward just-in-time or other means of reducing their investment in inventories, LIFO liquidations have become common. Such liquidations are usually disclosed in the inventory footnote of the financial statements. *As profits from LIFO liquidations are nonoperating in nature, they should be excluded from earnings for purposes of analysis.*

EXAMPLE 4

Oilgear

Exhibit 7 presents data from the inventory footnote for Oilgear, a manufacturer and distributor of systems and value-engineered components for a broad range of industrial machinery and industrial processes. The company uses the LIFO method of inventory for more than two-thirds of its inventory and reported inventory declines and LIFO liquidations in each of the years 1995–1999.[28] The motivation for the inventory declines (reported in the company's Management Discussion and Analysis) was to "align inventory levels with current (lower) customer demand."

LIFO liquidations added to Oilgear's reported earnings in each of the years 1995 to 1999. As the effect of LIFO liquidations is completely nonoperating in nature, operating results (COGS) should be adjusted to exclude it. Adjustments for each year follow (data in $000):

	1995	1996	1997	1998	1999
Sales	$82,157	$89,621	$90,904	$96,455	$90,709
COGS	(55,858)	(60,184)	(62,507)	(70,634)	(65,521)
Gross margin (reported)	**$26,299**	**$29,437**	**$28,397**	**$25,821**	**$25,188**
LIFO liquidation	800	1,350	750	740	850
Adjusted gross margin	**$25,499**	**$28,087**	**$27,647**	**$25,081**	**$24,338**
Liquidation effect:					
Gross margin increases	3%	5%	3%	3%	3%
Pretax income (reported)	**$ 3,070**	**$ 3,620**	**$ 3,363**	**$ 1,284**	**$ 1,864**
LIFO liquidation	800	1,350	750	740	850
Adjusted pretax income	**$ 2,270**	**$ 2,270**	**$ 2,613**	**$ 544**	**$ 1,014**

[27] A LIFO liquidation may not be a one-time, random occurrence but a signal that a company is entering an extended period of decline. Stober (1986) found that over 60% of his sample of firms had liquidations in more than one year and 33% experienced liquidations in three or more years. Similarly, Davis et al. (1984) found that liquidations were industry related, indicating a systematic effect, and Fried et al. (1989) found that writedowns and/or restructurings were often preceded by LIFO liquidations.

[28] Exhibit 7, from the *1999 Annual Report*, provides information only about 1997–1999 liquidations. Information as to prior-year liquidations was obtained from prior-year annual reports.

Liquidation effect:					
Pretax income increases	**35%**	**59%**	**29%**	**136%**	**84%**

Removing the LIFO liquidation effectively adjusts reported LIFO COGS to a current cost basis. Although the effects on gross margin are relatively small (3% to 5%), the effects on income are significant. As a result of the liquidation, Oilgear's reported (pretax) income was 29% to 136% higher than without the liquidation!

EXHIBIT 7 Oilgear: LIFO Liquidations

From Notes to Financial Statements

Inventories

Inventories at December 31, 1999 and 1998, consist of the following:

	1998	1999
Raw materials	$ 2,601,718	$ 2,447,402
Work in process	21,773,524	17,634,558
Finished goods	6,281,776	4,777,960
Total	$30,657,018	$24,859,920
LIFO reserve	(1,996,000)	(1,627,000)
Total (net of LIFO reserve)	$28,661,018	$23,232,920

During 1999, 1998, and 1997, LIFO inventory layers were reduced. These reductions resulted in charging lower inventory costs prevailing in previous years to cost of sales, thus reducing cost of sales by approximately $850,000, $740,000, and $750,000 below the amount that would have resulted from liquidating inventory recorded at December 31, 1999, 1998, and 1997 prices, respectively.

From Income Statement (in $millions)

	1997	1998	1999
Sales	$90,904	$96,455	$90,709
COGS	(62,507)	(70,634)	(65,521)
Gross margin	28,397	25,821	25,188
Pretax income	3,363	1,284	1,864

Source: Oilgear, *1999 Annual Report.*

Declining Prices

Our discussion thus far has assumed rising price levels. In the analysis of Sunoco, we saw that the LIFO reserve declines when prices fall. In some industries (notably those that are technology related), input prices decline steadily over time; in others (mainly commodity-based industries such as metals and petroleum), prices may fluctuate cyclically.

Declines in LIFO reserves occur whenever inventory costs fall as the lower-cost current purchases enter reported LIFO COGS, decreasing the cost difference between LIFO and FIFO ending inventories. Such declines are not considered LIFO liquidations, and disclosure of their impact is not required.

The theoretical arguments as to which accounting method provides better information still hold. LIFO provides more recent (or current) cost on the income statement and outdated costs on the balance sheet. The direction of the LIFO versus FIFO differences, however, reverses when prices decline. LIFO closing inventories are overstated, and FIFO COGS tends to be higher. Thus, although the pragmatic incentives to use LIFO for tax purposes are lost in an environment of declining prices[29] (LIFO results in higher taxes and lower cash flow), the nature of the information provided does not change. *The LIFO amounts on the balance sheet are not current and require adjustment, whereas the income statement amounts are current and do not need adjustment.*

EXAMPLE 5

Wyman-Gordon

Exhibit 8 presents data from the inventory footnote for Wyman-Gordon,[30] a producer of components for the aerospace industry. Wyman-Gordon used the LIFO method for many years and had a large LIFO reserve on its balance sheet. Weak industry conditions led to inventory declines, resulting in significant LIFO liquidations; declining prices also reduced the LIFO reserve. The exhibit indicates that in 1992 and 1993 the LIFO reserve declined $22,838 and $7,917 million, respectively. Wyman-Gordon separated the effects of liquidations and price declines:

	(in $thousands)	
	1992	**1993**
Effect of LIFO liquidation	$(18,388)	$(5,469)
Effect of lower prices	(4,450)	(2,448)
Total LIFO effect	$(22,838)	$(7,917)

When analyzing Wyman-Gordon, the LIFO liquidation effect and the declining **price effect** should be treated differently. If the analyst's objec-

[29] In addition, companies whose inventories are subject to obsolescence often take advantage of the ability (not available, for tax purposes, under LIFO) to write down inventory to market value.

[30] Wyman-Gordon is no longer a public company.

tive is to obtain a more accurate estimate of current cost income, then (*just*) the LIFO liquidation effect should be removed; the effects of declining prices on current purchases and sales, which are operating in nature, should not be removed. However, *for purposes of comparison with firms using FIFO* (i.e., calculating COGS on a FIFO basis), adjustment should be made for the total LIFO effect (liquidations *and* declining prices).

EXHIBIT 8 Wyman-Gordon: Inventories and Declines in LIFO Reserve

		in ($thousands)	
	1991	**1992**	**1993**
Inventory		$ 53,688	$42,388
LIFO reserve	64,203	41,365	33,448
Change in LIFO reserve (LIFO effect)		$(22,838)	$ (7,917)

If all inventories valued at LIFO cost had been valued at FIFO cost or market, which approximates current replacement cost, inventories would have been $41,365,000 and $33,448,000 higher than reported at December 31, 1992 and 1993, respectively.

Inventory quantities were reduced in 1991, 1992, and 1993, resulting in the liquidation of LIFO inventories carried at lower costs prevailing in prior years as compared with the cost of current purchases. The effect of lower quantities decreased 1991 loss from operations by $1,529,000, increased 1992 income from operations by $18,388,000, and decreased 1993 loss from operations by $5,469,000, whereas the effect of **deflation** had no impact on 1991 loss from operations, increased 1992 income from operations by $4,450,000, and decreased 1993 loss from operations by $2,448,000.

Source: Wyman-Gordon, *1993 Annual Report.*

INITIAL ADOPTION OF LIFO AND CHANGES TO AND FROM LIFO

9

Changes in the inventory accounting method require examination for two reasons:

1. Reporting methods for these changes are not symmetric; changing from FIFO to LIFO is not accorded the same treatment as a LIFO to FIFO switch.
2. The implications and motivation behind the accounting change are equally important; the change itself may convey information about the company's operations.

Initial Adoption of LIFO

In the United States the change to LIFO is made only on a prospective basis: GAAP do not require either retroactive restatement or the disclosure of any cumulative effect of the adoption of LIFO. Records necessary for restatement or *pro forma* disclosures often do not exist. Opening inventory in the year of adoption is the base-period inventory for subsequent LIFO computations.

When LIFO is adopted, required footnote disclosures include the impact of the adoption on the period's income before extraordinary items, net income, and related earnings per share amounts. A brief explanation of the reasons for the change in method must be provided and the absence of any cumulative effect disclosures or retroactive adjustment must be noted.

Exhibit 9 provides an example of the required disclosures. Effective January 1, 1999, Amerada Hess adopted the LIFO method for its crude oil and refined petroleum products. As Amerada Hess reported earnings per share of $4.88 for that year, the LIFO adoption reduced reported earnings by 18% from the $5.96 that would have been reported without the change. On the other hand, the change to LIFO resulted in a substantial tax saving as calculated below:

From inventory note: LIFO adjustment (effect)	$149,309,000
From accounting change note: effect on net income	97,051,000
Tax savings	$ 52,258,000

Amerada Hess was the last major U.S. oil refiner to adopt LIFO. In its footnote the company states that it switched to LIFO because the "LIFO method more closely matches current costs and revenues and will improve comparability with other oil companies." That may be so but the $52.3 million tax savings may also have had something to do with the company's decision. Note that the company chose to adopt LIFO in 1999, a year in which oil prices rose significantly, justifying the cost of changing accounting methods.

Indeed, adoptions of LIFO are often made to take advantage of the tax benefits inherent in the LIFO method and the propensity to switch is often a function of inflationary conditions. For example, in the early 1970s, over 400 firms switched to LIFO, reflecting double-digit inflation. Interestingly, the stock market has not always regarded such switches favorably despite their (positive) cash flow implications. The empirical section of the reading examines the reasons for this market reaction more closely.

Change from LIFO Method

Unlike changes to LIFO, changes from LIFO to other methods require retroactive restatement of reported earnings to the new method for prior years. The cumulative effect of adopting the new inventory accounting method is credited to retained earnings at the beginning of the earliest restated year to avoid a misstatement of current period income.

SEC regulations require a preferability letter from the firm's independent auditor stating its concurrence with and the rationale for the change. Additionally, a change from LIFO requires Internal Revenue Service approval.[31] The IRS considers changes from LIFO as a loss of tax deferral privileges, and the previous

[31] Firms switching from LIFO to another method also agree not to switch back to LIFO for at least 10 years, except under "extraordinary circumstances."

EXHIBIT 9 **Amerada Hess: Initial Adoption of LIFO**

Accounting Changes

Effective January 1, 1999, the Corporation adopted the last-in, first-out (LIFO) inventory method for valuing its refining and marketing inventories. The corporation believes that the LIFO method more closely matches current costs and revenues and will improve comparability with other oil companies. The change to LIFO decreased net income by $97,051,000 for the year ended December 31, 1999 ($1.08 per share basic and diluted). There is no cumulative effect adjustment as of the beginning of the year for this type of accounting change.

Inventories

Inventories at December 31 are as follows:

	Thousands of Dollars	
	1998	**1999**
Crude oil and other charge stocks	$ 35,818	$ 67,539
Refined and other finished products	386,917	393,064
	$422,735	$460,603
Less: LIFO adjustment		(149,309)
		$311,294
Materials and supplies	59,447	61,419
Total	$482,182	$372,713

Source: Amerada Hess, *Annual Report 1999.*

LIFO reserve becomes immediately taxable. Thus, a change from LIFO may bring significant adverse tax and cash flow consequences and requires evaluation of the impact on operations as well as management incentives for the switch. These motivations are also discussed in the following section.

10 LIFO: A HISTORICAL AND EMPIRICAL PERSPECTIVE

Overview of FIFO/LIFO Choice

Out of 600 (generally very large) firms sampled in *Accounting Trends and Techniques*,[32] about half use LIFO for at least part of their inventories. Few firms use LIFO for all inventories. Use by industry classification varies widely. LIFO is used by all rubber and plastic product firms (in this sample) and virtually all firms in the food and drug store, petroleum refining, furniture, and textile industries. None of the firms in the computer and data services, computer software, semiconductors, or telecommunications sectors do so.

[32] American Institute of Certified Public Accountants, 2000 edition.

Given the powerful incentives to use LIFO (tax savings and cash flow), two interrelated[33] questions arise:

1. Why do some firms continue to use FIFO?
2. Are firms that use LIFO perceived as being "better off" by the market despite lower reported earnings?

Many empirical studies have examined these issues; in this section we summarize their findings. Before doing so, we note that empirical research related to inventories is not confined to the FIFO/LIFO choice. Box 2 shows how analysts can use trends in inventory balances as an aid in forecasting future sales and profitability.

BOX 2 USING INVENTORY BALANCES TO AID IN FORECASTING[a]

Changes in inventory balances can provide ambiguous signals about a firm's future sales and earnings prospects. An unanticipated (from the analyst's perspective) increase in the inventory balance may signal either:[b]

1. an unexpected decrease in recent demand, causing an unplanned increase in inventory that signals lower future demand; or[c]
2. a (planned) increase in inventory levels by management anticipating higher future demand.

These two arguments are, of course, mutually exclusive. Which condition prevails cannot be determined from changes in the inventory account itself. Rather, the change itself acts as a signal for the analyst to investigate (using other sources of information) which condition is most likely for the company in question.[d]

The previous dichotomy relates only to changes in finished goods inventory. In a manufacturing environment, changes in work-in-process inventory (and to some degree changes in raw materials inventory) may indicate that management is increasing production to meet an increase in actual or anticipated orders.

Consistent with the above, Bernard and Noel (1991) examined whether changes in inventory could be used to forecast future sales and earnings. They found that the implications of inventory changes are not homogeneous for all firms, but differ between retailers and manufacturers.

For retailers, inventory increases signal higher sales but lower earnings and profit margins. This may seem paradoxical but the explanation is straightforward; a drop in

[a] See Bernard and Noel (1991) for a more elaborate discussion of the issues discussed here.

[b] Unplanned inventory changes may also have a direct impact on future unit production costs. When excess inventory must be reduced, production levels decline and unit costs increase as fixed overhead is spread over fewer units. Conversely, inventory building reduces unit costs by spreading overhead over increased production.

[c] Throughout this section, a distinction between demand and sales must be kept in mind. Lower current demand can be associated with higher future sales if a company, in response to lower demand, cuts prices, thus stimulating sales.

[d] The analyst must also be sure that the change is not (1) a result of a change in accounting method, (2) due to acquisitions of other companies, or (3) management's acquisition of more inventory in an attempt to beat an anticipated price increase.

(continued)

[33] These questions are interrelated because if the market reacts (for whatever reason) negatively to a switch to LIFO, it may explain why some firms choose to remain on FIFO.

OPTIONAL SEGMENT

BOX 2 *(continued)*

demand results in increased inventory. To eliminate "excess" inventory, retailers reduce prices to stimulate sales ("dumping" inventory). Therefore, sales increase but with lower earnings. These effects generally are short-lived as the effect on sales dissipates over time.

For manufacturers, increases in finished goods inventory again indicate lower future demand; higher sales and lower earnings in the short run follow these increases as manufacturers dump unwanted inventory. However, unlike retailers, in the long run (once the initial increase is worked down) the drop in demand persists and future sales and earnings decrease. For raw materials and work in process, on the other hand, increases in inventory levels are consistent with higher future demand and higher future sales.

The foregoing discussion provides a different analytical application of information contained in financial reports. The lessons of the reading, however, must not be forgotten. Any changes in inventory balances must take into consideration the inventory method used. Thus, for a LIFO company, analysis of changes should be based on current cost inventory amounts. In addition, an effort should be made to ensure that the change in inventory balances is driven by quantity changes, not increased prices for the same inventory quantity.

The large number of studies devoted to the FIFO/LIFO choice is due to its richness as the choice has opposite effects on reported income and cash flow. Moreover, the ability to adjust from one method to the other permits "as-if" comparisons in research design. The main empirical findings are relevant to the analyst as they provide evidence that the implications of the FIFO/LIFO choice (or any other accounting choice) are often complex and go beyond the simple trade-off of lower taxes (higher cash flow) versus higher reported income articulated in research designs. We provide a synopsis of the findings in the next section, using the work of Cushing and LeClere (1992) to motivate the discussion.

Summary of FIFO/LIFO Choice

Cushing and LeClere (1992) asked 32 LIFO firms and 70 FIFO firms to rank their reasons for their choice of inventory method. For LIFO firms, the overwhelming primary reason was the favorable tax effect. This result is consistent with research findings that firms using LIFO are primarily motivated by its favorable tax effects and these firms stand to gain the most from using LIFO.

The market, however, does not always regard a switch to LIFO favorably. By switching to LIFO, the firm may be providing (unfavorable) information about its sensitivity to changing prices (or other firm characteristics). Thus, reaction to a change in accounting method may reflect this other information rather than the tax advantage alone.

Reasons for choosing FIFO are complex. Based on the responses in Cushing and LeClere, no single reason emerges as most important for FIFO firms. Over half suggested economic reasons as their motivation. Twenty of the 70 firms (approximately 30%) indicated that LIFO did not provide them with any tax benefits (e.g., declining prices). Others claimed that the accounting and administrative costs to maintain LIFO records and/or ensure that there are no LIFO liquidations kept them from using LIFO. However, just as many firms stated that they chose FIFO because it was a "better accounting method" as it better reflected the physical flow of goods. Close to 40% indicated, as one of

their two primary reasons, their concern about the lower earnings resulting from LIFO.[34]

Consistent with the tax effects argument, Dopuch and Pincus (1988) found that FIFO firms were less likely (relative to LIFO firms) to have significant tax savings from LIFO. With respect to the income-enhancing arguments, Hunt (1985) did find some evidence that supported the bonus plan hypothesis.

Many of the inventory studies found the choice of inventory method closely related to industry and size factors, with larger firms opting for LIFO. The industry factor is a consequence of similar production, operating, and *inflation conditions* faced by firms in the same industry. The size factor has been explained in two ways. As noted, adoption of LIFO increases inventory management and control costs, which mitigate the benefit received from tax savings. For large firms, these costs are more readily absorbed and small relative to the potential tax benefits. Alternatively, the size effect reflects the fact that, for political reasons, larger firms tend to choose accounting methods that lower reported earnings.

Exhibit 10, based on Cushing and LeClere (1992), summarizes their findings; the variables and the rationale behind them are indicated in the table. Seven of the eight variables that explain the FIFO/LIFO choice are significant in the predicted direction. The estimated tax savings are significantly greater for

EXHIBIT 10 Variables Hypothesized to Affect FIFO-LIFO Choice

1. *Estimated tax savings* from use of LIFO expected to be larger for LIFO companies.
2. *Inventory materiality:* The larger a firm's inventory balance, the greater the incentive to use LIFO as the potential tax savings is larger.
3. *Tax loss carryforward:* The larger a firm's tax loss carryforward, the less incentive it has to use LIFO.
4. *Inventory variability:* The more variable a firm's inventory balance, the more likely it is to face inventory liquidations. This would tend to favor choosing FIFO over LIFO.
5. *Inventory obsolescence:* If a firm's inventory tends to become obsolete because of new product innovation, then the replacement of old products by new ones raises a difficult LIFO accounting question for which there is no authoritative answer. Such companies may prefer FIFO.
6. *Size as proxy for bookkeeping costs:* The larger the accounting costs required to use LIFO, the less likely a firm would choose LIFO. Larger firms would be able to absorb these costs more readily.
7. *Leverage:* Under the debt covenant hypothesis, firms with higher leverage would prefer FIFO as it would improve their debt/equity ratios.
8. *Current ratio:* Under the debt covenant hypothesis, firms with low current ratios would prefer FIFO, which improves their current ratio.

Source: Barry E. Cushing and Marc J. LeClere, "Evidence on the Determinants of Inventory Accounting Policy Choice," *Accounting Review* (April 1992), pp. 355–366, Table 4, p. 363.

[34] These percentages are considerably higher than those reported by Granof and Short (1984) in an earlier survey.

LIFO firms. Consistent with this, FIFO firms have higher average loss carry-forwards. Inventory variability is higher for FIFO firms, increasing the chances of LIFO liquidations. FIFO firms tend to be smaller, more highly leveraged, and less liquid. Similarly, the likelihood of inventory **obsolescence** is also a significant factor. Only the materiality measure is not statistically significant.

These variables indicate possible motivations to stay on FIFO. For a given firm, the analyst should try to determine which of these motivations apply and, thus, whether the firm is justified in staying on FIFO or management is inefficient (or self-serving) by foregoing tax savings from the use of LIFO. Management that remains on FIFO for motives that are either selfish or based on the belief that the market can be fooled should not inspire confidence.

INTERNATIONAL ACCOUNTING AND REPORTING PRACTICES

11

FIFO and the weighted-average method are the most commonly used methods worldwide. Historically, the use of LIFO was essentially limited to companies in the United States, and the significant tax benefits this method can provide suggest that the method will continue to enjoy widespread acceptance. These benefits have resulted in gradual adoption of LIFO as a permitted alternative in countries such as Germany, Italy, and Japan.[35] In some countries, LIFO is allowed for financial reporting but not income taxes, which may account for its lack of popularity in these countries. In practice, LIFO is rarely used in these countries, perhaps because of the low inflation rates of recent years. Non-U.S. reporting standards do not require disclosure of LIFO reserves, reducing the analyst's ability to make the adjustments discussed in this reading.

In the United Kingdom, Statement of Standard Accounting Practice (SSAP) 9 holds that LIFO may not result in a true and fair valuation and, in addition, the method is not allowed for tax purposes.

Average cost is the most widely used method in Germany, although LIFO has been allowed for tax purposes since 1990, and it may change reporting habits.

IASB Standard 2

In 1993, the IASB issued revised International Accounting Standard (IAS) 2, designating FIFO and weighted-average costs as the benchmark treatments and LIFO as the allowed alternative. Firms using LIFO are required to provide FIFO/weighted-average or current cost disclosures, facilitating the adjustments discussed in this reading.

Inventories are reported at the lower of cost or market value; cost depends on the method used. Market is generally defined as the net realizable value with specific limitations in the United States;[36] any writedown is determined on an item-by-item basis. Revised IAS 2 limits itself to net realizable value (NRV), and it does not specify whether the cost versus NRV comparison should be made on an item-by-item basis or by groups of similar items. This standard is similar to those of most other countries.

[35] Financial reporting and tax reporting are identical in these countries.

[36] Generally, these limitations ensure that inventories are written down to approximate current cost.

SUMMARY

The choice of accounting method for inventories is one of the basic decisions made by nearly all companies engaged in the manufacturing and distribution of goods. Ideally, the method chosen should result in the best measure of income and financial condition. However, no single method accomplishes these objectives in most cases and, in an environment of changing prices, assumptions as to the flow of costs affect reported income, balance sheet amounts, and associated ratios.

For companies operating in the United States, under conditions of rising prices, the cash flow advantage of LIFO usually dictates the choice of that method. When LIFO is not chosen, therefore, the first question should be: Why not? As the empirical work indicates, managers offer a number of reasons for not using LIFO, only some of which appear valid. Thus, companies that should use LIFO but do not may appear unattractive to investors.

In many cases, the analytical techniques presented in this reading enable the analyst to approximate the effect of LIFO on a company using FIFO or average cost. Such analysis can provide estimates of both the cash savings foregone (relevant to the discussion in the previous paragraph) and the holding gains included in reported income. Similarly, the reading demonstrates how the analyst can adjust from LIFO to FIFO where appropriate. The reading also explores the effects of liquidations and the incentives for the FIFO/LIFO choice, and concludes with a review of inventory accounting standards applied internationally.

PRACTICE PROBLEMS FOR READING 35

1. [Allocation of purchase costs under different inventory methods; CFA® adapted] Assume the following:

Quarter	Units Purchased	Per Unit Cost	Dollar Purchases	Unit Sales
I	200	$22	$ 4,400	200
II	300	24	7,200	200
III	300	26	7,800	200
IV	200	28	5,600	200
Year	1,000		$25,000	800

Inventory at beginning of Quarter I: 400 units at $20 per unit = $ 8,000.
Inventory at end of Quarter IV: 600 units.

A. Calculate reported inventory at the end of the year under *each* of the following inventory methods:

i. FIFO

ii. LIFO

iii. Average cost

B. Calculate the cost of goods sold for the year under each method listed in Part A.

C. Discuss the effect of the differences among the three methods on:

i. Reported income for the year

ii. Stockholders' equity at the end of the year

2. [Effect of inventory methods on financial statements; CFA adapted] Compare the effect of the use of the LIFO inventory method with use of the FIFO method on each of the following, assuming rising prices and stable inventory quantities:

i. Gross profit margin

ii. Net income

iii. Cash from operations

iv. Inventories

v. Inventory turnover ratio

vi. Working capital

vii. Total assets

viii. Debt-to-equity ratio

3. [Inventory methods; basic relationships] The M&J Company begins operations on January 1, 20X0 with the following balance sheet:

Cash	$10,000	Common stock	$10,000

During the year, the company maintains its inventory accounts using the FIFO method. Before a provision for income tax, the balance sheet at December 31, 20X0, is:

Cash	$ 5,000	Common stock	$10,000
Inventory	10,000	Pretax income	5,000
	$15,000		$15,000

M&J has 20X0 sales of $25,000. The company sells half of the *units* purchased during the year. Operating expenses (excluding COGS) are $12,000.

Prior to issuing financial statements, the company considers its choice of inventory method. Assume a tax rate of 40% and a dividend payout ratio of 50%.

A. Using the information provided, complete the following table:

	FIFO	Weighted Average	LIFO
Sales	$25,000	$25,000	$25,000
COGS			
Other expenses	12,000	12,000	12,000
Pretax income			
Income tax expense			
Net income			
Dividends paid			
Retained earnings			
Cash from operations			
Closing cash balance			
Closing inventory			
Inventory purchases			

B. Prepare a balance sheet for M&J at December 31, 20X0, assuming use of the:

i. LIFO inventory method

ii. Weighted-average method

iii. FIFO inventory method

C. Discuss the advantages and disadvantages of each of the three possible choices of inventory method.

Problem 4 is based on the following data, adapted from the actual financial statements of two firms in the automobile replacement parts industry.

Zenab Distributors, Balance Sheets, at December 31

	20X1	20X2
Cash	$ 500	$ 100
Accounts receivable (net)	8,100	8,300
Inventory	24,900	25,200
Current assets	$33,500	$33,600
Current liabilities	11,600	12,700

Zenab Distributors uses the LIFO method of accounting for 70% of its inventories; it uses FIFO for the remainder. If all inventories were carried at FIFO, inventory would be higher by $3,600 and $5,100 in 20X1 and 20X2, respectively.

Faybech Parts, Balance Sheets, at December 31

	20X1	20X2
Cash	$ 1,000	$ 600
Accounts receivable (net)	11,400	13,900
Inventory	22,300	30,300
Current assets	$34,700	$44,800
Current liabilities	10,700	12,200

Faybech Parts uses FIFO accounting for all inventories.

Income Statements, Year Ended December 31, 20X2

	Zenab	Faybech
Sales	$92,700	$77,000
COGS	61,300	52,000
Gross profit	$31,400	$25,000
Selling and general expense	26,400	21,500
Pretax income	$ 5,000	$ 3,500
Income tax expense	2,000	1,400
Net income	$ 3,000	$ 2,100

4. [LIFO versus FIFO; effect on ratios; adjusting ratios]

A. Using *only reported* financial data, compute each of the following ratios for both Zenab and Faybech:

- **i.** Current ratio (20X1 and 20X2)
- **ii.** Inventory turnover (20X2)
- **iii.** Gross profit margin (20X2)
- **iv.** Pretax profit margin (EBT to sales) (20X2)

B. Briefly compare the performance of the two firms in 20X2 based on the ratios computed in Part A.

C. Recalculate each of the ratios in part a with both companies.

- **i.** On FIFO
- **ii.** On LIFO
- **iii.** Using the current cost method

D. Select the basis of comparison for *each* of the four ratios that you feel is most meaningful. Justify *each* choice.

5. [LIFO versus FIFO; effect on ratios; adjusting ratios; CFA adapted]
The Zeta Corp. uses LIFO inventory accounting. The footnotes to the 20X4 financial statements contain the following data as of December 31:

	20X3	20X4
Raw materials	$392,675	$369,725
Finished products	401,325	377,075
Inventory on FIFO basis	$794,000	$746,800
LIFO reserve	(46,000)	(50,000)
Inventory on LIFO basis	$748,000	$696,800

You are also provided with the following data:

- The company has a marginal tax rate of 35%.
- COGS for 20X4 is $3,800,000.
- Net income for 20X4 is $340,000.
- Return on equity for 20X4 is 4.6%.

A. Calculate 20X4 net income for Zeta, assuming that it uses the FIFO inventory method.

B. Calculate the company's inventory turnover ratio on both a FIFO and LIFO basis.

C. Calculate Zeta's return on equity on a FIFO basis. (Remember to adjust both the numerator and denominator.)

D. Discuss the usefulness of the adjustments made in parts a, b, and c to a financial analyst.

E. Describe alternative measures of inventory turnover and return on equity that would be more useful to assess Zeta's operating performance.

6. [Adjusting for alternative accounting methods; effects of liquidation]
The Noland Company [NOLD] reported the following operating results:

Years Ended December 31 in ($thousands)			
	1997	1998	1999
Sales	$464,965	$465,479	$482,830
COGS	371,212	372,033	385,892
Gross margin	$ 93,753	$ 93,446	$ 96,938

In its 1999 annual report, the company states that:

> 1999's gross profit margin suffered from the year-end LIFO adjustment which increased cost of goods sold by $1,391,000 compared to $381,000 a year ago.

Information from the company's inventory footnote is presented below:

December 31 (in $thousands)	1997	1998	1999
Inventory, at approximate replacement cost	$98,965	$103,446	$104,106
Reduction to LIFO	32,495	32,876	34,267
LIFO inventory	$66,470	$ 70,570	$ 69,839

Liquidation of certain inventory layers carried at the higher/lower costs that prevailed in prior years as compared with the costs of 1999, 1998, and 1997 purchases had the effect of increasing 1999 and 1997 net income $47 thousand and $393 thousand, respectively, and decreasing 1998 net income $150 thousand.

A. Describe the "year-end LIFO adjustment" and show how the company calculated it for both 1998 and 1999.

B. Compute the company's 1998 and 1999 COGS using the FIFO method.

C. Explain how it is possible for a LIFO liquidation to decrease income as in 1998.

D. Excluding the effects of the LIFO liquidation, compute COGS for 1998 and 1999 using:

- **i.** The company's current accounting method
- **ii.** The FIFO method

E. State and justify which of the following measures of COGS is most appropriate to use to measure Noland's profitability:

- **i.** As reported
- **ii.** As computed in part b
- **iii.** As computed in part d

F. Describe how to use the inventory footnote data to adjust Noland's net worth (book value) to a current cost basis for 1998 and 1999.

7. [Decline in LIFO reserve] The following footnote appeared in the annual report of A. T. Cross [ATX], a pen manufacturer:

Note B—Inventories

Domestic writing instrument inventories, approximating $13,404,000 and $5,695,000 at December 30, 2000 and January 1, 2000, respectively, are priced at the lower of LIFO cost or market. The remaining inventories are priced at the lower of FIFO cost or market. If the FIFO method of inventory valuation had been used for those inventories priced using the LIFO method, inventories would have been approximately $9,614,000 and $11,227,000 higher than reported at December 30, 2000 and January 1, 2000, respectively. The Company believes the LIFO method of inventory valuation ordinarily results in a more appropriate matching of its revenues to their related costs, since current costs are included in cost of goods sold, and distortions in reported income due to the effect of changing prices are reduced.

A. Cross did not report any LIFO liquidation for 2000. Explain how its LIFO reserve could decline.

B. State two reasons why Cross might choose to continue to use the LIFO method despite the decline in the LIFO reserve.

8. [Effect of LIFO liquidations on gross margins] The following data were obtained from annual reports of Stride-Rite [SRR], a shoe manufacturer and retailer:

Years Ended December 31 (in $thousands)

	1997	1998	1999
Sales	$515,728	$539,413	$572,696
COGS	(328,172)	(348,587)	(362,108)
Gross profit	$187,556	$190,826	$210,588
LIFO liquidation (net of tax)	$ 3,379	$ 1,733	0

A. Compute the gross margin percentage for each year, 1997–1999.

B. Stride-Rite disclosed the effect of LIFO liquidations net of income tax. Assuming a tax rate of 35%, recompute Stride-Rite's gross margin for the years 1997–1999 after removing the effect of LIFO liquidations.

C. Explain why the trend in gross margins shown in part b is a better indicator of Stride-Rite's performance than the reported gross margins.

9. [Effect of inventory methods on contracts] The Sechne Company has entered into a number of agreements in the past year. These agreements contain provisions that depend on the firm's reported financial statements:

i. *Management compensation plan.* Bonuses are based on a weighted average of reported net income and cash from operations.

ii. *Bond indenture.* Specifies that the firm must maintain a minimum level of working capital, and dividend payments to shareholders require a minimum level of retained earnings.

iii. *Labor contract.* Employees have a profit-sharing plan that pays them a share of reported net income in excess of a specified level.

Sechne's corporate controller, who is *both* a manager and a shareholder, must select the accounting methods used for financial reporting. Discuss how these agreements may affect the controller's choice of an inventory accounting method for Sechne.

ANALYSIS OF LONG-LIVED ASSETS: PART I—THE CAPITALIZATION DECISION

by Gerald I. White, Ashwinpaul C. Sondhi, and Dov Fried

READING 36

LEARNING OUTCOMES

The candidate should be able to:

a. demonstrate the effects of capitalizing versus expensing on net income, shareholders' equity, cash flow from operations, and financial ratios;

b. determine which intangible assets, including software development costs and research and development costs, should be capitalized, according to U.S. GAAP and international accounting standards.

INTRODUCTION 1

The long-lived operating assets of a firm, unlike inventory, are not held for resale but are used in the firm's manufacturing, sales, and administrative operations. Such assets include tangible fixed assets (plant, machinery, and office facilities) as well as intangible assets such as computer software, patents, and trademarks.

This reading examines financial reporting and analysis issues when these assets are originally acquired, with emphasis on:

- which costs are included in the carrying amount of fixed assets
- the financial statement effects of capitalization versus expensing
- the capitalization of interest
- the circumstances under which research and development, computer software, and other intangible costs can be capitalized

B/S:
{Asset: Lwr HC or FV
{Accum Depr / Reval Res: −ve, +ve asset line

- analytical adjustments required to compare companies with different capitalization policies
- the analysis of fixed asset disclosures

Reading 37 discusses the accounting for and analysis of the use, impairment, and disposal of these long-lived assets.

2 ACQUIRING THE ASSET: THE CAPITALIZATION DECISION

Is it an Operating Exp. If no then normal argum to cap

The costs of acquiring resources that provide services over more than one operating cycle are capitalized and carried as assets on the balance sheet. All costs incurred until the asset is ready for use must be capitalized, including the invoice price, applicable sales tax, freight and insurance costs incurred delivering the equipment, and any installation costs.[1]

However, considerable debate surrounds the application of these principles and significant differences remain (across countries and firms) with respect to three major issues:

1. Should some components of acquisition cost be included in the capitalized cost (e.g., interest during construction)?
2. Do some types of costs merit capitalization (e.g., software development and research and development costs)?
3. What accounting method should be used to determine the amount of costs capitalized (e.g., oil and gas properties)?

These choices affect the balance sheet, income and cash flow statements, and ratios both in the year the choice is made and over the life of the asset. Management discretion can result in smoothing or manipulation of reported income, cash flows, and other measures of financial performance. Moreover, unlike some accounting choices whose effects reverse over time, some effects of the decision to capitalize or expense may never reverse.

This reading is devoted to the controversial issue of capitalization versus expensing of expenditures for long-lived assets. We start with an overview of the conceptual issues and a review of the implications of capitalization for financial statement analysis. The remaining sections then examine the specific components and categories of cost where capitalization practices vary.

---

[1] In June 2001, the Accounting Standards Executive Committee (AcSEC) of the AICPA issued an exposure draft of a proposed Statement of Position: Accounting for Certain Costs and Activities Related to Property, Plant, and Equipment. The SOP would require that:

- Costs incurred prior to asset acquisition must be expensed, with the exception of option payments and other costs directly related to specific PPE assets.
- All repair and maintenance costs during the life of PPE assets must be expensed.
- Overhead costs (including general and administrative and other support costs) must be expensed.

CAPITALIZATION VERSUS EXPENSING: CONCEPTUAL ISSUES

3

The Financial Accounting Standards Board (FASB), in its Statement of Financial Accounting Concepts (SFAC) 6, defines accounting assets as probable future economic benefits. Analytically, the concept of long-lived assets can also serve as:

1. an index of initial investment outlays, used as a base for measuring profitability (return on assets)
2. a measure of the firm's wealth, used for valuation and to measure solvency
3. inputs in the firm's production function, used to measure capital intensity, leverage, and operating efficiency

Different analytical objectives require distinct definitions of what constitutes an asset. Although returns on research and development should be evaluated in the same way as returns on a purchased factory, measurement problems may preclude recognition of such expenditures as assets for assessment of shareholder wealth or collateral for bondholders.

For this reason, traditional, historical cost-based accounting rules cannot satisfy all contexts; analysts must evaluate asset definitions used for financial reporting and make necessary adjustments. The appropriate adjustment may require the capitalization of previously expensed costs, or the reverse. In some cases, particularly for intangible assets, there is no one "correct" choice that serves all analytical needs.

Financial Statement Effects of Capitalization

Box 1 (Figures 1 to 5) uses a simple illustration to demonstrate the financial statement effects of the capitalize-versus-expense choice on growing firms. That choice will have significant effects on reported cash flows, as well as on the balance sheet and income statement.

Income Variability

Firms that capitalize costs and depreciate them (systematically allocate them to income) over time show smoother patterns of reported income (Figure 2). Firms that expense costs as incurred have greater variance in reported income, as the variance in spending is transmitted directly to income. That variance declines as the firm matures and is lower for larger firms (or those with other sources of income).

Profitability

In the early years, expensing lowers profitability, both in absolute terms (as the cost of new assets exceeds depreciation of previously capitalized expenditures) and relative to assets, sales, etc. *Profitability remains lower for expensing firms as long*

BOX 1 COMPARISON OF FINANCIAL STATEMENT EFFECTS: CAPITALIZATION VERSUS EXPENSING

For our illustration we consider two hypothetical firms, each with an asset base of \$1,000 on which it earns \$150, which begin to grow. Growth requires the acquisition of an "asset," which has a three-year life. Each asset costs \$100 and generates cash flows of \$50 per year. The pattern of growth[a] (the number of assets acquired each year and the replacement of old assets) is illustrated in Figure 1.

Growth is assumed to continue for 15 years after which maturity is reached, and all subsequent acquisitions are for replacement only. We further assume that the asset cost may be capitalized or expensed at the discretion of management under the provisions of generally accepted accounting principles (GAAP). One firm capitalizes the acquisition cost; the other expenses it. The firms are otherwise operationally identical. Their reported income, cash flow from operations, and related ratios, however, will differ markedly.

Figure 2 compares the pattern of reported income. The "expensing" firm exhibits a fluctuating pattern of income growth through maturity. The "capitalizing" firm, on the other hand, exhibits a smooth pattern of income growth. For firms that are initially larger,[b] the fluctuations are not as great throughout the growth and maturity cycle because of the larger base.

Figure 3 compares the return on assets (ROA) ratio for the two firms. The choice of accounting method affects both the numerator and denominator of the ROA. The expensing firm, having fewer recorded assets, will have a smaller denominator, increasing its reported ROA. The numerator (earnings) is volatile, so that sometimes ROA increases but at other times decreases. At the early stage of growth, the

Figure 1

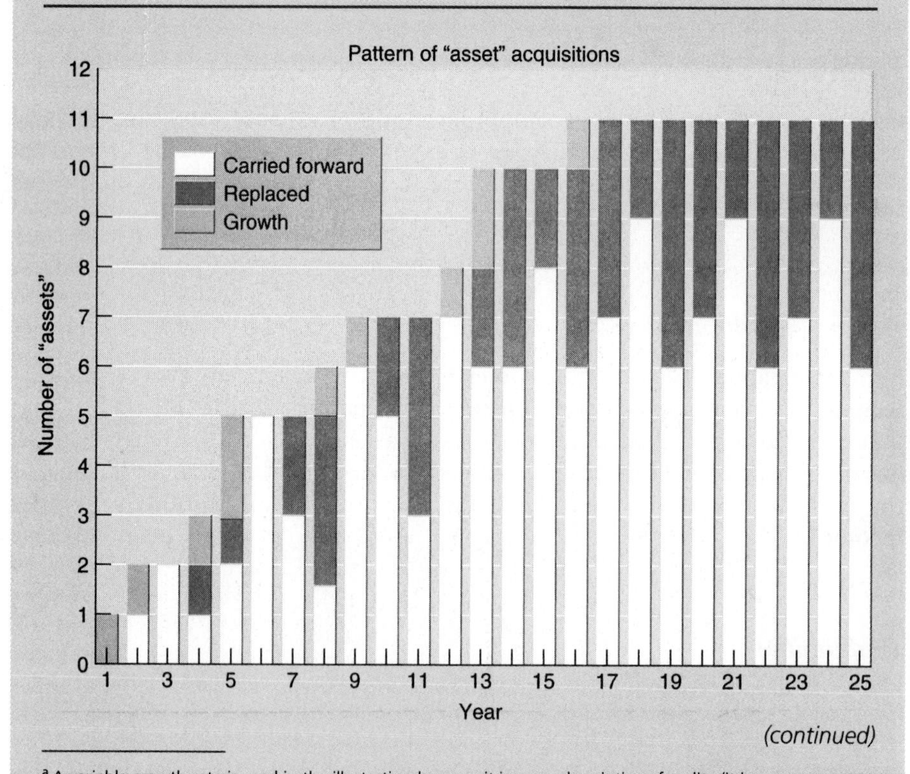

(continued)

[a] A variable growth rate is used in the illustration because it is more descriptive of reality (it has greater external validity). Any growth rate, other than a perfectly constant one, will create a similar pattern of differences between a capitalizing and expensing firm. At maturity or steady state, a constant growth rate generates identical (and constant) total expense for both firms. (ROA and cash flow from operations would still differ.)

[b] The term "larger" does not necessarily relate only to absolute size. It can also denote that the firm engages in other activities that offset the variability of the costs that are expensed.

BOX 1 (continued)

expensing firm's ROA gyrates about that of the capitalizing firm but will initially tend to be lower. As the expensing firm grows larger, the fluctuations persist, but its ROA is higher because the effect of lower reported assets on the denominator dominates.

Figure 4 compares reported cash from operations for the capitalizing and expensing firms. The capitalizing firm always shows higher cash from operations; the difference increases and does not reverse over the life of the asset (see Figure 5).

Figure 2

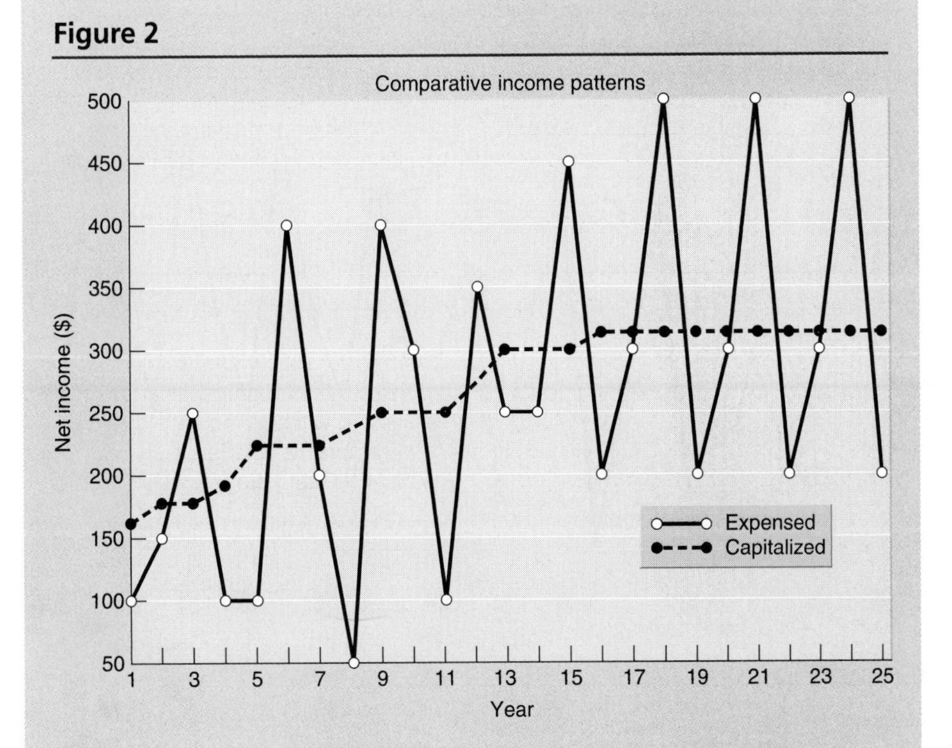

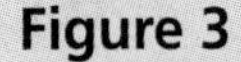

Figure 3

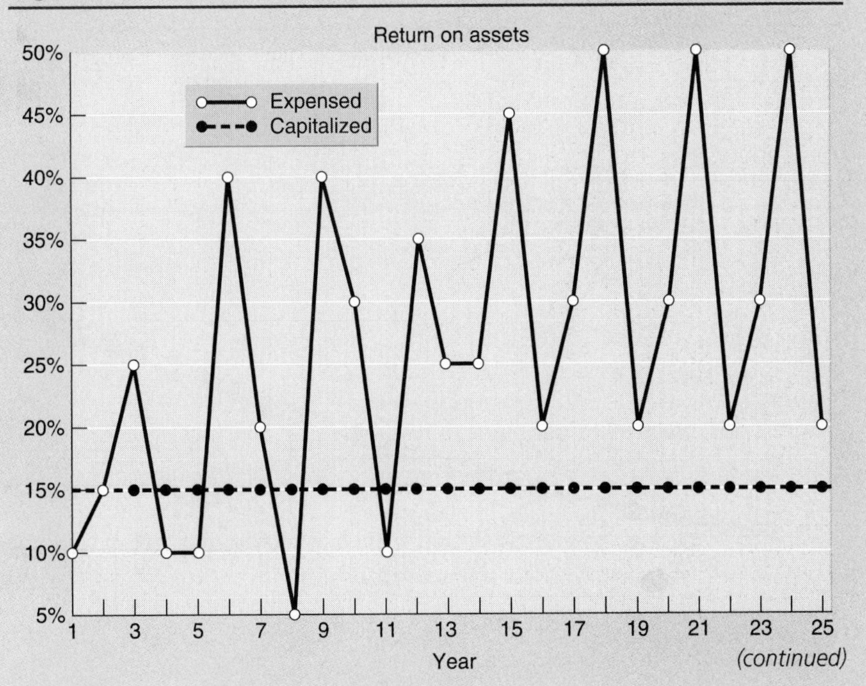

(continued)

BOX 1 (continued)

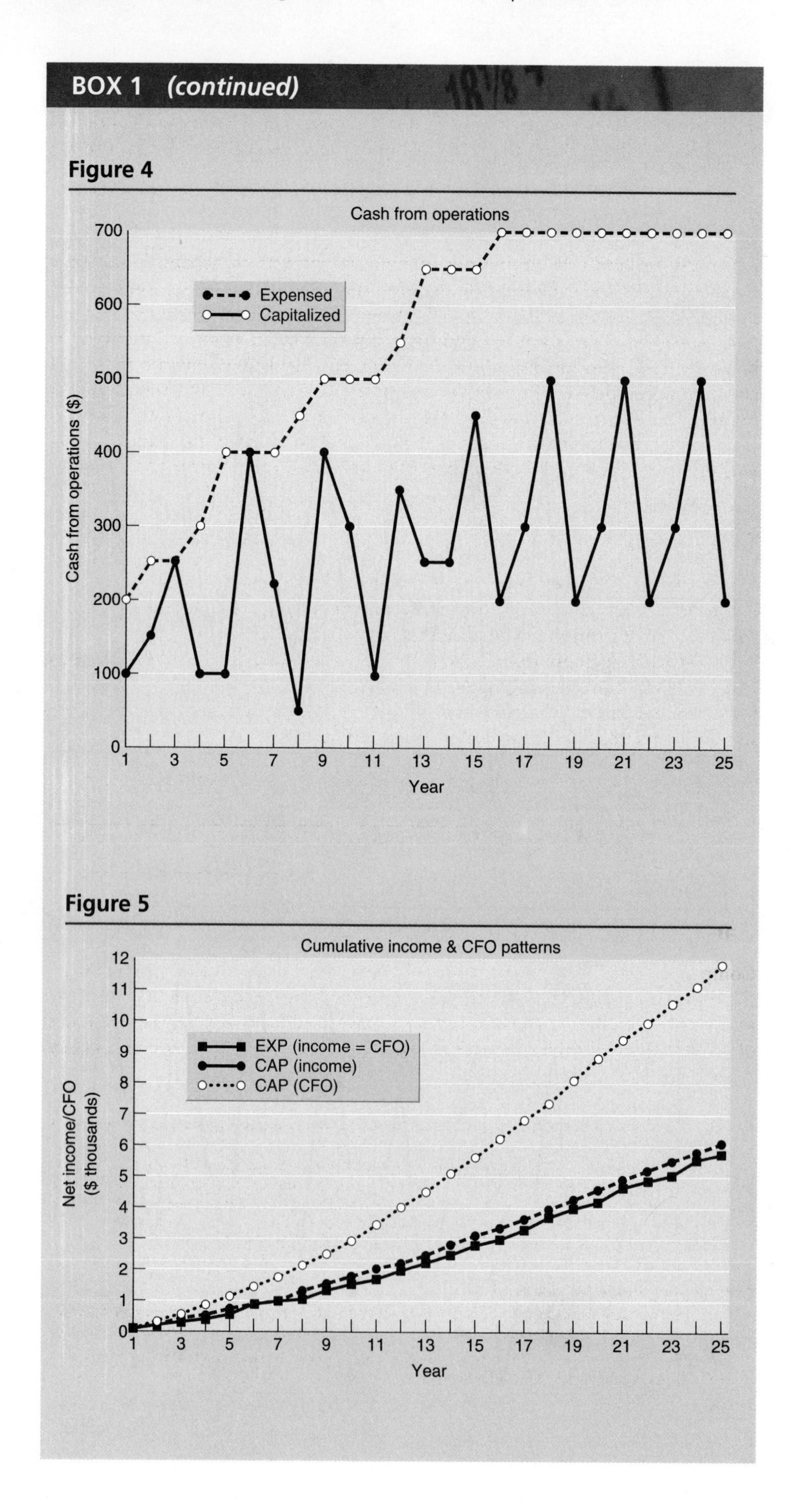

as the level of expenditures is increasing (positive growth). However, because they report lower assets (and equity), their ROA/ROE measures can be higher than those of firms that capitalize costs (Figure 3). In general, whether ROA and ROE will be higher depends on the relationship between profitability and growth.[2]

Cash Flow from Operations

Reported *net cash flow,* unlike net income, is immune to accounting alternatives.[3] However, the capitalization decision has a significant impact on the components of cash flow, with a trade-off between *cash from operations (CFO) and cash from investment (CFI).* Cash expenditures for capitalized assets are included in investing cash flow and *never* flow through CFO. Firms that expense these outlays, however, include these expenditures in CFO. Thus, CFO will always be higher for the capitalizing firm (Figure 4),[4] and the cumulative difference (rather than reversing) increases over time (Figure 5). *Thus, the capitalization of long-lived assets results in a permanent shift of expenditures from CFO to CFI.*

Leverage Ratios

Expensing firms report lower assets and equity balances.[5] As a result, debt-to-equity and debt-to-assets solvency ratios will appear worse for expensing firms as compared with firms that capitalize the same costs.

Given management discretion as to capitalization, a great deal of care must be exercised when assessing financial performance. The remainder of this reading considers particular areas where this problem occurs. Some issues are pervasive and cut across all industries; others are industry specific.

CAPITALIZATION VERSUS EXPENSING: GENERAL ISSUES 4

Capitalization of Interest Costs

Companies often construct long-lived assets, such as new operating facilities, for their own use and capitalize costs incurred during construction until the assets are ready to be placed in service. How should the firm measure the cost of these self-constructed assets? Should the interest cost on funds used for

[2] Sarath, Lev, and Sougiannis (2000) show that for a firm whose relevant expenditures are growing at a rate g, ROE on an expensing basis will be higher if that ROE $> g/(1 + g/2)$. For growth rates (in the relevant range) below 30%, that relationship is equivalent to comparing ROE and g. As long as they are close, there is little difference between ROE on an expense basis and ROE on a capitalized basis. The greater the difference between ROE and g, the greater the difference between ROE on an expense basis and ROE on a capitalized basis. (A similar relationship holds for pretax ROA.)

For (after-tax) ROA, ROA will be higher for the expensing firm if its ROA $> (1 - \text{tax rate})\ g/(1 + g/2)$.

[3] Ignoring any income tax effects.

[4] This affects the cash from operations/capital expenditures ratio that measures the degree to which the firm's internally generated funds finance the replacement and expansion of productive capacity.

[5] These effects are not directly shown in Box 1. However, they can be deduced from the discussion of the return-on-investment (ROA/ROE) measures.

construction be capitalized or expensed? Should interest capitalization require specific borrowing to finance construction? Should the firm capitalize a return on equity when there is no debt or the firm has borrowed less than the total construction cost? The answers to these questions vary from country to country.

In the United States, SFAS 34 (1979) requires the capitalization of interest costs incurred during the construction period. When a specific borrowing is associated with the construction, the interest cost incurred on that borrowing is capitalized. If no specific borrowing is identifiable, the weighted-average interest rate on outstanding debt (up to the amount invested in the project) is capitalized. When the firm has no interest expense, no borrowing costs may be capitalized. Capitalization of the cost of equity is not permitted under any circumstances. SFAS 34 requires the disclosure of the amount of interest capitalized.

The argument for interest capitalization is that the cost of a self-constructed asset should equal the cost of one purchased after completion. In the latter case, the purchase price would presumably include the cost of capital of the seller. Capitalization of interest for self-constructed assets, it is argued, replicates this process. This argument should apply even when the firm has no debt; in that case, return on equity capital used for construction should be capitalized.

On the other hand, there are strong arguments against the capitalization of interest in general and SFAS 34 in particular. On a conceptual level, interest, as a financing cost, is different from the other costs of acquiring and getting the asset ready for service. It results from a financing decision rather than an operating decision.

Under SFAS 34, interest is capitalized only if the firm is leveraged. It seems illogical that two identical assets should be carried at different costs, depending on the firm's financing decisions. Further, the capitalization of interest creates differences between reported earnings and cash flow. Given these arguments, we believe that expensing of all interest is the preferable treatment.

For purposes of analysis, therefore, the income statement capitalization of interest should be reversed, resulting in the following effects:

1. *Capitalized interest should be added back to interest expense.* The adjusted interest expense provides a better representation of the level and trend of a firm's financing costs.
2. *Adding capitalized interest back to interest expense reduces net income.* Unfortunately, although the amount of interest capitalized in the current year must be disclosed, disclosure of the amortization of previously capitalized interest (included in the fixed asset account) is not required and is rarely provided.[6] This amortization must be deducted from depreciation expense to accurately determine the net effect of interest capitalization on net income. *However, if the amount of interest capitalization in previous years is not large and asset lives are long, the amortization (over the asset life) is likely to be immaterial and can be ignored.* If interest capitalization has been large, the analyst must estimate the amortization.[7]

[6] See Problem 1, based on Chevron, which does disclose the amortization of previously capitalized interest.

[7] The amortization of capitalized interest is included in depreciation expense. Thus, one can use the historical ratio of interest capitalized to total capital expenditures to estimate the portion of depreciation applicable to capitalized interest expense.

3. *The capitalization of interest also distorts the classification of cash flows. Interest capitalized as part of the cost of fixed assets will never be reported as CFO, but as an investment outflow. To restore comparability with firms that do not capitalize interest, the amount of interest capitalized should be added back to cash for investment and subtracted from CFO.* The cash flows for capitalized interest are then included with other interest payments.[8]

4. *The interest coverage ratio should be calculated with interest expense adjusted to add back capitalized interest.* Otherwise, it is overstated.[9]

These adjustments tend to be small relative to cash flows but may be significant for interest expense and net income. The following example illustrates how adding back capitalized interest affects profitability and the interest coverage ratio.

EXAMPLE 1

Westvaco

Note F in Westvaco's fiscal 1999 financial statements reports capitalized interest, which can be used to adjust the interest coverage ratio:[10]

Westvaco, Years Ended October 31 (in $thousands)

	1997	1998	1999	% Change 1997–1999
As reported:				
EBIT	$339,872	$314,575	$271,514	(20%)
Interest expense	93,272	110,162	123,538	32%
Pretax income	$246,600	$204,413	$147,976	(40%)
Interest coverage	3.64X	2.86X	2.20X	(39%)
Interest capitalized	$ 25,962	$ 20,752	$ 8,890	(66%)
After adjustment:				
EBIT (unchanged)	$339,872	$314,575	$271,514	(20%)
Interest expense	119,234	130,914	132,428	11%
Pretax income	$220,638	$183,661	$139,086	(37%)
Interest coverage	2.85X	2.40X	2.05X	(28%)

[8] These interest payments would be deducted from cash from operations, as required by SFAS 95. Alternatively, interest payments should be considered financing cash flows and thus excluded from both CFO and cash for investment regardless of capitalization.

[9] The SFAS 95 requirement for the disclosure of interest paid makes it possible to make this adjustment and compute interest coverage accurately on a cash flow basis. On an accrual basis, the numerator, EBIT (and hence the coverage ratio), will be underestimated if the amortization of previous years' capitalized interest is not removed. However, as noted, this effect is relatively insignificant.

[10] Due to lack of disclosure, no adjustment has been made for the amortization of previously capitalized interest.

Based on Westvaco's reported data, the interest coverage ratio fell 39% due to declining earnings before interest and taxes (EBIT) and rising interest expense. While adding back capitalized interest does not radically change the data, it does show that:

- Adjusted interest coverage, based on interest incurred before capitalization, is, as expected, below the (reported) ratio based on interest expense after capitalization.
- Interest expense over the period rose only 11% rather than 32% as reported.
- Interest coverage fell 28% based on interest incurred, a smaller decline than the 39% decline based on reported data.
- While pretax income is lower each year, the two-year decline in pretax income was slightly lower after adjustment.

Capitalization of interest provides additional information. Despite rising interest costs, capitalized interest declined 66%, apparently due to a lower level of qualifying assets. *A significant change in capitalized interest may signal a shift in the amount or nature of capital spending, and should be investigated by the analyst.*

Interest Capitalization outside the United States

IAS 23, Borrowing Costs (revised 1993), makes expensing all borrowing costs the benchmark treatment. Alternatively, borrowing costs that are directly attributable to the acquisition, construction, or production of qualifying assets may be capitalized. Interest capitalization is also permitted in many jurisdictions worldwide. When comparing firms that capitalize interest with those that do not, adjustment is required to achieve a base for proper valuation.

Intangible Assets

Growth of the computer, Internet, telecommunications, and service industries has led to significantly increased investment in and use of intangible assets. Licenses, computer software, patents, **leasehold** rights, brand names, and copyrights are among the more familiar examples of assets without tangible, physical substance. As a result of their increased use, the financial reporting and analysis of such intangible assets have gained importance; for some firms they are important on- or off-balance-sheet revenue-producing assets that account for a substantial portion of the value of a firm.

Intangible assets are identifiable, nonmonetary resources controlled by firms.[11] When acquired in an arm's-length transaction, recognition and measurement rules are similar to those for tangible assets. However, practice is diverse with respect to the recognition and measurement of such assets when they are internally developed. In addition, practices differ with respect to the revaluation, amortization, and impairment of intangible assets, regardless of their origin.

[11] Goodwill is an intangible asset although it is not identifiable.

The decision whether to capitalize or expense the cost of asset acquisition is especially difficult when applied to intangible resources. The variations in legal protection available for intellectual property and other intangible assets in many countries also make the assessment of value more difficult than for tangible assets. We begin, therefore, with a review of the recognition and measurement issues associated with intangible assets.

Recognition and Measurement Issues

The cost of acquiring intangible assets from unrelated entities is capitalized at acquisition, measured by the amount paid to acquire them. Given an arm's-length transaction, the acquisition price is assumed to equal the market value of the assets acquired.

Intangible assets may also be received through government grants or generated internally by the firm. Few, if any, costs may be incurred in obtaining assets through government grants. Financial statement recognition of such assets would be informative, but in the absence of secondary markets it is difficult to defend any measurement basis other than cost. When active secondary markets do exist (such as for broadcast properties and cellular licenses), then market price can be a reliable measure of the value of these assets.

Internally generated intangible assets are the most troublesome category because:

- The costs incurred in developing these assets may not be easily separable.
- It is difficult to measure the amount and duration of benefits from such expenditures as advertising when they are made, or even later.
- There may be little relationship between the costs incurred and the value of the asset created.

For many internally generated intangible assets, discounted cash flow analysis may be the only way to measure their fair value. However, such measurement is subject to accurate forecasting of the amount and timing of cash flows and the choice of discount rates.

To illustrate these issues, we turn to a discussion of capitalization issues for specific intangible assets.

Research and Development

Companies invest in research and development (R&D) because they expect the investment to produce profitable future products. However, absent a resultant commercial product, these expenditures may have no value to the firm. Further, the value of the resulting product may be unrelated to the amount spent on R&D. Due to such valuation uncertainties, R&D is generally unacceptable to creditors as security for loans.

SFAS 2, Accounting for Research and Development Costs SFAS 2 (1974) requires that virtually all R&D costs be expensed[12] in the period incurred and the amount disclosed. In effect, assets with uncertain future economic benefits are barred from the balance sheet. The impact of SFAS 2 on the financial

[12] The main exception is contract R&D performed for unrelated entities. In this case, R&D is carried as an asset (similar to inventory) until completion of the contract.

statements of firms with significant R&D is substantial, and there is some evidence of a decrease in R&D expenditures when SFAS 2 was adopted. Accounting aside, R&D expenditures are clearly investments in the economic sense, albeit risky ones. Further, empirical evidence[13] suggests that benefits from R&D expenditures last, on average, seven to nine years (depending on the industry), supporting the argument that R&D is an economic asset. Pfizer, for example, spent nearly $2.8 billion (17.1% of revenue) on R&D in 1999.

Accounting for Research and Development Costs Outside the United States
IAS 9 (1993) requires the expensing of research costs but requires capitalization of development costs[14] when all of the following criteria are met:

1. The product (process) is clearly defined.
2. Costs can be clearly identified.
3. Technical feasibility has been established.
4. The firm intends to produce the product (use the process).
5. The market has been clearly defined.
6. The firm has sufficient resources to complete the project.

Capitalized costs must be reviewed periodically to ensure that these conditions are still operable and that capitalized costs do not exceed net realizable value.[15] The standard also requires disclosure of the accounting methods followed, amortization methods and lives, and a reconciliation of the carrying amount.

EXAMPLE 2

Nokia

Nokia, an international telecommunications manufacturer, follows IASB GAAP and capitalized R&D costs in its 1998 and 1999 financial statements.

As expensing research and development costs is the dominant accounting method worldwide, financial statements of companies such as Nokia that capitalize R&D must be restated (by expensing all such expenditures) to make them comparable with similar companies that expense these costs. Alternatively (or for other analytical purposes), it may be desirable to restate another firm's financial statements by capitalizing previously expensed R&D costs. Box 2 describes the procedures required to make the adjustments in both directions. Next we illustrate the capitalization-to-expense adjustment, using Nokia as an example. Later (see Microsoft example) we adjust from expense to capitalization.

[13] Research in this area can be found in both the accounting and economics literature. Lev and Sougiannis (1996) provide a brief review of the literature in this area. See also the discussion of valuation in Box 3.

[14] IAS 9 defines development costs as expenditures incurred to translate research output into the production of materials, devices, products, processes, systems, and services.

[15] See Reading 37 for a discussion of impairment.

Nokia: Capitalized R&D Costs

	Years Ended December 31 (millions of euros)		
	1997	**1998**	**1999**
Opening balance	€426	€469	€650
Additions	156	182	271
Disposals	(113)	(1)	(110)
Closing balance	€469	€650	€811
Accumulated depreciation (year-end)[a]	(242)	(361)	(398)
Closing balance (net)	€227	€289	€413
Depreciation expense		119	110

[a] Note that the 1998 depreciation expense equals the change in accumulated depreciation; in 1999 accumulated depreciation has been reduced by the amount allocated to the disposal of R&D. We can deduce that reduction to equal €73 (361 + 110 − 398).

We can use these disclosures to compute the effect of capitalization compared to expense.

Adjustment to Pretax Income: Subtract the difference between R&D expenditure (additions) and depreciation/writedowns from reported income. This adjustment essentially amounts to subtracting the change in net (unamortized) closing balance from reported income:

(Millions of Euros)	1998	1999
Pretax income (reported)	€2,456	€3,845
Less: change in net (unamortized) closing balance	62	124
Pretax income (adjusted)	€2,394	€3,721
% reduction	2.5%	3.2%

We can also adjust reported cash flows:

Adjustment to Cash Flows: Subtract R&D expenditure (additions) from CFO and add back to CFI:

(Millions of Euros)	1998	1999
Cash from operations	€1,687	€3,102
Cash flow from investing	(780)	(1,341)
Additions (R&D expenditures)	182	271
After adjustment		
Cash from operations	1,505	2,831
% reduction	10.8%	8.7%
Cash flow from investing	€(598)	€(1,070)

Finally, to make Nokia comparable to companies that expense all R&D, we must reduce equity[16] by the closing balance of unamortized R&D expense, net of tax effect:

(Millions of Euros)	1998	1999
Shareholders' equity (as reported)	€5,109	€7,378
Closing R&D balance (net of depreciation)	289	413
Less tax @ 28% (rate in Finland)	(81)	(116)
Net reduction in equity	€208	€297
Shareholders' equity (adjusted)	4,901	7,081
% reduction	4.1%	4.0%

These adjustments vary from 2% to 10% depending on the item being adjusted. Nokia is a very large company (1999 sales were nearly €20 billion). Depending on the size of the firm and the variability in expenditures, the effect on other firms may be more significant.[17]

One additional benefit of this analysis is that it highlights the actual expenditures on R&D activities. Changes in amount or trend (note the large 1999 increase for Nokia) should be examined for implications regarding the company's future sales and earnings.

BOX 2 ADJUSTING FINANCING STATEMENTS FOR CAPITALIZATION VERSUS EXPENSING

The capitalization-versus-expense decision has pervasive effects on firms' financial statements and ratios. In this box, we illustrate the adjustments from one method to the other. For convenience we use research and development (R&D) as the expenditure that can either be capitalized or expensed.

Adjusting from Capitalization to Expense

Income statement:

Pretax income	Deduct difference between R&D additions (expenditures) and amount amortized (or written off). This adjustment is equivalent to the *change in the net (unamortized) R&D asset.*
Net income	Deduct (1 − tax rate) × (change in the net (unamortized) R&D asset).

(continued)

[16] To adjust assets, we would deduct the closing balance of unamortized R&D expense.

[17] Nokia's 20-F report, in the required reconciliation between IASB and U.S. GAAP, shows somewhat different amounts for the income statement and balance sheet adjustments. These differences reflect the fact that, even under U.S. GAAP, Nokia could have capitalized a portion of these expenditures (computer software). The adjustments shown here eliminate the entire capitalized amount, facilitating comparison with firms that expense all R&D.

BOX 2 (continued)

Balance sheet:

Assets	Deduct net (unamortized) R&D asset from assets.
Liabilities	Deduct (tax rate) × (decrease in assets) from deferred tax liability.[a]
Equity	Deduct (1 − tax rate) × (decrease in assets) from equity.
Cash flow statement	Deduct R&D expenditures from CFO and add same amount to CFI

Adjusting from Expense to Capitalization

To capitalize expenditures, we need an assumption as to the period of amortization. This illustration assumes amortization over three years beginning in the year of the expenditure (year t).

Income statement:

Pretax income[b]	In year t, increase pretax income by $R\&D_t - 1/3(R\&D_t + R\&D_{t-1} + R\&D_{t-2})$.
Net income	Add (1 − tax rate) × (pretax income adjustment).

Balance sheet:[c]

Assets	Increase by $[2/3\ R\&D_t + 1/3\ R\&D_{t-1}]$.
Liabilities	Add (tax rate) × (increase in assets) to deferred tax liability.[d]
Equity	Increase by (1 − tax rate) × (increase in assets).
Cash flow statement:	Add $R\&D_t$ to CFO and deduct same amount from CFI.

[a] Assumes that R&D was expensed for tax purposes, creating a deferred tax liability (see Reading 38).

[b] General case, for amortization over n years: Increase pretax income by $[R\&D_t - 1/n\ (R\&D_t + R\&D_{t-1} + \ldots\ R\&D_{t-(n-1)})]$.

[c] Increase assets by $[(n-1)/n\ R\&D_t + (n-2)/n\ R\&D_{t-1} + \ldots\ 1/n\ R\&D_{t-(n-2)}]$.

[d] Assumes that R&D is expensed for tax purposes, so that capitalization results in a deferred tax liability (see Reading 38).

Research and Development Affiliates Although SFAS 2 does not permit the capitalization of R&D costs, companies have found ways to defer the recognition of such costs. One method is the R&D partnership. Another involves the issuance of "callable common" shares to the public.

Patents and Copyrights

All costs incurred in developing patents and copyrights are expensed in conformity with the treatment of R&D costs.[18] Only the legal fees incurred in registering internally developed patents and copyrights can be capitalized. However, the full acquisition cost is capitalized when such assets are purchased from other entities.

[18] However, publishers and motion picture producers capitalize all costs of creating their inventory.

Generally, patents have a legal life of 20 years under U.S. patent law; new copyrights have a legal life of 70 years beyond the creator's life. However, these periods should be viewed as upper limits. Successful patented products invite competition and the development of comparable or improved products that can diminish the value of the patent or make it obsolete. In addition, there is often a gap between the time that a patent is registered and the time the product comes to market.

In the pharmaceutical industry, for example, even after a patent is registered, the product cannot be marketed in most countries until it obtains regulatory approval, which can take a number of years. The analysis of companies that are heavily dependent on patented or proprietary products must consider the remaining legal life of patents on existing products and the number of patents in the pipeline.

Franchises and Licenses

Companies may sell the right to use their name, products, processes, or management expertise to others for some negotiated time period or market. The franchisee or licensee capitalizes the cost of purchasing these rights.

Brands and Trademarks

The cost of acquiring brands and trademarks in arm's-length transactions is capitalized. However, as in the case of other intangibles, U.S. GAAP prohibit recognition of the value of *internally created* brands or trademarks. IAS 38 also prohibits recognition of internally generated brands, mastheads, publishing titles, customer lists, and similar items. Some national accounting standards do permit recognition of such assets.

Advertising Costs

Successful advertising campaigns can contribute to generating a customer base and establishing brand or firm loyalty for many years. However, as with R&D, these benefits are uncertain and difficult to measure, and hence advertising costs are expensed as incurred. Even though there may be economic benefits, no asset is recorded because of measurement problems.

In December 1994, the Accounting Standards Executive Committee (AcSEC) of the AICPA issued Practice Bulletin 13,[19] Direct-Response Advertising and Probable Future Benefits, requiring capitalization of the costs of direct-response advertising that result in probable future benefits.[20] These costs are amortized over the estimated life of the future benefits. Capitalization is not allowed when the advertising produces leads that require additional marketing efforts to convert into sales.[21]

Goodwill

The difference between the cost of an acquired firm and the fair market value of its net assets is accounted for as an intangible asset, goodwill. It represents the

[19] This bulletin provides an interpretation of AICPA SOP 93-7, Reporting on Advertising Costs.

[20] An example would be advertising that results in a telephone response with an order.

[21] America On Line (AOL) capitalized marketing costs prior to 1996 as "deferred subscriber acquisition costs." After pressure from the SEC and analysts, AOL took a $385 million write-off in 1997 to eliminate these assets from its financial statements. In March 2000, AOL paid a $3.5 million fine to the SEC to settle charges that it had inflated profits in the years prior to 1997.

amount paid for the acquired firm's ability to earn excess profits, or value that cannot be assigned to tangible assets like property. The United States and most other GAAP limit the recognition of goodwill to cases where it is acquired in purchase method transactions.

Asset Revaluation

OPTIONAL SEGMENT BEGINS

The balance sheet is more informative when assets and liabilities are stated at market value rather than historical cost. Although the recognition of changes in fixed asset value is not permitted under U.S. GAAP, IASB standards do permit such revaluations.

IAS 16 (revised 1998), Property, Plant, and Equipment, allows firms to report fixed assets at fair value less accumulated depreciation.[22] Revaluations must be made with sufficient regularity to keep them current. All items in an asset class must be revalued if any are. Revaluation decreases that place the asset value below historical cost must be included in reported earnings. Revaluations are credited directly to equity except when they reverse writedowns that were included in reported income. IAS 16 has extensive disclosure provisions regarding revaluations and requires a full reconciliation of fixed assets. Footnote 12 to the Roche 2000 financial statements is a typical reconciliation.

IAS 41 (2000), Agriculture, requires that agricultural produce (e.g. cotton, milk, and logs) and biological assets (plants and animals) be measured at fair value for financial reporting. This standard became effective in 2003.

Revaluation is permitted under some non-U.S. GAAP as well.[23] Unfortunately, revaluation is applied inconsistently as standards in most countries do not specify either the method(s) to be used for revaluations or the intervals at which they must be made. The resulting balance sheet accounts are not comparable and, in some cases, may be misleading.

EXAMPLE 3

Holmen

Footnote 10 to Holmen's 1999 financial statements reports total revaluation surplus of SKr 4,372, almost all of which reflects the revaluation of forest land. No other data are provided although this item exceeds 27% of equity.

The revaluation of forest land has the following effects on Holmen compared with firms that do not revalue:

- lower asset turnover due to the higher asset value for land
- lower return on assets (ROA) due to higher assets
- higher reported book value per share
- lower return on equity (ROE) due to higher equity
- lower debt ratios due to higher equity

[22] Although historical cost is the benchmark treatment, revaluation is an allowed alternative.

[23] Australian GAAP, for example, permits revaluations. Barth and Clinch (1998) examined a sample of revaluations in Australia and found that both tangible and intangible revaluations tended to be value relevant.

OPTIONAL SEGMENT

As forestland is not depreciated, there is no effect on reported income. For assets that are depreciated, revaluation has the following additional effects:

- lower earnings due to higher depreciation expense
- lower interest coverage due to reduced EBIT

The earnings reduction further reduces ROA and ROE and dilutes the positive impact of the revaluation on book value per share.

5

CAPITALIZATION VERSUS EXPENSING: INDUSTRY ISSUES

Regulated Utilities

Even prior to the issuance of SFAS 34, almost all U.S. regulated utilities capitalized interest on construction work in progress. In addition, utilities capitalize many cash outflows that unregulated companies cannot. The reason is that accounting rules have direct economic impact for utilities. Rates charged to customers are largely a function of accounting-generated numbers.[24]

Regulators allow utilities to earn profits equal to a specified allowable rate of return on assets (rate base). Adding expenses to this allowable profit yields the rates they can charge their customers. Revenues are derived as follows:

$$\text{Revenues} = \text{Expenses} + (\text{Rate of Return} \times \text{Rate Base})$$

Using interest for a self-constructed asset as an example, expensing increases revenue immediately as the interest expense is recovered in the year incurred. Capitalizing results in recovery of the expense over time as depreciation of the additional fixed asset. However, the total allowable profit is increased due to the fact that the asset base has been increased. Hence, although revenues are deferred, the total amount collected over the life of the asset is greater. As the average life of utility fixed assets (mainly generating plants) is quite long, the incentive to capitalize costs in fixed assets (increasing the rate base) is powerful.

Fairness to customers is often one argument for capitalization; as current customers do not (yet) benefit from investments in capacity growth, they should not bear the cost. Thus, the cost of financing new capacity is capitalized and spread over time, matching the costs with the benefits (service to ratepayers). This logic is also appealing to regulators who prefer (for political reasons) to defer rate increases to future time periods. Logic and fairness aside, utilities have a direct economic incentive to capitalize.[25]

---

[24] For this reason, virtually all regulators that set prices also mandate the accounting principles followed by the companies that they regulate. This has given rise to so-called RAP (regulatory accounting principles), which may differ materially from GAAP.

[25] This discussion assumes that the capitalized interest will, in fact, be recovered from future revenues. In practice, "regulatory lag" often results in actual rates of return below the "allowable" rate of return. In addition, by capitalizing interest, the recovery of that interest is delayed to a later period and thus current period cash flow is reduced. For these reasons, some utilities have successfully petitioned regulators to allow some portion of the interest on construction work in progress (CWIP) to be recovered currently (expensed) rather than capitalized.

Regulatory accounting results in the creation of *regulatory assets* and *regulatory liabilities*. Regulatory assets are expenditures that regulators will permit the utility to recover in future periods, even though these expenditures do not qualify as assets for unregulated companies under GAAP. Examples include:

- Capitalization (as part of fixed assets) of return on equity as well as interest. These are called the allowance for funds used during construction (AFUDC).
- Capitalization (as part of fixed assets) of employee costs and other overhead.
- Demand-side management costs (expenditures to reduce demand).
- Costs to buy out coal or gas purchase contracts.

Under SFAS 71, such expenditures can be recorded as regulatory assets (regulatory liabilities) as long as recovery (settlement) is expected. If an adverse regulatory ruling is made, such assets must be written off.

When deregulation occurs, the company must reassess the carrying value of its assets and liabilities under these new circumstances. In the United States, deregulation of the telephone industry resulted in significant write-offs by companies in that industry as they:

- wrote down fixed assets to reflect shorter economic lives
- wrote off regulatory assets that were no longer recoverable

The use of shorter asset lives as a result of the accounting change increases depreciation expense, somewhat offset by the elimination of depreciation on older assets that were fully written off as part of the change. The change also sharply reduces reported stockholders' equity, increasing the reported debt-to-equity ratio.

The deregulation of the electric utility industry in the United States is in its early stages. Such deregulation is likely to result in similar write-offs of regulatory assets and the use of shorter lives for fixed assets.[26]

Computer Software Development Costs

The growing importance of computer software led the FASB to issue SFAS 86 (1985), which applies to software intended for sale or lease to others. SFAS 86 requires that all costs incurred to establish the technological and/or economic feasibility of software be viewed as R&D costs and expensed as incurred. Once economic feasibility has been established, subsequent costs can be capitalized as part of product inventory and amortized based on product revenues or on a straight-line basis.

Although this provision allows software firms to increase reported assets and income, some software firms[27] (most notably, Microsoft[28]) have not taken advantage

---

[26] Deregulation also eliminates the incentives for investments in generating plants by eliminating the guaranteed recovery of the investment and a return on investment. Shortages of generating capacity started to appear in 1999.

[27] In 1996, the Software Publishers Association (SPA) petitioned the FASB to abolish SFAS 86 and make expensing the required method of accounting. The SPA argued that the uncertainty surrounding eventual product sales made capitalization both inappropriate and not beneficial to investors. As noted in Box 3, Aboody and Lev (1998) found, on the contrary, that software capitalization was indeed value relevant to investors. Aboody and Lev suggested (using recent trends in software development costs) that perhaps the SPA was motivated by the fact that software development expenditures had declined to a low level and that expensing would now show higher income than capitalization. By eliminating the previous years' capitalization overhang with a onetime accounting charge, software developers could (under the SPA's proposal) get the best of both worlds, using capitalization when costs were growing and expensing when costs declined.

[28] Microsoft's fiscal 2000 annual report states that it adopted SOP 98-1 (discussed shortly) in 2000 but provides no disclosure of the effects. On page 22 it states that SFAS 86 "does not materially affect the Company."

of the provisions of SFAS 86. Disparate accounting for software hinders the comparison of computer software firms, requiring restatement to the same accounting method. SFAS 86 disclosures are sufficient to evaluate (and eliminate) the impact of capitalization. For some firms, the effect may be significant, as illustrated by the following example.

EXAMPLE 4

Lucent

The following data were obtained from Lucent's annual report for fiscal 1999:

Capitalized Software

(in $millions)	1998	1999
Opening balance	$293	$298
Closing balance	298	470
Amortization	234	249

where the balances were obtained from Lucent's balance sheet and the amortization amount from the statement of cash flows. By adding the year-to-year increase in the balance to the amortization, we can deduce the amount invested during the year (which is included in capital expenditures under investing activities):

(in $millions)	1998	1999
New investment	$239	$421

If Lucent expensed this amount each year (as does Microsoft), its income would have been reduced by:

	(in $millions)	1998	1999
Income adjustment	Investment less amortization	$ 5	$ 172
	Tax offset (35%)	(2)	(60)
	Net adjustment	$ 3	$ 112
Net income	Reported	$1,035	$3,458
	Adjusted	1,032	3,346
	% reduction	−0.3%	−3.2%

Note that the 1999 effect is much greater than the 1998 effect, reflecting the substantial increase in expenditures. Capitalization and amortization smoothes the effect of spending changes on reported income. It also obscures the large increase, which may suggest that Lucent hopes to expand its software sales.

Perhaps more important, however, is that amounts capitalized are included in cash for investing activities rather than cash from operations. By subtracting the new investment amount, we can adjust cash from operations:

Cash from Operations

(in $millions)	1998	1999
Reported	$1,860	$(276)
Adjusted	1,621	(697)
% reduction	−12.8%	−152.5%

While reported CFO turned negative in 1999, the effect is even greater when software expenditures are reclassified from investing to operating activities.

SOP 98-1 governs accounting for the cost of developing computer software for internal use (rather than sale or lease).[29] This standard requires the capitalization and subsequent amortization of the cost of developing internal-use software once technical feasibility has been established. EITF Issue 00-2[30] extends SOP 98-1 to website development costs, allowing capitalization of costs to develop or add applications for websites. IBM, for example, capitalized $81 million of website development costs in 2000.

EXAMPLE 5

Lucent

The 10-Q report filed by Lucent for the first quarter of fiscal 2000 (ending December 31, 1999) states:

> Effective October 1, 1999, Lucent adopted Statement of Position 98-1, "Accounting for the Costs of Computer Software Developed or Obtained for Internal Use" ("SOP 98-1"). As a result, certain costs of computer software developed or obtained for internal use have been capitalized and will be amortized over a three-year period. The impact of adopting SOP 98-1 was a reduction of costs and operating expenses of $80 million during the three months ended December 31, 1999.

[29] Issued by the Accounting Standards Executive Committee of the American Institute of Certified Public Accountants. For full discussion of SOP 98-1, see Daniel Noll, "Accounting for Internal Use Software," *Journal of Accountancy* (September 1998), pp. 95–98.

[30] Accounting for Web Site Development Costs, issued by the Emerging Issues Task Force based on discussions in January and March 2000. EITF 00-2 was effective for costs incurred after June 30, 2000.

The impact of the new standard increased pretax income by $80 million, equal to nearly 5% of pretax income excluding "one-time items." If not for the accounting change, that adjusted pretax income would have declined by more than 28% instead of the reported decline of 25%. The effect of the accounting change was not reported in the January 20, 2000 press release announcing Lucent's first quarter earnings, providing an illustration of the importance of reviewing SEC filings.

Accounting for Oil and Gas Exploration

Oil and gas exploration results in drilling both productive wells and dry holes.[31] As failure is an integral part of successful exploration, the cost of dry holes can be considered part of the cost of drilling productive ones. As in the case of R&D, the value of an oil discovery is frequently unrelated to the cost of drilling.

The FASB, in SFAS 19 (1977), required all firms to use the successful efforts (SE) accounting method that expenses all dry hole costs. Like the FASB's R&D reporting standard, this rule was conservative and eliminated assets with uncertain future benefits from the balance sheet. The Securities and Exchange Commission (SEC), fearing that the adoption of this rule would result in the curtailment of oil exploration (especially by smaller companies), forced the FASB to suspend SFAS 19 (SFAS 25, 1979). The SEC (ASR 253, 1978) permits public companies to use either SE or full cost (FC) methods of accounting. The latter permits the capitalization of dry hole costs.

Under current accounting practice, therefore, firms have the option of capitalizing the cost of dry holes (FC method) or expensing them as they occur (SE method). The choice between these two methods has a significant impact on the financial statements of oil and gas exploration companies and on many ratios as well. Exhibit 1 illustrates the difference between the SE and FC methods of accounting for oil and gas exploration costs. The balance sheet carrying amount of reserves, $4,000, is higher under the FC method because of the inclusion of the cost of dry holes ($3,000). The SE firm carries its reserves at only $1,000.[32]

The reported profitability (both levels and trends over time) of production is also affected. The SE firm reports a net loss of $250 in year 1 but net income of $2,750 per year for years 2 through 4, for a total net income of $8,000. The FC firm shows constant net income of $2,000 per year, again for a total of $8,000 over the four years. The effect of the FC method is to defer (capitalize) exploration costs and, therefore, accelerate the recognition of profit.

CFO may also differ. As previously discussed, although the income difference reverses over time, the difference in CFO does not. The cumulative CFO over the life of the well is higher for the FC firm by the cost of the capitalized dry holes ($12,000 − $9,000 = $3,000).

[31] Dry holes are wells drilled that do not find commercial quantities of oil or gas.

[32] Using a sample of oil and gas companies, Harris and Ohlson (1987) found that the market distinguished between SE and FC companies in a rational fashion. Book values of full cost companies were given less weight than those of SE companies. Additionally, they found that FC book values had less explanatory power than those of SE companies. This finding is consistent with a survey that indicated analysts prefer SE.

OPTIONAL SEGMENT

The differences between the methods cause SE firms to report:

- Lower carrying costs of oil and gas reserves than FC firms
- Lower stockholders' equity due to lower asset values
- Lower earnings than FC firms when exploration efforts are rising
- Lower cash from operations than FC firms

EXHIBIT 1 **Comparison of Successful Efforts and Full Cost Impact on Net Income and Cash from Operations**

Assumptions:

1. $1,000 cost of drilling well (dry or productive).
2. Four wells are drilled: One is productive, the other three are dry.
3. The productive well has a four-year life, with revenues (net of cost of production) of $3,000 per year.

Successful Efforts Method

The $3,000 cost of dry holes is expensed immediately. Only the $1,000 cost of the productive well is capitalized and amortized over its four-year life.

Year	1	2	3	4	Total
Net revenues	$ 3,000	$3,000	$3,000	$3,000	$12,000
Dry hole expense	(3,000)	0	0	0	(3,000)
Amortization	(250)	(250)	(250)	(250)	(1,000)
Net income	$ (250)	$2,750	$2,750	$2,750	$ 8,000
Cash Flows					
Operations[a]	$ 0	$3,000	$3,000	$3,000	$ 9,000
Investment	(1,000)	0	0	0	(1,000)
Total	$(1,000)	$3,000	$3,000	$3,000	$ 8,000

[a] Net revenues less dry hole expense.

Full Cost Method

The entire $4,000 drilling cost ($3,000 for dry holes and $1,000 for the productive well) is capitalized and amortized over the four-year life of the productive well.

Year	1	2	3	4	Total
Net revenues	$ 3,000	$3,000	$3,000	$3,000	$12,000
Amortization	(1,000)	(1,000)	(1,000)	(1,000)	(4,000)
Net income	$ 2,000	$2,000	$2,000	$2,000	$ 8,000
Cash Flows					
Operations[a]	$ 3,000	$3,000	$3,000	$3,000	$12,000
Investment	(4,000)	0	0	0	(4,000)
Total	$(1,000)	$3,000	$3,000	$3,000	$ 8,000

[a] Net revenues.

In practice, however, oil and gas firms using the SE method adjust their reported cash flow statements for this difference. They add exploration costs expensed back to net income (assuming use of the indirect method) and include those costs in capital expenditures. For example, Texaco's 1999 annual report states:

> We present cash flows from operating activities using the indirect method. We exclude exploratory expenses from cash flows of operating activities and apply them to cash flows of investing activities. On this basis, we reflect all capital and exploratory expenditures as investing activities.

However, Repsol, the large Spanish oil company, does not appear to make this adjustment. As a result, its reported cash flow components are not comparable with those of companies that make the adjustment.

6 ANALYTICAL ADJUSTMENTS FOR CAPITALIZATION AND EXPENSING

Need for Analytical Adjustments

Because the choices between capitalization and expensing discussed in this reading affect reported corporate performance, analysts must sometimes adjust reported data to facilitate analysis and comparisons.

Software companies, as noted earlier, are allowed to capitalize software costs, and most do so. A notable exception is Microsoft. Comparisons with other (software) companies can be facilitated and insight as to Microsoft's motivations can be gained by comparing Microsoft's reported income with income had it capitalized R&D. In our analysis, we assume a three-year amortization period.

(in $millions)

	1996	1997	1998	1999	2000
Net income as reported			$4,490	$7,785	$9,421
Adjustment					
R&D as reported	$1,432	$1,925	2,601	2,970	3,775
Amortization of R&D[a]			(1,986)	(2,499)	(3,115)
Pretax adjustment			$ 615	$ 471	$ 660
After-tax @ 35% tax rate			400	306	429
Adjusted income			4,890	8,091	9,850
% increase in income			8.9%	3.9%	4.6%

[a] For example, for 2000: ($2,601 + $2,970 + $3,775)/3 = $3,115.

Note that, as Microsoft's R&D is increasing, expensing R&D reduces reported income by 4% to 9%. Although one cannot be sure, it is possible that Microsoft opted not to capitalize costs in order to lessen pressure from antitrust authorities by reporting lower income.

In Microsoft's case, the adjustments to R&D do not significantly affect ROE and ROA.[33] However, that is a function of Microsoft's profitability and pattern of R&D expenditures. For other industries, the effects on ROE and ROA can be considerable.

The pharmaceutical industry, for example, reports ROE that is among the highest of all U.S. industries. Some suggest that this reflects a higher return for the risks inherent in R&D. Others contend that the industry simply earns excess profits, and drug prices have periodically become a political issue. To some extent, however, high drug-industry returns reflect the accounting method used for R&D. Expensing these costs understates equity, the denominator of the ROE ratio. Capitalizing R&D costs (treating them as an investment) would give a more accurate measure of ROE.

Figure 6 illustrates this point. Sougiannis (1994) and Lev and Sougiannis (1996) examined the effect on return on equity (ROE) of recalculating the financial results of Merck as if the company capitalized R&D expense and amortized the capitalized amounts over seven years.[34] Using the implied amortization schedule for Merck,[35] Figure 6 shows the effects of their conversion process graphically for the period 1982 to 1991. Adjusted ROE is significantly lower for all years, although the trend is unchanged.[36]

From the analyst's perspective, the problem is that accounting does not (and probably cannot) accurately measure the value of expenditures on research and development.[37] Thus the analyst must perform two tasks:

1. Adjust financial data to reflect differences in capitalization policy among firms.
2. Evaluate the flow of new products resulting from R&D expenditures.

The Merck example shows the effects of restating by capitalizing an expense. At times, it may be more appropriate to restate capitalized expenditures to expenses. Westvaco (capitalized interest) and Nokia (capitalized development costs) are examples of such restatements. The second task, far more difficult, is beyond the scope of financial statement analysis.

Similar adjustments are required for firms that differ in the extent to which they buy operating assets or lease them. Airlines, for example, may buy or lease airplanes. Similarly, retail store chains may own or lease stores. This choice has financial statement effects similar to those stemming from capitalizing or expensing. Reported ROA may be misleading; adjustments are required for comparability. Reading 40 discusses leasing and other off-balance-sheet financing techniques in detail.

---

[33] In 2000, average equity was $34,903 million, yielding ROE of 27.0%. Capitalizing R&D would increase equity for

$$1999\left[.65x\left(\left(\frac{2}{3}\right)2{,}970+\left(\frac{1}{3}\right)2{,}601\right)\right]=1{,}851 \text{ and for } 2000\left[.65x\left(\left(\frac{2}{3}\right)3{,}775+\left(\frac{1}{3}\right)2{,}970\right)\right]=2{,}280$$

Average equity would increase by [.5 × ($1,851 + $2,280) = $2,065] to $36,968 and adjusted ROE would be ($9,850/$36,968) = 26.6%. The reason for the small adjustment is related to the discussion in footnote 3. Note the growth rate in Microsoft's R&D expenditures for 2000 is 27.1%. As that growth rate is almost identical to the ROE of 27.0%, the differences in reported and adjusted ROE (ROA) will be negligible.

[34] Their analysis suggests that R&D has (on average) a seven-year duration for the pharmaceutical industry.

[35] The amortization schedule is neither straight-line nor declining balance. Rather, it amortizes capitalized R&D in proportion to the benefits received. As there is a lag between the time of the expenditure and benefits received, amortization increases over the first three years and declines thereafter.

[36] In this case, Merck's profitability as measured by ROE was in the 40% range whereas growth in R&D expenditures was considerably smaller at 15%.

[37] It is precisely this difficulty that prompted the FASB to require the expensing of R&D expenditures.

OPTIONAL SEGMENT

FIGURE 6 Recalculation of Profitability Ratios Assuming Capitalization of R&D Expenditures

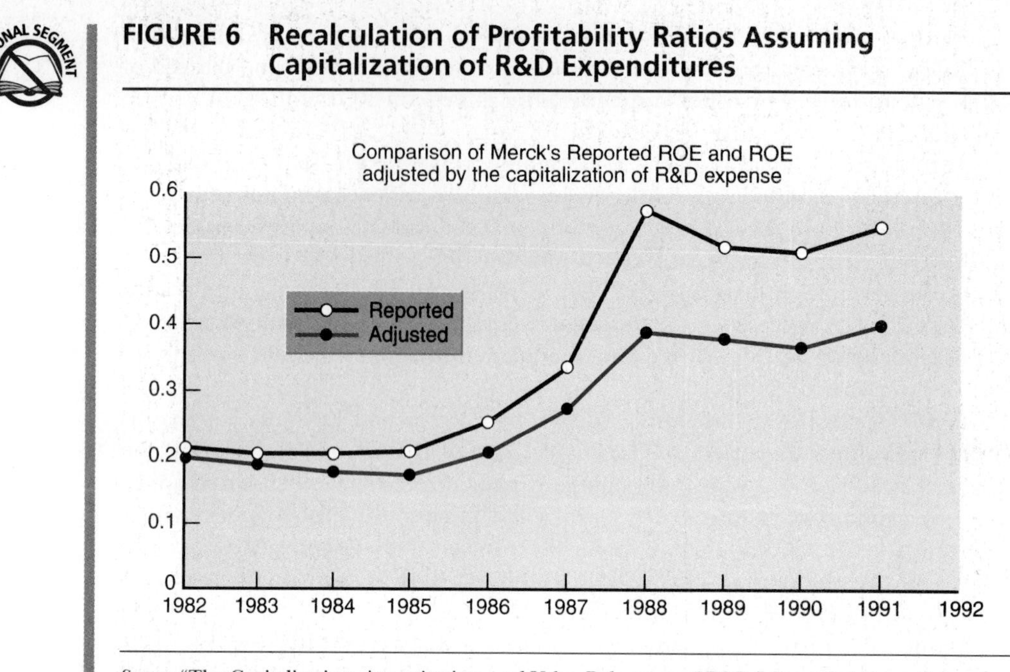

Source: "The Capitalization, Amortization, and Value-Relevance of R&D," *Journal of Accounting and Economics*, Baruch Lev and Theodore Sougiannis, Table 6 (Feb. 1996), pp. 107–138.

Valuation Implications

Expenditures for R&D and advertising are generally expensed because it is difficult, if not impossible, to reliably estimate their future benefits. That does not mean that these expenditures do not affect firm valuation. An outflow that is truly an expense reduces stockholder wealth; an outflow that generates future cash flows may actually increase it.

There are two types of valuation models: earnings based and asset based. Box 3 discusses how the capitalization decision affects these valuation models and presents empirical evidence that the market recognizes the asset characteristics of outflows in categories such as R&D, advertising, and oil and gas wells. These results suggest that the analyst cannot apply either capitalization or expensing mechanically, but must try to forecast the future benefits of these expenditures.

Other Economic Consequences

Although differences in accounting methods are cosmetic, they can have real consequences, as suggested by positive theory.

First, a firm's borrowing ability may be limited by unfavorable profitability or leverage ratios resulting from, for example, expensing R&D expenditures. Second, because of these unfavorable ratios, a firm may curtail these expenditures, effectively scaling back operations. Finally, whether or not managers actually reduce R&D, the fact that the market perceives such a possibility can cause negative market reaction.

Mandated accounting changes is one area where such effects can be examined, as they provide a laboratory environment permitting before-and-after comparisons. Box 4 reviews empirical evidence regarding mandated accounting changes for R&D and oil and gas accounting.

BOX 3 CAPTALIZATION AND VALUATION

Consider the following simplified valuation model:

$$\text{Value} = p \times \text{Net Inflows}$$

The model can be used to represent a (constant) discounted earnings model, where net inflows represent revenue and expense flows and the coefficient p is simply the **price/earnings (P/E)** ratio. Disaggregating the net inflows into inflows and outflows yields

$$\text{Value} = p \times \text{Inflows} - p \times \text{Expense Outflows} + b \times \text{Asset Outflows}$$

where asset outflows represent expenditures for such categories as R&D. If these outflows are actually expenses, then $b = -p$.

From a valuation perspective, the difference between asset and expense outflows should be whether the associated outflow has expected future benefits. The level and sign of the coefficient b measure whether the outflow should be considered an expense. An expense benefits only the period of occurrence, and the outlay reduces value by $-p$ times the outflow.[a] An asset outflow benefits future periods and, therefore, the coefficient b should be positive.[b]

Bublitz and Ettredge (1989) compared the market valuation of unexpected changes in advertising, R&D, and other expenses. Advertising was included because, like R&D, it is expected to provide benefits for more than one period, albeit for a shorter term than R&D. They expected the coefficient for R&D to be larger (more positive) than the coefficient for advertising, and both larger than the coefficient for other expenses. The results were mixed, but on balance they were consistent with a market assessment of advertising as short-lived and R&D as long-lived.[c]

Their valuation model used a discounted earnings-based perspective. Shevlin (1991) used an asset-based valuation model for R&D partnerships. In such a model, the value of the firm is defined as

$$\text{Value} = \text{Assets} - \text{Liabilities}$$

Shevlin[d] found that when R&D expenditures were considered assets, they contributed to firm value. Moreover, the market weighting given these expenditures was larger than for other assets, indicating that the expected benefit from these expenditures exceeds their book value.

Lev and Sougiannis (1996) and Sougiannis (1994) estimated stock prices and returns as functions of *both* earnings and book values. They also found that the capitalized components of R&D have value relevance[e] and are associated with current-period stock returns. More important, Lev and Sougiannis found a significant association between capitalized R&D and *subsequent* stock returns. This implied either a (systematic) mispricing by the market of R&D-intensive companies or compensation for (extra-market) risk associated with R&D.

Aboody and Lev (1998) compared companies that capitalized software development costs with those that chose not to. They found software capitalization (as well as the subsequent amortization) to be value relevant. Amounts capitalized were strongly associated with (contemporaneous) market prices and returns and were also positively associated with subsequent earnings changes. Moreover, consistent with the reasoning underlying SFAS 86,

> the coefficient of capitalized software . . . is larger than the coefficient of the development costs expensed by "expensers" . . . which in turn is larger than

(continued)

BOX 3 *(continued)*

the coefficient of the development costs expensed by "capitalizers". . . . *This order of coefficient sizes is consistent with the reasoning of SFAS No. 86 that capitalized software reflects the costs of projects close to fruition and should be strongly associated with near-term earnings, whereas the development costs of "expensers" reflect the costs of both feasible and prefeasibility projects, which should not be as strongly associated with near-term earnings. The development costs expensed by "capitalizers" reflect both prefeasibility costs and costs of failed projects, consistent with little or no association with subsequent earnings.*[f]

Lev, in a series of publications,[g] attempts to arrive at capitalization values in an indirect manner. Rather than capitalizing intangible expenditures, he capitalizes *intangible-driven earnings*. More specifically, Lev argues that a firm's earnings are a function of its physical, financial, and intangible assets; i.e.,

$$\text{Earnings} = f\,(\text{Physical Assets, Financial Assets, Intangible Assets})$$

Using a combination of past and forecasted earnings as well as "normal" returns on (known) physical and financial assets, he imputes *intangible-driven earnings* (i.e., earnings above those normally generated by a firm's physical and financial assets). Forecasted values of these intangible-driven earnings are then discounted to arrive at a capitalized value of intangible assets.

Such assets, known alternatively as "knowledge," "intellectual," or "intangible" capital, are not confined to technology companies. Lev shows that in addition to industries such as aerospace, telecommunications, computer hardware/software, and pharmaceuticals, the home products and food and beverage industries are also rich in intangible capital. This intangible capital he attributes to strong brand recognition.

Gu and Lev (2001) also test the valuation relevance of intangibles-driven earnings. They argue that their findings indicate that intangibles-driven earnings provide more relevant information to investors than conventional earnings and cash flows.

---

[a] The current benefits are reflected in the inflows.

[b] The asset outflows representing future benefits can be thought of as a growth component. For a firm with growth, its value can be expressed as

$$\text{Value} = \frac{E}{r} + \left[\frac{1}{r}\left(\frac{r^* - r}{r - ar^*}\right)\right]\text{aE}$$

where E is earnings, r the appropriate discount rate, r^* the amount the firm earns on its investment, and aE the amount the firm reinvests. In our example, $p = 1/r$ and b is the coefficient of the asset investment aE. That is, b is equal to the term in brackets. On the margin, it may be zero (if $r^* = r$) as the firm undertakes zero or break-even net present value investments.

[c] Their R&D results are consistent with those of Hirschey and Weygandt (1985), who found that the market valuation of R&D implies it is an asset outflow. Hirschey and Weygandt also found that advertising had characteristics similar to a long-lived asset.

[d] Shevlin applied option-pricing models to the valuation of R&D partnerships.

[e] Sougiannis, for example, shows that (on average) a one-dollar increase in R&D expenditures produces a five-dollar increase in market value.

[f] David Aboody and Baruch Lev, "The Value Relevance of Intangibles: The Case of Software Capitalization, *Journal of Accounting Research* (Supplement 1998), p. 178, emphasis added.

[g] See, for example, Lev (2001), Gu and Lev (2001), and articles published in *Fortune* ("Accounting Gets Radical," by Thomas A. Stewart, April 16, 2001) and *CFO* ("Knowledge Capital Scorecard: Treasures Revealed," by Andrew Osterland, April 2001) for a general description of the methodology and results. The exact methodology is proprietary.

The research confirms that, even if an accounting change has no direct economic impact, the effects of the change on reported income can have real indirect consequences, such as the curtailment of expenditures and negative market reaction. Indirect effects may also result from debt covenant constraints or the influence of management compensation contracts. Accounting choices may also be motivated by firm characteristics.

Additional Analysis of Fixed Asset Data

Changes in the balance sheet cost of fixed assets result from four types of events:

1. capital spending (acquisition of fixed assets)
2. sale, impairment, or retirement (no longer in use) of fixed assets
3. increases (decreases) in fixed assets due to acquisitions (disposals)
4. changes due to the effects of foreign currency translation

The following sections discuss capital expenditures and the sale/retirement of assets.

Capital Expenditures

The capital expenditure decision provides information to the investor as to a firm's future profitability and growth prospects. Management often announces major capital expenditure plans separately. McConnell and Muscarella (1986) and Kerstein and Kim (1995) provide evidence that there is positive (negative) market reaction to unexpected increases (decreases) in capital expenditures. Similarly, Lev and Thiagarajan (1993) show that firms with higher (lower) changes in capital expenditures than their industry average experience positive (negative) market reaction. Thus, it is important to monitor (changes in) the level of a firm's capital expenditures.

In doing so, note that capital expenditures tend to be seasonal, with the majority of such expenditures being carried out in the fourth quarter. Different

BOX 4 MANDATED ACCOUNTING CHANGES: ECONOMIC CONSEQUENCES AND MARKET REACTION

The capitalization-versus-expense issue has proved a fruitful area of empirical research. The issues examined provide interesting parallels between R&D (SFAS 2) and oil and gas accounting (SFAS 19). In both cases, mandated accounting changes favored expensing over capitalization (albeit in the case of SFAS 19, the standard was suspended).

Economic Consequences

Proponents of capitalization argued that the accounting change would lead to a reduction of risk-taking activities such as expenditures for R&D and exploration activities, as the cost of risk taking would increase. These fears were generally expressed for smaller companies[a] who feared that markets (at least private lenders) would focus on the effects on reported income (both amounts and variability). The change would thus impair their ability to raise capital.

As SFAS 19 was never implemented, the validity of these claims could not be verified. However, for SFAS 2, a number of studies attempted to verify whether the new standard curtailed R&D.

(continued)

BOX 4 *(continued)*

Horwitz and Kolodny (1980) reported that a majority of firms (58% to 67%) believed that small firms reduced planned R&D expenditures as a consequence of SFAS 2. Using a sample of small high-technology firms, they found evidence that the actual levels of R&D expenditures dropped following the introduction of SFAS 2.

In contrast, Dukes et al. (1980) found no evidence of curtailment of R&D subsequent to the adoption of SFAS 2. Their sample, however, consisted of larger companies, and in a subsequent study Elliott et al. (1984) confirmed the finding that small companies that had previously capitalized R&D curtailed R&D expenditures after the issuance of SFAS 2. However, they noted that the downward trend in R&D expenditures for these companies had already begun years prior to the issuance of SFAS 2. Comparing the operating performance of the "capitalizers" with a control sample of firms that had always expensed R&D, they found that the operating performance of the capitalizers was worse. They conjectured that financial difficulties, rather than the accounting change, may have caused the curtailment of R&D. In fact, it could be argued that the original decision to capitalize R&D by these firms may have been motivated by an effort to improve reported financial performance in the face of financial stress.

Selto and Clouse (1985) argued that firms would be likely to anticipate the effects of an accounting change such as SFAS 2 and adapt to it. Thus, if divisional managers would be motivated to reduce R&D expenditures because of the effect on their compensation (through earnings-based compensation plans), firms would adjust their compensation plans accordingly or, alternatively, take steps to centralize the R&D decision-making process. They found that although not all firms made such changes, those that did were the ones most likely to be affected by the provisions of SFAS 2. Thus, to the extent accounting changes have economic consequences, they may be manifested internally rather than externally.

Market Reaction

Vigeland (1981) found no market reaction to the mandated accounting change for R&D expenditures. There is little controversy with respect to this mandated accounting change. This is not true with respect to the mandated change(s) affecting accounting for oil and gas exploration. This issue spawned a cottage industry of research with studies examining the reaction to the announcement of (the exposure draft of) SFAS 19 and Accounting Series Release (ASR) 253, issued by the SEC, that suspended SFAS 19.

The research examined whether firms using the full cost method (FC) had negative (positive) returns when SFAS 19 (ASR 253) was announced. Generally negative reaction was found around the time of the announcement of the SFAS 19 exposure draft. Not everyone, however, agreed with its significance[b] and the results were found to be sensitive to the time period examined and (at the time of the exposure draft announcement) "confounding" news affecting the oil industry. Thus, even though negative market reaction was found, its cause was not clear.

With respect to the ASR 253 announcement, Collins et al. (1982) compared the market reaction at the time the SFAS 19 exposure draft was announced with the reaction experienced when ASR 253 was announced. They found that there was a significant negative correlation for the FC firms; that is, negative reaction to the first announcement was followed by positive reaction to the subsequent (suspension) announcement.

These studies tested market reaction without considering any factors that might cause differential market reactions across firms due to differential impacts on income and equity. Such factors might include firm size, the relative importance of exploration, firm leverage, and the existence of debt covenants and accounting-based management compensation schemes. Collins et al. (1981) and Lys (1984) tested for such factors with some success, finding, for example, that the degree of market reaction was related to (1) the size of the reduction in owner's equity that would result

(continued)

BOX 4 *(continued)*

from SFAS 19, (2) the existence of debt covenants, and (3) management compensation schemes based on reported income.

[a] The standards primarily affected smaller firms, as for both R&D and exploration costs, larger firms generally used the expensing method. See Reading 35, Box 1 for further discussion of the differential impact of the capitalize-versus-expense decision on larger and small firms.

[b] Collins and Dent (1979) and Lev (1979) claimed that the results were statistically significant, whereas Dyckman and Smith (1979) argued that the market reaction was not statistically different from that experienced by firms using successful efforts (SE).

theories exist as to whether this phenomenon is tied to a firm's budgetary cycle [Callen et al. (1996)] or the timing is tax related [Kinney and Trezevant (1993)].

Sale, Impairment, or Retirement of Assets

The sale or retirement of fixed assets removes these assets from the balance sheet. For most firms, sale or retirement also generates gains or losses, included in reported income.

In the case of Westvaco, gains on asset sales are included in other income (see financial statement Note B). In 1999, such gains accounted for 12% of pretax income. Some companies report gains or losses on a separate line in the income statement, whereas others include them elsewhere.[38] The analyst should examine such gains or losses for several reasons.

First, gains and losses resulting from asset sales are considered nonrecurring and the inclusion of such gains in reported income lowers the quality of earnings. However, if such gains or losses occur in most years, it is difficult to consider them "nonrecurring." As asset sales are to a great extent subject to management discretion, their timing and variation from year to year must be closely monitored as they can be used to distort operating trends. Bartov (1993) reported that firms use gains or losses from asset sales to smooth reported income.[39] Additionally, highly leveraged firms sell more long-lived assets than less leveraged firms in an effort to improve their reported debt-to-equity ratios.

A second reason for looking at asset sales is more fundamental. Sale of a significant portion of fixed assets is an indicator of change—in product line or production location. The examination of trends in capital spending and fixed asset sales can help the analyst ask perceptive questions regarding changes in future operations.

Finally, a pattern of gains suggests that the company's depreciation method is conservative, understating reported income and the net carrying amounts of fixed assets. A pattern of losses suggests that depreciation expense is understated (income is overstated) and fixed assets are overvalued on the balance sheet. In extreme cases, such losses are recognized as "impairments." Issues relating to depreciation and impairments are discussed in Reading 37.

[38] Undisclosed gains and losses can sometimes be deduced from the statement of cash flows. Gains and losses from asset sales are non-operating in nature, and must be subtracted from cash from operations. The proceeds from asset sales must be reported in cash from investment.

[39] Whether this constitutes "good" or "bad" behavior depends on whether one views income smoothing (see Reading 34) as "variance reducing" (providing information to investors as to a firm's expected performance) or manipulative behavior that hides a firm's actual performance.

SUMMARY

This reading considers the financial statement effects of the capitalize-versus-expense decision for long-lived assets. This decision is significant not only for firms with large investments in buildings and machinery, but also for those who have large expenditures on research, development, and computer software. The reading reviews the analytical techniques that can be used to restore comparability despite the use of differing accounting methods for similar transactions.

Once the capitalized amount is determined, the firm must choose an appropriate pattern of depreciation or amortization. Analysts must also contend with financial reporting for impairments and disposal of these assets. We discuss these issues in the next reading.

PRACTICE PROBLEMS FOR READING 36

1. [Capitalization of interest] The following data were obtained from the annual reports of Chevron, a multinational oil company (all data in $millions):

	1995	1996	1997	1998	1999
Interest expense	$ 401	$ 364	$ 312	$ 405	$ 472
Pretax income	1,789	4,740	5,502	1,834	3,648
Net income	930	2,607	3,256	1,339	2,070
Capitalized interest	141	108	82	39	59
Amortization of capitalized interest	47	24	28	35	9

A. Using reported interest expense, compute the earnings coverage ratio (times interest earned) for each year, 1995 to 1999.

B. Assuming that Chevron had always expensed interest as incurred:

i. Recompute the earnings coverage ratio for each year.

ii. Compare the two ratios (based on reported versus restated data).

iii. Recompute income (assume a 35% tax rate each year).

iv. Discuss the effect on net income of restatement to expense all interest.

C. Discuss the effect of restatement on the five-year trend of Chevron's:

i. Interest expense

ii. Interest coverage ratio

iii. Pretax and net income

D. State which calculation of the interest coverage ratio is better for financial analysis and justify your choice.

2. [Capitalization of computer software expenditure] Ericsson [ERICA], a multinational producer of wireless telephone equipment, produces its financial statements in accordance with Swedish GAAP but reconciles net income and shareholders' equity to U.S. GAAP. Swedish GAAP does not permit the capitalization of the cost of software development cost for either:

- software to be sold externally
- software developed for internal use

Ericsson's 1999 reconciliation, however, shows the effect of applying SFAS 86 (capitalization of software to be sold) for all years and SOP 98-1 (capitalization of software for internal use) starting in 1999 as shown in the following data.

Ericsson: 1999 Financial Data (SEK millions)

Under U.S. GAAP	1997	1998	1999
Development costs for software to be sold:			
Opening balance	6,100	7,398	10,744
Capitalization	5,232	7,170	7,898
Amortization	(3,934)	(3,824)	(4,460)
Writedown			(989)
Year-end balance	7,398	10,744	13,193
Development costs for software for internal use:			
Opening balance			
Capitalization			1,463
Amortization			(152)
Year-end balance			1,311
Under Swedish GAAP:			
Net sales	167,740	184,438	215,403
Pretax income	17,218	18,210	16,386
Total assets	147,440	167,456	202,628
Stockholders' equity	52,624	63,112	69,176

A. Compute each of the following ratios under Swedish GAAP for 1998 and 1999:

i. Asset turnover (on average assets)

ii. Pretax return on average equity

B. Using the data provided, adjust the 1997-1999 Swedish GAAP amounts assuming the capitalization of software development costs to be sold and for internal use. Using the adjusted data, compute the percentage change from the amounts originally reported for:

i. Pretax income

ii. Total assets

iii. Shareholders' equity

(Assume a 35% tax rate.)

C. Recompute each of the following ratios using the adjusted data for 1998 and 1999:

i. Asset turnover (on average assets)

ii. Pretax return on average equity

D. Discuss the implications of your analysis for the comparison of firms that capitalize software development costs with those that do not.

E. Discuss whether the capitalization and amortizaiton of software development costs under U.S. GAAP has any usefulness for investment analysis.

3. [Capitalization versus expensing] American Woodmark [AMWD] is a manufacturer of kitchen cabinets and similar items. Its fiscal year 2000 annual report contains the following footnote under Significant Accounting Policies:

> *Promotisonal Displays:* The Company's investment in promotional displays is carried at cost less applicable amortization. Amortizaiton is provided by the straight-line method on an individual display basis over the estimated period of benefit (approximately 30 months).

Financial Data at April 30 (in $thousands)

	1999	2000
Promotional displays	$ 8,451	$ 10,099
Total assets	140,609	166,656
Shareholders' equity	78,337	92,612
Sales	327,013	387,301
Net income	17,509	14,467

A. Explain why American Woodmark may have chosen to capitalize the cost of promotional displays rather than expense them.

B. Calculate the effect of that accounting choice on the following reported amounts for fiscal year 2000:

i. Net income

ii. Shareholders' equity

iii. Return on assets

(Assume a 35% tax rate.)

ANALYSIS OF LONG-LIVED ASSETS: PART II—ANALYSIS OF DEPRECIATION AND IMPAIRMENT

by Gerald I. White, Ashwinpaul C. Sondhi, and Dov Fried

READING

37

LEARNING OUTCOMES

The candidate should be able to:

a. demonstrate the different depreciation methods and explain how the choice of depreciation method affects a company's financial statements, ratios, and taxes;

b. demonstrate how modifying the depreciation method, the estimated useful life, and/or the salvage value used in accounting for long-lived assets affect financial statements and ratios;

c. determine the average age and average depreciable life of a company's assets using the company's fixed asset disclosures;

d. explain and illustrate the use of impairment charges on long-lived assets, and analyze the effects of taking such impairment charges on a company's financial statements and ratios;

e. discuss accounting requirements related to remedying environmental damage caused by operating assets and explain the financial statement and ratio effects that result from the application of those requirements.

INTRODUCTION 1

This reading continues the analysis of long-lived assets begun in the previous reading where we examined financial reporting and analysis issues arising at acquisition. We now consider the reporting and analysis of long-lived assets:

1. Over their useful lives, with emphasis on:
   - ▶ depreciation methods
   - ▶ depreciable lives and salvage values
   - ▶ impact of choices on financial statements

2. when they are disposed of, or written off when impaired, or at the end of their useful lives, with particular attention to the effects of impairment write-downs on financial statements and ratios

Amortization, depletion, and depreciation are all terms used for the systematic allocation of the capitalized cost of an asset to income over its useful life. Depreciation, the most frequently used of these terms, is often used generically in discussions of the concept. Strictly speaking, *depreciation* represents the allocation of the cost of tangible fixed assets, *amortization* refers to the cost of intangible assets, and *depletion* applies to natural resource assets.

2 THE DEPRECIATION CONCEPT

For accountants, depreciation is an allocation process, not a valuation process. It is important, therefore, for analysts to differentiate between accounting depreciation and economic depreciation. Although the accounting process may be purely allocative, the concept of depreciation also has economic meaning.

Income can be defined as the amount that can be distributed during the period without impairing the productive capacity of the firm. The cash flows generated by an asset over its life, therefore, cannot be considered income until a provision is made for its replacement. These cash flows must be reduced by the amount required to replace the asset to determine the earnings generated by that asset.

This is the underlying principle of economic depreciation; profits are overstated if no allowance is made for the replacement of the asset. The periodic depreciation expense, therefore, segregates a portion of cash flows for reinvestment, preserving that sum from distribution as dividends and taxes.[1]

Continuing this conceptual argument, suppose an asset costs $240 and is expected to generate net cash flows of $100 per year over its three-year life. Over the life of the asset, income equals $60 ($300 − $240) as $240 is required to replace the asset (if we assume that the asset is worthless at the end of the three-year period and price levels do not change). As financial statements report income annually, it is necessary to determine how much income (how much depreciation) to report each year. This requires the allocation of a portion of the multiperiod return to each period.

The next section describes the depreciation methods used in financial reporting, followed by a discussion of the impact of depreciation methods on financial statements. A separate analysis of accelerated depreciation methods used for income taxes is followed by a discussion of the interaction of inflation and depreciation methods. Analysis of financial statement depreciation disclosures, changes in depreciation methods, and a comprehensive examination of fixed asset disclosures round out the discussion.

Depreciation Methods

Annuity or Sinking Fund Depreciation

From an economic perspective, the income reported each year should reflect the rate of return earned by the asset. For example, the asset just described generates

[1] This does not mean that cash equal to depreciation expense is set aside for reinvestment but, rather, that the definition of income requires a subtraction for asset replacement.

EXHIBIT 1 Sinking Fund Depreciation

Year	(1) Opening Balance Asset	(2) Cash Flow	(3) Depreciation Expense	(4) = (2) − (3) Net Income	(5) = (4)/(1) Rate of Return
1	$240	$100	$ 71	$29	12%
2	169	100	80	20	12
3	89	100	89	11	12
Totals		$300	$240	$60	

a return of 12% over its three-year life.[2] To report a 12% return for each year requires the pattern of depreciation shown in Exhibit 1.

This pattern, with the amount of depreciation increasing every year, is known as *annuity or sinking fund depreciation.* U.S. GAAP, however, do not permit this form of depreciation. In Canada, increasing charge methods are used for income-producing properties in the real estate industry and by a few utilities, but they are not generally acceptable depreciation methods.

Straight-line and accelerated depreciation (discussed shortly) can also produce a constant rate of return when cash flows generated by the asset decline over time. Exhibit 2 illustrates this case; the rate of return is constant and reflects the true return earned by the asset.

Instead of depreciation patterns that generate a constant rate of return, accountants generally use depreciation patterns that result in constant or declining expense. These patterns are sometimes justified by the matching principle. Generally, however, they are arbitrary, their sole purpose being a systematic allocation of the asset cost over time.

Straight-Line Depreciation

Given the same asset and the pattern of constant cash flows shown in Exhibit 1, accountants (using the matching principle) argue that since the revenues (cash

EXHIBIT 2 Straight-Line Depreciation with Declining Cash Flows

Year	(1) Opening Balance Asset	(2) Cash Flow	(3) Depreciation Expense	(4) = (2) − (3) Net Income	(5) = (4)/(1) Rate of Return
1	$240	$109	$ 80	$29	12%
2	160	99	80	19	12
3	80	90	80	10	12
Totals		$298	$240	$58	

[2] The present value of a three-year annuity of $100 per year discounted at 12% is (approximately) equal to $240.

flows of $100) generated by the asset are the same each year, the income shown each year should also be the same. The result of this line of reasoning is the *straight-line method,* the pattern of depreciation expense exhibited in Exhibit 3. *Straight-line depreciation is the dominant method in the United States and most countries worldwide.* Westvaco, for example, states in the summary of significant accounting policies in its fiscal 1999 annual report:

> The cost of plant and equipment is depreciated, generally by the straight-line method, over the estimated useful lives of the respective assets. . . .

Note that the use of this method results in an *increasing* rate of return rather than the actual rate of return earned over the life of the asset.

Accelerated Depreciation Methods

The matching principle can also justify accelerated depreciation patterns, with higher depreciation charges in early years and smaller amounts in later years. There are two arguments:

1. Benefits (revenues) from an asset may be higher in early years, declining in later years as efficiency falls (the asset wears out). The matching process suggests that depreciation should decline with benefits.
2. Even if revenues are constant over time, an asset requires maintenance and repairs over time, costs that tend to increase as the asset ages. Accelerated depreciation methods compensate for the rising trend of maintenance and repair costs so that total asset costs are level over the asset's life.

However, both the efficiency and maintenance of an asset are difficult to forecast, and, in any case, accelerated depreciation methods are (like straight-line) arbitrary procedures designed to yield the desired pattern of higher depreciation amounts in earlier years. **Accelerated methods** have historically been used for tax reporting, where they are justified by the desire to promote capital investment, rather than accounting theory.

The two most common accelerated methods are the *sum-of-years' digits* (SYD) method and the family of *declining-balance* methods. A comparison of these methods (using the **double-declining-balance method**) with straight-line (SL) depreciation

EXHIBIT 3 Straight-Line Depreciation with Constant Cash Flows

	(1)	(2)	(3)	(4) = (2) − (3)	(5) = (4)/(1)
Year	Opening Balance Asset	Cash Flow	Depreciation Expense	Net Income	Rate of Return
1	$240	$100	$ 80	$20	8.3%
2	160	100	80	20	12.5
3	80	100	80	20	25.0
Totals		$300	$240	$60	

is presented in Exhibit 4. In the example used, the concept of *salvage value*, the estimated amount for which the asset can be sold at the end of its useful life, is introduced into the calculations.

While U.S. firms rarely use accelerated methods, they are more widely used outside of the United States. Takeda, for example, states in its summary of significant accounting policies (Note 2 in fiscal 1999 annual report) that:

> Depreciation is primarily computed by the declining balance method. . . .

EXHIBIT 4 **Comparison of Straight-Line and Accelerated Depreciation Methods**

Original Cost = $18,000

Salvage Value = $3,000

Depreciable Life $n = 5$

A. Straight-Line Depreciation

$$\text{Depreciation in Year } i = \frac{1}{n} \times (\text{Original Cost} - \text{Salvage Value})$$

Depreciation expense is constant each year; at the end of the five-year period, the net book value of the asset equals its salvage value of $3,000.

Year	Rate	(Original Cost— Salvage Value)	Depreciation Expense	Accumulated Depreciation	Net Book Value
0					$18,000
1	1/5	$15,000	$ 3,000	$ 3,000	15,000
2	1/5	15,000	3,000	6,000	12,000
3	1/5	15,000	3,000	9,000	9,000
4	1/5	15,000	3,000	12,000	6,000
5	1/5	15,000	3,000	15,000	3,000
Total			$15,000		

Accelerated Depreciation Methods

B. Sum-of-Years' Digits (SYD) Method

$$\text{Depreciation in Year } i = \frac{(n - i + 1)}{\text{SYD}} \times (\text{Original Cost} - \text{Salvage Value})$$

where SYD = $1 + 2 + 3 + \ldots + n$ the summation over the depreciable life of n years or simply SYD = $n(n + 1)/2$. For our example, $n = 5$.

SYD = $1 + 2 + 3 + 4 + 5 = 15$

or, alternatively, $SYD = \frac{(5)(5 + 1)}{2} = 15$

The rate of depreciation thus varies from year to year (as i varies) in reverse counting order of the years; that is, the pattern is 5/15, 4/15, 3/15, 2/15, and 1/15 and is depicted as follows:

(Exhibit continued on next page . . .)

EXHIBIT 4 (continued)

Year	Rate	(Original Cost—Salvage Value)	Depreciation Expense	Accumulated Depreciation	Net Book Value
0					$18,000
1	5/15	$15,000	$ 5,000	$5,000	13,000
2	4/15	15,000	4,000	9,000	9,000
3	3/15	15,000	3,000	12,000	6,000
4	2/15	15,000	2,000	14,000	4,000
5	1/15	15,000	1,000	15,000	3,000
Total			$15,000		

C. Double-Declining-Balance

$$\text{Depreciation in Year } i = \frac{2}{n} \times (\text{Original Cost} - \text{Accumulated Depreciation})$$

or

$$\frac{2}{n} \times (\textit{Net Book Value})$$

The rate of $(2/n)$ is what gives the double-declining-balance (DDB) method its name. The depreciation rate is double[a] the straight-line rate. The declining pattern occurs because the fixed rate is applied to an ever-decreasing asset balance (net book value),[b] and in our example it is calculated as follows:

Year	Rate	Net Book Value	Depreciation Expense	Accumulated Depreciation	Net Book Value
0					$18,000
1	2/5	$18,000	$ 7,200	$ 7,200	10,800
2	2/5	10,800	4,320	11,520	6,480
3	2/5	6,480	2,592	14,112	3,888
4	NA	NA	888	15,000	3,000
5	NA	NA	0	15,000	3,000
Total			$15,000		

NA = not applicable.

[a] The DDB method is actually only one case of the family of declining-balance methods. The same principle can be applied to other multiples of the straight-line rate (e.g., 150% declining balance). Higher multiples result in more accelerated patterns of depreciation expense.

[b] Note that salvage value is not used to calculate depreciation under declining-balance methods but acts as a floor for net book value.

Note that in year 4 the DDB procedure is discontinued. This is because depreciation can be taken only until the salvage value is reached. Following DDB in year 4 and beyond would have reduced net book value below salvage. When the DDB method is applied to longer-lived assets, a switch to the straight-line method often occurs in later years, when the latter method results in higher depreciation expense.

Units-of-Production and Service Hours Method

These methods depreciate assets in proportion to their actual use rather than as a function of the passage of time. Thus, more depreciation is recognized in years of higher production. Measurement requires an initial estimate of the total number of units of output or service hours expected over the life of the machine. The methods differ in whether asset usage is measured by output or hours used.

Assume that the asset described in Exhibit 4 is expected to produce 60,000 units of output over its life and have a service life of 150,000 hours. The actual hours of service and output, and the resultant depreciation schedules, are presented in Exhibit 5.

These methods make depreciation expense a variable rather than a fixed cost, decreasing the volatility of reported earnings as compared to straight-line or accelerated methods. Some companies use a mix of depreciation methods.

International Paper, for example, reports on its depreciation methods as follows:

> **Plants, Properties and Equipment**
>
> Plants, properties and equipment are stated at cost, less accumulated depreciation. For financial reporting purposes, we use the units-of-production method of depreciation for our major pulp and paper mills and certain wood products facilities and the straight-line method for other plants and equipment.[3]

EXHIBIT 5 Service Hours and Units-of-Production Methods

Original Cost = $18,000

Salvage Value = $3,000

	Service Hours Method Expected Service Hours = 150,000 Cost/Service Hour = $0.10[a]			Units-of-Production Method Expected Output = 60,000 Cost/Unit of Output = $0.25[b]		
Year	**Hours Worked**	**Depreciation**	**Net Book Value**	**Units of Output**	**Depreciation**	**Net Book Value**
0			$18,000			$18,000
1	40,000	$ 4,000	14,000	15,000	$ 3,750	14,250
2	35,000	3,500	10,500	16,000	4,000	10,250
3	45,000	4,500	6,000	20,000	5,000	5,250
4	20,000	2,000	4,000	10,000	2,250[c]	3,000
5	40,000	1,000[c]	3,000	12,500	0[c]	3,000
Total		$15,000			$15,000	

[a] ($18,000 − $3,000)/150,000.

[b] ($18,000 − $3,000)/60,000.

[c] Note that in both cases, the asset is never depreciated below the salvage value even when actual use exceeds estimated use.

[3] *Source:* International Paper, 10-K report, year ended December 31, 1999.

A significant drawback of these two methods occurs when the firm's productive capacity becomes obsolete as it loses business to more efficient competitors. The units-of-production and service hours methods decrease depreciation expense during periods of low production. The result is to overstate reported income and asset values at the same time as the asset's economic value declines. This danger is particularly acute for mature industries facing increased competition from new entrants or imports. Competition frequently increases the rate of economic depreciation of fixed assets. However, the corporate response is often to relieve the pressure on earnings by decreasing depreciation expense by changing to a method such as units-of-production. Alternatively, firms may get the same effect by lengthening lives.

Sooner or later, however, the firm will recognize the impairment (see the discussion later in this reading) of its productive capacity. Once impairment exists, companies report "restructuring" or similar charges to correct the overvaluation of fixed assets. Analysts often exclude such "nonrecurring" charges when evaluating corporate earnings. But to the extent that these charges represent an adjustment for past underdepreciation of assets, they correct a systematic overstatement of past earnings. As past earnings are used to forecast the future, this issue should not be ignored.

The following footnote from the 1992 financial statements of Brown & Sharpe, a machine tool manufacturer, illustrates this phenomenon:

> In 1992, the Company extended the estimated useful lives of machinery and equipment at its Swiss subsidiary, based upon the current low rate of utilization. The effect of this change was to reduce 1992 depreciation expense and net loss by $921,000 or $.19 per share.

Total depreciation expense for Brown & Sharpe fell from $8 million in 1992 to $6.8 million in 1993; the change in accounting estimate was apparently the major factor in that decline. In 1994, however, Brown & Sharpe reported restructuring charges that included: "costs . . . for . . . property, plant, and equipment . . . writeoffs . . . due to a plant closing in Switzerland."

Although the corporate temptation to change accounting methods when business is weak is understandable, that change can mislead investors. Furthermore, on occasion, a company recognizes the impairment of fixed assets gradually, by accelerating depreciation on a group of assets in danger of becoming obsolete. From an analytical point of view, it is preferable to recognize the impairment immediately. Because accounting depreciation is a systematic allocation of cost, its acceleration when the asset is impaired (and its use has declined or it has been temporarily idled) fails to match costs and revenues and misstates the earning power of the company.

Group and Composite Depreciation Methods

Depreciation methods described in the preceding sections apply to single assets; they may be impractical when firms use large numbers of similar assets in their operations. Group (composite) depreciation methods allocate the costs of similar (dissimilar) assets using depreciation rates based on a weighted average of the service lives of the assets.

Gains or losses on the disposal of assets depreciated using group or composite methods are either:

- ▶ recognized in reported income; or
- ▶ reported instead as a component of accumulated depreciation.[4]

Example Texaco uses group methods for most assets (see the Description of Significant Accounting Policies). Gains and losses are recognized only when a complete unit is disposed of.

Depletion

Financial reporting requirements for natural resources are similar to those for tangible assets. The carrying costs of natural resources include the costs of acquiring the land or mines and the costs of exploration and development of the resources. These costs may be capitalized or expensed as a function of the firm's accounting policies (such as successful efforts or full cost for oil and gas exploration).

The carrying costs of natural resources (excluding costs of machinery and equipment used in extraction or production) are allocated to accounting periods using the units-of-production method. This method requires an initial estimate of the units (of oil, coal, gold, or timber) in the resource base to compute a unit cost, which is then applied to the actual units produced, extracted, or harvested.

Amortization

Amortization of intangible assets may be based on useful lives as defined by law (e.g., patents) or regulation, or such assets may be depreciated over the period during which the firm expects to receive benefits from them (computer software). Companies use either straight-line or units-of-production methods. Goodwill and indefinite-term franchises and licenses may be amortized over periods not exceeding 40 years. Note that SFAS 142 (2001) eliminated the amortization of goodwill and certain intangible assets.

Example In Reading 36 we examined Lucent's capitalization of software development costs; now we discuss amortization. The accounting policies footnote is vague about amortization periods.

Lucent's financial statements show the following (in $millions):

Years Ended September 30			
	1997	**1998**	**1999**
Capitalized software costs (net)	293	298	470
Amortization	380	234	249

[4] At the time of the sale, the proceeds are added to cash, the original asset cost is removed from gross PPE, and the accumulated depreciation for the asset is removed from that account. The difference between the cash proceeds and the net book value of the assets sold is then credited-debited to the accumulated depreciation account; no gain or loss is recorded.

Amortization of capitalized software declined sharply in fiscal 1998. Amortization rose only slightly in fiscal 1999 despite the large increase in capitalized cost. There is no discussion of amortization in Lucent's Management Discussion and Analysis.

Depreciation Method Disclosures

As we have shown, the choice of the depreciation method can greatly affect the pattern of reported income. Disclosure of the depreciation method used is required and can usually be found in the footnote listing accounting policies. Most (more than 90%) American firms use straight-line depreciation, but accelerated methods are more widely used in other countries. The use of accelerated methods in the United States has declined in recent years as firms have changed to straight-line depreciation.

Depreciation Lives and Salvage Values

Even when the same depreciation method is used, comparability for a firm over time and among companies at a given point in time may be lacking. The *useful life* (the period over which the asset is depreciated) can vary from firm to firm, and excessively long lives understate reported depreciation expense. Although companies are required to disclose depreciation lives, in practice such disclosures are often vague, providing ranges rather than precise data. In such cases, the analyst must use available data to compute approximate depreciation lives (see the analysis of fixed asset disclosures later in the reading).

EXAMPLE 1

Westvaco

Westvaco's summary of significant accounting policies states that:

> The cost of plant and equipment is depreciated . . . over the estimated useful lives . . . which range from 20 to 40 years for buildings and 5 to 30 years for machinery and equipment.

Although usually a less significant factor, *salvage values* also affect comparisons; they (like asset lives) are also management estimates. High estimates reduce the depreciation base (cost less salvage value) and, therefore, reduce depreciation expense. (Note that salvage values are not employed in declining-balance depreciation methods.) In practice, companies rarely disclose data regarding salvage values, except when estimates are changed.[5]

[5] Changes in accounting estimates receive less disclosure than changes in method. APB 20 (para. 33) requires disclosure of the effect of a change that affects future periods, such as changes in depreciable lives.

Impact of Depreciation Methods on Financial Statements

The choice of depreciation method impacts both the income statement and balance sheet; for capital-intensive companies, the impact can be significant. As depreciation is an allocation of past cash flows, the method chosen for financial reporting purposes has no impact on the statement of cash flows.[6]

Accelerated depreciation methods, with higher depreciation expense in the early years of asset life, tend to depress both net income and stockholders' equity when compared with the straight-line method. As the percentage effect on net income is usually greater than the effect on net assets, return ratios tend to be lower when accelerated depreciation methods are used. Consequently, these methods are considered more conservative.

Toward the end of an asset's life, however, the effect on net income reverses. In Exhibit 4, depreciation expense in years 4 and 5 is lower using accelerated methods than under the straight-line method. This is true for individual assets. However, for companies with stable or rising capital expenditures, the early-year impact of new assets acquired dominates, and depreciation expense on a total firm basis is higher under an accelerated method. When capital expenditures decline, however, accelerated depreciation decreases depreciation expense as the later-year effect on older assets dominates.

Depreciable lives and salvage values impact both depreciation expense and stated asset values. Shorter lives and lower salvage values are considered conservative in that they lead to higher depreciation expense. These factors interact with the depreciation method to determine the expense; for example, use of the straight-line method with short depreciation lives may result in depreciation expense similar to that obtained from the use of an accelerated method with longer lives. Conservative depreciation practices also increase asset turnover ratios by decreasing the denominator of that ratio. Fixed-asset turnover ratios should be computed using gross fixed-asset investment in the denominator, although that is not done in practice.

Accelerated Depreciation and Taxes

Notwithstanding the theoretical arguments and the financial statement effects discussed, the primary reason for accelerated depreciation methods is their beneficial effect on the firm's tax burden. At the onset of an asset's life, the total amount of depreciable cost available is fixed. Depreciation acts as a tax shield by reducing the amount of taxes paid in any given year. Given a positive interest rate, firms are better off using accelerated depreciation methods to obtain the benefit of increased cash flows (from reduced taxes) in the earlier years.

Governments have long used the tax code to encourage investment, and this was the intent of the U.S. government when it first allowed accelerated depreciation methods for tax purposes in 1954. Many foreign governments also permit the use of accelerated depreciation methods. Since 1954, the U.S. government has frequently changed tax depreciation regulations to increase or decrease investment incentives in certain types of fixed assets or simply to raise revenues. The present system is known as MACRS—modified accelerated cost recovery system—which consists of specified depreciation patterns and depreciable lives (generally shorter than actual useful service lives) for different property classes.

---

[6] This assumes that the method chosen for tax purposes is independent of the method chosen for financial statement purposes.

MACRS uses the double-declining-balance and 150% declining-balance methods, which few companies use for financial reporting purposes. Thus, in the United States the depreciation method and lives used for financial statements almost always differ from those used for tax purposes. The implications of these differences are discussed in Reading 38, which also illustrates the use of tax disclosures to obtain insights into the depreciation practices used for financial reporting.

Impact of Inflation on Depreciation

Historical cost-based depreciation expense may be used to define income as long as the total expense over the asset's life is enough to replace the asset after it has been fully utilized. If, however, the replacement cost of the asset increases, then depreciation expense based on the original cost will be insufficient.

Returning to the example in Exhibit 1, assume that after three years the firm requires $300 to replace the asset. Now the total economic income earned by the firm is $0, as total cash flows equal the cost to replace. If we use the historical cost basis, however, total depreciation is limited to the original $240 cost, and reported income is overstated. In addition, because firms are only allowed to use historical cost basis depreciation for tax reporting, the resultant taxes are too high. Income taxes become, in effect, a tax on capital rather than a tax on income. Box 1 illustrates the resulting disincentives for investment in the context of a simple capital budgeting model.

Accelerated depreciation methods partially compensate for this inflation effect by shortening the (tax) recovery period. Depreciating the asset over a shorter life serves a similar purpose. A number of studies have examined whether accelerated methods compensate for inflation and/or reflect economic depreciation (variously defined).

Kim and Moore (1988), for example, report that, for the Canadian trucking industry, tax depreciation exceeded economic depreciation, resulting in a tax subsidy. Most (1984), focusing on reported income, found that in the United States the useful life (used for financial reporting) is generally longer than the economic life of the asset, understating reported depreciation and overstating reported income. Skinner (1982), on the other hand, reported the opposite phenomenon in the United Kingdom.

Beaver and Dukes (1973) examined firm price/earnings ratios and found that market prices, on average:

> assign a more accelerated form of depreciation than is implied by reported earnings.[7]

They did not attempt to discern the reasons for this result but recognized that it was consistent with either a constant rate of return depreciation model (with declining cash flows) or depreciation based on current costs rather than a historical cost system.

Generalizing these results to other time periods, particularly for studies that examined whether depreciation practices (whether for tax or book purposes) compensated for the actual economic or physical depreciation of assets, requires a great deal of caution, given changing economic environments. These comparisons are a function of the provisions of the tax code, the inflation rate, and varying degrees of technological obsolescence across industries during the comparison

[7] William H. Beaver and Roland E. Dukes, "Interperiod Tax Allocation and δ-Depreciation Methods: Some Empirical Results," *Accounting Review* (July 1973), pp. 549–559.

OPTIONAL SEGMENT BEGINS

BOX 1 DISINCENTIVES FOR INVESTMENT ARISING FROM HISTORICAL COST DEPRECIATION

We begin by assuming that the inflation rate p is equal to zero. A project is profitable if the net present value (NPV) of the cash flows of the investment:

$$\mathbf{NPV}_{(p=0)} = -I + (1-t)\sum \frac{C_i}{(1+r)^i} + t\sum \frac{d_i I}{(1+r)^i}$$

is greater than zero (i.e., NPV > 0), where C_i is the pretax (real) cash flow in period i, t is the marginal tax rate, d_i is the rate of depreciation in period i, I is the cost of the original investment, and r is the appropriate real discount rate.[a] The summation on the right reflects the depreciation tax shelter, and the NPV can be disaggregated into

NPV = −investment + present value (after-tax cash flows)
+ present value (depreciation tax shelter)

If we introduce an annual inflation rate of $p > 0$, then the expected (nominal) cash flows in any period will increase. In addition, the discount rate will change to reflect inflation. The depreciation deduction based on historical costs will not change. The expression for net present value now becomes

$$\mathbf{NPV}_{(p>0)} = -I + (1-t)\sum \frac{(1+p)^i C_i}{(1+p)^i(1+r)^i} + t\sum \frac{d_i I}{(1+p)^i(1+r)^i}$$

As the $(1 + p)^i$ terms in the first summation cancel, inflation (when it is expected) will not affect the after-tax cash flows. However, the depreciation tax shelter will now be worth less as

$$t\sum \frac{d_i I}{(1+r)^i} > t\sum \frac{d_i I}{(1+p)^i(1+r)^i}$$

The decline in the depreciation tax shelter will reduce the profitability of the project:

$$\mathbf{NPV}_{(p>0)} < \mathbf{NPV}_{(p=0)}$$

and ***ceteris paribus***, there is less likelihood that the project will be undertaken.

---

[a] Generally, the depreciation tax shelter would be discounted at a rate lower than the cash flows themselves as the tax deduction is "riskless." We do not make the distinction here for the sake of simplification. Alternatively, one can view this problem in the context of certainty, and r is the risk-free rate.

OPTIONAL SEGMENT ENDS

period. During the 1980s, the depreciation provisions of the U.S. tax code were changed three times, inflation declined to approximately 4% from double-digit rates, and technological change was rapid in many industries. International differences are an additional difficulty.

The benchmark issue emerging from these studies is: How does one determine the "correct" useful life and economic depreciation rate? This is an important question for analytical purposes. Estimates of economic lives on an aggregate industry basis can be derived from Department of Commerce data.

In 1982, the FASB issued SFAS 33 (Changing Prices), which required very large firms[8] to disclose supplementary, unaudited data on the effects of changing prices. Among the required disclosures were:

- the current cost of fixed assets
- depreciation expense on a current cost basis

These disclosures were intended to help financial statement users adjust for the shortcomings of historical cost depreciation discussed earlier. However, studies that examined the informational content of the replacement cost data found that, although historical cost earnings had informational content above and beyond that of current cost data provided by SFAS 33, the reverse did not hold.[9] Inflation-adjusted data did not appear to have any marginal information content above that provided by historical cost data. The reasons offered for this surprising result were that the data were:

- too difficult to comprehend, and the market had not yet learned how to use them
- not new, as the market knew how to adjust historical costs for inflation without SFAS 33 disclosures[10]
- irrelevant, either from a conceptual point of view or in the manner in which they were prepared and reported

Whatever the reason, in practice the data were difficult to prepare and use. Facing intense complaints regarding the cost of the disclosures and empirical research that seemed to belie the usefulness of the data, the FASB subsequently made the disclosures voluntary.

Changes in Depreciation Method

Companies may change the reported depreciation of fixed assets in different ways:

- change in method applicable only to newly acquired assets
- change in method applicable to all assets
- changes in asset lives or salvage value

Change in Method Applicable Only to Newly Acquired Assets A company can change its depreciation method only for newly acquired assets and continue to depreciate previously acquired similar assets using the same method(s) as in the past. The impact of the new method will be gradual, increasing as fixed assets acquired after the change grow in relative importance.

---

[8] SFAS 33 applied to firms with inventories and gross (before deducting depreciation) property exceeding $125 million (in the aggregate) or with total assets exceeding $1 billion.

[9] Some studies [e.g., Beaver et al. (1980, 1982)] found little information content, focusing on ASR 190 disclosures. Others [Beaver and Landsman (1983)] examined the SFAS 33 data with similar results. Although the consensus was that these data did not have information content, the conclusions were by no means unanimous [see, e.g., Easman et al. (1979) and Murdoch (1986)].

[10] One example is the work of Angela Falkenstein and Roman L. Weil, "Replacement Cost Accounting: What Will Income Statements Based on the SEC Disclosures Show?—Part I," *Financial Analysts Journal* (January–February 1977), pp. 46–57 and "Replacement Cost Accounting: What Will Income Statements Based on the SEC Disclosures Show?—Part II," *Financial Analysts Journal* (March–April 1977), pp. 48–57.

DuPont, for example, changed from the sum-of-the-years' digits method (for nonpetroleum properties) to the straight-line method for properties placed in service in 1995, with the following footnote disclosure:

> Property, plant and equipment (PP&E) is carried at cost and, except for petroleum PP&E, PP&E placed in service prior to 1995 is depreciated under the sum-of-the-years' digits method and other substantially similar methods. PP&E placed in service after 1994 is depreciated using the straight-line method. This change in accounting was made to reflect management's belief that the productivity of such PP&E will not appreciably diminish in the early years of its useful life, and it will not be subject to significant additional maintenance in the later years of its useful life. In these circumstances, straight-line depreciation is preferable in that it provides a better matching of costs with revenues. Additionally, the change to the straight-line method conforms to predominant industry practice. The effect of this change on net income will be dependent on the level of future capital spending; it did not have a material effect in 1995.[11]

This is a common method of changing accounting principles, as it does not require the restatement of past earnings.

The company made the uninformative statement that "the change is not expected to have a material effect on 1995 results." Nonetheless, *the change increased subsequent reported income* as depreciation charges for new PPE were lower (depreciation charges on old PPE continued to be computed using the SYD method).

Exhibit 6 contains an extract from DuPont's segment disclosures for the years 1994 to 1996. As petroleum assets are depreciated by the units of production method, we must remove the capital spending and depreciation for that segment:

	1994	1995	1996
Capital spending	$3,151	$3,394	$3,317
Petroleum segment	(1,635)	(1,714)	(1,616)
All nonpetroleum	$1,516	$1,680	$1,701
% change		10.8%	1.3%
Total depreciation	$3,106	$2,823	$2,719
Petroleum segment	(1,266)	(1,111)	(1,128)
All nonpetroleum	$1,840	$1,712	$1,591
% change		−7.0%	−7.1%

Although nonpetroleum capital spending rose in both 1995 and 1996, depreciation expense fell 7% in both years. The decline is clearly due to the combined effect of straight-line (lower than SYD) depreciation expense relating to new assets and declining SYD depreciation on old assets.

Change in Method Applicable to All Assets Instead of being implemented prospectively, the new method can be applied retroactively so that all fixed assets are depreciated using the new method. In this case, the effect is greater and can be significant in the year of the switch as well as in future years. For a sample of

[11] *Source:* DuPont 10-K report, 1995.

EXHIBIT 6 **DuPont Segment Disclosures ($millions)**

	Chemicals	Fibers	Polymers	Petroleum	Life Sciences	Diversified Businesses	Consolidated
1996:							
Depreciation, etc.	$330	$609	$350	$1,128	$70	$232	$2,719
Capital expenditures	338	611	446	1,616	93	213	3,317
1995:							
Depreciation, etc.	352	626	362	1,111	78	294	2,823
Capital expenditures	417	593	399	1,714	73	198	3,394
1994:							
Depreciation, etc.	405	686	386	1,266	79	284	3,106
Capital expenditures	258	640	356	1,635	47	215	3,151

Source: DuPont 10-K report, December 31, 1996.

38 companies that switched to straight-line depreciation, Healy et al. (1987) estimated that the median increase in income was 8% to 10% in the 10-year period following the change. In addition to the effect on current and future depreciation expense (and net income), there is a cumulative effect, given the retroactive nature of the change: the cumulative difference between originally reported depreciation and the restated depreciation for all past periods. When the new method is applied retroactively, companies must also disclose the pro forma impact of the new method on prior periods.

A change in depreciation method for all assets is considered a change in accounting principle under APB 20, Accounting Changes. *The cumulative effect of the change must be reported separately and net of taxes.*

Changes in Asset Lives or Salvage Value *Changes in asset lives and salvage values are changes in accounting estimates and are not considered changes in accounting principle.* Their impact is only prospective, and no retroactive or cumulative effects are recognized. Estimate changes attract much less notice than do changes in depreciation methods (see footnote 5). They are not, for example, referred to in the auditor's opinion. Thus, it is important to read financial statement footnotes carefully to be sure that no changes in accounting estimates have been made.

EXAMPLE 2

AMR

Exhibit 7 contains extracts from the *1999 Annual Report* of AMR, the parent of American Airlines, which changed the estimated useful lives *and* the salvage values used to compute depreciation on its flight equipment, effective January 1, 1999. Given the asset intensity of airlines, this change had a significant impact on reported earnings, as shown in the following table:

AMR (in $millions)			
Years Ended December 31	**1997**	**1998**	**1999**
As reported (with depreciation changes)			
Depreciation expense	$1,040	$1,040	$1,092
% Change from previous year		0.0%	5.0%
Operating income	$1,595	$1,988	$1,156
% Change from previous year		24.6%	−41.9%
After adjustment for depreciation change			
Depreciation expense	$1,040	$1,040	$1,250
% Change from previous year		0.0%	20.2%
Operating income	$1,595	$1,988	$ 998
% Change from previous year		24.6%	−49.8%

Despite the accounting change, depreciation expense rose 5% in 1991 due to new equipment. If not for the change, depreciation expense would have been more than 20% higher. Without the accounting change, the 1999 decline in operating income would have been steeper, 50% instead of 42%. This may have been the motivation for the change. *When analyzing firms that change depreciation methods or assumptions, it is important to remember that the effect of such changes persists, as depreciation on both old and new fixed assets is stretched out, increasing reported income.*

Increases in asset lives have been common in recent years. The effect of such increases is, of course, to increase reported earnings. Such changes are often made by more than one firm in an industry, as firms compete to show higher reported earnings and ROE. For example, in the airline industry, Delta Airlines changed both the estimated lives and the salvage values used to compute depreciation on flight equipment in 1993. Both Southwest Airlines and UAL (United Airlines) extended aircraft depreciable lives in 1999.

Box 2 examines the motivation for and reaction to depreciation changes. Whenever a change in depreciation method or lives is reported, the effect of the change on current year reported earnings should be removed to evaluate operating performance on a comparable basis. The change should also be factored into estimates of future reported income.

ANALYSIS OF FIXED ASSET DISCLOSURES 3

In practice, firms use varying accounting methods, lives, and residual value assumptions for fixed assets, hampering comparisons between firms. To improve comparability, the analyst must use financial statement disclosures to gain insight into a company's depreciation accounting. Unfortunately, in 1994 the SEC

EXHIBIT 7 AMR Corporation Change in Depreciation Lives of Flight Equipment

A. Extract from Depreciation Footnote

Effective January 1, 1999, in order to more accurately reflect the expected useful life of its aircraft, the Company changed its estimate of the depreciable lives of certain aircraft types from 20 to 25 years and increased the residual value from five to 10 percent. It also established a 30-year life for its new Boeing 777 aircraft, first delivered in the first quarter of 1999. As a result of this change, depreciation and amortization expense was reduced by approximately $158 million and net earnings were increased by approximately $99 million, or $0.63 per common share diluted, for the year ended December 31, 1999.

B. Extract from Income Statement

	Years Ended December 31 (in $millions)		
	1999	**1998**	**1997**
Revenues	$17,730	$17,516	$16,957
Expenses			
Depreciation and amortization	1,092	1,040	1,040
Total operating expenses	16,574	15,528	15,362
Operating income	1,156	1,988	1,595

C. Extract from Management Discussion and Analysis

Depreciation and amortization expense increased $52 million, or 5.0 percent, due primarily to the addition of new aircraft, partially offset by the change in depreciable lives and residual values for certain types of aircraft in 1999 (see Note 1 to the consolidated financial statements).

Source: AMR Corp. 10-K Report, December 31, 1999.

deleted the requirement for firms to disclose details of their property accounts.[12] However, the Commission has proposed restoring the requirement following complaints from financial analysts regarding the loss of these useful data. As a result, for American firms, only a broad analysis is possible except when detailed data are made available by the company. However, IAS 16 and many foreign GAAP require detailed disclosures about fixed assets, permitting detailed analysis as shown later in this reading.

[12] Financial Reporting Release (FRR) 44 (December 13, 1994) amended Rule 5-04 of Regulation S-X to eliminate Schedule V, Property, Plant and Equipment, and Schedule VI, Accumulated Depreciation, Depletion and Amortization of Property, Plant and Equipment. See FRR 44 for a listing of other schedules eliminated.

BOX 2 CHANGES IN DEPRECIATION METHODS: MOTIVATION AND REACTION

When the Internal Revenue Code of 1954 permitted the use of accelerated depreciation for tax purposes, many firms also adopted these methods for financial statement purposes. Subsequently, many of these firms "switched back" to straight-line depreciation for financial reporting purposes. The effect of the switch-back was to increase the firm's reported net income, (tangible) assets, and retained earnings.

Unlike the FIFO-LIFO switch discussed in Reading 35, the depreciation switch-back was a "pure accounting" change without any direct cash flow consequences as accelerated depreciation was retained for tax purposes. The phenomenon was originally studied by Archibald (1972) and Kaplan and Roll (1972) as a test of whether the efficient market hypothesis (EMH) or the functional fixation hypothesis prevailed with respect to financial statements; that is, was the market "fooled" by the numbers, or did it see through the accounting change, realizing that it had no economic consequence? The results of these studies (using weekly and monthly data) were consistent with the EMH, finding no market reaction to the switch.

With the advent of positive accounting research, the assumption of no economic consequences to a "pure accounting" change was reexamined. Management compensation contracts as well as debt covenants based on accounting numbers are affected by accounting changes. Holthausen (1981) examined the accounting switch-backs in this framework. He argued that an accounting change that increases reported income, given earnings-based management contracts, should result in negative market reaction, as there would be a wealth transfer from the owners of the firm to the managers. Conversely, the presence of debt covenants should result in a positive market reaction, as the increase in reported earnings and assets would generally increase the slack associated with any leverage constraints. Empirical results did not confirm these hypotheses.

Studies of market reaction to voluntary accounting changes have generally not found results consistent with the positive accounting framework, as (it is argued that) by the time the change is made, it has been generally anticipated that the firm (or its managers) will make the change to improve reported performance. Thus, although the motivation for the change (compensation, debt covenants) is as specified, the market has already taken it into account.

Evidence consistent with the compensation motivation for depreciation switch-backs is reported by Dhaliwal et al. (1982), who found that management-controlled firms are more likely to adopt straight-line depreciation methods. Furthermore, Healy et al. (1987) found that when firms changed reporting methods to straight-line depreciation,

> the CEO's bonus and salary awards are based on reported earnings both before and after the accounting changes. We find no evidence that subsequent to either the inventory change or the depreciation change, reported earnings are transformed to earnings under the original accounting method for computing compensation awards.[a]

Generally, however, they note that the percentage of the CEO's compensation attributable to the accounting change is small relative to their overall compensation package. On average, these results do not find a debt covenant or (significant) management compensation motivation for the change in depreciation method. For a given company, however, an analyst would be wise to check these factors whenever an income-increasing accounting change is implemented.

---

[a] Paul H. Healy, Sok-Hyon Kang, and Krishna Palepu, "The Effect of Accounting Procedure Changes on CEO's Cash Salary and Bonus Compensation," *Journal of Accounting and Economics* (1987), pp. 7–34.

OPTIONAL SEGMENT ENDS

Estimating Relative Age and Useful Lives

Fixed-asset data can be used to estimate the relative age of companies' property, plant, and equipment. The relative age as a percentage of depreciable ("useful") life is calculated as

Relative Age (%) = Accumulated Depreciation/Ending Gross Investment

As long as straight-line depreciation is used,[13] this is an accurate estimate of asset age as a percentage of depreciable life. Neither changes in asset mix (additions with longer or shorter lives than existing assets) nor the timing of purchases affect the calculation. The relative age is a useful measure of whether the firm's fixed-asset base is old or new. Newer assets are likely to be more efficient; when relative age is high, the firm has not been adding to (or modernizing) its capital stock and may find it difficult to compete with firms that have more modern facilities. Remember, however, that this calculation is affected by the firm's accounting methods in the following areas:

- depreciation lives[14]
- salvage values

Another useful calculation is the average depreciable life of fixed assets:

Average Depreciable Life = Ending Gross Investment/Depreciation Expense

This calculation is only a rough approximation as it can be affected by changes in asset mix. During periods of rapid growth in fixed assets, the time (within the year) when assets are placed into service can also affect the ratio. Over longer time periods, however, this ratio is a useful measure of a firm's depreciation policy and can be used for comparisons with competitors.

Estimating the Age of Assets

We can also calculate the approximate age (in years) of a firm's fixed assets by comparing accumulated depreciation with depreciation expense:[15]

Average Age = Accumulated Depreciation/Depreciation Expense

As in the case of depreciable life, average age calculations may be distorted by changes in asset mix and by acquisitions. Nonetheless, these data are useful for comparison purposes and can suggest a useful line of questioning when meeting with management.

Average age data, either as a percentage of gross cost or in absolute terms, are useful for two reasons. First, older assets tend to be less efficient; inefficient or obsolete fixed assets may make the firm uncompetitive. Second, knowing past

[13] The use of accelerated depreciation methods invalidates this analysis. However, since more than 90% of companies use straight-line depreciation, the method has general application.

[14] As noted earlier, depreciable lives and economic lives for reporting purposes are not equivalent. See the earlier reference to Most (1984).

[15] Average age can also be computed as relative age multiplied by average depreciable life.

patterns of capital replacement helps the analyst estimate when major capital expenditures will be required. The financing implications of capital expenditure requirements may be significant. Furthermore, when forecasting capital expenditures, the data should be compared with benchmark data on the useful (economic) life of fixed assets for that industry.

EXAMPLE 3

Forest Products Industry Comparison

Exhibit 8 contains average age and average depreciable life statistics for four Scandinavian companies in the forest products industry for 1999. Statistics for buildings and for machinery and equipment are shown separately, as required by Swedish GAAP.[16]

The statistics show significant differences among these four companies:

- SCA's fixed assets appear youngest and Assidoman's appear oldest.
- Holmen appears to use the shortest depreciable lives, followed by SCA.

These statistics are, however, only the starting point for analysis. They assume that all four firms have comparable assets when in fact they may have differing mixes of assets with different depreciable lives. Differences in product mix (requiring different fixed-asset mixes) and acquisitions and divestitures also affect the comparison. These statistics should be used to ask questions of management rather than to make decisions.

Several of these firms had major acquisitions or divestitures over the 1997–1999 period, making three-year comparisons meaningless. However data for SCA follow:

SCA: Analysis of Fixed Asset Disclosures by Property Class (SEK millions)

	1997	1998	1999
Buildings et al.			
Gross investment	12,566	13,986	12,513
Accumulated depreciation	(3,299)	(3,909)	(3,680)
Net investment	9,267	10,077	8,833
Depreciation expense	519	515	513
Average age %	26.3%	27.9%	29.4%
Average depreciable life years	24.2	27.2	24.4
Average age years	6.4	7.6	7.2

[16] IAS 16 requirements are similar.

	1997	1998	1999
Machinery and equipment			
Gross investment	42,404	47,256	47,487
Accumulated depreciation	(17,488)	(20,729)	(20,289)
Net investment	24,916	26,527	27,198
Depreciation expense	3,117	2,912	3,117
Average age %	41.2%	43.9%	42.7%
Average depreciable life years	13.6	16.2	15.2
Average age years	5.6	7.1	6.5

Even within one company, the fixed asset statistics can show significant change over short periods. The apparent increase in average depreciable life in 1998 and the 1999 decline may be due to significant asset acquisitions and dispositions in those years (note the changes in gross investment and accumulated depreciation). As in the case of comparisons with other companies, these statistics are a means rather than an end.

EXHIBIT 8 Analysis of Fixed Assets for Scandinavian Forest Products Industry

1999	Assidoman	Holmen	SCA	Stora Enso
Buildings				
Average age %	41.6	49.1	29.4	35.1
Average depreciable life years	27.3	21.0	24.4	27.6
Average age years	11.3	10.3	7.2	9.7
Machinery and equipment				
Average age %	55.7	50.0	42.7	48.3
Average depreciable life years	16.3	13.4	15.2	17.4
Average age years	9.1	6.7	6.5	8.4

Source: Data from 1999 annual reports.

4 IMPAIRMENT OF LONG-LIVED ASSETS

Fixed assets used in continuing operations are carried at acquisition cost less accumulated depreciation. The carrying amount of fixed assets may also be affected by changes in market conditions and technology. These changes may increase or decrease the fair value of fixed assets. Unlike some foreign countries (and the IASB), U.S. GAAP do not allow firms to recognize increases in value.

This section is concerned with the recognition, measurement, and disclosure problems associated with decreases in fair value, often called impairment, of long-lived assets. Impairment means that some or all of the carrying cost cannot be recovered from expected levels of operations. Due to unfavorable economic conditions, technological developments, or declines in market demand, firms may temporarily idle, continue to operate at a significantly reduced level, sell, or abandon impaired assets. These economic conditions may also call for fewer employees or those with different skills.

Financial Reporting of Impaired Assets

Impairments are sometimes reported as part of "restructuring" provisions. Such provisions contain elements that fall into two general categories. Some elements, including impairment writedowns, write off past cash flows.[17] Others reflect a major restructuring of the firm and may result in current and expected future cash outflows for such items as employee severance and lease payments. Restructuring provisions must, therefore, be separated into impairment (noncash writedowns of past cash outflows) and those with cash flow implications.

In October 2001, the FASB issued SFAS 144, Accounting for the Impairment or Disposal of Long-Lived Assets. The new standard superseded SFAS 121 (Accounting for Impairment) and APB 30,[18] and also nullified most of the guidance (EITF 94-3) on obligations associated with disposal activities.

SFAS 144 broadened the application of "discontinued operation" accounting and changed the treatment of assets intended for disposal. SFAS 121 (1995) had distinguished between assets held for sale and those remaining in use.

Impairment of Assets Held for Sale

The new standard requires that long-lived assets held for sale:

- Be written down to fair value less cost to sell when lower than the carrying amount. In most cases estimated fair value would be the present value of expected cash flows, discounted at the credit-adjusted risk-free rate. Costs to sell exclude costs associated with the ongoing operations of assets held for sale.
- Cease to be depreciated after reclassification as held for sale.

Subsequent increases in fair value less cost to sell would be recognized as gains only to the extent of previously recognized writedowns.

Impairment of Assets Remaining in Use

The standard requires the recognition of impairment when there is evidence that the carrying amount of an asset or a group of assets still in use can no longer be recovered. One or more of the following indicators may signal lack of recoverability:

---

[17] However, they may signal departure from a business segment or the need for significant capital expenditures for investments in new and improved technologies.

[18] APB 30 deals with disposal of a segment and the classification of items as extraordinary.

- a significant decrease in the market value, physical change, or use of the assets
- adverse changes in the legal or business climate
- significant cost overruns
- current period operating or cash flow losses combined with a history of operating or cash flow losses and a forecast of a significant decline in the long-term profitability of the asset

SFAS 144 provides a two-step process. First is the recoverability test: Impairment must be recognized when the carrying value of the assets exceeds the *undiscounted* expected future cash flows from their use and disposal. The second stage is loss measurement: the excess of the carrying amount over the fair value of the assets. When fair value cannot be determined, the *discounted* present value of future cash flows (discounted at the firm's incremental borrowing rate) must be used.[19]

For assets to be held and used, the new standard permits either a probability-weighted or a best-estimate approach when applying the undiscounted cash flows recoverability test. Estimates of future cash flows used in these tests would be based on the remaining useful life of the primary asset of the group, which may be recognized identifiable intangible assets that are being amortized. The standard includes guidance on the present value methods described in SFAC 7.

The recoverability test and loss measurement are based on assets grouped at the lowest level for which cash flows can be identified independently of cash flows of other asset groups. The impairment loss is reported pretax as a component of income from continuing operations.

The standard prohibits restoration of previous impairments. It requires disclosure of the amount of the loss, segments affected, events and circumstances surrounding the impairment, and how fair value was determined.

SFAS 144 does not require firms to disclose cash flows and discount rates used to measure impairment. Firms do not have to disclose impaired assets (even though one or more impairment indicators are present) as long as their gross *undiscounted* cash flows exceed their carrying amount (even when the discounted cash flows are below the carrying amount). Thus, there is no disclosure of early-warning signals.

SFAS 144 was effective in fiscal years beginning after December 15, 2001. The new standard applied prospectively to new disposal activities. Retroactive application was prohibited except for restatement for comparative purposes.

Analysts must develop supplementary techniques to counter inadequate disclosure requirements and the absence of early-warning signals. Significant declines in market value, abnormal technological changes, and overcapacity are good indicators of possible asset impairments. Research indicates that managers are slow to report impairments.

The telecommunications industry provides a good example; the three indicators mentioned earlier in the preceding paragraph were present during 2001. A June 25, 2001, article in the *Wall Street Journal* asked whether companies had delayed impairment announcements because asset writedowns would violate bond covenants based on minimum levels of fixed assets relative to debt. Impairment recognition would have reduced access to capital markets and risked technical insolvency.

[19] When the recoverability test is applied to assets acquired in purchase method business combinations, the standard requires the elimination of goodwill before recording writedowns of related impaired tangible and identifiable intangible assets. When only some of the acquired assets are subject to the recoverability test, goodwill must be allocated to the affected assets on a pro-rata basis using the relative fair values of all assets acquired. SFAS 142 (2001) made significant changes in accounting for the impairment of goodwill.

The need to evaluate recoverability periodically may result in the review of depreciation methods, lives, and salvage values. Changes in depreciation may precede or accompany a firm's reporting of asset impairment.

EXAMPLE 4

Texaco

Note 6 of Texaco's 1999 financial statements provides an example of impairment recognition and disclosure. Texaco, a multinational oil company, reported asset impairments (included in unusual items) in 1997, 1998, and 1999. While the impairment amounts are small compared to Texaco's net income, the disclosures illustrate the poor quality of disclosures in this area. Texaco's disclosures are very broad and uninformative. The statement that "fair value was determined by discounting expected future cash flows" provides no detail regarding the assumptions used.

Financial Statement Impact of Impairments

Impairment writedowns of long-lived assets have pervasive and significant effects on financial statements and financial ratios.

The principal balance sheet impacts of the writedowns are reductions in the:

- carrying value of plant, equipment, and other production assets
- deferred tax liabilities
- stockholders' equity

The lower level of fixed assets is a direct consequence of the impairment writedown. As a result, the firm's fixed-asset and total-asset turnover increases, affecting any comparison with firms that have not recognized impairments.

The reduction in deferred tax liabilities reflects the fact that the impairment loss is not recognized for tax purposes until the property is disposed of. However, because virtually all firms depreciate fixed assets more quickly for tax purposes than for financial reporting, the impairment has the effect of reducing the difference between the tax basis and reporting basis of these assets. Thus, previously established deferred tax liabilities are reduced (see Reading 38 for further discussion of deferred taxes).

The reduction in equity is the net effect of the impairment provision. This reduction increases the firm's debt-to-equity ratio and decreases reported book value per share. The price-to-book value ratio is increased.

Future financial statements are also affected by the writedown. Depreciation expense declines as a direct result of the reduction in the carrying value of fixed assets; reported earnings are higher than if no impairment were recognized. With higher earnings and lower assets and equity, return ratios (ROA and ROE) also increase.

The ratios used to evaluate fixed assets and depreciation policy earlier in this reading are also distorted by the impairment writedown. For example, the apparent average age of fixed assets increases, and fixed assets appear older than they really are.

Effect of SFAS 121 on Analysis of Impairment

The lack of reporting guidelines for impairments prior to SFAS 121 resulted in widely divergent timing, measurement, and reporting practices. Fried, Schiff, and Sondhi (FSS) (1989) and two Financial Executives Institute surveys[20] found that a majority of companies used net realizable values (NRV) to measure impairments. However, NRV meant different things to different firms, and the definition used was rarely disclosed.[21] The use of undiscounted cash flows under SFAS 121 reduces the probability of recognition of impairments and overstates asset values because of the failure to recognize the time value of money.

It is difficult to forecast impairment writedowns because managements have so much discretion as to timing. Substandard profitability, especially when persistent, is probably the surest sign of impaired assets. LIFO liquidations and changes in depreciation methods, estimated useful lives, and salvage values provide useful but very imprecise signals. Segment data can help the analyst spot underperforming operations.

The cash flow and tax implications of write-offs are also unclear in some cases. Generally, impairments recognized for financial reporting are not deductible for tax purposes until the affected assets are disposed of. Recognition of the impairment, therefore, leads to a deferred tax asset (a probable future tax benefit), not a current refund. Beneficial cash flow impacts may occur only in the future, when tax deductions are realized. Close attention to the income tax footnote should be helpful, but a complete understanding may require posing questions to management.

Timely recognition of impairments may correct understated past depreciation or permit recognition of the effect of changes in markets or technology on operating assets. Higher frequency of impairment announcements and the absence of reporting guidelines resulted in diverse accounting practices that were not comparable across companies and inconsistently applied within firms over time. The FASB recognized this problem when it placed asset impairment on its agenda. SFAS 144, and SEC efforts to improve disclosures regarding "restructuring" provisions have improved disclosure.

Empirical Findings

The frequency and dollar amount of writedowns have increased considerably in the last 25 years.[22] Elliott and Hanna (1996) report that fewer than 200 (5%) firms in the Compustat database reported write-offs in 1975, almost 800 (14%) did so in 1985, and over 1,200 (21%) in 1993. Moreover, in a phenomenon dubbed by Bleakley (1995) as a "recurring nonrecurring item," firms that report write-offs in one year tend to report write-offs again in subsequent years.[23]

---

[20] Financial Executives Institute, Committee on Corporate Reporting, "Survey on Unusual Charges," 1986 and 1991.

[21] The problem is compounded by SFAC 5, in which NRV is defined as a short-term, gross, undiscounted cash flow.

[22] The majority of write-offs (55%–60%) are taken in the fourth quarter. Given the detailed review (both by management and auditors) during preparation of the annual report, it is likely that the fourth quarter will always contain the largest number of write-offs.

[23] Elliott and Hanna found that 27% of the companies that take a write-off report a subsequent one the next year and approximately 60% do so within three years. Fried et al. (1990) also document multiple write-offs. Their probabilities, however, are higher (45% within one year and approximately 70% within three years).

The analysis of write-offs has been confounded by the existence of conflicting beliefs as to the nature and motivations behind such actions. Some view managers as manipulating earnings[24] by recognizing impairments only when it is to their benefit rather than as they occur. Others view impairment announcements as information provided by managers as to declines in asset values due to poor performance, technological shifts, and/or changes in the firm's objectives.

Articles in the financial and popular press as well as in academic journals often talk about the "big bath"—a tendency to take large write-offs during adverse times—and about "house cleaning"—large write-offs assumed to accompany changes in senior management. Consequently, write-off announcements often are viewed as a signal of improvement in future reported performance. However, debate lingers as to whether the subsequent improvement (should it materialize) is evidence that the upturn is real or merely a consequence of earnings management.

A number of studies have examined the write-off phenomenon. These studies document a number of recurring characteristics of write-offs.

1. *Poor financial as well as stock market performance usually precede write-offs.* Francis, Hanna, and Vincent (1996), Rees, Gill, and Gore (1996), and Elliott and Shaw (1988) all report poor stock market performance of write-off firms from three to five years prior to the write-off. Consistent with the foregoing, within their respective industries, firms with write-offs had lower operating performance as measured by ROA (Rees et al.), earnings, and ROE (Elliott and Shaw). These results hold for the year of the write-off[25] as well as the three-year period preceding the write-off.[26] Francis et al. showed similar results (with respect to ROA) but only for firms classifying their write-offs as restructurings.
2. *Overall, negative returns occur around the time of the write-off and for up to 18 months following the write-off. These results, however, depend on the nature of the write-off.* Elliott and Shaw reported that the negative return experienced around the time of the write-off was directly related to the size of the write-off; the larger the write-off, the more negative the reaction. On the other hand, Francis et al., as well as Lindhal and Ricks (1990), indicate that although, in general, market reaction to write-offs was negative, the results depend on whether the event is:
   a. a *writedown* comprising purely accounting decisions to reduce the carrying value of assets with no (apparent) change in operations; or
   b. a *restructuring* that consists of decisions to modify operations (e.g., asset sales, employee layoffs, plant closings).

   For the latter type of event, they report positive market reaction. Francis et al. argue that restructurings are associated with positive returns because they indicate decisions taken to modify and improve future operations and corporate strategy.[27]

---

[24] Earnings management can operate in both directions. Zucca and Campbell (1992) argue that firms may engage in big-bath behavior, taking write-offs when earnings are severely depressed, as well as smoothing behavior by taking write-offs when earnings are "too high."

[25] These conditions hold even without taking the write-off into consideration.

[26] FSS (1989), using a control group of firms matched by industry and size, found similar results. Strong and Meyer (1987), however, reported that although the write-off firms were not the best performers in their industry, they were not the worst either, but tended to cluster in the middle quintiles.

[27] Bartov, Lindhal, and Ricks (1996) similarly partitioned their write-off sample into a *writedown category* and an *operating decision category*. Although they found negative returns for both categories, the stock performance of the writedown category was much worse than that of the operating decision category.

3. *Problems leading to write-offs are rarely short-lived and generally persist after the write-off.* This persistence is especially true for firms taking multiple write-offs. Rees et al. show that such firms had market-adjusted returns that were significantly negative for up to two years after the initial write-off. Furthermore, (industry-adjusted) ROA for these firms did not recover after the write-off. These results are consistent with Elliott and Hanna, who found that bond ratings were lower and default probability higher for firms with sequential write-offs.

Taken together, the evidence seems to indicate that firms write down assets during periods of poor performance. However, the assumption of big-bath behavior may not be well founded. The writedown may also be a response to the (negative) change in the firm's economic situation. The prevalence of multiple write-offs and their increasing size is inconsistent with big-bath behavior, usually associated with a once-and-for-all write-off.[28] Similarly, the persistent negative financial performance and market returns following writedowns are consistent not with an expected reversal following a big-bath but rather with a permanent deterioration in the firm's prospects. Furthermore, positive returns following write-offs are generally confined to those situations where the firm has made explicit operating decisions (restructurings) to modify operations.

Given the significance and frequency of impairments, it is unfortunate that indicators of initial write-offs other than poor financial condition are hard to find.[29] Better disclosure in financial statements (or the Management Discussion and Analysis) of problems with particular segments would make it easier to predict write-offs. However, the evidence indicates that care must be taken to distinguish whether the write-off is purely an accounting decision or is coupled with corrective operating decisions.

5

LIABILITIES FOR ASSET RETIREMENT OBLIGATIONS

Governments often require that owners of operating assets remedy the environmental damage caused by operating those assets or restore land to its preexisting condition. Common examples include:

- restoration of strip mines after mining is completed
- dismantlement of an offshore oil platform after the end of its useful life
- removal of toxic wastes caused by production
- decontamination of site when a nuclear power plant is decommissioned

Prior to SFAS 143, current period costs of these activities were often expensed except for capital expenditures that were capitalized.[30] As no standards have

[28] In effect, if anything, firms seem to warehouse bad news and report it through multiple write-offs.

[29] FSS (1989) do report that LIFO liquidations are leading indicators of writedowns.

[30] SFAS 19 required the accrual of an asset retirement obligation in some cases. Under SFAS 19, ARO was recognized over the life of the asset and measured using a cost-accumulation approach; it was not discounted, and was often recorded as a contra asset with no recognition of a separate liability. In addition, many electricity producers accrued for the decontamination of nuclear facilities.

existed for the accrual of future expenditures, practice has been inconsistent with respect to:

- whether (or when) accrual takes place
- whether accruals increase the carrying amount of the related asset (and whether they must be depreciated)
- whether accruals are included in depreciation expense
- measurement of the liability (whether or not discounted, and at what rate)
- disclosure

Because of inconsistent accounting practice, the FASB issued SFAS 143, Accounting for Asset Retirement Obligations (AROs), in June 2001.

Provisions of SFAS 143

The requirements of SFAS 143 become effective for fiscal years starting after June 15, 2002 (calendar 2003 for most companies). However some companies will apply the standard earlier.

This standard changes accounting standards for ARO in the following ways:

- It applies to all entities[31] and to all legal obligations (including contractual obligations[32]) connected with the retirement of tangible fixed assets.
- Affected firms must recognize the fair value of an ARO liability in the period in which it is incurred (normally at acquisition).
- Absent a market value, fair value is the present value of the expected cash flows required to extinguish the liability.[33]
- As the liability is carried at its present value, the firm must recognize accretion expense in its income statement each period.
- An amount equal to the initial liability must be added to the carrying value of the asset, and depreciated over its useful life.
- Changes in the estimated liability are accounted for prospectively; prior period amounts are not restated.
- Required disclosures include:
  - description of the ARO and associated asset
  - reconciliation of the ARO liability, showing the effect of:
    - new liabilities incurred
    - liabilities extinguished
    - accretion expense
    - revisions of the estimated AROs
  - fair value of any restricted assets (such as funds) set aside for ARO obligations

Further detail regarding SFAS 143 is contained in Box 3.

[31] Paragraph 17 of SFAS 143 governs its application to leased assets.

[32] The standard also applies to legally enforceable contracts arising from promises made. One example would be a company's publicly stated promise to restore a site it is not required to restore by existing laws.

[33] See Box 3 for details.

BOX 3 SFAS 143 (2001): ACCOUNTING FOR ASSET RETIREMENT OBLIGATIONS

Explanation of Accounting Method

Initial Recognition and Measurement

SFAS 143 requires the recognition of the fair value of the ARO liability in the period it is incurred if a reasonable estimate of fair value can be made. The fair value of the liability is defined as the amount at which the liability can be settled in a current transaction between willing parties. Quoted market prices are presumed to be the best evidence of fair value. In their absence, firms must estimate fair value using the best available information on prices of similar liabilities and present value (or other valuation) methods.

For present value techniques, SFAS 143 applies the provisions of SFAC 7 to the measurement of ARO liabilities:

A. Estimate the expected (gross) cash flows required to extinguish the obligation, assuming an outside contractor is hired. Given uncertainty regarding future costs, the firm uses the expected value. Other assumptions (such as inflation rates) may be required.

B. The present value of the expected cash flows is computed using an interest rate based on the risk-free rate, but increased to reflect the **credit risk** of the firm (credit-adjusted risk-free rate).

C. The resulting measure of the ARO is recognized on the balance sheet, with periodic accretion (using the interest method) so that the liability equals the expected gross cash flows at the expected payment date. Use of the interest method means that accretion increases each year.

D. An equal amount is added to the carrying basis of the related asset and depreciated over that asset's useful life, using the same method used to depreciate the cost of the asset.

Subsequent Recognition and Measurement

E. If the timing or the amount of estimated gross cash flows change after the initial recognition, the ARO (and the related asset) is increased or decreased accordingly. Any increase is discounted using interest rates at the date of change; any decrease is discounted at the original interest rate. Accretion and depreciation charges change prospectively; there is no restatement of prior periods.

F. When the liability is extinguished (the cash flows occur), any difference between the amount paid and the carrying amount of the ARO liability is recognized as a gain or loss in the income statement.

Transition Method

The provisions of SFAS 143 were effective in fiscal years beginning after June 15, 2001, with earlier application encouraged. The new standard required use of the cumulative change method to recognize existing AROs. Such recognition was accomplished as follows:

1. Estimate gross obligation based on information available at the (current) transition date.
2. Discount to present value using current interest rates.
3. Replace any previous accrual with the following:
   a. asset equal to ARO at date of asset acquisition

(continued)

BOX 3 *(continued)*

b. accumulated depreciation to transition date, assuming SFAS 143 implemented at asset acquisition date

c. ARO liability at transition date

4. Record the difference between any previous accruals and those listed in the previous paragraph as the *cumulative effect* of implementing the new standard, shown in the income statement on a separate line.
5. Provide pro forma disclosure of the ARO liability for each year presented in the financial statement.

OPTIONAL SEGMENT ENDS

Effects of SFAS 143

Implementation of the new standard will result in the following financial statement effects for most firms:[34]

- Increase in the carrying value of fixed assets.
- Increase in liabilities due to recognition of the ARO.
- Lower net income due to recognition of additional depreciation (higher fixed assets) and accretion expense (on the ARO). Due to the nature of the accretion process, this expense will increase every year.

The following ratio effects will also occur:

- lower asset turnover (higher asset levels)
- higher debt-to-equity ratio as equity is depressed by lower net income[35]
- lower return on assets (lower income, higher assets)
- lower interest coverage (lower income due to higher depreciation, higher interest expense)

Bond covenants that rely on these ratios will also be affected, unless rewritten to ignore the accounting change. Disclosures will be improved in almost all cases. Cash flows will be unaffected.

IAS 16 (1998) requires firms that recognize the liability for remediation costs to include such cost in the carrying amount of fixed assets and depreciate it. The liability recognition is governed by IAS 37 (1998), which (similar to SFAS 143) requires that companies recognize the present value of asset retirement obligations.

[34] For firms that have already recognized ARO liabilities (based on expected gross cash outflows), it is possible that the ARO liability will decrease under SFAS 143 because that standard measures the ARO at its present value.

[35] The debt-to-equity ratio is also affected by whether AROs are considered debt or operating liabilities.

EXAMPLE 5

Texaco

In the Management Discussion and Analysis section of its 1999 annual report, Texaco reports (p. 29):

> **Restoration and Abandonment Costs and Liabilities**
> Expenditures in 1999 for restoration and abandonment of our oil and gas producing properties amounted to $26 million. At year-end 1999, accruals to cover the cost of restoration and abandonment were $911 million.

Further, in its accounting policy section (p. 30), Texaco states that:

> We include estimated future restoration and abandonment costs in determining amortization and depreciation rates of productive properties.

These minimal disclosures are representative of practice prior to SFAS 143. The December 31, 1999, total accrual equals 7.6% of stockholders' equity. Note that the accrual is undiscounted and may be offset by expected recoveries from state funds. While it appears that accruals are made through depreciation charges, Texaco does not write up fixed assets. The accounting effect of the proposed accounting standard cannot be estimated due to the complexity of the transition requirements.

SUMMARY

The capitalization decision is only the start of the accounting cycle for long-lived assets. Depreciation expense depends on the choice of accounting method and asset life and salvage value assumptions. Thus, the same asset can produce different amounts of depreciation expense, limiting the comparability of reported income. Economic depreciation may be entirely different from accounting depreciation.

Economic changes often result in asset lives that differ from those anticipated by accounting conventions. In such cases, asset impairment may require accounting recognition. Although SFAS 144 provides standards for impairment writedowns in the United States, management retains considerable discretion over their timing and amounts. The accrual (if any) for future environmental costs related to long-lived assets is another area where practice is highly inconsistent.

PRACTICE PROBLEMS FOR READING 37

1. [Depreciation methods; CFA® adapted] An analyst gathered the following information about a fixed asset purchased by a company:
   - Purchase price: $12,000,000
   - Estimated useful life: 5 years
   - Estimated salvage value: $2,000,000

   Compute the depreciation expense for this asset over its useful life using *each* of the following methods:

   i. Straight-line
   ii. Sum-of-years' digits (SYD)
   iii. Double-declining balance

2. [Effect of depreciation methods; CFA adapted] Compare the straight-line method of depreciation with accelerated methods with respect to their impact on:

   i. Trend of depreciation expense
   ii. Trend of net income
   iii. Reported return on equity
   iv. Reported return on assets
   v. Reported cash from operations
   vi. Asset turnover

3. [Depreciation methods and cash flows, courtesy of Professor Stephen Ryan] The Capital Company considers investing in either of two assets. Cash flows of these assets are:

Year	Asset A	Asset B
1	$36	$26
2	23	24
3	11	22

   A. At an interest rate of 10%, how much should Capital be willing to pay for each asset?

   B. Assuming that the amount calculated in part a is paid for each asset, calculate the depreciation schedule for each asset that results in a constant rate of return.

   C. What type of historical cost depreciation is equal to present value depreciation for Asset A? Asset B?

4. [Effects of accelerated depreciation] Exhibit P-1 contains data from the 1999 annual report of Boeing [BA], a leading manufacturer of aviation equipment.

   A. Despite more than $5 billion of capital expenditures over the four years 1996–1999, Boeing's net plant and equipment rose by barely 4%. One explanation is the sale of fixed assets in 1999 (proceeds $359 million). Discuss *two* other reasons for the slow growth in net plant and equipment.

EXHIBIT P-1 **Boeing Extracts from 1999 Financial Statements ($millions)**

Note 1. Summary of Significant Accounting Policies

Property, plant and equipment

Property, plant and equipment are recorded at cost, including applicable construction-period interest, and depreciated principally over the following estimated useful lives: new buildings and land improvements, form 20 to 45 years; and machinery and equipment, from 3 to 13 years. The principal methods of depreciation are as follows: buildings and land improvements, 150% declining balance; and machinery and equipment, sum-of-the-years' digits. The Company periodically evaluates the appropriateness of remaining depreciable lives assigned to long-lived assets subject to management's plan for use and disposition.

Note 11. Property, Plant and Equipment

Property, plant and equipment at December 31 consisted of the following:

	1999	1998
Land	$ 430	$ 499
Buildings	8,148	8,244
Machinery and equipment	10,411	10,521
Construction in progress	1,130	977
	$20,119	$20,241
Less accumulated depreciation	(11,874)	(11,652)
	$ 8,245	$ 8,589

Balances are net of impairment asset valuation reserve adjustments for real property available for sale of $76 and $64 for December 31, 1999 and 1998.

Depreciation expense was $1,330, $1,386 and $1,266 for 1999, 1998 and 1997, respectively. Interest capitalized as construction-period property, plant and equipment costs amounted to $64, $45 and $28 in 1999, 1998 and 1997, respectively.

Five-Year Summary

	1999	1998	1997	1996	1995
Total sales	$57,993	$56,154	$45,800	$35,453	$32,960
Net earnings (loss)	2,309	1,120	(178)	1,818	(36)
Additions to plant and equipment, net	1,236	1,665	1,391	971	747
Depreciation of plant and equipment	1,330	1,386	1,266	1,132	1,172
NEt plant and equipment at year-end	8,245	8,589	8,391	8,266	7,927

Source: Boeing, 10-K report, December 31, 1999.

B. Boeing reported gains on the disposition of fixed assets of $100 million over the 1998–99 period. Discuss how that gain was affected by Boeing's depreciation method.

C. Assume that in 1999 Boeing adopted the straight-line depreciation method retroactively, with no change in depreciable lives. Describe the expected effect of that change on Boeing's:

i. Net income for 1998 and 1999 (*Hint:* Consider the trend of capital expenditures for those two years.)

ii. Stockholders' equity at December 31, 1999

iii. Cash from operations for 1998 and 1999

iv. Fixed-asset turnover for 1999

D. Assume that Boeing adopted the straight-line depreciation method prospectively as of January 1, 2000, with no change in depreciable lives. Describe the expected effect of that change on Boeing's:

i. Net income for 2000 compared with net income assuming no accounting change

ii. Trend of depreciation expense over the 1999 to 2004 period

E. As a financial analyst, what conclusions might you draw form either change (part c or d)?

5. [Change in depreciation lives] On March 6, 2000, Pepsi Bottling Group (PBG) issued a press release containing the following:

> In recognition of its long-standing success in preventive maintenance programs, The Pepsi Bottling Group, Inc. (NYSE: PBG) today announced a change in the depreciation lives of certain categories of assets. This change will result in a reduction of about $58 million in depreciation expense, an increase in earnings per share of $0.22 and an increase in return on invested capital of 0.6% in the year 2000.

Exhibit P-2 contains extracts for the first-quarter 10-Q issued by PBG.

A. Compute each of the following ratios for the first quarter of 1999 and 2000, using reported data:

i. Gross profit margin

ii. Operating margin

B. Compute each of the following ratios for the first quarter of 1999 and 2000, after adjusting reported data for the depreciation change:

i. Gross profit margin

ii. Operating margin

C. Compute how much of the apparent improvement of each of these two ratios was due to the depreciation change.

D. Discuss the effect of the depreciation change on PBG's:

i. Fixed-asset turnover ratio

ii. Trend of reported earnings, 1999–2004

iii. Quality of earnings

iv. Cash from operations

EXHIBIT P-2 Pepsi Bottling Group

The Pepsi Bottling Group, Inc.
Condensed Consolidated Statements of Operations
(in millions, unaudited)

	12 Weeks Ended	
	March 20, 1999	March 18, 2000
Net revenues	$1,452	$1,545
Cost of sales	(835)	(845)
Gross profit	$ 617	$ 700
Selling, delivery and administrative expenses	(575)	(625)
Operating income	$ 42	$ 75

Note 6. Comparability of Results

Asset Lives

At the beginning of fiscal year 2000, we changed the estimated useful lives of certain categories of assets to reflect the success of our preventive maintenance programs in extending the useful lives of these assets. The changes, which are detailed in the table below, lowered total depreciation cost for the quarter by $14 million ($8 million after tax and minority interest, or $0.05 per share) reducing cost of sales by $8 million and selling, delivery and administrative expenses by $6 million.

Estimated Useful Lives

	1999	2000
Manufacturing equipment	10	15
Heavy fleet	8	10
Fountain dispensing equipment	5	7
Small specialty coolers and marketing equipment	5 to 7	3

Source: Pepsi Bottling Group, 10-Q Report, March 18, 2000.

The March 6 press release also contained the following statement:

> "We maintain that cash profits remain the best method of tracking our performance. However, since some investors look at us and other bottlers in terms of reported earnings, we thought it was important to reflect our depreciation expenses and reported profit more accurately," said John Cahill, Executive Vice President and Chief Financial Officer for PBG. "Even with these changes, the new policies still present our financial results conservatively."

E. Evaluate the benefits to PBG of making the depreciation change.

6. [Analysis of fixed assets] Roche's summary of significant accounting policies states:

> Property, plant and equipment are initially recorded at cost of purchase or construction and are depreciated on a straight-line basis, except for land, which is not depreciated. Estimated useful lives of major classes of depreciable assets are as follows:

Buildings and land improvements	40 years
Machinery and equipment	5–15 years
Office equipment	3 years
Motor vehicles	5 years

The following data were obtained from Roche's annual reports (the 1999 data are located in Note 12 of its 2000 annual report):

Property, plant, and equipment (CHF millions)

	1997	1998	1999
Buildings and land improvements:			
Gross investment	$ 7,576	$ 7,947	$ 8,578
Accumulated depreciation	(2,580)	(2,695)	(2,944)
Net investment	$ 4,996	$ 5,252	$ 5,634
Depreciation expense	233	195	210
Machinery and equipment:			
Gross investment	$10,529	$11,350	$13,174
Accumulated depreciation	(5,755)	(6,079)	(7,015)
Net investment	$ 4,774	$ 5,271	$ 6,159
Depreciation expense	692	948	1,036

A. Using the above data, compute each of the following ratios for all three years:

i. Average depreciable life (years)

ii. Average age (years)

iii. Average age (%)

B. Compare the result of part a (i) with the accounting policy statement above.

C. Discuss the three-year trend of the three ratios in part a for both fixed-asset classes.

D. State the questions you would ask management after reviewing parts A through C above.

7. [Impairment] Roche, in its report for the half-year ended June 30, 2000, adopted IAS 36 (Impairment), with the following disclosure:

> **'Impairment of assets'** When the recoverable amount of an asset, being the higher of its net selling price and its value in use, is less than its carrying amount, then the carrying amount is reduced to its recoverable value. This reduction is reported as an impairment loss. Value in use is calculated using estimated cash flows, generally over a five-year period, with extrapolating projections for subsequent years. These are discounted using an appropriate long-term interest rate. Previously the permitted alternative method for calculating value in use was applied, whereby it was calculated using cash flow projections on an undiscounted basis.
>
> As a result, the Group recognized impairment charges of 1,161 million Swiss francs relating to acquired intangible assets. A reduction in deferred tax liabilities of 348 million Swiss francs was also recorded, giving a net charge of 813 million Swiss francs in the consolidated results. Also included within this is a minor amount relating to impairment on a small number of products acquired in an earlier acquisition as a consequence of reduced market expectations. Under the Group's previous accounting policy, no impairment would have arisen. As a result of the impairment, the net book value of intangible assets was reduced by the amount of the impairment charge, and consequently amortization in the first half of 2000 was 64 million Swiss francs lower than it would have been under the previous policy.

A. Describe the effect of the accounting change on the year 2000:
- **i.** Income before the effect of accounting changes
- **ii.** Net income
- **iii.** Stockholders' equity
- **iv.** Cash from operations

B. Describe the effect of the accounting change on the year 2001:
- **i.** Net income
- **ii.** Return on equity
- **iii.** Cash from operations

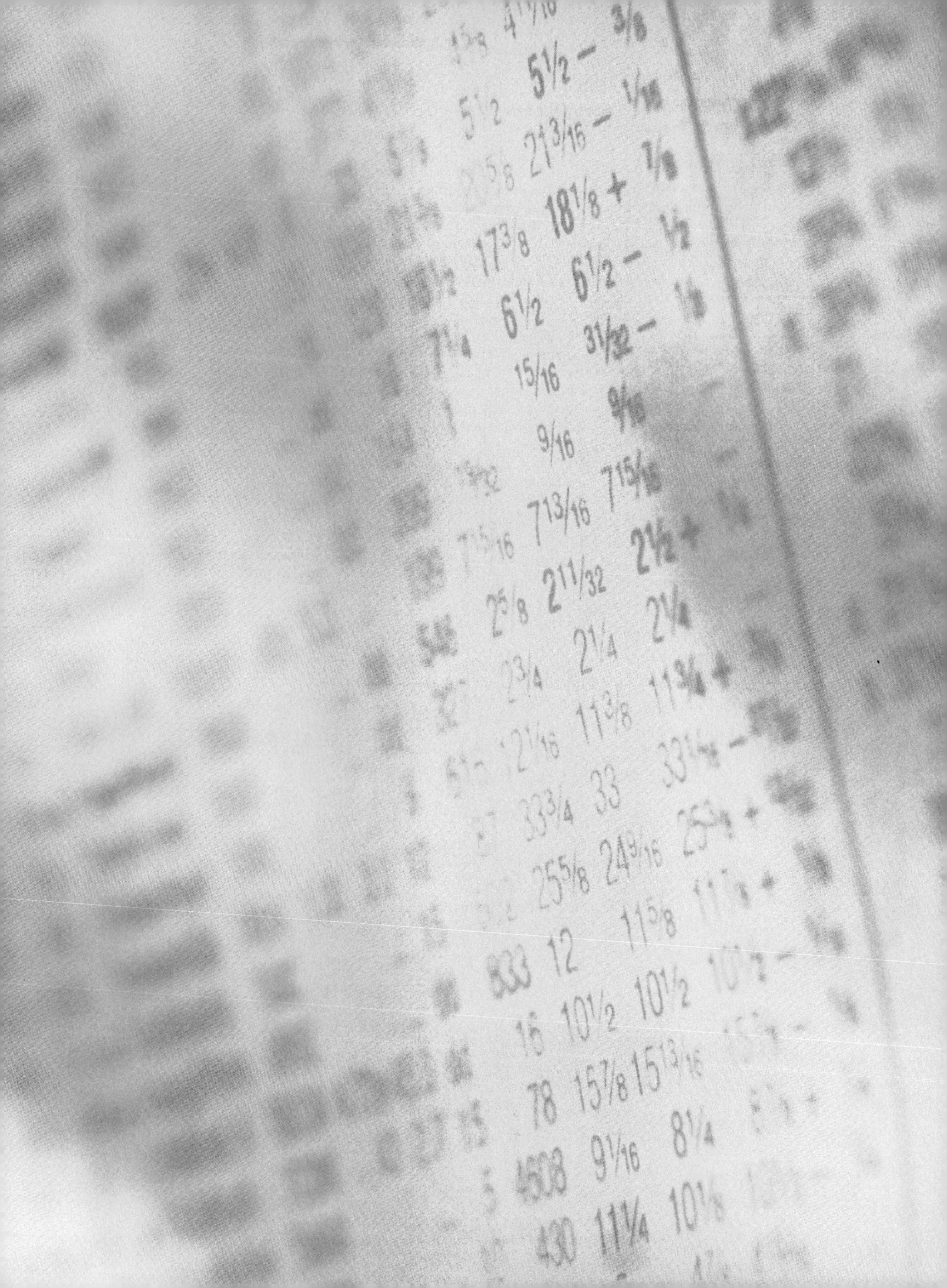

5½ –
5½ 21 3/16 –
18 1/8 +
17 3/8
6½ 6½ –
6½ 31/32 –
15/16
9/16
7 13/16 7 15/16
2 5/8 2 11/32 2½ +
2¼ 2¼
2¾ 11 3/8
33 3/4 33
25 5/8 24 9/16
12 11 5/8
10½ 10½
78 15 7/8 15 13/16
9 1/16 8¼
430 11¼

ANALYSIS OF INCOME TAXES

by Gerald I. White, Ashwinpaul C. Sondhi, and Dov Fried

READING 38

LEARNING OUTCOMES

The candidate should be able to:

a. explain the key terms related to income tax accounting and the origin of deferred tax liabilities and assets;

b. demonstrate the liability method of accounting for deferred taxes;

c. discuss the use of valuation allowances for deferred tax assets, and their implications for financial statement analysis;

d. explain the factors that determine whether a company's deferred tax liabilities should be treated as a liability or as equity for purposes of financial analysis;

e. distinguish between temporary and permanent items in pretax financial income and taxable income;

f. calculate and interpret income tax expense, income taxes payable, deferred tax assets, and deferred tax liabilities;

g. calculate and interpret the adjustment(s) to the deferred tax accounts related to a change in the tax rate;

h. interpret a deferred tax footnote disclosure that reconciles the effective and statutory tax rates;

i. analyze disclosures relating to, and the effect of, deferred taxes on a company's financial statements and financial ratios;

j. compare and contrast a company's deferred tax items and effective tax rate reconciliation 1) between reporting periods and 2) with the comparable items reported by other companies.

INTRODUCTION 1

Differences in the objectives of financial and tax reporting make income taxes a troublesome issue in financial reporting. The objective of financial reporting is to provide users with information needed to evaluate a firm's financial position, performance, and cash flows. The accrual basis of financial reporting allows management to select revenue and expense recognition methods that best reflect performance and smooth or otherwise manage (maximize or minimize) reported net income. As discussed throughout the text, management incentives to manage reported income result from management compensation contracts, bond covenants, political considerations, and the (presumed) effect of those factors on financial markets.

Tax reporting, in contrast, is the product of political and social objectives. Current-period *taxable income* is measured using the modified cash basis; revenue and expense recognition methods used in tax reporting often differ from those used for financial reporting as the firm has strong incentives to select methods allowing it to minimize taxable income and, therefore, taxes paid, maximizing cash from operations.[1]

Thus, differences between *taxes payable* for the period and reported *income tax expense* result from:

- the difference between accrual and modified cash bases of accounting
- differences in reporting methods and estimates

These differences create *deferred tax liabilities* (credits) and prepaid taxes or *deferred tax assets* (debits) that are difficult to interpret. There are disagreements as to (1) whether they are true assets or liabilities and (2) their usefulness as indicators of future cash flows. When these deferrals become very large, their interpretation can have a significant effect on the financial analysis of a firm or group of firms.

Note: Terminology related to income tax accounting can be confusing because two terms that seem similar can have very different meanings. A glossary of terms used in this reading is therefore provided in Box 1. Each term in the glossary is shown in italics when first used in the reading.

2 BASIC INCOME TAX ACCOUNTING ISSUES

Basic accounting issues are discussed in Box 2. There we provide a discussion and an illustration of how temporary differences between tax and financial reporting affect the balance sheet and the income statement. The box also contains a review of the impact of tax law and rate changes on deferred tax assets and liabilities. This permits us to focus on analytical issues in the reading.

[1] In countries such as Japan, Germany, and Switzerland, statutory financial reporting is required to conform to tax reporting. In these countries, the problems discussed in this reading do not occur for statutory (usually, parent company only) statements. However, consolidated financial statements, for example, those prepared under IAS GAAP, do not conform to tax reporting and deferred tax issues must be dealt with. See the discussion of financial reporting practices outside the United States later in this reading.

BOX 1 GLOSSARY: INCOME TAX ACCOUNTING

Amounts in Tax Return:

Taxable income	Income subject to tax.
Taxes payable (current tax expense)	Tax return liability resulting from current period taxable income. SFAS 109 calls this "current tax expense or benefit."
Income tax paid	Actual cash outflow for income taxes, including payments (refunds) for other years.
Tax loss carryforward	Tax return loss that can be used to reduce taxable income in future years.

Amounts in Financial Statements:

Pretax income	Income before income tax expense.
Income tax expense	Expense based on current period pre-tax income; includes taxes payable and deferred income tax expense.
Deferred income tax expense	Accrued income tax expense expected to be paid (or recovered) in future years; difference between taxes payable and income tax expense. Under SFAS 109, the amount depends on changes in deferred tax assets and liabilities.
Deferred tax asset (debit)	Balance sheet amounts; expected to be recovered from future operations.
Deferred tax liability (credit)	Balance sheet amounts; expected to result in future cash outflows.
Valuation allowance	Reserve against deferred tax assets (debits) based on likelihood that those assets will not be realized.
Timing difference	The difference between tax return and financial statement treatment (timing or amount) of a transaction.
Temporary difference	Difference between tax and financial statement reporting, which will affect taxable income when those differences reverse; similar to but broader than timing differences.

Note: SFAS 109 contains a more technical glossary of terms used in that standard.

BOX 2 BASIC INCOME TAX ACCOUNTING ISSUES

We use a simple example to illustrate the issues faced when tax accounting differs from accounting for financial statements. We begin this example assuming that depreciation is the only item of expense. Part A of Exhibit B1 depicts income tax reporting where the company depreciates a $6,000 asset over two years, giving rise to *taxes payable* of $800, $800, and $2,000 over the three-year period.

For financial reporting (Part B of Exhibit B1), the firm depreciates the asset over three years. *Pretax income* exceeds taxable income in the first two years; taxable income is higher in year 3.[a] What *tax expense* should the company report in its financial statements?

Part B1 of Exhibit B1 displays one approach (not permitted under U.S. GAAP) where the tax expense equals taxes payable. Pretax income is the same for all three years, but tax expense differs as the tax deferred in earlier years is paid in year 3. As a result, tax expense, as a percentage of pretax income, does not reflect the prevailing statutory tax rate, 40%. The reported tax rate is 26.7% for the first two years and 66.7% for year 3.

Timing Differences: Deferred Tax Liabilities

Part B2 of Exhibit B1 illustrates the U.S. GAAP treatment, SFAS 109, which requires the recognition of deferred tax liabilities when future taxable income is expected to exceed pretax income. IAS 12 has the same requirement. In our example, pretax income exceeds taxable income in years 1 and 2, but year 3 taxable income is expected to exceed pretax income by $2,000. At the end of years 1 and 2, a deferred tax liability of $400 (timing difference of $1,000 × 40% tax rate) is recognized to reflect the tax on the $1,000 *timing difference* that will be paid in year 3. This liability is reported each year as a portion of that year's tax expense. Thus, income tax expense is $1,200 in both years 1 and 2: tax payable or current tax expense ($800) plus *deferred income tax expense* ($400). The matching principle is satisfied as the relationship between revenues and expenses (40% tax rate) is maintained. At the end of year 2, the cumulative timing difference is $2,000 and the aggregate deferred tax liability is $800.

No tax depreciation remains to be recorded in year 3, but book depreciation expense equals $2,000. At the end of year 3, the machine has been fully depreciated for both tax and financial reporting purposes. The effect of the year 1 and 2 timing differences must be reversed; year 3 income tax expense equals $1,200 or taxes payable ($2,000) *less* the reversal of the deferred tax liability of $800 accumulated over the first two years.

Timing Differences: Deferred Tax Assets

Differences between financial accounting and tax accounting can also give rise to *deferred tax assets* (debits) when future pretax income is expected to exceed taxable income. Part B3 of Exhibit B1 introduces another timing difference, warranty expense, which gives rise to a deferred tax asset in years 1 and 2. As warranty payments are tax-deductible when paid rather than when accrued, larger amounts are charged to warranty expense earlier for financial statement purposes; tax deductions occur in later periods when the repairs or replacement services are provided.

As shown in part B3,[b] the firm recognizes a warranty expense of $500 in each of years 1 and 2, but receives no tax deduction because no expenditures are incurred in those years. The higher taxable income results in a prepayment of taxes; tax expense in the financial statements reflects lower pretax income. The difference of $500 in each of the first two years generates a deferred tax debit of $200 ($500 × 0.40) each year and decreases tax expense by that amount each year. At the end of year 2, there is a deferred tax asset of $400.

In year 3, tax-deductible expenditures of $1,500 are incurred for repairs, reducing taxable income and tax payments. These expenditures exceed the $500 of financial statement warranty expense of year 3 by $1,000; equal to the total additional expense accrued in the first two years. The temporary difference reverses, deferred income tax expense is reduced by $400 ($1,000 × 0.40), and the deferred tax debit generated during the first two years is eliminated.[c]

Comprehensive Example: Deferred Tax Liabilities and Deferred Tax Assets

Exhibit B1 separately illustrates the treatment of timing differences that gave rise to a deferred tax liability and a deferred tax asset. In practice, firms report both deferred tax assets and liabilities, resulting from multiple timing differences. Exhibit B2 shows the accounting when a firm has both types of timing differences.

---

[a] Of the $3,000 pretax income reported in years 1 and 2, $1,000 (the excess tax depreciation) is not subject to taxes in those years. The $2,000 (2 × $1,000) deferred in the first two years is subject to taxation in the third as taxable income ($5,000) exceeds pretax income ($3,000) by $2,000.

b In part B3, we ignore depreciation expense to illustrate the accounting treatment of timing differences that generate deferred tax assets.

c In these examples, income tax expense could also have been computed by applying the income tax rate of 40% directly to pretax income in each year. However, in more complex situations, discussed later, this approach would produce a different result.

(continued)

BOX 2 *(continued)*

Taxes payable equal the tax rate multiplied by taxable income and reflect the effects of tax depreciation and allowable warranty deductions on the tax return. Income tax expense is based on pretax income, which reflects financial statement depreciation and estimated warranty expense for products sold. Over the three-year period, total revenues are $15,000, total depreciation expense is $6,000, and total warranty expense is $1,500 for both financial and tax reporting. The timing of expense recognition differs, but the total amount is the same.[d]

EXHIBIT B1 Alternative Approaches to Reported Income Tax Expense

Assumptions:

- The firm purchases a machine costing $6,000 with a three-year estimated service life and no salvage value.
- For financial reporting purposes, the firm uses straight-line depreciation over the three-year life.
- For income tax reporting, the machine is depreciated over two years using the straight-line depreciation method.
- Products manufactured using the machine generate annual revenues of $5,000 for three years.
- The statutory tax rate is 40% in all three years.

Part A. Income Tax Reporting: Straight-Line Depreciation over Two Years

	Year 1	Year 2	Year 3	Total
Revenues	$5,000	$5,000	$5,000	$15,000
Depreciation expense	(3,000)	(3,000)	0	(6,000)
Taxable income	$2,000	$2,000	$5,000	$ 9,000
Taxes payable @ 40%	(800)	(800)	(2,000)	(3,600)
Net income	$1,200	$1,200	$3,000	$ 5,400

Part B. Financial Statements: Straight-Line Depreciation over Three Years

B1: Flow-Through Method—Not Permitted by GAAP

- No recognition of deferred taxes.
- Tax expense defined as taxes payable.

	Year 1	Year 2	Year 3	Total
Revenues	$5,000	$5,000	$5,000	$15,000
Depreciation expense	(2,000)	(2,000)	(2,000)	(6,000)
Pretax income	$3,000	$3,000	$3,000	$ 9,000
Tax expense = taxes payable	(800)	(800)	(2,000)	(3,600)
Net income	$2,200	$2,200	$1,000	$ 5,400

(Exhibit B1 continued on next page . . .)

[d] Warranty expense and actual repair costs are assumed to be identical for illustration only; it is difficult to predict the frequency and level of repair costs perfectly. Bad debt expenses and litigation losses are other examples of timing differences where predictions are uncertain.

(continued)

BOX 2 (continued)

EXHIBIT B1 (continued)

B2: SFAS 109 and IAS 12—Deferred Tax Liabilities

- Recognition of deferred taxes.
- Tax expense differs from taxes payable.

	Year 1	Year 2	Year 3	Total
Revenues	$5,000	$5,000	$5,000	$15,000
Depreciation expense	(2,000)	(2,000)	(2,000)	(6,000)
Pretax income	$3,000	$3,000	$3,000	$ 9,000
Tax expense @ 40%	(1,200)	(1,200)	(1,200)	(3,600)
Net income	$1,800	$1,800	$1,800	$ 5,400
Taxes payable (from part A)	800	800	2,000	3,600
Deferred tax expense	400	400	(800)	0
Balance sheet deferred tax liability	400	800	0	N.A.

Journal Entries

Years 1 and 2: Origination of the Deferred Tax Liability

Tax expense	$1,200	
Deferred tax liability		$ 400
Taxes payable		800

Year 3: Reversal of the Deferred Tax Liability

Tax expense	$1,200	
Deferred tax liability	800	
Taxes payable		$2,000

B3: SFAS 109 and IAS 12—Deferred Tax Assets

Assumption: Warranty expenses estimated at 10% of revenues each year; all repairs provided in year 3.

Income Tax Reporting	Year 1	Year 2	Year 3	Total
Revenues	$5,000	$5,000	$5,000	$15,000
Warranty expense	0	0	(1,500)	(1,500)
Taxable income	$5,000	$5,000	$3,500	$13,500
Tax payable @ 40%	(2,000)	(2,000)	(1,400)	(5,400)
Net income	$3,000	$3,000	$2,100	$ 8,100

(Exhibit B1 continued on next page . . .)

(continued)

BOX 2 *(continued)*

EXHIBIT B1 (continued)

Financial Statements

Revenues	$5,000	$5,000	$5,000	$15,000
Warranty expense	(500)	(500)	(500)	(1,500)
Pretax income	$4,500	$4,500	$4,500	$13,500
Tax expense @ 40%	(1,800)	(1,800)	(1,800)	(5,400)
Net income	$2,700	$2,700	$2,700	$ 8,100
Prepaid (deferred) tax	200	200	(400)	0
Balance sheet deferred tax asset	200	400	(400)	N.A.

Journal Entries

Years 1 and 2: Origination of Deferred Tax Assets

Tax expense	$1,800	
Deferred tax asset	200	
Taxes payable		$2,000

Year 3: Reversal of Deferred Tax Asset

Tax expense	$1,800	
Deferred tax asset		$ 0
Taxes payable		1,400

Do the deferred tax liabilities at the end of years 1 and 2 actually represent a liability for tax payments due in year 3? Similarly, does the deferred tax asset qualify as an asset? In this simple case, they do, as the forecast reversals occurred as expected and the firm did not engage in any other transactions with timing differences. In the real world, the answer is not so clear; these are important issues from an analytical perspective and the reading provides a comprehensive discussion of those issues.

Effect of Tax Rate and Tax Law Changes

The balance sheet orientation of SFAS 109 requires adjustments to deferred tax assets and liabilities to reflect the impact of a change in tax rates or tax laws. Using the example in Exhibit B2, Exhibit B3 depicts the impact of a tax rate decrease from 40% to 35% at the beginning of year 2. In panel A, we assume that the future tax decrease *was enacted before* the year 1 financial statements were prepared. Panel B illustrates the accounting under the assumption that the year 2 tax decrease *was enacted after* year 1 financial statements were prepared.

(continued)

BOX 2 (continued)

Panel A: Future Tax Rate Change Enacted in Current Year

Taxes payable for year 1 are based on the current tax rate of 40%, and the deferred tax assets and liabilities are based on the tax rate expected to be in effect when the differences reverse, 35%.

Note that year 1 tax expense as a percentage of pretax income (the effective tax rate) is 39% ($975/$2,500): a weighted average of the current tax rate of 40% and the 35% rate that will be in effect when the timing differences that gave rise to the deferred taxes reverse. There is no attempt to match income tax expense directly with pretax income, and one cannot calculate tax expense directly by multiplying pretax income by the current tax rate. For years 2 and 3, the calculations are similar to those in Exhibit B2 except that the new tax rate of 35% (rather than 40%) is used for all calculations.

EXHIBIT B2 Financial Reporting under SFAS 109

Income Tax Reporting	**Year 1**	**Year 2**	**Year 3**	**Total**
Revenues	$5,000	$5,000	$5,000	$15,000
Depreciation expense	(3,000)	(3,000)	0	(6,000)
Warranty expense	0	0	(1,500)	(1,500)
Taxable income	$2,000	$2,000	$3,500	$ 7,500
Tax payable @ 40%	(800)	(800)	(1,400)	(3,000)
Net Income	$1,200	$1,200	$2,100	$ 4,500
Financial Statements				
Revenues	$5,000	$5,000	$5,000	$15,000
Depreciation expense	(2,000)	(2,000)	(2,000)	(6,000)
Warranty expense	(500)	(500)	(500)	(1,500)
Pretax income	$2,500	$2,500	$2,500	$ 7,500
Tax expense @ 40%	(1,000)	(1,000)	(1,000)	(3,000)
Net Income	$1,500	$1,500	$1,500	$ 4,500
Deferred tax expense	400	400	(800)	0
Balance sheet deferred tax liability	400	800	0	N.A.
Prepaid tax	200	200	(400)	0
Balance sheet deferred tax asset	200	400	0	N.A.

(Exhibit B2 continued on next page . . .)

(continued)

BOX 2 (continued)

EXHIBIT B2 (continued)

Journal Entries

Years 1 and 2: Origination of Deferred Tax Liabilities and Deferred Tax Assets

Tax expense	$1,000	
Deferred tax asset	200	
Deferred tax liability		$ 400
Taxes payable		800

Year 3: Reversal of Deferred Tax Liabilities and Deferred Tax Assets

Tax expense	$1,000	
Deferred tax liability	800	
Deferred tax asset		$ 400
Taxes payable		1,400

EXHIBIT B3 Impact of Tax Rate Change: The Liability Method

Assumptions:

Identical to Exhibit B2

- A firm purchases a machine costing $6,000 with a three-year estimated service life and no salvage value.
- For financial reporting purposes, the firm uses straight-line depreciation with a three-year life.
- For income tax reporting, the machine is depreciated straight-line over two years.
- The machine is used to manufacture a product that will generate annual revenue of $5,000 for three years.
- Warranty expenses are estimated at 10% of revenues each year; all repairs are provided in year 3.

A. Year 2 Tax Rate Change Enacted in Year 1

Year 1: Tax Rate = 40%

Year 2 Tax Rate Will Be 35%

Income tax expense	975	
Deferred tax asset	175	
Deferred tax liability		350
Taxes payable		800

Selected T-Accounts

Deferred Tax Asset		Deferred Tax Liability	
$175			$350
$175			$350

Year 2: Tax Rate = 35%

(Exhibit B3 continued on next page . . .)

(continued)

BOX 2 *(continued)*

EXHIBIT B3 (continued)

			Deferred Tax Asset		Deferred Tax Liability	
Income tax expense	875		$175			$350
Deferred tax asset	175		175			
Deferred tax liability		350				350
Taxes payable		700	$350			$700

Year 3: Tax Rate = 35%

			Deferred Tax Asset		Deferred Tax Liability	
Income tax expense	875		$350			$700
Deferred tax liability	700				700	
Deferred tax asset		350		350		
Taxes payable		1,225	$ 0			$ 0

Calculations

	Temporary Differences			
	Depreciation (Liability)	Warranty (Asset)	Taxes Payable	Income Tax Expense
Year 1	35% × $1,000	35% × $(500)	40% × $2,000	$350 − $175 + $ 800
Year 2	35% × 1,000	35% × (500)	35% × 2,000	350 − 175 + 700
Year 3	35% × (2,000)	35% × 1,000	35% × 3,500	− 700 + 350 + 1,225

B. Year 2 Tax Rate Change Enacted in Year 2

Year 1: Tax Rate = 40%

Selected T-Accounts

			Deferred Tax Asset		Deferred Tax Liability	
Income tax expense	1,000					
Deferred tax asset	200					
Deferred tax liability		400	$200			$400
Taxes payable		800	$200			$400

Year 2: Tax Rate Reduced to 35%

(i) *Adjustment of Prior-Year Deferrals*

			Deferred Tax Asset		Deferred Tax Liability	
Deferred tax liability	50		$200			$400
Deferred tax asset		25		25	50	
Income tax expense		25	$175			$350

(Exhibit B3 continued on next page . . .)

(continued)

BOX 2 *(continued)*

EXHIBIT B3 (continued)

(ii) Current Year Operations

			Deferred Tax Asset		Deferred Tax Liability	
Income tax expense	875		$175			$350
Deferred tax asset	175		175			
Deferred tax liability		350				350
Taxes payable		700	$350			$700

Year 3: Tax Rate = 35%

			Deferred Tax Asset		Deferred Tax Liability	
Income tax expense	875		$350			$700
Deferred tax liability	700				700	
Deferred tax asset		350		350		
Taxes payable		1,225	$ 0			$ 0

Calculations

	Temporary Differences: Depreciation (Liability)	Temporary Differences: Warranty (Asset)	Taxes Payable	Income Tax Expense
Year 1	40% × $1,000	40% × $(500)	40% × $2,000	$400 − $200 + $ 800
Year 2	(5%) × 1,000	(5%) × (500)		−50 + 25
	35% × 1,000	35% × (500)	35% × 2,000	350 − 175 + 700
Year 3	35% × (2,000)	35% × 1,000	35% × 3,500	−700 + 350 + 1,225

Panel B: Future Tax Rate Change Enacted after Year 1 Statements Have Been Prepared

Calculations for year 1 tax expense, taxes payable, and deferred taxes are based on the year 1 tax rate of 40% and are identical to those in Exhibit B2. A deferred tax asset of $200 and a deferred tax liability of $400 are created.
In year 2, when the rate decrease is effective, two steps are necessary to calculate the current year's tax expense:

1. Exhibit B3 illustrates the restatement of end of year 1 deferred tax asset and liability balances to the new (lower) tax rate of 35% (assumed to be in effect when the deferred taxes will be paid). Year 2 tax expense is reduced (income is increased) since the lower rate reduces the expected tax payment when the depreciation difference reverses, partially offset by a lower expected tax benefit when the warranty expense difference reverses. The adjustment results in a deferred tax asset of $175 and liability of $350.[e]
2. The taxes payable and deferred taxes arising from current year operations are calculated using the new rate of 35%.

[e] These balances are now identical to those shown in panel A of the exhibit when the tax law change was known prior to the issuance of the year 1 financial statements. The only difference between the two panels is the timing of the restatement at the lower rate.

(continued)

BOX 2 (continued)

Tax expense for year 2 is calculated as follows:

Adjustment of Year 1 Balances to New Rate:	
Deferred tax asset of \$200 restated to \$175	\$ 25
Deferred tax liability of \$400 restated to \$350	(50)
Year 2 Taxes Payable and New Temporary Differences:	
Taxes payable = \$2,000 taxable income × 35%	700
Deferred tax asset = \$500 temporary difference × 35%	(175)
Deferred tax liability = \$1,000 temporary difference × 35%	350
Income tax expense	\$850

Note that, as in panel A, the income tax expense of \$850 is affected by changes in the deferred tax liability and asset accounts and there is no attempt to directly match the relationship of tax expense to pretax income.

3 THE LIABILITY METHOD: SFAS 109 AND IAS 12

The central accounting issue is whether the tax effects of transactions for which GAAP-based and tax-based accounting rules differ should be recognized in the period(s) in which they affect taxable income (in which case no deferred taxes would be recognized) or in the period(s) in which they are recognized in the financial statements (giving rise to deferred taxes). These alternatives produce different measures of operating and financial performance, affecting the evaluation of a firm's operating performance and earning power. Cash flows for taxes are not affected by financial reporting choices except when conformity between tax and financial reporting is required.

Both U.S. and IAS standards are based on the liability method, which is consistent with the second alternative.[2] This method measures the balance sheet deferred tax assets and liabilities first, under the assumption that temporary differences will reverse. Income tax expense reflects both the effect of any current period pretax income and future changes in the tax rate used to measure the tax effect of tax expense resulting from those reversals.

Accounting for taxes in the United States is based on SFAS 109 (1992), whose two objectives are to recognize:

1. taxes payable or refundable for the current year; and
2. the deferred tax liabilities and assets (adjusted for recoverability) measured as the future tax consequences of events that have been recognized in financial statements or tax returns.

[2] The deferral method (also consistent with the second alternative) measures income tax expense first. Changes in deferred tax assets and liabilities result *only* from current year deferred tax expense. These assets and liabilities are based on tax rates when they originated; the effect of tax rate changes is recognized only when timing differences actually reverse.

SFAS 109 recognizes the deferred tax consequences of *temporary differences*.[3] Deferred tax assets (adjusted for recoverability) and liabilities are calculated directly and reported on the balance sheet; *deferred income tax expense* used to determine reported income is a consequence of the resulting balance sheet amounts.

IAS 12 (2000) is also based on the liability method, with minor differences. Those differences are explained in the "Financial Reporting Outside the United States" section of this reading.

Deferred Tax Liabilities

SFAS 109 emphasizes tax liabilities, focusing on the balance sheet. *The standard mandates the recognition of deferred tax liabilities for all temporary differences expected to generate net taxable amounts in future years.*

The FASB argued that deferred tax consequences of temporary differences that will result in net taxable amounts in future years meet the SFAC 6 definition of liabilities.[4] The board contended that deferred taxes are legal obligations imposed by tax laws and temporary differences will affect taxable income in future years as they reverse.

Treatment of Operating Losses

Operating losses are due to an excess of tax deductions over taxable revenues. Tax losses can be carried back to prior years to obtain refunds of taxes paid; the impact of the carryback on income tax expense is recognized in the loss period because it can be measured and is recoverable.

Tax losses may also be carried forward to future periods if insufficient taxes were paid during the carryback period or the firm would lose valuable tax credits if losses were carried back to that period. Because the realization of *tax loss carryforwards* depends on future taxable income, the expected benefits are recognized as deferred tax assets. Under SFAS 109, such assets are recognized in full but a *valuation allowance* may be required if recoverability is unlikely.

Deferred Tax Assets and the Valuation Allowance

SFAS 109 is permissive regarding the recognition of deferred tax assets whenever deductible temporary differences generate an operating loss or tax credit carryforward. However, management (and its auditors) must defend recognition of

[3] This concept extends beyond chronological (timing) differences (e.g., earlier recognition of revenues and expenses on either the financial statements or tax returns), and also includes certain other events that result in differences between the tax bases of assets and liabilities and their carrying amounts in financial statements. Such differences arise when:

1. The tax basis of an asset is reduced by tax credits.
2. Investment tax credits are deferred and amortized.
3. The tax basis of a foreign subsidiary's assets is increased as a result of indexing.
4. The carrying amounts and tax bases of assets differ in purchase method acquisitions.

[4] A common temporary difference is a firm's use of longer depreciation lives for financial reporting than for tax return reporting, creating a difference between the carrying amount of the asset and its tax basis. Use of the asset in operations results in taxable income in the year(s) no depreciation can be recorded on the tax return. The board acknowledged that other events may offset the net taxable amounts that would be generated when temporary differences reverse, but because those events have not yet occurred, and they are not assumed in the financial statements, their tax consequences should not be recognized. See SFAS 109 (paras. 75–79) for more discussion of this issue.

all deferred tax assets. A valuation allowance reducing the deferred tax asset is required if an analysis of the sources of future taxable income suggests that it is more likely than not that some portion or all of the deferred tax asset will not be realized.[5]

EXAMPLE 1

Bethlehem Steel [BS] reported a net deferred tax asset at December 31, 2000 of about $985 million ($1,325 million less a valuation allowance of $340 million). This asset equaled 88% of stockholders' equity on that date. The company provided a valuation allowance equal to 50% of the deferred tax asset related to operating loss carryforwards and some temporary differences. BS stated,

> Based on our current outlook for 2001 and beyond, we believe that our net deferred tax asset will be realized by future operating results, asset sales, and tax planning opportunities.[6]

In the quarter ended June 30, 2001, however, BS recognized a 100% valuation allowance for its deferred tax assets, increasing income tax expense and net loss for the quarter by $1,009 million ($7.77 per diluted share) and for the first half of 2001 by $984 million ($7.58 per diluted share). Mainly due to the increased valuation allowance, Bethlehem's equity at June 30, 2001 became negative. The company stated that it now expected a financial accounting and tax loss in 2001 and that the outlook for the balance of 2001 was worse than earlier anticipated. Given its record of cumulative financial accounting losses, excluding unusual items, SFAS 109 required the increased valuation allowance. This is an excellent example of how management discretion with respect to the amount and timing of recognition of the valuation allowance affords management significant opportunity to manage earnings.

Tax-planning strategies can be used to reduce required valuation allowances, but they must be disclosed. SFAS 109 provides examples of positive and negative evidence that must be weighed to determine the need for a valuation allowance and to measure the amount of the allowance.[7] *Changes in the valuation allowance are included in income from continuing operations except when they are generated by unrecognized changes in the carrying amount of assets or liabilities.*[8]

Bethlehem reported that it expected to realize the deferred tax assets from future operating results and tax planning opportunities. The

[5] Sources of future taxable income include existing taxable temporary differences, future taxable income net of reversing temporary differences, taxable income recognized during qualifying carryback periods, and applicable tax-planning strategies.

[6] Note D to 2000 financial statements.

[7] Existing contracts or backlogs expected to be profitable, appreciated assets, earnings over the past few years, and the nature (nonrecurring) of the loss would suggest that a valuation allowance is not needed. Examples of negative evidence include cumulative losses in recent years and the past inability to use loss or tax credit carryforwards.

[8] The most common example is the deferred tax assets that arise when the market value of "available-for-sale" securities is less than cost; the unrealized loss is included in equity, under SFAS 115, net of the related deferred income tax assets.

company included choices of depreciation methods and lives, sales of assets, and the timing of contributions to the pension trust fund as examples of tax-planning opportunities.

When there are significant deferred tax assets, the analyst should review the company's financial performance and its accounting choices to assess the likelihood of realization of those assets.

Financial Statement Presentation and Disclosure Requirements

Large multinational companies operate in dozens of tax jurisdictions and their financial reports must summarize their tax position for all consolidated entities. Such firms often generate deferred tax assets and liabilities in different tax jurisdictions. *SFAS 109 permits offsets of deferred tax effects only within each tax-paying component and tax jurisdiction of the firm.*

EXAMPLE 2

Texaco reported (Note 8) a valuation allowance of $800 million at December 31, 1999, mostly related to foreign tax loss carryforwards and related book versus tax asset differences stemming from operations in Denmark. The company notes that the valuation allowance was required because these loss carryforwards are based on individual (oil and gas) fields and cannot be netted against taxable income from other fields.

Deferred tax assets and liabilities must be separated into current and noncurrent components based on the types of the assets and liabilities generating the deferral. However, deferred tax assets due to carryforwards are classified by reference to expected reversal dates. SFAS 109 specifically requires:

1. Separate disclosure of all deferred tax assets and liabilities, any valuation allowance, and the net change in that allowance for each reporting period.
2. Disclosure of any unrecognized deferred tax liability for the undistributed earnings of domestic or foreign subsidiaries and joint ventures. These disclosures should facilitate the comparison of the operating results of firms that have different policies with respect to deferred tax recognition or the remission of income from such affiliates.
3. Disclosure of the current-year tax effect of each type of temporary difference.
4. Disclosure of the components of income tax expense.
5. Reconciliation of reported income tax expense with the amount based on the statutory income tax rate (the reconciliation can use either amounts or percentages of pre-tax income).
6. Disclosure of tax loss carryforwards and credits.

These six requirements determine income tax disclosures in financial statements, the raw material for the analysis provided later in this reading.

4 DEFERRED TAXES: ANALYTICAL ISSUES

Estimates of the firm's future cash flows and earning power and the analysis of financial leverage must consider changes in deferred tax assets and liabilities, deferred tax expense, and any changes in the valuation allowance. *The key analytic issue is whether the deferred tax assets and liabilities will reverse in the future. If they will not, then it is highly debatable whether deferred taxes are assets or liabilities (that is, have cash flow consequences); it may be more appropriate to consider them as decreases or increases to equity.*

To resolve that issue, we need to understand the factors that determine the level of and trends in reported deferred taxes, to decide whether they are assets (or liabilities) and to evaluate their expected cash consequences.

Factors Influencing the Level and Trend of Deferred Taxes

In general, temporary differences originated by individual transactions will reverse and offset future taxable income and tax payments. However, *these reversals may be offset by other transactions, for example, newly originating temporary differences.* The cash consequences of deferred tax debits and credits depend on the following factors:

- future tax rates and tax laws
- changes in accounting methods
- the firm's growth rate (real or nominal)
- nonrecurring items and equity adjustments

We discuss these factors next.

Effects of Changes in Tax Laws and Accounting Methods

Management incentives for choosing revenue and expense recognition methods on the tax return and financial statements differ, as mentioned previously. Choices (and subsequent changes) of tax and/or accounting methods determine taxes payable, income tax expense, and both the amounts and rate of change of reported deferred tax balances.

Under the liability method,[9] when a new tax law is enacted its effects must be recognized immediately. Thus, lower tax rates will reduce deferred tax liabilities and assets, and the adjustment is included in current-period income tax expense. Assuming a net deferred tax liability, equity will increase. The larger the net deferred tax liability, the greater the impact of the tax cut, as previous-year deferrals are adjusted to the lower rate. For analytical purposes, one need not wait for the actual tax change to be enacted; estimates can be made when legislation is proposed.

Changes in GAAP can also significantly impact deferred taxes. For example, in 1992, many companies adopted SFAS 106, Accounting for Postretirement Benefits Other Than Pensions. That standard required accrual accounting for postretirement costs (mainly medical benefits for current employees after retire-

[9] See the illustration in Exhibit B3 of Box 2.

ment) rather than cash-basis accounting. As cash-basis accounting was used for income tax purposes, there was no temporary difference associated with these benefits prior to the adoption of SFAS 106.

EXAMPLE 3

Upon adoption of SFAS 106 in 1992, DuPont recognized a postretirement benefit liability of $5.9 billion and deferred tax asset of $2.1 billion. Was this $2.1 billion an asset? Would it reduce future taxes? The answers depend on the $5.9 billion liability associated with it. Eight years later, at December 31, 2000, DuPont's postretirement benefit liability was $5.76 billion. Benefits paid exceeded cost recognized in both 1999 and 2000, reducing the liability. Assuming this trend continues, DuPont will realize the deferred tax asset, but over a very long time period. A fair-value balance sheet should recognize the discounted present value of the deferred tax asset rather than its gross amount.

Thus, *realization of a deferred tax asset or liability depends on the realization of the temporary difference that created it.*

Effect of the Growth Rate of the Firm

For most firms, the deferred tax liability grows over time; temporary differences do not reverse on balance.[10] For growing firms, increased or higher-cost investments in fixed assets result in ever-increasing deferred tax liabilities due to the use of accelerated depreciation methods for tax reporting.

Exhibit 1 illustrates this effect by focusing on the deferred tax consequences of depreciation differences. Assume that a firm purchases one machine each year for $6,000 and uses the straight-line depreciation method over two years on its tax return and over three years in its financial statements. If we assume a 40% tax rate and zero residual value on both the tax return and the financial statements, the depreciation differences will produce a deferred tax expense (a deferred tax liability) of $400 in each year during the first two years of each machine's operation, with a reversal of $800 in its third year to eliminate the deferred tax liability generated over the first two years.

The acquisition of a second machine in year 2 generates another difference of $400; the deferred tax liability increases to $1,200 at the end of year 2. In year 3, the firm acquires and uses the third machine, originating its first-year temporary difference, and the asset acquired in year 2 originates its second-year difference. However, these originating differences are offset by the reversal of the

[10] This statement may not apply to deferred tax assets. Deferred tax assets (more precisely, prepaid taxes) stem from both recurring transactions (such as deferred revenues, warranty expenses, management compensation, employee benefits, and bad-debt reserves), and from more irregular events (such as restructuring costs, impairments, environmental remediation obligations, and provisions for litigation losses) that are accrued on the financial statements prior to their deduction on the tax return.

Management often has substantial discretion over the amount and timing of the origination of these debit balances as it controls the recognition of these expenses. However, the amount and timing of their reversal may not be as discretionary or predictable as the temporary differences (such as depreciation differences) that generate deferred tax liabilities.

EXHIBIT 1 Impact of Growth on Deferred Tax Liability

Assumptions

A firm purchases one machine during each year of operation. All other assumptions are identical to those used in Exhibit B1. Most important, temporary differences are originated and reversed as in Exhibit B1 and at the same tax rate, which is assumed to remain constant over time.

Deferred Tax Liability

Year 1	$ 400	Machine 1 (origination)
Year 2	400	Beginning balance
	400	Machine 1 (origination)
	400	Machine 2 (origination)
Year 3	$1,200	Beginning balance
	(800)	Machine 1 (reversal)
	400	Machine 2 (origination)
	400	Machine 3 (origination)
Year 4	$1,200	Beginning balance
	(800)	Machine 2 (reversal)
	400	Machine 3 (origination)
	400	Machine 4 (origination)
Year 5	$1,200	Beginning balance

Note: The balance stabilizes at $1,200 in this example at the end of year 3, with the originations exactly offset by the reversals. This result assumes constant levels of asset acquisitions, price levels, tax rates, and regulations. Increases in either price levels or acquisitions would result in rising balances of deferred tax liabilities.

accumulated temporary differences on the machine acquired in year 1 as it is depreciated in the financial statements, but no depreciation remains to be recorded for the asset on the tax return.

The deferred tax liability remains $1,200 and *stabilizes at that level* if asset acquisitions, depreciation methods, and tax rates and tax laws remain unchanged. Increased asset purchases above present levels (either in physical quantity or due to higher prices) would result in a growing deferred tax liability as originations exceeded reversals. Thus, as a result of growth, either in real or nominal terms, the net deferred tax liability will increase over time; *in effect, it will never be paid.*

If the firm reduces its acquisition of fixed assets and reversals exceed originations, the related deferred tax liability will decline. The cash consequences of this scenario, however, are uncertain. If the decrease in asset acquisitions results from declining product demand, then lower asset acquisitions may be accompanied by poor profitability. Without taxable income, the deferred taxes will never be paid. Alternatively, the firm may originate other temporary differences that offset depreciation reversals; in the aggregate, deferred tax liabilities may not decline.

The cash consequences of reversing temporary differences, therefore, depend on both future profitability and other activities of the firm that affect future taxable income.

Effects of Nonrecurring Items and Equity Adjustments

The following may also affect income tax expense, taxes paid, and deferred tax assets and liabilities:

- nonrecurring items
- extraordinary items
- accounting changes
- equity adjustments

Nonrecurring items (such as restructuring charges) may have future as well as current-period tax consequences, and complicate the analysis of the firm's tax position. Texaco, for example, reported restructuring changes in 1999, as detailed throughout its MD&A. These charges generated deferred tax assets.

Extraordinary items, such as a loss from the early retirement of debt, are reported after tax; the tax effect is often shown separately in the tax footnote. Transition effects of accounting changes often generate deferred tax effects, especially when the new method is not a permitted method of tax reporting. The large deferred tax asset resulting from the adoption of SFAS 106 (as discussed using DuPont) is a typical example.

Finally, equity adjustments that bypass the income statement may have current and deferred tax consequences. Common examples include:

- unrealized gains or losses on marketable securities
- currency translation adjustments

The items discussed previously may obscure the cash and deferred tax effects of continuing operations. Although firms generally disclose their associated tax effect, discerning their cash and deferred tax impact may require careful reading of the tax footnote supplemented by discussions with management.

Liability or Equity?

How should analysts treat deferred tax liabilities in the analysis of a firm's solvency?

As indicated previously, changes in a firm's operations or tax laws may result in deferred taxes that are never paid (or recovered). Moreover, a firm's growth may continually generate deferred tax liabilities. Even if temporary differences do reverse, future losses may forestall tax payments. These factors suggest that, in many cases, deferred taxes are unlikely to be paid.

Even if deferred taxes are eventually paid, the present value of those payments is considerably lower than the stated amounts. Thus, the deferred tax liability should be discounted at an appropriate interest rate.[11]

These arguments suggest that the components of the deferred tax liability should be analyzed to evaluate the likelihood of reversal or continued growth. Only those components that are likely to reverse should be considered a liability.[12] In addition, the liability should be discounted to its present value based on

[11] Discounting of deferred taxes is not allowed under either U.S. or IAS GAAP and is rare elsewhere. It is currently allowed in the Netherlands; however, few firms discount. The UK accounting standard FRS 19, Deferred Tax, permits but does not require discounting of deferred tax liabilities (only for the time value of money) that are not expected to settle for some time.

[12] Prior to the issuance of FRS 19, Deferred Tax, the United Kingdom allowed partial allocation and deferred taxes were recognized only when reversal was expected within the foreseeable future.

an estimate of the year(s) of reversal. If the temporary differences giving rise to deferred tax liabilities are not expected to reverse, those amounts should not be considered liabilities.

SFAS 109 requires disclosure of the components of the deferred tax liability at each year-end. These components should be examined over time to see which tend to reverse and which do not. For example, the effect of using accelerated depreciation methods for tax reporting tends not to reverse.[13] If reversal is expected, as capital expenditures decline, the liability should be discounted to present value. Similar analysis can be applied to other major differences, keeping in mind any expected tax law changes.

To the extent that deferred taxes are not a liability, then they are stockholders' equity. Had they not been recorded, prior-period tax expense would have been lower and both net income and equity higher. This adjustment reduces the debt-to-equity ratio, in some cases considerably.[14]

In some cases, however, deferred taxes are neither liability nor equity. For example, if tax depreciation is a better measure of economic depreciation than financial statement depreciation, adding the deferred tax liability to equity overstates the value of the firm. However, if the deferred tax liability is unlikely to result in a cash outflow, it is not a liability either. Ultimately, the financial analyst must decide on the appropriate treatment of deferred taxes on a case-by-case basis.

In practice, the analytical treatment of deferred tax liabilities varies. Some creditors, notably banks, do not consider them to be liabilities (but neither do they include them as part of equity). In calculating solvency and other ratios, many analysts ignore deferred taxes altogether.

Standard and Poor's, a major U.S. rating agency, includes noncurrent deferred taxes in permanent capital for its computation of pretax return on permanent capital. However, it does not consider deferred tax liabilities as debt.[15]

Box 3 discusses evidence provided by market research regarding the relevance of deferred taxes to securities valuation. The evidence indicates that the market incorporates the growth rate of an entity, the probability of reversal of deferred taxes, and the time value of money in its assessment of deferred taxes as liability or equity.

Analysis of Deferred Tax Assets and the Valuation Allowance

Deferred tax assets may be indicators of future cash flow, reported income, or both. Therefore, as with liabilities, one should examine the source of those assets and evaluate the likelihood and timing of reversal. Any valuation allowance should also be reviewed. To the extent that deferred tax assets have been offset by a valuation

[13] However, the recognition of fixed asset impairment (see the discussion in Reading 37) may instantaneously offset many years of accelerated depreciation. Such writedowns do not affect tax reporting unless the affected assets are sold. As a result, previously established deferred tax liabilities relating to these assets reverse. If the carrying value of the impaired assets is reduced below their tax basis, deferred tax assets must be established. But this reversal has no effect on taxable income or, therefore, taxes payable. This is another case where the reversal of temporary differences may not generate income tax cash outflows.

[14] Some creditors treat deferred tax liabilities as debt. In this case, there is a double effect; debt is decreased and equity increased by the same amount, with an even greater decrease in the debt-to-equity ratio.

[15] See Standard and Poor's "Formulas for Key Ratios," *Corporate Ratings Criteria* (New York: McGraw-Hill, 2000), p. 55.

BOX 3 VALUATION OF DEFERRED TAXES

Surprisingly, not many empirical studies have examined whether the market as a whole treats deferred taxes as debt. However, the results of those few studies that examined this issue are consistent with our view that the extent to which deferred tax liabilities should be treated as debt is a function of the probability that the deferrals will be reversed and the debt (if considered) should be discounted to its present value.

Amir, Kirschenheiter, and Willard (1997) found that, overall, deferred taxes are value relevant in explaining the cross-sectional variation in market values of equity. However, the degree of value relevance was related to the probability of future reversal. For example, the valuation coefficient on deferred tax liabilities arising from depreciation was close to zero, reflecting investors' expectations that firms would continue to invest in depreciable assets, increasing the likelihood that tax deferrals would not reverse in the future. On the other hand, deferred tax components related to restructurings had the highest valuation coefficients, consistent with an expectation that they would reverse in the short run (as written-down plants are sold at a loss and/or severance payments are made to employees).

Givoly and Hayn (1992) examined these issues in the context of the Tax Reform Act (TRA) of 1986. The TRA cut the statutory tax rate for U.S. corporations from 46% to 34%. This rate reduction reduced both the current tax obligation and the amount that would have to be repaid if and when future reversals of temporary differences occurred.

The TRA was debated for over two years in Congress. Givoly and Hayn examined the effects on stock prices of events that increased (decreased) the chance of the measure passing. After controlling for the effects on current tax payments, they argued that if the market treated the deferred tax liability as debt, then:

1. The larger the deferred tax liability, the more positive the impact of the TRA on the firm's market price.
2. If temporary differences will not be reversed, or future tax losses will result in nonpayment of the tax at reversal, the effects of the TRA should be minimal regardless of the liability amount. Thus, they argued that the larger the growth rate in the deferred tax account and the greater the probability of tax losses; the less likely there would be a positive impact on stock prices.

If the market ignored the deferred tax liability, none of these factors would have any impact. Overall, their results confirmed that the market incorporated the deferred tax liability into valuation.

When chances of the TRA adoption increased (decreased), then:

1. The larger the deferred tax liability, the more positive (negative) the market reaction.
2. A high liability growth rate and increased probability of losses decreased (increased) the abnormal return.

Givoly and Hayn also found that the market incorporated a discount factor in valuing the deferred tax liability. The deferred tax accounts of high-risk[a] firms tended to affect market valuation less than low-risk firms. This result is consistent with a higher discount rate being applied to the higher-risk firms.

[a] Based on the firm's market beta.

(continued)

BOX 3 (continued)

Sansing (1998), and Guenther and Sansing (2000), however, using a theoretical model, demonstrate analytically that deferred taxes should have value-relevance[b] *irrespective of the probability of eventual reversal*. However, the valuation coefficient on deferred taxes (which in their model is a function of the tax depreciation rate and the (market) rate of interest) is *considerably less than one*. Thus, they argue that the findings of Amir et al. and Givoly and Hayn should not be interpreted as reflecting the effects of the expected timing of the reversal of deferred taxes.

The above studies took a balance sheet perspective and found that deferred taxes are incorporated in valuation. Beaver and Dukes (1972), with an income statement perspective, had also found that market prices reflect the deferral method. They found that market reaction was more closely associated with income that incorporated deferred income taxes than with current tax expense.[c] Rayburn (1986), however, found that the association between deferred tax accruals and security returns was dependent on the expectations model assumed.

---

[b] Their reasoning is that, according to their model, the market (resale) value of the asset includes the tax basis of the asset. Deferred taxes reflect this factor, although not on a dollar-for-dollar basis.

[c] The authors found this result surprising as they expected the measure closer to cash flow (earnings without deferral) to be more closely associated with security prices. In a subsequent paper (Beaver and Dukes, 1973) the authors offered a different explanation. They demonstrated (see the discussion in Reading 37) that the market generally imputes accelerated depreciation rather than straight-line depreciation. As deferred taxes increase total expense for firms using straight-line depreciation, they argued that the observed results may be due to deferred taxes masking as a form of accelerated depreciation.

allowance, realization of those assets will increase reported income (and stockholders' equity) as well as generate cash flow. If no valuation allowance has been provided, then realization will have no effect on reported income or equity, although cash flow will still benefit.

Conversely, when deferred tax assets are no longer realizable, if no valuation allowance had been provided, then the establishment of such an allowance reduces reported income and equity (see the discussion of Bethlehem Steel in Example 1).

Given management discretion, the valuation allowance has become another factor used to evaluate the quality of earnings. Some firms are conservative, offsetting most or all deferred tax assets with valuation allowances. Other firms are more optimistic and assume that no valuation allowance is necessary.

The important point is that changes in the valuation allowance often affect reported earnings and can be used to manage them.

EXAMPLE 4

Apple Computer had recorded a significant valuation allowance against its deferred tax assets due to losses in the mid-1990s. With its return to profitability, it realized its loss carryforwards, reducing both deferred tax assets and the valuation allowance. The result was to lower the effective tax rate, as seen on the following page:

Apple Computer	**Years Ended September 30**			**Percent Change**	
Amounts in $millions	**1998**	**1999**	**2000**	**1999**	**2000**
As reported:					
Pretax income	$329	$ 676	$1,092	105%	62%
Income tax expense	(20)	(75)	(306)		
Net income	$309	$ 601	$ 786	94%	31%
Tax rate	6.1%	11.1%	28.0%		
Change in valuation allowance	$(97)	$(153)	$ (27)		
Excluding valuation allowance:					
Pretax income	$329	$ 676	$1,092	105%	62%
Income tax expense	(117)	(228)	(333)		
Net income	$212	$ 448	$ 759	111%	69%
Tax rate	35.6%	33.7%	30.5%		

Apple's pretax income increased by 105% in 1999 and 62% in 2000. The growth rate of net income was lower due to the diminishing effect of the valuation allowance. However, net income was inflated by the valuation allowance reductions. To eliminate these distortions, analysis should be based on net income excluding changes in the valuation allowance.

Effective Tax Rates

Valuation models that forecast future income or cash flows use the firm's effective tax rate as one input. Moreover, trends in effective tax rates over time for a firm and the relative effective tax rates for comparable firms within an industry can help assess operating performance and the income available for stockholders. Several alternative measures can be used to assess the firm's effective tax rate. The *reported* effective tax rate is measured as:

$$\frac{\text{Income tax expense}}{\text{Pretax income}}$$

However, both reported tax expense and pretax income are affected by management choices of revenue and expense recognition methods. Although pretax income is a key indicator of financial performance and is an appropriate denominator, other numerators generate tax rates that provide additional information.[16]

[16] Some empirical evidence (see Zimmerman, 1983) indicates that effective tax rates calculated using income tax paid and/or current tax expense tend to be higher for large firms. This is cited as evidence of the political cost hypothesis as large firms, being more politically sensitive, are required to make (relatively) larger wealth transfers than smaller firms. As the research results are largely due to the oil and gas industry, it is difficult to tell whether political costs result from size or industrial classification. Wang (1991) notes that because smaller firms are more likely to have operating losses than larger firms, their effective tax rate is more likely to be zero. Ignoring these losses may bias Zimmerman's research results.

The first alternative tax rate uses taxes payable (current tax expense) for the period, based on the revenue and the expense recognition methods used on the tax return:

$$\frac{\text{Taxes payable}}{\text{Pretax income}}$$

This ratio may also be used with cash taxes paid instead of taxes payable. The resulting ratio focuses more on cash flows:

$$\frac{\text{Income tax paid}}{\text{Pretax income}}$$

The amount of cash taxes paid can be easily obtained as both SFAS 95 (Statement of Cash Flows) and IAS 7 (Cash Flow Statements) require separate disclosure of this amount. Due to interim tax payments and refunds, cash taxes paid may be quite different from taxes payable.

Exhibit 2 calculates these differing measures of the effective tax rate for Pfizer.

Pfizer's reported effective tax rate (income tax expense/pretax income) rose from 27.0% in 1997 to 28% in 1999; the three-year average rate is 26.9%. All these rates are below the U.S. statutory rate for the period.[17]

Two questions are suggested by these data:

1. Why is Pfizer's effective tax rate below the statutory rate?
2. What is Pfizer's effective tax rate likely to be in the future?

We seek answers to these questions shortly.

EXHIBIT 2 Pfizer

Effective Tax Rates

	1997	1998	1999	Total
Taxes payable	$ 815	$ 918	$1,265	$2,998
Deferred tax expense	(40)	(276)	(21)	(337)
Income tax expense	$ 775	$ 642	$1,244	$2,661
Income taxes paid	809	1,073	1,293	3,175
Pretax income	2,867	2,594	4,448	9,909
Statutory tax rate	35.0%	35.0%	35.0%	35.0%
Income tax expense/pretax income	27.0%	24.7%	28.0%	26.9%
Taxes payable/pretax income	28.4%	35.4%	28.4%	30.3%
Taxes paid/pretax income	28.2%	41.4%	29.1%	32.0%

Source: Data from Pfizer annual reports.

[17] The average statutory rate for a multiyear period should be a weighted average, with pretax income providing the weights.

The second effective tax rate (taxes payable/pretax income) calculated in Exhibit 2 was 35.4% in 1998 and 28.4% in both 1997 and 1999. The average rate is 30.3% over the three-year period, above the first effective rate and below the statutory rate. Again, we will try to understand the factors causing these differences and the likelihood that they will persist in the future.

The third measure of the effective tax rate, which compares income tax paid with pretax income, is also variable over the three-year period. The average rate of 32.0% is close to the average rate for taxes payable. This congruence should be expected as the timing of taxes paid is affected by technical payment requirements and by errors in management's forecast of tax liability in each jurisdiction. Over time, these factors should cancel out.

We return to the analysis of Pfizer's income tax position shortly. To provide additional background for that analysis, we must first discuss the effect of temporary versus permanent differences on effective tax rates and other specialized issues that highlight differences between tax and financial reporting.

ACCOUNTING FOR TAXES: SPECIALIZED ISSUES 5

Temporary versus Permanent Differences

The different objectives of financial and tax reporting generate temporary differences between pretax financial income and taxable income. In addition, *permanent differences* result from revenues and expenses that are reportable either on tax returns or in financial statements but not both. In the United States, for example, interest income on tax-exempt bonds, premiums paid on officers' life insurance, and amortization of goodwill (in some cases) are included in financial statements but are never reported on the tax return. Similarly, certain dividends are not fully taxed, and tax or statutory depletion may exceed cost-based depletion reported in the financial statements.

Tax credits are another type of permanent difference. Such credits directly reduce taxes payable and are different from tax deductions that reduce taxable income. The Puerto Rico operations credit reported by Pfizer is one example. It partially exempts Pfizer from income, property, and municipal taxes.

No deferred tax consequences are recognized for permanent differences; however, they result in a difference between the effective tax rate and the statutory tax rate that should be considered in the analysis of effective tax rates.

Indefinite Reversals

The amount and timing of the reversal of some temporary differences are subject to management influence or control. Some differences may never reverse. The accounting for these differences is especially troublesome. The uncertainty as to the amount and timing of their cash consequences affects the estimation of cash flows and firm valuation.

The undistributed earnings of unconsolidated subsidiaries and joint ventures are the most common example of this problem. The U.S. tax code requires 80% ownership to consolidate for tax purposes, excluding joint ventures and many subsidiaries that are consolidated for accounting purposes. In addition, foreign subsidiaries are not consolidated in the U.S. tax return.[18]

[18] In some cases, even wholly owned U.S. subsidiaries may not be consolidated for tax purposes. Insurance subsidiaries, which are governed by special tax regulations, are one example.

As a result, the income of these affiliates is taxable on the parent's (U.S.) tax return only when dividends are received or the affiliate is sold, not when earnings are recognized. There is a difference between (tax return) taxable income and (financial reporting) pretax income. If the affiliate earnings are permanently reinvested, then affiliate earnings may never be taxable on the parent company's tax return.

SFAS 109 requires the recognition of deferred tax liabilities for temporary differences due to the undistributed earnings of essentially permanent domestic subsidiaries and joint ventures for fiscal years beginning on or after December 15, 1992.[19] SFAS 109 does not, however, require deferred tax provisions in the following cases:

- Undistributed earnings of a foreign subsidiary or joint venture that are considered to be permanently reinvested.
- Undistributed earnings of a domestic subsidiary or joint venture for fiscal years prior to December 15, 1992.

In its income tax note (Note 9), Pfizer reports that the firm has not recorded a U.S. tax provision of $1.9 billion on $8.2 billion of undistributed earnings of foreign affiliates at December 31, 1999. If the indefinite reversal assumption had not been applicable, the firm would have reported $1.9 billion of additional deferred tax liabilities, reducing equity by 21%. Earnings would also have been reduced in the years during which those provisions were not made.

Accounting for Acquisitions

SFAS 109 requires separate recognition of the deferred tax effects of any differences between the financial statement carrying amounts and tax bases of assets and liabilities recognized in purchase method acquisitions.

In some cases, a valuation allowance must be recorded for deferred tax assets due to the acquired firm's temporary differences or its operating loss or tax credit carryforwards. The tax benefits of subsequent reversals of the valuation allowance must be used, first, to reduce all related goodwill, second, to eliminate all other related noncurrent intangible assets, and third, to reduce reported income tax expense.

6 ANALYSIS OF INCOME TAX DISCLOSURES: PFIZER

Accounting for income taxes is complex; a large company may have many permanent and temporary differences between financial statement income and taxable income. A large multinational pays taxes in a number of jurisdictions, further complicating the process. From an analyst's perspective, unraveling these layers can seem daunting indeed.

Some analysts respond to this complexity by ignoring the issues. They analyze corporate performance on a pretax basis and simply accept that variations in the reported tax rate occur. We agree that analysis on a pretax basis is sound, but also believe that a firm's income tax accounting is too important to ignore.

---

[19] But if the parent has the statutory ability to realize those earnings tax free, no deferred tax provision is required (para. 33, SFAS 109).

The goals of income tax analysis are to:

1. Understand why the firm's effective tax rate differs (or does not differ) from the statutory rate in its home country.
2. Forecast changes in the effective tax rate, improving forecasts of earnings.
3. Review the historical differences between income tax expense and income taxes paid.
4. Forecast the future relationship between income tax expense and income tax payments.
5. Examine deferred tax liabilities and assets, including any valuation allowance, for:
   - possible effects on future earnings and cash flows
   - their relevance to firm valuation
   - their relevance in assessing a firm's capital structure

We pursue these five goals, using Pfizer as an example, and illustrate the insights regarding a firm that can be derived from its income tax disclosures.

Analysis of the Effective Tax Rate

The first step is an examination of the firm's tax rate, the trend in that rate, and the rate relative to similar companies. Variations are generally the consequence of:

- Different statutory tax rates in different jurisdictions; analysis can offer important clues as to the sources of income.
- Tax holidays that some countries offer; earnings from such operations usually cannot be remitted without payment of tax. Be alert to possible changes in the operations in such countries or the need to remit the accumulated earnings.
- Permanent differences between financial and taxable income: tax-exempt income, tax credits, and nondeductible expenses.
- The effect of tax rate and other tax law changes which, under SFAS 109, are included in income tax expense (a separate disclosure of this effect is required).
- Deferred taxes provided on the reinvested earnings of foreign affiliates and unconsolidated domestic affiliates.

As noted earlier, Pfizer's effective tax rate averaged 26.9% over the 1997 to 1999 period. Pfizer's tax footnote provides the required reconciliation between its statutory rate and effective rate for each year.[20] Because of the significance of some of these differences and variation in pretax income over the period, the rate-based disclosures are difficult to analyze. For that reason, Exhibit 3 converts them to dollar-based disclosures.

Starting with the three-year totals, the lower tax rate on non-U.S. earnings is the largest single factor in Pfizer's low effective tax rate, deducting nearly $500 million or 5 percentage points over the three-year period. Pfizer's international

[20] The reconciliation can be done in either percentages (relative to the statutory tax rate) or monetary amounts (relative to "statutory" income tax expense equal to pretax income multiplied by the statutory rate).

EXHIBIT 3 Pfizer

Reconciliation of Effective and Statutory Tax Rates

				1997 to 1999	
	1997	**1998**	**1999**	**Total**	**Rate**
Pretax income	$2,867	$2,594	$4,448	$9,909	
Statutory rate	35.0%	35.0%	35.0%		35.0%
Variations from statutory rate (in percent)					
Partially tax-exempt operations in Puerto Rico	−1.8%	−2.2%	−1.5%		
International operations	−5.0%	−5.5%	−4.8%		
Other-net	−1.2%	−2.5%	−0.7%		
Net difference	−8.0%	−10.2%	−7.0%		
Effective tax rate (Income tax expense/pretax income)	27.0%	24.7%	28.0%		
Tax in millions of dollars = Rate × Pretax Income					
At statutory rate	$1,003.5	$ 907.9	$1,556.8	$3,468.1	
Effect of					
Partially tax-exempt operations in Puerto Rico	$ (51.6)	$ (57.1)	$ (66.7)	$ (175.4)	−1.8%
International operations	(143.4)	(142.7)	(213.5)	(499.5)	−5.0%
Other-net	(34.4)	(64.9)	(31.1)	(130.4)	−1.3%
Net effect	$ (229.4)	$(264.6)	$ (311.4)	$ (805.3)	−8.1%
Income tax expense	$ 774.1	$ 643.3	$1,245.4	$2,662.8	26.9%

Source: Adapted from Pfizer, Note 9, 1999 annual report.

operations accounted for 39% of revenues and 42.5% of income from continuing operations in 1999, as shown in Pfizer's segment data. Thus, Pfizer's low effective tax rate is largely a function of its non-U.S. operations. Forecasting future effective tax rates, therefore, requires explicit forecasts of the earnings of these operations.

Pfizer's effective tax rate also benefits from lower tax rates paid by partially tax-exempt operations in Puerto Rico. This factor reduced the composite three-year tax rate by nearly two percentage points, adding $175 million to net income. Pfizer provides additional data regarding these operations, permitting a determination of the remaining benefits. Unexplained "other" benefits averaging 1.5 percentage points per year (but with considerable variability) further reduce the effective tax rate. Discussion with management should result in a better understanding of the source and likelihood of continuation of these benefits.

The Belgian tax assessment[21] and the limited term of the Puerto Rican tax exemption suggest that significant contributors to Pfizer's lower effective tax rate may not be available in the future.

Now that we understand the reasons for Pfizer's low effective tax rate in the past, we turn to the future. A forecast of future income tax expense should start with estimated pretax income and apply the statutory rate of 35%. The analyst should then adjust for:

- effects of the lower tax rate on foreign income
- effects of the lower tax rate on U.S. possession operations
- "other" effects

These adjustments may require input from Pfizer management or trade publications. Some firms provide periodic forecasts of their tax rate because of the difficulty of making such forecasts externally.

Analysis of Deferred Income Tax Expense

We now examine the effects of temporary differences on income tax expense. Companies are required to provide details of these differences, although formats vary. Pfizer's disclosure is typical, showing a breakdown in dollars for each year.

Temporary differences are generally the result of the use of different accounting policies or estimates for tax purposes than for financial reporting differences. Some of these differences are systematic; others are transaction specific. Frequent examples include:

- *Depreciation.* Different methods and/or lives result in different measures of depreciation expense.
- *Impairment.* Financial reporting writedowns do not generate tax deductions unless assets are sold.
- *Restructuring costs.* Usually tax-deductible when paid rather than when accrued.
- *Inventories.* Companies using last-in, first-out (LIFO) accounting for tax purposes in the United States must also use LIFO for reporting purposes; but when other methods are used, differences may occur.
- *Postemployment benefits.* The accruals required by SFAS 87 (pensions), SFAS 106 (other retiree benefits), and SFAS 112 (other post-employment benefits) are discussed elsewhere. Tax treatment of these costs is generally cash based, generating deferred tax effects.
- *Deferred compensation.* Tax-deductible only when payments are made.

On a cumulative basis, Pfizer generated negative deferred tax expense (taxes payable $>$ income tax expense) over the 1997 to 1999 period.[22] Depreciation generated positive deferred tax expense over this period, reflected in a rising level of deferred tax liabilities for property, plant, and equipment (PP&E). Pfizer used accelerated depreciation methods for most property on its tax return and the straight-line method on its financial statements.

[21] However, Pfizer may have benefited from the allocation and transfers of property to selected foreign operations. In 1994, Belgian tax authorities assessed additional taxes ($432 million) and interest ($97 million), claiming jurisdiction on certain income related to property transferred from non-Belgian subsidiaries to Pfizer's operations in Ireland.

[22] See Note 9 in Pfizer's financial statements and data in Exhibit 2.

Pfizer also reports deferred tax debits from PP&E, likely due to its asset impairments in both 1997 and 1998. Pfizer reports that, in 1999, it had substantially completed the restructuring announced in 1998; the deferred tax debits due to restructuring and PP&E declined in 1999 after increasing in 1998. *When a restructuring charge is taken, the tax effects generally occur as expenditures are made, with significant effects on deferred tax expense both in the year of the charge and the year(s) of payment.*

Pfizer's Note 9 also shows numerous other sources of deferred tax assets and liabilities, some of them poorly explained. Significant year-to-changes in deferred tax balances reflect differences between the tax and financial reporting treatment of transactions, and should be examined for their implications for cash flow and quality of earnings. The most significant deferred tax assets relate to inventories and employee benefits. There is a significant deferred tax liability for "unremitted earnings." These items are discussed in the next section as part of the analysis of deferred tax assets and liabilities.

Because Pfizer's deferred tax expense was negative over the 1997 to 1999 period, taxes payable (and income tax paid) exceeded income tax expense. Given increasing deferred tax debits for inventories, employee benefits, foreign tax credit, and other carryforwards, deferred tax expense may remain negative in the future.

Using Deferred Taxes to Estimate Taxable Income

Deferred tax expense reflects the difference between taxable income reported to tax authorities and pretax income reported to shareholders. This relationship can be used to estimate components of taxable income. The difference between taxable income and pretax income equals

$$\frac{\text{Deferred tax expense}}{\text{Statutory tax rate}}$$

For example, Pfizer's 1999 financial statement depreciation expense was $499 million (depreciation and amortization expense of $542 reported in the statement of cash flows less amortization of $43 million for goodwill and other intangibles in Note 8). The deferred tax liability related to depreciation was $514 million in 1999, an increase of $81 million over the amount reported in 1998 (Note 9). Using that amount and the statutory tax rate of 35%, we estimate that the additional depreciation expense under tax reporting was $231 million ($81 million divided by 0.35) and tax basis depreciation was $730 million ($499 + $231).

These calculations should be viewed as estimates. They are most reliable when they relate to a single tax jurisdiction as the appropriate tax rate and the difference between tax and financial reporting rules are clear. Although this method can, in theory, be used to calculate taxable income for the entire firm, such calculations for large multinationals are less reliable.

Similar calculations can be made for the cumulative financial reporting-tax differences using deferred tax asset and liability data. The calculation for Pfizer's fixed assets is shown in the next section of this reading.

Deferred tax disclosures can also be used, in some cases, to estimate the taxes paid associated with components of income and expense.

Analysis of Deferred Tax Assets and Liabilities

Our final step is an examination of the balance sheet consequences of Pfizer's income tax accounting. As required by SFAS 109, Note 9 contains a table of significant deferred tax assets and liabilities, as well as the valuation allowance, at each balance sheet date.

The most significant deferred tax asset relates to accrued employee benefits. Financial reporting rules for pension and postretirement benefits often result in large deferred tax assets. The second-largest deferred tax asset is associated with inventories, probably due to the 1999 Trovan write-off. Other contributors include prepaid/deferred items, restructuring charges, and various carryforwards. Pfizer reports a valuation allowance of $27 million at December 31, 1999 ($30 million at December 31, 1998). Note 9 says that tax credit carryforwards are the source of that allowance.

Pfizer's largest single source of deferred tax liabilities, as for most firms, is depreciation. If we assume a 35% tax rate for all depreciation-related deferred tax credits, the reporting difference can be estimated as $1.47 billion ($514/0.35) or 55% of accumulated depreciation of $2.7 billion. This is due to Pfizer's use of accelerated depreciation for tax purposes compared with straight-line for financial reporting.

Another source of large deferred tax credits is unremitted earnings of subsidiaries and joint venture affiliates that are included in financial statement income; the tax return only reflects dividends received.

Pfizer's net balance sheet debit (asset) for income tax is:

Deferred tax debits	$2,109
Less: Valuation allowance	(27)
Less: Deferred tax credits	(1,456)
Net debits	$ 626

Where do these debits and credits appear on Pfizer's balance sheet? The answer is: *in several places.* As required by SFAS 109, Note 9 discloses their location (in $millions):

Assets		Liabilities	
Prepaid expenses and taxes	$744		
Other assets, deferred taxes, and deferred charges	183	Deferred taxes on income	$301
Totals	$927		$301
		Net debit	$626

Is this $626 million a real asset? Or, to rephrase the question, What are the likely future cash flow effects of Pfizer's deferred tax assets and liabilities?

We begin with the largest deferred tax liability associated with accumulated depreciation. Capital expenditures have been rising (79% since 1997); unless there are decreases in capital spending, it seems unlikely that the deferred tax liability from depreciation will decline over the next few years. The trend in capital spending must, however, be monitored. Based on data available in the annual report, deferred tax credits due to unremitted earnings and other sources seem unlikely to reverse.

Pfizer's largest deferred tax asset, related to accrued employee benefits, might start to reverse at some point if employee levels stabilize or decrease. As retiree benefit payments increase, they may exceed the accrual for additional benefits earned (as in the case of DuPont, discussed earlier). The deferred tax debit from restructuring charges will reduce tax payments as severance payments are made and impaired PP&E is sold.

In total, therefore, it appears unlikely that Pfizer's deferred tax accruals will generate any significant cash flows over the next few years. In addition, given the unlikelihood of near-term reversal, the deferred tax credit should be discounted for the time value of money. The combination of these factors suggests that neither an asset nor a liability should be recognized for valuation purposes.

Other Issues in Income Tax Analysis

The following issues, although not relevant to an analysis of Pfizer, occur frequently enough to warrant brief mention:

- Watch for companies that report substantial income for financial reporting purposes but little or no taxes payable (implying little or no taxable income). Such differences often reflect aggressive revenue and expense recognition methods used for financial reporting, and low quality of earnings. In such cases, caution is indicated as the methods used for financial reporting purposes may be based on optimistic assumptions.[23]
- Look for current or pending reversals of past temporary differences. For example, a decline in capital spending may result in a greater proportion of depreciation coming from old assets that have already been heavily depreciated for tax purposes. Thus, financial reporting depreciation may exceed tax depreciation, generating a tax liability.
- Remember that deferred tax assets and liabilities may point to near-term cash consequences. Restructuring provisions often generate little cash or tax effect in the year they occur, but substantial effects in following years.
- Tax law changes may also result in the reversal of past temporary differences. In the United States, tax law changes in recent years have curtailed the use of the completed contract and installment methods for tax purposes, generating substantial tax liabilities for affected companies.

7

FINANCIAL REPORTING OUTSIDE THE UNITED STATES

As already noted, many foreign jurisdictions require conformity between financial reporting and tax reporting in separate (parent company) financial statements. In such cases, the issues discussed in this reading do not occur. That statement is no longer true, however, once consolidated statements include subsidiaries that are not consolidated for tax purposes. Given the worldwide tendency toward consolidated reporting, even firms in tax-conformity countries must grapple with the question of deferred tax accounting.

IASB Standards

IAS 12 (revised 2000) requires use of the liability method but *permits* companies to use "indefinite reversal" criteria to avoid recognizing deferred taxes on the reinvested earnings of subsidiaries, associates, and joint ventures, when both of the following conditions are met:

[23] Empirical evidence also suggests that firms cannot costlessly increase financial reporting income and at the same time keep taxable income very low. Mills (1998) shows that IRS audit adjustments increase as book—tax differences increase; that is, "The more book income (or tax expense) exceeds taxable income (or tax payable), the greater the proposed IRS audit adjustments."

1. The parent, investor, or venturer can control the manner and timing of the reversal of the temporary difference.
2. It is probable that the temporary difference will not reverse in the foreseeable future.

As a result, there are significant differences in the recognition of deferred tax liabilities among firms using IAS and U.S. GAAP; the latter group must record deferred taxes for the reinvested earnings of domestic affiliates. In addition, deferred taxes are based on enacted laws and rates whereas IAS 12 uses substantially enacted rates (tax rate changes that have been announced by the government but not yet enacted).

Other National Standards

Virtually all countries require the recognition of deferred taxes on temporary differences. Germany and the United Kingdom use the liability method, whereas France and Japan allow either the deferral (see footnote 2) or liability method. Most countries limit the recognition of deferred tax liabilities and few address the issue of deferred tax assets. In Switzerland, deferred taxes not expected to reverse need not be recognized and the recognition of certain deferred tax assets is discretionary.

German GAAP permits the recognition of deferred tax assets for the elimination of intercompany profits. In general, deferred taxes are computed under the liability method, but the amounts recognized are limited to the excess of consolidated deferred tax liabilities over consolidated deferred tax assets.

The accounting differences among U.S., IAS, and foreign GAAP affect reported net income and stockholders' equity (lower when deferred tax assets are unrecognized or offset by a valuation allowance). Another difficulty when comparing firms using different GAAP is the paucity of disclosure requirements in many cases. Both SFAS 109 and IAS 12 have substantial disclosure requirements; similar information is rarely available in the financial statements of most foreign countries.

Form 20-F reconciliations of reported net income and stockholders' equity show the adjustments due to differences in deferred tax accounting. These differences can be used to restore comparability between U.S. firms and foreign firms that file Form 20-F. In some cases, these adjustments can be used to approximate adjustments for firms not providing Form 20-F reconciliations, when they are similar to firms that do provide them.

Exhibit 4 contains disclosures provided by Cadbury Schweppes in its 2000 Form 20-F. Applying UK GAAP, the company calculated deferred tax liabilities of £105 million (1999: £93) using the partial allocation method.[24] Had it used comprehensive allocation (U.S. GAAP), it would have recorded an additional deferred tax liability of £58 million in 2000 (1999: £62 million); most of the difference is attributed to the accelerated depreciation method. No deferred tax is recorded for the effect of accelerated depreciation because it is not expected to reverse.

Although we have recommended this approach in the section "Liability or Equity" and agree that partial allocation is a logical alternative to the comprehensive allocation method, it presents two analytical problems. First, it makes Cadbury's

[24] The partial allocation method in UK GAAP limits the recognition of net deferred tax assets to amounts expected to be recovered without the assumption of future taxable income. The standard is permissive regarding deferred tax consequences of pension and postretirement benefits; firms may use either comprehensive or partial allocation with disclosure of the method selected.

EXHIBIT 4 Cadbury Schweppes

Panel A. Deferred Taxes: Partial Allocation

The analysis of the deferred tax liabilities/(assets) included in the financial statements at the end of the year is as follows:

In £millions	1999	2000
Accelerated capital allowances	£ 2	£ 3
Other timing differences	91	102
Deferred taxation liability	£93	£105

The deferred taxation liability is included in provisions for liabilities and charges. Gross deferred tax assets at year-end are £15 million (1999: £18 million). The potential liability for deferred taxation not provided comprised:

In £millions	1999	2000
UK accelerated capital allowances	£48	£77
UK property values	5	5
Other timing differences	9	(30)
	£62	£52

To the extent that dividends from overseas undertakings are expected to result in additional taxes, appropriate amounts have been provided. No taxes have been provided for other unremitted earnings since these amounts are considered permanently reinvested by subsidiary undertakings and in the case of associated undertakings the taxes would not be material. Distributable earnings retained by overseas subsidiary undertakings and the principal associated undertakings totaled approximately £846 million at 31 December 2000. The remittance of these amounts would incur tax at varying rates depending on available foreign tax credits.

Tax losses carried forward as at 31 December 2000 for offset against future earnings of overseas companies were approximately £103 million (1999: £103 million). The utilization of losses is dependent upon the level of future earnings and other limiting factors within the countries concerned. Tax losses totaling £22 million have expiration periods in 2001 and 2002, tax losses of £25 million expire in 2003 to 2012 and tax losses totaling £56 million have no **expiry** date.

(Exhibit continued on next page . . .)

EXHIBIT 4 (continued)

Panel B. U.S. GAAP

The U.S. GAAP analysis of deferred tax liability is as follows:

In £millions	1999	2000
Liabilities		
Fixed asset timing differences	£ 84	£ 84
Other timing differences	71	79
	£155	£163
Assets		
Operating loss carryforwards	(37)	(37)
Less: Valuation allowance	37	37
Net deferred tax liability	£155	£163

Source: Cadbury *20-F*, December 31, 2000.

financial statements not comparable to its U.S. competitors, Coca-Cola and PepsiCo, who use comprehensive allocation. Comparability can be restored either by adjusting Cadbury's income statement provision, its deferred taxes (and equity), or by converting its competitors' financial statements to the partial allocation method.

The second problem with partial allocation is management discretion that can be used to manage earnings. This discretion is comparable to that available in the application of valuation allowances under SFAS 109 and IAS 12.

In December 2000, the UK Accounting Standards Board issued FRS 19, Deferred Tax, requiring comprehensive allocation. Cadbury will most likely adopt this standard in 2002 and the resulting financial statements will be more comparable to its U.S. competitors. The UK–U.S. GAAP reconciliation in the form 20-F as it relates to deferred taxes is reproduced in Panel B of Exhibit 4. On December 31, 2000, the U.S. GAAP-based deferred tax liability is £163 million (1999: £152 million). This information can be used to make Cadbury's financial statements comparable to those of its U.S. competitors.

SUMMARY

In this reading, we have seen how income tax expense and deferred tax assets and liabilities are affected by the accounting method used and by management choices and assumptions. As all business enterprises are subject to income tax, no financial analysis is complete until the issues raised in this reading have been examined. Analysts must examine, in particular, the effective tax rate, the cash flow effects of deferred tax accruals, and the relevance of such accruals for valuation.

PRACTICE PROBLEMS FOR READING 38

1. [Deferred tax classification; CFA® adapted] Explain in which of the following categories deferred taxes can be found. Provide an example for each category in your answer.
   - i. Current liabilities
   - ii. Long-term liabilities
   - iii. Stockholders' equity
   - iv. Current assets
   - v. Long-term assets
2. [Deferred taxes; CFA adapted] State which of the following statements are correct under SFAS 109. Explain why.
   - i. The deferred tax liability account must be adjusted for the effect of enacted changes in tax laws or rates in the period of enactment.
   - ii. The deferred tax asset account must be adjusted for the effect of enacted changes in tax laws or rates in the period of enactment
   - iii. The tax consequences of an event must not be recognized until that event is recognized in the financial statements.
   - iv. Both deferred tax liabilities and deferred tax assets must be accounted for based on the tax laws and rates in effect at their origin.
   - v. Changes in deferred tax assets and liabilities are classified as extraordinary items in the income statement.
3. [Permanent versus temporary differences; CFA adapted]
   - A. Define *permanent differences* and describe two events or transactions that generate such differences.
   - B. Describe the impact of permanent differences on a firm's effective tax rate.
4. [Treatment of deferred tax liability; CFA adapted]
   - A. When computing a firm's debt-to-equity ratio, describe the conditions for treating the deferred tax liability:
     - i. As equity
     - ii. As debt
   - B. Provide arguments for excluding deferred tax liabilities from both the numerator and the denominator of the debt-to-equity ratio.
   - C. Describe the arguments for including a portion of the deferred taxes as equity and a portion as debt.
5. [Depreciation methods and deferred taxes] The Incurious George Company acquires assets K, L, and M at the beginning of year 1. Each asset has the same cost, a five-year life, and an expected salvage value of $3,000. For financial reporting, the firm uses the straight-line, sum-of-the-years' digits, and double-declining-balance depreciation methods for assets K, L, and M, respectively. It uses the double-declining-balance method for all assets on its tax return; its tax rate is 34%. Depreciation expense of $12,000 was reported for asset L for financial reporting purposes in year 2. Using this information:
   - A. Calculate the tax return depreciation expense for each asset in year 2.
   - B. Calculate the financial statement depreciation expense for assets K and M in year 2.

C. Calculate the deferred tax credit (liability) or debit (asset) for each asset at the end of:

i. Year 2

ii. Year 5

6. [Analysis of deferred tax; CFA adapted] On December 29, 2000, Mother Prewitt's Handmade Cookies Corp. acquires a numerically controlled chocolate chip milling machine. Due to differences in tax and financial accounting, depreciation for tax purposes is $150,000 more than depreciation in the financial statements, adding $52,500 to deferred taxes. At the same time, Mother Prewitt's sells $200,000 worth of cookies on an installment contract, recognizing the $100,000 profit immediately. For tax purposes, however, $80,000 of the profit will be recognized in 2001, requiring $27,200 of deferred taxes.

A. Compare the expected cash consequences of the two deferred tax items just described.

B. Explain your treatment of deferred taxes when calculating Mother Prewitt's solvency and leverage ratios.

C. In 2001, Mother Prewitt's tax rate will be 40%. Discuss the adjustments to *each* of the two deferred tax items in 2001 because of the change in the tax rate, assuming the use of SFAS 109.

7. [Tax effect of restructuring] Silicon Graphics [SGI] made the following announcements:

- 1998: restructuring charges of $144 million, including a $47 million write down of operating assets; additional $47 million impairment of long-lived assets.
- 1999: $4.2 million of operating asset write downs and a $16 million write-down of capitalized internal use software.
- 2000: Operating asset write downs of $26.6 million.

The company reported the following deferred tax assets ($ thousands):

Years Ended June 30	1997	1998	1999	2000
Depreciation	$57,675	$40,435	$49,226	$37,659

A. Using the U.S. statutory tax rates of 34% for 1998 and 35% for 1999 and 2000, estimate the changes in 1998, 1999, and 2000 deferred tax asset balances resulting from the write downs of operating assets.

B. Explain why your answer to part a differs from the actual changes in the deferred tax asset during those three years.

8. [Analysis of income tax footnote data] Exhibit P-1 contains the income tax footnote from the *2001 Annual Report* of Honda [7267], a multinational automobile manufacturer based in Japan. *Note that these data are prepared under U.S. GAAP.*

A. Calculate the differences (in yen) between Honda's income tax expense and that expense based on the statutory rate.

B. Using your answer to part a, compute the impact on Honda's income tax expense over the 1999 to 2001 period of:

i. Changes in the valuation allowance
ii. Tax law changes
iii. Undistributed earnings of subsidiaries

C. Lower non-Japanese tax rates reduced Honda's tax expense in each year, 1999 to 2001.
i. Discuss the trend in that reduction.
ii. Discuss the likely explanation for that trend.

D. Discuss the factors that an analyst must consider when forecasting Honda's effective tax rate for 2002.

9. [Deferred taxes and interim reports] State Auto Financial [STFC] reported the following operating results for the first three quarters of 1991 and 1992 ($ in thousands):

		1991	
	Q1	Q2	Q3
Pretax income	$4,797	$2,600	$3,244
Income tax expense	(1,224)	(624)	(848)
Net income	$3,573	$1,976	$2,396
		1992	
	Q1	Q2	Q3
Pretax income	$1,123	$3,723	$ 98
Income tax expense	(232)	(934)	583
Net income	$ 891	$2,789	$681

State Auto's 1992 third-quarter 10-Q reported that:

> the estimated annual effective tax rate was revised during the third quarter of 1992 from 25% to 17% to reflect the estimated tax impact of a decrease in taxable earnings, as prescribed by generally accepted accounting principles. The effect of this adjustment in the current quarter was a benefit of approximately $600,000.

A. Compute the tax rate used to compute net income for each quarter.

B. Using the data given, show how the change in the estimated tax rate increased third-quarter 1992 income by approximately $600,000.

C. Describe how the changed tax rate assumption distorted the comparison of third-quarter net income for 1991 and 1992.

D. Suggest two ways by which analysis can offset the distortion discussed in Part C.

E. Assume that State Auto had estimated a tax rate of 17% for the first two quarters of 1992.
i. Compute the effect of that assumption on reported net income for those quarters.
ii. Discuss how that assumption would have affected the year-to-year comparison of operating results for the first two quarters.

EXHIBIT P-1 Honda Motor

Income Tax Disclosures

The income before income taxes and equity in income of affiliates ("Income before income taxes") and income tax expense (benefit) for each of the years in the three-year period ended March 31, 2001 consist of the following:

	Yen (millions)			
		Income Taxes		
	Income before Income Taxes	Current	Deferred	Total
1999				
Japanese	¥199,848	¥125,423	¥ 15,144	¥140,567
Foreign[a]	320,663	107,875	(18,818)	89,057
	¥520,511	¥233,298	¥ (3,674)	¥229,624
2000				
Japanese	¥127,562	¥ 76,015	¥(22,160)	¥ 53,855
Foreign[a]	288,501	136,963	(20,384)	116,579
	¥416,063	¥212,978	¥(42,544)	¥170,434
2001				
Japanese	**¥133,166**	**¥ 65,444**	**¥ (4,697)**	**¥ 60,747**
Foreign[a]	**251,810**	**131,419**	**(13,727)**	**117,692**
	¥384,976	**¥196,863**	**¥(18,424)**	**¥178,439**

[a] Foreign includes income taxes provided on undistributed earnings of foreign subsidiaries and affiliates.

The effective tax rate of Honda for each of the years in the three-year period ended March 31, 2001, differs from the normal Japanese income tax rate for the following reasons.

	1999	2000	2001
Normal income tax rate	48.0%	41.0%	**41.0%**
Valuation allowance provided for current year operating losses of subsidiaries	1.2	2.8	**5.2**
Difference in normal tax rates of foreign subsidiaries	(3.0)	(1.3)	**(1.0)**
Adjustments to deferred tax assets and liabilities for enacted changes in tax laws and rates	(4.2)	—	—
Reversal of valuation allowance due to utilization of operating loss carryforwards	(0.1)	(0.1)	**(0.1)**
Other	2.2	(1.4)	**1.3**
Effective tax rate	44.1%	41.0%	**46.4%**

(Exhibit continued on next page . . .)

EXHIBIT P-1 (continued)

At March 31, 2001, certain of the company's subsidiaries have operating loss carryforwards for income tax purposes of approximately ¥112,857 million ($910,872 thousand), which are available to offset future taxable income, if any. Periods available to offset future taxable income vary in each tax jurisdiction and range from one year to an indefinite period as follows:

	Yen (millions)
Within 1 year	¥ 510
1 to 5 years	11,528
5 to 15 years	4,147
Indefinite periods	96,672
	¥112,857

At March 31, 2000 and 2001, Honda did not recognize deferred tax liabilities of ¥5,131 million and ¥5,987 million ($48,321 thousand) respectively, for certain portions of the undistributed earnings of the company's subsidiaries because such portions were reinvested or were determined to be reinvested. At March 31, 2000 and 2001, the undistributed earnings not subject to deferred tax liabilities were ¥649,929 million and ¥663,540 million ($5,355,448 thousand), respectively. Honda has recognized deferred tax liabilities for undistributed earnings for which decisions of reinvestment have not been made.

ANALYSIS OF FINANCING LIABILITIES

by Gerald I. White, Ashwinpaul C. Sondhi, and Dov Fried

READING 39

LEARNING OUTCOMES

The candidate should be able to:

a. distinguish between operating and trade debt related to operating activities and debt generated by financing activities, and discuss the analytical implications of a shift between the two types of liabilities;

b. determine the effects of debt issuance and amortization of bond discounts and premiums on financial statements and financial ratios;

c. analyze the effect on financial statements and financial ratios of issuing zero-coupon debt;

d. classify a debt security with equity features as a debt or equity security and demonstrate the effect of issuing debt with equity features on the financial statements and ratios;

e. describe the disclosures relating to financing liabilities, and discuss the advantages/disadvantages to the company of selecting a given financing instrument and the effect of the selection on a company's financial statements and ratios;

f. determine the effects of changing interest rates on the market value of debt and on financial statements and ratios;

g. calculate and describe the accounting treatment of, and economic gains and losses resulting from, the various methods of retiring debt prior to its maturity;

h. analyze the implications of debt covenants for creditors and the issuing company.

INTRODUCTION 1

The assessment of a firm's liabilities is crucial to the analysis of its long-run viability and growth. A firm can incur obligations in myriad ways; some are a consequence of the firm's operating activities, whereas others result from its financing decisions. The former are characterized by exchanges of goods and services for the later payment of cash (or vice versa), whereas debt arising from financing decisions generally involves current receipts of cash in exchange for later payments of cash. Both forms of debt are generally reported "on balance sheet," and our focus in this reading is on their measurement, interpretation, and analysis.

More complex arrangements, often based on contracts rather than immediate cash exchanges, involve promises to purchase (or use) products, services, or distribution systems in return for specified future payments of cash or equivalent resources. Such contractual arrangements are usually not recorded on the firm's balance sheet but may receive footnote disclosure. A thorough analysis of the firm's financial structure requires recognition of these liabilities as well. Such "off-balance-sheet" debt must first be identified, then measured, interpreted, and analyzed.

The analysis of a firm's short-term liquidity and long-term solvency position requires evaluation of both on- and off-balance-sheet debt. Debt-to-equity and interest coverage ratios based on reported financial data, for example, are affected by the form of transactions (rather than their substance), which determines whether they are recognized and how they are accounted for. This analysis must also consider incentives for management decisions regarding the proportion of on- versus off-balance-sheet debt.

An additional focus of analysis is debt covenants, used by creditors to protect themselves. These restrictions limit the firm's operations, its distributions to shareholders, and the amount of additional debt or leverage the firm can assume. Firms may alter their operating and financing activities and change accounting policies in an effort to operate within the confines of these covenants.

2 BALANCE SHEET DEBT

The liability amount reported on the balance sheet does not equal the total cash outflow required to satisfy the debt. Only the principal portion, that is, the present value of the future cash flow, is recorded. For example, if a firm borrows \$100 at an interest rate of 10%, the actual amount payable at year-end is \$110. The balance sheet liability equals the present value of the future payment or \$100.

Current Liabilities

Current liabilities are defined as those due within one year or one operating cycle; they result from both operating and financing activities. Analysis must distinguish among different types of current operating and financing liabilities:

Consequences of Operating Activities

1. *Operating and trade liabilities*, the most frequent type, are the result of credit granted to the company by its suppliers and employees.
2. *Advances from customers* arise when customers pay in advance for services to be rendered by the company. The firm is obligated to render the service and/or deliver a product to the customer in the near future.

Consequences of Financing Activities

3. *Short-term debt* represents amounts borrowed from banks or the credit markets that are expected to be repaid within one year or less.
4. *Current portion of long-term debt* identifies the portion of long-term debt that is payable within the next year; it is excluded from the long-term liability section of the balance sheet.

Operating and trade debt is reported at the expected (undiscounted) cash flow and is an important exception to the rule that liabilities are recorded at present value. A purchase of goods for $100 on credit, to be paid for within the normal operating cycle of the firm, is recorded at $100 even though its present value is lower. This treatment is justified by the short period between the incurrence of the debt and its payment, rendering the adjustment to present value immaterial.

When analyzing a firm's liquidity, advances from customers should be distinguished from other payables. Payables require a future outlay of cash. Advances from customers, on the other hand, are satisfied by delivery of goods or services,[1] requiring a cash outlay lower[2] than the advances recorded; otherwise, the firm would be selling below cost. Increases in advances should be viewed favorably as *advances are a prediction of future revenues rather than of cash outflows.*

Short-term debt and the current portion of long-term debt are the result of prior financing cash inflows. They indicate the firm's need for either cash or a means of refinancing the debt. The inability to repay short-term credit is a sign of financial distress.

It is important to monitor the relative levels of debt from operating as compared to financing activities. The former arise from the normal course of business activities and represent the required operating capital for a given level of production and sales: *A shift from operating to financing liabilities may signal the beginning of a liquidity crisis, as reduced access to* ***trade credit*** *results in increased reliance on borrowings.*

EXAMPLE 1

Warnaco

The following data for Warnaco Group, a major clothing manufacturer, illustrates this point:

Warnaco Group Amounts in $000

	1/1/00	12/30/00	Change
Accounts payable	$ 599,768	$ 413,786	$(185,982)
Total debt	1,332,755	1,493,483	160,728

Over one year Warnaco's trade credit fell 31%, requiring borrowing that increased the company's already-large debt burden. The company filed for bankruptcy on June 11, 2001.

[1] The firm will have a cash obligation only if the goods and services are not delivered. Thus, the primary liability does not require cash.

[2] This is especially true in industries with high fixed/low variable cost structures (e.g., airlines). The marginal cost for any individual customer is low relative to the selling cost.

Long-Term Debt

Firms obtain long-term debt financing from public issuance; from private placements with insurance companies, pension plans, and other institutional investors; or from long-term bank credit agreements. Creditors may receive a claim on specific assets pledged as security for the debt (e.g., mortgages), or they may have only general claims on the assets of the firm. Some debt, known as *project financing,* is repaid solely from the operations of a particular activity (e.g., a coal mine or office building). Some creditor claims are *subordinated,* in that they rank below those of *senior* creditors, whose claims have priority.

Long-term liabilities are interest-bearing in nature, but the structure of interest and principal payments varies widely. The different payment terms are, however, conceptually identical. As the subtleties of the financing equation(s) can be overwhelming and obscure the sight of the forest for the trees, *we suggest that the reader keep two basic principles in mind:*

1. Debt equals the present value of the remaining future stream of (interest and principal) payments. The book value reported in the financial statements uses the discount rate (market interest rate) in effect when the debt was incurred. Market value measurements use the current market interest rate.
2. Interest expense is the amount paid by the debtor to the creditor in excess of the amount borrowed. Even when the *total* amount of interest paid over time is known, its allocation to individual time periods (both cash outflows and accrual of expense in periodic income statements) may vary with the form of the debt.

These points seem simplistic but reference to them from time to time may help focus the discussions that follow.

Although bonds are only part of the debt universe, they are used for convenience to illustrate the accounting and analysis issues.

A bond is a "contract" or written agreement that obligates the borrower (bond issuer) to make certain payments to the lender (bondholder) over the life of the bond. A typical bond promises two types of payments: periodic interest payments (usually semiannual in the United States but annual in other countries) and a lump-sum payment when the bond matures.

The *face value* of the bond is the lump-sum payment due at maturity. The *coupon rate* is the stated cash interest rate (but not necessarily the actual rate of return).

$$\text{Periodic Payment} = \text{“Coupon Rate”} \times \text{Face Value}$$

The coupon rate is in quotation marks because it is stated on an annual basis, whereas payments are made semiannually. The coupon rate (CR) used for the payment calculation is therefore equal to one-half the stated coupon rate.

The example in Exhibit 1 is based on a three-year bond[3] with the following terms:

Face value (FV)	\$100,000
Coupon	10%
Interest payment	Semiannual

[3] Bonds issued for periods of 10 years or less are usually called notes. There is no analytical distinction, and we call all debt issues bonds for convenience.

EXHIBIT 1 Comparison of Bond Issued at Par, Premium, and Discount

Face Value (FV) of bond = $100,000
Coupon (CR) = 5% (semiannual payment; 10% annual rate)
Maturity = 3 years
Semiannual payments of $5,000 (0.5 × 10% × $100,000)

A. Bond Issued at Par: Market Rate = 10% (MR = 5%)

Period Ending	(1) Liability Opening	(2) (1) × MR Interest Expense	(3) FV × CR Coupon Payment	(4) (2) − (3) Change in Liability	(5) (1) + (4) Liability Closing	(6) FV Face Value of Bond
01/01/01	Proceeds (see below)				$100,000	$100,000
06/30/01	$100,000	$ 5,000	$ 5,000	$0	100,000	100,000
12/31/01	100,000	5,000	5,000	0	100,000	100,000
06/30/02	100,000	5,000	5,000	0	100,000	100,000
12/31/02	100,000	5,000	5,000	0	100,000	100,000
06/30/03	100,000	5,000	5,000	0	100,000	100,000
12/31/03	100,000	5,000	5,000	0	100,000	100,000
Totals		$30,000	$30,000			

Calculation of Proceeds

Present value of annuity of $5,000 for 6 periods, discounted at 5%:	
$5,000 × 5.0756 =	$ 25,378
Present value of $100,000 in 6 periods, discounted at 5%:	
$100,000 × 0.74622 =	74,622
Total	$100,000

B. Bond Issued at Premium: Market Rate = 8% (MR = 4%)

Period Ending	(1) Liability Opening	(2) (1) × MR Interest Expense	(3) FV × CR Coupon Payment	(4) (2) − (3) Change in Liability	(5) (1) + (4) Liability Closing	(6) FV Face Value of Bond	(7) (5) − (6) Closing Premium
01/01/01	Proceeds (see below)				$105,242	$100,000	$5,242
06/30/01	$105,242	$ 4,210	$ 5,000	$ (790)	104,452	100,000	4,452
12/31/01	104,452	4,178	5,000	(822)	103,630	100,000	3,630
06/30/02	103,630	4,145	5,000	(855)	102,775	100,000	2,775
12/31/02	102,775	4,111	5,000	(889)	101,886	100,000	1,886
06/30/03	101,886	4,075	5,000	(925)	100,961	100,000	961
12/31/03	100,961	4,039	5,000	(961)	100,000	100,000	0
Totals		$24,759	$30,000	$(5,242)			

(Exhibit continued on next page . . .)

EXHIBIT 1 (continued)

Calculation of Proceeds

Present value of annuity of $5,000 for 6 periods, discounted at 4%:	
$5,000 × 5.2421 =	$ 26,211
Present value of $100,000 in 6 periods, discounted at 4%:	
$100,000 × 0.79031 =	79,031
Total	$105,242

C. Bond Issued at Discount: Market Rate = 12% (MR = 6%)

Period Ending	(1) Liability Opening	(2) (1) × MR Interest Expense	(3) FV × CR Coupon Payment	(4) (2) − (3) Change in Liability	(5) (1) + (4) Liability Closing	(6) FV Face Value of Bond	(7) (5) − (6) Discount
01/01/01	Proceeds (see below)				$95,083	$100,000	$(4,917)
06/30/01	$95,083	$ 5,705	$ 5,000	$ 705	95,788	100,000	(4,212)
12/31/01	95,788	5,747	5,000	747	96,535	100,000	(3,465)
06/30/02	96,535	5,792	5,000	792	97,327	100,000	(2,673)
12/31/02	97,327	5,840	5,000	840	98,167	100,000	(1,833)
06/30/03	98,167	5,890	5,000	890	99,057	100,000	(943)
12/31/03	99,057	5,943	5,000	943	100,000	100,000	0
Totals		$34,917	$30,000	$4,917			

Calculation of Proceeds

Present value of annuity of $5,000 for 6 periods, discounted at 6%:	
$5,000 × 4.9173 =	$24,587
Present value of $100,000 in 6 periods, discounted at 6%:	
$100,000 × 0.70496 =	70,496
Total	$95,083

The purchaser of the bond expects six payments of interest (each payment is $5,000) and a final principal payment of $100,000 for a total of $130,000. Note that this stream of payments does not uniquely determine the principal amount borrowed by the bond issuer. *The amount borrowed (the proceeds received on issuance) depends on the market rate of interest for bonds of a similar maturity and risk as well as the payment stream.*

The market rate may be less than, equal to, or greater than the coupon rate. *It is the current market interest rate that allocates payments between interest and principal.*

Exhibit 1, parts A through C, shows how the economics of the bond and the accounting treatment of the payments are affected by the relationship between the market and coupon rates. The following points should be noted:

1. The initial liability is the amount paid to the issuer by the creditor (present value of the stream of payments discounted at the market rate), not necessarily the face value of the debt.
2. The *effective interest rate* on the bond is the market (not the coupon) rate at the time of issuance, and interest expense is that market rate times the bond liability.
3. The coupon rate and face value determine the actual cash flows (stream of payments from the issuer).
4. Total interest expense is equal to the payments by the issuer to the creditor in excess of the amount received. (Thus, total interest expense = \$130,000 − initial liability.)
5. The balance sheet liability over time is a function of (a) the initial liability and the relationship of (b) periodic interest expense to (c) the actual cash payments.
6. The balance sheet liability at any point in time is equal to the present value of the remaining payments, discounted at the market rate in effect at the time of the issuance of the bonds.

Exhibit 1A: Market Rate = Coupon Rate When the market rate equals the coupon rate of 10% (compounded semiannually), the bond is issued at par; that is, the proceeds equal the face value.[4] The creditor is willing to pay \$100,000, the present value of the stream of payments and the face value of the bond. In this case, the initial liability equals the face value.

Since the debt has been issued at a market rate of 10% (equal to the coupon rate), periodic interest expense (Exhibit 1A, column 2) equals the periodic cash payments (column 3). The liability remains \$100,000 (column 5) throughout the life of the bond.

Exhibit 1B: Market Rate < Coupon Rate When the market rate is less than the coupon rate, the creditor is willing to pay (and the bond issuer will demand) a premium above the face value of \$100,000.[5] If we assume a market rate of 8%, the proceeds and initial liability (Exhibit 1B) equal \$105,242 (face value of \$100,000 plus premium of \$5,242).

After six months, the bondholder earns interest of \$4,210 (4% × \$105,242) but receives a payment of \$5,000 (coupon rate times face value). This \$5,000 payment includes interest expense of \$4,210 and a \$790 principal payment, reducing the liability to \$104,452. For the second period, interest expense is \$4,178 (4% × \$104,452), lower than the first period expense since the liability has been reduced. After the second payment of \$5,000, the liability is further reduced. This process is continued until the bond matures. At that time, as shown in Exhibit 1B, the liability is reduced to \$100,000, the face value of the bond, which is repaid at maturity.

The process by which a bond premium (or discount) is amortized over the life of the bond is known as the *effective interest method*. This process, which results in a constant rate of interest over the life of the obligation, is widely used in financial reporting.

---

[4] We ignore, for simplicity, the underwriting costs and expenses associated with the bond issuance. These costs are generally capitalized and amortized over the life of the bond issue.

[5] Assuming a market interest rate of 8%, the bond issuer could find an investor willing to lend \$100,000 in exchange for a semiannual annuity stream of \$4,000 (4% × \$100,000) in addition to the lump-sum payment at maturity. For the borrower to obligate itself to pay the higher annuity of \$5,000 requires additional proceeds above the face value.

Exhibit 1C: Market Rate > Coupon Rate When the market rate exceeds the coupon rate, the bond buyer is unwilling to pay the full face value of the bond.[6] At a market rate of 12%, the bond would be issued at a discount of $4,917, and the proceeds and initial liability equal $95,083.

Interest expense for the first six months is $5,705 (6% × $95,083), but cash interest paid is only $5,000; the shortfall of $705 is added to the balance sheet liability. As a result, a higher liability is used to calculate interest expense for the second period, increasing interest expense, increasing the shortfall, and further increasing the liability. This cycle is repeated for all remaining periods until the bond matures. At that point, the initial principal of $95,083 plus the accumulated (unpaid) interest of $4,917 equals $100,000, the face value payment that retires the debt. The zero-coupon bond, discussed shortly, is the extreme case; all interest is unpaid until the bond matures.

Financial Statement Effects

Interest expense reported in the income statement (column 2 of Exhibit 1) is the effective interest on the loan based on the market rate in effect at issuance times the balance sheet liability at the beginning of the period. The actual cash payments (column 3) may not equal interest expense, but do equal the reduction in cash from operations (CFO). The balance sheet liability is shown in column 5. The initial cash received and the final face value payment of $100,000 are both treated as cash from financing (CFF). The financial statement effects on an annual basis (if we assume a December fiscal year-end) are summarized in Exhibit 2. Note that for bonds issued at a premium (discount), the interest expense decreases (increases) over time. This is a direct function of the declining (rising) balance sheet liability; for each period, interest expense is the product of the beginning liability and the effective interest rate. At any point in time, the balance sheet liability equals the present value of the remaining payments discounted at the effective interest rate at the issuance date.[7,8]

The reported cash flows for each period over the life of the bond (Exhibit 2) are identical across all three scenarios; the $100,000 face value payment is treated as cash from financing, and the periodic cash payments of $5,000 are reported as reductions in CFO.[9] For bonds issued at a premium or discount, however, these cash flows *incorrectly* describe the economics of the bond transaction.

The misclassification of cash flows results from reporting the coupon payments rather than interest expense as CFO. For bonds sold at a premium, part of the coupon payment is a reduction of principal and should be treated as a

[6] The bondholder can purchase a 12% bond and receive periodic payments of $6,000. The periodic payments from this bond are only $5,000. Thus, an investor would only purchase this bond at a *discount*.

[7] To illustrate this property, compute the balance sheet liability of $96,535 at December 31, 2001, for the bond issued at a discount. The present value of the remaining four periodic payments and lump-sum payment equals:

Present value of annuity of $5,000 for 4 periods discounted at 6%: $5,000 × 3.46511 =	$17,326
Present value of $100,000 for 4 periods discounted at 6%: $100,000 × 0.79209 =	79,209
	$96,535

[8] The *market* value of the debt, however, is equal to the present value of all remaining payments discounted at the *current market* interest rate.

[9] Under the indirect method, net income is adjusted by the change in bond discount/premium (the periodic amortization of the bond/discount premium) to derive CFO. Thus for the first year, the cash flow statement will show an addback of $1,612 in the premium case and a deduction of $1,452 in the discount case.

EXHIBIT 2 Comparison of Financial Statement Effects of Bonds Issued at Par, Premium, and Discount

Bond Face Value = $100,000
Maturity = 3 years
Coupon Rate = 10% (semiannual payments)

Premium Case: Market Rate = 8%
Discount Case: Market Rate = 12%

	Interest Expense Bond Issued at			Balance Sheet Liability Bond Issued at			Cash Flow from	
Year	Par	Premium	Discount	Par	Premium	Discount	Operations	Financing (for all cases)
2001	$10,000	$ 8,388	$11,452	$100,000	$103,630	$ 96,535	$10,000	
2002[a]	10,000	8,256	11,632	100,000	101,886	98,167	10,000	
2003[a]	10,000	8,114	11,833	100,000	100,000	100,000	10,000	$100,000
Totals	$30,000	$24,758	$34,917				$30,000	$100,000

[a]Interest expense and cash flow total of June 30 and December 31 amounts for each year. All data from Exhibit 1.

financing cash (out)flow. CFO is understated and financing cash flow is overstated by an equal amount. Similarly, when bonds are issued at a discount, part of the discount amortization represents additional interest expense. Consequently, CFO is overstated and financing cash flow is understated by that amount.

In summary, the cash flow classification of the debt payments depends on the coupon rates, not the effective interest rate. When these differ, CFO is misstated.

Exhibit 3 presents two cash flow reclassifications. The first correctly allocates cash outflows based on interest expense. After reallocation, the cash flows reflect the economics of the debt rather than the coupon payments alone.

The second reclassification, however, goes much further. We argue that all debt-related cash flows should be separated from operating cash flows. The "functional" reclassification in Exhibit 3 makes that separation so CFO is unaffected by borrowing. All debt-related cash flows are included in financing cash flow regardless of the coupon or effective interest rates.

Most debt is issued at or close to par (face value), making the distortion from bond premium or discount immaterial. However, when the discount is large, for example, with zero-coupon bonds, the difference between coupon and effective interest rates leads to the significant distortion of reported cash flows.

Zero-Coupon Debt

A zero-coupon bond has no periodic payments (coupon = 0).[10] For that reason, it must be issued at a deep discount to face value. The lump-sum payment at maturity includes all unpaid interest (equal to the face value minus the proceeds) from the time of issuance.

[10] The following discussion also applies to bonds sold at deep discounts, that is, with coupons that are far below market interest rates, and to bonds issued with attached warrants that generate debt discount (discussed later in the reading).

EXHIBIT 3 Reclassification of Cash Flows for Bonds in Exhibits 1 and 2

		SFAS 95		Reclassification Based on Interest Expense				Functional Reclassification for All Bonds	
		Cash Flow for All Bonds		Premium Bond		Discount Bond			
Year	Actual Cash Flow	Operations	Financing	Operations	Financing	Operations	Financing	Operations	Financing
2001	$ 10,000	$10,000	0	$ 8,388	$ 1,612	$11,452	$(1,452)	0	$ 10,000
2002	10,000	10,000	0	8,256	1,744	11,632	(1,632)	0	10,000
2003	110,000	10,000	100,000	8,114	101,886	11,833	98,167	0	110,000
Totals	$130,000	$30,000	$100,000	$24,758	$105,242	$34,917	$95,083	0	$130,000

SFAS 95 requires that cash flows be allocated between operations and financing based on the coupon interest rate.

The first reclassification allocates cash outflows based on interest expense. In 2001, for the premium case, $8,388 is shown as operating cash flow and the balance of $1,612 ($10,000 − $8,388) as financing. The interest expense reported for the discount issue, $11,452, is shown as operating cash flow and the excess over interest paid $1,452 ($11,452 − $10,000) is reported as a financing cash inflow. The 2003 financing cash flow for the discount issue, therefore, equals the outflow of $100,000 to repay the debt less $1,833 (interest expense in excess of interest paid).

The second reclassification is based on the authors' view that financing cash flow should include both principal and interest paid. Regardless of whether debt is issued at par, premium, or discount, financing cash flow reflects all payments made in the year of the actual payments.

The proceeds at issuance equal the present value of the face amount, discounted at the market interest rate. Thus, at a market rate of 10%, a $100,000 face value zero-coupon bond payable in three years will be issued at $74,622.

Exhibit 4 shows the income statement, cash flow, and balance sheet effects for this bond. Note that the repayment of $100,000 includes $25,378 of interest that is *never* reported as CFO; the full $100,000 payment is treated as cash from financing. The contrast with the bond issued at par (Exhibit 1A) is striking.

The interest on a zero-coupon bond never reduces operating cash flow. This surprising result has important analytic consequences. *One is that reported CFO is systematically overstated when a zero-coupon (or deep discount) bond is issued.* Furthermore, solvency ratios, such as cash-basis interest coverage, are improved relative to the issuance of par bonds. Finally, the cash eventually required to repay the obligation may become a significant burden.[11]

EQK Realty Investors (EQK), a real estate investment trust, illustrates this phenomenon. The company issued zero-coupon mortgage notes in 1985 and 1988. Adjustment of reported cash flow for the effect of interest on these zero-coupon bonds results in a quite different CFO trend.

[11] In fact, interest expense increases cash flow by generating income tax deductions. (Zero-coupon bond interest expense is tax-deductible even though it is not paid.) This result can have real-world consequences. When valuing a company for leveraged buyout (LBO) purposes, the use of zero-coupon or low-coupon debt (issued at a discount) can result in the following anomaly: The higher the interest rate, the higher the cash flow, mistakenly resulting in a higher price for the company. An investment banker commented to one of the authors that this factor contributed to overbidding in the late 1980s. Of course, when the zero-coupon bond comes due, the cash must be found to repay the (much higher) face amount.

EXHIBIT 4 Zero-Coupon Bond Analysis

Bond: Face Value (FV) = $100,000 Coupon 0%
Maturity = 3 years
Market Rate = 10% (MR = 5%)

	(1) Liability Opening	(2) (1) × MR Interest Expense	(3) FV × CR Coupon Payment	(4) (2) − (3) Change in Liability	(5) (1) + (4) Liability Closing	(6) FV Face Value of Bond	(7) (5) − (6) Discount
01/01/01	Proceeds (see below)				$ 74,622	$100,000	$(25,378)
06/30/01	$74,622	$ 3,731	$0	$ 3,731	78,353	100,000	(21,647)
12/31/01	78,353	3,917	0	3,917	82,270	100,000	(17,730)
06/30/02	82,270	4,114	0	4,114	86,384	100,000	(13,616)
12/31/02	86,384	4,319	0	4,319	90,703	100,000	(9,297)
06/30/03	90,703	4,535	0	4,535	95,238	100,000	(4,762)
12/31/03	95,238	4,762	0	4,762	100,000	100,000	(0)
Totals		$25,378	$0	$25,378			

Calculation of Proceeds

Present value of $100,000 in 6 periods, discounted at 5%:
$100,000 × 0.74622 = $74,622
Cash flow from operations: Zero in all periods
Cash flow from financing: $74,622 inflow at 1/1/01; $100,000 outflow at 12/31/03

Exhibit 5 presents excerpts from EQK's 1992 Balance Sheet, Cash Flow Statement, and Financial Statement Notes. The zero-coupon notes were retired in December 1992, using cash and a new (conventional) mortgage bond.

Given the opening (January 1, 1992) balance of $89,410 on the zero-coupon bond and the issuance of a mortgage bond having a face value of $75,716 ($75,324 + $392 debt discount), the cash required to retire the bond should have been $13,694 ($89,410 − $75,716). Why then did EQK report a cash payment of $23,038, an excess of $9,344, as cash from financing?

The answer can be found in the cash flows from operating activities section of the statement of cash flows. "Amortization of discount on zero-coupon mortgage notes" of $9,344 appears as an addback to net income, thereby *removing it from CFO;* $9,344 is the amount of interest that accrued on the zero-coupon bond from January 1992 through its retirement in December 1992. This interest, paid in 1992, was treated as a financing rather than an operating cash outflow. The impact of this misclassification on CFO is significant. Reclassifying the interest expense as CFO turns a positive cash flow of over $8 million into a negative $1.276 million:

Reported CFO	$8,068
Reclassify 1992 interest portion	(9,344)
Adjusted CFO	($1,276)

EXHIBIT 5 **EQK Realty Zero-Coupon Financing, Financial Statement Excerpts**

Balance Sheet

Year Ended December 31	1991	1992
Liabilities		
Mortgage note payable, net of debt discount of $392	—	$75,324
Zero-coupon mortgage notes, net of unamortized discount of $9,574	$89,410	—

Statement of Cash Flows

Year Ended December 31	1992
Cash flows from operating activities	
Net loss	$ (8,850)
Adjustments to reconcile net loss to net cash provided by operating activities	
Amortization of discount on zero-coupon mortgage notes	9,344
Other adjustments	7,574
Net cash provided by operating activities	$ 8,068
Cash flows from financing activities	
Prepayment of zero-coupon note	$(23,038)
Other adjustments	1,572
Net cash provided by (used in) financing activities	$(21,466)

Note 2. Debt Restructuring

In December 1992, the Company refinanced $75,689,000 representing the balance of its zero-coupon mortgage note that remained after reducing this indebtedness with the proceeds from the sale of properties. . . . The new financing, which is collateralized by first mortgage liens . . . matures in December 1995.

Source: EQK Realty Investors, *1992 Annual Report.*

Similar reclassification can be extended to previous years, when the company accrued (but did not pay) interest cost (amortization of discount) on these notes. Reported CFO obscured the fact that at some point the accrued interest must be repaid. As the maturity of the debt approached, the company faced a liquidity crisis.[12]

The following table presents reported and adjusted CFO for the period 1989 to 1994. The treatment of the interest on the zero-coupon bond causes significant distortions both prior to and following the 1992 refinancing.[13]

[12] In 1991 EQK's auditors issued a "going concern qualification" due to the impending maturity of the zero-coupon bond.

[13] The adjustment ignores small amounts of amortization of other discount notes.

EQK Realty Investors Adjustment of Operating Cash Flow (CFO), Years Ending December 31, 1989 to 1994 (in $thousands)

	1989	1990	1991	1992	1993	1994
Reported CFO	$10,458	$9,795	$ 5,728	$ 8,068	$4,087	$2,184
Less: Zero-coupon interest	7,486	8,318	9,229	9,344	0	0
Adjusted CFO	$ 2,972	$1,477	$(3,501)	$(1,276)	$4,087	$2,184

After adjustment, the 1989 to 1991 deterioration in CFO is even more striking as 1991 CFO is negative.[14] The 1992 recovery is less impressive as adjusted CFO remains negative. In 1993, CFO rises despite the burden of full-coupon debt; the unadjusted data obscure this improvement. The adjusted CFO data provide better information regarding the operating cash flow trend.

Variable-Rate Debt

Some debt issues do not have a fixed coupon payment; the periodic interest payment varies with the level of interest rates. Such debt instruments are generally designed to trade at their face value. To achieve this objective, the interest rate "floats" above the rate on a specified-maturity U.S. Treasury obligation or some other benchmark rate such as the prime rate or LIBOR (London InterBank Offered Rate). The "spread" above the benchmark depends on the credit rating of the issuer.

Fixed- versus Variable-Rate Debt and Interest Rate Swaps

Borrowers can issue fixed-rate or variable-rate debt directly; alternatively, they can enter into **interest rate swap** agreements that convert a fixed-rate obligation to a floating-rate obligation or vice versa.

Whether a firm prefers to incur fixed-rate or variable-rate debt depends on a number of factors. Variable-rate debt exposes the firm's interest expense, cash flows, and related ratios to higher volatility due to interest rate changes.[15] On the other hand, when the firm's operating cash flows are correlated with movements in interest rates, variable-rate debt minimizes risk. The common notion that fixed rates minimize risk by reducing the volatility of a firm's income and cash flows is, thus, only a half-truth.[16]

Financial intermediaries (banks, finance companies) generally issue a high proportion of variable-rate debt, as their assets tend to be variable-rate in nature. Thus, they match the variability of their assets and liabilities.

[14] Note the increasing trend of interest expense on the zero-coupon debt, similar to the trend in Exhibit 4.

[15] The impact of interest rate changes can, of course, be either positive or negative.

[16] The investor point of view, however, is different. Variable-rate debt has low price risk; interest rate changes should have minimal impact on its market price. Significant market fluctuation should result only from perceived changes in credit quality. However, the variability of income is higher than for fixed-rate debt.

However, a nonfinancial firm may also view variable-rate debt as hedging variable operating cash flows. For example, the 1996 financial statements of AMR (American Airlines) state:

> Because American's operating results tend to be better in economic cycles with relatively high interest rates and its capital instruments tend to be financed with long-term fixed-rate instruments, interest rate swaps in which American pays the floating rate and receives the fixed rate are used to reduce the impact of economic cycles on American's net income.[17]

Alternatively, a firm may prefer to issue variable-rate debt because management believes that interest rates will fall or short-term rates (the usual basis for variable debt) will remain below long-term rates charged on fixed-rate loans. The analysis of a firm's debt should include a consideration of whether management's choice of financing alternatives is based on the inherent economics of the business or management speculation on future interest rate changes.

Debtors use interest rate swaps to manage the fixed- and variable-rate mix of total borrowings. Box 1 presents the mechanics of interest rate swaps.

EXAMPLE 2

Nash-Finch

Nash-Finch [NAFC] is a food wholesaler with annual sales exceeding $4 billion. The company's debt at December 31, 1998 and 1999 was $300 million and $315 million, respectively. For both years, the variable-rate debt was approximately 42% of the total debt ($128 million in 1998 and $132 million in 1999).

The company engaged in interest rate swaps, converting variable-rate to fixed-rate debt. The company disclosed the following information regarding interest rate swaps outstanding at the 1998 and 1999 year-ends (amounts in $thousands):

	Years Ended December 31	
	1998	**1999**
Receive variable/pay fixed	$90,000	$30,000
Average receive rate	5.5%	5.3%
Average pay rate	6.5%	6.5%

Note that Nash remains liable for the original principal and interest payments on the fixed-rate debt (see Box 1). *At the inception of the swap, no accounting recognition is required although Nash has altered its debt obligation.* Presumably at that time, the swap was "fair," that is, the net present value of the swap payments was zero. The transaction is an *off-balance-sheet contract.*

[17] AMR Corporation, 1996 Financial Statements, Note 6.

The effect of the **swap** was to reduce the sensitivity of Nash to changes in interest rates:

Effect of Swap on Debt Structure (amounts in $thousands)

	1998		1999	
	Before Swap	**After Swap**	**Before Swap**	**After Swap**
Fixed	$172,125	$262,125	$183,609	$213,609
Variable	127,665	37,665	131,990	101,990
Total	$299,790	$299,790	$315,599	$315,599
% Variable	42.6%	12.6%	41.8%	32.3%

The swap has also affected Nash's interest expense as the required payments (fixed) exceeded the amounts received (based on variable rates):

	Years Ended December 31	
	1998	**1999**
Swap	$90,000	$30,000
Interest received	4,950	1,590
Interest paid	(5,850)	(1,950)
Net payment	$ (900)	$ (360)
Interest expense:		
Reported	$29,034	$31,213
Ex-swap	28,134	30,853
Increase due to swap	3.2%	1.2%

What conclusions can we draw from these data?

1. Nash entered into the swaps to reduce its vulnerability to higher interest rates. It did not replace swaps expiring in 1999, thus increasing its exposure. Yet total debt (and variable debt) increased from 1998 to 1999.
2. The swaps increased Nash's interest expense as the fixed-rate payments exceeded the variable rate payments. The net payments can be viewed as the cost of insurance against the effect of higher interest rates.
3. While the fair value of the swaps at inception (net present value) can be assumed to be zero, the fair value will fluctuate over the swap term. If the changes are favorable, Nash-Finch will have an unrealized gain; if unfavorable there will be an unrealized loss.
4. Nash also assumed *counterparty risk,* the risk that the other party will default. When Nash must make net payments (as in 1998 and 1999) there is no risk. If variable rates rose sharply, resulting in payments to

Nash, then default risk would be present.[18] *When a company enters into swaps that are material to its financial position, the analyst should ensure that the counterparties are sufficiently strong so that the likelihood of default is insignificant.*[19]

These conclusions result in questions that the analyst may want to pursue by discussing them with management. Especially in the first case, the answer might yield useful insights regarding management's strategy regarding interest rate risk.

BOX 1 INTEREST RATE SWAPS

Firms use interest rate swaps[a] to exchange variable- (floating-) rate debt for obligations with fixed interest rates or, alternatively, to exchange fixed-rate debt for obligations with variable rates.

Swaps are contractual obligations that supplement existing debt agreements. Each firm remains liable for its original debt, makes all payments on that debt, and carries that debt on its books. The firm with variable-rate debt agrees to pay, at specified intervals, amounts equal to a fixed rate times the *notional principal amount*. In return, the counterparty pays variable amounts equal to the variable interest rate (pegged to a specified rate or index) times that same notional principal amount.

Because firms wish to minimize credit risk, they do not engage in swaps with other industrial firms, even when a swap would meet the objectives of both parties. The **counterparty** is normally a bank or other financial institution with a high credit rating. Money center banks, as a result, have large portfolios of swaps.

Given that some firms prefer variable-rate debt and others fixed-rate debt, why do they not arrange their preferred form of financing directly with their creditors? Why incur the additional costs and/or risks of swaps? Frictions in the credit markets and/or the institutional setting of the firm may result in differential borrowing costs that make it cheaper to borrow in the non-preferred mode and swap into the preferred mode of borrowing rather than borrowing directly in the preferred mode. For example, some "household name" American firms can borrow at very low rates in certain foreign markets. A second factor leading to swaps is that preferences change over time. This is especially true of firms that use swaps to "match" assets and liabilities.

Illustration

The Triple A and Triple B companies each want to borrow $100 million. Assume that the Triple A company prefers variable-rate debt, whereas the Triple B company prefers fixed-rate debt. The companies' respective borrowing rates and preferences are:

(continued)

[a] For a further elaboration of these issues, see James Bicksler and Andrew Chen, "An Economic Analysis of Interest Rate Swaps," *Journal of Finance*, July 1986 and John Hull, *Introduction to Futures and Options Markets* (Englewood Cliffs, NJ: Prentice-Hall, 1995), Chapter 6.

[18] When the fair value of the swap changes so that Nash-Finch has an unrealized gain, realization of that gain depends on the creditworthiness of the counterparty.

[19] If we assume that the counterparty is a highly rated financial institution, it would not provide collateral to protect Nash against default.

OPTIONAL SEGMENT

BOX 1 *(continued)*

Company	Fixed Rate	Variable Rate	Preferred Mode
Triple A	8%	Prime	Variable
Triple B	10%	Prime + 1%	Fixed

The Triple-A company is considered to be more creditworthy than the Triple B company and, hence, is offered more favorable borrowing terms. Note that the rate differential on fixed-rate debt (2%) is greater than the differential (1%) on floating-rate debt. This discrepancy makes it profitable for firms to enter into swaps.

Based on these rates, we demonstrate that the combined borrowing cost for the two firms is 1% lower when each company *borrows in its nonpreferred mode*. This 1% difference is independent of changes in the prime rate.

Company	Borrow Preferred Mode	Borrow Nonpreferred Mode
Triple A	Prime	8%
Triple B	10%	Prime + 1%
Total cost	Prime + 10%	Prime + 9%

The two firms are both better off borrowing in their nonpreferred mode, "swapping" the debt and splitting the 1% savings. The swap agreement requires the following payments:

- The Triple A company pays the Triple B company the prime rate (times the notional amount of $100 million).
- The Triple B company pays the Triple A company 8.5% (times the notional amount of $100 million).

The cost of the original borrowing and the swap for each company is:

	Original Loan	To Swap +Counter-party	From Swap −Counter-party	=	Net Cost
Triple A	8%	Prime	(8.5%)		Prime − 0.5%
Triple B	Prime + 1%	8.5%	(Prime)		9.5%

Each company has obtained debt in its preferred mode at a rate one-half percent below the rate available on its preferred mode of borrowing.

(continued)

BOX 1 (continued)

Economic Effects of the Swap

Assume that the swap illustrated has a five-year term, the prime rate is 6% at inception, payments are made semiannually, and adjustments for changes in the prime rate are also semiannual. The first semiannual assessment results in a net payment of \$1.25 million [0.5 × (8.5% − 6%) × \$100 million] from Triple B to Triple A. If, for the second semiannual period, the prime rate increases to 7%, then the second scheduled payment will be \$0.75 million [0.5 × (8.5% − 7%) × \$100 million]. *Although Triple B has borrowed at a variable rate, increases in that rate are passed on to Triple A as Triple B's payments decline. Thus, Triple B's economic cost is the fixed rate of 9.5%. Conversely, Triple A is exposed to rising interest rates although it has incurred only fixed-rate debt. The swap has changed the economic position of both firms.*

Economic Effects of Termination

Now assume that Triple A, expecting increases in interest rates, wishes to terminate the swap agreement after the first payment. How much should Triple A pay to do so? The required payment should equal the fair value of the swap agreement, calculated as follows.[b]

Triple B is liable for 9 semiannual payments of \$4.25 million (0.5 × 8.5% × \$100 million). If Triple B enters into another swap agreement, it would be based on current interest rates. If the fixed rate has increased by 0.5% (while the prime rate has increased by 1%), Triple B would have to make 9 payments of \$4.5 million (0.5 × 9% × \$100 million), an increase of \$250 thousand. The present value of the increase discounted at the *new* rate of 9% is equal to approximately \$1.8 million. Thus, to terminate the swap, Triple A must pay Triple B that amount.

[b] In our simplified example, we assume that the swap is terminated at the same time when the floating rate is reset. Were this not the case, then a similar calculation would have to be made for the variable-rate bond to compensate for the fact that if Triple B entered into a new swap agreement, while it is true that it would pay a higher fixed rate, it would receive immediately floating-rate payments based on the higher floating rate and not have to wait for the next adjustment date. This calculation, however, is usually not very material; it is for only one payment and the discounting period is less than six months (from the termination date to the interest rate adjustment date).

Debt Denominated in a Foreign Currency

Companies sometimes issue debt for which all interest and principal payments are made in a foreign currency. There are three motivations for such issuance:

1. More favorable terms in foreign markets than domestic ones.[20]
2. Assets denominated in the foreign currency and debt denominated in that currency can hedge[21] against exchange rate movements.
3. Need for foreign currency for a particular investment or other transaction.

The carrying value of foreign currency debt is adjusted for changes in exchange rates. For example, Note 24 of the 2000 financial statements of Roche reports debt in Japanese yen and U.S. dollars as well as Roche's parent currency of Swiss

[20] For example, in July 1998, Pepsico issued one-year notes in Japan (to retail investors) and swapped the fixed-rate obligation for floating rate U.S. dollar payments. The company stated that its net borrowing cost was *comfortably below one-month LIBOR.*

[21] If the parent currency strengthens relative to the foreign currency, then the carrying amount of assets denominated in foreign currencies decreases. This decrease is offset by the decrease (in the parent currency) of the debt to be repaid.

francs. Note that the carrying amounts for the yen and U.S. dollar bonds[22] rose in 2000 due to appreciation of those currencies against the Swiss franc.[23]

This adjustment for exchange rate changes is distinct from any adjustment to current market value. Market value adjustments are based on changes in interest rates.[24] The market value of this debt in local currencies may have increased if interest rates declined since the debt was issued; this change is *not* reflected on the balance sheet. *Thus, the balance sheet liability has been adjusted for exchange rate changes but not interest rate changes.*

Project Debt

Some debt is issued to finance a single project, such as a factory, pipeline, or real estate. In these cases, the debt terms are tailored to the expected cash flows generated by the project. Project debt may be *nonrecourse*, meaning that the lender will be paid only from project cash flows and cannot demand payment from the debtor if the project is unsuccessful. Mortgages on real estate are the major example of nonrecourse debt. Even though such debt is shown on the debtor's balance sheet, the debt is a claim only against the project cash flows and assets. Some project debt is incurred by joint ventures, discussed in Reading 40.

EXAMPLE 3

Forest City Enterprises

Forest City [FCE], a U.S. developer of commercial and residential real estate, finances most of its projects with nonrecourse mortgage debt. The company's capital structure at January 31, 2000 was (in $millions):

Mortgage debt, nonrecourse	$2,382.4	74.5%
Recourse debt	429.9	13.4%
Shareholders' equity	386.5	12.1%
Total capital	$3,198.8	100.0%

The large proportion of nonrecourse debt protects the company from adversity. The effects of one poorly performing project cannot jeopardize others, as the company cannot lose more than its total investment in that project.

[22] The rise in the carrying amount of the zero coupon U.S. dollar obligations is due to accretion of discount as well as the appreciation of the U.S. dollar.

[23] See the financial review (p. 51 of the Roche annual report) for foreign currency data.

[24] In theory, exchange rates are also affected by interest rates. However, that influence is based on the *difference* in interest rate levels between the two countries, *not the level* of interest rates.

Debt with Equity Features

Convertible Bonds and Warrants

To reduce borrowing costs, many companies issue debt convertible into their common shares or issue a combination of bonds and warrants to purchase common shares. Although conceptually these two types of "equity-linked" debt are identical, their accounting consequences may differ.[25]

Convertible Bonds Under APB 14 (1969), the conversion feature of a bond is completely ignored when the bond is issued. Thus, the entire proceeds of the bond are recorded as a liability, and interest expense is recorded as if the bond were nonconvertible. However, the conversion feature lowers interest expense. When the bondholder converts the convertible bond into common stock, the entire proceeds are reclassified from debt to equity. As discussed in Box 2, however, the FASB issued an exposure draft that would change the accounting for convertible debt.

From an analytic perspective, however, recognition should be given to the equity feature prior to the conversion. When the stock price is (significantly) greater than the conversion price, it is likely that the debt will not have to be repaid, and the convertible bond should be treated as equity rather than debt when calculating solvency ratios such as debt-to-equity. When the stock price is significantly below the conversion price, the bond should be treated as debt. At levels close to the conversion price, the instrument has both debt and equity features, and its treatment becomes a more difficult issue.

One possibility is to separate the debt and equity values of the convertible bond, using option pricing models. This analysis is complex, however, and beyond the scope of this book. IAS 32 (2000) requires issuers to split compound instruments into their component parts. The FASB ED would require such separation. Alternatively, the analyst can examine the sensitivity of key ratios to bond classification, first treating the bond as debt and then as equity to see whether the differences are significant. If they are, then the question of whether the debt will be ultimately converted becomes a key issue, which may depend on the purpose of the analysis.[26]

EXAMPLE 4

Holmen

Note 18 of Holmen's annual report shows that in 1998, the company issued debt of SKr 361 million, convertible into class B common shares in 2004 at a price of SKr 148.10. As the market price of Holmen's class B

[25] A convertible bond can be disaggregated into a bond plus an option to convert the bond into common shares. An important difference between a convertible and a debt-plus-warrant issue is that, in the former case, the bond must be surrendered to exercise the option, whereas in the latter case, the bond and warrant are not linked. Thus, the issuer can use the proceeds of exercised warrants for purposes other than the retirement of the associated debt. Another difference is their impact on earnings-per-share calculations. The interest expense on the convertible issue is eliminated when diluted earnings per share are computed, whereas the interest on the debt component of the bond-plus-option alternative will never affect earnings-per-share calculations (however, there is an adjustment for the exercise of dilutive warrants).

[26] For example, in takeover analysis, the intended purchase price will determine whether convertible bonds will be converted to common or remain outstanding debt.

shares was SKr 307 at December 31, 1999, these bonds should be considered equity. The reclassification decreases the debt/total capital ratio:

Holmen Capital Structure
December 31, 1999

	Reported	Reclassification	Adjusted
SKr millions			
Financial liabilities	6,845	(361)	6,484
Equity	15,883	361	16,244
Total capital	22,728		22,728
Financial liabilities	30.1%		28.5%
Equity	69.9%		71.5%

Exchangeable Bonds Some bond issues are convertible into shares of another firm rather than those of the issuing firm. The analysis of such issues is more complex than the analysis of convertible debt. Exercise of the conversion privilege results in:

- extinguishment of the debt
- elimination of the investment in the underlying shares
- recognition of gain or loss from the "sale" (via debt conversion) of the underlying shares

The motivation for such debt issues may include:

1. The desire to obtain cash while retaining the underlying shares for strategic reasons.
2. Minimizing the market effect of sales; the underlying shares are sold over time as bonds are exchanged.
3. Financial benefits: The interest rate on the exchangeable bonds will be lower (because of the exchange feature) than on straight debt, and the exercise price will contain a premium over the current market price.
4. Delayed recognition of a large unrealized gain; recognition is postponed until the exchange privilege is exercised. This delays the income tax recognition of the gain and may permit management some control over the timing of the gain (it can call the bonds, forcing exchange, when it wishes to report the gain).
5. Hedging the investment. SFAS 133 changed the accounting for such hedges.

BOX 2 FASB EXPOSURE DRAFT: ACCOUNTING FOR FINANCIAL INSTRUMENTS WITH CHARACTERISTICS OF LIABILITIES, EQUITY, OR BOTH

On October 27, 2000, the Board issued an exposure draft (ED) that would change the accounting for:

- convertible debt
- redeemable preferred shares

In general, the ED would classify as equity all financial instruments components that establish an ownership relationship with the issuer. A component establishes an ownership relationship if it:

1. Is an outstanding equity share not subject to redemption, or
2. Is an obligation that can or must be settled by the issuance of equity shares, and all changes in the monetary value of the obligation are attributable to, equal to, and in the same direction as the change in the fair value of the issuer's equity shares.

The new standard would require that proceeds of issuance of securities with both liability and equity components be allocated between the value of the liability component and that of the equity component. The most important example is the issuance of convertible debt, which would be accounted for as if the company sold a combination of debt and warrants.

When a company issued convertible debt, it would be required to allocate the proceeds (net of underwriting fees and other direct costs of issuance) between the debt (liability) component and the warrant (equity) component using their relative fair values. If the warrant could not be valued, the issuer would estimate the fair value of the debt component, and allocate the remaining proceeds to the equity component.[a]

Further, if the debt is repurchased or converted, the issuer must recognize gain or loss[b] equal to the difference between the fair value of the debt component and the carrying amount of the liability.

There would also be a gain or loss on the equity component at the date of repurchase or conversion. This gain or loss would be excluded from income but would affect stockholders' equity.

The accounting change would have the following effects:

1. The difference between the fair value of the debt component and its face value would be amortized over the life of the debt, using the effective interest method. This would result in higher interest expense and lower income than under current accounting.
2. Only the debt component would be shown as a liability; the equity component would be recorded in stockholders' equity. As a result, the debt-to-equity ratio would be lower than under the current accounting method.
3. At redemption or conversion, the company would recognize a gain or loss on the liability component. In general, companies would recognize a loss when interest rates were lower at the time of repurchase or conversion than when the debt was issued. In the case of conversion, the fair value of the liability component would be added to equity, rather than the carrying amount under current accounting.

(continued)

[a] This method is styled the "with-and-without method" in the ED.
[b] Under SFAS 145 (2002), gains and losses from the extinguishment of debt are treated as extraordinary items only when they meet the APB 30 criteria for classification as an extraordinary item.

BOX 2 (continued)

4. At redemption or conversion, stockholders' equity would reflect the change in value of the equity component. When the underlying shares have risen in value, equity would rise, reducing the debt-to-equity ratio. Under current accounting, the market value at redemption or conversion date has no effect on the balance sheet.

The ED would also change the classification of redeemable preferred shares (and similar instruments such as Trust Preferreds) by requiring that they be recorded as debt in the issuer's balance sheet. Similarly, the "dividends" paid on such shares would be included in interest expense.

The effect of this change would be to increase the reported debt-equity ratio and reduce the interest coverage ratio of affected firms.

A final standard was expected to be issued prior to the end of 2002. It is likely that affected companies would be required to restate their financial statements for the accounting change.

EXAMPLE 5

Times Mirror

In March 1996, Times Mirror [TMC] sold 1.3 million shares of Premium Equity Participating Securities (PEPS) redeemable for shares of Netscape. TMC had purchased Netscape shares less than one year earlier, before Netscape's initial public offering, at a price of $2.25 per share. TMC's Netscape shares were restricted from public sale. The PEPS were sold at a price of $39.25 with a 4.25% coupon and a March 15, 2001 maturity. At that date, each PEPS was redeemable for the cash equivalent of:

- one Netscape share if that share's price was below $39.25
- .87 Netscape share if its price was $45.15 or higher
- $39.25 cash if Netscape's share price was between $45.15 and $39.25

The advantages to TMC of offering PEPS were that TMC:

1. Received the fair market value of its Netscape shares, at a low interest rate of 4.25%, despite the fact that the shares could not be legally sold.
2. Hedged its investment; if Netscape shares declined, the PEPS holders would receive smaller payments at maturity.
3. Maintained part of the upside potential given the reduced conversion rate if Netscape shares exceeded $45.15 in price at maturity.
4. Postponed capital gains tax until the actual sale of Netscape shares was effected through conversion of the PEPS.
5. Enabled TMC to control the timing of its realization of the large gain on the Netscape investment.

The last two advantages are illustrated by events in 1998 and 1999:

- In 1998, TMC sold part of its Netscape holding, redeemed a corresponding portion of the PEPS, and realized a pretax gain of $16 million.[27]
- In 1999, TMC sold shares of AOL (which had acquired Netscape) and redeemed additional PEPS, reporting a pretax gain of nearly $17 million.

Bonds with Warrants When warrants and bonds are issued together, the accounting treatment differs from that of convertible bonds. The proceeds must be allocated between the two financial instruments.[28] The fair value of the bond portion is the recorded liability. As a result, the bond is issued at a discount, and interest expense includes amortization of that discount. The fair value of the warrants is included in equity and has no income statement impact. When warrants are exercised, the additional cash increases equity capital.

Roche has made extensive use of bonds with equity features (see Note 24 and pages 99–101 of the Roche annual report).

Comparison of Convertible Bonds and Bonds with Warrants As bonds with warrants are accounted for as if they were issued at a discount, the reported liability is lower (but increases as the discount is amortized) as compared to that of a convertible bond. However, reported interest expense is higher.[29] As discussed earlier in this reading, reported cash flow from operations is the same, equal to the coupon interest.

These differences are summarized in the list below, which also includes a comparison with a conventional bond. Note that issuing debt with equity features:

- lowers interest expense
- increases operating cash flows
- results in a balance sheet liability equal to or below that of a conventional bond

In all respects, such debt appears less costly.

Interest Expense	Balance Sheet Liability	Operating Cash Flow
Conventional bond	Conventional bond	Conventional bond
greater than	*equal to*	*less than*
Bond with warrants	Convertible bond	Convertible bond
greater than	*greater than*	*equal to*
Convertible bond	Bond with warrants	Bond with warrants

[27] This gain was previously reflected in equity as TMC carried its investment in Netscape at market value.

[28] As discussed in Box 2, the FASB has proposed extending this accounting treatment to convertible bonds as well.

[29] Because of the accounting difference, American companies rarely issue debt/warrant combinations. However, such issues are common outside of the United States.

However, the financial statement effects are misleading as the cost of the equity feature is ignored. When convertible debt is issued, there is a systematic understatement of interest expense.[30]

Commodity Bonds

The interest and principal payments on bond issues are sometimes tied to the price of a commodity, such as gold, silver, or oil. Firms producing the commodity, as part of a hedge strategy, may issue such bonds. A higher commodity price increases the payments to bondholders but is offset by higher operating profitability. These bonds, therefore, convert interest from a fixed to a variable cost. Such bonds were issued during time periods when commodity prices were rising, making the bonds attractive to purchasers. A recent variation on this theme is the issuance of bonds whose payoff depends on losses due to insurance losses resulting from natural catastrophes.

Perpetual Debt

Some debt issues have no stated maturity. When debt does not have a maturity date, it may be considered preferred equity rather than a liability for analytic purposes. An exception would be cases where debt covenants are likely to force repayment or refinancing of the debt.

EXAMPLE 6

SAS

In 1986, SAS (Scandinavian Airlines) issued a perpetual 200 million Swiss franc–denominated subordinated loan, with the interest rate fixed for 10 years and reset every 10 years. While there is no set maturity date, SAS has the exclusive right to terminate the loan once every five years.

In 1994, SAS repurchased SFR 55.35 million at a price of 72. This repurchase shows that perpetual notes are not the same as equity, as changes in market conditions may lead the issuer to refinance them. However, given management control over the refinancing decision, treatment as preferred equity is appropriate absent evidence of refinancing intent.

When long-term interest rates were at low levels, some firms issued debt with a maturity of 100 years. Although such issues are technically debt, their long maturity suggests that, for all practical purposes, they represent permanent capital and should be treated as equity when computing the debt-to-equity ratio. For example, Walt Disney issued 100-year bonds in 1993.[31]

---

[30] Moreover, the impact of equity-linked bonds on earnings per share must always be taken into consideration.

[31] These bonds have a fixed interest rate of 7.55%, protecting Disney against future interest rate increases. As the bonds are not callable until 2023, the buyers were protected against lower interest rates for 30 years.

Preferred Stock

Many companies issue more than one class of shares. Preferred (or preference) shares have priority over common shares with respect to dividends and entitlement to the proceeds of sale or liquidation. In exchange for this privileged position, preferred shareholders usually give up their right to participate fully in the success of the company.

Preferred shares generally have a fixed dividend payment and a fixed preference on liquidation. Dividend payments are almost always *cumulative;* if not paid when due, they remain a liability (but one that is not recorded). Dividend arrears must be paid before any dividend can be paid to common shareholders. When calculating the net worth of a company with preferred shares outstanding, the analyst should:

1. Subtract the liquidating value of the preferred, not the par or stated value, which may be lower.
2. Subtract any cumulative dividends that are in arrears.

Some preferred shares have a variable interest rate. "Auction rate" preferred shares have interest rates that change frequently, making them attractive to buyers seeking "money-market"-type investments.[32] From an analytical perspective, these preferred shares function as short-term liabilities and should be treated as such. They are often called when market conditions change, making them a less permanent source of funds.

Preferred shares are almost always callable by the issuer. Many issues are, however, redeemable by the preferred shareholder, often over a period of years.[33] Because of these "sinking fund" provisions, redeemable preferreds should be treated as debt for analysis; they should be included as debt in solvency ratios, and dividend payments should be treated as interest. The FASB has issued an exposure draft (see Box 2) that would require redeemable preferred shares to be reported as debt, and the "dividends" on such shares included in interest expense, as required by IAS 32 (2000).

Consistent with this view, the SEC requires that redeemable preferred shares be excluded from stockholders' equity. However, at the same time, the SEC does not require their classification as debt. The argument against debt classification is that, ultimately, *firms cannot be forced to pay the dividends or redeem the preferred shares. Unlike creditors, preferred shareholders do not have the power to force the firm into bankruptcy for noncompliance* with the terms of the agreement.[34] Often, when dividends are in arrears, they do gain representation on the board of directors.

The ambiguity as to whether these shares are debt or equity was shown in two studies by Kimmel and Warfield (1993, 1995). They found that only 60% of redeemable preferred shares are actually redeemed; the other 40% are eventually converted to common shares, arguing against treating these hybrids as debt. Furthermore, as a firm's systematic risk (its beta) is related to a firm's debt-to-equity ratio, they tested whether the relationship had a better "fit" with the redeemables treated as debt or equity. They found that they *did not fit into either category unless the redeemables had voting rights and were convertible.* Only when these

[32] For U.S. corporate buyers, preferred dividends are 70% tax-free when ownership is below 20%, making these issues more attractive on an after-tax basis than many other short-term investments. The exclusion is 80% for ownership of 20% but below 80%.

[33] These provisions provide preferred shareholders with a guaranteed future value for the shares.

[34] In many states, a firm cannot pay dividends or redeem shares if such payments will jeopardize the company's survival.

attributes were present did the securities exhibit equitylike qualities. Thus, on average, one cannot generalize as to the nature of these hybrid securities.

The line between debt and equity has become increasingly blurred in recent years. Companies prefer to issue securities that minimize the after-tax cost of financing yet provide maximum flexibility.[35] Some issues are designated preferreds but are really debt; others are called debt but are functionally equity. Although help from accounting standards setters is on the way, analysts must evaluate such instruments on a case-by-case basis and decide whether to treat them as debt or equity.

Effects of Changes in Interest Rates

Debt reported on the balance sheet is equal to the present value of future cash payments discounted at the *market rate on the date of issuance*. Increases (decreases) in the *current market rate* decrease (increase) the *market value* of the debt. A company that issues fixed-rate debt prior to an increase (decrease) in market rates experiences an economic gain (loss) as a result of the rate change. This economic gain or loss is not reflected in either the income statement or balance sheet.

For some analytical purposes, however, the market value of a company's debt may be more relevant than its book value. It better reflects the firm's economic position and is as important as the current market values of a firm's assets. Analysis of a firm's absolute and relative level of debt and borrowing capacity should be based on current market conditions. Consider two firms reporting the same book value of debt. One firm issued the debt when interest rates were low; the other at higher current interest rates. Debt-to-equity ratios based on book values may be the same. However, the firm that issued the bonds at the lower interest rate has higher borrowing capacity as the economic value of its debt is lower.[36] Ratios calculated using the market value of debt would reflect the stronger solvency position.

Furthermore, in valuation models that deduct the value of debt from the value of the firm (or of its assets), that debt should be measured at market value rather than book value.[37] Firms that issued debt at lower rates are relatively better off when interest rates increase, and this advantage should increase the equity value of the firm.

In the United States, SFAS 107, Disclosures about Fair Value of Financial Instruments, requires that firms report the fair value of outstanding debt. IAS 32 (1998) has similar requirements. Box 3 restates the debt of Westvaco from book to market value. This exercise is useful for several reasons.

First, financial statement disclosures are based on year-end (or quarter) prices. When interest rates have changed significantly since the last report date, the analyst may need to recalculate the market value of the firm's debt. Second, most non-U.S. firms, and firms in the United States that are not subject to FASB disclosure requirements, do not provide market value disclosures; analysts must know how to estimate the market value of debt for such firms. Finally, market valuation requires assumptions and (especially for firms with complex financial

[35] Trust Preferred Securities (TPS) are an example of such securities. For tax purposes, they are treated as debt. While they cannot be classified as equity, they are not reported as debt but rather as preferred shares or minority interest. Similarly, "dividend" payments are reported as preferred dividends or minority interest. Frischmann, Kimmel, and Warfield (1999) refer to TPSs as the "Holy Grail" of financial instruments and report that, since their introduction in 1993, they have become the primary mode of new issues of preferred shares.

[36] Theoretically, it could refinance its current debt at the same interest rate as the other firm, lowering the book value of debt.

[37] Similarly, in discounted cash flow valuation analysis, the calculation of a firm's (weighted-average) cost of capital is based on market rather than book values of debt (and equity).

instruments) often there are competing valuation methods. In some cases, analysts may want to perform their own market value calculations. To do so, they must disaggregate management's aggregate fair value disclosure; this requires an understanding of how market values are estimated.

EXAMPLE 7

Westvaco

The book value of Westvaco's long-term debt was $1,477 million at October 31, 1999; its market value was $1,494 million, or 1% higher. The October 31, 1998 book value was $1,557 million; its market value was $1,636 million, or 5% higher. Thus, during the 1999 fiscal year, market value relative to book value declined 4%. This decline reflected the rise in interest rates (see Box 3), which reduced the fair value. The decline reflects the structure of Westvaco's debt, which is mostly fixed-rate debt with long maturities.

The Westvaco example above is not unique. The market value of the long-term debt of Mead [MEA] was 6.6% higher than book value at December 31, 1998 (Mead was on a calendar year). One year later, the market value was 2.9% below the book value; during calendar 1999, therefore, market value relative to book value declined by 9.5% as interest rates rose. Mead, which merged with Westvaco early in 2002, had a similar debt structure, mostly fixed rate debt with long maturities.

BOX 3 ESTIMATING THE MARKET VALUE OF DEBT

In many cases, the replacement of book value with market value is simple. For publicly traded debt, market values are readily available.[a] If the debt is not publicly traded, its present value can be calculated by applying the current market rate to the original debt terms. The maturity, coupon rate, and other terms of long-term debt are generally disclosed for each debt security issued.

The appropriate current market rate can be obtained from:

1. Other publicly traded debt of the company having approximately the same maturity; estimate the rate used by the market to discount that debt.
2. Publicly traded debt of equivalent companies in the same industry; estimate the rate used to discount that debt.
3. Estimating the risk premium over the rate on government debt of the same maturity. The risk premium depends on the bond-rating "risk" class of the company's bonds.

Calculating the Market Value of Debt

Footnote J in Westvaco's financial statements shows notes payable and long-term obligations at October 31, 1999. The company reports the fair value as required by SFAS 107.[b] The book and fair values for the three years ended October 31, 2000 are (in $thousands):

(continued)

[a] Sources include rating service publications (such as Standard & Poor's *Bond Guide*), newspapers, and electronic quotation services.

[b] The book value does not match the total of current and noncurrent obligations in footnote J. The company has apparently excluded some long-term obligations that it considers not to be financial instruments.

BOX 3 (continued)

October 31	1998	1999	2000
Book value	$1,557,477	$1,477,162	$2,716,772
Fair value	1,636,093	1,494,290	2,627,696
Difference	$ 78,616	$ 17,128	$ (89,076)

Source: Westvaco *Annual Reports, 1999 and 2000.*

The maturities, coupon rates, and carrying amounts for most obligations are listed in footnote J. Some obligations are publicly traded while others are not.

As Westvaco discloses the fair (market) value of its debt, we forgo the laborious task of calculating the estimated market value for each issue. The following comments are intended as a guide for use when such calculations are required.

Most of Westvaco's debt at October 31, 1999 consists of fixed-rate long-term debentures, some of which have sinking funds. Because the rate is fixed and the duration is long, the fair value of these bonds fluctuates with interest rates.

Example

In 1990 Westvaco, which was A rated, issued $100 million of 9.75% bonds due June 15, 2020. At the issue date, the yield[c] was 130 basis points (1.3%) above the yield on the U.S. Treasury 8.75% bonds due in May, 2020. The price and yield to maturity of the U.S. Treasury 8.75% issue at October 31, 1998–2001 was reported by Bloomberg as follows:

October 31	1998	1999	2000	2001
Price	142-11[d]	124-30	131-4	145-11
Yield-to-maturity	5.40%	6.53%	6.02%	4.98%

[d] U.S. government securities with maturities longer than one year are quoted as a % of face value in 32nds. Thus 142-11 means 142 11/32% of face value or $1,423.44 per $1,000 bond.

Source: Price and yield data from Bloomberg.

Estimation of the fair value of the Westvaco 9¾% bonds requires an estimate of the spread over the U.S. **Treasury bond**. That spread is a function of the rating of the corporate issuer (Westvaco) and the spread between bonds of different ratings classes. Bond quality spreads are variable over time, tending to compress when the economy is strong (and concerns about credit quality are low) and to widen when economic conditions weaken.

Westvaco was A rated by Standard & Poor's at October 31, 1997 and A rated at October 31, 1998. Standard & Poor's data show little change in quality spreads in 1998 and 1999. Thus, our calculations assume that the Westvaco bonds had a yield to maturity of 130 basis points for both years.

(continued)

[c] Throughout this box, yield means yield-to-maturity.

BOX 3 *(continued)*

Extending this analysis to 2000 and 2001, we find two changes:

1. Westvaco's S&P rating was reduced from A− to BBB+ in May 2000 and further reduced to BBB in June 2001. These rating reductions reflected Westvaco's higher leverage.
2. Quality spreads started to widen in 2000 and 2001 as concerns grew about the economic outlook and the possible effect of recession on corporate credit quality. The September 11, 2001, terrorist attacks accelerated this trend.

Thus our estimated **yield spread** for the Westvaco bonds is 180 basis points at October 31, 2000, and 220 basis points at October 31, 2001.

The following table shows the results of these assumptions and the calculated fair value of the Westvaco bonds. These fair value estimates differ from the actual market value reported in Bloomberg by less than 2% each year.

October 31	1998	1999	2000	2001
Yield on U.S. 8.75% bond	5.40%	6.53%	6.02%	4.98%
Assumed spread	1.30%	1.30%	1.80%	2.20%
Assumed yield on Westvaco 9.75% bond	6.70%	7.83%	7.82%	7.18%
Calculated value of Westvaco bond	$1,344.85	$1,194.43	$1,191.50	$1,260.88
Bloomberg value of Westvaco bond	1,369.80	1,217.40	1,169.30	1,245.60
Difference	−1.8%	−1.9%	1.9%	1.2%

Source: Price and yield data from Bloomberg.

Complexities in Market Value Estimation

Because of the conventional nature of Westvaco's debt, the calculation of its market value is straightforward. Westvaco's debt is virtually all fixed rate and dollar denominated. Simple debt structures, however, are becoming the exception rather than the rule for large companies, given globalization and the increased sophistication of financial markets.

Some complexities make the calculation of market values almost impossible as the requisite information is lacking. A few of the complexities summarized below have been discussed earlier, others will be addressed in later sections of the text, and some remain beyond the scope of our book.

Convertible Bonds

Market prices are readily available for most convertible debt issues. However, these prices incorporate both the debt and equity features of the security. Only the debt component of the market value should be included as part of debt.

(continued)

BOX 3 *(continued)*

Variable-Rate Debt

Variable-rate debt usually requires no market value adjustment. Because of the continuous adjustment of the interest rate on the debt, market value approximates book value.[e]

Debt Denominated in a Foreign Currency

For debt denominated in a foreign currency, the present value calculations should be based on current interest rates for the currency in which the debt is denominated.

Hedges and Derivatives

Firms can protect themselves against changes in interest rates and/or currency exchange rates using instruments such as options or **forward contracts** (including swap agreements). In this reading we confine ourselves to a discussion of *interest rate swaps*.

As previously discussed, *the original debt instrument with its original parameters remains in effect and is reported in the firm's financial statements; if publicly traded, market prices are available*. However, the estimated market value of the underlying debt instrument must reflect any interest rate swap.

When fixed-rate debt has been converted to floating-rate debt with an interest rate swap covering its full term, no adjustment to market value is required. If a swap does not cover the full term of fixed-rate debt, changes in interest rates after the end of the swap term will affect market values. Thus, it is important to discern the terms of any swaps by careful reading of footnotes.

When a swap converts floating-rate debt to fixed-rate debt, however, the market value is exposed to changes in interest rates. Even though the market value of the original obligation does not change, the fair value of the effective (because of the swap) obligation does and should be calculated.

---

[e] This is not precisely accurate. The variable-rate adjustment may lag the interest rate change. Nevertheless, given the short period until adjustment, the effect of any lag on present value is usually immaterial. Because of this, SFAS 107 states that, for variable-rate debt, the book value can be used to approximate the market or fair value.

These factors (confirmed by empirical results discussed in Box 4) suggest the conditions to be considered before deciding whether the restatement of debt to market value is a useful exercise. All of the following factors should be considered.

Debt: Market or Book Value?

Given the effort and assumptions required to estimate market values when they are not provided, we now turn to a discussion of the factors that determine whether the adjustment from book value to market value is a useful exercise. Empirical results with respect to these factors are discussed in Box 4.

Debt Maturities The effect of interest rate changes on the market value of debt increases with the maturity of the debt. If a firm's debt is mostly short-term, changes in interest rates will not appreciably affect its market value.[38]

---

[38] Thus, even if its long-term debt is adjusted by 10%, total debt will only be affected by 10% times the percentage of long-term debt. The lower the percentage of long-term debt, the smaller the overall adjustment.

Interest Rates on Debt For adjustable-rate debt, whose interest rate varies with the market rate of interest, book value approximates market value and no adjustment is required. On the other hand, the market value of fixed-rate debt issues does change with interest rates. This is especially true of zero-coupon and other discount debt, due to their longer duration relative to debt of the same maturity issued at par.

When a firm has swapped its fixed debt for floating-rate debt, there should be no adjustment, as the value of that debt is no longer exposed to interest rate changes. Conversely, when a firm swaps variable rates for fixed rates, the market value of that portion of its debt will vary with interest rates and adjustment is required.

Changes in Market Interest Rates The adjustment to market value depends on changes in the market rate of interest. As long as there is no long-term trend, fluctuations in market value tend to offset, leaving the difference between book and market values small. However, when rates rise or fall greatly over several years, the differences between book and market value can be significant.

Embedded Interest Rate Westvaco issued debt at various times and its (weighted) average outstanding coupon rate (*embedded rate*) was approximately 8.39%,[39] within the range of interest rates over the late 1990s. The adjustment from book value does not depend on the change in interest rates itself, but rate changes relative to the imbedded rate. As interest rates were below the embedded rate for both 1998 and 1999, the fair value exceeds book value.

Unless there are limits on the firm's ability to refinance (noncallable debt or deterioration in credit quality), the embedded rate should decline (with some lag) as interest rates fall. The reverse is not true; firms with long-term fixed-rate debt can enjoy low interest costs for many years even though interest rates in general have risen.

BOX 4 MARKET OR BOOK VALUES: EMPIRICAL EVIDENCE

Bowman (1980) examined the relationship between firms' market betas and the debt-to-equity ratio. Finance theory predicts that the higher a firm's debt-to-equity ratio (using market values), the higher the firm's beta.

Letting the superscripts M and B refer to the market and book value, respectively, Bowman examined which of the following four measures of the debt-to-equity ratio, D^M/E^M, D^M/E^B, D^B/E^M, and D^B/E^M, were more closely associated with the firm's beta.

Bowman obtained the best results when he used the market value of equity in the denominator. Whether debt was measured on a market basis or book basis made little difference as the ratios D^B/E^M and D^M/E^M yielded similar results. The pure book value ratio D^B/E^B did not perform as well; the measure of the market value of the debt-to-book value of equity (D^M/E^B) performed the poorest.

These results can be partly attributable to the fact that for close to 60% of the debt in Bowman's sample, book value and market value were equivalent. Furthermore, the correlation between the market value of debt and the book value of debt

(continued)

[39] Calculated as interest incurred (from Westvaco footnote F) divided by the average debt level. For 1999, the calculation is

$$\frac{\$132,428}{(\$1,552,377 + \$1,605,415)/2} = 8.39\%$$

BOX 4 *(continued)*

was close to 100%. As the study ranked debtors by relative rather than absolute levels of debt, changes in the market rates of interest shifted debt valuations without changing ranks.

Mulford (1986) replicated Bowman's study by using a later time period. Bowman's analysis was based on 1973 data, predating the dramatic rise in market interest rates of the late 1970s. Mulford, referring to Bowman's study, noted:

> His failure to find evidence of superior performance for a debt-to-equity ratio based on market values of debt may have been due to small differences between the book and market values of debt which accompanied the general level of interest rates at that time.[a]

To remedy this deficiency, Mulford focused on 1980, when market rates of interest were historically high. In addition, to alleviate potential measurement problems arising from the conversion of book to market values, he examined the performance of portfolios of firms in addition to individual firms. Mulford's results were more in line with theory, but only on a portfolio basis. No matter which variation was used to measure the relationship between beta and debt-to-equity, the market-based debt-to-equity ratio was always the most closely associated with beta on a portfolio basis. On an individual basis, D^M/E^M did not always perform as well, but the differences between it and the best performing ratio were minimal.

These results suggest, not surprisingly, that the market value of debt is not superior to book value when the difference between the stated and market rates of interest is small; the additional cost of obtaining market values is not worthwhile.[b] Adjustment is necessary only when the gap between the historic and market rates of interest is large. Even then, potential measurement problems[c] in estimating market values may offset any benefits from the adjustment process.

---

[a] Charles W. Mulford, "The Importance of a Market Value Measurement of Debt in Leverage Ratios: Replications and Extensions," *Journal of Accounting Research*, Autumn 1984, pp. 897–906.

[b] Given the high correlation between market and book values of debt, this is especially true for analyses that focus on relative rather than absolute debt burdens.

[c] The issue of a measurement problem also calls into question the results of both Bowman and Mulford from a different perspective. They adjusted only on-balance-sheet debt, ignoring any "off-balance-sheet" debt. As Reading 40 will make clear, the latter can be significant.

Debt of Firms in Distress

When the credit quality of a firm changes significantly (in either direction), the market price of debt will follow, independent of interest rate trends. When credit quality and the market value of debt decline, there appears to be a gain to the firm, yet it is difficult to argue that shareholders are better off. This apparent paradox reflects simultaneous changes in the value of assets as credit quality changes. It is reasonable to assume that some assets of such troubled companies are impaired (see the discussion in Reading 37).

Accounting for Restructured and Impaired Debt

When a debtor is in financial difficulty, creditors may agree to accept assets in payment of the debt or to "restructure" the obligation by modifying its terms (e.g., reducing the interest rate or deferring principal payments). When debt is extinguished, both the debtor and creditor will recognize gain or loss measured as the difference between the fair value of the assets (cash or other assets) used to repay the debt and its carrying amount. This accounting treatment raises neither accounting nor analysis issues.

When the obligation is restructured, however, different accounting rules apply to creditors and debtors. Creditors adhere to SFAS 114 (1993), as amended by SFAS 118 (1994), whereas debtors use SFAS 15 (1977) to account for these transactions.

Under SFAS 114, the creditor must recognize a loss equal to the difference between the carrying value of the loan and the present value of the restructured payment stream *discounted at the original discount rate* (effective interest rate). Thus, if a 12% coupon loan with a face value of $100,000 and three years remaining to maturity is restructured by reducing the interest rate to 8%, the creditor recognizes a loss of $9,610 as the new carrying value of the loan is $90,390.[40] The loan **impairment** may also be measured using the observable market price of the loan or the fair value of collateral when the loan is collateral dependent.[41]

The FASB was reluctant, however, to allow debtors to record gains resulting from financial distress. SFAS 15 provides that the debtor's carrying amount of the debt be compared with the *undiscounted gross cash flows* (principal and interest) due after restructuring. As long as the gross cash flows exceed the carrying amount, the debtor recognizes no gain. In our example, the future payments are ($100,000 + 3 × $8,000) = $124,000. No gain is recognized.[42]

However, the present value of the cash flows has been reduced; in economic terms, the debtor has gained at the expense of the creditor. The accounting mandated by SFAS 15 recognizes this transfer only over the life of the loan as payments are made; the debtor will show lower interest expense as the loan is amortized at the implicit interest rate of the loan. In our example, interest expense is now calculated at an interest rate of 8% rather than 12%.

A similar approach is mandated by the FASB for loans considered to be "impaired." Creditors are required to recognize the probable loss, but recognition of gains by debtors is not allowed. Under SFAS 114, creditors are required to carry impaired loans at the present value of cash flows expected after modification of the loan terms, *discounted at the original effective interest rate.* For the debtor, however, no gain recognition is permitted.

For purposes of analysis, however, both impaired and restructured debt should be restated to fair market value using a *current market interest rate* to discount the cash flows required by the (actual or expected) restructured obligation. However, as noted earlier, debtor "gains" should be viewed warily; gains resulting from an inability to repay loans are almost certainly offset by asset impairment.

Retirement of Debt Prior to Maturity

Firms generally choose the initial debt maturity of their obligations based on such considerations as cost and investment horizon (when projects funded with debt are expected to generate cash flows). Subsequently, conditions may change and a firm may wish to refinance or retire debt prior to the original maturity. Examples include:

---

[40] If we assume annual payments, the present value of a three-year annuity of $8,000 discounted at 12% + present value of $100,000 in three years discounted at 12% equals $90,390.

[41] SFAS 118 amended SFAS 114 to allow creditors to continue income-recognition methods for impaired loans that had been used prior to the adoption of SFAS 114. For example, cost-recovery or cash-basis methods report investments in impaired loans at less than the present value of expected future cash flows. In these cases, no additional impairment needs to be recognized under SFAS 118. SFAS 114 was also amended to require additional disclosures regarding the investment in certain impaired loans and the recognition of interest income on those loans.

[42] If the payments do not exceed the carrying value, then the gain is limited to the difference between those amounts; the debt is discounted at an implicit interest rate of zero.

- Declining interest rates permit the reduction of interest cost.
- Increasing cash from operations permits debt retirement earlier than expected.
- Sale of assets or additional equity generates funds and the firm decides to reduce **financial leverage**.

In such cases, the firm can reduce bank debt, commercial paper, and other short-term debt quickly and at small expense. For longer-maturity debt, the firm may exercise **call provisions**, tender offers, or in-substance defeasance. We examine the economic and accounting effects of these choices shortly.

Accounting for Debt Retirement

When firms retire debt prior to maturity, the gain or loss (difference between the book value of the liability and the amount paid at retirement) is treated as a component of continuing operations.[43]

Using the par bond example in Exhibit 1A, assume that on December 31, 2001, the market interest rate for the firm is 12%. As a result, the market price of the bonds should be $96,535.[44] If the firm paid $96,535 to retire the bond, the resulting gain on the bond retirement is $3,465 since the book value is $100,000.[45] While this gain must be included in income from continuing operations, there are two reasons why an analyst should consider treating it as a non-operating item:

- In reality, the firm is no better off as a result of the refinancing. To finance the retirement of the bond, it must issue new debt[46] bearing at least the same effective interest rate (and must incur transaction costs). Effectively, over the remaining life of the original bond, the net borrowing cost would be identical; the company has simply replaced 10% coupon debt with 12% coupon debt. In economic terms, the gain took place as interest rates rose, not when the refinancing took place. Because of the use of historical cost as a measure of the bond liability, however, only refinancing results in a recognized gain.[47]
- The decision to refinance is a function of the change in market interest rates. The analyst should evaluate the transaction to determine whether the gain or loss should be considered as part of normal operations or treated analytically as an extraordinary item.

In the early 1970s, interest rates rose sharply at the same time the U.S. economy entered recession. Firms found their outstanding low-coupon bonds selling at deep discounts. Many of these firms had poor operating profitability, but were

---

[43] SFAS 145 (2002) rescinded both SFAS 4 (1975), which mandated extraordinary item treatment for these gains and losses, and SFAS 64 (1982), which provided an exemption from extraordinary item reporting for gains and losses on normal sinking fund repurchases. Under SFAS 145, gains and losses on retirement of debt are reported as extraordinary items only if they meet APB 30 criteria.

[44] This can be seen from Exhibit 1C as the carrying amount of the discount bond is the present value at the (original) 12% interest rate.

[45] We have ignored unamortized debt issuance costs. When bonds are retired, the firm must write off these costs that were capitalized when the bonds were issued. This write-off becomes a component of the gain or loss on retirement.

[46] Even if it did not issue new debt to retire the bond but rather used internal funds, the firm would experience an opportunity cost equal to the forgone interest revenue.

[47] If the gain or loss is recognized at all, it should be in the period in which interest rates change, not in the year in which the refinancing takes place. In our example, the year is the same, but that coincidence is rare in practice.

able to increase reported income by retiring bonds. The issuance of SFAS 4 in 1975 was partially a response to this income manipulation activity.

In the late 1990s, lower interest rates resulted in the refinancing of higher coupon debt, resulting in a recognized loss. That loss should be viewed, however, as a signal of lower future interest expense, as high-coupon debt is replaced by lower-coupon debt (also see the following discussion of callable bonds).

EXAMPLE 8

DaimlerChrysler

In 1990, predecessor Chrysler had issued $1.1 billion of 12% debt, due in 2020. The high interest rate was due to the higher level of interest rates and Chrysler's poor debt rating. As a result of lower interest rates and improved financial condition, the bonds sold at a large premium in the late 1990s. Late in 1996, Chrysler repurchased half of the issue, recording an extraordinary pretax loss of $309 million. In 1998, DaimlerChrysler repurchased an additional $300 million of the bonds, recording an extraordinary pretax loss of $230 million (€203 million). The company replaced this high-cost debt with lower coupon debt, reducing interest expense significantly. The combined effect of the extraordinary loss from debt retirement (decreasing equity) and reduced future interest expense (increasing earnings) is a higher reported future return on equity.

Our discussion of discretionary debt retirements indicates that the amounts and timing of the accounting gain and the economic gain from debt retirement are quite different. This especially applies to callable bonds, whose retirement may give rise to economic profit but may generate a loss for accounting purposes.

Callable Bonds

When a bond is callable, the issuer has the option to buy back (call) the bond from bondholders at predetermined dates and prices. This differs from the case in which the issuer retires the old bond at a market price equal to the present value of the future payment stream. The call price is usually set at a premium over the face value of the bond, but is independent of the present value of the payment stream at the time the call is made. However, the actual exercise does depend on the relationship of the call price to that present value.

Exhibit 6 contains an analysis of a callable bond. The decline in interest rates constitutes an economic loss at the time of the rate change, as the market value of the bond rises. In the absence of the call provision, a decision to refinance would not impact Cole, which would incur new debt equal to $106,624 to refinance the debt at market rates. However, the call provision permits the firm to retire the bonds for only $102,000; the economic gain is the difference.[48]

[48] When bonds are issued, the call provisions are often an important ingredient in the market reception. As call provisions benefit only the issuer, bond buyers will bargain against them. Option-adjusted bond analysis is now routine. See, for example, Frank J. Fabozzi, *Fixed Income Analysis for the Chartered Financial Analyst Program*, New Hope, Pennsylvania; Frank J. Fabozzi Associates, 2000 (pp. 347ff). Many shorter-term issues are noncallable.

EXHIBIT 6 Analysis of Callable Bond

On January 1, 2001, Cole issues the following bond:

Face value	\$100,000
Coupon	10% (annual payments assumed for simplicity
Maturity	5 years
Call provision	Callable at any time after one year at 102

If the market interest rate applicable to Cole is 10%, then the bonds will be issued at par.

Reported Liability = \$100,000
Annual Interest Expense = \$10,000 (10% × \$100,000)

Assume that, on December 31, 2001, the market rate applicable to Cole has declined to 8%. The rate change has no accounting impact on the company. However, the present value of the cash flows associated with the debt rises to \$106,624 (discounted at 8%). Absent the call provision, the expected market price of the bonds is 106.624.

By calling the bonds at a price of 102, Cole realizes an economic gain of \$4,624 [(106.624 − 102) × (\$100,000)].

However, the call results in an accounting loss of \$2,000 [(100 − 102) × (\$100,000)].

Economically, it is beneficial to refinance the debt, but the income statement reports a loss. One can only speculate as to how many firms have not refinanced under such conditions because of the financial statement impact. This is yet another reason why analysts should ignore gains and losses from the retirement of debt.

Defeasance

In some cases, the firm wishes to retire debt but is unable to do so because the debt is non-callable. *In-substance defeasance* involves setting aside riskless securities sufficient to pay all remaining **installments** of principal and interest. The cash flow characteristics of the securities used must match those of the debt being defeased and must be placed in a trust fund restricted for that purpose.

Although the original debt remained outstanding, U.S. GAAP permitted debtor firms to derecognize the defeased obligations through December 31, 1996.[49] However, SFAS 125 (1996)[50] disallows in-substance defeasance and debt may be extinguished only on repayment or when the debtor is legally released from being the primary obligor. IAS 32 (2000) disallowed defeasance for firms following IAS GAAP.

---

[49] See SFAS 76 (1983) and FASB Technical Bulletin 84-4 for accounting and disclosure requirements related to defeasance.

[50] See SFAS 125, Accounting for the Transfers and Servicing of Financial Assets and Extinguishments of Liabilities.

3 BOND COVENANTS

Creditors use debt covenants in lending agreements to protect their interests by restricting activities of the debtor that could jeopardize the creditor's position. Auditors and management must certify that the firm has not violated the covenants. If any covenant is violated, the firm is in *technical default* of its lending agreement, and the creditor can demand repayment of the debt after the stated grace period. Generally, however, as we shall see, the terms are renegotiated but at a cost to the debtor as the lender demands concessions. The analysis of a firm's debt position must therefore take into consideration the nature of these covenants and the risk that the firm may violate them.

Information on debt covenants is important both to evaluate the firm's credit risk as well as to understand the implications of such restrictions for the firm's dividend and growth (investment) prospects. In addition, to the extent these covenants are accounting-based, they may affect the choice of accounting policies.

Nature of Covenants

Smith and Warner (1979) characterize debt covenants as placing limits on one or more of the following activities:

1. payment of dividends (includes share repurchases)
2. production and investment (includes mergers and acquisitions, sale and leaseback, or outright disposal of certain assets)
3. issuance of new debt (or incurrence of other liabilities)
4. payoff patterns (includes sinking fund requirements and the priorities of claims on assets)

In addition to direct restrictions on activities, covenants may require maintenance of certain levels of such accounting-based financial variables as stockholders' equity (or retained earnings), working capital, interest coverage, and debt-to-equity ratios. These levels are often related to the four types of activities listed above by restricting a certain activity if the accounting variable violates the specified target level. In some cases, the violation itself may signal a breach of the covenant even without any subsequent firm activity.

Bond covenants may also require that interest rates depend on certain financial ratios.

EXAMPLE 9

Luby's

Based in Texas, Luby's [LUB] operates cafeterias. It entered into a credit agreement with a group of banks early in 1996. That agreement was subsequently amended four times:

1. January 24, 1997
2. July 3, 1997
3. October 27, 2000
4. June 29, 2001

The second and third amendments are of particular interest. The second amendment increased the credit line from $100 million to $125 million but added the following provision with respect to the spread over the LIBOR rate ("applicable margin"):

Applicable margin means the following per-annum percentages, applicable in the following situations:

***Applicability* If the Leverage Is:**	**LIBOR Basis for Advances of One, Two, Three, or Six Months**	**LIBOR Basis for Advances of Seven to Fourteen Days**
not less than 2 to 1	0.225	0.325
less than 2 to 1	0.200	0.300
Difference	0.025	0.025

This provision gives the lender an additional margin over LIBOR of 2.5 basis points (.025%) if the leverage ratio (debt-to-equity ratio as defined in the original credit agreement) exceeds 2.0. This additional margin was presumably intended to compensate the lender for the additional risk.

The third amendment, adopted when Luby's earnings had fallen sharply, changed the *applicable margin* as follows:

***Applicability* If the Leverage Is:**	**LIBOR Basis for Advances of One, Two, Three, or Six Months**	**LIBOR Basis for Advances of Seven to Fourteen Days**
greater than or equal to 2.75 to 1	0.500	2.500
greater than or equal to 2.50 to 1 but less than 2.75 to 1	0.375	2.125
greater than or equal to 2.25 to 1 but less than 2.50 to 1	0.000	1.750
less than 2.25 to 1	0.000	1.250

This amendment increased the lending spread to reflect the higher leverage ratio, and provided a sliding scale under which the spread increases and decreases with the leverage ratio (a measure of risk).

Additionally, as detailed in Exhibit 7, the third amendment introduced a covenant based on the fixed-charge coverage ratio as well as imposing restrictions on net worth (stockholders' equity) and the leverage ratio. Note the extent to which the ratios as well as their components are defined by the agreement.

These provisions had several effects:

1. To restrict the ability of Luby's to incur additional debt that would dilute the interest of the creditors.

2. To require Luby's to maintain stockholders' equity, limiting its ability to pay dividends (it eliminated its dividend in October 2000) or buy back stock, either of which would reduce cash and the equity cushion.
3. To reward creditors for the level of risk by increasing the interest rate margin as the leverage ratio increases.

Luby's provides an example of bond covenants. Additional discussion regarding the nature of accounting-based debt covenants can be found in Box 5.

EXHIBIT 7 Excerpts from Luby's Bond Covenants

Fixed Charge Coverage Provision

"Earnings Available for Fixed Charges" means, for any period, calculated for the Borrower and its Subsidiaries on a consolidated basis in accordance with GAAP, the sum of (a) EBITDA, plus (b) all lease and rental expense pursuant to Operating Leases, minus (c) cash taxes paid, minus (d) Capital Expenditures.

"Fixed Charges" means, for any period, calculated for the Borrower and its Subsidiaries on a consolidated basis in accordance with GAAP, the sum of (a) all interest, premium payments, fees, charges and related expenses (including, but not limited to, interest expense pursuant to Capitalized Lease Obligations) in connection with borrowed money or in connection with the deferred purchase price of assets, in each case to the extent treated as interest in accordance with GAAP, (b) all dividends and distributions paid in respect of Capital Stock and (c) all lease and rental expenses pursuant to Operating Leases.

"Fixed Charges Coverage Ratio" means, for any date of determination, the ratio of (a) Earnings Available for Fixed Charges for the period of four consecutive fiscal quarters ending on such date to (b) Fixed Charges for the period of four consecutive fiscal quarters ending on such date.

The Borrower covenants and agrees that it will not allow the Fixed Charges Coverage Ratio to be less than 1.20 to 1 at the fiscal quarter ending November 30, 2000 or at the end of any fiscal quarter thereafter.

Net Worth Provision

The Borrower covenants and agrees that it will not allow its Net Worth at any time to be less than the sum of (i) $190,000,000 plus (ii) 50% of Consolidated Net Income (excluding Consolidated Net Income for any fiscal quarter in which Consolidated Net Income was a negative number) earned on or after September 1, 2000, plus (iii) 75% of the Net Cash Proceeds of any equity issues of the Borrower's Capital Stock in an underwritten public offering pursuant to an effective registration statement under the Securities Act of 1933, as amended, after September 1, 2000.

Leverage Ratio Provision

The Borrower covenants and agrees that it will not allow the Leverage Ratio to be greater than (a) 3.00 to 1 at the fiscal quarters ending November 30, 2000, February 28, 2001 and May 31, 2001, (b) 2.60 to 1 at the fiscal quarter ending August 31, 2001 and (c) 2.50 to 1 at the fiscal quarter ending November 30, 2001 and each fiscal quarter thereafter.

Source: Third Amendment to Credit Agreement, dated October 27, 2000, Exhibit 4(j) to Luby's Form 10-K for year ended August 31, 2000.

BOX 5 ACCOUNTING-BASED DEBT COVENANTS

Exhibit 8 contains a summary of the nature of accounting-based debt covenant restrictions, adapted from Duke and Hunt (1990). *Restricted retained earnings* as a constraint on dividend payments, one of the most common forms used, is outlined in Exhibit 9. The Luby's covenants discussed in the text are examples of these restrictions.

Information regarding these covenants was obtained by Smith and Warner (1979) and Duke and Hunt (1990) from the American Bar Foundation's *Commentaries on Debentures*, which summarizes typical covenants found in lending agreements. A cursory examination of these restrictions makes it clear that creditors seek to limit the firm's level of risk (investment and debt restrictions) and preserve the assets of the firm to ensure that debts are repaid (payment restrictions). Thus, covenants attempt to limit shareholders' ability to transfer assets to themselves (dividend restrictions), new shareholders (merger and acquisition restrictions), or new creditors (debt restrictions).

The best source of information on specific covenants (and other terms of the bond issue) for publicly issued bonds is the bond indenture, the legal document created when the bond is issued and filed with the registration statement filed with the SEC. The trustee (normally a bank) will have a copy of the **indenture** and is responsible for the enforcement of its terms. The bond prospectus should contain a good summary of these terms. Bank credit agreements entered into by public companies are filed with SEC annual (10-K) or quarterly (10-Q) reports.

For all debt issues, summarized data can be found in:

- services such as Moody's Industrial Manual
- annual reports
- SEC filings by debtors

Press and Weintrop (1990 and 1991) contend that information obtained from annual reports and Moody's is not comprehensive, especially with respect to covenants relating to privately placed debt, and that in these cases, it is necessary to access the original SEC filings.

Calculation of Accounting-Based Constraints

Each type of constraint is defined in the covenants. In addition, the covenants specify:

- Whether GAAP definitions are to be used or GAAP is to be modified. Leftwich (1983) noted that such modifications are most often associated with private rather than public debt indentures.
- Whether GAAP in effect at the time of the debt issuance are maintained throughout the life of the bond ("frozen" GAAP), or calculations in subsequent years are to be based on GAAP in effect at the date of the calculation ("rolling" GAAP). This is important when important new accounting standards are adopted.

Mohrman (1996) examined a sample of 174 lending agreements that contained covenants based on financial statement information. She found that over half (90) the covenants were based on *fixed* GAAP specified in the agreements. That is, the covenants were not affected by voluntary or FASB-mandated accounting changes, nor were they originally designed to mimic GAAP in effect at the time the contract was signed. Additionally, she found that contracts that contained more accounting-based covenants were more likely to specify fixed GAAP provisions and the use of such provisions in contracts was increasing over time.

(continued)

BOX 5 *(continued)*

EXHIBIT 8 Common Accounting-Based Debt Covenant Restrictions

Attribute:	Retained earnings
Measured as:	Restricted retained earnings
Limits:	Payments of dividends or stock repurchase below minimum level of restricted retained earnings
Attribute:	Net assets
Measured as:	Net tangible assets or net assets
Limits:	Investments, dividend payments, and new debt issues if net assets fall below a certain level
Attribute:	Working capital
Measured as:	Minimum working capital or current ratio
Limits:	Mergers and acquisitions, dividend payments, and new debt issues if the working capital or the current ratio fall below a certain level
Attribute:	Debt-to-equity
Measured as:	Debt divided by net tangible assets or debt divided by net assets
Limits:	Issuance of additional debt

Source: Joanne C. Duke and Herbert G. Hunt III, "An Empirical Examination of Debt Covenant Restrictions and Accounting-Related Debt Proxies," *Journal of Accounting and Economics*, Jan. 1990, adapted from Table 1, p. 52.

EXHIBIT 9 Unrestricted Retained Earnings: Inventory of Payable Funds

The most frequent accounting-based restriction specified is the dividend constraint. Dividends cannot be paid out of restricted retained earnings. Only unrestricted retained earnings, often referred to as the inventory of payable funds (IPF), are available for dividends. The general formulation of IPF is defined (see Smith and Warner, 1979) as the sum of:

1. a specified percentage k of earnings E from the date of the debt issuance to the present period, plus
2. proceeds from the sale of common shares CS from the date of the debt issuance to the present period, plus
3. a prespecified constant F, less
4. the sum of dividends DV and stock repurchases from the date of the debt issuance to the present period.

(Exhibit continued on next page . . .)

BOX 5 (continued)

EXHIBIT 9 (continued)

Algebraically, this is equal to

$$\text{IPF}_t = k \sum_{i=0}^{t} E_i + \sum_{i=0}^{t} CS_i + F - \sum_{i=0}^{t} DV_i$$

where period 0 represents the date of the debt issuance and period t refers to the current date. The prespecified constant F is usually set at approximately one year's earnings.[a] This builds some slack into the system in the event the firm has a loss.

[a]See Smith and Warner (1979), Note 36.

Costs and Effects of Covenant Violations

Although creditors have a right to demand immediate payment when an accounting-based debt covenant is violated, they do not usually do so. This does not mean that violating such covenants is costless. Waivers of such violations often come with strings attached. Creditors may renegotiate the terms of the debt to demand:

- accelerated principal payments
- an increased interest rate
- liens on assets (such as accounts receivable)
- new covenants increasing restrictions on the firm's investing, borrowing, and dividend-paying ability

Chen and Wei (1993) examined a sample of 128 companies that disclosed violations of their accounting-based debt covenants. For 71 of these firms, the creditors did not waive the violation but demanded accelerated payments or higher interest rates. Beneish and Press (1993) found the median interest rate increase to be 80 basis points; they estimated that the overall cost of such renegotiations averaged from 1 to 2% of the market value of the firm's equity or 4 to 7% of the balance on the loan.

When waivers were granted, not surprisingly, they were more often granted for secured debt and for smaller-size loans. Similarly, waivers were more likely to be granted to "healthier" firms considered less likely to become bankrupt. When waivers were granted, they were often (24 of the 57 companies) given only for limited time periods.

Successful renegotiation of the debt terms or receipt of a waiver may not be the last word. Chen and Wei found that by the following year creditors demanded payment of the debt for 39 companies (30% of the sample), forcing 13 companies into bankruptcy.

Beneish and Press found that accounting-based covenants were often relaxed as a result of renegotiation. However, they were supplanted with more direct covenants restricting capital expenditures, mergers, assets sales, stock repurchases, and future borrowings.

These results indicate the importance of monitoring debt covenants to ensure that the firm is not close to violating them. Such violations can expose the firm to direct out-of-pocket costs in the form of higher borrowing costs and/or limit the scope of a firm's investing and financing choices.[b]

[b] Given these costs, one can understand why DeFond and Jiambalvo (1994) reported that managements engage in (accounting) manipulations in an effort to satisfy the covenants.

SUMMARY

In this reading, we have examined the different forms that debt financing can take. The choice of debt issue can have significant effects on the pattern of reported income, cash flows, and financial position. In addition, different debt instruments respond differently to changes in interest rates. The reader should now have an understanding of the following issues:

1. The effects of zero-coupon or low-coupon debt, variable rate debt, and foreign currency debt on the firm's financial statements.
2. The economic and financial statement effects of interest rate swaps.
3. The implications for financial analysis of variable-rate debt versus fixed-rate debt.
4. The economic and accounting effects of debt with equity features.
5. The analyst's need to classify between debt and equity based on the essence of the financial instrument rather than its form.
6. The effect of changes in interest rates on the market value of debt and when the market value should be used instead of carrying value.
7. The accounting effects of debt retirement and analytical adjustments required.
8. The importance of debt covenants to the analysis of the firm.

Debt can also take forms that do not require recognition on the balance sheet. Such off-balance-sheet debt is the subject of the next reading.

PRACTICE PROBLEMS FOR READING 39

1. [Zero-coupon debt; CFA® adapted] Compare the effect of issuing zero-coupon debt with that of issuing full-coupon debt with the same effective interest rate on a company's:

A. Cash flow from operations over the life of the debt

B. Cash flow from financing in the year of issuance, the year of maturity, and over the life of the debt.

C. Cash flow from investing over the life of the debt

D. Trend of net income over the life of the debt

2. [Zero-coupon bonds] The Null Company issued a zero-coupon bond on January 1, 2000, due December 31, 2004. The face value of the bond was $100,000. The bond was issued at an effective rate of 12% (compounded annually).

A. Calculate the cash proceeds of the bond issue.

B. Complete the following table on a *pretax* basis, assuming that all interest is paid in the year it is due:

	2000	2001	2002	2003	2004
Earnings before interest and taxes	$50,000	$50,000	$50,000	$50,000	$50,000
Cash flow from operations before interest and taxes	60,000	60,000	60,000	60,000	60,000
Cash flow from operations					
Times interest earned					
Times interest earned (cash basis)					

C. Assume that Null had raised the same cash proceeds with a conventional bond issued at par, paying interest annually and the principal at maturity. Complete the following table, under the assumptions in Part B:

	2000	2001	2002	2003	2004
Earnings before interest and taxes	$50,000	$50,000	$50,000	$50,000	$50,000
Cash flow from operations before interest and taxes	60,000	60,000	60,000	60,000	60,000
Cash flow from operations					
Times interest earned					
Times interest earned (cash basis)					

D. Using the results of parts b and c, discuss the impact on reported cash flow from operations and interest coverage of Null's choice of bond.

E. Explain how consideration of income taxes would change your answers to Parts B through D.

3. [Zero-coupon bond; foreign currency debt] Roche has outstanding zero-coupon U.S. dollar notes, with a $2.15 billion face value due 2010, that were issued with a 7% yield to maturity. They are carried at the following amounts:

	12-31-98	12-31-99
Carrying amount (CHF millions)	1,282	1,618
Exchange rate (CHF/dollar)	1.37	1.60

A. Compute the carrying amount of the bonds in $U.S. at December 31, 1998.

B. Explain the difference between your answer to part a and the $2.15 billion face amounts of the notes.

C. Estimate the interest expense (in CHF) for those notes for 1999.

D. Using your answer for part c and the December 31, 1998 carrying value, estimate the carrying amount of the notes (in CHF) at December 31, 1999.

E. Provide two possible explanations for the difference between your answer to part d and the actual carrying amount in Swiss francs at December 31, 1999.

F. Describe the effect of issuing these notes, instead of full coupon notes, on Roche's:

i. Cash from operations

ii. Trend of interest expense

G. Describe the effect of the change in the value of the dollar during 1999 on Roche's interest expense on these notes.

4. [Understanding bond relationships; coupon versus effective interest] The Walk & Field Co. has outstanding bonds originally issued at a discount. During 2000, the unamortized bond discount decreased from $8,652 to $7,290. Annual interest paid was $7,200. The market rate of interest was 12% when the bond was issued.

Using the data provided, calculate:

i. Interest expense for 2000

ii. The face value of the bond

iii. The coupon rate of the bond

Note: You do not need present value calculations or tables to solve this problem.

5. [Foreign currency debt] Bristol-Myers [BMY] reported the following components of its long-term debt (in $millions):

December 31	1998	1999
2.14% yen notes, due 2005	$55	$62
1.73% yen notes, due 2003	54	62

The $U.S. equaled 113.60 Japanese yen at December 31, 1998, and 102.51 at December 31, 1999.

A. Compute the outstanding debt in Japanese yen at December 31, 1998 and 1999 for both issues.

B. Compute the percentage change in the outstanding debt in yen during 1999 for both issues.

C. Assuming that no new bonds were issued, state one conclusion that can be drawn from your answers to parts a and b.

D. State two possible motivations for Bristol-Myers, an American company, to issue debt in Japanese yen.

6. [Convertible debt] Note 5 of Takeda's annual report states that the company had convertible bonds outstanding at March 31, 1998 but none outstanding at March 31, 1999. From the statement of stockholders' equity and cash flow statement we can deduce that most of the bonds (more than 22 billion yen) were converted into approximately 11 million shares, implying a conversion price of approximately 2,000 yen per share. The market price of Takeda shares exceeded 3,000 yen during all of calendar 1998.

Years Ended March 31	1998	1999
As reported in ¥ millions		
Bank loans	9,509	9,361
Current debt	24,077	2,119
Long-term debt	10,896	9,858
Total debt	44,482	21,338
Equity	829,381	907,373
Total capital	873,863	928,711

A. Describe the advantages to Takeda of having issued these convertible notes rather than nonconvertible notes. State one disadvantage.

B. Compute Takeda's debt-to-total capital ratio at March 31, 1998, and March 31, 1999. State the factor that accounted for most of the change in that ratio.

C. State the appropriate classification for the convertible notes at March 31, 1998 (debt or equity) and justify your choice.

7. [Market value of debt versus book value; interest rate sensitivity] AMR [AMR] is the parent company of American Airlines. Exhibit P-1 contains extracts from Note 6 of AMR's 1999 annual report.

A. Based on the fair value data, state whether the long-term rates used to determine fair value rose or fell in 1999. Justify your choice.

B. State whether the interest rate used to determine the fair value of the $437 million "9.0%–10.20% debentures" (due through 2021) at December 31, 1999, was:

i. Below 10.20%

ii. Above 10.20%

Justify your choice.

C. Explain why the fair value of the $86 million variable-rate indebtedness equals the carrying value for both years.

EXHIBIT P-1 AMR Corp.

Amounts in $millions

6. Financial Instruments and Risk Management Fair Values of Financial Instruments

The fair values of the Company's long-term debt were estimated using quoted market prices where available. For long-term debt not actively traded, fair values were estimated using discounted cash flow analyses, based on the Company's current incremental borrowing rates for similar types of borrowing arrangements. The carrying amounts and estimated fair values of the Company's long-term debt, including current maturities, were (in millions):

	December 31			
	1999		1998	
	Carrying Value	Fair Value	Carrying Value	Fair Value
Secured variable and fixed-rate indebtedness	$2,651	$2,613	$890	$1,013
7.875% – 10.62% notes	1,014	1,024	875	973
9.0% – 10.20% debentures	437	469	437	531
6.0% – 7.10% bonds	176	174	176	189
Variable rate indebtedness	86	86	86	86
Other	16	16	20	20
	$4,380	$4,382	$2,484	$2,812

(Exhibit continued on next page . . .)

EXHIBIT P-1 (continued)

Interest Rate Risk Management

American enters into interest rate swap contracts to effectively convert a portion of its fixed-rate obligations to floating-rate obligations. These agreements involve the exchange of amounts based on a floating interest rate for amounts based on fixed interest rates over the life of the agreement without an exchange of the notional amount upon which the payments are based. The differential to be paid or received as interest rates change is accrued and recognized as an adjustment of interest expense related to the obligation. The related amount payable to or receivable from counterparties is included in current liabilities or assets. The fair values of the swap agreements are not recognized in the financial statements. Gains and losses on terminations of interest rate swap agreements are deferred as an adjustment to the carrying amount of the outstanding obligation and amortized as an adjustment to interest expense related to the obligation over the remaining term of the original contract life of the terminated swap agreement. In the event of the early extinguishment of a designated obligation, any realized or unrealized gain or loss from the swap would be recognized in income coincident with the extinguishment.

The following table indicates the notional amounts and fair values of the Company's interest rate swap agreements (in millions):

	December 31			
	1999		1998	
	Notional Amount	Fair Value	Notional Amount	Fair Value
Interest rate swap agreements	$696	$(9)	$1,054	$38

The fair values represent the amount the Company would pay or receive if the agreements were terminated at December 31, 1999 and 1998, respectively.

At December 31, 1999, the weighted-average remaining life of the interest rate swap agreements in effect was 5.1 years. The weighted-average floating rates and fixed rates on the contracts outstanding were:

	December 31	
	1999	1998
Average floating rate	5.855%	5.599%
Average fixed rate	6.593%	6.277%

Floating rates are based primarily on LIBOR and may change significantly, affecting future cash flows.

Source: AMR 10-K Report, December 31, 1999.

8. [Debt refinancing] On July 14, 2000, the *Wall Street Journal* reported on the earnings report by Fannie Mae [FNM], the largest mortgage lender in the United States. Fannie Mae has substantial outstanding debt and uses hedging techniques to manage its exposure to changing interest rates. Excerpts form that article follow:

> *Fannie Mae Posts 15% Earnings Gain for the Quarter*
> by Patrick Barta
>
> Fannie Mae overcame a cooling housing market to report double-digit earnings growth for the second quarter. . . .
>
> However, some pointed out that the company's results included a one-time after-tax gain of $32.7 million from the retirement of debt that helped compensate for a one-time trading loss. Typically, such gains are omitted when a company calculates its earnings-per-share results.
>
> "In our mind, [the gain] should be excluded," says Charles L. Hill, First Call's director of research.
>
> Fannie Mae says the company has long included retirement of debt in its earnings-per-share calculations, because it considers retirement of debt to be part of its continuing operations. The company notes that it reported gains and losses from debt retirement in its earnings-per-share calculations in 27 of the last 40 quarters. "It's something we do on a regular basis," says Mary Lou Christy, vice-president of investor relations.
>
> At the heart of the debate was a one-time loss of about $60 million, attributed to a hedging strategy that lost money after interest rates for Fannie Mae debt rose unexpectedly.
>
> The company was able to offset much of the loss by repurchasing debt at favorable rates, which produced the $32.7 million gain.[51]

A. Present one reason why the gain from debt retirement should be considered part of Fannie Mae's operating earnings and one reason why it should not.

B. Present one reason why the loss from the hedging strategy should be considered part of Fannie Mae's operating earnings and one reason why it should not.

C. Recommend the proper treatment for both items, from an analyst viewpoint, and justify your recommendation.

9. [Debt covenants] Exhibit P-2 contains information from NorAm Energy's 1994 Annual Report regarding debt covenants imposed by its creditors. The covenants restrict new borrowings and dividend payments. The exhibit states that as of December 31, 1994 the company has dividend capacity equal to $43.3 million. This amount was computed after reflecting the annual dividend of $42 million declared in 1994.

[51] *Wall Street Journal*, July 14, 2000, p. A2.

EXHIBIT P-2 NorAm Energy Corp.

Stockholders' Equity and Debt Covenants

Condensed Shareholders' Equity

	1994	1993
Capital Stock		
Preferred	$130,000	$130,000
Common stock including paid-in capital	944,870	944,118
	$1,074,870	$1,074,118
Retained Deficit		
Balance at beginning of year	(366,080)	(360,121)
Net income (loss)	48,066	36,087
Cash dividends		
Preferred stock, $3.00 per share	(7,800)	(7,800)
Common stock, $0.28 per share in 1994 and $0.28 per share in 1993	(34,265)	(34,246)
Balance at end of year	$(360,079)	$(366,080)
Unrealized gain on Itron investment, net of tax	2,586	
Total stockholders' equity	$717,377	$708,037

Note 5. Restrictions on Stockholders' Equity and Debt

Stockholders' Equity and Debt Covenants

Under the provisions of the Company's revolving credit facility as described in Note 3, and under similar provisions in certain of the Company's other financial arrangements, the Company's total debt capacity is limited and it is required to maintain a minimum level of stockholders' equity. The required minimum level of stockholders' equity was initially set at $650 million at December 31, 1993, increasing annually thereafter by (1) 50% of positive consolidated net income and (2) 50% of the proceeds (in excess of the first $50 million) of any incremental equity offering made after June 30, 1994. The Company's total debt is limited to $2.055 million. Based on these restrictions, the Company had incremental debt issuance and dividend capacity of $321.2 million and $43.3 million, respectively, at December 31, 1994. The Company's revolving credit facility also contains a provision which limits the Company's ability to reacquire, retire or otherwise prepay its long-term debt prior to its maturity to a total of $100 million.

Source: NorAm Energy, *1994 Annual Report.*

A. Show how the dividend capacity of $43.3 million as of December 31, 1994 was computed.

B. State whether the debt covenants restrict NorAm's ability to maintain its annual dividend through 1998. Justify your answer by preparing a schedule for the years 1995–1998 showing NorAm's expected and minimum shareholders' equity given current income and dividend levels.

C. Compute the level of income that would be required to maintain current dividend levels through 1998.

D. In 1995, NorAm approached its shareholders with a proposal to issue new shares. Suggest why the company was motivated to make this proposal and whether you, as a shareholder, would have supported the proposal.

LEASES AND OFF-BALANCE-SHEET DEBT

by Gerald I. White, Ashwinpaul C. Sondhi, and Dov Fried

READING

40

LEARNING OUTCOMES

The candidate should be able to:

a. discuss the incentives for leasing assets instead of purchasing them, and the incentives for reporting the leases as operating leases rather than capital leases;

b. contrast the effects of capital and operating leases on the financial statements and ratios of lessees and lessors;

c. describe the types of off-balance-sheet financing and analyze their effects on selected financial ratios;

d. distinguish between sales-type leases and direct financing leases and explain the effects of these types of leases on the financial statements of lessors.

INTRODUCTION 1

Rapid changes in manufacturing and information technology and expanding international trade and capital markets have resulted in the growth of multinational corporations that must cope with increasingly mobile capital, labor, and product markets. Volatile commodity and other factor price levels, fluctuating interest and foreign currency exchange rates, and continuous tax and regulatory changes have accompanied these changes. In addition, general inflation and industry-specific price changes have raised many asset prices and have increased the risks of operations and investments.

This economic climate has required increasing amounts of capital as firms acquire operating capacity (both for expansion and replacement purposes) at ever-higher prices. Because of the volatility of prices and cash flows, the risks of owning operating assets have also increased. These trends have driven firms to seek methods of:

1. acquiring the rights to assets through methods other than traditional direct purchases (financed by debt)
2. controlling the risks of operation through derivative and hedging transactions

Executory contracts are the primary alternative form of transactions used by firms to acquire operating capacity, supplies of raw materials, and other inputs. Such contracts or arrangements are the subject of this reading.

The increased use of these financing techniques and hedging transactions has been encouraged by drawbacks in the historical cost-based financial reporting system, in which recognition and measurement depend primarily on actual transactions. As contracts are considered legal promises, and neither cash nor goods may be exchanged at the inception of these contracts, accounting recognition is not required in many cases. The emphasis on accounting assets and liabilities rather than the recognition of economic resources and obligations further encourages firms to keep resources and obligations off the balance sheet.

Firms may engage in these transactions to avoid reporting high debt levels and leverage ratios and to reduce the probability of technical default under restrictive covenants in debt indentures. Off-balance-sheet transactions may also keep assets and potential gains out of the financial statements but under the control of management, which can orchestrate the timing of gain recognition to offset periods of poor operating performance.

Footnote disclosures constitute the best source of information about off-balance-sheet activities. Additional information may be available from disclosures in 10-K filings and from other company publications. In some cases, the economic meaning behind the disclosures requires explanation from management. Thus, a complete analysis of the firm must include a review of all financial statement disclosures to obtain data on off-balance-sheet activities. In many cases, straightforward adjustments can be used to reflect off-balance-sheet assets and liabilities on the balance sheet. Such adjustments result in a balance sheet that presents a more complete portrait of the firm's resources and obligations and financial ratios that are more comparable to those of competitors whose use of off-balance-sheet techniques is different.

The reading begins with a discussion of leases, the most common form of executory contract entered into by firms. The methods used to analyze and adjust for leases serve as a model for the analysis of other off-balance-sheet activities that comprise the second part of the reading.

LEASES 2

Accounting policy makers have grappled with leases for years to develop reporting requirements that emphasize the economic substance rather than the legal form of the leasing transaction. We begin our discussion of leases with a review of incentives for leases. A discussion of reporting requirements and the analysis of leases complete this section of the reading.

Incentives for Leasing

Firms generally acquire rights to use property, plant, and equipment by outright purchase, partially or fully funded by internal resources or externally borrowed funds. In a purchase transaction, the buyer acquires (and the seller surrenders) ownership, which includes all the benefits and risks embodied in the asset. Alternatively, firms may also acquire the use of property, including some or all of the benefits and risks of ownership, for specific periods of time and stipulated rental payments through contractual arrangements called *leases.*

Short-term, or *operating,* leases allow the lessee to use leased property for only a portion of its economic life. The lessee accounts for such leases as contracts, reporting (as rental expense) only the required rental payments as they are made. Because the lessor retains substantially all the risks of ownership of leased property, the leased assets remain on its balance sheet and are depreciated over their estimated economic lives; rental payments are recognized as revenues over time according to the terms of the lease.

However, longer-term leases may effectively transfer all (or substantially all) the risks and rewards of the leased property to the lessee. Such leases are the economic equivalent of sales with financing arrangements designed to effect the purchase (by the lessee) and sale (by the lessor) of the leased property. *Such leases, referred to as finance or capital leases, are treated for accounting purposes as sales.* The asset and associated debt are carried on the books of the lessee, and the lessor records a gain on "sale" at the inception of the lease. The lessee depreciates the asset over its life, and treats lease payments as payments of principal and interest.[1] The lessor records a financing profit over the lease term. The financial reporting differences between accounting for a lease as an operating or capital lease are far-reaching and affect the balance sheet, income statement, cash flow statement, and associated ratios.

One motivation for leasing rather than borrowing and buying an asset is to avoid recognition of the debt and asset on the lessee's financial statements.[2] Lease capitalization eliminates this advantage. Whether a lease is reported as operating or capitalized depends, as we shall see, on the terms of the lease and their relationship to criteria specified by SFAS 13 and IAS 17.

Notwithstanding these financial reporting requirements, leases may be structured to qualify as operating leases to achieve desired financial reporting effects and capital structure benefits. Operating leases allow lessees to avoid recognition of the asset and report higher profitability ratios and indicators of operating efficiency. Reported leverage is also lower because the related liability for contractual payments is not recognized.

[1] The lease payments made by the lessee to the lessor are recorded by the latter as receipts of principal and interest.

[2] Firms may believe that investors, lenders, and rating services do not adjust for leases. However, debt covenants sometimes explicitly include operating leases. Ratings services also incorporate leases when setting debt ratings (see, for example, Moody's Investors Service, *Off-Balance-Sheet Leases: Capitalization and Ratings Implications,* October 1999).

Extensive use of operating leases needs careful evaluation, and the analyst must adjust financial statements (to reflect unrecognized assets and liabilities) and the leverage, coverage, and profitability ratios for the effects of operating leases.

Box 1 reviews the finance literature on the competing incentives of the lease-versus-purchase decision. The impact of the financial reporting alternatives (operating vs. capitalization) on this decision is also discussed.

Lease Classification: Lessees

The preceding discussion suggests that lessees prefer to structure and report leases as operating leases. Their counterparts, lessors, however, prefer to structure leases as capital leases. This allows earlier recognition of revenue and income by reporting transactions that are in substance installment sales or financing arrangements as completed sales. The resulting higher profitability and turnover ratios are powerful incentives for lessors. The final section of the reading is devoted to a discussion of lease accounting from the perspective of the lessor. The discussion that follows retains the lessee perspective.

Lease classifications are not intended to be alternative reporting methods. However, management actively negotiates the provisions of lease agreements and the preferred accounting treatment is an important element of these contractual negotiations.

SFAS 13 (1976) and IAS 17 (revised 1997) attempt to promulgate "objective" and "reliable" criteria to facilitate the evaluation of the economic substance of lease agreements. One goal was to discourage off-balance-sheet financing by lessees and front-end loading of income by lessors. The criteria are designed to ensure that either the lessee or lessor recognize the leased assets on their books.

Capital Leases

A lease that, in economic substance, transfers to the lessee substantially all the risks and rewards inherent in the leased property is a financing or capital lease and should be capitalized. Under U.S. GAAP, the lessee must classify a lease meeting any one of the following SFAS 13 criteria at the inception of the lease as a capital lease:

1. The lease transfers ownership of the property to the lessee at the end of the lease term.
2. The lease contains a bargain purchase option.
3. The lease term is equal to 75% or more of the estimated economic life of the leased property (not applicable to land or when the lease term begins within the final 25% of the economic life of the asset).
4. The present value[3] of the minimum lease payments[4] (MLPs) equals or exceeds 90% of the fair value of leased property to the lessor.

The ownership and bargain purchase criteria imply a transfer of all the risks and benefits of the leased property to the lessee; in economic substance, such leases are financing arrangements. Lease terms extending to at least 75% of the

[3] The discount rate used to compute the present values should be the lessee's incremental borrowing rate or the implicit interest rate of the lessor, whichever is *lower*. The use of the lower rate generates the higher of two present values, increasing the probability that this criterion will be met and the lease capitalized. Under IAS 17, there is a similar (but less precise) requirement.

[4] MLPs include residual values when they are guaranteed by lessees since the guarantee results in a contractually fixed residual value and effectively transfers the risk of changes in residual values to the lessee.

BOX 1 INCENTIVES FOR LEASING AND THEIR EFFECT ON THE CAPITAL VERSUS OPERATING LEASE CHOICE

Management may have a number of reasons to prefer leasing compared to outright asset purchases. The choice may be a function of strategic investment and capital structure objectives, the comparative costs[a] of leasing versus equity or debt financing, the availability of tax benefits, and perceived financial reporting advantages. Some of these factors influence whether the lease will be treated as an operating or capital lease; others are unrelated to reporting methods.

Tax Incentives

The tax benefits of owning assets are exploited best by transferring them to the party in the higher marginal tax bracket. Firms with low effective tax rates more readily engage in leasing than firms in high tax brackets as the tax benefits can be passed on to the lessor. El-Gazzar et al. (1986) found that, consistent with this hypothesis, firms with lower effective tax rates had a higher proportion of lease debt to total assets than did firms with higher effective tax rates. Moreover, lessees with high effective tax rates tended to capitalize their leases for financial statement purposes. El-Gazzar et al. argue that tax effects also influence the choice of accounting method as the lessee attempts to influence the tax interpretation (by the IRS) of lease contracts. That is, it is more difficult to argue for capital lease treatment for tax purposes if the lease is treated as an operating lease for book purposes.

Nontax Incentives

Smith and Wakeman (1985) analyzed nontax incentives related to the lease-versus-purchase decision. Their list of eight nontax factors that make leasing more likely than purchasing is presented here. Some of these factors are not directly related to the lessee's choice, but are motivated by the manufacturer or lessor and/or the type of asset involved. We have sorted these conditions by their potential impact on the operating-versus-capitalization accounting choice.

Nontax Incentives for Leasing versus Purchase: Incentives Classified by Potential Impact on Operating versus Capital Lease Choice

Favors Operating Lease per SFAS 13

1. Period of use is short relative to the overall life of the asset.
2. Lessor has comparative advantage in reselling the asset.

Favors Structuring Lease as Operating Lease

3. Corporate bond covenants contain specific covenants relating to financial policies that the firm must follow.
4. Management compensation contracts contain provisions expressing compensation as a function of returns on invested capital.

Not Relevant to Operating versus Capital Lease Decision

5. Lessee ownership is closely held so that risk reduction is important.
6. Lessor (manufacturer) has market power and can thus generate higher profits by leasing the asset (and controlling the terms of the lease) rather than selling it.

(continued)

[a] Related to these costs are the risks related to residual values and obsolescence.

BOX 1 *(continued)*

7. Asset is not specialized to the firm.
8. Asset's value is not sensitive to use or abuse (owner takes better care of asset than lessee).

Short periods of use and the resale factor favor the use of operating leases, and under GAAP, these conditions would lead to lease agreements consistent with operating leases. The bond covenant and management compensation incentives also favor the negotiated structuring of the agreement as an operating lease.

Consistent with the foregoing, both Abdel-Khalik (1981) and Nakayama et al. (1981) note that the expected covenant violations resulting from SFAS 13 influenced firms to lobby against its adoption. Furthermore, Abdel-Khalik notes that firms renegotiated the terms of their leases during SFAS 13's transition period to make them eligible for treatment as operating leases. Imhoff and Thomas (1988) found that subsequent to SFAS 13, there was a general decline in leases as a form of financing.[b] Taken together, these results confirm that debt covenant and compensation factors affect both the choice of leasing as a form of financing as well as the choice of accounting treatment of the lease.

Based on Smith and Wakeman (1985).

[b] Further evidence is provided by El-Gazzar et al., who note that in the pre-SFAS 13 period, firms that had high debt-to-equity ratios and/or had incentive-based contracts based on income after interest expense were more likely to have leases classified as operating leases.

economic life of the leased asset are also considered to achieve such a transfer; there is an implicit assumption that most of the value of an asset accrues to the user within that period. Finally, a lease must be capitalized when the present value of the minimum lease payments is equal to or exceeds 90% of the fair value of the leased property at the inception of the lease. In effect, the lessee has contractually agreed to payments ensuring that the lessor will recover its investment along with a reasonable return. The transaction is, therefore, an installment purchase for the lessee financed by the lessor, and capitalization reflects this economic interpretation of the leasing transaction.[5]

The provisions of IAS 17 are less precise. That standard defines a finance lease (the IAS term for a capital lease) as one:

> that transfers substantially all of the risks and rewards incident to ownership of an asset. Title may or may not eventually be transferred.[6]

As IAS 17 lacks the quantitative criteria of SFAS 13, it is easier for a lease to be classified as an operating lease under IAS standards than under U.S. GAAP.

Operating Leases

Under U.S. GAAP, leases not meeting any of the four SFAS 13 criteria listed above are not capitalized and no asset or obligation is reported in the financial

[5] Leases are classified at the inception of the lease; the classification is not changed when the lessee or lessor is acquired unless the provisions of the lease agreement are changed. See FASB Interpretation 21 (1978).

[6] IAS 17, para. 3. An operating lease is defined as a "lease other than a finance lease."

statements of the lessee since no purchase is deemed to have occurred. Such leases are classified as operating leases, and payments are reported as rental expense. SFAS 13 mandates the use of the **straight-line method** of recognizing periodic rental payments unless another, systematic basis provides a better representation of the use of leased property. As a result, for leases with rising rental payments, lease expense and cash flow will not be identical.

Financial Reporting by Lessees: Capital versus Operating Leases

Financial reporting by lessees will be illustrated using a noncancellable lease beginning December 31, 2000, with annual MLPs of $10,000 made at the end of each year for four years. Ten percent is assumed to be the appropriate discount rate.

Operating Lease If the lease does not meet any criteria requiring capitalization:

- No entry is made at the inception of the lease.
- Over the life of the lease, only the annual rental expense of $10,000 will be charged to income and CFO.

Capital Lease If the lease meets any one of the four criteria of a capital lease:

- At the inception of the lease, an asset (leasehold asset) and liability (leasehold liability) equal to the present value of the lease payments, $31,700, is recognized.
- Over the life of the lease:

1. The annual rental expense of $10,000 will be allocated between interest and principal payments on the $31,700 leasehold liability according to the following amortization schedule:

Allocation of Payment of $10,000

Year	Opening Liability	Interest[a]	Principal	Closing Liability[b]
2000				$31,700
2001	$31,700	$3,170	$6,830	24,870
2002	24,870	2,487	7,513	17,357
2003	17,357	1,735	8,265	9,092
2004	9,092	909	9,092	0

[a] 10% of the opening liability.

[b] Equals the opening liability less the periodic amortization of the lease obligation. Also equals the present value of the remaining MLPs discounted at the interest rate in effect at the inception of the lease.

2. The cost of the leasehold asset of $31,700 is charged to operations (annual depreciation is $7,925) using the straight-line method over the term of the lease.[7]

[7] Generally, depreciation methods used for similar purchased property are applied to leased assets over their estimated economic lives when one of the transfer of ownership criteria (1 or 2) is met and over the lease term when one of the other capitalization criteria (3 or 4) is satisfied.

Comparative Analysis of Capitalized and Operating Leases

Balance Sheet Effects No assets or liabilities are recognized if the lease is treated as an operating lease. When leases are capitalized, there is a major impact on a firm's balance sheet at inception and throughout the life of the lease. At the inception of the lease, an asset and a liability equal to the present value of the lease payments are recognized.

Balance Sheet Effects of Lease Capitalization

	2000	2001	2002	2003	2004
Assets					
Leased assets	$31,700	$31,700	$31,700	$31,700	$31,700
Accumulated depreciation	0	7,925	15,850	23,775	31,700
Leased assets, net	$31,700	$23,775	$15,850	$ 7,925	$ 0
Liabilities					
Current portion of lease obligation	6,830	7,513	8,265	9,092	0
Long-term debt: lease obligation	24,870	17,357	9,092	0	0
	$31,700	$24,870	$17,357	$ 9,092	$ 0

The gross and net (of accumulated depreciation) amounts are reported at each balance sheet date. The current and noncurrent components of the lease obligation are reported as liabilities under capitalization. The current component is the principal portion of the lease payment to be made in the following year. Note that, at the inception of the lease, the leased asset and liability are equal at $31,700. Since the asset and liability are amortized using different methods, this equality is not again observed until the end of the lease term when both asset and liability are equal to zero.

Effect on Financial Ratios Lease capitalization increases asset balances, resulting in lower asset turnover and return on asset ratios, as compared with the operating lease method, which does not record leased assets.

The most important effect of lease capitalization, however, is its impact on leverage ratios. As lease obligations are not recognized for operating leases, leverage ratios are understated. Lease capitalization adds both current and noncurrent liabilities to debt, resulting in a corresponding decrease in working capital and increases in the debt-to-equity and other leverage ratios.

Income Statement Effects The income statement effects of lease reporting are also significant and impact operating income as well as net income. The operating lease method charges the periodic rental payments to expense as accrued, whereas capitalization recognizes depreciation and interest expense over the lease term.

Income Effects of Lease Classification

	Operating Lease	Capital Lease		
	Operating = Total Expense	Operating Expense	Nonoperating Expense	
Year	Rent	Depreciation	Interest	Total Expense
2001	$10,000	$ 7,925	$3,170	$11,095
2002	10,000	7,925	2,487	10,412
2003	10,000	7,925	1,735	9,660
2004	10,000	7,925	909	8,834
Totals	$40,000	$31,700	$8,300	$40,000

Operating Income Capitalization results in higher operating income (earnings before interest and taxes, or EBIT) since the annual straight-line depreciation expense of $7,925 is lower than the annual rental expense of $10,000 reported under the operating lease method. For an individual lease, this difference is never reversed and remains constant over the lease term given use of the straight-line depreciation method. Accelerated depreciation methods would generate smaller differences in early years, with an increasing difference as depreciation declines, increasing both the level and trend of EBIT.

Total Expense and Net Income Under capitalization, lease expense includes interest expense and depreciation of the leased asset. Initially, total expense for a capital lease exceeds rental expense reported for an operating lease, but declines over the lease term as interest expense falls.[8] In later years, total lease expense will be less than rental expense reported for an operating lease.

Note that total expense (interest plus depreciation) for a capital lease must equal total rental expense for an operating lease over the life of the lease.[9] Consequently, although total net income over the lease term is not affected by capitalization, the timing of income recognition is changed; lower net income is reported in the early years, followed by higher income in later years. This relationship holds for individual leases, but the effect on a firm depends on any additional leases entered into in subsequent periods. When asset prices (and lease rentals) are rising, the impact of old leases nearing expiration may be swamped by the impact of new leases. If a firm enters into new leases at the same or increasing rate over time, reported net income will remain lower under capitalization.

Effect on Financial Ratios In general, firms with operating leases report higher profitability, interest coverage (as interest expense is lower), return on equity, and return on assets ratios. The higher ROE ratios are due to the higher profitability (numerator effect), whereas the higher ROA is due primarily to the lower assets (denominator effect).

[8] If the company uses accelerated depreciation, then the difference in earlier years will be greater but the subsequent decline will also be rapid.

[9] This equality does not hold when the residual value is not zero.

Cash Flow Effects of Lease Classification Lease classification provides another example where accounting methods affect the classification of cash flows.[10] Under the operating lease method, all cash flows are operating and there is an operating cash outflow of $10,000 per year. However, lease capitalization results in both operating and financing cash flows as the rental payments of $10,000 are allocated between interest expense (treated as CFO) and amortization of the lease obligation (reported as cash from financing).

Cash Flow Effects of Lease Classification

	Operating Lease	Capital Lease	
Year	Operations	Operations	Financing
2001	$10,000	$3,170	$6,830
2002	10,000	2,487	7,513
2003	10,000	1,735	8,265
2004	10,000	909	9,091

In 2001, for example, CFO differs between the two methods by $6,830, the amortization of the lease obligation. Because interest expense declines over the lease term and an increasing proportion of the annual payment is allocated to the lease obligation, the difference in CFO increases over the lease term. Thus, lease capitalization systematically decreases the operating cash outflow while increasing the financing cash outflow.

Therefore, although the capital lease method adversely affects some financial statement ratios, it allows firms to report higher operating cash flows compared to those reported using the operating lease method.

Before proceeding, it is important to point out that *at the inception of the lease (year 2000), no cash flows are reported.* This is true even though a capital lease implies the purchase of an asset (cash outflow for investment) financed by the issuance of new debt (cash inflow from financing). Disclosure of the event is reported as part of the "significant noncash financing and investing activities." Analysts attempting to estimate a firm's cash flow requirements for operating capacity should, however, include the present value of such leases as a cash requirement. *Moreover, free cash flow calculations for valuation purposes should incorporate the present value of leases as a cash outflow for investment at the inception of the lease.*

Analysis of Lease Disclosures

A noncancellable lease, whether reported as a capital or operating lease, in effect, constitutes debt and the right to use an asset. If the lease is reported as a capital lease, this information is on-balance-sheet. If it is reported as an operating lease, then the debt and asset are off-balance-sheet and the analyst must adjust accordingly.

[10] We discuss only the classification of cash flows. After-tax cash flows are not affected by lease classification as *generally* firms that use the capital lease method for financial reporting purposes use the operating lease method for tax purposes. Tax payments and actual cash flows are therefore identical. Under the capital lease method, the lease expense under financial reporting exceeds the lease expense reported for tax purposes, resulting in a deferred tax asset.

This is especially true in industries such as airlines and retailers where some firms own operating assets (i.e., airplanes or stores), other firms lease them and report the leases as capital leases, and still other lessees account for them as operating leases. Given the same conditions, the firms using operating leases may report the "best" results as they will show minimal debt and their higher profits will appear to be generated by a relatively smaller investment in assets.

However, the disclosure requirements of firms with leases, capital or operating, are sufficiently detailed to provide the information required for adjustments.

Lease Disclosure Requirements

SFAS 13 requires the disclosure of gross amounts of capitalized lease assets as of each balance sheet date, by major classes or grouped by their nature or function; they may be combined with owned assets.

Lessees must also disclose future MLPs for each of the five succeeding fiscal years and the aggregate thereafter as well as the net present value of the capitalized leases.

Lessees reporting operating leases must also disclose future MLPs for each of the five succeeding fiscal years and in the aggregate thereafter (see Exhibit 46-1 for an example). The present value of the MLPs is not required but is occasionally provided. The rental expense under operating leases (classified as to minimum, contingent, and sublease rentals) for each period for which an income statement is presented must be disclosed as of the balance sheet date.

For both operating and capital leases, lessees must also disclose aggregate minimum rentals receivable under noncancellable subleases. Information regarding renewal terms, purchase options, contingent rentals, any escalation clauses, and restrictions on dividends, additional debt, and leasing is also required. However, rather than being informative, such disclosure is usually vague and general in nature.

IAS 17 disclosure requirements are far less extensive:

- MLPs due within one year
- MLPs due in more than one but less than five years
- MLPs due after five years

This abbreviated disclosure (for an example, see Note 12 of the Roche 2000 annual report) makes the analysis that follows less precise, but does permit approximations.

Financial Reporting by Lessees: An Example

Exhibit 1 contains balance sheet information and the lease footnote of AMR Corp. [AMR], the parent of American Airlines. From the balance sheet alone, it would seem that AMR primarily purchases rather than leases its equipment. The carrying value of purchased equipment is over seven times that of leased equipment.

The footnote paints an entirely different picture. AMR has substantial leases that are mostly structured as operating leases. As required by GAAP, capital lease obligations and operating leases are shown separately. Future MLPs for the next five years, and the aggregate thereafter, are disclosed for both capital and operating leases. For capital leases, interest has been deducted to report their present value of $1,847 million ($236 million is reported as current and $1,611 million as long-term debt).

EXHIBIT 1 AMR Excerpts from Balance Sheet and Lease Footnote, December 31, 1999 (in $millions)

Assets		
Equipment and property (net of accumulated depreciation of 7,403)		$14,338
Equipment and property under capital leases (net of accumulated amortization of 1,347)		1,949
Total assets		24,374
Liabilities		
Long-term debt		
Current maturity	$ 302	
Noncurrent	4,078	4,380
Capital lease obligations		
Current	$ 236	
Noncurrent	1,611	1,847
Total long-term debt and capital lease obligations		$ 6,227
Shareholders' equity		6,858

Leases

AMR's subsidiaries lease various types of equipment and property, including aircraft and airport and off-airport facilities. The future minimum lease payments required under capital leases, together with the present value of net minimum lease payments, and future minimum lease payments required under operating leases that have initial or remaining noncancellable lease terms in excess of one year as of December 31, 1999, were (in millions):

Years Ending December 31	Capital Leases	Operating Leases
2000	$ 347	$ 1,015
2001	329	1,006
2002	280	952
2003	198	965
2004	249	954
2005 and subsequent	1,081	12,169
	$2,484	$17,061
Less amount representing interest	(637)	
Present value of net minimum lease payments	$1,847	

At December 31, 1999, the Company had 205 jet aircraft and 71 turboprop aircraft under operating leases, and 79 jet aircraft and 61 turboprop aircraft under capital leases.

Source: AMR, *1999 Annual Report.*

Note that the (aggregate) operating lease payments of $17,061 million are almost seven times the capital lease payments ($2,484 million). Moreover, the data suggest that the operating leases are of longer term than the capital leases!

Aggregate MLPs of the capital leases for the next five years are about 56% of total future MLPs, or $1,403 million. Total MLPs for the remaining years are $1,081 million, or 44% of the total MLPs of $2,484 million over the lease terms. The average lease term of the capitalized leases can be estimated by computing the number of payments included in the "later years" amount of $1,081 million; that is, ($1,081 million/$249 million) if we assume that annual payments remain at the 2004 level. This suggests a lease term of approximately 9 (initial five plus the estimated remaining four) years.

For operating leases, the proportion of payments after the first five years is ($12,169/ $17,061) 71% of total payments. This suggests a longer term than for the capital leases. Dividing the remaining payments of $12,169 by the 2004 payment of $954 yields 13, suggesting a lease term of 18 years (5 plus 13) or *twice as long as the term of the capital leases.*

The note indicates that 205 jet aircraft and 71 turboprops are under operating leases. *Neither these assets nor the debt associated with them appear on the balance sheet.*

Investors and analysts can use the lease disclosures to adjust the balance sheet appropriately. The present value of the operating leases can be estimated by discounting the future minimum lease payments. This estimate requires assumptions about the pattern of MLPs after the first five years and the discount rate. The estimation procedure (described below) is "robust," with the calculated present value relatively invariant to the assumptions.

Assumed Pattern of MLPs Footnote disclosures reflect the payments to be made over each of the next five years and the total payments thereafter. The present value computation requires an estimate of the number of payments implicit in the latter lump sum. Either the rate of decline suggested by the cash outflows for the next five years or a constant amount over the remaining term may be used to derive the present value of the operating lease payments.

Discount Rate The discount rate should reflect the risk class of the leased assets as well as the company being analyzed. The interest rate implicit in the reported capital leases is a good approximation of that rate.[11]

Box 2 uses AMR to illustrate the estimation method(s). The procedure yields a rate of between 6.0% and 6.5% depending on the assumptions made; we use 6.4%. The two assumptions regarding pattern of cash flows over the lease term generate present value estimates of $10.1 and $9.9 billion, a difference of only 2%.

Impact of Operating Lease Adjustments

Liabilities The impact of the adjustment is highly significant. AMR's reported long-term debt and capital leases total $6.2 billion. Adding approximately $10 billion for off-balance-sheet operating leases increases debt by more than 160% to approximately $16.2 billion. *AMR has more debt off the balance sheet than on the balance sheet.* With equity of $6.9 billion, the debt-to-equity ratio of 0.9 mushrooms to 2.3.

---

[11] Because the implicit rate is an average rate based on terms at inception, it may be significantly different from either the reported or marginal long-term borrowing rate the company faces in the capital markets. The analyst may use a long-term borrowing rate estimated from the debt footnote or based on current market conditions.

BOX 2 ESTIMATION OF THE PRESENT VALUE OF OPERATING LEASES

A. The Implicit Discount Rate of a Firm's Capital Leases

Two approaches may be employed to estimate the average discount rate used to capitalize a firm's capital leases. The first uses only the next period's MLP; the second incorporates all future MLPs in the estimation procedure.

1. Using Next Period's MLP

The 2000 MLP for AMR's capital leases is \$347 million. That payment includes interest and principal. The principal portion is shown in AMR's current liabilities section as \$236 million. The difference, \$111 million, represents the interest component of the MLP. As the present value of AMR's capital leases equals \$1,847, the interest rate on the capitalized leases can be estimated as (\$111/\$1,847) 6.01%.

This calculation assumes that the principal payment of \$236 million will be made at the end of the year. If it is made early in the year, then the interest expense is based on the principal outstanding after payment of the current portion. The results can be biased if the current portion is a significant portion of the overall liability. An alternative estimate of the implicit interest rate may be derived using the average liability balance; that is, \$111/[0.5 × (\$1,847 + \$1,611)] = 6.42%.

2. Using All Future MLPs

The interest rate can also be estimated by solving for the implicit interest rate (internal rate of return) that equates the MLPs and their present value. This calculation requires an assumption about the pattern of MLPs after the first five years as the MLPs for the first five years (2000 to 2004) are given. From 2004 and on, two assumptions are possible:

1. constant rate, or
2. declining rate.

Constant Rate

Under the simpler constant rate assumption, it is assumed that the payment level (\$249 million) in the fifth year (2004) continues into the future, implying the following payment stream:

Year	2000	2001	2002	2003	2004	2005
MLP	\$347	\$329	\$280	\$198	\$249	\$249
Year	2006	2007	2008	2009[r]	Total	
MLP	\$249	\$249	\$249	\$85	\$2,484	

[r] Residual.

The internal rate of return that equates this stream to the present value of \$1,847 is 6.55%.

Declining Rate

Alternatively, and more realistically, one would expect the payments to decline over time. The rate of decline implicit in the MLPs reported individually for the first five years may be used to estimate the payment pattern after the initial five years. In AMR's case, payments decrease initially and then jump in 2004. On average, the

(continued)

BOX 2 *(continued)*

payments are approximately 94% of the previous year.[a] Using this rate we obtain the following pattern of payments:

Year	2000	2001	2002	2003	2004	2005
MLP	$347	$329	$280	$198	$249	$234
Year	2006	2007	2008	2009	2010[r]	Total
MLP	$220	$207	$194	$183	$43	$2,484

[r] Residual.

The internal rate of return that equates this stream to the present value of $1,847 is 6.40%; a rate close to the 6.55% based on the constant rate assumption. Generally, the differences are not significant and unless the rate of decline is very steep, the constant rate assumption simplifies the computation. *The first procedure yields an estimate of 6.0 to 6.4%; the second yields estimates of 6.40 to 6.55%. Based on these estimates, we use 6.4% for our analysis of AMR's operating leases.*

B. Finding the Present Value of the Operating Leases

For operating leases the MLPs for the first five years (2000 to 2004) are given. Again we can make two assumptions as to the pattern of payments for 2005 and on.

Under the constant rate assumption, it is assumed that MLPs from the year 2005 and on equal the 2004 payment of $954. Alternatively, based on the payment pattern of the operating lease MLPs over the first five years, one would expect the payments to decline at a rate of 1.5% a year. The assumed patterns and the resultant present values using the discount rate of 6.4% are presented below.

Constant Rate

Year	2000	2001	2002	2003	2004
MLP	$1,015	$1,006	$952	$965	$954
Year	2005–2016	2017[r]	Total	Present Value	
MLP	$954	$721	$17,061	$10,060	

[r] Residual.

Declining Rate

Year	2000	2001	2002	2003	2004	2005
MLP	$1,015	$1,006	$952	$965	$954	$940
Year	2006 ...	2018	2019[r]	Total	Present Value	
MLP	$926 ...	$772	$221	$17,061	$9,911	

[r] Residual.

(continued)

[a] We have used the arithmetic mean. The geometric mean is 92%.

BOX 2 (continued)

Note that the two present value estimates of $10.1 and $9.9 billion are within 2% of each other.

C. Executory Costs

Reported MLPs at times include such executory costs as maintenance, taxes, and insurance on the leased assets. These costs are not financing costs and should be excluded from the calculation of the lease present value. However, because footnote disclosures generally do not reduce MLPs by executory costs, the present value calculation described previously is biased.

In most cases that bias is small and can be ignored. However, the estimation method can be modified to adjust for this bias. When the firm discloses the total of the executory costs, we can assume that the pattern of the executory costs follows that of the MLPs. If we define p as the proportion of total executory costs to total MLPs,

$$p = \frac{\text{Total executory costs}}{\text{Total MLPs}}$$

then the procedures described above can be applied[b] to a pattern of *adjusted MLPs*, where the

$$\text{Adjusted MLP (for any year)} = (1 - p) \times \text{unadjusted MLP (for that year)}$$

[b] Alternatively, one can use the unadjusted MLPs and make the following two adjustments:

1. In calculating the implicit interest rate of the capital leases, gross up the present value of the capital leases by *dividing* by $(1 - p)$.
2. Using the interest rate calculated in step 1, find the present value of the unadjusted MLPs. *Multiply* that present value by $(1 - p)$.

AMR: Effects of Operating Lease Adjustments (in $billions)

	Reported	+	Operating Leases	=	Adjusted
Debt	$ 6.2		$10.0		$16.2
Equity	6.9				6.9
Debt/equity ratio	0.9X				2.3X
Assets	$24.4		$10.0		$34.4

Assets Exhibit 1 reports total assets of $24.4 billion. Capitalization of the operating leases increases total assets by $10 billion. AMR is operating 41% more assets than reported on its balance sheet. *Efficiency measures such as turnover or ROA use total assets in the denominator and are highly overstated; adjusted ratios more accurately portray AMR's asset efficiency.*

Income and Cash Flow Effects Adjustments for operating leases also affect the income and cash flow statements (as well as related ratios). These effects can be illustrated using the 2000 MLP of $1,015 million as an example. Under the operating lease method, both rent expense and the CFO outflow equal $1,015 million. Capitalization results in allocation of that $1,015 million between interest expense and principal payments; in addition, the leased asset must be depreciated. These changes reduce reported income but increase CFO.

AMR: Effects of Operating Lease Adjustment, 2000 (in $millions)

	As Reported	Adjusted
Income Statement		
Rent expense	$1,015	
Interest expense		$ 640[a]
Amortization expense		555[b]
Total expense	$1,015	$1,195
Cash Flow Statement		
If interest payments are treated as CFO (per SFAS 95)		
CFO outflow	$1,015	$ 640
CFF outflow	0	$ 375
If interest payments are treated as CFF (per Reading 33)		
CFO outflow	$1,015	0
CFF outflow	0	$1,015

[a] Interest expense = interest rate × PV of leases = 0.064 × $10 billion = $640 million.

[b] Amortization expense = PV of leases divided by lease term = $10 billion/18 = $555 million.

Other Lease-Related Issues

While lease classification affects how leases are reported in financial statements, it is not the only issue that affects financial analysis. The following may also be significant for some companies:

1. *Lease impairment.* Because of changes in market conditions, leased assets can become uneconomic to the firm. In such cases, the firm may recognize an impairment charge similar to the impairment charges for fixed assets. For example, OMI [OMM], an operator of oil tankers, recorded a loss of $6.3 million in June 1999 when it "determined that its current lease obligations for vessels exceeded its undiscounted forecasted future net cash flows."
2. *Sale and leaseback of assets.* Such sales can be a cost-effective source of funds, especially for firms with low credit ratings. Because the assets sold secure the obligation, lenders charge a lower interest rate than for unsecured borrowings. Both SFAS 13 and IAS 17 require the lessee to defer any gain on the asset sale, and recognize it over the lease term, when the lease is a capital (finance) lease. Amortization over the lease term is also required for sale/leasebacks classified as operating leases under SFAS 13. However, under IAS 17, gains on sale/leasebacks classified as operating leases are recognized immediately.[12]

[12] The accounting for sale/leasebacks can be quite complex, with numerous variations and exceptions under both U.S. and IAS GAAP. See Box 4 for further discussion.

3. *Lease guarantees.* Firms may guarantee leases for affiliates (see discussion of Texaco later in the reading). Companies may also remain obligated for leases when operating units are sold. For example, Kmart [KM] sold its Builders Square subsidiary in 1997 to Hechinger, another chain of home improvement stores. When Hechinger filed for bankruptcy in June 1999, Kmart recognized a pretax charge of $350 million for its guarantees of long-term leases with a net present value of $711 million.
4. *Straight-line recognition.* Both SFAS 13 and IAS 17 require both lessors and lessees to recognize operating lease payments over the life of the lease on a straight-line basis (equal amounts in each year). However, the lease payments may take a different form, resulting in either prepaid rent or rent receivable.

   For example, in the first quarter of 2001, Cisco [CSCO] paid Catellus [CDX] $68 million in connection with a California ground lease. Catellus reported that this sum would be amortized over the 34-year lease term.
5. *Synthetic leases.* Such leases use a special purpose entity to finance an asset purchase. The asset is then leased to the user. While the user receives the tax benefits of ownership, the transaction is accounted for as an operating lease, keeping it off-balance-sheet.

   For example, AOL Time Warner [AOL] used a synthetic lease to finance the construction of its New York headquarters, keeping a reported one billion dollars of debt off its balance sheet.

3 OFF-BALANCE-SHEET FINANCING ACTIVITIES

Leases are but one example of contractual arrangements that give rise to off-balance-sheet debt. In this section, we discuss other such arrangements and show how financial statements should be adjusted to reflect the underlying economic consequences. Like leases, some of these off-balance-sheet activities are commonplace and can be found in many firms and industries. Others tend to be industry specific or are the product of specific market conditions.

Take-or-Pay and Throughput Arrangements

Firms use take-or-pay contracts to ensure the long-term availability of raw materials and other inputs necessary for operations.[13] These agreements are common in the energy, chemical, paper, and metal industries. Under these arrangements, the purchasing firm commits to buy a minimum quantity of an input over a specified time period. Input prices may be fixed by contract or may be related to market prices. Energy companies use throughput arrangements with pipelines or processors (such as refiners) to ensure future distribution or processing requirements.

These contracts are often used as collateral for bank or other financing by unrelated suppliers or by investors in joint ventures. The contract serves as an

[13] Inventories can also be financed through product financing arrangements under which inventories are sold and later repurchased. SFAS 49 (1981) requires that such arrangements that do not effectively transfer the risk of ownership to the buyer must be accounted for as debt financing rather than sale of inventory. In such cases, the cost of holding inventories (storage and insurance) and interest cost on the imputed debt must be recognized as incurred. Prior to SFAS 49, companies sometimes used these arrangements to defer these costs and accelerate the recognition of profit. Product financing arrangements may still be accounted for as sales outside of the United States.

indirect guarantee of the related debt. However, neither the assets nor the debt incurred to obtain (or guarantee availability of) operating capacity are reflected on the balance sheet of the purchaser. SFAS 47 (1981) requires that, when a long-term commitment is used to obtain financing, the purchaser must disclose the nature of the commitment and the minimum required payments in its financial statement footnotes.

As take-or-pay contracts and throughput agreements effectively keep some operating assets and liabilities off the balance sheet, the analyst should add the present value of minimum future commitments to both property and debt.

Exhibit 2 contains the commitments and contingencies footnote from the 1999 annual report of Alcoa [AA], disclosing a take-or-pay obligation of Alcoa of Australia, a consolidated subsidiary. Note that the disclosure is similar to that required for (capital and operating) leases. We can apply the method used earlier to compute the present value of the debt. The calculation is shown in panel B of the exhibit.

The take-or-pay contracts reported by Alcoa represent $1,780 million of off-balance-sheet assets and debt. The impact of this adjustment on the leverage ratio is as follows:

Alcoa Balance Sheet, at December 31, 1999 (in $millions)

	Reported	Adjusted	Increase
Total debt	$3,067	$4,847	58%
Stockholders' equity	6,318	6,318	None
Debt-to-equity ratio	0.49X	0.77X	58%

Sale of Receivables

Receivables are sometimes financed by their sale (or securitization) to unrelated parties. That is, the firm sells the receivables to a buyer (normally a financial institution or investor group). Depending on the interest (if any) paid by customers and the effective interest rate on the sale transaction, the seller may recognize a gain or loss on the receivables sold. The seller uses the proceeds from the sale for operations or to reduce existing or planned debt. The firm continues to service the original receivables; customer payments are transferred to the new owner of the receivables. Some arrangements are revolving in nature as collected receivables are periodically replaced by new ones.

Such transactions are recorded as sales under SFAS 140, Accounting for Transfers and Servicing of Financial Assets and Extinguishments of Liabilities (2000), as long as there has been a *legal* transfer of ownership from the seller to the buyer.[14] To effect such transactions, firms often set up distinct (nonconsolidated) trusts or subsidiaries (often referred to as a *qualifying special-purpose entity, QSPE*) that the firm's creditors cannot access in the event of bankruptcy.[15] By

[14] SFAS 140 states that the transferor (seller) accounts for the transfer as a sale when it surrenders effective control over those assets (see SFAS 140 for details).

[15] LTV, a steel company, filed for bankruptcy late in 2000. LTV argued that the transfer of receivables (and a similar transfer of inventories) to a QSPE was a "disguised finance transaction" and that it still had an interest in the transferred assets. However, the bankruptcy court ruled against the company in March 2001.

EXHIBIT 2 Alcoa
Analysis of Take-or-Pay Contracts

A. Footnote: Contingent Liabilities

Alcoa of Australia (AofA) is party to a number of natural gas and electricity contracts that expire between 2001 and 2022. Under these take-or-pay contracts, AofA is obligated to pay for a minimum amount of natural gas or electricity even if these commodities are not required for operations. Commitments related to these contracts total $190 in 2000, $182 in 2001, $179 in 2002, $176 in 2003, $176 in 2004, and $2,222 thereafter.

Source: Alcoa, *1999 Annual Report.*

B. Analysis: Take-or-Pay Contracts, 2000 to 2004 and Beyond (in $millions)

Year	Take-or-Pay Obligation
2000	$ 190
2001	182
2002	179
2003	176
2004	176
Thereafter	2,222

Using the technique for capitalizing operating leases discussed earlier in the reading, the above payment stream can be discounted to its present value. Estimated payments continue after 2004 (using, for simplifying purposes, the constant rate assumption) for

$$\frac{\$2{,}222 \text{ million}}{\$176 \text{ million}} = 12.63 \text{ years}$$

Given this payment stream, the present value can be arrived at using an estimated cost of debt (based on capitalized lease disclosures or other long-term debt). For Alcoa, we estimate an interest rate of 7%. When applied to the minimum payments shown above, the resulting present value equals $1,780 million for take-or-pay obligations. Thus approximately $1.8 billion should be added as an adjustment to Alcoa's consolidated property and total debt.

selling the receivables through such entities, the firm has adhered to the strict legal definition of ownership transfer. Exhibit 3 provides examples of such arrangements from the financial statements of Lucent Technologies [LU]. Note that in 2000, Lucent's receivables and loans were sold through a "bankruptcy-remote subsidiary," as required by GAAP for sale recognition.

By reporting such transactions as sales, the company decreases accounts receivable and increases cash from operations in the period of sale. However, most such receivable sales and/or securitizations provide that the seller retains the effective credit risk by either:

EXHIBIT 3 **Lucent Technologies Receivable Securitization Activities (Years Ended September 30)**

1999

- Subsidiary of Lucent sold approximately $625 million of accounts receivable to a nonconsolidated qualified special-purpose entity (QSPE).
- The QSPE resold the receivables to an unaffiliated financial institution.
- Lucent transferred $700 million of other receivables to the QSPE as collateral.

2000

- Lucent and a third-party financial institution arranged for the creation of a nonconsolidated Special Purpose Trust.
- Trust purchases, from a wholly owned (bankruptcy-remote) subsidiary of Lucent, customer finance loans, and receivables on a limited-recourse basis.
- Balance of receivables sold but uncollected was $1,329 million.

Source: Information from Lucent Technologies, *2000 Annual Report.*

- Retaining a portion of the receivables and receiving payment only after the securitized amount has been repaid. If the retained percentage exceeds the historic loss ratio, the seller has retained the effective risk.
- Providing other collateral, or agreeing to replace delinquent receivables with current receivables.

As shown in Exhibit 3, Lucent provided the second form of implicit guarantee. *When the seller retains the entire expected loss experience, these transactions are effectively collateralized borrowings with the receivables serving as collateral.* Sales of receivables are another form of off-balance-sheet financing and should be adjusted as follows:

1. *Balance Sheet.* Both accounts receivable and current liabilities should be increased by the amount of receivables sold that have not yet been collected.
2. *Cash Flow Statement.* CFO must be adjusted; the change in the uncollected amount should be classified as cash from financing rather than CFO.

These two adjustments usually capture the analytical effects of receivable sales. However, as sales/securitizations of receivables transactions can be quite complex, other aspects of the financial statements may also be affected. Moreover, to the extent amounts received from receivable sales are not equal to the "face value" of receivables sold, the (cash flow) adjustment is only an approximation, albeit a reasonably accurate one.

Box 3 illustrates the effects of sales/securitizations on the income statement. Treating the transaction as a sale results in earlier income recognition as compared to treating it as a collateralized borrowing.

BOX 3 INCOME STATEMENT EFFECTS OF RECEIVABLE SALES AND SECURIZATIONS

Our illustration assumes that the company is selling (credit) receivables that it carries on its books at $1,000,000. Depending on the interest rate structure of the credit receivables and the risk, the buyer may pay more or less than $1,000,000.

Buyer Pays Less: $900,000

Transaction qualifies as a sale: The seller will *immediately* recognize a $100,000 loss on the sale.[a]

Transaction does not qualify as a sale and is treated as a financing: The $100,000 is treated as a "discount" on the loan payable taken by the seller.[b] The income statement is not affected at the time of the sale. Over time (as the receivables are collected) the discount is amortized as additional interest expense.[c]

Buyer Pays More: $1,100,000

Transaction qualifies as a sale: The mirror image of the previous transaction occurs (i.e., the seller will *immediately* recognize a $100,000 gain on the sale).

Transaction does not qualify as a sale and is treated as a financing: The $100,000 is treated as a "premium" on the loan payable taken by the seller.[d] The income statement is not affected at the time of the sale. Over time (as the receivables are collected) the premium is amortized and interest expense is reduced.[e]

Analytical procedures: From an analytical perspective, the two approaches result in different timing of income or loss recognition. Thus, if a company recognized a securitization as a sale and the analyst felt that it would be more appropriate to view the transaction as a financing event, then the financial statement adjustments would be as follows:

- Remove gain/loss from current period income.
- Add the securitized receivables to the balance sheet amount.
- Classify the securitization proceeds as debt.

---

[a] The entry would be

Cash	$900,000	
Loss on sale	100,000	
Accounts receivable		$1,000,000

[b] The entry would be

Cash	$900,000	
Loan payable (net of discount)		$900,000

[c] For example, when $200,000 of the receivables are collected, the entry for the "passthrough" would be

Amortization of discount	$ 20,000	
Loan payable	180,000	
Cash		200,000

Note, if the transaction were treated as a sale, there would be no entry at the time of collection.

[d] The entry would be

Cash	$1,100,000	
Loan payable (includes premium)		$1,100,000

[e] For example, when $200,000 of the receivables are collected, the entry would be

Loan payable	220,000	
Amortization of premium		20,000
Cash		200,000

Note: If the transaction were treated as a sale, there would be no entry at the time of collection.

EXAMPLE 1

Lucent Technologies

Exhibit 4 continues with our Lucent example. Panel A summarizes data from the financial statements. As indicated in Exhibit 3, Lucent engaged in receivables securitization and reported balances of $625 and $1,329 million of outstanding uncollected receivables in 1999 and 2000, respectively. In both years, the receivables were sold through an entity established specifically for this purpose.

Balance sheet. Lucent recorded the securitizations as sales as they were structured to satisfy the (legalistic) requirements of SFAS 125 and 140. Lucent, however, transferred other (not sold) receivables to the subsidiary as collateral for the receivables sold and therefore ultimately bears the credit risk.

The sale proceeds should therefore not be viewed as a reduction of accounts receivable, but rather as an increase in (short-term) borrowing. As panel B of Exhibit 4 indicates, Lucent's 1999 (2000) accounts receivable, current assets, and current liabilities should be increased by $625 ($1,329) million.[16]

Cash flow classification. Accounting for these transactions as sales distorts the amount and timing of CFO as the firm received cash earlier than if the receivables had been collected in the normal course of business. An adjustment is required to reclassify *the change in the uncollected receivables sold*[17] from CFO to cash from financing.

Since 1999 was the first year Lucent engaged in sales securitization, the full $625 million should be deducted from CFO (and classified as CFF). For 2000, the adjustment should be the change in sold but uncollected receivables; that is, ($1,329 − $625 =) $704 million. These adjustments are made in Exhibit 4, panel B.

Effects of adjustments. The effects of these adjustments are also demonstrated in Exhibit 4. Relative to 1998, sales in 1999 and 2000 increased 26% and 39%, respectively. *Reported* accounts receivable, however, increased only 16% and 26% over that same period; an apparent improvement in receivables management. This improvement is reflected in the receivable turnover with days receivables outstanding improving by 14 days from 117 to 103 days over the 1998–2000 period.

However, after adjustment for receivables sold, the improvement disappears. Restoring the $625 million of receivables sold in 1999 results in an (adjusted) increase of 24% in receivables relative to 1998, similar to the 26% sales increase over the same period. For 2000, we find that, after adjustment, receivables increased 46%, greater than the 39%

[16] The manner in which Lucent set up its QSPE in 1999 results in another, more subtle "off-balance-sheet activity." (See subsequent section entitled "Joint Ventures, Finance Subsidiaries, and Investment in Affiliates.") By transferring $700 million of its receivables to the subsidiary as collateral, Lucent effectively removed this amount from its receivables balances (where they belong) and buried it within the investment in subsidiary accounts. Total assets are not affected but the composition of those assets is. To keep the exposition for sale of receivables straightforward, we have ignored this factor in our presentation.

[17] The change in accounts receivable is an adjustment to net income when deriving CFO. Because the uncollected balance of the receivables sold must be added to the reported balance of accounts receivable, calculation of the adjusted CFO requires exclusion of any change in the balance of uncollected receivables sold.

EXHIBIT 4 **Lucent Technologies Analysis of Receivables Securization**

	A. Reported Data				B. Adjusted Data	
	1998	1999	2000		1999	2000
From Footnotes						
Balance of uncollected receivables	$ 0	$ 625	$ 1,329			
From Balance Sheet				*Adjustment:*	***Add $625***	***Add $1,329***
Accounts receivable	7,821	**9,097**	**10,059**		**9,722**	**11,388**
Current assets		**19,240**	**21,490**		**19,865**	**22,819**
Current liabilities		**9,150**	**10,877**		**9,775**	**12,206**
From Cash Flow Statement				*Adjustment:*	***Deduct $625***	***Deduct $704***
CFO	1,452	**(962)**	**304**		**(1,587)**	**(400)**
From Income Statement						
Sales	24,367	**30,617**	**33,813**			
Selected Trends and Ratios						
% Change in sales from 1998		**26%**	**39%**		**26%**	**39%**
% Change in A/R from 1998		**16%**	**26%**		**24%**	**46%**
# of days A/R outstanding	117	**101**	**103**		**105**	**114**
Current ratio	1.45	**2.10**	**1.98**		**2.03**	**1.87**
CFO/Current liabilities	0.13	**(0.11)**	**0.03**		**(0.16)**	**(0.03)**

Source: Data from Lucent Technologies, *1998–2000 Annual Reports.*

increase in sales. After adjustment, the number of days of outstanding receivables, which declined on a reported basis, rose to 114 in 2000, similar to the 1998 level.[18]

Moving to Lucent's liquidity ratios, we note that both the adjusted current ratio and the CFO/current liabilities ratio are below the reported amounts. For these ratios, there is an adjustment to both the numerator and denominator. For the current ratio, the same amount is added to both; the numerator adjustment improves the ratio whereas the denominator adjustment reduces the ratio. It is only because the (reported) ratio is greater than 1 that the net effect is a lower ratio. Were the ratio less than 1 to begin with, the effect of the adjustment would be to improve the ratio. Both adjustments to the CFO/current liabilities ratio, on the other hand, reduce the ratio as CFO is decreased and current liabilities are increased.

[18] Sales of receivables should be added back when assessing the provision for bad debts.

Turning to CFO, we find that the receivables sales masked the deterioration of the company's operating cash flow: 1998 CFO was $1,452 million; 1999 reported CFO plunged to ($962) million, recovering to $304 million in 2000.

After adjustment for receivables sold, CFO was considerably below the amounts reported. For 1999, adjusted CFO was ($1,587) million, an outflow two-thirds greater than the reported amount of ($962) million. Although 2000 CFO improved, on an adjusted basis it remained negative at ($400) million.

The cash flow trend may have been the motivation for Lucent beginning a program of receivable securitization in 1999; as CFO deteriorated, the company needed another source of cash.

Other Securitizations

While the securitization of accounts receivable remains a major source of financing, other forms of securitization have emerged. A few examples follow:

1. PolyGram, the Dutch film producer, issued bonds in 1998 backed by expected revenues from films.
2. Marne et Champagne issued bonds in 2000 backed by its champagne inventories.
3. Toys "R" Us [TOY] issued bonds in 2000 secured by license-fee income from its Japanese affiliate.
4. Yasuda Fire & Marine Insurance [8755] used auto and mortgage loans and leasing credits to back bonds issued in 2000.

Such issues are a growing form of off-balance-sheet financing, used worldwide, with significant implications for current and future period cash flows. The financial analyst must be alert to such transactions and make the appropriate analytical adjustments.[19]

Joint Ventures, Finance Subsidiaries, and Investment in Affiliates

Firms may acquire manufacturing and distribution capacity through investments in affiliated firms, including suppliers and end users. Joint ventures with other firms may offer economies of scale and provide opportunities to share operating, technological, and financial risks. To obtain financing, the venture may enter into take-or-pay or throughput contracts with minimum payments designed to meet the venture's debt service requirements. Direct or indirect guarantees of the joint venture debt may also be present. Generally, firms account for their investments in joint ventures and affiliates (where they have 20 to 50% ownership) using the equity method whereby the balance sheet reports the firm's **net investment** in the affiliate. The net investment reflects the parent's proportionate share of the assets minus the liabilities of the subsidiary (*i.e., the parent's financial statements do not report its share of the debt of these affiliates*).

[19] Bond ratings services recognize the effect of securitizations on a company's debt structure. For example, Moody's March 2000 analysis of Federal-Mogul [FMO] included $450 million of securitized receivables in its calculation of Federal Mogul's total debt.

For example, Micron [MU] stated in its August 31, 2000 10-K report that it participated in two joint ventures (in Singapore and Japan). Micron entered into take-or-pay contracts requiring it to purchase all of the output of the joint ventures and to provide technology, systems support, and other services. These joint ventures are not consolidated although they are clearly part of Micron operationally. They supplied more than one-third of all memory produced by Micron in fiscal 2001 and Micron reported all transactions with the venture as part of cost of goods sold.

Similarly, many firms have long used legally separate finance subsidiaries to borrow funds to finance parent-company receivables. Such debt is often lower-cost than general-purpose borrowings because of the well-defined collateral. Finance subsidiaries enable the parent to generate sales by granting credit to dealers and customers for purchases of its goods and services. Until 1987, most firms used the equity method to account for finance subsidiaries.[20] The FASB eliminated the nonconsolidation option (SFAS 94) and firms must now consolidate the assets and liabilities of controlled financial subsidiaries. As a result, some parent firms reduced their ownership of finance subsidiaries below 50% to gain the benefit of "debt suppression" afforded by the equity method.

From an overall economic entity (parent firm plus share in the affiliate) perspective, however, affiliate debt should be considered explicitly because it is clearly required to maintain the parent's operations. Additionally, the parent firm generally supports affiliate borrowings through extensive income maintenance agreements and direct or indirect guarantees of debt.

The information required for these adjustments to debt and related interest coverage and leverage ratios can be obtained from the footnotes, which may

EXHIBIT 5 Georgia-Pacific Joint Venture Financing

Note 13: Related Party Transactions

The Corporation is a 50% partner in a joint venture (GA-MET) with Metropolitan Life Insurance Company (Metropolitan). GA-MET owns and operates the Corporation's main office building in Atlanta, Georgia. The Corporation accounts for its investment in GA-MET under the equity method.

At January 1, 2000, GA-MET had an outstanding mortgage loan payable to Metropolitan in the amount of $144 million. The note bears interest at 9½%, requires monthly payments of principal and interest through 2011, and is secured by the land and building owned by the joint venture. In the event of foreclosure, each partner has severally guaranteed payment of one-half of any shortfall of collateral value to the outstanding secured indebtedness. Based on the present market conditions and building occupancy, the likelihood of any obligation to the Corporation with respect to this guarantee is considered remote.

Source: Georgia-Pacific, *1999 Annual Report.*

[20] Livnat and Sondhi (1986) showed that the exclusion of finance subsidiary debt allowed firms to report higher coverage and lower leverage ratios, stabilized reported debt ratios over time, and reduced the probability of a technical violation of bond covenants. Heian and Thies (1989) identified 182 companies (in 35 industry groups) reporting unconsolidated finance subsidiaries in 1985. Supplementary disclosures provided by 140 of these companies indicated a total of $205 billion in subsidiary debt that had not been reported on the parent's balance sheet. The authors also computed debt-to-capital ratios on the basis of pro forma consolidation and compared them to the pre-consolidation ratios; the average increase in the ratio for the sample was 34%, but nearly 90% for the firms with the 21 largest finance units.

disclose the assets, liabilities, and results of operations of finance subsidiaries in a summarized format.[21]

Exhibit 5 contains an excerpt from the footnote on commitments and contingencies in the *1999 Annual Report* issued by Georgia Pacific [GP]. It discloses a joint venture with Metropolitan Life [MET]. GP is clearly liable for one-half of this off-balance-sheet debt, and $72 million should be added to GP's (property and) debt. In the GP example, the parent explicitly guaranteed the debt of the affiliate. Even in the absence of such guarantees, the proportionate share of the affiliate's debt should be added to the reported debt of the investor and the financial statements should be adjusted accordingly. These adjustments will be illustrated shortly in the analysis of Texaco and Exhibits 6 and 7.

ANALYSIS OF OBS ACTIVITIES: TEXACO

4

Texaco is a major worldwide refiner, marketer, and distributor of oil products. Exhibit 6 contains excerpts from footnotes to Texaco's 1999 financial statements relating to its unconsolidated subsidiaries, leases, and commitments and contingencies. *A complete assessment of a company's off-balance-sheet activities requires a review of all financial statement disclosures.*

EXHIBIT 6 Texaco Off-Balance-Sheet Activities

Excerpts from 1999 Notes to Financial Statements
Note 5: Investments and Advances

We account for our investments in affiliates, including corporate joint ventures and partnerships owned 50% or less, on the equity method. . . . The following table provides summarized financial information on a 100% basis for the Caltex Group, Equilon, Motiva, Star and all other affiliates that we account for on the equity method, as well as Texaco's total share of the information.

As of December 31, 1999
(millions of dollars)

	Equilon	Motiva	Caltex Group	Other Affiliates	Texaco's Total Share
Current assets	$ 4,209	$ 1,271	$ 2,705	$ 801	$ 3,796
Noncurrent assets	7,208	5,307	7,604	2,230	9,321
Current liabilities	(5,636)	(1,278)	(3,395)	(736)	(4,916)
Noncurrent liabilities	(735)	(2,095)	(2,639)	(792)	(2,638)
Net equity	$ 5,046	$ 3,205	$ 4,275	$1,503	$ 5,563

(Exhibit continued on next page . . .)

[21] When the subsidiary or joint venture issues publicly traded debt, then full financial statements are available and can be used for more accurate adjustments.

EXHIBIT 6 (continued)

Note 10: Lease Commitments and Rental Expense

We have leasing arrangements involving service stations, tanker charters, crude oil production and processing equipment and other facilities. We reflect amounts due under capital leases in our balance sheet as obligations, while we reflect our interest in the related assets as properties, plant and equipment. The remaining lease commitments are operating leases, and we record payments on such leases as rental expense.

As of December 31, 1999, we had estimated minimum commitments for payment of rentals (net of noncancelable sublease rentals) under leases which, at inception, had a noncancellable term of more than one year, as follows:

(millions of dollars)

	Operating Leases	Capital Leases
2000	$ 134	$ 9
2001	93	9
2002	416	8
2003	50	7
2004	54	7
After 2004	315	14
Total lease commitments	$1,062	$54
Less interest		(8)
Present value of total capital lease obligations		$46

Note 15: Other Financial Information, Commitments and Contingencies

Preferred Shares of Subsidiaries

Minority holders own $602 million of preferred shares of our subsidiary companies, which is reflected as minority interest in subsidiary companies in the Consolidated Balance Sheet.

The above preferred stock issues currently require annual dividend payments of approximately $34 million. We are required to redeem $75 million of this preferred stock in 2003, $65 million (plus accreted dividends of $59 million) in 2005, $112 million in 2024 and $350 million in 2043. We have the ability to extend the required redemption dates for the $112 million and $350 million of preferred stock beyond 2024 and 2043.

Financial Guarantees

We have guaranteed the payment of certain debt, lease commitments and other obligations of third parties and affiliate companies. These guarantees totaled $716 million and $797 million at December 31, 1999 and 1998. The year-end 1999 and 1998 amounts include $336 million and $387 million of operating lease commitments of Equilon, our affiliate.

(Exhibit continued on next page . . .)

OPTIONAL SEGMENT

EXHIBIT 6 (continued)

Throughput Agreements

Texaco Inc. and certain of its subsidiary companies previously entered into certain long-term agreements wherein we committed to ship through affiliated pipeline companies and an offshore oil port sufficient volume of crude oil or petroleum products to enable these affiliated companies to meet a specified portion of their individual debt obligations, or, in lieu thereof, to advance sufficient funds to enable these affiliated companies to meet these obligations. In 1998, we assigned the shipping obligations to Equilon, our affiliate, but Texaco remains responsible for deficiency payments on virtually all of these agreements. Additionally, Texaco has entered into long-term purchase commitments with third parties for take or pay gas transportation. At December 31, 1999 and 1998, our maximum exposure to loss was estimated to be $445 million and $500 million.

However, based on our right of counterclaim against Equilon and unaffiliated third parties in the event of non-performance, our net exposure was estimated to be $173 million and $195 million at December 31, 1999 and 1998.

No significant losses are anticipated as a result of these obligations.

Litigation

Texaco and approximately 50 other oil companies are defendants in 17 purported class actions. The actions are pending in Texas, New Mexico, Oklahoma, Louisiana, Utah, Mississippi, and Alabama. . . . Plaintiffs seek to recover royalty underpayments and interest. In some cases plaintiffs also seek to recover severance taxes and treble and punitive damages. Texaco and 24 other defendants have executed a settlement agreement with most of the plaintiffs that will resolve many of these disputes. The federal court in Texas gave final approval to the settlement in April 1999 and the matter is now pending before the U.S. Fifth Circuit Court of Appeal.

Texaco has reached an agreement with the federal government to resolve similar claims. The claims of various state governments remain unresolved.

It is impossible for us to ascertain the ultimate legal and financial liability with respect to contingencies and commitments. However, we do not anticipate that the aggregate amount of such liability in excess of accrued liabilities will be materially important in relation to our consolidated financial position or results of operations.

Source: Texaco, *1999 Annual Report.*

Exhibit 7 illustrates the adjustments for off-balance-sheet financing activities discussed in this reading. Panel A presents Texaco's reported and adjusted debt, total liabilities, and equity. Panel B shows each adjustment to the reported amounts, based on the information provided in Exhibit 6. The result is a more comprehensive measure of the firm's leverage.

EXHIBIT 7 Texaco Adjusted Long-Term Debt, Liabilities, and Solvency Analysis (amounts in $millions)

A. Reported and Adjusted Debt, Liabilities, and Capitalization Ratios

	Reported	Adjustments (Panel B below)	Adjusted	% Increase
Debt	$ 7,647	$4,613	$12,260	60%
Total liabilities	16,930	8,927	25,857	53%
Shareholders' equity	12,042		12,042	
Capitalization Ratios				
Debt to equity	0.64		1.02	60%
Total liabilities to equity	1.41		2.15	53%

B. Adjustments for Off-Balance-Sheet Data

	Debt	Liabilities
Share of affiliate debt	$2,638	$7,554
Capitalization of operating leases	864	864
Redeemable preferred shares	602	—
Guarantees	336	336
Throughput agreements	173	173
Total Adjustments to Debt and Liabilities	**$4,613**	**$8,927**

Adjustments to 1999 Debt

Share of Affiliate Debt. Texaco has entered into a number of joint ventures with other major oil companies. The three primary ones are:

Joint Venture	Partners	Texaco's Share
Equilon	Shell Oil	44.0%
Motiva	Shell Oil, Saudi Refining	32.5%
Caltex	Chevron	50.0%

As Texaco is not the majority owner of any of these ventures, their financial results are not consolidated with Texaco's financial statements and (Texaco's portion of) the debt and liabilities of these joint ventures remains off-balance-sheet. Texaco, however, reports its proportionate share of its joint ventures' assets and liabilities in the final column of Note 5. The adjustment to debt equals Texaco's share in the noncurrent[22] liabilities of its joint ventures; Texaco's liabilities are increased by its share of total (current plus noncurrent) liabilities of its joint ventures.

[22] Current liabilities may include financing obligations, but they are excluded in calculating the debt adjustment as no disclosures were provided. This "undercounting" may be partially offset by the "overcount" implied in including all noncurrent liabilities as certain noncurrent liabilities (e.g., deferred taxes) may not constitute debt.

Capitalization of Operating Leases Note 10 (in Exhibit 6) provides information on Texaco's operating and capital leases. The interest rate implicit in the 1999 capital leases is 4.5%, relatively low even considering the low interest rate levels prevalent in the late 1990s. Texaco's long-term debt footnote (not shown) indicated a cost of debt of about 5.5% for new 10-year debt issued in 1999. We used a discount rate of 5% (and a straight-line assumption for payments after 2004), resulting in a present value adjustment of $864 million.

Redeemable Preferred Shares Redeemable preferred shares should be treated as debt. Note 15 (in Exhibit 6) states that Texaco includes $602 million of such preferred shares as part of minority interest. As minority interest is included in total liabilities, no adjustment is required there. However, debt must be increased by $602 million.

Financial Guarantees As a portion of the $716 million of guarantees relates to affiliate debt, including it would result in double counting as we have already adjusted for Texaco's share of affiliate debt. Thus, we adjust only for $336 million of guarantees of Equilon's operating leases, as that amount is off-balance-sheet for Equilon as well. Note that Texaco's guarantee includes a guarantee of lease residual values.

Throughput Agreements We have used the net exposure of $173 million, although a conservative approach would use the gross exposure of $445 million.

Litigation We note only that potential liabilities related to litigation exist. However, a numeric adjustment is not possible based on the information provided.

The effect of these adjustments is summarized in Exhibit 7, panel A. Adjusted debt is 60% higher than reported debt in 1999 and total liabilities increase by 53%. The adjusted debt-to-equity and liabilities-to-equity ratios are significantly higher than the reported ratios.

FINANCIAL REPORTING BY LESSORS

5

Many manufacturers and dealers offer customers leases to market their products. Such *sales-type leases* include both a manufacturing or merchandising profit (the difference between the fair value at the inception of the lease and the cost or carrying value of the leased property) and interest income due to the financing nature of the transaction. Financial institutions and leasing intermediaries offer direct financing leases that generate interest income only. Either class of lessors may create operating leases.

The remainder of the reading discusses the accounting by lessors for sales-type and direct financing leases. Leveraged leases are beyond the scope of this text and sales with leasebacks are discussed in Box 4.

Lessor financial reporting is illustrated using the lessee example of the beginning of the reading with the additional assumptions that the leased equipment cost $20,000 to manufacture and the expected residual value (not guaranteed by the lessee) is $2,500 after four years.

Lease Classification: Lessors

Lease capitalization by lessors is required when the lease meets *any one* of the four criteria specified for capitalization by lessees and *both* of the following revenue-recognition criteria:

BOX 4 FINANCIAL REPORTING FOR SALES WITH LEASEBACKS

Sale leaseback transactions are sales of property by the owner who then leases it back from the buyer-lessor. Financial reporting for these transactions is governed by SFAS 28, Accounting for Sales with Leasebacks (1979), as amended by SFAS 66, Accounting for Sales of Real Estate (1982).

The amount and timing of profit (or loss) recognized on a sale leaseback transaction are determined by the proportion of the rights to use the leased property retained by the owner-lessee after the sale. If all or substantially all the use rights are retained by the owner-lessee, it is a financing transaction, and no profit or loss on the transaction should be recognized.

The extent of continuing use is determined by the proportion of the present value of reasonable rentals relative to the fair value of assets sold and leased back. This proportion is used to assign sale leaseback transactions to the following financial reporting categories.

Minor leasebacks. Present value of reasonable rentals is less than 10% of the fair value of the leased property; the buyer-lessor obtains substantially all the rights to use the leased property. Any gain (or loss) on the transaction is recognized in full at the inception of the lease.

More than minor but less than "substantially all" leasebacks. Present value of reasonable rentals exceeds 10% but is less than 90% of the fair value of the asset sold; depending on specific criteria, some or all of the gain or loss must be deferred and amortized over the lease term.

Substantially all leasebacks. Present value of MLPs equals or exceeds 90% of the fair value of property sold; the total gain (loss) must be deferred and amortized over the lease term. The leaseback is a financing transaction, and the gain (loss) is recognized as the leased property is used.

Example

OMI [OMM], an oil tanker operator, sold a vessel in May 1997 for $39.9 million and leased it back for five years. The $15.7 million gain was deferred and recognized as an adjustment to lease expense over the five-year lease term. Had the gain been recognized immediately, 1997 pretax income would have been more than twice the reported level.

IAS Standards for Sales with Leasebacks

IAS 17, the accounting standard for these transactions, is significantly different from U.S. GAAP as it requires that:

- When a sale/leaseback results in a finance lease, any profit on the sale must be deferred and recognized over the lease term.
- When a sale/leaseback results in an operating lease, and the sales price equals the asset's fair value, the seller recognizes any gain or loss.
- When a sale/leaseback results in an operating lease, and the sales price is below fair value, the seller recognizes any gain or loss. The exception is that any loss is deferred and amortized when the lease provides for payments that are below market.
- When a sale/leaseback results in an operating lease, and the sales price exceeds fair value, the seller defers any gain and amortizes it over the lease term.

1. Collectibility of the MLPs is reasonably predictable.
2. There are no significant uncertainties regarding the amount of unreimbursable costs yet to be incurred by the lessor under the provisions of the lease agreement.

Leases not meeting these criteria must be reported as operating leases since either the risks and benefits of leased assets have not been transferred, or the earnings process is not complete.

Sales-Type Leases

Exhibit 8 presents financial reporting by a lessor for a sales-type lease using the lessee example. Part A illustrates the accounting recognition at inception and the determination of gross and net investment in the lease; part B provides the lessor's amortization schedule for the sales-type lease.

The lessor recognizes sales revenue of $31,700, the present value of the MLPs. The cost of goods sold is the carrying amount of the leased property. The present value of the unguaranteed residual value of the leased property constitutes continuing investment by the lessor and is not included in costs charged against income; that is, it is deducted from cost to manufacture.

The lessor's gross investment in the lease is $42,500, the sum of the MLPs and the unguaranteed residual value. Net investment in the lease is $33,407, determined by discounting the MLPs and the unguaranteed residual value at the interest rate implicit in the lease (10%), as shown in Part A.

EXHIBIT 8 Lessor Financial Reporting

A. Sales-Type Lease

*Lessor's **Gross Investment** in Leased Equipment*		
MLPs: $10,000 × 4		$40,000
Unguaranteed residual value		2,500
		$42,500
Lessor's Net Investment in Leased Equipment		
Present value at 10% of an annuity of 4 payments of $10,000		$31,700
Present value at 10% of $2,500, 4 periods hence		1,707
		$33,407
Unearned Income		
Gross investment in lease		$42,500
Less: Net investment		33,407
		$ 9,093
Accounting Recognition at Lease Inception		
Sales revenue[a]	$ 31,700	
Cost of goods sold[b]	(18,293)	
Gross profit on sale		$13,407
Gross investment in lease	$ 42,500	
Unearned income	(9,093)	
Net investment in lease		$33,407

[a] Present value of lease payments, excluding residual value.

[b] Cost to manufacture (assumed to be $20,000) less PV of residual value.

(Exhibit continued on next page . . .)

EXHIBIT 8 (continued)

B. Lessor Amortization Schedule: Sales-Type Lease

Year	Annual Payment Received (A)	Interest Income (B)	Reduction in Investment (C) = (A) − (B)	Net Investment (D)
2000				$33,407
2001	$10,000	$3,340	$ 6,660	26,747
2002	10,000	2,675	7,325	19,422
2003	10,000	1,942	8,058	11,364
2004	10,000	1,136	8,864	2,500
Totals	$40,000	$9,093	$30,907	

C. Balance Sheet Effects

	Capital (Sales-Type) Lease			Operating Lease		
	Net Investment in Leases					
Year	Current	Long-Term	Total	Assets Under Lease	Accumulated Depreciation	Net
2000	$6,660	$26,747	$33,407	$20,000	$ 0	$20,000
2001	7,325	19,422	26,747	20,000	4,375	15,625
2002	8,058	11,364	19,422	20,000	8,750	11,250
2003	8,864	2,500	11,364	20,000	13,125	6,875
2004	2,500	0	2,500	20,000	17,500	2,500

D. Income Statement Effects

	Capital (Sales-Type) Lease		Operating Lease		
Year		Income	Rental Revenue	Depreciation	Income
2000	Gain on Sale	$13,407			
2001	Interest	3,340	$10,000	$ 4,375	$ 5,625
2002	Interest	2,675	10,000	4,375	5,625
2003	Interest	1,942	10,000	4,375	5,625
2004	Interest	1,136	10,000	4,375	5,625
Totals		$22,500	$40,000	$17,500	$22,500

(Exhibit continued on next page . . .)

EXHIBIT 8 (continued)

E. Cash Flow Statement Effects

	Capital (Sales-Type) Lease			Operating Lease
Year	CFO	Cash from Investment	Total	CFO
2000	$13,407	$(13,407)	$ 0	$ 0
2001	3,340	6,660	10,000	10,000
2002	2,675	7,325	10,000	10,000
2003	1,942	8,058	10,000	10,000
2004	1,136	8,864	10,000	10,000
Totals	$22,500	$ 17,500	$40,000	$40,000

The difference between the gross and net investment represents unearned income, the interest component of the transaction. Unearned income is systematically amortized to income over the lease term, using the interest method that reports a constant rate of return of 10% on the net investment in the lease. The lessor reports its net investment in the lease on the balance sheet (see the next section). Contingent rentals, if any, are reported as they are earned. SFAS 13 requires an annual review of the estimated residual value. Nontemporary declines must be recognized; however, increases in value or subsequent reversals of declines cannot be reported.

Balance Sheet Effects (Exhibit 8C) The lessor reports the current and noncurrent components of its net investment in sales-type leases. Lessors using the operating lease method do not report any investment in leases, but they continue to report the assets on the balance sheet as long-term assets, net of accumulated depreciation. These amounts assume straight-line depreciation over four years of the original cost of the asset less estimated residual value ($20,000 − $2,500). Note that the operating lease method reports lower net assets each year and, ignoring income effects, tends to increase return on assets relative to the sales-type lease method.

Income Statement Effects (Exhibit 8D) For the sales-type lease, the lessor records profit at inception of $13,407. The annual rental of $10,000 is allocated to interest income and return of principal. Reported interest income reflects a constant 10% return on the declining net investment in the lease. The balance of the rental payment is applied to amortize (reduce principal) the net investment systematically over the lease term.

The operating lease method reports constant income over the lease term as straight-line depreciation is charged against the constant annual rental. The use of accelerated depreciation would result in a pattern of increasing income over the lease term as depreciation declines.

The sales-type lease reports substantially higher income in the first year of the lease due to recognition of manufacturing profit at the inception of the lease. However, reported income declines thereafter due to declining interest income over the remainder of the lease term, relative to constant or increasing income under the operating lease method. In our example, reported net income is higher under the operating lease method after the initial year. *Over the lease term, the total net income is the same under both methods.*

Cash Flow Effects (Exhibit 8E) At the inception of the lease, no cash changes hands. The operating lease method reports no cash flow effects on the statement of cash flows. In contrast, the sales-type lease method reports 2000 operating cash flow of $13,407, equal to the sales profit at the inception of the lease. This cash inflow is offset by a net cash outflow for investment equal to $13,407 (the investment of $33,407 less the $20,000 prior carrying amount of the leased property). Net cash flow remains zero.

In subsequent years, under the operating lease method, CFO is equal to the rental payment of $10,000/year. Under the sale-type lease method, the $10,000 payment is allocated between CFO and cash from investment; CFO is equal to interest income and cash from investment is equal to the reduction in the net investment. Thus, after inception, the operating lease method reports higher CFO and, since interest income declines over the lease term, this difference in CFO increases. Simultaneously, a correspondingly larger reduction in net investment is reported in investment cash flow.

Note that total cash flow (operating plus investing) is unaffected by the method of lease accounting. The actual cash flow in each year is $10,000, the lease payment received. Only under the operating lease method does CFO equal the cash flows associated with the lease. Capitalization of the lease by the lessor reclassifies reported cash flows between operating and investing activities.

The use of sales-type lease accounting allows firms to recognize income earlier than the operating lease method. Lease capitalization also allows firms to report higher CFO at the inception of the lease. This aggressive recognition of income and cash flows ("front-end loading") improves financial ratios; it accurately reflects the firm's operations only if the risks and benefits of leased property have been fully transferred to the lessee and the lessor has no further performance obligation.

Footnote Disclosures Footnote disclosure for lessors under U.S. GAAP is similar to that of lessees. The sales-type lease method requires the disclosure of gross MLPs receivable, unearned income, and the current and noncurrent components of the net investment in leases. Lessors must also provide information on lease terms, future MLPs receivable over the next five years, and the aggregate thereafter. Disclosure for operating leases is limited to MLPs receivable over the next five years and the aggregate thereafter.

Direct Financing Leases

In a direct financing lease, the lessor's original cost or carrying value (prior to the lease) of the asset approximates the market value of the leased asset (the present value of the MLPs). Such leases are pure financing transactions and financial reporting for direct financing leases reflects this fact. *No sale is recognized at the inception of the lease, and there is no manufacturing or dealer profit. Only financing income is reported.*

Unearned income is the difference between the gross investment in the lease and the cost or carrying amount of the leased property. It is amortized to report a constant periodic return (effective interest method) on the net investment in the lease (gross investment plus initial direct costs less unearned income). Thus, in our example, the lessor would report (interest) income and cash flows similar to those reported for the sales-type lease over the period 2001–2004. There are no income or cash flow consequences at the inception of the lease in 2000.

Disclosure requirements for financing leases are similar to those for sales-type leases. Lessors must disclose MLPs receivable over the next five fiscal years and the aggregate thereafter. Any allowance for uncollectibles, executory costs, unguaranteed residual value, and unearned income must also be reported.

The income reported on financing leases depends on assumptions made, particularly those regarding uncollectible payments and residual values. When uncollectibles are underestimated, or residual values overestimated, income is overstated. For example, the *New York Times* reported[23] that automobile lessors would lose more than $10 billion in 2000 because they overestimated the residual values of cars and trucks that they had leased to customers.

Financial Reporting by Lessors: An Example

Exhibit 9 contains IBM Credit Corp.'s footnote on its activities as lessor. The company finances customer purchases of information-handling equipment through direct financing leases; shorter-term leases of such equipment are treated as operating leases.

EXHIBIT 9 IBM Credit Corp. Net Investment in Capital Leases

The Company's capital lease portfolio includes direct financing and leveraged leases. The Company originates financing for customers in a variety of industries and throughout the United States. The Company has a diversified portfolio of capital equipment financing for end users.

Direct financing leases consist principally of IBM advanced information processing products with terms generally from two to three years. The components of the net investment in direct financing leases at December 31, 1999 and 1998, are as follows:

(In $thousands)

	1999	1998
Gross lease payments receivable	$5,335,352	$5,278,060
Estimated unguaranteed residual values	442,288	397,529
Deferred initial direct costs	18,339	30,634
Unearned income	(604,035)	(571,168)
Allowance for receivable losses	(47,220)	(65,644)
Total	$5,144,724	$5,069,411

(Exhibit continued on next page . . .)

[23] December 15, 2000, p. F1.

EXHIBIT 9 (continued)

The scheduled maturities of minimum lease payments outstanding at December 31, 1999, expressed as a percentage of the total, are due approximately as follows:

Within 12 months	50%
13 to 24 months	33
25 to 36 months	13
37 to 48 months	3
After 48 months	1
	100%

Included in the net investment in capital leases is $17.7 million of seller interest at December 31, 1998, relating to the securitization of such leases. These securitizations were terminated and settled in 1999.

Refer to the note, Allowance for Receivable Losses, for a reconciliation of the direct financing leases and leveraged leases allowances for receivable losses.

Equipment on Operating Leases

Operating leases consist principally of IBM advanced information processing products with terms generally from two to three years. The components of equipment on operating leases at December 31, 1999 and 1998, are as follows:

(In $thousands)

	1999	1998
Cost	$ 7,166,892	$ 7,046,757
Accumulated depreciation	(3,780,206)	(3,427,172)
Total	$ 3,386,686	$ 3,619,585

Minimum future rentals were approximately $3,094.2 million at December 31, 1999. The scheduled maturities of the minimum future rentals at December 31, 1999, expressed as a percentage of the total, are due approximately as follows:

Within 12 months	57%
13 to 24 months	30
25 to 36 months	10
37 to 48 months	2
After 48 months	1
	100%

Source: IBM Credit Corp., *1999 Annual Report.*

IBM discloses aggregate MLPs receivable and reports the periodic payments in each of the next five years and in the aggregate thereafter as a percentage of this total. The terms of both the direct financing leases and operating leases range from two to three years.[24] However, the operating leases generally have shorter terms: 57% of the operating leases are due within one year, higher than the 50% of direct financing leases due within 12 months of the financial statement date.

Additional disclosures are required for the capitalized direct financing leases: current and noncurrent components, allowance for uncollectibles, estimated unguaranteed residual values, and unearned interest. IBM Credit provides most applicable disclosures. No contingent rentals are reported; they may not be significant. However, the current and noncurrent components have not been reported separately. Computation of the implicit interest rate requires additional assumptions.

The footnote disclosure includes the securitization of direct financing lease receivables and reference to a reconciliation of the allowance for losses.

Going beyond the financial effects of IBM's lessor activities, the footnote data indicate that the company is experiencing minimal lease growth. Direct financing leases increased by 1% (using MLPs) during 1999 while operating leases grew at a rate less than 2%. These patterns may represent stable volume and prices, or higher volume offset by lower lease prices, or a shift from leases to sales (reflecting changes in relative prices or customer preferences). This is another example of how attention to footnote detail can suggest worthwhile questions about changes in operations to ask management.

IAS Standards for Lessors

IAS 17 provides accounting standards for lessors that are broadly similar to those of U.S. GAAP. The most significant differences are:

- Lease classification as a finance lease depends on broad principles (see discussion for lessees earlier in the reading) rather than the SFAS 13 rules.
- Disclosure requirements are the same as for lessees, with MLPs disclosed for amounts due:
  1. within one year
  2. one to five years
  3. In more than five years

[24] In its 1994 annual report, IBM Credit reported financing lease terms ranging three to five years and operating leases that spanned two to four years. The shortening of lease terms is consistent with the rapid technological changes in the computer industry.

SUMMARY

Financial liabilities can take many forms, from simple, full-coupon debt to leasing and other more esoteric forms of off-balance-sheet activities. This reading and the previous one illustrated the far-reaching effects of such transactions on a firm's income, cash flow, and capital structure. The principal points made in this reading are:

1. Operating leases are the most common form of off-balance-sheet financing. Such leases should be capitalized and adjustments made to reported financial data.
2. In addition to leases, there are other means of acquiring the use of assets without reflecting them on the balance sheet, such as:
   - joint ventures
   - take-or-pay and throughput agreements
   - sales of receivables

   The reading illustrates techniques that can be used to adjust financial statements for these activities as well.

The discussion and analysis of OBS activities is not yet complete.

PRACTICE PROBLEMS FOR READING 40

1. [Lease classification and financial statement effects; CFA® adapted] On January 1, 2001, a company entered into a capital lease, recording a balance sheet obligation of $10,000, using an interest rate of 12%. The lease payment for 2001 was $1,300. Compute each of the following:
   i. Interest expense for 2001
   ii. The lease obligation at the end of 2001
   iii. The effect of the lease payments on each of the three components of cash flow for 2001
   iv. Each of items (i) through (iii) if the lease had been recorded as an operating lease
2. [Analysis of lessee] The Tolrem Company has decided to lease an airplane on January 1, 2002. The firm and its lessor have not yet decided the terms of the lease. Assume that the terms can be adjusted to permit Tolrem to either capitalize the lease or record it as an operating lease.
   A. State the effect (higher, lower, or equal) of the choice of capitalizing the lease on the following for 2002 (the initial year of the lease):
      i. Cash flow from operations
      ii. Financing cash flow
      iii. Investing cash flow
      iv. Net cash flow
      v. Debt-to-equity ratio
      vi. Interest coverage ratio
      vii. Operating income
      viii. Net income
      ix. Deferred tax asset or liability
      x. Taxes paid
      xi. Pre- and posttax return on assets
      xii. Pre- and posttax return on equity
   B. Recall that the difference between net income under the two methods changes direction at some point during the lease term. State which answers to part a will change in the year after the switch occurs and describe the change.
   C. Assume that Tolrem enters into new aircraft leases at a constant annual rate. Describe the effect of the choice of accounting method on the items in Part A.
3. [Lease capitalization] In 1999, Liberty Bancorp [LIBB] leased new property and accounted for the lease as a capital lease. Until 1999, it had reported all of its leased assets as operating leases. The following information with respect to the capital lease was obtained form the company's 1999 annual report:

Capital lease assets (net of amortization)	$2,479,570
Capitalized lease obligations	2,596,031
Interest on capitalized leases	223,733
Repayment of capital lease obligations	3,969

Minimum lease payments over the next five years and thereafter (in $thousands):

	2000	2001	2002	2003
Capital Lease MLPs	$272	$280	$288	$297
	2004	**Thereafter**		**Total**
Capital Lease MLPs	$305	$4,596		$6,038

A. Determine the amount of the capital lease at its inception.

B. The company states that it amortizes its capital leases over the term of the lease. Determine the amortization expense for 1999 and the term of the lease. Compute the total expense for 1999 as a result of the capital lease.

C. Explain how the capital lease affected the 1999 cash flow statement.

D. Describe the adjustment to the company's 1999 free cash flows that should be made for the capital lease.

E. Assuming that the lease was reported as an operating lease, determine:

  i. Lease expense for 1999

  ii. The effect on the cash flow statement

4. [Effect of lease capitalization on ratios] Exhibit P-1 presents selected 1999 financial data provided by The Limited [LTD]. (*Note:* Use 6% as the appropriate interest rate for present-value calculations.)

A. In its 10-K filing, The Limited provides an adjusted "earnings to fixed charge coverage" ratio.

  i. Calculate the ratio without the adjustment.

  ii. Explain why the adjusted ratio is a better measure of the company's interest coverage.

B. Compute the debt-to-equity ratio for The Limited based on reported data.

C. In its MD&A, the company provides a summary of its working capital position and capitalization. Adjust each of the following for the effect of (capitalization of) the firm's operating leases:

  i. Working capital

  ii. Long-term debt

  iii. Debt-to-equity ratio

EXHIBIT P-1 **The Limited Inc.**

Selected Financial Data

Liquidity and Capital Resources (MD&A)

A summary of the Company's working capital position and capitalization follows (in $thousands):

	Year Ended January 30, 1999
Cash provided by operating activities	$ 571,014
Working capital	1,070,249
Capitalization:	
Long-term debt	550,000
Shareholders' equity	2,233,303
Total capitalization	$2,783,303

Leased Facilities and Commitments (Notes to Financial Statements)

Minimum Rent Commitments Under Noncancellable Operating Leases

Year	2000	2001	2002	2003	2004	Thereafter
MLP	$643,828	$632,785	$602,868	$563,468	$502,880	$1,427,862

Ratio of Earnings to Fixed Charges (10-K)

Year Ended January 30, 1999		
Adjusted Earnings		
Pretax earnings		$2,363,646
Fixed Charges		
Portion of minimum rent of $689,240 representative of interest	$229,747	
Interest on indebtedness	68, 528	298,275
Minority interest		64,564
Total earnings as adjusted		$2,726,485
Ratio of earnings to fixed charges	9.1X	

Source: The Limited, *1999 Annual Report* and 10-K.

5. [Sale of receivables; ratio and cash flow effects] Foster Wheeler [FWC] entered into arrangements to sell receivables in 1998 and 1999. The accounts receivable footnote in the firm's *1999 Annual Report* noted that

> As of December 31, 1999, and December 25, 1998, $50 million and $38.4 million, respectively, in receivables were sold under the agreement and are therefore not reflected in the accounts receivable-trade balance in the Consolidated Balance Sheet.

Selected reported financial data for the company follow:

Years Ended December (in $millions)			
	1997	1998	1999
Sales	$4,060	$4,537	$3,867
Trade accounts receivable	664	720	739
Current assets		1,673	1,615
Current liabilities		1,492	1,472
Total short- and long-term debt		963	961
Stockholders' equity		572	376
Cash flow from operations	(113)	(59)	(6)

A. Compute the impact of the sale of receivables on FWC's receivable turnover ratio and cash cycle for 1998 and 1999.

B. Compute the reported and adjusted (for the sale of receivables) current and debt-to-equity ratios for 1998 and 1999.

C. Discuss the impact of the sale on (the trend of) the firm's cash flow from operations over the period 1997 to 1999.

6. [Off-balance-sheet obligations; CFA adapted] Extracts from The Bowie Company's December 31, 2001, balance sheet and income statement are presented in the following schedule, along with its interest coverage ratio:

Debt	$12 million
Equity	20
Interest expense	1
Times interest earned	5.0X

The Bowie Corporation's financial statement footnotes include the following:

i. At the beginning of 2001, Bowie entered into an operating lease with future payments of $40 million ($5 million/year) with a discounted present value of $20 million.

ii. Bowie has guaranteed a $5 million, 10% bond issue, due in 2007, issued by Crockett, a nonconsolidated 30%-owned affiliate.

iii. Bowie has committed itself (starting in 2002) to purchase a total of $12 million of phosphorus from PEPE, Inc., its major supplier, over the next five years. The estimated present value of these payments is $7 million.

A. Adjust Bowie's debt and equity and recompute the debt-to-equity ratio, using the information in footnotes (i) to (iii).

B. Adjust the times-interest-earned ratio for 2001 for these commitments.

C. Discuss the reasons (both financial and operating) why Bowie may have entered into these arrangements.

D. Describe the additional information required to fully evaluate the impact of these commitments on Bowie's current financial condition and future operating trends.

7. [Analysis of lessor] Carignane Corp., a manufacturer/lessor, enters into a sales-type lease agreement with Mourvedre, Inc., as lessee. The lessor capitalizes the lease rather than reporting it as an operating lease.

Describe the effect (lower, higher, or none) of this choice on the following accounts and ratios of Carignane (the lessor) in the first and ninth years of a 10-year lease:

i. Total assets
ii. Revenues
iii. Expenses
iv. Asset turnover ratio
v. Interest income
vi. Cost of goods sold
vii. Net income
viii. Retained earnings
ix. Income taxes paid
x. Posttax return on assets
xi. Cash flow form operations
xii. Investment cash flow

8. [Analysis of lessor and lessee] On January 1, 2001, the Malbec Company leases a Willmess winepress to the Baldes Group under the following conditions:

i. Annual lease payments are $20,000 for 20 years.
ii. At the end of the lease term, the press is expected to have a value of $5,500.
iii. The fair market value of the press is $185,250.
iv. The estimated economic life of the press is 30 years.
v. Malbec's implicit interest rate is 12%; Baldes' incremental borrowing rate is 10%.
vi. Malbec reports similar presses at $150,000 in finished-goods inventory.

A. Based on the data given, state whether Baldes should treat this lease as an operating or a capital lease. Justify your answer. What additional information would help to answer the question?

B. Assume that Baldes capitalizes the lease. List the financial statement accounts affected (at January 1, 2001) by that decision and calculate each effect.

C. Assume that Baldes uses straight-line depreciation for financial reporting purposes. Compute the income statement, balance sheet, and statement of cash flows effects of the lease for 2001 and 2002 under each lease accounting method.

D. Based on the data given, state whether Malbec should treat this lease as an operating or a sales-type lease. Justify your answer. What additional information would help to answer the question?

E. Assume that Malbec treats the lease as an operating lease. List the financial statement accounts affected (at January 1, 2001) by that decision and calculate each effect.

F. Assume that Malbec treats the lease as a sales-type lease and the lessee does not guarantee the residual value of the winepress. List the financial statement accounts affected (at January 1, 2001) by that decision and calculate each effect.

G. Assume that Malbec uses straight-line depreciation for financial reporting purposes. Compute the income statement, balance sheet, and statement of cash flows effects of the lease for 2001 and 2002 under each lease accounting method.

STUDY SESSION 10
FINANCIAL STATEMENT ANALYSIS:
Techniques, Applications, and International Standards Convergence

The readings in this study session discuss financial analysis techniques, financial statement analysis applications, and the international convergence of accounting standards.

The first reading presents the most frequently used tools and techniques used to evaluate companies, including common size analysis, cross-sectional analysis, trend analysis, and ratio analysis. The second reading then shows the application of financial analysis techniques to major analyst tasks including the evaluation of past and future financial performance, credit risk, and the screening of potential equity investments. The reading also discusses analyst adjustments to reported financials. Such adjustments are often needed to put companies' reported results on a comparable basis.

This study session concludes with a reading on convergence of international and U.S. accounting standards. Although there has been much progress in harmonizing accounting standards globally, as this reading discusses, there are still significant variations between generally accepted accounting principles from one country to another.

READING ASSIGNMENTS

Reading 41 Financial Analysis Techniques
Reading 42 Financial Statement Analysis: Applications
Reading 43 International Standards Convergence

LEARNING OUTCOMES

Reading 41: Financial Analysis Techniques

The candidate should be able to:

a. evaluate and compare companies using ratio analysis, common-size financial statements, and charts in financial analysis;

b. describe the limitations of ratio analysis;

c. explain and demonstrate the classification of financial ratios;

d. calculate and interpret activity, liquidity, solvency, profitability, and valuation ratios;

e. demonstrate how ratios are related and how to evaluate a company using a combination of different ratios;

f. demonstrate the application of DuPont analysis (the decomposition of return on equity);

g. calculate and interpret the ratios used in equity analysis, credit analysis, and segment analysis;

h. describe how the results of common-size and ratio analysis can be used to model and forecast earnings.

Reading 42: Financial Statement Analysis: Applications

The candidate should be able to:

a. evaluate a company's past financial performance and explain how a company's strategy is reflected in past financial performance;

b. prepare a basic projection of a company's future net income and cash flow;

c. describe the role of financial statement analysis in assessing the credit quality of a potential debt investment;

d. discuss the use of financial statement analysis in screening for potential equity investments;

e. determine and justify appropriate analyst adjustments to a company's financial statements to facilitate comparison with another company.

Reading 43: International Standards Convergence

The candidate should be able to:

a. identify and explain the major international accounting standards for each asset and liability category on the balance sheet and the key differences from U.S. generally accepted accounting principles (GAAP);

b. identify and explain the major international accounting standards for major revenue and expense categories on the income statement, and the key differences from U.S. GAAP;

c. identify and explain the major differences between international and U.S. GAAP accounting standards concerning the treatment of interest and dividends on the cash flow statement;

d. interpret the effect of differences between international and U.S. GAAP accounting standards on the balance sheet, income statement, and the statement of changes in equity for some commonly used financial ratios.

FINANCIAL ANALYSIS TECHNIQUES

by Thomas R. Robinson, Hennie van Greuning, Elaine Henry, and Michael A. Broihahn

READING

41

LEARNING OUTCOMES

The candidate should be able to:

a. evaluate and compare companies using ratio analysis, common-size financial statements, and charts in financial analysis;

b. describe the limitations of ratio analysis;

c. explain and demonstrate the classification of financial ratios;

d. calculate and interpret activity, liquidity, solvency, profitability, and valuation ratios;

e. demonstrate how ratios are related and how to evaluate a company using a combination of different ratios;

f. demonstrate the application of DuPont analysis (the decomposition of return on equity);

g. calculate and interpret the ratios used in equity analysis, credit analysis, and segment analysis;

h. describe how the results of common-size and ratio analysis can be used to model and forecast earnings.

THEME

Financial analysis techniques—such as ratio analysis and common-size financial statements—can provide valuable insight into a company's operations, risk characteristics, and valuation beyond what is readily apparent by examining raw data. When data are presented analytically, differences across time periods, interrelationships of financial statement accounts, and comparisons among companies are more easily understood. Furthermore, trends and relationships become more visible, thereby assisting in equity valuation and credit analysis.

1 INTRODUCTION

Financial analysis applies analytical tools to financial data to assess a company's performance and trends in that performance. In essence, an analyst converts data into financial metrics that assist in decision making. Analysts seek to answer such questions as: How successfully has the company performed, relative to its own past performance and relative to its competitors? How is the company likely to perform in the future? Based on expectations about future performance, what is the value of this company or the securities it issues?

A primary source of data is a company's financial reports, including the financial statements, footnotes, and management's discussion and analysis. This reading focuses on data presented in financial reports prepared under international financial reporting standards (IFRS) and United States generally accepted accounting principles (U.S. GAAP). However, even financial reports prepared under these standards do not contain all the information needed to perform effective financial analysis. Although financial statements do contain data about the *past* performance of a company (its income and cash flows) as well as its *current* financial condition (assets, liabilities, and owners' equity), such statements may not provide some important nonfinancial information nor do they forecast *future* results. The financial analyst must be capable of using financial statements in conjunction with other information in order to reach valid conclusions and make projections. Accordingly, an analyst will most likely need to supplement the information found in a company's financial reports with industry and economic data.

The purpose of this reading is to describe various techniques used to analyze a company's financial statements. Financial analysis of a company may be performed for a variety of reasons, such as valuing equity securities, assessing credit risk, conducting due diligence related to an acquisition, or assessing a subsidiary's performance. This reading will describe the techniques common to any financial analysis and then discuss more specific aspects for the two most common categories: equity analysis and credit analysis.

Equity analysis incorporates an owner's perspective, either for valuation or performance evaluation. Credit analysis incorporates a creditor's (such as a banker or bondholder) perspective. In either case, there is a need to gather and analyze information to make a decision (ownership or credit); the focus of analysis varies due to the differing interest of owners and creditors. Both equity and credit analysis assess the entity's ability to generate and grow earnings and cash flow, as well as any associated risks. Equity analysis usually places a greater emphasis on growth, whereas credit analysis usually places a greater emphasis on risks. The difference in emphasis reflects the different fundamentals of these types of investments: The value of a company's equity generally increases as the company's earnings and cash flow increase, whereas the value of a company's debt has an upper limit.[1]

The balance of this reading is organized as follows: Section 2 recaps the framework for financial statements and the place of financial analysis techniques within it. Section 3 provides a description of analytical tools and techniques. Section 4 explains how to compute, analyze, and interpret common financial ratios. Sections 4 through 8 explain the use of ratios and other analytical data in equity analysis, debt analysis, segment analysis, and forecasting, respectively. A summary of the key points and practice problems in the CFA Institute multiple-choice format conclude the reading.

THE FINANCIAL ANALYSIS PROCESS 2

In financial analysis, as in any business task, a clear understanding of the end goal and the steps required to get there is essential. In addition, the analyst needs to know the typical questions to address when interpreting financial data and how to communicate the analysis and conclusions.

2.1 The Objectives of the Financial Analysis Process

Due to the variety of reasons for performing financial analysis, the numerous available techniques, and the often substantial amount of data, it is important that the analytical approach be tailored to the specific situation. Prior to embarking on any financial analysis, the analyst should clarify purpose and context, and clearly understand the following:

- What is the purpose of the analysis? What questions will this analysis answer?
- What level of detail will be needed to accomplish this purpose?
- What data are available for the analysis?
- What are the factors or relationships that will influence the analysis?
- What are the analytical limitations, and will these limitations potentially impair the analysis?

Having clarified the purpose and context of the analysis, the analyst can select the techniques (e.g., ratios) that will best assist in making a decision. Although there is no single approach to structuring the analysis process, a general framework is set forth in Exhibit 1.[2] The steps in this process were discussed in more detail in Reading 29. The primary focus of this reading is on Phases 3 and 4, processing and analyzing data.

[1] The upper limit is equal to the undiscounted sum of the principal and remaining interest payments (i.e., the present value of these contractual payments at a zero percent discount rate).

[2] Components of this framework have been adapted from van Greuning and Bratanovic (2003, p. 300) and Benninga and Sarig (1997, pp. 134–156).

EXHIBIT 1 A Financial Statement Analysis Framework

Phase	Sources of Information	Output
1. Articulate the purpose and context of the analysis	▶ The nature of the analyst's function, such as evaluating an equity or debt investment or issuing a credit rating. ▶ Communication with client or superior on needs and concerns. ▶ Institutional guidelines related to developing specific work product.	▶ Statement of the purpose or objective of analysis. ▶ A list (written or unwritten) of specific questions to be answered by the analysis. ▶ Nature and content of report to be provided. ▶ Timetable and budgeted resources for completion.
2. Collect input data	▶ Financial statements, other financial data, questionnaires, and industry/economic data. ▶ Discussions with management, suppliers, customers, and competitors. ▶ Company site visits (e.g., to production facilities or retail stores).	▶ Organized financial statements. ▶ Financial data tables. ▶ Completed questionnaires, if applicable.
3. Process data	▶ Data from the previous phase.	▶ Adjusted financial statements. ▶ Common-size statements. ▶ Ratios and graphs. ▶ Forecasts.
4. Analyze/interpret the processed data	▶ Input data as well as processed data.	▶ Analytical results.
5. Develop and communicate conclusions and recommendations (e.g., with an analysis report)	▶ Analytical results and previous reports. ▶ Institutional guidelines for published reports.	▶ Analytical report answering questions posed in Phase 1. ▶ Recommendation regarding the purpose of the analysis, such as whether to make an investment or grant credit.
6. Follow up	▶ Information gathered by periodically repeating above steps as necessary to determine whether changes to holdings or recommendations are necessary.	▶ Updated reports and recommendations.

2.2 Distinguishing between Computations and Analysis

An effective analysis encompasses both computations and interpretations. A well-reasoned analysis differs from a mere compilation of various pieces of information, computations, tables, and graphs by integrating the data collected into a cohesive whole. Analysis of past performance, for example, should address not only what happened but also why it happened and whether it advanced the company's strategy. Some of the key questions to address include:

- What aspects of performance are critical for this company to successfully compete in this industry?

- How well did the company's performance meet these critical aspects? (This is established through computation and comparison with appropriate benchmarks, such as the company's own historical performance or competitors' performance.)
- What were the key causes of this performance, and how does this performance reflect the company's strategy? (This is established through analysis.)

If the analysis is forward looking, additional questions include:

- What is the likely impact of an event or trend? (Established through interpretation of analysis.)
- What is the likely response of management to this trend? (Established through evaluation of quality of management and corporate governance.)
- What is the likely impact of trends in the company, industry, and economy on future cash flows? (Established through assessment of corporate strategy and through forecasts.)
- What are the recommendations of the analyst? (Established through interpretation and forecasting of results of analysis.)
- What risks should be highlighted? (Established by an evaluation of major uncertainties in the forecast.)

Example 1 demonstrates how a company's financial data can be analyzed in the context of its business strategy and changes in that strategy. An analyst must be able to understand the "why" behind the numbers and ratios, not just what the numbers and ratios are.

EXAMPLE 1

Change in Strategy Reflected in Financial Performance

Motorola (NYSE:MOT) and Nokia (NYSE:NOK) engage in the design, manufacture, and sale of mobility products worldwide. Selected financial data for 2003 through 2005 for these two competitors are given below.

Selected Financial Data for Motorola (in $millions)

Years ended 31 December	2005	2004	2003
Net sales	36,843	31,323	23,155
Operating earnings	4,696	3,132	1,273

Selected Financial Data for Nokia Corporation (in €millions)

Years ended 31 December	2005	2004	2003
Net sales	34,191	29,371	29,533
Operating profit	4,639	4,326	4,960

Source: Motorola 10-K and Nokia 20-F, both filed 2 March 2006.

Although the raw numbers for Motorola and Nokia are not directly comparable because Motorola reports in U.S. dollars and Nokia in euros, the relative changes can be compared. Motorola reported a 35 percent increase in net sales from 2003 to 2004 and a further increase in 2005 of approximately 18 percent. Also, the company's operating earnings more than doubled from 2003 to 2004 and grew another 50 percent in 2005. Over the 2003 to 2004 time period, industry leader Nokia reported a decrease in both sales and operating profits, although sales growth was about 16 percent in 2005.

What caused Motorola's dramatic growth in sales and operating profits? One of the most important factors was the introduction of new products, such as the stylish RAZR cell phone in 2004. Motorola's 2005 10-K indicates that more than 23 million RAZRs had been sold since the product was launched. The handset segment represents 54 percent of the company's 2004 sales and nearly 58 percent of 2005 sales, so the impact on sales and profitability of the successful product introduction was significant. The introduction of branded, differentiated products not only increased demand but also increased the potential for higher pricing. The introduction of the new products was one result of the company's strategic shift to develop a consumer marketing orientation as a complement to its historically strong technological position.

Analysts often need to communicate the findings of their analysis in a written report. Their reports should, therefore, communicate how conclusions were reached and why recommendations were made. For example, a report might present the following:[3]

- the purpose of the report, unless it is readily apparent
- relevant aspects of the business context
  - economic environment (country, macro economy, sector)
  - financial and other infrastructure (accounting, auditing, rating agencies)
  - legal and regulatory environment (and any other material limitations on the company being analyzed)
- evaluation of corporate governance
- assessment of financial and operational data
- conclusions and recommendations (including risks and limitations to the analysis)

An effective storyline and well-supported conclusions and recommendations are normally enhanced by using 3–10 years of data, as well as analytic techniques appropriate to the purpose of the report.

[3] The nature and content of reports will vary depending upon the purpose of the analysis and the ultimate recipient of the report. For an example of the contents of an equity research report, see Stowe, Robinson, Pinto, and McLeavey (2002, pages 22–28).

ANALYSIS TOOLS AND TECHNIQUES 3

The tools and techniques presented in this section facilitate evaluations of company data. Evaluations require comparisons. It is difficult to say that a company's financial performance was "good" without clarifying the basis for comparison.

In assessing a company's ability to generate and grow earnings and cash flow, and the risks related to those earnings and cash flows, the analyst draws comparisons to other companies (cross-sectional analysis) and over time (trend or time-series analysis).

For example, an analyst may wish to compare the profitability in 2004 of Dell and Gateway. These companies differ significantly in size, so comparing net income in raw dollars is not useful. Instead, ratios (which express one number in relation to another) and common-size financial statements can remove size as a factor and enable a more relevant comparison.

The analyst may also want to examine Dell's performance relative to its own historic performance. Again, the raw dollar amounts of sales or net income may not highlight significant changes. However, using ratios (see Example 2), horizontal financial statements, and graphs can make such changes more apparent.

EXAMPLE 2

Ratio Analysis

Dell computer reported the following data for three recent fiscal years:

Fiscal Year Ended (FY)	Net Income (millions of USD)
1/31/2003	$2,122
1/30/2004	$2,645
1/28/2005	$3,043

Overall net income has grown steadily over the three-year period. Net income for FY2005 is 43 percent higher than net income in 2003, which is a good sign. However, has profitability also steadily increased? We can obtain some insight by looking at the net profit margin (net income divided by revenue) for each year.

Fiscal Year Ended	Net Profit Margin
1/31/2003	5.99%
1/30/2004	6.38%
1/28/2005	6.18%

The net profit margin indicates that profitability improved from FY2003 to FY2004 but deteriorated slightly from FY2004 to FY2005. Further analysis is needed to determine the cause of the profitability decline and assess whether this decline is likely to persist in future years.

The following paragraphs describe the tools and techniques of ratio analysis in more detail.

3.1 Ratios

There are many relationships between financial accounts and between expected relationships from one point in time to another. Ratios are a useful way of expressing these relationships. Ratios express one quantity in relation to another (usually as a quotient).

Notable academic research has examined the importance of ratios in predicting stock returns (Ou and Penman, 1989; Abarbanell and Bushee, 1998) or credit failure (Altman, 1968; Ohlson, 1980; Hopwood et al., 1994). This research has found that financial statement ratios are effective in selecting investments and in predicting financial distress. Practitioners routinely use ratios to communicate the value of companies and securities.

Several aspects of ratio analysis are important to understand. First, the computed ratio is not "the answer." The ratio is an *indicator* of some aspect of a company's performance, telling what happened but not why it happened. For example, an analyst might want to answer the question: Which of two companies was more profitable? The net profit margin, which expresses profit relative to revenue, can provide insight into this question. Net profit margin is calculated by dividing net income by revenue:[4]

$$\frac{\text{Net income}}{\text{Revenue}}$$

Assume Company A has €100,000 of net income and €2,000,000 of revenue, and thus a net profit margin of 5 percent. Company B has €200,000 of net income and €6,000,000 of revenue, and thus a net profit margin of 3.33 percent. Expressing net income as a percentage of revenue clarifies the relationship: For each €100 of revenue, Company A earns €5 in net income, while Company B earns only €3.33 for each €100 of revenue. So, we can now answer the question of which company was more profitable in percentage terms: Company A was more profitable, as indicated by its higher net profit margin of 5 percent. We also note that Company A was more profitable despite the fact that Company B reported higher absolute amounts of net income and revenue. However, this ratio by itself does not tell us *why* Company A has a higher profit margin. Further analysis is required to determine the reason (perhaps higher relative sales prices or better cost control).

Company size sometimes confers economies of scale, so the absolute amounts of net income and revenue are useful in financial analysis. However, ratios reduce the effect of size, which enhances comparisons between companies and over time.

A second important aspect of ratio analysis is that differences in accounting policies (across companies and across time) can distort ratios, and a meaningful comparison may, therefore, involve adjustments to the financial data. Third, not all ratios are necessarily relevant to a particular analysis. The ability to select a

[4] The term "sales" is often used interchangeably with the term "revenues." Other times it is used to refer to revenues derived from sales of products versus services. Furthermore, the income statement usually reflects "revenues" or "sales" after returns and allowances (e.g., returns of products or discounts offered after a sale to induce the customer to not return a product). Additionally, in some countries including the United Kingdom, the term "turnover" is used in the sense of "revenue."

relevant ratio or ratios to answer the research question is an analytical skill. Finally, as with financial analysis in general, ratio analysis does not stop with computation; interpretation of the result is essential. In practice, differences in ratios across time and across companies can be subtle, and interpretation is situation specific.

3.1.1 The Universe of Ratios

There are no authoritative bodies specifying exact formulas for computing ratios or providing a standard, comprehensive list of ratios. Formulas and even names of ratios often differ from analyst to analyst or from database to database. The number of different ratios that can be created is practically limitless. There are, however, widely accepted ratios that have been found to be useful. Section 4 of this reading will focus primarily on these broad classes and commonly accepted definitions of key ratios. However, the analyst should be aware that different ratios may be used in practice and that certain industries have unique ratios tailored to the characteristics of that industry. When faced with an unfamiliar ratio, the analyst can examine the underlying formula to gain insight into what the ratio is measuring. For example, consider the following ratio formula:

$$\frac{\text{Operating income}}{\text{Average total assets}}$$

Never having seen this ratio, an analyst might question whether a result of 12 percent is better than 8 percent. The answer can be found in the ratio itself. The numerator is operating income and the denominator is average total assets, so the ratio can be interpreted as the amount of operating income generated per unit of assets. For every €100 of average total assets, generating €12 of operating income is better than generating €8 of operating income. Furthermore, it is apparent that this particular ratio is an indicator of profitability (and, to a lesser extent, efficiency in use of assets in generating operating profits). When facing a ratio for the first time, the analyst should evaluate the numerator and denominator to assess what the ratio is attempting to measure and how it should be interpreted. This is demonstrated in Example 3.

EXAMPLE 3

Interpreting a Financial Ratio

An insurance company reports that its "combined ratio" is determined by dividing losses and expenses incurred by net premiums earned. It reports the following combined ratios:

	2005	2004	2003	2002	2001
Combined ratio	90.1%	104.0%	98.5%	104.1%	101.1%

Explain what this ratio is measuring and compare and contrast the results reported for each of the years shown in the chart. What other information might an analyst want to review before concluding on this information?

Solution: The combined ratio is a profitability measure. The ratio is explaining how much the costs (losses and expenses) were for every dollar of revenue (net premiums earned). The underlying formula indicates that a lower ratio is better. The 2005 ratio of 90.1 percent means that for every dollar of net premiums earned, the costs were $.901, yielding a gross profit of $.099. Ratios greater than 100 percent indicate an overall loss. A review of the data indicates that there does not seem to be a consistent trend in this ratio. Profits were achieved in 2005 and 2003. The results for 2004 and 2002 show the most significant losses at 104 percent.

The analyst would want to discuss this data further with management and understand the characteristics of the underlying business. He or she would want to understand why the results are so volatile. The analyst would also want to determine what ratio should be used as a benchmark.

The Operating income/Average total assets ratio shown above is one of many versions of the return on assets (ROA) ratio. Note that there are other ways of specifying this formula based on how assets are defined. Some financial ratio databases compute ROA using the ending value of assets rather than average assets. In limited cases, one may also see beginning assets in the denominator. Which one is right? It depends upon what you are trying to measure and the underlying company trends. If the company has a stable level of assets, the answer will not differ greatly under the three measures of assets (beginning, average, and ending). If, however, the assets are growing (or shrinking), the results will differ. When assets are growing, operating income divided by ending assets may not make sense because some of the income would have been generated before some assets were purchased, and this would understate the company's performance. Similarly, if beginning assets are used, some of the operating income later in the year may have been generated only because of the addition of assets; therefore, the ratio would overstate the company's performance. Because operating income occurs throughout the period, it generally makes sense to use some average measure of assets. A good general rule is that when an income statement or cash flow statement number is in the numerator of a ratio and a balance sheet number is in the denominator, then an average should be used for the denominator. It is generally not necessary to use averages when only balance sheet numbers are used in both the numerator and denominator because both are determined as of the same date. However, as we shall see later, there are occasions when even balance sheet data may be averages, e.g., in analyzing the components of return on equity (ROE), which is defined as net income divided by average shareholders' equity.

If an average is used, there is also judgment required as to what average should be used. For simplicity, most ratio databases use a simple average of the beginning and end-of-year balance sheet amounts. If the company's business is seasonable so that levels of assets vary by interim period (semiannual or quarterly), then it may be beneficial to take an average over all interim periods, if available (if the analyst is working within a company and has access to monthly data, this can also be used).

3.1.2 Value, Purposes, and Limitations of Ratio Analysis

The value of ratio analysis is that it enables the equity or credit analyst to evaluate past performance, assess the current financial position of the company, and gain insights useful for projecting future results. As noted previously, the ratio itself is not "the answer" but an indicator of some aspect of a company's performance. Financial ratios provide insights into:

- microeconomic relationships within a company that help analysts project earnings and free cash flow;
- a company's financial flexibility, or ability to obtain the cash required to grow and meet its obligations, even if unexpected circumstances develop; and
- management's ability.

There are also limitations to ratio analysis:

- *The homogeneity of a company's operating activities.* Companies may have divisions operating in many different industries. This can make it difficult to find comparable industry ratios to use for comparison purposes.
- *The need to determine whether the results of the ratio analysis are consistent.* One set of ratios may indicate a problem, whereas another set may prove that the potential problem is only short term in nature.
- *The need to use judgment.* A key issue is whether a ratio for a company is within a reasonable range. Although financial ratios are used to help assess the growth potential and risk of a company, they cannot be used alone to directly value a company or its securities, or to determine its creditworthiness. The entire operation of the company must be examined, and the external economic and industry setting in which it is operating must be considered when interpreting financial ratios.
- *The use of alternative accounting methods.* Companies frequently have latitude when choosing certain accounting methods. Ratios taken from financial statements that employ different accounting choices may not be comparable unless adjustments are made. Some important accounting considerations include the following:
    - FIFO (first in, first out), LIFO (last in, first out), or average cost inventory valuation methods (IFRS no longer allow LIFO);
    - Cost or equity methods of accounting for unconsolidated affiliates;
    - Straight line or accelerated methods of depreciation; and
    - Capital or operating lease treatment.

  The expanding use of IFRS and the planned convergence between U.S. GAAP and IFRS seeks to make the financial statements of different companies comparable and so overcome some of these difficulties. Nonetheless, there will remain accounting choices that the analyst must consider.

3.1.3 Sources of Ratios

Ratios may be computed using data directly from companies' financial statements or from a database such as Reuters, Bloomberg, Baseline, FactSet, or Thomson Financial. These databases are popular because they provide easy access to many years of historical data so that trends over time can be examined. They also allow for ratio calculations based on periods other than the company's fiscal year, such as for the trailing 12 months (TTM) or most recent quarter (MRQ).

Analysts should be aware that the underlying formulas may differ by vendor. The formula used should be obtained from the vendor, and the analyst should determine whether any adjustments are necessary. Furthermore, database providers often exercise judgment when classifying items. For example, operating income may not appear directly on a company's income statement, and the vendor may use judgment to classify income statement items as "operating" or "nonoperating." Variation in such judgments would affect any computation involving operating income. It is, therefore, a good practice to use the same source for data when comparing different companies or when evaluating the historical record of a single given company. Analysts should verify the consistency of formulas and data classifications of the data source. Analysts should also be mindful of the judgments made by a vendor in data classifications and refer back to the source financial statements until they are comfortable that the classifications are appropriate.

Systems are under development that collect financial data from regulatory filings and can automatically compute ratios. The eXtensible Business Reporting Language (XBRL) is a mechanism that attaches "smart tags" to financial information (e.g., total assets), so that software can automatically collect the data and perform desired computations. The organization developing XBRL (www.xbrl.org) is a worldwide nonprofit consortium of organizations, including the International Accounting Standards Board.

Analysts can compare a subject company to similar (peer) companies in these databases or use aggregate industry data. For nonpubic companies, aggregate industry data can be obtained from such sources as Annual Statement Studies by the Risk Management Association or Dun & Bradstreet. These publications provide industry data with companies sorted into quartiles. Twenty-five percent of companies' ratios fall within the lowest quartile, 25 percent have ratios between the lower quartile and median value, and so on. Analysts can then determine a company's relative standing in the industry.

3.2 Common-Size Analysis

Common-size analysis involves expressing financial data, including entire financial statements, in relation to a single financial statement item, or base. Items used most frequently as the bases are total assets or revenue. In essence, common-size analysis creates a ratio between every financial statement item and the base item.

Common-size analysis was demonstrated in readings for the income statement, balance sheet, and cash flow statement. In this section, we present common-size analysis of financial statements in greater detail and include further discussion of their interpretation.

3.2.1 Common-Size Analysis of the Balance Sheet

A vertical[5] common-size balance sheet, prepared by dividing each item on the balance sheet by the same period's total assets and expressing the results as percentages, highlights the composition of the balance sheet. What is the mix of assets being used? How is the company financing itself? How does one company's balance sheet composition compare with that of peer companies, and what is behind any differences?

A horizontal common-size balance sheet, prepared by computing the increase or decrease in percentage terms of each balance sheet item from the

[5] The term **vertical analysis** is used to denote a common-size analysis using only one reporting period or one base financial statement, whereas **horizontal analysis** can refer either to an analysis comparing a specific financial statement with prior or future time periods or to a cross-sectional analysis of one company with another.

prior year, highlights items that have changed unexpectedly or have unexpectedly remained unchanged.

For example, Exhibit 2 presents a vertical common-size (partial) balance sheet for a hypothetical company in two different time periods. In this example, receivables have increased from 35 percent to 57 percent of total assets. What are possible reasons for such an increase? The increase might indicate that the company is making more of its sales on a credit basis rather than a cash basis, perhaps in response to some action taken by a competitor. Alternatively, the increase in receivables as a percentage of assets may have occurred because of a change in another current asset category, for example, a decrease in the level of inventory; the analyst would then need to investigate why that asset category had changed. Another possible reason for the increase in receivables as a percentage of assets is that the company has lowered its credit standards, relaxed its collection procedures, or adopted more aggressive revenue recognition policies. The analyst can turn to other comparisons and ratios (e.g., comparing the rate of growth in accounts receivable with the rate of growth in sales to help determine which explanation is most likely).

EXHIBIT 2 **Vertical Common-Size (Partial) Balance Sheet for a Hypothetical Company**

	Period 1 % of Total Assets	Period 2 % of Total Assets
Cash	25	15
Receivables	35	57
Inventory	35	20
Fixed assets, net of depreciation	5	8
Total assets	100	100

3.2.2 Common-Size Analysis of the Income Statement

A vertical common-size income statement divides each income statement item by revenue, or sometimes by total assets (especially in the case of financial institutions). If there are multiple revenue sources, a decomposition of revenue in percentage terms is useful. For example, Exhibit 3 presents a hypothetical company's vertical common-size income statement in two different time periods. Revenue is separated into the company's four services, each shown as a percentage of total revenue. In this example, revenues from Service A have become a far greater percentage of the company's total revenue (45 percent in Period 2). What are possible reasons for and implications of this change in business mix? Did the company make a strategic decision to sell more of Service A, perhaps because it is more profitable? Apparently not, because the company's earnings before interest, taxes, depreciation, and amortization (EBITDA) declined from 53 percent of sales to 45 percent, so other possible explanations should be examined. In addition, we note from the composition of operating expenses that the main reason for this decline in profitability is that salaries and employee benefits have increased from 15 percent to 25 percent of total revenue. Are more highly compensated employees required for Service A? Were higher training costs incurred in order to increase Service A revenues? If the analyst wants to predict future performance, the causes of these changes must be understood.

In addition, Exhibit 3 shows that the company's income tax as a percentage of sales has declined dramatically (from 15 percent to 8 percent). Furthermore, as a percentage of earnings before tax (EBT) (usually the more relevant comparison), taxes have decreased from 36 percent to 23 percent. Is Service A provided in a jurisdiction with lower tax rates? If not, what is the explanation?

The observations based on Exhibit 3 summarize the issues that can be raised through analysis of the vertical common-size income statement.

EXHIBIT 3 Vertical Common-Size Income Statement for Hypothetical Company

	Period 1 % of Total Revenue	Period 2 % of Total Revenue
Revenue source: Service A	30	45
Revenue source: Service B	23	20
Revenue source: Service C	30	30
Revenue source: Service D	17	5
Total revenue	**100**	**100**
Operating expenses (excluding depreciation)		
Salaries and employee benefits	15	25
Administrative expenses	22	20
Rent expense	10	10
EBITDA	**53**	**45**
Depreciation and amortization	4	4
EBIT	**49**	**41**
Interest paid	7	7
EBT	**42**	**34**
Income tax provision	15	8
Net income	**27**	**26**

Note: EBIT = earnings before interest and tax.

3.2.3 Cross-Sectional Analysis

As noted previously, ratios and common-size statements derive part of their meaning through comparison to some benchmark. Cross-sectional analysis (sometimes called "relative analysis") compares a specific metric for one company with the same metric for another company or group of companies, allowing comparisons even though the companies might be of significantly different sizes and/or operate in different currencies.

Exhibit 4 presents a vertical common-size (partial) balance sheet for two hypothetical companies at the same point in time. Company 1 is clearly more liquid (liquidity is a function of how quickly assets can be converted into cash) than Company 2, which has only 12 percent of assets available as cash, compared with the highly liquid Company 1, where cash is 38 percent of assets. Given that cash

EXHIBIT 4 Vertical Common-Size (Partial) Balance Sheet for Two Hypothetical Companies

	Company 1 % of Total Assets	Company 2 % of Total Assets
Cash	38	12
Receivables	33	55
Inventory	27	24
Fixed assets net of depreciation	1	2
Investments	1	7
Total Assets	**100**	**100**

is generally a relatively low-yielding asset and thus not a particularly efficient use of the balance sheet, why does Company 1 hold such a large percentage of total assets in cash? Perhaps the company is preparing for an acquisition, or maintains a large cash position as insulation from a particularly volatile operating environment. Another issue highlighted by the comparison in this example is the relatively high percentage of receivables in Company 2's assets, which (as discussed in Section 3.2.1) may indicate a greater proportion of credit sales, overall changes in asset composition, lower credit or collection standards, or aggressive accounting policies.

3.2.4 Trend Analysis[6]

When looking at financial statements and ratios, trends in the data, whether they are improving or deteriorating, are as important as the current absolute or relative levels. Trend analysis provides important information regarding historical performance and growth and, given a sufficiently long history of accurate seasonal information, can be of great assistance as a planning and forecasting tool for management and analysts.

Exhibit 5A presents a partial balance sheet for a hypothetical company over five periods. The last two columns of the table show the changes for Period 5 compared with Period 4, expressed both in absolute currency (in this case, dollars) and in percentages. A small percentage change could hide a significant currency change and vice versa, prompting the analyst to investigate the reasons despite one of the changes being relatively small. In this example, the largest percentage change was in investments, which decreased by 33.3 percent.[7] However, an examination of the absolute currency amount of changes shows that investments changed by only $2 million and the more significant change was the $12 million increase in receivables.

Another way to present data covering a period of time is to show each item in relation to the same item in a base year (i.e., a horizontal common-size balance

[6] In financial statement analysis, the term "trend analysis" usually refers to comparisons across time periods of 3–10 years not involving statistical tools. This differs from the use of the term in the quantitative methods portion of the CFA curriculum, where "trend analysis" refers to statistical methods of measuring patterns in time-series data.

[7] Percentage change is calculated as: (Ending value − Beginning value)/Beginning value, or equivalently, (Ending value/Beginning value) − 1.

sheet). Exhibit 5B presents the same partial balance sheet as in Exhibit 5A but with each item indexed relative to the same item in Period 1. For example, in Period 2, the company had $29 million cash, which is 75 percent of the amount of cash it had in Period 1, or expressed as an index relative to Period 1, 75 ($\$29/\$39 = 0.75 \times 100 = 75$). Presenting data this way highlights significant changes. In this example, we see easily that the company has less than half the amount of cash in Period 1, four times the amount of investments, and eight times the amount of property, plant, and equipment.

An analysis of horizontal common-size balance sheets highlights structural changes that have occurred in a business. Past trends are obviously not necessarily an accurate predictor of the future, especially when the economic or competitive environment changes. An examination of past trends is more valuable when the macroeconomic and competitive environments are relatively stable and when the analyst is reviewing a stable or mature business. However, even in less stable contexts, historical analysis can serve as a basis for developing expecta-

EXHIBIT 5A Partial Balance Sheet for a Hypothetical Company over Five Periods

Assets ($ millions)	Period 1	2	3	4	5	Change 4 to 5 ($ million)	Change 4 to 5 (%)
Cash	39	29	27	19	16	−3	−15.8%
Investments	1	7	7	6	4	−2	−33.3%
Receivables	44	41	37	67	79	12	17.9%
Inventory	15	25	36	25	27	2	8%
Fixed assets net of depreciation	1	2	6	9	8	−1	−11.1%
Total assets	100	105	112	126	133	8	5.6%

EXHIBIT 5B Horizontal Common-Size (Partial) Balance Sheet for a Hypothetical Company over Five Periods, with Each Item Expressed Relative to the Same Item in Period One

Assets	Period 1	2	3	4	5
Cash	1.00	0.75	0.69	0.48	0.41
Investments	1.00	7.35	6.74	6.29	4.00
Receivables	1.00	0.93	0.84	1.52	1.79
Inventory	1.00	1.68	2.40	1.68	1.78
Fixed assets net of depreciation	1.00	2.10	5.62	8.81	8.00
Total assets	1.00	1.05	1.12	1.26	1.33

tions. Understanding past trends is helpful in assessing whether these trends are likely to continue or if the trend is likely to change direction.

One measure of success is for a company to grow at a rate greater than the rate of the overall market in which it operates. Companies that grow slowly may find themselves unable to attract equity capital. Conversely, companies that grow too quickly may find that their administrative and management information systems cannot keep up with the rate of expansion.

3.2.5 Relationships among Financial Statements

Trend data generated by a horizontal common-size analysis can be compared across financial statements. For example, the growth rate of assets for the hypothetical company in Exhibit 5 can be compared with the company's growth in revenue over the same period of time. If revenue is growing more quickly than assets, the company may be increasing its efficiency (i.e., generating more revenue for every dollar invested in assets).

As another example, consider the following year-over-year percentage changes for a hypothetical company:

Revenue	+20%
Net income	+25%
Operating cash flow	−10%
Total assets	+30%

Net income is growing faster than revenue, which indicates increasing profitability. However, the analyst would need to determine whether the faster growth in net income resulted from continuing operations or from nonoperating, nonrecurring items. In addition, the 10 percent decline in operating cash flow despite increasing revenue and net income clearly warrants further investigation because it could indicate a problem with earnings quality (perhaps aggressive reporting of revenue). Lastly, the fact that assets have grown faster than revenue indicates the company's efficiency may be declining. The analyst should examine the composition of the increase in assets and the reasons for the changes. Example 4 provides a recent example of a company where comparisons of trend data from different financial statements can indicate aggressive accounting policies.

EXAMPLE 4

Use of Comparative Growth Information[8]

Sunbeam, a U.S. company, brought in new management to turn the company around during July 1996. For the following year, 1997, the following common-size trends were apparent:

Revenue	+19%
Inventory	+58%
Receivables	+38%

[8] Adapted from Robinson and Munter (2004, pp. 2–15).

It is generally more desirable to observe inventory and receivables growing at a slower (or similar) rate to revenue growth. Receivables growing faster than revenue can indicate operational issues, such as lower credit standards or aggressive accounting policies for revenue recognition. Similarly, inventory growing faster than revenue can indicate an operational problem with obsolescence or aggressive accounting policies, such as an improper overstatement of inventory to increase profits.

In this case, the explanation lay in aggressive accounting policies. Sunbeam was later charged by the U.S. SEC with improperly accelerating the recognition of revenue and engaging in other practices, such as billing customers for inventory prior to shipment.

3.3 The Use of Graphs as an Analytical Tool

Graphs facilitate comparison of performance and financial structure over time, highlighting changes in significant aspects of business operations. In addition, graphs provide the analyst (and management) with a visual overview of risk trends in a business. Graphs may also be used effectively to communicate the analyst's conclusions regarding financial condition and risk management aspects.

Exhibit 6 presents the information from Exhibit 5A in a stacked column format. The graph makes the significant decline in cash and growth in receivables (both in absolute terms and as a percentage of assets) readily apparent.

Choosing the appropriate graph to communicate the most significant conclusions of a financial analysis is a skill. In general, pie graphs are most useful to communicate the composition of a total value (e.g., assets over a limited amount of time, say one or two periods). Line graphs are useful when the focus is on the

EXHIBIT 6 Stacked Column Graph of Asset Composition of Hypothetical Company over Five Periods

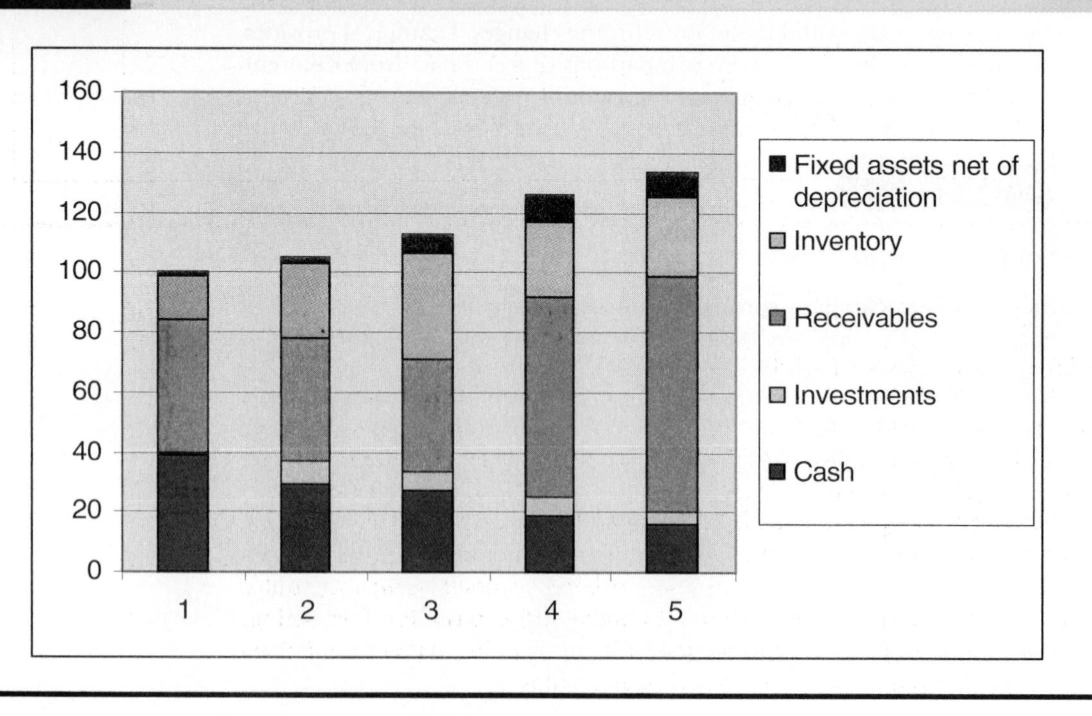

change in amount for a limited number of items over a relatively longer time period. When the composition and amounts, as well as their change over time, are all important, a stacked column graph can be useful.

When comparing Period 5 with Period 4, the growth in receivables appears to be within normal bounds, but when comparing Period 5 with earlier periods, the dramatic growth becomes apparent. In the same manner, a simple line graph will also illustrate the growth trends in key financial variables. Exhibit 7 presents the information from Exhibit 5 as a line graph, illustrating the growth of assets of a hypothetical company over five periods. The steady decline in cash, volatile movements of inventory, and dramatic growth of receivables is clearly illustrated.

EXHIBIT 7 **Line Graph of Growth of Assets of Hypothetical Company over Five Periods**

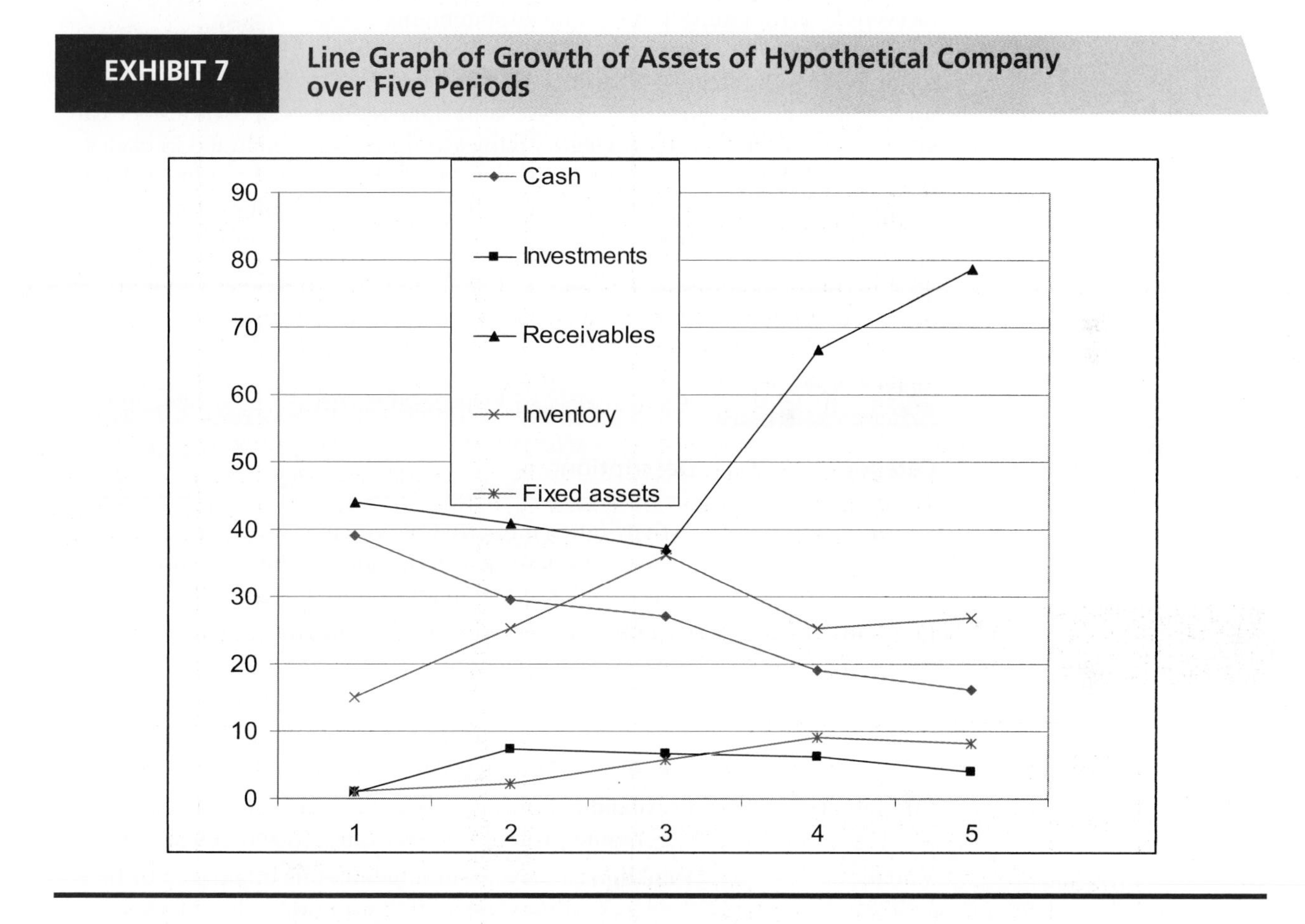

3.4 Regression Analysis

When analyzing the trend in a specific line item or ratio, frequently it is possible simply to visually evaluate the changes. For more complex situations, regression analysis can help identify relationships (or correlation) between variables. For example, a regression analysis could relate a company's sales to GDP over time, providing insight into whether the company is cyclical. In addition, the statistical relationship between sales and GDP could be used as a basis for forecasting sales.

Other examples of such relationships are the relation between a company's sales and inventory over time, or the relation between hotel occupancy and a company's hotel revenues. In addition to providing a basis for forecasting, regression analysis facilitates identification of items or ratios that are not behaving as expected, given historical statistical relationships.

4 COMMON RATIOS USED IN FINANCIAL ANALYSIS

In the previous section, we focused on ratios resulting from common-size analysis. In this section, we expand the discussion to include other commonly used financial ratios and the broad classes into which they are categorized. There is some overlap with common-size financial statement ratios. For example, a common indicator of profitability is the net profit margin, which is calculated as net income divided by sales. This ratio appears on a common-size vertical income statement. Other ratios involve information from multiple financial statements or even data from outside the financial statements.

Due to the large number of ratios, it is helpful to think about ratios in terms of broad categories based on what aspects of performance a ratio is intended to detect. Financial analysts and data vendors use a variety of categories to classify ratios. The category names and the ratios included in each category can differ. Common ratio categories include activity, liquidity, solvency, and profitability. These categories are summarized in Exhibit 8. Each category measures a different aspect of analysis, but all are useful in evaluating a company's overall ability to generate cash flows from operating its business and the associated risks.

EXHIBIT 8 Categories of Financial Ratios

Category	Description
Activity	**Activity ratios** measure how efficiently a company performs day-to-day tasks, such as the collection of receivables and management of inventory.
Liquidity	**Liquidity ratios** measure the company's ability to meet its short-term obligations.
Solvency	**Solvency ratios** measure a company's ability to meet long-term obligations. Subsets of these ratios are also known as "leverage" and "long-term debt" ratios.
Profitability	**Profitability ratios** measure the company's ability to generate profitable sales from its resources (assets).
Valuation	**Valuation ratios** measure the quantity of an asset or flow (e.g., earnings) associated with ownership of a specified claim (e.g., a share or ownership of the enterprise).

These categories are not mutually exclusive; some ratios are useful in measuring multiple aspects of the business. For example, an activity ratio measuring how quickly a company collects accounts receivable is also useful in assessing the company's liquidity because collection of revenues increases cash. Some profitability ratios also reflect the operating efficiency of the business. In summary, analysts appropriately use certain ratios to evaluate multiple aspects of the business. Analysts also need to be aware of variations in industry practice in the calculation of financial ratios. In the text that follows, alternative views on ratio calculations are often provided.

4.1 Interpretation and Context

Financial ratios can only be interpreted in the context of other information, including benchmarks. In general, the financial ratios of a company are compared with those of its major competitors (cross-sectional and trend analysis) and to the company's prior periods (trend analysis). The goal is to understand the underlying causes of divergence between a company's ratios and those of the industry. Even ratios that remain consistent require understanding because consistency can sometimes indicate accounting policies selected to smooth earnings. An analyst should evaluate financial ratios based on the following:

1. *Company goals and strategy.* Actual ratios can be compared with company objectives to determine whether objectives are being attained and whether the results are consistent with the company's strategy.
2. *Industry norms (cross-sectional analysis).* A company can be compared with others in its industry by relating its financial ratios to industry norms or to a subset of the companies in an industry. When industry norms are used to make judgments, care must be taken because:
   - Many ratios are industry specific, and not all ratios are important to all industries.
   - Companies may have several different lines of business. This will cause aggregate financial ratios to be distorted. It is better to examine industry-specific ratios by lines of business.
   - Differences in accounting methods used by companies can distort financial ratios.
   - Differences in corporate strategies can affect certain financial ratios.
3. *Economic conditions.* For cyclical companies, financial ratios tend to improve when the economy is strong and weaken during recessions. Therefore, financial ratios should be examined in light of the current phase of the business cycle.

The following sections discuss activity, liquidity, solvency, and profitability ratios in turn. Selected valuation ratios are presented later in the section on equity analysis.

4.2 Activity Ratios

Activity ratios are also known as asset utilization ratios or **operating efficiency ratios**. This category is intended to measure how well a company manages various activities, particularly how efficiently it manages its various assets. Activity ratios are analyzed as indicators of ongoing operational performance—how effectively assets are used by a company. These ratios reflect the efficient management of both working capital and longer-term assets. As noted, efficiency has a direct impact on liquidity (the ability of a company to meet its short-term obligations), so some activity ratios are also useful in assessing liquidity.

4.2.1 Calculation of Activity Ratios

Exhibit 9 presents the most commonly used activity ratios. The exhibit shows the numerator and denominator of each ratio.

EXHIBIT 9 Definitions of Commonly Used Activity Ratios

Activity Ratios	Numerator	Denominator
Inventory turnover	Cost of goods sold	Average inventory
Days of inventory on hand (DOH)	Number of days in period	Inventory turnover
Receivables turnover	Revenue	Average receivables
Days of sales outstanding (DSO)	Number of days in period	Receivables turnover
Payables turnover	Purchases	Average trade payables
Number of days of payables	Number of days in period	Payables turnover
Working capital turnover	Revenue	Average working capital
Fixed asset turnover	Revenue	Average net fixed assets
Total asset turnover	Revenue	Average total assets

Activity ratios measure how efficiently the company utilizes assets. They generally combine information from the income statement in the numerator with balance sheet items in the denominator. Because the income statement measures what happened *during* a period whereas the balance sheet shows the condition only at the end of the period, average balance sheet data are normally used for consistency. For example, to measure inventory management efficiency, cost of goods sold (from the income statement) is divided by average inventory (from the balance sheet). Most databases, such as Bloomberg and Baseline, use this averaging convention when income statement and balance sheet data are combined. These databases typically average only two points: the beginning of the year and the end of the year. The examples that follow based on annual financial statements illustrate that practice. However, some analysts prefer to average more observations if they are available, especially if the business is seasonal. If a semiannual report is prepared, an average can be taken over three data points (beginning, middle, and end of year). If quarterly data are available, a five-point average can be computed (beginning of year and end of each quarterly period) or a four-point average using the end of each quarterly period. Note that if the company's year ends at a low or high point for inventory for the year, there can still be bias in using three or five data points, because the beginning and end of year occur at the same time of the year and are effectively double counted.

Because cost of goods sold measures the cost of inventory that has been sold, this ratio measures how many times per year the entire inventory was theoretically turned over, or sold. (We say that the entire inventory was "theoretically" sold because in practice companies do not generally sell out their entire inventory.) If, for example, a company's cost of goods sold for a recent year was €120,000 and its average inventory was €10,000, the inventory turnover ratio would be 12. The company theoretically turns over (i.e., sells) its entire inventory 12 times per year (i.e., once a month). (Again, we say "theoretically" because in practice the company likely carries some inventory from one month into another.) Turnover can then be converted to **days of inventory on hand (DOH)** by dividing inventory turnover into the number of days in the accounting period. In this example, the result is a DOH of 30.42 (365/12), meaning that, on average, the company's inventory was on hand for about 30 days, or, equivalently, the company kept on hand about 30 days' worth of inventory, on average, during the period.

Activity ratios can be computed for any annual or interim period, but care must be taken in the interpretation and comparison across periods. For example, if the same company had cost of goods sold for the first quarter (90 days) of the following year of €35,000 and average inventory of €11,000, the inventory turnover would be 3.18 times. However, this turnover rate is 3.18 times per quarter, which is not directly comparable to the 12 times per year in the preceding year. In this case, we can annualize the quarterly inventory turnover rate by multiplying the quarterly turnover by 4 (12 months/3 months; or by 4.06, using 365 days/90 days) for comparison to the annual turnover rate. So, the quarterly inventory turnover is equivalent to a 12.72 annual inventory turnover (or 12.91 if we annualize the ratio using a 90-day quarter and a 365-day year). To compute the DOH using quarterly data, we can use the quarterly turnover rate and the number of days in the quarter for the numerator—or, we can use the annualized turnover rate and 365 days; either results in DOH of around 28.3, with slight differences due to rounding (90/3.18 = 28.30 and 365/12.91 = 28.27). Another time-related computational detail is that for companies using a 52/53-week annual period and for leap years, the actual days in the year should be used rather than 365.

In some cases, an analyst may want to know how many days of inventory are on hand at the end of the year rather than the average for the year. In this case, it would be appropriate to use the year-end inventory balance in the computation rather than the average. If the company is growing rapidly or if costs are increasing rapidly, analysts should consider using cost of goods sold just for the fourth quarter in this computation because the cost of goods sold of earlier quarters may not be relevant. Example 5 further demonstrates computation of activity ratios using Hong Kong Exchange-listed Lenovo Group Limited.

EXAMPLE 5

Computation of Activity Ratios

Ya-Wen Yang would like to evaluate how efficient Lenovo Group Limited is at collecting its trade accounts receivable on average during the fiscal year ended 31 March 2005. Yang has gathered the following information from Lenovo's annual and interim reports:

	HK$ in Thousands
Trade receivables as of 31 March 2004	1,230,944
Trade receivables as of 31 March 2005	851,337
Revenue for year ended 31 March 2005	22,554,678

What is Lenovo's receivables turnover and number of **days of sales outstanding (DSO)** for the fiscal year ended 31 March 2005?

Solution:

Receivables turnover = Revenue/Average receivables
= 22,554,678/[(1,230,944 + 851,337)/2]
= 22,554,678/1,041,140.50
= 21.6634 times

DSO = Number of days in period/Receivables turnover
= 365/21.6634
= 16.85 days

On average, it took Lenovo 16.85 days to collect receivables during the fiscal year ended 31 March 2005.

4.2.2 Interpretation of Activity Ratios

In the following, we discuss the activity ratios that were defined in Exhibit 9.

Inventory Turnover and DOH Inventory turnover lies at the heart of operations for many entities. It indicates the resources (money) tied up in inventory (i.e., the carrying costs) and can, therefore, be used to indicate inventory management effectiveness. The higher the inventory turnover ratio, the shorter the period that inventory is held and so the lower DOH. In general, inventory turnover (and DOH) should be benchmarked against industry norms.

A high inventory turnover ratio relative to industry norms might indicate highly effective inventory management. Alternatively, a high inventory turnover ratio (and commensurately low DOH) could possibly indicate the company does not carry adequate inventory, so shortages could potentially hurt revenue. To assess which explanation is more likely, the analyst can compare the company's revenue growth with that of the industry. Slower growth combined with higher inventory turnover could indicate inadequate inventory levels. Revenue growth at or above the industry's growth supports the interpretation that the higher turnover reflects greater inventory management efficiency.

A low inventory turnover ratio (and commensurately high DOH) relative to the rest of the industry could be an indicator of slow-moving inventory, perhaps due to technological obsolescence or a change in fashion. Again, comparing the company's sales growth with the industry can offer insight.

Receivables Turnover and DSO The number of DSO represents the elapsed time between a sale and cash collection, reflecting how fast the company collects cash from customers it offers credit. Although limiting the numerator to sales made on credit would be more appropriate, credit sales information is not always available to analysts; therefore, revenue as reported in the income statement is generally used as an approximation.

A relatively high **receivables turnover** ratio (and commensurately low DSO) might indicate highly efficient credit and collection. Alternatively, a high receivables turnover ratio could indicate that the company's credit or collection policies are too stringent, suggesting the possibility of sales being lost to competitors offering more lenient terms. A relatively low receivables turnover ratio would typically raise questions about the efficiency of the company's credit and collections procedures. As with inventory management, comparison of the company's sales growth relative to the industry can help the analyst assess whether sales are being lost due to stringent credit policies. In addition, comparing the company's estimates of uncollectible accounts receivable and actual credit losses with past experience and with peer companies can help assess whether low turnover reflects credit management issues. Companies often provide details of receivables aging (how much receivables have been outstanding by age). This can be used along with DSO to understand trends in collection, as demonstrated in Example 6.

EXAMPLE 6

Evaluation of an Activity Ratio

Ya-Wen Yang has computed the average DSO for fiscal years ended 31 March 2004 and 2005:

	2005	2004
Days of sales outstanding	16.85	14.05

Yang would like to better understand why, on average, it took almost 17 days to collect receivables in 2005 versus 14 days in 2004. He collects accounts receivable aging information from Lenovo's annual reports and computes the percentage of accounts receivable by days outstanding. This information is presented below:

	31 March 2005		31 March 2004		31 March 2003	
	HK$000	Percent	HK$000	Percent	HK$000	Percent
0–30 days	588,389	69.11%	944,212	76.71%	490,851	88.68%
31–60 days	56,966	6.69%	84,481	6.86%	27,213	4.92%
61–90 days	40,702	4.78%	20,862	1.69%	10,680	1.93%
Over 90 days	165,280	19.41%	181,389	14.74%	24,772	4.48%
Total	851,337	100.00%	1,230,944	100.00%	553,516	100.00%

From these data, it appears that over the past three years there has been a trend of fewer receivables due within 30 days and more due for periods of longer than 90 days. Lenovo's footnotes disclose that general trade customers are provided with 30-day credit terms but that systems integration customers (consulting jobs) are given 180 days. Furthermore, the footnotes reveal that consulting revenues increased dramatically over the 2003 to 2004 period. In the third quarter of fiscal year ending 31 March 2005, Lenovo spun off its systems integration business to another company, retaining a small percentage interest. Yang concludes that the higher DSO in fiscal year ending 31 March 2005 appears to be due to the higher revenue in systems integration, which has longer credit terms. Yang may further surmise that DSO should drop in the next fiscal year since this business has been spun off.

Payables Turnover and the Number of Days of Payables The **number of days of payables** reflects the average number of days the company takes to pay its suppliers, and the **payables turnover** ratio measures how many times per year the company theoretically pays off all its creditors. For purposes of calculating these ratios, an implicit assumption is that the company makes all its purchases using credit. If the amount of purchases is not directly available, it can be computed as cost of goods sold plus ending inventory less beginning inventory. Alternatively, cost of goods sold is sometimes used as an approximation of purchases.

A payables turnover ratio that is high (low days payable) relative to the industry could indicate that the company is not making full use of available credit facilities; alternatively, it could result from a company taking advantage of early payment discounts. An excessively low turnover ratio (high days payable) could indicate trouble making payments on time, or alternatively, exploitation of lenient supplier terms. This is another example where it is useful to look simultaneously at other ratios. If liquidity ratios indicate that the company has sufficient cash and other short-term assets to pay obligations and yet the days payable ratio is relatively high, the analyst would favor the lenient supplier credit and collection policies as an explanation.

Working Capital Turnover Working capital is defined as current (expected to be consumed or converted into cash within one year) assets minus current liabilities. **Working capital turnover** indicates how efficiently the company generates revenue with its working capital. For example, a working capital turnover ratio of 4.0 indicates that the company generates €4 of revenue for every €1 of working capital. A high working capital turnover ratio indicates greater efficiency (i.e., the company is generating a high level of revenues relative to working capital). For some companies, working capital can be near zero or negative, rendering this ratio incapable of being interpreted. The following two ratios are more useful in those circumstances.

Fixed Asset Turnover This ratio measures how efficiently the company generates revenues from its investments in fixed assets. Generally, a higher **fixed asset turnover** ratio indicates more efficient use of fixed assets in generating revenue. A low ratio can indicate inefficiency, a capital-intensive business environment, or a new business not yet operating at full capacity—in which case the analyst will not be able to link the ratio directly to efficiency. In addition, asset turnover can be affected by factors other than a company's efficiency. The fixed asset turnover ratio would be lower for a company whose assets are newer (and, therefore, less depreciated and so reflected in the financial statements at a higher carrying value) than the ratio for a company with older assets (that are thus more depreciated and so reflected at a lower carrying value). The fixed asset ratio can be erratic because, although revenue may have a steady growth rate, increases in fixed assets may not follow a smooth pattern; so, every year-to-year change in the ratio does not necessarily indicate important changes in the company's efficiency.

Total Asset Turnover The **total asset turnover** ratio measures the company's overall ability to generate revenues with a given level of assets. A ratio of 1.20 would indicate that the company is generating €1.20 of revenues for every €1 of average assets. A higher ratio indicates greater efficiency. Because this ratio includes both fixed and current assets, inefficient working capital management can distort overall interpretations. It is, therefore, helpful to analyze working capital and fixed asset turnover ratios separately.

A low asset turnover ratio can be an indicator of inefficiency or of relative capital intensity of the business. The ratio also reflects strategic decisions by management: for example, the decision whether to use a more labor-intensive (and less capital-intensive) approach to its business or a more capital-intensive (and less labor-intensive) approach.

When interpreting activity ratios, the analysts should examine not only the individual ratios but also the collection of relevant ratios to determine the overall efficiency of a company. Example 7 demonstrates the evaluation of activity ratios, both narrow (e.g., number of days inventory) and broad (total asset turnover) for a Taiwanese semiconductor manufacturer.

EXAMPLE 7

Evaluation of Activity Ratios

United Microelectronics Corp. (UMC) is a semiconductor foundry company based in Taiwan. As part of an analysis of management's operating efficiency, an analyst collects the following activity ratios from Bloomberg:

Ratio	2004	2003	2002	2001
DOH	35.68	40.70	40.47	48.51
DSO	45.07	58.28	51.27	76.98
Total asset turnover	0.35	0.28	0.23	0.22

These ratios indicate that the company has improved on all three measures of activity over the four-year period. The company has fewer DOH, is collecting receivables faster, and is generating a higher level of revenues relative to total assets. The overall trend is good, but thus far, the analyst has only determined *what* happened. A more important question is *why* the ratios improved, because understanding good changes as well as bad ones facilitates judgments about the company's future performance. To answer this question, the analyst examines company financial reports as well as external information about the industry and economy. In examining the annual report, the analyst notes that in the fourth quarter of 2004, the company experienced an "inventory correction" and that the company recorded an allowance for the decline in market value and obsolescence of inventory of TWD 1,786,493, or about 15 percent of year-end inventory value (compared with about a 5.9 percent allowance in the prior year). This reduction in the value of inventory accounts for a large portion of the decline in DOH from 40.7 in 2003 to 35.68 in 2004. Management claims that this inventory obsolescence is a short-term issue; analysts can watch DOH in future interim periods to confirm this assertion. In any event, all else being equal, the analyst would likely expect DOH to return to a level closer to 40 days going forward.

More positive interpretations can be drawn from the total asset turnover. The analyst finds that the company's revenues increased more than 35 percent while total assets only increased by about 6 percent. Based on external information about the industry and economy, the analyst attributes the increased revenues largely to the recovery of the semiconductor industry in 2004. However, management was able to achieve this growth in revenues with a comparatively modest increase in assets, leading to an improvement in total asset turnover. Note further that part of the reason for the modest increase in assets is lower DOH and DSO.

4.3 Liquidity Ratios

Liquidity analysis, which focuses on cash flows, measures a company's ability to meet its short-term obligations. Liquidity measures how quickly assets are converted into cash. Liquidity ratios also measure the ability to pay off short-term obligations. In day-to-day operations, liquidity management is typically achieved through efficient use of assets. In the medium term, liquidity in the nonfinancial sector is also addressed by managing the structure of liabilities. (See discussion on financial sector below.)

The level of liquidity needed differs from one industry to another. A particular company's liquidity position may also vary according to the anticipated need for funds at any given time. Judging whether a company has adequate liquidity requires analysis of its historical funding requirements, current liquidity position, anticipated future funding needs, and options for reducing funding needs or attracting additional funds (including actual and potential sources of such funding).

Larger companies are usually better able to control the level and composition of their liabilities than smaller companies. Therefore, they may have more potential funding sources, including public capital and money markets. Greater discretionary access to capital markets also reduces the size of the liquidity buffer needed relative to companies without such access.

Contingent liabilities, such as letters of credit or financial guarantees, can also be relevant when assessing liquidity. The importance of contingent liabilities varies for the nonbanking and banking sector. In the nonbanking sector, contingent liabilities (usually disclosed in the footnotes to the company's financial statements) represent potential cash outflows, and when appropriate, should be included in an assessment of a company's liquidity. In the banking sector, contingent liabilities represent potentially significant cash outflows that are not dependent on the bank's financial condition. Although outflows in normal market circumstances typically may be low, a general macroeconomic or market crisis can trigger a substantial increase in cash outflows related to contingent liabilities because of the increase in defaults and business bankruptcies that often accompany such events. In addition, such crises are usually characterized by diminished levels of overall liquidity, which can further exacerbate funding shortfalls. Therefore, for the banking sector, the effect of contingent liabilities on liquidity warrants particular attention.

4.3.1 Calculation of Liquidity Ratios

Common liquidity ratios are presented in Exhibit 10. These liquidity ratios reflect a company's position at a point in time and, therefore, typically use data from the ending balance sheet rather than averages. The current, quick, and cash ratios reflect three measures of a company's ability to pay current liabilities. Each uses a progressively stricter definition of liquid assets.

The **defensive interval ratio** measures how long a company can pay its daily cash expenditures using only its existing liquid assets, without additional cash flow coming in. This ratio is similar to the "burn rate" often computed for start-up internet companies in the late 1990s or for biotechnology companies. The numerator of this ratio includes the same liquid assets used in the quick ratio, and the denominator is an estimate of daily cash expenditures. To obtain daily cash expenditures, the total of cash expenditures for the period is divided by the number of days in the period. Total cash expenditures for a period can be approximated by summing all expenses on the income statement—such as cost

EXHIBIT 10 Definitions of Commonly Used Liquidity Ratios

Liquidity Ratios	Numerator	Denominator
Current ratio	Current assets	Current liabilities
Quick ratio	Cash + short-term marketable investments + receivables	Current liabilities
Cash ratio	Cash + short-term marketable investments	Current liabilities
Defensive interval ratio	Cash + short-term marketable investments + receivables	Daily cash expenditures
Additional Liquidity Measure		
Cash conversion cycle (net operating cycle)	DOH + DSO − number of days of payables	

of goods sold; selling, general, and administrative expenses; and research and development expenses—and then subtracting any noncash expenses, such as depreciation and amortization. (Typically, taxes are not included.)

The **cash conversion cycle**, a financial metric not in ratio form, measures the length of time required for a company to go from cash (invested in its operations) to cash received (as a result of its operations). During this period of time, the company needs to finance its investment in operations through other sources (i.e., through debt or equity).

4.3.2 Interpretation of Liquidity Ratios

In the following, we discuss the interpretation of the five basic liquidity ratios presented in Exhibit 10.

Current Ratio This ratio expresses current assets (assets expected to be consumed or converted into cash within one year) in relation to current liabilities (liabilities falling due within one year). A higher ratio indicates a higher level of liquidity (i.e., a greater ability to meet short-term obligations). A current ratio of 1.0 would indicate that the book value of its current assets exactly equals the book value of its current liabilities.

A lower ratio indicates less liquidity, implying a greater reliance on operating cash flow and outside financing to meet short-term obligations. Liquidity affects the company's capacity to take on debt. The current ratio implicitly assumes that inventories and accounts receivable are indeed liquid (which is presumably not the case when related turnover ratios are low).

Quick Ratio The **quick ratio** is more conservative than the current ratio because it includes only the more liquid current assets (sometimes referred to as "**quick assets**") in relation to current liabilities. Like the current ratio, a higher quick ratio indicates greater liquidity.

The quick ratio reflects the fact that certain current assets—such as prepaid expenses, some taxes, and employee-related prepayments—represent costs of the current period that have been paid in advance and cannot usually be converted back into cash. This ratio also reflects the fact that inventory might not be easily and quickly converted into cash, and furthermore, that a company would probably not be able to sell all of its inventory for an amount equal to its carrying value, especially if it were required to sell the inventory quickly. In situations where inventories are illiquid (as indicated, for example, by low inventory turnover ratios), the quick ratio may be a better indicator of liquidity than the current ratio.

Cash Ratio The cash ratio normally represents a reliable measure of an individual entity's liquidity in a crisis situation. Only highly marketable short-term investments and cash are included. In a general market crisis, the fair value of marketable securities could decrease significantly as a result of market factors, in which case even this ratio might not provide reliable information.

Defensive Interval Ratio This ratio measures how long the company can continue to pay its expenses from its existing liquid assets without receiving any additional cash inflow. A defensive interval ratio of 50 would indicate that the company can continue to pay its operating expenses for 50 days before running out of quick assets, assuming no additional cash inflows. A higher defensive interval ratio indicates greater liquidity. If a company's defensive interval ratio is very low relative to peer companies or to the company's own history, the analyst would want to ascertain whether there is sufficient cash inflow expected to mitigate the low defensive interval ratio.

Cash Conversion Cycle (Net Operating Cycle) This metric indicates the amount of time that elapses from the point when a company invests in working capital until the point at which the company collects cash. In the typical course of events, a merchandising company acquires inventory on credit, incurring accounts payable. The company then sells that inventory on credit, increasing accounts receivable. Afterwards, it pays out cash to settle its accounts payable, and it collects cash in settlement of its accounts receivable. The time between the outlay of cash and the collection of cash is called the "cash conversion cycle." A shorter cash conversion cycle indicates greater liquidity. The short cash conversion cycle implies that the company only needs to finance its inventory and accounts receivable for a short period of time. A longer cash conversion cycle indicates lower liquidity; it implies that the company must finance its inventory and accounts receivable for a longer period of time, possibly indicating a need for a higher level of capital to fund current assets. Example 8 demonstrates the advantages of a short cash conversion cycle as well as how a company's business strategies are reflected in financial ratios.

EXAMPLE 8

Evaluation of Liquidity Ratios

An analyst is evaluating the liquidity of Dell and finds that Dell provides a computation of the **number of days of receivables**, inventory, and accounts payable, as well as the overall cash conversion cycle, as follows:

Fiscal Year Ended	28 Jan 2005	30 Jan 2004	31 Jan 2003
DSO	32	31	28
DOH	4	3	3
Less: Number of days of payables	73	70	68
Equals: Cash conversion cycle	(37)	(36)	(37)

The minimal DOH indicates that Dell maintains lean inventories, which is attributable to key aspects of the company's business model—namely, the company does not build a computer until it is ordered. Furthermore, Dell has a sophisticated just-in-time manufacturing system. In isolation, the increase in number of days payable (from 68 days in 2003 to 73 days in 2005) might suggest an inability to pay suppliers; however, in Dell's case, the balance sheet indicates that the company has almost $10 billion of cash and short-term investments, which would be more than enough to pay suppliers sooner if Dell chose to do so. Instead, Dell takes advantage of the favorable credit terms granted by its suppliers. The overall effect is a negative cash cycle, a somewhat unusual result. Instead of requiring additional capital to fund working capital as is the case for most companies, Dell has excess cash to invest for about 37 days (reflected on the balance sheet as short-term investments) on which it is earning, rather than paying, interest.

For comparison, the analyst computes the cash conversion cycle for three of Dell's competitors:

Fiscal Year	2004	2003	2002
HP Compaq	27	37	61
Gateway	(7)	(9)	(3)
Apple	(40)	(41)	(40)

The analyst notes that of the group, only HP Compaq has to raise capital for working capital purposes. Dell is outperforming HP Compaq and Gateway on this metric, its negative cash conversion cycle of minus 37 days indicating stronger liquidity than either of those two competitors. Apple, however, is slightly more liquid than Dell, evidenced by its slightly more negative cash conversion cycle, and Apple also has a similarly stable negative cash conversion cycle.

4.4 Solvency Ratios

Solvency refers to a company's ability to fulfill its long-term debt obligations. Assessment of a company's ability to pay its long-term obligations (i.e., to make interest and principal payments) generally includes an in-depth analysis of the components of its financial structure. Solvency ratios provide information regarding the relative amount of debt in the company's capital structure and the adequacy of earnings and cash flow to cover interest expenses and other fixed charges (such as lease or rental payments) as they come due.

Analysts seek to understand a company's use of debt for several main reasons. One reason is that the amount of debt in a company's capital structure is important for assessing the company's risk and return characteristics, specifically its financial leverage. Leverage is a magnifying effect that results from the use of **fixed costs**—costs that stay the same within some range of activity—and can take two forms: **operating leverage** and financial leverage. Operating leverage results from the use of fixed costs in conducting the company's business. Operating leverage magnifies the effect of changes in sales on operating income. Profitable companies may use operating leverage because when revenues increase, with operating leverage, their operating income increases at a faster rate. The explanation is that, although **variable costs** will rise proportionally with revenue, fixed costs will not. When financing a firm (i.e., raising capital for it), the use of debt constitutes financial leverage because interest payments are essentially fixed financing costs. As a result of interest payments, a given percent change in EBIT results in a larger percent change in earnings before taxes (EBT). Thus, financial leverage tends to magnify the effect of changes in EBIT on returns flowing to equityholders. Assuming that a company can earn more on the funds than it pays in interest, the inclusion of some level of debt in a company's capital structure may lower a company's overall cost of capital and increase returns to equityholders. However, a higher level of debt in a company's capital structure increases the risk of default and results in higher borrowing costs for the company to compensate lenders for assuming greater credit risk. Starting with Modigliani and Miller (1958, 1963), a substantial amount of research has focused on a company's optimal capital structure and the subject remains an important one in corporate finance. In analyzing financial statements, an analyst aims to understand levels and trends in a company's use of financial leverage in relation to past practices and the practices of peer companies. Analysts also need to be aware of the relationship between operating leverage and financial leverage. The greater a company's use of operating leverage, the greater the risk of the operating income stream available to cover debt payments; operating leverage can thus limit a company's capacity to use financial leverage.

A company's relative solvency is fundamental to valuation of its debt securities and its creditworthiness. Finally, understanding a company's use of debt can provide analysts with insight into the company's future business prospects because management's decisions about financing often signal their beliefs about a company's future.

4.4.1 Calculation of Solvency Ratios

Solvency ratios are primarily of two types. Debt ratios, the first type, focus on the balance sheet and measure the amount of debt capital relative to equity capital. Coverage ratios, the second type, focus on the income statement and measure the ability of a company to cover its debt payments. All of these ratios are useful in assessing a company's solvency and, therefore, in evaluating the quality of a company's bonds and other debt obligations.

Exhibit 11 describes commonly used solvency ratios. The first three of the debt ratios presented use total debt in the numerator. The definition of total debt used in these ratios varies among informed analysts and financial data vendors, with some using the total of interest-bearing short-term and long-term debt, excluding liabilities such as accrued expenses and accounts payable. (For calculations in this reading, we use this definition.) Other analysts use defini-

EXHIBIT 11 Definitions of Commonly Used Solvency Ratios

Solvency Ratios	Numerator	Denominator
Debt Ratios		
Debt-to-assets ratio[a]	Total debt[b]	Total assets
Debt-to-capital ratio	Total debt[b]	Total debt[b] + Total shareholders' equity
Debt-to-equity ratio	Total debt[b]	Total shareholders' equity
Financial leverage ratio	Average total assets	Average total equity
Coverage Ratios		
Interest coverage	EBIT	Interest payments
Fixed charge coverage	EBIT + lease payments	Interest payments + lease payments

[a] "Total debt ratio" is another name sometimes used for this ratio.

[b] In this reading, we take total debt in this context to be the sum of interest-bearing short-term and long-term debt.

tions that are more inclusive (e.g., all liabilities) or restrictive (e.g., long-term debt only, in which case the ratio is sometimes qualified as "long-term," as in "long-term debt-to-equity ratio"). If using different definitions of total debt materially changes conclusions about a company's solvency, the reasons for the discrepancies warrant further investigation.

4.4.2 Interpretation of Solvency Ratios

In the following, we discuss the interpretation of the basic solvency ratios presented in Exhibit 11.

Debt-to-Assets Ratio This ratio measures the percentage of total assets financed with debt. For example, a **debt-to-assets ratio** of 0.40 or 40 percent indicates that 40 percent of the company's assets are financed with debt. Generally, higher debt means higher financial risk and thus weaker solvency.

Debt-to-Capital Ratio The **debt-to-capital ratio** measures the percentage of a company's capital (debt plus equity) represented by debt. As with the previous ratio, a higher ratio generally means higher financial risk and thus indicates weaker solvency.

Debt-to-Equity Ratio The **debt-to-equity ratio** measures the amount of debt capital relative to equity capital. Interpretation is similar to the preceding two ratios (i.e., a higher ratio indicates weaker solvency). A ratio of 1.0 would indicate equal amounts of debt and equity, which is equivalent to a debt-to-capital ratio of 50 percent. Alternative definitions of this ratio use the market value of stockholders' equity rather than its book value (or use the market values of both stockholders' equity and debt).

Financial Leverage Ratio This ratio (often called simply the "leverage ratio") measures the amount of total assets supported for each one money unit of equity. For example, a value of 3 for this ratio means that each €1 of equity supports €3 of total assets. The higher the financial leverage ratio, the more leveraged the company is in the sense of using debt and other liabilities to finance assets. This ratio is often defined in terms of average total assets and average total equity and plays an important role in the DuPont decomposition of return on equity that will be presented in Section 4.6.2.

Interest Coverage This ratio measures the number of times a company's EBIT could cover its interest payments. A higher interest coverage ratio indicates stronger solvency, offering greater assurance that the company can service its debt (i.e., bank debt, bonds, notes) from operating earnings.

Fixed Charge Coverage This ratio relates fixed charges, or obligations, to the cash flow generated by the company. It measures the number of times a company's earnings (before interest, taxes, and lease payments) can cover the company's interest and lease payments.[9] Similar to the interest coverage ratio, a higher fixed charge coverage ratio implies stronger solvency, offering greater assurance that the company can service its debt (i.e., bank debt, bonds, notes, and leases) from normal earnings. The ratio is sometimes used as an indication of the quality of the preferred dividend, with a higher ratio indicating a more secure preferred dividend.

Example 9 demonstrates the use of solvency ratios in evaluating the creditworthiness of a company.

EXAMPLE 9

Evaluation of Solvency Ratios

A credit analyst is evaluating the solvency of Alcatel (now known as Alcatel-Lucent) as of the beginning of 2005. The following data are gathered from the company's 2005 annual report (in € millions):

	2004	2003
Total equity	4,389	4,038
Accrued pension	1,144	1,010
Other reserves	2,278	3,049
Total financial debt	4,359	5,293
Other liabilities	6,867	7,742
Total assets	19,037	21,132

[9] For computing this ratio, an assumption sometimes made is that one-third of the lease payment amount represents interest on the lease obligation and that the rest is a repayment of principal on the obligation. For this variant of the fixed charge coverage ratio, the numerator is EBIT plus one-third of lease payments and the denominator is interest payments plus one-third of lease payments.

The analyst concludes that, as used by Alcatel in its 2005 annual report, "total financial debt" consists of noncurrent debt and the interest-bearing, borrowed portion of current liabilities.

1. **A.** Calculate the company's financial leverage ratio for 2004.
   B. Interpret the financial leverage ratio calculated in Part A.
2. **A.** What are the company's debt-to-assets, debt-to-capital, and debt-to-equity ratios for the two years?
   B. Is there any discernable trend over the two years?

Solution to 1:

A. Average total assets was (19,037 + 21,132)/2 = 20,084.50 and average total equity was (4,389 + 4,038)/2 = 4,213.5. Thus, financial leverage was 20,084.50/4,213.5 = 4.77.

B. For 2004, every €1 in total equity supported €4.77 in total assets, on average.

Solution to 2:

A. Debt-to-assets for 2003 = 5,293/21,132 = 25.05%

Debt-to-assets for 2004 = 4,359/19,037 = 22.90%

Debt-to-capital for 2003 = 5,293/(5,293 + 4,038) = 56.72%

Debt-to-capital for 2004 = 4,359/(4,359 + 4,389) = 49.83%

Debt-to-equity for 2003 = 5,293/4,038 = 1.31

Debt-to-equity for 2004 = 4,359/4,389 = 0.99

B. On all three metrics, the company's level of debt has declined. This decrease in debt as part of the company's capital structure indicates that the company's solvency has improved. From a creditor's perspective, higher solvency (lower debt) indicates lower risk of default on obligations.

4.5 Profitability Ratios

The ability to generate profit on capital invested is a key determinant of a company's overall value and the value of the securities it issues. Consequently, many equity analysts would consider profitability to be a key focus of their analytical efforts.

Profitability reflects a company's competitive position in the market, and by extension, the quality of its management. The income statement reveals the sources of earnings and the components of revenue and expenses. Earnings can be distributed to shareholders or reinvested in the company. Reinvested earnings enhance solvency and provide a cushion against short-term problems.

4.5.1 Calculation of Profitability Ratios

Profitability ratios measure the return earned by the company during a period. Exhibit 12 provides the definitions of a selection of commonly used profitability

EXHIBIT 12 **Definitions of Commonly Used Profitability Ratios**

Profitability Ratios	Numerator	Denominator
Return on Sales[10]		
Gross profit margin	Gross profit	Revenue
Operating profit margin	Operating income[11]	Revenue
Pretax margin	EBT (earnings before tax but after interest)	Revenue
Net profit margin	Net income	Revenue
Return on Investment		
Operating ROA	Operating income	Average total assets
ROA	Net income	Average total assets
Return on total capital	EBIT	Short- and long-term debt and equity
ROE	Net income	Average total equity
Return on common equity	Net income − Preferred dividends	Average common equity

ratios. Return-on-sales profitability ratios express various subtotals on the income statement (e.g., gross profit, operating profit, net profit) as a percentage of revenue. Essentially, these ratios constitute part of a common-size income statement discussed earlier. Return on investment profitability ratios measure income relative to assets, equity, or total capital employed by the company. For operating ROA, returns are measured as operating income, i.e., prior to deducting interest on debt capital. For ROA and ROE, returns are measured as net income, i.e., after deducting interest paid on debt capital. For **return on common equity**, returns are measured as net income minus preferred dividends (because preferred dividends are a return to preferred equity).

4.5.2 Interpretation of Profitability Ratios

In the following, we discuss the interpretation of the profitability ratios presented in Exhibit 12. For each of the profitability ratios, a higher ratio indicates greater profitability.

Gross Profit Margin Gross profit margin indicates the percentage of revenue available to cover operating and other expenditures. Higher gross profit margin indicates some combination of higher product pricing and lower product costs.

[10] "Sales" is being used as a synonym for "revenue."

[11] Some analysts use EBIT as a shortcut representation of operating income. Note that EBIT, strictly speaking, includes nonoperating items such as dividends received and gains and losses on investment securities. Of utmost importance is that the analyst compute ratios consistently whether comparing different companies or analyzing one company over time.

The ability to charge a higher price is constrained by competition, so gross profits are affected by (and usually inversely related to) competition. If a product has a competitive advantage (e.g., superior branding, better quality, or exclusive technology), the company is better able to charge more for it. On the cost side, higher gross profit margin can also indicate that a company has a competitive advantage in product costs.

Operating Profit Margin Operating profit is calculated as gross margin minus operating costs. So, an operating margin increasing faster than the gross margin can indicate improvements in controlling operating costs, such as administrative overheads. In contrast, a declining operating profit margin could be an indicator of deteriorating control over operating costs.

Pretax Margin Pretax income (also called "earnings before tax") is calculated as operating profit minus interest, so this ratio reflects the effects on profitability of leverage and other (nonoperating) income and expenses. If a company's pretax margin is rising primarily as a result of increasing nonoperating income, the analyst should evaluate whether this increase reflects a deliberate change in a company's business focus and, therefore, the likelihood that the increase will continue.

Net Profit Margin Net profit, or net income, is calculated as revenue minus all expenses. Net income includes both recurring and nonrecurring components. Generally, the net profit margin adjusted for nonrecurring items offers a better view of a company's potential future profitability.

ROA ROA measures the return earned by a company on its assets. The higher the ratio, the more income is generated by a given level of assets. Most databases compute this ratio as:

$$\frac{\text{Net income}}{\text{Average total assets}}$$

The problem with this computation is net income is the return to equityholders, whereas assets are financed by both equityholders and creditors. Interest expense (the return to creditors) has already been subtracted in the numerator. Some analysts, therefore, prefer to add back interest expense in the numerator. In such cases, interest must be adjusted for income taxes because net income is determined after taxes. With this adjustment, the ratio would be computed as:

$$\frac{\text{Net income} + \text{Interest expense}\ (1 - \text{Tax rate})}{\text{Average total assets}}$$

Alternatively, some analysts elect to compute ROA on a pre-interest and pretax basis as:

$$\frac{\text{Operating income or EBIT}}{\text{Average total assets}}$$

As noted, returns are measured prior to deducting interest on debt capital (i.e., as operating income or EBIT). This measure reflects the return on all assets invested in the company, whether financed with liabilities, debt, or equity. Whichever form of ROA that is chosen, the analyst must use it consistently in comparisons to other companies or time periods.

Return on Total Capital **Return on total capital** measures the profits a company earns on all of the capital that it employs (short-term debt, long-term debt, and equity). As with ROA, returns are measured prior to deducting interest on debt capital (i.e., as operating income or EBIT).

ROE ROE measures the return earned by a company on its equity capital, including minority equity, preferred equity, and common equity. As noted, return is measured as net income (i.e., interest on debt capital is not included in the return on equity capital). A variation of ROE is return on common equity, which measures the return earned by a company only on its common equity.

Both ROA and ROE are important measures of profitability and will be explored in more detail below. As with other ratios, profitability ratios should be evaluated individually and as a group to gain an understanding of what is driving profitability (operating versus nonoperating activities). Example 10 demonstrates the evaluation of profitability ratios and the use of management's discussion that accompanies financial statements to explain the trend in ratios.

EXAMPLE 10

Evaluation of Profitability Ratios

An analyst is evaluating the profitability of DaimlerChrysler (NYSE: DCX) over a recent three-year period and collects the following profitability ratios:

	2004	2003	2002
Gross profit margin	19.35%	19.49%	18.99%
Operating profit margin	3.19%	2.83%	3.35%
Pretax margin	2.49%	0.44%	4.06%
Net profit margin	1.74%	0.33%	3.15%

DCX's 2003 Annual Report indicates that revenue declined in 2003. Furthermore, management's discussion of results in that report notes the following:

> General administrative expenses of €5.4 billion remained virtually flat on the prior-year level. General administrative expenses as a percentage of revenues were 3.9 percent in 2003 and 3.6 percent in 2002, reflecting the limited variability of these expenses. Slightly higher personnel expenses, primarily caused by higher net periodic pension and post-retirement benefit costs, resulted in a moderate increase of general administrative expenses.

1. Contrast gross profit margins and operating profit margins over 2002 to 2004.
2. Explain the decline in operating profit margin in 2003.
3. Explain why the pretax margin might decrease to a greater extent than the operating profit margin in 2003.

4. Compare and contrast net profit margins and pretax margins over 2002 to 2004.

Solution to 1: Gross margin improved from 2002 to 2003 as a result of some combination of price increases and/or cost control. However, gross margin declined slightly in 2004. Operating profit margin, on the other hand, declined from 2002 to 2003, and then improved in 2004.

Solution to 2: The decline in operating profit from 3.35 percent in 2002 to 2.83 percent in 2003 appears to be the result of DCX's operating leverage, discussed in management's discussion. Revenue declined in 2003 but, according to management, general administrative expenses were virtually flat compared with 2002. These expenses thus increased as a proportion of revenue in 2003, lowering the operating profit margin. This is an example of the effects of fixed cost on profitability. In general, as revenues rise, to the extent that costs remain fixed, operating margins should increase. However, if revenue declines, the opposite occurs.

Solution to 3: Pretax margin was down substantially in 2003, indicating that the company may have had some nonoperating losses or high interest expense in that year. A review of the company's financial statement footnotes confirms that the cause was nonoperating losses: Specifically, the company had a significant impairment loss on investments in 2003.

Solution to 4: Net profit margin followed the same pattern as pretax margin, declining substantially in 2003, then improving in 2004 but not reaching 2002 levels. In the absence of major variation in the applicable tax rates, this would be the expected as net income is EBT(1 − tax rate).

4.6 Integrated Financial Ratio Analysis

In prior sections, the text presented separately activity, liquidity, solvency, and profitability ratios. In the following, we illustrate the importance of examining a portfolio of ratios, not a single ratio or category of ratios in isolation, to ascertain the overall position and performance of a company. Experience shows that the information from one ratio category can be helpful in answering questions raised by another category and that the most accurate overall picture comes from integrating information from all sources. Section 4.6.1 provides some introductory examples of such analysis and Section 4.6.2 shows how return on equity can be analyzed into components related to profit margin, asset utilization (activity), and financial leverage.

4.6.1 The Overall Ratio Picture: Examples

This section presents two simple illustrations to introduce the use of a portfolio of ratios to address an analytical task. Example 11 shows how the analysis of a pair of activity ratios resolves an issue concerning a company's liquidity. Example 12 shows that examining the overall ratios of multiple companies can assist an analyst in drawing conclusions about their relative performances.

EXAMPLE 11

A Portfolio of Ratios

An analyst is evaluating the liquidity of a Canadian manufacturing company and obtains the following liquidity ratios:

	2005	2004	2003
Current ratio	2.1	1.9	1.6
Quick ratio	0.8	0.9	1.0

The ratios present a contradictory picture of the company's liquidity. Based on the increase in its current ratio from 1.6 to 2.1, the company appears to have strong and improving liquidity; however, based on the decline of the quick ratio from 1.0 to 0.8, its liquidity appears to be deteriorating. Because both ratios have exactly the same denominator, current liabilities, the difference must be the result of changes in some asset that is included in the current ratio but not in the quick ratio (e.g., inventories). The analyst collects the following activity ratios:

DOH	55	45	30
DSO	24	28	30

The company's DOH has deteriorated from 30 days to 55 days, meaning that the company is holding increasingly greater amounts of inventory relative to sales. The decrease in DSO implies that the company is collecting receivables faster. If the proceeds from these collections were held as cash, there would be no effect on either the current ratio or the quick ratio. However, if the proceeds from the collections were used to purchase inventory, there would be no effect on the current ratio and a decline in the quick ratio (i.e., the pattern shown in this example). Collectively, the ratios suggest that liquidity is declining and that the company may have an inventory problem that needs to be addressed.

EXAMPLE 12

A Comparison of Two Companies (1)

An analyst collects the following information for two companies:

Anson Industries	2005	2004	2003	2002
Inventory turnover	76.69	89.09	147.82	187.64
DOH	4.76	4.10	2.47	1.95

Anson Industries	2005	2004	2003	2002
Receivables turnover	10.75	9.33	11.14	7.56
DSO	33.95	39.13	32.77	48.29
Accounts payable turnover	4.62	4.36	4.84	4.22
Days payable	78.97	83.77	75.49	86.56
Cash from operations/ Total liabilities	31.41%	11.15%	4.04%	8.81%
ROE	5.92%	1.66%	1.62%	−0.62%
ROA	3.70%	1.05%	1.05%	−0.39%
Net profit margin (Net income/Revenue)	3.33%	1.11%	1.13%	−0.47%
Total asset turnover (Revenue/Average assets)	1.11	0.95	0.93	0.84
Leverage (Average assets/ Average equity)	1.60	1.58	1.54	1.60

Clarence Corporation	2005	2004	2003	2002
Inventory turnover	9.19	9.08	7.52	14.84
DOH	39.73	40.20	48.51	24.59
Receivables turnover	8.35	7.01	6.09	5.16
DSO	43.73	52.03	59.92	70.79
Accounts payable turnover	6.47	6.61	7.66	6.52
Days payable	56.44	55.22	47.64	56.00
Cash from operations/ Total liabilities	13.19%	16.39%	15.80%	11.79%
ROE	9.28%	6.82%	−3.63%	−6.75%
ROA	4.64%	3.48%	−1.76%	3.23%
Net profit margin (Net income/Revenue)	4.38%	3.48%	−1.60%	−2.34%
Total asset turnover (Revenue/Average assets)	1.06	1.00	1.10	1.38
Leverage (Average assets/ Average equity)	2.00	1.96	2.06	2.09

Which of the following choices best describes reasonable conclusions an analyst might make about the companies' efficiency?

A. Over the past four years, Anson has shown greater improvement in efficiency than Clarence, as indicated by its total asset turnover ratio increasing from 0.84 to 1.11.

B. In 2004, Anson's DOH of only 4.76 indicated that it was less efficient at inventory management than Clarence, which had DOH of 39.73.

C. In 2004, Clarence's receivables turnover of 8.35 times indicated that it was more efficient at receivables management than Anson, which had receivables turnover of 10.75.

D. Over the past four years, Clarence has shown greater improvement in efficiency than Anson, as indicated by its net profit margin of 4.38 percent.

Solution: A is correct. Over the past four years, Anson has shown greater improvement in efficiency than Clarence, as indicated by its total asset turnover ratio increasing from 0.84 to 1.11. Over the same period of time, Clarence's total asset turnover ratio has declined from 1.38 to 1.06. Choice B is incorrect because it misinterprets DOH. Choice C is incorrect because it misinterprets receivables turnover. Choice D is incorrect because net profit margin is not an indicator of efficiency.

4.6.2 DuPont Analysis: The Decomposition of ROE

As noted earlier, ROE measures the return a company generates on its equity capital. To understand what drives a company's ROE, a useful technique is to decompose ROE into its component parts. (Decomposition of ROE is sometimes referred to as **DuPont analysis** because it was developed originally at that company.) Decomposing ROE involves expressing the basic ratio (i.e., net income divided by average shareholders' equity) as the product of component ratios. Because each of these component ratios is an indicator of a distinct aspect of a company's performance that affects ROE, the decomposition allows us to evaluate how these different aspects of performance affected the company's profitability as measured by ROE.[12]

Decomposing ROE is useful in determining the reasons for changes in ROE over time for a given company and for differences in ROE for different companies in a given time period. The information gained can also be used by management to determine which areas they should focus on to improve ROE. This decomposition will also show why a company's overall profitability, measured by ROE, is a function of its efficiency, operating profitability, taxes, and use of financial leverage. DuPont analysis shows the relationship between the various categories of ratios discussed in this reading and how they all influence the return to the investment of the owners.

Analysts have developed several different methods of decomposing ROE. The decomposition presented here is one of the most commonly used and the one found in popular research databases, such as Bloomberg. Return on equity is calculated as:

$$\text{ROE} = \text{Net income}/\text{Average shareholders' equity}$$

[12] For purposes of analyzing ROE, this method usually uses average balance sheet factors; however, the math will work out if beginning or ending balances are used throughout. For certain purposes, these alternative methods may be appropriate. See Stowe et al. (2002, pp. 85–88).

The decomposition of ROE makes use of simple algebra and illustrates the relationship between ROE and ROA. Expressing ROE as a product of only two of its components, we can write:

$$\text{ROE} = \frac{\text{Net income}}{\text{Average shareholders' equity}}$$

$$= \frac{\text{Net income}}{\text{Average total assets}} \times \frac{\text{Average total assets}}{\text{Average shareholders' equity}} \quad \textbf{(41-1a)}$$

which can be interpreted as:

$$\text{ROE} = \text{ROA} \times \text{Leverage}$$

In other words, ROE is a function of a company's ROA and its use of financial leverage ("leverage" for short, in this discussion). A company can improve its ROE by improving ROA or making more effective use of leverage. Consistent with the definition given earlier, leverage is measured as average total assets divided by average shareholders' equity. If a company had no leverage (no liabilities), its leverage ratio would equal 1.0 and ROE would exactly equal ROA. As a company takes on liabilities, its leverage increases. As long as a company is able to borrow at a rate lower than the marginal rate it can earn investing the borrowed money in its business, the company is making an effective use of leverage and ROE would increase as leverage increases. If a company's borrowing cost exceeds the marginal rate it can earn on investing, ROE would decline as leverage increased because the effect of borrowing would be to depress ROA.

Using the data from Example 12 for Anson Industries, an analyst can examine the trend in ROE and determine whether the increase from an ROE of −0.625 percent in 2002 to 5.925 percent in 2005 is a function of ROA or the use of leverage:

	ROE	=	ROA	×	Leverage
2005	5.92%		3.70%		1.60
2004	1.66%		1.05%		1.58
2003	1.62%		1.05%		1.54
2002	−0.62%		−0.39%		1.60

Over the four-year period, the company's leverage factor was relatively stable. The primary reason for the increase in ROE is the increase in profitability measured by ROA.

Just as ROE can be decomposed, the individual components such as ROA can be decomposed. Further decomposing ROA, we can express ROE as a product of three component ratios:

$$\frac{\text{Net income}}{\text{Average shareholders' equity}} = \frac{\text{Net income}}{\text{Revenue}} \times \frac{\text{Revenue}}{\text{Average total assets}}$$

$$\times \frac{\text{Average total assets}}{\text{Average shareholders' equity}} \quad \textbf{(41-1b)}$$

which can be interpreted as:

$$\text{ROE} = \text{Net profit margin} \times \text{Asset turnover} \times \text{Leverage}$$

The first term on the right-hand side of this equation is the net profit margin, an indicator of profitability: how much income a company derives per one money unit (e.g., euro or dollar) of sales. The second term on the right is the asset turnover ratio, an indicator of efficiency: how much revenue a company generates per one money unit of assets. Note that ROA is decomposed into these two components: net profit margin and asset turnover. A company's ROA is a function of profitability (net profit margin) and efficiency (asset turnover). The third term on the right-hand side of Equation 41-1b is a measure of financial leverage, an indicator of solvency: the total amount of a company's assets relative to its equity capital. This decomposition illustrates that a company's ROE is a function of its net profit margin, its efficiency, and its leverage. Again, using the data from Example 12 for Anson Industries, the analyst can evaluate in more detail the reasons behind the trend in ROE:[13]

	ROE	=	Net profit margin	×	Asset turnover	×	Leverage
2005	5.92%		3.33%		1.11		1.60
2004	1.66%		1.11%		0.95		1.58
2003	1.62%		1.13%		0.93		1.54
2002	−0.62%		−0.47%		0.84		1.60

This further decomposition confirms that increases in profitability (measured here as net profit margin) are indeed an important contributor to the increase in ROE over the four-year period. However, Anson's asset turnover has also increased steadily. The increase in ROE is, therefore, a function of improving profitability and improving efficiency. As noted above, ROE decomposition can also be used to compare the ROEs of peer companies, as demonstrated in Example 13.

EXAMPLE 13

A Comparison of Two Companies (2)

Referring to the data for Anson Industries and Clarence Corporation in Example 12, which of the following choices best describes reasonable conclusions an analyst might make about the companies' ROE?

A. Anson's inventory turnover of 76.69 indicates it is more profitable than Clarence.

B. The main drivers of Clarence's superior ROE in 2004 are its greater use of debt financing and higher net profit margin.

C. The main driver of Clarence's superior ROE in 2004 is its more efficient use of assets.

D. Anson's days payable of 78.97 indicates it is more profitable than Clarence.

[13] Please note that ratios are expressed in terms of two decimal places and are rounded. Therefore, ROE may not be the exact product of the three ratios.

Solution: B is correct. The main driver of Clarence's superior ROE (9.29 percent compared with only 5.94 percent for Anson) in 2004 is its greater use of debt financing (leverage of 2.00 compared with Anson's leverage of 1.60) and higher net profit margin (4.38 percent compared with only 3.33 percent for Anson). A and D are incorrect because neither inventory turnover nor days payable is an indicator of profitability. C is incorrect because Clarence has less-efficient use of assets than Anson, indicated by turnover of 1.06 for Clarence compared with Anson's turnover of 1.11.

To separate the effects of taxes and interest, we can further decompose the net profit margin and write:

$$\frac{\text{Net income}}{\text{Average shareholders' equity}} = \frac{\text{Net income}}{\text{EBT}} \times \frac{\text{EBT}}{\text{EBIT}} \times \frac{\text{EBIT}}{\text{Revenue}} \times \frac{\text{Revenue}}{\text{Average total assets}} \times \frac{\text{Average total assets}}{\text{Average shareholders' equity}} \quad \textbf{(41-1c)}$$

which can be interpreted as:

$$\text{ROE} = \text{Tax burden} \times \text{Interest burden} \times \text{EBIT margin} \times \text{Asset turnover} \times \text{Leverage}$$

This five-way decomposition is the one found in financial databases such as Bloomberg. The first term on the right-hand side of this equation measures the effect of taxes on ROE. Essentially, it reflects one minus the **average tax rate**, or how much of a company's pretax profits it gets to keep. This can be expressed in decimal or percentage form. So, a 30 percent tax rate would yield a factor of 0.70 or 70 percent. A higher value for the tax burden implies that the company can keep a higher percentage of its pretax profits, indicating a lower tax rate. A decrease in the tax burden ratio implies the opposite (i.e., a higher tax rate leaving the company with less of its pretax profits).

The second term on the right-hand side captures the effect of interest on ROE. Higher borrowing costs reduce ROE. Some analysts prefer to use operating income instead of EBIT for this factor and the following one (consistency is required!). In such a case, the second factor would measure both the effect of interest expense and nonoperating income.

The third term on the right-hand side captures the effect of operating margin (if operating income is used in the numerator) or EBIT margin (if EBIT is used) on ROE. In either case, this factor primarily measures the effect of operating profitability on ROE.

The fourth term on the right-hand side is again the asset turnover ratio, an indicator of the overall efficiency of the company (i.e., how much revenue it generates per unit of assets). The fifth term on the right-hand side is the financial leverage ratio described above—the total amount of a company's assets relative to its equity capital.

This decomposition expresses a company's ROE as a function of its tax rate, interest burden, operating profitability, efficiency, and leverage. An analyst can use this framework to determine what factors are driving a company's ROE. The decomposition of ROE can also be useful in forecasting ROE based upon expected efficiency, profitability, financing activities, and tax rates. The relationship of the individual factors, such as ROA to the overall ROE, can also be expressed in the form of an ROE tree to study the contribution of each of the five factors, as shown in Exhibit 13 for Anson Industries.[14]

Exhibit 13 shows that Anson's ROE of 5.92 percent in 2005 can be decomposed into ROA of 3.7 percent and leverage of 1.60. ROA can further be decomposed into a net profit margin of 3.33 percent and total asset turnover of 1.11. Net profit margin can be decomposed into a tax burden of 0.70 (an average tax rate of 30 percent), an interest burden of 0.90, and an EBIT margin of 5.29 percent. Overall ROE is decomposed into five components.

EXHIBIT 13 DuPont Analysis of Anson Industries' ROE: 2005

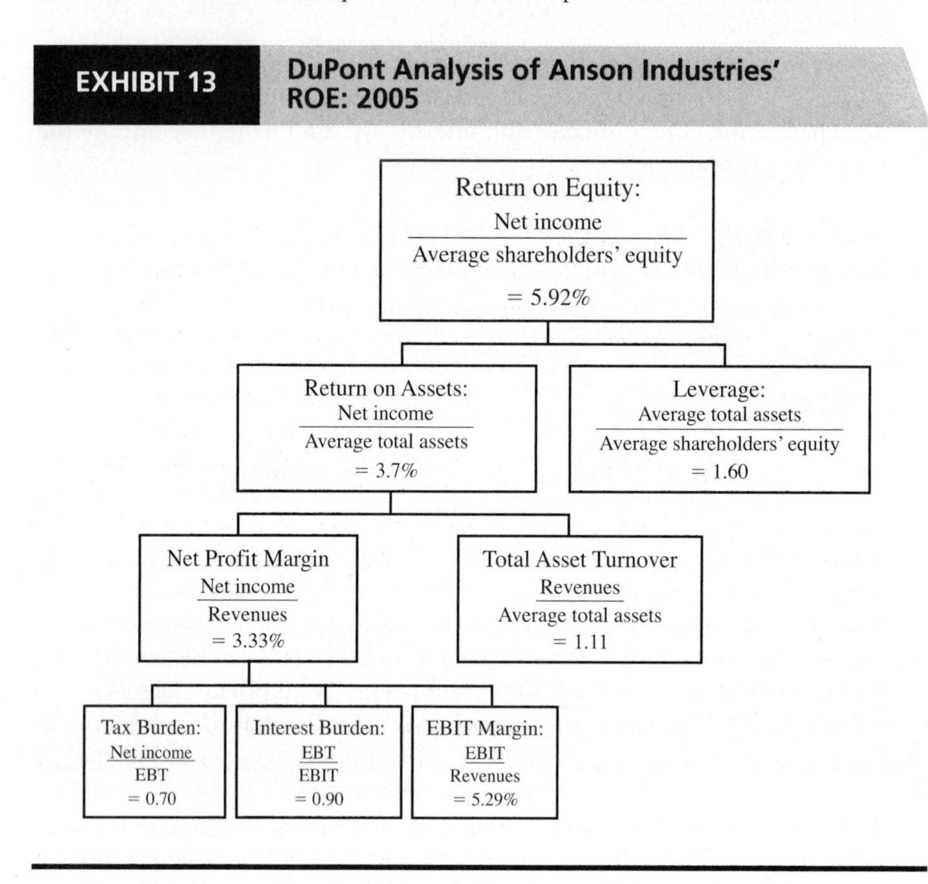

Example 14 demonstrates how the five-component decomposition can be used to determine reasons behind the trend in a company's ROE.

EXAMPLE 14

Five-Way Decomposition of ROE

An analyst examining BP PLC (BP) wishes to understand the factors driving the trend in ROE over a recent three-year period. The analyst obtains the following data from Bloomberg and ascertains that Bloomberg has included nonoperating income in the interest burden factor:

[14] Note that a breakdown of net profit margin was not provided in Example 12, but is added here.

	2004	2003	2002
ROE	20.62%	14.42%	10.17%
Tax burden	64.88%	62.52%	60.67%
Interest burden	130.54%	112.60%	130.50%
EBIT margin	6.51%	6.40%	4.84%
Asset turnover	1.55	1.38	1.19
Leverage	2.42	2.32	2.24

What might the analyst conclude?

Solution: Because the tax burden reflects the relation of after-tax profits to pretax profits, the increase from 60.67 percent to 64.88 percent indicates that taxes declined as a percentage of pretax profits. This decline in average tax rates could be due to lower tax rates from new legislation or revenue in a lower tax jurisdiction. An interest burden factor greater than 100 percent means that nonoperating income exceeded interest expense in all three years. Operating margin (EBIT margin) improved, particularly from 2002 to 2003, indicating the company's operations were more profitable. The company's efficiency (asset turnover) increased each year as did its leverage. Overall, the trend in ROE (doubling in three years) did not result from a single aspect of the company's performance, but instead was a function of lower average tax rates, increasing operating profits, greater efficiency, and increased use of leverage. Additional research on the causes of the various changes is required in order to develop expectations about the company's future performance.

The most detailed decomposition of ROE that we have presented is a five-way decomposition. Nevertheless, an analyst could further decompose individual components of a five-way analysis. For example, EBIT margin (EBIT/Revenue) could be further decomposed into a nonoperating component (EBIT/Operating income) and an operating component (Operating income/Revenues). The analyst can also examine which other factors contributed to these five components. For example, an improvement in efficiency (total asset turnover) may have resulted from better management of inventory (DOH) or better collection of receivables (DSO).

EQUITY ANALYSIS 5

One application of financial analysis is to select securities as part of the equity portfolio management process. Analysts are interested in valuing a security to assess its merits for inclusion or retention in a portfolio. The valuation process has several steps, including:[15]

[15] Stowe et al. (2002, p. 6).

1. understanding the business and the existing financial profile
2. forecasting company performance
3. selecting the appropriate valuation model
4. converting forecasts to a valuation
5. making the investment decision

Financial analysis assists in providing the core information to complete the first two steps of this valuation process: understanding the business and forecasting performance.

Fundamental equity analysis involves evaluating a company's performance and valuing its equity in order to assess its relative attractiveness as an investment. Analysts use a variety of methods to value a company's equity, including valuation ratios (e.g., the price-to-earnings or P/E ratio), discounted cash flow approaches, and residual income approaches (ROE compared with the cost of capital), among others. The following section addresses the first of these approaches—the use of valuation ratios.

5.1 Valuation Ratios

Valuation ratios have long been used in investment decision making. A well-known example is the P/E ratio—probably the most widely used indicator in discussing the value of equity securities—which relates share price to the earnings per share (EPS). Additionally, some analysts use other market multiples, such as price to book value (P/B) and price to cash flow (P/CF). The following sections explore valuation ratios and other quantities related to valuing equities.

5.1.1 Calculation of Valuation Ratios and Related Quantities

Exhibit 14 describes the calculation of some common **valuation ratios** and related quantities.

The P/E ratio expresses the relationship between the price per share and the amount of earnings attributable to a single share. In other words, the P/E ratio tells us how much an investor in common stock pays per dollar of current earnings.

Because P/E ratios are calculated using net income, the ratios can be sensitive to nonrecurring earnings or one-off earnings events. In addition, because net income is generally considered to be more susceptible to manipulation than are cash flows, analysts may use **price to cash flow** as an alternative measure—particularly in situations where earnings quality may be an issue. EBITDA per share, because it is calculated using income before interest, taxes, and depreciation, can be used to eliminate the effect of different levels of fixed asset investment across companies. It facilitates comparison between companies in the same sector but at different stages of infrastructure maturity. **Price to sales** is calculated in a similar manner and is sometimes used as a comparative price metric when a company does not have positive net income.

Another price-based ratio that facilitates useful comparisons of companies' stock prices is **price to book value**, or P/B, which is the ratio of price to book value per share. This ratio is often interpreted as an indicator of market judgment about the relationship between a company's required rate of return and its actual rate of return. Assuming that book values reflect the fair values of the assets, a price to book ratio of one can be interpreted as an indicator that the company's future returns are expected to be exactly equal to the returns required by the market. A

EXHIBIT 14 Definitions of Selected Valuation Ratios and Related Quantities

	Numerator	Denominator
Valuation Ratios		
P/E	Price per share	Earnings per share
P/CF	Price per share	Cash flow per share
P/S	Price per share	Sales per share
P/BV	Price per share	Book value per share
Per-Share Quantities		
Basic EPS	Net income minus preferred dividends	Weighted average number of ordinary shares outstanding
Diluted EPS	Adjusted income available for ordinary shares, reflecting conversion of dilutive securities	Weighted average number of ordinary and potential ordinary shares outstanding
Cash flow per share	Cash flow from operations	Average number of shares outstanding
EBITDA per share	EBITDA	Average number of shares outstanding
Dividends per share	Common dividends declared	Weighted average number of ordinary shares outstanding
Dividend-Related Quantities		
Dividend payout ratio	Common share dividends	Net income attributable to common shares
Retention rate (b)	Net income attributable to common shares − Common share dividends	Net income attributable to common shares
Sustainable growth rate	$b \times$ ROE	

ratio greater than one would indicate that the future profitability of the company is expected to exceed the required rate of return, and values of this ratio less than one indicate that the company is not expected to earn excess returns.[16]

5.1.2 Interpretation of Earnings per Share

Exhibit 14 presented a number of per-share quantities that can be used in valuation ratios. In the following, we discuss the interpretation of one such critical quantity, EPS.

[16] For more detail on valuation ratios as used in equity analysis, see Stowe et al. (2002).

EPS is simply the amount of earnings attributable to each share of common stock. In isolation, EPS does not provide adequate information for comparison of one company with another. For example, assume that two companies have only common stock outstanding and no dilutive securities outstanding. In addition, assume the two companies have identical net income of $10 million, identical book equity of $100 million and, therefore, identical profitability (10 percent, using ending equity in this case for simplicity). Furthermore, assume that Company A has 100 million weighted average common shares outstanding, whereas Company B has 10 million weighted average common shares outstanding. So, Company A will report EPS of $1 per share, and Company B will report EPS of $10 per share. The difference in EPS does not reflect a difference in profitability—the companies have identical profits and profitability. The difference reflects only a different number of common shares outstanding.

Analysts should understand in detail the types of EPS information that companies report:

Basic EPS provides information regarding the earnings attributable to each share of common stock. International Accounting Standards (IAS) No. 33 contains the international principles for the determination and presentation of EPS. This standard applies to entities whose shares are publicly traded or in the process of being issued in public securities markets, and other entities that choose to disclose EPS. U.S. Financial Accounting Standards Board Statement No. 128 contains the standards for computing and presenting EPS.

To calculate basic EPS, the weighted average number of shares outstanding during the period is first calculated. The weighted average number of shares consists of the number of ordinary shares outstanding at the beginning of the period, adjusted by those bought back or issued during the period, multiplied by a time-weighting factor.

Accounting standards generally require the disclosure of basic as well as diluted EPS (**diluted EPS** includes the effect of all the company's securities whose conversion or exercise would result in a reduction of basic EPS; dilutive securities include convertible debt, convertible preferred, warrants, and options). Basic EPS and diluted EPS must be shown with equal prominence on the face of the income statement for each class of ordinary share. Disclosure includes the amounts used as the numerators in calculating basic and diluted EPS, and a reconciliation of those amounts to the company's profit or loss for the period. Because both basic and diluted EPS are presented in a company's financial statements, an analyst does not need to calculate these measures for reported financial statements. Understanding the calculations is, however, helpful for situations requiring an analyst to calculate expected future EPS.

To calculate diluted EPS, earnings are adjusted for the after-tax effects assuming conversion, and the following adjustments are made to the weighted number of shares:

- The weighted average number of shares for basic EPS, *plus* those that would be issued on conversion of all dilutive potential ordinary shares. Potential ordinary shares are treated as dilutive when their conversion would decrease net profit per share from continuing ordinary operations.
- These shares are deemed to have been converted into ordinary shares at the beginning of the period or, if later, at the date of the issue of the shares.
- Options, warrants (and their equivalents), convertible instruments, contingently issuable shares, contracts that can be settled in ordinary shares or cash, purchased options, and written put options should be considered.

5.1.3 Dividend-Related Quantities

In the following, we discuss the interpretation of the dividend-related quantities presented in Exhibit 14. These quantities play a role in some present value models for valuing equities.

Dividend Payout Ratio The **dividend payout ratio** measures the percentage of earnings that the company pays out as dividends to shareholders. The amount of dividends per share tends to be relatively fixed because any reduction in dividends has been shown to result in a disproportionately large reduction in share price. Because dividend amounts are relatively fixed, the dividend payout ratio tends to fluctuate with earnings. Therefore, conclusions about a company's dividend payout policies should be based on examination of payout over a number of periods. Optimal dividend policy, similar to optimal capital structure, has been examined in academic research and continues to be a topic of significant interest in corporate finance.

Retention Rate The retention rate is the complement of the payout ratio (i.e., 1 − payout ratio). Whereas the payout ratio measures the percentage of earnings that a company pays out as dividends, the retention rate is the percentage of earnings that a company retains. It is simply one minus the payout ratio. (Note that both the dividend payout ratio and retention rate are both percentages of earnings. The difference in terminology—"ratio" versus "rate" versus "percentage"—reflects common usage rather than any substantive differences.)

Sustainable Growth Rate A company's **sustainable growth rate** is viewed as a function of its profitability (measured as ROE) and its ability to finance itself from internally generated funds (measured as the retention rate). A higher ROE and a higher retention rate result in a higher sustainable growth rate. This calculation can be used to estimate a company's growth rate, a factor commonly used in equity valuation.

5.2 Industry-Specific Ratios

As stated earlier in this reading, a universally accepted definition and classification of ratios do not exist. The purpose of ratios is to serve as indicators of important aspects of a company's performance and value. Aspects of performance that are considered important in one industry may be irrelevant in another, and industry-specific ratios reflect these differences. For example, companies in the retail industry may report same-store sales changes because, in the retail industry, it is important to distinguish between growth that results from opening new stores and growth that results from generating more sales at existing stores. Industry-specific metrics can be especially important to the value of equity in early stage industries, where companies are not yet profitable.

In addition, regulated industries—especially in the financial sector—often are required to comply with specific regulatory ratios. For example, the banking sector's liquidity and cash reserve ratios provide an indication of banking liquidity and reflect monetary and political requirements. Banking capital adequacy requirements, although not perfect, do relate banks' solvency requirements directly to their specific levels of risk exposure.

Exhibit 15 presents some industry-specific and task-specific ratios.[17]

[17] These are provided for illustrative purposes only. There are many other industry-specific ratios that are outside the scope of this reading. Resources such as Standard and Poor's Industry Surveys present useful ratios for each industry.

EXHIBIT 15 Definitions of Some Common Industry and Task-Specific Ratios

Ratios	Numerator	Denominator
Business Risk		
Coefficient of variation of operating income	Standard deviation of operating income	Average operating income
Coefficient of variation of net income	Standard deviation of net income	Average net income
Coefficient of variation of revenues	Standard deviation of revenue	Average revenue
Financial Sector Ratios		
Capital adequacy—banks	Various components of capital	Risk-weighted assets, market risk exposure, and level of operational risk assumed
Monetary reserve requirement	Reserves held at central bank	Specified deposit liabilities
Liquid asset requirement	Approved "readily marketable" securities	Specified deposit liabilities
Net interest margin	Net interest income	Total interest-earning assets
Retail Ratios		
Same (or comparable) store sales	Average revenue growth year over year for stores open in both periods	Not applicable
Sales per square foot (meter)	Revenue	Total retail space in feet or meters
Service Companies		
Revenue per employee	Revenue	Total number of employees
Net income per employee	Net income	Total number of employees
Hotel		
Average daily rate	Room revenue	Number of rooms sold
Occupancy rate	Number of rooms sold	Number of rooms available

5.3 Research on Ratios in Equity Analysis

Some ratios should be expected to be particularly useful in equity analysis. The end product of equity analysis is often a valuation and investment recommendation. Theoretical valuation models are useful in selecting ratios that would be useful in this process. For example, a company's P/B is theoretically linked to ROE, growth, and the required return. ROE is also a primary determinate of residual income in a residual income valuation model. In both cases, higher ROE relative to the required return denotes a higher valuation. Similarly, profit margin is related to justified price-to-sales (P/S) ratios. Another common valuation method involves forecasts of future cash flows that are discounted back to the present. Trends in ratios can be useful in forecasting future earnings and cash flows (e.g., trends operating profit margin and collection of customer receivables). Future growth expectations are a key component of all of these valuation models. Trends may be useful in assessing growth prospects (when used in conjunction with overall economic and industry trends). The variability in ratios and common-size data can be useful in assessing risk, an important component of the required rate of return in valuation models. A great deal of academic research has focused on the use of these fundamental ratios in evaluating equity investments.

A classic study, Ou and Penman (1989a and 1989b), found that ratios and common-size metrics generated from accounting data were useful in forecasting earnings and stock returns. Ou and Penman examined a variety of 68 such metrics and found that these variables could be reduced to a more parsimonious list and combined in a statistical model that was particularly useful for selecting investments. These variables included:

- percentage change in current ratio
- percentage change in quick ratio
- percentage change in inventory turnover
- inventory/Total assets (a common-size measure) and the percentage change in this metric
- percentage change in inventory
- percentage change in sales
- percentage change in depreciation
- change in dividend per share
- percentage change in depreciation to plant assets ratio
- ROE
- change in ROE
- percentage change in capital expenditures to total assets ratio (contemporaneously and lagged)
- debt-to-equity ratio and the percentage change in this ratio
- percentage change in total asset turnover
- ROA
- gross margin
- pretax margin
- sales to total cash
- percentage change in total assets
- cash flow to debt
- working capital to total assets

- operating ROA
- repayment of long-term debt to total long-term debt
- cash dividend to cash flows

Subsequent studies have also demonstrated the use of ratios in evaluation of equity investments and valuation. Lev and Thiagarajan (1993) examined fundamental financial variables used by analysts to assess whether they are useful in security valuation. They found that fundamental variables add about 70 percent to the explanatory power of earnings alone in predicting excess returns (stock returns in excess of those expected). The fundamental variables they found useful included percentage changes in inventory and receivables relative to sales, gross margin, sales per employee, and the change in bad debts relative to the change in accounts receivable, among others. Abarbanell and Bushee (1997) found some of the same variables useful in predicting future accounting earnings. Abarbanell and Bushee (1998) devised an investment strategy using these same variables and found that they can generate excess returns under this strategy.

Piotroski (2000) used financial ratios to supplement a value investing strategy and found that he can generate significant excess returns. Variables used by Piotroski include ROA, cash flow ROA, change in ROA, change in leverage, change in liquidity, change in gross margin, and change in inventory turnover.

This research shows that in addition to being useful in evaluating the past performance of a company, ratios can be useful in predicting future earnings and equity returns.

6 CREDIT ANALYSIS

Credit risk is the risk of loss caused by a counterparty's or debtor's failure to make a promised payment. For example, credit risk with respect to a bond is the risk that the obligor (the issuer of the bond) is not able to pay interest and principal according to the terms of the bond indenture (contract). Credit analysis is the evaluation of credit risk.

Approaches to credit analysis vary and, as with all financial analysis, depend on the purpose of the analysis and the context in which it is done. Credit analysis for specific types of debt (e.g., acquisition financing and other highly leveraged financing) often involves projections of period-by-period cash flows similar to projections made by equity analysts. Whereas the equity analyst may discount projected cash flows to determine the value of the company's equity, a credit analyst would use the projected cash flows to assess the likelihood of a company complying with its financial covenants in each period and paying interest and principal as due.[18] The analysis would also include expectations about asset sales and refinancing options open to the company.

Credit analysis may relate to the borrower's credit risk in a particular transaction or to its overall creditworthiness. In assessing overall creditworthiness, one general approach is credit scoring, a statistical analysis of the determinants of credit default.

Another general approach to credit analysis is the credit rating process that is used, for example, by credit rating agencies to assess and communicate the proba-

[18] Financial covenants are clauses in bond indentures relating to the financial condition of the bond issuer.

bility of default by an issuer on its debt obligations (e.g., commercial paper, notes, and bonds). A credit rating can be either long term or short term and is an indication of the rating agency's opinion of the creditworthiness of a debt issuer with respect to a specific debt security or other obligation. Where a company has no debt outstanding, a rating agency can also provide an issuer credit rating that expresses an opinion of the issuer's overall capacity and willingness to meet its financial obligations. The following sections review research on the use of ratios in credit analysis and the ratios commonly used in credit analysis.

6.1 The Credit Rating Process

The rating process involves both the analysis of a company's financial reports as well as a broad assessment of a company's operations. The credit rating process includes many of the following procedures:[19]

- Meeting with management, typically including the chief financial officer, to discuss, for example, industry outlook, overview of major business segments, financial policies and goals, distinctive accounting practices, capital spending plans, and financial contingency plans.
- Tours of major facilities, time permitting.
- Meeting of a ratings committee where the analyst's recommendations are voted on, after considering factors that include:
  - **Business risk**, including the evaluation of:
    - operating environment
    - industry characteristics (e.g., cyclicality and capital intensity)
    - success factors and areas of vulnerability
    - company's competitive position, including size and diversification
  - Financial risk, including:
    - the evaluation of capital structure, interest coverage, and profitability using ratio analysis
    - the examination of debt covenants
  - Evaluation of management
- Monitoring of publicly distributed ratings—including reconsideration of ratings due to changing conditions.

In assigning credit ratings, rating agencies emphasize the importance of the relationship between a company's business risk profile and its financial risk. "The company's business risk profile determines the level of financial risk appropriate for any rating category."[20]

When analyzing financial ratios, rating agencies normally investigate deviations of ratios from the median ratios of the universe of companies for which such ratios have been calculated and also use the median ratings as an indicator for the ratings grade given to a specific debt issuer. This so-called universe of rated companies changes constantly, and any calculations are obviously affected by economic factors as well as by mergers and acquisitions. International ratings include the influence of country and economic risk factors. Exhibit 16 presents

[19] Based on Standard & Poor's Corporate Ratings Criteria (2006).

[20] Standard & Poor's Corporate Ratings Criteria (2006), p. 23.

EXHIBIT 16 Selected Credit Ratios Used by Standard & Poor's

Credit Ratio	Numerator[a]	Denominator[b]
EBIT interest coverage	EBIT	Gross interest (prior to deductions for capitalized interest or interest income)
EBITDA interest coverage	EBITDA	Gross interest (prior to deductions for capitalized interest or interest income)
Funds from operations to total debt	FFO (net income adjusted for non-cash items)[c]	Total debt
Free operating cash flow to total debt	CFO (adjusted) less capital expenditures[d]	Total debt
Total debt to EBITDA	Total debt	EBITDA
Return on capital	EBIT	Capital = Average equity (common and preferred stock) and short-term portions of debt, noncurrent deferred taxes, minority interest
Total debt to total debt plus equity	Total debt	Total debt plus equity

Source: Based on data from Standard & Poor's Corporate Ratings Criteria 2006, p. 43.

[a] Emphasis is on earnings from *continuing* operations.

[b] Note that both the numerator and denominator definitions are adjusted from ratio to ratio and may not correspond to the definitions used in this reading.

[c] FFO = funds from operations.

[d] CFO = cash flow from operations.

key financial ratios used by Standard & Poor's in evaluating industrial companies. Note that before calculating ratios, rating agencies make certain adjustments to reported financials such as adjusting debt to include off-balance sheet debt in a company's total debt.

6.2 Research on Ratios in Credit Analysis

A great deal of academic and practitioner research has focused on determining which ratios are useful in assessing the credit risk of a company, including the risk of bankruptcy.

One of the earliest studies examined individual ratios to assess their ability to predict failure of a company up to five years in advance. Beaver (1967) found that six ratios could correctly predict company failure one year in advance 90 percent of the time and five years in advance at least 65 percent of the time. The ratios found effective by Beaver were cash flow to total debt, ROA, total debt to total assets, working capital to total assets, the current ratio, and the no-credit interval ratio (the length of time a company could go without borrowing).

Altman (1968) and Altman, Haldeman, and Narayanan (1977) found that financial ratios could be combined in an effective model for predicting bankruptcy. Altman's initial work involved creation of a *Z*-score that was able to correctly predict financial distress. The *Z*-score was computed as

$$\begin{aligned} Z = & \ 1.2 \times (\text{Current assets} - \text{Current liabilities})/\text{Total assets} \\ & + 1.4 \times (\text{Retained earnings}/\text{Total assets}) \\ & + 3.3 \times (\text{EBIT}/\text{Total assets}) \\ & + 0.6 \times (\text{Market value of stock}/\text{Book value of liabilities}) \\ & + 1.0 \times (\text{Sales}/\text{Total assets}) \end{aligned}$$

In his initial study, a *Z*-score of lower than 1.81 predicted failure, and the model was able to accurately classify 95 percent of companies studied into a failure group and a nonfailure group. The original model was designed for manufacturing companies. Subsequent refinements to the models allow for other company types and time periods. Generally, the variables found to be useful in prediction include profitability ratios, coverage ratios, liquidity ratios, capitalization ratios, and earnings variability (Altman 2000).

Similar research has been performed on the ability of ratios to predict bond ratings and bond yields. For example, Ederington, Yawtiz, and Roberts (1987) found that a small number of variables (total assets, interest coverage, leverage, variability of coverage, and subordination status) were effective in explaining bond yields. Similarly, Ederington (1986) found that nine variables in combination could correctly classify more than 70 percent of bond ratings. These variables included ROA, long-term debt to assets, interest coverage, cash flow to debt, variability of coverage and cash flow, total assets, and subordination status. These studies have shown that ratios are effective in evaluating credit risk, bond yields, and bond ratings.

BUSINESS AND GEOGRAPHIC SEGMENTS 7

Analysts often need to evaluate the performance underlying business segments (subsidiary companies, operating units, or simply operations in different geographic areas) to understand in detail the company as a whole. Unfortunately, companies are not required to provide full financial statements for segments for which all of the traditional ratios can be computed. Publicly traded companies are required to provide limited segment information under both IFRS and U.S. GAAP.

7.1 IAS 14 Requirements

Under IAS 14 (Segment Reporting), disclosures are required for reportable segments. U.S. GAAP requirements are similar to IFRS but less detailed. One noticeable omission under U.S. GAAP is the disclosure of segment liabilities.

A reportable segment is defined as a business or geographical segment where both of the following apply:

- the majority (greater than 50 percent) of its revenue is earned externally; and
- its income from sales, segment result, or assets is greater than or equal to 10 percent of the appropriate total amount of all segments.

A business segment is a distinguishable component of a company that is engaged in providing an individual product or service or a group of related products or services and that is subject to risks and returns that are different from those of other business segments. A geographical segment is a distinguishable component of a company that is engaged in providing products or services within a particular economic environment.

Different business and geographical segments should be identified. A company's business and geographical segments for external reporting purposes should be those organizational units for which information is reported to the board of directors and to the chief executive officer. If a company's internal organizational and management structure and its system of internal financial reporting to the board of directors and the chief executive officer are not based on individual products, services, groups of related products or services, nor on geography, the directors and management of the company should choose either business segments or geographical segments as the company's primary segment reporting format, based on their assessment of which type of segment reflects the primary source of the company's risks and returns. Under this standard, most entities would identify their business and geographical segments as the organizational units for which information is reported to the nonexecutive board of directors and senior management.

If the total revenue from external customers for all reportable segments combined is less than 75 percent of the total company revenue, additional reportable segments should be identified until the 75 percent level is reached. Small segments might be combined as one if they share a substantial number of factors that define a business or geographical segment, or they might be combined with a similar significant reportable segment. If they are not separately reported or combined, they are included as an unallocated reconciling item.

The company must identify a primary segment reporting format (either business or geographical) with the other segment used for the secondary reporting format. The dominant source and nature of risks and returns govern whether a company's primary segment reporting format will be its business segments or its geographical segments. The company's internal organization and management structure, and its system of internal financial reporting to the board of directors and the chief executive officer, are normally the basis for identifying the predominant source and nature of risks and differing rates of return facing the company.

For each primary segment, the following should be disclosed:

- segment revenue, distinguishing between revenue to external customers and revenue from other segments
- segment result (segment revenue minus segment expenses)
- carrying amount of segment assets
- segment liabilities
- cost of property, plant, and equipment, and intangible assets acquired
- depreciation and amortization expense
- other noncash expenses
- share of the net profit or loss of an investment accounted for under the equity method
- reconciliation between the information of reportable segments and the consolidated financial statements in terms of segment revenue, result, assets, and liabilities

For each secondary segment, the following should be disclosed:

- revenue from external customers
- carrying amount of segment assets
- cost of property, plant, and equipment, and intangible assets acquired

Other required disclosures are as follows:

- revenue of any segment whereby the external revenue of the segment is greater than or equal to 10 percent of company revenue but that is not a reportable segment (because a majority of its revenue is from internal transfers)
- basis of pricing intersegment transfers
- changes in segment accounting policies
- types of products and services in each business segment
- composition of each geographical segment

7.2 Segment Ratios

Based on the limited segment information that companies are required to present, a variety of useful ratios can be computed, as shown in Exhibit 17.

EXHIBIT 17 Definitions of Segment Ratios

Segment Ratios	Numerator	Denominator
Segment margin	Segment profit (loss)	Segment revenue
Segment turnover	Segment revenue	Segment assets
Segment ROA	Segment profit (loss)	Segment assets
Segment debt ratio	Segment liabilities	Segment assets

The **segment margin** measures the operating profitability of the segment relative to revenues, whereas the **segment ROA** measures the operating profitability relative to assets. **Segment turnover** measures the overall efficiency of the segment: how much revenue is generated per unit of assets. The **segment debt ratio** examines the level of liabilities (hence solvency) of the segment. Example 15 demonstrates the evaluation of segment ratios.

EXAMPLE 15

The Evaluation of Segment Ratios

The following information relates to the business segments of Nokia for 2004 in millions of euros. Evaluate the performance of the segments using the segment margin, segment ROA, and segment turnover.

	Revenue	Operating Profit	Segment Assets
Mobile phones	18,429	3,768	3,758
Multimedia	3,636	179	787
Enterprise solutions	806	−199	210
Networks	6,367	878	3,055

	Segment Margin	Segment ROA	Segment Turnover
Mobile phones	20.45%	100.27%	4.90
Multimedia	4.92%	22.74%	4.62
Enterprise solutions	−24.69%	−94.76%	3.84
Networks	13.79%	28.74%	2.08

Solution: Mobile Phones is the best performing segment with the highest segment margin, segment ROA, and efficiency. Networks is the second highest in terms of profitability but lowest in efficiency (the ability to generate revenue from assets). Enterprise Solutions is not profitable; however, it is the smallest segment and may still be in the development stage.

8 MODEL BUILDING AND FORECASTING

Analysts often need to forecast future financial performance. For example, EPS forecasts of analysts are widely followed by Wall Street. Analysts use data about the economy, industry, and company in arriving at a company's forecast. The results of an analyst's financial analysis, including common-size and ratio analysis, are integral to this process, along with the judgment of the analysts.

Based upon forecasts of growth and expected relationships among the financial statement data, the analyst can build a model (sometimes referred to as an "earnings model") to forecast future performance. In addition to budgets, pro forma financial statements are widely used in financial forecasting within companies, especially for use by senior executives and boards of directors. Last but not least, these budgets and forecasts are also used in presentations to credit analysts and others in obtaining external financing.

For example, based on a revenue forecast, an analyst may budget expenses based on expected common-size data. Forecasts of balance sheet and cash flow statements can be derived from expected ratio data, such as DSO. Forecasts are not limited to a single point estimate but should involve a range of possibilities. This can involve several techniques:

- **Sensitivity analysis**: Also known as "what if" analysis, sensitivity analysis shows the range of possible outcomes as specific assumptions are changed; this could, in turn, influence financing needs or investment in fixed assets.

- **Scenario analysis**: Scenario analysis shows the changes in key financial quantities that result from given (economic) events, such as the loss of customers, the loss of a supply source, or a catastrophic event. If the list of events is mutually exclusive and exhaustive and the events can be assigned probabilities, the analyst can evaluate not only the range of outcomes but also standard statistical measures such as the mean and median value for various quantities of interest.
- **Simulation**: This is computer-generated sensitivity or scenario analysis based on probability models for the factors that drive outcomes. Each event or possible outcome is assigned a probability. Multiple scenarios are then run using the probability factors assigned to the possible values of a variable.

SUMMARY

Financial analysis techniques, including common-size and ratio analysis, are useful in summarizing financial reporting data and evaluating the performance and financial position of a company. The results of financial analysis techniques provide important inputs into security valuation. Key facets of financial analysis include the following:

- Common-size financial statements and financial ratios remove the effect of size, allowing comparisons of a company with peer companies (cross-sectional analysis) and comparison of a company's results over time (trend or time-series analysis).
- Activity ratios measure the efficiency of a company's operations, such as collection of receivables or management of inventory. Major activity ratios include inventory turnover, days of inventory on hand, receivables turnover, days of sales outstanding, payables turnover, number of days of payables, working capital turnover, fixed asset turnover, and total asset turnover.
- Liquidity ratios measure the ability of a company to meet short-term obligations. Major liquidity ratios include the current ratio, quick ratio, cash ratio, and defensive interval ratio.
- Solvency ratios measure the ability of a company to meet long-term obligations. Major solvency ratios include debt ratios (including the debt-to-assets ratio, debt-to-capital ratio, debt-to-equity ratio, and financial leverage ratio) and coverage ratios (including interest coverage and fixed charge coverage).
- Profitability ratios measure the ability of a company to generate profits from revenue and assets. Major profitability ratios include return on sales ratios (including gross profit margin, operating profit margin, pretax margin, and net profit margin) and return on investment ratios (including operating ROA, ROA, ROE, and return on common equity).
- Ratios can also be combined and evaluated as a group to better understand how they fit together and how efficiency and leverage are tied to profitability.
- ROE can be analyzed as the product of the net profit margin, asset turnover, and financial leverage.
- Ratio analysis is useful in the selection and valuation of debt and equity securities and is a part of the credit rating process.
- Ratios can also be computed for business segments to evaluate how units within a business are doing.
- The results of financial analysis provide valuable inputs into forecasts of future earnings and cash flow.

PRACTICE PROBLEMS FOR READING 41

1. Comparison of a company's financial results to other peer companies for the same time period is called
   A. credit analysis.
   B. horizontal analysis.
   C. time-series analysis.
   D. cross-sectional analysis.
2. In order to assess a company's ability to fulfill its long-term obligations, an analyst would *most likely* examine
   A. activity ratios.
   B. liquidity ratios.
   C. solvency ratios.
   D. profitability ratios.
3. Which ratio would a company *most likely* use to measure its ability to meet short-term obligations?
   A. Current ratio.
   B. Payables turnover.
   C. Gross profit margin.
   D. Days of inventory on hand.
4. Which of the following ratios would be *most useful* in determining a company's ability to cover its debt payments?
   A. ROA.
   B. Total asset turnover.
   C. Receivables turnover.
   D. Fixed charge coverage.
5. John Chan is interested in assessing both the efficiency and liquidity of Spherion PLC. Chan has collected the following data for Spherion:

	2005	2004	2003
Days of inventory on hand	32	34	40
Days sales outstanding	28	25	23
Number of days of payables	40	35	35

   Based on this data, what is Chan *least likely* to conclude?
   A. Inventory management has contributed to improved liquidity.
   B. Management of payables has contributed to improved liquidity.
   C. Management of receivables has contributed to improved liquidity.
   D. The company's cash conversion cycle has decreased, indicating improved liquidity.

6. Marcus Lee is examining the solvency of Apex Manufacturing and has collected the following data (in millions of euros):

	2005	2004	2003
Total debt	€2,000	€1,900	€1,750
Total equity	€4,000	€4,500	€5,000

Which of the following would be the *most appropriate* conclusion for Lee?

A. The company is becoming increasingly less solvent, as evidenced by the increase in its debt-to-equity ratio from 0.35 to 0.50 from 2003 to 2005.

B. The company is becoming less liquid, as evidenced by the increase in its debt-to-equity ratio from 0.35 to 0.50 from 2003 to 2005.

C. The company is becoming increasingly more liquid, as evidenced by the increase in its debt-to-equity ratio from 0.35 to 0.50 from 2003 to 2005.

D. The company is becoming increasingly more solvent, as evidenced by the increase in its debt-to-equity ratio from 0.35 to 0.50 from 2003 to 2005.

7. With regard to the data in Problem 6, what would be a reasonable explanation of these financial results?

A. The decline in the company's equity results from a decline in the market value of this company's common shares.

B. The increase in the company's debt of €250 from 2003 to 2005 indicates that lenders are viewing the company as increasingly creditworthy.

C. The increase in the company's debt indicates that the company refinanced its short-term debt with long-term debt to lock-in low interest rates.

D. The decline in the company's equity indicates that the company may be incurring losses on its operations, paying dividends greater than income, and/or repurchasing shares.

8. Linda Roper observes a decrease in a company's inventory turnover. Which of the following would explain this trend?

A. The company installed a new inventory management system, allowing more efficient inventory management.

B. Due to problems with obsolescent inventory last year, the company wrote off a large amount of its inventory at the beginning of the period.

C. Due to problems with obsolescent inventory last year, the company has renegotiated its supplier contracts, allowing purchases to better track demand.

D. The company installed a new inventory management system but experienced some operational difficulties resulting in duplicate orders being placed with suppliers.

9. Which of the following would best explain an increase in receivables turnover?

A. The company adopted new credit policies last year and began offering credit to customers with weak credit histories.

B. Due to problems with an error in its old credit scoring system, the company had accumulated a substantial amount of uncollectible accounts and wrote off a large amount of its receivables.

C. To match the terms offered by its closest competitor, the company adopted new payment terms now requiring net payment within 30 days rather than 15 days, which had been its previous requirement.

D. The company's former collections manager had excessively stringent approaches to collecting accounts receivable, resulting in deteriorating customer relationships; therefore, the manager was replaced last year by a manager with a more lenient approach.

10. Brown Corporation had an average days sales outstanding of 19 days in 2005. Brown wants to decrease its collection period in 2006 to match the industry average of 15 days. Credit sales in 2005 were \$300 million, and Brown expects credit sales to increase to \$390 million in 2006. To achieve Brown's goal of decreasing the collection period, the change in the average accounts receivable balance from 2005 to 2006 that must occur is *closest* to

A. −\$1.22 million.

B. −\$0.42 million.

C. \$0.42 million.

D. \$1.22 million.

11. An analyst gathered the following data for a company:

	2003	2004	2005
ROE	19.8%	20.0%	22.0%
Return on total assets	8.1%	8.0%	7.9%
Total asset turnover	2.0	2.0	2.1

Based only on the information above, the *most* appropriate conclusion is that, over the period 2003 to 2005, the company's

A. net profit margin and financial leverage has decreased.

B. net profit margin and financial leverage has increased.

C. net profit margin has decreased but its financial leverage has increased.

D. net profit margin has increased but its financial leverage has decreased.

12. A decomposition of ROE for Integra SA is as follows:

	2005	2004
ROE	18.90%	18.90%
Tax burden	0.70	0.75
Interest burden	0.90	0.90
EBIT margin	10.00%	10.00%
Asset turnover	1.50	1.40
Leverage	2.00	2.00

Which of the following choices *best* describes reasonable conclusions an analyst might make based on this ROE decomposition?

A. Profitability and the liquidity position both improved in 2005.

B. The higher average tax rate in 2005 offset the improvement in profitability, leaving ROE unchanged.

C. The higher average tax rate in 2005 offset the improvement in efficiency, leaving ROE unchanged.

D. The lower average tax rate in 2005 offset the deterioration in efficiency, leaving ROE unchanged.

13. A decomposition of ROE for Company A and Company B is as follows:

	Company A		Company B	
	2005	2004	2005	2004
ROE	26.46%	18.90%	26.33%	18.90%
Tax burden	0.7	0.75	0.75	0.75
Interest burden	0.9	0.9	0.9	0.9
EBIT margin	7.00%	10.00%	13.00%	10.00%
Asset turnover	1.5	1.4	1.5	1.4
Leverage	4	2	2	2

Which of the following choices best describes reasonable conclusions an analyst might make based on this ROE decomposition?

A. Company A's ROE is higher than Company B's in 2005, but the difference between the two companies' ROE is very small and was mainly the result of Company A's increase in its financial leverage.

B. Company A's ROE is higher than Company B's in 2005, apparently reflecting a strategic shift by Company A to a product mix with higher profit margins.

C. Company A's ROE is higher than Company B's in 2005, which suggests that Company A may have purchased new, more efficient equipment.

D. Company A's ROE is higher than Company B's in 2005, and this reflects more efficient inventory management by Company A.

14. Rent-A-Center reported the following information related to total debt and shareholders' equity in its 2003 annual report.

	As of 31 December				
(in $ thousands)	**2003**	**2002**	**2001**	**2000**	**1999**
Total debt	698,000	521,330	702,506	741,051	847,160
Stockholders' equity	794,830	842,400	405,378	309,371	206,690

What would an analyst's most appropriate conclusion be based on this data?

A. The company's solvency has improved from 1999 to 2002.

B. The company's solvency has improved from 2002 to 2003.

C. The data suggest the company increased debt in 2002.

D. The data suggest the company has been profitable and that the total income and new share issuance of this company has been about equal to the amount of dividend payments and share repurchases made by the company from 1999 to 2003.

15. Frank Collins observes the following data for two companies:

	Company A	**Company B**
Revenue	$4,500	$6,000
Net income	$50	$1,000
Current assets	$40,000	$60,000
Total assets	$100,000	$700,000
Current liabilities	$10,000	$50,000
Total debt	$60,000	$150,000
Shareholders' equity	$30,000	$500,000

Which of the following choices best describes reasonable conclusions that Collins might make about the two companies' ability to pay their current and long-term obligations?

A. Company A's current ratio of 4.0x indicates it is more liquid than Company B, whose current ratio is only 1.2x, but Company B is more solvent, as indicated by its lower debt-to-equity ratio.

B. Company A's current ratio of 25 percent indicates it is less liquid than Company B, whose current ratio is 83 percent, and Company A is also less solvent, as indicated by a debt-to-equity ratio of 200 percent compared with Company B's debt-to-equity ratio of only 30 percent.

C. Company A's current ratio of 4.0x indicates it is more liquid than Company B, whose current ratio is only 1.2x, and Company A is also more solvent, as indicated by a debt-to-equity ratio of 200 percent compared with Company B's debt-to-equity ratio of only 30 percent.

D. Company A's current ratio of 25 percent indicates it is less liquid than Company B, whose current ratio is 83 percent, but Company A is more solvent, as indicated by a debt-to-equity ratio of 200 percent compared with Company B's debt-to-equity ratio of only 30 percent.

The following information relates to Questions 16–19

The data below appear in the five-year summary of a major international company. A business combination with another major manufacturer took place in 2003. The term "turnover" in this financial data is a synonym for revenue.

	2000	2001	2002	2003	2004
Financial statements	GBP m	GBP m	GBP m	GBP m	GBP m
Income statements					
Turnover (i.e., revenue)	4,390	3,624	3,717	8,167	11,366
Profit before interest and taxation (EBIT)	844	700	704	933	1,579
Net interest payable	−80	−54	−98	−163	−188
Taxation	−186	−195	−208	−349	−579
Minorities	−94	−99	−105	−125	−167
Profit for the year	484	352	293	296	645
Balance sheets					
Fixed assets	3,510	3,667	4,758	10,431	11,483
Current asset investments, cash at bank and in hand	316	218	290	561	682
Other current assets	558	514	643	1,258	1,634
Total assets	4,384	4,399	5,691	12,250	13,799
Interest bearing debt (long term)	−602	−1,053	−1,535	−3,523	−3,707
Other creditors and provisions (current)	−1,223	−1,054	−1,102	−2,377	−3,108
Total liabilities	−1,825	−2,107	−2,637	−5,900	−6,815
Net assets	2,559	2,292	3,054	6,350	6,984
Shareholders' funds	2,161	2,006	2,309	5,572	6,165
Equity minority interests	398	286	745	778	819
Capital employed	2,559	2,292	3,054	6,350	6,984
Cash flow					
Working capital movements	−53	5	71	85	107
Net cash inflow from operating activities	864	859	975	1,568	2,292

16. The company's total assets at year-end 1999 were GBP 3,500 million. Which of the following choices *best* describes reasonable conclusions an analyst might make about the company's efficiency?

A. Comparing 2004 with 2000, the company's efficiency improved, as indicated by a total asset turnover ratio of 0.86 compared with 0.64.

B. Comparing 2004 with 2000, the company's efficiency deteriorated, as indicated by its current ratio.

C. Comparing 2004 with 2000, the company's efficiency improved, as indicated by the growth in its assets to GBP 13,799 million.

D. Comparing 2004 with 2000, the company's efficiency deteriorated due to asset growth faster than turnover (i.e., revenue) growth.

17. Which of the following choices *best* describes reasonable conclusions an analyst might make about the company's solvency?

A. Comparing 2004 with 2000, the company's solvency improved, as indicated by an increase in its debt-to-assets ratio from 0.14 to 0.27.

B. Comparing 2004 with 2000, the company's solvency deteriorated, as indicated by a decrease in interest coverage from 10.6 to 8.4.

C. Comparing 2004 with 2000, the company's solvency improved, as indicated by the growth in its profits to GBP 645 million.

D. Comparing 2004 with 2000, the company's solvency deteriorated, as indicated by a decrease in its debt-to-equity ratio from 4.2 to 1.9.

18. Which of the following choices *best* describes reasonable conclusions an analyst might make about the company's liquidity?

A. Comparing 2004 with 2000, the company's liquidity improved, as indicated by an increase in its debt-to-assets ratio from 0.14 to 0.27.

B. Comparing 2004 with 2000, the company's liquidity deteriorated, as indicated by a decrease in interest coverage from 10.6 to 8.4.

C. Comparing 2004 with 2000, the company's liquidity improved, as indicated by the growth in its current assets to GBP 2,316 million.

D. Comparing 2004 with 2000, the company's liquidity improved, as indicated by an increase in its current ratio from 0.71 to 0.75.

19. Which of the following choices *best* describes reasonable conclusions an analyst might make about the company's profitability?

A. Comparing 2004 with 2000, the company's profitability improved, as indicated by an increase in its debt-to-assets ratio from 0.14 to 0.27.

B. Comparing 2004 with 2000, the company's profitability deteriorated, as indicated by a decrease in its net profit margin from 11.0 percent to 5.7 percent.

C. Comparing 2004 with 2000, the company's profitability improved, as indicated by the growth in its shareholders' equity to GBP 6,165 million.

D. Comparing 2004 with 2000, the company's profitability deteriorated, as indicated by a decrease in its operating margin from 2.44 to 1.74.

20. In general, a creditor would consider a decrease in which of the following ratios to be positive news?

A. Interest coverage (times interest earned).

B. Debt to total assets.

C. Return on assets.

D. Receivables turnover.

21. Assuming no changes in other variables, which of the following would decrease ROA?

A. A decrease in the effective tax rate.

B. A decrease in interest expense.

C. An increase in net operating margin.

D. An increase in average assets.

22. What does the P/E ratio measure?

A. The "multiple" that the stock market places on a company's EPS.

B. The relationship between dividends and market prices.

C. The earnings for one common share of stock.

D. The percentage of the company's net earnings paid out as dividends.

FINANCIAL STATEMENT ANALYSIS: APPLICATIONS

by Thomas R. Robinson, Hennie van Greuning, Elaine Henry, and Michael A. Broihahn

READING 42

LEARNING OUTCOMES

The candidate should be able to:

a. evaluate a company's past financial performance and explain how a company's strategy is reflected in past financial performance;

b. prepare a basic projection of a company's future net income and cash flow;

c. describe the role of financial statement analysis in assessing the credit quality of a potential debt investment;

d. discuss the use of financial statement analysis in screening for potential equity investments;

e. determine and justify appropriate analyst adjustments to a company's financial statements to facilitate comparison with another company.

THEME

Although certain steps are common to almost all analyses of financial statements, given the variety of purposes and contexts, no single approach is uniformly applicable. This reading examines several basic applications of financial statement analysis.

INTRODUCTION 1

This reading presents several important applications of financial statement analysis. Among the issues we will address are the following:

- What are the key questions to address in evaluating a company's past financial performance?

- How can an analyst approach forecasting a company's future net income and cash flow?
- How can financial statement analysis be used to evaluate the credit quality of a potential fixed-income investment?
- How can financial statement analysis be used to screen for potential equity investments?
- How can differences in accounting methods affect financial ratio comparisons between companies, and what are some adjustments analysts make to reported financials in the interests of comparability?

Prior to undertaking any analysis, an analyst should explore the purpose and context of the analysis because purpose and context guide further decisions about the approach, the tools, the data sources, and the format in which to report results of the analysis, and also suggest which aspects of the analysis are most important. The analyst should then be able to formulate the key questions that the analysis must address. The questions will suggest the data the analyst needs to collect to objectively address the questions. The analyst then processes and analyzes the data to answer these questions. Conclusions and decisions based on the analysis are communicated in a format appropriate to the context, and follow-up is undertaken as required. Although this reading will not formally present applications as a series of steps, the process just described is generally applicable.

Section 2 describes the use of financial statement analysis to evaluate a company's past financial performance, and Section 3 describes basic approaches to projecting a company's future financial performance. Section 4 presents the use of financial statement analysis in assessing the credit quality of a potential debt investment. Section 5 concludes the survey of applications by describing the use of financial statement analysis in screening for potential equity investments. Analysts often encounter situations in which they must make adjustments to a company's reported financial results to increase their accuracy or comparability with the financials of other companies. Section 6 illustrates several typical types of analyst adjustments. A summary of the key points and practice problems in the CFA Institute multiple-choice format conclude the reading.

2 APPLICATION: EVALUATING PAST FINANCIAL PERFORMANCE

Analysts often analyze a company's past financial performance to determine the comparability of companies for a market-based valuation,[1] to provide a basis for

[1] Stowe, Robinson, Pinto, and McLeavey (2002) describe market-based valuation as using price multiples ratios of a stock's market price to some measure of value per share (e.g., price-to-earnings ratios). Although the valuation method may be used independently of an analysis of a company's past financial performance, such an analysis may explain reasons for differences in companies' price multiples.

a forward-looking analysis of the company, or to obtain information for evaluating the company's management.

An evaluation of a company's past performance addresses not only *what* happened (i.e., how the company performed) but also *why* it happened—the causes behind the performance and how the performance reflects the company's strategy. Evaluative judgments assess whether the performance is better or worse, compared with a relevant benchmark such as the company's own historical performance, a competitor's performance, or market expectations. Some of the key analytical questions include:

- How have corporate measures of profitability, efficiency, liquidity, and solvency changed over the period being analyzed? Why?
- How do the level and trend in a company's profitability, efficiency, liquidity, and solvency compare with the corresponding results of other companies in the same industry? What explains any differences?
- What aspects of performance are critical for a company to successfully compete in its industry, and how did the company perform relative to those critical performance aspects?
- What are the company's business model and strategy, and how did they influence the company's performance as reflected, for example, in its sales growth, efficiency, and profitability?

Data available to answer these questions include the company's (and its competitors') financial statements, materials from the company's investor relations department, corporate press releases, and nonfinancial statement regulatory filings, such as proxies. Useful data also include industry information (e.g., from industry surveys, trade publications, and government sources), consumer information (e.g., from consumer satisfaction surveys), and information that is gathered by the analyst firsthand (e.g., through on-site visits). Processing the data will typically involve creating common-size financial statements, calculating financial ratios, and reviewing or calculating industry-specific metrics. Example 1 illustrates the effects of strategy on performance and the use of basic economic reasoning in interpreting results.

EXAMPLE 1

A Change in Strategy Reflected in a Change in Financial Performance

In analyzing the historical performance of Motorola (NYSE: MOT) as of the beginning of 2006, an analyst might refer to the information presented in Exhibit 1. Panel A presents selected data for Motorola from 2003 to 2005. Panel B presents an excerpt from the segment footnote, giving data for Motorola's mobile device business segment (the segment that manufactures and sells cellular phones). Panel C presents excerpts from the Management Discussion and Analysis (MD&A) describing the results of the segment.

Looking back to 1996, Motorola was the market leader with its StarTAC cellular phone, but since 1998, Nokia had become the largest player in the global mobile phone market. "The mood inside Motorola was grim in early 2003. Nokia, whose 'candy bar' phone designs were all the rage had snatched Motorola's No. 1 worldwide market share" (*Fortune*, 12 June 2006, p. 126).

Following the arrival of new CEO Edward Zander at the end of 2003, Motorola radically revamped its strategy for new products: "Design leads, and engineering follows" (*Business Week*, 8 August 2005, p. 68). Motorola's strategy thereafter evolved to include a strong consumer marketing orientation to complement its historically strong technological position. The company launched 60 new products in 2004, an important one of which was the RAZR cellular phone with an ultra-thin profile that served to differentiate it from competitors' offerings. The successful introduction of new products in 2004 enabled the company to gain market share and increase profitability.

The changes at Motorola extended beyond the product strategy. An article in *Barron's* noted that in addition to the shift in product strategy, "Motorola has undergone a financial overhaul. . . The company has reduced the percentage of working capital to sales to less than 12 percent from about 22 percent, a sign of increased efficiency" (*Barron's* 25 July 2005, p. 23).

EXHIBIT 1 Selected Data for Motorola (Years Ended 31 December)

Panel A: Data for Motorola (dollars in millions)	2005	2004	2003
Net sales	$36,843	$31,323	$23,155
Gross margin	11,777	10,354	7,503
Operating earnings	4,696	3,132	1,273
Total assets	35,649	30,922	26,809

Panel B: Data for Motorola's Mobile Device Segment from Segment Footnote (dollars in millions)	2005	2004	2003
Net sales	21,455	17,108	11,238
Operating earnings	2,198	1,728	511
Assets	7,548	5,442	3,900

Panel C: Excerpt from MD&A

2004 "Our wireless handset business had a very strong year in 2004, reflected by a 53% increase in net sales, a 257% increase in operating earnings and increased market share. The increase in net sales was driven by an increase in unit shipments, which increased 39% in 2004 compared to 2003, and improved ASP [average selling price], which increased 15% in 2004 compared to 2003. . . This increase in net sales, accompanied by process improvements in the supply chain and benefits from ongoing

(Exhibit continued on next page . . .)

EXHIBIT 1 (continued)

cost reduction activities resulted in increased gross margin, which drove the increase in overall operating earnings for the business. . . ."

2005 "Net sales increased by $4.3 billion, or 25%, to $21.5 billion and operating earnings increased by 27% to $2.2 billion. We shipped 146 million handsets in 2005, up 40% from 2004. . . The increase in unit shipments was attributed to an increase in the size of the total market and a gain in the segment's market share. The gain in market share reflected strong demand for GSM handsets and consumers' desire for the segment's compelling products that combine innovative style leading technology. The segment had increased net sales in all regions of the world as a result of an improved product portfolio, strong market growth in emerging markets, and high replacement sales in more mature markets. Average selling price ("ASP") decreased approximately 10% compared to 2004, driven primarily by a higher percentage of lower-tier, lower-priced handsets in the overall sales mix."

Source: Motorola's 2005 10-K filed 2 March 2006 and 2004 10-K filed 4 March 2005.

Using the information provided, address the following:

1. Typically, products that are differentiated either through recognizable brand names, proprietary technology, or both can be sold at a higher price than commodity products.
   - **A.** In general, would the selling prices of differentiated products be more directly reflected in a company's operating profit margin or gross profit margin?
   - **B.** Does Motorola's segment footnote (Panel B) reflect a successful differentiation strategy in its mobile devices business?
   - **C.** Based on the excerpts from Motorola's MD&A (Panel C), compare and contrast the drivers of the growth in sales in Motorola's mobile device business in 2005 with the drivers in 2004.
2. The *Barron's* article refers to working capital as a percentage of sales, an indicator of efficiency.
   - **A.** In general, what other ratios indicate a company's efficiency?
   - **B.** Does the financial data for Motorola shown in this example reflect increased efficiency?

Solution to 1:

A. Sales of differentiated products at premium prices would generally be reflected more directly in the gross profit margin, increasing it, all else equal. The effect of premium pricing generally would also be reflected in a higher operating margin. However, expenditures on advertising and/or research in support of differentiating features mean that the effect on operating profit margins is often weaker than the effect on gross profit margins.

B. Although Motorola's segment footnote does not include information on gross margins by segment, it does include sufficient information for calculating operating profit margins, which should also be positively correlated with premium pricing. Dividing operating earnings by net sales, we find that operating margins in the mobile devices business increased from 4.5 percent ($511/11,238) in 2003 to 10.1 percent ($1,728/17,108) in 2004 and 10.2 percent ($2,198/21,455) in 2005. The data indicate successful results from the differentiation strategy in 2004, but no further meaningful improvement in 2005.

C. In both years, the MD&A attributes sales growth to an increase in Motorola's share of the handset market. The 2005 MD&A explicitly mentions growth of the total wireless handset market as another factor in sales growth for that year. The 2004 results benefited from both a 39 percent increase in units sales (compared with 2003) and a 15 percent increase in ASP. The sources of growth shifted somewhat from 2004 to 2005. Lower-tier, lower-price handsets became a larger part of Motorola's product mix in 2005, and ASP declined by 10 percent. Because sales grew by 25.4 percent [= (21,455 − 17,108)/17,108] in 2005, it is clear, however, that the growth in handset unit sales more than overcame the decline in ASP.

Solution to 2:

A. Other ratios that indicate a company's efficiency include asset turnover, fixed asset turnover, working capital turnover, receivables turnover, and inventory turnover. In addition, efficiency is indicated by days of inventory on hand, days of sales outstanding, and days of payables.

B. Yes, they do indicate increased efficiency. The data given permit the calculation of one efficiency ratio, total asset turnover. Motorola's total asset turnover improved from 0.864 (23,155/26,809) for 2003 to 1.013 (31,323/30,922) for 2004 to 1.033 (36,843/35,649) for 2005.

In calculating financial statement ratios, an analyst needs to be aware of the potential impact of companies reporting under different accounting standards, such as U.S. generally accepted accounting principles (U.S. GAAP) and international financial reporting standards (IFRS). Furthermore, even within a given set of accounting standards, companies still have discretion to choose among acceptable methods and also must make certain estimates even when applying the same method. Therefore, it may be useful to make selected adjustments to a company's financial statement data in order to facilitate comparisons with other companies or with the industry overall. Examples of such analyst adjustments will be discussed in Section 6. Example 2 illustrates how differences in accounting standards can affect financial ratio comparisons.

EXAMPLE 2

The Effect of U.S. GAAP versus IFRS on ROE Comparisons

Despite convergence between U.S. GAAP and IFRS, differences remain. Non-U.S. companies that use IFRS (or any other acceptable body of accounting standards) and file with the U.S. Securities and Exchange Commission (because their shares or depositary receipts based on their shares trade in the United States) are required to reconcile their net income and shareholders' equity accounts to U.S. GAAP. In comparing the historical performance of Motorola and Nokia, you have prepared Exhibit 2 to evaluate whether the difference in accounting standards affects the comparison of the two companies' return on equity (ROE). Panel A presents selected data for Motorola for 2004 and 2005, and Panel B presents data for Nokia under IFRS and under U.S. GAAP.

EXHIBIT 2 Data for Motorola and Nokia for a ROE Calculation (Years Ended 31 December)

Panel A: Selected Data for Motorola (dollars in millions)	2005	2004
U.S. GAAP		
Net income	4,599	2,191
Shareholders' equity	16,676	13,331

Panel B: Selected Data for Nokia Corporation (euros in millions)	2005	2004
IFRS		
Net income	3,616	3,192
Shareholders' equity	12,155	14,231
U.S. GAAP		
Net income	3,582	3,343
Shareholders' equity	12,558	14,576

Source: Motorola's 10-K and Nokia's 20-F, both filed 2 March 2006.

Does the difference in accounting standards affect the ROE comparison?

Solution: Motorola's return on average shareholders' equity for 2005 at 30.7 percent [net income of $4,599 divided by average shareholders' equity, calculated as ($16,676 + $13,331)/2] was higher than Nokia's, whether calculated under IFRS or U.S. GAAP. The difference in accounting standards does *not* affect the conclusion, though it does affect the magnitude of the difference in profitability. Under IFRS, Nokia's ROE was 27.4 percent [net income of €3,616 divided by average shareholders' equity, calculated as (€12,155+ €14,231)/2]. Under U.S. GAAP, Nokia's ROE was slightly lower at 26.4 percent [net income of €3,582 divided by average shareholders' equity, calculated as (€12,558 + €14,576)/2]. Results of the calculations are summarized in the following table:

Panel A: Motorola	
U.S. GAAP	
Return on average shareholders' equity	30.7%
Panel B: Nokia Corporation	
IFRS	
Return on average shareholders' equity	27.4%
U.S. GAAP	
Return on average shareholders' equity	26.4%

In Example 2, Nokia's ROE for 2005 under IFRS and U.S. GAAP differed only slightly. In some cases, the effect of applying IFRS and U.S. GAAP on ROE and other profitability ratios can be substantial. For example, the Swiss drug company Novartis, which has undertaken historically numerous business combinations, shows a return on average shareholders' equity of 19.0 percent in 2005 under IFRS compared with 13.7 percent under U.S. GAAP; the differences are largely due to differences in accounting for business combinations.[2] Research indicates that for most non-U.S. companies filing with the U.S. Securities and Exchange Commission (SEC), differences between U.S. GAAP and home-country GAAP net income average around 1 to 2 percent of market value of equity, but with large variation.[3]

Comparison of the levels and trends in the company's performance provide information for statements about *how* the company performed. The company's management presents its view about causes underlying its performance in the MD&A section of its annual report and during periodic conference calls. To gain additional understanding on the causes underlying a company's performance, an analyst can review industry information or seek additional sources of information.

The results of an analysis of past performance provide a basis for reaching conclusions and making recommendations. For example, an analysis undertaken as the basis for a forward-looking study might result in conclusions about whether a company's future performance is likely to reflect continuation of recent historical trends or not. As another example, an analysis to support a market-based valuation of a company might focus on whether the company's better (worse) profitability and growth outlook compared with the peer group median justify its relatively high (low) valuation, as judged by market multiples such as price-to-earnings ratio (P/E), market-to-book ratio (MV/BV), and total invested capital to

[2] Henry and Yang (2006).

[3] Pownall and Schipper (1999). "Home country GAAP" can refer to IFRS in addition to non-IFRS GAAP other than U.S. GAAP.

earnings before interest, taxes, depreciation, and amortization (TIC/EBITDA).[4] As another example, an analysis undertaken as a component of an evaluation of the company's management might result in conclusions about whether the company has grown as fast as another company, or as the industry overall, and whether the company has maintained profitability while growing.

3 APPLICATION: PROJECTING FUTURE FINANCIAL PERFORMANCE

In some cases, evaluating a company's past performance provides a basis for forward-looking analyses. An evaluation of a company's environment and history may persuade the analyst that historical data constitute a valid basis for such analyses and that the analyst's projections may be based on the continuance of past trends, perhaps with some adjustments. Alternatively, in the case of a major acquisition or divestiture, or for a start-up company, or for a company operating in a volatile industry, past performance may be less relevant to future performance.

Projections of future financial performance are used in determining the value of a company or of its equity component. Projections of future financial performance are also used in credit analysis—particularly in project finance or acquisition finance—to determine whether a company's cash flows will be adequate to pay the interest and principal on its debt and to evaluate whether a company will likely be in compliance with its financial covenants.

Sources of data for analysts' projections include some or all of the following: the company's projections; the company's previous financial statements; industry structure and outlook; and macroeconomic forecasts.

Projections of a company's near-term performance may be used as an input to market-based valuation (valuation based on price multiples). Such projections may involve projecting next years' sales and using the common-size income statement to project major expense items or particular margins on sales (e.g., gross profit margin or operating profit margin). More complex projections of a company's future performance involve developing a more detailed analysis of components across multiple periods—for example, projections of sales and gross margin by product line, projection of operating expenses based on historical patterns, and projection of interest expense based on requisite debt funding, interest rates, and applicable taxes. Furthermore, a projection should include sensitivity analyses related to the major assumptions.

3.1 Projecting Performance: An Input to Market-Based Valuation

One application of financial statement analysis involves projecting a company's near-term performance as an input to market-based valuation. For example, one might project a company's sales and profit margin to estimate earnings per share (EPS) and then apply a projected P/E to establish a target price for a company's stock.

Analysts often take a top-down approach to projecting a company's sales.[5] First, industry sales are projected based on their historical relation with some

[4] **Total invested capital** is the sum of market value of common equity, book value of preferred equity, and face value of debt.

[5] The discussion in this paragraph is indebted to Benninga and Sarig (1997).

macroeconomic indicator or indicators such as real **gross domestic product**. In researching the automobile industry, for example, the analyst may find that the industry's annual domestic unit automobile sales (numbers of cars sold in domestic markets) bears a relation to annual changes in real GDP. Regression analysis is often used in establishing the parameters of such relations. Other factors in projecting sales may include consumer income or tastes, technological developments, and the availability of substitute products or services. After industry sales are projected, a company's market share is projected. Company-level market share projections may be based on historical market share and a forward-looking assessment of the company's competitive position. The company's sales are then estimated as its projected market share multiplied by projected total industry sales.

After developing a sales forecast for a company, an analyst can choose among various methods for forecasting income and cash flow. One decision is the level of detail in forecasts. For example, separate forecasts may be made for individual expense items or for more aggregated expense items, such as total operating expenses. Rather than stating a forecast in terms of expenses, the forecast might be stated in terms of a forecasted profit margin (gross, operating, or net). The net profit margin, in contrast to the gross or operating profit margins, is affected by financial leverage and tax rates, which are subject to managerial and legal/ regulatory revisions; therefore, historical data may sometimes be more relevant for projecting gross or operating margins. Whatever the margin used, the forecasted amount of profit for a given period is the product of the forecasted amount of sales and the forecast of the selected profit margin.

As Example 3 illustrates, for relatively mature companies operating in non-volatile product markets, historical information on operating profit margins can provide a useful starting point for forecasting future operating profits (at least over short forecasting horizons). For a new or relatively volatile business, or one with significant fixed costs (which can magnify the volatility of operating margins), historical operating profit margins are typically less reliable for projecting future margins.

EXAMPLE 3

Using Historical Operating Profit Margins to Forecast Operating Profit

One approach to projecting operating profit is to determine a company's average operating profit margin over the previous three years and apply that margin to a forecast of the company's sales. Consider the following three companies:

- Johnson & Johnson (JNJ). This U.S. health care conglomerate founded in 1887 had 2005 sales of around $50.5 billion from its three main businesses: pharmaceuticals, medical devices and diagnostics, and consumer products.
- BHP Billiton (BHP). This company, with group headquarters in Australia and secondary headquarters in London, is the world's largest natural resources company, reporting revenue of approximately US$32 billion for the fiscal year ended June 2006. The company mines, processes, and markets coal, copper, nickel, iron, bauxite, and silver and also has substantial petroleum operations.

decline to match the industry average of 15 days in 2006. Total sales (all on credit) in 2005 were $300 million, and Brown expects total sales (all on credit) to increase to $320 million in 2006. To achieve the lower DSO, the change in the average accounts receivable balance from 2005 to 2006 that must occur is *closest* to

A. −$3.51 million.

B. −$2.46 million.

C. $2.46 million.

D. $3.51 million.

Solution: B is correct. The first step is to calculate **accounts receivable turnover** from the DSO collection period. Receivable turnover equals 365/19 (DSO) = 19.2 for 2005, and 365/15 = 24.3 in 2006. Next, we use the fact that the average accounts receivable balance equals sales/receivable turnover to conclude that for 2005, average accounts receivable was $300,000,000/19.2 = $15,625,000, and for 2006, it must equal $320,000,000/24.3 = $13,168,724. The difference is a reduction in receivables of $2,456,276.

The next section illustrates the application of financial statement analysis to credit risk analysis.

APPLICATION: ASSESSING CREDIT RISK

4

Credit risk is the risk of loss caused by a counterparty's or debtor's failure to make a promised payment. For example, credit risk with respect to a bond is the risk that the obligor (the issuer of the bond) is not able to pay interest and principal according to the terms of the bond indenture (contract). Credit analysis is the evaluation of credit risk. Credit analysis may relate to the credit risk of an obligor in a particular transaction or to an obligor's overall creditworthiness.

In assessing an obligor's overall creditworthiness, one general approach is credit scoring, a statistical analysis of the determinants of credit default. As noted above, credit analysis for specific types of debt (e.g., acquisition financing and other highly leveraged financing) typically involves projections of period-by-period cash flows.

Whatever the techniques adopted, the analytical focus of credit analysis is on debt-paying ability. Unlike payments to equity investors, payments to debt investors are limited by the agreed contractual interest. If a company experiences financial success, its debt becomes less risky, but its success does not increase the amount of payments to its debtholders. In contrast, if a company experiences financial distress, it may be unable to pay interest and principal on its debt obligations. Thus, credit analysis has a special concern with the sensitivity of debt-paying ability to adverse events and economic conditions—cases in which the creditor's promised returns may be most at risk. Because those returns are generally paid in cash, credit analysis usually focuses on cash flow rather than accrual-income returns. Typically, credit analysts use return measures related to operating cash flow because it represents cash generated internally, which is available to pay creditors.

These themes are reflected in Example 7, which illustrates the application of four groups of quantitative factors in credit analysis to an industry group: scale and diversification, tolerance for leverage, operational stability, and margin stability. Scale and diversification relate to a company's sensitivity to adverse events and economic conditions as well as to other factors—such as market leadership, purchasing power with suppliers, and access to capital markets—that can affect debt-paying ability. Financial policies or tolerance for leverage relates to the obligor's ability to service its indebtedness (i.e., make the promised payments on debt). In the example, various solvency ratios are used to measure tolerance for leverage. One set of tolerance-for-leverage measures is based on retained cash flow (RCF). RCF is defined by Moody's as operating cash flow before working capital changes less dividends. A ratio of RCF/total debt of 0.5, for example, indicates that the company may be able to pay off debt in approximately 1/0.5 = 2 years from cash flow retained in the business (at current levels of RCF and debt), assuming no capital expenditures; a ratio adjusting for capital expenditures is also used. Other factors include interest coverage ratios based on EBITDA, which is also chosen by Moody's in specifying factors for operational efficiency and margin stability. "Operational efficiency" as defined by Moody's relates to cost structure: Companies with lower costs are better positioned to deal with financial stress. "Margin stability" relates to the past volatility of profit margins: Higher stability should be associated with lower credit risk.

EXAMPLE 7

Moody's Evaluation of Quantifiable Rating Factors[9]

Moody's Investors Service indicates that when assigning credit ratings for the global paper and forest products industry, they look at a number of factors, including quantitative measures of four broad factors. These factors are weighted and aggregated in determining the overall credit rating assigned. The four broad factors, the subfactors, and weightings are as follows:

Broad Factor	Subfactors	Subfactor Weighting (%)	Broad Factor Weighting (%)
Scale and diversification	Average annual revenues	6.00	15
	Segment diversification	4.50	
	Geographic diversification	4.50	
Financial policies (tolerance for leverage)	Retained cash flow (RCF)/Total debt	11.00	55
	(RCF − Capital expenditures)/Total debt	11.00	
	Total debt/EBITDA	11.00	
	(EBITDA − Capital expenditures)/Interest	11.00	
	EBITDA/Interest	11.00	
Operational efficiency	Vertical integration	5.25	15
	EBITDA margin	5.25	
	EBITDA/Average assets	4.50	
Margin stability	Average percentage change in EBITDA margin	15.00	15
Total		100.00	100

[9] Moody's Investors Service, "Rating Methodology: Global Paper & Forest Products Industry," June 2006, pp. 8–19.

1. What are some reasons why Moody's may have selected these four broad factors as being important in assigning a credit rating?
2. Why might financial policies be weighted so heavily?

Solution to 1:

Scale and Diversification:

- Large scale can result in purchasing power over suppliers, leading to cost savings.
- Product and geographic diversification should lower risk.

Financial Policies:

- Strong financial policies should be associated with the ability of cash flow to service debt.

Operational Efficiency:

- Companies with high operational efficiency should have lower costs and higher margins than less efficient companies and so be able to withstand a downturn easier.

Margin Stability:

- Lower volatility in margins would imply lower risk relative to economic conditions.

Solution to 2: The level of debt relative to earnings and cash flow is a critical factor in assessing creditworthiness. The higher the current level of debt, the higher the risk of default.

A point to note regarding Example 7 is that the rating factors and the metrics used to represent each can vary by industry group. For example, for heavy manufacturing (manufacturing of the capital assets used in manufacturing and production processes), Moody's distinguishes order trends and quality as distinctive credit factors affecting future revenues, factory load, and profitability patterns.

Analyses of a company's historical and projected financial statements are an integral part of the credit evaluation process. As noted by Moody's, the rating process makes:

> . . . extensive use of historic financial statements. Historic results help with understanding the pattern of a company's results and how the company compares to others. They also provide perspective, helping to ensure that estimated future results are grounded in reality.[10]

As noted in the above example, Moody's computes a variety of ratios in assessing creditworthiness. A comparison of a company's ratios to its peers is informative in evaluating relative creditworthiness, as demonstrated in Example 8.

[10] Ibid., p. 6.

EXAMPLE 8

Peer Comparison of Ratios

A credit analyst is assessing the tolerance for leverage for two paper companies based on the following subfactors identified by Moody's:[11]

	International Paper	Louisiana-Pacific
RCF/Debt	8.2 %	59.1%
(RCF − Capital expenditures)/Debt	0.2%	39.8%
Debt/EBITDA	5.6x	1.0x
(EBITDA − Capital expenditures)/Interest	1.7x	8.1x
EBITDA/Interest	3.1x	10.0x

Based solely on the data given, which company is more likely to be assigned a higher credit rating?

Solution: The ratio comparisons are all in favor of Louisiana-Pacific. Louisiana-Pacific has a much higher level of retained cash flow relative to debt whether capital expenditures are netted from RCF or not. Louisiana-Pacific has a lower level of debt relative to EBITDA and a higher level of EBITDA relative to interest expense. Louisiana-Pacific is likely to be assigned a higher credit rating.

Before calculating ratios such as those presented in Example 8, rating agencies make certain adjustments to reported financial statements, such as adjusting debt to include off-balance-sheet debt in a company's total debt.[12] A later section will describe some common adjustments. Financial statement analysis, especially financial ratio analysis, can also be an important tool used in selecting equity investments, as discussed in the next section.

5 APPLICATION: SCREENING FOR POTENTIAL EQUITY INVESTMENTS

Ratios using financial statement data and market data are used to screen for potential equity investments. **Screening** is the application of a set of criteria to reduce a set of potential investments to a smaller set having certain desired characteristics. Criteria involving financial ratios generally involve comparing one or more ratios with some prespecified cutoff values.

[11] Ibid., p. 12; the values reported are based on average historical data.

[12] Ibid., p. 6.

EXHIBIT 3 (continued)

	Time					
	0	1	2	3	4	5
(15) Plus noncash items		0.0	0.0	0.0	0.0	0.0
(16) Less: investment in working capital		−10.0	9.0	9.9	10.9	12.0
(17) Less: investment in fixed capital		0.0	0.0	0.0	0.0	0.0
(18) Change in cash		17.0	−0.7	−0.9	−1.0	−1.3
(19) Beginning cash		0.0	17.0	16.3	15.4	14.4
(20) Ending cash		17.0	16.3	15.4	14.4	13.1

To explain the exhibit, at time zero, the company is formed with $100 of equity capital (Line 12). All of the company's capital is assumed to be immediately invested in working capital (Line 9). In future periods, because it is assumed that no dividends are paid, equity increases each year by the amount of net income. Future periods' working capital is assumed to be 90 percent of annual sales.

Sales are assumed to be $100 in the first period and to grow at a constant rate of 10 percent per annum (Line 1). The cost of goods sold is assumed constant at 20 percent of sales (Line 2), so the gross profit margin is 80 percent. Operating expenses are assumed to be 70 percent of sales each year (Line 3). Interest income (Line 4) is calculated as 5 percent of the beginning cash/borrowing balance (Line 8) and is an income item when there is a cash balance, as it is in this example. (If available cash is inadequate to cover required cash outflows, the shortfall is presumed to be covered by borrowing. This borrowing would be shown as a negative balance on Line 8 and an associated interest expense on Line 4. Alternatively, a forecast can be presented with separate lines for cash and borrowing.) Taxes of 30 percent are deducted to obtain net income (Line 7).

To calculate each period's cash flow, we begin with net income (Line 7 = Line 14), add back any noncash items such as depreciation (Line 15), deduct investment in working capital (Line 16), and deduct investment in fixed capital (Line 17).[7] In this simple example, we are assuming that the company does not invest in any fixed capital (long-term assets) but, rather, rents furnished office space. Therefore, there is no depreciation, and thus noncash items are zero. Each period's change in cash (Line 18) is added to the beginning cash balance (Line 19) to obtain the ending cash balance (Line 20 = Line 8).

Example 5 is simplified to demonstrate some principles of forecasting. In practice, each aspect of a forecast presents substantial challenges. Sales forecasts may be very detailed, with separate forecasts for each year of each product line, and/or

[7] Working capital represents funds that must be invested in the daily operations of a business such as to carry inventory and accounts receivable. The term "investment" in this context means "the addition to" or "increase." The "investment in fixed capital" is also referred to as "capital expenditure" or "capex." See Stowe et al. (2002), Chapter 3, for further information.

each geographical or business segment. Sales forecasts may be based on past results (for relative stable businesses), management forecasts, industry studies, and/or macroeconomic forecasts. Similarly, gross margins may be detailed and may be based on past results or forecast relationships. Expenses other than cost of goods sold may be broken down into more detailed line items, each of which may be forecasted based on its relationship with sales (if variable) or on its historical levels. Working capital requirements may be estimated as a proportion of the amount of sales (as in the example) or the change in sales, or as a compilation of specific forecasts for inventory, receivables, and payables. Most forecasts will involve some investment in fixed assets, in which case depreciation amounts affect taxable income and net income but not cash flow. Example 5 makes the simplifying assumption that interest is paid on the beginning-of-year cash balance.

Example 5 developed a series of point estimates for future net income and cash flow. In practice, forecasting generally includes an analysis of the risk in forecasts—in this case, an assessment of the impact on income and cash flow if the realized values of variables differ significantly from the assumptions used in the base case or if actual sales are much different from forecasts. Quantifying the risk in forecasts requires an analysis of the economics of the company's businesses and expense structures, and the potential impact of events affecting the company, the industry, and the economy in general. That investigation done, the analyst can assess risk using scenario analysis or Monte Carlo simulation. Scenario analysis involves specifying assumptions that differ from those included as the base case assumptions. In the above example, the projections of net income and cash flow could be recast using a more pessimistic scenario, with assumptions changed to reflect slower sales growth and higher costs. A Monte Carlo simulation involves specifying probability distributions of values for variables and random sampling from those distributions. In the above analysis, the projections would be repeatedly recast using randomly selected values for the drivers of net income and cash flow, thus permitting the analyst to evaluate the range of results possible and the probability of simulating the possible actual outcomes.

An understanding of financial statements and ratios can enable an analyst to make more detailed projections of income statement, balance sheet, and cash flow statement items. For example, an analyst may collect information on normal inventory and receivables turnover ratios and use this information to forecast accounts receivable, inventory, and cash flows based on sales projections rather than use a composite working capital investment assumption, as in the above example.

As the analyst makes detailed forecasts, he or she must ensure that they are mutually consistent. For instance, in Example 6, the analyst's forecast concerning days of sales outstanding (which is an estimate of the average time to collect payment from sales made on credit) should flow from a model of the company that yields a forecast of the change in the average accounts receivable balance given as the solution to the problem. Otherwise, predicted days of sales outstanding and accounts receivable would not be mutually consistent.

EXAMPLE 6

Consistency of Forecasts[8]

Brown Corporation had an average days-of-sales-outstanding (DSO) period of 19 days in 2005. An analyst thinks that Brown's DSO will

[8] Adapted from a past CFA Institute examination question.

decline to match the industry average of 15 days in 2006. Total sales (all on credit) in 2005 were $300 million, and Brown expects total sales (all on credit) to increase to $320 million in 2006. To achieve the lower DSO, the change in the average accounts receivable balance from 2005 to 2006 that must occur is *closest* to

A. −$3.51 million.

B. −$2.46 million.

C. $2.46 million.

D. $3.51 million.

Solution: B is correct. The first step is to calculate **accounts receivable turnover** from the DSO collection period. Receivable turnover equals 365/19 (DSO) = 19.2 for 2005, and 365/15 = 24.3 in 2006. Next, we use the fact that the average accounts receivable balance equals sales/receivable turnover to conclude that for 2005, average accounts receivable was $300,000,000/19.2 = $15,625,000, and for 2006, it must equal $320,000,000/24.3 = $13,168,724. The difference is a reduction in receivables of $2,456,276.

The next section illustrates the application of financial statement analysis to credit risk analysis.

APPLICATION: ASSESSING CREDIT RISK 4

Credit risk is the risk of loss caused by a counterparty's or debtor's failure to make a promised payment. For example, credit risk with respect to a bond is the risk that the obligor (the issuer of the bond) is not able to pay interest and principal according to the terms of the bond indenture (contract). Credit analysis is the evaluation of credit risk. Credit analysis may relate to the credit risk of an obligor in a particular transaction or to an obligor's overall creditworthiness.

In assessing an obligor's overall creditworthiness, one general approach is credit scoring, a statistical analysis of the determinants of credit default. As noted above, credit analysis for specific types of debt (e.g., acquisition financing and other highly leveraged financing) typically involves projections of period-by-period cash flows.

Whatever the techniques adopted, the analytical focus of credit analysis is on debt-paying ability. Unlike payments to equity investors, payments to debt investors are limited by the agreed contractual interest. If a company experiences financial success, its debt becomes less risky, but its success does not increase the amount of payments to its debtholders. In contrast, if a company experiences financial distress, it may be unable to pay interest and principal on its debt obligations. Thus, credit analysis has a special concern with the sensitivity of debt-paying ability to adverse events and economic conditions—cases in which the creditor's promised returns may be most at risk. Because those returns are generally paid in cash, credit analysis usually focuses on cash flow rather than accrual-income returns. Typically, credit analysts use return measures related to operating cash flow because it represents cash generated internally, which is available to pay creditors.

These themes are reflected in Example 7, which illustrates the application of four groups of quantitative factors in credit analysis to an industry group: scale and diversification, tolerance for leverage, operational stability, and margin stability. Scale and diversification relate to a company's sensitivity to adverse events and economic conditions as well as to other factors—such as market leadership, purchasing power with suppliers, and access to capital markets—that can affect debt-paying ability. Financial policies or tolerance for leverage relates to the obligor's ability to service its indebtedness (i.e., make the promised payments on debt). In the example, various solvency ratios are used to measure tolerance for leverage. One set of tolerance-for-leverage measures is based on retained cash flow (RCF). RCF is defined by Moody's as operating cash flow before working capital changes less dividends. A ratio of RCF/total debt of 0.5, for example, indicates that the company may be able to pay off debt in approximately 1/0.5 = 2 years from cash flow retained in the business (at current levels of RCF and debt), assuming no capital expenditures; a ratio adjusting for capital expenditures is also used. Other factors include interest coverage ratios based on EBITDA, which is also chosen by Moody's in specifying factors for operational efficiency and margin stability. "Operational efficiency" as defined by Moody's relates to cost structure: Companies with lower costs are better positioned to deal with financial stress. "Margin stability" relates to the past volatility of profit margins: Higher stability should be associated with lower credit risk.

EXAMPLE 7

Moody's Evaluation of Quantifiable Rating Factors[9]

Moody's Investors Service indicates that when assigning credit ratings for the global paper and forest products industry, they look at a number of factors, including quantitative measures of four broad factors. These factors are weighted and aggregated in determining the overall credit rating assigned. The four broad factors, the subfactors, and weightings are as follows:

Broad Factor	Subfactors	Subfactor Weighting (%)	Broad Factor Weighting (%)
Scale and diversification	Average annual revenues	6.00	15
	Segment diversification	4.50	
	Geographic diversification	4.50	
Financial policies (tolerance for leverage)	Retained cash flow (RCF)/Total debt	11.00	55
	(RCF − Capital expenditures)/Total debt	11.00	
	Total debt/EBITDA	11.00	
	(EBITDA − Capital expenditures)/Interest	11.00	
	EBITDA/Interest	11.00	
Operational efficiency	Vertical integration	5.25	15
	EBITDA margin	5.25	
	EBITDA/Average assets	4.50	
Margin stability	Average percentage change in EBITDA margin	15.00	15
Total		100.00	100

[9] Moody's Investors Service, "Rating Methodology: Global Paper & Forest Products Industry," June 2006, pp. 8–19.

1. What are some reasons why Moody's may have selected these four broad factors as being important in assigning a credit rating?
2. Why might financial policies be weighted so heavily?

Solution to 1:

Scale and Diversification:

- Large scale can result in purchasing power over suppliers, leading to cost savings.
- Product and geographic diversification should lower risk.

Financial Policies:

- Strong financial policies should be associated with the ability of cash flow to service debt.

Operational Efficiency:

- Companies with high operational efficiency should have lower costs and higher margins than less efficient companies and so be able to withstand a downturn easier.

Margin Stability:

- Lower volatility in margins would imply lower risk relative to economic conditions.

Solution to 2: The level of debt relative to earnings and cash flow is a critical factor in assessing creditworthiness. The higher the current level of debt, the higher the risk of default.

A point to note regarding Example 7 is that the rating factors and the metrics used to represent each can vary by industry group. For example, for heavy manufacturing (manufacturing of the capital assets used in manufacturing and production processes), Moody's distinguishes order trends and quality as distinctive credit factors affecting future revenues, factory load, and profitability patterns.

Analyses of a company's historical and projected financial statements are an integral part of the credit evaluation process. As noted by Moody's, the rating process makes:

> . . . extensive use of historic financial statements. Historic results help with understanding the pattern of a company's results and how the company compares to others. They also provide perspective, helping to ensure that estimated future results are grounded in reality.[10]

As noted in the above example, Moody's computes a variety of ratios in assessing creditworthiness. A comparison of a company's ratios to its peers is informative in evaluating relative creditworthiness, as demonstrated in Example 8.

[10] Ibid., p. 6.

EXAMPLE 8

Peer Comparison of Ratios

A credit analyst is assessing the tolerance for leverage for two paper companies based on the following subfactors identified by Moody's:[11]

	International Paper	Louisiana-Pacific
RCF/Debt	8.2 %	59.1%
(RCF − Capital expenditures)/Debt	0.2%	39.8%
Debt/EBITDA	5.6x	1.0x
(EBITDA − Capital expenditures)/Interest	1.7x	8.1x
EBITDA/Interest	3.1x	10.0x

Based solely on the data given, which company is more likely to be assigned a higher credit rating?

Solution: The ratio comparisons are all in favor of Louisiana-Pacific. Louisiana-Pacific has a much higher level of retained cash flow relative to debt whether capital expenditures are netted from RCF or not. Louisiana-Pacific has a lower level of debt relative to EBITDA and a higher level of EBITDA relative to interest expense. Louisiana-Pacific is likely to be assigned a higher credit rating.

Before calculating ratios such as those presented in Example 8, rating agencies make certain adjustments to reported financial statements, such as adjusting debt to include off-balance-sheet debt in a company's total debt.[12] A later section will describe some common adjustments. Financial statement analysis, especially financial ratio analysis, can also be an important tool used in selecting equity investments, as discussed in the next section.

5 APPLICATION: SCREENING FOR POTENTIAL EQUITY INVESTMENTS

Ratios using financial statement data and market data are used to screen for potential equity investments. **Screening** is the application of a set of criteria to reduce a set of potential investments to a smaller set having certain desired characteristics. Criteria involving financial ratios generally involve comparing one or more ratios with some prespecified cutoff values.

[11] Ibid., p. 12; the values reported are based on average historical data.

[12] Ibid., p. 6.

A security selection approach incorporating financial ratios may be used whether the investor uses top-down analysis or bottom-up analysis. **Top-down analysis** involves identifying attractive geographic segments and/or industry segments and then the most attractive investments within those segments. **Bottom-up analysis** involves selection from all companies within a specified investment universe. Regardless of the direction, screening for potential equity investments aims to identify companies that meet specific criteria. An analysis of this type may be used as the basis for directly forming a portfolio, or it may be undertaken as a preliminary part of a more thorough analysis of potential investment targets.

Fundamental to this type of analysis are decisions about which metrics to use as screens, how many metrics to include, what values of those metrics to use as cutoff points, and what weighting to give each metric. Metrics can include not only financial ratios but also characteristics such as market capitalization or membership as a component security in a specified index. Exhibit 4 is an example of a hypothetical simple stock screen based on the following criteria: a valuation ratio (price-to-sales) less than a specified value; a solvency ratio measuring financial leverage (total assets/equity) not exceeding a specified value; dividend payments; and positive one-year-ahead forecast EPS. The exhibit shows the results of applying the screen to a set of 4,203 U.S. securities that comprise a hypothetical equity manager's investment universe.

EXHIBIT 4 Example of a Stock Screen

	Stocks Meeting Criterion	
Criterion	**Number**	**Percent of Total**
Price per share/Sales per share < 1.5	1,560	37.1%
Total assets/Equity ≤ 2.0	2,123	50.5%
Dividends > 0	2,497	59.4%
Consensus forecast EPS > 0	2,956	70.3%
Meeting all four criteria simultaneously	473	11.3%

Source: http://finance.yahoo.com.

Several points about the screen in Exhibit 4 are observed in many screens seen in practice:

- Some criteria serve as checks on the interpretation of other criteria. In this hypothetical example, the first criterion selects stocks that are relatively cheaply valued. However, the stocks might be cheap for a good reason, such as poor profitability or excessive financial leverage. So, the criteria requiring forecast EPS and dividends to be positive serve as checks on profitability, and the criterion limiting financial leverage serves as a check on financial risk. Of course, financial ratios or other statistics cannot generally control for exposure to certain types of risk (e.g., related to regulatory developments or technological innovation).

- If all the criteria were completely independent of each other, the set of stocks meeting all four criteria would be 329, equal to 4,203 times 7.8 percent—the product of the fraction of stocks satisfying the four criteria individually (i.e., $0.371 \times 0.505 \times 0.594 \times 0.703 = 0.078$, or 7.8 percent). As the screen illustrates, criteria are often not independent, and the result is more securities passing the screen. In this example, 473 (or 11.3 percent) of the securities passed all four screens. As an example of the lack of independence, dividend-paying status is probably positively correlated with the ability to generate positive earnings and the value of the fourth criterion. If stocks that pass one test tend to also pass the other, fewer would be eliminated after the application of the second test.
- The results of screens can sometimes be relatively concentrated in a subset of the sectors represented in the benchmark. The financial leverage criterion in Exhibit 4 would exclude all banking stocks, for example. What constitutes a high or low value of a measure of a financial characteristic can be sensitive to the industry in which a company operates.

Screens can be used by both **growth investors** (focused on investing in high-earnings-growth companies), **value investors** (focused on paying a relatively low share price in relation to earnings or assets per share), and **market-oriented investors** (an intermediate grouping for investors whose investment disciplines cannot be clearly categorized as value or growth). The criteria of growth screens would typically feature criteria related to earnings growth and/or momentum. Value screens, as a rule, feature criteria setting upper limits for the value of one or more valuation ratios. Market-oriented screens would not strongly emphasize valuation or growth criteria. The use of screens involving financial ratios may be most common among value investors.

There have been many studies researching the most effective items of accounting information for screening equity investments. Some research suggests that certain items of accounting information can help explain (and potentially predict) market returns (e.g., Chan et al. 1991; Lev and Thiagarajan 1993; Lakonishok et al. 1994; Davis 1994; Arbanell and Bushee 1998). Representative of such investigations is Piotroski (2000), whose screen uses nine accounting-based fundamentals that aim to identify financially strong and profitable companies among those with high book value/market value ratios. For example, the profitability measures relate to whether the company reported positive net income, positive cash flow, and an increase in return on assets (ROA).

An analyst may want to evaluate how a portfolio based on a particular screen would have performed historically, using a process known as "backtesting." **Backtesting** applies the portfolio selection rules to historical data and calculates what returns would have been earned if a particular strategy had been used. The relevance of backtesting to investment success in practice can, however, be limited. Haugen and Baker (1996) describe some of these limitations:

- Survivorship bias: If the database used in backtesting eliminates companies that cease to exist because of a merger or bankruptcy, then the remaining companies collectively will appear to have performed better.
- Look-ahead bias: If a database includes financial data updated for restatements (where companies have restated previously issued financial statements to correct errors or reflect changes in accounting principles),[13] then there is

[13] In the United States, restatements of previously issued financial statements have increased in recent years. The U.S. Government Accounting Office (2002) reports 919 restatements by 834 public companies in the period from January 1997 to June 2002. The number of restatements increased from 613 in 2004 to 1,195 in 2005 (*Wall Street Journal*, 2006).

a mismatch between what investors would have actually known at the time of the investment decision and the information used in backtesting.

- Data-snooping bias: If researchers build models based on previous researchers' findings, then using the same data base to test the model is not actually a test. Under this scenario, the same rules may or may not produce similar results in the future. One academic study argues that the apparent ability of value strategies to generate excess returns is largely explainable as the result of collective data snooping (Conrad, Cooper, and Kaul, 2003).

EXAMPLE 9

Ratio-Based Screening for Potential Equity Investments

Below are two alternative strategies under consideration by an investment firm:

> *Strategy A* invests in stocks that are components of a global equity index, have a ROE above the median ROE of all stocks in the index, and a P/E ratio less than the median P/E.
> *Strategy B* invests in stocks that are components of a broad-based U.S. equity index, have price to operating cash flow in the lowest quartile of companies in the index, and have shown increases in sales for at least the past three years.

Both strategies were developed with the use of backtesting.

1. How would you characterize the two strategies?
2. What concerns might you have about using such strategies?

Solution to 1: Strategy A appears to aim for global diversification and combines a requirement for profitability with a traditional measure of value (low P/E). Strategy B focuses on both large and small companies in a single market and apparently aims to identify companies that are growing and yet managing to generate positive cash flow from operations.

Solution to 2: The use of *any* approach to investment decisions depends on the objectives and risk profile of the investor. With that crucial consideration in mind, ratio-based benchmarks can offer an efficient way to screen for potential equity investments. However, in doing so, many types of questions arise.

First, unintentional selections can be made if criteria are not specified carefully. For example, Strategy A might unintentionally select a loss-making company with negative shareholders' equity because negative net income divided by negative shareholders' equity would arithmetically result in a positive ROE. Strategy B might unintentionally select a company with negative operating cash flow because price to operating cash flow would be negative and thus very low in the ranking. In both cases, the analyst can add additional screening criteria to avoid unintentional selection (e.g., criteria requiring positive shareholders' equity and operating cash flow).

Second, the inputs to ratio analysis are derived from financial statements, and companies may differ in the financial standards applied (e.g., IFRS versus U.S. GAAP); the specific accounting method chosen within those allowed under any body of reporting standards; and/or the estimates made in applying an accounting method.

Third, backtesting may not provide a reliable indication of future performance because of survivorship bias, look-ahead bias, or data snooping; furthermore, as suggested by finance theory and by common sense, the past is not necessarily indicative of the future. Fourth, implementation decisions can crucially affect returns. For example, decisions about frequency and timing of portfolio selection and reevaluation affect transaction costs and taxes paid out of the portfolio.

6 ANALYST ADJUSTMENTS TO REPORTED FINANCIALS

When comparing companies that use different accounting methods or estimate key accounting inputs in different ways, analysts frequently adjust a company's financials. In this section, we first provide a framework for considering potential analyst adjustments to facilitate such comparisons and then provide examples of such adjustments. In practice, required adjustments vary widely. The examples presented here are not intended to be comprehensive, but rather to illustrate the use of adjustments to facilitate comparison.

6.1 A Framework for Analyst Adjustments

In this discussion of potential analyst adjustments to a company's financial statements, we employ a balance sheet focused framework. Of course, because the financial statements are interrelated, adjustments to items reported on one statement must also be reflected in adjustments to items on another statement. For example, an analyst adjustment to the balance sheet item inventory affects the income statement item cost of goods sold; and the owners' equity amount is affected by analyst adjustments relating to expense or revenue recognition.

Regardless of the particular order in which an analyst considers the items that may require adjustment for comparability, the following considerations are appropriate:

- *Importance.* Is an adjustment to this item likely to affect my conclusions? In other words, does it matter? For example, in an industry where companies require minimal inventory, does it matter that two companies use different inventory accounting methods?
- *Body of standards.* Is there a difference in the body of standards being used (U.S. GAAP versus IFRS)? If so, in which areas is the difference likely to affect a comparison?
- *Methods.* Is there a difference in methods?
- *Estimates.* Is there a difference in important estimates?

The following sections illustrate analyst adjustments—first those relating to the asset side of the balance sheet and then those relating to the liability side.

6.2 Analyst Adjustments Related to Investments

Accounting for investments in the debt and equity securities of other companies (other than investments accounted for under the equity method and investments in consolidated subsidiaries) depends on management's intention (i.e., to actively trade the securities, make them available for sale, or, in the case of debt securities, to hold them to maturity). When securities are classified as "trading" securities, unrealized gains and losses are reported in the income statement. When securities are classified as "available-for-sale" securities, unrealized gains and losses are not reported in the income statement and instead are recognized in equity. If two otherwise comparable companies have significant differences in the classification of investments, analyst adjustments may be useful to facilitate comparison.

Also, IFRS requires that those unrealized gains and losses on available-for-sale debt securities that arise due to exchange rate movements be recognized in the income statement, whereas U.S. GAAP does not. To facilitate comparison across companies, increases (decreases) in the value of available-for-sale debt securities arising from exchange rate movements can be deducted from (added to) the amount of income reported by the IFRS-reporting company.

6.3 Analyst Adjustments Related to Inventory

With inventory, adjustments may be required for different accounting methods. As described in previous readings, a company's decision about the inventory method will affect the value of inventory shown on the balance sheet as well as the value of inventory that is sold (cost of goods sold). If one company, not reporting under IFRS[14], uses LIFO (last in, first out) and another uses FIFO (first in, first out), comparison of the two companies may be difficult. However, companies that use the LIFO method must also disclose the value of their inventory under the FIFO method. To place inventory values for a company using LIFO reporting on a FIFO basis, the analyst would add the ending balance of the LIFO reserve to the ending value of inventory under LIFO accounting; to adjust cost of goods sold to a FIFO basis, the analyst would subtract the change in the LIFO reserve from the reported cost of goods sold under LIFO accounting. Example 10 illustrates the use of a disclosure of the value of inventory under the FIFO method to make a valid current ratio comparison between companies reporting on a LIFO and FIFO basis.

EXAMPLE 10

Adjustment for a Company Using LIFO Method of Accounting for Inventories

An analyst is comparing the financial performance of SL Industries (AMEX: SLI), a U.S. company operating in the electric lighting and wiring industry, with a company that reports using IFRS. The IFRS company uses the FIFO method of inventory accounting, and you therefore must convert SLI's results to a comparable basis.

[14] IAS No. 2 does not permit the use of LIFO.

EXHIBIT 5 **Data for SL Industries**

	31 December	
	2005	2004
Total current assets	$44,194,000	$37,990,000
Total current liabilities	18,387,000	18,494,000

NOTE 6. INVENTORIES

Inventories consist of the following ($ in thousands):

	31 December	
	2005	2004
Raw materials	$ 9,774	$ 9,669
Work in process	4,699	5,000
Finished goods	1,926	3,633
	16,399	18,302
Less: Allowances	(1,829)	(2,463)
	$14,570	$15,839

The above includes certain inventories that are valued using the LIFO method, which aggregated $4,746,000 and $3,832,000 as of December 31, 2005 and December 31, 2004, respectively. The excess of FIFO cost over LIFO cost as of December 31, 2005 and December 31, 2004 was approximately $502,000 and $565,000, respectively.

Source: 10-K for SL Industries, Inc. for the year ended 31 December 2005; filed with the SEC 24 March 2006.

1. Based on the information in Exhibit 5, calculate SLI's current ratio under FIFO and LIFO for 2004 and 2005.
2. Interpret the results of adjusting the current ratio to be consistent with inventory on a FIFO basis.

Solution to 1: The calculations of SLI's current ratio (current assets divided by current liabilities) are given below.

	2005	2004
I. Current Ratio (Unadjusted)		
Total current assets	$44,194,000	$37,990,000
Total current liabilities	18,387,000	18,494,000
Current ratio (unadjusted)	2.40	2.05

	2005	2004
II. Current Ratio (Adjusted)		
Adjust the inventory to FIFO, add	502,000	565,000
Total current assets (adjusted)	$44,696,000	$38,555,000
Total current liabilities	18,387,000	18,494,000
Current ratio (adjusted)	2.43	2.08

To adjust the LIFO inventory to FIFO, the excess amounts of FIFO cost over LIFO cost are added to LIFO inventory, increasing current assets by an equal amount. The effect of adjusting inventory on the current ratio is to increase it from 2.05 to 2.08 in 2004 and from 2.40 to 2.43 in 2005.

Solution to 2: SLI appears to be somewhat more liquid based on the adjusted current ratio. However, the year-over-year improvement in the current ratio on an adjusted basis at 16.8 percent (2.43/2.08 − 1) was slightly less favorable than the improvement of 17.1 percent (2.40/2.05 − 1) on an adjusted basis.

In summary, the information disclosed by companies using LIFO allows an analyst to calculate the value of the company's inventory as if it were using the FIFO method. In the example above, the portion of inventory valued using the LIFO method was a relatively small portion of total inventory, and the LIFO reserve (excess of FIFO cost over LIFO) was also relatively small. However, if the LIFO method is used for a substantial part of a company's inventory and the LIFO reserve is large relative to reported inventory, the adjustment to a FIFO basis can be important for comparison of the LIFO-reporting company with another company that uses the FIFO method of inventory valuation. Example 11 illustrates a case in which such an adjustment would have a major impact on an analyst's conclusions.

EXAMPLE 11

Analyst Adjustment to Inventory Value for Comparability in a Current Ratio Comparison

Company A reports under IFRS and uses the FIFO method of inventory accounting for its entire inventory. Company B reports under U.S. GAAP and uses the LIFO method. Exhibit 6 gives data pertaining to current assets, LIFO reserves, and current liabilities of these companies.

Based on the data given in Exhibit 6, compare the liquidity of the two companies as measured by the current ratio.

EXHIBIT 6 **Data for Companies Accounting for Inventory on Different Bases**

	Company A (FIFO)	Company B (LIFO)
Current assets (includes inventory)	$ 300,000	$ 80,000
LIFO reserve	N/A	$ 20,000
Current liabilities	$ 150,000	$ 45,000

Solution: Company A's current ratio is 2.0. Based on unadjusted balance sheet data, Company B's current ratio is 1.78. Company A's higher current ratio indicates that Company A appears to be more liquid than Company B; however, the use of unadjusted data for Company B is not appropriate for making comparisons with Company A.

After adjusting Company B's inventory to a comparable basis (i.e., to a FIFO basis), the conclusion changes. The table below summarizes the results when Company B's inventory is left on a LIFO basis and when it is placed on a FIFO basis for comparability with Company A.

		Company B	
	Company A (FIFO)	Unadjusted (LIFO basis)	Adjusted (FIFO basis)
Current assets (includes inventory)	$ 300,000	$ 80,000	$ 100,000
Current liabilities	$ 150,000	$ 45,000	$ 45,000
Current ratio	2.00	1.78	2.22

When both companies' inventories are stated on a FIFO basis, Company B appears to be more liquid, as indicated by its current ratio of 2.22 versus Company A's ratio of 2.00. The adjustment to place Company B's inventory on a FIFO basis was significant because Company B was assumed to use LIFO for its entire inventory and its inventory reserve was $20,000/$80,000 = 0.25, or 25 percent of its reported inventory.

As mentioned earlier, an analyst can also adjust the cost of goods sold for a company using LIFO to a FIFO basis by subtracting the change in the amount of the LIFO reserve from cost of goods sold. Such an adjustment would be appropriate for making profitability comparisons with a company reporting on a FIFO basis and would be important to make when the impact of the adjustment would be material.

6.4 Analyst Adjustments Related to Property, Plant, and Equipment

Management generally has considerable discretion in the determination of depreciation expense. Depreciation expense affects reported net income and reported net fixed asset values. Analysts often consider management's choices related to depreciation as one qualitative factor in evaluating the quality of a company's financial reporting and, in some cases, they may adjust reported depreciation expense for a specific analytic purpose.

The amount of depreciation expense depends on both the accounting method and the estimates used in the calculations. Companies can depreciate fixed assets (other than land) using the straight-line method, an accelerated method, or a usage method. The straight-line method reports an equal amount of depreciation expense each period, computed as the depreciable cost divided by the estimated useful life of the asset (when acquired, an asset's depreciable cost is calculated as its total cost minus its estimated salvage value). Accelerated methods depreciate the asset more quickly, apportioning a greater amount of the depreciable cost to depreciation expense in the earlier periods. Usage-based methods depreciate an asset in proportion to its usage. Apart from selecting a depreciation method, companies must estimate an asset's salvage value and useful life to compute depreciation.

Disclosures required for depreciation often do not facilitate specific adjustments, so comparisons across companies concerning their decisions in depreciating assets are often qualitative and general. The accounts that are associated with depreciation include the balance sheet accounts for gross property, plant, and equipment (gross PPE); accumulated depreciation; the income statement account for depreciation expense; and the statement of cash flows disclosure of capital expenditure (capex) and asset disposals. The relationships between these items can reveal various pieces of information:

- accumulated depreciation divided by gross PPE, from the balance sheet, suggests how much of its useful life the company's overall asset base has passed;
- accumulated depreciation divided by depreciation expense suggests how many years' worth of depreciation expense has already been recognized (i.e., the average age of the asset base);
- net PPE (net of accumulated depreciation) divided by deprecation expense is an approximate indicator of how many years of useful life remain for the company's overall asset base;
- gross PPE divided by depreciation expense can suggest the average life of the assets at installation;
- capex divided by the sum of gross PPE plus capex can suggest what percentage of the asset base is being renewed through new capital investment; and
- capex in relation to asset disposal provides information on growth of the asset base.

These relationships can be evaluated across companies in an industry to suggest differences in strategies for asset utilization or areas for further investigation.

EXAMPLE 12

Differences in Depreciation

An analyst is evaluating the financial statements for two companies in the same industry. The companies have similar strategies with respect to the use of equipment in manufacturing their products. The following information is provided (amounts in millions):

	Company A	Company B
Net PPE	$1,200	$750
Depreciation expense	$120	$50

1. Based on the information given, estimate the average remaining useful lives of the asset bases of Company A and Company B.
2. Suppose that, based on a physical inspection of the companies' plants and other industry information, the analyst believes that the actual remaining useful lives of Company A's and Company B's assets is roughly equal at 10 years. Based only on the facts given, what might the analyst conclude concerning Company B's reported net income?

Solution to 1: The estimated average remaining useful life of Company A's asset base, calculated as net PPE divided by depreciation expense, is $1,200/$120 = 10 years. For Company B, the average remaining useful life of the asset base appears to be far longer at 15 years ($750/$50).

Solution to 2: If Company B's depreciation expense were calculated using 10 years, it would be $75 million (i.e., $25 million higher than reported) and higher depreciation expense would decrease net income. The analyst might conclude that Company B's reported net income reflects relatively aggressive accounting estimates compared with Company A's reported net income.

6.5 Analyst Adjustments Related to Goodwill

Goodwill is an example of an intangible asset (i.e., one without physical substance). Goodwill arises when one company purchases another for a price that exceeds the fair value of the assets acquired. Goodwill is recorded as an asset. For example, assume ParentCo purchases TargetCo for a purchase price of $400 million, the fair value of TargetCo's identifiable assets is $300 million, and the excess of the purchase price is attributed to TargetCo's valuable brands and well-trained workforce. ParentCo will record total assets of $400 million, consisting of $300 million in identifiable assets and $100 million of goodwill. The goodwill is tested annually for impairment, and if its value has declined, ParentCo will reduce the amount of the asset and report a write-off due to impairment.

One of the conceptual difficulties with goodwill arises in comparative financial statement analysis. Consider, for example, two hypothetical U.S. companies, one of which has grown by making an acquisition and the other one of which has grown internally. Assume that the economic value of the two companies is identical: Each has an identically valuable branded product, well-trained workforce, and proprietary technology. The company that has grown by acquisition will incur a related expenditure and will report assets on its balance sheet equal to the amount of the expenditure (assuming no write-offs). The company that has grown internally will have done so by incurring expenditures for advertising, staff training, and research, all of which are expensed as incurred under U.S. GAAP and are thus not directly reflected on the company's balance sheet. Ratios based on asset values and/or income, including profitability ratios such as return on assets and MV/BV, will generally differ for the two companies because of differences in the accounting values of assets and income related to goodwill, although by assumption the economic value of the companies is identical.

EXAMPLE 13

Ratio Comparisons for Goodwill

Miano Marseglia is an analyst who is evaluating the relative valuation of two footwear manufacturing companies: Phoenix Footwear Group (AMEX: PXG) and Rocky Brands (NASDAQ: RCKY). As one part of an overall analysis, Marseglia would like to see how the two companies compare with each other and with the industry based on price/book (P/B) ratios.[15] Because both companies are nondiversified, are small, and have high risk relative to larger, more diversified companies in the industry, Marseglia expects them to sell at a lower P/B ratio than the industry average of 3.68. Marseglia collects the following data on the two companies.

	PXG	RCKY
Market capitalization at 11 October 2006 (Market price per share times the number of shares outstanding)	$37.22 million	$67.57 million
Total shareholders' equity as of the most recent quarter (MRQ)	$54.99 million	$100.35 million
Goodwill	$33.67 million	$24.87 million
Other intangible assets	$33.22 million	$38.09 million

Marseglia computes the P/B ratios as follows:

PXG $37.22/$54.99 = 0.68

RCKY $67.57/$100.35 = 0.67

The companies have similar P/B ratios (i.e., they are approximately equally valued relative to MRQ shareholders' equity). As expected, each company also appears to be selling at a significant discount to the industry average P/B multiple of 3.68. Marseglia is concerned, however, because he notes that both companies have significant intangible assets, particularly goodwill. He wonders what the relative value would be if the P/B ratio were computed after adjusting book value first to remove goodwill and then to remove all intangible assets. Book value reduced by all intangible assets is known as "tangible book value." The average price/tangible book value for the industry is 4.19.

1. Compute the P/B ratio adjusted for goodwill and the price/tangible book value ratio for each company.

[15] Price/book, or P/B, is the price per share divided by stockholders' equity per share. It is also referred to as a market/book, or MV/BV, ratio because it can also be calculated as total market value of the stock (market capitalization) divided by total stockholders' equity.

2. Which company appears to be a better value based *solely* on this data? (Note that the P/B ratio is only one part of a broader analysis. Much more evidence on the valuation and the comparability of the companies would be required to reach a conclusion about whether one company is a better value.)

Solution to 1:

	PXG	RCKY
Total stockholders' equity	$54.99 million	$100.35 million
Less: Goodwill	$33.67 million	$24.87 million
Book value, adjusted	$21.32 million	$75.48 million
Adjusted P/B ratio	$37.22/$21.32 = 1.75	$67.57/$75.48 = 0.90

	PXG	RCKY
Total stockholders' equity	$54.99 million	$100.35 million
Less: Goodwill	$33.67 million	$24.87 million
Less: Other intangible assets	$33.22 million	$38.09 million
Tangible book value	$(11.90) million	$37.39 million
Price/tangible book value ratio	NM (not meaningful)	$67.57/$37.39 = 1.81

Solution to 2: Based on an adjustment for goodwill accumulated in acquisitions, RCKY appears to be selling for a lower price relative to book value than PXG (0.90 versus 1.75). Both companies are selling at a significant discount to the industry, even after adjusting for goodwill.

Based on price/tangible book value, RCKY is also selling for a lower multiple than the industry (1.81 versus 4.19). PXG has a negative tangible book value, and its price/tangible book value ratio is not meaningful with a negative denominator. Based on this interpretation and based *solely* on this information, PXG appears relatively expensive compared with RCKY.

6.6 Analyst Adjustments Related to Off-Balance-Sheet Financing

A number of business activities give rise to obligations which, although they are economically liabilities of a company, are not required to be reported on a company's balance sheet. Including such off-balance-sheet obligations in a company's liabilities can affect ratios and conclusions based on such ratios. In this section, we describe adjustments to financial statements related to one type of off-balance-sheet obligation, the operating lease.

The rights of a lessee (the party that is leasing some asset) may be very similar to the rights of an owner, but if the terms of the lease can be structured so it can be accounted for as an operating lease, the lease is treated like a rental contract, and neither the leased asset nor the associated liability is reported on the balance sheet.[16] The lessee simply records the periodic lease payment as a rental expense in its income statement. In contrast, when a company actually owns an asset, the asset is shown on the balance sheet along with any corresponding liability, such as financing for the asset. Similarly, if a lease is accounted for as a capital lease—essentially equivalent to ownership—the leased asset and associated liability appear on the lessee's balance sheet. The issue of concern to analysts arises when a lease conveys to the lessee most of the benefits and risks of ownership, but the lease is accounted for as an operating lease—the case of off-balance-sheet financing. International accounting standard setters have stated that the entities should not avoid balance sheet recording of leases through artificial leasing structures, seeking to avoid the substance of the transaction.

A 2005 report by the U.S. SEC on off-balance-sheet financing estimates that more than 63 percent of companies in the United States report having an operating lease. The SEC estimate of total future lease payments under operating leases was $1.2 trillion.

Because companies are required to disclose in their financial statements the amount and timing of lease payments, an analyst can use this information to answer the question: How would a company's financial position look if operating lease obligations were included in its total liabilities?

Exhibit 7 presents selected items from the balance sheet of AMR Corporation (the parent of American Airlines) and the text of the footnote from the financial statements about the company's leases. We can use the information in this exhibit to illustrate analyst adjustments:

EXHIBIT 7 **Lease Arrangements of AMR Corporation (NYSE: AMR) Selected Items from Balance Sheet ($ millions)**

	31 December	
	2005	**2004**
Total Assets	**$29,495**	**$28,773**
Current maturities of long-term debt	$ 1,077	$ 659
Long-term debt, less current maturities	12,530	12,436
Total long-term debt	13,607	13,095
Current obligations under capital leases	162	147
Obligations under capital leases, less current obligations	926	1,088
Total long-term debt and capital leases	$14,695	$14,330

From Footnote 5. Leases

AMR's subsidiaries lease various types of equipment and property, primarily aircraft and airport facilities. The future minimum lease payments required under capital leases, together with the present value of such payments, and future minimum lease payments required under operating leases that have initial or

(Exhibit continued on next page . . .)

[16] A lessee classifies a lease as an operating lease if certain guidelines concerning the term of the lease, the present value of the lease payments, and the ownership of the asset at the end of the lease term are satisfied. Under U.S. GAAP, FAS No. 13 specifies the criteria for classification.

EXHIBIT 7 (continued)

remaining non-cancelable lease terms in excess of one year as of December 31, 2005, were (in millions):

Year Ending December 31	Capital Leases	Operating Leases
2006	$263	$1,065
2007	196	1,039
2008	236	973
2009	175	872
2010	140	815
2011 and thereafter	794	7,453
	$1,804	$12,217[a]
Less amount representing interest	716	
Present value of net minimum lease payments	$1,088	

[a] As of December 31, 2005, included in Accrued liabilities and Other liabilities and deferred credits on the accompanying consolidated balance sheet is approximately $1.4 billion relating to rent expense being recorded in advance of future operating lease payments.

Source: AMR Corporation's Form 10-K for period ending 31 December 2005, filed 24 February 2006.

To evaluate the company's solvency position, we can calculate the debt-to-assets ratio, defined in Reading 41 as the ratio of total debt to total assets. Excluding obligations under capital leases (amounting to $1,088 in 2005) from the definition of total debt, we would calculate the ratio for 2005 as 46.1 percent (total long-term debt/total assets = $13,607/$29,495). Properly including obligations under capital leases in the definition of total debt, we would calculate the ratio as 49.8 percent ($14,695/$29,495).

The company's footnote on leases discloses a total of $12.2 billion of future payments for operating leases on an undiscounted basis. The footnote also indicates that, of this amount, only $1.4 billion is shown on the balance sheet. To determine the impact of including operating lease obligations in the total liabilities, we will calculate the present value of the future operating lease payments. Calculating the present value of the future operating lease payments requires a discount rate. We can estimate an appropriate discount rate from the information about the present value of the capital lease payments. The discount rate is the internal rate of return implied by the stream of lease payments and their present value.

For AMR, the present value of the capital lease payments is $1,088 million. Using the stream of payments shown in the footnote and assuming that all of the $794 million payments are made in the year 2011 would give an internal rate of return of 13.7 percent. However, based on the schedule of payments shown, a better assumption is that the $794 million payments do not all occur in a single year. One approach to estimating the timing of these payments is to assume that the payments in 2011 and subsequent years equal the average annual payments in years 2006 to 2010 of $202 = ($263 + $196 + $236 + $175 + $140)/5. Using this approach, there are four annual payments in 2011 and thereafter, and the internal rate of return of the capital lease is 12.1 percent. Given that lease payments have been generally declining over 2006 to 2010, another approach resulting in lower lease payments after 2010 would be to assume that the $794 million is paid equally over some longer time span, such as 10 years. Using this assumption, the internal rate of return of the capital lease payments is 10.0 percent.[17]

EXHIBIT 8 Present Value of Operating Lease Payments Using Discount Rate Derived from Present Value of Capital Lease Payments ($millions)

	Capital Lease			Operating Lease	
	Payments (As Given)	Payments Incl. Estimated Annual Payments for 2011 and Thereafter	Payments Incl. Estimated Annual Payments for 2011 and Thereafter	Payments (As Given)	Payments Incl. Estimated Annual Payments for 2011 and Thereafter
Present value, *given*	−$1,088	−$1,088	−$1,088		
Year 2006	$263	$263	$263	$1,065	$1,065
2007	$196	$196	$196	$1,039	$1,039
2008	$236	$236	$236	$973	$973
2009	$175	$175	$175	$872	$872
2010	$140	$140	$140	$815	$815
2011 and thereafter	$794	$202	$79	$7,453	$953
		$202	$79		$953
		$202	$79		$953
		$188	$79		$953
			$79		$953
			$79		$953
			$79		$953
			$79		$782
			$79		
			$79		
Internal rate of return	13.7%	12.1%	10.0%		
Present value of operating lease payments using a 13.7% discount rate:					$5,671
Present value of operating lease payments using a 12.1% discount rate:					$6,106
Present value of operating lease payments using a 10.0% discount rate:					$6,767

[17] If the term structure of the capital and operating leases can be assumed to be similar, an alternative, shortcut, way to estimate the present value of future operating lease payments that do not appear on the balance sheet is to assume that the relationship between the discounted and undiscounted operating lease payments is approximately the same as the relationship between the discounted and undiscounted capital lease payments. The discounted capital lease payments of $926 million as reported on the balance sheet are 56.4 percent of the undiscounted noncurrent capital lease payments of $1,642 million ($1,804 million total minus $162 million current payments). Applying the same relationship to operating lease payments, 56.4 percent of the undiscounted noncurrent operating lease payments of $10,817 million ($12,217 million total minus $1,400 million current) equals $6.1 billion, close to the estimate of the present value of future operating lease payments given in Exhibit 8 using a 12.1 percent discount rate.

Having estimated an appropriate discount rate, we can calculate the present value of the future operating lease payments. Exhibit 8 presents the results of these calculations and illustrates the sensitivity of the analysis to assumptions about the timing of cash flows. We developed discount rate estimates of 12.1 percent and 10 percent. Using a discount rate of 12.1 percent, the present value of future operating lease payments would be roughly $6.1 billion, and using a discount rate of 10.0 percent, the present value would be around $6.8 billion. Because $1.4 billion of the amounts related to operating leases already appear on the balance sheet (as disclosed in the company's lease footnote), the value of the future operating lease payments that do not appear on the balance sheet are estimated to be in the range of $6,106 million − $1,400 million = $4,706 million, or about $4.7 billion, to $6,767 million − $1,400 million = $5,367 million, or about $5.4 billion. The lower the assumed discount rate, the higher the present value of the lease payments.

We now add the present value of the off-balance-sheet future operating lease payments to the company's total assets and total debt. Making this adjustment increases the debt-to-assets ratio to an amount between ($14,695 + $4,706)/($29,495 + $4,706) = 56.7 percent and ($14,695 + $5,367)/($29,495 + $5,367) = 57.5 percent. If a point estimate of the debt-to-assets ratio were needed, in this case, the analyst might select the 57.5 percent estimate based on the lower discount rate because that discount rate is more consistent with yields on investment-grade bonds as of the date of the example.

EXAMPLE 14

Analyst Adjustment to Debt for Operating Lease Payments

An analyst is evaluating the capital structure of two (hypothetical) companies, Koller Semiconductor and MacRae Manufacturing, as of the beginning of 2006. Koller Semiconductor makes somewhat less use of operating leases than MacRae Manufacturing. The analyst has the following additional information:

	Koller Semiconductor	MacRae Manufacturing
Total debt	$1,200	$2,400
Total equity	$2,000	$4,000
Average interest rate on debt	10%	8%
Lease payments on operating leases:		
2006	10	90
2007	18	105
2008	22	115
2009	25	128
2010 and thereafter	75	384

Based on the information given, discuss how adjusting for operating leases affects the companies' solvency based on their debt to debt-plus-equity ratios, assuming no adjustment to equity. (Assume payments after 2009 occur at the same rate as for 2009. For example, for Koller Semiconductor, the payments for 2010 through 2012 are assumed to be $25 each year.)

Solution: Before making the adjustment, the companies' debt to debt-plus-equity ratios are identical, both at 37.5 percent. To make the adjustment for operating leases, the first step is to calculate the present value of the operating lease payments. Assuming that payments after 2009 occur at the same rate as for 2009, Koller's payment would be $25 in 2010, 2011, and 2012. The present value of $25 discounted for five years at 10 percent is $15.52. MacRae's payment is assumed to be $128 in each of 2010, 2011, and 2012. The present value of $128 discounted for five years at 8 percent is $87.11. Calculations for the following two years are made in the same manner, resulting in the present values shown in the following table:

	Koller Semiconductor	MacRae Manufacturing
2006	$9.09	$83.33
2007	$14.88	$90.02
2008	$16.53	$91.29
2009	$17.08	$94.08
2010	$15.52	$87.11
2011	$14.11	$80.66
2012	$12.83	$74.69
Total present value (PV)	$100.04	$601.18

After adding the present value of capitalized lease obligations to total debt, MacRae Manufacturing's debt to debt-plus-equity ratio is significantly higher, at 42.9 percent, as shown in the following table. The higher ratio reflects the impact of lease obligations on MacRae's solvency:

	Koller Semiconductor		MacRae Manufacturing	
	Before Capitalizing	After Capitalizing	Before Capitalizing	After Capitalizing
Total debt	$1,200	$1,300	$2,400	$3,001
Total equity	$2,000	$2,000	$4,000	$4,000
Debt/ (Debt + Equity)	37.5%	39.4%	37.5%	42.9%

The adjustment for operating leases essentially treats the transaction as if the asset had been purchased rather than leased. The present value of the capitalized lease obligations is the amount owed and the amount at which the asset is valued. Further adjustments reflect the reduction of rent expenses (if the asset is owned, rent would not be paid), the related interest expense on the amount owed, and a depreciation expense for the asset. The reduction of rent expense can be estimated as the average of two years of rent expense. Interest expense is estimated as the interest rate times the PV of the lease payments. Depreciation is estimated on a straight-line basis based on the number of years of future lease payments.

EXAMPLE 15

Stylized Example of Effect on Coverage Ratio for Operating Lease Adjustment

The analyst is also evaluating the interest coverage ratio of the companies in the previous example, Koller Semiconductor and MacRae Manufacturing.

	Koller Semiconductor	MacRae Manufacturing
EBIT before adjustment	\$850	\$1,350
Interest expense before adjustment	\$120	\$192

The prior-year (2005) rent expense was \$11 for Koller Semiconductor and \$90 for MacRae Manufacturing.

Using the information in Example 14 and the additional information given above, discuss how adjustment for operating leases affects the companies' solvency as measured by their coverage ratios.

Solution: Interest coverage is calculated as EBIT divided by interest. For the adjustments, rent expense is the average of two years' rent. For Koller Semiconductor, rent expense is calculated as (\$11 + \$10)/2. The cost of interest on lease obligations is estimated as the interest rate multiplied by the present value of the lease payments. For Koller Semiconductor, this interest expense is calculated as 10% × \$100.04, and for MacRae Manufacturing, it is calculated as 8% × \$601.18. Depreciation is estimated on a straight-line basis by dividing the PV of lease payments by the number of years of lease payments (seven years). After the adjustment, both companies show a decline in interest coverage ratio, reflecting the increased obligation associated with the operating lease obligations. There is also a larger apparent difference in the coverage between the two companies.

	Koller Semiconductor	MacRae Manufacturing
Interest coverage before adjustment	7.1	7.0
EBIT before adjustment	**850**	**1,350**
Rent expense; an add-back to EBIT	10.5	90.0
Depreciation; a deduction from EBIT	(14.3)	(85.9)
EBIT after adjustment	846.2	1354.1
Interest expense before adjustment	120	192
Assumed cost of interest on lease obligation (to add to interest)	10.0	48.1
Interest expense after adjustment	130.0	240.1
Interest coverage after adjustment	**6.5**	**5.6**

In summary, adjusting a company's financial statements to include amounts of lease payments gives a more complete picture of the company's financial condition and enables the comparison of companies with varying arrangements for financing assets. It may additionally be necessary to adjust for amounts associated with other off-balance-sheet financing arrangements.

SUMMARY

This reading described selected applications of financial statement analysis, including the evaluation of past financial performance, the projection of future financial performance, the assessment of credit risk, and the screening of potential equity investments. In addition, the reading introduced analyst adjustments to reported financials. In all cases, the analyst needs to have a good understanding of the financial reporting standards under which financial statements are prepared. Because standards evolve over time, analysts must stay current in order to make good investment decisions. The main points in the reading include the following:

- Evaluating a company's historical performance addresses not only what happened but also the causes behind the company's performance and how the performance reflects the company's strategy.
- The projection of a company's future net income and cash flow often begins with a top-down sales forecast in which the analyst forecasts industry sales and the company's market share. By projecting profit margins or expenses and the level of investment in working and fixed capital needed to support projected sales, the analyst can forecast net income and cash flow.
- Projections of future performance are needed for discounted cash flow valuation of equity and are often needed in credit analysis to assess a borrower's ability to repay interest and principal of a debt obligation.
- Credit analysis uses financial statement analysis to evaluate credit-relevant factors, including tolerance for leverage, operational stability, and margin stability.
- When ratios using financial statement data and market data are used to screen for potential equity investments, fundamental decisions include which metrics to use as screens, how many metrics to include, what values of those metrics to use as cutoff points, and what weighting to give each metric.
- Analyst adjustments to a company's reported financial statements are sometimes necessary (e.g., when comparing companies that use different accounting methods or assumptions). Adjustments include those related to investments; inventory; property, plant, and equipment; goodwill; and off-balance-sheet financing.

PRACTICE PROBLEMS FOR READING 42

1. Projecting profit margins into the future on the basis of past results would be *most* reliable when the company
   - **A.** is a large, diversified company operating in mature industries.
   - **B.** is in the commodities business.
   - **C.** operates in a single business segment.
   - **D.** is a small, rapidly growing company.
2. Galambos Corporation had an average receivable collection period of 19 days in 2003. Galambos has stated that it wants to decrease its collection period in 2004 to match the industry average of 15 days. Credit sales in 2003 were $300 million, and analysts expect credit sales to increase to $400 million in 2004. To achieve the company's goal of decreasing the collection period, the change in the average accounts receivable balance from 2003 to 2004 that must occur is *closest* to
   - **A.** −$836,000.
   - **B.** −$420,000.
   - **C.** $420,000.
   - **D.** $836,000.
3. Credit analysts are likely to consider which of the following in making a rating recommendation?
   - **A.** Business risk, but not financial risk.
   - **B.** Financial risk, but not business risk.
   - **C.** Both business risk and financial risk.
   - **D.** Neither business risk nor financial risk.
4. When screening for potential equity investments based on return on equity, to control risk an analyst would be *most likely* to include a criterion that requires
   - **A.** positive net income.
   - **B.** negative net income.
   - **C.** positive total assets.
   - **D.** negative shareholders' equity.
5. One concern when screening for low price-to-earnings stocks is that companies with low price-to-earnings ratios may be financially weak. What criteria might an analyst include to avoid inadvertently selecting weak companies?
   - **A.** Current-year sales growth lower than prior-year sales growth.
   - **B.** Net income less than zero.
   - **C.** Debt-to-equity ratio above a certain cutoff point.
   - **D.** Debt-to-total assets ratio below a certain cutoff point.
6. When a database eliminates companies that cease to exist because of a merger or bankruptcy, this can result in
   - **A.** look-ahead bias.
   - **B.** backtesting bias.
   - **C.** survivorship bias.
   - **D.** data-snooping bias.

7. In a comprehensive financial analysis, financial statements should be
A. used as reported without adjustment.
B. adjusted after completing ratio analysis.
C. adjusted after completing common-size analysis.
D. adjusted for differences in accounting standards, such as international financial reporting standards and U.S. generally accepted accounting principles.

8. When comparing financial statements prepared under IFRS with those prepared under U.S. generally accepted accounting principles, analysts may need to make adjustments related to
A. realized gains.
B. realized losses.
C. unrealized gains and losses for trading securities.
D. unrealized gains and losses for available-for-sale securities.

9. When comparing a U.S. company using the last in, first out (LIFO) method of inventory to companies preparing their financial statements under international financial reporting standards (IFRS), analysts should be aware that according to IFRS, the LIFO method of inventory
A. is never acceptable.
B. is always acceptable.
C. is acceptable when applied to finished goods inventory only.
D. is acceptable for raw materials inventory only.

10. An analyst is evaluating the balance sheet of a U.S. company that uses last in, first out (LIFO) accounting for inventory. The analyst collects the following data:

	31 Dec 05	31 Dec 06
Inventory reported on balance sheet	$500,000	$600,000
LIFO reserve	$50,000	$70,000
Average tax rate	30%	30%

After adjustment to convert to first in, first out (FIFO), inventory at 31 December 2006 would be closest to
A. $600,000.
B. $620,000.
C. $649,000.
D. $670,000.

11. An analyst gathered the following data for a company ($ in millions):

	31 Dec 2000	31 Dec 2001
Gross investment in fixed assets	$2.8	$2.8
Accumulated depreciation	$1.2	$1.6

The average age and average depreciable life, respectively, of the company's fixed assets at the end of 2001 are *closest* to

Average Age	Average Depreciable Life
A. 1.75 years	7 years
B. 1.75 years	14 years
C. 4.00 years	7 years
D. 4.00 years	14 years

12. To compute tangible book value, an analyst would

A. add goodwill to stockholders' equity.
B. subtract only goodwill from stockholders' equity.
C. add all intangible assets to stockholders' equity.
D. subtract all intangible assets from stockholders' equity.

13. Which of the following is an off-balance-sheet financing technique? The use of

A. the FIFO inventory method.
B. the LIFO inventory method.
C. capital leases.
D. operating leases.

14. To better evaluate the solvency of a company, an analyst would most likely add to total liabilities

A. the total amount of future capital lease payments.
B. the present value of future capital lease payments.
C. the total amount of future operating lease payments.
D. the present value of future operating lease payments.

INTERNATIONAL STANDARDS CONVERGENCE

by Thomas R. Robinson, Hennie van Greuning, Elaine Henry, and Michael A. Broihahn

READING 43

LEARNING OUTCOMES

The candidate should be able to:

a. identify and explain the major international accounting standards for each asset and liability category on the balance sheet and the key differences from U.S. generally accepted accounting principles (GAAP);

b. identify and explain the major international accounting standards for major revenue and expense categories on the income statement, and the key differences from U.S. GAAP;

c. identify and explain the major differences between international and U.S. GAAP accounting standards concerning the treatment of interest and dividends on the cash flow statement;

d. interpret the effect of differences between international and U.S. GAAP accounting standards on the balance sheet, income statement, and the statement of changes in equity for some commonly used financial ratios.

THEME

The momentum for the convergence between international financial reporting standards (IFRS) and U.S. generally accepted accounting principles has increased significantly over the past few years. The two bodies now issue joint exposure drafts for a number of standards. Around the world, many national accounting standard setters have adopted, or are in the process of adopting, IFRS.

This reading describes the context within which IFRS are issued and objectives for their application in various financial statements. However, the fact that convergence is ongoing implies that standards are frequently changing. Although this text presents basic principles and issues, analysts should also be aware of available resources to find the timeliest information on IFRS.

1 INTRODUCTION

The International Accounting Standards Board (IASB) is the standard-setting body of the International Accounting Standards Committee (IASC) Foundation. The objectives of the IASC Foundation are to develop a single set of global financial reporting standards and to promote the use of those standards. In accomplishing these objectives, the IASC Foundation explicitly aims to bring about convergence between national standards and international standards.

Around the world, many national accounting standard setters have adopted, or are in the process of adopting, the standards issued by the IASB: International Financial Reporting Standards, or IFRS.[1]

Over the past few years, convergence between IFRS and U.S. generally accepted accounting principles (U.S. GAAP), which are issued by the Financial Accounting Standards Board (FASB), has increased significantly. The two accounting standards boards now issue joint exposure drafts for a number of standards. In February 2006, the FASB and IASB published a memorandum of understanding outlining a "roadmap for convergence" over the next several years.

The IFRS *Framework for the Preparation and Presentation of Financial Statements* (referred to here as the "Framework") was introduced in Reading 31. In this reading, we review certain key aspects of the Framework. Section 2 provides an overview of the Framework. Sections 3, 4, and 5 provide additional descriptions of the IFRS relevant to each of the financial statements, noting some of the differences currently remaining between IFRS and U.S. GAAP. Section 6 summarizes the standard setters' agenda for convergence. Section 7 describes the effect on selected financial ratios of current differences between U.S. and international standards. A summary of key points and practice problems in the CFA Institute multiple-choice format conclude the reading.

A note of caution: The stated objective of the IASB/FASB convergence project is to eliminate differences between IFRS and U.S. GAAP. The convergence project implies that frequent changes to accounting standards are bound to continue for a number of years. Because a detailed comparison of current differences between IFRS and U.S. GAAP would be of limited practical value, this reading aims to present basic principles and issues. Analysts should be aware of resources available to find the timeliest information on IFRS, including the website of the IASB (www.iasb.org) and the website of the FASB (www.fasb.org).

---

[1] International accounting standards also include standards with a numbering system identified as "IAS" (international accounting standards), which were issued by the board of the IASC prior to the formation of the IASB in 2001 and the hand-over of standard-setting functions from the IASC's board to the IASB.

THE IFRS FRAMEWORK 2

The IFRS Framework, which is currently being re-examined as part of the international convergence project, was originally published in 1989 and was designed to assist the IASB in developing standards as well as to assist users of financial statements in interpreting the information contained therein. The Framework sets forth the concepts that underlie the preparation and presentation of financial statements and provides guidance on the definition, recognition, and measurement of the elements from which financial statements are constructed. In addition, the Framework discusses the concepts of capital and capital maintenance.

2.1 Key Aspects of the IFRS Framework

The objectives of financial statements, as stated in the Framework, are "to provide information about the financial position, performance, and changes in financial position of an entity; this information should be useful to a wide range of users for the purpose of making economic decisions."[2] The definition, therefore, covers the balance sheet (including the statement of changes in equity), income statement, and cash flow statement.

To achieve the objective of providing useful information, financial statements should have certain characteristics. Recent IASB updates emphasize the following qualitative characteristics related to the usefulness of information in financial statements:

- relevance
- predictive value
- faithful representation (an emphasis on economic substance over form, reliability, and completeness)
- neutrality (absence of bias)
- verifiability

Financial statements provide information on the financial position and performance of an entity by grouping the effects of transactions and other events into the following five broad classes or elements:

Balance Sheet Elements (Financial Position):

- Assets. Resources controlled by an entity as a result of past events and from which future economic benefits are expected to flow to the entity.
- Liabilities. Present obligations of an entity arising from past events, the settlement of which is expected to result in an outflow of resources from the entity.
- Equity. Assets less liabilities (for companies, shareholders' equity), which is the residual interest in the assets of the entity.

[2] *Framework for the Preparation and Presentation of Financial Statements,* IASC, 1989, adopted by IASB 2001, paragraph 12.

Income Statement Elements (Performance):

- Income. Increases in economic benefits that result in an increase in equity, other than increases resulting from contributions by owners. The increases in economic benefits may be in the form of inflows of assets, enhancements to assets, or decreases in liabilities. Income includes both revenues and gains. Revenues are income from the ordinary activities of the entity (e.g., the sale of products). Gains result from activities other than ordinary activities (e.g., the sale of equipment no longer needed).
- Expenses. Decreases in economic benefits that result in decreases in equity, other than decreases because of distributions to owners. The decreases in economic benefits may be in the form of outflows of assets, depletions of assets, or increases in liabilities. (Expenses include losses as well as those items normally thought of as expenses, such as the cost of goods sold or wages.)

Changes in these five basic elements are portrayed in the statement of cash flow and the statement of changes in equity.

2.2 Challenges in Financial Statement Preparation: Timing and Amounts

Two key challenges for preparers of financial statements are determining when to recognize financial events and how to measure the financial effect of these events.

Recognition is the process of incorporating into the financial statement an item that meets the definition of a financial statement element (i.e., assets, liabilities, equity, income, and expenses) and satisfies the criteria for recognition. The IFRS criteria for recognition of an item are that it should be recognized in the financial statements if:

- it is *probable* that any future economic benefit associated with the item will flow to or from the entity; and
- the item has a cost or value that can be *measured with reliability*.

Measurement is the process of determining the monetary effect of financial events and thus the amounts that are to be recognized and presented in the financial statements.

In meeting the challenges of recognition and measurement, financial statement preparers employ judgment about appropriate methods—many of which are constrained by IFRS requirements to use specific methods—and the estimation of relevant parameters. Such judgments and estimates can vary across companies and across time; therefore, analysts should develop awareness of the potential effect of these variations on financial statements.

3 THE BALANCE SHEET

A number of standards, including the Framework described above, apply to the majority of the components of the balance sheet. These include standards describing requirements for companies adopting international financial stan-

dards for the first time,[3] requirements for presenting financial statements under **international financial** standards,[4] and accounting for changes in accounting **principles and estimates.**[5]

Other standards apply more directly to specific components of the balance sheet. The sections below describe the key aspects of the standards relevant to each component of the balance sheet.

3.1 Marketable Securities

The international standards of accounting for marketable securities, contained in IAS No. 39, require that companies recognize securities initially at fair market value; for investments in marketable securities, this is typically the cost to acquire securities.

The fair market value of securities changes over time, and the central issue in accounting for securities is: Should securities continue to be presented at cost or adjusted as changes occur in their fair market value? Under the accounting standards, the answer depends on how the security is categorized.

Securities with fixed maturities and payments (e.g., bonds) that the company intends to hold until maturity (and has the ability to do so) can be categorized as "held to maturity." **Held-to-maturity** securities are presented at their original cost, updated for any amortization of discount or premium. A debt security purchased for an amount greater than its principal value is said to have been purchased at a premium; if purchased for an amount less than its principal value it is said to have been purchased at a discount. Any premium or discount is amortized (i.e., reduced) over the remaining life of the security so that at maturity, the value of the security in the accounting records equals the principal value.

Securities that do not have fixed maturities (e.g., equity) and bonds that a company does not intend to hold until maturity are presented at their fair market value, and the reported value continues to be adjusted as changes occur in the fair market value. Such changes in a security's fair market value during an accounting period, assuming the security is not sold, give rise to unrealized gains or losses. An unrealized gain results from an increase in a security's value over the accounting period, and an unrealized loss results from a decrease in a security's value. If the security is sold, the gain or loss is said to be realized. When securities are sold, a company realizes a gain (loss) if the sale price is greater than (less than) the value of the security in the company's books.

The accounting for unrealized holding gains or losses differs for **held-for-trading securities** (trading securities) versus available-for-sale securities. Trading securities are simply those securities that the company intends to trade, and available-for-sale securities are those that do not fall into any other category. The category "trading securities" also includes derivatives.

Unrealized holding gains or losses on trading securities are recorded in the income statement. Unrealized holding gains or losses on available-for-sale securities are recorded in equity (as part of other comprehensive income) until the securities are sold. So, both trading and available-for-sale securities are valued at market value, but only the unrealized holding gains or losses on trading securities flow directly through the income statement. As a result, the performance of trading securities portfolios is more transparently reflected in the financial statements.

---

[3] IFRS No. 1.

[4] IAS No. 1.

[5] IAS No. 8.

Exhibit 1 summarizes the different categories of marketable securities and their accounting treatment.

EXHIBIT 1 Categories of Marketable Securities and Accounting Treatment

Category	How Measured	Unrealized and Realized Gains and Losses	Income (Interest and Dividends) Reported
Held to maturity	Amortized cost	Unrealized: not reported Realized: reported in income statement	In income statement
Trading	Fair value	Unrealized: reported in income statement Realized: reported in income statement	In income statement
Available for sale	Fair value	Unrealized: reported in equity Realized: reported in income statement	In income statement

EXAMPLE 1

Accounting for Marketable Securities

Assume a company has the following portfolio of marketable securities:

Category	Value at Fiscal Year End 2005	Value at Fiscal Year End 2006
Held to maturity	$10,000,000	$10,000,000
Held for trading	$5,000,000	$5,500,000
Available for sale	$8,000,000	$7,000,000

1. What amount of unrealized holding gains or losses would the company report in total?
2. How much unrealized holding gains or losses would the company report in its income statement?

Solution to 1: The total amount of unrealized holding gains or losses that the company would report is determined by comparing the end-of-period value of held-for-trading and available-for-sale securities with their values as reported at the end of the previous period. In this example, the company would report a total of $500,000 as unrealized holding *losses*, calculated as the value of the held-for-trading and available-for-sale securities at the end of the period ($12,500,000) minus their value at the beginning of the period ($13,000,000).

Solution to 2: The company would report an unrealized holding *gain* of $500,000 in its income statement. The change in the market value of the available-for-sale securities (the unrealized loss of $1,000,000) would not be reported in the income statement. Instead, it would be shown as part of comprehensive income.

An analyst should obtain an understanding of management's rationale for categorizing securities as "trading securities" or as "available for sale." The performance of trading securities portfolios is more transparently reflected in the financial statements because the income statement shows both income (interest and dividends) and changes in value, whether realized or unrealized. In contrast, with available-for-sale securities, there is an asymmetrical treatment of income and changes in value. This asymmetrical treatment can cause an unsophisticated user of financial statements to misinterpret the performance of a company's marketable securities portfolio. It is possible, for example, that unrealized losses could accumulate in equity without affecting the income statement.

An additional standard relevant to marketable securities is the requirement that risk exposures arising from financial instruments be disclosed; requirements include specified minimum qualitative and quantitative disclosures about credit risk, **liquidity risk**, and market risk.[6] Qualitative disclosures require a description of management's objectives, policies, and processes for managing those risks. Quantitative disclosures refer to the provision of information regarding the *extent* to which an entity is exposed to risk. Together, these disclosures provide an overview of the entity's use of financial instruments and the resulting risk exposures.

3.2 Inventories

The reading on balance sheets describes various methods by which companies determine the cost of goods in inventory. Unlike U.S. GAAP, international accounting standards[7] require that the choice of the accounting method used to value inventories should be based upon the order in which products are sold, relative to when they are put into inventory. Therefore, whenever possible, the cost of a unit of inventory should be assigned by specific identification of the unit's costs. In many cases, however, it is necessary to use a formula to calculate inventory costs.

International standards permit the use of two alternative formulas for assigning the cost of inventory: (1) weighted average cost, in which the cost per unit of inventory is determined as a weighted average of the cost of all units of inventory, and (2) first in, first out (FIFO), in which it is assumed that the costs associated with the first units purchased (first in) are considered to be the cost of the first units sold (first out).

---

[6] IFRS No. 7.

[7] IAS No. 2.

Unlike U.S. GAAP, international standards do not allow the use of the LIFO (last in, first out) method to calculate the cost of inventory because the method is not considered a faithful model of inventory flows. The IASB has noted that the use of LIFO is often tax driven because this method results in lower taxable income during periods of rising prices; however, they concluded that tax considerations do not provide a conceptual basis for selecting an appropriate treatment.

Like U.S. GAAP, international standards require inventory to be reported at the lower of cost or net realizable value. However, IFRS permits the reversal of inventory writedowns, but no such provision exists in U.S. GAAP.

3.3 Property, Plant, and Equipment

The international standards of accounting for property, plant, and equipment, contained in IAS No. 16, require companies to recognize these assets initially at cost.

Like U.S. GAAP, international standards allow property, plant, and equipment to be reported in the financial statements at cost less accumulated depreciation. "Depreciation" is the systematic allocation of the cost of the asset over its useful life, and "accumulated depreciation" is the cumulative amount of depreciation expense recorded in relation to the asset.

Unlike U.S. GAAP, international accounting standards allow another alternative: reporting property, plant, and equipment at a revalued amount. When property, plant, and equipment are revalued, they are reported in the financial statements at fair value as of the revaluation date, less accumulated depreciation subsequent to the revaluation. Any revaluation increase is reported as part of equity, unless it is reversing a previous revaluation decrease. (The reason for this is that the previous decrease was reported as a reduction in the company's net income.) Any revaluation decrease is reported in profit and loss unless it is reversing a previous revaluation increase.

3.4 Long-Term Investments

The overall IFRS Framework for accounting for a company's investments in the securities of another company is based on the extent of control that the investing company has on the investee company. In the discussion of marketable securities above, it was assumed that the equity investment gave the investing company no control over the investee. As discussed, in such cases, the investments are designated as "trading" or "available for sale" and reflected at fair value.

If, however, an equity investment *did* give the investing company some control over the investee, the accounting standards require a different treatment. The specific treatment depends on the amount of control. If an investor owns 20 percent or more of the voting power of an investee, such an ownership stake would provide significant influence, where significant influence is defined as "power to participate in financial and operating policy decisions of the investee but is not control or joint control over those policies."[8] When an investor has significant influence, international standards require that the investment be reported using the equity method of accounting. The equity method of accounting means that the investor reports its pro rata share of the investee's profits as an increase in the amount of investment.

[8] IAS No. 28.

If an investor owns more than 50 percent of the voting power of the investee, such an ownership stake would provide significant control and the investee's financial statements would be consolidated with those of the investor. Consolidation roughly means that the investee's assets, liabilities, and income are combined into those of the investor. *Note:* The IFRS standard on business combinations is an active agenda item of the convergence project and is, therefore, subject to change during the 2006–2007 timeframe.

When an investor shares the ownership of an investee, as in a joint venture, control is shared and the investor would account for the investment using a proportionate consolidation method, with the equity method as an alternative. Proportionate consolidation roughly means that the investor's financial statements include its proportionate share of the investee's assets, liabilities, and income.

Exhibit 2 summarizes the different levels of control associated with each level of ownership and the accounting treatment used in each situation.

EXHIBIT 2 Accounting Treatment for Different Levels of an Investor's Percentage Ownership in an Investee and Related Extent of Control

Extent of Control	Percent Ownership	Accounting Treatment	IFRS Reference
Significant influence	Between 20–50%	Equity accounting	IAS No. 28
Control	More than 50%	Business combinations/consolidation	IAS No. 27/IFRS No. 3/SIC 12
Joint control	Shared	Joint ventures/proportionate consolidation or equity accounting	IAS No. 31/SIC 13

Note: SIC = Standing Interpretations Committee.

Like U.S. GAAP, international standards use extent of control as a factor determining whether an investee should be consolidated. U.S. GAAP differs from IFRS in that it allows a dual model: one model based on extent of voting control and one model based on an alternative assessment of economic control. The model based on economic control depends first on the economic substance of the investee and second on the investor's economic interests in the investee (liability for the investee's losses and opportunity to benefit from the investee's gains).

Unlike U.S. GAAP, international standards prescribe that interests in joint ventures should be accounted for using the proportionate consolidation method. International standards allow the equity method as a nonrecommended alternative,[9] whereas U.S. GAAP requires the equity method of accounting.

3.5 Goodwill

IFRS defines goodwill as the amount an acquirer pays to buy another company, minus the fair value of the net identifiable assets acquired. Goodwill is intended

[9] IAS No. 31.

to represent future economic benefits arising from assets that are not capable of being individually identified and separately recognized. Goodwill is considered an intangible asset (i.e., an asset without physical substance). Whereas some intangible assets—so-called identifiable intangible assets, such as patents and trademarks—can be bought and sold individually, goodwill cannot. Goodwill is an unidentifiable intangible.

Under IFRS No. 3, goodwill is capitalized as an asset and tested for impairment annually. Impairment means diminishment in value. Impairment of goodwill is a noncash expense; however, the impairment of goodwill does affect reported net income. When impairment of goodwill is charged against income in the current period, current reported income decreases. This charge against income also leads to reduced net assets and reduced shareholders' equity, but potentially improved return on assets, asset turnover ratios, return on equity, and equity turnover ratios because equity, the denominator in these ratios, is smaller. Even if the market reacts indifferently to an impairment write-off, an analyst should understand the implications of a goodwill write-off and, more generally, evaluate whether reported goodwill has been impaired. Example 2 presents a partial goodwill impairment footnote for Prudential PLC.

EXAMPLE 2

Goodwill Impairment Testing

Susan Lee is examining the financial statements of Prudential PLC and notes that the income statement shows a goodwill impairment charge of £120 million. Lee finds the following footnote to Prudential's financial statements.

Prudential PLC
2005 Annual Report Footnote H1

Impairment Testing

Goodwill does not generate cash flows independently of other groups of assets and thus is assigned to cash generating units (CGUs) for the purposes of impairment testing. These CGUs are based upon how management monitors the business and represent the lowest level to which goodwill can be allocated on a reasonable basis. An allocation of the Group's goodwill to CGUs is shown below:

	2005 £millions	2004 £millions
M&G	1,153	1,153
Japan life company	—	120
Venture investment subsidiaries of the PAC with-profits fund	607	784
Other	188	188
	1,948	2,245

'Other' represents goodwill amounts allocated across cash generating units in Asia and U.S. operations. These goodwill amounts are not individually material. There are no other intangible assets with indefinite useful lives other than goodwill.

Assessment of Whether Goodwill May Be Impaired

With the exception of M&G and venture investment subsidiaries of the PAC with-profits fund the goodwill in the balance sheet relates to acquired life businesses. The Company routinely compares the aggregate of net asset value and acquired goodwill on an IFRS basis of acquired life business with the value of the business as determined using the EEV methodology, as described in section D1. Any excess of IFRS over EEV carrying value is then compared with EEV basis value of current and projected future new business to determine whether there is any indication that the goodwill in the IFRS balance sheet may be impaired.

Goodwill is tested for impairment by comparing the CGUs carrying amount, excluding any goodwill, with its recoverable amount.

M&G

The recoverable amount for the M&G CGU has been determined by calculating its value in use. This has been calculated by aggregating the present value of future cash flows expected to be derived from the component businesses of M&G (based upon management projections) and its current surplus capital.

The discounted cash flow valuation has been based on a three-year plan prepared by M&G, and approved by the directors of Prudential plc, and cash flow projections for later years.

As a cross check to the discounted cash flow analysis, a review was undertaken of publicly available information for companies engaged in businesses comparable to the component businesses, including reported market prices for such companies' shares. In addition, a review was undertaken of publicly available terms of transactions involving companies comparable to the component businesses. In particular, comparison has been made of the valuation multiples implied by the discounted cash flow analysis to current trading multiples of companies comparable to the component businesses, as well as to multiples achieved in precedent transactions.

The value in use is particularly sensitive to a number of key assumptions, as follows:

i. The assumed growth rate on forecast cash flows beyond the terminal year of the budget. A growth rate of 2.5 percent has been used to extrapolate beyond the plan period.

ii. The risk discount rate. Differing discount rates have been applied in accordance with the nature of the individual component businesses. For retail and institutional business a risk discount rate of 12 percent has been applied. This represents the average implied discount rate for comparable UK listed asset managers calculated by reference to risk-free rates, equity risk premiums of 5 percent and an average 'beta' factor for relative market risk of comparable UK listed asset managers. A similarly granular approach has been applied for the other component businesses of M&G.

iii. That asset management contracts continue on similar terms.

Management believes that any reasonable change in the key assumptions would not cause the carrying amount of M&G to exceed its recoverable amount.

Japanese Life Company

As noted above, the entire goodwill relating to the Japanese life operation of £120 million has been deemed to be impaired following impairment testing carried out in 2005. This testing was based on a recoverable amount for the Japanese company that was determined by calculating its value in use based on net present value cash flow projections. Such projections reflected existing business over the expected duration of the contracts and expected new business. A risk discount rate of 5 percent was applied to the projected cash flows. On the basis of the results of this exercise it was determined that all goodwill held in relation to the Japanese business should be written off in 2005.

PAC With-Profits Fund Venture Investment Subsidiaries

The recoverable amount for the ventures entities controlled by the Group through PPM Capital has been determined on a portfolio CGU basis by aggregating fair values calculated for each entity less costs to sell these entities.

The fair value of each entity is calculated by PPM Capital in accordance with the International Private Equity and Venture Capital Valuation Guidelines which set out industry best practice for determining the fair value of private equity investments. The guidelines require that an enterprise value is calculated for each investment, typically using an appropriate multiple applied to the Company's maintainable earnings. All amounts relating to financial instruments ranking higher in a liquidation than those controlled by PPM Capital are then deducted from the enterprise value and a marketability discount applied to the result to give a fair value attributable to the instruments controlled by PPM Capital. The marketability discount ranges from 10 percent to 30 percent, depending on PPM Capital's level of control over a realization process.

Management believes that any reasonable change in the key assumptions would not give rise to an impairment charge.

1. What operating unit resulted in a goodwill impairment charge, and how was the charge computed?
2. For the operating unit identified in Part 1, would an analyst anticipate subsequent goodwill impairments?

Solution to 1: The entire impairment charge for 2005 was related to the Japanese life company operating unit. The loss was determined by projecting future cash flows for this unit and discounting them at a rate of 5 percent.

Solution to 2: Because the impairment charge for 2005 represented all of the goodwill of the Japanese life company operating unit, subsequent goodwill impairments for this operating unit should not occur.

Because goodwill can significantly influence the comparability of financial statements between companies using different accounting methods, analysts sometimes make certain goodwill-related adjustments to a company's financial statements. The objective of such adjustments is to remove any distortion that goodwill and its recognition, amortization, and impairment might create. Adjustments include the following:

- subtracting goodwill from assets and use of this adjusted data to compute financial ratios;
- excluding goodwill impairment charges from income and use of this adjusted data when reviewing operating trends; and
- evaluating future business acquisitions by taking into account the purchase price paid relative to the net assets and earnings prospects of the acquired company.

If the amount an acquirer pays to buy another company is less than the fair value of the net identifiable assets acquired, it is not recognized as "negative goodwill." Instead, a gain is recognized. However, before any gain is recognized, the acquirer should reassess the cost of acquisition and the fair values attributed to the acquiree's identifiable assets, liabilities, and contingent liabilities.

As noted, goodwill arises in connection with acquisitions. Several other aspects of international accounting for acquisitions may be noted. Under the purchase method of accounting,[10] the acquisition price must be allocated to all of the acquired company's identifiable tangible and intangible assets, liabilities, and contingent liabilities. The assets and liabilities of the acquired entity are combined into the financial statements of the acquiring company at their fair values on the acquisition date. Because the acquirer's assets and liabilities, measured at their historical costs, are combined with the acquired company's assets and liabilities, measured at their fair market value on the acquisition date, the acquirer's pre- and post-merger balance sheets are often not easily compared.

Furthermore, under the purchase method, the income statement and the cash flow statements include the operating performance of the acquiree from the date of the acquisition forward. Operating results prior to the acquisition are not restated and remain the same as historically reported by the acquirer. Consequently, although the financial statements of the acquirer will reflect the reality of the acquisition, they will not be comparable before and after the acquisition.

3.6 Intangible Assets Other Than Goodwill

IAS No. 38 includes standards for reporting certain intangible assets other than goodwill. These intangible assets are referred to as "identifiable intangible assets." Identifiable intangible assets arise either from contractual or other legal rights, or must be capable of being separated from the company and sold, transferred, licensed, rented, or exchanged.

The standards for reporting identifiable intangible assets, contained in IAS No. 38, provide that an intangible asset is recognized—at cost—if it is probable

[10] IFRS No. 3.

that the future economic benefits attributable to the asset will flow to the company and if the cost of the asset can be measured reliably. Only those intangibles that have been purchased or manufactured (in limited instances) may be recognized as assets. Internally produced items, such as customer lists, are not recognized as assets.

Given that it meets the criteria for recognition, an intangible asset with a finite useful life is amortized on a systematic basis over the best estimate of its useful life. In other words, the cost of the identifiable intangible asset is allocated systematically over the asset's useful life. If the identifiable intangible asset does not have a finite useful life, it is not amortized. Instead, the asset is tested at least annually for impairment as with goodwill. Testing for impairment involves evaluating whether the current value of an asset is materially lower than its carrying value.

Like U.S. GAAP, international standards allow identifiable intangibles to be reported in the financial statements at cost less amortization and less any impairment charges.

Unlike U.S. GAAP, international accounting standards allow another alternative: reporting identifiable intangible assets at a revalued amount. When identifiable intangible assets are revalued, they are reported in the financial statements at fair value as of the revaluation date, less accumulated amortization subsequent to the revaluation. Any revaluation increase is reported as part of equity, unless it is reversing a previous revaluation decrease. Any revaluation decrease is reported in profit and loss unless it is reversing a previous revaluation increase. U.S. GAAP prohibits revaluations.

Companies also have intangible assets that accounting rules do not include as items that can be recorded in financial statements; these intangible assets include management skill, a positive corporate culture, trademarks, name recognition, a good reputation, proprietary products, and so forth. However, the costs related to these intangible assets—such as training, advertising, and research—must be expensed. An analyst must be aware of the potential value of such unrecorded assets.

3.7 Provisions (Nonfinancial Liabilities)

Nonfinancial liabilities include **provisions**, which are liabilities of uncertain timing or amount, such as warranty obligations, and contingent liabilities, which are liabilities contingent on the occurrence of some event. The standards for reporting nonfinancial liabilities, contained in IAS No. 37, provide that a company should recognize nonfinancial liabilities when it has a present obligation as a result of a past event and the company can reliably estimate the cost to settle the obligation.

The amount recognized as a nonfinancial liability should be the best estimate, as of the balance sheet date, of the cost that will be required to settle the obligation.

4 THE INCOME STATEMENT

A number of standards, including the Framework (described above), apply to the majority of the components of the income statement. These include standards describing requirements for companies adopting international financial standards for the first time, requirements for presenting financial statements under international financial standards, and accounting for changes in accounting principles and estimates.[11]

Other standards apply more directly to specific components of the income statement. The sections below describe the key aspects of the standards relevant to each component in the same order as the components described in the reading discussing the income statement.

4.1 Revenue Recognition: General

The IASB Framework defines income as including both revenue and gains. In IAS No. 18, revenue is defined as the gross inflow of economic benefits during the period, arising in the ordinary course of activities, or resulting in increases in equity other than contributions by equity participants.

IAS No. 18 addresses how revenue is to be measured, namely, at the fair value of consideration received. The standard also addresses the timing of revenue recognition.

Some criteria for recognizing revenue are common to both the sale of goods and the provision of services: It must be possible to reliably measure the amount of revenue and costs of the transaction, and it must be probable that economic benefits of the transaction will flow to the seller. In addition, to recognize revenue from the sale of goods, it is necessary that the risks and rewards of ownership pass to the buyer and that the seller not have continued control over the goods sold. To recognize revenue from the provision of services, it is necessary that the stage of completion of the service can be measured reliably.

U.S. GAAP defines revenue in terms of actual or expected cash flows, and, for revenue recognition, U.S. GAAP focuses extensively on realization and earned status. U.S. GAAP also provides more extensive guidance than IFRS regarding industry-specific issues. Despite such differences, the key principles are similar in U.S. GAAP and IFRS.

4.2 Revenue Recognition for Construction Contracts

IAS No. 11 deals with the recognition of construction contract revenue and costs—in particular, the allocation of contract revenue and costs to the accounting periods in which construction work is performed. The standard applies to the accounting for construction contracts in the financial statements of contractors.

A construction contract is a contract specifically negotiated for the construction of an asset or a combination of assets that are closely interrelated or interdependent in terms of their design, technology, and function, or their ultimate purpose or use. Construction contracts include those for the construction or restoration of assets and the restoration of the environment.

When the outcome of a construction contract can be estimated reliably, revenue and costs (and, therefore, profit) should be recognized based on the stage of completion (percentage of completion method). When the outcome of a contract *cannot* be reliably estimated, revenue should be recognized to the extent that it is probable to recover contract costs. This requirement differs from U.S. GAAP, which requires that the completed contract method be used in such cases.

---

[11] IFRS No. 1, IAS No. 1, and IAS No. 8, respectively.

4.3 Cost of Sales

Two international accounting standards, IAS No. 2 (accounting for the cost of inventories) and IAS No. 18 (revenue recognition), have an effect on cost of sales. As noted, under international standards, LIFO is not an acceptable method for the valuation of inventory. Consequently, financial statements prepared according to U.S. GAAP may differ significantly from those prepared under IFRS.

U.S. GAAP does, however, require that companies using LIFO disclose the information required to enable a user of financial statements to adjust the inventory and cost of sales figures to a basis comparable with financial statements prepared using IFRS.

4.4 Administrative Expenses (Including Employee Benefits)

Administrative (or operating) expenses typically include overheads related to employee costs. The IASB Framework defines expenses to include losses because expenses are decreases in economic benefits that result in a decrease in equity. The inclusion of losses as expenses contrasts with U.S. GAAP, which differentiates expenses from losses by restricting the term "expenses" to refer to those outflows (of cash or the equivalent) that relate to the entity's ongoing primary business operations.

One type of administrative expense with specific international accounting principles is the expense related to employee benefits, such as salaries, bonuses, post-employment benefits, and termination benefits. Recognition and measurement principles, as well as the disclosure requirements, are provided in IAS No. 19. IFRS No. 2 deals with equity compensation benefits, such as share options.

4.5 Depreciation Expenses

As discussed above, depreciation is the process of recognizing the costs of fixed assets over time by systematically decreasing the assets' value and reporting a commensurate expense on the income statement. The term "**depletion**" is used for this process when the asset is a natural resource, and the term "amortization" is used for this process when the asset is an intangible asset. The cost of acquiring land is not depreciated.

International standards require companies to review the depreciation method applied to an asset at least at each financial year-end. If there has been a significant change in the expected pattern of consumption of the future economic benefits embodied in the asset, companies must change the depreciation method to reflect the changed pattern. Similar to U.S. GAAP, such a change is accounted for as a change in accounting estimate[12] and thus reflected on future financial statements.

Various depreciation methods exist, including the straight line method (which allocates evenly the cost of a long-lived asset over its estimated useful life) and accelerated methods (which allocate a greater proportion of the

[12] IAS No. 8.

asset's cost in the earlier years of its useful life, thus accelerating the timing of the depreciation expense). In choosing the appropriate depreciation method, IFRS requires:

- the depreciable amount is allocated on a *systematic* basis over the useful life; and
- the method used must reflect the pattern of expected *consumption*.

Whether the straight line depreciation method or an accelerated method is used, the method complies with IFRS *only* if it reflects the pattern of the expected consumption of the assets.

4.6 Finance Costs

In general, borrowing costs—defined as interest and other costs incurred by an entity in connection with the borrowing of funds—are expensed in the period incurred.

IFRS offers an alternative to expensing borrowing costs immediately. When borrowing costs are incurred in connection with the acquisition, construction, or production of an asset that takes a long time to be ready for its intended use, such borrowing costs can be added to the total cost of the asset.[13] In other words, rather than expensing these costs immediately, a company has the alternative to capitalize these borrowing costs and depreciate them over time. This topic is an item on the list of IASB's short-term convergence projects as of December 2006.

U.S. GAAP requires the capitalization of interest costs for assets that take a substantial time to complete.

4.7 Income Tax Expense

IAS No. 12 prescribes the accounting treatment for income taxes and specifically addresses issues relating to the carrying amount of assets as well as transactions and other events of the current period, which are recognized in the entity's financial statements.

As with U.S. GAAP, international standards provide for the accounting treatment when differences exist between accounting methods allowed by the relevant taxing authority and accounting methods allowed for financial statement reporting (i.e., IFRS). Where differences exist between methods allowable by taxing authorities and by IFRS, differences will exist between taxable profit and financial statement pretax profit (also referred to as "accounting profit"). Such differences give rise to differences in the value of a company's assets and liabilities recorded in its financial statements (balance sheet) and the tax bases of those assets and liabilities. In turn, these differences can result in future taxes payable or receivable, so-called deferred tax liabilities and deferred tax assets.

The primary differences between U.S. GAAP and IFRS are attributable to differences in exceptions to the application of the principles (i.e., differences in the scope of coverage of the principles).

---

[13] IAS No. 23.

4.8 Nonrecurring Items

Nonrecurring items generally include discontinued operations, accounting changes, and unusual or infrequent items. As noted, analysts typically find it useful to break reported earnings down into recurring and nonrecurring components. Recurring earnings are viewed as permanent or sustainable, whereas nonrecurring earnings are considered to be somewhat random and unsustainable. Therefore, analysts often exclude the effects of nonrecurring items when performing a short-term analysis of an entity (e.g., estimating next year's earnings). However, even so-called nonrecurring events, such as sales of a part of a business, tend to recur from time to time, so analysts may include some average (per year) amount of nonrecurring items for longer-term analyses.

IFRS and U.S. GAAP differ in their treatment of these issues, although as with other areas, convergence is occurring.[14]

For discontinued operations, IFRS changed to align with U.S. GAAP. IFRS No. 5 generally converges with SFAS No. 144. The new international guidance, like the U.S. standards, requires that discontinued operations be reported when a company disposes of one of its business components (or when the component is being held for sale) and will no longer have management involvement.

For accounting changes, U.S. GAAP changed to align with IFRS. SFAS No. 154, issued in June 2005, generally converges with IAS No. 8. Changes in accounting principles are accounted for retrospectively, and changes in accounting estimates are accounted for prospectively.

For extraordinary items, convergence has not yet been achieved. U.S. GAAP continues to allow extraordinary items (i.e., items that are both unusual in nature and infrequent in occurrence) to be reported separately from net income.

Unlike U.S. GAAP, IFRS do not distinguish between items that are and are not likely to recur. Furthermore, IFRS do not permit any items to be classified as "extraordinary items." However, IFRS do require the disclosure of all material information that is relevant to understanding a company's performance. The analyst generally can use this information, together with information from outside sources, to estimate amounts of recurring and nonrecurring items.

5 THE CASH FLOW STATEMENT

Both international standards and U.S. GAAP require that a statement of cash flows be included among a company's full set of financial statements (FASB Statement No. 95, *Statement of Cash Flows,* and IAS No. 7, *Cash Flow Statements*) showing the changes in cash and cash equivalents over an accounting period.

Both sets of standards require that the cash flow statement include sections covering operating, investing, and financing activities of the company. The differences between international and U.S. standards arise in the classification of certain cash flows.

International standards allow companies to report cash inflows from interest and dividends as either operating or investing activities and cash outflows for interest and dividends as either operating or financing activities (see Exhibit 3).

[14] This topic is discussed in "Convergence: In Search of the Best," D. Herrmann and I.P.N. Hauge, *Journal of Accountancy* online edition, January 2006: www.aicpa.org/PUBS/JOFA/jan2006/herrmann.htm.

In contrast, U.S. standards require the following: Interest and dividends received are classified as inflows from operating activities; interest paid is classified as an outflow for operating activities; and dividends paid are classified as financing activities.

EXHIBIT 3 Statement of Cash Flows

Classification of Interest and Dividends under International and U.S. Standards

Category	Classification in IFRS vs. U.S. GAAP
Cash Flows from *Operating* Activities	
Cash from principal revenue-producing activities of the entity (i.e., cash receipts from customers less cash payments to suppliers and employees).	
Interest received	IFRS alternatives: operating or investing section
	U.S. GAAP: mandated operating section
Dividends received	IFRS alternatives: operating or investing section
	U.S. GAAP: mandated operating section
Interest paid	IFRS alternatives: operating or financing section
	U.S. GAAP: mandated operating section
Dividends paid (IFRS only)	IFRS alternatives: operating or financing section
Cash Flows from *Investing* Activities	
Purchases of long-term assets and other investments not included in cash equivalents; proceeds on sale.	
Interest received (IFRS only)	IFRS alternatives: operating or investing section
Dividends received (IFRS only)	IFRS alternatives: operating or investing section
Cash Flows from *Financing* Activities	
Cash from issuance or repayment of equity capital and/or long-term debt.	
Dividends paid	IFRS alternatives: operating or financing section
	U.S. GAAP: mandated financing section
Interest paid	IFRS alternatives: operating or financing section

6 STANDARD SETTERS' AGENDA FOR CONVERGENCE

As noted in the introduction to this reading, in February 2006, the FASB and IASB published a memorandum of understanding outlining a "roadmap for convergence" over the next several years. This section summarizes the standard setters' agenda for convergence over the period 2006 to 2008.

By 2008, the IASB and FASB aim to conclude whether any major differences should be eliminated in the following topics for short-term convergence, and if so, to complete the work to do so: fair value option (allow companies to report financial assets and liabilities at fair value on a contract-by-contract basis, converging to IFRS); borrowing costs (eliminate alternative to expense immediately when in connection with longer-term projects, converging to U.S. GAAP); research and development; impairment; segment reporting; subsequent events; and income taxes.

Topics that are already on an active agenda for IASB and/or FASB include business combinations, consolidations, fair value measurement guidance, liabilities and equity distinctions, performance reporting, post-retirement benefits (including pensions), and revenue recognition. Joint IASB and FASB goals for 2008 have been established for each of these topics.

7 EFFECT OF DIFFERENCES BETWEEN ACCOUNTING STANDARDS

As we note throughout this reading, differences between international and U.S. accounting standards are decreasing as convergence between the two sets of standards occurs. Differences that do exist have an effect on commonly used financial ratios. We discuss several major differences here.

If comparing a U.S. company that uses LIFO accounting with an international company for whom this method is not allowable, an analyst will make adjustments. Specifically, using financial statement note disclosures, the analyst will adjust the U.S. company's profits (gross, operating, and net), ending inventory, and total assets. These adjustments will affect certain profitability, solvency, liquidity, and activity ratios. For comparison purposes, inventory is adjusted from LIFO to FIFO by adding the LIFO reserve to the LIFO inventory value on the balance sheet. Under U.S. GAAP, a company must disclose the LIFO reserve amount in the financial statement notes if the LIFO method is followed. In addition, cost of goods sold is adjusted from LIFO to FIFO by subtracting the net increase in the LIFO reserve that occurred during the fiscal year. Example 3 illustrates a LIFO to FIFO conversion.

EXAMPLE 3

LIFO Effects on Financial Statements and Ratios

Buccaneer Corporation prepares its financial statements (Exhibits 4 and 5) in accordance with U.S. GAAP and uses the LIFO inventory method. During the year, Buccaneer's LIFO reserve increased from $40 million to $64 million. The income tax rate is 30 percent.

EXHIBIT 4 **Income Statement and Balance Sheet under LIFO and FIFO Inventory Accounting ($ millions)**

Account	LIFO Method	LIFO to FIFO Adjustment	FIFO Method
Sales	1,800.0	—	1,800.0
Cost of sales	1,060.0	(24.0)	1,036.0
Gross profit	740.0	24.0	764.0
Operating expenses	534.0	—	534.0
Income before taxes	206.0	24.0	230.0
Income taxes	61.8	(7.2)	69.0
Net income	144.2	(16.8)	161.0
Cash	80.0	—	80.0
Inventory	356.0	64.0	420.0
Other current assets	344.0	—	344.0
Fixed assets, net	1,120.0	—	1,120.0
Total assets	1,900.0	64.0	1,964.0
Current liabilities	200.0	—	200.0
Noncurrent liabilities	424.0	19.2	443.2
Common stock	840.0	—	840.0
Retained earnings	436.0	44.8	480.8
Total liabilities and equity	1,900.0	64.0	1,964.0

The net increase in Buccaneer's LIFO reserve during the fiscal year was $24 million ($64 million − $40 million). To adjust from LIFO to FIFO, the net increase in the LIFO reserve must be subtracted from the LIFO reported cost of sales. (A net decrease in the LIFO reserve during the year would be added to LIFO reported cost of sales in a LIFO to FIFO conversion.) Accordingly, because reported gross profits are $24 million higher after the FIFO conversion, income tax expense will increase by $7.2 million ($24 million × 30% income tax rate), resulting in an increase to net income of $16.8 million. For the balance sheet conversion, the year-end LIFO reserve of $64 million is added to the LIFO reported inventory, resulting in an increase of $64 million to both inventory and total assets under FIFO. In addition, the deferred income tax liabilities will increase by $19.2 million ($64 million × 30% income tax rate), and retained earnings will increase by $44.8 million ($64 million × 70% after-tax retention).

Comparative selected profitability, solvency, liquidity, and activity ratios for Buccaneer Corporation under the two inventory methods are given in Exhibit 5.

EXHIBIT 5 Financial Ratios under LIFO and FIFO Inventory Accounting

Ratio	Formula	LIFO Method	FIFO Method
Net profit margin	Net income ÷ Net sales	8.01%	8.94%
Financial leverage	Total assets ÷ Total equity	1.489	1.487
Current ratio	Current assets ÷ Current liabilities	3.90	4.22
Inventory turnover	Cost of sales ÷ Ending inventory	2.98 turns	2.47 turns

If comparing an IFRS company with a U.S. company that reports extraordinary items separately from net income but which reports certain unusual items as part of operating income, an analyst will examine the financial statement notes to identify similar items that have received different reporting treatment.

If comparing an IFRS company, which has written up the value of its intangible or tangible long-term assets, with a U.S. company, an analyst will eliminate the effect of the write-ups in calculating asset-based ratios. Example 4 illustrates a revaluation adjustment conversion.

EXAMPLE 4

Analyst Adjustments to Revaluations in IFRS/U.S. GAAP Comparisons

Aramis Ltd. prepares its financial statements in accordance with IFRS. During the current year, Aramis revalued its fixed assets upward by a total of €75 million to better reflect its present fair market value.

The analyst must reverse the revaluation adjustments that Aramis has made if Aramis is to be compared with a company that complies with U.S. GAAP. For Aramis, the analyst will reduce both fixed assets and other equity by the upward revaluation of €75 million. Exhibit 6 shows these adjustments.

EXHIBIT 6 Analyst Adjustments to Revaluation (€ millions)

Account	Unadjusted	Reversal of Revaluation	Post-Adjustment
Sales	1,700.0	—	1,700.0
Cost of sales	1,040.0	—	1,040.0
Gross profit	660.0	—	660.0
Operating expenses	475.0	—	475.0
Income before taxes	185.0	—	185.0
Income taxes	74.0	—	74.0
Net income	111.0	—	111.0

(Exhibit continued on next page . . .)

EXHIBIT 6 (continued)

Account	Unadjusted	Reversal of Revaluation	Post-Adjustment
Fixed assets, net	1,150.0	(75.0)	1,075.0
Inventory	310.0	—	310.0
Other current assets	120.0	—	120.0
Cash	20.0	—	20.0
Total assets	1,600.0	(75.0)	1,525.0
Noncurrent liabilities	370.0	—	370.0
Current liabilities	225.0	—	225.0
Contributed capital	550.0	—	550.0
Earned and other equity	455.0	(75.0)	380.0
Total liabilities and equity	1,600.0	(75.0)	1,525.0

Selected comparative performance ratios for Aramis under the two approaches are given in Exhibit 7.

EXHIBIT 7 Financial Ratios Pre- and Post-Adjustment

Ratio	Formula	Unadjusted	Post-Adjustment
Return on assets	Net income ÷ Total assets	6.94%	7.28%
Return on equity	Net income ÷ Total equity	11.04%	11.94%
Asset turnover	Net sales ÷ Total assets	1.063 turns	1.115 turns
Equity turnover	Net sales ÷ Total equity	1.692 turns	1.828 turns
Financial leverage	Total assets ÷ Total equity	1.592	1.640

SUMMARY

The IASB is the standard-setting body of the IASC Foundation. The objectives of the IASC Foundation are to develop a single set of global financial reporting standards and to promote the use of those standards. In accomplishing these objectives, the IASC Foundation explicitly aims to bring about convergence between national standards and international standards. Many national accounting standard setters have adopted, or are in the process of adopting, the IFRS.

This reading discussed both the IFRS Framework and the IFRS standards for reporting accounting items on the balance sheet, income statement, and cash flow statement. Key points include the following:

- The objectives of financial statements, as stated in the Framework, are "to provide information about the financial position, performance, and changes in financial position of an entity; this information should be useful to a wide range of users for the purpose of making economic decisions."
- To achieve the objective of providing useful information, financial statements should have the following qualitative characteristics: relevance, predictive value, faithful representation, neutrality, and verifiability.
- Financial statements provide information on the financial position and performance of an entity by grouping the effects of transactions and other events into the following five broad elements: assets, liabilities, equity, income, and expenses.
- Both IFRS and U.S. GAAP require companies to present basic financial statements: balance sheet, income statement, statement of cash flows, and statement of changes in equity.
- One major difference between IFRS and U.S. GAAP affecting all three statements involves inventories: U.S. GAAP allows the LIFO method for inventory costing, whereas IFRS does not.
- Another major balance sheet difference between IFRS and U.S. GAAP is that IFRS allows companies to revalue property, plant, and equipment as well as intangible assets.
- Accounting for investments is another area of difference: IFRS uses a voting control model to determine need for consolidation, whereas U.S. GAAP uses a dual model based on voting control and economic control.
- An important difference between IFRS and U.S. GAAP is the treatment of some nonrecurring items. IFRS does not permit any items to be classified as "extraordinary items."
- International standards allow companies to report cash inflows from interest and dividends as relating to either "operating" or "investing activities," and cash outflows for interest and dividends as relating to either "operating" or "financing activities."
- Convergence between IFRS and U.S. GAAP has increased significantly over the past few years and is continuing.
- Analysts should know how to make financial statement adjustments to better compare IFRS reporting companies with those companies reporting under U.S. GAAP.

PRACTICE PROBLEMS FOR READING 43

1. According to the IFRS Framework, which of the following is a qualitative characteristic related to the usefulness of information in financial statements?

A. Neutrality.

B. Timeliness.

C. Accrual basis.

D. Going concern.

2. Under the IFRS Framework, changes in the elements of financial statements are *most likely* portrayed in the

A. balance sheet.

B. income statement.

C. cash flow statement.

D. accounting policies and notes.

3. Under IASB standards, which of the following categories of marketable securities is *most likely* to incur an asymmetrical treatment of income and changes in value?

A. Held for trading.

B. Held to maturity.

C. Available for sale.

D. Joint venture interests.

4. According to IASB standards, which of the following inventory methods is *most preferred*?

A. Specific identification.

B. Weighted average cost.

C. First in, first out (FIFO).

D. Last in, first out (LIFO).

5. According to IASB standards, which of the following inventory methods is not acceptable?

A. Specific identification.

B. Weighted average cost.

C. First in, first out (FIFO).

D. Last in, first out (LIFO).

6. Under IASB standards, inventory writedowns are

A. not allowed.

B. allowed but not reversible.

C. allowed and subject to reversal.

D. treated similarly to U.S. GAAP.

7. According to IASB standards, property, plant, and equipment revaluations are

A. not allowed.

B. allowed for decreases only.

C. treated similarly to U.S. GAAP.

D. allowed for both increases and decreases.

8. Under IASB standards, a joint venture interest is accounted for by using
   A. consolidation.
   B. the equity method or consolidation.
   C. consolidation or proportionate consolidation.
   D. the equity method or proportionate consolidation.
9. Under IASB standards, goodwill
   A. may be written off when acquired.
   B. is subject to an annual impairment test.
   C. is amortized over its expected useful life.
   D. may be recorded when excess industry profits are generated.
10. Under IASB standards, negative goodwill
    A. must be recorded as a gain.
    B. is prorated to the noncurrent assets.
    C. is accounted for as an extraordinary item.
    D. is amortized to income over a 10-year period.
11. Under IASB standards, an identifiable intangible asset with an indefinite life
    A. may be written off when acquired.
    B. is amortized over a 20-year period.
    C. is accounted for in the same manner as goodwill.
    D. remains unadjusted until its life becomes determinable.
12. Under IASB standards, identifiable intangible assets are
    A. only revalued downward, with the decrease reported to equity.
    B. only revalued downward, with the decrease reported to profit and loss.
    C. revalued upward and reported to equity when reversing a previous revaluation decrease.
    D. revalued upward and reported to profit and loss when reversing a previous revaluation decrease.
13. Under IASB standards, when the outcome of a construction contract cannot be estimated reliably, revenue and costs should be
    A. recognized by using the completed contract method.
    B. deferred until the outcome can be estimated reliably.
    C. recognized by using the percentage of completion contract method.
    D. recognized to the extent that it is probable to recover contract costs.
14. Under IASB standards, fixed asset depreciation methods must be
    A. rational and systematic.
    B. rational and reviewed at least annually.
    C. rational and reflect the pattern of expected consumption.
    D. systematic and reflect the pattern of expected consumption.
15. Under IASB standards, cash inflows for the receipt of interest and dividends are
    A. operating cash flows.
    B. either operating or investing cash flows.
    C. either investing or financing cash flows.
    D. either operating or financing cash flows.

16. Under IASB standards, cash outflows for the payment of interest are

A. operating cash flows.

B. either operating or investing cash flows.

C. either investing or financing cash flows.

D. either operating or financing cash flows.

17. Under IASB standards, cash outflows for the payment of dividends are

A. financing cash flows.

B. either operating or investing cash flows.

C. either investing or financing cash flows.

D. either operating or financing cash flows.

18. When comparing a U.S. company that uses LIFO accounting with an IFRS company that uses FIFO accounting, an analyst will

A. make no adjustment if the adjustment data are unavailable.

B. adjust either company to achieve comparability with the other.

C. adjust the U.S. company to achieve comparability with the IFRS company.

D. adjust the IFRS company to achieve comparability with the U.S. company.

19. When comparing an IFRS company that has written up the value of its intangible assets with a U.S. company, an analyst will eliminate the effect of the write-ups in calculating the

A. gross margin.

B. earnings per share.

C. fixed asset turnover ratio.

D. financial leverage multiplier.

APPENDIX

SOLUTIONS FOR READING 29

1. B is correct. This is the role of financial reporting. The role of financial analysis is to evaluate the financial reports.
2. A is correct. The balance sheet portrays the current financial position. The income statement and cash flow statement present different aspects of performance, and the statement of owners' equity presents changes in equity (one aspect of financial position).
3. B is correct. Profitability is the performance aspect measured by the income statement. The balance sheet portrays the current financial position. The cash flow statement presents a different aspect of performance, and the statement of owners' equity presents changes in equity (one aspect of financial position).
4. A is correct. The footnotes disclose choices in accounting methods, estimates, and assumptions.
5. C is correct. Although some aspects of management compensation would be found in the footnotes, this is a required disclosure in the proxy statement.
6. D is correct. This is a component of management's discussion and analysis.
7. D is correct. An unqualified opinion is a "clean" opinion and indicates that the financial statements present the company's performance and financial position fairly.
8. C is correct. Ratios are an output of the process data step but are an input into the analyze/interpret data step.

SOLUTIONS FOR READING 30

1. C is correct. Sales of products, a primary business activity, are classified as an operating activity. Issuance of debt would be a financing activity. Acquisition of a competitor and the sale of surplus equipment would both be classified as investing activities.
2. A is correct. Issuance of debt would be classified as a financing activity. B is incorrect because payment of income taxes would be classified as an operating activity. Both C and D are incorrect because the receipt of dividends and investments in common stock would be generally classified as investing activities.
3. A is correct. An asset is an economic resource of an entity that will either be converted into cash or consumed.
4. D is correct. Owners' equity is a residual claim on the resources of a business.
5. A is correct. Assets must equal liabilities plus owners' equity and, therefore, €2,000 = €1,200 + Owners' equity. Owners' equity must be €800.
6. C is correct.

Beginning retained earnings	\$1,400
+ Net income	200
− Distributions to owners	(100)
= Ending retained earnings	\$1,500

7. D is correct.

Assets = Liabilities + Contributed capital + Beginning retained earnings − Distributions to owners + Revenues − Expenses

Liabilities	\$1,000
+ Contributed capital	500
+ Beginning retained earnings	600
− Distributions to owners	(0)
+ Revenues	5,000
− Expenses	(4,300)
= Assets	\$2,800

8. D is correct. This is a contribution of capital by the owners. Assets would increase by \$500,000 and contributed capital would increase by \$500,000, maintaining the balance of the accounting equation.
9. A is correct. The payment of January rent represents prepaid rent (an asset), which will be adjusted at the end of January to record rent expense. Cash (an asset) decreases by \$12,000. Deposits (an asset) increase by \$4,000. Prepaid rent (an asset) increases by \$8,000. There is no net change in assets.
10. C is correct. The sale of products without receipt of cash results in an increase in accounts receivable (an asset) of €10,000. The balance in inventory (an asset) decreases by €8,000. The net increase in assets is €2,000. This would be balanced by an increase in revenue of €10,000 and an increase in expenses (costs of goods sold) of €8,000.
11. D is correct. The receipt of cash in advance of delivering goods or services results in unearned revenue, which is a liability. The company has an obligation to deliver \$30,000 in goods in the future. This balances the increase in cash (an asset) of \$30,000.

12. B is correct. Depreciation is an expense and increases accumulated depreciation. Accumulated depreciation is a contra account which reduces property, plant, and equipment (an asset) by €250,000. Assets decrease by €250,000, and expenses increase by €250,000.
13. A is correct. The balance sheet shows the financial position of a company at a particular point in time. The balance sheet is also known as a "statement of financial position."
14. B is correct. The three sections of the statement of cash flows are operating, investing, and financing activities.
15. D is correct. Cash received prior to revenue recognition increases cash and deferred or unearned revenue. This is a liability until the company provides the promised goods or services.
16. A is correct. When cash is to be received after revenue has been recognized but no billing has actually occurred, an unbilled (accrued) revenue is recorded. Such accruals would usually occur when an accounting period ends prior to a company billing its customer. This type of accrual can be contrasted with a simple credit sale, which is reflected as an increase in revenue and an increase in accounts receivable. No accrual is necessary.
17. B is correct. Payment of expenses in advance is called a prepaid expense which is classified as an asset.
18. C is correct. When an expense is incurred but not yet recognized and no cash has been paid, expenses are increased and a liability ("accrued expense") is established for the same amount.
19. B is correct. The general ledger is the collection of all business transactions sorted by account in an accounting system. The general journal is the collection of all business activities sorted by date.
20. C is correct. In order to balance the accounting equation, the company would either need to increase assets or decrease liabilities. Creating a fictitious asset would be one way of attempting to cover up the fraud.

SOLUTIONS FOR READING 31

1. C is correct. An objective of financial statements is not to provide information about users. The objectives are to provide information about the entity's financial position, performance, and changes in financial position.
2. C is correct. The IASB is currently charged with developing International Accounting Standards. The IASC was the predecessor organization to the IASB.
3. C is correct. U.S. Financial Accounting Standards are developed by the FASB.
4. D is correct. The SEC requires that shareholders of a company receive a proxy statement prior to a shareholder meeting. Such meetings are held at least once a year, but any special meetings would also require a proxy.
5. D is correct. The qualitative characteristics of financial statements according to the IFRS Framework are understandability, relevance, reliability, and comparability.
6. B is correct. The Framework recognizes the following constraints on providing relevant, reliable information: timeliness, benefit versus cost, and balancing of the qualitative characteristics.
7. C is correct. The IFRS Framework identifies two important underlying assumptions of financial statements: accrual basis and going concern. Going concern is the assumption that the entity will continue to operate for the foreseeable future. Enterprises with the intent to liquidate or materially curtail operations would require different information for a fair presentation.
8. A is correct. The IFRS Framework identifies two important underlying assumptions of financial statements: accrual basis and going concern. Accrual basis reflects the effects of transactions and other events being recognized when they occur, not when the cash flows. These effects are recorded and reported in the financial statements of the periods to which they relate.
9. B is correct. The qualitative characteristic of reliability is contributed to by faithful representation, substance over form, neutrality, prudence, and completeness.
10. D is correct. Fair presentation involves both full disclosure and transparency.
11. D is correct. Historical cost is the consideration paid to acquire an asset.
12. D is correct. The amount that would be received in an orderly disposal is realizable value.
13. D is correct. Under IAS No. 1, a complete set of financial statements includes: a balance sheet, an income statement, a statement of changes in equity, a cash flow statement, and notes comprising a summary of significant accounting policies and other explanatory notes.
14. C is correct. The elements of financial statements related to the measure of performance are income and expenses.
15. A is correct. The elements of financial statements related to the measurement of financial position are assets, liabilities, and equity.
16. A is correct. Timeliness is not a characteristic of a coherent financial reporting framework. Consistency, transparency, and comprehensiveness are characteristics of a coherent financial reporting framework.

17. A is correct. The FASB has been criticized in the past as having a rules-based approach; however, it has indicated that it is moving toward an objectives-oriented approach.

18. B is correct. A discussion of the impact would be the most meaningful, although A and C would also be useful.

SOLUTIONS FOR READING 32

1. C is correct. IAS No. 1 states that expenses may be categorized by either nature or function.
2. D is correct. Cost of goods sold is a classification by function. The other three expenses represent classifications by nature.
3. D is correct. Gross margin is revenue minus cost of goods sold. A represents net income; B represents pretax income; and C represents operating income.
4. D is correct. Under IFRS, income includes increases in economic benefits from increases in assets, enhancement of assets, and decreases in liabilities.
5. C is correct. Net revenue is revenue for goods sold during the period less any returns and allowances, or $1,000,000 minus $100.000 = $900,000. A is incorrect; this represents gross profit. B is incorrect; this is the cash collected that is not used under the accrual basis. D is incorrect; this is revenue before subtracting the returns.
6. D is correct. The preferred method is the percentage-of-completion method. The completed contract method should be used only when the outcome cannot be measured reliably. The other two methods do not relate to long-term contracts.
7. A is correct. Under the completed contract method, no revenue would be reported until the project is completed. B is incorrect. This is the profit under the percentage-of-completion method. C is incorrect. This is the revenue under the percentage-of-completion method. D is incorrect. This is the revenue to be reported upon contract completion.
8. B is correct. The installment method apportions the cash receipt between cost recovered and profit using the ratio of profit to sales value (i.e., $3,000,000 ÷ $5,000,000 = 60 percent). Argo will, therefore, recognize $600,000 in profit for 2006 ($1,000,000 cash received × 60 percent). A uses the cost recovery method, C is the cash received, and D is the total profit that will be realized for 2006 and 2007 when all the cash ($5,000,000) is collected.
9. A is correct. Under the cost recovery method, the company would not recognize any profit until the cash amounts paid by the buyer exceeded Argo's cost of $2,000,000.
10. D is correct. Revenue for barter transactions should be measured based on the fair value of revenue from similar nonbarter transactions with unrelated parties.
11. B is correct. Apex is not the owner of the goods and should only report its net commission as revenue. D is the amount paid to the owners. C is the total amount collected on behalf of the owners.
12. C is correct. Under the First In, First Out (FIFO) method, the first 10,000 units sold came from the October purchases at $10, and the next 2,000 units sold came from the November purchases at $11. A is incorrect; this is cost of goods sold under the Last In, First Out (LIFO) method. B is incorrect because it places a cost of $10 on all units. D is incorrect because it uses the weighted average cost method.

13. D is correct. Under the weighted average cost method:

October purchases	10,000 units	\$100,000
November purchases	5,000 units	\$55,000
Total	15,000 units	\$155,000

\$155,000/15,000 units = \$10.3333 × 12,000 units = \$124,000.

14. B is correct. The Last In, First Out (LIFO) method is not permitted under IFRS. The other three methods are permitted.

15. B is correct. Straight-line depreciation would be (\$600,000 − \$50,000)/10, or \$55,000. A assumes the machine was totally expensed in 2007. C ignores the \$50,000 residual value. D improperly adds (rather than subtracts) the \$50,000 residual value.

16. C is correct. Double-declining balance depreciation would be \$600,000 × 20 percent (twice the straight-line rate). A uses 10 percent instead of 20 percent. B applies the depreciation percentage after the residual value has been subtracted from the initial book value. D assumes the full depreciable amount is expensed in the first year.

17. D is correct. This would result in the highest amount of depreciation in the first year and hence the lowest amount of net income relative to the other choices.

18. A is correct. A fire may be infrequent, but it would still be part of continuing operations. IFRS does not permit classification of an item as extraordinary. Discontinued operations relate to a decision to dispose of an operating division, and a prior period adjustment involves correction of an error.

19. D is correct. The weighted average number of shares outstanding for 2007 is 1,050,000. Basic earnings per share would be \$1,000,000 divided by 1,050,000, or \$0.95. A subtracts the common dividends from net income and uses 1,100,000 shares. B subtracts common dividends from net income and uses 1,000,000 shares. C uses the proper net income but 1,100,000 shares.

20. B is correct. With stock options, the treasury stock method must be used. Under that method, the company would receive \$100,000 (10,000 × \$10) and would repurchase 6,667 shares (\$100,000/\$15). The shares for the denominator would be:

Shares outstanding	1,000,000
Options exercises	10,000
Treasury shares purchased	(6,667)
Denominator	1,003,333

SOLUTIONS FOR READING 33

1. B is correct. Assets are resources controlled by a company as a result of past events.
2. A is correct. Assets = Liabilities + Equity and, therefore, Assets − Liabilities = Equity.
3. C is correct. A classified balance sheet is one that classifies assets and liabilities as current or noncurrent and provides a subtotal for current assets and current liabilities.
4. B is correct. Goodwill is a long-term asset, and the others are all current assets.
5. A is correct. Current liabilities are those liabilities, including debt, due within one year. Long-term liabilities are not due within the current year.
6. B is correct. The cash received from customers represents an asset. The obligation to provide a product in the future is a liability called "unearned income" or "unearned revenue." Once the product is delivered, the liability will be converted into revenue.
7. C is correct. Inventories are carried at historical cost, unless the current replacement cost of the inventory is less.
8. D is correct. Paying rent in advance will reduce cash and increase prepaid expenses, both of which are assets.
9. D is correct. Accrued liabilities are expenses that have been reported on a company's income statement but have not yet been paid.
10. B is correct. Initially, goodwill is measured as the difference between the purchase price paid for an acquisition and the fair value of the acquired company's net assets.
11. C is correct. Impairment write downs reduce equity in the denominator of the debt-to-equity ratio but do not affect debt, so the debt-to-equity ratio is expected to increase. Impairment write downs reduce total assets but do not affect revenue. Thus, total asset turnover is expected to increase.
12. C is correct. For financial assets classified as trading securities, unrealized gains and losses are reported on the income statement and flow to shareholders' equity as part of retained earnings.
13. D is correct. For financial assets classified as available for sale, unrealized gains and losses are not recorded on the income statement but do appear on the balance sheet. Shareholders' equity is adjusted through a separate line item for valuation gains and losses termed "other comprehensive income."
14. A is correct. When financial assets are classified as held to maturity, gains and losses are recognized only when realized.
15. B is correct. IFRS requires that minority interest in consolidated subsidiaries be classified as shareholders' equity.
16. D is correct. Retained earnings are a component of owners' equity.
17. B is correct. Share repurchases reduce the company's cash (an asset). Shareholders' equity is reduced because there are fewer shares outstanding and treasury stock is an offset to owners' equity.
18. C is correct. Common-size analysis (as presented in the reading) tells investors how the composition of assets is changing over time. As a result, it can signal when the company is becoming more leveraged.

19. A is correct. The current ratio compares assets that can quickly be turned into cash to liabilities that need to be paid within one year. The other ratios are more suited to longer-term concerns.

20. A is correct. The cash ratio determines how much of a company's near-term obligations can be settled with existing cash balances.

21. C is correct. The debt-to-equity ratio tells how much financial risk a company is exposed to.

22. B is correct. The quick ratio ([Cash + Marketable securities + Receivables] ÷ Current liabilities) is 0.81 ([¥779,103 + ¥1,492 + ¥460,202 + ¥1,113,071 − ¥87,709] ÷ ¥2,809,368).

23. D is correct. Deferred insurance acquisition costs increased as a percentage of total assets from 3.84 percent in 2004 (¥349,194 ÷ ¥9,090,662) to 3.95 percent in 2005 (¥374,805 ÷ ¥9,499,100). Although the accounts given in choices A, B, and C increased in absolute Japanese yen terms during 2005, these accounts declined as a percentage of total assets in 2005.

24. C is correct. The financial leverage ratio (Total assets ÷ Total equity) is 3.31 (¥9,499,100 ÷ ¥2,870,338).

SOLUTIONS FOR READING 34

1. D is correct. Answer A is incorrect because these are elements of the income statement. Answers B and C are incorrect: These are items of information involved in making calculations for the statement of cash flows.
2. B is correct. Purchases and sales of long-term assets are considered investing activities. Note: Absent information to the contrary, it is assumed that the sale of a building involves cash. If, for example, the transaction had involved the exchange of a building for common stock or the exchange of a building for a long-term note payable, it would have been considered a significant noncash activity.
3. A is correct. Answers B, C, and D are all items that are included in operating cash flows. Note: International accounting standards allow companies to include receipt of interest and dividends as either operating or investing cash flows, and international accounting standards allow companies to include payment of interest and dividends as either operating or financing cash flows.
4. B is correct. Noncash transactions, if significant, are reported as supplementary information, not in the investing or financing sections of the cash flow statement.
5. C is correct. Interest expense is always classified as an operating cash flow under U.S. GAAP but may be classified as either an operating or financing cash flow under IFRS.
6. A is correct. Taxes are only required to be separately disclosed on the cash flow statement under IFRS.
7. A is correct. The operating section may be prepared under the indirect method. The other sections are always prepared under the direct method.
8. A is correct. Under the indirect method, the operating section would begin with net income and adjust it to arrive at operating cash flow. The other three items would appear under the direct method as a cash flow statement prepared under U.S. GAAP. Note that cash paid for interest may appear on an indirect cash flow statement under IFRS if classified as a financing activity.
9. C is correct. Revenues of $100 million minus the increase in accounts receivable of $10 million equal $90 million cash received from customers. The increase in accounts receivable means that the company received less in cash than it reported as revenue.
10. B is correct. Cost of goods sold of $80 million plus the increase in inventory of $5 million equals purchases from suppliers of $85 million. The increase in accounts payable of $2 million means that the company paid $83 million in cash ($85 million minus $2 million) to its suppliers.
11. D is correct. Cost of goods sold of $75 million less the decrease in inventory of $6 million equals purchases from suppliers of $69 million. The increase in accounts payable of $2 million means that the company paid $67 million in cash ($69 million minus $2 million).
12. C is correct. Beginning wages payable of $3 million plus wage expense of $20 million, minus ending wages payable of $1 million equals $22 million. The expense of $20 million plus the $2 million decrease in wages payable equals $22 million.

13. D is correct. Cash received from customers = sales + the decrease in accounts receivable = 254.6 + 4.9 = 259.5. Cash paid to suppliers = cost of goods sold + the increase in inventory − increase in accounts payable = 175.9 + 8.8 − 2.6 = 182.1

14. D is correct. Interest expense of $19 million less the increase in interest payable of $3 million equals $16 million. Tax expense of $6 million plus the decrease in taxes payable of $4 million equals $10 million.

15. C is correct. Net income (NI) for 2005 can be computed as the change in retained earnings, $25, plus the dividends paid in 2005, $10. NI can also be calculated from the formula: beginning retained earnings + NI − dividends paid = ending retained earnings. Depreciation of $25 would be added back to net income while the increases in accounts receivable, $5, and in inventory, $3, would be subtracted from net income because they are uses of cash. The decrease in accounts payable is also a use of cash and, therefore, a subtraction from net income. Thus, cash flow from operations for 2005 is $25 + $10 + $25 − $5 − $3 − $7 = $45 ($ millions).

16. C is correct. Selling price (cash inflow) minus book value equals gain or loss on sale; therefore, gain or loss on sale plus book value equals selling price (cash inflow). The amount of loss is given, $2 million. To calculate the book value of the equipment sold, find the historical cost of the equipment and the accumulated depreciation on the equipment.

- Beginning balance of equipment of $100 million plus equipment purchased of $10 million minus ending balance of equipment of $105 million equals the historical cost of equipment sold, or $5 million.
- Beginning accumulated depreciation of $40 million plus depreciation expense for the year of $8 million minus ending balance of accumulated depreciation of $46 million equals accumulated depreciation on the equipment sold, or $2 million.
- Therefore, the book value of the equipment sold was $5 million minus $2 million, or $3 million.
- Because the loss on the sale of equipment was $2 million, the amount of cash received must have been $1 million.

17. A is correct. The increase of $42 million in common stock and additional paid-in capital indicates that the company issued stock during the year. The increase in retained earnings of $15 million indicates that the company paid $10 million in cash dividends during the year, determined as beginning retained earnings of $100 million plus net income of $25 million, minus ending retained earnings of $115, which equals $10 million in cash dividends.

18. A is correct. To derive operating cash flow, the company would make the following adjustments to net income: add depreciation (a noncash expense) of $2 million; add the decrease in accounts receivable of $3 million; add the increase in accounts payable of $5 million; and subtract the increase in inventory of $4 million. Total additions would be $10 million, and total subtractions would be $4 million for net additions of $6 million.

19. D is correct. Before examining individual cash flows, the major sources and uses of cash should be evaluated.

20. C is correct. The primary source of cash is operating activities. An examination of the financing section indicates that the company pays dividends. The primary use of cash is investing activities. Interest received for Telefónica is classified as an investing activity.

21. B is correct. Answer A is a description of the indirect method of determining cash flow from operations. Answer C is a description of the way to prepare a common-size income statement. Answer D is incomplete; the other alternative way to prepare a statement of cash flows is to show each item of cash inflow as a percentage of total inflows and each item of cash outflows as a percentage of total outflows.
22. B is correct. Free cash flow to the firm can be computed as operating cash flows plus after-tax interest expense less capital expenditures.
23. A is correct. This is the interest coverage ratio using operating cash flow rather than earnings before interest, tax, depreciation, and amortization (EBITDA).

SOLUTIONS FOR READING 35

1. A. Start with the basic inventory relationship

$$BI + P = COGS + EI$$

Opening inventory	400 units @ \$20	\$ 8,000
Purchases	1,000	25,000
Total	1,400 units	\$33,000

i. Under FIFO, ending inventory consists of 600 units:

100 purchased in second quarter at \$24	\$ 2,400
300 purchased in third quarter at \$26	7,800
200 purchased in fourth quarter at \$28	5,600
600 units total	\$15,800

ii. Under LIFO, ending inventory consists of 600 units:

400 inventory at January 1 at \$20	\$ 8,000
200 purchased in first quarter at \$22	4,400
600 units total	\$12,400

iii. Under average cost, ending inventory consists of 600 units with an average cost of \$33,000/1,400 = \$23.5714 per unit or \$14,142.84 total.

B. COGS for the year equals the \$33,000 total of opening inventory plus purchases, less closing inventory under the method chosen:

i. FIFO: \$33,000 less \$15,800 = \$17,200

ii. LIFO: \$33,000 less \$12,400 = \$20,600

iii. Average cost: \$33,000 less \$14,142.84 = \$18,857.16

C. i. Reported income is highest under FIFO (lowest COGS) and lowest under LIFO (highest COGS). Average cost is in between FIFO and LIFO.

ii. Stockholders' equity is highest under FIFO (highest inventory and retained earnings) and lowest under LIFO (lowest inventory and retained earnings), with average cost in between.

2. Using FIFO instead of LIFO when prices are rising and inventory quantities are stable has the following effects:

i. Gross profit margins are higher under FIFO than under LIFO because revenues at higher current prices are matched with cost-of-goods-sold measured using older (lower) prices.

ii. Net income is lower under LIFO than under FIFO because cost-of-goods-sold is higher.

iii. Cash from operations is higher under LIFO than under FIFO because income tax paid is lower.

iv. Inventory balances are lower under LIFO than under FIFO because cost-of-goods-sold is higher and lower prices remain in inventory.

v. Inventory turnover is lower under FIFO than under LIFO because cost-of-goods-sold is lower and inventory balances higher. Both factors decrease the inventory turnover ratio.

vi. Working capital is lower under LIFO than under FIFO because inventory balances are lower, despite partial offset from higher cash balances (because of lower tax payments).

vii. Total assets are higher under FIFO because FIFO inventory balances are higher.

viii. The debt-to-equity ratio is lower under FIFO than under LIFO because equity is higher, reflecting higher retained earnings.

3. A. The first step is to obtain FIFO cost-of-goods-sold:

Pretax income = sales − COGS − other expenses

$5,000 = $25,000 − COGS − $12,000

Solving: COGS = $8,000

Purchases are equal to COGS + Closing Inventory = $8,000 + $10,000 = $18,000.

The key to this problem is to distinguish between the flow of units and the flow of costs. Purchases are independent of the accounting method used.

Since half the units were sold, half remain in inventory. Under LIFO, therefore, the cost allocations to inventory and COGS are the reverse of those allocated under FIFO. That is, under LIFO, COGS = $10,000 and Closing Inventory = $8,000.

Under the weighted average method, as total purchases equal $18,000, the allocation between COGS and closing inventory will be equal: COGS = Closing Inventory = $9,000.

Recalling that pretax CFO depends on purchases, not COGS, we can now fill in the rest of the table.

	FIFO	Weighted Average	LIFO
Sales	$25,000	$25,000	$25,000
COGS	8,000	9,000	10,000
Other expenses	12,000	12,000	12,000
Pretax income	5,000	4,000	3,000
Income tax expense	2,000	1,600	1,200
Net income	3,000	2,400	1,800
Dividends paid	1,500	1,200	900
Retained earnings	1,500	1,200	900
Cash from operations[a]	(7,000)	(6,600)	(6,200)
Closing cash balance[b]	1,500	2,200	2,900
Closing inventory	10,000	9,000	8,000
Inventory purchases	18,000	18,000	18,000

[a] Cash from operations = Sales − Other expenses − Purchases − Tax expense.

[b] Cash balance = $10,000 + Cash from operations.

B. M & J Company
Balance Sheet, December 31, 20X0

	FIFO	Weighted Average	LIFO
Cash	$ 3,000	$ 3,400	$ 3,800
Inventory	10,000	9,000	8,000
Total assets	$13,000	$12,400	$11,800
Common stock	$10,000	$10,000	$10,000
Retained earnings	3,000	2,400	1,800
Total equities	$13,000	$12,400	$11,800

C. The advantages of LIFO are that it results in the highest cash flow (by reducing income taxes) and it best measures net income by matching the cost of sales with most recent costs to replace inventory sold. The disadvantage of LIFO is that inventory on the balance sheet is understated.

The advantage of FIFO is that inventory is measured at most recent costs. Its disadvantages are the reduced cash flow and overstatement of reported income.

Average cost has the disadvantage of misreporting both the balance sheet inventory and net income. Income taxes are higher than under the LIFO method (but lower than under FIFO). The "advantage" of average cost is that it is "less wrong" than LIFO on the balance sheet and "less wrong" than FIFO on the income statement.

4. A.

Year	Zenab 20X1	(LIFO) 20X2	Faybech 20X1	(FIFO) 20X2
Current ratio	2.89	2.65	3.24	3.68
Inventory turnover		2.45		1.98
Gross profit margin		.339		.32
Pretax income/sales		.054		.045

B. Faybech's liquidity (as measured by the current ratio) appears to be better. Its inventory turnover is lower, however, implying lower efficiency. Faybech appears to be slightly less profitable as well.

C. i. Using the FIFO income statements below, we compute the following ratios:

Year	Zenab 20X1	(FIFO) 20X2	Faybech 20X1	(FIFO) 20X2
Current ratio[a]	3.20	3.04	3.24	3.68
Inventory turnover[b]		2.03		1.98
Gross profit margin		.355		.32
Pretax income/sales		.070		.045

[a] 20X1 = ($33,500 + $3,600)/$11,600
20X2 = ($33,600 + $5,100)/$12,700

[b] $\frac{\$59{,}800}{(\$25{,}200 + \$5{,}100 + \$24{,}400 + \$3{,}600)/2}$

A comparision of both companies on a FIFO basis is presented below:

	Zenab	Faybech
Sales	$92,700	$77,000
Cost of goods sold	59,800	52,000
Gross profit	32,900	25,000
Selling and general expense	26,400	21,500
Pretax income	$ 6,500	$ 3,500

ii. Using the LIFO income statements below (using the Zenab statement after conversion to 100% LIFO), we compute the following profitability ratios:

Year	Zenab (100% LIFO) 20X2	Faybech (LIFO) 20X2
Gross profit margin	.332	.303
Pretax income/sales	.047	.024

Balance sheet adjustments are not possible for Faybech and the 30% of Zenab inventories on FIFO. Thus adjusted current and inventory turnover ratios cannot be computed.

A comparision of both companies on a LIFO basis is presented below:

	Zenab	Faybech
Sales	$92,700	$77,000
Cost of goods sold	61,300	53,675
Gross profit	31,400	23,325
Selling and general expense	26,400	21,500
Pretax income	$ 5,000	$ 1,825

iii. The current cost method of computing the inventory turnover ratio uses the FIFO measure of inventory and the LIFO measure of COGS. The ratios are:

	Zenab	Faybech
LIFO costs of goods sold	$61,943	$53,675
FIFO average inventory	29,400	26,300
Inventory turnover ratio	2.11X	2.04X

D. Balance sheet values are most meaningful when FIFO is used. For the income statement, however, LIFO should be used. Therefore for the current ratio, we use the FIFO amounts. For the gross profit margin, and pretax/sales we use the 100% LIFO amounts. For the inventory turnover ratio, the current cost approach is preferred. However that ratio and the FIFO based ratio are similar in this case:

	Zenab		Faybech	
Year	20X1	20X2	20X1	20X2
FIFO current ratio	3.20	3.04	3.24	3.68
FIFO inventory turnover		2.03		1.98
Current cost turnover		2.11		2.04
LIFO gross profit margin		.332		.303
LIFO pretax income/sales		.047		.024

Notice that, based on these ratios, Zenab is clearly more profitable than Faybech. The inventory turnover ratios are, however, virtually identical. While Faybech still has a higher current ratio, the difference is smaller than it appears based on the reported balance sheet data.

5. A. The LIFO Reserve increased by $4,000. If the company used FIFO, its pretax income would be $4,000 higher. After-tax income would be higher by .65 × $4,000 = $2,600.

B. Inventory turnover is COGS/average inventory:

LIFO $3,800,000/[.5($748,000 + $696,800)] = 5.26X

FIFO $3,796,000/[.5($794,000 + $746,800)] = 4.93X

C. Since the firm's ROE is 4.6% and net income is $340,000, then average equity = $340,000/.046 = $7,391,304

If the company used FIFO, equity would be higher by the LIFO reserve amount adjusted for taxes. The average LIFO reserve is $48,000. Therefore, average equity should be higher by $31,200 (.65 × $48,000) after tax.

FIFO average equity = $7,391,304 + $31,200 = $7,422,504 ROE_{FIFO} = $342,600/$7,422,504 = 4.62%

The adjustment of ROE is insignificant in this case because the increase in the numerator (income) and denominator (equity) are proportionate.

D. There are two reasons to make adjustments for accounting methods:

1. to more accurately measure the firm's operations

2. to facilitate comparisons of different firms on the same basis

For inventory turnover, the adjustment results in a more accurate measure of performance. However, the main purpose of the LIFO to FIFO adjustment is to enable the analyst to compare Zeta to other firms that use FIFO.

E. The current cost method (inventory and equity at FIFO, COGS and net income at LIFO) should be used for both inventory turnover and ROE. For inventory turnover, this method better approximates the actual (physical) turnover. The argument for ROE is that FIFO equity better reflects the Company's current value, while LIFO income reflects the current operating profits earned on that equity. For Zeta, these adjustments offset. In some cases, however, the current cost method ratios are quite different.

6. A. The LIFO adjustment refers to the change in the LIFO reserve (or as Noland calls it 'Reduction to LIFO')

	1997	1998	1999
LIFO reserve	$32,495	$32,876	$34,267
Change in LIFO reserve		381	1,391

B. $COGS_{FIFO} = COGS_{LIFO}$ − change in LIFO reserve

For 1998: $372,033 − $381 = $371,652

For 1999: 385,892 − 1,391 = 384,501

C. Income would decline if prices in previous years were higher than current prices and the higher priced layer was liquidated.

D. i. 1998: COGS = $372,033 − $150 = $371,883

1999: COGS = 385,892 + 47 = 385,939

ii. For FIFO, COGS is the same as in part b—"liquidations" do not affect FIFO COGS

E. The most appropriate measure is the calculation computed in part d(i): LIFO COGS after eliminating effects of liquidation. That measure of COGS is closest to replacement cost.

F. By adding the LIFO reserve to equity: i.e. add $32,876,000 to 1998 equity and $34,267,000 to 1999 equity. Depending on the purpose of analysis, it may be appropriate to tax-adjust these values i.e. add [$32,876,000 × (1-tax rate)] to 1998 equity and [$34,267,000 × (1-tax rate)] to 1999 equity.

7. A. The cost of inventory may have declined due to deflation.

B. 1. They might believe that the price decrease is temporary and in the future prices will increase again.

2. Since the LIFO reserve is large, a switch to FIFO would require a large tax expense (equal to tax rate times the LIFO reserve) immediately. Thus, even if they felt that prices would continue to decrease in the future, they are still better off paying the higher taxes slowly over time (as the LIFO reserve declines) rather than paying the full amount immediately.

8.

	1997	1998	1999
A. Sales	$515,728	$539,413	$572,696
Gross margin	187,556	190,826	210,588
Gross margin %	**36.4%**	**35.4%**	**36.8%**
B. LIFO liquidation	$ 3,379	$ 1,733	none
Pretax liquidation[a]	**5,198**	**2,666**	
Adjusted			
Gross margin	$182,358	$188,160	$210,588
Gross margin %	**35.4%**	**34.9%**	**36.8%**

[a] Equals LIFO liquidation (net of tax)/.65

C. The adjusted gross margin percentage is more indicative of the longer-term trend of the company. By removing the effects of the LIFO liquidation(s), COGS and subsequently gross margin are more reflective of current cost income. Removing the effect of the liquidation shows that gross margins improved significantly from 1997–1998 to 1999.

9. Contracts can provide strong incentives that affect the choice of inventory method. However different contracts may provide incentives for different choices. The following discussion assumes rising prices.

The management compensation plan provides a mixed incentive. Use of LIFO reduces income but increases cash from operations. Assuming a tax rate t, and a LIFO effect L, net income decreases by $(1-t)L$ while cash from operations increases by tL. The net effect $(2t-1)L$ is positive only at tax rates above 50%. Thus management contracts argue against use of LIFO.

Bond convenants also argue against LIFO. Working capital is reduced by the LIFO reserve less taxes saved. The annual amount is $(t-1)L$ which is always negative. Retained earnings are also lower under LIFO.

Union employee profit sharing payments are lower under LIFO, assuming that profits would exceed the minimum level. This would seem to argue for LIFO, to reduce compensation paid.

However, there are also second and third order effects that must be considered. Lower profit sharing payments, for example, increase net income (and cash from operations), increasing management compensation and easing the effect of bond covenants. These effects require complex calculations and are highly firm-specific.

Some effects are non-quantitative. Lower profit sharing payments may result in higher wage demands from workers. For management, use of FIFO may raise questions about why they failed to obtain tax savings by using LIFO.

Thus, while we can identify many of the factors that motivate the choice of inventory method, the controller's choice will depend on how these factors affect Sechne; there is no simple answer.

SOLUTIONS FOR READING 36

1. Exhibit S-1 contains the calculations required for Parts A through B(iii).

EXHIBIT S-1 Chevron

Adjustments for Capitalization of Interest

Amounts in $millions Year	**1995**	**1996**	**1997**	**1998**	**1999**	***Part C* *1999/95***
As reported						
Interest expense	$ 401	$ 364	$ 312	$ 405	$ 472	**1.18**
Pretax income	1,789	4,740	5,502	1,834	3,648	**2.04**
Net income	930	2,607	3,256	1,339	2,070	**2.23**
Capitalized interest	141	108	82	39	59	
Amortization of capitalized interest	47	24	28	35	9	
A. ***Calculations***						
EBIT	$2,190	$5,104	$5,814	$2,239	$4,120	
Times interest earned	**5.46**	**14.02**	**18.63**	**5.53**	**8.73**	**1.60**
B. ***Adjusted***						
Net capitalized interest	$ 94	$ 84	$ 54	$ 4	$ 50	
After 35% income tax	61	55	35	3	33	
Interest expense	542	472	394	444	531	**0.98**
EBIT	2,237	5,128	5,842	2,274	4,129	
i. Times interest earned	**4.13**	**10.86**	**14.83**	**5.12**	**7.78**	**1.88**
ii. % reduction from reported ratio	**−24.4%**	**−22.5%**	**−20.4%**	**−7.4%**	**−10.9%**	
Pretax income	$1,695	$4,656	$5,448	$1,830	$3,598	**2.12**
iii. Net income	**869**	**2,552**	**3,221**	**1,336**	**2,038**	**2.34**
% reduction from reported	−6.6%	−2.1%	−1.1%	−0.2%	−1.6%	

B. iv. Expensing all interest reduces net income for each year. However the effect diminishes over time.

C. i. Because the amount of interest capitalized declined over time, restatement reduces the rate of increase in interest expense.

ii. While the interest coverage ratio is lower after restatement, its trend improves due to the lower growth rate of interest expense.

iii. Both pretax and net income are lower after restatement but their growth rate improves due to the lower growth rate of interest expense.

D. The restated data are more useful for financial analysis because they are based on actual interest expense. They provide better comparability with firms that do not capitalize interest.

2. Exhibit S-2 contains the calculations required by Parts A through C.

EXHIBIT S-2 Ericsson

Amounts in SEK millions	1997	1998	1999
A. Under Swedish GAAP:			
Net sales	167,740	184,438	215,403
Pretax income	17,218	18,210	16,386
Total assets	147,440	167,456	202,628
Stockholders' equity	52,624	63,112	69,176
Average total assets		157,448	185,042
Average stockholders' equity		57,868	66,144
i. Asset turnover		**1.17**	**1.16**
ii. Pretax ROE		**0.31**	**0.25**
B. Adjustments:			
Development costs for software to be sold:			
Capitalization	5,232	7,170	7,898
Amortization	(3,934)	(3,824)	(4,460)
Write down			(989)
Net effect	1,298	3,346	2,449
Development costs for software for internal use:			
Capitalization			1,463
Amortization			(152)
Net effect	—	—	1,311
Total pretax effect	1,298	3,346	3,760
Adjusted pretax income	18,516	21,556	20,146
i. % change	**8%**	**18%**	**23%**
Year-end balances:			
Software to be sold	7,398	10,744	13,193
Internal use software			1,311
Total	7,398	10,744	14,504
Less: deferred tax @ 35%	(2,589)	(3,760)	(5,076)
Increase in equity	4,809	6,984	9,428

(Exhibit continued on next page . . .)

EXHIBIT S-2 (continued)

Adjusted total assets	154,838	178,200	217,132
ii. % change	**5.0%**	**6.4%**	**7.2%**
Adjusted equity	57,433	70,096	78,604
iii. % change	**9.1%**	**11.1%**	**13.6%**
C.			
Adjusted average assets		166,519	197,666
Adjusted average equity		63,764	74,350
i. Adjusted asset turnover		**1.11**	**1.09**
ii. Adjusted pretax ROE		**0.34**	**0.27**

D. The adjustments for Ericsson show that capitalization of software development costs can have a significant effect on reported income and equity, and on financial ratios. Therefore comparability requires that all firms be restated to the same basis.

E. The amounts capitalized highlight expenditures and enable the analyst to inquire about the new products under development. The amortization period used may be useful as a forecast of the useful life of the product. In both cases (capitalization and amortization) significant changes from prior periods may provide useful signals of impending change.

3. A. The capitalization of the investment in displays delays their impact on income as compared with expensing. In addition, cash from operations is permanently increased as the expenditures are classified as cash flows for investment. Finally, if these expenditures are volatile, capitalization and amortization smoothes the impact on reported income.

B. **i.** In 2000, the capitalized amount increased by $1,648,000. Had promotional displays been expensed, net income would be $1,071,200 (after 35% tax) lower. Expensing would have reduced net income by 7.4% ($1,071.2/$14,467).

ii. Shareholders' equity would be reduced by 65% of $10,099,000 equal to $6,564,350 or 7.1%.

iii. Reported return on (average) assets equals $14,467[($166,656 + $140,609)/2] = 9.42%

Adjusted return on (average) assets equals ($14,467 – $1,071)/[($166,656 – $10,099) + ($140,609 – $8,451)/2] = 9.28% as assets must be reduced by the investment in promotional displays.

SOLUTIONS FOR READING 37

1. **i.** Straight-line depreciation
   ii. Sum-of-years' digits

Depreciable base	$10,000,000	$10,000,000
Sum-of-years' digits		15
Year	**Straight Line Method**	**Sum-of-Years' Digits**
1	$ 2,000,000	$ 3,333,333
2	2,000,000	2,666,667
3	2,000,000	2,000,000
4	2,000,000	1,333,333
5	2,000,000	666,667
Total	$10,000,000	$10,000,000

   iii. Double-declining balance

Depreciable base	$12,000,000	Rate = 40%
	Double-Declining Balance	
Year	**Depreciation**	**Balance**
1	$ 4,800,000	$ 7,200,000
2	2,880,000	4,320,000
3	1,728,000	2,592,000
4	592,000	2,000,000
5		2,000,000
Total	$10,000,000	

2. **i.** Straight-line methods report constant depreciation expense throughout the life of the asset. Accelerated methods result in higher depreciation expense initially, but a declining trend thereafter. The effect on total depreciation expense depends on the growth rate of capital spending (whether the effect of higher depreciation expense on new assets offsets the impact of declining depreciation expense on old ones). Using the same economic life, accelerated methods will report higher depreciation expense than the straight-line method during the early years and lower expense thereafter.

   ii. The effect on net income is the reverse of the above. Net income is lower initially. Its reversal will depend on the level and growth of capital expenditures in the future.

iii. Accelerated depreciation methods report lower net income (higher depreciation expense), lower assets, and lower equity (higher accumulated depreciation) than the straight-line method. The numerator effect may dominate, producing lower return ratios. For a growing firm with increasing capital expenditures, the early years' depreciation expense difference will persist, resulting in lower return ratios.

iv. Accelerated depreciation methods report lower income in the first year but higher income in later years as depreciation expense declines. Reported assets are lower throughout. Companies with rapidly growing capital expenditures are likely to report lower ROA as the income effect dominates. As they mature, however, slowing capital expenditures and the growing effect of the reduced denominator (assets) is likely to result in higher ROA than under the straight-line method.

v. For financial reporting purposes, the choice of method has no effect on reported cash flows, as depreciation is a noncash expense. However, for tax purposes, the use of accelerated methods rather than the straight-line method reduces taxes paid, increasing cash from operations.

vi. As depreciation expense has no effect on revenues, accelerated depreciation methods increase reported asset turnover, as the denominator is lower.

3. A. The present value of the cash flows, discounted at 10%, is $60 for each asset.

B. Asset A:

Year	Net Asset	Cash Flow	Depreciation Expense	Income	ROA
1	$60	$36	$30	$6	10%
2	30	23	20	3	10%
3	10	11	10	1	10%

Asset B:

Year	Net Asset	Cash Flow	Depreciation Expense	Income	ROA
1	$60	$26	$20	$6	10%
2	40	24	20	4	10%
3	20	22	20	2	10%

C. The pattern for Asset A is the sum-of-the-years' digits method. The pattern for Asset B is the straight-line method.

4. A. Boeing uses accelerated depreciation methods: 150% declining balance for buildings and land improvements and sum-of-the-years digits for machinery and equipment. As a result early year depreciation resulting from capital expenditures is high keeping net plant and equipment low. The second reason is that, from 1995 to 1999, total depreciation expense was $6,286 while net additions to plant and equipment were $6,010 or $176 lower.

B. Accelerated depreciation methods result in low balance sheet carrying values for fixed assets, increasing the likelihood that asset sales will result in gains.

C. **i.** If Boeing adopted the straight-line method in 1999, depreciation expense for both 1998 and 1999 will most likely be reduced. Depreciation on assets acquired in recent years will be reduced although depreciation on older assets will be higher under the straight-line method. As 1998 capital spending was relatively high, the more recent year effects are likely to be greater than the older year effects of the accounting change. As 1999 capital spending was reduced, the effect on that year's depreciation will be less than on 1998.

ii. Stockholders' equity at December 31, 1999 will be higher due to lower prior year depreciation that increases net income and, therefore, retained earnings.

iii. Cash from operations is unaffected by the choice of depreciation method.

iv. Fixed asset turnover for 1999 will be decreased by the accounting change as lower prior year depreciation expense increases net fixed assets.

D. **i.** If Boeing adopted the straight-line depreciation method prospectively at January 1, 2000, net income for 2000 would increase as depreciation of current year capital additions is lower under the new method.

ii. Depreciation expense would be likely to decline due to the combined effect of lower depreciation expense on current year capital additions and the declining trend of depreciation expense on older assets for which accelerated methods remain in use.

E. As the accounting change would increase reported income without any effect on cash flows, an analyst might include that the company expects

i. future earnings trends to be negative

ii. capital spending to rise sharply

Either of these expectations might lead the company to change its accounting method to improve near-term reported earnings.

5. A.–C. As shown in the table below, the accounting change improved the 2000 gross margin ratio by 0.5% and the operating ratio by 0.9%.

	As Reported		Accounting Change	Adjusted 2000
	1999	2000		
Net revenues	$1,452	$1,545		$1,545
Cost of sales	(835)	(845)	$ 8	(853)
Gross profit	$ 617	$ 700	$ 8	$ 692
S, D, & A expense	(575)	(625)	6	(631)
Operating income	$ 42	$ 75	$14	$ 61
% of Sales				
Net revenues	100.0%	100.0%		100.0%
Cost of sales	−57.5%	−54.7%	0.5%	−55.2%
Gross margin	**42.5%**	**45.3%**	**0.5%**	**44.8%**
S, D, & A expense	−39.6%	−40.5%	0.4%	−40.8%
Operating margin	**2.9%**	**4.9%**	**0.9%**	**3.9%**

D. **i.** Fixed asset turnover is reduced as lower depreciation expense increases the net carrying amount of fixed assets.

ii. The accounting change improves the reported income trend as 2000 and following years benefit from the reduced depreciation expense.

iii. PBG's quality of earnings is reduced as the accounting change increases reported earnings.

iv. Cash from operations is unchanged as depreciation is a noncash expense.

E. If the company believes that its performance is best measured using cash flow data, the accounting change has no benefit whatsoever. However reported income is increased, reducing the reported price-earnings ratio.

6. A. Calculations below use the following definitions:

i. Average depreciable life (years) = Gross investment/ depreciation expense

ii. Average age (years) = Accumulated depreciation/depreciation expense

iii. Average age (%) = Accumulated depreciation/gross investment

	1997	1998	1999
Buildings and land improvements			
i. Average depreciable life (years)	32.5	40.8	40.8
ii. Average age (years)	11.1	13.8	14.0
iii. Average age (%)	34.1%	33.9%	34.3%
Machinery and equipment			
i. Average depreciable life (years)	15.2	12.0	12.7
ii. Average age (years)	8.3	6.4	6.8
iii. Average age (%)	54.7%	53.6%	53.2%

B. The average depreciable life for buildings and land improvements is just over 40 years for 1998 and 1999, very close to the 40 years stated life. The 1997 ratio is much lower. The high depreciation for that year suggests that there was some special factor accounting for the discrepancy.

The average for machinery and equipment varies over the three-year period but is consistent with the 15-year maximum stated life. The ratio suggests that most assets in this category are depreciated over 15 years despite the stated policy of 5–15 years.

C. The average age (years) of buildings and land improvements has been increasing but is still low (and stable) compared with the average depreciable life (average age (%)). For machinery and equipment the average age fell in 1998 and was stable in 1999. These ratios suggest that Roche's physical facilities are modern, although it would be useful to compare the ratios with those of Roche competitors.

D. Questions worth asking include:

- Why was 1997 depreciation on buildings and land improvements abnormally high?
- Was 1997 depreciation on machinery and equipment abnormally low and, if so, why?
- What types of machinery and equipment are depreciated over 15 years versus shorter time periods?
- What is the breakdown of future capital expenditures between land improvements and machinery and equipment?
- Will future capital expenditures change the average depreciable life due to changes in the asset mix?

7. A. **i.** Income before the effect of accounting changes was increased because intangible amortization was reduced.

ii. Net income was reduced by the impairment charge, partly offset by reduced amortization.

iii. Stockholders' equity was reduced by lower net income.

iv. Cash from operations was unchanged as both the impairment charge and amortization are noncash expenses.

B. **i.** 2001 net income will be increased as amortization of the reduced intangible assets is lower as a result of the accounting change.

ii. Return on equity is increased by the accounting change as net income is increased and equity is reduced (see answer to A(iii)).

iii. Cash from operations is unchanged as amortization is a noncash expense.

SOLUTIONS FOR READING 38

1. Deferred taxes can be found in all of the categories listed. Examples are:
   - i. Current liabilities may include deferred tax liabilities arising from an installment sale with cash payments expected within one year.
   - ii. Deferred income tax credits resulting from the use of accelerated depreciation for tax purposes and straight line for financial reporting are reported in long-term liabilities.
   - iii. The stockholders' equity account may include the deferred tax offset to the valuation allowance for available-for-sale securities or the cumulative translation adjustment account.
   - iv. The deferred tax asset (debit) due to accrued compensation with cash payment expected within one year is a component of current assets.
   - v. Long-term assets would include deferred tax assets (debits) recognized, (for example, for postretirement benefits or restructuring charges), but not expected to be funded within one year.
2. i. Correct: Under SFAS 109, changes in tax laws must be reflected in the deferred tax liability in the period of enactment.
   - ii. Correct: Answer to (i) also applies to deferred tax assets.
   - iii. Correct: The tax consequences of events that have not been reflected in the financial statements (such as future earnings or losses) are not recognized.
   - iv. Incorrect: See answers to (i) and (ii) above. This statement is true for the deferral method (see footnote 2 in Reading 38).
   - v. Incorrect: Changes in deferred tax assets and liabilities are included in income tax expense except for those charged directly to stockholders' equity.
3. A. Permanent differences are items of income or expense that affect *either tax return income or financial income, but not both.* Examples include:
   - ▶ tax-exempt interest income (not reported on the tax return);
   - ▶ interest expense on amounts borrowed to purchase tax-exempt securities (not deductible on the tax return);
   - ▶ tax or other nondeductible government penalties (not reported on the tax return);
   - ▶ statutory mineral depletion in excess of cost basis depletion (not reported in the financial statements);
   - ▶ premiums on key-person life insurance policies (not deductible on the tax return);
   - ▶ proceeds from key-person life insurance policies (not reported on the tax return).

   B. Permanent differences, depending on their nature, either increase or decrease the firm's effective tax rate relative to the statutory rate. For example, tax-exempt interest income (the first example listed) reduces the effective tax rate as there is no tax expense associated with this income.

4. A. i. If the deferred tax liability is not expected to reverse, there is no expectation of a cash outflow and the liability should be considered as equity.

ii. If the deferred tax liability is the result of a temporary difference that is expected to reverse, with consequent tax payment, it should be treated as a liability.

B. Because both the amounts and timing of tax payments resulting form the reversals of temporary differences are uncertain, deferred taxes should be excluded from both liabilities and equity.

C. The portion of the deferred tax liability that represents (the present value of) expected payments should be treated as debt. Accounting-based timing differences that are not expected to reverse should be treated as equity.

5. We begin by determining the cost of each asset using the information about asset L. Year 2 depreciation under the sum-of-the-years' digits method with a five-year life is 4/15ths. Therefore, the depreciable base (cost − salvage value) must be \$12,000/(4/15) = \$45,000 and the cost must be \$48,000 because salvage value is \$3,000. We can now prepare a depreciation schedule for each method:

Depreciation Expense

Year	Asset K Straight-line[a]	Asset L SYD[b]	Asset M DDB[c]
1	$ 9,000	$15,000	$19,200
2	9,000	12,000	11,520
3	9,000	9,000	6,912
4	9,000	6,000	4,147
5	9,000	3,000	3,221
Total	$45,000	$45,000	$45,000

[a] Base = \$45,000 (cost − salvage value); expense = \$45,000/5 = \$9,000.

[b] Base = \$45,000; expense = 5/15ths, 4/15ths, 3/15ths, etc.

[c] Base = \$48,000 (salvage value ignored); rate = 40%

Year 1 expense = .40 × \$48,000 = \$19,200, leaving \$28,800

Year 2 expense = .40 × \$28,800 = \$11,520, leaving \$17,280

Year 3 expense = .40 × \$17,280 = \$6,912, leaving \$10,368

Year 4 expense = .40 × \$10,368 = \$4,147, leaving \$6,221

Year 5 expense = \$3,221 leaving \$3,000

A. The double-declining-balance method is used on the tax return for all three assets; year 2 depreciation expense under that method is **\$11,520**.

B. Financial statement depreciation expense in year two (from table above) is:

Asset K (straight line)	**$ 9,000**
Asset M (double-declining-balance)	**11,520**

C. **i.** At the end of year two, accumulated depreciation equals (from table on previous page):

Asset K (straight line)	$18,000
Asset L (SYD)	27,000
Asset M (DDB)	30,720
Tax return (DDB)	30,720

Therefore, the deferred tax liability is:

Asset K: .34 ($30,720 − $18,000) = **$4,324.80**
Asset L: .34 ($30,720 − $27,000) = **1,264.80**
Asset M: No deferred tax as the same method is used for financial and tax reporting.

ii. At the end of year five, accumulated depreciation is the same under all methods and there is no deferred tax asset or liability.

6. A.–B. Assuming that Mother Prewitt continues to buy machines in the future, the depreciation timing difference will never reverse and there is no expected cash consequence. In this case, the deferred tax can be treated as equity.

If the installment sale is not expected to recur, the tax on that sale will be paid in 2001 and will require cash. For that reason, the $27,200 of deferred taxes should be considered a liability when calculating liquidity, solvency, and leverage ratios.

If, on the other hand, installment sales are expected to recur, such sales are no different from the depreciation case. The cash consequences of deferred tax items depend on the probability of their reversal, not on their nature.

C. Under SFAS 109 (liability method), enacted changes in tax rates are recognized, and the deferred tax liabilities must be restated to amounts based on the 40% tax rate. The incremental liability is recorded as a component of income tax expense regardless of when (or if) paid.

7.

	Years Ended June 30			
Amounts in $millions	**1997**	**1998**	**1999**	**2000**
Deferred tax assets due to depreciation	$57.7	$40.4	$49.2	$37.7
Effect on fixed assets of:				
Impairment of long-lived assets		47.0		
Write downs of operating assets		47.0	4.2	26.6
Write downs of capitalized software		—	16.0	—
Total effect on fixed assets		$94.0	$20.2	$26.6
Tax rate		34%	35%	35%
A. Expected effect on deferred tax asset		**$32.0**	**$ 7.1**	**$ 9.3**
Reported change in deferred tax asset		(17.3)	8.9	(11.6)
Difference between expected effect and reported change in deferred tax asset		$49.3	$(1.8)	$20.9

B. Write downs reduce the carrying amount of the assets on the financial statements but have no effect on the tax basis. Even if the company uses the straight-line depreciation method for both tax and financial reporting, tax depreciation would be higher than book depreciation after a write-off, generating deferred tax liabilities (credits) or lowering deferred tax assets (debits). In each year, therefore, write downs increase the deferred tax asset but depreciation expense tends to reduce it.

In the table on the previous page, we compute the effect of the asset changes on the deferred tax asset for each year by multiplying the impairment plus the write-off amount by the tax rate for that year. We then compare that effect with the reported change in the deferred tax asset related to depreciation.

For 1998, the non-cash impairment of long-lived assets and the write down of operating assets would generate a $32 million *increase* in deferred tax assets. However, the company reported a *decrease* of $17.3 million in deferred tax assets due to depreciation. The difference is much too high to result from current year depreciation expense. The most likely explanation is that the company sold fixed assets during the year, eliminating the book-tax difference relating to those assets. If those assets had a higher tax basis than book basis, sale would reduce the deferred tax asset by that difference multiplied by the tax rate.

In 1999, the difference is smaller and in the right direction, since we have an expected $7.1 million increase due to write downs and a reported increase of $8.9 million. Regardless of whether internal-use software was capitalized on the tax return, its write-off should generate a deferred tax debit. This difference is probably due to a combination of current year depreciation (reducing the deferred tax asset) and asset sales (increasing the deferred tax asset).

In 2000, instead of an increase of $9.3 million, the company reports a decrease of $11.6 million in deferred tax assets. As for 1998, asset sales provide the most likely explanation.

8. A. The first step converts the effective tax rate analysis from Exhibit 1 into a pretax income-based reconciliation, following the format of Exhibit 3. Exhibit S-2 shows the results for each year and three-year totals.

B. The reconciliation in Exhibit S-2 shows the following:

i. Net changes in the valuation allowance increased tax expense by ¥36,593 (37,915 − 1,322) million over the three-year period increasing from ¥5,725 (¥6,246 − ¥521) million in 1999 to ¥19,634 (¥20,019 − ¥385) in 2001.

ii. Changes in tax law decreased 1999 income tax expense by ¥21,861 million. There were no changes in tax laws and rates for other years.

iii. Honda's disclosures are unclear. It appears that the decision not to recognize deferred taxes on reinvested subsidiary earnings decreased 2001 tax expense by ¥856 million [5,987 − 5,131] or 0.2% of pretax income. However the reported amounts are extremely low relative to the reported reinvested earnings (¥663,540 million at 3/31/01). A better understanding of this issue is required before meaningful adjustments can be made.

EXHIBIT S-2 Honda Motor

Reconciliation of Effective and Statutory Rates

In ¥ Millions Except Percentages	Years Ended March 31 1999	2000	2001	3-Year Total
Pretax income — Japanese	199,848	127,562	133,166	460,576
Pretax income — Foreign	320,663	288,501	251,810	860,974
Pretax income — Total	520,511	416,063	384,976	1,321,550
Statutory tax rate	48.0%	41.0%	41.0%	43.3%
Valuation allowance	1.2	2.8	5.2	
Difference in normal foreign tax rates	(3.0)	(1.3)	(1.0)	
Changes in tax laws and rates	(4.2)	0.0	0.0	
Reversal of valuation allowance	(0.1)	(0.1)	(0.1)	
Other	2.2	(1.4)	1.3	
Effective tax rate	44.1%	41.0%	46.4%	43.8%
Income tax expense at statutory rate	249,845	170,586	157,840	578,271
Effects of:				
Valuation allowance	6,246	11,650	20,019	37,915
Difference in tax rates of foreign subsidiaries	(15,615)	(5,409)	(3,850)	(24,874)
Changes in tax laws and rates	(21,861)	0	0	(21,861)
Reversal of valuation allowance due to operating loss carryforwards	(521)	(416)	(385)	(1,322)
Other	11,451	(5,825)	5,005	10,631
Income tax expense[a]	229,545	170,586	178,629	578,760
Calculation below required for Part C.				
Pretax income — Foreign	320,663	288,501	251,810	860,974
Foreign tax expense[b]	(138,303)	(112,877)	(99,392)	(348,215)
Foreign net income	182,360	175,624	152,418	512,759
Foreign tax rate	43.1%	39.1%	39.5%	40.4%

[a] Numbers differ from Exhibit P-1 due to rounding.

[b] Calculated as (statutory rate × foreign pretax income) − differences in tax rates of foreign subsidiaries. Using 1999 as an example: (48% × $320,663) − $15,615 = $138,303.

C. **i.** Although lower non-Japanese tax rates reduced Honda's tax expense in each year, 1999–2001, that reduction declined from 1999 to 2001.

ii. As Japanese tax rates declined from 48% in 1999 to 41% in 2000 and 2001, they are now closer to non-Japanese rates reducing the difference.

D. Factors an analyst must consider when forecasting Honda's effective tax rate for 2002 include the following:

- the mix of Japanese and foreign pretax income;
- any possible changes in Japanese and foreign tax rates;
- the impact of the valuation allowance; and
- the composition of and trends in "other" tax differences.

9. A.

	1991 Tax Rate	1992 Tax Rate
Q1	$1,224/$4,797 = 25.5%	$232/$1,123 = 20.7%
Q2	$624/$2,600 = 24.0	$934/$3,723 = 25.1
Q3	$848/$3,244 = 26.1	$583/$98 = (594.9)

B. Using a tax rate of 17% for 1992 Q3 alone, tax expense would have been $16,660. The actual tax credit for Q3 was $583,000, for a difference of $600,000.

C. On a pretax basis, 1992 Q3 declined by 97% from 1991 Q3 ($98 versus $3,224). Net income, however, declined by only 72% ($681 versus $2,396) because 1992 Q3 included the tax benefit of revising the tax rate on earnings already reported for the first two quarters of 1992.

D. One possibility is to make comparisons only on a pretax basis to avoid distortions due to changes in the estimated tax rates. Another approach would use post-tax data to analyze the trends by applying the change to each quarter of 1992.

E. **i.**

	1992		
	Q1	Q2	Q3
Pretax income	$1,123	$3,723	$98
Income tax expense @17%	(191)	(633)	(17)
Net income	$ 932	$3,090	$81

ii. The assumption has a marginal effect on Q1; it continues to reflect a significant decline relative to 1991 Q1. For Q2, we see the improvement in performance augmented by a lower tax rate (17% compared to 25%, but presumably a better indicator of future tax rates). The analyst should attempt to determine the causes of the decline in income in Q1 and Q3, the recovery in Q2 and better understand the implications for future performance.

SOLUTIONS FOR READING 39

1. **A.** When full-coupon debt is issued, interest paid reduces cash from operations (CFO). When zero-coupon debt is issued, however, no cash interest is paid. CFO is unaffected, and is therefore higher than when full-coupon debt is issued. In addition, when imputed interest on zero-coupon debt is tax deductible, CFO is further increased by the tax benefit.

   B. When full-coupon debt is issued, the proceeds are included in cash from financing (CFF). When that debt matures, the amount paid reduces CFF. Assuming the debt is issued and redeemed at par, the net effect on CFF is zero over the life of the debt.

   Zero-coupon debt is issued at a discount; CFF is below the full-coupon case. However at maturity the full face amount is paid (same as full-coupon case). The net amount of CFF (outflow) is therefore greater than when full-coupon debt is issued.

   C. No effect.

   D. Interest on the zero-coupon bond rises each year as the carrying amount rises, increasing the base on which each year's interest expense is computed. All other things being equal, net income declines each year.

2. **A.** Proceeds equal $\$100{,}000/(1.12)^5 = \mathbf{\$56{,}742}$

   B.

	2000	2001	2002	2003	2004
EBIT	$50,000	$50,000	$50,000	$50,000	$50,000
CFO before interest & taxes	60,000	60,000	60,000	60,000	60,000
Interest expense	6,809	7,626	8,541	9,566	10,714
CFO	60,000	60,000	60,000	60,000	60,000
Times interest earned	7.34	6.56	5.85	5.23	4.67
Times interest earned (cash basis)	[Infinite, since no interest is paid. In 2004, when the bond is retired, the payment will be reported as a financing cash outflow.]				

C. For a full-coupon bond, annual interest expense paid in cash would be $56,742 × .12 = $6.809.

	2000	2001	2002	2003	2004
EBIT	$50,000	$50,000	$50,000	$50,000	$50,000
CFO before interest & taxes	60,000	60,000	60,000	60,000	60,000
Interest expense	6,809	6,809	6,809	6,809	6,809
CFO	53,191	53,191	53,191	53,191	53,191
Times interest earned	7.34	7.34	7.34	7.34	7.34
Times interest earned (cash basis)	8.81	8.81	8.81	8.81	8.81

D. Cash flow form operations is higher when zero-coupon bonds are issued because interest is never reported as an operating cash outflow. [Note the infinite cash-basis coverage ratio.] Interest coverage, however, is lower after the first year, and declines as interest expense increases over time, reflecting the steadily increasing principal amount. Full-coupon bonds (if sold at par) result in a constant cash outflow from operations and constant interest expense. Given the Null Company's "steady state," the interest coverage ratio is constant on both accrual and cash flow bases.

E. Given the tax deductibility of accrued but unpaid interest on zero-coupon bonds, cash flow form operations will be higher for both cases. The reported cash flow differences will remain unchanged. For the zero-coupon case, cash flow form operations is even more misleading as the firm must generate sufficient cash from operations to repay the debt at maturity. The obligation must be repaid, regardless of its cash flow classification.

3. A. The $US carrying amount = 1,282/1.37 = **$936 million**.

B. Because the notes have no coupon, they were issued at a discount. The difference between the face amount and the amount computed in part a must be unamortized discount.

C. Interest expense (CHF millions) would be 7% × 1,282 = **CHF 90**.

D. Adding the 1999 interest computed in part c to the carrying amount at December 31, 1998: 90 + 1,282 = **CHF 1,372 million**.

E. The most obvious explanation is the change in the exchange rate from 1.37 to 1.60.

In $US, 1999 interest expense = 7% × $936 = $65 million, making the carrying amount at December 31, 1999 equal to $1,001 million [$936 + $65]. This is much closer to the carrying amount computed at 1,618/1.60 = $1,011 million.

A second factor is that interest expense in CHF is computed quarterly, based on average rates for each period. The CHF carrying value at December 31, 1999 equals the 1998 carrying value + 1999 interest expense + translation loss [Swiss franc decline increases the CHF debt amount].

F. **i.** Cash from operations is higher each year when zero coupon notes are issued because there is no cash interest.

ii. Interest expense rises each year (excluding the effect of exchange rates) because it is based on a (rising) $US carrying amount.

G. The rise in the value of the dollar (decline in Swiss franc) increases interest expense in CHF.

4. **i.** Interest expense = Interest paid + change in bond discount

$8,562 = $7,200 + $1,362

ii. = Market rate × [face value − discount]
= .12 × [face value − $8,652]

Therefore, face value = ($8,562/.12) + $8,652 = **$80,000**.

iii. Coupon rate = interest paid/face value
= $7,200/$80,000 = **9%**

5. A.–B.

In ¥ millions	Years	1998	1999	% Increase
Issue				
2.14%	2005	6,248	6,356	1.72%
1.73%	2003	6,134	6,356	3.61%

The yen amounts were obtained by multiplying the dollar amounts by the exchange rate. For example, for the 2.14% bond at December 31, 1998, $55 × 113.60 = 6,248. [*Note:* the yen amounts are rounded.]

C. It appears that both bonds were issued at a discount, creating amortization that increases the carrying amount each year. If we add the 1999 increase to the coupon rate, it appears that the effective interest rates are 3.86% and 5.34% respectively.

D. One possible motivation is to finance Japanese operations that are conducted in yen. A second is that, as a well-known company, BMY may be able to borrow more cheaply by borrowing in yen and swapping the yen proceeds into U.S. dollars.

6. A. The advantage is that, when Takeda's share price rose, the debt was converted into equity, strengthening the balance sheet. As convertible notes are issued with a conversion price that exceeds the then market price, the company effectively sold common shares at a premium. In addition, because of the conversion feature, the interest rate would have been below the rate required by nonconvertible notes.

The disadvantage is that the debt was converted into common shares at a time when Takeda could have sold new shares at a much higher price, obtaining the same capital at a lower cost.

B. Reported data

In ¥ millions	1998	1999
Total debt	44,482	21,338
Equity	829,381	907,373
Total capital	873,863	928,711
Debt/total capital	5.1%	2.3%

The more than 50% debt decrease was the largest factor reducing the debt total capital ratio.

C. As the market price of Takeda shares was well above the conversion price in 1998, the convertible debt should be classified as equity. After that adjustment (subtracting 22,000 from debt and adding the same amount to equity) Takeda's debt was virtually unchanged from 1998 to 1999 and the decline in the debt/total capital ratio was small:

Adjusted Data

In ¥ millions	1998
Total debt	22,482
Equity	851,381
Total capital	873,863
Debt/total capital	2.6%

This analysis underscores the discussion in the reading; the analyst must classify convertible debt based on market considerations. Proper classification results in a more appropriate leverage measure.

7. A. The market value of AMR's fixed rate debt issues fell relative to book value at December 31, 1999, implying that interest rates must have risen. Higher rates reduce the present value of payments associated with fixed rate debt.

B. The interest rate must have been below 10.2% as the present value exceeds book value.

C. Because the interest rate on variable rate debt floats, fair value should not change except as a result of changes in credit quality.

8. A. An argument for inclusion is that, for Fannie Mae, the issuance and retirement of debt are recurring operating activities whose consequences should be included in operating earnings.

An argument for exclusion is that gains or losses from debt repurchase reflect economic changes during the entire period the debt was outstanding and should not be included in operating earnings for the period in which management chose to realize the gain.

B. An argument for including the hedging loss is that hedging activities are part of Fannie Mae's normal operating activities.

An argument for exclusion is that the hedging loss was unusually large and inclusion distorts the trend of operating earnings.

C. We believe that gains and losses from debt retirement should be excluded from operating earnings for most firms. These gains and losses result form management decisions and because (as discussed in the reading) refinancing may not yield any economic gain or loss despite the accounting gain or loss. Hedging results should be included in operating earnings as hedging gains and losses should offset other economic effects that are also included.

However, Fannie Mae may be an exception. As stated in Part A, the company routinely issues and retires debt, suggesting that gains and losses should be included in operating earnings. Before doing so, the analyst should try to determine whether the gains or losses for the particular quarter are unusual or reflect interest rate changes over multiple periods, suggesting that the gains or losses should (analytically) be spread over several quarters.

9. A. The calculated dividend capacity equals:

Minimum shareholders' equity, 12/31/93	$650.0 million
50% of 1994 net income of $48 million	24.0
Minimum shareholders' equity, 12/31/94	$674.0 million
Actual shareholders' equity, 12/31/94	717.3
Unrestricted amount	$ 43.3 million

B. Without any increase in income, the current dividend can be maintained for only two years:

Estimated Stockholders' Equity ($millions)	1995	1996	1997
Opening	$717.3	$723.3	$729.3
Income	48.0	48.0	48.0
Dividend	(42.0)	(42.0)	(42.0)
Closing	$723.3	$729.3	$735.3[a]

[a] Below minimum stockholders' equity required.

Minimum Stockholders' Equity ($millions)			
Opening	$674.0	$698.0	$722.0
Addition (50% of income)	24.0	24.0	24.0
Closing	$698.0	$722.0	$746.0

As the table above shows, in 1997 the minimum equity requirement will be violated.

C. To maintain dividend payments at the 1994 level through 1998, income would have to increase. The required income for 1997 and 1998 is $69.4 million and $84.0 million respectively.[a] These amounts result in the following table for those years:

Estimated Stockholders' Equity ($millions)	1997	1998
Opening	$729.3	$756.7
Income	69.4	84.0
Dividend	(42.0)	(42.0)
Closing	$756.7	$798.7

Minimum Stockholders' Equity ($millions)		
Opening	$722.0	$756.7
50% of income	34.7	42.0
Closing	$756.7	$798.7

[a] These amounts can be calculated as follows:

1997: Increase = 2 × shortfall in equity = 2 × ($746.0 − 735.3)
= 2 × $10.7 = $21.4 million

1998: Income must equal $84 million, twice the dividend, to maintain equity at the required level.

D. The answer would depend on the shareholder's view of the market price of NorAm's shares. Issuance of new shares to maintain the current dividend makes no sense given finance theory, which states that the two are equivalent. In an imperfect world, however, NorAm's shares may have been fully valued but the shareholder may not have wished to sell and incur capital gains taxes. If NorAm had attractive investment opportunities not reflected in its stock price, then issuing new shares to increase the firm's borrowing capacity would have been desirable.

SOLUTIONS FOR READING 40

1. **i.** Interest expense = 12% × $10,000 (beginning balance of lease obligation) = $1,200.

   ii. The lease obligation will be reduced by $100 ($1,300 − $1,200) leaving an obligation of $9,900.

   iii. Cash form Operations will be reduced by the interest payment of $1,200. Cash from investing activities will not be affected. (However, the firm will report the capital lease as a "noncash investment and financing activity.") Cash from financing will be reduced by the amount of the principal payment of $100.

   iv. Under an operating lease there is no lease obligation on the balance sheet. The only effect on income is Rent Expense of $1,300. Similarly, CFO is reduced by $1,300. (CFI and CFF are not affected.)

2. **A.** The following states the effects of Tolrem using the capital lease method as compared with the operating lease method.

   i. Cash from operations is higher as only the interest portion of lease expense is deducted from operating cash flows; total lease expense is deducted for operating leases.

   ii. Financing cash flow is lower for capital lease, as part of lease rental is treated as amortization of liability and classified as financing cash outflow.

   iii. Investing cash flow is not affected by the lease treatment. However, the firm will report capital leases in the statement of cash flows (or a footnote) as noncash investment activities.

   iv. Net cash flow reflects the actual rental payment and is unaffected by the financial reporting treatment of the lease.

   v. Debt/equity ratio is higher for capital lease, as it records the present value of minimum lease payments as debt *and* reduces net income (and therefore equity) in first year.

   vi. Interest coverage ratio is usually (not always) lower for capital lease method, which reports interest expense but also higher EBIT, see (vii). For coverage ratios well above 1.0, the ratio will decline. If the increase in interest expense exceeds the increase in EBIT, the ratio will decline even for firms with very low coverage ratios.

   vii. Operating income is lower for operating lease because the total lease payment is an operating expense; for capital lease, interest portion of lease expense is nonoperating.

   viii. Net income is higher for operating lease; total lease expense (interest plus depreciation) is higher for capital lease.

   ix. Deferred tax assets are higher for capital lease; as lease treatment for tax purposes is unaffected by accounting choice, capital lease will generate a deferred tax asset as taxable income (operating lease) exceeds pretax income (capital lease).

   x. Taxes paid are unaffected by choice of method.

xi. Pretax return on assets is higher for operating leases as pretax income is higher and no assets are reported as the result of the lease; a capital lease reduces income and reports lease assets. Post-tax return on assets is higher for the same reasons.

xii. Pretax return on equity: both pretax income and equity are higher for operating than for capital leases. The higher pretax income should increase the ratio in all but exceptional cases. Post-tax return on equity should be higher for same reason. However as increase in post-tax income equals (for first year) increase inequity, there may be more exceptional cases.

B. Net income (viii) will be lower for the operating lease after the "crossover" point. As total net income over the life of the lease is unaffected by the accounting choice, higher net income (operating lease) in the early years must be offset by lower net income in later years.

C. Consistent use of the operating lease method in place of capitalization will not change the direction of the effects shown in part A, but will increase their magnitude. In aggregate, new leases will keep Tolrem from reaching the crossover point for net income, keeping net income and return ratios higher than if the leases were capitalized.

3. A. Since it is the first year:

Capital lease obligations	\$2,596,031
Repayment of capital lease obligations	3,969
Capital lease at inception	\$2,600,000

B. Amortization expense = \$2,600,000 − \$2,479,570 = \$120,430

Assuming the asset is being amortized on a straight line basis over the lease term, the lease term = \$2,600,000/\$120,430 = 21.6 or 22 years

Total expense = interest + amortization = \$120,430 + \$223,733 = \$344,163

C. CFO was reduced by the interest expense of \$223,733 and CFF was reduced by the "repayment of capital lease obligations" of \$3,969

D. Free cash flows should be reduced by \$2,600,000 − the "cost" of the leased asset.

E. **i.** Lease expense would be lease payment = \$223,733 + \$3,969 = \$227,702

ii. CFO would be reduced by lease payment of \$227,702

4. A. The adjustment involves the addition of the interest component of minimum lease payments to stated interest expense. The adjustment reflects a partial, *de facto* capitalization of operating leases.

i. Unadjusted ratio of earnings to fixed charges:

Pretax earnings	$2,363,646
Interest on indebtedness	68,528
Earnings before interest and taxes (EBIT)	$2,432,174
Fixed Charges:	
Interest on indebtedness	$68,528
Unadjusted Ratio of Earnings to Fixed Charges	35.5X

ii. The unadjusted ratio is almost four times the adjusted ratio. *Note:* The SEC rule that governs this calculation assumes that the interest component is one-third of the MLP. The true interest component may be higher or lower, changing the coverage ratio.

B. Reported debt-to-equity = $550,000/$2,233,303 = **0.25**.

C. Calculation of amounts adjusted for lease capitalization:

The Limited, Inc.
1999 Working Capital Position and Capitalization Table

	Reported	Adjusted
i. Working capital	**$1,070,249**	**$633,579[a]**
Capitalization:		
Long-term debt	550,000	550,000
Add: Capitalized lease payments		3,452,628[b]
ii. Adjusted long-term debt		**$4,002,628**
Shareholders' equity	2,233,303	2,233,303
Total capitalization	$2,783,303	$6,235,931
iii. Debt-to-equity	**0.25**	**1.80**

[a] Working capital is reduced by the principal component of the 2000 MLPs calculated as

$$\$436,670 = [\$643,828 - (0.6 \times \$3,452,628)]$$

where $3,452,628 is the present value calculated in note 2 below.

[b] Present value of MLPs using an interest rate of 6%. The "thereafter" MLPs are spread using the constant rate assumption; ($502,880 in 2005 and 2006 and $422,102 in 2007).

5. A.

In $millions	1997	1998	1999
Receivables reported	$664.0	$ 720.0	$ 739.0
Receivables sold	—	38.4	50.0
Adjusted receivables	$664.0	$ 758.4	$ 789.0
Average receivables			
as reported		692.0	729.5
adjusted		711.2	773.7
Sales		$4,537.0	$3,867.0
Receivable turnover			
Reported		6.56	5.30
Adjusted		6.38	5.00
# of days receivable			
Reported		56 days	69 days
Adjusted		57 days	73 days
Cash cycle effect		**1 day**	**4 days**

The sale of receivables allowed the company to show an improved receivable turnover and cash cycle; the improvement was more significant for 1999 as the amount of receivables sold increased and sales declined.

B. The effect on the current ratio is minimal as the same amount is added to both numerator and denominator of the ratio and that ratio is close to 1. The debt-to-equity ratio adjustment is more significant in 1999 due to the increase in receivables sold and the lower equity amount.

	1998	1999
Current assets	$1,673.0	$1,615.0
Current liabilities	1,492.0	1,472.0
Current ratio	**1.121**	**1.097**
Adjusted (add receivables sold)		
Current assets	$1,711.4	$1,665.0
Current liabilities	1,530.4	1,522.0
Current ratio adjusted	**1.118**	**1.094**
Debt reported	$ 963.0	$ 961.0
Debt adjusted	1,001.4	1,011.0
Equity	572.0	376.0
Debt-to-equity reported	**1.68**	**2.56**
Debt-to-equity adjusted	**1.75**	**2.69**

C. As the calculation below indicates, both the level and trend in CFO are overstated as a result of the sale of receivables.

	1997	**1998**	**1999**
CFO as reported	$(113.0)	$(59.0)	$ (6.0)
Change in receivables sold	—	38.4	11.6
CFO adjusted	$(113.0)	$(97.4)	$(17.6)

6. A. Debt should be increased by:

$20 million	(present value of operating lease)
5	(guarantee)
7	(present value of take-or-pay agreement)
$32 million	

There is no effect on equity as each obligation is offset by a corresponding asset:

Leased assets for operating lease
Receivable for Crockett's obligation to repay debt
Supply agreement

The recomputed debt-to-equity ratio is:

($12 + $32)/$20 = **2.2X** as compared to .6X before adjustment.

B. Additional interest expense is:

Lease (effective interest rate is about 18%)

	.18 × $20 =	$3.6 million
Bond guarantee	.10 × 5 =	0.5
Total		$4.1 million

Before adjustment, the interest expense is $1.0 million and the times interest earned ratio is 5.0, implying EBIT of $5.0 million.

After adjustment, the ratio is:

($5.0 + $4.1)/($1.0 + $4.1) = **1.78X.**

No adjustment has been made for the take-or-pay contract, as it does not affect 1993 interest expense. Adjustments in future years will be based on the implicit interest rate of 21%.

C. Reasons for entering into off-balance-sheet obligations:

1. Avoidance of or mitigation of the risk of violating debt covenant restrictions.

2. Leased assets revert to lessor after eight years, limiting risk of obsolescence.

3. Guarantee of Crockett's debt may lower interest costs, increasing profitability of investment.

4. Contract with PEPE secures source of supply and possibly advantageous pricing.

D. Additional information needed for full evaluation:

1. (Lease) Useful life of leased assets; conditions under which lease can be canceled; nature of leased assets.
2. (Guarantee) Financial condition of Crockett; bond covenants.
3. (Take-or-pay) Alternate sources of supply; quantity to be purchased relative to total needs; price provisions of contract.

7.

	1st Year	9th Year
i. Assets	Higher	Higher
ii. Revenues	Higher	Lower
iii. Expenses	Higher	Lower
iv. Asset turnover ratio	Higher	Lower
v. Interest income	Higher	Higher
vi. Cost of goods sold	Higher	No effect
vii. Net income	Higher	Lower
viii. Retained earnings	Higher	Higher
ix. Taxes paid	No effect	No effect
x. Post-tax ROA	Higher	Lower
xi. Cash from operations	Higher	Lower
xii. Investment cash flow	Lower	Higher

Assets are higher because inventory is replaced with (higher) receivables because of the recognition of manufacturing profit. Assets remain higher throughout the lease term.

Revenues are higher in Year 1 as the sales-type lease recognizes a sale whereas the operating lease method does not. In later years, interest revenue from the sales-type lease should be lower than lease revenue for the operating lease. This effect is more pronounced over time; in year 9, interest income is low given the small remaining receivable. The revenue effect increases the asset turnover ratio in the first year. But the revenue effect reduces turnover in the ninth year.

Expenses are higher in year 1 due to the recognition of cost of goods sold. In later years, there is no expense for the sales-type lease; the operating lease method reports depreciation expense in every year, however.

Initial period income and income-related ratios are higher for the sales-type lease because the sale (and income) is recognized at the inception of the lease. In later years, however, income is higher for the operating lease.

Income taxes paid are the same since the lease cannot be considered a completed sale for tax purposes.

Cash from operations is higher for the first year due to recognition of the sale (the investment in the lease is classified as an investing cash outflow). In later years the operating lease method shows higher cash from operations as rental income exceeds the interest income recorded for the sales-type lease (income taxes paid are the same).

[See Exhibit 8 and the accompanying text for further explanation of these effects.]

8. A. The present value of the minimum lease payments receivable of $170,271 (at 10%, the lower of lessee and lessor rates) is more than 90% of the fair market value of $185,250. Therefore, the lessee, Baldes, should capitalize the lease. It would be useful to know whether the lessee has guaranteed the residual value of the leased asset.

B. Leased assets $170,271

Long-term lease obligation	167,298
Current portion of lease obligation	2,973
Total lease obligation	$170,271

Note that there are no income or cash flow statement effects at the inception of the lease.

C. i. Balance sheet effects of capital lease:

	01/01/01	12/31/01	12/31/02
Leased assets	$170,271	$170,271	$170,271
Accumulated depreciation	0	(8,514)	(17,028)
Leased assets (net)	$170,271	$161,757	$153,243
Current portion of lease obligation	$ 2,973	$ 3,270	$ 3,597
Long-term portion of lease obligation	167,298	164,028	160,431
Total lease obligation	$170,271	$167,298	$164,028

No impact on balance sheet if operating lease method applied. [Deferred tax assets reflecting the difference between total expense under the two methods would also be reported.]

ii. Income statement effects of capital lease:

Years Ended December 31	2001	2002
Interest expense[a]	$17,027	$16,730
Depreciation expense[b]	8,514	8,514
Total expense	$25,541	$25,244

[a] Interest expense for: 2001 = .10 × $170,271
2002 = .10 × $167,298

[b] Depreciation expense = $170,271/20 for each year

Note: The income statement would show lease expense of $20,000 each year under the operating lease method.

iii. Statement of cash flow effects of capital lease:

Years Ended December 31	2001	2002
Cash from operations	$(17,027)	$(16,730)
Financing cash flow	(2,973)	(3,270)

The operating lease method reports $20,000 cash outflow from operations for each year.

D. As in part A, the PV of the MLPs is more than 90% of the fair market value, permitting capitalization. However, for the lessor to capitalize the lease, revenue recognition criteria must be satisfied as well. These conditions are:

i. Collectibility of MLPs is reasonably assured, and

ii. There are no significant uncertainties regarding the amount of costs yet to be incurred by the lessor or other obligations under the provisions of the lease agreement.

To evaluate these issues, information would be needed regarding the financial condition of Baldes and any remaining obligations of Malbec.

E. The operating lease method has no effect on Malbec's balance sheet at the inception of the lease since the lessor has merely entered into a rental arrangement—an executory contract.

F. Sales-type lease reporting by lessor:

Malbec's gross investment in the lease:		
MLPs ($20,000 × 20)	$400,000	
Unguaranteed residual value	5,500	
Gross investment	$405,500	
Net investment:		
Present value of 20 payments at 10%	$170,271	
PV of $5,500, 20 periods hence at 10%	818	
Net investment	$171,089	
Unearned income: $405,500 − $171,089 =	$234,411	
Journal entry at inception (1/1/01):		
Gross investment	$405,500	
Cost of goods sold	149,182	
Sales revenue		$170,271
Inventory		150,000
Unearned income		234,411

Balance sheet effects, January 1, 2001:

Inventory (reduction due to sale)	$(150,000)
Gross investment in sales-type lease	$405,500
Less: unearned interest income	(234,411)
Net investment	$171,089

Income statement effects, year ended December 31, 2001:

Sales revenue	$170,271
Cost of goods sold	(149,182)
Income effect	$ 21,089

G.

Balance Sheet Effects	12/31/01	12/31/02
Sales-type lease:		
Net investment in lease, current	$ 3,180	$ 3,498
Net investment in lease, long-term	159,518	156,020
Operating lease:		
Assets under lease	$ 150,000	$150,000
Accumulated depreciation	(7,225)	(14,450)
Net assets	$142,775	$135,550

Income Statement Effects	12/31/01	12/31/02
Sales-type lease:		
Sales revenue	$ 170,271	$ —
Cost of goods sold	(149,182)	—
Sales profit	$ 21,089	—
Interest income	17,109	$ 16,820
Pretax income	$ 38,198	$ 16,820
Operating lease:		
Rental income	$ 20,000	$ 20,000
Depreciation expense	(7,225)	(7,225)
Pretax income	$ 12,775	$ 12,775

(continued on next page . . .)

Cash Flow Statement Effects	12/31/01	12/31/02
Sales-type lease:		
Cash from operations:		
Sales profit	$ 21,089	$ —
Inventory reduction	150,000	—
Interest income	17,109	16,820
Cash from operations	$ 188,198	$ 16,820
Investment cash flow:		
Net investment in lease	$(171,089)	$ —
Reduction in net investment	2,891	3,180
Investment cash flow	$(168,198)	$ 3,180
Net cash flow	$ 20,000	$ 20,000
Operating lease:		
Rental income	$ 20,000	$ 20,000
Cash from operations	$ 20,000	$ 20,000

Note: There is no effect on investment cash flow when the operating lease method is used.

CFO—Indirect Method	12/31/01	12/31/02
Sales-type lease:		
Pretax income	$ 38,198	$16,820
Inventory reduction	150,000	—
Cash from operations	$ 188,198	$ 16,820
Operating lease:		
Pretax income	$12,775	$12,775
Depreciation expense	7,225	7,225
Cash from operations	$ 20,000	$ 20,000

SOLUTIONS FOR READING 41

1. D is correct. Cross-sectional analysis involved the comparison of companies with each other for the same time period. Time-series analysis is the comparison of financial data across different time periods.
2. C is correct. Solvency ratios are used to evaluate the ability of a company to meet its long-term obligations.
3. A is correct. The current ratio is a liquidity ratio. It compares the net amount of current assets expected to be converted into cash within the year, compared with liabilities falling due in the same period. A current ratio of 1.0 would indicate that the company would have just enough current assets to pay current liabilities.
4. D is correct. Solvency ratios measure the ability to cover debt payments. There are two main types of solvency ratios. Debt ratios focus on the balance sheet and measure the amount of capital raised by debt relative to equity. Coverage ratios focus on the income statement and measure the ability of a company to cover its debt payments. The fixed charge coverage ratio is a coverage ratio that relates known fixed obligations to the cash flow generated by the entity.
5. C is correct. Chan is very *unlikely* to reach the conclusion given in Statement C because days sales outstanding increased from 23 days in 2003 to 25 days in 2004 to 28 days in 2005, indicating that the time required to collect receivables has increased over the period, which is a negative factor for Spherion's liquidity. By contrast, days of inventory on hand dropped over the period 2003 to 2005, a positive for liquidity. Thus Statement A is an appropriate conclusion. The company's increase in days payable from 35 days to 40 days shorted its cash collection cycle, thus contributing to improved liquidity; therefore, Statement B is also an appropriate conclusion. Over the period, the company's cash conversion cycle has decreased from 28 days to 20 days (calculation below), indicating improved liquidity, so Statement D is an appropriate conclusion.

Calculation of Cash Conversion Cycle	2005	2004	2003
Days of inventory on hand	32	34	40
+ Days of sales outstanding	28	25	23
− Number of days of payables	(40)	(35)	(35)
= Cash conversion cycle	20	24	28

6. A is correct. The company is becoming increasingly less solvent, as evidenced by its debt-to-equity ratio increasing from 0.35 to 0.50 from 2003 to 2005. B is incorrect because it incorrectly interprets the debt-to-equity ratio as a measure of liquidity. C and D are incorrect because they incorrectly interpret the direction of the trend and misinterpret the ratio as an indicator of liquidity.

Debt to equity:

2005	2,000/4,000 = 0.5000
2004	1,900/4,500 = 0.4222
2003	1,750/5,000 = 0.3500

7. D is correct. The decline in the company's equity indicates that the company may be incurring losses on its operations, paying dividends greater than income, or repurchasing shares. Recall that beginning equity + new shares issuance − shares repurchased + net income − dividends = ending equity. A is incorrect because the book value of a company's equity is not affected by changes in the market value of its common stock. B is incorrect because an increased amount of lending does not necessarily indicate that lenders view a company as increasingly creditworthy. Creditworthiness is not evaluated based on how much a company has increased its debt but rather on its willingness to pay its obligations and its ability to pay. (Its financial strength is indicated by its solvency, liquidity, profitability, efficiency, and other aspects of credit analysis.) C is incorrect because refinancing short-term debt with long-term debt does not affect the amount of total debt.
8. D is correct. The company's problems with its inventory management system causing duplicate orders would result in a higher amount of inventory than needed and would, therefore, likely result in a decrease in inventory turnover. A is incorrect because a more efficient inventory management system would likely be reflected in the inventory turnover ratio, an indicator of more efficient inventory management. B is incorrect because a write-off of inventory at the beginning of the period would decrease the average inventory for the period (the denominator of the inventory turnover ratio), thus increasing the ratio rather than decreasing it. C is incorrect because the ability to make purchases from its suppliers that better track demand suggests that inventory turnover would have increased (improved) relative to the prior year when there were inventory problems.
9. B is correct. A write-off of receivables would decrease the average amount of accounts receivable (the denominator of the receivables turnover ratio), thus increasing this ratio. A is incorrect because weaker credit customers are more likely to make payments more slowly or to pose collection difficulties, which would likely increase the average amount of accounts receivable and thus decrease receivables turnover. C is incorrect because a longer payment period would likely increase the average amount of accounts receivable and thus decrease receivables turnover. D is incorrect because more lenient collections policies would increase the average amount of accounts receivable and thus decrease receivables turnover.
10. C is correct because accounts receivable turnover can be calculated to determine the average DSO. Turnovers are equal to 365/19 (DSO) = 19.2 for 2005 and 365/15 = 24.3 in 2004. Sales/turnovers are equal to accounts receivable balances. For 2005, $300,000,000/19.2 = $15,625,000, and for 2006, $390,000,000/24.3 = $16,049,383. The difference is an increase in receivables of $424,383.

    A is incorrect because the accounts receivable balance must increase.
    B is incorrect because the accounts receivable balance must increase.
    D is incorrect because it has no basis at all.
11. C is correct. ROE = Return on assets × Financial leverage. ROA can be decomposed into the product of net profit margin (net income divided by revenue) and total asset turnover (revenue divided by average total assets). Because ROA has been decreasing over 2003 to 2005 while total asset turnover has been increasing, it must be the case that the net profit margin has been declining. Furthermore, because ROE has increased despite the drop in ROA, financial leverage must have increased. Statement C is the only statement that correctly identifies the trends in net profit margin and financial leverage.

12. C is correct. The increase in the average tax rate in 2005, as indicated by the decrease in the value of the tax burden (the tax burden equals one minus the average tax rate), offset the improvement in efficiency indicated by higher asset turnover; as a result, ROE remained unchanged at 18.90 percent. Statement A is not correct because the EBIT margin, measuring profitability, was unchanged in 2005; furthermore, no information is given on liquidity. Statement B is not correct because profitability was unchanged in 2005. Statement D is not correct because the average tax rate was higher not lower in 2005; furthermore, efficiency improved rather than deteriorated in 2005.
13. A is correct. The difference between the two companies' ROE in 2005 is very small and is mainly the result of Company A's increase in its financial leverage, indicated by the increase in its Assets/Equity ratio from 2 to 4. B is incorrect because Company A has experienced a significant decline in its operating margin, from 10 percent to 7 percent which, all else equal, would not suggest that it is selling more of products with higher profit margin. C is incorrect because the impact of efficiency on ROE is identical for the two companies, as indicated by both companies' asset turnover ratios of 1.5. Furthermore, if Company A had purchased newer equipment to replace older, depreciated equipment, then the company's asset turnover ratio (computed as sales/assets) would have declined, assuming constant sales. D is also incorrect because the impact of efficiency on ROE is identical for the two companies, as indicated by both companies' asset turnover ratios of 1.5. If more efficient inventory management had caused Company A's increase in ROE, this would have been evidenced by a change in its asset turnover ratio.
14. A is correct. The debt-to-equity ratio has improved from 1999 to 2002 from 410 percent to 88 percent (calculations below). The decrease in total debt implies that debt has been repaid, not borrowed. B is incorrect because the company's solvency has deteriorated from 2002 to 2003, as indicated by the higher debt-to-equity ratio. C is incorrect because lower total debt in 2002 suggests repayment of debt. D is incorrect because the company's stockholders' equity increased between 1999 and 2003. An increase in stockholders' equity results from increases in shareholders' equity (which result from income and/or new share issuance) greater than the amount of reductions (which result from losses and/or dividend payments and/or share repurchases). If the amount of total income and new share issuance of this company had been about equal to the amount of dividend payments and share repurchases made by the company from 1999 to 2003, total stockholders' equity would have remained approximately unchanged.

	2003	2002	2001	2000	1999
Total debt	698,000	521,330	702,506	741,051	847,160
Stockholders' equity	794,830	842,400	405,378	309,371	206,690
Total debt-to-equity ratio	88%	62%	173%	240%	410%

15. A is correct. Company A's current ratio of 4.0x ($40,000/$10,000 = 4.0) indicates it is more liquid than Company B, whose current ratio is only 1.2x ($60,000/$50,000 = 1.2). Company B is more solvent, as indicated by its lower debt-to-equity ratio of 30 percent ($150,000/$500,000 = 0.30) compared with Company A's debt-to-equity ratio of 200 percent

($60,000/$30,000 = 2.0). The other choices are incorrect either because the current ratio is incorrectly calculated (as in choices B and D), and/or because the debt-to-equity ratio was incorrectly interpreted (as in choices C and D).

16. D is correct. The company's efficiency deteriorated, as indicated by the decline in its total asset turnover ratio from 1.11 (GBP 4,390/[(GBP 4,384 + 3,500)/2 = 1.11] for the year 2000 to 0.87 (GBP 11,366/[(GBP 12,250 + GBP 13,799)/2] = 0.87) for the year 2004. The decline in the total asset turnover ratio resulted from an increase in average assets from GBP 3,942 (GBP 4,384 + 3,500)/2 = GBP 3,942) in 2000 to GBP 13,024.5 in 2004, an increase of 330 percent, compared with an increase in turnover (i.e., revenues) from GBP 4,390 in 2000 to GBP 11,366 in 2004, an increase of only 259 percent. A is incorrect because the asset turnover ratio is calculated incorrectly. B is incorrect because the current ratio is not an indicator of efficiency. C is incorrect because, in isolation, growth in assets does not provide enough information to assess efficiency.

17. B is correct. Comparing 2004 with 2000, the company's solvency deteriorated, as indicated by a decrease in interest coverage from 10.6 (GBP 844/GBP 80 = 10.6) in 2000 to 8.4 (GBP 1,579/GBP 188 = 8.4). A is incorrect because it misinterprets the debt-to-asset ratio. C is incorrect because, in isolation, the amount of profits does not provide enough information to assess solvency. D is incorrect because the debt-to-equity ratio is miscalculated and misinterpreted.

18. D is correct. Comparing 2004 with 2000, the company's liquidity improved, as indicated by an increase in its current ratio from 0.71 ([GBP 316 + GBP 558]/GBP 1,223 = 0.71) in 2000 to 0.75 ([GBP 682 + GBP 1,634]/GBP 3,108 = 0.75) in 2004. Note, however, comparing only current investments with the level of current liabilities shows a decline in liquidity from 0.25 (316/1223 = 0.25) in 2000 to 0.22 (GBP 682/GBP 3,108 = 0.22) in 2004. A is incorrect because the debt-to-assets ratio is not an indicator of liquidity. B is incorrect because interest coverage is not an indicator of liquidity. C is incorrect because, in isolation, the amount of current assets does not provide enough information to assess liquidity.

19. B is correct. Comparing 2004 with 2000, the company's profitability deteriorated, as indicated by a decrease in its net profit margin from 11 percent (484/4,390 = 0.11) to 5.7 percent (645/11,366 = 0.057). A is incorrect because the debt-to-assets ratio is not an indicator of profitability. C is incorrect because growth in shareholders' equity, in isolation, does not provide enough information to assess profitability. D is incorrect because the operating margin is incorrectly calculated.

20. B is correct. In general, a creditor would consider a decrease in debt to total assets as positive news. As noted in Section 4, a higher level of debt in a company's capital structure increases the risk of default and will result in higher borrowing costs for the company to compensate lenders for assuming greater credit risk.

21. D is correct. Assuming no changes in other variables, an increase in average assets would decrease ROA.

22. A is correct. The P/E ratio measures the "multiple" that the stock market places on a company's EPS.

SOLUTIONS FOR READING 42

1. A is correct. For a large, diversified company, margin changes in different business segments may offset each other. Furthermore, margins are most likely to be stable in mature industries.
2. D is correct. Accounts receivable turnover is equal to 365/19 (collection period in days) = 19.2 for 2003 and needs to equal 365/15 = 24.3 in 2004 for Galambos to meet its goal. Sales/turnover equals the accounts receivable balance. For 2003, $300,000,000/19.2 = $15,625,000, and for 2004, $400,000,000/24.3 = $16,460,905. The difference of $835,905 is the increase in receivables needed for Galambos to achieve its goal.
3. C is correct. Credit analysts consider both business risk and financial risk.
4. A is correct. Requiring that net income be positive would avoid selecting companies that report positive return on equity because both net income and shareholders' equity are negative.
5. D is correct. A lower debt-to-total assets ratio indicates greater financial strength. Requiring that a company's debt-to-total assets ratio be below a certain cutoff point would allow the analyst to screen out highly leveraged and, therefore, potentially financially weak companies. Requiring declining sales growth (answer A), negative income (answer B), or high leverage (answer C) would not be appropriate for screening out financially weak companies.
6. C is correct. Survivorship bias exists when companies that merge or go bankrupt are dropped from the database and only surviving companies remain. Look-ahead bias involves using updated financial information in backtesting that would not have been available at the time the decision was made. Data-snooping bias involves developing and testing models on the same database, potentially finding a model that works only for that data set. Backtesting involves testing models in prior periods and is not a bias itself.
7. D is correct. Financial statements should be adjusted for differences in accounting standards (as well as accounting and operating choices). These adjustments should be made prior to common-size and ratio analysis.
8. D is correct. IFRS makes a distinction between unrealized gains and losses on available-for-sale debt securities that arise due to exchange rate movements and requires these changes in value to be recognized in the income statement, whereas U.S. GAAP does not make this distinction.
9. A is correct. LIFO is not permitted under international financial reporting standards.
10. D is correct. To convert LIFO inventory to FIFO inventory, the entire LIFO reserve must be added back: $600,000 + $70,000 = $670,000.
11. C is correct. There were no additions or deletions to the fixed asset account during the year, so depreciation expense is equal to the difference in accumulated depreciation at the beginning of the year and the end of the year, or 0.4 million. Average age is equal to accumulated depreciation/depreciation expense, or 1.6/0.4 = 4 years. Average depreciable life is equal to ending gross investment/depreciation expense = 2.8/0.4 = 7 years.
12. D is correct. Tangible book value removes all intangible assets, including goodwill, from the balance sheet.

13. D is correct. Operating leases can be used as an off-balance-sheet financing technique because neither the asset nor liability appears on the balance sheet. Inventory and capital leases are reported on the balance sheet.

14. D is correct. The present value of future operating lease payments would be added to total assets and total liabilities.

SOLUTIONS FOR READING 43

1. A is correct. Neutrality is a qualitative characteristic. (Timeliness is a constraint; accrual basis and going concern are assumptions.)
2. C is correct. Changes in the five basic elements (assets, liabilities, equity, income, and expenses) are portrayed in the cash flow statement and the statement of changes in equity.
3. C is correct. For available-for-sale securities, there is an asymmetrical treatment of income and changes in value. Under this classification, unrealized gains and losses can accumulate in equity without affecting the income statement.
4. A is correct. Whenever possible, the cost of inventory should be assigned by specific identification of the unit's costs. Two alternative formulas for assigning the cost of inventory are weighted average cost and FIFO.
5. D is correct. LIFO is not an acceptable inventory costing method.
6. C is correct. Like U.S. GAAP, international standards require inventory to be reported at the lower of cost or net realizable value. However, IFRS permit the reversal of inventory write downs, but no such provision exists in U.S. GAAP.
7. D is correct. Unlike U.S. GAAP, international accounting standards allow revaluations (both increases and decreases) for property, plant, and equipment.
8. D is correct. When an investor shares the ownership of an investee, as in a joint venture, control is shared and the investor would account for the investment using a proportionate consolidation method, with the equity method as an alternative.
9. B is correct. Under IFRS No. 3, goodwill is capitalized and tested for impairment annually.
10. A is correct. A gain is recognized if the amount an acquirer pays to buy another company is less than the fair value of the identifiable net assets acquired. Extraordinary gains are not allowed under IASB GAAP.
11. C is correct. If an intangible asset does not have a finite life, it is not amortized. Instead, the asset is tested at least annually for impairment (like goodwill).
12. D is correct. Any upward revaluation is reported as part of equity, unless it is reversing a previous revaluation decrease.
13. D is correct. When the outcome of a contract cannot be reliably estimated, revenue should be recognized to the extent that it is probable to recover contract costs. This differs from U.S. GAAP, which requires that the completed contract method be used in such cases.
14. D is correct. In choosing the appropriate depreciation method, IFRS requires that (1) the depreciable amount is allocated on a systematic basis over the useful life, and (2) the method used must reflect the pattern of expected consumption.
15. B is correct. IASB GAAP allows cash flows from interest and dividends to be reported as either "operating" or "investing cash inflows." Under U.S. GAAP, these must be reported as "operating cash inflows."
16. D is correct. IASB GAAP allows cash payments for interest to be reported as either "operating" or "financing cash outflows." Under U.S. GAAP, these must be reported as "operating cash outflows."

17. D is correct. IASB GAAP allows cash payments for dividends to be reported as either "operating" or "financing cash outflows." Under U.S. GAAP, these must be reported as "financing cash outflows."
18. C is correct. If comparing a U.S. company that uses LIFO accounting with an international company for whom this method is not allowable, an analyst will make adjustments. Specifically, using LIFO reserve note disclosures, the analyst will adjust the U.S. company's profits, ending inventory, and total assets.
19. D is correct. If comparing an IFRS company, which has written up the value of its intangible assets, with a U.S. company, an analyst will eliminate the effect of the write-ups in calculating any affected asset-based ratios, which, in this case, includes the financial leverage multiplier (Total assets ÷ Total common equity).

GLOSSARY

A priori probability A probability based on logical analysis rather than on observation or personal judgment.

Abandonment option The ability to terminate a project at some future time if the financial results are disappointing.

Abnormal rate of return The amount by which a security's actual return differs from its expected rate of return which is based on the market's rate of return and the security's relationship with the market.

Above full-employment equilibrium A macroeconomic equilibrium in which real GDP exceeds potential GDP.

Absolute dispersion The amount of variability present without comparison to any reference point or benchmark.

Absolute frequency The number of observations in a given interval (for grouped data).

Accelerated method A method of depreciation that allocates relatively large amounts of the depreciable cost of an asset to earlier years and reduced amounts to later years.

Accelerated methods of depreciation Depreciation methods that allocate a relatively large proportion of the cost of an asset to the early years of the asset's useful life.

Account With the accounting systems, a formal record of increases and decreases in a specific asset, liability, component of owners' equity, revenue, or expense.

Account format A method of presentation of accounting transactions in which effects on assets appear at the left and effects on liabilities and equity appear at the right of a central dividing line; also known as T-account format.

Accounting risk The risk associated with accounting standards that vary from country to country or with any uncertainty about how certain transactions should be recorded.

Accounts payable Amounts that a business owes to its vendors for goods and services that were purchased from them but which have not yet been paid.

Accounts receivable turnover Ratio of sales on credit to the average balance in accounts receivable.

Accrual accounting The system of recording financial transactions as they come into existence as a legally enforceable claim, rather than when they settle.

Accrued expenses (accrued liabilities) Liabilities related to expenses that have been incurred but not yet paid as of the end of an accounting period—an example of an accrued expense is rent that has been incurred but not yet paid, resulting in a liability "rent payable."

Accrued interest Interest earned but not yet paid.

Accumulated depreciation An offset to property, plant, and equipment (PPE) reflecting the amount of the cost of PPE that has been allocated to current and previous accounting periods.

Active factor risk The contribution to active risk squared resulting from the portfolio's different-than-benchmark exposures relative to factors specified in the risk model.

Active return The return on a portfolio minus the return on the portfolio's benchmark.

Active risk The standard deviation of active returns.

Active risk squared The variance of active returns; active risk raised to the second power.

Active specific risk or asset selection risk The contribution to active risk squared resulting from the portfolio's active weights on individual assets as those weights interact with assets' residual risk.

Active strategy In reference to short-term cash management, an investment strategy characterized by monitoring and attempting to capitalize on market conditions to optimize the risk and return relationship of short-term investments.

Activity ratios (asset utilization or operating efficiency ratios) Ratios that measure how efficiently a company performs day-to-day tasks, such as the collection of receivables and management of inventory.

Addition rule for probabilities A principle stating that the probability that *A* or *B* occurs (both occur) equals the probability that *A* occurs, plus the probability that *B* occurs, minus the probability that both *A* and *B* occur.

Additional information Information that is required or recommended under the GIPS standards and is not considered as "supplemental information" for the purposes of compliance.

Additions Enlargements to the physical layout of a plant asset.

Add-on interest A procedure for determining the interest on a bond or loan in which the interest is added onto the face value of a contract.

Adjusted beta Historical beta adjusted to reflect the tendency of beta to be mean reverting.

Adjusted R^2 A measure of goodness-of-fit of a regression that is adjusted for degrees of freedom and hence does not automatically increase when another independent variable is added to a regression.

Administrative fees All fees other than the trading expenses and the investment management fee. Administrative fees include custody fees, accounting fees, consulting fees, legal fees, performance measurement fees, or other related fees. These administrative fees are typically outside the control of the investment management firm and are not included in either the gross-of-fees return or the net-of-fees return. However, there are some markets and investment vehicles where administrative fees are controlled by the firm. (See the term "bundled fee.")

Aggregate demand The relationship between the quantity of real GDP demanded and the price level.

Aggregate hours The total number of hours worked by all the people employed, both full time and part time, during a year.

Aggregate production function The relationship between the quantity of real GDP supplied and the quantities of labor and capital and the state of technology.

Aging schedule In the context of accounts receivable, it is an analysis of accounts receivable categorized by days outstanding.

Allocative efficiency A situation in which we cannot produce more of any good without giving up some of another good that we value more highly.

Allowance for bad debts An offset to accounts receivable for the amount of accounts receivable that are estimated to be uncollectible.

Alpha A term commonly used to describe a manager's abnormal rate of return, which is the difference between the return the portfolio actually produced and the expected return given its risk level.

Alternative hypothesis The hypothesis accepted when the null hypothesis is rejected.

American Depository Receipts (ADRs) Certificates of ownership issued by a U.S. bank that represent indirect ownership of a certain number of shares of a specific foreign firm. Shares are held on deposit in a bank in the firm's home country.

American option An option contract that can be exercised at any time until its expiration date

American terms With reference to U.S. dollar exchange rate quotations, the U.S. dollar price of a unit of another currency.

Amortization The process of allocating the cost of intangible long-term assets having a finite useful life to accounting periods; the allocation of the amount of a bond premium or discount to the periods remaining until bond maturity.

Amortizing and accreting swaps A swap in which the notional principal changes according to a formula related to changes in the underlying.

Analysis of variance (ANOVA) The analysis of the total variability of a dataset (such as observations on the dependent variable in a regression) into components representing different sources of variation; with reference to regression, ANOVA provides the inputs for an *F*-test of the significance of the regression as a whole.

Annual percentage rate The cost of borrowing expressed as a yearly rate.

Annuity A finite set of level sequential cash flows.

Annuity due An annuity having a first cash flow that is paid immediately.

Anomalies Security price relationships that appear to contradict a well-regarded hypothesis; in this case, the efficient market hypothesis.

Anticipation stock Excess inventory that is held in anticipation of increased demand, often because of seasonal patterns of demand.

Antidilutive With reference to a transaction or a security, one that would increase earnings per share (EPS) or result in EPS higher than the company's basic EPS—antidilutive securities are not included in the calculation of diluted EPS.

Arbitrage (1) The simultaneous purchase of an undervalued asset or portfolio and sale of an overvalued but equivalent asset or portfolio, in order to obtain a riskless profit on the price differential. Taking advantage of a market inefficiency in a risk-free manner. (2) A trading strategy designed to generate a guaranteed profit from a transaction that requires no capital commitment or risk bearing on the part of the trader. A simple example of an arbitrage trade would be the simultaneous purchase and sale of the same security in different markets at different prices. (3) The condition in a financial market in which equivalent assets or combinations of assets sell for two different prices, creating an opportunity to profit at no risk with no commitment of money. In a well-functioning financial market, few arbitrage opportunities are possible. (4) A risk-free operation that earns an expected positive net profit but requires no net investment of money.

Arbitrage opportunity An opportunity to conduct an arbitrage; an opportunity to earn an expected positive net profit without risk and with no net investment of money.

Arbitrage portfolio The portfolio that exploits an arbitrage opportunity.

Arbitrage pricing theory (APT) A theory that posits that the expected return to a financial asset can be described by its relationship with several common risk factors. The multifactor APT can be contrasted with the single-factor CAPM.

Arithmetic mean The sum of the observations divided by the number of observations.

Arrears swap A type of interest rate swap in which the floating payment is set at the end of the period and the interest is paid at that same time.

Asian call option A European-style option with a value at maturity equal to the difference between the stock price at maturity and the average stock price during the life of the option, or $0, whichever is greater.

Asset allocation The process of deciding how to distribute an investor's wealth among different asset classes for investment purposes.

Asset beta The unlevered beta; reflects the business risk of the assets.

Asset class Securities that have similar characteristics, attributes, and risk/return relationships.

Asset impairment Loss of revenue-generating potential of a long-lived asset before the end of its useful life; the difference between an asset's carrying value and its fair value, as measured by the present value of the expected cash flows.

Asset-based loans A loan that is secured with company assets.

Assets under management (AUM) The total market value of the assets managed by an investment firm.

Assets Resources controlled by an enterprise as a result of past events and from which future economic benefits to the enterprise are expected to flow.

Assignment of accounts receivable The use of accounts receivable as collateral for a loan

At the money An option in which the underlying value equals the exercise price.

At-the-money option An option for which the strike (or exercise) price is close to (at) the current market price of the underlying asset.

Autocorrelation The correlation of a time series with its own past values.

Automated Clearing House An electronic payment network available to businesses, individuals, and financial institutions in the United States, U.S. Territories, and Canada.

Automatic fiscal policy A change in fiscal policy that is triggered by the state of the economy.

Automatic stabilizers Mechanisms that stabilize real GDP without explicit action by the government.

Autonomous expenditure The sum of those components of aggregate planned expenditure that are not influenced by real GDP. Autonomous expenditure equals investment, government purchases, exports, and the autonomous parts of consumption expenditure and imports.

Autoregressive (AR) model A time series regressed on its own past values, in which the independent variable is a lagged value of the dependent variable.

Available-for-sale securities Securities that a company does not intend to actively trade or (in the case of debt securities) hold to maturity.

Average cost pricing rule A rule that sets price to cover cost including normal profit, which means setting the price equal to average total cost.

Average fixed cost Total fixed cost per unit of output—total fixed cost divided by output.

Average product The average product of a resource. It equals total product divided by the quantity of the resource employed.

Average tax rate A person's total tax payment divided by his or her total income.

Average total cost Total cost per unit of output.

Average variable cost Total variable cost per unit of output.

Backtesting With reference to portfolio strategies, the application of a strategy's portfolio selection rules to historical data to assess what would have been the strategy's historical performance.

Backwardation A condition in the futures markets in which the benefits of holding an asset exceed the costs, leaving the futures price less than the spot price.

Balance of payments (1) A summary of all economic transactions between a country and all other countries for a specific time period, usually a year. The balance-of-payments account reflects all payments and liabilities to foreigners (debits) and all payments and obligations received from foreigners (credits). (2) A record of all financial flows crossing the borders of a country during a given time period (a quarter or a year).

Balance of payments accounts A country's record of international trading, borrowing, and lending.

Balance of trade *See* Trade balance.

Balance sheet A financial statement that shows what assets the firm controls at a fixed point in time and how it has financed these assets.

Balance sheet ratios Financial ratios involving balance sheet items only.

Balance sheet (statement of financial position or statement of financial condition) The financial statement that presents an entity's current financial position by disclosing resources the entity controls (its assets) and the claims on those resources (its liabilities and equity claims), as of a particular point in time (the date of the balance sheet).

Balanced budget A government budget in which tax revenues and expenditures are equal.

Balanced budget multiplier The magnification on aggregate demand of a *simultaneous* change in government purchases and taxes that leaves the budget balance unchanged.

Balanced fund A mutual fund with, generally, a three-part investment objective: (1) to conserve the investor's principal, (2) to pay current income, and (3) to increase both principal and income. The fund aims to achieve this by owning a mixture of bonds, preferred stocks, and common stocks.

Bank discount basis A quoting convention that annualizes, on a 360-day year, the discount as a percentage of face value.

Barriers to entry Legal or natural constraints that protect a firm from potential competitors.

Barter The direct exchange of one good or service for other goods and services.

Basic earnings per share Net earnings available to common shareholders (i.e., net income minus preferred dividends) divided by the weighted average number of common shares outstanding during the period.

Basis The difference between the spot price of the underlying asset and the futures contract price at any point in time (e.g., the *initial* basis at the time of contract origination, the *cover* basis at the time of contract termination).

Basis point value (BPV) Also called *present value of a basis point* or *price value of a basis point* (PVBP), the change in the bond price for a 1 basis point change in yield.

Basis swap (1) An interest rate swap involving two floating rates. (2) A swap in which both parties pay a floating rate.

Bayes' formula A method for updating probabilities based on new information.

Bear spread An option strategy that involves selling a put with a lower exercise price and buying a put with a higher exercise price. It can also be executed with calls.

Behavioral finance Involves the analysis of various psychological traits of individuals and how these traits affect how they act as investors, analysts, and portfolio managers.

Below full-employment equilibrium A macroeconomic equilibrium in which potential GDP exceeds real GDP.

Benchmark A comparison portfolio; a point of reference or comparison.

Benchmark bond A bond representative of current market conditions and used for performance comparison.

Benchmark error Situation where an inappropriate or incorrect benchmark is used to compare and assess portfolio returns and management.

Benchmark portfolio A comparison standard of risk and assets included in the policy statement and similar to the investor's risk preference and investment needs, which can be used to evaluate the investment performance of the portfolio manager.

Bernoulli random variable A random variable having the outcomes 0 and 1.

Bernoulli trial An experiment that can produce one of two outcomes.

Beta A standardized measure of systematic risk based upon an asset's covariance with the market portfolio.

Betterments Improvements that do not add to the physical layout of a plant asset.

Bid-ask spread The difference between the quoted ask and the bid prices.

Big tradeoff A tradeoff between equity and efficiency.

Bill-and-hold basis Sales on a bill-and-hold basis involve selling products but not delivering those products until a later date.

Binomial model A model for pricing options in which the underlying price can move to only one of two possible new prices.

Binomial option pricing model A valuation equation that assumes the price of the underlying asset changes through a series of discrete upward or downward movements.

Binomial random variable The number of successes in n Bernoulli trials for which the probability of success is constant for all trials and the trials are independent.

Binomial tree The graphical representation of a model of asset price dynamics in which, at each period, the asset moves up with probability p or down with probability $(1 - p)$.

Black market An illegal trading arrangement in which the price exceeds the legally imposed price ceiling.

Black-Scholes option pricing model A valuation equation that assumes the price of the underlying asset changes continuously through the option's expiration date by a statistical process known as *geometric Brownian motion.*

Block Orders to buy or sell that are too large for the liquidity ordinarily available in dealer networks or stock exchanges.

Bond A long-term debt security with contractual obligations regarding interest payments and redemption.

Bond-equivalent basis A basis for stating an annual yield that annualizes a semiannual yield by doubling it.

Bond-equivalent yield The yield to maturity on a basis that ignores compounding.

Bond equivalent yield A calculation of yield that is annualized using the ratio of 365 to the number of days to maturity. Bond equivalent yield allows for the restatement and comparison of securities with different compounding periods.

Bond option An option in which the underlying is a bond; primarily traded in over-the-counter markets.

Bond price volatility The percentage changes in bond prices over time.

Bond yield plus risk premium approach An estimate of the cost of common equity that is produced by summing the before-tax cost of debt and a risk premium that captures the additional yield on a company's stock relative to its bonds. The additional yield is often estimated using historical spreads between bond yields and stock yields.

Book value equity per share The amount of the book value (also called carrying value) of common equity per share of common stock, calculated by dividing the book value of shareholders' equity by the number of shares of common stock outstanding.

Book value of equity (or book value) (1) Shareholders' equity (total assets minus total liabilities) minus the value of preferred stock; common shareholders' equity. (2) The accounting value of a firm.

Book value per share Book value of equity divided by the number of common shares outstanding.

Bottom-up analysis With reference to investment selection processes, an approach that involves selection from all securities within a specified investment universe, i.e., without prior narrowing of the universe on the basis of macroeconomic or overall market considerations.

Box spread An option strategy that combines a bull spread and a bear spread having two different exercise prices, which produces a risk-free payoff of the difference in the exercise prices.

Brady bonds Bonds issued by emerging countries under a debt-reduction plan named after Mr. Brady, former U.S. Secretary of the Treasury.

Brand name A registered name that can be used only by its owner to identify a product or service.

Break point In the context of the weighted average cost of capital (WACC), a break point is the amount of capital at which the cost of one or more of the sources of capital changes, leading to a change in the WACC.

Breusch-Pagan test A test for conditional heteroskedasticity in the error term of a regression.

Broker (1) An agent who executes orders to buy or sell securities on behalf of a client in exchange for a commission. (2) *See* Futures commission merchants.

Budget deficit A government's budget balance that is negative—expenditures exceed tax revenues.

Budget surplus A government's budget balance that is positive—tax revenues exceed expenditures.

Bull spread An option strategy that involves buying a call with a lower exercise price and selling a call with a higher exercise price. It can also be executed with puts.

Bundled fee A fee that combines multiple fees into one "bundled" fee. Bundled fees can include any combination of management, transaction, custody, and other administrative fees. Two specific examples of bundled fees are the wrap fee and the all-in fee.

All-in fee Due to the universal banking system in some countries, asset management, brokerage, and custody are often part of the same company. This allows banks to offer a variety of choices to customers regarding how the fee will be charged. Customers are offered numerous fee models in which fees may be bundled together or charged separately. All-in fees can include any combination of investment management, trading expenses, custody, and other administrative fees.

Wrap fee Wrap fees are specific to a particular investment product. The U.S. Securities and Exchange Commission (SEC) defines a wrap fee account (now more commonly known as a separately managed account or SMA) as "any advisory program under which a specified fee or fees not based upon transactions in a client's account is charged for investment advisory services (which may include portfolio management or advice concerning the selection of other investment advisers) and execution of client transactions." A typical separately managed account has a contract or contracts (and fee) involving a sponsor (usually a broker or independent provider) acting as the investment advisor, an investment management firm typically as the subadvisor, other services (custody, consulting, reporting, performance, manager selection, monitoring, and execution of trades), distributor, and the client (brokerage customer). Wrap fees can be all-inclusive, asset-based fees (which may include any combination of management, transaction, custody, and other administrative fees).

Business cycle The periodic but irregular up-and-down movement in production.

Business risk (or sales risk) Risk that is related to the uncertainty of revenues

Butterfly spread An option strategy that combines two bull or bear spreads and has three exercise prices.

Buy-and-hold strategy A passive portfolio management strategy in which securities (bonds or stocks) are bought and held to maturity.

Call An option that gives the holder the right to buy an underlying asset from another party at a fixed price over a specific period of time.

Call market A market in which trading for individual stocks only takes place at specified times. All the bids and asks available at the time are combined and the market administrators specify a single price that will possibly clear the market at that time.

Call option Option to buy an asset within a certain period at a specified price called the *exercise price.*

Call premium Amount above par that an issuer must pay to a bondholder for retiring the bond before its stated maturity.

Call provisions Specifies when and how a firm can issue a call for bonds outstanding prior to their maturity.

Cannibalization Cannibalization occurs when an investment takes customers and sales away from another part of the company.

Cap (1) A contract on an interest rate, whereby at periodic payment dates, the writer of the cap pays the difference between the market interest rate and a specified cap rate if, and only if, this difference is positive. This is equivalent to a stream of call options on the interest rate. (2) A combination of interest rate call options designed to hedge a borrower against rate increases on a floating-rate loan.

Capital The tools, equipment, buildings, and other constructions that businesses now use to produce goods and services.

Capital account (1) The record of transactions with foreigners that involve either (a) the exchange of ownership rights to real or financial assets or (b) the extension of loans. (2) A component of the balance of payments that reflects unrequited (or unilateral) transfers corresponding to capital flows entailing no compensation (in the form of goods, services, or assets). Examples include investment capital given (without future repayment) in favor of poor countries, debt forgiveness, and expropriation losses.

Capital accumulation The growth of capital resources.

Capital allocation line (CAL) A graph line that describes the combinations of expected return and standard deviation of return available to an investor from combining the optimal portfolio of risky assets with the risk-free asset.

Capital appreciation A return objective in which the investor seeks to increase the portfolio value, primarily through capital gains, over time to meet a future need rather than dividend yield.

Capital asset pricing model (CAPM) An equation describing the expected return on any asset (or portfolio) as a linear function of its beta relative to the market portfolio.

Capital budgeting The allocation of funds to relatively long-range projects or investments.

Capital Employed (Real Estate) The denominator of the return expressions, defined as the "weighted-average equity" (weighted-average capital) during the measurement period. Capital employed should not include any income or capital return accrued during the measurement period. Beginning capital is adjusted by weighting the cash flows (contributions and distributions) that occurred during the period. Cash flows are typically weighted based on the actual days the flows are in or out of the portfolio. Other weighting methods are acceptable; however, once a methodology is chosen, it should be consistently applied.

Capital expenditure An expenditure for the purchase or expansion of a long-term asset, recorded in an asset account.

Capital market line (CML) The line with an intercept point equal to the risk-free rate that is tangent to the efficient frontier of risky assets; represents the efficient frontier when a risk-free asset is available for investment.

Capital preservation A return objective in which the investor seeks to minimize the risk of loss; generally a goal of the risk-averse investor.

Capital rationing A capital rationing environment assumes that the company has a fixed amount of funds to invest.

Capital return (real estate) The change in the market value of the real estate investments and cash/cash equivalent assets held throughout the measurement period (ending market value less beginning market value) adjusted for all capital expenditures (subtracted) and the net proceeds from sales (added). The return is computed as a percentage of the capital employed through the measurement period. Synonyms: capital appreciation return, appreciation return.

Capital stock The total quantity of plant, equipment, buildings, and inventories.

Capital structure A company's specific mixture of long-term financing.

Caplet Each component call option in a cap.

Capped swap A swap in which the floating payments have an upper limit.

Captive finance subsidiary A wholly-owned subsidiary of a company that is established to provide financing of the sales of the parent company.

Carried interest (private equity) The profits that general partners earn from the profits of the investments made by the fund (generally 20-25%). Also known as "carry."

Carrying value The unexpired part of an asset's cost. Also called *book value.*

Cartel A group of firms that has entered into a collusive agreement to limit output and increase prices and profits.

Carve-Out A single or multiple asset class segment of a multiple asset class portfolio.

Cash In accounting contexts, cash on hand (e.g., petty cash and cash not yet deposited to the bank) and demand deposits held in banks and similar accounts that can be used in payment of obligations.

Cash conversion cycle (net operating cycle) A financial metric that measures the length of time required for a company to convert cash invested in its operations to cash received as a result of its operations; equal to days of inventory on hand + days of sales outstanding − number of days of payables.

Cash equivalents Very liquid short-term investments, usually maturing in 90 days or less.

Cash flow additivity principle The principle that dollar amounts indexed at the same point in time are additive.

Cash flow at risk (CFAR) A variation of VAR that reflects the risk of a company's cash flow instead of its market value.

Cash flow coverage ratio Ratio of cash flow from operations + interest payments + tax payments to interest payments; a comparison of the cash flows available to meet interest obligations with existing interest obligations.

Cash flow from operations (cash flow from operating activities or operating cash flow) The net amount of cash provided from operating activities.

Cash flow statement (statement of cash flows) A financial statement that reconciles beginning-of-period and end-of-period balance sheet values of cash; consists of three parts: cash flows from operating activities, cash flows from investing activities, and cash flows from financing activities.

Cash-flow-to-debt ratio Ratio of cash flow from operations to total debt; a measure of debt coverage that estimates the length of time it would take for the company to repay its debt if it were to apply all of its cash flow from operations toward debt repayment.

Cash-generating efficiency A company's ability to generate cash from its current or continuing operations.

Cash price or spot price The price for immediate purchase of the underlying asset.

Cash ratio The ratio of cash+ short-term marketable investments to current liabilities; provides an indication of a company's ability to satisfy current liabilities with just the cash and cash equivalents on hand.

Cash settlement A procedure used in certain derivative transactions that specifies that the long and short parties engage in the equivalent cash value of a delivery transaction.

CD equivalent yield *See* Money market yield.

Central bank A bank's bank and a public authority that regulates a nation's depository institutions and controls the quantity of money.

Central limit theorem A result in statistics that states that the sample mean computed from large samples of size n from a population with finite variance will follow an approximate normal distribution with a mean equal to the population mean and a variance equal to the population variance divided by n.

Centralized risk management or companywide risk management When a company has a single risk management group that monitors and controls all of the risk-taking activities of the organization. Centralization permits economies of scale and allows a company to use some of its risks to offset other risks. See also *enterprise risk management.*

Certificates of deposit (CDs) Instruments issued by banks and S&Ls that require minimum deposits for specified terms and that pay higher rates of interest than deposit accounts.

Ceteris paribus Other things being equal—all other relevant things remaining the same.

Chain rule of forecasting A forecasting process in which the next period's value as predicted by the forecasting equation is substituted into the right-hand side of the equation to give a predicted value two periods ahead.

Change in demand A change in buyers' plans that occurs when some influence on those plans other than the price of the good changes. It is illustrated by a shift of the demand curve.

Change in supply A change in sellers' plans that occurs when some influence on those plans other than the price of the good changes. It is illustrated by a shift of the supply curve.

Change in the quantity demanded A change in buyers' plans that occurs when the price of a good changes but all other influences on buyers' plans remain unchanged. It is illustrated by a movement along the demand curve.

Characteristic line Regression line that indicates the systematic risk (beta) of a risky asset.

Chart of accounts A list of accounts used in an entity's accounting system.

Cheapest to deliver A bond in which the amount received for delivering the bond is largest compared with the amount paid in the market for the bond.

Cherry-picking When a bankrupt company is allowed to enforce contracts that are favorable to it while walking away from contracts that are unfavorable to it.

Classical A macroeconomist who believes that the economy is self-regulating and that it is always at full employment.

Classified balance sheet A balance sheet organized so as to group together the various assets and liabilities into subcategories (e.g., current and noncurrent).

Clean price The price of a bond obtained as the total price of the bond minus accrued interest. Most bonds are traded on the basis of their clean price.

Clearinghouse An entity associated with a futures market that acts as middleman between the contracting parties and guarantees to each party the performance of the other.

Closed-end fund (private equity) A type of investment fund where the number of investors and the total committed capital is fixed and not open for subscriptions and/or redemptions.

Closed-end investment company An investment company that issues only a limited number of shares, which it does not redeem (buy back). Instead, shares of a closed-end fund are traded in securities markets at prices determined by supply and demand.

Closeout netting Netting the market values of *all* derivative contracts between two parties to determine one overall value owed by one party to another in the event of bankruptcy.

Coefficient of variation (CV) The ratio of a set of observations' standard deviation to the observations' mean value.

Cointegrated Describes two time series that have a long-term financial or economic relationship such that they do not diverge from each other without bound in the long run.

Collar An option strategy involving the purchase of a put and sale of a call in which the holder of an asset gains protection below a certain level, the exercise price of the put, and pays for it by giving up gains above a certain level, the exercise price of the call. Collars also can be used to provide protection against rising interest rates on a floating-rate loan by giving up gains from lower interest rates.

Collateral trust bonds A mortgage bond wherein the assets backing the bond are financial assets like stocks and bonds.

Collateralized mortgage obligation (CMO) A debt security based on a pool of mortgage loans that provides a relatively stable stream of payments for a relatively predictable term.

Collusive agreement An agreement between two (or more) producers to restrict output, raise the price, and increase profits.

Combination A listing in which the order of the listed items does not matter.

Command system A method of organizing production that uses a managerial hierarchy.

Commercial bank A firm that is licensed by the Comptroller of the Currency in the U.S. Treasury or by a state agency to receive deposits and make loans.

Commercial paper Unsecured short-term corporate debt that is characterized by a single payment at maturity.

Commission brokers Employees of a member firm who buy or sell securities for the customers of the firm.

Committed capital (private equity) Pledges of capital to a venture capital fund. This money is typically not received at once but drawn down over three to five years, starting in the year the fund is formed. Also known as "commitments."

Committed lines of credit A bank commitment to extend credit up to a pre-specified amount; the commitment is considered a short-term liability and is usually in effect for 364 days (one day short of a full year)

Commodity forward A contract in which the underlying asset is oil, a precious metal, or some other commodity.

Commodity futures Futures contracts in which the underlying is a traditional agricultural, metal, or petroleum product.

Commodity option An option in which the asset underlying the futures is a commodity, such as oil, gold, wheat, or soybeans.

Commodity swap A swap in which the underlying is a commodity such as oil, gold, or an agricultural product.

Common size statements Financial statements in which all elements (accounts) are stated as a percentage of a key figure such as revenue for an income statement or total assets for a balance sheet.

Common-size analysis The restatement of financial statement items using a common denominator or reference item; an example is an income statement in which all items are expressed as a percent of revenue.

Common stock An equity investment that represents ownership of a firm, with full participation in its success or failure. The firm's directors must approve dividend payments.

Company fundamental factors Factors related to the company's internal performance, such as factors relating to earnings growth, earnings variability, earnings momentum, and financial leverage.

Company share-related factors Valuation measures and other factors related to share price or the trading characteristics of the shares, such as earnings yield, dividend yield, and book-to-market value.

Comparable company A company that has similar business risk; usually in the same industry and preferably with a single line of business.

Comparative advantage A person or country has a comparative advantage in an activity if that person or country can perform the activity at a lower opportunity cost than anyone else or any other country.

Competitive bid An underwriting alternative wherein an issuing entity (governmental body or a corporation) specifies the type of security to be offered (bonds or stocks) and the general characteristics of the issue, and the issuer solicits bids from competing investment banking firms with the understanding that the issuer will accept the highest bid from the bankers.

Competitive environment The level of intensity of competition among firms in an industry, determined by an examination of five competitive forces.

Competitive market A market that has many buyers and many sellers, so no single buyer or seller can influence the price.

Competitive strategy The search by a firm for a favorable competitive position within an industry within the known competitive environment.

Complement In probability, with reference to an event *S*, the event that *S* does not occur; in economics, a good that is used in conjunction with another good.

Completed contract A method of revenue recognition in which the company does not recognize any revenue until the contract is completed; used particularly in long-term construction contracts.

Completely diversified portfolio A portfolio in which all unsystematic risk has been eliminated by diversification.

Component cost of capital The rate of return required by suppliers capital for an individual source of a company's funding, such as debt or equity.

Composite Aggregation of individual portfolios representing a similar investment mandate, objective, or strategy.

Composite creation date The date when the firm first groups the portfolios to create a composite. The composite creation date is not necessarily the earliest date for which performance is reported for the composite. (See composite inception date.)

Composite definition Detailed criteria that determine the allocation of portfolios to composites. Composite definitions must be documented in the firm's policies and procedures.

Composite description General information regarding the strategy of the composite. A description may be more abbreviated than the composite definition but includes all salient features of the composite.

Compounding The process of accumulating interest on interest.

Comprehensive income The change in equity of a business enterprise during a period from nonowner sources; includes all changes in equity during a period except those resulting from investments by owners and distributions to owners; comprehensive income equals net income plus other comprehensive income.

Computer-Assisted Execution System (CAES) A service created by Nasdaq that automates order routing and execution for securities listed on domestic stock exchanges and involved on the Intermarket Trading System (ITS).

Conditional expected value (1) Expected value of a variable conditional on some available information set. The expected value changes over time with changes in the information set. (2) The expected value of a stated event given that another event has occurred.

Conditional heteroskedasticity Heteroskedasticity in the error variance that is correlated with the values of the independent variable(s) in the regression.

Conditional probability The probability of an event given (conditioned on) another event.

Conditional variance (1) Variance of a variable conditional on some available information set. (2) The variance of one variable, given the outcome of another.

Conditional variances The variance of one variable, given the outcome of another.

Confidence interval A range that has a given probability that it will contain the population parameter it is intended to estimate.

Consistency A desirable property of estimators; a consistent estimator is one for which the probability of estimates close to the value of the population parameter increases as sample size increases.

Consistent With reference to estimators, describes an estimator for which the probability of estimates close to the value of the population parameter increases as sample size increases.

Consolidated Quotation System (CQS) An electronic quotation service for issues listed on the NYSE, the AMEX, or regional exchanges and traded on the Nasdaq InterMarket.

Constant maturity swap or CMT swap A swap in which the floating rate is the rate on a security known as a constant maturity treasury or CMT security.

Constant maturity treasury or CMT A hypothetical U.S. Treasury note with a constant maturity. A CMT exists for various years in the range of 2 to 10.

Constant returns to scale Features of a firm's technology that leads to constant long-run average cost as output increases. When constant returns to scale are present, the *LRAC* curve is horizontal.

Consumer Price Index (CPI) An index that measures the average of the prices paid by urban consumers for a fixed "basket" of the consumer goods and services.

Consumer surplus The value of a good minus the price paid for it, summed over the quantity bought.

Consumption expenditure The total payment for consumer goods and services.

Contango A situation in a futures market where the current futures price is greater than the current spot price for the underlying asset.

Contestable market A market in which firms can enter and leave so easily that firms in the market face competition from potential entrants.

Contingent claims Derivatives in which the payoffs occur if a specific event occurs; generally referred to as options.

Continuous market A market where stocks are priced and traded continuously by an auction process or by dealers when the market is open.

Continuous random variable A random variable for which the range of possible outcomes is the real line (all real numbers between $-\infty$ and ∞) or some subset of the real line.

Continuous time Time thought of as advancing in extremely small increments.

Continuously compounded return The natural logarithm of 1 plus the holding period return, or equivalently, the natural logarithm of the ending price over the beginning price.

Contra account An account that offsets another account.

Contract price The transaction price specified in a forward or futures contract.

Convenience yield The nonmonetary return offered by an asset when the asset is in short supply, often associated with assets with seasonal production processes.

Conventional cash flow A conventional cash flow pattern is one with an initial outflow followed by a series of inflows.

Conversion factor An adjustment used to facilitate delivery on bond futures contracts in which any of a number of bonds with different characteristics are eligible for delivery.

Conversion value The value of the convertible security if converted into common stock at the stock's current market price.

Convertible bonds A bond with the added feature that the bondholder has the option to turn the bond back to the firm in exchange for a specified number of common shares of the firm.

Convexity (1) A measure of the change in duration with respect to changes in interest rates. (2) A measure of the degree to which a bond's price-yield curve departs from a straight line. This characteristic affects estimates of a bond's price volatility for a given change in yields.

Cooperative equilibrium The outcome of a game in which the players make and share the monopoly profit.

Copyright A government-sanctioned exclusive right granted to the inventor of a good, service, or productive process to produce, use, and sell the invention for a given number of years.

Correlation A number between −1 and 1 that measures the co-movement (linear association) between two random variables.

Correlation analysis The analysis of the strength of the linear relationship between two data series.

Correlation coefficient A standardized measure of the relationship between two variables that ranges from 2 1.00 to 1 1.00.

Cost averaging The periodic investment of a fixed amount of money.

Cost of capital The rate of return that the suppliers of capital-bondholders and owners-require as compensation for their contribution of capital.

Cost of carry The cost associated with holding some asset, including financing, storage, and insurance costs. Any yield received on the asset is treated as a negative carrying cost.

Cost of carry model A model for pricing futures contracts in which the futures price is determined by adding the cost of carry to the spot price.

Cost of debt The cost of debt financing to a company, such as when it issues a bond or takes out a bank loan.

Cost of goods sold For a given period, equal to beginning inventory minus ending inventory plus the cost of goods acquired or produced during the period.

Cost of preferred stock The cost to a company of issuing preferred stock; the dividend yield that a company must commit to pay preferred stock holders.

Cost recovery method A method of revenue recognition in which is the seller does not report any profit until the cash amounts paid by the buyer—including principal and interest on any financing from the seller—are greater than all the seller's costs for the merchandise sold.

Cost-push inflation An inflation that results from an initial increase in costs.

Council of Economic Advisers In the executive branch of the U.S. government, a council whose main work is to monitor the economy and keep the President and the public well informed about the current state of the economy and the best available forecasts of where it is heading.

Counterparty A participant to a derivative transaction.

Country risk Uncertainty due to the possibility of major political or economic change in the country where an investment is located. Also called *political risk.*

Coupon Indicates the interest payment on a debt security. It is the coupon rate times the par value that indicates the interest payments on a debt security.

Covariance A measure of the co-movement (linear association) between two random variables.

Covariance matrix A matrix or square array whose entries are covariances; also known as a variance-covariance matrix.

Covariance stationary Describes a time series when its expected value and variance are constant and finite in all periods and when its covariance with itself for a fixed number of periods in the past or future is constant and finite in all periods.

Covered call An option strategy involving the holding of an asset and sale of a call on the asset.

Covered interest arbitrage A transaction executed in the foreign exchange market in which a currency is purchased (sold) and a forward contract is sold (purchased) to lock in the exchange rate for future delivery of the currency. This transaction should earn the risk-free rate of the investor's home country.

Credit With respect to double-entry accounting, a credit records increases in liability, owners' equity, and revenue accounts or decreases in asset accounts; with respect to borrowing, the willingness and ability of the borrower to make promised payments on the borrowing.

Credit analysis The evaluation of credit risk; the evaluation of the creditworthiness of a borrower or counterparty.

Credit derivatives A contract in which one party has the right to claim a payment from another party in the event that a specific credit event occurs over the life of the contract.

Credit-linked notes Fixed-income securities in which the holder of the security has the right to withhold payment of the full amount due at maturity if a credit event occurs.

Credit risk (or default risk) The risk of loss caused by a counterparty's or debtor's failure to make a promised payment.

Credit scoring model A statistical model used to classify the creditworthiness of borrowers.

Credit spread option An option on the yield spread on a bond.

Credit swap A type of swap transaction used as a credit derivative in which one party makes periodic payments to the other and receives the promise of a payoff if a third party defaults.

Credit union A depository institution owned by a social or economic group such as firm's employees that accepts savings deposits and makes mostly consumer loans.

Credit VAR, Default VAR, or Credit at risk A variation of VAR that reflects credit risk.

Creditor nation A country that during its entire history has invested more in the rest of the world than other countries have invested in it.

Creditworthiness The perceived ability of the borrower to pay what is owed on the borrowing in a timely manner; it represents the ability of a company to withstand adverse impacts on its cash flows.

Cross elasticity of demand The responsiveness of the demand for a good to the price of a substitute or complement, other things remaining the same. It is calculated as the percentage change in the quantity demanded of the good divided by the percentage change in the price of the substitute or complement.

Cross-product netting Netting the market values of all contracts, not just derivatives, between parties.

Cross-sectional analysis Analysis that involves comparisons across individuals in a group over a given time period or at a given point in time.

Cross-sectional data Observations over individual units at a point in time, as opposed to time-series data.

Crowding-out effect The tendency for a government budget deficit to decrease in investment.

Cumulative distribution function A function giving the probability that a random variable is less than or equal to a specified value.

Cumulative relative frequency For data grouped into intervals, the fraction of total observations that are less than the value of the upper limit of a stated interval.

Currency The bills and coins that we use today.
A record of the payments for imports of goods and services, receipts from exports of goods and services, interest income, and net transfers.

Currency appreciation The rise in the value of one currency in terms of another currency.

Currency depreciation The fall in the value of one currency in terms of another currency.

Currency drain An increase in currency held outside the banks.

Currency forward A forward contract in which the underlying is a foreign currency.

Currency option An option that allows the holder to buy (if a call) or sell (if a put) an underlying currency at a fixed exercise rate, expressed as an exchange rate.

Currency swap A swap in which each party makes interest payments to the other in different currencies.

Current assets Assets that are expected to be consumed or converted into cash in the near future, typically one year or less.

Current cost With reference to assets, the amount of cash or cash equivalents that would have to be paid to buy the same or an equivalent asset today; with reference to liabilities, the undiscounted amount of cash or cash equivalents that would be required to settle the obligation today.

Current credit risk The risk associated with the possibility that a payment currently due will not be made.

Current income A return objective in which the investor seeks to generate income rather than capital gains; generally a goal of an investor who wants to supplement earnings with income to meet living expenses.

Current liabilities Those liabilities that are expected to be settled in the near future, typically one year or less (e.g. accounts payable, wages payable).

Current P/E *See* Trailing P/E.

Current ratio The ratio of current assets to current liabilities; a measure of a company's ability to satisfy its current liabilities with its current assets.

Current taxes payable Tax expenses that have been recognized and recorded on a company's income statement but which have not yet been paid.

Current yield A bond's yield as measured by its current income (coupon) as a percentage of its market price.

Customer list A list of customers or subscribers.

Cyclical businesses Businesses with high sensitivity to business- or industry-cycle influences.

Cyclical company A firm whose earnings rise and fall with general economic activity.

Cyclical stock A stock with a high beta; its gains typically exceed those of a rising market and its losses typically exceed those of a falling market.

Cyclical surplus or deficit The actual surplus or deficit minus the structural surplus or deficit.

Cyclical unemployment The fluctuations in unemployment over the business cycle.

Daily settlement See *marking to market.*

Data mining The practice of determining a model by extensive searching through a dataset for statistically significant patterns.

Day trader A trader holding a position open somewhat longer than a scalper but closing all positions at the end of the day.

Days of inventory on hand (DOH) An activity ratio equal to the number of days in the period divided by inventory turnover over the period.

Days of sales outstanding (DSO) An activity ratio equal to the number of days in period divided by receivables turnover.

Deadweight loss A measure of inefficiency. It is equal to the decrease in consumer surplus and producer surplus that results from an inefficient level of production.

Dealing securities Securities held by banks or other financial intermediaries for trading purposes.

Debentures Bonds that promise payments of interest and principal but pledge no specific assets. Holders have first claim on the issuer's income and unpledged assets. Also known as *unsecured bonds*.

Debit With respect to double-entry accounting, a debit records increases of asset and expense accounts or decreases in liability and owners' equity accounts.

Debt incurrence test A financial covenant made in conjunction with existing debt that restricts a company's ability to incur additional debt at the same seniority based on one or more financial tests or conditions.

Debtor nation A country that during its entire history has borrowed more from the rest of the world than it has lent to it.

Debt-rating approach A method for estimating a company's before-tax cost of debt based upon the yield on comparably rated bonds for maturities that closely match that of the company's existing debt.

Debt-to-assets ratio A solvency ratio calculated as total debt divided by total assets; a measure of the proportion of assets that is financed with debt (both short-term and long-term debt).

Debt-to-capital ratio A solvency ratio calculated as total debt divided by total debt plus total shareholders' equity.

Debt-to-equity ratio A solvency ratio calculated as total debt divided by total shareholders' equity; compares the proportions of a company's assets that are financed through the use of debt relative to equity, evaluated using book values of the capital sources.

Decentralized risk management A system that allows individual units within an organization to manage risk. Decentralization results in duplication of effort but has the advantage of having people closer to the risk be more directly involved in its management.

Deciles Quantiles that divide a distribution into 10 equal parts.

Decision rule With respect to hypothesis testing, the rule according to which the null hypothesis will be rejected or not rejected; involves the comparison of the test statistic to rejection point(s).

Declining-balance method An accelerated method of depreciation in which depreciation is computed by applying a fixed rate to the carrying value (the declining balance) of a tangible long-lived asset.

Declining trend channel The range defined by security prices as they move progressively lower.

Deep in the money Options that are far in-the-money.

Deep out of the money Options that are far out-of-the-money.

Default risk The risk that an issuer will be unable to make interest and principal payments on time.

Default risk premium An extra return that compensates investors for the possibility that the borrower will fail to make a promised payment at the contracted time and in the contracted amount.

Defensive competitive strategy Positioning the firm so that its capabilities provide the best means to deflect the effect of the competitive forces in the industry.

Defensive interval ratio A liquidity ratio that estimates the number of days that an entity could meet cash needs from liquid assets; calculated as (cash + short-term marketable investments + receivables) divided by daily cash expenditures.

Defensive stock A stock whose return is not expected to decline as much as that of the overall market during a bear market (a beta less than one).

Deflation A process in which the price level falls—a negative inflation.

Degree of confidence The probability that a confidence interval includes the unknown population parameter.

Degrees of freedom (df) The number of independent observations used.

Delivery A process used in a deliverable forward contract in which the long pays the agreed-upon price to the short, which in turn delivers the underlying asset to the long.

Delivery option The feature of a futures contract giving the short the right to make decisions about what, when, and where to deliver.

Delta The relationship between the option price and the underlying price, which reflects the sensitivity of the price of the option to changes in the price of the underlying.

Delta hedge An option strategy in which a position in an asset is converted to a risk-free position with a position in a specific number of options. The number of options per unit of the underlying changes through time, and the position must be revised to maintain the hedge.

Delta-normal method A measure of VAR equivalent to the analytical method but that refers to the use of delta to estimate the option's price sensitivity.

Demand The relationship between the quantity of a good that consumers plan to buy and the price of the good when all other influences on buyers' plans remain the same. It is described by a demand schedule and illustrated by a demand curve.

Demand curve A curve that shows the relationship between the quantity demanded of a good and its price when all other influences on consumers' planned purchases remain the same.

Demand for labor The relationship between the quantity of labor demanded and the real wage rate when all other influences on firm's hiring plans remain the same.

Demand-pull inflation An inflation that results from an initial increase in aggregate demand.

Dependent With reference to events, the property that the probability of one event occurring depends on (is related to) the occurrence of another event.

Dependent variable The variable whose variation about its mean is to be explained by the regression; the left-hand-side variable in a regression equation.

Depletion The exhaustion of a natural resource through mining, cutting, pumping, or other extraction, and the way in which the cost is allocated.

Depository institution A firm that takes deposits from households and firms and makes loans to other households and firms.

Depreciable cost The cost of an asset less its residual value.

Depreciation The process of systematically allocating the cost of long-lived (tangible) assets to the periods during which the assets are expected to provide economic benefits.

Derivative A financial instrument that offers a return based on the return of some other underlying asset or factor (e.g., a stock price, an interest rate, or exchange rate).

Derivative security An instrument whose market value ultimately depends upon, or derives from, the value of a more fundamental investment vehicle called the underlying asset or security.

Derivatives (1) Securities bearing a contractual relation to some underlying asset or rate. Options, futures, forward, and swap contracts, as well as many forms of bonds, are derivative securities. (2) A financial instrument that offers a return based on the return of some other underlying asset.

Derivatives dealers Commercial and investment banks that make markets in derivatives. .

Derived demand The demand for a productive resource, which is derived from the demand for the goods and services produced by the resource.

Descriptive statistics The study of how data can be summarized effectively.

Diff swaps A swap in which the payments are based on the difference between interest rates in two countries but payments are made in only a single currency.

Diffuse prior The assumption of equal prior probabilities.

Diluted earnings per share Net income, minus preferred dividends, divided by the number of common shares outstanding considering all dilutive securities (e.g., convertible debt and options); the EPS that would result if all dilutive securities were converted into common shares.

Diluted shares The number of shares that would be outstanding if all potentially dilutive claims on common shares (e.g., convertible debt, convertible preferred stock, and employee stock options) were exercised.

Diminishing balance method An accelerated depreciation method, i.e., one that allocates a relatively large proportion of the cost of an asset to the early years of the asset's useful life.

Diminishing marginal returns The tendency for the marginal product of an additional unit of a factor of production to be less than the marginal product of the previous unit of the factor.

Diminishing marginal utility The decrease in marginal utility as the quantity consumed increases.

Direct debit program An arrangement whereby a customer authorizes a debit to a demand account; typically used by companies to collect routine payments for services.

Direct format (direct method) With reference to the cash flow statement, a format for the presentation of the statement in which cash flow from operating activities is shown as operating cash receipts less operating cash disbursements.

Direct method The procedure for converting the income statement from an accrual basis to a cash basis by adjusting each item on the income statement.

Direct write-off method An approach to recognizing credit losses on customer receivables in which the company waits until such time as a customer has defaulted and only then recognizes the loss.

Disbursement float The amount of time between check issuance and a check's clearing back against the company's account.

Discount To reduce the value of a future payment in allowance for how far away it is in time; to calculate the present value of some future amount. Also, the amount by which an instrument is priced below its face value.

Discount interest A procedure for determining the interest on a loan or bond in which the interest is deducted from the face value in advance.

Discounting The conversion of a future amount of money to its present value.

Discouraged workers People who are available and willing to work but have not made specific efforts to find a job within the previous four weeks.

Discrete random variable A random variable that can take on at most a countable number of possible values.

Discrete time Time thought of as advancing in distinct finite increments.

Discretionary fiscal policy A policy action that is initiated by an act of Congress.

Discretionary policy A policy that responds to the state of the economy in a possibly unique way that uses all the information available, including perceived lessons from past "mistakes."

Discriminant analysis A multivariate classification technique used to discriminate between groups, such as companies that either will or will not become bankrupt during some time frame.

Diseconomies of scale Features of a firm's technology that leads to rising long-run average cost as output increases.

Dispersion The variability around the central tendency.

Disposable income Aggregate income minus taxes plus transfer payments.

Distinct business entity A unit, division, department, or office that is organizationally and functionally segregated from other units, divisions, departments, or offices and retains discretion over the assets it manages and autonomy over the investment decision-making process. Possible criteria that can be used to determine this include: (a) being a legal entity; (b) having a distinct market or client type (e.g., institutional, retail, private client, etc.); (c) using a separate and distinct investment process.

Dividend discount model (DDM) A technique for estimating the value of a stock issue as the present value of all future dividends.

Dividend discount model based approach or implied risk premium approach An approach for estimating a country's equity risk premium. The market rate of return is estimated as the sum of the dividend yield and the growth rate in dividends for a market index. Subtracting the risk-free rate of return from the estimated market return produces an estimate for the equity risk premium.

Dividend payout ratio The ratio of dividends paid to earnings for a period; more specifically, the ratio of dividends paid to common shareholders to net income attributable to common shares.

Dividends per share The dollar amount of cash dividends paid during a period per share of common stock.

Dominant strategy equilibrium A Nash equilibrium in which the best strategy of each player is to cheat (deny) regardless of the strategy of the other player.

Double declining balance depreciation An accelerated depreciation method that involves depreciating the asset at double the straight-line rate.

Double-declining-balance method An accelerated method of depreciation in which a fixed rate equal to twice the straight-line percentage is applied to the carrying value (the declining balance) of a tangible long-lived asset.

Double-entry accounting The accounting system of recording transactions in which every recorded transaction affects at least two accounts so as to keep the basic accounting equation (assets = liabilities + owners' equity) in balance.

Down transition probability The probability that an asset's value moves down in a model of asset price dynamics.

Drag on liquidity When receipts lag, creating pressure from the decreased available funds.

Dummy variable A type of qualitative variable that takes on a value of 1 if a particular condition is true and 0 if that condition is false.

Dumping The sale by a foreign firm of exports at a lower price that the cost of production.

Duopoly A market structure in which two producers of a good or service compete.

DuPont analysis An approach to decomposing return on investment, e.g., return on equity, as the product of other financial ratios.

DuPont system A method of examining ROE by breaking it down into three component parts: (1) profit margin, (2) total asset turnover, and (3) financial leverage.

Duration A measure of an option-free bond's average maturity. Specifically, the weighted average maturity of all future cash flows paid by a security, in which the weights are the present value of these cash flows as a fraction of the bond's price. A measure of a bond's price sensitivity to interest rate movements.

Dutch Book Theorem A result in probability theory stating that inconsistent probabilities create profit opportunities.

Dynamic comparative advantage A comparative advantage that a person or country possesses as a result of having specialized in a particular activity and then, as a result of learning-by-doing, having become the producer with the lowest opportunity cost.

Dynamic hedging A strategy in which a position is hedged by making frequent adjustments to the quantity of the instrument used for hedging in relation to the instrument being hedged.

Earnings at risk (EAR) A variation of VAR that reflects the risk of a company's earnings instead of its market value.

Earnings momentum A strategy in which portfolios are constructed of stocks of firms with rising earnings.

Earnings multiplier model A technique for estimating the value of a stock issue as a multiple of its earnings per share.

Earnings per share (EPS) The amount of income earned during a period per share of common stock; (net income − preferred dividends) divided by the weighted average number of common shares outstanding.

Earnings surprise A company announcement of earnings that differ from analysts' prevailing expectations.

Earnings yield Earnings per share divided by price; the reciprocal of the P/E ratio.

EBITDA Earnings before interest, taxes, depreciation, and amortization.

Economic depreciation The change in the market value of capital over a given period.

Economic efficiency A situation that occurs when the firm produces a given output at the least cost.

Economic exposure The risk associated with changes in the relative attractiveness of products and services offered for sale, arising out of the competitive effects of changes in exchange rates.

Economic growth The expansion of production possibilities that results from capital accumulation and technological change.

Economic information Data on prices, quantities, and qualities of goods and services and factors of production.

Economic model A description of some aspect of the economic world that includes only those features of the world that are needed for the purpose at hand.

Economic order quantity-reorder point An approach to managing inventory based on expected demand and the predictability of demand; the ordering point for new inventory is determined based on the costs of ordering and carrying inventory, such that the total cost associated with inventory is minimized.

Economic profit A firm's total revenue minus its opportunity cost.

Economic rent The income received by the owner of a factor of production over and above the amount required to induce that owner to offer the factor for use.

Economic theory A generalization that summarizes what we think we understand about the economic choices that people make and the performance of industries and entire economies.

Economic value added (EVA) Internal management performance measure that compares net operating profit to total cost of capital. Indicates how profitable company projects are as a sign of management performance.

Economics The social science that studies the *choices* that individuals, businesses, governments, and entire societies make and how they cope with *scarcity* and the *incentives* that influence and reconcile those choices.

Economies of scale Features of a firm's technology that leads to a falling long-run average cost as output increases.

Economies of scope Decreases in average total cost that occur when a firm uses specialized resources to produce a range of goods and services.

Effective annual rate The amount by which a unit of currency will grow in a year with interest on interest included.

Effective annual yield (EAY) An annualized return that accounts for the effect of interest on interest; EAY is computed by compounding 1 plus the holding period yield forward to one year, then subtracting 1.

Effective duration Direct measure of the interest rate sensitivity of a bond (or any financial instrument) based upon price changes derived from a pricing model.

Efficiency In statistics, a desirable property of estimators; an efficient estimator is the unbiased estimator with the smallest variance among unbiased estimators of the same parameter.

Efficient capital market A market in which security prices rapidly reflect all information about securities.

Efficient frontier The portion of the minimum-variance frontier beginning with the global minimum-variance portfolio and continuing above it; the graph of the set of portfolios offering the maximum expected return for their level of variance of return.

Efficient market A market in which the actual price embodies all currently available relevant information. Resources are sent to their highest valued use.

Efficient portfolio A portfolio offering the highest expected return for a given level of risk as measured by variance or standard deviation of return.

Elastic demand Demand with a price elasticity greater than 1; other things remaining the same, the percentage change in the quantity demanded exceeds the percentage change in price.

Elasticity of demand The responsiveness of the quantity demanded of a good to a change in its price, other things remaining the same.

Elasticity of supply The responsiveness of the quantity supplied of a good to a change in its price, other things remaining the same.

Electronic funds transfer The use of computer networks to conduct financial transactions electronically.

Empirical probability The probability of an event estimated as a relative frequency of occurrence.

Employment Act of 1946 A landmark Congressional act that recognized a role for government actions to keep unemployment, keep the economy expanding, and keep inflation in check.

Employment-to-population ratio The percentage of people of working age who have jobs.

Ending market value (private equity) The remaining equity that a limited partner has in a fund. Also referred to as net asset value or residual value.

Enhanced derivatives products companies (EDPC or special purpose vehicles SPVs) A type of subsidiary engaged in derivatives transactions that is separated from the parent company in order to have a higher credit rating than the parent company.

Enterprise risk management A form of *centralized risk management* that typically encompasses the management of a broad variety of risks, including insurance risk.

Entrepreneurship The human resource that organizes labor, land, and capital. Entrepreneurs come up with new ideas about what and how to produce, make business decisions, and bear the risks that arise from their decisions.

Equation of exchange An equation that states that the quantity of money multiplied by the velocity of circulation equals GDP.

Equilibrium price The price at which the quantity demanded equals the quantity supplied.

Equilibrium quantity The quantity bought and sold at the equilibrium price.

Equitizing cash A strategy used to replicate an index. It is also used to take a given amount of cash and turn it into an equity position while maintaining the liquidity provided by the cash.

Equity Assets less liabilities; the residual interest in the assets after subtracting the liabilities.

Equity forward A contract calling for the purchase of an individual stock, a stock portfolio, or a stock index at a later date at an agreed-upon price.

Equity options Options on individual stocks; also known as stock options.

Equity risk premium The expected return on equities minus the risk-free rate; the premium that investors demand for investing in equities.

Equity swap A swap transaction in which at least one cash flow is tied to the return to an equity portfolio position, often an equity index.

Error autocorrelation The autocorrelation of the error term.

Error term The portion of the dependent variable that is not explained by the independent variable(s) in the regression.

Estimate The particular value calculated from sample observations using an estimator.

Estimated (or fitted) parameters With reference to regression analysis, the estimated values of the population intercept and population slope coefficient(s) in a regression.

Estimated rate of return The rate of return an investor anticipates earning from a specific investment over a particular future holding period.

Estimated useful life The total number of service units expected from a long-term asset.

Estimation With reference to statistical inference, the subdivision dealing with estimating the value of a population parameter.

Estimator An estimation formula; the formula used to compute the sample mean and other sample statistics are examples of estimators.

Eurobonds Bonds denominated in a currency not native to the country in which they are issued.

Eurodollar A dollar deposited outside the United States.

European option An option contract that can only be exercised on its expiration date.

European terms With reference to U.S. dollar exchange rate quotations, the price of a U.S. dollar in terms of another currency.

European-style option or European option An option exercisable only at maturity.

European Union (EU) A formal association of European countries founded by the Treaty of Rome in 1957. Formerly known as the EEC.

Event Any outcome or specified set of outcomes of a random variable.

Event study Research that examines the reaction of a security's price to a specific company, world event, or news announcement.

Ex-ante Before the fact.

Excess kurtosis Degree of peakedness (fatness of tails) in excess of the peakedness of the normal distribution.

Excess reserves A bank's actual reserves minus its required reserves.

Exchange for physicals (EFP) A permissible delivery procedure used by futures market participants, in which the long and short arrange a delivery procedure other than the normal procedures stipulated by the futures exchange.

Exchange rate risk Uncertainty due to the denomination of an investment in a currency other than that of the investor's own country.

Exchange-traded fund (ETF) A tradable depository receipt that gives investors a pro rata claim to the returns associated with a portfolio of securities (often designed to mimic an index, such as the Standard & Poor's 500) held in trust by a financial institution.

Exercise (or exercising the option) The process of using an option to buy or sell the underlying.

Exercise price (or strike price or striking price, or strike) The fixed price at which an option holder can buy or sell the underlying.

Exercise rate or strike rate The fixed rate at which the holder of an interest rate option can buy or sell the underlying.

Exhaustive Covering or containing all possible outcomes.

Expansion A business cycle phase between a trough and a peak-phase in which real GDP increases.

Expected rate of return The return that analysts' calculations suggest a security should provide, based on the market's rate of return during the period and the security's relationship to the market.

Expected return The rate of return that an investor expects to get on an investment.

Expected utility The average utility arising from all possible outcomes.

Expected value The probability-weighted average of the possible outcomes of a random variable.

Expenditure A payment or obligation to make future payment for an asset or a service.

Expensed Taken as a deduction in arriving at net income.

Expenses Outflows of economic resources or increases in liabilities that result in decreases in equity (other than decreases because of distributions to owners).

Expiration date The date on which a derivative contract expires.

Expiry The expiration date of a derivative security.

Exports The goods and services that we sell to people in other countries.

Extended DuPont System A method of examining *ROE* by breaking it down into five component parts.

External benefits Benefits that accrue to people other than the buyer of the good.

External cash flow Cash, securities, or assets that enter or exit a portfolio.

External costs Costs that are not borne by the producer of the good but borne by someone else.

External diseconomies Factors outside the control of a firm that raise the firm's costs as the industry produces a larger output.

External economies Factors beyond the control of a firm that lower the firm's costs as the industry produces a larger output.

External valuation (real estate) An external valuation is an assessment of market value performed by a third party who is a qualified, professionally designated, certified, or licensed commercial property valuer/appraiser. External valuations must be completed following the valuation standards of the local governing appraisal body.

Externality A cost or a benefit that arises from production that falls on someone other than the producer or a cost or a benefit that arises from consumption that falls on someone other than the consumer.

Extraordinary repairs Repairs that affect the estimated residual value or estimated useful life of an asset thereby increasing its carrying value.

Face value The promised payment at maturity separate from any coupon payment.

Factor A common or underlying element with which several variables are correlated.

Factor risk premium (or factor price) The expected return in excess of the risk-free rate for a portfolio with a sensitivity of 1 to one factor and a sensitivity of 0 to all other factors.

Factor sensitivity (also factor betas or factor loadings) A measure of the response of return to each unit of increase in a factor, holding all other factors constant.

Factors of production The productive resources that businesses use to produce goods and services.

Fair market value The market price of an asset or liability that trades regularly.

Fair value The amount at which an asset could be exchanged or a liability settled, between knowledgeable, willing parties in an arm's-length transaction.

Federal budget The annual statement of the expenditures and tax revenues of the government of the United States together with the laws and regulations that approve and support those expenditures and taxes.

Federal funds rate The interest rate that banks charge each other on overnight loans of reserves.

Federal Open Market Committee The main policy-making organ of the Federal Reserve System.

Federal Reserve System The central bank of the United States.

Fee Schedule The firm's current investment management fees or bundled fees for a particular presentation. This schedule is typically listed by asset level ranges and should be appropriate to the particular prospective client.

Feedback-rule policy A rule that specifies how policy actions respond to changes in the state of the economy.

Fiduciary A person who supervises or oversees the investment portfolio of a third party, such as in a trust account, and makes investment decisions in accordance with the owner's wishes.

Fiduciary call A combination of a European call and a risk-free bond that matures on the option expiration day and has a face value equal to the exercise price of the call.

FIFO method The first in, first out, method of accounting for inventory, which matches sales against the costs of items of inventory in the order in which they were placed in inventory.

Financial account A component of the balance of payments covering investments by residents abroad and investments by nonresidents in the home country. Examples include direct investment made by companies, portfolio investments in equity and bonds, and other investments and liabilities.

Financial analysis The process of selecting, evaluating, and interpreting financial data, along with other pertinent information, in order to formulate an assessment of the company's present and future financial condition and performance.

Financial flexibility The ability to react and adapt to financial adversities and opportunities.

Financial futures Futures contracts in which the underlying is a stock, bond, or currency.

Financial innovation The development of new financial products—new ways of borrowing and lending.

Financial leverage The extent to which a company can effect, through the use of debt, a proportional change in the return on common equity that is greater than a given proportional change in operating income; also, short for the financial leverage ratio.

Financial leverage ratio (or equity multiplier) A measure of financial leverage calculated as average total assets divided by average total equity; indicates the extent to which assets are financed with debt relative to equity.

Financial risk Uncertainty of net income and net cash flows attributed to the use of financing that has a fixed cost, such as debt and leases.

Financing activities Activities related to obtaining or repaying capital to be used in the business (e.g., equity and long-term debt).

Firm (1) For purposes of the GIPS standards, the term "firm" refers to the entity defined for compliance with the GIPS standards. See the term "distinct business entity." (2) An economic unit that hires factors of production and organizes those factors to produce and sell goods and services.

First-differencing A transformation that subtracts the value of the time series in period $t - 1$ from its value in period t.

First-order serial correlation Correlation between adjacent observations in a time series.

Fiscal imbalance The present value of the government's commitments to pay benefits minus the present value of its tax revenues.

Fiscal policy The government's attempt to achieve macroeconomic objectives such as full employment, sustained economic growth, and price level stability by setting and changing taxes, making transfer payments, and purchasing goods and services.

Fixed asset turnover An activity ratio calculated as total revenue divided by average net fixed assets.

Fixed charge coverage A solvency ratio measuring the number of times interest and lease payments are covered by operating income, calculated as (EBIT + lease payments) divided by (interest payments + lease payments).

Fixed costs Costs that stay the same within some range of activity.

Fixed exchange rate An exchange rate that is set at a determined amount by government policy.

Fixed exchange rate regime A system in which the exchange rate between two currencies remains fixed at a preset level, known as official parity.

Fixed rate perpetual preferred stock Nonconvertible, noncallable preferred stock that has a fixed dividend rate and no maturity date.

Fixed-income forward A forward contract in which the underlying is a bond.

Fixed-income investments Loans with contractually mandated payment schedules from firms or governments to investors.

Fixed-rule policy A rule that specifies an action to be pursued independently of the state of the economy.

Flat trend channel The range defined by security prices as they maintain a relatively steady level.

Flexible exchange rate system A system in which exchange rates are determined by supply and demand.

Flexible exchange rates Exchange rates that are determined by the market forces of supply and demand. They are sometimes called floating exchange rates.

Float In the context of customer receipts, the amount of money that is in transit between payments made by customers and the funds that are usable by the company.

Float factor An estimate of the average number of days it takes deposited checks to clear; average daily float divided by average daily deposit.

Floating-rate loan A loan in which the interest rate is reset at least once after the starting date.

Floor A combination of interest rate put options designed to hedge a lender against lower rates on a floating-rate loan.

Floor brokers Independent members of an exchange who act as brokers for other members.

Floor traders or locals Market makers that buy and sell by quoting a bid and an ask price. They are the primary providers of liquidity to the market.

Floored swap A swap in which the floating payments have a lower limit.

Floorlet Each component put option in a floor.

Flotation cost Fees charged to companies by investment bankers and other costs associated with raising new capital.

Flow A quantity per unit of time.

Foreign bond A bond issued by a foreign company on the local market and in the local currency (e.g., Yankee bonds in the United States, Bulldog bonds in the United Kingdom, or Samurai bonds in Japan).

Foreign exchange expectation A relation that states that the forward exchange rate, quoted at time 0 for delivery at time 1, is equal to the expected value of the spot exchange rate at time 1. When stated relative to the current spot exchange rate, the relation states that the forward discount (premium) is equal to the expected exchange rate movement.

Foreign exchange market The market in which the currency of one country is exchanged for the currency of another.

Foreign exchange rate The price at which one currency exchanges for another.

Forward contract An agreement between two parties in which one party, the buyer, agrees to buy from the other party, the seller, an underlying asset at a later date for a price established at the start of the contract.

Forward discount A situation where, from the perspective of the domestic country, the spot exchange rate is smaller than the forward exchange rate with a foreign country.

Forward P/E *See* Leading P/E.

Forward premium A situation where, from the perspective of the domestic country, the spot exchange rate is larger than the forward exchange rate with a foreign country.

Forward price or forward rate The fixed price or rate at which the transaction scheduled to occur at the expiration of a forward contract will take place. This price is agreed on at the initiation date of the contract.

Forward rate A short-term yield for a future holding period implied by the spot rates of two securities with different maturities.

Forward rate agreement (FRA) A forward contract calling for one party to make a fixed interest payment and the other to make an interest payment at a rate to be determined at the contract expiration.

Forward swap A forward contract to enter into a swap.

Four-firm concentration ratio A measure of market power that is calculated as the percentage of the value of sales accounted for by the four largest firms in an industry.

Franchise The right or license to an exclusive territory or market.

Franchise factor A firm's unique competitive advantage that makes it possible for a firm to earn excess returns (rates of return above a firm's cost of capital) on its capital projects. In turn, these excess returns and the franchise factor cause the firm's stock price to have a *P/E* ratio above its base *P/E* ratio that is equal to $1/k$.

Free cash flow The excess of operating cash flow over capital expenditures.

Free cash flow to equity The cash flow available to holders of the company's common equity after all operating expenses, interest, and principal payments have been paid and necessary investments in working capital and fixed capital have been made.

Free cash flow to the firm The cash flow available to the company's suppliers of capital after all operating expenses (including taxes) have been paid and necessary investments in working capital (e.g., inventory) and fixed capital (e.g., plant and equipment) have been made.

Free-rider problem The absence of an incentive for people to pay for what they consume.

Frequency distribution A tabular display of data summarized into a relatively small number of intervals.

Frequency polygon A graph of a frequency distribution obtained by drawing straight lines joining successive points representing the class frequencies.

Frictional unemployment The unemployment that arises from normal labor turnover-from people entering and leaving the labor force and from the ongoing creation and destruction of jobs.

Full employment A situation in which the quantity of labor demanded equal the quantity supplied. At full employment, there is no cyclical unemployment—all unemployment is frictional and structural.

Full price The price of a security including accrued interest.

Full-costing A method of accounting for the costs of exploring and developing oil and gas resources in which all costs are recorded as assets and depleted over the estimated life of the producing resources.

Full-costing method A method of accounting for the costs of exploring and developing oil and gas resources in which all costs are recorded as assets and depleted over the estimated life of the producing resources.

Fundamental beta A beta that is based at least in part on fundamental data for a company.

Fundamental factor models A multifactor model in which the factors are attributes of stocks or companies that are important in explaining cross-sectional differences in stock prices.

Future value (FV) The amount to which a payment or series of payments will grow by a stated future date.

Futures commission merchants (FCMs) Individuals or companies that execute futures transactions for other parties off the exchange.

Futures contract A variation of a forward contract that has essentially the same basic definition but with some additional features, such as a clearinghouse guarantee against credit losses, a daily settlement of gains and losses, and an organized electronic or floor trading facility.

Futures exchange A legal corporate entity whose shareholders are its members. The members of the exchange have the privilege of executing transactions directly on the exchange.

Gains Asset inflows not directly related to the ordinary activities of the business.

Game theory A tool that economists use to analyze strategic behavior—behavior that takes into account the expected behavior of others and the mutual recognition of independence.

Gamma A numerical measure of how sensitive an option's delta is to a change in the underlying.

GDP deflator One measure of the price level, which is the average of current-year prices as a percentage of base-year prices.

General Agreement on Tariffs and Trade An international agreement signed in 1947 to reduce tariffs on international trade.

Generalized least squares A regression estimation technique that addresses heteroskedasticity of the error term.

Generally accepted accounting principles (GAAP) Accounting principles formulated by the Financial Accounting Standards Board and used to construct financial statements.

Generational accounting An accounting system that measures the lifetime tax burden and benefits of each generation.

Generational imbalance The division of the fiscal imbalance between the current and future generations, assuming that the current generation will enjoy the existing levels of taxes and benefits

Generic *See* Plain-vanilla.

Geometric mean A measure of central tendency computed by taking the nth root of the product of n non-negative values.

Giro system An electronic payment system used widely in Europe and Japan.

Goods and services The objects that people value and produce to satisfy their wants.

Goodwill An intangible asset that represents the excess of the purchase price of an acquired company over the fair value of the net assets acquired.

Government budget deficit The deficit that arises when federal government spends more than it collects in taxes.

Government budget surplus The surplus that arises when the federal government collects more in taxes than it spends.

Government debt The total amount of borrowing that the government has borrowed. It equals the sum of past budget deficits minus budget surpluses.

Government purchases Goods and services bought by the government.

Government purchases multiplier The magnification effect of a change in government purchases of goods and services on aggregate demand.

Government sector surplus or deficit An amount equal to net taxes minus government purchases of goods and services.

Great Depression A decade (1929-1939) of high unemployment and stagnant production throughout the world economy.

Gross domestic product (GDP) The market value of all the final goods and services produced within a country during a given time period—usually a year.

Gross investment The total amount spent on purchases of new capital and on replacing depreciated capital.

Gross-Of-Fees Return The return on assets reduced by any trading expenses incurred during the period.

Gross profit (gross margin) Sales minus the cost of sales (i.e., the cost of goods sold for a manufacturing company).

Gross profit margin A profitability ratio calculated as gross profit divided by revenue; indicates how much of every dollar of revenues is left after the cost of goods sold.

Group depreciation The grouping of similar items to calculate depreciation.

Grouping by function With reference to the presentation of expenses in an income statement, the grouping together of expenses serving the same function, e.g. all items that are costs of good sold.

Grouping by nature With reference to the presentation of expenses in an income statement, the grouping together of expenses by similar nature, e.g., all depreciation expenses.

Growth company A company that consistently has the opportunities and ability to invest in projects that provide rates of return that exceed the firm's cost of capital. Because of these investment opportunities, it retains a high proportion of earnings, and its earnings grow faster than those of average firms.

Growth investors With reference to equity investors, investors who seek to invest in high-earnings-growth companies.

Growth option or expansion option The ability to make additional investments in a project at some future time if the financial results are strong.

Growth stock A stock issue that generates a higher rate of return than other stocks in the market with similar risk characteristics.

Harmonic mean A type of weighted mean computed by averaging the reciprocals of the observations, then taking the reciprocal of that average.

Hedge A trading strategy in which derivative securities are used to reduce or completely offset a counter-party's risk exposure to an underlying asset.

Hedge fund An investment vehicle designed to manage a private, unregistered portfolio of assets according to any of several strategies. The investment strategy often employs arbitrage trading and significant financial leverage (e.g., short selling, borrowing, derivatives) while the compensation arrangement for the manager typically specifies considerable profit participation.

Hedge ratio The relationship of the quantity of an asset being hedged to the quantity of the derivative used for hedging.

Hedging A general strategy usually thought of as reducing, if not eliminating, risk.

Held-for-trading securities (trading securities) Securities that a company intends to trade.

Held-to-maturity securities (Fixed-income) Securities that a company intends to hold to maturity; these are presented at their original cost, updated for any amortization of discounts or premiums.

Herfindahl-Hirschman Index A measure of market power that is calculated as the square of the market share of each firm (as a percentage) summed over the largest 50 firms (or over all firms if there are fewer than 50) in a market.

Heteroskedastic With reference to the error term of a regression, having a variance that differs across observations.

Heteroskedasticity The property of having a nonconstant variance; refers to an error term with the property that its variance differs across observations.

Heteroskedasticity-consistent standard errors Standard errors of the estimated parameters of a regression that correct for the presence of heteroskedasticity in the regression's error term.

High-yield bond A bond rated below investment grade. Also referred to as *speculative-grade bonds* or *junk bonds*.

Histogram A bar chart of data that have been grouped into a frequency distribution.

Historical cost In reference to assets, the amount paid to purchase an asset, including any costs of acquisition and/or preparation; with reference to liabilities, the amount of proceeds received in exchange in issuing the liability.

Historical equity risk premium approach An estimate of a country's equity risk premium that is based upon the historical averages of the risk-free rate and the rate of return on the market portfolio.

Historical method A method of estimating VAR that uses data from the returns of the portfolio over a recent past period and compiles this data in the form of a histogram.

Historical simulation (or back simulation) method Another term for the historical method of estimating VAR. This method involves not a *simulation* of the past but rather what *actually happened* in the past, sometimes adjusted to reflect the fact that a different portfolio may have existed in the past than is planned for the future.

Holding period return (HPR) The return that an investor earns during a specified holding period; a synonym for total return.

Holding period yield (HPY) The return that an investor earns during a specified holding period; holding period return with reference to a fixed-income instrument.

Homogenization Creating a contract with standard and generally accepted terms, which makes it more acceptable to a broader group of participants.

Homoskedasticity The property of having a constant variance; refers to an error term that is constant across observations.

Horizontal analysis Common-size analysis that involves comparing a specific financial statement with that statement in prior or future time periods; also, cross-sectional analysis of one company with another.

Horizontal common-size analysis An analysis in which financial statement accounts are compared to a benchmark in a different reporting period. Accounts in subsequent periods are restated as a percentage of the base period's value for the same account.

Human capital The value of skills and knowledge possessed by the workforce.

Hurdle rate The rate of return that must be met for a project to be accepted.

Hypothesis With reference to statistical inference, a statement about one or more populations.

Hypothesis testing With reference to statistical inference, the subdivision dealing with the testing of hypotheses about one or more populations.

Identifiable intangible An intangible that can be acquired singly and is typically linked to specific rights or privileges having finite benefit periods (e.g., a patent or trademark).

If-converted method A method for accounting for the effect of convertible securities on earnings per share (EPS) that specifies what EPS would have been if the convertible securities had been converted at the beginning of the period, taking account of the effects of conversion on net income and the weighted average number of shares outstanding.

Impairment Diminishment in value.

Implicit rental rate The firm's opportunity cost of using its own capital.

Implied repo rate The rate of return from a cash-and-carry transaction implied by the futures price relative to the spot price.

Implied volatility The volatility that option traders use to price an option, implied by the price of the option and a particular option-pricing model.

Implied yield A measure of the yield on the underlying bond of a futures contract implied by pricing it as though the underlying will be delivered at the futures expiration.

Imports The goods and services that we buy from people in other countries.

In the money An option that has positive intrinsic value.

Incentive A reward that encourages or a penalty that discourages an action.

Incentive system A method of organizing production that uses a market-like mechanism inside the firm.

Income Increases in economic benefits in the form of inflows or enhancements of assets, or decreases of liabilities that result in an increase in equity (other than increases resulting from contributions by owners).

Income effect The effect of a change in income on consumption, other things remaining the same.

Income elasticity of demand The responsiveness of demand to a change in income, other things remaining the same. It is calculated as the percentage change in the quantity demanded divided by the percentage change in income.

Income statement (statement of operations or profit and loss statement) A financial statement that provides information about a company's profitability over a stated period of time.

Income statement A financial statement that shows the flow of the firm's sales, expenses, and earnings over a period of time.

Incremental cash flows The changes or increments to cash flows resulting from a decision or action;

the cash flow with a decision minus the cash flow without that decision.

Indenture The legal agreement that lists the obligations of the issuer of a bond to the bondholder, including payment schedules, call provisions, and sinking funds.

Independent With reference to events, the property that the occurrence of one event does not affect the probability of another event occurring.

Independent and identically distributed (IID) With respect to random variables, the property of random variables that are independent of each other but follow the identical probability distribution.

Independent projects Independent projects are projects whose cash flows are independent of each other.

Independent variable A variable used to explain the dependent variable in a regression; a right-hand-side variable in a regression equation.

Index amortizing swap An interest rate swap in which the notional principal is indexed to the level of interest rates and declines with the level of interest rates according to a predefined scheduled. This type of swap is frequently used to hedge securities that are prepaid as interest rates decline, such as mortgage-backed securities.

Index option An option in which the underlying is a stock index.

Indexing An investment strategy in which an investor constructs a portfolio to mirror the performance of a specified index.

Indirect format (indirect method) With reference to cash flow statements, a format for the presentation of the statement which, in the operating cash flow section, begins with net income then shows additions and subtractions to arrive at operating cash flow.

Indirect method The procedure for converting the income statement from an accrual basis to a cash basis by adjusting net income for items that do not affect cash flows, including depreciation, amortization, depletion, gains, losses, and changes in current assets and current liabilities.

Individual transferable quota (ITQ) A production limit that is assigned to an individual who is free to transfer the quota to someone else.

Induced taxes Taxes that vary with real GDP.

Industry life cycle analysis An analysis that focuses on the industry's stage of development.

Inelastic demand A demand with a price elasticity between 0 and 1; the percentage change in the quantity demanded is less than the percentage change in price.

Infant-industry argument The argument that it is necessary to protect a new industry to enable it to grow into a mature industry that can compete in world markets.

Inferior good A good for which demand decreases as income increases.

Inflation A process in which the price level is rising and money is losing value.

Inflation premium An extra return that compensates investors for expected inflation.

Inflation rate The percentage change in the price level from one year to the next.

Inflationary gap The amount by which real GDP exceeds potential GDP.

Information An attribute of a good market that includes providing buyers and sellers with timely, accurate information on the volume and prices of past transactions and on all currently outstanding bids and offers.

Information ratio (IR) Mean active return divided by active risk.

Information ratio Statistic used to measure a portfolio's average return in excess of a comparison, benchmark portfolio divided by the standard deviation of this excess return.

Informationally efficient market A more technical term for an efficient capital market that emphasizes the role of information in setting the market price.

Initial margin requirement The margin requirement on the first day of a transaction as well as on any day in which additional margin funds must be deposited.

Initial public offering (IPO) A new issue by a firm that has no existing public market.

In-sample forecast errors The residuals from a fitted time-series model within the sample period used to fit the model.

Instability in the minimum-variance frontier The characteristic of minimum-variance frontiers that they are sensitive to small changes in inputs.

Installment Said of a sale in which proceeds are to be paid in installments over an extended period of time.

Installment method (installment-sales method) With respect to revenue recognition, a method that specifies that the portion of the total profit of the sale that is recognized in each period is determined by the percentage of the total sales price for which the seller has received cash.

Intangible asset An asset without physical substance.

Intellectual property rights Property rights for discoveries owned by the creators of knowledge.

Interest coverage A solvency ratio calculated as EBIT divided by interest payments.

Interest coverage ratio (or times-interest-earned ratio) Ratio of EBIT to interest payments; a comparison of the earnings available to meet interest obligations with existing interest obligations.

Interest rate A rate of return that reflects the relationship between differently dated cash flows; a discount rate.

Interest rate call An option in which the holder has the right to make a known interest payment and receive an unknown interest payment.

Interest rate cap or cap A series of call options on an interest rate, with each option expiring at the date on which the floating loan rate will be reset, and with each option having the same exercise rate. A cap in general can have an underlying other than an interest rate.

Interest rate collar A combination of a long cap and a short floor, or a short cap and a long floor. A collar in general can have an underlying other than an interest rate.

Interest rate floor or floor A series of put options on an interest rate, with each option expiring at the date on which the floating loan rate will be reset, and with each option having the same exercise rate. A floor in general can have an underlying other than the interest rate.

Interest rate forward (See *forward rate agreement*)

Interest rate option An option in which the underlying is an interest rate.

Interest rate parity A formula that expresses the equivalence or parity of spot and forward rates, after adjusting for differences in the interest rates.

Interest rate put An option in which the holder has the right to make an unknown interest payment and receive a known interest payment.

Interest rate risk The uncertainty of returns on an investment due to possible changes in interest rates over time.

Interest rate swap A swap in which the underlying is an interest rate. Can be viewed as a currency swap in which both currencies are the same and can be created as a combination of currency swaps.

Interest The income that capital earns.

Interest-on-interest Bond income from reinvestment of coupon payments.

Intergenerational data mining A form of data mining that applies information developed by previous researchers using a dataset to guide current research using the same or a related dataset.

Intermarket Trading System (ITS) A computerized system that connects competing exchanges and dealers who trade stocks listed on a U.S. exchange. Its purpose is to help customers find the best market for these stocks at a point in time.

Internal liquidity (solvency) ratios Financial ratios that measure the ability of the firm to meet future short-term financial obligations.

Internal rate of return (IRR) The discount rate that makes net present value equal 0; the discount rate that makes the present value of an investment's costs (outflows) equal to the present value of the investment's benefits (inflows).

Internal Rate of Return (Private Equity) (IRR) IRR is the annualized implied discount rate (effective compounded rate) that equates the present value of all the appropriate cash inflows (paid-in capital, such as drawdowns for net investments) associated with an investment with the sum of the present value of all the appropriate cash outflows (such as distributions) accruing from it and the present value of the unrealized residual portfolio (unliquidated holdings). For an interim cumulative return measurement, any IRR depends on the valuation of the residual assets.

Internal Valuation (Real Estate) An internal valuation is an advisor's or underlying third-party manager's best estimate of market value based on the most current and accurate information available under the circumstances. An internal valuation could include industry practice techniques, such as discounted cash flow, sales comparison, replacement cost, or a review of all significant events (both general market and asset specific) that could have a material impact on the investment. Prudent assumptions and estimates must be used, and the process must be applied consistently from period to period, except where a change would result in better estimates of market value.

International Fisher relation The assertion that the interest rate differential between two countries should equal the expected inflation rate differential over the term of the interest rates.

Interquartile range The difference between the third and first quartiles of a dataset.

Interval With reference to grouped data, a set of values within which an observation falls.

Interval scale A measurement scale that not only ranks data but also gives assurance that the differences between scale values are equal.

In-the-money option An option that, if exercised, would result in the value received being worth more than the payment required to exercise (apart from transaction costs).

Intrinsic value The portion of a call option's total value equal to the greater of either zero or the difference between the current value of the underlying asset and the exercise price; for a put option, intrinsic value is the greater of either zero or the exercise price less the underlying asset price. For a stock, it is the value derived from fundamental analysis of the stock's expected returns or cash flows.

Intrinsic value or exercise value The value obtained if an option is exercised based on current conditions.

Inventory The unsold units of product on hand.

Inventory blanket lien The use of inventory as collateral for a loan. Though the lender has claim to some or all of the company's inventory, the company may still sell or use the inventory in the ordinary course of business.

Inventory turnover An activity ratio calculated as cost of goods sold divided by average inventory; an indication of the resources tied up in inventory relative to the speed at which inventory is sold during the period.

Inverse floater A floating-rate note or bond in which the coupon is adjusted to move opposite to a benchmark interest rate.

Inverse relationship A relationship between variables that move in opposite directions.

Invested Capital (Private Equity) The amount of paid-in capital that has been invested in portfolio companies.

Investing activities Activities which are associated with the acquisition and disposal of property, plant, and equipment; intangible assets; other long-term assets; and both long-term and short-term investments in the equity and debt (bonds and loans) issued by other companies.

Investment The purchase of new plant, equipment, and buildings and additions to inventories.

Investment Advisor (Private Equity) Any individual or institution that supplies investment advice to clients on a per fee basis. The investment advisor inherently has no role in the management of the underlying portfolio companies of a partnership/fund.

Investment company A firm that sells shares of the company and uses the proceeds to buy portfolios of stock, bonds, or other financial instruments.

Investment decision process Estimation of intrinsic value for comparison with market price to determine whether or not to invest.

Investment demand The relationship between investment and real interest rate, other things remaining the same.

Investment horizon The time period used for planning and forecasting purposes or the future time at which the investor requires the invested funds.

Investment management company A company separate from the investment company that manages the portfolio and performs administrative functions.

Investment Management Fee The fee payable to the investment management firm for the on-going management of a portfolio. Investment management fees are typically asset based (percentage of assets), performance based (based on performance relative to a benchmark), or a combination of the two but may take different forms as well.

Investment Multiple (TVPI Multiple) (Private Equity) The ratio of total value to paid-in-capital. It represents the total return of the investment to the original investment not taking into consideration the time invested. Total value can be found by adding the residual value and distributed capital together.

Investment opportunity schedule A graphical depiction of a company's investment opportunities ordered from highest to lowest expected return. A company's optimal capital budget is found where the investment opportunity schedule intersects with the company's marginal cost of capital.

Investment strategy A decision by a portfolio manager regarding how he or she will manage the portfolio to meet the goals and objectives of the client. This will include either active or passive management and, if active, what style in terms of top-down or buttom-up or fundamental versus technical.

IRR The discount rate which forces the PV of a project's inflows to equal the PV of its costs.

IRR rule An investment decision rule that accepts projects or investments for which the IRR is greater than the opportunity cost of capital.

January effect A frequent empirical anomaly where risk-adjusted stock returns in the month of January are significantly larger than those occurring in any other month of the year.

Job search The activity of looking for acceptable vacant jobs.

Joint probability The probability of the joint occurrence of stated events.

Joint probability function A function giving the probability of joint occurrences of values of stated random variables.

Just-in-time method (JIT) Method of managing inventory that minimizes in-process inventory stocks.

Keynesian An economist who believes that left alone, the economy would rarely operate at full employment and that to achieve full employment, active help from fiscal policy and monetary policy is required.

***k*th Order autocorrelation** The correlation between observations in a time series separated by *k* periods.

Kurtosis The statistical measure that indicates the peakedness of a distribution.

Labor The work time and work effort that people devote to producing goods and services.

Labor force The sum of the people who are employed and who are unemployed.

Labor force participation rate The percentage of the working-age population who are members of the labor force.

Labor productivity Real GDP per hour of work.

Labor union An organized group of workers whose purpose is to increase wages and to influence other job conditions.

Laddering strategy A form of active strategy which entails scheduling maturities on a systematic basis within the investment portfolio such that investments are spread out equally over the term of the ladder.

Laffer curve The relationship between the tax rate and the amount of tax revenue collected.

Land The gifts of nature that we use to produce goods and services.

Law of demand Other things remaining the same, the higher the price of a good, the smaller is the quantity demanded of it.

Law of diminishing returns As a firm uses more of a variable input, with a given quantity of other inputs (fixed inputs), the marginal product of the variable input eventually diminishes.

Law of one price The condition in a financial market in which two financial instruments or combinations of financial instruments can sell for only one price. Equivalent to the principle that no arbitrage opportunities are possible.

Law of supply Other things remaining the same, the higher the price of a good, the greater is the quantity supplied of it.

Leading indicators A set of economic variables whose values reach peaks and troughs in advance of the aggregate economy.

Leading P/E (or forward P/E or prospective P/E) A stock's current price divided by the next year's expected earnings.

Learning-by-doing People become more productive in an activity (learn) just by repeatedly producing a particular good or service (doing).

Leasehold A right to occupy land or buildings under a long-term rental contract.

Leasehold improvements Improvements to leased property that become the property of the lessor at the end of the lease.

Legal monopoly A market structure in which there is one firm and entry is restricted by the granting of a public franchise, government license, patent, or copyright.

Legal risk The risk that the legal system will not enforce a contract in case of dispute or fraud.

Leptokurtic Describes a distribution that is more peaked than a normal distribution.

Level of significance The probability of a Type I error in testing a hypothesis.

Leveraged floating-rate note or leveraged floater A floating-rate note or bond in which the coupon is adjusted at a multiple of a benchmark interest rate.

Liabilities Present obligations of an enterprise arising from past events, the settlement of which is expected to result in an outflow of resources embodying economic benefits; creditors' claims on the resources of a company.

License The right to use a formula, technique, process, or design.

LIFO layer liquidation With respect to the application of the LIFO inventory method, the liquidation of old, relatively low-priced inventory; happens when the volume of sales rises above the volume of recent purchases so that some sales are made from relatively old, low-priced inventory.

LIFO method The last in, first out, method of accounting for inventory, which matches sales against the costs of items of inventory in the reverse order the items were placed in inventory (i.e., inventory produced or acquired last are assumed to be sold first).

Likelihood The probability of an observation, given a particular set of conditions.

Limit down A limit move in the futures market in which the price at which a transaction would be made is at or below the lower limit.

Limit move A condition in the futures markets in which the price at which a transaction would be made is at or beyond the price limits.

Limit order An order that lasts for a specified time to buy or sell a security when and if it trades at a specified price.

Limit pricing The practice of setting the price at the highest level that inflicts a loss on an entrant.

Limit up A limit move in the futures market in which the price at which a transaction would be made is at or above the upper limit.

Limited Partnership (Private Equity) The legal structure used by most venture and private equity funds. Usually fixed life investment vehicles. The general partner or management firm manages the partnership using the policy laid down in a partnership agreement. The agreement also covers terms, fees, structures, and other items agreed between the limited partners and the general partner.

Linear association A straight-line relationship, as opposed to a relationship that cannot be graphed as a straight line.

Linear interpolation The estimation of an unknown value on the basis of two known values that bracket it, using a straight line between the two known values.

Linear regression Regression that models the straight-line relationship between the dependent and independent variable(s).

Linear relationship A relationship between two variables that is illustrated by a straight line.

Linear trend A trend in which the dependent variable changes at a constant rate with time.

Liquid Term used to describe an asset that can be quickly converted to cash at a price close to fair market value.

Liquid assets Those company assets that are most readily converted to cash.

Liquidity In the context of financial analysis, a company's ability to satisfy its short-term obligations using assets that are most readily converted into cash.

Liquidity premium An extra return that compensates investors for the risk of loss relative to an investment's fair value if the investment needs to be converted to cash quickly.

Liquidity ratios Financial ratios measuring a company's ability to meet its short-term obligations.

Liquidity risk The risk that a financial instrument cannot be purchased or sold without a significant concession in price due to the size of the market.

Living wage An hourly wage rate that enables a person who works a 40-hour week to rent adequate housing for not more than 30 percent of the amount earned.

Lockbox system A payment system in which customer payments are mailed to a post office box and the banking institution retrieves and deposits these payments several times a day, enabling the company to have use of the fund sooner than in a centralized system in which customer payments are sent to the company.

Locked limit A condition in the futures markets in which a transaction cannot take place because the price would be beyond the limits.

Logit model A qualitative-dependent-variable multiple regression model based on the logistic probability distribution.

Log-linear model With reference to time-series models, a model in which the growth rate of the time series as a function of time is constant.

Log-log regression model A regression that expresses the dependent and independent variables as natural logarithms.

London Interbank Offer Rate (LIBOR) The Eurodollar rate at which London banks lend dollars to other London banks; considered to be the best representative rate on a dollar borrowed by a private, high-quality borrower.

Long The buyer of a derivative contract. Also refers to the position of owning a derivative.

Long position The buyer of a commodity or security or, for a forward contract, the counterparty who will be the eventual buyer of the underlying asset.

Long run A period of time in which the quantities of all resources can be varied.

Longitudinal data Observations on characteristic(s) of the same observational unit through time.

Long-lived assets Assets that are expected to provide economic benefits over a future period of time greater than one year.

Long-run aggregate supply curve The relationship between the real GDP supplied and the price level in the long run when real GDP equals potential GDP.

Long-run average cost curve The relationship between the lowest attainable average total cost and output when both capital and labor are varied.

Long-run industry supply curve A curve that shows how the quantity supplied by an industry varies as the market price varies after all the possible adjustments have been made, including changes in plant size and the number of firms in the industry.

Long-run macroeconomic equilibrium A situation that occurs when real GDP equals potential GDP-the economy is on its long-run aggregate supply curve.

Long-run Phillips curve Inflation rate equals the expected inflation rate.

Long-term assets Assets that have a useful life of more than one year, are used in the operation of a business, and are not intended for resale. Less commonly called *fixed assets*.

Long-term contract A contract that spans a number of accounting periods.

Long-term debt-to-assets ratio Ratio of long-term debt to total assets; the proportion of the company's assets that is financed with long-term debt.

Long-term equity anticipatory securities (LEAPS) Options originally created with expirations of several years.

Look-ahead bias A bias caused by using information that was unavailable on the test date.

Losses Asset outflows not directly related to the ordinary activities of the business.

Lower bound The lowest possible value of an option.

Lucas wedge The accumulated loss of output that results from a slowdown in the growth rate of real GDP per person.

M1 A measure of money that consists of currency and traveler's checks plus checking deposits owned by individuals and businesses.

M2 A measure of money that consists of M1 plus time deposits, savings deposits, and money market mutual funds and other deposits.

Macaulay duration The duration without dividing by 1 plus the bond's yield to maturity. The term, named for one of the economists who first derived it, is used to distinguish the calculation from modified duration. See also *modified duration.*

Macroeconomic factor A factor related to the economy, such as the inflation rate, industrial production, or economic sector membership.

Macroeconomic factor model A multifactor model in which the factors are surprises in macroeconomic variables that significantly explain equity returns.

Macroeconomic long run A time frame that is sufficiently long for real GDP to return to potential GDP so that full employment prevails.

Macroeconomic short run A period during which some money prices are sticky and real GDP might be below, above, or at potential GDP and unemployment might be above, below, or at the natural rate of unemployment.

Macroeconomics The study of the performance of the national economy and the global economy.

Maintenance margin The required proportion that the investor's equity value must be to the total market value of the stock. If the proportion drops below this percent, the investor will receive a margin call.

Maintenance margin requirement The margin requirement on any day other than the first day of a transaction.

Management fee The compensation an investment company pays to the investment management company for its services. The average annual fee is about 0.5 percent of fund assets.

Manufacturing resource planning (MRP) The incorporation of production planning into inventory management. A MRP analysis provides both a materials acquisition schedule and a production schedule.

Margin The amount of money that a trader deposits in a margin account. The term is derived from the stock market practice in which an investor borrows a portion of the money required to purchase a certain amount of stock. In futures markets, there is no borrowing so the margin is more of a down payment or performance bond.

Margin account The collateral posted with the futures exchange clearinghouse by an outside counterparty to insure its eventual performance; the *initial* margin is the deposit required at contract origination while the *maintenance* margin is the minimum collateral necessary at all times.

Margin call A request by an investor's broker for additional capital for a security bought on margin if the investor's equity value declines below the required maintenance margin.

Marginal benefit curve A curve that shows the relationship between the marginal benefit of a good and the quantity of that good consumed.

Marginal benefit The benefit that a person receives from consuming one more unit of a good or service. It is measured as the maximum amount that a person is willing to pay for one more unit of the good or service.

Marginal cost The opportunity cost of producing one more unit of a good or service. It is the best alternative forgone. It is calculated as the increase in total cost divided by the increase in output.

Marginal cost pricing rule A rule that sets the price of a good or service equal to the marginal cost of producing it.

Marginal probability *See* Unconditional probability.

Marginal product The increase in total product that results from a one-unit increase in the variable input, with all other inputs remaining the same. It is calculated as the increase in total product divided by the increase in the variable input employed, when the quantities of all other inputs are constant.

Marginal product of labor The additional real GDP produced by an additional hour of labor when all other influences on production remain the same.

Marginal propensity to consume The fraction of a change in disposable income that is consumed. It is calculated as the change in consumption expenditure divided by the change in disposable income.

Marginal revenue The change in total revenue that results from a one-unit increase in the quantity sold. It is calculated as the change in total revenue divided by the change in quantity sold.

Marginal revenue product The change in total revenue that results from employing one more unit of a resource (labor) while the quantity of all other resources remains the same. It is calculated as the increase in total revenue divided by the increase in the quantity of the resource (labor).

Marginal social benefit The marginal benefit enjoyed by society-by the consumer of a good or service (marginal private benefit) plus the marginal benefit enjoyed by others (marginal external benefit).

Marginal social cost The marginal cost incurred by the entire society-by the producer and by everyone else on whom the cost falls-and is the sum of marginal private cost and the marginal external cost.

Marginal tax rate The part of each additional dollar in income that is paid as tax.

Margins (or profit margin ratios and return-on-sales ratios) Ratios that are useful for evaluating a company's ability to manage its expenses to generate profits from its sales.

Marked to market The settlement process used to adjust the margin account of a futures contract for daily changes in the price of the underlying asset.

Market demand The relationship between the total quantity demanded of a good and its price. It is illustrated by the market demand curve.

Market failure A state in which the market does not allocate resources efficiently.

Market order An order to buy or sell a security immediately at the best price available.

Market portfolio The portfolio that includes all risky assets with relative weights equal to their proportional market values.

Market power The ability to influence the market, and in particular the market price, by influencing the total quantity offered for sale.

Market price of risk The slope of the capital market line, indicating the market risk premium for each unit of market risk.

Market risk premium The expected excess return on the market over the risk-free rate.

Market risk The risk associated with interest rates, exchange rates, and equity prices.

Market Value The current listed price at which investors buy or sell securities at a given time.

Market Value (Real Estate) The most probable price that a property should bring in a competitive and open market under all conditions requisite to a fair sale, the buyer and seller each acting prudently and knowledgeably, and assuming the price is not affected by undue stimulus. Implicit in this definition is the consummation of a sale as of a specified date and the passing of title from seller to buyer under conditions whereby: (a) Buyer and seller are typically motivated. (b) Both parties are well informed or well advised and each acting in what they consider their own best interests. (c) A reasonable time is allowed for exposure in the open market. (d) Payment is made in terms of currency or in terms of financial arrangements comparable thereto. (e) The price represents the normal consideration for the property sold unaffected by special or creative financing or sales concessions granted by anyone associated with the sale.

Market value added (MVA) External management performance measure to compare the market value of the company's debt and equity with the total capital invested in the firm.

Market-oriented investors With reference to equity investors, investors whose investment disciplines cannot be clearly categorized as value or growth.

Marking to market A procedure used primarily in futures markets in which the parties to a contract settle the amount owed daily. Also known as the *daily settlement.*

Markowitz decision rule A decision rule for choosing between two investments based on their means and variances.

Mark-to-market The revaluation of a financial asset or liability to its current market value or fair value.

Matching principle The accounting principle that expenses should be recognized when the associated revenue is recognized.

Matching strategy An active investment strategy that includes intentional matching of the timing of cash outflows with investment maturities.

Materiality The condition of being of sufficient importance so that omission or misstatement of the item in a financial report could make a difference to users' decisions.

Matrix pricing In the fixed income markets, to price a security on the basis of valuation-relevant characteristics (e.g. debt-rating approach).

Maturity premium An extra return that compensates investors for the increased sensitivity of the market value of debt to a change in market interest rates as maturity is extended.

McCallum rule A rule that adjusts the growth rate of the monetary base to target the inflation rate but also to take into account changes in the trend productivity growth rate and fluctuations in aggregate demand.

Mean The sum of all values in a distribution or dataset, divided by the number of values summed; a synonym of arithmetic mean.

Mean absolute deviation With reference to a sample, the mean of the absolute values of deviations from the sample mean.

Mean excess return The average rate of return in excess of the risk-free rate.

Mean reversion The tendency of a time series to fall when its level is above its mean and rise when its level is below its mean; a mean-reverting time series tends to return to its long-term mean.

Mean–variance analysis An approach to portfolio analysis using expected means, variances, and covariances of asset returns.

Means of payment A method of settling a debt.

Mean-variance analysis An approach to portfolio analysis using expected means, variances, and covariances of asset returns.

Measure of central tendency A quantitative measure that specifies where data are centered.

Measure of location A quantitative measure that describes the location or distribution of data; includes not only measures of central tendency but also other measures such as percentiles.

Measurement scales A scheme of measuring differences. The four types of measurement scales are nominal, ordinal, interval, and ratio.

Median The value of the middle item of a set of items that has been sorted into ascending or descending order; the 50th percentile.

Mesokurtic Describes a distribution with kurtosis identical to that of the normal distribution.

Microeconomics The study of the choices that individuals and businesses make, the way those choices interact, and the influence governments exert on them.

Minimum efficient scale The smallest quantity of output at which the long-run average cost curve reaches its lowest level.

Minimum wage A regulation that makes the hiring of labor below a specified wage rate illegal.

Minimum-variance frontier The graph of the set of portfolios that have minimum variance for their level of expected return.

Minimum-variance portfolio The portfolio with the minimum variance for each given level of expected return.

Minority interest The portion of consolidated subsidiaries' net assets not owned by the parent.

Mismatching strategy An active investment strategy whereby the timing of cash outflows is not matched with investment maturities.

Mixed factor models Factor models that combine features of more than one type of factor model.

Modal interval With reference to grouped data, the most frequently occurring interval.

Mode The most frequently occurring value in a set of observations.

Model risk The use of an inaccurate pricing model for a particular investment, or the improper use of the right model.

Model specification With reference to regression, the set of variables included in the regression and the regression equation's functional form.

Modified duration A measure of a bond's price sensitivity to interest rate movements. Equal to the Macaulay duration of a bond divided by one plus its yield to maturity.

Monetarist An economist who believes that the economy is self regulating and that it will normally operate at full employment, provided that monetary policy is not erratic and that the pace of money growth is kept steady.

Monetary base The sum of the Federal Reserve notes, coins, and banks' deposits at the Fed.

Monetary policy The Fed conducts the nation's monetary policy by changing interest rates and adjusting the quantity of money.

Money Any commodity or token that is generally acceptable as a means of payment.

Money market fund A fund that invests in short-term securities sold in the money market. (Large companies, banks, and other institutions also invest their surplus cash in the money market for short periods of time.) In the entire investment spectrum, these are generally the safest, most stable securities available. They include Treasury bills, certificates of deposit of large banks, and commercial paper (short-term IOUs of large corporations).

Money market mutual fund A fund operated by a financial institution that sells shares in the fund and holds liquid assets such as U.S. Treasury bills and short-term commercial bills.

Money market yield (or CD equivalent yield) A yield on a basis comparable to the quoted yield on an interest-bearing money market instrument that pays interest on a 360-day basis; the annualized holding period yield, assuming a 360-day year.

Money market The market for short-term debt instruments (one-year maturity or less).

Money multiplier The amount by which a change in the monetary base is multiplied to determine the resulting change in the quantity of money.

Money price The number of dollars that must be given up in exchange for a good or service.

Money wage rate The number of dollars that an hour of labor earns.

Moneyness The relationship between the price of the underlying and an option's exercise price.

Money-weighted rate of return The internal rate of return on a portfolio, taking account of all cash flows.

Monopolistic competition A market structure in which a large number of firms compete by making similar but slightly different products.

Monopoly A market structure in which there is one firm, which produces a good or service that has no close substitute and in which the firm is protected from competition by a barrier preventing the entry of new firms.

Monte Carlo simulation A risk analysis technique in which probable future events are simulated on a computer, generating estimated rates of return and risk indexes.

Monte Carlo simulation method An approach to estimating VAR that produces random outcomes to examine what might happen if a particular risk is faced. This method is widely used in the sciences as well as in business to study a variety of problems.

Mortgage bonds Bonds that pledge specific assets such as buildings and equipment. The proceeds from the sale of these assets are used to pay off bondholders in case of bankruptcy.

Moving average The continually recalculating average of security prices for a period, often 200 days, to serve as an indication of the general trend of prices and also as a benchmark price.

Multicollinearity A regression assumption violation that occurs when two or more independent variables (or combinations of independent variables) are highly but not perfectly correlated with each other.

Multifactor model An empirical version of the APT where the investor chooses the exact number and identity of the common risk factors used to describe an asset's risk-return relationship. Risk factors are often designated as *macroeconomic* variables (e.g., inflation, changes in gross domestic product) or *microeconomic* variables (e.g., security-specific characteristics like firm size or book-to-market ratios).

Multiple linear regression Linear regression involving two or more independent variables.

Multiple linear regression model A linear regression model with two or more independent variables.

Multiple *R* The correlation between the actual and forecasted values of the dependent variable in a regression.

Multiplication rule for probabilities The rule that the joint probability of events *A* and *B* equals the probability of *A* given *B* times the probability of *B*.

Multiplier The amount by which a change in autonomous expenditure is magnified or multiplied to determine the change in equilibrium expenditure and real GDP.

*Multi-step format** With respect to the format of the income statement, a format that presents a subtotal for gross profit (revenue minus cost of goods sold).

Multivariate distribution A probability distribution that specifies the probabilities for a group of related random variables.

Multivariate normal distribution A probability distribution for a group of random variables that is completely defined by the means and variances of the variables plus all the correlations between pairs of the variables.

Must A required provision for claiming compliance with the GIPS standards.

Mutual fund An investment company that pools money from shareholders and invests in a variety of securities, including stocks, bonds, and money market securities. A mutual fund ordinarily stands ready to buy back (redeem) its shares at their current net asset value, which depends on the market value of the fund's portfolio of securities at the time. Mutual funds generally continuously offer new shares to investors.

Mutually exclusive events Events such that only one can occur at a time.

Mutually exclusive projects Mutually exclusive projects compete directly with each other. For example, if Projects A and B are mutually exclusive, you can choose A or B, but you cannot choose both.

***n* Factorial** For a positive integer *n*, the product of the first *n* positive integers; 0 factorial equals 1 by definition. *n* factorial is written as *n*!.

Nasdaq InterMarket A trading system that includes Nasdaq market makers and ECNs that quote and trade stocks listed on the NYSE and the AMEX. It involves dealers from the Nasdaq market and the Intermarket Trading System (ITS). In many ways, this has become what had been labeled the third market.

Nash equilibrium The outcome of a game that occurs when player A takes the best possible action given the action of player B and player B takes the best possible action given the action of player A.

National saving The sum of private saving (saving by households and businesses) and government saving.

Natural monopoly A monopoly that occurs when one firm can supply the entire market at a lower price than two or more firms can.

Natural rate of unemployment The unemployment rate when the economy is at full employment. There is no cyclical unemployment; all unemployment is frictional and structural.

Natural resources Long-term assets purchased for the economic value that can be taken from the land and used up.

Near-term, high-priority goal A short-term financial investment goal of personal importance, such as accumulating funds for making a house down payment or buying a car.

Needs-tested spending Government spending on programs that pay benefits to suitably qualified people and businesses.

Negative relationship A relationship between variables that move in opposite directions.

Negative serial correlation Serial correlation in which a positive error for one observation increases the chance of a negative error for another observation, and vice versa.

Negotiated sales An underwriting arrangement wherein the sale of a security issue by an issuing entity (governmental body or a corporation) is done using an investment banking firm that maintains an ongoing relationship with the issuer. The characteristics of the security issue are determined by the issuer in consultation with the investment banker.

Neoclassical growth theory A theory of economic growth that proposes that real GDP grows because technological change induces a level of saving and investment that makes capital per hour of labor grow.

Net asset value The market value of the assets owned by a fund.

Net book value The remaining (undepreciated) balance of an asset's purchase cost.

Net borrower A country that is borrowing more from the rest of the world than it is lending to it.

Net exports The value of exports minus the value of imports.

Net income (loss) The difference between revenue and expenses; what remains after subtracting all expenses (including depreciation, interest, and taxes) from revenue.

Net investment Net increase in the capital stock–gross investment minus depreciation.

Net lender A country that is lending more to the rest of the world than it is borrowing from it.

Net operating cycle (or cash conversion cycle) An estimate of the average time that elapses between paying suppliers for materials and collecting cash from the subsequent sale of goods produced.

Net present value (NPV) The present value of an investment's cash inflows (benefits) minus the present value of its cash outflows (costs).

Net profit margin (profit margin or return on sales) An indicator of profitability, calculated as net income divided by revenue; indicates how much of each dollar of revenues is left after all costs and expenses.

Net revenue Revenue after adjustments (e.g., for estimated returns or for amounts unlikely to be collected).

Net taxes Taxes paid to governments minus transfer payments received from governments.

Net-of-Fees Return The gross-of-fees return reduced by the investment management fee.

Netting When parties agree to exchange only the net amount owed from one party to the other.

New issue Common stocks or bonds offered by companies for public sale.

New Keynesian A Keynesian who holds the view that not only is the money wage rate sticky but that prices of goods and services are also sticky.

Node Each value on a binomial tree from which successive moves or outcomes branch.

No-load fund A mutual fund that sells its shares at net asset value without adding sales charges.

Nominal GDP The value of the final goods and services produced in a given year valued at the prices that prevailed in that same year. It is a more precise name for GDP.

Nominal rate Rate of interest based on the security's face value.

Nominal risk-free interest rate The sum of the real risk-free interest rate and the inflation premium.

Nominal scale A measurement scale that categorizes data but does not rank them.

Nominal yield A bond's yield as measured by its coupon rate.

Noncash investing and financing transactions Significant investing and financing transactions involving only long-term assets, long-term liabilities, or stockholders' equity that do not affect current cash inflows or outflows.

Nonconventional cash flow In a nonconventional cash flow pattern, the initial outflow is not followed by inflows only, but the cash flows can flip from positive (inflows) to negative (outflows) again (or even change signs several times).

Noncurrent Not due to be consumed, converted into cash, or settled within one year after the balance sheet date.

Noncurrent assets Assets that are expected to benefit the company over an extended period of time (usually more than one year).

Nondeliverable forwards (NDFs) Cash-settled forward contracts, used predominately with respect to foreign exchange forwards.

Nonlinear relation An association or relationship between variables that cannot be graphed as a straight line.

Nonparametric test A test that is not concerned with a parameter, or that makes minimal assumptions about the population from which a sample comes.

Nonrenewable natural resources Natural resources that can be used only once and that cannot be replaced once they have been used.

Nonstationarity With reference to a random variable, the property of having characteristics such as mean and variance that are not constant through time.

Nontariff barrier Any action other than a tariff that restricts international trade.

Normal backwardation The condition in futures markets in which futures prices are lower than expected spot prices.

Normal contango The condition in futures markets in which futures prices are higher than expected spot prices.

Normal distribution A continuous, symmetric probability distribution that is completely described by its mean and its variance.

Normal good A good for which demand increases as income increases.

Normal profit The expected return for supplying entrepreneurial ability.

North American Free Trade Agreement An agreement, which became effective on January 1, 1994, to eliminate all barriers to international trade between the United States, Canada, and Mexico after a 15-year phasing in period.

Notes Intermediate-term debt securities with maturities longer than 1 year but less than 10 years.

Notes payable Amounts owed by a business to creditors as a result of borrowings that are evidenced by (short-term) loan agreements.

Notional principal The principal value of a swap transaction, which is not exchanged but is used as a scale factor to translate interest rate differentials into cash settlement payments.

***n*-Period moving average** The average of the current and immediately prior $n - 1$ values of a time series.

NPV rule An investment decision rule that states that an investment should be undertaken if its NPV is positive but not undertaken if its NPV is negative.

Null hypothesis The hypothesis to be tested.

Number of days of inventory Ratio of the amount of inventory on hand to the average day's cost of goods sold; an indication of the number of days a company ties up funds in inventory.

Number of days of payables An activity ratio equal to the number of days in a period divided by the payables turnover ratio for the period; an estimate of the average number of days it takes a company to pay its suppliers.

Number of days of receivables Ratio of accounts receivable to average day's revenue; an indication of the length of time between a sale (i.e. an account receivable is created) and the collection of the account receivable in cash.

Objective probabilities Probabilities that generally do not vary from person to person; includes a priori and objective probabilities.

Objectives The investor's goals expressed in terms of risk and return and included in the policy statement.

Obsolescence The process of becoming out of date, which is a factor in the limited useful life of tangible assets.

Offensive competitive strategy A strategy whereby a firm attempts to use its strengths to affect the competitive forces in the industry and, in so doing, improves the firm's relative position in the industry.

Official reserves The amount of reserves owned by the central bank of a government in the form of gold, Special Drawing Rights, and foreign cash or marketable securities.

Official settlements account A record of the change in a country's official reserves.

Off-market FRA A contract in which the initial value is intentionally set at a value other than zero and therefore requires a cash payment at the start from one party to the other.

Offsetting A transaction in exchange-listed derivative markets in which a party re-enters the market to close out a position.

Okun gap The gap between real GDP and potential GDP, and so is another name for the output gap.

Oligopoly A market structure in which a small number of firms compete.

One-sided hypothesis test (or one-tailed hypothesis test) A test in which the null hypothesis is rejected only if the evidence indicates that the population parameter is greater than (smaller than) θ_0. The alternative hypothesis also has one side.

Open market operation The purchase or sale of government securities—U.S. Treasury bills and bonds—by the Federal Reserve System in the open market.

Open-End Fund (Private Equity) A type of investment fund where the number of investors and the total committed capital is not fixed (i.e., open for subscriptions and/or redemptions).

Operating activities Activities that are part of the day-to-day business functioning of an entity, such as selling inventory and providing services.

Operating cycle An estimate of the average time needed for a company to convert raw materials into cash from a sale.

Operating efficiency ratios Financial ratios intended to indicate how efficiently management is utilizing the firm's assets in terms of dollar sales generated per dollar of assets. Primary examples would be: total asset turnover, fixed asset turnover, or equity turnover.

Operating leverage The use of fixed costs in operations.

Operating profit (operating income) A company's profits on its usual business activities before deducting taxes.

Operating profit margin A profitability ratio calculated as operating income divided by revenue; indicates how much of each dollar of revenues is left after both cost of goods sold and operating expenses are considered.

Operating profitability ratios Financial ratios intended to indicate how profitable the firm is in terms of the percent of profit generated from sales. Alternative measures would include: operating profit (EBIT)/net sales; pretax profit (EBT)/net sales; and net profit/sales.

Operating return on assets A profitability ratio calculated as operating income divided by average total assets; a measure of the operating income resulting from the company's investment in total assets.

Operating risk Risk that is attributable to a company's operating cost structure.

Operations risk or operational risk The risk of loss from failures in a company's systems and procedures (for example, due to computer failures or human failures) or events completely outside of the control of organizations (which would include "acts of God" and terrorist actions).

Opportunity cost The value that investors forgo by choosing a particular course of action; the value of something in its best alternative use.

Opportunity set The set of assets available for investment.

Optimal portfolio The portfolio on the efficient frontier that has the highest utility for a given investor. It lies at the point of tangency between the efficient frontier and the curve with the investor's highest possible utility.

Optimizer A specialized computer program or a spreadsheet that solves for the portfolio weights that will result in the lowest risk for a specified level of expected return.

Option A financial instrument that gives one party the right, but not the obligation, to buy or sell an underlying asset from or to another party at a fixed price over a specific period of time. Also referred to as contingent claims.

Option contract An agreement that grants the owner the right, but not the obligation, to make a future transaction in an underlying commodity or security at a fixed price and within a predetermined time in the future.

Option premium The initial price that the option buyer must pay to the option seller to acquire the contract.

Option price, option premium, or premium The amount of money a buyer pays and seller receives to engage in an option transaction.

Option-adjusted spread A type of yield spread that considers changes in the term structure and alternative estimates of the volatility of interest rates.

Ordinal scale A measurement scale that sorts data into categories that are ordered (ranked) with respect to some characteristic.

Ordinary annuity An annuity with a first cash flow that is paid one period from the present.

Ordinary least squares (OLS) An estimation method based on the criterion of minimizing the sum of the squared residuals of a regression.

Ordinary shares (common stock or common shares) Equity shares that are subordinate to all other types of equity (e.g., preferred equity).

Orthogonal Uncorrelated; at a right angle.

OTC Electronic Bulletin Board (OTCBB) A regulated quotation service that displays real-time quotes, last-sale prices, and volume information for a specified set of over-the-counter (OTC) securities that are not traded on the formal Nasdaq market.

Other comprehensive income Items of comprehensive income that are not reported on the income statement; comprehensive income minus net income.

Other receivables Amounts owed to the company from parties other than customers.

Outcome A possible value of a random variable.

Outliers Small numbers of observations at either extreme (small or large) of a sample.

Out-of-sample forecast errors The differences between actual and predicted value of time series outside the sample period used to fit the model.

Out-of-sample test A test of a strategy or model using a sample outside the time period on which the strategy or model was developed.

Out-of-the-money Options that, if exercised, would require the payment of more money than the value received and therefore would not be currently exercised.

Out-of-the-money option (1) An option that has no value if exercised immediately. For example, a call when the strike price is above the current price of the underlying asset, or a put when the strike price is below the current price of the underlying asset. (2) An option that has no intrinsic value. (3) Options that, if exercised, would require the payment of more money than the value received and therefore would not be currently exercised.

Overnight index swap (OIS) A swap in which the floating rate is the cumulative value of a single unit of currency invested at an overnight rate during the settlement period.

Overweighted A condition in which a portfolio, for whatever reason, includes more of a class of securities than the relative market value alone would justify.

Owners' equity The excess of assets over liabilities; the residual interest of shareholders in the assets of an entity after deducting the entity's liabilities.

Paid-In Capital (Private Equity) The amount of committed capital a limited partner has actually transferred to a venture fund. Also known as the cumulative drawdown amount.

Paired comparisons test A statistical test for differences based on paired observations drawn from samples that are dependent on each other.

Paired observations Observations that are dependent on each other.

Pairs arbitrage trade A trade in two closely related stocks involving the short sale of one and the purchase of the other.

Panel data Observations through time on a single characteristic of multiple observational units.

Par value *See* Principal.

The principal amount repaid at maturity of a bond. Also called face value.

Parameter A descriptive measure computed from or used to describe a population of data, conventionally represented by Greek letters.

Parameter instability The problem or issue of population regression parameters that have changed over time.

Parametric test Any test (or procedure) concerned with parameters or whose validity depends on assumptions concerning the population generating the sample.

Partial regression coefficients or partial slope coefficients The slope coefficients in a multiple regression.

Passive strategy In reference to short-term cash management, it is an investment strategy characterized by simple decision rules for making daily investments.

Patent A government-sanctioned exclusive right granted to the inventor of a good, service, or productive process to produce, use, and sell the invention for a given number of years.

Payables turnover An activity ratio calculated as purchases divided by average trade payables.

Payback The time required for the added income from the convertible security relative to the stock to offset the conversion premium.

Payer swaption A swaption that allows the holder to enter into a swap as the fixed-rate payer and floating-rate receiver.

Payment date The date on which a firm actually mails dividend checks.

Payment netting A means of settling payments in which the amount owed by the first party to the second is netted with the amount owed by the second party to the first; only the net difference is paid.

Payoff The value of an option at expiration.

Payoff matrix A table that shows the payoffs for every possible action by each player for every possible action by each other player.

Pegged exchange rate regime A system in which a country's exchange rate in relation to a major currency is set at a target value (the peg) but allowed to fluctuate within a small band around the target.

Percentage-of-completion A method of revenue recognition in which, in each accounting period, the company estimates what percentage of the contract is complete and then reports that percentage of the total contract revenue in its income statement.

Percentiles Quantiles that divide a distribution into 100 equal parts.

Perfect collinearity The existence of an exact linear relation between two or more independent variables or combinations of independent variables.

Perfect competition A market in which there are many firms each selling an identical product; there are many buyers; there are no restrictions on entry into the industry; firms in the industry have no advantage over potential new entrants; and firms and buyers are well informed about the price of each firm's product.

Perfect price discrimination Price discrimination that extracts the entire consumer surplus.

Perfectly elastic demand Demand with an infinite price elasticity; the quantity demanded changes by an infinitely large percentage in response to a tiny price change.

Perfectly inelastic demand Demand with a price elasticity of zero; the quantity demanded remains constant when the price changes.

Performance appraisal The evaluation of risk-adjusted performance; the evaluation of investment skill.

Performance guarantee A guarantee from the clearinghouse that if one party makes money on a transaction, the clearinghouse ensures it will be paid.

Performance measurement The calculation of returns in a logical and consistent manner.

Period costs Costs (e.g., executives' salaries) that cannot be directly matched with the timing of revenues and which are thus expensed immediately.

Periodic rate The quoted interest rate per period; the stated annual interest rate divided by the number of compounding periods per year.

Permutation An ordered listing.

Perpetuity A perpetual annuity, or a set of never-ending level sequential cash flows, with the first cash flow occurring one period from now.

Personal trust An amount of money set aside by a grantor and often managed by a third party, the trustee. Often constructed so one party receives income from the trust's investments and another party receives the residual value of the trust after the income beneficiaries' death.

Pet projects Projects in which influential managers want the corporation to invest. Often, unfortunately, pet projects are selected without undergoing normal capital budgeting analysis.

Phillips curve A curve that shows a relationship between inflation and unemployment.

Physical deterioration A decline in the useful life of a depreciable asset resulting from use and from exposure to the elements.

Plain-vanilla Refers to a security, especially a bond or a swap, issued with standard features. Sometimes called generic.

Plain vanilla swap An interest rate swap in which one party pays a fixed rate and the other pays a floating rate, with both sets of payments in the same currency.

Platykurtic Describes a distribution that is less peaked than the normal distribution.

Plowback ratio An indication of the proportion of earnings that are reinvested in the company rather than paid out as dividends; calculated as 1 − dividend payout ratio.

Point estimate A single numerical estimate of an unknown quantity, such as a population parameter.

Point of sale Systems that capture transaction data at the physical location in which the sale is made.

Policy statement A statement in which the investor specifies investment goals, constraints, and risk preferences.

Pooled estimate An estimate of a parameter that involves combining (pooling) observations from two or more samples.

Population All members of a specified group.

Population mean The arithmetic mean value of a population; the arithmetic mean of all the observations or values in the population.

Population standard deviation A measure of dispersion relating to a population in the same unit of measurement as the observations, calculated as the positive square root of the population variance.

Population variance A measure of dispersion relating to a population, calculated as the mean of the squared deviations around the population mean.

Portfolio An individually managed pool of assets. A portfolio may be a subportfolio, account, or pooled fund.

Portfolio performance attribution The analysis of portfolio performance in terms of the contributions from various sources of risk.

Portfolio possibilities curve A graphical representation of the expected return and risk of all portfolios that can be formed using two assets.

Position trader A trader who typically holds positions open overnight.

Positive relationship A relationship between two variables that move in the same direction.

Positive serial correlation Serial correlation in which a positive error for one observation increases the chance of a positive error for another observation, and a negative error for one observation increases the chance of a negative error for another observation.

Posterior probability An updated probability that reflects or comes after new information.

Potential credit risk The risk associated with the possibility that a payment due at a later date will not be made.

Potential GDP The quantity of real GDP at full employment.

Poverty A situation in which a household's income is too low to be able to buy the quantities of food, shelter, and clothing that are deemed necessary.

Power of a test The probability of correctly rejecting the null-that is, rejecting the null hypothesis when it is false.

Precautionary stocks A level of inventory beyond anticipated needs that provides a cushion in the event that it takes longer to replenish inventory than expected or in the case of greater than expected demand.

Predatory pricing Setting a low price to drive competitors out of business with the intention of setting a monopoly price when the competition has gone.

Preferences A description of a person's likes and dislikes.

Preferred stock An equity investment that stipulates the dividend payment either as a coupon or a stated dollar amount. The firm's directors may withhold payments.

Pre-investing The strategy of using futures contracts to enter the market without an immediate outlay of cash.

Premium A bond selling at a price above par value due to capital market conditions.

Prepaid expense A normal operating expense that has been paid in advance of when it is due.

Present (price) value of a basis point (PVBP) The change in the bond price for a 1 basis point change in yield. Also called *basis point value* (BPV).

Present value The amount of money that, if invested today, will grow to be as large as a given future amount when the interest that it will earn is taken into account.

Present value (PV) The present discounted value of future cash flows: for assets, the present discounted value of the future net cash inflows that the asset is expected to generate; for liabilities, the present discounted value of the future net cash outflows that are expected to be required to settle the liabilities.

Pretax profit margin A profitability ratio calculated as earnings before taxes divided by revenue; useful for isolating the effects of taxes on a company's profitability.

Price ceiling A regulation that makes it illegal to charge a price higher than a specified level.

Price continuity A feature of a liquid market in which there are small price changes from one transaction to the next due to the depth of the market.

Price discovery A feature of futures markets in which futures prices provide valuable information about the price of the underlying asset.

Price discrimination The practice of selling different units of a good or service for different prices or of charging one customer different prices for different quantities bought.

Price effect The effect of a change in the price on the quantity of a good consumed, other things remaining the same.

Price elasticity of demand A units-free measure of the responsiveness of the quantity demanded of a good to a change in its price, when all other influences on buyers' plans remain the same.

Price floor A regulation that makes it illegal to charge a price lower than a specified level.

Price level The average level of prices as measured by a price index.

Price limits Limits imposed by a futures exchange on the price change that can occur from one day to the next.

Price momentum A portfolio strategy in which you acquire stocks that have enjoyed above-market stock price increases.

Price multiple The ratio of a stock's market price to some measure of value per share.

Price relative A ratio of an ending price over a beginning price; it is equal to 1 plus the holding period return on the asset.

Price risk The component of interest rate risk due to the uncertainty of the market price of a bond caused by changes in market interest rates.

Price taker A firm that cannot influence the price of the good or service it produces.

Price to book value A valuation ratio calculated as price per share divided by book value per share.

Price to cash flow A valuation ratio calculated as price per share divided by cash flow per share.

Price to sales A valuation ratio calculated as price per share divided by sales per share.

Price/earnings (P/E) ratio The number by which expected earnings per share is multiplied to estimate a stock's value; also called the *earnings multiplier.*

Priced risk Risk for which investors demand compensation for bearing (e.g. equity risk, company-specific factors, macroeconomic factors).

Price-setting option The operational flexibility to adjust prices when demand varies from forecast. For example, when demand exceeds capacity, the company could benefit from the excess demand by increasing prices.

Price-weighted index An index calculated as an arithmetic mean of the current prices of the sampled securities.

Primary market The market in which newly issued securities are sold by their issuers, who receive the proceeds.

Principal The amount of funds originally invested in a project or instrument; the face value to be paid at maturity.

Principal-agent problem The problem of devising compensation rules that induce an agent to act in the best interest of a principal.

Prior probabilities Probabilities reflecting beliefs prior to the arrival of new information.

Private Equity Private equity includes, but is not limited to, organizations devoted to venture capital, leveraged buyouts, consolidations, mezzanine and distressed debt investments, and a variety of hybrids, such as venture leasing and venture factoring.

Private information Information that is available to one person but is too costly for anyone else to obtain.

Private placement A new issue sold directly to a small group of investors, usually institutions

Private sector surplus or deficit An amount equal to saving minus investment.

Probability A number between 0 and 1 describing the chance that a stated event will occur.

Probability density function A function with non-negative values such that probability can be described by areas under the curve graphing the function.

Probability distribution A distribution that specifies the probabilities of a random variable's possible outcomes.

Probability function A function that specifies the probability that the random variable takes on a specific value.

Probit model A qualitative-dependent-variable multiple regression model based on the normal distribution.

Producer surplus The price of a good minus the opportunity cost of producing it, summed over the quantity sold.

Product differentiation Making a product slightly different from the product of a competing firm.

Production efficiency A situation in which the economy cannot produce more of one good without producing less of some other good.

Production-flexibility The operational flexibility to alter production when demand varies from forecast. For example, if demand is strong, a company may profit from employees working overtime or from adding additional shifts.

Production function The relationship between real GDP and the quantity of labor when all other influences on production remain the same.

Production method A method of depreciation that assumes depreciation is solely the result of use and that allocates depreciation based on the units of use or output during each period of an asset's useful life.

Production possibilities frontier The boundary between the combinations of goods and services that can be produced and the combinations that cannot.

Production quota An upper limit to the quantity of a good that may be produced in a specified period.

Productivity growth slowdown A slowdown in the growth rate of output per person.

Profit The income earned by entrepreneurship.

Profitability ratios Ratios that measure a company's ability to generate profitable sales from its resources (assets).

Project sequencing To defer the decision to invest in a future project until the outcome of some or all of a current project is known. Projects are sequenced through time, so that investing in a project creates the option to invest in future projects.

Property rights Social arrangements that govern the ownership, use, and disposal of resources or factors of production, goods, and services that are enforceable in the courts.

Prospective P/E *See* Leading P/E.

Protective put An option strategy in which a long position in an asset is combined with a long position in a put.

Provision In accounting, a liability of uncertain timing or amount.

Pseudo-random numbers Numbers produced by random number generators.

Public good A good or service that is both nonrival and nonexcludable—it can be consumed simultaneously by everyone and from which no one can be excluded.

Pull on liquidity When disbursements are paid too quickly or trade credit availability is limited, requiring companies to expend funds before they receive funds from sales that could cover the liability.

Purchasing power parity The equal value of different monies.

Purchasing power parity (PPP) A theory stating that the exchange rate between two currencies will exactly reflect the purchasing power of the two currencies.

Pure discount instruments Instruments that pay interest as the difference between the amount borrowed and the amount paid back.

Pure factor portfolio A portfolio with sensitivity of 1 to the factor in question and a sensitivity of 0 to all other factors.

Pure-play method A method for estimating the beta for a company or project; it requires using a comparable company's beta and adjusting it for financial leverage differences.

Put An option that gives the holder the right to sell an underlying asset to another party at a fixed price over a specific period of time.

Put-call parity An equation expressing the equivalence (parity) of a portfolio of a call and a bond with a portfolio of a put and the underlying, which leads to the relationship between put and call prices

Put-call-forward parity The relationship among puts, calls, and forward contracts.

Put option A contract giving the right to sell an asset at a specified price, on or before a specified date.

***p*-Value** The smallest level of significance at which the null hypothesis can be rejected; also called the marginal significance level.

Qualitative dependent variables Dummy variables used as dependent variables rather than as independent variables.

Quality financial statements Financial statements that most knowledgeable observers (analysts, portfolio managers) would consider conservatively prepared in terms of sales, expenses, earnings, and asset valuations. The results reported would reflect reasonable estimates and indicate what truly happened during the period and the legitimate value of assets and liabilities on the balance sheet.

Quantile (or fractile) A value at or below which a stated fraction of the data lies.

Quantity demanded The amount of a good or service that consumers plan to buy during a given time period at a particular price.

Quantity of labor demanded The labor hours hired by the firms in the economy.

Quantity of labor supplied The number of labor hours that all households in the economy plan to work.

Quantity supplied The amount of a good or service that producers plan to sell during a given time period at a particular price.

Quantity theory of money The proposition that in the long run, an increase in the quantity of money brings an equal percentage increase in the price level.

Quartiles Quantiles that divide a distribution into four equal parts.

Quick assets Assets that can be most readily converted to cash (e.g., cash, short-term marketable investments, receivables).

Quick ratio (or acid test ratio) A liquidity ratio calculated as quick assets (cash + short-term marketable investments + receivables) divided by current liabilities; provides an indication of a company's ability to satisfy current liabilities with its most liquid assets.

Quintiles Quantiles that divide a distribution into five equal parts.

Quota A quantitative restriction on the import of a particular good, which specifies the maximum amount that can be imported in a given time period.

Random number An observation drawn from a uniform distribution.

Random number generator An algorithm that produces uniformly distributed random numbers between 0 and 1.

Random variable A quantity whose future outcomes are uncertain.

Random walk A time series in which the value of the series in one period is the value of the series in the previous period plus an unpredictable random error.

Random walk theory (1) The theory that current stock prices already reflect known information about the future. Therefore, the future movement of stock prices will be determined by surprise occurrences. This will cause them to change in a random fashion. (2) A theory stating that all current information is reflected in current security prices and that future price movements are random because they are caused by unexpected news.

Range The difference between the maximum and minimum values in a dataset.

Range forward A trading strategy based on a variation of the put-call parity model where, for the same underlying asset but different exercise prices, a call option is purchased and a put option is sold (or vice versa).

Ratio scales A measurement scale that has all the characteristics of interval measurement scales as well as a true zero point as the origin.

Ratio spread An option strategy in which a long position in a certain number of options is offset by a short position in a certain number of other options on the same underlying, resulting in a risk-free position.

Rational expectation The most accurate forecast possible, a forecast that uses all the available information, including knowledge of the relevant economic forces that influence the variable being forecasted.

Real business cycle theory A theory that regards random fluctuations in productivity as the main source of economic fluctuations.

Real Estate Real estate Investments include: (a) Wholly owned or partially owned properties, (b) Commingled funds, property unit trusts, and insurance company separate accounts, (c) Unlisted, private placement securities issued by private real estate investment trusts (REITs) and real estate operating companies (REOCs), and (d) Equity-oriented debt, such as participating mortgage loans or any private interest in a property where some portion of return to the investor at the time of investment is related to the performance of the underlying real estate.

Real estate investment trusts (REITs) Investment funds that hold portfolios of real estate investments.

Real income A household's income expressed as a quantity of goods that the household can afford to buy.

Real interest rate The nominal interest rate adjusted for inflation; the nominal interest rate minus the inflation rate.

Real options Options embedded in a firm's real assets that give managers valuable decision-making flexibility, such as the right to either undertake or abandon an investment project.

Real rate of interest The money rate of interest minus the expected rate of inflation. The real rate of interest indicates the interest premium, in terms of real goods and services, that one must pay for earlier availability.

Real risk-free interest rate The single-period interest rate for a completely risk-free security if no inflation were expected.

Real risk-free rate (RRFR) The basic interest rate with no accommodation for inflation or uncertainty. The pure time value of money.

Real wage rate The quantity of goods ands services that an hour's work can buy. It is equal to the money wage rate divided by the price level.

Realizable value (settlement value) With reference to assets, the amount of cash or cash equivalents that could currently be obtained by selling the asset in an orderly disposal; with reference to liabilities, the undiscounted amount of cash or cash equivalents expected to be paid to satisfy the liabilities in the normal course of business.

Realization Multiple (Private Equity) The realization multiple (DPI) is calculated by dividing the cumulative distributions by the paid-in-capital.

Realized capital gains Capital gains that result when an appreciated asset is sold; realized capital gains are taxable.

Receivables turnover An activity ratio equal to revenue divided by average receivables; an indication of the resources tied up in accounts receivable and the speed at which receivables are collected during the period.

Receiver swaption A swaption that allows the holder to enter into a swap as the fixed-rate receiver and floating-rate payer.

Recession There are two common definitions of recession. They are (1) A business cycle phase in which real GDP decreases for at least two successive quarters. (2) A significant decline in activity spread across the economy, lasting for more than a few months, visible in industrial production, employment, real income, and wholesale-retail trade.

Recessionary gap The amount by which potential GDP exceeds real GDP.

Reference base period The period in which the CPI is defined to be 100.

Regime With reference to a time series, the underlying model generating the times series.

Registered competitive market makers (RCMMs) Members of an exchange who are allowed to use their memberships to buy or sell for their own account within the specific trading obligations set down by the exchange.

Registered traders Members of the stock exchange who are allowed to use their memberships to buy and sell for their own account, which means they save commissions on their trading but they provide liquidity to the market, and they abide by exchange regulations on how they can trade.

Regression coefficients The intercept and slope coefficient(s) of a regression.

Regulation Rules administrated by a government agency to influence economic activity by determining prices, product standards and types, and conditions under which new firms may enter an industry.

Regulatory risk The risk associated with the uncertainty of how derivative transactions will be regulated or with changes in regulations.

Rejection point (or critical value) A value against which a computed test statistic is compared to decide whether to reject or not reject the null hypothesis.

Relative dispersion The amount of dispersion relative to a reference value or benchmark.

Relative frequency With reference to an interval of grouped data, the number of observations in the interval divided by the total number of observations in the sample.

Relative price The ratio of the price of one good or service to the price of another good or service. A relative price is an opportunity cost.

Renewable natural resources Natural resources that can be used repeatedly without depleting what is available for future use.

Rent The income that land earns.

Rent ceiling A regulation that makes it illegal to charge a rent higher than a specified level.

Rent seeking Any attempt to capture a consumer surplus, a producer surplus, or an economic profit.

Replacement value The market value of a swap.

Report format With respect to the format of a balance sheet, a format in which assets, liabilities, and equity are listed in a single column.

Required rate of return The return that compensates investors for their time, the expected rate of inflation, and the uncertainty of the return.

Required reserve ratio The ratio of reserves to deposits that banks are required, by regulation, to hold.

Reserve ratio The fraction of a bank's total deposits that are held in reserves.

Reserves Cash in a bank's vault plus the bank's deposits at Federal Reserve banks.

Residual autocorrelations The sample autocorrelations of the residuals.

Residual claim The owners' remaining claim on the company's assets after the liabilities are deducted.

Residual value The estimated net scrap, salvage, or trade-in value of a tangible asset at the estimated date of its disposal. Also called *salvage value* or *disposal value.*

Resistance level A price at which a technician would expect a substantial increase in the supply of a stock to reverse a rising trend.

Retail method An inventory accounting method in which the sales value of an item is reduced by the gross margin to calculate the item's cost.

Return on assets (ROA) A profitability ratio calculated as net income divided by average total assets; indicates the company's net profit generated per dollar invested in total assets.

Return on common equity A profitability ratio calculated as (net income − preferred dividends) divided by average common equity; equal to the return on equity ratio when no preferred equity is outstanding.

Return on equity (ROE) A profitability ratio calculated as net income divided by average shareholders' equity; indicates the return generated per dollar of shareholders' investment in the company.

Return-on-investment ratios Ratios that are useful for comparing the net benefits generated from investments.

Return on total capital A profitability ratio of net income to total capital (i.e., average interest-bearing debt + average total equity); indicates the return to the investments made by both creditors and shareholders.

Return prediction studies Studies wherein investigations attempt to predict the time series of future rates of return using public information. An example would be predicting above-average returns for the stock market based on the aggregate dividend yield—e.g., high dividend yield indicates above average future market returns.

Revenue The amount charged for the delivery of goods or services in the ordinary activities of a business over a stated period; the inflows of economic resources to a company over a stated period.

Revenue bond A bond that is serviced by the income generated from specific revenue-producing projects of the municipality.

Revenue expenditure An expenditure for ordinary repairs and maintenance of a long-term asset, which is recorded by a debit to an expense account.

Revolving credit agreements The strongest form of short-term bank borrowing facilities; they are in effect for multiple years (e.g., 3–5 years) and may have optional medium-term loan features

Rho The sensitivity of the option price to the risk-free rate.

Ricardo-Barro effect The equivalence of financing government purchases by taxes or by borrowing.

Rising trend channel The range defined by security prices as they move progressively higher.

Risk averse The assumption about investors that they will choose the least risky alternative, all else being equal.

Risk budgeting The establishment of objectives for individuals, groups, or divisions of an organization that takes into account the allocation of an acceptable level of risk.

Risk governance The setting of overall policies and standards in risk management

Risk management The process of identifying the level of risk an entity wants, measuring the level of risk the entity currently has, taking actions that bring the actual level of risk to the desired level of risk, and monitoring the new actual level of risk so that it continues to be aligned with the desired level of risk.

Risk premium The expected return on an investment minus the risk-free rate.

Risk premium (RP) (1) The difference between the expected return on an asset and the risk-free interest rate. (2) The increase over the nominal risk-free rate that investors demand as compensation for an investment's uncertainty. (3) The expected return on an investment minus the risk-free rate.

Risk-free asset An asset with returns that exhibit zero variance.

Risk-neutral probabilities Weights that are used to compute a binomial option price. They are the probabilities that would apply if a risk-neutral investor valued an option.

Risk-neutral valuation The process by which options and other derivatives are priced by treating investors as though they were risk neutral.

Risky asset An asset with uncertain future returns.

Rival A good or services or a resource is rival if its use by one person decreases the quantity available for someone else.

Robust The quality of being relatively unaffected by a violation of assumptions.

Robust standard errors Standard errors of the estimated parameters of a regression that correct for the presence of heteroskedasticity in the regression's error term.

Root mean squared error (RMSE) The square root of the average squared forecast error; used to compare the out-of-sample forecasting performance of forecasting models.

Roy's safety first criterion A criterion asserting that the optimal portfolio is the one that minimizes the probability that portfolio return falls below a threshold level.

Rule of 72 The principle that the approximate number of years necessary for an investment to double is 72 divided by the stated interest rate.

Runs test A test of the weak-form efficient market hypothesis that checks for trends that persist longer in terms of positive or negative price changes than one would expect for a random series.

Safety stock A level of inventory beyond anticipated needs that provides a cushion in the event that it takes longer to replenish inventory than expected or in the case of greater than expected demand.

Safety-first rules Rules for portfolio selection that focus on the risk that portfolio value will fall below some minimum acceptable level over some time horizon.

Sales Generally, a synonym for revenue; "sales" is generally understood to refer to the sale of goods, whereas "revenue" is understood to include the sale of goods or services.

Sales returns and allowances An offset to revenue reflecting any cash refunds, credits on account, and discounts from sales prices given to customers who purchased defective or unsatisfactory items.

Salvage value The amount the company estimates that it can sell the asset for at the end of its useful life.

Sample A subset of a population.

Sample excess kurtosis A sample measure of the degree of a distribution's peakedness in excess of the normal distribution's peakedness.

Sample kurtosis A sample measure of the degree of a distribution's peakedness.

Sample mean The sum of the sample observations, divided by the sample size.

Sample selection bias Bias introduced by systematically excluding some members of the population according to a particular attribute-for example, the bias introduced when data availability leads to certain observations being excluded from the analysis.

Sample skewness A sample measure of degree of asymmetry of a distribution.

Sample standard deviation The positive square root of the sample variance.

Sample statistic or statistic A quantity computed from or used to describe a sample.

Sample variance A sample measure of the degree of dispersion of a distribution, calculated by dividing the sum of the squared deviations from the sample mean by the sample size (n) minus 1.

Sampling The process of obtaining a sample.

Sampling distribution The distribution of all distinct possible values that a statistic can assume when computed from samples of the same size randomly drawn from the same population.

Sampling error The difference between the observed value of a statistic and the quantity it is intended to estimate.

Sampling plan The set of rules used to select a sample.

Sandwich spread An option strategy that is equivalent to a short butterfly spread.

Sarbanes-Oxley Act An act passed by the U.S. Congress in 2002 that created the Public Company Accounting Oversight Board (PCAOB) to oversee auditors.

Saving The amount of income that households have left after they have paid their taxes and bought their consumption goods and services.

Saving supply The relationship between saving and the real interest rate, other things remaining the same.

Savings and loan association (S&L) A depository institution that receives checking deposits and savings deposits and that makes personal, commercial, and home-purchase loans.

Savings bank A depository institution, owned by its depositors, that accepts savings deposits and makes mortgage loans.

Scalper A trader who offers to buy or sell futures contracts, holding the position for only a brief period of time. Scalpers attempt to profit by buying at the bid price and selling at the higher ask price.

Scarcity Our inability to satisfy all our wants.

Scatter diagram A diagram that plots the value of one economic variable against the value of another.

Scatter plot A two-dimensional plot of pairs of observations on two data series.

Scenario analysis A risk management technique involving the examination of the performance of a portfolio under specified situations. Closely related to stress testing.

Screening The application of a set of criteria to reduce a set of potential investments to a smaller set having certain desired characteristics.

Search activity The time spent looking for someone with whom to do business.

Seasoned equity issues New equity shares offered by firms that already have stock outstanding.

Seats Memberships in a derivatives exchange.

Secondary market The market in which outstanding securities are bought and sold by owners other than the issuers. Purpose is to provide liquidity for investors.

Sector rotation strategy An active strategy that involves purchasing stocks in specific industries or stocks with specific characteristics (low *P/E*, growth, value) that are anticipated to rise in value more than the overall market.

Securities Act of 1933 An act passed by the U.S. Congress in 1933 that specifies the financial and other significant information that investors must receive when securities are sold, prohibits misrepresentations, and requires initial registration of all public issuances of securities.

Securities Exchange Act of 1934 An act passed by the U.S. Congress in 1934 that created the Securities and Exchange Commission (SEC), gave the SEC authority over all aspects of the securities industry, and empowered the SEC to require periodic reporting by companies with publicly traded securities.

Security market line (SML) The graph of the capital asset pricing model.

Segment debt ratio Segment liabilities divided by segment assets.

Segment margin Segment profit (loss) divided by segment revenue.

Segment ROA Segment profit (loss) divided by segment assets.

Segment turnover Segment revenue divided by segment assets.

SelectNet An order-routing and trade-execution system for institutional investors (brokers and dealers) that allows communication through the Nasdaq system rather than by phone.

Self-interest The choices that you think are the best for you.

Semideviation The positive square root of semivariance (sometimes called semistandard deviation).

Semilogarithmic Describes a scale constructed so that equal intervals on the vertical scale represent equal rates of change, and equal intervals on the horizontal scale represent equal amounts of change.

Semivariance The average squared deviation below the mean.

Sensitivity analysis Analysis that shows the range of possible outcomes as specific assumptions are changed.

Separation theorem The proposition that the investment decision, which involves investing in the market portfolio on the capital market line, is separate from the financing decision, which targets a specific point on the CML based on the investor's risk preference.

Serially correlated With reference to regression errors, errors that are correlated across observations.

Settlement date or payment date The date on which the parties to a swap make payments.

Settlement period The time between settlement dates.

Settlement price The official price, designated by the clearinghouse, from which daily gains and losses will be determined and marked to market.

Settlement risk When settling a contract, the risk that one party could be in the process of paying the counterparty while the counterparty is declaring bankruptcy.

Shareholders' equity Total assets minus total liabilities.

Sharpe measure A relative measure of a portfolio's benefit-to-risk ratio, calculated as its average return in excess of the risk-free rate divided by the standard deviation of portfolio returns.

Sharpe ratio The average return in excess of the risk-free rate divided by the standard deviation of return; a measure of the average excess return earned per unit of standard deviation of return.

Short The seller of a derivative contract. Also refers to the position of being short a derivative.

Short hedge A short position in a forward or futures contract used to offset the price volatility of a long position in the underlying asset.

Short position The seller of a commodity or security or, for a forward contract, the counterparty who will be the eventual seller of the underlying asset.

Short run The short run in microeconomics has two meanings. For the firm, it is the period of time in which the quantity of at least one input is fixed and the quantities of the other inputs can be varied. The fixed input is usually capital-that is, the firm has a given plant size. For the industry, the short run is the period of time in which each firm has a given plant size and the number of firms in the industry is fixed.

Short sale The sale of borrowed securities with the intention of repurchasing them later at a lower price and earning the difference.

Shortfall risk The risk that portfolio value will fall below some minimum acceptable level over some time horizon.

Short-run aggregate supply curve A curve that shows the relationship between the quantity of real GDP supplied and the price level in the short run when the money wage rate, other resource prices, and potential GDP remain constant.

Short-run industry supply curve A curve that shows the quantity supplied by the industry at each price varies when the plant size of each firm and the number of firms in the industry remain the same.

Short-run macroeconomic equilibrium A situation that occurs when the quantity of real GDP demanded equals quantity of real GDP supplied—at the point of intersection of the *AD* curve and the *SAS* curve.

Short-run Phillips curve A curve that shows the tradeoff between inflation and unemployment, when the expected inflation rate and the natural rate of unemployment remain the same.

Should Encouraged (recommended) to follow the recommendation of the GIPS standards but not required.

Shutdown point The output and price at which the firm just covers its total variable cost. In the short run, the firm is indifferent between producing the profit-maximizing output and shutting down temporarily.

Signal An action taken by an informed person (or firm) to send a message to uninformed people or an action taken outside a market that conveys information that can be used by that market.

Simple interest The interest earned each period on the original investment; interest calculated on the principal only.

Simple random sample A subset of a larger population created in such a way that each element of the population has an equal probability of being selected to the subset.

Simple random sampling The procedure of drawing a sample to satisfy the definition of a simple random sample.

Simulation Computer-generated sensitivity or scenario analysis that is based on probability models for the factors that drive outcomes.

Simulation trial A complete pass through the steps of a simulation.

Single-payment loan A loan in which the borrower receives a sum of money at the start and pays back the entire amount with interest in a single payment at maturity.

Single-price monopoly A monopoly that must sell each unit of its output for a same price to all its customers.

Single-step format With respect to the format of the income statement, a format that does not subtotal for gross profit (revenue minus cost of goods sold).

Sinking fund (1) Bond provision that requires the bond to be paid off progressively rather than in full at maturity. (2) Bond provision that requires the issuer to redeem some or all of the bond systematically over the term of the bond rather than in full at maturity.

Skewed Not symmetrical.

Skewness A quantitative measure of skew (lack of symmetry); a synonym of skew.

Slope The change in the value of the variable measured on the *y*-axis divided by the change in the value of the variable measured on the *x*-axis.

Small-firm effect A frequent empirical anomaly where risk-adjusted stock returns for companies with low market capitalization (i.e., share price multiplied by number of outstanding shares) are significantly larger than those generated by high market capitalization (large cap) firms.

Small-Order Execution System (SOES) A quotation and execution system for retail (nonprofessional) investors who place orders with brokers who must honor their prevailing bid-ask for automatic execution up to 1,000 shares.

Social interest Choices that are the best for society as a whole.

Soft dollars A form of compensation to a money manager generated when the manager commits the investor to paying higher brokerage fees in exchange for the manager receiving additional services (e.g., stock research) from the broker.

Software Capitalized costs associated with computer programs developed for sale, lease, or internal use and amortized over the estimated economic life of the programs.

Solvency With respect to financial statement analysis, the ability of a company to fulfill its long-term obligations.

Solvency ratios Ratios that measure a company's ability to meet its long-term obligations.

Sovereign risk The risk that a government may default on its debt.

Sovereign yield spread An estimate of the country spread (country equity premium) for a developing nation that is based on a comparison of bonds yields in country being analyzed and a developed country. The sovereign yield spread is the difference between a government bond yield in the country being analyzed, denominated in the currency of the developed country, and the Treasury bond yield on a similar maturity bond in the developed country.

Spearman rank correlation coefficient A measure of correlation applied to ranked data.

Specialist The major market maker on U.S. stock exchanges who acts as a broker or dealer to ensure the liquidity and smooth functions of the secondary stock market.

Specific identification method An inventory accounting method that identifies which specific inventory items were sold and which remained in inventory to be carried over to later periods.

Speculative company A firm with a great degree of business and/or financial risk, with commensurate high earnings potential.

Speculative stock A stock that appears to be highly overpriced compared to its intrinsic valuation.

Spending phase Phase in the investment life cycle during which individuals' earning years end as they retire. They pay for expenses with income from social security and returns from prior investments and invest to protect against inflation.

Spot price Current market price of an asset. Also called cash price.

Spot rate The required yield for a cash flow to be received at some specific date in the future—for example, the spot rate for a flow to be received in one year, for a cash flow in two years, and so on.

Spread An option strategy involving the purchase of one option and sale of another option that is identical to the first in all respects except either exercise price or expiration.

Spurious correlation A correlation that misleadingly points towards associations between variables.

Stagflation The combination of recession and inflation.

Standard cost With respect to inventory accounting, the planned or target unit cost of inventory items or services.

Standard deviation The positive square root of the variance; a measure of dispersion in the same units as the original data.

Standard normal distribution (or unit normal distribution) The normal density with mean (μ) equal to 0 and standard deviation (σ) equal to 1.

Standardized beta With reference to fundamental factor models, the value of the attribute for an asset minus the average value of the attribute across all stocks, divided by the standard deviation of the attribute across all stocks.

Standardizing A transformation that involves subtracting the mean and dividing the result by the standard deviation.

Stated annual interest rate or quoted interest rate A quoted interest rate that does not account for compounding within the year.

Statement of cash flows (cash flow statement) A financial statement that reconciles beginning-of-period and end-of-period balance sheet values of cash; provides information about an entity's cash inflows and cash outflows as they pertain to operating, investing, and financing activities.

Statement of changes in shareholders' equity (statement of owners' equity) A financial statement that reconciles the beginning-of-period and end-of-period balance sheet values of shareholders' equity; provides information about all factors affecting shareholders' equity.

Statement of retained earnings A financial statement that reconciles beginning-of-period and end-of-period balance sheet values of retained income; shows the linkage between the balance sheet and income statement.

Statistic A quantity computed from or used to describe a sample of data.

Statistical factor models A multifactor model in which statistical methods are applied to a set of historical returns to determine portfolios that best explain either historical return covariances or variances.

Statistical inference Making forecasts, estimates, or judgments about a larger group from a smaller group actually observed; using a sample statistic to infer the value of an unknown population parameter.

Statistically significant A result indicating that the null hypothesis can be rejected; with reference to an estimated regression coefficient, frequently understood to mean a result indicating that the corresponding population regression coefficient is different from 0.

Statistics The science of describing, analyzing, and drawing conclusions from data; also, a collection of numerical data.

Stock A quantity that exists at a point in time.

Stock dividend A dividend paid in the form of additional shares rather than in cash.

Stock split An action taken by a firm to increase the number of shares outstanding, such as doubling the number of shares outstanding by giving each stockholder two new shares for each one formerly held.

Stock-out losses Profits lost from not having sufficient inventory on hand to satisfy demand.

Storage costs or carrying costs The costs of holding an asset, generally a function of the physical characteristics of the underlying asset.

Straddle An option strategy involving the purchase of a put and a call with the same exercise price. A straddle is based on the expectation of high volatility of the underlying.

Straight-line method A method of depreciation that assumes depreciation depends only on the passage of time and that allocates an equal amount of depreciation to each accounting period in an asset's useful life.

Straight-line method A depreciation method that allocates evenly the cost of a long-lived asset less its estimated residual value over the estimated useful life of the asset.

Strangle A variation of a straddle in which the put and call have different exercise prices.

Strap An option strategy involving the purchase of two calls and one put.

Strategies All the possible actions of each player in a game.

Stratified random sampling A procedure by which a population is divided into subpopulations (strata) based on one or more classification criteria. Simple random samples are then drawn from each stratum in sizes proportional to the relative size of each stratum in the population. These samples are then pooled.

Stress testing/scenario analysis A set of techniques for estimating losses in extremely unfavorable combinations of events or scenarios.

Strike price Price at which an option can be exercised (same as exercise price).

Strip An option strategy involving the purchase of two puts and one call.

Structural change Economic trend occurring when the economy is undergoing a major change in organization or in how it functions.

Structural surplus or deficit The budget balance that would occur if the economy were at full employment and real GDP were equal to potential GDP.

Structural unemployment The unemployment that arises when changes in technology or international competition change the skills needed to perform jobs or change the locations of jobs.

Structured note (1) A bond or note issued with some unusual, often option-like, clause. (2) A bond with an embedded derivative designed to create a payoff distribution that satisfies the needs of a specific investor clientele. (3) A variation of a floating-rate note that has some type of unusual characteristic such as a leverage factor or in which the rate moves opposite to interest rates.

Style analysis An attempt to explain the variability in the observed returns to a security portfolio in terms of the movements in the returns to a series of benchmark portfolios designed to capture the essence of a particular security characteristic such as size, value, and growth.

Subjective probability A probability drawing on personal or subjective judgment.

Subsidy A payment that the government makes to a producer.

Substitute A good that can be used in place of another good.

Substitution effect The effect of a change in price of a good or service on the quantity bought when the consumer (hypothetically) remains indifferent between the original and the new consumption situations—that is, the consumer remains on the same indifference curve.

Successful efforts accounting A method of accounting for the costs of exploring and developing oil and gas resources in which successful exploration is recorded as an asset and depleted over the estimated life of the resource and all unsuccessful efforts are immediately written off as losses.

Sunk cost A cost that has already been incurred.

Supplemental Information Any performance-related information included as part of a compliant performance presentation that supplements or enhances the required and/or recommended disclosure and presentation provisions of the GIPS standards.

Supply The relationship between the quantity of a good that producers plan to sell and the price of the good when all other influences on sellers' plans remain the same. It is described by a supply schedule and illustrated by a supply curve.

Supply curve A curve that shows the relationship between the quantity supplied and the price of a good when all other influences on producers' planned sales remain the same.

Supply of labor The relationship between the quantity of labor supplied and the real wage rate when all other influences on work plans remain the same.

Supply-side effects The effects of fiscal policy on employment, potential GDP, and aggregate supply.

Support level A price at which a technician would expect a substantial increase in price and volume for a stock to reverse a declining trend that was due to profit taking.

Surprise The actual value of a variable minus its predicted (or expected) value.

Survey approach An estimate of the equity risk premium that is based upon estimates provided by a panel of finance experts.

Survivorship bias The bias resulting from a test design that fails to account for companies that have gone bankrupt, merged, or are otherwise no longer reported in a database.

Sustainable growth rate The rate of dividend (and earnings) growth that can be sustained over time for a given level of return on equity, keeping the capital structure constant and without issuing additional common stock.

Swap An agreement between two parties to exchange a series of future cash flows.

Swap spread The difference between the fixed rate on an interest rate swap and the rate on a Treasury note with equivalent maturity; it reflects the general level of credit risk in the market.

Swaption An option to enter into a swap.

SWOT analysis An examination of a firm's *S*trengths, *W*eaknesses, *O*pportunities, and *T*hreats. This analysis helps an analyst evaluate a firm's strategies to exploit its competitive advantages or defend against its weaknesses.

Symmetry principle A requirement that people in similar situations be treated similarly.

Synthetic call The combination of puts, the underlying, and risk-free bonds that replicates a call option.

Synthetic forward contract The combination of the underlying, puts, calls, and risk-free bonds that replicates a forward contract.

Synthetic index fund An index fund position created by combining risk-free bonds and futures on the desired index.

Synthetic put The combination of calls, the underlying, and risk-free bonds that replicates a put option.

Systematic factors Factors that affect the average returns of a large number of different assets.

Systematic risk The variability of returns that is due to macroeconomic factors that affect all risky assets. Because it affects all risky assets, it cannot be eliminated by diversification.

Systematic sampling A procedure of selecting every *k*th member until reaching a sample of the desired size. The sample that results from this procedure should be approximately random.

Tangible assets Long-term assets that have physical substance.

Tangible book value per share Common shareholders' equity minus intangible assets from the balance sheet, divided by the number of shares outstanding.

Tap Procedure by which a borrower can keep issuing additional amounts of an old bond at its current market value. This procedure is used for bond issues, notably by the British and French governments, as well as for some short-term debt instruments.

Target balance A minimum level of cash to be held available—estimated in advance and adjusted for known funds transfers, seasonality, or other factors.

Target capital structure The proportion of component sources of capital (e.g. equity, debt) that a company strives to maintain

Target semideviation The positive square root of target semivariance.

Target semivariance The average squared deviation below a target value.

Tariff A tax that is imposed by the importing country when an imported good crosses its international boundary.

Tax incidence The division of the burden of a tax between the buyer and the seller.

Tax multiplier The magnification effect of a change in taxes on aggregate demand.

Tax risk The uncertainty associated with tax laws.

Tax wedge The gap between the before-tax and after-tax wage rates.

Taylor rule A rule that adjusts the federal funds rate to target the inflation rate and to take into account deviations of the inflation rate from its target and deviations of real GDP from potential GDP.

***t*-Distribution** A symmetrical distribution defined by a single parameter, degrees of freedom, that is largely used to make inferences concerning the mean of a normal distribution whose variance is unknown.

Technical analysis Estimation of future security price movements based on past price and volume movements.

Technological change The development of new goods and better ways of producing goods and services.

Technological efficiency A situation that occurs when the firm produces a given output by using the least amount of inputs.

Technology Any method of producing a good or service.

Temporary New Account A tool that firms can use to remove the effect of significant cash flows on a portfolio. When a significant cash flow occurs in a portfolio, the firm may treat this cash flow as a "temporary new account," allowing the firm to implement the mandate of the portfolio without the impact of the cash flow on the performance of the portfolio.

Tenor The original time to maturity on a swap.

Term structure of interest rates The relationship between term to maturity and yield to maturity for a sample of comparable bonds at a given time. Popularly known as the *yield curve.*

Term to maturity Specifies the date or the number of years before a bond matures or expires.

Termination date The date of the final payment on a swap; also, the swap's expiration date.

Terms of trade The quantity of goods and services that a country exports to pay for its imports of goods and services.

Test statistic A quantity, calculated based on a sample, whose value is the basis for deciding whether or not to reject the null hypothesis.

Theta The rate at which an option's time value decays.

Third market Over-the-counter trading of securities listed on an exchange.

Thrift institutions Thrift institutions include savings and loan associations, savings banks, and credit unions.

Tick The minimum price movement for the asset underlying a forward or futures contract; for Treasury bonds, one tick equals 1/32 of 1 percent of par value.

Time series A set of observations on a variable's outcomes in different time periods.

Time to expiration The time remaining in the life of a derivative, typically expressed in years.

Time value decay The loss in the value of an option resulting from movement of the option price toward its payoff value as the expiration day approaches.

Time value of money The principles governing equivalence relationships between cash flows with different dates.

Time value or speculative value The difference between the market price of the option and its intrinsic value, determined by the uncertainty of the underlying over the remaining life of the option.

Time-period bias The possibility that when we use a time-series sample, our statistical conclusion may be sensitive to the starting and ending dates of the sample.

Time-series analysis An examination of a firm's performance data over a period of time.

Time-series data Observations of a variable over time.

Time-series graph A graph that measures time (for example, months or years) on the *x*-axis and the variable or variables in which we are interested on the *y*-axis.

Time-weighted rate of return The compound rate of growth of one unit of currency invested in a portfolio during a stated measurement period; a measure of investment performance that is not sensitive to the timing and amount of withdrawals or additions to the portfolio.

Top-down analysis With reference to investment selection processes, an approach that starts with macro selection (i.e., identifying attractive geographic segments and/or industry segments) and then addresses selection of the most attractive investments within those segments.

Total asset turnover An activity ratio calculated as revenue divided by average total assets; indicates the extent to which the investment in total assets results in revenues.

Total cost The cost of all the productive resources that a firm uses.

Total Firm Assets Total firm assets are all assets for which a firm has investment management responsibility. Total firm assets include assets managed outside the firm (e.g., by subadvisors) for which the firm has asset allocation authority.

Total fixed cost The cost of the firm's fixed inputs.

Total invested capital The sum of market value of common equity, book value of preferred equity, and face value of debt.

Total probability rule for expected value A rule explaining the expected value of a random variable in terms of expected values of the random variable conditional on mutually exclusive and exhaustive scenarios.

Total probability rule A rule explaining the unconditional probability of an event in terms of probabilities of the event conditional on mutually exclusive and exhaustive scenarios.

Total product The maximum output that a given quantity of factors of production can produce.

Total return A return objective in which the investor wants to increase the portfolio value to meet a future need by both capital gains and current income reinvestment.

Total return swap A swap in which one party agrees to pay the total return on a security. Often used as a credit derivative, in which the underlying is a bond.

Total revenue The value of a firm's sales. It is calculated as the price of the good multiplied by the quantity sold.

Total revenue test A method of estimating the price elasticity of demand by observing the change in total revenue that results from a change in the price, when all other influences on the quantity sold remain the same.

Total variable cost The cost of all the firm's variable inputs.

Tracking error The standard deviation of the difference in returns between an active investment portfolio and its benchmark portfolio; also called tracking error volatility, tracking risk, and active risk.

Tracking portfolio A portfolio having factor sensitivities that are matched to those of a benchmark or other portfolio.

Tracking risk The standard deviation of the differences between a portfolio's returns and its benchmark's returns; a synonym of active risk.

Trade balance The balance of a country's exports and imports; part of the current account.

Trade credit A spontaneous form of credit in which a purchaser of the goods or service is, effectively, financing its purchase by delaying the date on which payment is made.

Trade Date Accounting The transaction is reflected in the portfolio on the date of the purchase or sale, and not on the settlement date. Recognizing the asset or liability within at least 3 days of the date the transaction is entered into (Trade Date, T 1 1, T 1 2 or T 1 3) all satisfy the trade date accounting requirement for purposes of the GIPS standards. (See settlement date accounting.)

Trade receivables (commercial receivables or accounts receivable) Amounts customers owe the company for products that have been sold as well as amounts that may be due from suppliers (such as for returns of merchandise).

Trademark A registered symbol that can be used only by its owner to identify a product or service.

Tradeoff An exchange–giving up one thing to get something else.

Trading effect The difference in performance of a bond portfolio from that of a chosen index due to short-run changes in the composition of the portfolio.

Trading Expenses The costs of buying or selling a security. These costs typically take the form of brokerage commissions or spreads from either internal or external brokers. Custody fees charged per transaction should be considered custody fees and not direct transaction costs. Estimated trading expenses are not permitted.

Trading rule A formula for deciding on current transactions based on historical data.

Trading securities (held-for-trading securities) Securities held by a company with the intent to trade them.

Trading turnover The percentage of outstanding shares traded during a period of time.

Trailing P/E (or current P/E) A stock's current market price divided by the most recent four quarters of earnings per share.

Tranche Refers to a portion of an issue that is designed for a specific category of investors. French for "slice."

Transaction cost The cost of executing a trade. Low costs characterize an operationally efficient market.

Transaction Expenses (Private Equity) Include all legal, financial, advisory, and investment banking fees related to buying, selling, restructuring, and recapitalizing portfolio companies.

Transaction exposure The risk associated with a foreign exchange rate on a specific business transaction such as a purchase or sale.

Transactions costs The costs that arise from finding someone with whom to do business, of reaching an agreement about the price and other aspects of the exchange, and of ensuring that the terms of the agreement are fulfilled. The opportunity costs of conducting a transaction.

Transactions motive In the context of inventory management, it refers to the need for inventory as part of the routine production–sales cycle.

Translation exposure The risk associated with the conversion of foreign financial statements into domestic currency.

Treasury bill A negotiable U.S. government security with a maturity of less than one year that pays no periodic interest but yields the difference between its par value and its discounted purchase price.

Treasury bond A U.S. government security with a maturity of more than 10 years that pays interest periodically.

Treasury note A U.S. government security with maturities of 1 to 10 years that pays interest periodically.

Treasury stock method A method for accounting for the effect of options (and warrants) on earnings per share (EPS) that specifies what EPS would have been if the options and warrants had been exercised and the company had used the proceeds to repurchase common stock.

Tree diagram A diagram with branches emanating from nodes representing either mutually exclusive chance events or mutually exclusive decisions.

Trend A long-term pattern of movement in a particular direction.

Trimmed mean A mean computed after excluding a stated small percentage of the lowest and highest observations.

Trust receipt arrangement The use of inventory as collateral for a loan. The inventory is segregated and held in trust, and the proceeds of any sale must be remitted to the lender immediately.

***t*-Test** A hypothesis test using a statistic (*t*-statistic) that follows a *t*-distribution.

Two-sided hypothesis test (or two-tailed hypothesis test) A test in which the null hypothesis is rejected in favor of the alternative hypothesis if the evidence indicates that the population parameter is either smaller or larger than a hypothesized value.

Type I error The error of rejecting a true null hypothesis.

Type II error The error of not rejecting a false null hypothesis.

U.S. interest rate differential A gap equal to the U.S. interest rate minus the foreign interest rate.

U.S. Official reserves The government's holdings of foreign currency.

Unbiasedness Lack of bias. A desirable property of estimators, an unbiased estimator is one whose expected value (the mean of its sampling distribution) equals the parameter it is intended to estimate.

Unbilled revenue (accrued revenue) Revenue that has been earned but not yet billed to customers as of the end of an accounting period.

Uncertainty A situation in which more than one event might occur but it is not known which one.

Unclassified balance sheet A balance sheet that does not show subtotals for current assets and current liabilities.

Unconditional heteroskedasticity Heteroskedasticity of the error term that is not correlated with the values of the independent variable(s) in the regression.

Unconditional probability (or marginal probability) The probability of an event *not* conditioned on another event.

Uncovered interest rate parity The assertion that expected currency depreciation should offset the interest differential between two countries over the term of the interest rate.

Underlying An asset that trades in a market in which buyers and sellers meet, decide on a price, and the seller then delivers the asset to the buyer and receives payment. The underlying is the asset or other derivative on which a particular derivative is based. The market for the underlying is also referred to as the spot market.

Underweighted A condition in which a portfolio, for whatever reason, includes less of a class of securities than the relative market value alone would justify.

Unearned fees Unearned fees are recognized when a company receives cash payment for fees prior to earning them.

Unearned revenue (deferred revenue) A liability account for money that has been collected for goods or services that have not yet been delivered.

Unemployment rate The percentage of the people in the labor force who are unemployed.

Unidentifiable intangible An intangible that cannot be acquired singly and that typically possesses an indefinite benefit period; an example is accounting goodwill.

Unit elastic demand Demand with a price elasticity of 1; the percentage change in the quantity demanded equals the percentage change in price.

Unit normal distribution *See* Standard normal distribution.

Unit root A time series that is not covariance stationary is said to have a unit root.

Univariate distribution A distribution that specifies the probabilities for a single random variable.

Unlimited funds An unlimited funds environment assumes that the company can raise the funds it wants for all profitable projects simply by paying the required rate of return.

Unrealized capital gains Capital gains that reflect the price appreciation of currently held unsold assets.

Unsystematic risk Risk that is unique to an asset, derived from its particular characteristics. It can be eliminated in a diversified portfolio.

Unweighted index An indicator series affected equally by the performance of each security in the sample regardless of price or market value. Also referred to as an *equal-weighted series.*

Unwind The negotiated termination of a forward or futures position before contract maturity.

Up transition probability The probability that an asset's value moves up.

Utilitarianism A principle that states that we should strive to achieve "the greatest happiness for the greatest number of people."

Utility The benefit or satisfaction that a person gets from the consumption of a good or service.

Utility of wealth The amount of utility that a person attaches to a given amount of wealth.

Valuation The process of determining the value of an asset or service.

Valuation analysis An active bond portfolio management strategy designed to capitalize on expected price increases in temporarily undervalued issues.

Valuation process Part of the investment decision process in which you estimate the value of a security.

Valuation ratios Ratios that measure the quantity of an asset or flow (e.g., earnings) in relation to the price associated with a specified claim (e.g., a share or ownership of the enterprise).

Value The amount for which one can sell something, or the amount one must pay to acquire something.

Value at risk (VAR) A money measure of the minimum value of losses expected during a specified time period at a given level of probability.

Value chain The set of transformations to move from raw material to product or service delivery.

Value investors With reference to equity investors, investors who are focused on paying a relatively low share price in relation to earnings or assets per share.

Value stocks Stocks that appear to be undervalued for reasons besides earnings growth potential. These stocks are usually identified based on high dividend yields, low *P/E* ratios, or low price-to-book ratios.

Value-weighted index An index calculated as the total market value of the securities in the sample. Market value is equal to the number of shares or bonds outstanding times the market price of the security.

Variable costs Costs that rise proportionally with revenue.

Variance The expected value (the probability-weighted average) of squared deviations from a random variable's expected value.

Variation margin Additional margin that must be deposited in an amount sufficient to bring the balance up to the initial margin requirement.

Vega The relationship between option price and volatility.

Velocity of circulation The average number of times a dollar of money is used annually to buy the goods and services that make up GDP.

Venture Capital (Private Equity) Risk capital in the form of equity and/or loan capital that is provided by an investment institution to back a business venture that is expected to grow in value.

Vertical analysis Common-size analysis using only one reporting period or one base financial statement; for example, an income statement in which all items are stated as percentages of sales.

Vertical common-size analysis An analysis in which financial statement accounts are compared to a benchmark item in that same year. For the income statement, all items are restated as a percentage of revenues; for the balance sheet, all items are restated as a percentage of total assets.

Vintage Year (Private Equity) The year that the venture capital or private equity fund or partnership first draws down or calls capital from its investors.

Volatility As used in option pricing, the standard deviation of the continuously compounded returns on the underlying asset.

Voluntary export restraint An agreement between two governments in which the government of the exporting country agrees to restrain the volume of its own exports.

Wages The income that labor earns.

Warehouse receipt arrangement The use of inventory as collateral for a loan. . It is similar to a trust receipt arrangement except that there is a third part (i.e., a warehouse company) that supervises the inventory.

Warrant An instrument that allows the holder to purchase a specified number of shares of the firm's common stock from the firm at a specified price for a given period of time.

Weak-form efficient market hypothesis The belief that security prices fully reflect all security market information.

Wealth The market value of all the things that people own.

Weighted average cost method An inventory accounting method that averages the total cost of available inventory items over the total units available for sale.

Weighted-average cost of capital A weighted average of the after-tax required rates of return on a company's common stock, preferred stock, and long-term debt, where the weights are the fraction of each source of financing in the company's target capital structure.

Weighted average cost of capital (or marginal cost of capital) The required rate of return that investors demand for the average-risk investment of a company and the cost that a company incurs for additional capital. Found as the average of the company's component costs of capital, weighted by their proportions in the company's capital structure.

Weighted mean An average in which each observation is weighted by an index of its relative importance.

White-corrected standard errors A synonym for robust standard errors.

Winsorized mean A mean computed after assigning a stated percent of the lowest values equal to one specified low value, and a stated percent of the highest values equal to one specified high value.

Working capital The excess of current assets over current liabilities.

Working capital management The management of a company's short-term assets (such as inventory) and short-term liabilities (such as money owed to suppliers).

Working capital turnover An activity ratio calculated as revenue divided by average working capital; an indication of the efficiency with which working capital is employed to produce revenues.

Working-age population The total number of people aged 16 years and over who are not in jail, hospital, or some other form of institutional care.

World Trade Organization An international organization that places greater obligations on its member countries to observe the GATT rules.

Yankee bonds Bonds sold in the United States and denominated in U.S. dollars but issued by a foreign firm or government.

Yield The promised rate of return on an investment under certain assumptions.

Yield beta A measure of the sensitivity of a bond's yield to a general measure of bond yields in the market that is used to refine the hedge ratio.

Yield spread The difference between the yield on a bond and the yield on a default-free security, usually a government note, of the same maturity. The yield spread is primarily determined by the market's perception of the credit risk on the bond.

Yield to maturity The total yield on a bond obtained by equating the bond's current market value to the discounted cash flows promised by the bond.

Yield to worst Given a bond with multiple potential maturity dates and prices due to embedded call options, the practice is to calculate a yield to maturity for each of the call dates and prices and select the lowest yield (the most conservative possible yield) as yield to worst.

Zero-cost collar A transaction in which a position in the underlying is protected by buying a put and selling a call with the premium from the sale of the call offsetting the premium from the purchase of the put. It can also be used to protect a floating-rate borrower against interest rate increases with the premium on a long cap offsetting the premium on a short floor.

INDEX

Page numbers followed by n refer to footnotes.

B

exercised and the company had used the proceeds to repurchase common stock.

Tree diagram A diagram with branches emanating from nodes representing either mutually exclusive chance events or mutually exclusive decisions.

Trend A long-term pattern of movement in a particular direction.

Trimmed mean A mean computed after excluding a stated small percentage of the lowest and highest observations.

Trust receipt arrangement The use of inventory as collateral for a loan. The inventory is segregated and held in trust, and the proceeds of any sale must be remitted to the lender immediately.

***t*-Test** A hypothesis test using a statistic (*t*-statistic) that follows a *t*-distribution.

Two-sided hypothesis test (or two-tailed hypothesis test) A test in which the null hypothesis is rejected in favor of the alternative hypothesis if the evidence indicates that the population parameter is either smaller or larger than a hypothesized value.

Type I error The error of rejecting a true null hypothesis.

Type II error The error of not rejecting a false null hypothesis.

U.S. interest rate differential A gap equal to the U.S. interest rate minus the foreign interest rate.

U.S. Official reserves The government's holdings of foreign currency.

Unbiasedness Lack of bias. A desirable property of estimators, an unbiased estimator is one whose expected value (the mean of its sampling distribution) equals the parameter it is intended to estimate.

Unbilled revenue (accrued revenue) Revenue that has been earned but not yet billed to customers as of the end of an accounting period.

Uncertainty A situation in which more than one event might occur but it is not known which one.

Unclassified balance sheet A balance sheet that does not show subtotals for current assets and current liabilities.

Unconditional heteroskedasticity Heteroskedasticity of the error term that is not correlated with the values of the independent variable(s) in the regression.

Unconditional probability (or marginal probability) The probability of an event *not* conditioned on another event.

Uncovered interest rate parity The assertion that expected currency depreciation should offset the interest differential between two countries over the term of the interest rate.

Underlying An asset that trades in a market in which buyers and sellers meet, decide on a price, and the seller then delivers the asset to the buyer and receives payment. The underlying is the asset or other derivative on which a particular derivative is based. The market for the underlying is also referred to as the spot market.

Underweighted A condition in which a portfolio, for whatever reason, includes less of a class of securities than the relative market value alone would justify.

Unearned fees Unearned fees are recognized when a company receives cash payment for fees prior to earning them.

Unearned revenue (deferred revenue) A liability account for money that has been collected for goods or services that have not yet been delivered.

Unemployment rate The percentage of the people in the labor force who are unemployed.

Unidentifiable intangible An intangible that cannot be acquired singly and that typically possesses an indefinite benefit period; an example is accounting goodwill.

Unit elastic demand Demand with a price elasticity of 1; the percentage change in the quantity demanded equals the percentage change in price.

Unit normal distribution *See* Standard normal distribution.

Unit root A time series that is not covariance stationary is said to have a unit root.

Univariate distribution A distribution that specifies the probabilities for a single random variable.

Unlimited funds An unlimited funds environment assumes that the company can raise the funds it wants for all profitable projects simply by paying the required rate of return.

Unrealized capital gains Capital gains that reflect the price appreciation of currently held unsold assets.

Unsystematic risk Risk that is unique to an asset, derived from its particular characteristics. It can be eliminated in a diversified portfolio.

Unweighted index An indicator series affected equally by the performance of each security in the sample regardless of price or market value. Also referred to as an *equal-weighted series*.

Unwind The negotiated termination of a forward or futures position before contract maturity.

Up transition probability The probability that an asset's value moves up.

Utilitarianism A principle that states that we should strive to achieve "the greatest happiness for the greatest number of people."

Utility The benefit or satisfaction that a person gets from the consumption of a good or service.

Utility of wealth The amount of utility that a person attaches to a given amount of wealth.

Valuation The process of determining the value of an asset or service.

Valuation analysis An active bond portfolio management strategy designed to capitalize on expected price increases in temporarily undervalued issues.

Valuation process Part of the investment decision process in which you estimate the value of a security.

Valuation ratios Ratios that measure the quantity of an asset or flow (e.g., earnings) in relation to the price associated with a specified claim (e.g., a share or ownership of the enterprise).

Value The amount for which one can sell something, or the amount one must pay to acquire something.

Value at risk (VAR) A money measure of the minimum value of losses expected during a specified time period at a given level of probability.

Value chain The set of transformations to move from raw material to product or service delivery.

Value investors With reference to equity investors, investors who are focused on paying a relatively low share price in relation to earnings or assets per share.

Value stocks Stocks that appear to be undervalued for reasons besides earnings growth potential. These stocks are usually identified based on high dividend yields, low *P/E* ratios, or low price-to-book ratios.

Value-weighted index An index calculated as the total market value of the securities in the sample. Market value is equal to the number of shares or bonds outstanding times the market price of the security.

Variable costs Costs that rise proportionally with revenue.

Variance The expected value (the probability-weighted average) of squared deviations from a random variable's expected value.

Variation margin Additional margin that must be deposited in an amount sufficient to bring the balance up to the initial margin requirement.

Vega The relationship between option price and volatility.

Velocity of circulation The average number of times a dollar of money is used annually to buy the goods and services that make up GDP.

Venture Capital (Private Equity) Risk capital in the form of equity and/or loan capital that is provided by an investment institution to back a business venture that is expected to grow in value.

Vertical analysis Common-size analysis using only one reporting period or one base financial statement; for example, an income statement in which all items are stated as percentages of sales.

Vertical common-size analysis An analysis in which financial statement accounts are compared to a benchmark item in that same year. For the income statement, all items are restated as a percentage of revenues; for the balance sheet, all items are restated as a percentage of total assets.

Vintage Year (Private Equity) The year that the venture capital or private equity fund or partnership first draws down or calls capital from its investors.

Volatility As used in option pricing, the standard deviation of the continuously compounded returns on the underlying asset.

Voluntary export restraint An agreement between two governments in which the government of the exporting country agrees to restrain the volume of its own exports.

Wages The income that labor earns.

Warehouse receipt arrangement The use of inventory as collateral for a loan. . It is similar to a trust receipt arrangement except that there is a third part (i.e., a warehouse company) that supervises the inventory.

Warrant An instrument that allows the holder to purchase a specified number of shares of the firm's common stock from the firm at a specified price for a given period of time.

Weak-form efficient market hypothesis The belief that security prices fully reflect all security market information.

Wealth The market value of all the things that people own.

Weighted average cost method An inventory accounting method that averages the total cost of available inventory items over the total units available for sale.

Weighted-average cost of capital A weighted average of the after-tax required rates of return on a company's common stock, preferred stock, and long-term debt, where the weights are the fraction of each source of financing in the company's target capital structure.

Weighted average cost of capital (or marginal cost of capital) The required rate of return that investors demand for the average-risk investment of a company and the cost that a company incurs for additional capital. Found as the average of the company's component costs of capital, weighted by their proportions in the company's capital structure.

Weighted mean An average in which each observation is weighted by an index of its relative importance.

White-corrected standard errors A synonym for robust standard errors.

Winsorized mean A mean computed after assigning a stated percent of the lowest values equal to one specified low value, and a stated percent of the highest values equal to one specified high value.

Working capital The excess of current assets over current liabilities.

Working capital management The management of a company's short-term assets (such as inventory) and short-term liabilities (such as money owed to suppliers).

Working capital turnover An activity ratio calculated as revenue divided by average working capital; an indication of the efficiency with which working capital is employed to produce revenues.

Working-age population The total number of people aged 16 years and over who are not in jail, hospital, or some other form of institutional care.

World Trade Organization An international organization that places greater obligations on its member countries to observe the GATT rules.

Yankee bonds Bonds sold in the United States and denominated in U.S. dollars but issued by a foreign firm or government.

Yield The promised rate of return on an investment under certain assumptions.

Yield beta A measure of the sensitivity of a bond's yield to a general measure of bond yields in the market that is used to refine the hedge ratio.

Yield spread The difference between the yield on a bond and the yield on a default-free security, usually a government note, of the same maturity. The yield spread is primarily determined by the market's perception of the credit risk on the bond.

Yield to maturity The total yield on a bond obtained by equating the bond's current market value to the discounted cash flows promised by the bond.

Yield to worst Given a bond with multiple potential maturity dates and prices due to embedded call options, the practice is to calculate a yield to maturity for each of the call dates and prices and select the lowest yield (the most conservative possible yield) as yield to worst.

Zero-cost collar A transaction in which a position in the underlying is protected by buying a put and selling a call with the premium from the sale of the call offsetting the premium from the purchase of the put. It can also be used to protect a floating-rate borrower against interest rate increases with the premium on a long cap offsetting the premium on a short floor.

INDEX

Page numbers followed by n refer to footnotes.

E

G

H

J

K

L

V

W

X

Y

Z

P

V

W